An Exegetical
Bibliography
of the
New Testament

MATTHEW AND MARK

MERCER UNIVERSITY PRESS • MACON, GEORGIA

An
Exegetical
Bibliography
of the
New Testament

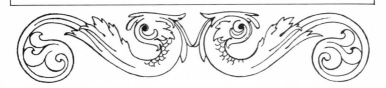

EDITED BY

GÜNTER WAGNER

ISBN 0-86554-013-6

Library of Congress Cataloging in Publication Data

An Exegetical bibliography of the New Testament.

1. Bible. N.T.—Bibliography.   I. Wagner, Günter, 1928-

Z7772.L1E93   1983   [BS2361.2]   016.225   83-969
ISBN   0-86554-013-6

To Margaret and Floyd Patterson

Preface

This bibliography is an "unwanted child," but it may well deserve its place. When I started teaching in 1958, I devised a detailed system for the collection of bibliographical information relevant for New Testtament studies, ranging from the Old Testament background to the theology of the Early Church. Year after year I used—or misused—all available student help and secretarial assistance to work through our library holdings and current additions to glean references to all sorts of materials and to type each individual reference that was considered useful on a separate card. The card was then filed under its proper heading, so that it would take me—or any student who wished to use the file—no more than a minute to pick up a sizable pile of cards representing a basic bibliography on any topic in the entire New Testament field. The purpose of the whole undertaking was to enable the student as quickly as possible to get down to research without wasting days, even weeks, on the search for literature.

The students who helped me represented more than a dozen nation-alities and spoke as many different mother tongues. Knowing or not knowing French, German, Spanish, Danish, Italian, Polish, etc., naturally proved to be both an asset and a liability, in regard to accuracy and consistency; however, as the whole collection was intended to be nothing but a tool for our research, perfectionism in matters of form did not plague us. Postgraduate students who majored in the field of New Testament and later started teaching in various parts of the world got "homesick" for that monstrous steel cabinet in my office and wondered how they could still have access to it. We decided to type up the data of the exegetical section and to fotocopy a reduced size of the condensed text, again on separate cards—so that everyone could add further references to his own card file.

Between 1973 and 1979 we made available "Bibliographical Aids" on all New Testament writings. Since 1981 I am editing the Second Series, copied by off-set printing, again in a postcard size, loose-leaf edition; upon request we are adding the place of publication from the Second Series onward and hope that our customers will not mind the inconsistency. We are most grateful to Mercer University Press for publishing at this time Series One and Two together in book form in one text. Updates/supplements for the card editions (Series Three) will continue to be available from Rüschlikon in the future.

I want to express my appreciation to all who have assisted in the production of these bibliographies, especially to Emanuel Wieser, Martin Scott and my wife Doris, who have helped with the editing, typing and proofreading of the manuscripts for the Second Series. I am grateful for the support given me by the administration of the Baptist Theological Seminary, Rüschlikon, and in particular to my friends, Margaret and Floyd Patterson (Washington, D. C.), whose encouragement and help have been invaluable throughout the years.

Baptist Theological Seminary   Günter Wagner
Rüschlikon-Zürich
September 8, 1982

List of Abbreviations

ABenR	American Benedictine Review (Atchison, Kansas)
ACR	Australasian Catholic Record (Sydney)
AER	American Ecclesiastical Review (Washington)
AfrER	African Ecclesiastical Review (Kampala)
AJA	American Journal of Archaeology (New York)
AJBA	Australian Journal of Biblical Archaelogy (Sydney)
ALUOS	Annual of Leeds University Oriental Society (Leeds)
AnBib	Analecta Biblica (Rome)
ANQ	Andover Newton Quarterly (Newton Centre, Massachusetts)
AssS	Assemblées du Seigneur (Paris)
ASThI	Annual of the Swedish Theological Institute (Jerusalem)
AThR	Anglican Theological Review (Evanston, Illinois)
AusBR	Australian Biblical Review (Melbourne)
AUSS	Andrews University Seminary Studies (Berrien Springs, Michigan)
BA	Biblical Archaeologist (Cambridge, Massachusetts)
BASOR	Bulletin of the American Schools of Oriental Research (Cambridge, Massachusetts)
Biblica	Biblica (Rome)
BiblOr	Bibliotheca Orientalis (Leiden)
BiblSa	Bibliotheca Sacra (Dallas)
BibW	Biblical World (Chicago)
BiLe	Bibel und Leben (Düsseldorf)
BiOr	Bibbia e Oriente (Genoa)
BiRe	Bible Revue (Ravenna)
BJRL	Bulletin of the John Rylands Library (Manchester)
BLE	Bulletin de Littérature Ecclésiastique (Toulouse)
BR	Biblical Research (Chicago)

BTh	Biblical Theology (Belfast)
BThB	Biblical Theology Bulletin (Rome)
BTr	Bible Translator (London)
BTS	Bible et Terre Sainte (Paris)
BuK	Bibel und Kirche (Stuttgart)
BuL	Bibel und Liturgie (Klosterneuburg)
BVieC	Bible et Vie Chrétienne (Bruges)
BZ	Biblische Zeitschrift (Paderborn)
CahCER	Cahiers du Cercle Ernest-Renan (Paris)
CahJos	Cahiers de Joséphologie (Montreal)
CBQ	Catholic Biblical Quarterly (Washington)
ChrC	Christian Century (Chicago)
ChrTo	Christianity Today (Washington)
ChSt	Chicago Studies (Mundelein, Illinois)
CiCa	Civiltà Cattolica (Rome)
CiDi	Ciudad de Dios (Madrid)
ClM	Clergy Monthly (Ranchi)
ClR	Clergy Review (London)
CoTh	Collectanea Theologica (Warsaw)
CrCu	Cross Currents (West Nyack, New Jersey)
CrQ	Crozer Quarterly (Chester, Pennsylvania)
CSR	Christian Scholar's Review (St. Paul, Minnesota)
CThJ	Calvin Theological Journal (Grand Rapids, Michigan)
CThM	Concordia Theological Monthly (St. Louis, Missouri)
CV	Communio Viatorum (Praque)
DBM	Deltion Biblikon Meleton (Athens)
DDSR	Duke Divinity School Review (Durham, North Carolina)
DiThom	Divus Thomas (Poscenza)
DoLi	Doctrine and Life (Dublin)
DRev	Downside Review (Bath)
DTT	Dansk Teologisk Tidsskrift (Copenhagen)
DuRev	Dunwoodie Review (New York)
EFr	Estudios Fransiscanos (Madrid)
EphC	Ephemerides Carmeliticae (Rome)
EphL	Ephemerides Liturgicae (Rome)
EphM	Ephemerides Mariologicae (Madrid)
EphT	Ephemerides Theologicae Lovanienses (Louvain)
EQ	Evangelical Quarterly (London)
ER	Ecumenical Review (Geneva)
EstBi	Estudios Biblicos (Madrid)
EstEc	Estudios Eclesiásticos (Madrid)
EsVe	Escritos del Vedat (Torrente)
EsVie	Espirit et Vie (Langres)
ET	Expository Times (Birmingham)
ETh	Église et Théologie (Ottawa)

EThR	Études Théologiques et Religieuses (Montpelliar)
EuA	Erbe und Auftrag (Beuren)
EuD	Euntes Docete (Rome)
EvKomm	Evangelische Kommentare (Stuttgart)
EvTh	Evangelische Theologie (München)
Exp	The Expositor (London)
FrR	Freiburger Rundbrief (Freiburg)
FSt	Franziskanische Studien (Münster)
FZPhTh	Freiburger Zeitschrift für Philosphie und Theologie (Fribourg)
GOThR	Greek Orthodox Theological Review (Brookline, Massachusetts)
GPM	Göttinger Predigtmeditationen (Göttingen)
GRBS	Greek, Roman and Byzantine Studies (Durham, North Carolina)
GThT	Gereformeerd Theologisch Tijdschrift (Amsterdam)
GuL	Geist und Leben (München)
HerKor	Herder Korrespondenz (Freiburg)
Herm	Hermathena (Dublin)
HeyJ	Heythrop Journal (London)
HPR	Homiletic and Pastoral Review (New York)
HR	History of Religion (Chicago)
HThR	Harvard Theological Review (Cambridge, Massachusetts)
HUCA	Hebrew Union College Annual (Cincinnati)
IEJ	Israel Exploration Journal (Jerusalem)
IES	Indian Ecclesiastical Studies (Bangalore)
IJTh	Indian Journal of Theology (Serampore)
IKiZ	Internationale Kirchliche Zeitschrift (Bern)
IKZ	Internationale Katholische Zeitschrift (Rodenkirchen)
IndTheol Stu	Indian Theological Studies (Bangalore)
Interp	Interpretation (Richmond)
IThQ	Irish Theological Quarterly (Marynooth)
JAAR	Journal of the American Academy of Religion (Chambersburg, Pennsylvania)
JAC	Jahrbuch für Antike und Christentum (Münster)
JAOS	Journal of the American Oriental Society (Baltimore)
JBL	Journal of Biblical Literature (Missoula, Montana)
JEH	Journal of Ecclesiastical History (London)
JES	Journal of Ecumenical Studies (Philadelphia)
JEThS	Journal of the Evangelical Theological Society (Wheaton)
JHebS	Journal of Hebraic Studies (New York)
JHS	Journal of Hellenic Studies (London)
JJS	Journal of Jewish Studies (London)
JR	Journal of Religion (Chicago)
JRomS	Journal of Roman Studies (London)
JRTh	Journal of Religious Thought (Washington)

JSJ	Journal for the Study of Judaism (Leiden)
JSS	Journal of Semitic Studies (Manchester)
JThS	Journal of Theological Studies (Oxford)
KG	Katholische Gedanke (Bonn)
KuD	Kerygma und Dogma (Göttingen)
LiBi	Linguistica Biblica (Bonn)
LM	Lutherische Monatshefte (Hamburg)
LQ	Lutheran Quarterly (Gettysburg)
LR	Lutherische Rundschau (Geneva)
LSt	Louvain Studies (Louvain)
LThPh	Laval Théologique et Philosophique (Quebec)
LThQ	Lexington Theological Quarterly (Lexington, Kentucky)
LuVie	Lumière et Vie (Lyons)
LuVit	Lumen Vitae (Brussels)
LW	Lutheran World (Geneva)
MCh	Modern Churchman (Ludlow)
MisC	Miscelánea Comillas (Madrid)
MSR	Mélanges de Science Religieuse (Lille)
MTh	Melita Theologica (LaValetta)
MThZ	Münchener Theologische Zeitschrift (München)
NEAJTh	North East Asia Journal of Theology (Tokyo)
NedThT	Nederlands Theologisch Tijdschrift (The Hague)
NGTT	Nederuits Gereformeerde Teologiese Tydskrif (Stellenbosch)
NKZ	Neue kirchliche Zeitschrift (Erlangen)
NovT	Novum Testamentum (Leiden)
NRTh	Nouvelle Revue Théologique (Louvain)
NTS	New Testament Studies (Cambridge)
NTT	Norsk Teologisk Tidsskrift (Oslo)
NV	Nova et Vetera (Geneva)
NW	Neue Weg (Zürich)
OCP	Orientalia Christiana Periodica (Rome)
OKS	Ostkirchliche Studien (Würzburg)
OLZ	Orientalistische Literaturzeitung (Berlin)
PaCl	Palestra del Clero (Rovigo)
PEQ	Palestine Exploration Quarterly (London)
PSThJ	Perkins School of Theology Journal (Dallas)
PThR	Princeton Theological Review (Princeton)
RAM	Rassegna di Ascetica y Mistica (Florence)
RB	Revue Biblique (Jerusalem)
RBen	Revue Bénédictine (Maredsous)
RBL	Ruch Biblijny i Liturgiczny (Cracow)
RBR	Ricerche Bibliche e Religiose (Milan)
RCB	Revista de Cultura Biblica (São Paulo)
RCIA	Revue de Clerge African (Inkisi, Zaire)

RCT	Revista de Cultura Teologica (São Paulo)
REA	Revue des Études Augustiniennes (Paris)
REB	Revista Eclesiástica Brasileira (Petropolis)
RechSR	Recherches de Science Religieuse (Paris)
ReL	Religion in Life (Nashville)
REsp	Revista de Espiritualidad (Madrid)
RestQ	Restoration Quarterly (Abilene, Texas)
RET	Revista Española de Teología (Madrid)
RevBi	Revista Biblica (Buenos Aires)
RevEx	Review and Expositor (Louisville)
RevQ	Revue de Qumran (Paris)
RevR	Revue Réformée (Saint-Germain-en-Laye)
RevSR	Revue des Sciences Religieuses (Strasbourg)
RHE	Revue d'Histoire Ecclésiastique (Strasbourg)
RHPR	Revue d'Histoire et de Philosophie Religieuses (Strasbourg)
RHR	Revue de l'Histoire des Religions (Paris)
RHSp	Revue d'Histoire de la Spiritualité (Paris)
RivAC	Rivista di Archeologia Cristiana (Rome)
RivB	Rivista Biblica (Brescia)
RQ	Römische Quartalschrift (Freiburg)
RSLR	Rivista di Storia e Letteratura Religiosa (Turin)
RSPhTh	Revue des Sciences Philosophiques et Théologiques (Paris)
RSt	Religious Studies (London)
RT	Rassegna di Teologia (Naples)
RThAM	Recherches de Théologie Ancienne et Médiévale (Louvain)
RThL	Revue Théologique de Louvain (Louvain)
RThom	Revue Thomiste (Toulouse)
RThPh	Revue de Théologie et de Philosophie (Lausanne)
RThR	Reformed Theological Review (Hawthorn, Victoria)
RTK	Roczniki Teologiczno-Kanoniczne (Lublin)
RUO	Revue de l'Université d'Ottawa (Ottawa)
SaDo	Sacra Dottrina (Bologna)
SaDoBB	Sacra Dottrina Bolletino Bibliografico (Bologna)
SBFLA	Studii Biblici Franciscani Liber Annuus (Jerusalem)
SciE	Science et Esprit (Montreal)
ScrB	Scripture Bulletin (London)
ScrTh	Scripta Theologica (Pamplona)
ScuC	Scuola Cattolica (Milan)
SEA	Svensk Exegetisk Arsbok (Uppsala)
SEAJTh	South East Asia Journal of Theology (Singapore)
SJTh	Scottish Journal of Theology (Edinburgh)
SouJTh	Southwestern Journal of Theology (Fort Worth)
SThV	Studia Theologica Varsaviensia (Warsaw)

StLit	Studia Liturgica (Rotterdam)
StPa	Studia Patavina (Padua)
StPh	Studia Philonica (Chicago)
StR/SciR	Studies in Religion/Sciences Religieuses (Toronto)
StTh	Studia Theologica (Lund)
StZ	Stimmen der Zeit (München)
SVThQ	St. Vladimir's Theological Quarterly (Crestwood, New York)
SvTK	Svensk Teologisk Kvartalskrift (Lund)
TAik	Teologinen Aikakauskirja (Helsinki)
TB	Tyndale Bulletin (Cambridge)
Th	Theology: A Journal of Historic Christianity (London)
ThG	Theologie und Glaube (Paderborn)
ThLZ	Theologische Literaturzeitung (Leipzig)
ThPh	Theologie und Philosophie (Frankfurt)
ThQ	Theologische Quartalschrift (Tübingen)
ThR	Theologische Rundschau (Tübingen)
ThRv	Theologische Revue (Münster)
ThSK	Theologische Studien und Kritiken (Hamburg)
ThSt	Theological Studies (New York)
ThT	Theology Today (Princeton)
ThZ	Theologische Zeitschrift (Basel)
TRE	Theologische Realenzyklopädie (Berlin/New York: Walter de Gruyter)
TsTK	Tidsskrift for Teologi og Kirke (Oslo)
TT	Theologisch Tidschrift (Amsterdam)
TThZ	Trierer Theologische Zeitschrift (Trier)
TvTh	Tijdschrift voor Theologie (Nijmegen)
US	Una Sancta (Niederaltaich)
USQR	Union Seminary Quarterly Review (New York)
VChr	Vetera Christianorum (Bari)
VD	Verbum Domini (Rome)
VE	Vox Evangelica (London)
VF	Verkündigung und Forschung (München)
VieS	Vie Spirituelle (Paris)
VigChr	Vigiliae Christianae (Amsterdam)
VR	Vox Reformata (Geelong, Victoria)
VT	Vetus Testamentum (Leiden)
WThJ	Westminster Theological Journal (Philadelphia)
WuW	Wissenschaft und Weisheit (Düsseldorf)
ZAW	Zeitschrift für die Alttestamentliche Wissenschaft (Berlin)
ZDMG	Zeitschrift der Deutschen Morgenländischen Gesellschaft (Wiesbaden)

ZKG	Zeitschrift für Kirchengeschichte (Stuttgart)
ZKTh	Zeitschrift für Katholische Theologie (Innsbruck)
ZNW	Zeitschrift für die Neutestamentliche Wissenschaft (Berlin)
ZRGG	Zeitschrift für Religions-und Geistesgeschichte (Erlangen)
ZThK	Zeitschrift für Theologie und Kirche (Tübingen)
ZyMy	Zycie i Mysl (Warsaw)

Matthew

1-28 GAECHTER, P. Die literarische Kunst im Matthäus-Evangelium (1968) 12-14.

SELBY, D. J., Introduction to the New Testament (New York 1971) 121-124. ELLIS, P. F., Matthew: His Mind and His Message (Minnesota 1974) 28-31.

1:1-4:16 FRANZMANN, M. H., "Studies in Discipleship. I: The Calling of the Disciples (Mt. 4:18-22; 1:1-4:16)" CThM 31 (1960) 607-625. *KRENTZ, E. "The Extent of Matthew's Prologue. Toward the Structure of the First Gospel," JBL 83 (4, '64) 409-414. SCHWEIZER, E., Matthäus und seine Gemeinde (Stuttgart 1974) 1.3.1., 1.3.2.1, 1.3.2.2. KINGSBURY, J. D., Matthew: Structure, Christology, Kingdom (Philadelphia 1975) 11-17, 50-53.

1f EWALD, H. Die drei ersten Evangelien (1850) 168ff. VöGTLE, A. Das Evangelium und die Evangelien (1971) 65-68, 84-87.

1:1-25 *HOFMANS, F. "Maria altijd maagd," CollBrugGand 8 (4, '62) 475-94; 9 (1, '63) 53-78. *KRäMER, M. "Die Menschenwerdung Jesu Christi nach Matthäus (Mt 1). Sein Anliegen und sein literarisches Verfahren," Biblica 45 (1, '64) 1-50. *PASCUAL, E. "La Genealogia de Jesus segun S. Mateo," EstBib 23 (2, '64) 109-149.

1:1-18 *NEWMAN, B. M., Jr., "Matthew 1.1-18: Some Comments and a Suggested Restructuring" BTr 27 (1976) 209-12.

1:1-17 *LEMBERTZ, M. "Die Toledoth in Mt. 1, 1-17 und Lk 3, 33b ff" in: Festschrift Franz Dornseiff (1953) 201-225. M'NEILE, A. H. The Gospel According to St. Matthew (1955) 5f. *DUPONT, J. "La genealogia di Gesu secondo Matteo 1,1-17," BiOr 4 (1, '62) 3-6. STRECKER, G. Der Weg der Gerechtigkeit (1962) 90. HAHN, F. Christologische Hoheitstitel (1963) 242f, 373, 402. *SCHELKLE, K. H. "Die Frauen im Stammbaum Jesu," BuK 18 (4, '63) 113-15. *BRUNS, J. E. "Matthew's Genealogy of Jesus," BibleToday 1 (15, '64) 980-985. HENNECKE, E. & SCHNEEMELCHER, W. Neutestamentliche Apokryphen (1964) 320. *MORETON, M. J. "The Genealogy of Jesus," Studia Evangelica II (1964) 219-224. *RAMLOT, L. "Les généalogies bibliques. Un genre littéraire oriental," BVieC 60 ('64) 53-70. *LéON-DUFOUR, X. "Libro della Genesi di Gesu Cristo," RivB 13 (3, '65) 223-237. WARMERS, E. "Der Name über allen Namen," in: Kleine Predigt-Typologie III (1965) Schmidt, L. (ed.) 23-26. GAECHTER, P. Die literarische Kunst im Matthäus-Evangelium (1968) 16-18. SASS, G. Ungereimtes bei Matthäus (1968) 1-3. *SCHöLLIG, H. "Die Zählung der Generationen im matthäischen Stammbaum," ZNW 59 (3-4, '68) 261-268. JOHNSON, M.D. The Purpose of the Biblical Genealogies (1969) 146-228. BURGER, C. Jesus als Davidssohn (1970) 91-102. STEGEMANN, H. "Die des Uria," in: Tradition und Glaube (1971) Jeremias, G. (ed.) 246-76. SCHUBERT, K., Jesus im Lichte der Religionsgeschichte des Judentums (München 1973) 28-30. *ABEL, E. L. "The Genealogies of Jesus HO CHRISTOS" NTS 20 (1974) 203-210. *NINEHAM, D. E., "The Genealogy in St. Matthew's Gospel and its Significance for the Study of the Gospels" BJRL 58 (1976) 421-44. "Adam" in: TRE I (1977) 416. *LACH, J., "Historyczność genealogii Chrystusa w Mt. 1, 1-17 (Geschichtlichkeit des Stammbaumes Jesu bei Mt. 1, 1-17)" SThV 15 (1977) 19-35. NINEHAM, D. E. Explorations in Theology 1 (London 1977). *SCHNIDER, F. and STENGER, W., "Die Frauen im Stammbaum Jesu nach Matthäus. Strukturale Beobachtungen zu Mt. 1, 1-17" BZ 23 (1979) 187-96. SWIDLER, L., Biblical Affirmations of Woman (Philadelphia 1979) 246, 278.

1:1-16　*SEETHALER, P. "Eine kleine Bemerkung zu den Stammbäumen Jesu nach Matthäus und Lukas," BZ 16 (2, '72) 256-257. *GORDON, C. H., "Paternity at Two Levels" JBL 96 (1977) 101. *GORDON, C. H., "The Double Paternity of Jesus" Biblical Archeology Review 4 (1978) 26-27.

1:1-8a　*GRYGLEWICZ, F. "The St. Adalbert Codex of the Gospels," NTS 11 ('64-65) 259f.

1:1-7　*WALKER, N. "The Alleged Matthean Errata," NTS 9 ('62-63) 391f.

1:1　STONEHOUSE, N. B. The Witness of Matthew and Mark to Christ (1944) 124, 224. KILPATRICK, G. D. The Origins of the Gospel According to St. Matthew (1950) 52. *BARTINA, S. "Jesus, el Cristo, ben David ben Abraham (Mt 1, 1). Los appelidos de la Biblia y su traduccion al castellano," EstBib 18 (4, '59) 375-393. STRECKER, G. Der Weg der Gerechtigkeit (1962) 118, 126. HAHN, F. Christologische Hoheitstitel (1963) 208, 245, 319, 402. HUMMEL, R. Die Auseinandersetzung zwischen Kirche und Judentum im Matthäusevangelium (1963) 116, 112ff. MARXSEN, W. Mark the Evangelist (1969) 25, 50, 141, 142. *MALINA, B. J. "Literary Structure and Form of Mt 28:16-20," NTS 17 ('70-71) 99f. FRANKEMöLLE, H. Jahwebund und Kirche Christi. Studien zur Form- und Traditionsgeschichte des "Evangeliums" nach Matthäus (Münster 1974) 167, 170, 217, 311-14, 318-21, 360-65. TALBERT, C. H., Literary Patterns, Theological Themes and the Genre of Luke-Acts (Missoula 1974) 123. KINGSBURY, J. D., Matthew: Structure, Christology, Kingdom (Philadelphia

1975) 9-12. *TATUM, W. B., "The Origin of Jesus Messiah' (Matt. 1:1, 18a): Matthew's Use of the Infancy Traditions" JBL 96 (1977) 523-535. *CHOPINEAU, J., "Un notarikon en Matthieu 1/1. NOTE sur la généalogie de l'évangile de Matthieu" EThR 53 (1978) 269-70.

1:2-2:23 SCHUBERT, K., Jesus im Lichte der Religionsgeschichte des Judentums (München 1973) 28-33.

1:2-17 BLASS, F. Philosophy of the Gospels (1898) 171f. WILKENS, J. Einführung in das Evangelium nach Matthäus I (1934) 25-27. STRECKER, G. Der Weg der Gerechtigkeit (1962) 38, 89. *MALINA, B. J. "Literary Structure and Form of Mt 28:16-20," NTS 17 ('70-71) 99f.

1:2-16 FARRER, A. St. Matthew and St. Mark (1954) 183. *VöGTLE, A. "Die Genealogie Mt. 1, 2-16 und die matthäische Kindheitsgeschichte (I. Teil)," BZ 8 (1, '64) 45-58. VöGTLE, A. Das Evangelium und die Evangelien (1971) 57-137.

1:2ff VöGTLE, A., "Die Genealogie und die matthäische Kindheitsgeschichte (II. Teil)" BZ 9 (1965) 32-49. FRANKEMöLLE, H., Jahwebund und Kirche Christi. Studien zur Form- und Traditionsgeschichte des "Evangeliums" nach Matthäus (Münster 1974) 309, 311-18. "Apokalyptik" in: TRE III (1978) 253.

1:2 CONZELMANN, H. and LINDEMANN, A., Arbeitsbuch zum Neuen Testament (Tübingen 1975) 92, 335-37. METZGER, B. M., The Early Versions of the New Testament. Their Origin, Transmission, and Limitations (Oxford) 1977) 172, 243.

1:3 HAHN, F. Christologische Hoheitstitel (1963) 243. McNAMARA, M. The New Testament and the Palestinian Targum to the Pentateuch (1966) 140. NICKELS, P. Targum and the New Testament (1967) 15. METZGER, B. M., The Early Versions of the New Testament. Their Origin Transmission, and Limitations (Oxford 1977) 242.

1:4 HAHN, F. Christologische Hoheitstitel (1963) 243.

1:5 *YAKOWITCH, Y., "Rahab als Mutter des Boas in der Jesus-Genealogie (Matth. I 5)" NovT 17 (1975) 1-5. METZGER, B. M., The Early Versions of the New Testament. Their Origin, Transmission, and Limitations (Oxford 1977) 172. HANSON, A. T., "Rahab the Harlot in Early Christian Tradition" Journal for the Study of the New Testament 1 (1978) 53-60.

1:6 HAHN, F. Christologische Hoheitstitel (1963) 243. HUMMEL, R. Die Auseinandersetzung zwischen Kirche and Judentum im Matthäusevangelium (1963) 114.

1:7-11   HUMMEL, R. Die Auseinandersetzung zwischen Kirche und Judentum im Matthäusevangelium (1963) 114.

1:7   HAHN, F. Christologische Hoheitstitel (1963) 243.

1:8-10:42   *GRYGLEWICZ, F. "The St. Adalbert Codex of the Gospels," NTS 11 ('64-65) 269f.

1:8-6:5   *GRYGLEWICZ, F. "The St. Adalbert Codex of the Gospels," NTS 11 ('64-65) 259f.

1:8   KILPATRICK, G. D. The Origins of the Gospel According to St. Matthew (1950) 52. METZER, B. M., The Early Versions of the New Testament. Their Origin, Transmission, and Limitations (Oxford 1977) 42.

1:11f   VöGTLE, A. Das Evangelium und die Evangelien (1971) 97-99.

1:11   KILPATRICK, G. D. The Origins of the Gospel According to St. Matthew (1950) 52. STRECKER, G. Der Weg der Gerechtigkeit (1962) 383. VöGTLE, A. Das Evangelium und die Evangelien (1971) 95-97.

1:12-15   KILPATRICK, G. D. The Origins of the Gospel According to St. Matthew (1950) 52.

1:12   METZGER, B. M., The Early Versions of the New Testament. Their Origin, Transmission, and Limitations (Oxford 1977) 172.

1:14   YATES, J. E. The Spirit and the Kingdom (1963) 181ff.

1:15, 18   RAYAN, S., The Holy Spirit: Heart of the Gospel and Christian Hope (New York 1978) 32f.

1:16f   *LEANEY, R. "The Birth Narratives in St. Luke and St. Matthew," NTS 8 ('61-62) 164f.

1:16.18.20   BETZ, H. D. Lukian von Samosata und das Neue Testament (1961) 53, 56, 105, 106.

1:16   CONYBEARE, F. C., "Note on Mt. 1:16" ZNW 13 (1912) 171. KILPATRICK, G. D. The Origins of the Gospel According to St. Matthew (1950) 52. KOEHLER, L. Eine Handvoll Neues Testament, Ehrfurcht vor dem Leben (1954) 80. M'NEILE, A. H. The Gospel According to St. Matthew (1955) 4f. *METZGER, B. M. "On the Citation of Variant Readings of Matt. 1:16," JBL 77 (4, '58) 361-363. BLAIR, E. P. Jesus in the Gospel of Matthew (1960) 55. STRECKER, G. Der Weg der Gerechtigkeit (1962) 53,126. HAHN, F. Christologische Hoheitstitel (1963) 208,319. HUMMEL, F. Die Auseinandersetzung zwischen Kirche und Judentum im Matthäusevangelium (1963) 112ff. BLAIR, H. A. "Matthew 1, 16 and the Matthean Geneaology," in: Studia Evangelica II (1964) Cross, F. L. (ed.) 149-154. VöGTLE, A. Das Evangelium und die Evangelien (1971) 99-102. *PESCH, R.

"Der Gottessohn im matthäischen Evangelienprolog (Mt 1-2). Beobachtungen zu den Zitationsformeln der Reflexionszitate," Biblica 48 ('67) 409-11. *METZGER, B. M. "The Text of Matthew 1:16," in: New Testament and Early Christian Literature (1972) Aune, D. E. (ed.) 16-24. CONZELMANN, H. and LINDEMANN, A., Arbeitsbuch zum Neuen Testament (Tübingen 1975) 60. METZGER, B. M., The Early Versions of the New Testament. Their Origin, Transmission, and Limitations (Oxford 1977) 40, 150.

1:17 STAEHELIN, E. Die Verkündigung des Reiches Gottes in der Kirche Jesu Christi I (1951) 347, 373. HAHN, F. Christologische Hoheitstitel (1963) 224. HUMMEL, F. Die Auseinandersetzung zwischen Kirche und Judentum im Matthäusevangelium (1963) 113ff. *DRIVER, G. "The Number of the Beast," in: Bibel und Qumran (1968) Wagner, S. (ed.) 77. VöGTLE, A. Das Evangelium und die Evangelien (1971) 87-92. FRANKEMöLLE, H., Jahwebund und Kirche Christi. Studien zur Form und Traditionsgeschichte des "Evangeliums" nach Matthäus (Münster 1974) 311-14, 318-21. METZGER, B. M., The Early Versions of the New Testament (Oxford 1977) 178.

1:18-2:23 TAYLOR, V. The Formation of the Gospel Tradition (1949) 152f. PARKER, P. The Gospel Before Mark (1953) 121-122. *CROSSAN, D. M. "Structure & Theology of Mt. 1:18-23," CahJos 16 (1, '68) 119-135. STRECKER, G. Der Weg der Gerechtigkeit (1962) 51-54, 58, 147. GAECHTER, P. Die literarische Kunst im Matthäus-Evangelium (1968) 24-25. *DAVIS, C. T. "Tradition and Redaction in Matthew 1:18-23," JBL 90 (4, '71) 404-21. SAITO, T., Die Mosevorstellungen im Neuen Testament (Bern 1977) 58-71, 137, 142f, 146f, 166f. *DOWN, M. J., "The Matthaean Birth Narratives: Matthew 1:18-2:23" ET 90 (1978) 51-52. RUETHER, R. R., Mary-The Feminine Face of the Church (London 1979) 25-30.

1:18ff *USENER, H. ZNW 4 (1903) 1-21. CLEMEN, C. Primitive Christianity and Its Non-Jewish Sources (1912) 288f. BLAIR, E. P. Jesus in the Gospel of Matthew (1960) 79. STRECKER, G. Der Weg der Gerechtigkeit (1962) 77. HAHN, F. Christologische Hoheitstitel (1963) 278. BRUNNER, E. Dogmatik II (1946) 415ff.

1:18-25 BüCHSEL, D. F. Der Geist Gottes im Neuen Testament (1926) 191-196. WILKENS, J. Einführung in das Evangelium nach Matthäus I (1934) 27-32. *ENSLIN, M. S. "The Christian Stories of the Nativity," JBL LIX ('40) 314-338. HIRSCH, E. Frühgeschichte des Evangeliums (1941) 324-326. KNOX, W. L. Some Hellenistic Elements in Primitive Christianity (1944) 22-25. STONEHOUSE, N. B. The Witness of Matthew and Mark to Christ (1944) 125. KILPATRICK, G. D. The Origins of the Gospel According to St. Matthew (1950) 52. *DELORME, J. "Marie habitait-elle chez Joseph?" AmiCler 66 (51, '56) 774. KNOX, W. L. The Sources of the Synoptic Gospels. Vol. II: St. Luke & St. Matthew (1957) 122-24. *RAHNER, K. "Nimm das Kind und seine Mutter,' GuL 30 (1, '57) 14-22. BORNKAMM-BARTH-HELD, UEberlieferung und Auslegung im Matthäus-Evangelium (1961) 127, 220, 226. HAHN, F. Christologische Hoheitstitel (1963) 268, 274f, 314f. HUMMEL, R. Die Auseinandersetzung zwischen Kirche und Judentum im Matthäusevangelium (1963) 111f. KRAEMER, M., "Zwei Probleme aus Mt. 1:18-25: Vers 20 und 25" Salesianum 26 (1964) 303-33. KRÄMER, M. "Die globale Analyse des Stiles in Mt 1, 18-25," Biblica 45 (1-2, '64) 4-22. MISKOTTE, K. H. in: Herr, tue meine Lippen auf (1964) Eichholz, G. (ed.) 34ff. PIPER, O. A. "The Virgin Birth. The Meaning of the Gospell Accounts" Interpretation 18 (2, '64) 132-48. WILKINSON, J. Apologetic Aspects of the Virgin Birth of Jesus Christ," SJTh 17 (2, '64) 159-81. JOHNSON, S. L. "The Genesis of Jesus," BiblSa 122 (488, '65) 331-42. ROBINSON, W. C. "A Re-study of the Virgin Birth of Christ. God's Son was born of a Woman: Mary's Son Prayed 'Abba Father'," EQ 37 (4, '65) 198-211. DAVIES, W. D., The Sermon on the Mount (Cambridge 1966) 13f. LOCHMAN, J. M., "Das Wunder der Weihnacht" Theologická příloha Křesť 'anská revue 5 (1967) 97-102. GERMANO, J., "Nova et vetera in pericopam de sancto Joseph" VD 46 (1968) 351-60. *DANIELI, G. "A proposito della origini della tradizione sinottica sulla concezione verginale," DiThom 72 (3, '69) 312-31. LORENZ, F. Streit um Jesus (1969) 27-30. TRILLING, W. Christusverkündigung in den Synoptischen Evangelien (1969) 13. BURGER, C. Jesus als Davidssohn (1970) 102-104. *MARTIN, F. CBQ 32 (1, '70) 131-34. *WANSBROUGH, H. "Event and Intrepretation: VIII. The Adoption of Jesus," ClR 55 (12, '70) 921-928. *BROER, I. "Die Bedeutung der 'Jungfrauengeburt' im Matthäusevangelium," BuL 12 (4, '71) 248-260. *RASCO, E. "El anuncio a José (Mt 1, 18-25)," CahJos 19 (1-4, '71) 84-103. VöGTLE, A. Das Evangelium und die Evangelien (1971) 70-73. LOCHMAN, J. M., Das Radikale Erbe (Zürich 1972) 264-73. *GRAYSTON, K., "Matthieu 1:18-25. Essai d'interprétation" RThPh 23 (1973) 221-32. *FORD, J. M., "Mary's Virginitas Post-Partum and Jewish Law" Biblica 54 (1973) 269-72. *STRAMARE, T., "Giuseppe, 'uomo giusto', in Mt 1, 18-25" RivB 21 (1973) 287-300. *VALLAURI, E., "L'esegesi moderna di fronte alla verginità di Maria" Laurentianum 14 (1973) 445-80. FRANKEMöLLE, H., Jahwebund und Kirche Christi (Münster 1974) 13-15, 166, 310, 321. GOULDER, M. D.,

Midrash and Lection in Matthew (London 1974) 234f. *DUBARLE, A. M., "La conception virginale et la citation d'Is., VII, 14 dans l'évangile de Matthieu" RevBi 85 (1978) 362-80. SWIDLER, L., Biblical Affirmations of Woman (Philadelphia 1979) 241, 264.

1:18-24   M'NEILE, A. H. The Gospel According to St Matthew (1955) 10-13. HENNECKE, E. & SCHNEEMELCHER, W. Neutestamentliche Apokryphen (1964) I: 284f, II: 467. *BOUTON, A. "C'est toi qui lui donneras le nom de Jésus. Mt 1, 18-24," AssS 8 ('72) 17-25. *RAHNER, K., Was sollen wir jetzt tun? Vier Meditationen (Freiburg - Vienna 1974).

1:18-22   *LéON-DUFOUR, X. "Le juste Joseph," NRTh 81 (3, '59) 225-31.

1:18-21   HOLLENWEGER, W. J./TONKS, H., in: Predigtstudien für das Kirchenjahr 1978/1979 (Berlin 1978) 56-62.

1:18-20   *PESCH, R. "Der Gottessohn im matthäischen Evangelienprolog (Mt 1-2). Beobachtungen zu den Zitationsformeln der Reflexionszitate," Biblica 48 ('67) 416-19. KILPATRICK, G. D. The Origins of the Gospel According to St. Matthew (1950) 52.

1:18   *FOURNELLE, G. G. "Our Lady's Marriage to Saint Joseph," MarSt 7 ('56) 122-129. KNOX, W. L. The Sources of the Synoptic Gospels. Vol. II: St. Luke & St. Matthew (1957) 122. DE KRUIJF, T., Der Sohn Des Lebendigen Gottes (Rome 1962) 106f, 109, 135. STRECKER, G. Der Weg der Gerechtigkeit (1962) 52f, 56f, 125f. HUMMEL, F. Die Auseinandersetzung zwischen Kirche und Judentum im Matthäusevangelium (1963) 112ff. SCHNEIDER, G., Anfragen an das Neue Testament (Essen 1971) 106-108. KINGSBURY, J. D., Matthew: Structure, Christology, Kingdom (Philadelphia 1975) 96, 98. *TATUM, W. B., " 'The Origin of Jesus Messiah' (Mt. 1:1· 18a): Matthew's Use of the Infancy Traditions" JBL 96 (1977) 523-35. SCHWEIZER, E., Heiliger Geist (Stuttgart 1978) 77-79. LAGRAND, J., "How was the Virgin Mary 'Like a Man' " NovT 22 (1980) 97-107.

1:19f   STRECKER, G. Der Weg der Gerechtigkeit (1962) 54.

1:19   *SOTTOCORNOLA, F. "Tradition and the doubt of St. Joseph concerning Mary's virginity," Marianum 19 (1, '57) 127-141. SPICO, C. " 'Joseph, son mari, étant juste. . .' (Mt. 1, 19)," RevBi 71 (2, '64) 206-214. HILL, D. "A Note on Matthew 1:19," ET 76 (4, '65) 133-134. GERMANO, J. M. "Nova et vetera in pericopam de sancto Ioseph (Mt 1, 18-25)," VerbDom 46 (6, '68) 351-360. SICARI, A. A. " 'Ioseph Iustus' (Matteo 1, 19): La storia dell'interpretazione e le nouve prospettive," CahJos 19 (1-4, '71) 62-83. FRANKEMöLLE, H., Jahwebund

und Kirche Christi (Münster 1974) 173, 277, 281, 283, 295. METZGER, B. M., The Early Versions of the New Testament (Oxford 1977) 34. *TOSATO, A., "Joseph, Being a Just Man (Matt 1:19)" CBQ 41 (1979) 547-51.

1:20ff   PETZKE, G. Die Traditionen über Apollonius von Tyana und das Neue Testament (1970) 137, 163, 206.

1:20-25   SCHILLE, G. Frühchristliche Hymnen (1965) 133.

1:20-23   DAVIES, W. D., The Sermon on the Mount (Cambridge 1966) 77f.

1:20f   STRECKER, G. Der Weg der Gerechtigkeit (1962) 55.

1:20-21   PELLETIER, A. "L'Annonce à Joseph," Rech SR 54 (1, '66) 67-68. BAGATTI, B., "L'interpretazione mariana di Apocalisse 12, 1-6 nel II secolo" Marianum 40 (1978) 153-159.

1:20   STONEHOUSE, N. B. The Witness of Matthew and Mark to Christ (1944) 124, 201, 224. STRECKER, G. Der Weg der Gerechtigkeit (1962) 52, 54f. HAHN, F. Christologische Hoheitstitel (1963) 73, 245, 274. KRäMER, M. "Die Menschenwerdung Jesu Christi nach Matthäus (Mt 1). Sein Anliegen und sein literarisches Verfahren," Biblica 45 (1-2, '64) 23-34. DAVIES, W. D., The Sermon on the Mount (Cambridge 1966) 15, 77. KINGSBURY, J. D., Matthew: Structure, Christology, Kingdom (Philadelphia 1975) 43-46. METZGER, B. M., The Early Versions of the New Testament (Oxford 1977) 315, 318. SWIDLER, L., Biblical Affirmations of Woman (Philadelphia 1979) 56.

1:21-23   BRENNAN, J. P. "Virgin and Child in Isaiah 7:14," Bible Today 1 (15, '64) 968-74.

1:21, 23, 25   GERMANO, J. M. "Privilegium nominis messianici a S. Joseph imponendi (Is 7, 14; Mt 1, 21, 23, 25)," VerbDom 47 (3, '69) 151-62.

1:21   KILPATRICK, G. D. The Origins of the Gospel According to St. Matthew (1950) 53, 54, 57, 93, 105, 107. FARRER, A. St. Matthew and St. Mark (1954) 178. BEST, E. One Body in Christ (1955) 124. NEPPER-CHRISTENSEN, P. Das Matthäusevangelium. Ein Judenchristliches Evangelium? (1958) 84, 85, 86, 87, 158, 159. BLAIR, E. P. Jesus in the Gospel of Matthew (1960) 57, 79. STRECKER, G. Der Weg der Gerechtigkeit (1962) 54-56, 74, 90, 115, 149. HAHN, F. Christologische Hoheitstitel (1963) 243. HUMMEL, F. Die Auseinandersetzung zwischen Kirche und Judentum im Matthäusevangelium (1963) 136f, 145. HAHN, F. Das Verständnis der Mission im Neuen Testament (1965) 108. BRAUN, H. Qumran und NT II (1966) 65, 76, 81. FRANKEMöLLE, H. Jahwebund und Kirche Christi

(Münster 1974) 71, 95, 109, 211-18 232, 309, 314. LUTHER, M., in: Luther's Works Vol. 52, Sermons II (Philadelphia 1974) 157f. KINGSBURY, J. D., Matthew: Structure, Christology, Kingdom (Philadelphia 1975) 42-44. METZGER, B. M., The Early Versions of the New Testament (Oxford 1977) 254, 458.

1:22f STONEHOUSE, N. B. The Witness of Matthew and Mark to Christ (1944) 190. ENSLIN, M. S. The Literature of the Christian Movement (1956) 397f. ROTHFUCHS, W. Die Erfüllungszitate des Matthäus-Evangeliums (1969) 57-60.

1:22 STONEHOUSE, N. B. The Witness of Matthew and Mark to Christ (1944) 201. KILPATRICK, G. D. The Origins of the Gospel According to St. Matthew (1950) 93. BLAIR, E. P. Jesus in the Gospel of Matthew (1960) 56, 90. STRECKER, G. Der Weg der Gerechtigkeit (1962) 50, 74. SCHWEIZER, E. Neotestamentica (1963) 399. HAHN, F. Christologische Hoheitstitel (1963) 73. HUMMEL, R. Die Auseinandersetzung zwischen Kirche und Judentum im Matthäusevangelium (1963) 131, 134. DAVIES, W. D., The Sermon on the Mount (Cambridge 1966) 77. PESCH, R. "Der Gottessohn im matthäischen Evangelienprolog (Mt 1-2). Beobachtungen zu den Zitationsformeln der Reflexionszitate," Biblica 48 ('67) 395-420. FRANKEMöLLE, H., Jahwebund und Kirche Christi (Münster 1974) 321, 389, 393. METZGER, B. M., The Early Versions of the New Testament (Oxford 1977) 146.

1:23-25 SPARKS, I. A. "A New Uncial Fragment of St. Matthew," JBL 88 (2, '69) 201-202. JUNACK, K. "Zu einem neuentdeckten Unzialfragment des Matthäus-Evangeliums," NTS 16 ('69-70) 284-88.

1:23 STONEHOUSE, N. B. The Witness of Matthew and Mark to Christ (1944) 127. KILPATRICK, G. D. The Origins of the Gospel According to St. Matthew (1950) 53, 54, 57, 93, 105. PARKER, P. The Gospel Before Mark (1953) 182-83. *BRATCHER, R. G. "A Study of Isaiah 7:15. Its Meaning and Use in the Masoretic Text, the Septuagint and the Gospel of Matthew," BTr 9 (3, '58) 98-125. TRILLING, W. Das wahre Israel (1959) 26f. BLAIR, E. P. Jesus in the Gospel of Matthew (1960) 39, 46, 68, 90. LINDARS, B. New Testament Apologetic (1961) 176, 213f, 260. STRECKER, G. Der Weg der Gerechtigkeit (1962) 29, 49, 50, 53, 55f, 58, 67, 71, 83f, 90, 213. WALKER, N. "The Alleged Matthaean Errata," NTS 9 ('62-63) 392. McNamara, M. "The Emmanuel Prophecy and Its Context-III," Scripture 15 (31, '63) 80-88. BRAUN, H. Qumran und NT II (1966) 80, 88, 267, 305, 306. BLACK, M. An Aramaic Approach to the Gospels and Acts (1967) 126f. MALINA, B. J. "Literary Structure and Form of Mt. 28:16-20," NTS 17 ('70-71) 99f. del OLMO LETE, G. "La profecia del

Emmanuel (Is. 7, 10-17). Estado actual de la interpretacion," EphM 22 (3-4, '72) 357-385. KLIJN, A. F. J./REININK, G. J., Patristic Evidence for Jewish-Christian Sects (Leiden 1973) 53. KüMMEL, W. G. Einleitung in das Neue Testament (1973) 81-83. LANGE, J. Das Erscheinen des Auferstandenen im Evangelium nach Mattäus (Würzburg 1973) 263, 328-30, 342, 344, 348, 495. FRANKEMöLLE, H., Jahwebund und Kirche Christi (Münster 1974) 12-21, 166, 212, 215, 217, 309, 314, 327. KINGSBURY, J. D., Matthew: Structure, Christology, Kingdom (Philadelphia 1975) 49-53, 77-80, 123-25, 161-63. *WILLIS, J. T., "The Meaning of Isaiah 7:14 and Its Application in Matthew 1:23" RestQ 21 (1978) 1-18.

1:24f STRECKER, G. Der Weg der Gerechtigkeit (1962) 54, 200. HAHN, F. Christologische Hoheitstitel (1963) 73.

1:25 BLASS, F. Philosophy of the Gospels (1898) 87ff. STRECKER, G. Der Weg der Gerechtigkeit (1962) 52, 53, 54, 90. KRäMER, M. "Die Menschenwerdung Jesu Christi nach Matthäus (Mt 1). Sein Anliegen und sein literarisches Verfahren," Biblica 45 (1-2, '64) 34-45. BLINZLER, J., Die Brüder und Schwestern Jesu (Stuttgart 1967) 50-56.*VöGTLE, A. "Mt 1, 25 und die Virginitas B. M. Virginis post partum," ThQ 147 (1, '67) 28-39. *TAVARES, A., Da Mariologia à Cristologia (Mt 1, 25) (Lisbon 1972). *TAVARES, A., Estudo de Mt. 1, 25 na tradicao patrística e nas perspectivas da exegese actual (Rome 1972). *GERMANO, J. M., "Et non cognoscebat eam donec. . . 'Inquisitio super sensu spirituali seu mystico Mt. 1, 25" Marianum 35 (1973) 184-240. OBERLINNER, L., Historische Ueberlieferung und christologische Aussage (Stuttgart 1975) 51-57. METZGER, B. M., The Early Versions of the New Testament (Oxford 1977) 39.

2-6 *SQUILLACI, D. "Il mistero di Betlem nel profeta Michea (5, 2-5a)," PaCl 41 (15, '62) 763-66.

2 FRAENKEL, S., "Zu Mt 2" ZNW 8 (1907) 241-42. NESTLE, E., "Zu Mt. 2" ZNW 8 (1907) 73-74. FEINE, D. P. & BEHM, D. J. Einleitung in das Neue Testament (1950) 43f. KILPATRICK, G. D. The Origins of the Gospel According to St. Matthew (1950) 53, 54. M'NEILE, A. H. The Gospel According to St Matthew (1955) 22-24. KNOX, W. L. The Sources of the Synoptic Gospels. Vol. II: St Luke & St Matthew (1957) 122-25. *BRUNS, J. E. "The Magi Episode in Matthew

2," CBQ 23 (1, '61) 51-54. DE KRUIJF, Th., Der Sohn des lebendigen Gottes (Rome 1962) 106, 107, 109, 135. VöGTLE, A. "Das Schicksal des Messiaskindes. Zur Auslegung und Theologie von Mt 2," BuL 6 (4, '65) 246-279. BRAUN, H. Qumran und NT II (1966) 77, 311. *BISHOP, E. F. F. "Some Reflections on Justin Martyr and the Nativity Narratives," EQ 39 (1, '67) 30-39. MALINA, B. "Matthew 2 and Is 41, 2-3: a possible relationship?" SBFLA 17 ('67) 290-302. NICKELS, P. Targum and New Testament (1967) 15. KAMPHAUS, F. Von der Exegese zur Predigt (1968) 236-240. VöGTLE, A., "Das Schicksal des Messiaskindes" also: Theologisches Jahrbuch Leipzig 11 (1968) 126-59. NELLESSEN, E. Das Kind und seine Mutter (1969). KüNZI, M. Das Naherwartungslogion Matthäus 10, 23 (1970) 44f. *WANSBROUGH, H. "Event and Interpretation: VI. The Childhood of Jesus," ClR 55 (2, '70) 112-19. VöGTLE, A. Messias und Gottessohn (1971) 20-41, 61-64, 65-80. VöGTLE, A. Das Evangelium und die Evangelien (1971) 75-84. HENGEL, M., and MERKEL, H., "Die Magier aus dem Osten und die Flucht nach Ägypten (Mt 2) im Rahmen der antiken Religionsgeschichte und der Theologie des Matthäus" in: Orientierungen an Jesus. Für Josef Schmid (Freiburg 1973) 139-69. DRURY, C., " 'Who's in, Who's out' " in: M. Hooker and C. Hickling (eds.) What about the New Testament (London 1975) 223-33. KINGSBURY, J. D., Matthew: Structure, Christology, Kingdom (Philadelphia 1975) 44-48. *SALVONI, F., "La visita dei Magi e la fuga in Egitto" RBR 14 (1979) 171-201.

2:1ff   NEPPER-CHRISTENSEN, P. Das Matthäuevangelium. Ein Judenchristliches Evangelium? (1958) 19, 22, 200. BLAIR, E. P. Jesus in the Gospel of Matthew (1960) 79. VISSER'T HOOFT, W. A. "Die Magier und die Mission," in: Basileia (1961) Schmidt, K. L. (ed.) 208-11. STRECKER, G. Der Weg der Gerechtigkeit (1962) 200. PETZKE, G. Die Traditionen über Apollonius von Tyana und das Neue Testament (1970) 138, 164, 192.

2:1-23   BULTMANN, R. The History of the Synoptic Tradition (1963) 292-293, 304. BETTENCOURT, E. "Os Magos, Herodes e Jesus," RCB 5 (10-11, '68) 30-42.

2:1-18   BURGER, C. Jesus als Davidssohn (1970) 104f.

2:1-12   DIETERICH, A. "Die Weisen aus dem Morgenlande," ZNW (1902) 1-14. WILKENS, J. Einführung in das Evangelium nach Matthäus I (1934) 34-46. MARSH-EDWARDS, J. C. "The Magi in Tradition and Art," IrER 85 ('56) 1-9. RICHARDS, H. J. "The Three Kings (Mt II 1-12)," Scripture 8 ('56) 23-28. EICHHOLZ, G. Herr, tue meine Lippen auf (1957) 44-47.

DENIS, A. -M. "L'adoration des Mages vue par S. Matthieu," NRTh 82 (1, '60) 32-39. SQUILLACI, D. "I Magi," PaCl 39 (1, '60) 16-20. MERKEL, F. GPM 15 ('60-61) 53ff. DOERNE, M. Er kommt auch noch Heute (1961) 31-33. GALBIATI, E. "Esegesi degli Evangeli festivi. L'Adorazione dei Magi (Matt. 2, 1-12). (Festa dell'Epifania)," BiOr 4 (1, '62) 20-29. *STRANGE, M. "King Herod the Great in a Representative Role," Bible Today 1 (3, '62) 188-93. HAHN, F. Christologische Hoheitstitel (1963) 268f, 275, 277f. SCHOENBERG, M. W. "Why Epiphany?" HPR 64 (3, '63) 222-230. GIBBS, J. M. "Purpose and Pattern in Matthew's use of the Title 'Son of David'," NTS 10 ('63-64) 463f. HAHN, F. Das Verständnis der Mission im Neuen Testament (1965) 31. RIEDL, J., "Sie fanden das Kind mit Maria, seiner Mutter" Am Tisch des Wortes 7 (1965) 27-43. HENRY, A., "La visite des Mages" Terre sainte 1 (1966) 2-4. *GAECHTER, P. "Die Magierperikope (Mt 2, 1-12)," ZKTh 90 (3, '68) 257-95. KAMPHAUS, F. Von der Exegese zur Predigt (1968) 280-96. McNAMARA, M. "Were the Magi Essenes?" IrER 110 (6, '68) 305-28. SOUBIGOU, L. "A Narracao da Epifania segundo Sao Mateus," RCB 5, (10-11, '68) 8-14. ROSENBERG, R. A. "The 'Star of the Messiah' Reconsidered," Biblica 53 (1, '72) 105-109. ZANI, L. "Influsso del genere letterario midrashico su Mt 2, 1-12," StPa 19 (2, '72) 257-320. STUHLMACHER, P. GPM 27/1 ('72-73) 63-70. SCHUBERT, K., Jesus im Lichte der Religionsgeschichte des Judentums (Wien 1973) 30-32. GOULDER, M. D. Midrash and Lection in Matthew (London 1974) 180, 236ff, 339. *PAX, E., "Spuren der Nabatäer im Neuen Testament" BiLe 15 (1974) 193-206. *BROWN, R. E., "The Meaning of the Magi; The Significance of the Star" Worship 49 (1975) 574-82. BLOCH, R., "Midrash" in: W. S. Green (ed.) Approaches to Ancient Judaism (Missoula 1978) 48. *SCHMAHL, G., "Magier aus dem Osten und die Heiligen Drei Könige" TThZ 87 (1978) 295-303. "Astrologie" in: TRE 4 (1979) 309. *WATSON, J. K., "La naissance du dieu chrétien et la nova de l'an - 5" CahCER 27 (1979) 2-8.

2:1-11   SCHMIDT, Ph. "Etwa über den Stern der Weisen," Klerusblatt 35 ('55) 507-508. TRUMPP, J. "Der Stern der Weisen aus dem Morgenland," Standard 12 ('57) ed. by the Standard Telephon und Radio AG., Zürich 12-15. J. S. "Der Stern von Betlehem," GuL 36 (6, '63) 462-65. SCHILLE, G. Frühchristliche Hymnen (1965) 136.

2:1-8   NICKELS, P. Targum and New Testament (1967) 15.

2:1-6   BLAIR, E. P. Jesus in the Gospel of Matthew (1960) 133. GOPPELT, L., Theologie des Neuen Testaments I (Göttingen 1975) 73-74.

2:1-5   HENNECKE, E, & SCHNEEMELCHER, W. Neutestamentliche Apokryphen I (1964) 91, 289, 309.

2:1f   JUNACK, K. "Zu einem neuentdeckten Unzialfragment des Matthäus-Evangeliums," NTS 16 ('69-70) 284-88.

2:1-2   BETZ, H. D. Lukian von Samosata und das Neue Testament (1961) 59, 105, 108. SWIDLER, L., Biblical Affirmations of Woman (Philadelphia 1979) 246.

2:1. 7   CHARBEL, A. "Mt 2, 1.7: Os Reis Magos eram Nabateus?" RCB 8 (1-2, '71) 96-103.

2:1   KILPATRICK, G. D. The Origins of the Gospel According to St. Matthew (1950) 54. STRECKER, G. Der Weg der Gerechtigkeit (1962) 51ff, 57, 90, 93. MALINA, B. J. "Literary Structure and Form of Mt. 28:16-20," NTS 17 ('70-71) 99f. *CHARBEL, A., "Mt. 2, 1.7: I Magi erano Nabatei?" RivB 20 (Suppl. 1972) 571-83. "Abendland" in: TRE 1 (1977) 17. SWIDLER, L., Biblical Affirmations of Woman (Philadelphia 1979) 268.

2:2   SCHAUMBERGER, J. Biblica 24 ('43) 162-69. STONEHOUSE, N. B. The Witness of Matthew and Mark to Christ (1944) 179. *TURNER, N. "The New-Born King-Mt 2:2," ET 68 ('57) 122. LEGRAND, L. "Vidimus Stellam Ejus in Oriente," ClM 23 (10, '59) 377-84. HAHN, F. Christologische Hoheitstitel (1963) 86, 319. HUMMEL, R. Die Auseinandersetzung zwischen Kirche und Judentum im Matthäusevangelium (1963) 114, 146. ANON. "What was the Star of Bethlehem?" ChrTo 9 ('64) 277-80. TESTA, E., "Nous avons vu son étoile en orient" Terre sainte 1 (1965) 5-12. BRAUN, H. Qumran und NT II (1966) 311. NICKELS, P. Targum and New Testament (1967) 16. CAVALLIN, H. C. C., Life after Death (Lund 1974) 7.2.1.1. FRANKEMöLLE, H., Jahwebund und Kirche Christi (Münster 1974) 167, 170, 211, 245, 313, 353. METZGER, B. M., The Early Versions of the New Testament (Oxford 1977) 324. "Astrologie" in: TRE 4 (1979) 306-307.

2:4   HAHN, F. Christologische Hoheitstitel (1963) 224, 319. HUMMEL, R. Die Auseinandersetzung zwischen Kirche und Judentum im Matthäusevangelium (1963) 145, 163. BOUSSET, W. Die Religion des Judentums im Späthellenistischen Zeitalter (1966⁻1926) 167. FRANKEMöLLE, H., Jahwebund und Kirche Christi (Münster 1974) 170, 195, 202-204, 309.

2:5f   STONEHOUSE, N. B. The Witness of Matthew and Mark to Christ (1944) 190. STRECKER, G. Der Weg der Gerechtigkeit (1962) 93. NICKELS, P. Targum and New Testament (1967)

16. TAGAWA, K. "People and Community in the Gospel of Matthew," NTS 16 ('69-70) 153f.

2:5 KILPATRICK, G. D. The Origins of the Gospel According to St. Matthew (1950) 53. BLAIR, E. P. Jesus in the Gospel of Matthew (1960) 56. STRECKER, G. Der Weg der Gerechtigkeit (1962) 57, 71.

2:6 GRILL, J., Untersuchungen über die Entstehung des vierten Evangeliums II (Leipzig 1923) 154-55. STONEHOUSE, N. B. The Witness of Matthew and Mark to Christ (1944) 127. KILPATRICK, G. D. The Origins of the Gospel According to St Matthew (1950) 54, 57. BLAIR, E. P. Jesus in the Gospel of Matthew (1960) 39. LINDARS, B. New Testament Apologetic (1961) 192-94. STRECKER, G. Der Weg der Gerechtigkeit (1962) 49, 57, 58, 84, 99. HUMMEL, R. Die Auseinandersetzung zwischen Kirche und Judentum im Matthäusevangelium (1963) 139, 144, 145. BRAUN, H. Qumran und NT II (1966) 267. NICKELS, P. Targum and New Testament (1967) 16. ROTHFUCHS, W. Die Erfüllungszitate des Matthäus-Evangeliums (1969) 60-61. HEER, J. "Der Bethlehemspruch Michas und die Geburt Jesu (Mich 5, 1-3)," BuK 25 (4 '70) 106-109. FRANKEMöLLE, H., Jahwebund und Kirche Christi (Münster 1974) 195, 199-200, 232, 246. *SALVONI, F., "Il vaticinio di Michea" RBR 10 (1975) 31-42.

2:7 *CHARBEL, A., "Mt 2, 1.7: I Magi erano Nabatei?" RivB 20 (Suppl. 1972) 571-83.

2:8-16 HENNECKE, E. & SCHNEEMELCHER, W. Neutestamentliche Apokryphen I (1964) 289.

2:8 STONEHOUSE, N. B. The Witness of Matthew and Mark to Christ (1944) 179. HAHN, F. Christologische Hoheitstitel (1963) 86. METZGER, B. M., The Early Versions of the New Testament (Oxford 1977) 177, 249.

2:9-10 CAVALLIN, H. C. C., Life after Death (Lund 1974) 7.2.1.1.

2:9 PETERS, C. Biblica 23 ('42) 323-32. STONEHOUSE, N. B. The Witness of Matthew and Mark to Christ (1944) 171. METZGER, B. M., The Early Versions of the New Testament (Oxford 1977) 180. "Astrologie" in: TRE 4 (1979) 307.

2:10-11 SWIDLER, L., Biblical Affirmations of Woman (Philadelphia 1979) 246.

2:11-14 BARTINA, S., "Casa o caserio? Los magos en Belén" EstBi 25 (1966) 355-57.

2:11-21 SWIDLER, L., Biblical Affirmations of Woman (Philadelphia 1979) 246.

2:11 STONEHOUSE, N. B. The Witness of Matthew and Mark to Christ (1944) 179. KILPATRICK, G. D. The Origins of the

Gospel According to St Matthew (1950) 22, 125. HAHN, F. Christologische Hoheitstitel (1963) 86. PESCH, R. "Der Gottessohn im matthäischen Evangelienprolog (Mt. 1-2). Beobachtungen zu den Zitationsformeln der Reflexionszitate," Biblica 48 ('67) 414-15. MALINA, B. J. "Literary Structure and Form of Mt. 28:16-20," NTS 17 ('70-71) 99f. KINGSBURY, J. D., Matthew: Structure, Christology, Kingdom (Philadelphia 1975) 45-47.

2:12f.16.19 BETZ, H. D. Lukian von Samosata und das Neue Testament (1961) 53, 56, 105, 108.

2:13ff NEPPER-CHRISTENSEN, P. Das Matthäusevangelium. Ein Judenchristliches Evangelium? (1958) 149, 151, 165.

2:13-23 WILKENS, J. Einführung in das Evangelium nach Matthäus I (1934) 36-43. HAHN, F. Christologische Hoheitstitel (1963) 278, 401.

2:13-18 DAUBE, D. "The Earliest Structure of the Gospels," NTS 5 ('58-59) 184ff. KIIVIT, GPM 17 ('62-63) 45ff. KRUSCHE, W. GPM 23/1 ('68-69) 50-55. PEISKER, C. H., GPM 29 (1974) 56-63. BERTHOLD, C./SCHOLZ, F., "Erster Sonntag nach Weihnachten: Matthäus 2:13-18. Randfiguren der Heilsgeschichte" Predigtstudien (1980/1981) 60-67.

2:13-16 STONEHOUSE, N. B. The Witness of Matthew and Mark to Christ (1944) 125.

2:13-15 WALKER, N. "The Alleged Matthaean Errata," NTS 9 ('62-63) 393. BLOCH, R., "Midrash" in: W. S. Green (ed.) Approaches to Ancient Judaism: Theory and Practice (Missoula 1978) 48. *BAGATTI, B., "La fuga in Egitto: prova per la S. Famiglia" SaDo 24 (1979) 131-41. SWIDLER, L., Biblical Affirmations of Woman (Philadelphia 1979) 247.

2:13f STRECKER, G. Der Weg der Gerechtigkeit (1962) 58. SCHILLE, G. Frühchristliche Hymnen (1965) 133.

2:13 BLAIR, E. P. Jesus in the Gospel of Matthew (1960) 134.

2:14f STRECKER, G. Der Weg der Gerechtigkeit (1962) 93.

2:14 KüNZI, M. Das Naherwartungslogion Matthäus 10, 23 (1970) 33f.

2:15-5:1 FARRER, A. St Matthew and St. Mark (1954) 193.

2:15 STONEHOUSE, N. B. The Witness of Matthew and Mark to Christ (1944) 127, 190. KILPATRICK, G. D. The Origins of the Gospel According to St Matthew (1950) 54, 57, 107. NEPPER-CHRISTENSEN, P. Das Matthäusevangelium. Ein Judenchristliches Evangelium? (1958) 21, 139, 140, 151, 167. BLAIR, E. P. Jesus in the Gospel of Matthew (1960) 39, 56, 60, 134. LINDARS, B. New Testament Apologetic (1961) 216f,

260. DE KRUIJF, T., Der Sohn Des Lebendigen Gottes (Rome 1962) 41, 51, 57, 105, 107, 108. STRECKER, G. Der Weg der Gerechtigkeit (1962) 49, 57f, 71, 84, 90, 125. HAHN, F. Christologische Hoheitstitel (1963) 73, 319. HUMMEL, R. Die Auseinandersetzung zwischen Kirche und Judentum im Matthäusevangelium (1963) 115, 130. PESCH, R. "Der Gottessohn im matthäischen Evangelienprolog (Mt 1-2). Beobachtungen zu den Zitationsformeln der Reflexionszitate," Biblica 48 ('67) 395-420. ROTHFUCHS, W. Die Erfüllungszitate des Matthäus-Evangeliums (1969) 62f. BARTINA, S. "Y desde Egipto lo he proclamado hijo mio (Mt 2, 15; Os 11, 1)," EstBib 29 (1-2, '70) 157-160. FRANKEMöLLE, H., Jahwebund und Kirche Christi (Münster 1974) 14, 165f., 321, 389, 393. BLOCH, R., "Methodological Note for the Study of Rabbinic Literature" in: W. S. Green (ed.) Approaches to Ancient Judaism: Theory and Practice (Missoula 1978) 75.

2:16ff FARRER, A. St Matthew and St Mark (1954) 182.

2:16-23 GOULDER, M. D., Midrash and Lection in Matthew (London 1974) 239ff.

2:16-18 SCHUBERT, K., Jesus im Lichte der Religionsgeschichte des Judentums (Wien/München 1973) 326. *MAIER, P. L., "The Infant Massacre-- History or Myth?" ChrTo 20 (1975) 299-302. BLOCH, R., "Midrash" in: W. S. Green (ed.) Approaches to Ancient Judaism: Theory and Practice (Missoula 1978) 48. *FRANCE, R. T., "Herod and the Children of Bethlehem" NovT (1979) 98-120.

2:16 STONEHOUSE, N. B. The Witness of Matthew and Mark to Christ (1944) 126. LOEWENICH, W. von, Luther als Ausleger der Synoptiker (1954) 59f. BLACK, M. An Aramaic Approach to the Gospels and Acts (1967) 117f. SCHALIT, A. König Herodes (1969) 648. MUELLER, U. B., "Die griechische Esra-Apokalypse" in: W. G. Kümmel (ed.) Jüdische Schriften aus hellenistisch-römischer Zeit V/2 (Gütersloh 1976) 95. METZGER, B. M., The Early Versions of the New Testament (Oxford 1977) 177.

2:17-18 GERSTENBERGER, G./SCHRAGE, W., Leiden (Stuttgart 1977) 122. (Engl. Tr.: Suffering, Nashville 1980, 142).

2:17f STONEHOUSE, N. B. The Witness of Matthew and Mark to Christ (1944) 190. HUMMEl, R. Die Auseinandersetzung zwischen Kirche und Judentum im Matthäusevangelium (1963) 131, 132.

2:17 STONEHOUSE, N. B. The Witness of Matthew and Mark to Christ (1944) 200. NEPPER-CHRISTENSEN, P. Das Matthäusevangelium. Ein Judenchristliches Evangelium?

(1958) 21, 139, 140, 151, 152. STRECKER, G. Der Weg der Gerechtigkeit (1962) 59, 106. BLAIR, E. P. Jesus in the Gospel of Matthew (1960) 56, 90. ROTHFUCHS, W. Die Erfüllungszitate des Matthäus-Evangeliums (1969) 63-65.

2:18-25 FILAS, F. L. "Karl Rahner, Saint Joseph's Doubt (in Theology Digest, 6, 1958, p. 169-73)," CahJos 7 (2, '59) 270-72.

2:18 STONEHOUSE, N. B. The Witness of Matthew and Mark to Christ (1944) 127. STRECKER, G. Der Weg der Gerechtigkeit (1962) 49, 58f. KILPATRICK, G. D. The Origins of the Gospel According to St Matthew (1950) 15, 54, 57. BLAIR, E. P. Jesus in the Gospel of Matthew (1960) 39, 90. LINDARS, B. New Testament Apologetic (1961) 217f, 260. DE KRUIJF, T., Der Sohn Des Lebendigen Gottes (Rome 1962) 105, 107, 109, 112, 136. METZGER, B. M., The Early Versions of the New Testament (Oxford 1977) 180. RIVKIN, E., A Hidden Revolution (Nashville 1978) 122.

2:19-23 FRANZ, GPM 9, ('54-55) 38ff. DOERNE, M. Er kommt auch noch heute (1961) 29-31. KIIVIT, GPM 17 ('62-63) 45ff. HUMMEL, R. Die Auseinandersetzung zwischen Kirche und Judentum im Matthäusevangelium (1963) 137. FRANZ, E. GPM 9/1 ('63) 38-41. MALINA, B. J. "Literary Structure and Form of Mt. 28:16-20," NTS 17 ('70-71) 99f. SWIDLER, L., Biblical Affirmations of Woman (Philadelphia 1979) 247.

2:19-21 SCHILLE, G. Frühchristliche Hymnen (1965) 133.

2:19 BLAIR, E. P. Jesus in the Gospel of Matthew (1960) 134. STRECKER, G. Der Weg der Gerechtigkeit (1962) 90. HAHN, F. Christologische Hoheitstitel (1963) 73, 274. METZGER, B. M., The Early Versions of the New Testament (Oxford 1977) 248.

2:20f STONEHOUSE, N. B. The Witness of Matthew and Mark to Christ (1944) 147. STRECKER, G. Der Weg der Gerechtigkeit (1962) 99.

2:20 BLAIR, E. P. Jesus in the Gospel of Matthew (1960) 134. GLASSON, T. F., Moses in the Fourth Gospel (London 1963) 21f. HUMMEL, R. Die Auseinandersetzung zwischen Kirche und Judentum im Matthäusevangelium (1963) 144. CAVALLIN, H. C. C., Life After Death (Lund 1974) 4, 3nI.I.

2:21 METZGER, B. M., The Early Versions of the New Testament (Oxford 1977) 242.

2:22f VANDERVORST, J. "Note sur Matthieu (II, 22, 23)," Misc. Bibl. B. Ubach. ('53) 329-331. STRECKER, G. Der Weg der Gerechtigkeit (1962) 65, 93.

2:22 STONEHOUSE, N. B. The Witness of Matthew and Mark to Christ (1944) 125. BLAIR, E. P. Jesus in the Gospel of Matthew

(1960) 134. HAHN, F. Christologische Hoheitstitel (1963) 274. METZGER, B. M., The Early Versions of the New Testament (Oxford 1977) 180, 248.

2:23 CASPARI, W. "Nazwraioc Mt. 2, 23 nach alttestamentlichen Voraussetzungen," ZNW 21 ('22) 122-27. LYONNET, S. Biblica 25 ('44) 196-206. STONEHOUSE, N. B. The Witness of Matthew and Mark to Christ (1944) 127, 160, 190. KILPATRICK, G. D. The Origins of the Gospel According to St Matthew (1950) 54, 57, 124. SCHMID, J. Das Evangelium nach Matthäus (1956) 52f. NEPPER-CHRISTENSEN, P. Das Matthäusevangelium. Ein Judenchristliches Evangelium? (1958) 139, 140, 141. ZOLLI, E. "Nazarenus Vocabitur," ZNW 49 (1-2, '58) 135, 136. BLAIR, E. P. Jesus in the Gospel of Matthew (1960) 39, 56. RUDOLF, K. Die Mandäer I (1960) 115. SCHWEIZER, E. Mk 1, 24 in: Judentum, Urchristentum, Kirche (1960) Eltester, W. (ed.) 90-93. DELLING, G. Die Zueignung des Heils in der Taufe (1961) 83. LINDARS, B. New Testament Apologetic (1961) 194-196, 220, 223, 261, 264. REMBRY, J. G., "Quoniam Nazaraeus vocabitur" in: ThSt 15 (1961) 113-27. REMBRY, J. G. "Quoniam Nazaraeus vocabitur' (Mt 2/23)," SBFLA 12 ('61-62) 46-65. DE KRUIJF, T., Der Sohn Des Lebendigen Gottes (Rome 1962) 49, 105, 106, 107, 134. STRECKER, G. Der Weg der Gerechtigkeit (1962) 42, 58, 59ff, 65, 84, 91, 96. WALKER, N. "The Alleged Matthaean Errata," NTS 9 ('62-63) 392f. HAHN, F. Christologische Hoheitstitel (1963) 237. GäRTNER, B. The Temple and the Community in Qumran and the New Testament (1965) 132. SCHWEIZER, E. Neotestamentica (1963) 51ff. HENNECKE, E. & SCHNEEMELCHER, W. Neutestamentliche Apokryphen II (1964) 467. SANDERS, J. A. "Nazoraios in Matt 2:23," JBL 84 (2, '65) 169-172. BRAUN, H. Qumran und NT II (1966) 324. DAVIES, W. D., The Sermon on the Mount (Cambridge 1966) 78. BLACK, M. An Aramaic Approach to the Gospels and Acts (1967) 197f. DALMAN, G. Orte und Wege Jesu (1967) 62f. NICKELS, P. Targum and New Testament (1967) 16. RESCH, A. Agrapha, Aussercanonische Schrift-Fragmente (1967) 23. REHM, M. Der königliche Messias (1968) 197. ROTHFUCHS, W. Die Erfüllungszitate des Matthäusevangeliums (1969) 65-67. KLIJN, A. F. J./REININK, G. J., Patristic Evidence for Jewish-Christian Sects (Leiden 1973) 44. GOULDER, M. D., Midrash and Lection in Matthew (London 1974) 129, 240f. LONGENECKER, R. N., Biblical Exegesis in the Apostolic Period (Grand Rapids 1975) 134, 137, 145-47. *ZUCKSCHWERDT, E., "Nazōraîos in Matth. 2, 23" ThZ 31

(1975) 65-77. *TATUM, W. B., "Matthew 2.23--Wordplay and Misleading Translations" BTr 27 (1976) 135-38. DUNN, J. D. G., Unity and Diversity in the New Testament (London 1977) 93. SANDMEL, S., We Jews and Jesus (New York 1977) 122. BLOCH, R., "Midrash" in: W. S. Green (ed.) Approaches to Ancient Judaism: Theory and Practice (Missoula 1978) 48.

3-25   KILPATRICK, G. D. The Origins of the Gospel According to St. Matthew (1950) 108, 135, 136. *BOUHOURS, J. F., "Une étude de l'ordonnance de la triple tradition" RechSR 60 (1972) 595-614.

3-20   DAVIS, W. H. Davis' Notes on Matthew (1962) 6-79.

3-18   SANDMEL, S., We Jews and Jesus (New York 1977) 19.

3-9   *TRUBLET, J., "Une loi pour être heureux. Étude de quelques textes du Deutéronome et de Matthieu" Christus 25 (1978) 474-81.

1-9:17   RIST, J. M., On the Independence of Matthew and Mark (Cambridge 1978) 17-33.

3:1-7:29   HAHN, F. Christologische Hoheitstitel (1963) 400.

3-4   KILPATRICK, G. D. The Origins of the Gospel According to St. Matthew (1950) 135.

3:1-4:25   GAECHTER, P. Die literarische Kunst im Matthäus-Evangelium (1968) 23-24.

3:1-4:22   RIDDERBOS, H. Matthew's Witness to Jesus Christ (1958) 22-26. CONZELMANN, H./LINDEMANN, A., Arbeitsbuch zum Neuen Testament (Tübingen 1875) 57.

3:1-4:18   EWALD, H. Die drei ersten Evangelien (1850) 154ff.

3:1-4:17   EGGER, W., Frohbotschaft und Lehre (Frankfurt 1976) 40.

3   M'NEILE, A. H. The Gospel According to St. Matthew (1955) 33ff, 35-37. GNILKA, J. "Der Täufer Johannes und der Ursprung der christlichen Taufe," BuL 4 (1, '63) 39-49. BRAUN, H. Qumran und NT II (1966) 18. FRANKEMöLLE, H., Jahwebund und Kirche Christi (Münster 1974) 212f. KINGSBURY, J. D., Matthew: Structure, Christology, Kingdom (Philadelphia 1975) 12-15. BöCHER, O., "Johannes der Täufer in der neutestamentlichen Ueberlieferung" in: G. Müller (ed.) Rechtfertigung Realismus Universalismus in Biblischer Sicht (Darmstadt 1978) 45-52.

3:1ff STAEHELIN, E. Die Verkündigung des Reiches Gottes in der Kirche Jesu Christi I (1951) 297. TRILLING, W. Die Täufertradition bei Matthäus BZ NF 3 ('59) 271-89.

3:1-12 WILKENS, J. Einführung in das Evangelium nach Matthäus I (1934) 69-73. HIRSCH, E. Frühgeschichte des Evangeliums (1941) 27-35. KILPATRICK, G. D. The Origins of the Gospel According to St Matthew (1950) 10. BORNKAMM-BARTH-HELD UEberlieferung und Auslegung im Matthäus-Evangelium (1961) 13f, 25, 56, 58, 71, 110, 153. BULTMANN, R. The History of the Synoptic Tradition (1963) 245-47. PRYKE, J. "John the Baptist and the Qumran Community," RevQ 4 (4, '64) 483-96. BIEDER, W., Die Verheissung der Taufe im Neuen Testament (Zürich 1966) 41-43. MARCONCINI, B. "Tradizione e redazione in Mt. 3, 1-12," RivB 19 (2, '71) 165-186. *MARCONCINI, B., "La predicazione del Battista. Interpretazione storica e applicazioni" BiOr 15 (1973) 49-60. GOULDER, M. D., Midrash and Lection in Matthew (London 1974) 242-44, 358. SAND, A., Das Gesetz und die Propheten (Regensburg 1974) 128-33. CONZELMANN, H./LINDEMANN, A., Arbeitsbuch zum Neuen Testament (Tübingen 1975) 61. FUCHS, A., "Die Ueberschneidungen von Mk und 'Q' nach B. H. Streeter und E. P. Sanders und ihre wahre Bedeutung (Mk 1, 1-8 par)" in: W. Haubeck/M. Backmann (eds.) Wort in der Zeith (Leiden 1980) 57-81. SCHRECKENBERG, H., "Flavius Josephus und die lukanischen Schriften" in: W. Haubeck/M. Bachmann (eds.) Wort in der Zeit (Leiden 1980) 187-90.

3:1-11 KRECK, W. in: Herr, tue meine Lippen auf Bd. 3 (1964) Eichholz, G. (ed.) 22ff. DINKLER, E. GPM 6/1 ('67) 11-13. "Anfechtung" in: TRE 2 (1978) 693.

3:1-6 KILPATRICK, G. D. The Origins of the Gospel According to St Matthew (1950) 107. SUHL, A. Die Funktion der alttestamentlichen Zitate und Anspielungen im Markusevangelium (1965) 133ff.

3:1-5 NICKELS, P. Targum and New Testament (1967) 16.

3:1-4 GAMBA, G., "Struttura letteraria e significato funzionale de Mt 3:1-4" Salesianum (1969) 234-64.

3:1-3 PARKER, P. The Gospel Before Mark (1953) 175-176. HAHN, F. Das Verständnis der Mission im Neuen Testament (1965) 106.

3:1 STONEHOUSE, N. B. The Witness of Matthew and Mark to Christ (1944) 127, 128. STRECKER, G. Der Weg der Gerechtigkeit (1962) 29, 90f, 187. SCHüTZ, R. Johannes der Täufer (1967). MARXSEN, W. Mark the Evangelist (1969) 36,

45f, 48, 50. KINGSBURY, J. D., Matthew: Structure, Christology, Kingdom (Philadelphia 1975) 28-31.

3:2ff STRECKER, G. Der Weg der Gerechtigkeit (1962) 216, 228.

3:2f BORNKAMM-BARTH-HELD, UEberlieferung und Auslegung im Matthäus-Evangelium (1961) 13, 109f.

3:2 VOLZ, P. Die Eschatologie der jüdischen Gemeinde (1934) 166. KILPATRICK, G. D. The Origins of the Gospel According to St Matthew (1950) 90, 92. STAEHELIN, E. Die Verkündigung des Reiches Gottes in der Kirche Jesu Christi I (1951) 257, 366. FLEW, R. N. Jesus and His Church (1956) 38. BLAIR, E. P. Jesus in the Gospel of Matthew (1960) 88f. STRECKER, G. Der Weg der Gerechtigkeit (1962) 149, 158f, 179, 187, 195, 227f. DELLING, G. Die Taufe im Neuen Testament (1963) 43, 50. HAHN, F. Christologische Hoheitstitel (1963) 380. HUMMEL, R. Die Auseinandersetzung zwischen Kirche und Judentum im Matthäusevangelium (1963) 134. ROMANIUK, K. "Repentez-vous car le Royaume des cieux est Tout Proche (Matt. IV. 17 par)," NTS 12 ('65-66) 259f. JüNGEL, E. Paulus und Jesus (1966) 174ff. SANFORD, J. A., The Kingdom Within (New York 1970) 51f. WILSON, S. G., The Gentiles and the Gentile Mission in Luke-Acts (Cambridge 1973) 60f. FRANKEMöLLE, H., Jahwebund und Kirche Christi (Münster 1974) 95, 267, 271. KINGSBURY, J. D., Matthew: Structure, Christology, Kingdom (Philadelphia 1975) 138-40. EGGER, W., Frohbotschaft und Lehre (Frankfurt 1976) 46, 53. McDONALD, J. I. R., Kerygma and Didache (Cambridge 1980) 18f.

3:3ff STRECKER, G. Der Weg der Gerechtigkeit (1962) 186f.

3:3-17 WILKENS, J. Einführung in das Evangelium nach Matthäus I (1934) 73-74.

3:3 STRECKER, G. Der Weg der Gerechtigkeit (1962) 22, 29, 63. DELLING, G. Die Taufe im Neuen Testament (1963) 47. HAHN, F. Christologische Hoheitstitel (1963) 380. HUMMEL, R. Die Auseinandersetzung zwischen Kirche und Judentum im Matthäusevangelium (1963) 132, 134. BRAUN, H. Qumran und NT II (1966) 12, 16, 80, 88, 139, 267, 306, 315. BLACK, M. An Aramaic Approach to the Gospels and Acts (1967) 98f.

3:4-5 MASSAUX, E. Influence de l'Evangile de saint Matthieu sur la littérature chrétienne avant saint Irénée (1950) 348-50.

3:4 KILPATRICK, G. D. The Origins of the Gospel According to St Matthew (1950) 39, 107.

3:5-10   *LACHS, S. T., "John the Baptist and His Audience" Gratz College Annual of Jewish Studies 4 (1975) 28-32.

3:5ff   KNOX, W. L. The Sources of the Synoptic Gospels. Vol. II: St Luke & St Matthew (1957) 4-5.

3:5   STONEHOUSE, N. B. The Witness of Matthew and Mark to Christ (1944) 128. NICKELS, P. Targum and New Testament (1967) 16. SMITH, M., Tannaitic Parallels to the Gospels (Philadelphia 1968) .7.21+.

3:6.7ff   RUDOLPH, K. Die Mandäer I (1960) 62, 105.

3:6   STONEHOUSE, N. B. The Witness of Matthew and Mark to Christ (1944) 128. STRECKER, G. Der Weg der Gerechtigkeit (1962) 29, 148, 227. DELLING, G. Die Taufe im Neuen Testament (1963) 43, 45. "Beichte" in: TRE 5 (1980) 483.

3:7-10:12   LüHRMANN, D. Die Redaktion der Logienquelle (1969) 24-31.

3:7 - 4:11   DRURY, J., Tradition and Design in Luke's Gospel (Atlanta 1976) 128-31.

3:7ff   DELLING, G. Die Taufe im Neuen Testament (1963) 49.

3:7-12   DILLON, R. J. "Towards a Tradition-History of the Parables of th True Israel (Matthew 21, 33-22, 14)," Biblica 47 ('66) 22-25. SALAS, A. "El mensaje del Bautista. Redaccion y teologia en Mt 3, 7-12," EstBib 29 (1-2, '70) 55-72. JEREMIAS, J. Neutestamentliche Theologie I (1971) 55, 173. HOFFMAN, P. Studien zur Theologie der Logienquelle (1972) Passim. SCHULZ, S., Q- Die Spruchquelle der Evangelisten (1972) 366-378. POLAG, A., Die Christologie der Logienquelle (Neukirchen-Vluyn 1977) 154-56. FRIEDRICH, G., "Beobachtungen zur messianischen Hohepriestererwartung in den Synoptikern" in: Auf das Wort kommt es an (Göttingen 1978) 73-75.

3:7-11   McDONALD, J. I. R., Kerygma and Didache (Cambridge 1980) 17f.

3:7-10   KILPATRICK, G. D. The Origins of the Gospel According to St Matthew (1950) 85. BARRETT, C. K. The New Testament Background: Selected Documents (1956) 198. STRECKER, G. Der Weg der Gerechtigkeit (1962) 149, 158, 187. DAVIES, W. D., The Gospel and the Land (Berkley 1974) 169. SAND, A., Das Gesetz und die Propheten (Regensburg 1974) 110f. TALBERT, C. H., Literary Patterns, Theological Themes and the Genre of Luke-Acts (Missoula 1974) 46. EDWARDS, R. A., A. Theology of Q (Philadelphia 1976) 80-82. FUCHS, A., "Intention und Adressatenzder Bußpredigt des Täufers bei Mt. 3:7-10" in: Jesus in der Verkündigung der Kirche (Freistadt

1976) 62-75. POLAG, A., Die Christologie der Logienquelle (Neukirchen-Vluyn 1977) 154.

3:7-9   MOORE, G. F. Judaism I (1946) 544.

3:7f   HUMMEL, R. Die Auseinandersetzung zwischen Kirche und Judentum im Matthäusevangelium (1963) 151, 152. JEREMIAS, J. Neutestamentliche Theologie I (1971) 51, 55.

3:7-8   SMITH, M., Tannaitic Parallels to the Gospels (Philadelphia 1968) 3bn11+. BETZ, O., "Rechtfertigung und Heiligung" in: G. Müller (ed.) Rechtfertigung Realismus Universalismus in Biblischer Sicht (Darmstadt 1978) 36.

3:7   KILPATRICK, G. D. The Origins of the Gospel According to St Matthew (1950) 75, 85, 92, 121. SCHLATTER, A. Johannes der Täufer (1956) 99ff. TREU, U. " 'Otterngezücht.' Ein patristischer Beitrag zur Quellen Kunde des Physiologus" ZNW 50 (1-2, '59) 113-22. DELLING, G. Die Taufe im Neuen Testament (1963) 49. BRAUN, H. Qumran und NT II (1966) 16, 17, 115. TALBERT, C. H., Literary Patterns, Theological Themes, and the Genre of Luke-Acts (Missoula 1974) 46. HOLZ, T., " 'Euer Glaube and Gott'. Zu Form und Inhalt von 1 Thess. 1:9f" in: Die Kirche des Anfangs (Freiburg/Wein 1978) 466, 479f. MEYER, B. F., The Aims of Jesus (London 1979) 116, 117-19. McDonald, J. I. R., Kerygma and Didache (Cambridge 1980) 80.

3:8ff   HUMMEL, R. Die Auseinandersetzung zwischen Kirche und Judentum im Matthäusevangelium (1963) 148.

3:8-10   FARRER, A. St Matthew and St Mark (1954) 175.

3:8-9   SEITZ, O. J. F. " 'What Do These Stones Mean'?" JBL 79 (3, '60) 247-254.

3:8.12   KLEIN, G. "Predigt des Johannes," ZNW 2 (1901) 343f.

3:8   STRECKER, G. Der Weg der Gerechtigkeit (1962) 228. JüNGEL, E. Paulus und Jesus (1966) 175ff.

3:9f   TOWNSEND, J. T. "Matthew xxiii,9," JThS 12 (1, '61) 56-59.

3:9   FLEW, R. N. Jesus and His Church (1956) 37. DELLING, G. Die Taufe im Neuen Testament (1963) 49. HAHN, F. Christologische Hoheitstitel (1963) 243. HUMMEL, R. Die Auseinandersetung zwischen Kirche und Judentum im Matthäusevangelium (1963) 150f. GäRTNER, B. The Temple and the Community in Qumran and the New Testament (1965) 75. BOUSSET, W. Die Religion des Judentums im Späthellenistischen Zeitalter (1966⁻1926) 199. BRAUN, H. Qumran und NT II (1966) 17, 18. HASLER, W. Amen (1969) 55. JEREMIAS, J. Neutestamentliche Theologie I (1971) 55, 170. CAVALLIN, H. C. C., Life After Death (Lund 1974)

5.2.4, 7.2.3.6. BRUCE, F. F., The Time is Fulfilled (Exeter 1979) 61. MEYER, B. F., The Aims of Jesus (London 1979) 116, 121.

3:10 KILPATRICK, G. D. The Origins of the Gospel According to St Matthew (1950) 85, 92(2). BLAIR, E. P. Jesus in the Gospel of Matthew (1960) 115. STRECKER;, G. Der Weg der Gerechtigkeit 1962) 228. JEREMIAS, J. Neutestamentliche Theologie I (1971) 51, 252. CAVALLIN, H. C. C., Life After Death (Lund 1974) 7.2.n26. METZGER, B. M., The Early Versions of the New Testament (Oxford 1977) 249. MEYER, B. F., The Aims of Jesus (London 1979) 117-19. McDONALD, J. I. H., Kerygma and Didache (Cambridge 1980) 80.

3:11f STAEHELIN, E. Die Verkündigung des Reiches Gottes in der Kirche Jesu Christi I (1951) 289. STREETER, B. H. The Four Gospels (1951) 250f.

3:11-12 *BEST, E. "Spirit-Baptism," NovTest 4 (3, '60) 236-43. SIMPSON, B. T. "Agreement of Matthew and Luke against Mark," NTS 12 ('65-66) 276f. BRAUN, H. Qumran und NT II (1966) 4, 9, 13, 18, 79, 253ff, 271ff. TALBERT, C. H., Literary Patterns, Theological Themes and the Genre of Luke-Acts (Missoula 1974) 46. GOPPELT, L., Theologie des Neuen Testaments (Göttingen 1975) 90f. EDWARDS, R. A., A Theology of Q (Philadelphia 1976) 81f. SCHWEIZER, E., Heiliger Geist (Stuttgart 1978) 76. MEYER, B. F., The Aims of Jesus (London 1979) 117-19. McDONALD, J. I. H., Kerygma and Didache (Cambridge 1980) 17.

3:11 VOLZ, P. Die Eschatologie der jüdischen Gemeinde (1934) 159. BARRETT, C. K. The Holy Spirit and the Gospel Tradition (1947) 29f, 125f. STAEHELIN E. Die Verkündigung des Reiches Gottes in der Kirche Jesu Christi I (1951) 289. GLASSON, T. F. "Water, Wind and Fire (Luke iii.6) and Orphic Initiation," NTS 3 (1, '56) 69-71. *KRIEGER, N. "Barfuss Busse Tun," NovTest 1 ('56) 227-28. SCHLATTER, A. Johannes der Täufer (1956) 103ff. BARNARD, L. W. "Matt. III.11//Luke III.6," JThS 8 (1, '57) 107. TRILLING, W. Das wahre Israel (1959) 18. TURRADO, L. "El bautismo 'in Spiritu sanct et igni'," EstEc 34 (134-35, '60) 807-17. BORNKAMM-BARTH-HELD, UEberlieferung und Auslegung im Matthäus-Evangelium (1961) 109f, 129. DIAZ, J. A. "El bautismo de fuego anunciado por el Bautista y su relacion con la profecia de Malaquias," MisC 37 ('62) 121-33. STRECKER, G. Der Weg der Gerechtigkeit (1962) 91, 126, 227, 237. DELLING, G. Die Taufe im Neuen Testament (1963) 46. HAHN, F. Christologische Hoheitstitel (1963) 393. DIAZ, J. A. "El bautismo de fuego anunciado por el Bautista y su relacion con la profecia de Malaquias," EstBib 23 (3-4, '64) 319-31. JüNGEL, E. Paulus und Jesus (1966) 175ff. SEEBERG, A. Der Katechismus der Urchristenheit (1966) 214, 220, 221. BRETSCHER, P. G. " 'Whose Sandals'? (Matt 3:11)," JBL 86 (1, '67) 81-87. STROBEL, A. Erkenntnis und Bekenntnis der Sünde in neutestamentlicher Zeit (1968) 45. PATZIA, A. G. "Did John the Baptist Preach a Baptism of Fire and the Holy Spirit?" EQ 40 (1, '68) 21-27. WINK, W. John the Baptist in the Gospel Tradition (1968) 36-38. DUNN, J. D. G. Baptism in the Holy Spirit (1970) 8-14, 18-21. BEUTLER, J., Martyria (Frankfurt 1972) 248, 285f. LADD, G. E., A Theology of the New Testament (Grand Rapids 1974) 36, 38, 163, 542. LOHSE, E., Grundriss der neutestamentlichen Theologie (Stuttgart 1974) 22f.. SANDMEL, S., We Jews and Jesus (New York 1977) 120. RAYAN, S., The Holy Spirit: Heart of the Gospel and Christian Hope (New York 1978) 2.

3:12 FLEW, R. N. Jesus and His Church (1956) 67. BLAIR, E. P. Jesus in the Gospel of Matthew (1960) 115. DELLING, G. Die Taufe im Neuen Testament (1963) 48. DAVIES, W. D., The Sermon on the Mount (Cambridge 1966) 106f. LADD, G. E., A Theology of the New Testament (Grand Rapids 1974) 37, 74, 88, 348. HOLM-NIELSEN, S., "Die Psalmen Salomons" in: W. G. Kümmel (ed.) Jüdische Schriften aus hellenistisch-römischer Zeit IV (Gütersloh 1977) 87.

3:13 - 4:11 *PRZYBYLSKI, B., "The Role of Mt 3:13-4:11 in the Structure and Theology of the Gospel of Matthew" BThB 4 (1974) 222-35.

3:13ff BLAIR, E. P. Jesus in the Gospel of Matthew (1960) 98.

3:13-17 SCHLATTER, A. Die Theologie des Neuen Testaments I (1909) 29-37. BARTH, M., Die Taufe - ein Sakrament? (Zürich 1951) 59-72. DENNEY, J. The Death of Christ (1956) 18f. GILS, F. Jésus Prophète D'Après Les Evangiles Synoptiques (1957) 49-73. BORNKAMM-BARTH-HELD, UEberlieferung und Auslegung im Matthäus-Evangelium (1961) 13, 33, 121, 129ff. STRECKER, G. Der Weg der Gerechtigkeit (1962) 150, 178ff. ROBINSON, J. A. T. "The one Baptism," Twelve New Testament Studies (1962) 158-75. "Verkündigt das angenehme Jahr des Herrn," Predigtgedanken aus Vergangenheit und Gegenwart (1962) 135-53. SABBE, M. "Het verhaal van Jezus' doopsel" (The Account of the Baptism of Jesus), CollBrugGand 8 (4, '62) 456-74; 9 (2, '63) 211-230; (3, '63) 333-65. BRUNNER, P. in: Herr, tue meine Lippen auf (1964) Eichholz, G. (ed.) 71ff. LINDIJER, C. H. "Jezus' doop in de Jordaan," NedThT 18 (3, '64) 177-192. BROMILEY, G. W. "The Baptism of Jesus," ChrTo 9 (12, '65) 599-600. BIEDER,

W., Die Verheissung der Taufe im Neuen Testament (Zürich 1966) 86f. BRAUN, H. Qumran und NT II (1966) 65f, 71, 76, 189, 312. JOHNSON, S. L. "The Baptism of Christ," BiblSa 123 (491, '66) 220-29. LUTHER, M. Predigten über die Christus-Botschaft (1966) 73-79. HROMADKA, J. L. GPM 23/1 ('68-69) 69-71. BORNKAMM, G. GPM 9/1 ('68-69) 41-45.` STECK, K. G. GPM 17/1 ('68-69) 65-72. LENTZEN-DEIS, F. Die Taufe Jesu nach den Synoptikern (1970) 282-84. FRANKEMöLLE, H., Jahwebund und Kirche Christi (Münster 1974) 92-95, 323. SCHROER, H., in: GPM 29 (1974/75) 92-101. STIERLE, B.,/HIRSCHLER, H., in: Predigtstudien für das Kirchenjahr 1978/79 (Stuttgart 1978) 103-109. "Berufung" in: TRE 5 (1980) 684.

3:13-15 SASS, G. Ungereimtes bei Matthäus (1968) 4-5.

3:13f KNOX, W. L. The Sources of the Synoptic Gospels. Vol. II: St. Luke & St. Matthew (1957) 43.

3:13 STONEHOUSE, N. B. The Witness of Matthew and Mark to Christ (1944) 128.

3:14-17 HENNECKE, E. & SCHNEEMELCHER, W. Neutestamentliche Apokryphen (1964) I 103, 394 II 482.

3:14f KILPATRICK, G. D. The Origins of the Gospel According to St. Matthew (1950) 37, 50, 96, 107. GILMORE, A. Christian Baptism (1959) 85ff. DELLING, G. Die Taufe im Neuen Testament (1963) 55. WREGE, H.-T. Die UEberlieferungsgeschichte der Bergpredigt (1968) 46.

3:14 KILPATRICK, G. D. The Origins of the Gospel According to St. Matthew (1950) 50. TRILLING, W. Das wahre Israel (1959) 18f. BLAIR, E. P. Jesus in the Gospel of Matthew (1960) 88. METZGER, B. M., The Early Versions of the New Testament (Oxford 1977) 180.

3:15 LJUNGMAN, H. Das Gesetz Erfüllen (1954) 97-126. KNOX, W. L. The Sources of the Synoptic Gospels. Vol. II: St. Luke & St. Matthew (1957) 125. TRILLING, W. Das wahre Israel (1959) 148. BLAIR, E. P. Jesus in the Gospel of Matthew (1960) 117, 118, 119, 120, 121. BORNKAMM-BARTH-HELD, UEberlieferung und Auslegung im Matthäus-Evangelium (1961) 47, 63, 65f, 121, 135, 137f. STRECKER, G. Der Weg der Gerechtigkeit (1962) 35, 134, 150, 153, 216. EISSFELDT, O. "Plerosai pasan dikaiosynen in Matthäus 3:15," ZNW 61 (3-4, '70) 209-15. ZIESLER, J. A. The Meaning of Righteousness in Paul (1972) 133f, 146. EISSFELDT, O. Kleine Schriften V (1973) 179-84. FRANKEMöLLE, H., Jahwebund und Kirche Christi (Münster 1974) 94, 96, 173, 280, 283f, 286, 288, 295, 299, 304, 389, 390. SAND, A., Das Gesetz und die Propheten (Regensburg 1974) 198f.

3:16 - 4:11 RAYAN, S., The Holy Spirit: Heart of the Gospel and Christian Hope (New York 1978) 127.

3:16f STRECKER, G. Der Weg der Gerechtigkeit (1962) 216. HAHN, F. Christologische Hoheitstitel (1963) 319. DUNN, J. D. G. Baptism in the Holy Spirit (1970) 26f, 34.

3:16-17 MASSAUX, E. Influence de l'Evangile de saint Matthieu sur la littérature chrétienne avant saint Irénée (1950) 350-52, 548-49. POLAG, A., Die Christologie der Logienquelle (Neukirchen-Vluyn 1977) 151, 154.

3:16 KILPATRICK, G. D. The Origins of the Gospel According to St Matthew (1950) 39. GILS, F. Jésus Prophète D'Après Les Evangiles Synoptiques (1957) 50-53. GILMORE, A. Christian Baptism (1959) 88f. BLAIR, E. P. Jesus in the Gospel of Matthew (1960) 79. KECK, L. E. "The Spirit and the Dove," NTS 17 ('70-71) 41-67. KLIJN, A. F. J., "Die syrische Baruch-Apokalypse" in: W. G. Kümmel (ed.) Jüdische Schriften aus hellenistisch-römischer Zeit V (Gütersloh 1976) 138. SWIDLER, L., Biblical Affirmations of Woman (Philadelphia 1979) 60. "Berufung" in: TRE 5 (1980) 685.

3:17 STONEHOUSE, N. B. The Witness of Matthew and Mark to Christ (1944) 19. KILPATRICK, G. D. The Origins of the Gospel According to St Matthew (1950) 107. GILS, F. Jésus Prophéte D-Après Les Evangiles Synoptiques (1957) 54-73. HOOKER, M. D. Jesus and the Servant (1959) 68-73. BLAIR, E. P. Jesus in the Gospel of Matthew (1960) 60. DE KRUIJF, Th., Der Sohn des lebendigen Gottes (Rome 1962) 41, 44, 46, 47, 49, 50. STRECKER, G. Der Weg der Gerechtigkeit (1962) 58, 125. HUMMEL, R. Die Auseinandersetzung zwischen Kirche und Judentum im Matthäusevangelium (1963) 115. JEREMIAS, J. Abba; Studien zur neutestamentlichen Theologie und Zeitgeschichte (1966) 192-94. LENTZEN-DEIS, F. Die Taufe Jesu nach den Synoptikern (1970) 109f. KINGSBURY, J. D., Matthew: Structure, Christology, Kingdom (Philadelphia 1975) 13-15. BLOCH, R., "Methodological Note for the Study of Rabbinic Literature" in: W. S. Green (ed.) Approaches to Ancient Judaism (Missoula 1978) 75. FRIEDRICH, G., "Beobachtungen zur messianischen Hohepriestererwartung in den Synoptikern" in: Auf das Wort kommt es an (Göttingen 1978) 73-75.

3:19 HOLM-NIELSEN, S., "Die Psalmen Salomons" in: W. G. Kümmel (ed.) Jüdische Schriften aus hellenistisch-römischer Zeit IV (Gütersloh 1977) 87.

4:1ff STRECKER, G. Der Weg der Gerechtigkeit (1962) 91, 137. PETZKE, G. Die Traditionen über Apollonius von Tyana und das Neue Testament (1970) 170, 177.

4:1-11 SCHLATTER, A. Die Theologie des Neuen Testaments (1909) 352-57. BöKLEN, E., "Zu der Versuchung Jesu" ZNW 18 (19171918) 244. BüCHSEL, D. F. Der Geist Gottes im Neuen Testament (1926) 171-76. WILKENS, J. Einführung in das Evangelium nach Matthäus I (1934) 74-77. BARRETT, C. K. The Holy Spirit and the Gospel Tradition (1947) 46-53. HIRSCH, E. Frühgeschichte des Evangeliums (1941) 73-77. MASSAUX, E. Influence de l'Evangile de saint Matthieu sur la littérature chrétienne avant saint Irénée (1950) 543-45. ARGYLE, A. W. "The Accounts of the Temptations of Jesus in Relation to the Q Hypothesis," ET 64 ('52-53) 382. DENNEY, J. The Death of Christ (1956) 20. LEIVESTAD, R. Christ the Conqueror (1954) 50ff. LOEWENICH, W. von, Luther als Ausleger der Synoptiker (1954) 67f, 80f, 176f, 245f. *DUPONT, J. "L'Arrier-fond Biblique du Recit des Tentations de Jesus," NTS 3 ('56-57) 287ff. EICHHOLZ, G. Herr, tue meine Lippen auf I (1957) 93ff. GILS, F. Jésus Prophète D'Après Les Evangiles Synoptiques (1957) 83-85. *DOUBLE, P. "The Temptations," ET 72 (3, '60) 91-93. *DUQUOC, C. "La tentation du Christ," LuVie 10 (53, '61) 21-41. BORNKAMM-BARTH-HELD, UEberlieferung und Auslegung im Matthäus-Evangelium (1961) 34. *GRAHAM, E. "The Temptation in the Wilderness," ChurchQuartRev 162 (342, '61) 17-32. *KESICH, V. "Christ's Temptation in the Apocryphal Gospels and Acts," SVThQ 5 (4, '61) 3-9. KöPPEN, K. -P. Die Auslegung der Versuchungsgeschichte unter besonderer Berücksichtigung der Alten Kirche (1961). *POWELL, W. "The Temptation," ET 72 (8, '61) 248. *COOKE, B. "The Hour of Temptation," Way 2 (3, '62) 177-87. ROBINSON, J. A. T. "The Temptations," Twelve New Testament Studies (1962) 39. STRECKER, G., Der Weg der Gerechtigkeit (1962) 39. BAUMBACH, G. Das Verständnis des Bösen in den synoptischen Evangelien (1963) 103ff. BULTMANN, R. The History of the Synoptic Tradition (1963) 254-56. HAHN, F. Christologische Hoheitstitel (1963) 72. HENNECKE, E. & SCHNEEMELCHER, W.

Neutestamentliche Apokryphen I (1964) 77, 95, 280. *KELLY,
H. A. "The Devil in the Desert," CBQ 26 (2, '64)190-220.
*BISHOP, E. F. F. " 'Scripture Says'," EQ 37 (4, '65) 218-20.
KASSING, A., "Die Glaubensentscheidungen Jesu" Am Tisch
des Wortes 8 (1965) 30-40. *KESICH, V. "Hypostatic and
Prosopic Union in the Exegesis of Christ's Temptation,"
SVThQ 9 (3, '65) 118-37. BRAUN, H. Qumran und NT II
(1966) 76, 106, 114. DIGNATH, W. & WIBBING, S. Taufe-
Versuchung-Verklärung (1966) 33-55. *DUPONT, J.
"L'origine du récit des tentations de Jésus au désert," RevBi 73
(1, '66) 30-76. GERHARDSSON, B., The Testing of God's Son
(Lund 1966) 7-83. JOHNSON, S. L. "The Temptation of
Christ," BiblSa 123 (492, '66) 342-52. FREY, F. "Die
Versuchung Jesu," in: Die Passionstexte (1967) Frey, F. (ed.)
129-34. *STEGNER, W. R. "Wilderness and Testing in the
Scrolls and in Matthew 4:1-11," BR 12 ('67) 18-27. WEBER, O.
Predigtmeditationen (1967) 134-38. DUPONT, J. Les
Tentations de Jésus au Désert (1968) 11-42. GERHARDSSON,
B. "The Parable of the Sower and its Interpretation," NTS 14
('68) 165-93. *LEONARDI, G. "Le tentazioni di Gesù nella
interpretazione patristica," StPa 15 (2, '68) 229-62. VAN
IERSEL, B. M. F., "Jesus, Teufel und Dämonen" Annalen van
het Thijmgenootschap 55 (1968) 5-22. BLANK, J.
Schriftauslegung in Theorie und Praxis (1969) 117-21.
DUPONT, J. Die Versuchungen Jesu in der Wüste (1969).
*HOFFMANN, P. "Die Versuchungsgeschichte in der
Logienquelle. Zur Auseinandersetzung der Judenchristen mit
dem politischen Messianismus," BZ 13 (2, '69) 207-23.
*LEONARDI, G. "Il racconto sinottico della tentazioni di
Gesù: fonti, ambiente e dottrina," StPa 16 (3, '69) 391-429.
*KNöRZER, W. ". . .dann wollen wir an dich glauben.
Kritische Sichtung heutiger Erlösungshoffnungen und
Zukunftsmodelle vor dem Hintergrund der Versuchungen
Jesu," BuK 25 (1, '70) 9-13. *MICHL, J. "Da trat der
Versucher an ihn heran. Die UEberlieferung von den
Versuchungen Jesu im Neuen Testament," BuK 25 (1, '70) 1-5.
*SCHIERSE, F. J. "Wenn du Gottes Sohn bist. . .Was sagen
die Versuchungsüberlieferungen des Neuen Testaments über
Jesus Christus?" BuK 25 (1, '70) 6-8. JEREMIAS, J.
Neutestamentliche Theologie I (1971) 74ff.
SCHNACKENBURG, R. Schriften zum Neuen Testament
(1971) 101-28. *FITZGERALD, J. T., "The Temptation of
Jesus: The Testing of the Messiah in Matthew" RestQ 15 (1972)
152-60. *KIRK, J. A. "The Messianic Role of Jesus and the
Temptation Narrative: A Contemporary Perspective

(concluded)," EQ 44 (2, '72) 91-102. SCHULZ, S. Q Die Spruchquelle der Evangelisten (1972) 177-190. THYEN, D., "Eine Unterrichtseinheit über Matthäus 4, 1-11" in: Bloth et al. (eds.) Mutuum Colloquium. Festschrift für Helmut Kittel (Dortmund 1972) 285-95. SEILER, D. & SCHARFENBERG, J. "Invokavit: Matthäus 4, 1-11," in: Predigtstudien ('72-73) Lange, E. (ed.) 137-48. *SMYTH-FLORENTIN, F. "Jésus, le Fils du Père, vainqueur de Satan. Mt 4, 1-11; Mc 1, 12-15; Lc 4, 1-13," AssS 14 ('73) 56-75. STANTON, G. N., "On the Christology of Q" in: B. Lindars and S. S. Smalley (eds.) Christ and the Spirit in the New Testament. In Honour of Ch.F.D. Moule (Cambridge 1973) 34f. COLLINS, R. F., The Temptation of Jesus" MTh 26 (1974) 32-45. GOULDER, M. D., Midrash and Lection in Matthew (London 1974) 185, 189, 245ff. TALBERT, C. H., Literary Patterns, Theological Themes, and the Genre of Luke-Acts (Missoula 1974) 47. DUNN, J. D. G., Jesus and the Spirit (London 1975) 27, 66, 85, 168. *KURICHIANIL, J., "The Temptations of Christ, Their Meaning" Biblehashyam 1 (1975) 106-25. CALLOUD, J. Structural Analysis of Narrative (Philadelphia 1976) 47-108. EDWARDS, R. A., A Theology of Q (Philadelphia 1976) 82-84. *MUSZYńSKI, H., "Kuszenie Chrystusa w tradycji synoptyczenej" CoTh 46 (1976) 17-41. BERGMAN, J., "Zum Zwei-Wege-Motiv. Religionsgeschichtliche und exegetische Bemerkungen" SEA 41-42 (1977) 27-56. *LUZARRAGA, J., "Discernimiento Espiritual en las Tentaciones de Jesús y de la Iglesia" Manresa 49 (1977) 129-42. POLAG, A., Die Christologie der Logienquelle (Neukirchen-Vluyn 1977) 146-51. SAITO, T., Die Mosevorstellungen im Neuen Testament (Bern (1977) 51-53. "Anfechtung" in: TRE 2 (1978) 693. RIST, J. M., On the Independence of Matthew and Mark (Cambridge 1978) 22-24. *FEUILLET, A., "Die Versuchungen Jesu" IKZ/Communio 8 (1979) 226-37. SCHRAGE, W., in: GPM 33 (1979) 130-38. *KESICH, V. "The Antiocheans and the Temptation Story," StPa VII, 496-502.

4:1-10 SURKAU, GPM ('60-61) 83ff. IWAND, H. J. Predigt-Meditationen (1964) 432-39.

4:1-7 HAHN, F. Christologische Hoheitstitel (1963) 303.

4:1 STONEHOUSE, N. B. The Witness of Matthew and Mark to Christ (1944) 128, 129. BRUNNER, E. Dogmatik II (1946) 126. STRECKER, G. Der Weg der Gerechtigkeit (1962) 180. McNAMARA, M. The New Testament and the Palestinian Targum to the Pentateuch (1966) 221f.

4:2-11 HOFFMANN, P. Studien zur Theologie der Logienquelle (1972) 4, 206.

4:2 KNOX, W. L. The Sources of the Synoptic Gospels. Vol II: St Luke & St Matthew (1957) 4. HAHN, F. Christologische Hoheitstitel (1963) 401. BOUSSET, W. Die Religion des Judentums im Späthellenistischen Zeitalter (1966‑1926) 180. FRIEDRICH, G., "Beobachtungen zur messianischen Hohepriestererwartung in den Synoptikern" in: Auf das Wort kommt es an (Göttingen 1978) 91f.

4:3-11 DAVIES, W. D., The Sermon on the Mount (Cambridge 1966) 73f.

4:3ff CULLMANN, O. Die Christologie des Neuen Testaments (1957) 291ff.

4:3f PARKER, P. The Gospel Before Mark (1953) 61ff.

4:3.6. BLAIR, E. P. Jesus in the Gospel of Matthew (1960) 61. *HOLST, R. "The Temptation of Jesus," ET 82 (11, '71) 343-44.

4:3 DE KRUIJF, Th., Der Sohn des lebendigen Gottes (Rome 1962) 41, 55, 85, 97, 104. MüLLER, U. B., "Die griechische Esra-Apokalypse" in: W. G. Kümmel (ed.) Jüdische Schriften aus hellenistisch-römischer Zeit V (Gütersloh 1976) 96. HUMMEL, R. Die Auseinandersetzung zwischen Kirche und Judentum im Matthäusevangelium (1963) 115.

4:4 STRECKER, G. Der Weg der Gerechtigkeit (1962) 24. JEREMIAS, J. Neutestamentliche Theologie I (1971) 25f, 75, 248f.

4:5-7 PARKER, P. The Gospel Before Mark (1953) 62-63. HYLDAHL, N. "Die Versuchung auf der Zinne des Tempels (Matth 4, 5-7‑Luke 4, 9-12)," StTh 15 (2, '61) 113-27. HAHN, F. Christologische Hoheitstitel (1963) 240.

4:5f McNAMARA, M. The New Testament and the Palestinian Targum to the New Testament (1966) 250.

4:5 STONEHOUSE, N. B. The Witness of Matthew and Mark to Christ (1944) 185. KILAPATRICK, G. D. The Origins of the Gospel According to St Matthew (1950) 47, 124.

4:6 DE KRUIJF, Th., Der Sohn des lebendigen Gottes (Rome 1962) 41, 55, 57, 85, 97, 104. STRECKER, G. Der Weg der Gerechtigkeit (1962) 24, 61. HUMMEL, R. Die Auseinandersetzung zwischen Kirche und Judentum im Matthäusevangelium (1963) 116. FRANKEMöLLE, H., Jahwebund und Kirche Christi (Münster 1974) 95, 165, 301.

4:7 STRECKER, G. Der Weg der Gerechtigkeit (1962) 24.

4:8-10 HAHN, F. Christologische Hoheitstitel (1963) 175f.

4:8ff FRIEDRICH, G. "Das Problem der Autorität im Neuen

Testament" in: Auf das Wort kommt es an (Göttingen 1978) 389.

4:8f WILLRICH, H. "Zur Versuchung Jesu," ZNW 4 (1903) 349f.

4:8 KLIJN, A. F. J., "Die syrische Baruch-Apokalypse" in: W. G. Kümmel (ed.) Jüdische Schriften aus hellenistisch-römischer Zeit V (Gütersloh 1976) 173. LIVIO, J.-B., "La signification théologique de la 'montagne' dans le premier evangile" Bulletin de Centre Protestant d'études (Geneve) 30 (1978)' 13-20. *KILPATRICK, G. D., "Three Problems of New Testament Text" NovT 21 (1979) 289-92.

4:9f STONEHOUSE, N. B. The Witness of Matthew and Mark to Christ (1944) 179. HAHN, F. Christologische Hoheitstitel (1963) 86.

4:10 STRECKER, G. Der Weg der Gerechtigkeit (1962) 24. HAHN, F. Christologische Hoheitstitel (1963) 72.

4:11 STONEHOUSE, N. B. The Witness of Matthew and Mark to Christ (1944) 127. BORNKAMM-BARTH-HELD, UEberlieferung und Auslegung im Matthäus-Evangelium (1961) 133.

4:12ff STONEHOUSE, N. B. The Witness of Matthew and Mark to Christ (1944) 129ff.

4:12 - 7:29 *DuBUIT, M., En tous les temps Jésus-Christ. Tome 3. Sermon sur la Montagne (Mulhouse 1977).

4:12-25 LöWE, H./ZIPPERT, Chr., in: Predigtstudien für das Kirchenjahr 1976/77 (Stuttgart 1976) 98-104. VOIGT, M., in: GPM 31 (1976/77) 85-89.

4:12-23 *DUPREZ, A., "Le programme de Jésus, selon Matthieu. Mt 4, 12-23" AssS 34 (1973) 9-18.

4:12-17 STECK, K. G. GPM 19 (1964/4) 81-87. BAUER, G. in:
23-25 Hören und Fragen (1967) Eichholz, G. & Falkenroth, A. (eds.) 132ff. KüNKEL, K. Göttinger Predigtmeditationen 25 (4, '70) 101-108. LANGE, E. Predigtstudien für das Kirchenjahr 1970/71 (1970) 113-18.

4:12-17 WILKENS, J. Einführung in das Evangelium nach Matthäus I (1934) 77-78. KILPATRICK, G. D. The Origins of the Gospel According to St Matthew (1950) 82. HAHN, F. Das Verständnis der Mission im Neuen Testament (1965) 106. SCHOTT, E. GPM 11/1 60-63. SCHüRMANN, H., "Zur Traditionsgeschichte der Nazareth-Perikope Lk 4, 16-30" in: A Descamps/A..de Halleux (eds.) Mélanges Bibliques en hommage au R. P. Béda Rigaux (Gembloux 1970) 201f. GLöCKNER, R., Die Verkündigung des Heils beim Evangelisten Lukas (Mainz 1975) 129f. EGGER, W.

Frohbotschaft und Lehre (Frankfurt a.M. 1976) 35, 45f. WENDLAND, G/STöHR, M., in: Predigtstudien für das Kirchenjahr 1980/81 (Stuttgart 1980) 90-97.

4:12-16 DAVIES, W. D., The Gospel and the Land (London 1974) 226. *GAMBA, G. G., "Gesù si stabilisce a Cafarnao. Annotazioni in margine all struttura letteraria ed al significato dottrinale e funzionale di Mt. 4, 12-16 ed al piano d'insieme de Vangelo di Matteo" BiOr 16 (1974) 109-132. KINGSBURY, J. D., Matthew: Structure, Christology, Kingdom (Philadelphia 1975) 15-17.

4:12f STRECKER, G. Der Weg der Gerechtigkeit (1962) 64f.

4:12-13 POLAG, A. Die Christologie der Logienquelle (Neukirchen-Vluyn 1977) 155.

4:12 STONEHOUSE, N. B. The Witness of Matthew and Mark to Christ (1944) 128. KILPATRICK, G. D. The Origins of the Gospel According to St Matthew (1950) 89, 93. BLAIR, E. P. Jesus in the Gospel of Matthew (1960) 86, 90. DELLING, G. Die Zueignung des Heils in der Taufe (1961) 83. STRECKER, G. Der Weg der Gerechtigkeit (1962) 186.

4:13-16 KILPATRICK, G. D. The Origins of the Gospel According to St Matthew (1950) 50, 96. DUPONT, J., Essais sur la Christologie de Saint Jean (Bruges 1951) 69, 70, 88.

4:13 STONEHOUSE, N. B. The Witness of Matthew and Mark to Christ (1944) 136, 141. KILPATRICK, G. D. The Origins of the Gospel According to St Matthew (1950) 93, 94. STRECKER, G. Der Weg der Gerechtigkeit (1962) 62, 66.

4:14ff STONEHOUSE, N. B. The Witness of Matthew and Mark to Christ (1944) 132, 185, 191, 223. KNOX, W. L. The Sources of the Synoptic Gospels. Vol. II: St Luke & St Matthew (1957) 126.

4:14-17 STRECKER, G. Der Weg der Gerechtigkeit (1962) 93.

4:14-16 KILPATRICK, G. D. The Origins of the Gospel According to St Matthew (1950) 57, 93. HAHN, F. Christologische Hoheitstitel (1963) 380. ROTHFUCHS, W. Die Erfüllungszitate des Matthäus-Evangeliums (1969) 67-70. *SOARES PRABHU, G. M. "Matthew 4:14-16. A Key to the Origin of the Formula Quotations of Matthew," IJTh 20 (1-2, '71) 70-91. FRANKEMöLLE, H., Jahwebund und Kirche Christi (Münster 1974) 200f, 345, 390.

4:14 KILAPATRICK, G. D. The Origins of the Gospel According to St Matthew (1950) 57. BLAIR, E. P. Jesus in the Gospel of Matthew (1960) 56. HUMMEL, R. Die Auseinandersetzung zwischen Kirche und Judentum im Matthäusevangelium (1963) 132.

4:15ff   BORNKAMM-BARTH-HELD, UEberlieferung und Auslegung im Matthäus-Evangelium (1961) 13, 34.

4:15f   TRILLING, W. Das wahre Israel (1959) 112f. STRECKER, G. Der Weg der Gerechtigkeit (1962) 492, 63ff, 83f, 195. LINDARS, B. New Testament Apologetic (1961) 196-99, 261.

4:15-16   KNOX, W. L. The Sources of the Synoptic Gospels I (1957) 128. BLAIR, E. P. Jesus in the Gospel of Matthew (1960) 39.

4:15   HAHN, F. Das Verständnis der Mission im Neuen Testament (1965) 109. *TAGAWA, K. People and Community in the Gospel of Matthew NTS 16 (1969-70) 153f.

4:16   HUMMEL, R. Die Auseinandersetzung zwischen Kirche und Judentum im Matthäusevangelium (1963) 145. FRANKEMöLLE, H., Jahwebund und Kirche Christi (Münster 1974) 195, 200f. "Allegorese" in: TRE 2 (1978) 278.

4:17-16:20   KINGSBURY, J. D., Matthew: Structure, Christology, Kingdom (Philadelphia 1975) 19-25.

4:17-11:30   SCHWEIZER, E., Matthäus und seine Gemeinde (Stuttgart 1974) I.3.1, I.3.3.

4:17-7:27   *SABOURIN, L., Il discorso della Montagna Nel Vangelo di Matteo (Marino 1976).

4:17   WINDISCH, H. The Meaning of the Sermon on the Mount (1937) 113f. STONEHOUSE, N. B. The Witness of Matthew and Mark to Christ (1944) 129, 131, 153, 227, 234. STAEHELIN, E. Die Verkündigung des Reiches Gottes in der Kirche Jesu Christi I (1951) 297, 366. BLAIR, E. P. Jesus in the Gospel of Matthew (1960) 88. McARTHUR, H. K. Understanding the Sermon on the Mount (1960) 86, 94, 99, 177, 178. ROBINSON, J. M. Kerygma und historischer Jesus (1960) 57. BORNKAMM-BARTH-HELD UEberlieferung und Auslegung im Matthäus-Evangelium (1961) 109f, 237f. STRECKER, G. Der Weg der Gerechtigkeit (1962) 91, 149, 158, 179, 187, 195, 196, 227f. DELLING, G. Die Taufe im Neuen Testament (1963) 43. HAHN, F. Christologische Hoheitstitel (1963) 380. HUMMEL, R. Die Auseinandersetzung zwischen Kirche und Judentum im Matthäusevangelium (1963) 134. JüNGEL, E. Paulus und Jesus (1966) 174ff. 191. *ROMANIUK, K. "Repentez-vous, car le Royaume des Cieux est tout proche (Matt. iv. 17 par.)," NTS (3, '66) 259-269. METZGER, B. M. "Explicit reference in the works of Origin to variant readings in New Testament manuscripts," Historical and Literary Studies (1968) 91. MARXSEN, W. Mark the Evangelist (1969) 49, 124, 138, 142. SANFORD, J. A., The Kingdom Within (New York 1970) 46f. GOPPELT, L., Theologie des Neuen Testaments I (Göttingen

1975) 91, 104, 106, 127f 255. KINGSBURY, J. D. Matthew: Structure, Christology, Kingdom (Philadelphia 1975) 16-21, 52-54, 138-40. EGGER, W. Frohbotschaft und Lehre (Frankfurt a.M. 1976) 52f. "Beichte" in: TRE 5 (1980) 429. McDONALD, J. I. H., Kerygma and Didache (Cambridge 1980) 20f.

4:18-13:58   PERRIN, N. The New Testament (New York 1974) 179-83.

4:18-5:5   FARRER, A. St Matthew and St Mark (1954) 181.

4:18-22   EWALD, H. Die drei ersten Evangelien (1850) 191ff. WILKENS, J. Einführung in das Evangelium nach Matthäus I (1934) 78-80. STONEHOUSE, N. B. The Witness of Matthew and Mark to Christ (1944) 133. GOODSPEED, E. J. A Life of Jesus (1950) 47-49. LOEWENICH, W. von, Luther als Ausleger des Synoptiker (1954) 171f. FRANZMANN, M. H., "Studies in Discipleship. I: The Calling of the Disciples (Mt 4:18-22, 1:1 - 4:16)" CThM 31 (1960) 607-25. ERNST, J., Anfänge der Christologie (Stuttgart 1972) 127f. RIST, J. M., On the Independence of Matthew and Mark (Cambridge 1978) 25-26. BORNKAMM-BARTH-HELD, UEberlieferung und Auslegung im Matthäus-Evangelium (1961) 99, 220. WUELLNER, W. H. The Meaning of 'Fishers of Men' (1967) 232f. ITTEL, G. W. Jesus und die Jünger (1970) 14-18. OTOMO, Y. Nachfolge Jesu und Anfänge der Kirche im Neuen Testament (1970) 29-34.

4:18-20   STRECKER, G. Der Weg der Gerechtigkeit (1962) 198, 231.

4:18   *BARTINA, S. "La red esparavel del Evangelio (Mt 4, 18; Mc 1, 16)," EstBi 19 (3, '60) 215-27. BLAIR, E. P. Jesus in the Gospel of Matthew (1960) 55. STRECKER, G. Der Weg der Gerechtigkeit (1962) 202, 204, 206. HUMMEL, R. Die Auseinandersetzung zwischen Kirche und Judentum im Matthäusevangelium (1963) 112ff.

4:19   STRECKER, G. Der Weg der Gerechtigkeit (1962) 212₃.

4:23-9:34   STONEHOUSE, N. B. The Witness of Matthew and Mark to Christ (1944) 143, 133ff.

4:23-ch. 7   EWALD, H. Die drei ersten Evangelien (1850) 207ff.

4:23-5:2   BOWMAN, J. W. & TAPP, R. W. The Gospel from the Mount (1958) 19-25.

4:23-5:1   FARRER, A. St Matthew and St Mark (1954) 106.

4:23ff   ARVEDSON, T. Das Mysterium Christi (1937) 226f.

4:23-25   WILKENS, J. Einführung in das Evangelium nach Matthäus I (1934) 80-82. TRILLING, W. Das wahre Israel (1959) 111f. PLOTZKE, U. Bergpredigt (1960) 9-12. STRECKER, G. Der Weg der Gerechtigkeit (1962) 195, 200₈. FREYNE, S. The

Twelve: Disciples and Apostles (1968) 73ff. GAECHTER, P. Die literarische Kunst im Matthäus-Evangelium (1968) 54-55. FüRST, W. GPM 11/1 63-69. KINGSBURY, J. D., Matthew: Structure, Christology, Kingdom (Philadelphia 1975) 20-25. EGGER, W., Frohbotschaft und Lehre (Frankfurt a.M. 1976) 35, 53, 70f, 77f, 99f.

4:23f STRECKER, G. Der Weg der Gerechtigkeit (1962) 173.

4:23 STONEHOUSE, N. B. The Witness of Matthew and Mark to Christ (1944) 144, 160, 227. BORNKAMM-BARTH-HELD, UEberlieferung und Auslegung im Matthäus-Evangelium (1961) 49, 102, 120, 161, 237, 247, 258. STRECKER, G. Der Weg der Gerechtigkeit (1962) 115, 121, 128f, 194. HUMMEL, R. Die Auseinandersetzung zwischen Kirche und Judentum im Matthäusevangelium (1963) 145. HAHN, F. Das Verständnis der Mission im Neuen Testament (1965) 104, 105, 106. MARXSEN, W. Mark the Evangelist (1969) 123f, 138, 142, 145. SANFORD, J. A., The Kingdom Within (New York 1970) 56. KüMMEL, W. G. Einleitung in das Neue Testament (1973) 78f. FENEBERG, W. Der Markusprolog (München 1974) 145f. FRANKEMöLLE, H., Jahwebund und Kirche Christi (Münster 1974) 91, 100, 102, 195, 203, 225, 253, 266, 267, 360, 378. LADD, G. E., A Theology of the New Testament (Grand Rapids 1974) 45, 57, 114. KINGSBURY, J. D., Matthew: Structure, Christology, Kingdom (Philadelphia 1975) 128-30, 163-65. RIST, J. M., On the Independence of Matthew and Mark (Cambridge 1978) 29. "Bergpredigt" in: TRE 5 (1980) 608.

4:24 PARKER, P. The Gospel Before Mark (1953) 89-90. KNOX, W. L. The Sources of the Synoptic Gospels II (1957) 125. BETZ, H. D. Lukian von samosata und das Neue Testament (1961) 146, 148. STRECKER, G. Der Weg der Gerechtigkeit (1962) 195. LANGE, J., Das Erscheinen des Auferstandenen im Evangelium nach Matthäus (Würzburg 1973) 71, 150, 358, 363-65, 372, 399f, 402, 494. *ROSS, J. M., "Epileptic or Moonstruck?" BTr 29 (1978) 126-28.

4:25-8:1 LUND, N. W. Chiasmus in the New Testament (1942) 242f.

4:25 DALMAN, G. Orte und Wege Jesu (1967) 5f.

5-9 BORNKAMM-BARTH-HELD, UEberlieferung und Auslegung im Matthäus-Evangelium (1961) 234, 243, 258.

5-7   SCHLATTER, A. Die Theologie des Neuen Testaments I
(1909) 137-140. FIEBIG, P. Jesu Bergpredigt (1924).
WINDISCH, H. Der Sinn der Bergpredigt (1929), Engl. Ed.:
The Meaning of the Sermon on the Mount (1951). HUBER, H.
Die Bergpredigt (1932). SCHMITZ, O., "Thurneysens
christologische Deutung der Bergpredigt" Jahrbuch der
Theologischen Schule Bethel 9 (1938) 17-36. DIBELIUS, M.
Botschaft und Geschichte I (1940) 79-174. DIBELIUS, M. The
Sermon on the Mount (1940). THIELICKE, H. "Ich aber sage
euch. . . ." Auslegung der Bergpredigt in Stuttgarter
Gottesdiensten (1946). THOMPSON, E. T. The Sermon on the
Mount and Its Meaning for Today (1946). SPRENGLER, P.
Die Bergpredigt (1947). MANSON, W. Jesus the Messiah
(1948) 78-93. SCHNIEWIND, J. Das Evangelium nach
Matthäus (1949) 37-39. BONHOEFFER, D. Nachfolge (1950)
55ff. GOODSPEED, E. J. A Life of Jesus (1950) 76-85.
*HUNTER, A. M. "The Meaning of the Sermon on the
Mount," ET LXIII (1952) 176-79. DIBELIUS, M. Botschaft
und Geschichte I (1953) 79-174. HUNTER, A. M. Design for
Life (1953). FARRER, A. St Matthew and St Mark (1954) 50,
ch. X passim. *MASSAUX, E. "Le texte du sermon sur la
montagne de Matthieu utilisé par Saint Justin. Contribution à
la critique textuelle du premier évangile," EphT XXVII (1954)
411-448. *RENWART, L. Augustiana, NRTh 87 (1955) 983-84.
EDDLEMAN, H. L. Teachings of Jesus in Matthew 5-7 (1955).
KEPLER, T. S. Jesus' Design for Living (1955). M'NEILE, A.
H. The Gospel According to St Matthew (1955) 99-101.
BORNKAMM, G. Jesus von Nazareth (1956) 92ff, 201ff.
GOPPELT, L. "Der Staat in der Sicht des Neuen Testaments,"
in: Macht und Recht. Beiträge zur lutherischen Staatslehre der
Gegenwart (1956) Dombois, H. & Wilkens, E. (eds.) 9-12.
NYGREN, A. Die Bergpredigt EKL I (1956) 392-95.
SCHMID, J. Das Evangelium nach Matthäus (1956) 154-60.
THIELICKE, H. Das Leben kann noch einmal beginnen
(1956). BORNKAMM, G. "Bergpredigt. I. Biblisch," RGG3 I
(1957) 1047-50. FASCHER, E. "Bergpredigt. II.
Auslegungsgeschichtlich," RGG3 I (1957) 1050-53.
BOWMAN, J. W. & Tapp, R. W. The Gospel from the Mount
(1957). KNOX, W. L. The Sources of the Synoptic Gospels II
(1957) 7ff. STAUDINGER, J. S. J. Die Bergpredigt (1957).
KING, G. H. New Order. An Expositional Study of the Sermon
on the Mount (1958). *PENTECOST, J. D. "The Purpose of
the Sermon on the Mount," BiblSa 115 (458, '58) 128-35; (459,
'58) 212-17· (460, '58) 313-19. *WULF, F. "Ist die Bergpredigt
für Christen in der Welt realisierbar?" GuL 31 (3, '58) 184-197.
*BATDORF, I. W. "How Shall We Interpret the Sermon on

the Mount?" Journ BibRel 27 (3, '59) 211-17. KARRENBERG, F. Gestalt und Kritik des Westens (1959) 38-40. *KüRZINGER, J. "Zur Komposition der Bergpredigt nach Matthäus," Biblica 40 (3, '59) 569-89. LLOYD-JONES, D. M. Studies in the Sermon on the Mount I (1959). BORNKAMM, G. Jesus von Nazareth (1960) 202-206. JEREMIAS, J., 'Die Bergpredigt" Calwer Hefte 27 (1960) 5-32. MANSON, T. W. Ethics and the Gospel (1960). McARTHUR, H. K. Understanding the Sermon on the Mount (1960). PLOTZKE, U. Bergpredigt. Von der Freiheit des Christlichen Lebens (1960). BORNKAMM-BARTH-HELD, UEberlieferung und Auslegung im Matthäus-Evangelium (1961) 234, 238, 243. DRUMWRIGHT, H. L., "The Ethical Motif in Mt 5-7" SouJTh 5 (1962) 65-76. *HERING, J. "Le Sermon sur la Montagne dans la nouvelle traduction anglaise de la Bible," RHPR 42 (2-3, '62) 122-32. JEREMIAS, J. Paroles de Jésus. Le Sermon sur la montagne, le Notre-Père dans l'exégèse actuelle (1963). LüTHI, W. & BRUNNER, R. The Sermon on the Mount (1963). *SCHOENBERG, M. "The Location of the Mount of Beatitudes," Bible Today 1 (4, '63) 232-39. THIELICKE, H. Life Can Begin Again. Sermons on the Sermon on the Mount (1963). DAVIES, W. D. The Setting of the Sermon on the Mount (1964). JEREMIAS, J. Il discorso della montagna (1964). LOOSLEY, E. G. The Challenge from the Mount (1964). *SCHMID, J. "Ich aber sage euch. Der Anruf der Bergpredigt," BuK 19 (3, '64) 75-79. THURNEYSEN, E. Die Bergpredigt (1964). EICHHOLZ, G. Auslegung der Bergpredigt (1965). EICHHOLZ, G. "Die Aufgabe einer Auslegung der Bergpredigt," in: Tradition und Interpretation (1965). HUNTER, A. M. A Pattern for Life (1965). *MOUNCE, R. H. "Synoptic Self-portraits," EQ 37 (4, '65) 212-17. DAVIES, W. D., The Sermon on the Mount (Cambridge 1966). JEREMIAS, J. Abba; Studien zur neutestamentlichen Theologie und Zeitgeschichte (1966). SCHARBERT, A. Die Bergpredigt (1966). SCHNACKENBURG, R., Present and Future III (Notre Dame 1966). *HäRING, B. "The Normative Value of the Sermon on the Mount," CBQ 29 (3, '67) 375-85. LOUW, J. P. "Dikaiosyne," Neotestamentica 1 ('67) 35-41. NORMAN, F. Christos Didaskalos (1967) 18, 26-27, 31-38, 42, 50, 79, 105. ROBERTS, J. H. "The Sermon on the Mount and the Idea of Liberty," Neotestamentica 1 ('67) 9-15. SCHNACKENBURG, R. Christliche Existenz nach dem N. T. (1967) 109-30. TOIT, A. B. du, "The Self-Revelation of Jesus in Matthew 5-7," Neotestamentica 1 ('67) 66-72. CERFAUX, L. Jésus aux origines de la Tradition (1968) 72-80. GOPPELT, L. Die

Bergpredigt und die Wirklichkeit dieser Welt (1968). HäRING, B. What Does Christ Want? (1968). KNöRZER, W. Die Bergpredigt. Modell einer neuen Welt (1968). SMITH, M. Tannaitic Parallels to the Gospels (Philadelphia 1968) 4bn27, 4A+, C+. *KRAUSE, C. "The Sermon on the Mount in Ecumenical Thought Since World War II," LV 15, (1, '68) 52-59; "Der Bergpredigt in den ökumenischen Studien seit dem Zweiten Weltkrieg," LR 18 (1, '68) 65-74. LUCK, U. Die Vollkommenheitsforderung der Bergpredigt. Ein aktuelles Kapitel der Theologie des Matthäus (1968). REUMANN, J. Jesus in the Church's Gospels (1968) 233-41. SCHNACKENBURG, R. Christian Existence in the New Testament (1968) 128-57. *SKIBBE, E. M. "Pentateuchal Themes in the Sermon on the Mount," LQ 20 (1, '68) 44-51. WREGE, H.-T. Die UEberlieferungsgeschichte der Bergpredigt (1968). BANNACH, H. Ich aber sage euch. Sechs Bibelarbeiten über die Bergpredigt (Matthäus 5-7) beim 14. Deutschen Evangelischen Kirchentag Stuttgart 1969 (1969). BLANK, J. Schriftauslegung in Theorie und Praxis (1969) 137, 141f. *COLLINS, R. F. "Christian Personalism and the Sermon on the Mount," ANQ, 10 (1, '69) 19-30. *HAWKINS, R. A. "Covenant Relations of the Sermon on the Mount," RestQ 12 (1, '69) 1-9. *CORBIN, M. "Nature et signification de la Loi évangélique," RechSR 57 (1, '69) 5-48. FRIEDLANDER, G. The Jewish Sources of the Sermon on the Mount (1969). HAENCHEN, E. "Neutestamentliche und gnostische Evangelien," in: Christentum und Gnosis (1969) Eltester, W. (ed.) 32. KUHN, J. (ed.) Die bessere Gerechtigkeit, Die Bergpredigt zwischen Utopie und Realität (1969). LüHRMANN, D. Die Redaktion der Logienquelle (1969) 53-56. MüSSLE, M .(ed.), Der "politische" Jesus. Seine Bergpredigt (1969). POKORNY, P. Der Kern der Bergpredigt. Eine Auslegung (1969). SCHNEIDER, G. Botschaft der Bergpredigt (1969), 7-22, 112-16. *GREENWOOD, D. "Moral Obligation in the Sermon on the Mount," ThSt 31 (2, '70) 301-309. *HENGEL, M. "Leben in der Veränderung. Ein Beitrag zum Verständnis der Bergpredigt," EvKomm 3 (11, '70) 647-51. *LERLE, E. "Realisierbare Forderungen der Bergpredigt?" KuD 16 (1, '70) 32-40. LOHSE, E. (ed.), Der Ruf Jesu und die Antwort der Gemeinde (1970) 99-104. SCHILLE, G. Das vorsynoptische Judenchristentum (1970) 65ff. KECK, L. E. "The Sermon on the Mount," in: Jesus and man's hope (1971). Miller, D. G. & Hadidian, D. Y. 311-22. RAGAZ, L., Die Bergpredigt Jesu (Hamburg 1971⁻1945). SELBY, D. J., Introduction to the New Testament (New York 1971) 112, 113, 124-28. *GIAVINI, G. "Le norme etiche della Bibbia e l'uomo d'oggi," ScuC 100 (1, '72) 5-15; (2, '72) 83-97. *KRAUTTER, B., Die Bergpredigt im Religionsunterricht (München/Stuttgart 1973). KüMMEL, W. G. Einleitung in das Neue Testament (1973) 18f. LANGE, J., Das Erscheinen des Auferstandenen im Evangelium nach Matthäus (Würzburg 1973) 387, 393, 404, 408, 424, 442-44, 493f. *SCHMAHL, G. "Gültigkeit und Verbindlichkeit der Bergpredigt" BiLe 14 (1973) 180-87. *SCHNEIDER, G., Botschaft der Bergpredigt (Leipzig 1973). *AGOURIDIS, S., "Hē epi tou Orous Homilia" DBM 2 (1974) 183-217. *ELLIS, P. F., "Matthew: His Mind and His Message. The Sermon on the Mount - the Authority of Jesus 'in Word'. Mt 5:1 - 7:29" Bible Today 70 (1974) 1483-91. ELLIS, P. F., Matthew: His Mind and His Message (Collegeville 1974) 31-40. SAND, A., Das Gesetz und die Propheten (Regensburg 1974) 46-56. BLIGH J., The Sermon on the Mount. A Discussion on Mt 5-7 (Slough 1975). CONZELMANN, H./LINDEMANN, A., Arbeitsbuch zum Neuen Testament (Tübingen 1975) 61f. *GIUSTOZZI, E., "Hay un sistema de normas en el Sermón de la Montãna?" RevBi 37 (1975) 235-43. HARNER, Ph.B., Understanding the Lord's Prayer (Philadelphia 1975) 5-7. *KISSINGER, W. S., The Sermon on the Mount: A History of Interpretation and Bibliography (Metuchen NJ 1975). BETZ, O., "Rechtfertigung in Qumran" in: J. Friedrich et al. (eds.) Rechtfertigung. Festschrift für Ernst Käsemann (Göttingen 1976) 131-38. DRURY, J., Tradition and Design in Luke's Gospel (Atlanta 1976) 131-38. *FISHER, F. L., The Sermon on the Mount (Nashville 1976). *LANG, H., "Verschränkung von narrativer Syntax und kommunikativen Einheiten und ihre Abhängigkeit vom soziokulturellen Kontext, dargestellt am Beispiel der Bergpredigt" LiBi 37 (1976) 16-30. *MENESTRINA, G., "Matteo 5-7 e Luca 6, 20-49 nell 'Evangelo di Tommaso" BiOr 18 (1976) 65-67. *BEYSCHLAG, K., "Zur Geschichte der Bergpredigt in der Alten Kirche" ZThK 74 (1977) 291-322. *TUTTLE, G. A., "The Sermon on the Mount: Its Wisdom Affinities and Their Relation to Its Structure" JEThS 20 (1977) 213-30. *BORNKAMM, G., "Der Aufbau der Bergpredigt" NTS 24 (1978) 419-32. *CARSON, D. A., The Sermon on the Mount (Grand Rapids 1978). *EGGER, W., "Faktoren der Textkonstitution in der Bergpredigt" Laurentianum 19 (1978) 177-98. *FEUILLET, A., "Die beiden Aspekte der Gerechtigkeit in der Bergpredigt" IKZ/Communio 7 (1978) 108-15. GRANT, R. M., "The Sermon on the Mount in Early Christianity" Semeia 12 (1978) 215-31. *LACHS, S. T., "Some

Textual Observations on the Sermon on the Mount" Jewish Quarterly Review 69 (1978) 98-111. MARXSEN, W., Christologie-praktisch (Gütersloh 1978) 94-106. RIST, J. M., On the Independence of Matthew and Mark (Cambridge 1978) 26. Zimmerli, W., "Die Seligpreisungen der Bergpredigt und das Alte Testament" in: E. Bammel/C. K. Barrett/W. D. Davies (eds.) Donum Gentilicium: New Testament Studies in Honour of David Daube (Oxford 1978) 8-26. *BERNER, U., Die Bergpredigt. Rezeption und Auslegung im 20. Jahrhundert (Göttingen 1979). *BETZ, H. D., "The Sermon on the Mount: Its Literary Genre and Function" JR 59 (1979) 285-97. *HENDRICKX, H., The Sermon on the Mount (Manila 1979). *McEleney, N. J., "the Principles of the Sermon on the Mount" CBQ 41 (1979) 552-70. SHINN, R. L., The Sermon on the Mount (Nashville 1979). "Bergpredigt" in: TRE 5 (1980) 603, 608, 611.

5-6   STRECKER, G. Der Weg der Gerechtigkeit (1962) 12.

5   FIEBIG, P. Jesu Bergpredigt (1924). MARRIOTT, H. The Sermon on the Mount (1925). BONHOEFFER, D. Nachfolge (1950) 55ff. SCHILLE, G. Bemerkungen zur Formgeschichte des Evangliums. NTS 4 (1957-58) 107ff. FUCHS, E. "Jesu Selbstzeugnis nach Matthäus 5," Zur Frage nach dem historischen Jesus (1960) 100-25. McARTHUR, H. K. Understanding the Sermon on the Mount (1960) 11, 15, 22, 30, 35, 87, 95, 118, 142, 143, 166. GIDEON, V. E., "Preaching Values in Mt 5" SouJTh 5 (1962) 77-88. GOULDER, M. D., Type and History in Acts (London 1964) 127f. KäSEMANN, E. Exegetische Versuche und Besinnungen II (1964) 84. BRAUN, H. Qumran und NT II (1966) 68, 79, 219, 270, 272, 277, 309, 311. KäSEMANN, E. New Testament Questions of Today (1969) 84. DUPONT, J. Les Béatitudes (1969). RAYAN, S., The Holy Spirit: Heart of the Gospel and Christian Hope (New York 1978) 39-51.

5:1ff   *WAITZ, H. "Eine Parallele zu den Seligpreisungen aus dem ausserkanonischen Evangelium," ZNW 4 (1903) 335-40.

5:1-20   CHAMBERS, O. Studies in the Sermon on the Mount (1941) 11-24.

5:1-16   RIDDERBOS, H. Matthew's Witness to Jesus Christ (1958) 27-33. PELIKAN, J. (ed.), The Preaching of Chrysostom (1967) 39-66.

5:1-12   THOMPSON, E. T. The Sermon on the Mount (1946) 33-47. HEIM, D. K. Die Bergpredigt (1949) 61-72. BUCHHOLZ, F. EvTh 14 (1954) 97-104. EICHHOLZ, G. Herr, tue meine Lippen auf (1957) 347-54. *SABBE, M. "De exegese van de zaligheden," CollBrugGand 5 (1, '59) 85-88. KNöRZER, W. Die Bergpredigt. Modell einer neuen Welt (1968), 26-37. BANNACH, H. "Die Seligpreisungen," Ich aber sage euch (1969) 8-16. DEMMER, H. "Matthäus 5, 1-12" Ich aber sage euch (1969) 33-40. EICHELE, E. "Matthäus 5, 1-12," Ich aber sage euch (1969) 54-62. LANGE, E. "Die Gerechtigkeit des Jüngers," Ich aber sage euch (1969) 81-90. VON OPPEN, D. "Friedfertigkeit - ein Hindernis zum Frieden?" Ich aber sage euch (1969), 112-15. ZAHRNT, H. "Matthäus 5, 1-12," Ich aber sage euch (1969) 122-35. *FRANKENMöLLE, H. "Die Makarismen (Mt 5, 1-12; Lk 6, 20-23). Motive und Umfang der redaktionelle Kompositionen," BZ 15 (1, '71) 52-75. *JAQUEMIN, P. E., "Les béatitudes selon saint Matthieu. Mt 5, 1-12a" AssS 66 (1973) 50-63. *NEWMAN, B. M., "Some Translational Notes on the Beautitudes. Matthew 5.1-12" BTr 26 (1975) 106-20.

5:1-11 BARDORF, I. W. Interpreting the Beatitudes (1966).

5:1-10 STECK, K. G. GPM 3/4 (1973) 461-69.
(11-12)

5:1-10 MüLHAUPT, E. (ed.), Martin Luthers Auslegung der Bergpredigt (1961) 52-61. *HINNEBUSCH, P. "The Messianic Meaning of the Beatitudes," Bible Today 59 ('72) 707-17.

5:1-3 SHINN, R. L. Sermon on the Mount (1962) 8-13.

5:1-2 THOLUCK, A. Die Bergrede Christi (1872) 35-43. WILKENS, J. Einführung in das Evangelium nach Matthäus I (1934) 82-84. HEIM, D. K. Die Bergpredigt Jesus (1949) 5-15. KEPLER, T. S. Jesus' Design for Living (1952) 11-13. KING, G. H. New Order (1954) 7-14. EICHHOLZ, G. Auslegung der Bergpredigt (1965) 20-25. SCHNEIDER, G. Botschaft der Bergpredigt (1969) 25-26.

5:1 WINDISCH, H. The Meaning of the Sermon on the Mount (1937) 63ff. STONEHOUSE, N. B. The Witness of Matthew and Mark to Christ (1944) 134, 176. MASSAUX, E. Influence de l'Evangile de saint Matthieu sur la littérature chrétienne avant saint Irénée (1950) 165-168. PARKER, P. The Gospel Before Mark (1953) 177-178. KNOX, W. L. The Sources of the Synoptic Gospels II (1957) 7. BLAIR, E. P. Jesus in the Gospel of Matthew (1960) 134. BORNKAMM-BARTH-HELD, UEberlieferung und Auslegung im Matthäus-Evangelium (1961) 123, 208. STRECKER, G. Der Weg der Gerechtigkeit (1962) 98, 106, 127, 147. HAHN, F. Christologische Hoheitstitel (1963) 401. *MANEK, J. "On the Mount-On the Plain (Mt. v 1-Lk. vi 17)," NovTest 9 (2, '67) 124-31. SCHREIBER, J. Theologie des Vertrauens (1967) 214-16.

SEITZ, O. J. F. Love your Enemies NTS 16 (1969-70) 39f.
LANGE, J., Das Erscheinen des Auferstandenen im Evangelium nach Matthäus (Würzburg 1973) 41, 317, 320, 392-94, 396, 403, 411f, 429, 436, 441, 444f, 472, 479. KINGSBURY, J. D., Matthew: Structure, Christology, Kingdom (Philadelphia 1975) 56-58. LIVIO, J.-B., "La signification théologique de la 'montagne' dans le premier évangile" Bulletin du Centre Protestant d'Études 30 (1978) 13-20. "Bergpredigt" in: TRE 5 (1980) 608.

5:2-7:27   HIRSCH, E. Frühgeschichte des Evangeliums (1941) 77-88.

5:2-12   HARBSMEIER, G., in: GPM 33 (1979) 410-15. *MAY, J., "Fehlt dem Christentum ein Verhältnis zur Natur? Eine Analyse der Seligpreisungen (Mt 5, 2-12) und der Feuerpredigt des Buddha (Samy. XXXV, 28)" US 34 (1979) 159-71.

5:2f   PLOTZKE, U. Bergpredigt (1960) 13-18.

5:3-7:27   STONEHOUSE, N. B. The Witness of Matthew and Mark to Christ (1944) 130, 134. BUTLER, B. C. The Originality of St Matthew (1951) 37ff. DUPONT, D. J. Les Béatitudes (1958) 175-184. BURCHARD, Chr., "The Theme of the Sermon on the Mount" in: L. Schottroff et al. (eds.) Essays in the Love Commandment (Philadelphia 1978) 57-91.

5:3ff   STAEHELIN, E. Die Verkündigung des Reiches Gottes in der Kirche Jesu Christi I (1951) 56, 210, 284, 385. KNOX, W. L. The Sources of the Synoptic Gospels II (1957) 12ff. BERTRANGS, A. Les Béatitudes (1962). HAHN, F. Christologische Hoheitstitel (1963) 402. CARRE, A. -M. Béatitudes pour aujourd'hui (1963). BRETSCHER, P. G. The World Upside Down or Right Side Up? (1964). PLOTZKE, U. God's Own Magna Charta (1964). WIRT, S. E. Magnificent Promise. A Fresh View of the Beatitudes-from the Cross (1964). RIFE, M .J. "Matthew's Beatitudes and the Septuagint," in: Studies in the History and Text of the New Testament (1967) Daniels, B. L. & Suggs, M. J. (eds.) 107-13. DODD, C. H. "The Beatitudes: a form-critical study," More New Testament Studies (1968). *LIPINSKI, E. "Macarismes et psaumes de congratulation," RB 75 (3, '68) 321-67. MIEGGE, G. Il Sermone sul monte. Commentario esegetico (1970). FRIEDLANDER. G. The Jewish Sources of the Sermon on the Mount (1969) 11-23.

5:3-48   GRANT, F. C. The Gospels (1957) 143f.

5:3-16   THOLUCK, A. Die Bergrede Christi (1862) 43-96. *HOFFMAN, P. " 'Selig sind die Armen. . .' Auslegung der Bergpredigt II (Mt 5, 3-16)," BuL 10 (2, '69) 111-22. SAND, A., Das Gesetz und die Propheten (Regensburg 1974) 175-77.

5:3-12 JüLICHER, D. A. Die Gleichnissreden Jesu (1910) 73-75. FIEBIG, P. "Die mündliche UEberlieferung als Quelle des Synoptikern," in: Neutestamentliche Studien Georg Heinrici zu seinem 70. Geburtstag (1914) Deissmann, A. & Windisch, H. (eds.) 85ff. HEINRICI, G. Neutestamentliche Studien (1914) 85ff. WILKENS, J. Einfürung in das Evangelium nach Matthäus I (1934) 84-87. HUGH, M. The Beatitudes (1952). HUNTER, A. M. Design for Life (1953) 29-37. BLACK, M. The Beatitudes ET 64/4 (1953) 125-26. KING, G. H. New Order (1954) 14-22. LOEWENICH, W. von, Luther als Ausleger der Synoptiker (1954) 158f. ZERWICK, M. on J. Dupont, Les Beatitudes, Le probleme littéraire, Le message doctrinal VD 33 (1955) 298-300. DUPONT, J. Les Béatitudes. Le Problème littéraire. Les deux versions du Sermon sur la montagne et des Béatitudes (1958). *BRAUMANN, G. "Zum traditionsgeschichtlichen Problem der Seligpreisungen Mt v 3-12," NovTest 4 (4, '60) 253-300. BORNKAMM-BARTH-HELD, UEberlieferung und Auslegung im Matthäus-Evangelium (1961) 14, 56, 115. BULTMANN, R. The History of the Synoptic Tradition (1963) 109f. PERRIN, N., The Kingdom of God in the Teaching of Jesus (Philadelphia 1963) 83, 85, 181-83. KAMLAH, E. Die Form der katalogischen Paränese im N. T. (1964) 24-27. EICHHOLZ, G. Auslegung der Bergpredigt (1965) 26-54. HUNTER, A. M. A Pattern for Life (1965) 33-41. DAVIES, W. D., The Sermon on the Mount (Cambridge 1966) 86. AGOURIDES, S., "La tradition des Béatitudes chez Matthieu et Luc" in: A. Descamps/A. de Halleux (eds.) Mélanges Bibliques en hommage au R. P. Béda Rigaux (Gembloux 1970) 9-27. *DUPONT, J. " 'Béatitudes' égyptiennes," Biblica 47 (2, '66) 185-222. DODD, C. H. "The Beatitudes: a form-critical study," More New Testament Studies (1968) 1-10. *TRUHLER, K. "The Earthly Cast of the Beatitudes," Concilium 39 ('68) 33-43. *KIEFFER, R. "Vishet och välsignelse som grundmotive i saligprisningarna hos Matteus och Lukas," SVA 34 ('69) 107-21. SCHNEIDER, G. Botschaft der Bergpredigt (1969) 27-39. TRILLING, W. "Heilsverheissung und Lebenslehre des Jüngers," in: Christusverkündigung in den Synoptischen Evangelien (1969) 64. *GROUNDS, V. C. "Mountain Manifesto," BiblSa 128 (510, '71) 135-41. *STRECKER, G. "Die Makarismen der Bergpredigt," NTS 17 (3, '71) 255-75. GOPPELT, L., Theologie des Neuen Testaments I (Göttingen 1975) 118ff. HOFFMANN, P.,/EID, V., Jesus von Nazareth und eine christliche Moral (Freiburg 1975) 29-35. *DUPONT, J., "Introduction aux Béatitudes" NRTh 98 (1976) 97-108. EDWARDS, R. A., A Theology of Q (Philadelphia 1976) 84-

85. *GUELICH, R. A., "The Matthean Beatitudes: 'Entrance-Requirements' or Eschatological Blessings?" JBL 95 (1976) 415-34. *STACHOWIAK, L., "Osiem blogoslawieństw na tle pojeć etycznych mieszkańców Palestyny w epoce Chrystusa (Die Seligpreisungen im Lichte der sittlichen Ideale der Palästina-Bewohner zur Zeit Jesu)" RTK 23 (1976) 49-59. POLAG, A., Die Christologie der Logienquelle (Neukirchen-Vluyn 1977) 10. *BETZ, H. D., "Die Makarismen der Bergpredigt (Matthäus 5, 3-12). Beobachtungen zur literarischen Form und theologischen Bedeutung" ZThK 75 (1978) 3-19. FLUSSER, D., "Some Notes on the Beatitudes (Matthew 5:3-12, Luke 6:20-26)" Immanuel 8 (1978) 37-47. ZIMMERLI, W., "Die Seligpreisungen der Bergpredigt und das Alte Testament" in: E. Bammel/C. K. Barrett/W. D. Davies (eds.) Donum Gentilicium: New Testament Studies in Honour of David Daube (Oxford 1978) 8-26. "Bergpredigt" in: TRE 5 (1980) 604f.

5:3-11 *STRAMARE, T. "Le beatitudini e la critica letteraria," RivB 13 (1, '65) 31-40. HENGEL, M., Was Jesus a Revolutionist? (Philadelphia 1971) 9. SANDERS, J. T., Ethics in the New Testament (Philadelphia 1975) 45f. SUGGS, M. J., "The Antithesis as Redactional Products" in: Essays in the Love Commandment (Philadelphia 1978) 93-107.

5:3-10 *d' A. S. J. "Les béatitudes, apprivoisement à la Béatitude," VieS 107 (487, '62) 356-67. *REGAMEY, P.-R. "Qui ne peut le moins peut le plus. La Providence et l'esprit des Béatitudes," VieS 106 (481, '62) 257-81. *BAUMANN, R. "Heil euch, ihr Armen! Die ursprüngliche Botschaft der Seligpreisungen," BuK 19 (3, '64) 79-85. HAHN, F. Das Verständnis der Mission im Neuen Testament (1965) 106. RIFE, J. M., "Matthew's Beatitudes and the Septuagint" in: B. L. Daniels/M. J. Suggs (eds.) Studies in the History and Text of the New Testament: in honor of Kenneth Willis Clark (Salt Lake City 1967) 107-12. GAECHTER, P. Die literarische Kunst im Matthäus-Evangelium (1968) 22-23. LORENZ, F. Streit um Jesus (1969) 5-12. BJöRCK, S., Valda Texter ur Nya Testamentet (Stockholm 1972) 3-4. CAVALLIN, H. C. C., Life After Death, Part I (Lund 1974) 4, II, n4. GOULDER, M. D., Midrash and Lection in Matthew (London 1974) 186, 252-69, 272-79. POLAG, A., Die Christologie der Logienquelle (Neukirchen-Vluyn 1977) 41f.

5:3-9 STRECKER, G. Der Weg der Gerechtigkeit (1962) 12, 38, 150f. KLEINE, R., "Die Seligpreisungen des Herrn" Anzeiger für die Katholische Geistlichkeit 72 (1963) 222-28, 526-34.

5:3-7 SCHÜRMANN, H., "Beobachtungen zum Menschensohn-

Titel in der Redenquelle" in: R. Pesch/E. Schnackenburg (eds.) Jesus und der Menschensohn (Freiburg 1975) 130f.

5:3-6 BOWMAN, J. W. & Tapp, R. W. The Gospel from the Mount (1958) 27-36. *MICHAELIS, C. "Die II-Alliteration der Subjektsworte der ersten Seligpreisungen in Mt. v 3-6 und ihre Bedeutung für den Aufbau der Seligpreisungen bei Mt., Lk. und in Q," NovTest 10 (2-3, '68) 148-61. DUNN, J., Jesus and the Spirit (London 1975) 54f. EDWARDS, R. A., A Theology of Q (Philadelphia 1976) 62f. "Bergpredigt" in: TRE 5 (1980) 605f.

5:3-5 VOLZ, P. Die Eschatologie der jüdischen Gemeinde (1934) 81, 380, 408, 413. *FLUSSER, D. "Blessed are the Poor in the Spirit. . .," IEJ 10 (1, '60) 1-13. BORNKAMM-BARTH-HELD, UEberlieferung und Auslegung im Matthäus-Evangelium (1961) 115f. *BöHL, F., "Die Demut (*'nwh*) als höchste der Tugenden. Bemerkungen zu Mt 5, 3.5" BZ 20 (1976) 217-23.

5:3f.6. SCHULZ, S. Q Die Spruchquelle der Evangelisten (1972) 76-84.

5:3f HOFFMANN, P. Studien zur Theologie der Logienquelle (1972) passim.

5:3-4 TALBERT, C. H., Literary Patterns, Theological Themes and the Genre of Luke-Acts (Missoula 1974) 42. DUNN, J. D. G., Jesus and the Spirit (London 1975) 376.

5:3 STONEHOUSE, N. B. The Witness of Matthew and Mark to Christ (1944) 228. STAEHELIN, E. Die Verkündigung des Reiches Gottes in der Kirche Jesu Christi I (1951) 268-85. KEPLER, T. S. Jesus' Design for Life (1952) 14-16. LLOYD-JONES, D. M. Studies in the Sermon on the Mount I (1954) 42-52. STAUDINGER, J. Die Bergpredigt (1957) 23, 43, 165, 190, 267. DUPONT, D. J. Les Béatitudes (1958) 209-17, 251-53, 261-63, 291-94. BEST, E. Matthew V.3. NTS 7 (1960-61) 255f. *McCARRIGLE, F. J. "The Humility of 'The Poor in Spirit'," AER 144 (5, '61) 313-19. LEGASSE, S. "Les Pauvres en Esprit et les 'Volontaires' de Qumran," NTS 8 (4, '62) 335-45. STRECKER, G. Der Weg der Gerechtigkeit (1962) 150f, 156, 232. BüRKI, H. "Die geistliche Armen", in: Abraham unser Vater (Festschr. für Otto Michel (1963) 58-64. DUPONT, J. "Les πτωχοὶ τῷ πνεύματι et les'nwj de Qumran," in: Neutestamentliche Aufsätze (1963) 53-64. HAHN, F. Christologische Hoheitstitel (1963) 402. RODZIANKO, V. "The Meaning of Matthew 5, 3," in: Studia Evangelica II (1964) Cross, F. L. (ed.) 118. *MANEK, J. "Vier Bibelstudien zur Problematik der sozialen Umwandlung," CommViat 10 (1, '67)

61-70; (2-3, '67) 179-82. *STRAMARE, T. "Beati i poveri," RivB 13 (2, '65) 179-86. BRAUN, H. Qumran und NT II (1966) 98, 104, 252, 256, 287f, 291. SASS, G. Ungereimtes bei Matthäus (1968) 6-7. *SHIBUTANI, O. "The Kingdom of God and the Kingdom of Heavens," KatorShin 7 (1, '68) 62-92. (In Japanese.) SUMMERS, R. The Secret Sayings of the Living Jesus (1968) 23. WREGE, H.-T. Die UEberlieferungsgeschichte der Bergpredigt (1968) 6. SANFORD, J. A., The Kingdom Within (New York 1970) 189f. JEREMIAS, J. Neutestamentliche Theologie I (1971) 40, 83, 100, 114, 118, 198. GRUNDMANN, W., "Weisheit im Horizont des Reiches Gottes. Eine Studie zur Verkündigung Jesu nach der Spruchüberlieferung Q" in: R. Schnackenburg/et al. (eds.) Die Kirche des Anfangs. Festschrift für Heinz Schürmann (Leipzig 1977) 182. *SCHWARZ, G., " 'Ihnen gehört das Himmelreich'? (Matthäus v. 3)" NTS 23 (1977) 341-43. *SIMON, M. L., " 'Bienaventurados los pobres de espiritu' (Mt 5, 3). Base y fundamento de la pobreza evangelica" Biblia y Fe 5 (1979) 148-62. "Bergpredigt" in: TRE 5 (1980) 605.

5:4-9   SHINN, R. L. Sermon on the Mount (1962) 14-20.

5:4, 6   BOERMA, C., Rich Man, Poor Man - and the Bible (London 1979) 46-48.

5:4   BORNHäUSER, D. K. Die Bergpredigt (1927) 30ff. KEPLER, T. S. Jesus' Design for Living (1952) 17-20. *TEBBE, W. EvTh 12 (1952/53) 121-28. LLOYD-JONES, D. M. Studies in the Sermon on the Mount I (1954) 53-62. DUPONT, D. J. Les Béatitudes (1958) 261-63. PLOTZKE, U. Bergpredigt (1960) 19-26. STRECKER, G. Der Weg der Gerechtigkeit (1962) 189?. WREGE, H.-T. Die UEberlieferungsgeschichte der Bergpredigt (1968) 16. BLANK, J. Schriftauslegung in Theorie und Praxis (1969) 26f. GOULDER, M. D., Midrash and Lection in Matthew (London 1974) 160, 254, 263, 264ff, 277f, 422. SWIDLER, L., Biblical Affirmations of Woman (Philadelphia 1979) 284.

5:5ff   STAEHELIN, E. Die Verkündigung des Reiches Gottes in der Kirche Jesu Christi I (1951) 386.

5:5-8   HENNECKE, E. & SCHNEEMELCHER, W. Neutestamentliche Apokryphen II (1964) 244, 345, 549f.

5:5-7   HEIM, D. K. Die Bergpredigt Jesu (1949) 50-60.

5:5   STAEHELIN, E. Die Verkündigung des Reiches Gottes in der Kirche Jesu Christi I (1951) 139, 247, 268, 301, 333, 396. KEPLER, T. S. Jesus' Design for Living (1952) 20-22. LLOYD-JONES, D. M. Studies in the Sermon on the Mount I (1954) 63-72. *COCAGNAC, A.-M. "Trois méditations sur la douceur

évangélique," LuVie 7 (38, '58) 98-112. DUPONT, D. J. Les
Béatitudes (1958) 251-57. McARTHUR, H. K. Understanding
the Sermon on the Mount (1960) 15, 84, 164, 171. PLOTZKE,
U. Bergpredigt (1960) 26-32. *COLUNGA, A.
"Bienaventurados los mansos ellos poseeran la tierra,"
Salmaticensis 9 (3, '62) 589-97. STRECKER, G. Der Weg der
Gerechtigkeit (1962) 232, 384, 74, 174, 232. SMITH, M.,
Tannaitic Parallels to the Gospels (Philadelphia 1968) 2bn64+.
WREGE, H.-T. Die UEberlieferungsgeschichte der
Bergpredigt (1968) 24. BEST, E. I Peter and the Gospel
Tradition NTS 16 (1969-70) 108f. DAVIES, W. D., The Gospel
and the Land (London 1974) 359, 360-63. CLARK, K. W.,
"The Making of the Twentieth Century New Testament" in:
The Gentile Bias and Other Essays (Leiden 1980) 151.

5:6-7   BRAUN, H. Qumran und NT II (1966) 17, 87, 287, 291, 299.

5:6   KEPLER, T. S. Jesus' Design for Living (1952) 22-25. LLOYD-
JONES, D. M. Studies in the Sermon on the Mount I (1954) 73-
83, 84-94. *VON RACZECK, E. "Selig, die hungern und
dursten nach der Gerechtigkeit, denn sie werden gesättigt
werden," BenMon 33 (1-2, '57) 46-49. STAUDINGER, J. Die
Bergpredigt (1957) 32-35. DUPONT, D. J. Les Béatitudes
(1958) 217, 223. BLAIR, E. P. Jesus in the Gospel of Matthew
(1960) 120. PLOTZKE, U. Bergpredigt (1960) 32-38.
BORNKAMM-BARTH-HELD, UEberlieferung und
Auslegung im Matthäus-Evangelium (1961) 116, 130f.
STRECKER, G. Der Weg der Gerechtigkeit (1962) 1483, 150f,
153f, 156f. SCHRAGE, W. Das Verhältnis des Thomas-
Evangeliums zur Synoptischen Tradition und zu den
Koptischen Evangelienübersetzung (1964) 149. JüNGEL, E.
Paulus und Jesus (1966) 39. SMITH, M., Tannaitic Parallels to
the Gospel (Philadelphia 1968) 2bn62+. WREGE, H.-T. Die
UEberlieferungsgeschichte der Bergpredigt (1968) 17.
ZIESLER, J. A. The Meaning of Righteousness in Paul (1972)
132f, 134, 142f. SAND, A., Das Gesetz und die Propheten
(Regensburg 1974) 201f. TALBERT, C. H., Literary Patterns,
Theological Themes, and the Genre of Luke - Acts (Missoula
1974) 42. SWIDLER, L., Biblical Affirmations of Woman
(Philadelphia 1979) 285. "Bergpredigt" in: TRE 5 (1980) 605.

5:7-10   BOWMAN, J. W. & TAPP, R. W. The Gospel from the Mount
(1958) 37-43. STRECKER, G. Der Weg der Gerechtigkeit
(1962) 156. "Bergpredigt" in: TRE 5 (1980) 605.

5:7-9   STRECKER, G. Der Weg der Gerechtigkeit (1962) 1576.

5:7   MOORE, G. F. Judaism II (1946) 170n. MASSAUX, E.
Influence de l'Evangile de saint Matthieu sur la littérature

chrétienne avant saint Irénée (1950) 1-13, 166-68. KEPLER, T.
S. Jesus' Design for Living (1952) 25-28. LLOYD-JONES, D.
M. Studies in the Sermon on the Mount I (1954) 95-105.
STAUDINGER, J. Die Bergpredigt (1957) 33-36. WREGE,
H.-T. Die UEberlieferungsgeschichte der Bergpredigt (1968)
25. SWIDLER, L., Biblical Affirmations of Woman
(Philadelphia 1979) 286. "Barmherzigkeit" in: TRE 5 (1980)
225, 227.

5:8 BORNHäUSER, D. K. Die Bergpredigt (1927) 40f.
STAEHELIN, E. Die Verkündigung des Reiches Gottes in der
Kirche Jesu Christi I (1951) 175, 188. KEPLER, T. S. Jesus'
Design for Living (1954) 28-31. LLOYD-JONES, D. M.
Studies in the Sermon on the Mount I (1954) 106-16.
STAUDINGER, J. Die Bergpredigt (1957) 36-38. PLOTZKE,
U. Bergpredigt (1960) 38-45. KäSEMANN, E. Exegetische
Versuche und Besinnungen I (1964) 310. NICKELS, P. Targum
and New Testament (1967) 16. WREGE, H.-T. Die
UEberlieferungsgeschichte der Bergpredigt (1968) 26.
NöTSCHER, F. "Das Angesicht Gottes schauen" nach
biblischer und babylonishcer Auffassung (1969). *PRETE, B.
"Il senso dell'espressione hoi katharoi te kardia (Mt. 5, 8),"
RivB 18 (3, '70) 253-68. BERKOUWER, G. C., The Return of
Christ (Grand Rapids 1972) 313, 360, 368, 377, 385.
BONNHOEFFER, D., Gesammelte Schriften 5 (München
1972) 109, 446ff.

5:9 VOLZ, P. Die Eschatologie der jüdischen Gemeinde (1934) 81.
MOORE, G. F. Judaism II (1946) 169n. STAEHELIN, E. Die
Verkündigung des Reiches Gottes in der Kirche Jesus Christi I
(1951) 185, 284. KEPLER, T. S. Jesus' Design for Living (1952)
31-34. LLOYD-JONES, D. M. Studies in the Sermon on the
Mount I (1954) 117-27. STAUDINGER, J. Die Bergpredigt
(1957) 38-40. PLOTZKE, U. Bergpredigt (1960) 45-50, 50-55.
*BRUPPACHER, H. "Kleine Beiträge zu einer kommenden
Revision der Züricher Bibel," KirchReformSchweiz (Mar. 31,
'66) 100-101. BROWN, M. P. "Matthew as EIPHOΠOIOΣ,"
in: Studies in the History and Text of the New Testament (1967)
Daniels, B. L. & Suggs, M. J. (eds.), 39-50. NICKELS, P.
Targum and New Testament (1967) 16. WREGE, H.-T. Die
UEberlieferungsgeschichte der Begpredigt (1968) 26.
*RIESENFELD, H., "Guds söner och de heligas församling"
SEA 41-42 (1976/77) 179-88. DELLING, G. "Die 'Söhne
(Kinder) Gottes' im Neuen Testament" in R. Schnackenburg et
al. (eds.) Die Kirche des Anfangs. Für Heinz Schürmann
(Freiburg 1978) 621. SWIDLER, L., Biblical Affirmations of
Woman (Philadelphia 1979) 284.

5:10ff STRECKER, G. Der Weg der Gerechtigkeit (1962) 157₆, 2394.

5:10-12 THIELICKE, H. Das Leben kann noch einmal beginnen (1956) 22-36. PLOTZKE, U. Bergpredigt (1960) 55-61. BORNKAMM-BARTH-HELD, UEberlieferung und Auslegung im Matthäus-Evangelium (1961) 94f, 98, 104, 130f. SHINN, R. L. Sermon on the Mount (1962) 21-26. TöDT, H. E. Der Menschensohn in der synoptischen UEberlieferung (1963) 232f, 308f. BRAUN, H. Qumran und NT II (1966) 104, 154, 196, 219, 253, 289, 294. STRECKER, G. Der Weg der Gerechtigkeit (1962) 231.

5:10f STUHLMACHER, P. Gerechtigkeit Gottes bei Paulus (1965) 190f.

5:10-11 KEPLER, T. S. Jesus' Design for Living (1952) 34-37.

5:10 STONEHOUSE, N. B. The Witness of Matthew and Mark to Christ (1944) 228. STAEHELIN, E. Die Verkündigung des Reiches Gottes in der Kirche Jesu Christi I (1951) 285. LLOYD-JONES, D. M. Studies in the Sermon on the Mount I (1954) 128-37. STAUDINGER, J. Die Bergpredigt (1957) 40-43. DUPONT, D. J. Les Béatitudes (1958) 223-27. PLOTZKE, U. Bergpredigt (1960) 187-91. STRECKER, G. Der Weg der Gerechtigkeit (1962) 30₅, 38, 151, 159, 201₄. SCHRAGE, W. Das Verhältnis des Thomas-Evangeliums zur Synoptischen Tradition und zu den Koptischen Evangelienübersetzungen (1964) 147. WREGE, H.-T. Die UEberlieferungsgeschichte der Bergpredigt (1968) 26. BEST, E. I Peter and the Gospel Tradition NTS 16 (1969-70) 109ff. SAND, A., Das Gesetz und die Propheten (Regensburg 1974) 201f. KLIJN, A. F. J., "Die syrische Baruch-Apokalypse" in: W. G. Kümmel (ed.) Jüdische Schriften aus hellenistisch-römischer Zeit V (Gütersloh 1976) 157.

5:11-16 BOWMAN, J. W. & TAPP, R. W. The Sermon from the Mount (1958) 44-54. GOULDER, M. D., Midrash and Lection in Matthew (London 1974) 254ff.

5:11f BORNHäUSSER, D. K, Die Bergpredigt (1927) 33f. HAHN, F. Christologische Hoheitstitel (1963) 43. SATAKE, A. Die Gemeindeordnung in der Johannesapokalypse (1966) 177-79. WREGE, H.-T. Die UEberlieferungsgeschichte der Bergpredigt (1968) 20. FRIEDLANDER, G. The Jewish Sources of the Sermon on the Mount (1969) 24, 26f, 88. JEREMIAS, J. Neutestamentliche Theologie I (1971) 179, 229, 231, 250. HOFFMANN, P. Studien zur Theologie der Logienquelle (1972) 99f, 114f, 182-87. SCHULZ, S. Q Die Spruchquelle der Evangelisten (1972) 452-57.

5:11-12 LLOYD-JONES, D. M. Studies in the Sermon on the Mount I

(1954) 138-48. DUPONT, D. J. Les Béatitudes (1958) 224-26.
MüLHAUPT, E. (ed.), D. Martin Luthers Auslegung der
Bergpredigt (1961) 61-66. SMITH, M., Tannaitic Parallels to
the Gospel (Philadelphia 1968) A+. GOULDER, M. D.,
Midrash and Lection in Matthew (London 1974) 279-81.
TALBERT, C. H., Literary Patterns, Theological Themes, and
the Genre of Luke-Acts (Missoula 1974) 42. EDWARDS, R.
A., A Theology of Q (Philadelphia 1976) 63.
GERSTENBERGER, G./SCHRAGE, W., Leiden (Stuttgart
1977) 126f; ET: J. E. Steely (transl.) Suffering (Nashville 1980)
147f. POLAG, A. Die Christologie der Logienquelle
(Neukirchen-Vluyn 1977) 97. GNILKA, J.,
"Martyriumsparänese und Sühnetod in synoptischen und
jüdischen Traditionen" in: R. Schnackenburg et al. (eds.) Die
Kirche des Anfangs. Für Heinz Schürmann (Freiburg 1978)
234f. "Bergpredigt" in: TRE 5 (1980) 605.

5:11   WINDISCH, H. The Meaning of the Sermon on the Mount
(1937) 129, 138, 152. DUPONT, D. J. Les Béatitudes (1958)
227-243. STRECKER, G. Der Weg der Gerechtigkeit (1962)
30, 150, 154. SCHRAGE, W. Das Verhältnis des Thomas-
Evangeliums zur Synoptischen Tradition und zu den
Koptischen Evangelienübersetzungen (1964) 147.
KäSEMANN, E. Exegetische Versuche und Besinnungen II
(1964) 99. DAVIES, W. D., The Sermon on the Mount
(Cambridge 1966) 86. BLACK, M. An Aramaic Approach to
the Gospels and Acts (1967) 191f. GREEVES, H. Ehe nach dem
Neuen Testament NTS 15 (1968-69) 370ff. KäSEMANN, E.
New Testament Questions of Today (1969) 100. BORSCH, F.
H. The Christian & Gnostic Son of Man (1970) 22-23.
GOULDER, M. D., Midrash and Lection in Matthew (London
1974) 152, 252, 282. *SATAKE, A., "Das Leiden der Jünger
'um meinetwillen' " ZNW 67 (1976) 4-19. WILLIAMS, J. A., A
Conceptual History of Deuteronomism in the Old Testament,
Judaism and the New Testament (Louisville 1976) 310.
METZGER, B. M., The Early Versions of the New Testament
(Oxford 1977) 247.

5:12   KEPLER, T. S. Jesus' Design for Living (1952) 37-40.
M'NEILE, A. H. The Gospel According to St. Matthew (1955)
54f. KNOX, W. L. The Sources of the Synoptic Gospels II
(1957) 125. TRILLING, W. Das wahre Israel (1959) 63.
STRECKER, G. Der Weg der Gerechtigkeit (1962) 1374, 156,
164, 235. HUMMEL, R. Die Auseinandersetzung zwischen
Kirche und Judentum im Matthäusevangelium (1963) 158.
HAHN, F. Christologische Hoheitstitel (1963) 366.
LOCKYER, H. All the Parables of the Bible (1963) 144ff.

KäSEMANN, E. Exegetische Versuche und Besinnungen II (1964) 90, 94. BLACK, M. An Aramaic Approach to the Gospels and Acts (1967) 191f. NICKELS, P. Targum and New Testament (1967) 16. KäSEMANN, E. New Testament Questions of Today (1969) 91, 96. JEREMIAS, J. Neutestamentliche Theologie I (1971) 20, 83, 208, 230. PATSCH, H. Abendmahl und historischer Jesus (1972) 204f. MINEAR, P. S., "False Prophecy and Hypocrisy in the Gospel of Matthew" in: J. Gnilka (ed.) Neues Testament und Kirche. Für Rudolf Schnackenburg (Freiburg 1974) 77f, 85. LADD, G. E., A Theology of the New Testament (Grand Rapids 1974) 133, 205, 236, 303. SAND, A., Das Gesetz und die Propheten (Regensburg 1974) 172f.

5:13-7:29   MüSSLE, M. (ed.) Die Humanität Jesu im Spiegel der Bergpredigt. Matthäus 5:13-7:29 und Lukas 6:27-49 (1971).

5:13ff   BORNHäUSSER, D. K, Die Bergpredigt (1927) 45ff.

5:13-26   LOEWENICH, W. von, Luther als Ausleger der Synoptiker (1954) 87f.

5:13-18   HEIM, K. D. Die Bergpredigt Jesu (1949) 5-15.

5:13-16   WILKENS, J. Einführung in das Evangelium nach Matthäus I (1934) 87-88. THOMPSON, E. T. The Sermon on the Mount (1946) 47-53. HUNTER, A. M. Design for Life (1953) 40-42. KING, G. H. New Order (1954) 22-29. LLOYD-JONES, D. M. Studies in the Sermon on the Mount I (1954) 170-79. THIELICKE, H. Das Leben kann noch einmal beginnen (1956) 37-48. *AALEN, L. "Lysets begrep i de synoptiske evangelier," SEA 22-23 ('57-'58) 17-31. McARTHUR, H. K. Understanding the Sermon on the Mount (1960) 71, 86, 90. BORNKAMM-BARTH-HELD, UEberlieferung und Auslegung im Matthäus-Evangelium (1961) 14, 56, 95. Also in Predigtgedanken . . . Gegenwart Reihe C, Band 3-4 (1963) 317ff. MüLHAUPT, E. (ed.), D. Martin Luthers Auslegung der Bergpredigt (1961) 66-81. SHINN, R. L. Sermon on the Mount (1962) 27-31. *SOUCEK, J. B. "Salz der Erde und Licht der Welt. Zur Exegese von Matth. 5,13-16," ThZ 19 (3, '63) 169-79. BROWN, J. P. Synoptic Parallels in the Epistles and Form-History NTS 10 (1963-64) 31f. OBENDIEK, H. in: Herr, tue meine Lippen auf (1964) Eichholz, G. (ed.) 314ff. EICHHOLZ, G. Auslegung der Bergpredigt (1965) 55-60. HUNTER, A. M. A Pattern for Life (1965) 44-46. BRAUN, H. Qumran und NT II (1966) 93, 229. DAVIES, W. D., The Sermon on the Mount (Cambridge 1966) 86f. DU TORR, A. B., "The Nature of the Witness of the Church" Ou testamentiese werkgemeenskap in Suid-Afrika (1966) 200-18. KNöRZER, W. Die Bergpredigt, Modell einer neuen Welt (1968) 38-39. WREGE, H.T. Die

UEberlieferungsgeschichte der Bergpredigt (1968) 27.
SCHNEIDER, G. Botschaft der Bergpredigt (1969) 39-42.
OTOMO, Y. Nachfolge Jesu und Anfänge der Kirche im Neuen
Testament (1970) 86f. SUGGS, M. J. Wisdom, Christology,
and Law in Matthew's Gospel (1970) 122ff.
SCHNACKENBURG, R. Schriften zum Neuen Testament
(1971) 177-200. GOLLWITZER, Veränderung im Diesseits
(1973) 139. HAHN, F., "Die Worte vom Licht Lk 11, 33-36" in:
P. Hoffman (ed.) Orientierung an Jesus. Für Josef Schmid
(Freiburg 1973) 117-19, 124, 127. SCHNACKENBURG, R.,
Aufsätze und Studien zum Neuen Testament (Leipzig 1973)
303-25. *LéGASSE, S., "Les chrétiens 'sel de la terre', 'lumière
du monde.' Mt 5:13-16" AssS 36 (1974) 17-25. *KRäMER, M.,
"Ihr seid das Salz der Erde . . . Ihr seid das Licht der Welt. Die
vielgestaltige Wirkkraft des Gotteswortes der Heiligen Schrift
für das Leben der Kirche aufgezeigt am Beispiel Mt 5, 13-16"
MThZ 28 (1977) 133-57. SCHWEIZER, E., in: GPM 33 (1979)
322-29.

5:13f   BULTMANN, R. The History of the Synoptic Tradition (1963)
91f. SCHWARZ, G. Matthaus V 13a und 14a NTS 17 (1970-71)
80-86.

5:13   JüLICHER, D. A. Die Gleichnisreden Jesu (1910) 67-79.
STONEHOUSE, N. B. The Witness of Matthew and Mark to
Christ (1944) 150. DODD, C. H. The Parables of the Kingdom
(1948) 139ff. KEPLER, T. S. Jesus' Design for Living (1952) 40-
43. LLOYD-JONES, D. M. Studies in the Sermon on the
Mount I (1954) 149-58. STAUDINGER, J. Die Bergpredigt
(1957) 63-66. DUPONT, D. J. Les Béatitudes (1958) 91-93.
MINEAR, P. S. Images of the Church in the New Testament
(1960) 29f. PLOTZKE, U. Bergpredigt (1960) 62-67.
*DEATRICK, E. P. "Salt, Soil, Savior," BA 25 (2, '62) 41-48.
*FENSHAM, F. C. "Salt as Curse in the Old Testament and
the Ancient Near East," BA 25 (2 '62) 48-50. *SOUCEK, J. B.
"Le sel de la terre et la lumière du monde," CommViat 6 (1, '63)
5-12. *LAMBRECHT, J. "Die Logia-Quellen von Markus 13,"
Biblica 47 (1966) 334-35. KARAVIDOPULOS, J., "Der Sinn
des 'Salzes' in den Worten Jesu" Th 39 (1968) 286-393.
JEREMIAS, J. Neutestamentliche Theologie I (1971) 18, 37f.
SCHULZ, S. Q Die Spruchquelle der Evangelisten (1972) 470-
72. TALBERT, C. H., Literary Patterns, Theological Themes,
and the Genre of Luke - Acts (Missoula 1974) 55. METZGER,
B. M., The Early Versions of the New Testament (Oxford 1977)
247, 368. KLAUCK, H.-J., Allegorie und Allegorese in
synoptischen Gleichnistexten (Münster 1978) 281.

5:14-16   JüLICHER, D. A. Die Gleichnisreden Jesu (1910) 79-88, 88-

91. MOORE, G. F. Judaism II (1946) 103. KEPLER, T. S. Jesus' Design for Living (1952) 43-45. DUPONT, D. J. Les Béatitudes (1958) 83-86. MINEAR, P. S. Images of the Church in the New Testament (1960) 128f. PLOTZKE, U. Bergpredigt (1960) 67-73. LOCKYER, H. All the Parables of the Bible (1963) 146ff. HENNECKE, E. & SCHNEEMELCHER, W. Neutestamentliche Apokryphen (1964) I 70, II 70, 75, 100, 389. FRIEDLANDER, G. The Jewish Sources of the Sermon on the Mount (1969) 30f. GOULDER, M. D., Midrash and Lection in Matthew (London 1974) 282f, 302, 332.

5:14f SCHRAGE, W. Das Verhältnis des Thomas-Evangeliums zur Synoptischen Tradition und zu den Koptischen Evangelienübersetzungen (1964) 77. REUMANN, J. Jesus in the Church's Gospels: Modern Scholarship and the Earliest Sources (1968) 402-403. JEREMIAS, J. Neutestamentliche Theologie I (1971) 34, 47, 108, 166, 221, 236.

5:14-15 MONTEFIORE, H. A comparison of the Parables of the Gospel according to Thomas and of the Synoptic Gospels NTS 7 (1960-61) 240f. SWIDLER, L., Biblical Affirmations of Woman (Philadelphia 1979) 166, 226, 258.

5:14 LLOYD-JONES, D. M. Studies in the Sermon on the Mount I (1954) 159-69. STAUDINGER, J. Die Bergpredigt (1957) 66-69, 69-70. PLOTZKE, U. Bergpredigt (1960) 73-78. *CAMPBELL, K. M., "The New Jerusalem in Matthew 5.14" SJTh 31 (1978) 335-63. BERGER, P.-R., "Die Stadt auf dem Berge. Zum kulturhistorischen Hintergrund von Lukas 1, 31" in: W. Haubeck/M. Bachmann (eds.) Wort in der Zeit. Für Karl Heinrich Rengstorff (Leiden 1980) 82-85.

5:15-20 LLOYD-JONES, D. M. Studies in the Sermon on the Mount II (1962) 251-60.

5:15f TRILLING, W. Das wahre Israel (1959) 118.

5:15-16 STAUDINGER, J. Die Bergpredigt (1957) 70-72.

5:15 DODD, C. H. The Parables of the Kingdom (1948) 142ff. DUPONT, D. J. Les Béatitudes (1958) 82-87. *DERRETT, J. D. M. "The Light under a Bushel: The Hanukkah Lamp?" ET 78 (1, '66) 18. JEREMIAS, J. Abba; Studien zur neutestamentlichen Theologie und Zeitgeschichte (1966) 99-102. STRECKER, G. Der Weg der Gerechtigkeit (1962) 55₉. SCHRAGE, W. Das Verhältnis des Thomas-Evangeliums zur Synoptischen Tradition und zu den Koptischen Evangelienübersetzungen (1964) 81. SUMMERS, R. The Secret Sayings of the Living Jesus (1968) 29. HOFFMANN, P. Studien zur Theologie der Logienquelle (1972) 5, 269. SCHULZ, S. Q Die Spruchquelle der Evangelisten (1972) 474-

76. HAHN, F., "Die Worte vom Licht Lk 11, 33-36" in: P. Hoffmann (ed.) Orientierung an Jesus. Für Josef Schmid (Freiburg 1973) 108, 110-13, 123, 128. TALBERT, C. H., Literary Patterns, Theological Themes, and the Genre of Luke-Acts (Missoula 1974) 54. CONZELMANN, H./LINDEMANN, A., Arbeitsbuch zum Neuen Testament (Tübingen 1975) 63. JANSSEN, E., "Testament Abrahams" in: W. G. Kümmel (ed.) Jüdische Schriften aus hellenistisch-römischer Zeit III (Gütersloh 1975) 215.

5:16-18 BOUSSET, W. Die Religion des Judentums im Späthellenistischen Zeitalter (1966⁻1926) 120, 144, 416.

5:16.45 McNAMARA, M. The New Testament and the Palestinian Targum to the Pentateuch (1966) 136.

5:16 WINDISCH, H. The Meaning of the Sermon on the Mount (1937) 66, 68, 113, 127, 201. MASSAUX, E. Influence de l'Evangile de saint Matthieu sur la littérature chrétienne avant saint Irénée (1950) 482-484. SPICQ, C. Dieu et L'Homme (1961) 49-50. BEST, E. I Peter and the Gospel Tradition NTS 16 (1969-70) 109ff. JEREMIAS, J. Neutestamentliche Theologie I (1971) 34, 47, 153, 221. *GRAYSTON, K., "Matthew 5:16: An Interpretation" Epworth Review 6 (1979) 61-63.

5:17ff BORNHäUSSER, D. K. Die Bergpredigt (1927) 59ff. STAEHELIN, E. Die Verkündigung des Reiches Gottes in der Kirche Jesu Christi I (1951) 56, 356. LJUNGMAN, H. Das Gesetz Erfüllen (1954) 5-36, 95f, 121f. KNOX, W. L. The Sources of the Synoptic Gospels II (1957) 9, 27. BULTMANN, R. Theologie des Neuen Testaments (1965) 16, 50, 58. GOGARTEN, F. Christ the Crisis (1967) 266f.

5:17-48 THOLUCK, A. Die Bergrede Christi (1872) 96-268. WINDISCH, H. The Meaning of the Sermon on the Mount (1937) 62, 68, 125. THOMPSON, E. T. The Sermon on the Mount (1946) 57-81. TAYLOR, V. The Formation of the Gospel Tradition (1949) 97-99. FARRER, A. St. Matthew and St. Mark (1954) 165. LJUNGMAN, H. Das Gesetz Erfüllen (1954) 91-96. *GEORGE, A. *Soyez parfaits comme votre Père céleste (Matth. 5, 17-48)," BVieC 19 ('57) 85-90. BLAIR, E. P. Jesus in the Gospel of Matthew (1960) 117ff, 122. JOö, O. A. W. Matthew's Understanding of the Law in Matt. 5:17-48 (1967). *MEIER, J. P., Law and History in Matthew's Gospel (Rome 1976).

5:17-37 SHINN, R. L. Sermon on the Mount (1962) 32-38. *HOFFMANN, P. "Die bessere Gerechtigkeit. Auslegung der Bergpredigt III (Mt 5, 17-37)," BuL 10 (3, '69) 175-89.

5:17-32 THIELICKE, H. Das Leben kann noch einmal beginnen (1956) 49-65.

5:17-26 PELIKAN, J. (ed.), The Preaching of Chrysostom (1967) 67-95.

5:17-22 BRAUN, GPM 4 (1949-50) 203ff. IWAND, GPM 9 (1954-55) 185ff. IWAND, GPM 15 (1960-61) 205ff.

5:17-20 WIESEN, ZNW 3 (1902) 336-52. WILKENS, J. Einführung in das Evangelium nach Matthäus I (1934) 89-91. MANSON, W. Jesus the Messiah (1948) 82-89. DAVIES, W. D., Torah in the Messianic Age and/or the Age to Come (Philadelphia 1952) 4. KEPLER, T. S. Jesus' Design for Living (1952) 45-48. HUNTER, A. M. Design for Life (1953) 42-44. KING, G. H. New Order (1954) 29-36. LJUNGMAN, H., Das Gesetz Erfüllen (1954) 8-10, 65-75, 102f. BOWMAN, J. W. & TAPP, R. W. The Sermon from the Mount (1958) 55-63. MUNCK, J. Paul and the Salvation of Mankind (1959) 253f. TRILLING. W. Das wahre Israel (1959) 138ff. BORNKAMM-BARTH-HELD, UEberlieferung und Auslegung im Matthäus-Evangelium (1961) 21, 60ff, 68, 87, 149, 243ff. STRECKER, G. Der Weg der Gerechtigkeit (1962) 135, 1374. HUMMEL, R. Die Auseinandersetzung zwischen Kirche und Judentum im Matthäusevangelium (1963) 64-75. SCHMITHALS, W. Paulus und Jakobus (1963) 92f. SCHWEIZER, E. Neotestamentica (1963) 399-406. KäSEMANN, E. Exegetische Versuche und Besinnungen II (1964) 85, 96. EICHHOLZ, G. Auslegung der Bergpredigt (1965) 61-68. HUNTER, A. M. A Pattern for Life (1965) 46-48. DAVIES, W. D., The Sermon on the Mount (Cambridge 1966) 29f. HARDER, G. "Jesus und das Gesetz (Matthäus 5, 17-20)," in: Antijudaismus im Neuen Testament? (1967) Eckert, W. P., Levinson, N. P. & Stöhr, M. (eds.) 105-18. MANEK, J. "Vier Bibelstudien zur Problematik der sozialen Umwandlung," CommViat 10 (1, '67) 61-70· (2-3, '67) 179-82. KNöRZER, W. Bergpredigt, Modell einer neuen Welt (1968) 40-43. WREGE, H.-T. Die UEberlieferungsgeschichte der Bergpredigt (1968) 35. (1968) 35. CARLSTON, C. The things that Defile (Mark VII. 14) and the Law in Matthew and Mark NTS 15 (1968-69) 77f, 82ff. KäSEMANN, E. New Testament Questions of Today (1969) 85. SCHNEIDER, G. Botschaft der Bergpredigt (1969) 42-45. SUGGS, M. J. Wisdom, Christology, and Law in Matthew's Gospel (1970) 115ff. FEUILLET, A. Morale Ancienne et Morale Chrétienne NTS 17 (1970-71) 123-37. BORNKAMM, G. Geschichte und Glaube II (1971) 73-80. KELLERMANN, U. Messias und Gesetz (1971) 13f. HüBNER, H., Das Gesetz in der synoptischen Tradition (Witten 1973) 15-112. SCHWEIZER, E., "Noch einmal Mt 5,

17-20" in: H. Balz/S. Schulz (eds.) Das Wort und die Wörter (Stuttgart 1973) 69-73. *BANKS, R., "Matthew's Understanding of the Law: Authenticity and Interpretation in Matthew 5:17-20" JBL 93 (1974) 226-42. FRANKEMöLLE, H., Jahwebund und Kirche Christi (Münster 1974) 94, 274f, 276. GOULDER, M. D., Midrash and Lection in Matthew (London 1974) 256, 261, 283-86, 421. SCHWEIZER, E., Matthäus und seine Gemeinde (Stuttgart 1974) GOPPELT, L., Theologie des Neuen Testaments. I (Göttingen 1975) 154ff. BURCHARD, C., "Versuch, das Thema der Bergpredigt zu finden" in: G. Strecker (ed.) Jesus Christus in Historie und Theologie: Neutestamentliche Festschrift für Hans Conzelmann (Tübingen 1975) 420-22, 426. ARENS, E., The HΛΘON - sayings in the Synoptic Tradition (Fribourg 1976) 91-116. GOPPELT, L., Theologie des Neuen Testaments II (Göttingen 1976) 558. *FUCHS, E., "L'imaginaire et le symbolique. Rèflexions hasardeuses sur Matthieu 5, 17-20" Bulletin du Centre Protestant d'études 30 (1978) 116-21. LANGE, H., "The Greater Righteousness: Theological Reflections on Matthew 5:17-20" Currents in Theology and Mission 5 (1978) 116-21. *LUZ, U., "Die Erfüllung des Gesetzes bei Matthäus (Mt 5, 17-20)" ZThK 75 (1978) 398-435. RIVKIN, E., A Hidden Revolution (Nashville 1978) 87f. SABOURIN, L., "Matthieu 5, 17-20 et le rôle prophétique de la Loi (cf. Mt 11, 13)" SciE 30 (1978) 303-11. WENHAM, D., "Jesus and the law: an exegesis on Matthew 5:17-20" Themelios 4 (1979) 92-96.

5:17-19   STONEHOUSE, N. B. The Witness of Matthew and Mark to Christ (1944) 197ff, 202. LLOYD-JONES, D. M. Studies in the Sermon on the Mount I (1954) 189-98. PLOTZKE, U. Bergpredigt (1960) 79-86. MüLHAUPT, E. (ed.) D Martin Luthers Auslegung der Bergpredigt (1961) 81-84. STRECKER, G. Der Weg der Gerechtigkeit (1962) 143ff. BULTMANN, R. The History of the Synoptic Tradition (1963) 138f, 146f. LONGENECKER, R. N. Paul Apostle of Liberty (1964) 138f. *STIASSNY, J. "Jesus accomplit la Promesse. Essai d'interprétation de Matthieu 5, 17-19," BVieC 59 ('64) 30-37. BRAUN, H. Qumran und NT II (1966) 86ff, 113. STECK, K. G. GPM 11/3 211-17. DUNN, J. D. G., Unity and Diversity in the New Testament (London 1977) 246f. SWIDLER, L., Biblical Affirmations of Woman (Philadelphia 1979) 285. "Bergpredigt" in: TRE 5 (1980) 604, 609f.

5:17f   REUMANN, J. Jesus in the Church's Gospels: Modern Scholarship and the Earliest Sources (1968) 406-407. TAGAWA, K. People and Community in the Gospel of

Matthew NTS 16 (1969-70) 153f. *TAVARD, G. H. "Christianity and Israel: How did Christ fulfill the Law?" DRev 75 ('57) 55-68. DAVIES, W. D. "Matthew 5, 17-18," in: Melanges Bibliques Rédigées en L'Honneur de Andre Robert (n.d.) 428-56. LOHSE, E. and others (eds.), Der Ruf Jesu und die Antwort der Gemeinde (1970) 94-111.

5:17-18 HANSSEN, O., "Zum Verständnis der Bergpredigt" in: Der Ruf Jesus und die Antwort der Gemeinde: Festschrift für J. Jeremias (Göttingen 1970) 94-111. SANFORD, J. A., The Kingdom Within (New York 1970) 50f. KLEINE, R., "Ich bin nicht gekommen aufzuheben sondern die Fülle zu bringen" Anzeige für die Katholische Geistlichkeit 71 (1962) 414-24.

5:17 WINDISCH, H. The Meaning of the Sermon on the Mount (1937) 74, 76, 138. BERGER, K. Die Gesetzauslegung Jesu (1940) 209-27. BRUNNER, E. Dogmatik II (1950) 414. MASSAUX, E. Influence de l'Evangile de saint Matthieu sur la littérature chrétienne avant saint Irénée (1950) 354-355, 13-14. FARRER, A. St Matthew and St Mark (1954) 179. *BOISMARD, M.-E. "La Loi et l'Espirit," LuVie XXI (1955) 65-82. KNOX, W. L. The Sources of the Synoptic Gospels II (1957) 19, 31, 35. *MITTON, C. L. "The Law and the Gospel," ET 68/10 (1957) 312-15. STAUDINGER, J. Die Bergpredigt (1957) 73-75. DUPONT, D. J. Les Béatitudes (1958) 138-45. NEPPER-CHRISTENSEN, P. Das Matthäusevangelium. Ein Judenchristliches Evangelium? (1958) 19, 140, 177. TRILLING, W. Das wahre Israel (1959) 143ff. BLAIR, E. P. Jesus in the Gospel of Matthew (1960) 94, 117, 119, 121. McARTHUR, H. K. Understanding the Sermon on the Mount (1960) 14, 26-28, 31, 32, 39, 40, 41, 48, 163-66, 169. BORNKAMM-BARTH-HELD, UEberlieferung und Auslegung im Matthäus-Evangelium (1961) 47, 58, 62ff, 138ff, 143, 148ff, 244. DE KRUIJF, T., Der Sohn Des Lebendigen Gottes (Rome 1962) 46, 127f, 153. STRECKER, G. Der Weg der Gerechtigkeit (1962) 607, 146f, 179. BULTMANN, R. The History of the Synoptic Tradition (1963) 155-56, 153. HUMMEL, R. Die Auseinandersetzung zwischen Kirche und Judentum im Matthäusevangelium (1963) 75, 132f, 135. *KOOREN, J. G. "Wet en Evangelie," HomBib 22 (9, '63) 200-205. KäSEMANN, E. New Testament Questions of Today (1969) 97. McCONNELL, R. S. Law and Prophecy in Matthew's Gospel (1969) 6-30. JEREMIAS, J. Neutestamentliche Theologie I (1971) 16, 26, 29, 36, 67, 87-89, 200, 204, 240, 242. *BURTNESS, J. H., "Life-Style and Law: Some Reflections on Matthew 5:17" Dialog 14 (1974) 13-20. FRANKEMöLLE, H., Jahwebund und Kirche Christi

(Münster 1974) 299, 304, 388, 390. SAND, A., Das Gesetz und die Propheten (Regensburg 1974) 183-87. BANKS, R., Jesus and the Law in the Synoptic Tradition (London 1975) 204-207. 250f. GOPPELT, L., Theologie des Neuen Testaments. II (Göttingen 1976) 556f. METZGER, B. M., The Early Versions of the New Testament (Oxford 1977) 250. *LACH, J., Logion Jezusa o przestrzeganiu starotestamentalnego prawa (Mt 5, 17)" SThV 16 (1978) 3-17. MEYER, B. F., The Aims of Jesus (London 1979) 147, 166f. "Bergpredigt" in: TRE 5 (1980) 608. LéGASSE, S., "Mt 5:17 et la Prétendue tradition paracanonique" in: J. Zmijewski/E. Nellessen (eds.) Begegnung mit dem Wort: Festschrift für Heinrich Zimmermann (Bonn 1980) 11-21.

5:18ff DAVIES, W. D., The Sermon on the Mount (Cambridge 1966) 92f.

5:18f WINDISCH, H. The Meaning of the Sermon on the Mount (1937) 68, 74, 200. NEPPER-CHRISTENSEN, P. Das Matthäusevangelium. Ein Judenchristliches Evangelium? (1958) 14, 19, 22, 139.

5:18-19 WENDLING, E., "Zu Matthäus, Miszellen" ZNW 5 (1904) 253. MOORE, G. F. Judaism (1946) I 269f, 472 II 9n. STRECKER, G. Der Weg der Gerechtigkeit (1962) 166. BLAIR, E. P. Jesus in the Gospel of Matthew (1960) 117. McCONNELL, R. S. Law and Prophecy in Matthew's Gospel (1969) 30-34. LANGE, L., Das Erscheinen des Auferstandenen im Evangelium nach Mattäus (Würzburg 1973) 31, 250, 270, 321-23. BEST, E., From Text to Sermon (Atlanta 1978) 23.

5:18 *SUTCLIFFE, E. F. Biblica 9 (1928) 458-60. DAVIES, W. D., Torah in the Messianic Age and/or the Age to Come (Philadelphia 1952) 52, 79, 893. *DIEZ, M. A. "Cesara la Tora en la Edad Messianica? II," EstBi XIII/1 (1954) 5-51. HONEYMAN, A. M. "Matthew V, 18 and the Validity of the Law," NTS 1/2 (1954) 141-42. LJUNGMAN, H. Das Gesetz Erfüllen (1954) 5-10, 14-16, 36-47, 48-52, 54-56, 58-60. KNOX, W. L. The Sources of the Synoptic Gospels II (1957) 27. ODEBERG, H., "Matth 5, 18 (schwed)" Eranos 14 (1957) 43-45. STAUDINGER, J. Die Bergpredigt (1957) 75-78. DUPONT, D. J. Les Béatitudes (1958) 134-38, 140-42. *AUER, W. "Iota unum aut unus apex non praeteribit a lege ... (Mt 5, 18)," BuK 14 (4, '59) 97-103. TRILLING, W. Das wahre Israel (1959) 138ff. BLAIR, E. P. Jesus in the Gospel of Matthew (1960) 121, 122. McARTHUR, H. K. Understanding the Sermon on the Mount (1960) 15, 86, 129, 164, 166, 178. STRECKER, G. Der Weg der Gerechtigkeit (1962) 13. NICKELS, P. Targum and New Testament (1967) 17.

HASLER, V. Amen (1969) 55. PESCH, R. Naherwartungen (1969) 182, 189. BERGER, K. Die Amen-Worte Jesus BZNW 39 (1970) 73-74. VöGTLE, A. Das Neue Testament und die Zukunft des Kosmos (1970) 28, 42, 43, 71, 99-107. *HAMERTON-KELLY, R. G. "Attitudes to the Law in Matthew's Gospel: A Discussion of Matthew 5:18," BR 17 ('72) 19-32. HOFFMANN, P. Studien zur Theologie der Logienquelle (1972) 5, 42, 49. SCHULZ, S. Q Die Spruchquelle der Evangelisten (1972) 114-16. GOULDER, M. D., Midrash and Lection in Matthew (London 1974) 128, 167, 284f, 288. SAND, A., Das Gesetz und die Propheten (Regensburg 1974) 36-39. TALBERT, C. H., Literary Patterns, Theological Themes, and the Genre of Luke-Acts (Missoula 1974) 55. BANKS, R., Jesus and the Law in the Synoptic Tradition (London 1975) 213f, 217f. POLAG, A., Die Christologie der Logienquelle (Neukirchen-Vluyn 1977) 79. "Bergpredigt" in: TRE 5 (1980) 606, 610. SCHWARZ, G., ZNW 66 (1975) 268f.

5:19ff PARKER, P. The Gospel Before Mark (1953) 91-92.

5:19-24 PARKER, P. The Gospel Before Mark (1953) 8-9.

5:19-20 STAUDINGER, J. Die Bergpredigt (1957) 78-81. BIEDER, W., Die Verheissung der Taufe im Neuen Testament (Zürich 1966) 278f.

5:19 DIBELIUS, F., "Zwei Worte Jesu" ZNW 11 (1910) 188. WINDISCH, H. The Meaning of the Sermon on the Mount (1937) 37, 74f. FEINE, D. P. & BEHM, D. J. Einleitung in das Neue Testament (1950) 52f. STAEHELIN, E. Die Verkündigung des Reiches Gottes in der Kirche Jesu Christi I (1951) 369. LJUNGMAN H., Das Gesetz Erfüllen (1954) 15-17, 33-35, 48-53, 60f. KNOX, W. L. The Sources of the Synoptic Gospels II (1957) 19f. DUPONT, D. J. Les Béatitudes (1958) 136-38, 142, 144s. TRILLING, W. Das wahre Israel (1959) 153ff. BLAIR, E. P. Jesus in the Gospel of Matthew (1960) 32, 122. McARTHUR, H. K. Understanding the Sermon on the Mount (1960) 39, 110, 169, 172, 174. *SCHüRMANN, H. " 'Wer daher eines dieser geringsten Gebote auflöst...' Wo fand Matthäus das Logion Mt 5, 19?" BZ 4 (2, '60) 238-50. STRECKER, G. Der Weg der Gerechtigkeit (1962) 40f, 151, 162. KäSEMANN, E. Exegetische Versuche und Besinnungen II (1964) 79. SMITH, M., Tannaitic Parallels to the Gospels (Philadelphia 1968) 2 b n 75+. KäSEMANN, E. New Testament Questions of Today (1969) 78. JEREMIAS, J. Neutestamentliche Theologie I. (1971), 22, 26, 40-42, 100, 204, 208. GOULDER, M. D., Midrash and Lection in Matthew (London 1974) 75, 284ff, 307, 357, 421. BANKS, R., Jesus and the Law in the Synoptic Tradition (London 1975) 220f.

SANDERS, J. T., Ethics in the New Testament (Philadelphia 1975) 43. POLAG, A., Die Christologie der Logienquelle (Neukirchen-Vluyn 1977) 163.

5:20-7:11 'Bergpredigt" in: TRE 5 (1980) 604f.

5:20ff BORNHäUSSER, D. K. Die Bergpredigt (1927) 69f.

5:20-48 *BROER, I., "Die Antithesen und der Evangelist Matthäus. Versuch, eine alte These zu revidieren" BZ 19 (1975) 50-63. SANDERS, J. T., Ethics in the New Testament (Philadelphia 1975) 40-42.

5:20-26 DOERNE, M. Er kommt auch noch heute (1961) 112-14. MüLHAUPT, E. (ed.), D Martin Luthers Auslegung der Bergpredigt (1961) 84-98. IWAND, H. J. Predigt-Meditationen (1964) 455-62. HEPHATA, Predigtgedanken aus Vergangenheit und Gegenwart (1966) 134-48. VööBUS, A., The Gospels in Study and Preaching (Philadelphia 1966) 173-202. PAKOZDY, L. M. GPM 2/3 (1973) 344-53.

5:20-24 DEISS, L., "Va d'abord te réconcillier avec ton frère" AssS (1966) 34-46.

5:20-22 PLOTZKE, U. Bergpredigt (1960) 92-98.

5:20 VOLZ, P. Die Eschatologie der jüdischen Gemeinde (1934) 167. WINDISCH, H. The Meaning of the Sermon on the Mount (1937) 26ff, 36f, 64, 71, 74, 95, 111, 113, 116 134, 138f, 168, 176, 199, 209. MANSON, W. Jesus the Messiah (1948) 82-84. LLOYD-JONES, D. M. Studies in the Sermon on the Mount I (1954) 190-209. STONEHOUSE, N. B. The Witness of Matthew and Mark to Christ (1944) 153, 201, 227. STAEHELIN, E. Die Verkündigung des Reiches Gottes in der Kirche Jesu Christi I (1951). KNOX, W. L. The Sources of the Synoptic Gospels II (1957) 16, 19f, 27, 33. STAUDINGER, J. Die Bergpredigt (1957) 32, 88, 109, 120, 133 134, 142. DUPONT, D. J. Les Béatitudes (1958) 131-33, 144d, 158s. TRILLING, W. Das wahre Israel (1959) 156f, 187. BLAIR, E. P. Jesus in the Gospel of Matthew (1960) 94, 117, 120. McARTHUR, H. K. Understanding the Sermon on the Mount (1960) 58, 60, 87, 106, 174. PLOTZKE, U. Bergpredigt (1960) 86-92. BORNKAMM-BARTH-HELD, UEberlieferung und Auslegung im Matthäus-Evangelium (1961) 14, 28, 56, 74, 87, 91, 130, 148. STRECKER, G. Der Weg der Gerechtigkeit (1962) 18, 140, 144, 146, 151f, 153, 155, 158f, 162s, 166s, 174s, 180, 232. HUMMEL, R. Die Auseinandersetzung zwischen Kirche und Judentum im Matthäusevangelium (1963) 156, 161. BRAUN, H. Qumran und NT II (1966) 86-89, 112, 299. KERTLEGE, K. 'Rechtfertigung' bei Paulus (1967) 46. WREGE, H.-T. Die UEberlieferung der Bergpredigt (1968)

42ff, 175. FRIEDLANDER, G. The Jewish Sources of the Sermon on the Mount (1969) 35, 40, 91. HASLER, V. Amen (1969) 77. McCONNELL, R. S. Law and Prophecy in Matthew's Gospel (1969) 34-41. SANFORD, J. A., The Kingdom Within (New York 1970) 50f, 98f, 147f. JEREMIAS, J. Neutestamentliche Theologie I (1971) 40f, 153. ZIESLER, J. A. The Meaning of Righteousness in Paul (1972) 133f, 141f, 144, 146. FRANKEMöLLE, H., Jahwebund und Kirche Christi (Münster 1974) 203, 268, 282f, 291f, 293, 295, 307. GOULDER, M. D., Midrash and Lection in Matthew (London 1974) 14, 262, 271, 274f, 421. LADD, G. E., A Theology of the New Testament (Grand Rapids 1974) 79, 103, 129, 278. SAND, A., Das Gesetz und die Propheten (Regensburg 1974) 203. BANKS, R., Jesus and the Law in the Synoptic Tradition (London 1975) 224f. BETZ, O., "Rechtfertigung in Qumran" in: J. Friedrich/W. Pöhlmann/P. Stuhlmacher (eds.) Rechtfertigung: Festschrift für Ernst Käsemann (Göttingen 1976) 27f. GOPPELT, L., Theologie des Neuen Testaments. II (Göttingen 1976) 559. METZGER, B. M., The Early Versions of the New Testament (Oxford 1977) 245, 438. "Bergpredigt" in: TRE 5 (1980) 605f, 607f, 610.

5:21-7:27   *AGOURIDIS, S., "He- epi tou Orous Homilia (synechia)" DBM 2 (1974) 271-328.

5:21ff   STONEHOUSE, N. B. The Witness of Matthew and Mark to Christ (1944) 198f. BORNKAMM, G. Jesus von Nazareth (1956) 95ff. KNOX, W. L. The Sources of the Synoptic Gospels II (1957) 20, 126. STRECKER, G. Der Weg der Gerechtigkeit (1962) 16, 244, 1412. KäSEMANN, E. Exegetische Versuche und Besinnungen I (1964) 206. DAVIES, W. D., The Sermon on the Mount (Cambridge 1966) 81f. THEISSEN, G., Soziologie der Jesusbewegung (München 1977) 75.

5:21-48   WILKENS, J. Einführung in das Evangelium nach Matthäus I (1934) 91-99. SCHNIEWIND, J. Das Evangelium nach Matthäus (1949) 57f, 73-75. LJUNGMAN, H. Das Gesetz Erfüllen (1954) 34-36, 76-91, 93f. DUPONT, D. J. "Les Béatitudes (1958) 130-32, 143-45, 156-59. *HASLER, V. "Das Herzstück der Bergpredigt. Zum Verständnis der Antithesen in Matth. 5, 21-48," ThZ 15 (2, '59) 90-106. TRILLING, W. Das wahre Israel (1959) 180ff. BLAIR, E. P. Jesus in the Gospel of Matthew (1960) 46, 120. BORNKAMM-BARTH-HELD, UEberlieferung und Auslegung im Matthäus-Evangelium (1961) 14, 22, 71, 87f, 89, 96, 148. STRECKER, G. Der Weg der Gerechtigkeit (1962) 38, 146, 2332. HUMMEL, R. Die Auseinandersetzung zwischen Kirche und Jundentum im Matthäusevangelium (1963) 72-75. BRAUN, H. Qumran und

NT II (1966) 86-89, 299. GAECHTER, P. Die literarische Kunst im Matthäus-Evangelium (1968) 18-19. *ELLIOTT, J. H. "Law and Eschatology: The Antitheses of the 'Sermon on the Mount'," LW 15 (1, '68) 16-24· "Die Antithesen der Bergpredigt: Gesetz und Eschatologie," LR 18 (1, '68) 19-29. CARLSTON, C. The Things that Defile (Mark VII. 14) and the Law in Matthew and Mark NTS 15 (1968-69) 79ff. JEREMIAS, J. Neutestamentliche Theologie I (1971) 87, 89, 207, 240f. Engl. ed.: New Testament Theology Part One (1971) 83, 85, 145, 214, 251ff. HOLTZCLAW, B., "A Note on Matthew 5, 21-48" in: E. H. Barth/R. E. Cocraft (eds.) Festschrift to Honor F. W. Gingrich (Leiden 1972) 161-63. LOHSE, E., Die Einheit des Neuen Testaments (Göttingen 1973) 73f. SAND, A., Das Gesetz und die Propheten Regensburg 1974) 46-56. *SCHMAHL, G., "Die Antithesen der Bergpredigt. Inhalt und Eigenart ihrer Forderungen" TThZ 83 (1974) 284-97. BANKS, R., Jesus and the Law in the Synoptic Tradition (London 1975) 243f. *DIETZFELBINGER, C., Die Antithesen der Bergpredigt (München 1975). GOPPELT, L., Theologie des Neuen Testaments I (Göttingen 1975) 150ff. HOFFMAN, P./EID, V., Jesus von Nazareth und eine christliche Moral (Freiburg 1975) 73-79. GOPPELT, L., Theologie des Neuen Testaments II (Göttingen 1976) 557 f. *GUELICH, R. A., "The Antitheses of Matthew v. 21-48: Traditional and/or Redactional" NTS 22 (1976) 444-57. SUGGS, M. J., "The Antitheses as Redactional Products" in: L. Schottroff et al. (eds.) Essays in the Love Commandment (Philadelphia 1978) 94-99. *STRECKER, G., "Die Antithesen der Bergpredigt (Mt 5:21-48 par)" ZNW 69 (1978) 36-72. *DIETZFELBINGER, C., "Die Antithesen der Bergpredigt im Verständnis des Matthäus" ZNW 70 (1979) 1-15. "Bergpredigt" in: TRE 5 (1980) 605-12.

5:21-44   *CONGDON, R. D., "Did Jesus Sustain the Law in Matthew 5?" BiblSa 135 (1978) 117-25.

5:21-42   CHAMBERS, O. Studies in the Sermon on the Mount (1941) 25-47.

5:21-28   BULTMANN, R. The History of the Synoptic Tradition (1963) 134-36, 147, 149, 325.

5:21-26   HEIM, K. D. Die Bergpredigt Jesu (1949) 5-15, 16-22. KEPLER, T. S. Jesus' Design for Living (1952) 48-51. HUNTER, A. M. Design for Life (1953) 45-47. KING, G. H. New Order (1954) 36-43. LLOYD-JONES, D. M. Studies in the Sermon on the Mount I (1954) 221-31. LJUNGMAN, H. Das Gesetz Erfüllen (1954) 76-78. EICHHOLZ, G. Herr, tue meine Lippen auf (1957) 233-37. BOWMAN, J. M. & TAPP, R. W.

The Sermon from the Mount (1958) 65-73. McARTHUR, H. K. Understanding the Sermon on the Mount (1960) 87, 91, 95. EICHHOLZ, G. Auslegung der Bergpredigt (1965) 69-77. HUNTER, A. M. A Pattern for Life (1965) 49-51. DAVIES, W. D., The Sermon on the Mount (Cambridge 1966) 81-83. KNöRZER, W. Die Bergpredigt, Modell einer neuen Welt (1968) 43-46. SCHNEIDER, G. Botschaft der Bergpredigt (1969) 48-51. GOULDER, M. D., Midrash and Lection in Matthew (London 1974) 256ff.

5:21-25 WREGE, H.-T. Die UEberlieferungsgeschichte der Bergpredigt (1968) 57.

5:21-24 BRAUN, H. Qumran und NT II (1966) 96, 101f, 105, 157, 287, 291, 295. "Bergpredigt" in: TRE 5 (1980) 604.

5:21.27.33.38.43 McNAMARA, M. The New Testament and the Palestinian Targum to the Pentateuch (1966) 126.

5:21f TRILLING, W. Das wahre Israel (1959) 182. JüNGEL, E. Paulus und Jesus (1966) 203-208. GOGARTEN, F. Christ the Crisis (1967) 106f. SASS, G. Ungereimtes bei Matthäus (1968) 8-9. *MOULE, C. F. D. "Uncomfortable Words I. The Angry Word: Matthew 5:21f.," ET 81 (1, '69) 10-13. SEITZ, O. J. F. Love your Enemies NTS 16 (1969-70) 39f. JEREMIAS, J. Neustestamentliche Theologie I (1971) 26, 148, 199, 212, 241.

5:21-22 MASSAUX, E. Influence de l'Evangile de saint Matthieu sur la litterature chrétienne avant saint Irénée (1950) 444-46. LLOYD-JONES, D. M. Studies in the Sermon on the Mount I (1954) 210-20. STAUDINGER, J. Die Bergpredigt (1957) 81-88. *WEISE, M. "Mt 5:21f.-ein Zeugnis sakraler Rechtsprechung in der Urgemeinde," ZNW 49 (1-2, '58) 116-23. SANFORD, J. A., The Kingdom Within (New York 1970) 120f. GOULDER, M. D., Midrash and Lection in Matthew (London 1974) 286f. HOFFMANN, P./EID, V., Jesus von Nazareth und eine christliche Moral (Freiburg 1975) 76f. MEYER, B. F., The Aims of Jesus (London 1979) 143-45.

5:21.43 McNAMARA, M. The New Testament and the Palestinian Targum to the Pentateuch (1966) 126.

5:21 STONEHOUSE, N. B. The Witness of Matthew and Mark to Christ (1944) 201. BLAIR, E. P. Jesus in the Gospel of Matthew (1960) 113. McARTHUR, H. K. Understanding the Sermon on the Mount (1960) 15, 36-38, 166. BORNKAMM-BARTH-HELD, UEberlieferung und Auslegung im Matthäus-Evangelium (1961) 83. STRECKER, G. Der Weg der Gerechtigkeit (1962) 23. McNAMARA, M. The New Testament and the Palestinian Targum to the Pentateuch (1966) 126-28, 130, 131, 256, 258. NICKELS, P. Targum and

New Testament (1967) 17. BRUNNER, E. Dogmatik II (1950) 239. BANKS, R., Jesus and the Law in the Synoptic Tradition (London 1975) 186f. METZGER, B. M., The Early Versions of the New Testament (Oxford 1977) 252.

5:22ff STONEHOUSE, N. B. The Witness of Matthew and Mark to Christ (1944) 175.

5:22.28.32. HASLER, V. Amen (1969) 79. LOHSE, E. and others (eds.)
34.39.44. Der Ruf Jesu und die Antwort der Gemeinde (1970) 190-203.

5:22 KöHLER, K., "Zu Mt 5:22" ZNW 19 (1919/20) 91. MOORE, G. F. Judaism II (1946) 148n. MASSAUX, E. Influence de l'Evangile de saint Matthieu sur la littérature chrétienne avant saint Irénée (1950) 482-84, 630-31. *WERNBERG-MOLLER, P. "A Semitic Idiom in Matt v. 22," NTS 3 (1, '56) 71-73. STAUDINGER, J. Die Bergpredigt (1957) 83, 85, 93, 124, 282. KNOX, W. L. The Sources of the Synoptic Gospels II (1957) 13, 20, 21, 75. McARTHUR, H. K. Understanding the Sermon on the Mount (1960) 15, 50, 87, 108, 109, 111, 121, 141, 142, 176, 177. STRECKER, G. Der Weg der Gerechtigkeit (1962) 21, 392. *BUSSBY, F. "A Note on raka (Matthew v. 22) and battologeo (Matthew vi. 7) in the Light of Qumran," ET 76 (1, '64) 26. HENNECKE, E. & SCHNEEMELCHER, W. Neutestamentliche Apokryphen (1964) I 95. NICKELS, P. Targum and New Testament (1967) 17. DAVIES, W. D., The Sermon on the Mount (Cambridge 1966) 82. JEREMIAS, J. Neutestamentliche Theologie I (1971) 17, 26, 34, 148. *GUELICH, R. A., "Mt 5:22: Its Meaning and Integrity" ZNW 64 (1973) 39-52. GOULDER, M. D., Midrash and Lection in Matthew (London 1974) 83, 257f, 286, 405. HOWARD, V. P., Das Ego in den synoptischen Evangelien (Marburg 1975) 185-98. "Aramäisch" in: TRE III (1978) 608. METZGER, B. M., "St. Jerome's explicit references to variant readings in manuscripts of the New Testament" in: E. Best et al., (eds.) Text and Interpretation. To Matthew Black (Cambridge 1979) 180.

5:23-26 PLOTZKE, U. Bergpredigt (1960) 98-104. LöWE, R. in: Hören und Fragen (1967) Eichholz, G. & Falkenroth, A. (eds.) 532ff. LOCHMAN, J. M. GPM 13/4 257-64.

5:23f BLAIR, E. P. Jesus in the Gospel of Matthew (1960) 148. STRECKER, G. Der Weg der Gerechtigkeit (1962) 166, 311. HUMMEL, R. Die Auseinandersetzung zwischen Kirche und Judentum im Matthäusevangelium (1963) 80f, 94. KäSEMANN, E. Exegetische Versuche und Besinnungen I (1964) 239. JEREMIAS, J. Abba; Studien zur neutestamentlichen Theologie und Zeitgeschichte (1966). FRIEDLANDER, G. The Jewish Sources of the Sermon on the

Mount (1969) 46f, 156. JEREMIAS, J. Neutestamentliche Theologie I (1971) 187f, 201.

5:23-24 DUPONT, D. J. Les Béatitudes (1958) 147-49. VööBUS, A., The Gospels in Study and Preaching (Philadelphia 1966) 185f. SANFORD, J. A., The Kingdom Within (New York 1970) 121. LOHSE, E., Grundriss der neutestamentlichen Theologie (Stuttgart 1974) 31, 63, 121. MOULE, C. F. D., "'As we forgive . . .'-A Note on the Distinction between Deserts and Capacity in the Understanding of Forgiveness" in: E. Bammel et al. (eds.) Donum Gentilicium. In Honour of David Daube (Oxford 1978) 75f. "Benediktionen" in: TRE 5 (1980) 567.

5:23 BUTLER, B. C. The Originality of St Matthew (1951) 134ff. STAUDINGER, J. Die Bergpredigt (1957) 85, 93, 182, 261, 265, 282. McNAMARA, M. The New Testament and the Palestinian Targum to the Pentateuch (1966) 126. GOULDER, M. D., Midrash and Lection in Matthew (London 1974) 16, 258, 325, 397, 421. "Abendmahlsfeier" in: TRE I (1977) 245.

5:24-25 MEURER, S., Das Recht im Dienst der Versöhnung und des Friedens (Zürich 1972) 76-79.

5:24 GOPPELT, L., Theologie des Neuen Testaments I (Göttingen 1975) 158f.

5:25f JüLICHER, D. A. Die Gleichnisreden Jesu (1910) 240-46. McARTHUR, H. K. Understaning the Sermon on the Mount (1960) 87, 92, 164, 165, 174. JEREMIAS, J. Die Gleichnisse Jesu (1962) 38, 39-41, 95, 179f, 209. *CAIRD, G. B. "Expounding the Parables: I. The Defendant (Matthew 5:25f.; Luke 12:58f.)," ET 77 (2, '65) 36-39. BOUSSET, W. Die Religion des Judentums im Späthellenistischen Zeitalter (1966-1926) 411. HOFFMAN, P. Studien zur Theologie der Logienquellen (1972) 5, 41. SCHULZ, S., Q- Spruchquelle der Evangelisten (1972) 421-24.

5:25-26 DODD, C. H. The Parables of the Kingdom (1948) 136ff. FARRER, A. St Matthew and St Mark (1954) 171. FLEW, R. N. Jesus and His Church (1956) 44. KNOX, W. L. The Sources of the Synoptic Gospels II (1957) 74. MOWRY, L. "Parable," IDB III (1962) 652a.b. STRECKER, G. Der Weg der Gerechtigkeit (1962) 311, 159, 2353. FRIEDLANDER, G. The Jewish Sources of the Sermon on the Mount (1969) 48f. SANFORD, J. A., The Kingdom Within (New York 1970) 116-18. DERRETT, J. D. M. Law in the New Testament: The Parable of the Unjust Judge NTS 18 (1971-72) 182ff. MEURER, S., Das Recht im Dienst der Versöhnung und des Friedens (Zürich 1972) 63-76. GOULDER, M. D., Midrash and Lection in Matthew (London 1974) 258, 287f,436.

TALBERT, C. H., Literary Patterns, Theological Themes, and the Genre of Luke-Acts (Missoula 1974) 55. CONZELMANN, H./LINDEMANN, A., Arbeitsbuch zum Neuen Testament (Tübingen 1975) 62. MANEK, J.... und brachte Frucht (Berlin 1977) 36f. TRITES, A. A., The New Testament Concept of Witness (Cambridge 1977) 190f.

5:25 STAEHELIN, E. Die Verkündigung des Reiches Gottes in der Kirche Jesu Christi (1951) 357. STAUDINGER, J. Die Bergpredigt (1957) 86-88.

5:26 HASLER, V. Amen (1969) 57.

5:27ff STONEHOUSE, N. B. The Witness of Matthew and Mark to Christ (1944) 198f. KNOX, W. L. The Sources of the Synoptic Gospels II (1957) 21-22. STRECKER, G. Der Weg der Gerechtigkeit (1962) 244.

5:27-37 PELIKAN, J. (ed.), The Preaching of Chrysostom (1967) 96-113.

5:27-32 HEIM, D. K. Die Bergpredigt Jesu (1949) 35-49. KING, G. H. New Order (1954) 43-50. LJUNGMAN, H. Das Gesetz Erfüllen (1954) 78-82. BOWMAN, J. M. & TAPP, R. W. The Sermon from the Mount (1958) 74-82. MüLHAUPT, E. (ed.), D Martin Luthers Auslegung der Bergpredigt (1961) 98-101. DAVIES, W. D., The Sermon on the Mount (Cambridge 1966) 109. BALTENSWEILER, H. Die Ehe im Neuen Testament (1967) 112ff. *DU PLESSIS, I. J., "The Ethics of Marriage according to Matt. 5:27-32" Neotestamentica 1 (1967) 16-27.

5:27-30 KEPLER, T. S. Jesus' Design for Living (1952) 51-53. HUNTER, A. M. Design for Life (1953) 47f. LLOYD-JONES, D. M. Studies in the Sermon on the Mount I (1954) 232-41. *McCASLAND, S. V. "Matthew Twists the Scriptures," JBL 80 (1961) 147-48. EICHHOLZ, G. Auslegung der Bergpredigt (1965) 78-80. HUNTER, A. M. A Pattern for Life (1965) 51f. KNöRZER, W. Die Bergpredigt, Modell einer neuen Welt (1968) 46-47. WREGE, H.-T. Die UEberlieferungsgeschichte der Bergpredigt (1968) 64. SCHNEIDER, G. Botschaft der Bergpredigt (1969) 51-52. HOFFMANN, P./VOLKER, E., Jesus von Nazareth und eine christliche Moral (Freiburg 1975) 75f. STAGG, E., and F., Woman in the World of Jesus (Philadelphia 1978) 218f. "Bergpredigt" in: TRE 5 (1980) 604.

5:27f MASSAUX, E. Influence de l'Evangile de saint Matthieu sur la littérature chrétienne avant saint Irénée (1950) 444-46. TRILLING, W. Das wahre Israel (1959) 182f. PLOTZKE, U. Bergpredigt (1960) 104-110. BULTMANN, R. The History of the Synoptic Tradition (1963) 134-38, 147, 149. JüNGEL, E. Paulus und Jesus (1966) 203-208. SEITZ, O. J. F. Love your

Enemies NTS 16 (1969-70) 39f. PHIPPS, W. E. Was Jesus married? (1970) 72-74.

5:27-28 SANFORD, J. A., The Kingdom Within (New York 1970) 169f. THEISSEN, G., Soziologie der Jesusbewegung (München 1977) 75. MEYER, B. F., The Aims of Jesus (London 1979) 143-45. SWIDLER, L., Biblical Affirmations of Woman (Philadelphia 1979) 247. "Bergpredigt" in: TRE 5 (1980) 606. GERSTENBERGER, E. S.,/SCHRAGE, W., Frau und Mann: Biblische Konfrontationen, Band 1013 (Stuttgart 1980) 166.

5:27.38 McNAMARA, M. The New Testament and the Palestinian Targum to the Pentateuch (1966) 126.

5:27 STONEHOUSE, N. B. The Witness of Matthew and Mark to Christ (1944) 200. BRUNNER, E. Dogmatik I (1946) 239. STRECKER, G. Der Weg der Gerechtigkeit (1962) 23. NICKELS, P. Targum and New Testament (1967) 17.

5:28-32 MOORE, G. F. Judaism II (1946) 123f, 267-69.

5:28-30 SCHEP, J. A., The Nature of the Resurrection Body (Grand Rapids 1976) 64f.

5:28 BONHöFFER, A. Epiktet und das Neue Testament (1911) 176, 318. HENNECKE, E. & SCHNEEMELCHER, W. Neutestamentliche Apokryphen (1964) II 98. BRAUN, H. Qumran und NT II (1966) 103, 288, 292. BERGER, K. Zu den Sogenannten Sätzen Heiligen Rechts NTS 17 (1970-71) 14-16, 28f. JEREMIAS, J. Neutestamentliche Theologie I (1971) 26, 118, 149, 218. HOWARD, V. P., Das Ego in den Synoptischen Evangelien (Marburg 1975) 185-98. *HAACKER, K., "Der Rectssahtz Jesu zum Thema Ehebruch (Mt 5, 28)" BZ 21 (1977) 113-16. STAGG, E. and F., Woman in the World of Jesus (Philadelphia 1978) 128-31. SWIDLER, L., Biblical Affirmations of Woman (Philadelphia 1979) 174.

5:29ff STROBEL, A. Erkenntnis und Bekenntnis der Sünde in neutestamentlicher Zeit (1968) 44.

5:29-31 PLOTZKE, U. Bergpredigt (1960) 116-22.

5:29f STONEHOUSE, N. B. The Witness of Matthew and Mark to Christ (1944) 208. LLOYD-JONES, D. M. Studies in the Sermon on the Mount I (1954) 242-251. BEST, E. One Body in Christ (1955) 221. STAUDINGER, J. Die Bergpredigt (1957) 92-95. DUPONT, D. J. Les Béatitudes (1958) 121-23, 149s. SUMMERS, R. The Secret Sayings of the Living Jesus (1968) 60.

5:29-30 SANFORD, J. A., The Kingdom Within (New York 1970) 186.

5:31ff WINDISCH, H. The Meaning of the Sermon on the Mount (1937) 74f.

5:31f STONEHOUSE, N. B. The Witness of Matthew and Mark to Christ (1944) 198, 203ff. TRILLING, W. Das wahre Israel (1959) 185. BORNKAMM-BARTH-HELD, UEberlieferung und Auslegung im Matthäus-Evangelium (1961) 23, 88f. *LöVESTAM, E. "Apolyein en gammalpalestinensisk skilsmässorterm" (Apolyein-An Old Palestinian Divorce Term), SVA 27 ('62) 132-35. STRECKER, G. Der Weg der Gerechtigkeit (1962) 133₁, 142₃. BULTMANN, R. The History of the Synoptic Tradition (1963) 134-36, 148. BORNKAMM, G. "Ehescheidung und Wiederverheiratung im Neuen Testament" in: Geschichte und Glaube I (1968) 56-59. KNöRZER, W. Die Bergpredigt, Modell einer neuen Welt (1968) 48-54. WREGE, H.-T. Die UEberlieferungsgeschichte der Bergpredigt (1968) 66. *SAND, A. "Die Unzuchtsklausel in Mt 5, 31, 32, und 19, 3-9," MThZ 20 (2, '69) 118-29. JEREMIAS, J. Neutestamentliche Theologie I (1971) 26, 199, 207, 240. SEITZ, O. J. F. Love your Enemies NTS 16 (1969-70) 39f. BERGER, K. Die Gesetzauslegung Jesu (1940) 508f, 517f, 557f, 561f, 567-70.

5:31-32 KEPLER, T. S. Jesus' Design for Living (1952) 54-57. HUNTER, A. M. Design for Life (1953) 49-51. LLOYD-JONES, D. M. Studies in the Sermon on the Mount I (1954) 252-261. SCHNACKENBURG, R. Die sittliche Botschaft des Neuen Testaments (1954) 88-92. *DELORME, J. "Sens du texte de S. Matthieu (V, 31-32) sur le divorce," AmiCler 66 (51, '56) 772-74. *VACCARI, A. "Indissolubilità del matrimonio nella Bibbia," CiCa 113 (2, '62) 259-62. *COINER, H. G. "Divorce and Remarriage. Toward Pastoral Practice," CThM 34 (9, '63) 541-54. EICHHOLZ, G. Auslegung der Bergpredigt (1965) 81-85. HUNTER, A. M. Pattern for Life (1965) 53-55. BAUER, J. B., "De coniugali foedere quid edixerit Matthaeus?" VD 44 (1966) 74-78. *LEENHARDT, F.-J. "Les femmes aussi. . .à propos du billet de répudiation," RThPh 19 (1, '69) 31-40. SAND, A., "Die Unzuchtsklausel in Mt 5:31, 32 und 19:3-9" MThZ 20 (1969) 118-29. SCHNEIDER, G. Botschaft der Bergpredigt (1969) 53-55. GOULDER, M. D., Midrash and Lection in Matthew (London 1974) 290f. *FITZMYER, J. A., "The Matthean Divorce Texts and Some New Palestinian Evidence" ThSt 37 (1976) 197-226. *PRZYBYLA, A. E., "List rozwodowy w prawie Mojzesza (Lettre de divorce dans la loi mosaïque)" ZyMy 26 (1976) 54-63. *VALLAURI, E., "Le clausole matteane sul divorzio. Tendenze esegetiche recenti" Laurentianum 17 (1976) 82-112.

STAGG, E. and F., Woman in the World of Jesus (Philadelphia 1978) 131f. *STOCK, A., "Matthean Divorce Texts" Biblical Theology Bulletin 8 (1978) 24-33. FURNISH, V. P., The Moral Teaching of Paul (Nashville 1979) 40. SCHüRMANN, H., "Neutestamentliche Marginalien zur Frage nach der Institutionalität, Unauflösbarkeit und Sakramentalität der Ehe" in: Kirche und Bibel: Festgabe für Bischof Eduard Schick (Paderborn 1979) 415-23. SWIDLER, L., Biblical Affirmations of Woman (Philadelphia 1979) 176.

5:31 STONEHOUSE, N. B. The Witness of Matthew and Mark to Christ (1944) 200. KNOX, W. L. The Sources of the Synoptic Gospels II (1957) 99. STRECKER, G. Der Weg der Gerechtigkeit (1962) 244, 28, 130f. *BAUER, J. B. "De coniugali foedere quid edixerit Matthaeus? (Mt 5, 31 s; 19, 3-9)," VerbDom 44 (2, '66) 74-78.

5:32 *BAUER, J. B. "Die matthäische Ehescheidungsklausel (Mt 5, 32 und 19, 9)," BuLit 38 (2, '64-'65) 101-106. *MOINGT, J. "Le divorce 'pour motif d'impudicité' (Matthieu, 5, 32; 19, 9)," RechSR 56 (3, '68) 337-84. CROUZEL, H. "Le texte patristique de Matthieu v. 32 et xix 9, " NTS 19 (1, '72) 98-119. *HOLZMEISTER, U. "Die Streitfrage über die Ehescheidungstexte bei Matthäus 5.32, 19.9," Biblica 26, (1945) 133-46. PARKER, P. The Gospel Before Mark (1953) 70-71. *VAWTER, B. "The Divorce in Mt 5, 32 and 19, 9," CBQ 76/XVI (1954) 155-67. VACCARI, A. "De matrimonio et divortio apud Matthaeum," Biblica 36 (1955) 149-51. *VACCARI, A. "La clausola sul divorzio in Matteo 5, 32· 19, 9," RivB III/2 (1955) 97-119. *CONSIDINE, T. "Except it be for Fornication," ACR 33 ('56) 214-23. *LEEMING, B. & DYSON, R. A. "Except it be for Fornication," Scripture 8 ('56) 75-82. *ALBERTI, A. "Il divorzio nel Vangelo di Matteo," DivThom 60 (4, '57) 398-410. STAUDINGER, J. Die Bergpredigt (1957) 284-88. FEGHALI, J., "A propos de l'incie de St. Matthieu (V, 32· XIX, 9)" L'Année Canonique 6 (1958) 117-19. *BALTENSWEILER, H. "Die Ehebruchsklauseln bei Matthäus. Zu Matth. 5, 32; 19, 9," TZ 15 (5, '59) 340-56. *DELLAGIACOMA, V. "Il matrimonio presso gli Ebrei," RivB 7 (3, '59) 230-41. *RICHARDS, H. J. "Christ on Divorce," Scripture 11 (13, '59) 22-32. McARTHUR, H. K. Understanding the Sermon on the Mount (1960) 15, 36, 51, 97, 108, 164. PLOTZKE, U. Bergpredigt (1960) 110-16. *ZERWICK, M., "De matrimonio et divortio in Evangelio," VerbDom 38 (4, '60) 193-212. *JERVELL, J. "Skilsmisse og gjengifte etter Det nye testamente," NTT 62 (4, '61) 195-210. SCHRAGE, W. Die Konkreten Einzelgebote in der

Paulinischen Paränese (1961) 244. STRECKER, G. Der Weg der Gerechtigkeit (1962) 17. 244, 130ff. FLEMING, T. V. "Christ and Divorce," ThS 24 (1963) 106-120. *DAUVILLIER, J., "L'indissolubilité du mariage dans la nouvelle Loi," OrSyr 9 (2-3, '64) 265-89. *DUBARLE, A. M. "Mariage et divorce dans l'Evangile," OrSyr 9 (1, '64) 61-73. *O'ROURKE, J. J. "A Note on an Exception: Mt 5:32 (19:9) and 1 Cor 7:12 Compared," HeyJ 5 (3, '64) 299-302. *KARPINSKI, R. "Nierozerwalnosé małżenstwa w Nowym Testamencie Mt 5, 32 i 19, 9," RBL 18 (2, '65) 77-88. STENDAHL, K., The Bible and the Role of Women (New York 1966) 26f. *COINER, H. G. "Those 'Divorce and Remarriage' Passages (Matt 5:32; 19:9; 1 Cor 7:10-16). With Brief Reference to the Mark and Luke Passages," CThM 39 (6, '68) 367-84. *MAHONEY, A., "A New Look at the Divorce Clauses in Mt 5, 32 and 19, 9," CBQ 30 (1, '68) 29-38. GREEVES, H. Ehe Nach dem Neuen Testament NTS 15 (1968-69) 381ff. EZECHIELE, D., "Eccetto in caso de fornicazione" PaCl 48 (1969) 1297-1300. *NEPPER-CHRISTENSEN, P. "Utugtsklausulen og Josef i Matthaeusevangeliet," SEA 34 ('69) 122-46. DELLING, G. Studien zum Neuen Testament und zum hellenistischen Judentum (1970) 229-31. DERRETT, J. D. M. Law in the New Testament (1970) 367-88. LOHSE, E., and others (eds.), Der Ruf Jesu und die Antwort der Gemeinde (1970) 226-46.*NEMBACH, U. "Ehescheidung nach alttestamentlich und jüdischen Recht," TZ 26 (3, '70) 161-71. *TAYLOR, R. J. "Divorce in Matthew 5:32; 19:9. Theological Research and Pastoral Care," ClR 55 (10, '70) 792-800. BERGER, K. Zu den Sogenannten Sätzen Heiligen Rechts NTS 17 (1970-71) 14-16, 28f. *GIAVINI, G. "Nuove e vecchie vie per la lettura delle clausole di Matteo sul divorzio," ScuC 99 (2, '71) 83-93. JEREMIAS, J. Neutestamentliche Theologie I (1971) 26, 152, 204, 207, 217. OLSEN, N. V. The New Testament Logia on Divorce (1971). *SCHNEIDER, G. "Jesu Wort über die Ehescheidung in der UEberlieferung des Neuen Testaments," TThZ 80 (2, '71) 65-87. *STRAMARE, T. "Causa fornicationis. Verso una soluzione del problema?" PaCl 5L (17, '71) 1028-32. *STRAMARE, T., "Matteo divorzista?" Divinitas 15 (2, '71) 213-35. BAUER, J. B., Scholia Biblica et Patristica (Graz 1972) 231. ERNST, J., Anfänge der Christologie (Stuttgart 1972) 150-52. HOFFMANN, P. Studien zur Theologie der Logienquelle (1972) 5, 42. *SABOURIN, L. "The Divorce Clauses (Mt 5:32; 19, 9)," BThB 2 (1, '72) 80-86. SCHULZ, S., Q Die Spruchquelle der Evangelisten (1972) 116-20. *BARTINA, S., "Jesús y el divorcio. La solución de

Tarcisio Stramare" EstBi 32 (1973) 385-88. GOULDER, M. D., Midrash and Lection in Matthew (London 1974) 18, 36, 39, 235, 291, 334. *DA SILVA, A. P., "Ainda uma teoria sobre Mt 5, 32 e 19, 9? (No atual debate sobre o divórcio)" RCB 11 (1974) 112-19. TALBERT, C. H., Literary Patterns, Theological Themes, and the Genre of Luke-Acts (Missoula 1974) 55. GOPPELT, L., Theologie des Neuen Testaments. I (Göttingen 1975) 161f. BANKS, R., Jesus and the Law in the Synoptic Tradition (London 1975) 192f. HOWARD, V. P., Das Ego in den Synoptischen Evangelien (Marburg 1975) 185-98. *STRAMARE, T., "Clausole di Matteo e indissolubilità del matrimonio" BiOr 17 (1975) 65-74. VARGAS-MACHUCA, A., "Los casos de 'divorcio' admitidos por S. Mateo (5, 32 y 19, 9). Consecuencias para la teologia actual" EstEc 50 (1975) 5-54. METZGER, B.M, The Early Versions of the New Testament (Oxford 1977) 179. *VAWTER, B., "Divorce and the New Testament" CBQ 39 (1977) 528-42. *ZALESKI, J., "Elementy egzegezy patrystycznej we wspòtszenych interpretacjach tekstu Mt 5, 32 czy 19, 9 (Elemente der patristischen Exegese in der gegenwärtigen Auslegung von Mt 5, 32 bzw. 19, 9)" CoTh 47 (1977) 43-63. BLOCH, R., "Midrash" in: W. S. Green (ed.) Approaches to Ancient Judiasm (Missoula 1978) 49. *GELDARD, M., "Jesus' Teaching on Divorce: thoughts on the meaning of *porneia* in Matthew 5:32 and 19:9" Churchman 92 (1978) 134-43. *MANRIQUE, A., "Jesús de Nazaret ante el divorcio" Biblia y Fe 4 (1978) 33-46. SWIDLER, L., Biblical Affirmations of Woman (Philadelphia 1979) 174, 231, 239, 259. BAUER, J. B., "Bemerkungen zu den matthäischen Unzuchtsklauseln (Mt 5, 32; 19, 9)" in: J. Zmijewski/E. Nellessen (eds.) Begegnung mit dem Wort: Festschrift für Heinrich Zimmermann (Bonn 1980) 23-33.

5:33ff STONEHOUSE, N. B. The Witness of Matthew and Mark to Christ (1944) 198, 206ff. BORNKAMM-BARTH-HELD, UEberlieferung und Auslegung im Matthäus-Evangelium (1961) 112, 135f.

5:33-39 BRAUN, H. Qumran und NT II (1966) 89, 99, 102, 105, 287, 289, 295f.

5:33-37 KEPLER, T. S. Jesus' Design for Living (1952) 57-60. HUNTER, A. M. Design for Life (1953) 51f. KING, G. H. New Order (1954) 50-55. LLOYD-JONES, D. M. Studies in the Sermon on the Mount I (1954) 262-70. LJUNGMAN, H. Das Gesetz Erfüllen (1954) 82-83. THIELICKE, H. Das Leben kann noch einmal beginnen (1956) 66-80. STAUDINGER, J. Die Bergpredigt (1957) 103-110. BOWMAN, J. W. & TAPP, R. W. The Sermon from the Mount (1958) 83-88. McARTHUR,

H. K. Understanding the Sermon on the Mount (1960) 37, 45, 91, 95, 120, 121, 137. PLOTZKE, U. Bergpredigt (1960) 122-28. MüLHAUPT, E. (ed.), D Martin Luthers Auslegung der Bergpredigt (1961) 101-103. STRECKER, G. Der Weg der Gerechtigkeit (1962) 133f, 152l. BULTMANN, R. The History of the Synoptic Tradition (1963) 134f, 147, 149. EICHHOLZ, G. Auslegung der Bergpredigt (1965) 86-91. HUNTER, A. M. A Pattern for Life (1965) 55f. KNöRZER, W. Die Bergpredigt, Modell einer neuen Welt (1968) 54-56. WREGE, H.-T. Die UEberlieferungsgeschichte der Bergpredigt (1968) 70. SCHNEIDER, G. Botschaft der Bergpredigt (1969) 55-57. SANFORD, J. A., The Kingdom Within (New York 1970) 108. JEREMIAS, J. Neutestamentliche Theologie I (1971) 26, 171, 175, 200, 207, 212, 241. *MINEAR, P. S. "Yes or No: The demand for honesty in the early Church," NovTest 13 (1, '71) 1-13. GOULDER, M. D., Midrash and Lection in Matthew (London 1974) 259f, 291ff, 421, 424. HOFFMANN, P./EID, V., Jesus von Nazareth und eine christlich Moral (Freiburg 1975) 77-79. WESTERHOLM, S., Jesus and Scribal Authority (Lund 1978) 106-108. "Bergpredigt" in: TRE 5 (1980) 604.

5:33f TRILLING, W. Das wahre Israel (1959) 183f. JüNGEL, E. Paulus und Jesus (1966) 203-208. MEYER, B. F., The Aims of Jesus (London 1979) 143-45.

5:33-34 MASSAUX, E. Influence de l'Evangile de saint Matthieu sur la littérature chrétienne avant saint Irénée (1950) 444-46.

5:33 STONEHOUSE, N. B. The Witness of Matthew and Mark to Christ (1944) 201. STRECKER, G. Der Weg der Gerechtigkeit (1962) 238. NICKELS, P. Targum and New Testament (1967) 17. *MILFORD, T. R. "Is All This Swearing Necessary?' Theology 68 (543, '65) 410-17. BANKS, R., Jesus and the Law in the Synoptic Tradition (London 1975) 193f.

5:34-37 STäHLIN, G. "Zum Gebrauch von Beteuerungsformeln im N. T.," in: Donum Gratulatorium (1962) 115-43.

5:34-36 BAUMBACH, G. Das Verständnis des Bösen in den synoptischen Evangelien (1963) 69ff. BANKS, R., Jesus and the Law in the Synoptic Tradition (London 1975) 194f.

5:34f STRECKER, G. Der Weg der Gerechtigkeit (1962) 232.

5:34 *SUTCLIFFE, E. F. "Not to swear at all (Mt. V, 34)," Scripture V/3 (1952) 68-69. McARTHUR, H. K. Understanding the Sermon on the Mount (1960) 36, 51, 141. SMITH, M., Tannaitic Parallels to the Gospels (Philadelphia 1968) 6 b n 4+. HOWARD, V. P., Das Ego in den Synoptischen Evangelien (Marburg 1975) 185-98. THEISSEN, G., Soziologie der Jesusbewegung (München 1977) 75.

5:35 KNOX, W. L. The Sources of the Synoptic Gospels II (1957) 41.

5:36 BOUSSET, W. Die Religion des Judentums im Späthellenistischen Zeitalter (1966⁻1926) 376.

5:37 MOORE, G. F. Judaism II (1946) 189n. *KUTSCH, E., " 'Eure Rede aber sei ja ja, nein nein'," EvTh 20 (5, '60) 206-18. STRECKER, G. Der Weg der Gerechtigkeit (1962) 183. BAUMBACH, G. Das Verständnis des Bösen in den Synoptischen Evangelien (1963) 67ff, 213f.

5:38ff STONEHOUSE, N. B. The Witness of Matthew and Mark to Christ (1944) 198, 208. STRECKER, G. Der Weg der Gerechtigkeit (1962) 1331. HUMMEL, R. Die Auseinandersetzung zwischen Kirche und Judentum im Matthäusevangelium (1963) 73. "Bergpredigt" in: TRE 5 (1980) 613.

5:38-48 HEIM, D. K. Die Bergpredigt Jesu (1949) 23-34. STREETER, B. H. The Four Gospels (1951) 251f. PIROT, J. Paraboles et Allégories Evangeliques (1949) 42-49. THIELICKE, H. Das Leben kann noch einmal beginnen (1956) 81-99. *NICOLAS, A. "Etude biblique. La relation avec l'ennemi," Foi et Vie 59 (4, '60) 235-51. SHINN, R. L. Sermon on the Mount (1962) 39-47. FALKENROTH, A. in: Hören und Fragen (1967) Eichholz, G. & Falkenroth, A. (eds.), 486ff. *RAUSCH, J. "The Principle of Nonresistence and Love of Enemy in Mt 5, 38-48," CBQ 28 (1, '66) 31-41. PELIKAN, J. (ed.), The Preaching of Chrysostom (1967) 114-29. *HOFFMANN, P. "Die bessere Gerechtigkeit. Die Auslegung der Bergpredigt IV (Mt 5,38-48)" BuL 10 (4, '69). BANNACH, H. "Die bessere Gerechtigkeit", Ich aber sage euch (1969) 16-24. DEMMER, H. "Matthäus 5, 38-48," Ich aber sage euch (1969) 40-47. EICHELE, E. "Matthäus 5, 38-48," Ich aber sage euch (1969) 62-71. LANGE, E. "Die Kosten des Freidens," Ich aber sage euch (1969) 90-101. LORENZ, F. Streit um Jesus (1969) 12-19. VON OPPEN, D. "Feindesliebe hat viele Gesichter," Ich aber sage euch (1969) 115-17. ZAHRNT, H. "Matthäus 5, 38-48," Ich aber sage euch (1969) 136-48. LANGE, E. (ed.), Predigtstudien für das Kirchenjahr 1970/71 (1970) 217-21. BRAUN, H. GPM 13₈4 239-44. EHRENBERG, H. P. GPM 6/4 217-19í SCHRAGE, W. GPM 25 (3, '71) 402-13. EDWARDS, R. A., A Theology of Q (Philadelphia 1976) 85-87. SCHOTTROFF, L., "Gewaltverzicht und Feindesliebe in der urchristlichen Jesus-tradition, Mt 5, 38-48; Lk 6, 27-36" in: G. Strecker (ed.) Jesus Christus in Historie und Theologie: Neutestamentliche Festschrift für Hans Conzelmann (Tübingen 1975) 197-221. *DíAZ, J. A., "Las 'Buenas obras' (o la 'justicia') dentro de la estructura de los principales temas de Teología Biblica" EstEc 52 (1977) 445-86. SCHMIDT, J./LüTCKE, K.-H., in: P. Krusche (ed.) Predigtstudien V, 2. Halbband (Stuttgart 1977) 209-15. *FULLER, R. H. (ed.), Essays on the Love Commandment (Philadelphia 1978). SCHOTTROFF, L., "Non-Violence and the Love of One's Enemy" in: L. Schottroff et al. (eds.) Essays in the Love Commandment (Philadelphia 1978) 9-39. BAUMBACH, G., GPM 33 (1979) 415-22.

5:38-42   KEPLER, T. S. Jesus' Design for Living (1952) 60-62. HUNTER, A. M. Design for Life (1953) 52-56. KING, G. H. New Order (1954) 55-61. LLOYD-JONES, D. M. Studies in the Sermon on the Mount I (1954) 271-79, 280-89, 290-98. LJUNGMAN, H. Das Gesetz Erfüllen (1954) 83-85. STAUDINGER, J. Die Bergpredigt (1957) 110-20. BOWMAN, J. W. & TAPP, R. W. The Sermon from the Mount (1958) 89-98. McARTHUR, H. K. Understanding the Sermon on the Mount (1960) 45, 91, 95, 118, 136, 178. PLOTZKE, U. Bergpredigt (1960) 128-34. MüLHAUPT, E. (ed.), D Martin Luthers Auslegung der Bergpredigt (1961) 103-124. EICHHOLZ, G. Auslegung der Bergpredigt (1965) 92-98. HUNTER, A. M. A Pattern for Life (1965) 56-59. KNöRZER, W. Die Bergpredigt, Modell einer neuen Welt (1968) 56-59. WREGE, H.-T. Die UEberlieferungsgeschichte der Bergpredigt (1968) 75. SCHNEIDER, G. Botschaft der Bergpredigt (1969) 58-60. MEURER, S., Das Recht im Dienst der Versöhnung und des Friedens (Zürich 1972) 63-76. GOULDER, M. D., Midrash and Lection in Matthew (London 1974) 159, 260f, 293, 445. *SAHLIN, H., "Traditionskritische Bemerkungen zu zwei Evangelienperikopen" StTh 33 (1979) 69-84.

5:38-41   BULTMANN, R. The History of the Synoptic Tradition (1963) 135f, 148f. MEYER, B. F., The Aims of Jesus (London 1979) 143-45.

5:38f   TRILLING, W. Das wahre Israel (1959) 185. BORNKAMM-BARTH-HELD, UEberlieferung und Auslegung im Matthäus-Evangelium (1961) 136, 148. STRECKER, G. Der Weg der Gerechtigkeit (1962) 142l. SEITZ, O. J. F. Love your Enemies NTS 16 (1969-70) 39f. JEREMIAS, J. Neutestamentliche Theologie I (1971) 26, 199, 230, 240f.

5:38   STONEHOUSE, N. B. The Witness of Matthew and Mark to Christ (1944) 200. KNOX, W. L. The Sources of the Synoptic Gospels II (1957) 35. STRECKER, G. Der Weg der Gerechtigkeit (1962) 24. CURRIE, S., "Matthew 5:38a" HThR 57 (1964) 140-45. McNAMARA, M. The New Testament and the Palestinian Targum to the Pentateuch (1966) 131 fn. 14. THEISSEN, G., Soziologie der Jesusbewegung (München 1977) 20.

5:39ff DAVIES, W. D., The Sermon on the Mount (Cambridge 1966) 97.

5:39-48 LüHRMANN, D., "Liebet eure Feinde" ZThK 69 (1972) 412-38. "Bergpredigt" in: TRE 5 (1980) 604.

5:39-44 POLAG, A., Die Christologie der Logienquelle (Neukirchen-Vluyn 1977) 77.

5:39-42 MOORE, G. F. Judaism II (1946) 143n, 151, 165, 168. STRECKER, G. Der Weg der Gerechtigkeit (1962) 183. *TANNEHILL, R. C. "The 'Focal Instance' as a Form of New Testament Speech: A Study of Matthew 5:39b-42," JR 50 (4 '70) 372-85. ERNST, J., Anfänge der Christologie (Stuttgart 1972) 154-58. SCHULZ, S. Q Die Spruchquelle der Evangelisten (1972) 120-27. TALBERT, C. H., Literary Patterns, Theological Themes, and the Genre of Luke-Acts (Missoula 1974) 42. HOFFMANN, P./EID, V., Jesus von Nazareth und eine christliche Moral (Freiburg 1975) 157-64. TANNEHILL, R., The Sword of His Mouth (Philadelphia 1975) 67-77.

5:39-41 PERRIN, N., Jesus and the Language of the Kingdom (London 1976) 41, 48, 51-62.

5:39-40 KNOX, W. L. The Sources of the Synoptic Gospels II (1957) 15, 17, 21.

5:39 KITTEL, G. Die Probleme des Palästinischen Spätjudentums und das Urchristentum (1926) 32. MANSON, W. Jesus the Messiah (1948) 30-32, 86-87. MASSAUX, E. Influence de l'Evangile de saint Matthieu sur la littérature chrétienne avant saint Irénée (1950) 584-85, 611-12, 482-84. *CLAVIER, H. "Matthieu 5:39 et la non-résistance," RHPhR 37 (1, '57) 44-57. GLOVER, R. The Didache's Quotations and the Synoptic Gospels NTS 5 (1958-59) 14ff. McARTHUR, H. K. Understanding the Sermon on the Mount (1960) 48, 106, 107, 111, 121, 128, 141, 147. SCHRAGE, W. Die konkreten Einzelgebote in der Paulinischen Paränese (1961) 234. BAUMBACH, G. Das Verständnis des Bösen in den synoptischen Evangelien (1963) 70ff. *CURRIE, S. D. "Matthew 5:39a-Resistance or Protest?" HThR 57 (2, '64) 140-45. JEREMIAS, J. Neutestamentliche Theologie I (1971) 229f. HOWARD, V. P., Das Ego in den Synoptischen Evangelien (Marburg 1975) 185-98. METZGER, B. M., The Early Versions of the New Testament (Oxford 1977) 437f. THEISSEN, G., Soziologie der Jesusbewegung (München 1977) 75.

5:40-41 BANKS, R., Jesus and the Law in the Synoptic Tradition (London 1975) 196f.

5:41 MASSAUX, E. Influence de l'Evangile de saint Matthieu sur la littérature chrétienne avant saint Irénée (1950) 482-84. KNOX, W. L. The Sources of the Synoptic Gospels II (1957) 15, 19. McARTHUR, H. K. Understanding the Sermon on the Mount (1960) 36, 121, 130, 164. THEUNISSEN, M., "ὁ αἰτῶν λαμβάνει. Der Gebetsglaube Jesu und die Zeitlichkeit des Christseins" in: Jesus, Ort der Erfahrung Gottes (Basel 1976) 57. THEISSEN, G., Soziologie der Jesusbewegung (München 1977) 20.

5:42.43 BARRETT, C. K. The New Testament Background: Selected Documents (1956) 223.

5:42 MASSAUX, E. Influence de l'Evangile de saint Matthieu sur la littérature chrétienne avant saint Irénée (1950) 473-74, 611-13. MUNCK, J. Jewish Christianity in Post Apostolic Times NTS 6 (1959-60) 109f. STRECKER, G. Der Weg der Gerechtigkeit (1962) 134.

5:43ff STONEHOUSE, N. B. The Witness of Matthew and Mark to Christ (1944) 198ff. BORNKAMM, G. Jesus von Nazareth (1956) 103ff.

5:43-48 BERGER, K. Die Gesetzauslegung Jesu (1940) 237-42, 444f, 452f et al. CHAMBERS, O. Studies in the Sermon on the Mount (1941) 48-74. KEPLER, T. S. Jesus' Design for Living (1952) 63-65. HUNTER, A. M. Design for Life (1953) 56-59. KING, G. H. New Order (1954) 61-65. LJUNGMAN, H. Das Gesetz Erfüllen (1954) 85-91. LLOYD-JONES, D. M. Studies in the Sermon on the Mount I (1954) 299-309, 310-20. BOWMAN, J. W. & TAPP, R. W. The Sermon from the Mount (1958) 99-105. DUPONT, D. J. Les Béatitudes (1958) 151-56, 191-93. McARTHUR, H. K. Understanding the Sermon on the Mount (1960) 37, 87, 91, 95, 121, 177. BORNKAMM-BARTH-HELD, UEberlieferung und Auslegung im Matthäus-Evangelium (1961) 74, 83, 87, 92f, 96, 148. MüLHAUPT, E. (ed.), D Martin Luthers Auslegung der Bergpredigt (1961) 124-25. DE BOER, W. P. The Imitation of Paul (1962) 71ff. STRECKER, G. Der Weg der Gerechtigkeit (1962) 1331, 135. EICHHOLZ, G. Auslegung der Bergpredigt (1965) 99-103. HUNTER, A. M. A Pattern for Life (1965) 60-63. DAVIES, W. D., The Sermon on the Mount (Cambridge 1966) 140f. McNAMARA, M. The New Testament and the Palestinian Targum to the Pentateuch (1966) 127 fn. 2. *DU PLESSIS, P. J. "Love and Perfection in Matt. 5:43-48," Neotestamentica 1 ('67) 28-34. KNöRZER, W. Die Bergpredigt, Modell einer neuen Welt (1968) 59-61. WREGE, H.-T. Die UEberlieferungsgeschichte der Bergpredigt (1968) 82. FURNISH, V. P. The Love Command in the New Testament (1972) 45-54. GOULDER, M. D., Midrash and Lection in

Matthew (London 1974) 89, 271, 294ff, 463. *BAYER, O., "Sprachbewegung und Weltveränderung. Ein systematischer Versuch als Auslegung von Mt 5, 43-48" EvTh 35 (1975) 309-21. CONZELMANN, H./LINDEMANN, A., Arbeitsbuch zum Neuen Testament (Tübingen 1975) 62. *BOUTTIER, M., "Hésiode et le sermon sur la montagne" NTS 25 (1978) 129f.

5:43-47 SCHNEIDER, G. Botschaft der Bergpredigt (1969) 60-63. SANFORD, J. A., The Kingdom Within (New York 1970) 124f.

5:43-45 PLOTZKE, U. Bergpredigt (1960) 135-41. DAVIES, W. D., The Sermon on the Mount (Cambridge 1966) 144f.

5:43f TRILLING, W. Das wahre Israel (1959) 185f. STRECKER, G. Der Weg der Gerechtigkeit (1962) 142₃. BRAUN, H. Qumran und NT II (1966) 89, 96, 107, 112, 153, 287, 295. SEITZ, O. J. F. Love your Enemies NTS 16 (1969-70) 39-54. JEREMIAS, J. Neutestamentliche Theologie I (1971) 26, 28, 118, 199, 206, 240. MEYER, B. F., The Aims of Jesus (London 1979) 143-45. SWIDLER, L., Biblical Affirmations of Woman (Philadelphia 1979) 286.

5:43 STONEHOUSE, N. B. The Witness of Matthew and Mark to Christ (1944) 200. KNOX, W. L. The Sources of the Synoptic Gospels II (1957) 35. BLAIR, E. P. Jesus in the Gospel of Matthew (1960) 113. STRECKER, G. Der Weg der Gerechtigkeit (1962) 18, 24. *LINTON, O. "St. Matthew 5, 43," StTh 18 (1, '64) 66-79. JüNGEL, E. Paulus und Jesus (1966) 213. McNAMARA, M. The New Testament and the Palestinian Targum to the Pentateuch (1966) 127. MOLIN, G. "Matthäus 5, 43 und das Schrifttum von Qumran," in: Bible und Qumran (1968) Wagner, S. (ed.), 150-52. SEITZ, O. J. F. "Love your Enemies. The Historical Setting of Matthew v. 43f.; Luke vi.27f." NTS 16 (1, '69) 39-54. STAUDINGER, J. Die Bergpredigt (1957) 121-23. DAVIES, W. D., The Sermon on the Mount (Cambridge 1966) 83. SANFORD, J. A., The Kingdom Within (New York 1970) 148f.

5:44ff LINTON, O., "Le parallelismus membrorum dans le Nouveau Testament grec" in: A. DESCAMPS/DE HALLEUX, A. (eds.) Mélanges Bibliques en hommage au R. P. Béda Rigaux (Gembloux 1970) 503-505.

5:44-48 KNOX, W. L. The Sources of the Synoptic Gospels II (1957) 9, 24. BULTMANN, R. The History of the Synoptic Gospels (1963) 148f. DAVIES, W. D., The Sermon on the Mount (Cambridge 1966) 104. SCHULZ, S. Q Die Spruchquelle der Evangelisten (1972) 127-39. TALBERT, C. H., Literary Patterns, Theological Themes, and the Genre of Luke-Acts

(Missoula 1974) 42. PERRIN, N., Jesus and the Language of the Kingdom (London 1976) 41, 53f.

5:44f   MASSAUX E. Influence de l'Evangile de saint Matthieu sur la littérature chrétienne avant saint Irénée (1950) 580-82. SCHULZ, A Nachfolgen und Nachnahmen (1962) 226-30, 248f. JüNGEL, E. Paulus und Jesus (1966) 213f.

5:44-45   CONZELMANN, H./LINDEMANN, A., Arbeitsbuch zum Neuen Testament (Tübingen 1975) 362. HOFFMANN, P./EID, V., Jesus von Nazareth und eine christliche Moral (Freiburg 1975) 151-55. DELLING, G., "Die 'Söhne (Kinder) Gottes' im Neuen Testament" in: R. Schnackenburg et al. (eds.) Die Kirche des Anfangs: Für Heinz Schürmann (Wien 1978) 620f.

5:44   MASSAUX, E. Influence de l'Evangile de saint Matthieu sur la littérature chrétienne avant saint Irénée (1950) 414-15, 471-72, 529-30, 584-85, 596-97, 608-11. STAEHELIN, E. Die Verkündigung des Reiches Gottes in der Kirche Jesu Christi I (1951) 144. BROWN, R. E., "The Qumran Scrolls and the Johannine Gospel and Epistles" CBQ 17 (1955) 403-19, 559-74, also in: K. Stendahl (ed.) The Scrolls and the New Testament (New York 1957) 198, GT: "Die Schriftrollen von Qumran und das Johannesevangelium und die Johannesbriefe" in: K. H. Rengstorf (ed.) Johannes und sein Evangelium (Darmstadt 1973) 512. KNOX, W. L. The Sources of the Synoptic Gospels II (1957) 14, 17. SCHRAGE, W. Die konkreten Einzelgebote in der Paulinischen Paränese (1961) 243. STRECKER, G. Der Weg der Gerechtigkeit (1962) 2394. STAUDINGER, J. Die Bergpredigt (1957) 122-25. HENNECKE, E. & SCHNEEMELCHER, W. Neutestamentliche Apokryphen (1964) I 135. DAVIES, W. D., The Sermon on the Mount (Cambridge 1966) 97. HASLER, V. Amen (1969) 59. BEST, E. I Peter and the Gospel Tradition NTS 16 (1969-70) 105f. JEREMIAS, J. Neutestamentliche Theologie I (1971) 187, 206, 209, 283. HOWARD, V. P., Das Ego in den Synoptischen Evangelien (Marburg 1975) 185-98. METZGER, B. M., The Early Versions of the New Testament (Oxford 1977) 39. "Agrapha" in: TRE 2 (1978) 108.

5:45-47   POLAG, A., Die Christologie der Logienquelle (Neukirchen-Vluyn 1977) 77.

5:45f   MANSON, W. Jesus the Messiah (1948) 106-108.

5:45   MOORE, G. F. Judaism II (1946) 378. PARKER, P. The Gospel Before Mark (1953) 136-37. KNOX, W. L. The Sources of the Synoptic Gospels II (1957) 15, 17. STAUDINGER, J. Die Bergpredigt (1957) 124-25. BLAIR, E. P. Jesus in the

Gospel of Matthew (1960) 91. McARTHUR, H. K. Understanding the Sermon on the Mount (1960) 60, 65, 87. *SCHRUERS, P. "La paternité divine dans Mt., V, 45 et VI, 26-32." EphT 36 (3-4, '60) 593-624. BORNKAMM-BARTH-HELD, UEberlieferung und Auslegung im Matthäus-Evangelium (1961) 23, 130. STRECKER, G. Der Weg der Gerechtigkeit (1962) 141s, 219. McNAMARA, M. The New Testament and the Palestinian Targum of the Pentateuch (1966) 136, 136 fn. 35. FRIEDLANDER, G. The Jewish Sources of the Sermon on the Mount (1969) 76, 78, 83. BEST, E. I Peter and the Gospel of Tradition NTS 16 (1969-70) 109f. PETZKE, G. Die Traditionen über Apollonius von Tyana und das Neue Testament (1970) 207, 228. SANFORD, J. A., The Kingdom Within (New York 1970) 134-36. JEREMIAS, J. Neutestamentliche Theologie I (1971) 71, 177f, 209. BRUNNER, E. Dogmatik I (1946) 202. BRUNNER, E. Dogmatik II (1956) 181. JANSSEN E., "Testament Abrahams" in: W. G. Kümmel (ed.) Jüdische Schriften aus hellenistisch-römischer Zeit III (Gütersloh 1975) 207.

5:46-48 PLOTZKE, U. Bergpredigt (1960) 141-47. SMITH, M., Tannaitic Parallels to the Gospels (Philadelphia 1968) A+, B 30.

5:46f MASSAUX, E. Influence de l'Evangile de saint Matthieu sur la littérature chrétienne avant saint Irénée (1950) 608-11. HUMMEL, R. Die Auseinandersetzung zwischen Kirche und Judentum im Matthäusevangelium (1963) 22. STRECKER, G. Der Weg der Gerechtigkeit (1962) 164.

5:46-47 HOFFMANN, P./EID, V., Jesus von Nazareth und eine christliche Moral (Freiburg 1975) 156f.

5:47 KNOX, W. L. The Sources of the Synoptic Gospels II (1957) 33, 133. *KETTEL, J. "Die christliche Botschaft über den Gruss," GuL 37 (3, '64) 165-71. BLACK, M. An Aramaic Approach to the Gospels and Acts (1967) 176f. TAGAWA, K. People and Community in the Gospel of Matthew NTS 16 (1969-70) 153f. *DAS NEVES, J. C., "Quem são os ethnikoi do Evangelho de Mateus?" Didaskalia 4 (1974) 229-35.

5:48 BONHöFFER, A. Epiktet und das Neue Testament (1911) 89, 31. WINDISCH, H. The Meaning of the Sermon on the Mount (1937) 68, 70, 84, 96, 92, 120, 132, 184f, 201ff. BRUNNER, E. Dogmatik I (1946) 314. MASSAUX, E. Influence de l'Evangile de saint Matthieu sur la littérature chrétienne avant saint Irénée (1950) 477-79. FUCHS, E. "Die vollkommene Gewissheit. Zur Auslegung von Matth. 5, 48," in: Neutestamentliche Studien für Rud. Bultmann zu seinem siebzigsten Geburtstag (1954) 130-36. LJUNGMAN, H. Das Gesetz Erfüllen (1954) 88-91. *SCHNACKENBURG, R. "Die Vollkommenheit des

Christen nach den Evangelien," GuL 32 (6, '59) 420-33.
TRILLING, W. Das wahre Israel (1959) 166ff. BLAIR, E. P.
Jesus in the Gospel of Matthew (1960) 136. FUCHS, E. "Die
vollkommene Gewissheit," in: Zur Frage nach dem
Historischen Jesus (1960) 126-35. BORNKAMM-BARTH-
HELD, UEberlieferung und Auslegung im Matthäus-
Evangelium (1961) 90f, 92, 96. SCHULZ, A. Nachfolgen und
Nachnahmen (1962) 231-34. STRECKER, G. Der Weg der
Gerechtigkeit (1962) 141, 232. HUMMEL, R. Die
Auseinandersetzung zwischen Kirche und Judentum im
Matthäusevangelium (1963) 152, 156. *LEE, E. K. "Hard
Sayings," Theology 66 (521, '63) 462. *ROBSON, G. A. "Hard
Sayings," Theology 66 (520, '63) 416-17. *BRUPPACHER, H.
"Ein neues Jesuswort," KirchReformSchweiz 121 (Aug. 12,
'65) 242-44. BRAUN, H. Qumran und NT II (1966) 86, 299.
*DUPONT, J. "L'appel à imiter Dieu en Matthieu 5, 48 et Luc
6, 36." RivB 14 (2, '66) 137-58. McNAMARA, M. The New
Testament and the Palestinian Targum to the Pentateuch
(1966) 56, 133-36. *BRUPPACHER, H. "Was sagte Jesu in
Matthäus 5:48?" ZNW 58 (1-2, '67) 145. NICKELS, P. Targum
and New Testament (1967) 17. SCHNACKENBURG, R.
Christian Existence in the New Testament (1968) 158-89.
SCHNEIDER, G. Botschaft der Bergpredigt (1969) 64-65.
BEST, E. I Peter and the Gospel Tradition NTS 16 (1969-70)
110f. SANFORD, J. A., The Kingdom Within (New York
1970) 47f, 127f. FRANKEMöLLE, H., Jahwebund und Kirche
Christi (Münster 1974) 160f, 163, 182, 277, 282, 288, 291,
307.SAND, A., Das Gesetz und die Propheten (Regensburg
1974) 54-56. POLAG, A., Die Christologie der Logienquelle
(Neukirchen-Vluyn 1977) 61f. "Amt" in: TRE 2 (1978) 516.
"Barmherzigkeit" in: TRE 5 (1980) 237.

6-7   *BLIGH, J. "Matching Passages, 5: The Sermon on the Mount
      II," Way 9 (4, '69) 321-30.

6:1-7:27   BUTLER, B. C. The Originality of St Matthew (1951) 37ff.
           *HOFFMANN, P. "Der ungeteilte Dienst. Die Auslegung der
           Bergpredigt V (Mt 6:1-7:27)," BuL 11 (2, '70) 89-104.

6:1-7:12   WINDISCH, H. The Meaning of the Sermon on the Mount
           (1937) 126f.

6   FIEBIG, P. Jesu Bergpredigt (1924). MARRIOTT, H. The
Sermon on the Mount (1925). BONHOEFFER, D. Nachfolge
(1950) 96ff. KNOX, W. L. The Sources of the Synoptic Gospels
II (1957) 4. McARTHUR, H. K. Understanding the Sermon on
the Mount (1960) 22, 87, 88, 89. FEUILLET, A. Morale
Ancienne et Morale Chrétienne d'après Mt. 5.17-20;
Comparison avec la Doctrine de L'Epître aux Ramains NTS 17
(1970-71) 132f.

6:1ff   KNOX, W. L. The Sources of the Synoptic Gospels II (1957) 9,
20, 25. STRECKER, G. Der Weg der Gerechtigkeit (1962) 134,
140, 174. BULTMANN, R. Theologie des Neuen Testaments
(1965) 16f. JEREMIAS, J. New Testament Theology I (1971)
216. FRIEDRICH, G., "Das Problem der Autorität im Neuen
Testament" in: Auf das Wort kommt es an. Gesammelte
Aufsätze (Göttingen 1978) 285-87. GARLAND, D. E., "The
Intention of Mark 23" Supplements to NovT LII (1979) 121.

6:1-18   THOLUCK, A. Die Bergrede Christi (1872) 269-346.
WILKENS, J. Einführung in das Evangelium nach Matthäus I
(1934) 99-103. WINDISCH, H. The Meaning of the Sermon on
the Mount (1937) 42, 63f. THOMPSON, E. T. The Sermon on
theMount (1946) 81-102. FARRER, A. St Matthew and St
Mark (1954) 165, 171. BLAIR, E. P. Jesus in the Gospel of
Matthew (1960) 111. SHINN, R. L. Sermon on the Mount
(1962) 27-31. EICHHOLZ, G. Auslegung der Bergpredigt
(1965) 104-33. BOUSSET, W. Die Religion des Judentums im
Späthellenistischen Zeitalter (1966‾1926) 141, 178, 180f, 380.
SUMMERS, R. The Secret Sayings of the Living Jesus (1968)
31, 58, 68. SCHNEIDER, G. Botschaft der Bergpredigt (1969)
65-77. JEREMIAS, J. Neutestamentliche Theologie I (1971)
144, 146f, 152, 173, 189. Eng. ed. New Testament Theology I
(1971) 145, 146, 148, 153, 177, 194. GOULDER, M. D.,
Midrash and Lection in Matthew (London 1974) 83, 158, 164f,
254, 262f, 270, 275, 292, 296, 301, 421, 423. SCHWEIZER, E.,
"Der Jude im Verborgenen. . ., dessen Lob nicht von
Menschen, sondern von Gott kommt" in: Neues Testament
und Kirche: Festschrift für Rudolf Schnackenburg (Freiburg
1974) 115-124. SCHWEIZER, E., Matthäus und seine
Gemeinde (Stuttgart 1974) I.5.5,IV. BETZ, H. D., "Eine
judenchristliche Kult-Didache in Mt 6:1-18" in: G. Strecker
(ed.) Jesus Christus in Historie und Theologie: Festschrift für
Hans Conzelmann (Tübingen 1975) 445-57. BURCHARD, C.,
"Versuch, das Thema der Bergpredigt zu finden" in: G.
Strecker (ed.) Jesus Christus in Historie und Theologie:
Festschrift für Hans Conzelmann (Tübingen 1975) 426-28.
SANDERS, J. T. Ethics in the New Testament (Philadelphia

1975) 45f. McDONALD, J. I. H., Kerygma and Didache (Cambridge 1980) 106.

6:1-15   PELIKAN, J. (ed.), The Preaching of Chrysostom (1967) 130-52. FRICK, R. GPM 11/2 137-42.

6:1-8.   KING, G. H. New Order (1954) 68-74.
16-18

6:1-8.   KNöRZER, W. Die Bergpredigt, Modell einer neuen Welt
14-18   (1968) 62-68.

6:1-6.   GERHARDSSON, B. "Andlig offertjänst enlight Matt. 6:1-6,
16-21   16-21," SEA 36 ('71) 117-25. GERHARDSSON, B. "Geistiger Opferdienst nach Matth. 6:1-6, 16-21," in: Neues Testament und Geschichte (1972) Baltensweiler, H. & Reicke, B. (eds.) 69-77.

6:1-6.   BOWMAN, J. W. & TAPP, R. W. The Sermon from the
16-18   Mount (1958) 107-18. GEORGE, A. "La Justice a faire dans le Secret (Matthieu 6, 1-6 et 16-18)," Biblica 40 (3-4, '59) 590-98. TANNEHILL, R. C., The Sword of His Mouth (Missoula 1975) 78-88.

6:1-8   RUDOLPH, K., Die Gnosis (Göttingen 1978) 280.

6:1-6   GEORGE, A. "La justice à faire dans le secret (Matthieu 6, 1-6 et 16-18)," Biblica 40 (3, '59) 590-98. RIVKIN, E., A Hidden Revolution (Nashville 1978) 121-22. SWIDLER, L., Biblical Affirmations of Woman (Philadelphia 1979) 288.

6:1-4   KEPLER, T. S. Jesus' Design for Living (1952) 65-68. HUNTER, A. M. Design for Life (1953) 60-62. THIELICKE, H. Das Leben kann noch einmal beginnen (1956) 100-17. McARTHUR, H. K. Understanding the Sermon on the Mount (1960) 51, 91, 176. MüLHAUPT, E. (ed.) D Martin Luthers Auslegung der Bergpredigt (1961) 125-31. LLOYD-JONES, D. M. Studies in the Sermon on the Mount II (1962) 9-20. ΚΡΑΘΣΕ, Γ. ΓΠΜ 17, (1963/2) 295-302. HUNTER, A. M. A Pattern for Life (1965) 64f. JüNGEL, E. Paulus und Jesus (1966) 208. BALTZER/BRANDENBURGER/MERKEL GPM 23/3 (1968/69) 319-23. JEREMIAS, J. Neutestamentliche Theologie I (1971) 26, 29, 189, 208. GOULDER, M. D., Midrash and Lection in Matthew (London 1974) 260f, 293. BLENDINGER, C./KUGLER, G. in: P. Krusche et al. (eds) Predigtstudien für das Kirchenjahr 1975. Perikopenreihe III-Zweiter Halbband (Stuttgart 1975) 184.-91. MARQUARD, F.-W., GPM 29 (1975) 378-86.

6:1-2   SMITH, M., Tannaitic Parallels to the Gospels (Philadelphia 1968) A+.

6:1.5f.   WREGE, H.-T. Die UEberlieferungsgeschichte der

Bergpredigt (1968) 94.

6:1.9.   McNAMARA, M. The New Testament and the Palestinian Targum to the Pentateuch (1966) 136.

6:1   KNOX, W. L. The Sources of the Synoptic Gospels II (1957) 19, 25. STAUDINGER, J. Die Bergpredigt (1957) 32, 133, 134, 136, 140, 142, 155, 183, 188. DUPONT, D. J. Les Béatitudes (1958) 159-61. BLAIR, E. P. Jesus in the Gospel of Matthew (1960) 120. PLOTZKE, U. Bergpredigt (1960) 148-53. BORNKAMM-BARTH-HELD, Ueberlieferung und Auslegung im Matthäus-Evangelium (1961) 130. *NAGEL, W. "Gerechtigkeit-oder Almosen? (Mt 6, 1)," VigChr 15 (3, '61) 141-45. STRECKER, G. Der Weg der Gerechtigkeit (1962) 152, 153f, 159, 165₂, 180. FRANKEMöLLE, H. Jahwebund und Kirche Christi (Münster 1974) 28, 94, 161, 173, 280, 282f. SAND, A., Das Gesetz und die Propheten. (Regensburg 1974) 203f. BETZ, O., "Rechfertigung in Qumran" in: J. Friedrich et al. (eds). Rechfertigung: Festschrift für E. Käsemann (Göttingen 1976) 27f. "Bergpredigt" in: TRE 5 (1980) 605.

6:2-18   STRECKER, G. Der Weg der Gerechtigkeit (1962) 39₂, 152, 158₄, 165₄. GAECHTER, P. Die literarische Kunst im Matthäus-Evangelium (1968) 19-20.

6:2-6   "Bergpredigt" in: TRE 5 (1980) 604.

6:2-4   STAUDINGER, J. Die Bergpredigt (1957) 133-39. PLOTZKE, U. Bergpredigt (1960) 153-59.

6:2.5.16   HASLER, V. Amen (1969) 83.

6:2   KLEIN, G., "Mt 6:2" ZNW 6 (1905) 203f. KLOSTERMANN, E. "Zum Verständnis von Mt 6:2," ZNW 47 ('56) 280-81. STAUDINGER, J. Die Bergpredigt (1957) 134-37. DAVIES, W. D., The Sermon on the Mount (Cambridge 1966) 87. SANFORD, J. A. The Kingdom Within (New York 1970) 96. GOPPELT, L., Theologie des Neuen Testaments (Göttingen 1975) 130, 172ff.

6:3-4   STAUDINGER, J. Die Bergpredigt (1957) 137-39. "Armenfürsorge" in: TRE 4 (1979) 15. MEYER, B. F., The Aims of Jesus (London 1979) 145-47.

6:3   RUDOLPH, K. Die Mandäer I (1960) 73, 106· II (1961) 284. STRECKER, G. Der Weg der Gerechtigkeit (1962) 164₇. SCHRAGE, W. Das Verhältnis des Thomas-Evangeliums zur Synoptischen Tradition und zu den Koptischen Evangelienübersetzungen (1964) 129. JEREMIAS, J. Neutestamentliche Theologie I (1971) 26, 152, 208f, 213. BERKOUWER, G. C., The Return of Christ (Grand Rapids 1972) 424f.

6:4-6 KäSEMANN, E. New Testament Questions of Today (1969) 95.

6:4, 6, 18 CLARK, K. W., "The Making of the Twentieth Century New Testament" in: J. L. Sharpe III (ed.) The Gentile Bias and other Essays (Leiden 1980) 151.

6:4 McARTHUR, H. K. Understanding the Sermon on the Mount (1960) 15, 88, 176. KäSEMANN, E. Exegetische Versuche und Besinnungen (1964) II 94.

6:5-7:12 *GIAVINI, G., "Lo schema di Mt. 6, 5-7, 12: una precisazione" RivB 20 (suppl., '72) 575-87.

6:5-26 GRYGLEWICZ, F. The St. Adalbert Codex of the Gospels NTS 11 (1964-65) 259f.

6:5-18 MASSAUX, E. Influence de l'Evangile de saint Matthieu sur la littérature chrétienne avant saint Irénée (1950) 615-18. GOULDER, M. D., Midrash and Lection in Matthew (London 1974) 262f.

6:5-15 MüLHAUPT, E. (ed.) D Martin Luthers Auslegung der Bergpredigt (1961) 131-52. SHINN, R. L. Sermon on the Mount (1962) 48-53.

6:5-14 BUTLER, B. C. The Originality of St Matthew (1951) 134ff.

6:5-13 STAUDINGER, J. Die Bergpredigt (1957) 147f. BRAUN, H. GPM 19 (1965/1) 200-205. BECKMANN, J. in: Hören und Fragen (1967) Eichholz, G. & Falkenroth, A. (eds.), 299ff. LANGE, E. (ed.) Predigtstudien für das Kirchenjahr 1970/71 (1970-71) 78-84. FüRST, W. GPM 25 (1, '71) 221-29. SCHMAUCH, W. GPM 13/2 127-31. KNOLL, G. et al. in: P. Krusche (ed.) Predigtstudien. Perikopenreihe V-Zweiter Halbband (Stuttgart 1977) 52-58. JOSUTTIS, M., GPM 31 (1976/1977) 217-23.

6:5-8 KEPLER, T. S. Jesus' Design for Living (1952) 68-71. HUNTER, A. M. Design for Life (1953) 62f. THIELICKE, H. Das Leben kann noch einmal beginnen (1956) 118-31. LLOYD-JONES, D. M. Studies in the Sermon on the Mount II (1962) 21-32. HUNTER, A. M. A Pattern for Life (1965) 65-67. *VOUGA, F. et al. "Providence et priere. Références bibliques" in: Bulletin du Centre Protestant d'Etudes 30 (1978) 31-39.

6:5f STAUDINGER, J. Die Bergpredigt (1957) 139-45. PLOTZKE, U. Bergpredigt (1960) 159-64. JüNGEL, E. Paulus und Jesus (1966) 208. JEREMIAS, J. Neutestamentliche Theologie I

(1971) 26, 44, 167, 182, 189, 208. SMITH, M., Tannaitic Parallels to the Gospels (Philadelphia 1968) A+. GOPPELT, L., Theologie des Neuen Testaments (Göttingen 1975) 130, 172ff. METZGER, B. M. The Early Versions of the New Testament (Oxford 1977) 254, 390.

6:6 STAUDINGER, J. Die Bergpredigt (1957) 143-45. McARTHUR, H. K. Understanding the Sermon on the Mount (1960) 15, 88, 128, 141, 176, 179. STRECKER, G. Der Weg der Gerechtigkeit (1962) 232. KäSEMANN, E. Exegetische Versuche und Besinnungen (1964) II 94. METZGER, B. M., The Early Versions of the New Testament (Oxford 1977) 242.

6:7-15 HIRSCH, E. Frühgeschichte des Evangeliums (1941) 100-102. LOHMEYER, E. Das Vater-Unser (1946). SCOTT, E. F. The Lord's Prayer (1951). FARRER, A. St Matthew and St Mark (1954) 169. LüTHI, W. The Lord's Prayer. An Exposition (1961). *BOTHA, F. J., "Recent Research on the Lord's Prayer" Neotestamentica 1 (1967) 42-50. WREGE, H.-T. Die UEberlieferungsgeschichte der Bergpredigt (1968) 97. SAND, A., Das Gesetz und die Propheten (Regensburg 1974) 121.

6:7-9 DAVIES, W. D., The Sermon on the Mount (Cambridge 1966) 87.

6:7-8 STAUDINGER, J. Die Bergpredigt (1957) 145-47. PLOTZKE, U. Bergpredigt (1960) 164-68.

6:7 KNOX, W. L. The Sources of the Synoptic Gospels II (1957) 25, 33, 34, 133. TRILLING, W. Das wahre Israel (1959) 94. *BUSSBY, F. "A Note on *raka* (Mt. v.22) and *battologeo* (Mt. vi.7) in the Light of Qumran," ET 76 (1, '64) 26. BLACK, M. An Aramaic Approach to the Gospels and Acts (1967) 177f. TAGAWA, K. People and Community in the Gospel of Matthew NTS 16 (1969-70) 153f.

6:8 BRUNNER, E. Dogmatik I (1946) 282. BLAIR, E. P. Jesus in the Gospel of Matthew (1960) 91. JANSSEN, E., "Testament Abrahams" in: W. G. Kümmel (ed.) Jüdische Schriften aus hellenistisch-römischer Zeit III (Gütersloh 1975) 218. METZGER, B. M., The Early Versions of the New Testament (Oxford 1977) 324.

6:9ff STREETER, B. H. The Four Gospels (1951) 276f. DAVIES, W. D., The Sermon on the Mount (Cambridge 1966) 4.

6:9-15 KING, G. H. New Order (1954) 74-78. BOWMAN, J. W. & TAPP, R. W. The Sermon from the Mount (1958) 119-29. FRIEDLANDER, G. The Jewish Sources of the Sermon on the

Mount (1969) 123, 164f. JEREMIAS, J., in: R. Batey (ed.) New Testament Issues (London 1970) 88-101. GOPPELT, L., Theologie des Neuen Testaments. I (Göttingen 1975) 120f.

6:9-13 KNOPF, R., "Eine Thonscherbe mit dem Texte des Vaterunsers," ZNW 2 (1901) 228-33. SEEBERG, A. "Vaterunser und Abendmahl," in: Neutestamentliche Studien Georg Heinrici zu seinem 70. Geburtstag (1914) Deissmann, A. & Windisch, H. (eds.) 108-14. THIELICKE, H. Das Gebet Das Die Welt Umspannt (1945). MAURER, K. Das Vater Unser (1947). SCHNIEWIND, J. Das Evangelium nach Matthäus (1949) 80f. HUGH, M. The Lord's Prayer (1951). STAEHELIN, E. Die Verkündigung des Reiches Gottes in der Kirche Jesu Christi I (1951) 58, 88. HUNTER, A. M. Design for Life (1953) 64-74. STEUERNAGEL, C. "Die ursprüngliche Zweckbestimmung des Vaterunser," Wissenschaftliche Zeitschr. d. Karl-Marx-Universität (1953/54) 217-20. *MANSON, T. W. "The Lord's Prayer," BJRL 38/1 (1955) 99-113; 38/2 (1956) 436-48. KNOX, W. L. The Sources of the Synoptic Gospels II (1957) 60. *RICHARDSON, R. D. "The Lord's Prayer as an Early Eucharist," AThR 39 (2, '57) 123-30. STAUDINGER, J. Die Bergpredigt (1957) 148-80. MAGNE, J. "Le Pater-Mt. 6, 9-13," Biblica 39 (1958) 196-97. SCHüRMANN, H. Das Gebet des Herrn (1958). *DIAZ, J. A. "El problema literario del Padre Neustro," EstBi 18 (1, '59) 63-75. FRESENIUS, W. "Beobachtungen und Gedanken zum Gebet des HERRN," EvTh 20 (5, '60) 235-39. JEREMIAS, J. "The Lord's Prayer in Modern Research," ET 71 (4, '60) 141-46. KELLOGG, A. L. & TALBERT, E. W. "The Wycliffe Pater Noster and Ten Commandments, with Special Reference to English MSS. 85 and 90 in the John Rylands Library," BJRL 42 (2, '60) 345-77. McARTHUR, H. K. Understanding the Sermon on the Mount (1960) 71, 88, 164. *MIEGGE, G. "Le 'Notre Père', prière du temps présent," EThR 35 (4, '60) 237-53. BAMMEL, E. "A New Text of the Lord's Pryaer," ET 73 (2, '61) 54. BROWN, R. E. "The Pater Noster as an Eschatological Prayer," ThSt 22 (2, '61) 175-208. CYSTER, R. F. "The Lord's Prayer and the Exodus Tradition," Theology 64 (495, '61) 377-81. LüTHI, W. The Lord's Prayer (1961⁻1946). SCOTT, E. F. The Lord's Prayer. Its Character, Purpose, and Interpretation (1961). *BLENKINSOPP, J. "The Lord's Prayer and the Hill of Olives," HeyJ 3 (2, '62) 169-71. *BLENKINSOPP, J. "The Lord's Prayer," HeyJ 3 (1, '62), 51-60. *BROWN, R. E. "Meaning of the Our Father," TheolDig 10 (1, '62) 3-10. JEREMIAS, J. Das Vater-Unser im Lichte der neueren Forschung (1962). JEREMIAS, J. "Fader var i den nyare forskningens ljus," SEA 27 ('62) 33-54. VAN DEN BUSSCHE, H. Das Vaterunser (1963). VAN DEN BUSSCHE, H. Understanding the Lord's Prayer (1963). EBELING, G. Vom Gebet. Predigten über das Unser-Vater (1963). EVANS, C. F. The Lord's Prayer (1963). *GOULDER, M. D. "The Composition of the Lord's Prayer," JThS 14 (1, '63) 32-45. MARCHEL, W. Abba, Père! La Priére du Christ et des chrétiens. Etude exégétique sur les origines et la signification de l'invocation à la divinité comme père, avant et dans le Nouveau Testament (1963). MARCHEL, W. Abba, Vater! Die Vaterbotschaft des Neuen Testaments (1963). SCHRöDER, R. A. et. al., Das Vaterunser. Eine Auslegung (1963). MARITAIN, R. Notes on the Lord's Prayer (1964). SCHüRMANN, H. Praying with Christ. The "Our Father" for Today (1964). WILLIS, G. G. "The Lord's Prayer in Irish Gospel Manuscripts," in: Studia Evangelica III (1964) Cross, F. L. (ed.) 282-88. *BAHR, G. J. "The Use of the Lord's Prayer in the Primitive Church," JBL 84 (2, '65) 153-59. BROWN, R. E. "The Pater Noster as an Eschatological Prayer," in: New Testament Essays (1965) 217-53. *CELADA, B. "El Padre Nuestro. Progresos en la inteligencia de la oracion de los cristianos," CultBib 22 (204, '65) 279-83. HUNTER, A. M. A Pattern for Life (1965) 67-78. JACOUEMIN, E., "La prière du Seigneur" AssS 48 (1965) 47-64. LOHMEYER, E. "Our Father." An Introduction to the Lord's Paryer (1965). STUHLMACHER, P. Gerechtigkeit Gottes bei Paulus (1965) 252-54. *TILLARD, J. M. R. "La prière des chrétiens," LuVie 14 (75, '65) 39-84. VICEDOM, G. Gebet für die Welt (1965). *ARON, R. "Les origines juives du Pater," Maison-Dieu 85 ('66) 36-40. *ANON, "Priére Oecuménique. Nouveau texte du 'Notre Père'," AmiCler 76 (Jan. 6, '66) 8-10. *BENOIT, J.-D. "Le Notre Père dans le culte et la prière des Eglises protestantes," Maison-Dieu 85 ('66) 101-16. *DALMAIS, I.-H. "L'introduction et l'emblisme de l'Orasion dominicale dans la célébration eucharistique," Maison-Dieu 85 ('66) 92-100. *DELORME, J. "La prière du Seigneur. Pour une catéchèse biblique du 'Notre Père.' A propos de la nouvelle traduction," AmiCler 76 (Apr. 14, '66) 225-36. *DENIS-BOULET, N. M. "La place du Notre Père dans la liturgie," Maison-Dieu 85 ('66) 69-91. *DUPONT, J. & BONNARD, P. "Le Notre Père: notes exégétiques," Maison-Dieu 85 ('66) 7-35. *HAMMAN, A. "Le Notre Père dans la catéchése des Pères de l'Eglise," Maison-Dieu 85 ('66) 41-68. *POLAERT, A. "La catéchèse du Notre Père aux hommes d'aujourd'hui," Maison-Dieu 85 ('66) 117-39. *ROGUET, A.-M. "Le nouveau texte français du Notre Père," VieS 114 (523, '66) 5-24. *WIENER, C. "La nouvella traduction française de la prière du Seigneur: Signification pastorale et oecuménique," 140-52. JEREMIAS, J. Abba; Studien zur neutestamentlichen Theologie und Zeitgeschichte (1966) 152-71. *YAMAUCHI, E. M. "The 'Daily Bread' Motif in Antiquity," WThJ 28 (2, '66) 145-56. Centre nationale de pastorale liturgique, "La traduction commune du 'Notre Père'," QuestLitPar 47 (2-3, '66) 141-45. *FRY, E. M. "A Provisional New Translation of the Lord's Prayer," BTr 18 (3, '67) 123-25. *KNöRZER, W. "Unser Vater im Himmel. Das Gebet des Herrn als Inbegriff des Evangeliums," BuK 22 (3, '67) 79-86. KUSS, O. Auslegung und Verkündigung (1967) 277-333. *MASSINGBERD, J. "Yom Kippur and the Matthean Form of the Pater Noster," Worship 41 (10, '67) 609-619. *SHRIVER, D. W. "The Prayer That Spans the World. An Exposition: Social Ethics and the Lord's Prayer," Interpretation 21 (3, '67) 274-88. KNöRZER, W. Die Bergpredigt, Modell einer neuen Welt (1968) 69-82. *KRUSE, H. "The Lord's Prayer and the Passion of Christ," KatorShin 7 (1, '68) 20-61. (In Japanese.) *KRUSE, H. "Pater Noster et Passio Christi," VerbDom 46 (1, '68) 3-29. MASSINGBERD, J. "The Forgiveness Clause in the Matthean Form of the Our Father," ZNW 59 (1-2, '68) 127-31. METZGER, B. M. "How many times does ἐπιούσιος occur outside the Lord's Prayer?" in: Historical and Literary Studies (1968) 64-66. REUMANN, J. Jesus in the Church's Gospel: Modern Scholarship and the Earliest Sources (1968) 92-108. SCHWARZ, G. Matthaus VI. 9-13/Lukas XI. 2-4, NTS 15 (1968-69) 233ff. *DU BUIT, F. M. "Notre Père," Evangile 50 (3, '69) 5-46. CARMIGNAC, J. Recherches sur le "Notre Père" (1969). KNöRZER, W. Vater Unser (1969). *ANGENIEUX, J. "Les différents types de structure du 'Pater' dans l'histoire de son exègèse," EphT 46 (3-4, '70) 325-59. *ANGENIEUX, J. "Les différents types du structure du 'Pater' dans l'histoire de son exégèse," EphT 46 (1, '70) 40-77. BAKER, A. RevQ 7 (3, '70) 431-33. *BROWN, R. E. CBQ 32 (2, '70) 264-66. DELCOR, M. "A propos de la traduction oecuménique du 'Notre Père'," BLE 71 (2, '70) 127-30. COTHENET, E. "La Prière du Seigneur," EsVie 80 (44, '70) 631-34. OTOMO, Y. Nachfolge Jesu und Anfänge der Kirche im Neuen Testament (1970) 70-80. RENGSTORF, K. H. "Das Vaterunsers in seiner Bedeutung für unser Zusammenleben," in: Kerygma und Melos (1970) 13-25. JEREMIAS, J. Neutestamentliche Theologie I (1971) 33, 188-96. JEREMIAS, J. New Testament Theology I (1971) 23, 193ff. LELOIR, L. RHE 66 (2, '71) 553-56. *SWETNAM, J. " 'Hallowed be Thy Name'," Biblica 52 (4, '72) 556-63. HOFFMANN, P. Studien zur Theologie der Logienquelle

(1972) 4, 39f. SCHULZ, S. Q Die Spruchquelle der Evangelisten (1972) 84-93. *Van TILBORG, S. "A Form-Criticism of the Lord's Prayer," NovTest 14 (2, '72) 94-105. GOULDER, M. D., Midrash and Lection in Matthew (London 1974) 262, 296ff. TALBERT, C. H., Literary Patterns, Theological Themes, and the Genre of Luke-Acts (Missoula 1974) 54. BLIGH, J., The Sermon on the Mount (Slough 1975) 124-30. CONZELMANN, H./LINDEMANN, A., Arbeitsbuch zum Neuen Testament (Tübingen 1975) 27. *HARNER, P. B., Understanding The Lord's Prayer (Philadelphia 1975). EDWARDS, R. A., A Theology of Q (Philadelphia 1976) 107f. *ASHTON, J., "Le Notre Père" Christus 24 (1977) 459-70. *ASHTON, J., "Our Father" Way 18 (1978) 83-91. *GERHARDSSON, B., "Fader var i Nya testamentet" SvTK 54 (1978) 93-102. *KISTEMAKER, S. J., "The Lord's Prayer in the First Century" JEThS 21 (1978) 323-28. *ASHLEY, B. M., "What Do We Pray in the Lord's Prayer?" Spirituality Today 31 (1979) 121-36. CAMBE, M./LUCAS, N., "Le 'Notre Père' (Matthieu 6, 9-13). Eléments d'analyse structurale" Foi et Vie 78 (1979) 113-17. MEYER, B. F., The Aims of Jesus (London 1979) 208. "Bergpredigt" in: TRE 5 (1980) 605, 607. FRANK, K. S., "Die Vaterunser-Erklärung der Regula Magistri" in: E. Dassmann/K. S. Frank (eds.) Pietas: Festschrift für Bernhard Kötting. JAC Erg. Bd. 8 (1980) 458-71.

6:9-12   VAN DEN BUSSCHE, H. "Het Onze Vader," CollBrugGand 5 (3, '59) 289-335; (4, '59) 467-95. DAVIES, W. D., The Sermon on the Mount (Cambridge 1966) 4. SMITH, M., Tannaitic Parallels to the Gospels (Philadelphia 1968) 6 b n 5+.

6:9-10   LLOYD-JONES, D. M. Studies in the Sermon on the Mount II (1962) 57-66. HENNECKE, E. & SCHNEEMELCHER, W. Neutestamentliche Apokryphen (1964) II 310, 364.

6:9   STAEHELIN, E. Die Verkündigung des Reiches Gottes in der Kirche Jesu Christi I (1951) 377. KEPLER, T. S. Jesus' Design for Living (1952) 71-74. SCHMID, J. Das Evangelium nach Matthäus (1956) 124-28. STAUDINGER, J. Die Bergpredigt (1957) 154f. PLOTZKE, U. Bergpredigt (1960) 182-87, 168-73. LLOYD-JONES, D. M. Studies in the Sermon on the Mount II (1962) 45-56. STRECKER, G. Der Weg der Gerechtigkeit (1962) 18. HAHN, F. Christologische Hoheitstitel (1963) 320. MARCHEL, W. Abba, Père! La Prière du Christ et des Chrétiens (1963) 191-202. NICKELS, P. Targum and New Testament (1967) 17. JEREMIAS, J. Neutestamentliche Theologie I (1971) 21f, 68, 191. METZGER, B. M., The Early Versions of the New Testament (Oxford 1977) 177. POLAG,

A., Die Christologie der Ligienquelle (Neukirchen-Vluyn 1977)
59. "Albert der Grosse" in: TRE 2 (1978) 182. THüSING, W.,
"Die Bitten des johanneischen Jesus in dem Gebet Joh 17 und
die Intentionen Jesu von Nazaret" in: R. Schnackenburg et al.
(eds.) Die Kirche des Anfangs: Für Heinz Schürmann
(Freiburg 1978) 316-19.

6:10-14 MOORE, G. F. Judaism (1946) I 401, II 95, 154.

6:10-12 BAMMEL, E. "Ein neuer Vater-Unser-Text," ZNW 52 (3-4,
'61) 280-81.

6:10.13 *SMITH, G. "The Matthaean 'Additions' to the Lord's
Prayer," ET 82 (2, '70) 54-55.

6:10 HANSON, S. The Unity of the Church in the New Testament
(1946) 41f. STAEHELIN, E. Die Verkündigung des Reiches
Gottes in der Kirche Jesu Christi I (1951) 192, 200, 298, 333,
391. KEPLER, T. S. Jesus' Design for Living (1952) 75-77, 77-
80. DIBELIUS, M. Botschaft und Geschichte I (1953) 175-77.
KNOX, W. L. The Sources of the Synoptic Gospels II (1957)
27. STAUDINGER, J. Die Bergpredigt (1957) 161-64.
TRILLING, W. Das wahre Israel (1959) 163f. PLOTZKE, U.
Bergpredigt (1960) 192-97. ROBINSON, J. M. Kerygma und
historischer Jesus (1960) 143. BORNKAMM-BARTH-HELD,
UEberlieferung und Auslegung im Matthäus-Evangelium
(1961) 65, 133, 135. STRECKER, G. Der Weg der
Gerechtigkeit (1962) 155, 183. *COLLINS, R. F. "'Thy Will Be
Done on Earth As It Is in Heaven'-Matthew 6:10," Bible Today
1 (14, '64) 911-17. *PYTEL, J. "Adveniat regnum tuum.
Historia interpretacji prosby," RTK 11 (1, '64) 57-69. HAHN,
F. Das Verständnis der Mission im Neuen Testament (1965)
107. *STEINMETZ, F. J. "'Dein Reich komme!' Zur zweiten
Bitte des Vaterunsers," GuL 41 (6, '68) 414-28.
FREUDENBERGER, R. "Zum Text der Zweiten
Vaterunserbitte," NTS 15 (1968-69) 423-26. JEREMIAS, J.
Neutestamentliche Theologie I (1971) 22, 40f, 103. HIERS, R.
H., The Historical Jesus and the Kingdom of God (Gainesville
1973) 67f. FRANKEMöLLE, H., Jahwebund und Kirche
Christi (Münster 1974) 268, 275-77, 389. LADD, G. E., A
Theology of the New Testament (Grand Rapids 1974) 63f, 85,
103. *MENESTRINA, G., "Sicut in caelo et in terra (Nota a
Matteo 6, 10)" BiOr 19 (1977) 5-8. METZGER, B. M., The
Early Versions of the New Testament (Oxford 1977) 178, 315.
CLARK, K. W., "Realized Eschatology" in: The Gentile Bias
and other Essays (Leiden 1980) 53. HARRINGTON, D. J.,
God's People in Christ (Philadelphia 1980) 25.

6:11-15 LLOYD-JONES, D.M. Studies in the Sermon on the Mount II (1962) 67-77.

6:11 HEINRICI, G. Neutestamentliche Studien (1914) 114-19. KEPLER, T. S. Jesus' Design for Living (1952) 81-84. VOGT, E. "De Initiis urbis Jericho," Biblica 35 (1954) 136-37. STAUDINGER, J. Die Bergpredigt (1957) 164-68. *THOMPSON, G. H. P. "Thy Will be Done in Earth, as it is in Heaven (Matthew vi, 11). A suggested Re-interpretation," ET 70 (12, '59) 379-81. *VAN DEN BUSSCHE, H. "Donne-nous aujourd-'hui notre pain quotidien," BVieC 32 ('60) 42-46. M'NEILE, A. H. The Gospel According to St Matthew (1955) 79f. PLOTZKE, U. Bergpredigt (1960) 197-203. NICKELS, P. Targum and New Testament (1967) 17. *STARCKY, J. "La quatrième demande du Pater," HThR 64 (2-3, '71) 401-409. HEMMERDINGER, B. "Un Elément Pythagoricien dans le Pater," ZNW 63 (1-2, '72) 121. *ORCHARD, B. "The Meaning of ton epiousion (Mt 6:11--Lk 11:3)" Biblical Theology Bulletin 3 (1973) 274-82. *BAKER, A. "What Sort of Bread did Jesus want us to Pray for?" New Blackfriars 54 (634, '73) 125-29. *JACOB, T., "The Daily Bread in the Teaching of Jesus" Jeevadhara 32 (1976) 187-97. *RORDORF, W., "Le 'pain quotidien' (Matth. 6, 11) dans l'histoire de l'exégèse" Didaskalia 6 (1976) 221-35. *BOURGOIN, H., "Le pain quotidien" CahCER 25 (1977) 1-17. METZGER, B. M., The Early Versions of the New Testament (Oxford 1977) 423. BRAUN, F. M., "Le pain dont nous avons besoin, Mt 6, 11; Lc 11,3" NRTh 100 (1978) 559-68. *TEN KATE, R., "Geef ons heden ons 'dagelijks' brood" NedThT 32 (1978) 125-39. *BOURGOIN, H., "Epiousios expliqué par la notion de préfixe vide" Biblica 60 (1979) 91-96. BRUCE, F. F., "The Gospel Text of Marius Victorinus" in: E. Best/R. M. Wilson (eds.) Text and Interpretation. Studies in the New Testament presented to Matthew Black (Cambridge 1979) 70. *GRELOT, P., "La Quatrième Demande du 'Pater' et son Arrière-Plan Sémitique" NTS 25 (1979) 299-314.

6:12ff KNOX, W. L. The Sources of the Synoptic Gospels II (1957) 36.

6:12-15 MASSAUX, E. Influence de l'Evangile de saint Matthieu sur la littérature chrétienne avant saint Irénée (1950) 9-13. KEPLER, T. S. Jesus' Design for Living (1952) 84-87.

6:12 STAUDINGER, J. Die Bergpredigt (1957) 168-73. FENSHAM, F. C., "The Legal Background of Mt VI 12" NovT 4 (1960) 1f. PLOTZKE, U. Bergpredigt (1960) 204-208, 209-16. STRECKER, G. Der Weg der Gerechtigkeit (1962) 149. HUMMEL, R. Die Auseinandersetzung zwischen Kirche

und Judentum im Matthäusevangelium (1963) 102.
*MEGIVERN, J. "Forgive Us Our Debts," Scripture 18 (42, '62) 33-47. BLACK, M. An Aramaic Approach to the Gospels and Acts (1967) 129f. SCHüRMANN, H. Ursprung und Gestalt (1970) 281, 284, 286, 288, 290, 292. JEREMIAS, J. Neutestamentliche Theologie I (1971) 18, 187f. *LACHS, S. T., "On Matthew VI.12" NovT 17 (1975) 6-8. MOULE, C. F. D., " '. . .As we forgive. . .' A Note on the Distinction between Deserts and Capacity in the Understanding of Forgiveness" in: E. Bammel et al. (eds.) Donum Gentilicium: New Testament Studies in Honour of David Daube (Oxford 1978) 68-77.

6:13ff   SMITH, M., Tannaitic Parallels to the Gospels (Philadelphia 1968) 6 b n 5+.

6:13b-20   VISCHER, W. Die evangelische Gemeindeordnung (1946) 9-28.

6:13   VOLZ, P. Die Eschatologie der jüdischen Gemeinde (1934) 385. VISCHER, W. Die evangelische Gemeindeordnung (1946) 7-9. MASSAUX, E. Influence de l'Evangile saint Matthieu sur la littérature chrétienne avant saint Irénée (1950) 169-70, 206-207, 624-26. STAEHELIN, E. Die Verkündigung des Reiches Gottes in der Kirche Jesu Christi I (1951) 166. KEPLER, T. S. Jesus' Design for Living (1952) 87-92. ANON, "Notes of Recent Exposition," ET 67 (1955) 62. BAUER, J. B. "Liberia nos a malo," VD 34 ('56) 12-15. POWELL, W. "Lead us not into Temptation," ET 67/7 (1956) 177-78. STAUDINGER, J. Die Bergpredigt (1957) 173-80. *SYKES, M. H. "And Do Not Bring Us to the Test," ET 73 (9, '62) 189f. *Walker, M. B. "Lead Us Not Into Temptation," ET 73 (9, '62) 287. TILLICH, P. Das Ewige im Jetzt (1964) 110-18. *CARMIGNAC, J. "Fais que nous n'entrions pas dans la tentation. La portée d'une négation devant un verbe au causatif," RevBi 72 (2, '65) 218-26. H. B., "Zur Auslegung der 6. Bitte. Und führe uns nicht in Versuchung. Matth. 6, 13a," KirchReformSchweiz 121 (Aug. 26, '65) 257-58. BRUPPACHER, H. "Kleine Beiträge zu einer kommenden Revision der Zürcher Bibel," KirchReform Schweiz 122 (May 12, '66) 150-51. *FLUSSER, D. "Qumran and Jewish 'Apotropaic' Prayers," IEJ 16 (3, '66) 194-205. *GEORGE, A. "Ne nous soumets pas à tentation. . . . Note sur la traduction nouvelle du Notre Père," BVieC 71 ('66) 74-79. *HOUK, C. B. "Peirasmos, The Lord's Prayer, and the Massah Tradition," SJTh 19 (2, '66) 216-25. SANFORD, J. A., The Kingdom Within (New York 1970) 134-36. BAKER, A. "Lead Us Not into Temptation," New Blackfriars 52 (609, '71) 64-69. JEREMIAS, J. Neutestamentliche Theologie I (1971) 26f, 28, 188, 196. *DAHMS, J. V., " 'Lead Us Not Into Temptation' "

JEThS 17 (1974) 223-30. MOULE, C. F. D., "An Unsolved Problem in the Temptation-Clause in the Lord's Prayer" RThR 33 (1974) 65-75. *WILLIS, G. G., "Lead Us Not Into Temptation" DRev 93 (1975) 281-88. THEUNISSEN, M., "ὁ αἰτῶν λαμβάνει. Der Gebetsglaube Jesu und die Zeitlichkeit des Christseins" in: Jesus, Ort der Erfahrung Gottes (Basel 1976) 60f. METZGER, B. M., The Early Versions of the New Testament (Oxford 1977) 42, 118, 135, 250. "Antichrist" in: TRE 3 (1978) 22.

6:14-15 MASSAUX, E. Influence de l'Evangile de saint Matthieu sur la littérature chrétienne avant saint Irénée (1950) 166-68. FARRER, A. St Matthew and St Mark (1954) 171. KNOX, W. L. The Sources of the Synoptic Gospels II (1957) 135. STAUDINGER, J. Die Bergpredigt (1957) 35, 210, 265, 282. *STENDAHL, K. "Prayer and Forgiveness," SEA 22-23 ('57-'58) 75-86. McARTHUR, H. K. Understanding the Sermon on the Mount (1960) 21, 72, 89, 124. PLOTZKE, U. Bergpredigt (1960) 216-20. STRECKER, G. Der Weg der Gerechtigkeit (1962) 149. HUMMEL, R. Die Auseinandersetzung zwischen Kirche und Judentum im Matthäusevangelium (1963) 102. KäSEMANN, E. Exegetische Versuche und Besinnungen (1964) II 79. KäSEMANN, E. New Testament Questions of Today (1969) 77. JEREMIAS, J. Neutestamentliche Theologie I (1971) 26, 29, 35, 187, 189. GOULDER, M. D., Midrash and Lection in Matthew (London 1974) 41, 75, 110, 285, 288, 298, 385, 403. SANDERS, J. T., Ethics in the New Testament (Philadelphia 1975) 42f. MOULE, C. F. D., "'... As we forgive...' A Note on the Distinction between Deserts and Capacity in the Understanding of Forgiveness" in: E. Bammel et al. (eds.) Donum Gentilicium: New Testament Studies in Honour of David Daube (Oxford 1978) 75. "Beichte" in: TRE 5 (1980) 430.

6:14 STAUDINGER, J. Die Bergpredigt (1957) 182-83. STROBEL, A. Erkenntnis und Bekenntnis der Sünde in neutestamentlicher Zeit (1968) 60.

6:15 METZGER, B. M., The Early Version of the New Testament (Oxford 1977) 255.

6:16ff KNOX, W. L. The Sources of the Synoptic Gospels II (1957) 125.

6:16-26ff BONHöFFER, A. Epiktet und das Neue Testament (1911) 60, 69, 290, 292, 298, 302, 307, 309.

6:16-23 PELIKAN, J. (ed.) The Preaching of Chrysostom (1967) 153-66.

6:16-18 KEPLER, T. S. Jesus' Design for Living (1952) 92-95.

HUNTER, A. M. Design for Life (1953) 74f. THIELICKE, H. Das Leben kann noch einmal beginnen (1956) 132-47. STAUDINGER, J. Die Bergpredigt (1957) 183-87. DUPONT, D. J. Les Béatitudes (1958) 160-62, 80s, 130s. *GEORGE, A. "La justice à faire dans le secret (Matthieu 6, 1-6 et 16-18)," Biblica 40 (3, '59) 590-98. PAKOZDY, GPM (1960/61) 213ff. PLOTZKE, U. Bergpredigt (1960) 220-26. MüLHAUPT, E. (ed.) D Martin Luthers Auslegung der Bergpredigt (1961) 153-62. LLOYD-JONES, D. M. Studies in the Sermon on the Mount II (1962) 33-44. STRECKER, G. Der Weg der Gerechtigkeit (1962) 1892. HUNTER, A. M. A Pattern for Life (1965) 78f. JüNGEL, E. Paulus und Jesus (1966) 208. *O'HARA, J. "Christian Fasting (Mt. 6, 16-18)," Scripture 19 (45, '67) 3-18. FRIEDLANDER, G. The Jewish Sources of the Sermon on the Mount (1969) 118f. JEREMIAS, J. Neutestamentliche Theologie I (1971) 26, 189, 208, 291. RIVKIN, E., A Hidden Revolution (Nashville 1978) 121f. "Bergpredigt" in: TRE 5 (1980) 604, 607, 624.

6:16   NESTLE, E., "Matth 6:16" ZNW 15 (1914) 94. GOPPELT, L., Theologie des Neuen Testaments. I (Göttingen 1975) 130, 172ff.

6:17-18   MEYER, B. F., The Aims of Jesus (London 1979) 145-47.

6:17   STAUDINGER, J. Die Bergpredigt (1957) 185-87.

6:18   McARTHUR, H. K. Understanding the Sermon on the Mount (1960) 15, 88, 176. KäSEMANN, E. Exegetische Versuche und Besinnungen (1964) II 94. FRIEDLANDER, G. The Jewish Sources of the Sermon on the Mount (1969) 263f. KäSEMANN, E. New Testament Questions of Today (1969) 95. CLARK, K. W., "The Making of the Twentieth Century New Testament" in: The Gentile Bias and other Essays (Leiden 1980) 151.

6:19-7:12   WILKENS, J. Einführung in das Evangelium nach Matthäus I (1934) 103-111.

6:19-7:11   *GIAVINI, G. "Abbiamo forse in Mt. 6, 19-7, 11 il primo commento al 'Pater Noster'?" RivB 13 (2, '65) 171-77.

6:19ff   BARRETT, C. K. The New Testament Background: Selected Documents (1956) 223. KNOX, W. L. The Sources of the Synoptic Gospels II (1957) 27-28. STRECKER, G. Der Weg der Gerechtigkeit (1962) 1421, 1647. THEISSEN, G., Soziologie der Jesusbewegung (München 1977) 18.

6:19-34   THOLUCK, A. Die Bergrede Christi (1872) 346-67. THOMPSON, E. T. The Sermon on the Mount (1946) 102-28. FARRER, A. St Matthew and St Mark (1954) 169, 175. BOWMAN, J. W. & TAPP, R. W. The Sermon from the Mount

(1958) 130-41. RIESENFELD, H. "Vom Schätzesammeln und Sorgen - ein Thema urchristlicher Paränese. Zu Mt. 6, 19-34," in: Neotestamentica et Patristica (Festschrift für Oscar Cullmann) (1962) 47-58. EICHHOLZ, G. Auslegung der Bergpredigt (1965) 134-46. KNöRZER, W. Die Bergpredigt, Modell einer neuen Welt (1968) 83-87. SCHNEIDER, G. Botschaft der Bergpredigt (1969) 77-86. GOULDER, M. D., Midrash and Lection in Matthew (London 1974) 158, 263f, 271, 275. GOPPELT, L., Theologie des Neuen Testaments. I (Göttingen 1975) 133f.

6:19-21.25-33 "Bergpredigt" in: TRE 5 (1980) 604.

6:19-24 KING, G. H. New Order (1954) 81-88. THIELICKE, H. Das Leben kann noch einmal beginnen (1956) 149-62. LLOYD-JONES, D. M. Studies in the Sermon on the Mount II (1962) 86-96, 97-106. SHINN, R. L. Sermon on the Mount (1962) 54-60. IWAND, H. J. Predigt-Meditationen (1964) 81-89. HOFFMANN, P. Studien zur Theologie der Logienquelle (1972) 5, 40ff, 114, 327f. HAHN, F., "Die Worte vom Licht Lk 11, 33-36" in: P. Hoffmann (ed.) Orientierung an Jesus: Für Josef Schmid (Freiburg 1973) 108, 124-27.

6:19-21 HIRSCH, E. Frühgeschichte des Evangeliums (1941) 118-20. KEPLER, T. S. Jesus' Design for Living (1952) 95-97. HUNTER, A. M. Design for Life (1953) 76f. FARRER, A. St Matthew and St Mark (1954) 168. DUPONT, D. J. Les Béatitudes (1958) 79-81. *PESCH, W. "Zur Exegese von Mt 6, 19-21 und Lk 12, 33-34," Biblica 40 (4, '60) 356-78. MüLHAUPT, E. (ed.) D Martin Luthers Auslegung der Bergpredigt (1961) 162-71. HUNTER, A. M. A Pattern for Life (1965) 80f. KOCH, K. "Der Schatz im Himmel" in: Leben angesichts des Todes. Festschrift für Helmut Thielicke (!968) Lohse, B. & Schmidt, H. P. (eds.) 47-60. WREGE, H.-T. Die Ueberlieferungsgeschichte der Bergpredigt (1968) 109. SCHNEIDER, G. Botschaft der Bergpredigt (1969) 78f. SANFORD, J. A., The Kingdom Within (New York 1970) 200f. SCHULZ, S. Q Die Spruchquelle der Evangelisten (1972) 142-45. GOULDER, M. D., Midrash and Lection in Matthew (London 1974) 74, 77, 80, 90, 276, 301f. TALBERT, C. H., Literary Patterns, Theological Themes, and the Genre of Luke-Acts (Missoula 1974) 55. BORSCH, F. H., "Jesus the Wandering Preacher?" in: M. Hooker/ C. Hickling (eds.) What about the New Testament?: Essays in Honour of Christopher Evans (London 1975) 50. SANDERS, J. T., Ethics in the New Testament (Philadelphia 1975) 46. EDWARDS, R. A., A Theology of Q (Philadelphia 1976) 124f.

6:19f PLOTZKE, U. Bergpredigt (1960) 227-33. LLOYD-JONES,

D. M. Studies in the Sermon on the Mount II (1962) 78-85.
SCHRAGE, W. Das Verhältnis des Thomas-Evangeliums zur
Synoptischen Tradition und zu den Koptischen
Evangelienübersetzungen (1964) 159. SUMMERS, R. The
Secret Sayings of the Living Jesus (1968) 30. JEREMIAS, J.
Neutestamentliche Theologie I (1971) 25f.

6:19-20 KLIJN, A. F., "Die syrische Baruch-Apokalypse" in: W. G.
Kümmel (ed.) Jüdische Schriften aus hellenistisch-römischer
Zeit. V/2 (Gütersloh 1976) 143.

6:19 MOORE, G.F. Judaism (1946) II 91. FARRER, A. St Matthew
and St Mark (1954) 171. BRAUN,H. Qumran und NT II (1966)
98, 288, 291. FRIEDLANDER, G. The Jewish Sources of the
Sermon on the Mount (1969) 181, 189, 236. METZGER, B. M.,
The Early Versions of the New Testament (Oxford 1977) 178.

6:20 STAEHELIN, E. Die Verkündigung des Reiches Gottes in der
Kirche Jesu Christi I (1951) 203. McARTHUR, H. K.
Understanding the Sermon on the Mount (1960) 89, 95, 164-65.
STRECKER, G. Der Weg der Gerechtigkeit (1962) 235. BEST,
E. "I Peter and the Gospel Tradition" NTS 16 (1969-70) 103f.
JEREMIAS, J. Neutestamentliche Theologie I (1971) 20, 25,
208, 213, 215. LADD, G. E., A Theology of the New Testament
(Grand Rapids 1974) 205, 236, 303. LANG, F. G., "Sola gratia
im Markusevangelium" in: J. Friedrich et al. (eds.)
Rechtfertigung: Festschrift für Ernst Käsemann (Tübingen
1976) 331f. HOLM-NEILSEN, S., "Die Psalmen Salomos" in:
W. G. Kümmel (ed.) Jüdische Schriften aus hellenistisch-
römischer Zeit. IV/2 (Gütersloh 1977) 83.

6:21 MASSAUX, E. Influence de l'Evangile de saint Matthieu sur la
littérature chrétienne avant saint Irénée (1950) 479-81.
FARRER, A. St Matthew and St Mark (1954) 171. *MEES, M.,
"Das Sprichtwort Mt 6, 21/Lk 12, 34 und seine
ausserkanonischen Parallelen" Augustinianum 14 (1974) 67-
89.

6:22-24 HUNTER, A.M. Design for Life (1953) 77f. HUNTER, A. M.
A Pattern for Life (1965) 81f.

6:22f JüLICHER, D. A. Die Gleichnisreden Jesu (1910) 98-108.
WINDISCH, H. The Meaning of the Sermon on the Mount
(1937) 41, 201, 212. *CADBURY, H. J. "The Single Eye,"
HThR XLVII (1954) 69-74. McARTHUR, H. K.
Understanding the Sermon on the Mount (1960) 91, 92, 144.
BAUMBACH, G. Das Verständnis des Bösen in den
synoptischen Evangelien (1963) 77ff. SASS, G. Ungereimtes bei
Matthäus (1968) 10-11. WREGE, H.-T. Die
Ueberlieferungsgeschichte der Bergpredigt (1968) 113.
JEREMIAS, J. Neutestamentliche Theologie I (1971) 25, 27,

35, 142, 153. SCHULZ, S. Q Die Spruchquelle der Evangelisten (1972) 468-70.

6:22-23 KEPLER, T. S. Jesus' Design for Living (1952) 98-100. STAUDINGER, J. Die Bergpredigt (1957) 193-96. MüLHAUPT, E. (ed.) D Martin Luthers Auslegung der Bergpredigt (1961) 171-78. *FENSHAM, F. C., "The Good and Evil Eye in the Sermon on the Mount" Neotestamentica 1 (1967) 51-58. SMITH, M., Tannaitic Parallels to the Gospels (Philadelphia 1968) 7 end+. SCHNEIDER, G. Botschaft der Bergpredigt (1969) 79-81. SANFORD, J. A., The Kingdom Within (New York 1970) 146-48. HAHN, F., "Die Worte vom Licht Lk 11, 33-36" in: P. Hoffmann (ed.) Orientierung an Jesus: Für Josef Schmid (Freiburg 1973) 108, 114-17, 126f, 128f. ΤΑΛΒΕΡΤ, Ψ. Η., Λιτεραρυ Παττερνσ, Τηεολογιψαλ Τηεμεσ, ανδ τηε Γενρε οφ Λθκε-Αψτσ (Μισσοθλα 1974) 54. JANSSEN, E., "Testament Abrahams" in: W. G. Kümmel (ed.) Jüdische Schriften aus hellenistisch-römischer Zeit III (Gütersloh 1975) 217. SANFORD, J. A., Healing and Wholeness (New York 1977) 25. BETZ, H. D., "Matthew 6:22f and ancient Greek theories of vision" in: E. Best/R. M. Wilson (eds.) Text and Interpretation. Studies presented to Matthew Black (Cambridge 1979) 43-56.

6:22 DANIELOU, J. on C. Edlund Das Auge der Einfalt (1952) RSR 43 (1955) 567-69. FARRER, A. St Matthew and St Mark (1954) 174. BOUSSET, W. Die Religion des Judentums im Späthellenistischen Zeitalter (1966‾1926) 419. METZGER, B. M., The Early Versions of the New Testament (Oxford 1977) 177.

6:23 PLOTZKE, U. Bergpredigt (1960) 233-38. *ROBERTS, R. L. "An Evil Eye (Matthew 6:23)," RestQ 7 (3, '63) 143-47. JüNGEL, E. Paulus und Jesus (1966) 164. STROBEL, A. Erkenntnis und Bekenntnis der Sünde in neutestamentlicher Zeit (1968) 44. METZGER, B. M., The Early Versions of the New Testament (Oxford 1977) 435.

6:24-34 FRIEDRICH, GPM 4 (1949/50) 244ff. SCHMAUCH, GPM 9 (1954/55) 220ff. EICHHOLZ, G. (ed.) Herr, tue meine Lippen auf (1957) 275-80. LUTHER, GPM 15 (1960/61) 259ff. DOERNE, M. Er kommt auch noch heute (1961) 133-36. MüLHAUPT, E. (ed.) D Martin Luthers Auslegung der Bergpredigt (1961) 178-92. Wir wissen weder Tag noch Stunde in: Predigtgedanken aus Vergangenheit und Gegenwart Reihe A, Band 6 (1966) 6-37. MARXSEN, W. Predigten (1968) 115-22. BORNKAMM, G. "Gerechtigkeit und Gesetz Christi," in: Zuwendung der Gerechtigkeit (1969) 36-42. LANGE, E. "Planung und Vertrauen," in: Ich aber sage euch (1969) 101-

111. VON OPPEN, D. "Das Reich Gottes und die kleinen Schritte," in: Ich aber sage euch (1969) 117-21. BOHREN, R., Predigtlehre (München 1971) 136, 509ff. *JACQUEMIN, P.-E. "Les options du Chrétien. Mt 6, 24-34," AssS 39 ('72) 18-27. LOCHMANN, J. M. GPM 3/4 (1973) 408-14. FüRST, Th., in: GPM 33 (1979) 364-74.

6:24-33   JACQUEMIN, E., "Les options du chrétien" AssS 68 (1964) 31-44.

6:24-27   PELIKAN, J. (ed.) The Preaching of Chrysostom (1967) 167-76.

6:24-25   BRAUN, H. Qumran und NT II (1966) 98, 288, 291.

6:24   JüLICHER, D. A. Die Gleichnisreden Jesu (1910) 108-15. WINDISCH, H. The Meaning of the Sermon on the Mount (1937) 33, 41, 88, 109, 202, 204. KEPLER, T. S. Jesus' Design for Living (1952) 100-103. LOEWENICH, W. von, Luther als Ausleger der Synoptiker (1954) 226f. KNOX, W. L. The Sources of the Synoptic Gospels II (1957) 28, 69, 129. STAUDINGER, J. Die Bergpredigt (1957) 196-201. DUPONT, D. J. Les Béatitudes (1958) 111-113. McARTHUR, H. K. Understanding the Sermon on the Mount (1960) 91, 92, 95, 109, 141. PLOTZKE, U. Bergpredigt (1960) 238-44. HENNECKE, E. & SCHNEEMELCHER, W. Neutestamentliche Apokryphen (1964) II 92. SCHRAGE, W. Das Verhältnis des Thomas-Evangeliums zur Synoptischen Tradition und zu den Koptischen Evangelienübersetzungen (1964) 109. JüNGEL, E. Paulus und Jesus (1966) 157. *GROENEWALD, E. P., "God and Mammon" Neotestamentica 1 (1967) 59-66. SUMMERS, R. The Secret Sayings of the Living Jesus (1968) 38. WREGE, H.-T. Die Ueberlieferungsgeschichte der Bergpredigt (1968) 115. SCHNEIDER, G. Botschaft der Bergpredigt (1969) 81f. JEREMIAS, J. Neutestamentliche Theologie I (1971) 17, 25f, 33, 175, 214. *NAGEL, W. "Neuer Wein in alten Schläuchen (Mt 9, 17), " VigChr 14 (1, '60) 1-8. SCHULZ, S. Q Die Spruchquelle der Evangelisten (1972) 459-61. *RüGER, H. P., *"Mamonas"* ZNW 64 (1973) 127-31. TALBERT, C. H., Literary Patterns, Theological Themes, and the Genre of Luke-Acts (Missoula 1974) 55. LANG, B., Frau Weisheit (Düsseldorf 1975) 169. *SAFRAI, S. and FLUSSER, D., "The Slave of Two Masters" Immanuel 6 (1976) 30-33. "Aramäisch" in: TRE 3 (1978) 607. "Armenfürsorge" in: TRE 4 (1979) 16.

6:25-7:6   BANNACH, H. "Nicht sorgen - nicht richten," in: Ich aber sage euch (1969) 25-32. DEMMER, H. "Matthäus 6, 25-7, 6," in: Ich aber sage euch (1969) 47-53. EICHELE, E. "Matthäus 6, 25-7, 6, " in: Ich aber sage euch (1969) 71-80. LORENZ, F.

Streit um Jesus (1969) 19-25. ZAHRNT, H. "Matthäus 6, 25-7, 6," in: Ich aber sage euch (1969) 148-60.

6:25ff KNOX, W. L. The Sources of the Synoptic Gospels II (1957) 69, 73. KäSEMANN, E. Exegetische Versuche und Besinnungen (1964) I 209. HIERS, R. H., The Historical Jesus and the Kingdom of God (Gainesville 1973) 19f, 38, 68, 83. GOULDER, M. D., Midrash and Lection in Matthew (London 1974) 86, 302ff, 349, 421. "Agrapha" in: TRE 2 (1978) 107. "Barmherzigkeit" in: TRE 5 (1980) 235.

6:25-34 HEIM, D. K. Die Bergpredigt Jesu (1949) 50-60. KEPLER, T. S. Jesus' Design for Living (1952) 103-106. HUNTER, A. M. Design for Life (1953) 78-81. KING, G. H. New Order (1954) 88-95. THIELICKE, H. Das Leben kann noch einmal beginnen (1956) 163-77. *SPADAFORA, F. "Montevergine: Il Santuario. L'anthemis è il 'giglio dei campi' di cui parla l'Evangelo," PaCl 37 (24, '58) 1277-79. SHINN, R. L. Sermon on the Mount (1962) 61-67. HUNTER, A. M. A Pattern for Life (1965) 82-86. BLACK, M. An Aramaic Approach to the Gospels and Acts (1967) 178f. WREGE, H.-T. Die Ueberlieferungsgeschichte der Bergpredigt (1968) 116. FRIEDLANDER, G. The Jewish Sources of the Sermon on the Mount (1969) 186f. SCHNEIDER, G. Botschaft der Bergpredigt (1969) 82-86. AGRELL, G., Work, Toil and Sustenance (Hägersten 1976). EDWARDS, R. A., A Theology of Q (Philadelphia 1976) 123-124.

6:25-33 HIRSCH, E. Frühgeschichte des Evangeliums (1941) 118-20. DUPONT, D. J. Les Béatitudes (1958) 74-80. GOPPELT, L. Christologie und Ethik (1968) 103f. MöLLER, C. Von der Predigt zum Text (1970) 147-64. *RIVAS, L. H. "Los bienes y la justicia. La pobreza: opcion de vida y precedencia de valores," RivB 32 (3, '70) 245-51. BOHREN: R., Predigtlehre (München 1971) 136, 511ff. SCHULZ, S. Q Die Spruchquelle der Evangelisten (1972) 149-57. TALBERT, C. H., Literary Patterns, Theological Themes, and the Genre of Luke-Acts (Missoula 1974) 55. BORSCH, F. H., "Jesus the Wandering Preacher?" in: M. Hooker/C. Hickling (eds.) What about the New Testament? In honour of Chris. Evans (London 1975) 50. *OLSTHOORN, M. F., The Jewish Background and the Synoptic Setting of Mt 6:25-33 and Lk12:22-31 (Jerusalem 1975). TANNEHILL, R. C., The Sword of His Mouth (Philadelphia 1976) 60-67. GRUNDMANN, W., "Weisheit im Horizont des Reiches Gottes" in: R. Schnackenburg (ed.) Die Kirche des Anfangs. Für H. Schürmann (Leipzig 1977) 195-96.

6:25-32 THEISSEN, G., Soziologie der Jesusbewegung (München 1977) 19.

6:25-31 DAVIES: W. D., The Sermon on the Mount (Cambridge 1966) 104.

6:25-30 LLOYD-JONES, D. M. Studies in the Sermon on the Mount II (1962) 107-116, 117-24.

6:25f PLOTZKE, U. Bergpredigt (1960) 244-50.

6:25-26 MASSAUX, E. Influence de l'Evangile de saint Matthieu sur la littérature chrétienne avant saint Irénée (1950) 479-81. HENNECKE, E. & SCHNEEMELCHER, W. Neutestamentliche Apokryphen (1964) II 320, 324.

6:25 WINDISCH, H. The Meaning of the Sermon on the Mount (1937) 126, 138, 212. BEST, E. One Body in Christ (1955) 216. STAUDINGER, J. Die Bergpredigt (1957) 201-202. SCHRAGE, W. Das Verhältnis des Thomas-Evangeliums zur Synoptischen Tradition und zu den Koptischen Evangelienübersetzungen (1964) 90. HASLER, V. Amen (1969) 59. CAVALLIN, H. C. C., Life after Death I (Lund 1974) 4.3.II. THEISSEN, G., Soziologie der Jesusbewegung (München 1977) 75. METZGER, B. M., "St. Jerome's explicit references to variant readings in manuscripts of the New Testament" in: E. Best/R. McL. Wilson (eds.) Text and Interpretation. Presented to M. Black (Cambridge 1979) 180.

6:26-26:55 GRYGLEWICZ, F. The St. Adalbert Codex of the Gospels NTS 11 (1964-65) 259f.

6:26ff BLAIR, E. P. Jesus in the Gospel of Matthew (1960) 91.

6:26-32 *SCHRUERS, P. "La paternité divine dans Mt, V, 45 et VI, 26-32," EphT 36 (3.4, '60) 593-624. DAVIES, W. D., The Sermon on the Mount (Cambridge 1966) 144f.

6:26 BRUNNER, E. Dogmatik II (1950) 181. PARKER, P. The Gospel Before Mark (1953) 136-37. STAUDINGER, J. Die Bergpredigt (1957) 202-203. FUCHS, E. "Die Verkündigung Jesu. Der Spruch von den Raben," in: Der historische Jesus und der kerygmatische Christus (1961) Ristow, H. & Matthiae, K. (eds.) 385-88. SMITH, M., Tannaitic Parallels to the Gospels (Philadelphia 1968) 6bn5+.

6:27-30 PLOTZKE, U. Bergpredigt (1960) 250-55.

6:28-34 PELIKAN, J. (ed.) The Preaching of Chrysostom (1967) 177-90.

6:28-30 STAUDINGER, J. Die Bergpredigt (1957) 203-205.

6:28 MASSAUX, E. Influence de l'Evangile de saint Matthieu sur la littérature chrétienne avant saint Irénée (1950) 412-13, 413-14, 479-81. *GLASSON, T. F. "Carding and Spinning: Oxyrhynchus Papyrus No. 655," JThS 13 (2, '62) 331-32. DALMAN, G. Orte und Wege Jesu (1967) 169f. *BRUNNER,

K., "Textkritisches zu Mt 6:28 *ou xainousin* statt *auxanousin* vorgeschlagen" ZKTh 100 (1978) 251-56.

6:29   HASLER, V. Amen (1969) 59.

6:30-44   *ROBINSON, D. F. "The Parable of the Loaves," AThR 39 (2, '57) 107-15.

6:30-34   SMITH, M., Tannaitic Parallels to the Gospels (Philadelphia 1968) 6bn5+.

6:30   MOORE, G.F. Judaism (1946) II 232n. BRUNNER, E. Dogmatik II (1950) 23. BORNKAMM-BARTH-HELD, Ueberlieferung und Auslegung im Matthäusevangelium (1961) 105, 280f. LLOYD-JONES, D. M. Studies in the Sermon on the Mount II (1962) 125-34. "Agrapha" in: TRE 2 (1978) 107.

6:31ff   STAEHELIN, E. Die Verkündigung des Reiches Gottes in der Kirche Jesu Christi I (1951) 57.

6:31-38   BORNKAMM, G. Geschichte und Glaube II (1971) 54-56.

6:31-33   STAUDINGER, J. Die Bergpredigt (1957) 205-206. LLOYD-JONES, D. M. Studies in the Sermon on the Mount II (1962) 135-45.

6:31f   MASSAUX, E. Influence de l'Evangile de saint Matthieu sur la littérature chrétienne avant saint Irénée (1950) 479-81. PLOTZKE, U. Bergpredigt (1960) 255-59. STRECKER, G. Der Weg der Gerechtigkeit (1962) 155.

6:31   JEREMIAS, J. Neutestamentliche Theologie I (1971) 25f.

6:32   TRILLING, W. Das wahre Israel (1959) 94. BLACK, M. An Aramaic Approach to the Gospels and Acts (1967) 176f. TAGAWA, K. "People and Community in the Gospel of Matthew" NTS 16 (1969-70) 153f.

6:33-34   ALAND, K. "Text von p7 bietet" NTS 3 (1957) 261-86. THEUNISSEN, M., "ὁ αἰτῶν λαμβάνει. Der Gebetsglaube Jesu und die Zeitlichkeit des Christseins" in: Jesus, Ort der Erfahrung Gottes (Basel 1976) 29.

6:33   GRILL, J., Untersuchungen über die Entstehung des vierten Evangeliums II (Leipzig 1923) 417, 424f. WINDISCH, H. The Meaning of the Sermon on the Mount (1937) 28, 36, 39, 42, 113. MOORE, G. F. Judaism (1946) II 100. MASSAUX, E. Influence de l'Evangile de saint Matthieu sur la littérature chrétienne avant saint Irénée (1950) 479-81. NöTSCHER, F. "Das Reich (Gottes) und seine Gerechtigkeit (Mt 6, 33 vgl. Lc 12, 31)," Biblica 31 (1950) 237-41. STAEHELIN, E. Die Verkündigung des Reiches Gottes in der Kirche Jesu Christi I (1951) 325. FARRER, A. St Matthew and St Mark (1954) 171. STAUDINGER, J. Die Bergpredigt (1957) 32, 33, 40, 167, 209, 223. TRILLING, W. Das wahre Israel (1959) 122f. BLAIR, E.

P. Jesus in the Gospel of Matthew (1960) 120. McARTHUR, H. K. Understanding the Sermon on the Mount (1960) 89, 91, 95. PLOTZKE, U. Bergpredigt (1960) 260-64. BORNKAMM-BARTH-HELD, Ueberlieferung und Auslegung im Matthäus-Evangelium (1961) 14, 28, 130f. NöTSCHER, F. "Das Reich (Gottes) und seine Gerechtigkeit," in: Vom Alten zum Neuen Testament. Gesammelte Aufsätze (1962) 226-30. STRECKER, G. Der Weg der Gerechtigkeit (1962) 152, 153, 154f, 157. HUMMEL, R. Die Auseinandersetzung zwischen Kirche und Judentum im Matthäusevangelium (1963) 156. KäSEMANN, E. Exegetische Versuche und Besinnungen (1964) II 185. HAHN, F. Das Verständnis der Mission im Neuen Testament (1965) 107. STUHLMACHER, P. Gerechtigkeit Gottes bei Paulus (1965) 188f. KERTELGE, K. "Rechtfertigung" bei Paulus (1967) 46f. REUMANN, J. Jesus in the Church's Gospels: Modern Scholarship and the Earliest Sources (1968) 47-48. FRIEDLANDER, G. The Jewish Sources of the Sermon on the Mount (1969) 188, 208, 263f. KäSEMANN, E. New Testament Questions of Today (1969) 172. SANFORD, J. A., The Kingdom Within (New York 1970) 57f, 201. FEUILLET, A. "Morale Ancienne et Morale Chrétienne" NTS 17 (1970-71) 132f. JEREMIAS, J. Neutestamentliche Theologie I (1971) 22, 25f, 40, 42, 100. ZIESLER, J. A. The Meaning of Righteousness in Paul (1972) 133ff, 143, 146. GOLLWITZER, H., Veränderung im Diesseits (München 1973) 39. GOULDER, M. D., Midrash and Lection in Matthew (London 1974) 63, 81, 262, 304, 332. LADD, G. E., A Theology of the New Testament (Grand Rapids 1974) 72, 79, 85, 103. SAND, A., Das Gesetz und die Propheten (Regensburg 1974) 204f. BETZ, O., "Rechtfertigung in Qumran" in: J. Friedrich et al., Rechtfertigung. Festschrift für E. Käsemann (Tübingen 1976) 27f. GOPPELT, L., Theologie des Neuen Testaments II (Göttingen 1976) 560. METZGER, B. M., The Early Versions of the New Testament (Oxford 1977) 118. THEISSEN, G., Soziologie der Jesusbewegung (München 1977) 19.

6:34-7:7 FARRER, A. St Matthew and St Mark (1954) 169. KNOX, W. L. The Sources of the Synoptic Gospels II (1957) 29, 70.

6:34 ZORELL, F. Biblica 1 (1920) 95f. STAUDINGER,J. Die Bergpredigt (1957) 165, 201, 207, 209, 266, 291, 305. McARTHUR, H. K. Understanding the Sermon on the Mount (1960) 91, 95, 164. MINEAR, P. S. Images of the Church in the New Testament (1960) 85f. PLOTZKE, U. Bergpredigt (1960) 264-68. LLOYD-JONES, D. M. Studies in the Sermon on the Mount II (1962) 146-57. BULTMANN, R. The History of the Synoptic Tradition (1963) 106f. HENNECKE, E. &

SCHNEEMELCHER, W. Neutestamentliche Apokryphen (1964) II 320. BOHREN,R., Predigtlehre (München 1971) 136. METZGER, B. M., The Early Versions of the New Testament (Oxford 1977) 267. THEISSEN, G., Soziologie der Jesusbewegung (München 1977) 19. McDONALD, J. I. H., Kerygma and Didache (Cambridge 1980) 81.

7   Fiebig, P. Jesu Bergpredigt (1924). BONHOEFFER, D. Nachfolge (1950) 118ff. KNöRZER, W. Die Bergpredigt, Modell einer neuen Welt (1968) 88-94.

7:1ff   THEISSEN, G., Soziologie der Jesusbewegung (München 1977) 75.

7:1-27   BUTLER, B. C. The Originality of St Matthew (1951) 37ff. EICHHOLZ, G. Auslegung de Bergpredigt (1965) 147-65. HOFFMANN, P. Studien zur Theologie der Logienquelle (1972) passim.

7:1-23   FARRER, A. St Matthew and St Mark (1954) 8. *AGOURDIDIS, S., "He epi tou Orous Homilia (synecheia)" DBM 3 (1975) 47-60.

7:1-20   PELIKAN, J. (ed.) The Preaching of Chrysostom (1967) 191-213.

7:1-12   THOLUCK, A. Die Bergrede Christi (1872) 368-85. CHAMBERS, O. Studies in the Sermon on the Mount (1941) 75-91. THOMPSON, E. T. The Sermon on the Mount (1946) 128-47.

7:1-11   GAECHTER, P. Die Literarische Kunst im Matthäus-Evangelium (1968) 43-44. BURCHARD, Chr., "Versuch, das Thema der Bergpredigt zu finden" in: G. Strecker (ed.) Jesus Christus in Historie und Theologie. Für H. Conzelmann (Tübingen 1975) 428-30.

7:1-6   KEPLER, T. S. Jesus' Design for Living (1952) 106-109. FARRER, A. St Matthew and St Mark (1954) 169. KING, G. H. New Order (1954) 95-102. THIELICKE, H. Das Leben kann noch einmal beginnen (1956) 178-93. BOWMAN, J. W. & TAPP, R. W. The Sermon from the Mount (1958) 143-50. SHINN, R. L. Sermon on the Mount (1962) 68-74. GOULDER, M. D., Midrash and Lection in Matthew (London 1974) 265f, 278, 304f,462.

7:1-5   HUNTER, A. M. Design for Life (1953) 82f. FARRER, A. St Matthew and St Mark (1954) 171, 173. VAGANAY, L. Existe-t-il Chez Marc Quelques Traces du Sermon sur la Montagne? NTS 1 (1954-55) 193ff. DUPONT, D. J. Les Béatitudes (1958) 126, 163-67. McARTHUR, H. K. Understanding the Sermon on the Mount (1960) 22, 72, 164. PLOTZKE, U. Bergpredigt (1960) 269-74. MüLHAUPT, E. (ed.) D Martin Luthers Auslegung der Bergpredigt (1961) 192-202. LLOYD-JONES, D. M. Studies in the Sermon on the Mount II (1962) 171-82. BULTMANN, R. The History of the Synoptic Tradition (1963) 79f. HUNTER, A. M. A Pattern for Life (1965) 86f. SCHNEIDER, G. Botschaft der Bergpredigt (1969) 86-89. SCHULZ, S. Q Die Spruchquelle der Evangelisten (1972) 146-49. TALBERT, C. H., Literary Patterns, Theological Themes, and the Genre of Luke-Acts (Missoula 1974) 42. EDWARDS, R. A., A Theology of Q (Philadelphia 1976) 87-90. GARLAND, D. E., The Intention of Matthew 23 (Leiden 1979) 121f. "Bergpredigt" in: TRE 5 (1980) 604, 605, 607.

7:1-2   MASSAUX, E. Influence de l'Evangile de saint Matthieu sur la littérature chrétienne avant saint Irénée (1950) 9-13. McARTHUR, H. K. Understanding the Sermon on the Mount (1960) 52, 90, 91, 95, 174. LLOYD-JONES, D. M. Studies in the Sermon on the Mount II (1962) 158-70. McNAMARA, M. The New Testament and the Palestinian Targum to the Pentateuch (1966) 139, 142. WREGE, H.-T. Die Ueberlieferungsgeschichte der Bergpredigt (1968) 124. LINTON, O., "Le parallelismus membrorum dans le Nouveau Testament grec" in: A. Descamps/A. de Halleux (eds.) Mélanges Bibliques en hommage au R. P. Béda Rigaux (Gembloux 1970) 502-503. SANFORD, J. A., The Kingdom Within (New York 1970) 122-23.

7:1   STRECKER, G. Der Weg der Gerechtigkeit (1962) 162. DAVIES, W. D., The Sermon on the Mount (Cambridge 1966) 99. MEURER, S., Das Recht im Dienst der Versöhnung und des Friedens (Zürich 1972) 63-76. METZGER, B. M., The Early Versions of the New Testament (Oxford 1977) 250, 254.

7:2   KNOX, W. L. The Sources of the Synoptic Gospels II (1957) 30. DUPONT, D. J. Les Béatitudes (1958) 50-52. KäSEMANN, E. Exegetische Versuche und Besinnungen (1964) II 96f. McNAMARA, M. The New Testament and the Palestinian Targum to the Pentateuch (1966) 138f, 256. NICKELS, P. Targum and New Testament (1967) 18. SMITH, M., Tannaitic Parallels to the Gospels (Philadelphia 1968) 6bnl+, 6bn5+. STROBEL, A. Erkenntnis und Bekenntnis der Sünde in neutestamentlicher Zeit (1968) 45. CARLSTON, C. The Things that Defile (Mark VII.14) and the Law in Matthew and Mark NTS 15 (1968-69) 79-80. KäSEMANN, E. New Testament Questions of Today (1969) 98, 99. RüGER, H. P. " 'Mit welchem Mass ihr messt, wird euch gemessen werden'," ZNW 60 (3-4, '69) 174-82. *COUROYER, B. " 'De la mesure dont vous mesurez il vous sera mesuré'," RevB 77 (3, '70) 366-70. JEREMIAS, J. Neutestamentliche Theologie I (1971) 22, 35, 175, 212.

7:3ff STONEHOUSE, N. B. The Witness of Matthew and Mark to Christ (1944) 175.

7:3-5 KNOX, W. L. The Sources of the Synoptic Gospels II (1957) 15. SUMMERS, R. The Secret Sayings of the Living Jesus (1968) 35, 36. WREGE, H.-T. Die Ueberlieferungsgeschichte der Bergpredigt (1968) 129. SANFORD, J. A., The Kingdom Within (New York 1970) 148. TANNEHILL, R. C., The Sword of His Mouth (Philadelphia 1975) 114-18.

7:3.5 SCHRAGE, W. Das Verhältnis des Thomas-Evangeliums zur Synoptischen Tradition und zu den Koptischen Evangelienübersetzungen (1964) 71.

7:3 FARRER, A. St Matthew and St Mark (1954) 174.

7:5-7 HENNECKE, E. & SCHNEEMELCHER, W. Neutestamentliche Apokryphen (1964) I 94f, 258; II 146, 327.

7:5 KNOX, W. L. The Sources of the Synoptic Gospels II (1957) 11.

7:6-11 FARRERm A. St Matthew and St Mark (1954) 172.
7:6 PERLES, F., "Zur Erklärung von Mt 7:6" ZNW 25 (1926) 163. STAEHELIN, E. Die Verkündigung des Reiches Gottes in der Kirche Jesu Christi I (1951) 88. *CASTELLINI, G. M. "Struttura letteraria di Mt 7, 6," RivB II (1954) 310-17. FARRER, A. St Matthew and St Mark (1954) 175. *GLASSON, T. F. "Chiasmus in St Matthew vii.6," ET 68 (10, '57) 302. *KAHANE, H. and R. "Pearls Before Swine? A Reinterpretation of Matt. 7, 6," Traditio 13 ('57) 421-24. KNOX, W. L. The Sources of the Synoptic Gospels II (1957) 34. PLOTZKE, U. Bergpredigt (1960) 274-78. MüLHAUPT, E. (ed.) D Martin Luthers Auslegung der Bergpredigt (1961) 203-207. LLOYD-JONES, D. M. Studies in the Sermon on the Mount II (1962) 183-94. JEREMIAS, J. "Matthäus 7, 6a," in: Abraham unser Vater (1963) 271-75. SCHRAGE, W. Das Verhältnis des Thomas-Evangeliums zur Synoptischen Tradition und zu den Koptischen Evangelienübersetzungen (1964) 179. HUNTER, A. M. A Pattern for Life (1965) 19, 21, 87f. BRAUN, H. Qumran und NT II (1966) 95. JEREMIAS, J. Abba; Studien zur neutestamentlichen Theologie und

Zeitgeschichte (1966) 83-87. BLACK, M. An Aramaic Approach to the Gospels and Acts (1967) 200f. NICKELS, P. Targum and New Testament (1967) 18. SASS, G. Ungereimtes bei Matthäus (1968) 12-13. FRIEDLANDER, G. The Jewish Sources of the Sermon on the Mount (1969) 76, 219, 223, 264. SCHNEIDER, G. Botschaft der Bergpredigt (1969) 90-92. ABEL, E. L. Who Wrote Matthew? NTS 17 (1970-71) 144f. *HJäRPE, J. " 'Pärlor at svin.' Ett 'Jesusord' i arabisk tradition," SEA 36 ('71) 126-35. JEREMIAS, J. Neutestamentliche Theologie I (1971) 34f. SCHWARZ, G. "Matthäus vii 6a. Emendation and Rückübersetzung," NovTest 14 (1, '72) 18-25. GOULDER, M. D., Midrash and Lection in Matthew (London 1974) 265f, 278, 282, 325. CONZELMANN, H., and LINDEMANN, A., Arbeitsbuch zum Neuen Testament (Tübingen 1975) 19. *MAXWELL-STUART, P. G., " 'Do not give what is holy to the dogs' Mt 7:6" ET 90 (1979) 341.

7:7ff KNOX, W. L. The Sources of the Synoptic Gospels II (1957) 30, 60. GERSTENBERGER, G., and SCHRAGE, W., Leiden (Stuttgart 1977) 254. ET: J. E. Steely (trans.) Suffering (Nashville 1980) 269f.

7:7-27 FARRER, A. St Matthew and St Mark (1954) 169.

7:7-12 KING, G. H. New Order (1954) 102-109. THIELICKE, H. Das Leben kann noch einmal beginnen (1956) 194-206. BOWMAN, J. W. & TAPP, R. W. The Sermon from the Mount (1958) 151-56.

7:7-11 WINDISCH, H. The Meaning of the Sermon on the Mount (1937) 39, 204, 206f. HIRSCH, E. Frühgeschichte des Evangeliums (1941) 100-102. KEPLER, T. S. Jesus' Design for Living (1952) 109-12. HUNTER, A. M. Design for Life (1953) 84-86. STAUDINGER, J. Die Bergpredigt (1957) 220-23. MüLHAUPT, E. (ed.) D Martin Luthers Auslegung der Bergpredigt (1961) 207-13. LLOYD-JONES, D. M. Studies in the Sermon on the Mount II (1962) 195-205. SHINN, R. L. Sermon on the Mount (1962) 61-67. HUNTER, A. M. A Pattern for Life (1965) 88-90. SCHNEIDER, G. Botschaft der Bergpredigt (1969) 92-94. KIRK, J. A. "The Meaning of Wisdom in James: Examination of a Hypothesis" NTS 16 (1969-70) 24f. SCHULZ, S. Q Die Spruchquelle der Evangelisten (1972) 161-64. GOULDER, M. D., Midrash and Lection in Matthew (London 1974) 266, 268, 278, 305f. TALBERT, C. H., Literary Patterns, Theological Themes, and the Genre of Luke-Acts (Missoula 1974) 54. EDWARDS, R. A., A Theology of Q (Philadelphia 1976) 108-109. GRUNDMANN, W., "Weisheit im Horizont des Reiches

Gottes" in: R. Schnackenburg (ed.) Die Kirche des Anfangs. Für H. Schürmann (Leipzig 1977) 187-88. "Bergpredigt" in: TRE 5 (1980) 604, 607. McDONALD, J. I. H., Kerygma and Didache (Cambridge 1980) 82.

7:7f   THEUNISSEN, M., "ὁ αἰτῶν λαμβάνει. Der Gebetsglaube Jesu und die Zeitlichkeit des Christseins" in: Jesus, Ort der Erfahrung Gottes (Basel 1976) 21f, 46, 50.

7:7-8   BLAIR, E. P. Jesus in the Gospel of Matthew (1960) 91. PLOTZKE, U. Bergpredigt (1960) 278-83. JEREMIAS, J. Neutestamentliche Theologie I (1971) 22, 34f, 186.

7:7   RUDOLPH, K. Die Mandäer (1960) I 106; ([1961]) II 232, 5. SCHRAGE, W. Das Verhältnis des Thomas-Evangeliums zur Synoptischen Tradition und zu den Koptischen Evangelienübersetzungen (1964) 177. BEYSCHLAG, K. Clemen Romanus und der Frühkatholizismus (1966) 94. SMITH, M., Tannaitic Parallels to the Gospels (Philadelphia 1968) 6bn5+. BOHREN, R. Wiedergeburt des Wunders (1972) 39-45. BROX, N., "Suchen und Finden. Zur Nachgeschichte von Mt 7:7b/Lk 11:9b" in: P. Hoffmann (ed.) Orientierung an Jesus (Freiburg 1973) 17-36. HOWARD, V. P., Das Ego in den Synoptischen Evangelien (Marburg 1975) 174-76.

7:8   SCHRAGE, W. Das Verhältnis des Thomas-Evangeliums zur Synoptischen Tradition und zu den Koptischen Evangelienübersetzungen (1964) 181. JEREMIAS, J. Neutestamentliche Theologie I (1971) 21f.

7:9-11 JüLICHER, D. A. Die Gleichnisreden Jesu (1910) 36-44. PLOTZKE, U. Bergpredigt (1960) 283-87.

7:11.21 McNAMARA, M. The New Testament and the Palestinian Targum to the Pentateuch (1966) 136.

7:11   WINDISCH, H. The Meaning of the Sermon on the Mount (1937) 113, 182, 184f., 205. BLAIR, E. P. Jesus in the Gospel of Matthew (1960) 91. WAINWRIGHT, A. W. The Trinity in the New Testament (1962) 210-211. HAHN, F. Christologische Hoheitstitel (1963) 107. SMITH, M., Tannaitic Parallels to the Gospels (Philadelphia 1968) 6bn5+. POLAG, A., Die Christologie der Logienquelle (NeukirchenVluyn 1977) 62.

7:12-27 BORNKAMM-BARTH-HELD, Ueberlieferung und Auslegung im Matthäus-Evangelium (1961) 68ff. HUMMEL, R. Die Auseinandersetzung zwischen Kirche und Judentum im Matthäusevangelium (1963) 65.

7:12-14 BRAUN, H. Qumran und NT II (1966) 18, 87, 189, 216, 287, 291, 299. *BERGMAN, J., "Zum Zwei-Wege-Motiv" SEA 41-42 (1976-1977) 27-56.

7:12 WINDISCH, H. The Meaning of the Sermon on the Mount (1937) 41, 54, 66f., 74, 76, 86, 99, 131, 145, 201, 212. BERGER, K. Die Gesetzauslegung Jesu (1940) 209-27, 242f. STONEHOUSE, N. B. The Witness of Matthew and Mark to Christ (1944) 200. BRUNNER, E. Dogmatik I (1946) 96. MASSAUX, E. Influence de l'Evangile de saint Matthieu sur la littérature chrétienne avant saint Irénée (1950) 9-13. KEPLER, T. S. Jesus' Design for Living (1952) 112-14. HUNTER, A. M. Design for Life (1953) 86f. FARRER, A. St Matthew and St Mark (1954) 179. BARRETT, C. K. The New Testament Background: Selected Documents (1956) 223. KNOX, W. L. The Sources of the Synoptic Gospels II (1957) 29-30, 125. STAUDINGER, J. Die Bergpredigt (1957) 224-25. DUPONT, D. J. Les Béatitudes (1958) 143s, 172-75. *METZGER, B. M. "The Designation 'The Golden Rule'," ET 69 (10, '58) 304. *GUY, H. A. "The Golden Rule," ET 70 (6, '59) 184. TILLICH, P. Das Neue Sein (1959) 37-40. TRILLING, W. Das wahre Israel (1959) 145f., 170f. BLAIR, E. P. Jesus in the Gospel of Matthew (1960) 93, 121, 123. PLOTZKE, U. Bergpredigt (1960) 287-91. BORNKAMM-BARTH-HELD, Ueberlieferung und Auslegung im Matthäus-Evangelium (1961) 23, 58, 60, 68, 74f., 92, 148. MüLHAUPT, E. (ed.) D Martin Luthers Auslegung der Bergpredigt (1961) 213-24. SCHRAGE, W. Die konkreten Einzelgebote in der paulinischen Paränese (1961) 237. DIHLE, A. Die goldene Regel; Eine Einführung in die Geschichte der antiken und frühchristlichen Vulgärethik (1962). LLOYD-JONES, D. M. Studies in the Sermon on the Mount II (1962) 206-16. SHINN, R. L. Sermon on the Mount (1962) 75-79. STRECKER, G. Der Weg der Gerechtigkeit (1962) 607, 135, 136, 144, 146. HUMMEL, R. Die Auseinandersetzung zwischen Kirche und Judentum im Matthäusevangelium (1963) 132, 133. HENNECKE, E. & SCHNEEMELCHER, W. Neutestamentliche Apokryphen (1964) II 393. HUNTER, A. M. A Pattern for Life (1965) 90f. *BORGEN, P. "Den sakalte gyldne regel (Matt. 7:12, Luk. 6.31), dens forekomst i det Nye Testamentes omverden og dens innhold i evangelienes kontekst," NTT 67 (3, '66) 129-46. BOUSSET, W. Die Religion des Judentums im Späthellenistischen Zeitalter (1966‾1926) 139, 144. SUMMERS, R. The Secret Sayings of the Living Jesus (1968) 69. FRIEDLANDER, G. The Jewish Sources of the Sermon on the Mount (1969) 67, 229ff. SCHNEIDER, G. Botschaft der Bergpredigt (1969) 95-98. BORNKAMM, G. Geschichte und Glaube II (1971) 94-96. SCHULZ, S. Q Die Spruchquelle der Evangelisten (1972) 139-41. GOLLWITZER, H., Veränderung im Diesseits (München 1973) 49.

FRANKEMöLLE, H., Jahwebund und Kirche Christi (Münster 1974) 278, 283, 295, 299, 302-304, 390. GOULDER, M. D., Midrash and Lection in Matthew (London 1974) 20, 25, 268. SAND, A., Das Gesetz und die Propheten (Regensburg 1974) 187-89. TALBERT, C. H., Literary Patterns, Theological Themes, and the Genre of Luke-Acts (Missoula 1974) 42. CONZELMANN, H., and LINDEMANN, A., Arbeitsbuch zum Neuen Testament (Tübingen 1975) 359f. HOFFMANN, P., and EID, V., Jesus von Nazareth und eine christliche Moral (Freiburg 1975) 148-50. POLAG, A., Die Christologie der Logienquelle (Neukirchen-Vluyn 1977) 77. "Bergpredigt" in: TRE 5 (1980) 604, 607, 610.

7:13ff NORDEN, E. Agnostos Theos (1956⁻1912) 362f. KNOX, W. L. The Sources of the Synoptic Gospels II (1957) 31-32. "Allegorese" in: TRE 2 (1978) 280.

7:13-29 CHAMBERS, O. Studies in the Sermon on the Mount (1941) 91-111.

7:13-27 THOLUCK, A. Die Bergrede Christi (1872) 385-406. BOWMAN, J. W. & TAPP, R. W. The Sermon from the Mount (1958) 157-64. STRECKER, G. Der Weg der Gerechtigkeit (1962) 135. BURCHARD, Chr., "Versuch, das Thema der Bergpredigt zu finden" in: G. Strecker (ed.) Jesus Christus in Historie und Theologie. Für H. Conzelmann (Tübingen 1975) 416, 430-32.

7:13-23 IWAND, H. J. "Hütet euch..." Eine Predigt, EvTh (1946) 169-78. KING, G. H. New Order (1954) 109-17.

7:13-20 SHINN, R. L. Sermon on the Mount (1962) 80-85.

7:13f WINDISCH, H. The Meaning of the Sermon on the Mount (1937) 26, 28, 37, 64, 97f., 100, 105, 199. HUNTER, A. M. Design for Life (1953) 87f. PLOTZKE, U. Bergpredigt (1960) 292-96. WREGE, H.-T. Die Ueberlieferungsgeschichte der Bergpredigt (1968) 132-35. SCHULZ, S. Q Die Spruchquelle der Evangelisten (1972) 309-12.

7:13-14 WILKENS, J. Einführung in das Evangelium nach Matthäus I (1934) 111-112. THOMPSON, E. T. The Sermon on the Mount (1946) 151. KEPLER, T. S. Jesus' Design for Living (1952) 115-18. FARRER, A. St Matthew and St Mark (1954) 174. THIELICKE, H. Das Leben kann noch einmal beginnen (1956) 207-23. KNOX, W. L. The Sources of the Synoptic Gospels II (1957) 79. STAUDINGER, J. Die Bergpredigt (1957) 226, 233. DUPONT, D. J. Les Béatitudes (1958) 94s, 98-101, 171s. BETZ, H. D. Lukian von Samosata und das Neue Testament (1961) 39, 205. MüLHAUPT, E. (ed.) D Martin Luthers Auslegung der Bergpredigt (1961) 225-30. LLOYD-

JONES, D. M. Studies in the Sermon on the Mount II (1962) 217-28, 229-39. STRECKER, G. Der Weg der Gerechtigkeit (1962) 158. LOCKYER, H. All the Parables of the Bible (1963) 154ff. HARDER, GPM (1964/65) 57ff. JüNGEL, E. Paulus und Jesus (1966) 184. TRAUB, H. in: Hören und Fragen (1967) Eichholz, G. & Falkenroth, A. (eds.) 93ff. MICHALKO, J. GPM 25 (4, '70) 76-81. SANFORD, J. A., The Kingdom Within (New York 1970) 65f, 190f. BOHREN, R. Wiedergeburt des Wunders (1972) 54-60. CAVALLIN, H. C. C., Life After Death I (Lund 1974) 3, I2, I, 3,I2, n7. TALBERT, C. H., Literary Patterns, Theological Themes, and the Genre of Luke-Acts (Missoula 1974) 56. EDWARDS, R. A., A Theology of Q (Philadelphia 1976) 130-32. PERRIN, N., Jesus and the Language of the Kingdom (London 1976) 41, 48, 53-54. STECK, K. G., in: GPM 31/1 (1976-1977) 64-70.

7:13 WINDISCH, H. The Meaning of the Sermon on the Mount (1937) 130, 170, 173, 187, 209. McARTHUR, H. K. Understanding the Sermon on the Mount (1960) 140, 165, 169. *SCHWARZ, G. "Matthäus vii 13a. Ein Alarmruf angesichts höchster Gefahr," NovTest 12 (2, '70) 229-32. JANSSEN, E., "Testament Abrahams" in: W. G. Kümmel (ed.) Jüdische Schriften aus Hellenistisch-römischer Zeit III (Gütersloh 1975) 228. KLIJN, A. F. J., "Die syrische Baruch-Apokalypse" in: W. G. Kümmel (ed.) Jüdische Schriften aus Hellenistisch-römischer Zeit V (Gütersloh 1976) 183.

7:14 VOLZ, P. Die Eschatologie der jüdischen Gemeinde (1934) 113.

7:15-27 STRECKER, G. Der Weg der Gerechtigkeit (1962) 137₄, 239₃. SMITH, M., Clement of Alexandria and a secret Gospel of Mark (Cambridge, Mass. 1973) 258-61. MINEAR, P. S., "False Prophecy and Hypocrisy in the Gospel of Matthew" in: J. Gnilka (ed.) Neues Testament und Kirche. Für R. Schnackenburg (Freiburg 1974) 80-86.

7:15-23 WILKENS, J. Einführung in das Evangelium nach Matthäus I (1934) 112-14. THOMPSON, E. T. The Sermon on the Mount (1946) 152-54. KEPLER, T. S. Jesus' Design for Living (1952) 118-20. HUNTER, A. M. Design for Life (1953) 88-90. EICHHOLZ, G. Herr, tue meine Lippen auf (1957) 242-46. FRICK, GPM 9 (1954/55) 195ff. HAMEL, GPM 15 (1960/61) 220ff. DOERNE, M. Er kommt auch noch heute (1961) 117-19. MüLHAUPT, E. (ed.) D Martin Luthers Auslegung der Bergpredigt (1961) 230-75. HUNTER, A. M. A Pattern for Life (1965) 93-95. "Hephata" in: Predigtgedanken aus Vergangenheit und Gegenwart A/5 (1966) 167-79. VööBUS, A., The Gospels in Study and Preaching (Philadelphia 1966)

235-58. SCHWEIZER, E., Matthäus und seine Gemeinde (Stuttgart 1974) 126-31. *HILL, D., "False Prophets and Charismatics: Structure and Interpretation in Mt. 7:15-23" Biblica 57 (1976) 327-48. *KRäMER, M., "Hütet euch vor den falschen Propheten" Biblica 57 (1976) 349-77. DUNN, J. D. G., Unity and Diversity in the New Testament (London 1977) 117.

7:15-22   SANDERS, J. T., Ethics in the New Testament (Philadelphia 1975) 44.

7:15-21   FRICK, R. GPM 9/3 195-200.

7:15-20   McARTHUR, H. K. Understanding the Sermon on the Mount (1960) 74, 85, 90, 91, 172. PLOTZKE, U. Bergpredigt (1960) 297-302. BORNKAMM-BARTH-HELD, Ueberlieferung und Auslegung im Matthäus-Evangelium (1961) 68, 149, 152f. BAUMBACH, G. Das Verständnis des Bösen in den synoptischen Evangelien (1963) 81ff. HAHN, F. Christologische Hoheitstitel (1963) 96. SATAKE, A. Die Gemeindeordnung in der Johannesapokalypse (1966) 190. *LEGASSE, S. "Les faux prophètes. Matthieu 7, 15-20," EFr 18 (47, '68) 205-18. SCHNEIDER, G. Botschaft der Bergpredigt (1969) 102-104. GOULDER, M. D., Midrash and Lection in Matthew (London 1974) 150, 307f. SAND, A., Das Gesetz und die Propheten (Regensburg 1974) 111-112. EDWARDS, R. A., A Theology of Q (Philadelphia 1976) 90-91.

7:15-16   DAVIES, W. D., The Sermon on the Mount (Cambridge 1966) 70.

7:15.16a   LLOYD-JONES, D. M. Studies in the Sermon on the Mount II (1962) 240-50.

7:15   FARRER, A. St Matthew and St Mark (1954) 174. KNOX, W. L. The Sources of the Synoptic Gospels II (1957) 16. BLAIR, E. P. Jesus in the Gospel of Matthew (1960) 92, 114, 165. HENNECKE, E. & SCHNEEMELCHER, W. Neutestamentliche Apokryphen (1964) II 340. KäSEMANN, E. Exegetische Versuche und Besinnungen (1964) II 84. *BöCHER, O. "Wölfe in Schafspelzen. Zum religionsgeschichtlichen Hintergrund von Matth. 7, 15," ThZ 24 (6, '68) 405-26. WREGE, H.-T. Die Ueberlieferungs- geschichte der Bergpredigt (1968) 136. FRIEDLANDER, G. The Jewish Sources of the Sermon on the Mount (1969) 250f. KäSEMANN, E. New Testament Questions of Today (1969) 83. PESCH, R. Naherwartungen (1969) 43, 116. BARRETT, C. K., "Ψευδαπόστολοι" in: A. Descamps and A. Halleux (eds.) Mélanges Bibliques en hommage au R. P. Béda Rigaux (Gembloux 1970) 381-82. LAMPE, G. W. H., "Grievous

Wolves (Acts 20:29)" in: B. Lindars and S. S. Smalley (eds.) Christ and the Spirit in the New Testament. In honour of C. F. D. Moule (Cambridge 1973) 255f. BEYSCHLAG, K., Simon Magnus und die Christliche Gnosis (Tübingen 1974) 13, 71, 129. MüLLER, U. B., Zur früchristlichen Theologiegeschichte (Gütersloh 1976) 36.

7:16ff   BLAIR, E. P. Jesus in the Gospel of Matthew (1960) 92.

7:16-21   TALBERT, C. H., Literary Patterns, Theological Themes, and the Genre of Luke-Acts (Missoula 1974) 42. "Bergpredigt" in: TRE 5 (1980) 604.

7:16-20   JüLICHER, D. A. Die Gleichnisreden Jesu (1910) 116-28. FARRER, A. St Matthew and St Mark (1954) 175. DUPONT, D. J. Les Béatitudes (1958) 44-50. 126s, 169-71. HÜMMEL, R. Die Auseinandersetzung zwischen Kirche und Judentum im Matthäusevangelium (1963) 123, 148, 156. WREGE, H.-T. Die Ueberlieferungsgeschichte der Bergpredigt (1968) 137. FRIEDLANDER, G. The Jewish Sources of the Sermon on the Mount (1969) 253ff. HOLST, R., "Re-examining Mk 3:28f and its Parallels" ZNW 63 (1972) 122-24. SCHULZ, S. Q Die Spruchquelle der Evangelisten (1972) 316-20.

7:16   KNOX, W. L. The Sources of the Synoptic Gospels II (1957) 11, 13, 14, 16. STRECKER, G. Der Weg der Gerechtigkeit (1962) 55₉. SCHRAGE, W. Das Verhältnis des Thomas-Evangeliums zur Synoptischen Tradition und zu den Koptischen Evangelienübersetzungen (1964) 100. SUMMERS, R. The Secret Sayings of the Living Jesus (1968) 37. METZGER, B. M., The Early Versions of the New Testament (Oxford 1977) 391.

7:17   BLAIR, E. P. Jesus in the Gospel of Matthew (1960) 114. BLACK, M. An Aramaic Approach to the Gospels and Acts (1967) 202f.

7:18   STRECKER, G. Der Weg der Gerechtigkeit (1962) 159. SCHRAGE, W. Das Verhältnis des Thomas-Evangeliums zur Synoptischen Tradition und zu den Koptischen Evangelienübersetzungen (1964) 168. JEREMIAS, J. Neutestamentliche Theologie I (1971) 25f, 29.

7:20   BULTMANN, R. The History of the Synoptic Tradition (1963) 90f. WRIGHT, J. H., "Discernment of spirits in the New Testament" International Catholic Review/Communio 1 (1974) 115-27.

7:21ff   STONEHOUSE, N. B. The Witness of Matthew and Mark to Christ (1944) 254. BLAIR, E. P. Jesus in the Gospel of Matthew (1960) 165. McARTHUR, H. K. Understanding the Sermon on the Mount (1960) 58, 71, 85, 91, 174. HÜMMEL, R. Die

Auseinandersetzung zwischen Kirche und Judentum im Matthäusevangelium (1963) 156.

7:21-29   PELIKAN, J. (ed.) The Preaching of Chrysostom (1967) 214-24.

7:21-27   *ORNELLA, A. "Les chrétiens seront jugés. Mt 7, 21-27," AssS 40 ('72) 16-27. EDWARDS, R. A., A Theology of Q (Philadelphia 1976) 91-93.

7:21-23   WINDISCH, H. The Meaning of the Sermon on the Mount (1937) 26, 37, 64, 126, 138. KNOX, W. L. The Sources of the Synoptic Gospels II (1957) 31. BORNKAMM-BARTH-HELD, Ueberlieferung und Auslegung im Matthäus-Evangelium (1961) 55, 58, 69, 152. STAUDINGER, J. Die Bergpredigt (1957) 237-38. LLOYD-JONES, D. M. Studies in the Sermon on the Mount II (1962) 261-71, 272-82, 283-93. SHINN, R. L. Sermon on the Mount (1962) 86-91. TöDT, H. E. Der Menschensohn in der synoptischen Ueberlieferung (1963) 233f. HENNECKE, E. & SCHNEEMELCHER, W. Neutestamentliche Apokryphen (1964) I 94f, 113. SATAKE, A. Die Gemeindeordnung in der Johannesapokalypse (1966) 188-90. WREGE, H.-T. Die Ueberlieferungsgeschichte der Bergpredigt (1968) 146. SCHNEIDER, G. Botschaft der Bergpredigt (1969) 104-106. O'NEILL, J. C., The Theology of Acts in its Historical Setting (London 1970) 39-40. BLANK, J., Verändert Interpretation den Glauben? (Freiburg 1972) 102-12. GOLLWITZER, H., Veränderung im Diesseits (München 1973) 147. *MEES, M., "Ausserkanonische Parallelstellen zu den Gerichtsworten Mt 7:21-23· Lk 6:46· 13:26-28 und ihre Bedeutung für die Formung der Jesusworte" VChr 10 (1973) 79-102.

7:21-22   KINGSBURY, J. D., Matthew: Structure, Christology, Kingdom (Philadelphia 1975) 104-107.

7:21f   HAHN, F. Christologische Hoheitstitel (1963) 83, 85, 98.

7:21   BONHöFFER, A. Epiktet und das Neue Testament (1911) 297, 318. WINDISCH, H. The Meaning of the Sermon on the Mount (1937) 28, 71, 73, 113, 129, 136, 138, 168, 187. STONEHOUSE, N. B. The Witness of Matthew and Mark to Christ (1944) 228. STAEHELIN, E. Die Verkündigung des Reiches Gottes in der Kirche Jesu Christi I (1951) 57. MOORE, G. F. Judaism (1946) II 205n. MASSAUX, E. Influence de l'Evangile de saint Matthieu sur la littérature chrétienne avant saint Irénée (1950) 14-17, 144-45, 489-90. DUPONT, D. J. Les Béatitudes (1958) 167-69. TRILLING, W. Das wahre Israel (1959) 162f. PLOTZKE, U. Bergpredigt (1960) 303-306. SCHWEIZER, E. Erniedrigung und Erhöhung bei Jesus und seinen Nachfolgern (1962) §7b. STRECKER, G. Der Weg der Gerechtigkeit (1962) 155, 160, 162₅, 166₆. BULTMANN, R. The History of the Synoptic Tradition (1963) 116f. HAHN, F. Christologische Hoheitstitel (1963) 96, 97f., 321. O'NEILL, J. C., The Theology of Acts in its Historical Setting (London 1970) 38-40. JEREMIAS, J. Neutestamentliche Theologie I (1971) 25f., 40f., 47, 153. SCHULZ, S. Q Die Spruchquelle der Evangelisten (1972) 427-30. LANGE, J., Das Erscheinen des Auferstandenen im Evangelium nach Matthäus (Würzburg 1973) 39, 45-47, 53, 72, 93, 106, 108, 137, 140, 150f, 208, 220-22, 240. SCHNACKENBURG, R., Aufsätze und Studien zum Neuen Testament (Leipzig 1973) 55ff. GOULDER, M. D., Midrash and Lection in Matthew (London 1974) 73, 308f. LADD, G. E., A Theology of the New Testament (Grand Rapids 1974) 103, 171, 216. SAND, A., Das Gesetz und die Propheten (Regensburg 1974) 123. SCHNEIDER, G., "Christusbekenntnis und Christliches Handeln" in: R. Schnackenburg et al. (eds.) Die Kirche des Anfangs. Für H. Schürmann (Leipzig 1977) 9-24.

7:22-18:35 WINK, W. P. CBQ 34 (1, '72) 242-43.

7:22ff KNOX, W. L. The Sources of the Synoptic Gospels II (1957) 80. DAVIES, W. D., The Sermon on the Mount (Cambridge 1966) 71.

7:22f WINDISCH, H. The Meaning of the Sermon on the Mount (1937) 71, 129, 138. PLOTZKE, U. Bergpredigt (1960) 307-311. STRECKER, G. Der Weg der Gerechtigkeit (1962) 176, 231₂. HAHN, F. Christologische Hoheitstitel (1963) 96f., 98. KäSEMANN, E. Exegetische Versuche und Besinnungen (1964) II 83f., 98. JEREMIAS, J. Neutestamentliche Theologie I (1971) 47, 96, 98. SCHULZ, S. Q Die Spruchquelle der Evangelisten (1972) 424-27.

7:22-23 DUPONT, D. J. Les Béatitudes (1958) 101-103. TRILLING, W., "Amt und Amtsverständnis bei Matthäus" in: A. Descamps and A. Halleux (eds.) Mélanges Bibliques en hommage au R. P. Béda Rigaux (Gembloux 1970) 34-38. TALBERT, C. H., Literary Patterns, Theological Themes, and the Genre of Luke-Acts (Missoula 1974) 56. EDWARDS, R. A., A Theology of Q (Philadelphia 1976) 130-32.

7:22 CLEMEN, C. Primitive Christianity and Its Non-Jewish Sources (1912) 234f. DELLING, G. Die Zueignung des Heils in der Taufe (1961) 46f 52. *DANIEL, C. " 'Faux Prophètes': surnom des Esséniens dans le Sermon sur la Montagne," RevQ 7 (1, '69) 45-79. KäSEMANN, E. New Testament Questions of Today (1969) 83, 100.

7:23ff   FINDLAY, J. A. Jesus and His Parables (1951) 95ff.

7:23-25   BRAUN, H. Qumran und NT II (1966) 105, 267.

7:23   FEINE, D. P. & BEHM, D. J. Einleitung in das Neue Testament (1950) 52f. BLAIR, E. P. Jesus in the Gospel of Matthew (1960) 107. STRECKER, G. Der Weg der Gerechtigkeit (1962) 24, 159, 239⁶. KäSEMANN, E. Exegetische Versuche und Besinnungen (1964) II 94. KäSEMANN, E. New Testament Questions of Today (1969) 96. LADD, G. E., A Theology of the New Testament (Grand Rapids 1974) 74, 196, 379.

7:24-29   THIELICKE, H. Das Leben kann noch einmal beginnen (1956) 240-53. MüLHAUPT, E. (ed.) D. Martin Luthers Auslegung der Bergpredigt (1961) 275-78. SHINN, R. L. Sermon on the Mount (1962) 92-98. STRECK, K. G. GPM 17 (1963/2) 274-81. Also in: Die Liebe Gottes (1963) 146-56. KLAAS, W. in: Herr, tue meine Lippen auf (1964) Eichholz, G. (ed.) 96ff. WINTER, F. GPM 23/3 (1968/69) 249-99. P. Krusche/E. Lange/D. & E. Rössler (eds.) Predigtstudien für das Kirchenjahr 1975 (Stuttgart 1975) 161-67. VOIGT, M., in: GPM 29 (1975) 354-58.

7:24-27   JüLICHER, D. A. Die Gleichnisreden Jesu (1910) 259-68. WILKENS, J. Einführung in das Evangelium nach Matthäus I (1934) 112. WINDISCH, H. The Meaning of the Sermon on the Mount (1937) 28, 42, 112, 126, 187, 199, 209. THOMPSON, E. T. The Sermon on the Mount (1946) 154-58. PIROT, J. Paraboles et Allégories Evangeliques (1949) 57-61. KEPLER, T. S. Jesus' Design for Living (1952) 121-24. HUNTER, A. M. Design for Life (1953) 90-92. FARRER, A. St Matthew and St Mark (1954) 165. KING, G. H. New Order (1954) 117-23. BORNKAMM-BARTH-HELD, Ueberlieferung und Auslegung im Matthäus-Evangelium (1961) 59, 69. LLOYD-JONES, D. M. Studies in the Sermon on the Mount II (1962) 294-304, 305-14, 315-25. HAHN, F. Christologische Hoheitstitel (1963) 96. BISER, E. Die Gleichnisse Jesu (1965) 71ff., 157. HUNTER, A. M. A Pattern for Life (1965) 95f. WREGE, H.-T. Die Ueberlieferungsgeschichte der Bergpredigt (1968) 152. FRIEDLANDER, G. The Jewish Sources of the Sermon on the Mount (1969) 257ff. SCHNEIDER, G. Botschaft der Bergpredigt (1969) 106-108. BARCLAY, W. And Jesus Said (1970) 217-22. JEREMIAS, J. Neutestamentliche Theologie I (1971) 26f., 29, 135, 152, 242. SANFORD, J. A. The Kingdom Within (New York 1970) 202f. SCHULZ, S. Q Die Spruchquelle der Evangelisten (1972) 312-16. GOULDER, M. D., Midrash and Lection in Matthew (London 1974) 50, 54, 56, 59, 61, 65, 88, 309. TALBERT, C. H., Literary Patterns,

Theological Themes, and the Genre of Luke-Acts (Missoula 1974) 42. MANEK, J., . . . und brachte Frucht. Die Gleichnisse Jesu (Berlin 1977) 37-39. VIELHAUER, Ph., "Oikodome" in: G. Klein, (ed.) Oikodome (München 1979) 55. "Bergpredigt" in: TRE 5 (1980) 604, 605, 607.

7:24-26　HAHN, F. Das Verständnis der Mission im Neuen Testament (1965) 106.

7:24-25　SANFORD, J. A., The Kingdom Within (New York 1970) 77.

7:24f　PLOTZKE, U. Bergpredigt (1960) 311-15.

7:24.　SCHWEIZER, E. "Zur Sondertradition der Gleichnisse bei Matthäus," in: Tradition und Glaube (1971) Jeremias, G., (ed.) 278-82.

7:24　KNOX, W. L. The Sources of the Synoptic Gospels II (1957) 29. STRECKER, G. Der Weg der Gerechtigkeit (1962) 214. BLACK, M. An Aramaic Approach to the Gospels and Acts (1967) 106f. SMITH, M., Tannaitic Parallels to the Gospels (Philadelphia 1968) 8bn7+. METZGER, B. M., The Early Versions of the New Testament (Oxford 1977) 178. "Amt" in: TRE 2 (1978) 516.

7:26f　PLOTZKE, U. Bergpredigt (1960) 315-19.

7:26　STRECKER, G. Der Weg der Gerechtigkeit (1962) 214. BLACK, M. An Aramaic Approach to the Gospels and Acts (1967) 106f.

7:28-8:1　FARRER, A. St Matthew and St Mark (1954) 179.

7:28f　WINDISCH, H. The Meaning of the Sermon on the Mount (1937) 63f., 136. STONEHOUSE, N. B. The Witness of Matthew and Mark to Christ (1944) 135. BUTLER, B. C. The Originality of St Matthew (1951) 126ff. FARRER, A. St Matthew and St Mark (1954) 196. PLOTZKE, U. Bergpredigt (1960) 320-23. HAHN, F. Christologische Hoheitstitel (1963) 400. SCHNEIDER, G. Botschaft der Bergpredigt (1969) 109-111.

7:28-29　KEPLER, T. S. Jesus' Design for Living (1952) 124-27. KING, G. H. New Order (1954) 124-25. STAUDINGER, J. Die Bergpredigt (1957) 244-47. BOWMAN, J. W. & TAPP, R. W. The Sermon from the Mount (1958) 165-67. LLOYD-JONES, D. M. Studies in the Sermon on the Mount II (1962) 326-37. HARTMANN, L., Testimonium Linguae (Lund 1963) 26. EICHHOLZ, G. Auslegung der Bergpredigt (1965) 20-25. SCHNEIDER, G. Botschaft der Bergpredigt (1969) 109-111. KINGSBURY, J. D., Matthew: Structure, Christology, Kingdom (Philadelphia 1975) 23-25.

7:28　STONEHOUSE, N. B. The Witness of Matthew and Mark to

Christ (1944) 130, 134f., 143, 176, 199. BLAIR, E. P. Jesus in the Gospel of Matthew (1960) 132. STRECKER, G. Der Weg der Gerechtigkeit (1962) 388, 130. SMITH, M., Tannaitic Parallels to the Gospels (Philadelphia 1968) 2.97+. EGGER, W., Frohbotschaft und Lehre (Frankfurt 1976) 35.

7:29   BLAIR, E. P. Jesus in the Gospel of Matthew (1960) 46. STRECKER, G. Der Weg der Gerechtigkeit (1962) 30, 127. DAVIES, W. D., The Sermon on the Mount (Cambridge 1966) 87. DUNN, J. D. G., Unity and Diversity in the New Testament (London 1977) 117. MEYER, B. F., The Aims of Jesus (London 1979) 158-162.

8:1-11:1   FRANSEN, I. "La Charte de l'apôtre (Matth. 8, i-11, i)." BVieC 37 ('61) 34-45.

8-10   FARRER, A. St Matthew and St Mark (1954) 41, 44.

8-9   RIDDERBOS, H. Matthew's Witness to Jesus Christ (1958) 34-39. BORNKAMM-BARTH-HELD, Ueberlieferung und Auslegung im Matthäus-Evangelium (1961) 234ff., 245, 254. DE KRUIJF, Th., Der Sohn des Lebendigen Gottes (Rome 1962) 61, 65, 70, 121, 129. HUMMEL, R. Die Auseinandersetzung zwischen Kirche und Judentum im Matthäusevangelium (1963) 139-41. *DREWES, B. F. "The Composition of Matthew 8-9," SEAJTh 12 (2, '71) 92-101. SELBY, D. J., Introduction to the New Testament (New York 1971) 115, 116, 128-30, 134. *BURGER, C. "Jesu Taten nach Matthäus 8 und 9," ZThK 70/3 (1973) 272-87. ELLIS, P. F., Matthew: His Mind and His Message (Collegeville 1974) 40-46. *KINGSBURY, J. D., "Observations on the 'Miracle Chapters' of Matthew 8-9" CBQ 40 (1978) 559-73. SEYBOLD, K. and MüLLER, U., Krankheit und Heilung (Stuttgart 1978) 145-47.

8:1-9:34   GAECHTER, P. Die literarische Kunst im Matthäus-Evangelium (1968) 20-21, 70-71. *THOMPSON, W. G. "Reflections on the Composition of Mt 8:1-9:34," CBQ 33 (3, '71) 365-88.

8   BJöRCK, S. et al., Valda Texter ur Nya Testamentet (Stockholm 1972) 5-9.

8:1-35   BUTLER, B. C. "M Vaganay and the 'Community Discourse'

" NTS 1 (1954-55) 283ff.

8:1-17 THOMPSON, W. G. Matthew's Advice to a Divided Community in Mt 17, 22-18, 35 (1970) 86-93.

8:1-13 SCHOTT, E. GPM 9/1 51-53. EICHHOLZ, G. Herr, tue meine Lippen auf (1957) 58-62. HUMMEL, R. Die Auseinandersetzung zwischen Kirche und Judentum im Matthäusevangelium (1963) 139.

8:1-11 HAHN, F. Christologische Hoheitstitel (1963) 400.

8:1-9.34. STONEHOUSE, N. B. The Witness of Matthew and Mark to Christ (1944) 134, 135ff. STRECKER, G. Der Weg der Gerechtigkeit (1962) 101, 175, 195, 220f.

8:1-9 WEBER, GPM 9 (1954/55) 192ff. DOERNE, M. Er kommt auch noch heute (1961) 114-17.

8:1-4 EWALD, H. Die drei ersten Evangelien (1850) 193ff. KNOX, W. L. The Sources of the Synoptic Gospels II (1957) 46. SCHEDL, C. Talmud, Evangelium, Synagoge (1969) 393f. CRIBBS, F. L., in: G. MacRae (ed.) SBL Seminar Papers 2 (Montana 1973) 12-13. GOULDER, M. D., Midrash and Lection in Matthew (London 1974) 316f, 319, 345. BARTLETT, D. L., Fact and Faith (Valley Forge 1975) 50. *KINGSBURY, J. D., "Retelling the 'Old, Old Story' " Currents in Theology and Mission 4 (1977) 342-49. RIST, J. M., On the Independence of Matthew and Mark (Cambridge 1978) 29-30. HEIL, J. P., "Significant aspects of the Healing Miracles in Matthew" CBQ 41 (1979) 274-87.

8:1 STONEHOUSE, N. B. The Witness of Matthew and Mark to Christ (1944) 134, 140. HAHN, F. Christologische Hoheitstitel (1963) 400. BLAIR, E. P. Jesus in the Gospel of Matthew (1960) 134. KNOX, W. L. The Sources of the Synoptic Gospels II (1957) 7.

8:2ff STRECKER, G. Der Weg der Gerechtigkeit (1962) 195.

8:2-17 BORNKAMM-BARTH-HELD, Ueberlieferung und Auslegung im Matthäus-Evangelium (1961) 160f., 236, 241f., 244, 246f., 250. CONNOLLY, D. "Ad miracula sanationum apud Matthaeum," VerbDom 45 (1967) 306-25.

8:2-16 PARKER, P. The Gospel Before Mark (1953) 176-77.

8:2-4 WILKENS, J. Einführung in das Evangelium nach Matthäus I (1934) 116-17. STONEHOUSE, N. B. The Witness of Matthew and Mark to Christ (1944) 135. BORNKAMM-BARTH-HELD, Ueberlieferung und Auslegung im Matthäus-Evangelium (1961) 202ff., 218, 221, 223f., 227f., 241, 243f., 272, 286. HENNECKE, E. & SCHNEEMELCHER, W. Neutestamentliche Apokryphen (1964) I 60. SUHL, A. Die

Funktion der alttestamentlichen Zitate und Anspielungen im Markusevangelium (1965) 120ff.

8:2 FARRER, A. St Matthew and St Mark (1954) 124. BORNKAMM-BARTH-HELD, Ueberlieferung und Auslegung im Matthäus-Evangelium (1961) 203, 214, 216f., 222f., 242, 269. HAHN, F. Christologische Hoheitstitel (1963) 85, 86. STONEHOUSE, N. B. The Witness of Matthew and Mark to Christ (1944) 166, 179. PESCH, R. Jesu ureigene Taten? Ein Beitrag zur Wunder-Frage in: Quaestiones Disputatae (1970) Rahner, K. & Schlier, H. (eds.) 90-93. LANGE, J., Das Erscheinen des Auferstandenen im Evangelium nach Matthäus (Würzburg 1973) 54, 219-21, 223, 370, 473, 479.

8:3ff SPAEMANN, H. "Jesus, das Gesetz und wir. Zum Generationenproblem in der Christenheit heute," Seelsorger 39 (2, '69) 84-92

8:3 STONEHOUSE, N. B. The Witness of Matthew and Mark to Christ (1944) 220. BORNKAMM-BARTH-HELD, Ueberlieferung und Auslegung im Matthäus-Evangelium (1961) 203f., 218, 223, 242, 262, 272f. PESCH, R. Jesu ureigene Taten? Ein Beitrag zur Wunder-Frage in: Quaestiones Disputatae (1970) Rahner, K. & Schlier, H., (eds.) 93-95. WESTERHOLM, S., Jesus and Scribal Authority (Lund 1978) 68.

8:4 STONEHOUSE, N. B. The Witness of Matthew and Mark to Christ (1944) 139. MOORE, G. F. Judaism (1946) II 9. PARKER, P. The Gospel Before Mark (1953) 63ff. TRILLING, W. Das wahre Israel (1959) 105. BORNKAMM-BARTH-HELD, Ueberlieferung und Auslegung im Matthäus-Evangelium (1961) 184, 203, 243f. BROX, N. Zeuge und Märtyrer (1961) 26f. STRECKER, G. Der Weg der Gerechtigkeit (1962) 121?. HUMMEL, R. Die Auseinandersetzung zwischen Kirche und Judentum im Matthäusevangelium (1963) 81f., 94. HAHN, F. Das Verständnis der Mission im Neuen Testament (1965) 110. PESCH, R. Jésu ureigene Taten? Ein Beitrag zur Wunder-Frage in: Quaestiones Disputatae (1970) Rahner, K. & Schlier, H. (eds.) 95-98. TRITES, A. A., The New Testament Concept of Witness (Cambridge 1977) 178.

8:5ff KNOX, W. L. The Sources of the Synoptic Gospels II (1957) 7. GOULDER, M. D., Type and History in Acts (London 1964) 128f.

8:5-13 EWALD, H. Die drei ersten Evangelien (1850) 224ff. WILKENS, J. Einführung in das Evangelium nach Matthäus I

(1934) 117-20. HIRSCH, E. Frühgeschichte des Evangeliums
(1941) 88-90. STONEHOUSE, N. B. The Witness of Matthew
and Mark to Christ (1944) 136, 230. SURKAU, GPM 4
(1949/50) 53ff. SCHOTT, GPM 9 (1954/55) 51ff. MOUSON,
J. "De sanatione pueri Centurionis (Mt. VIII, 5-13), " Coll
Mech 44 (6. '59) 633-36. TRILLING, W. Das wahre Israel
(1959) 83f. BLAIR, E. P. Jesus in the Gospel of Matthew (1960)
46. Zu Suchen Seine Herrlichkeit in: Predigtgedanken aus
Vergangenheit und Gegenwart Bd. 2 (1960) 80-108.
BORNKAMM-BARTH-HELD, Ueberlieferung und
Auslegung im Matthäus-Evangelium (1961) 94, 182ff., 199,
221ff., 227f., 242, 265, 267f., 273, 286. DOERNE, M. Er kommt
auch noch heute (1961) 38-40. GNILKA, J. Die Verstockung
Israels (1961) 97f. STRECKER, G. Der Weg der Gerechtigkeit
(1962) 94f., 99ff., 107, 108f., 117. HAHN, F. Christologische
Hoheitstitel (1963) 218. HODGES, Z. C. "The Centurion's
Faith in Matthew and Luke," BiblSa 121 (484, '64) 321-32.
BLANK, J. "Zur Christologie ausgewählter Wunderberichte,"
EvangErz 20 (1968) 470-83. WREGE, H.-T. Die
Ueberlieferungsgeschichte der Bergpredigt (1968) 47. BLANK,
J. Schriftauslegung in Theorie und Praxis (1969) 107, 112-17.
LüHRMANN, D. Die Redaktion der Logienquelle (1969) 57f.
SCHEDL, C. Talmud, Evangelium, Synagoge (1969) 294-97.
WEISER, A. Glaube und Wunder; Eine Heilung in
Kapharnaum in: Kleine Reihe zur Bibel 5 (1969). TAGAWA,
K. People and Community in the Gospel of Matthew NTS 16
(1969-70) 153f. JEREMIAS, J. Neutestamentliche Theologie I
(1971) 90, 110, 161, 235. E. T. New Testament Theology I
(1971). SCHNIDER, F./STENGER, W. Johannes und die
Synoptiker (1971) 54-88. DANTINE, J. GPM 27/1 (1972) 81-
86. HOFFMANN, P. Studien zur Theologie der Logienquelle
(1972) passim. SCHULZ, S. Q Die Spruchquelle der
Evangelisten (1972) 236-46. LANGE, E. "Dritter Sonntag nach
Epiphanias: Matthäus 8, 5-13," in: Predigtstudien (1972/73)
Lange, E. (ed.) 90-93. FRANKEMöLLE, H., Jahwebund und
Kirche Christi (Münster 1974) 108, 111-14, 118, 137, 173, 217,
254, 261, 264, 313, 319. GOULDER, M. D., Midrash and
Lection in Matthew (London 1974) 46, 142, 160, 317, 319-21,
328, 329, 343. TALBERT, C. H., Literary Patterns, Theological
Themes, and the Genre of Luke-Acts (Missoula 1974) 43.
ZINGG, P., Das Wachsen der Kirche (Freiburg 1974) 251.
BARTLETT, D. L., Fact and Faith (Valley Forge 1975) 51-52.
HOWARD, V. P., Das Ego in den Synoptischen Evangelien
(Marburg 1975) 168-74. EDWARDS, R. A., A Theology of Q
(Philadelphia 1976) 93-94. POLAG, A., Die Christologie der
Logienquelle (Neukirchen-Vluyn 1977) 158. MARTIN, R. P.,

"The Pericope of the Healing of the Centurion's Servant/son" in: R. A. Guelich (ed.) Unity and Diversity in New Testament Theology. In honour of G. E. Ladd (Grand Rapids 1978) 14-22.

8:5-10 *HOOKE, S. H. "Jesus and the Centurion: Matthew viii.5-10," ET 69 (3, '57) 79-80. SCHMITHALS, W. Paulus und Jakobus (1963) 93. TALBERT, C. H., Literary Patterns, Theological Themes, and the Genre of Luke-Acts (Missoula 1974) 19. SCHMITHALS, W., "Zur Herkunft der gnostischen Elemente in der Sprache des Paulus" in: B. Aland et al. (eds.) Gnosis. Für H. Jonas (Göttingen 1978) 401.

8:5-6 PARKER, P. The Gospel Before Mark (1953) 64-65.

8:5 FARRER, A. St Matthew and St Mark (1954) 124. SWIDLER, L., Biblical Affirmations of Woman (Philadelphia 1979) 197.

8:6 HAHN, F. Christologische Hoheitstitel (1963) 82, 86. LANGE, J., Das Erscheinen des Auferstandenen im Evangelium nach Matthäus (Würzburg 1973) 46f, 53f, 219-21.

8:7 BORNKAMM-BARTH-HELD, Ueberlieferung und Auslegung im Matthäus-Evangelium (1961) 184. HOWARD, V. P., Das Ego in den Synoptischen Evangelien (Marburg 1975) 168-74.

8:8f BORNKAMM-BARTH-HELD, Ueberlieferung und Auslegung im Matthäus-Evangelium (1961) 161, 183f., 218, 225, 241f., 273.

8:8 STRECKER, G. Der Weg der Gerechtigkeit (1962) 176. HAHN, F. Christologische Hoheitstitel (1963) 82f., 86, 94. HUMMEL, R. Die Auseinandersetzung zwischen Kirche und Judentum im Matthäusevangeliuum (1963) 140. METZGER, B. M., The Early Versions of the New Testament (Oxford 1977) 173. TALBERT, C. H., Literary Patterns, Theological Themes, and the Genre of Luke-Acts (Missoula 1974) 19.

8:9 HAHN, F. Christologische Hoheitstitel (1963) 82.

8:10ff STRECKER, G. Der Weg der Gerechtigkeit (1962) 1114.

8:10-12 STONEHOUSE, N. B. The Witness of Matthew and Mark to Christ (1944) 139. SCHWEIZER, E. Gemeinde und Gemeindeordnung im Neuen Testament (1959) §§4c, e 5b.

8:10-11 SANFORD, J. A., The Kingdom Within (New York 1970) 196-97.

8:10 KNOX, W. L. The Sources of the Synoptic Gospels II (1957) 87. BORNKAMM-BARTH-HELD, Ueberlieferung und Auslegung im Matthäus-Evangelium (1961) 105, 184f., 225, 264. HUMMEL, R. Die Auseinandersetzung zwischen Kirche und Judentum im Matthäusevangelium (1963) 144f. HASLER,

V. Amen (1969) 60. GOPPELT, L., Theologie des Neuen Testaments I (Göttingen 1975) 160, 183, 199, 201f.

8:11-21   RICHARDSON, A. The Miracle-Stories of the Gospels (1948) 94f.

8:11f   MOORE, G. F. Judaism (1946) II 365. NEPPER-CHRISTENSEN, P. Das Matthäusevangelium. Ein Judenchristliches Evangelium? (1958) 17, 19, 29, 197, 198. BULTMANN, R. The History of the Synoptic Tradition (1963) 128f. WREGE, H.-T. Die Ueberlieferungsgeschichte der Bergpredigt (1968) 47, 150f., 173, 178. *ZELLER, D. "Das Logion Mt 8, 11f/Lk 13, 28f und das Motiv der 'Völkerwallfahrt'," BZ 15 (2, '71) 222-37. GRIMM, W. "Zum Hintergrund von Mt 8, 11f/Lk 13, 28f," BZ 16 (2, '72) 255-56. SCHULZ, S. Q Die Spruchquelle der Evangelisten (1972) 232-330. ZELLER, D. "Das Logion Mt 8, 11f/Lk 13, 28f und das Motiv der 'Völkerwallfahrt' (Schluss)," BZ 16(1, '72) 84-93.

8:11-12   STONEHOUSE, N. B. The Witness of Matthew and Mark to Christ (1944) 232, 240. STAEHELIN, E. Die Verkündigung des Reiches Gottes in der Kirche Jesu Christi I (1951) 57, 123, 200. BEST, E. One Body in Christ (1955) 107. KNOX, W. L. The Sources of the Synoptic Gospels II (1957) 33, 80. TRILLING, W. Das wahre Israel (1959) 68ff. BORNKAMM-BARTH-HELD, Ueberlieferung und Auslegung im Matthäus-Evangelium (1961) 25f., 56, 94, 104, 157, 185f., 280. STRECKER, G. Der Weg der Gerechtigkeit (1962) 176г. HUMMEL, R. Die Auseinandersetzung zwischen Kirche und Judentum im Matthäusevangelium (1963) 146-48, 149-51, 153, 156n., 157. KäSEMANN, E. Exegetische Versuche und Besinnungen (1964) II 98. HAHN, F. Das Verständnis der Mission im Neuen Testament (1965) 26f., 28, 30f. *DUPONT, J. " 'Beaucoup viendront du levant et du couchant...' (Matthie 8, 11-12· Luc 13, 28-29)," SciEccl 19 (2, '67) 153-67. KäSEMANN, E. New Testament Questions of Today (1969) 100. VöGTLE, A. Das Neue Testament und die Zukunft des Kosmos (1970) 148f. JEREMIAS, J. Neutestamentliche Theologie I (1971) 55, 100, 134, 236, 238. FRANKEMöLLE, H., Jahwebund und Kirche Christi (Münster 1974) 37f, 108, 112f, 114, 166, 173, 217, 254, 261, 264, 313, 319. TALBERT, C. H., Literary Patterns, Theological Themes, and the Genre of Luke-Acts (Missoula 1974) 56. EDWARDS, R. A., A Theology of Q (Philadelphia 1976) 130-32. "Abraham" in: TRE 1 (1977) 378. BRUCE, F. F., The Time is Fulfilled (Exeter 1978) 62. POLAG, A., Die Christologie der Logienquelle (Neukirchen-Vluyn 1977) 92.

8:11 NöTSCHER, F., Altorientalischer und alttestamentlicher Auferstehungsglaube (Darmstadt 1970⁻1926) 280, 314. STONEHOUSE, N. B. The Witness of Matthew and Mark to Christ (1944) 186. STAEHELIN, E. Die Verkündigung Gottes in der Kirche Jesu Christi I (1951) 138. FLEW, R. N. Jesus and His Church (1956) 62. BLAIR, E. P. Jesus in the Gospel of Matthew (1960) 31. PERRIN, N., The Kingdom of God in the Teaching of Jesus (Philadelphia 1963) 61, 68, 80, 85, 183, 188. HENNECKE, E. & SCHNEEMELCHER, W. Neutestamentliche Apokryphen (1964) II 394. BRAUN, H. Qumran und NT II (1966) 39, 91, 271. HASLER, V. Amen (1969) 60. DELLING, G. Studien zum Neuen Testament und zum hellenistischen Judentum. Gesammelte Aufsätze 1950-1968 (1970) 224-34. SANFORD, J. A., The Kingdom Within (New York 1970) 49f. JEREMIAS, J. Neutestamentliche Theologie I (1971) 25, 40, 42, 117. CAVALLIN, H. C. C., Life After Death (Lund 1974) 4. 5. 5. 7. 2n23. LADD, G. E., A Theology of the New Testament (Grand Rapids 1974) 83, 103, 205, 231. WESTERMANN, C., Forschung am Alten Testament. Gesammelte Studien II (München 1974) 287f. "Abendmahl" in: TRE 1 (1977) 49, 213. "Abraham" in: TRE 1 (1977) 378. METZGER, B. M., The Early Versions of the New Testament (Oxford 1977) 172.

8:12-13 BETZ, H. D. Lukian von Samosata und das Neue Testament (1961) 81, 88, 159.

8:12 VOLZ, P. Die Eschatologie der jüdischen Gemeinde (1934) 167. STAEHELIN, E. Die Verkündigung des Reiches Gottes in der Kirche Jesu Christi I (1951) 238. KNOX, W. L. The Sources of the Synoptic Gospels II (1957) 81. BLAIR, E. P. Jesus in the Gospel of Matthew (1960) 30. STRECKER, G. Der Weg der Gerechtigkeit (1962) 115, 160₂. KäSEMANN, E. Exegetische Versuche und Besinnungen (1964) II 94. SMITH, M., Tannaitic Parallels to the Gospels (Philadelphia 1968) 3.9+. KäSEMANN, E. New Testament Questions of Today (1969) 95. JEREMIAS, J. Neutestamentliche Theologie I (1971) 22, 25, 40, 52f., 131, 291. SCHWANK, B. " 'Dort wird Heulen und Zähneknirschen sein,' " BZ 16 (1, '72) 121-22. GOULDER, M. D., Midrash and Lection in Matthew (London 1974) 119, 162, 282, 321, 429. LADD, G. E., A Theology of the New Testament (Grand Rapids 1974) 65, 74, 97, 107.

8:13 PARKER, P. The Gospel Before Mark (1953) 64-65. HAHN, F. Christologische Hoheitstitel (1963) 402. BORNKAMM-BARTH-HELD, Ueberlieferung und Auslegung im Matthäus-Evangelium (1961) 105, 107, 182, 185, 200, 205f., 209, 121, 218, 222, 225, 227f., 230, 256, 262, 268, 273f. HUMMEL, R. Die

Auseinandersetzung zwischen Kirche und Judentum im Matthäusevangelium (1963) 140. STRECKER, G. Der Weg der Gerechtigkeit (1962) 121l4. PETZKE, G. Die Traditionen über Appolonius von Tyana und das Neue Testament (1970) 136, 180. GOPPELT, L., Theologie des Neuen Testaments I (Göttingen 1975) 199ff, 204.

8:14-17   EWALD, H. Die drei ersten Evangelien (1850) 193ff. SCHEDL, C. Talmud, Evangelium, Synagoge (1969) 297-99.

8:14-15   WILKENS, J. Einführung in das Evangelium nach Matthäus I (1934) 117. BORNKAMM-BARTH-HELD, Ueberlieferung und Auslegung im Matthäus-Evangelium (1961) 159ff., 219, 221, 233, 241, 270, 286. STRECKER, G. Der Weg der Gerechtigkeit (1962) 2043. LEON-DUFOUR, X. "La Guérison de la Belle-Mère de Simon Pierre," EstBi 24 (3, '65) 193-216. LAMARCHE, P "La guérison de la belle-mère de Pierre et le genre littéraire des évangiles," NRTh 87 (5, '65) 515-26. PESCH, R. Neuere Exegese-Verlust oder Gewinn? (1968) 162-68. OLSSON, B., "Att umgås med texter" (To Communicate with Texts) SvTK 52 (1976) 49-58. RIST, J. M., On the Independence of Matthew and Mark (Cambridge 1978) 29. SWIDLER, L., Biblical Affirmations of Woman (Philadelphia 1979) 180, 184, 225, 236, 258.

8:14   STONEHOUSE, N. B. The Witness of Matthew and Mark to Christ (1944) 137, 160, 231. FARRER, A. St Matthew and St Mark (1954) 117, 124. STRECKER, G. Der Weg der Gerechtigkeit (1962) 94f., 198.

8:15ff   KNOX, W. L. The Sources of the Synoptic Gospels II (1957) 124ff.

8:16-17   BORNKAMM-BARTH-HELD, Ueberlieferung und Auslegung im Matthäus-Evangelium (1961) 160ff.

8:16   STONEHOUSE, N. B. The Witness of Matthew and Mark to Christ (1944) 137. BLAIR, E. P. Jesus in the Gospel of Matthew (1960) 46. BORNKAMM-BARTH-HELD, Ueberlieferung und Auslegung im Matthäus-Evangelium (1961) 120, 161, 218, 241f., 269. STRECKER, G. Der Weg der Gerechtigkeit (1962) 93, 121l7, 151l, 176, 195. HARTMAN, L., Testimonium Linguae (Lund 1963) 22f. DALTON, W. J., Christ's Proclamation to the Spirits (Rome 1965) 147f. EGGER, W., Frohbotschaft und Lehre (Frankfurt 1976) 35, 70f.

8:17f   STRECKER, G. Der Weg der Gerechtigkeit (1962) 94.

8:17   STONEHOUSE, N. B. The Witness of Matthew and Mark to Christ (1944) 191. PARKER, P. The Gospel Before Mark (1953) 10-11. BORNKAMM-BARTH-HELD, Ueberlieferung und Auslegung im Matthäus-Evangelium (1961) 34, 120f., 162, 233, 246ff. BLAIR, E. P. Jesus in the Gospel of Matthew (1960) 39, 56, 79. LINDARS, B. New Testament Apologetic (1961) 20, 86, 88, 153f., 158, 168, 261, 267. DE KRUIJF, T., Der Sohn Des Lebendigen Gottes (Rome 1962) 32, 48, 63, 105. STRECKER, G. Der Weg der Gerechtigkeit (1962) 36₃, 49₂, 66, 71₂, 74, 120₂, 176. SCHWEIZER, E. Erniedrigung und Erhöhung bei Jesus und seinen Nachfolgern (1962) §6b. HAHN, F. Christologische Hoheitstitel (1963) 54, 202. HUMMEL, R., Die Auseinandersetzung zwischen kirche und Judentum im Matthäusevangelium (1963) 124, 132, 139. NELLESSEN, E. Das Kind und seine Mutter (1969) 38f. ROTHFUCHS, W. Die Erfüllungszitate des Matthäus-Evangeliums (1969) 70-72. KüMMEL, W. G. Einleitung in das Neue Testament (1973) 81f. GERSTENBERGER, G./SCHRAGE, W., Leiden (Stuttgart 1977) 122f, 128f; ET: J. E. Steely (trans.) Suffering (Nashville 1980) 143, 150.

8:18-24:41   DRURY, J., Tradition and Design in Luke's Gospel (Atlanta 1976) 138-64.

8:18-23:27   BECKER, U./WIBBING, S., Wundergeschichten (Gütersloh 1965) 45ff.

8:18-9:17   BORNKAMM-BARTH-HELD, Ueberlieferung und Auslegung im Matthäus-Evangelium (1961) 236f., 241.

8:18ff   KNOX, W. L. The Sources of the Synoptic Gospels II (1957) 46-47. STRECKER, G. Der Weg der Gerechtigkeit (1962) 41, 94, 124, 176, 191, 230₄, 231.

8:18-34   EWALD, H. Die drei ersten Evangelien (1850) 237ff. MUSSNER, F. Die Wunder Jesu (1967) 50f.

8:18-27   BORNKAMM-BARTH-HELD, Ueberlieferung und Auslegung im Matthäus-Evangelium (1961) 27, 48ff., 93, 156, 171, 189ff., 199, 221, 233, 237, 253, 255, 271. ALONSO DIAZ, J., "Pasaje de la calma de la tormenta en el Evangelio, segun Mateo." CultBib 20 (190, '63) 149-57. LEON-DUFOUR, X. "La tempête apaisée," NRTh 87 (9, '65) 897-922.

8:18-22   WILKENS, J. Einführung in das Evangelium nach Matthäus I (1934) 121-22. ZIMMERMANN, H. Neutestamentliche Methodenlehre (1967) 116-19. DRESCHER, H.-G., Nachfolge und Begegnung (Gütersloh 1972) 94-121. EDWARDS, R. A., A Theology of Q (Philadelphia 1976) 100f.

8:18-20   SCHEDL, C. Talmud, Evangelium, Synagoge (1969) 299f. ELLIS, P. F., Matthew: His Mind and His Message (Minnesota 1974) 28-31.

8:18.23-27.   BECKER, U./WIBBING, S. Wundergeschichten (1965) 45-50.

SCHREINER, J. Gestalt und Anspruch des Neuen Testaments (1969) 180f.

8:18 STONEHOUSE, N. B. The Witness of Matthew and Mark to Christ (1944) 138, 139, 140. BORNKAMM-BARTH-HELD, Ueberlieferung und Auslegung im Matthäus-Evangelium (1961) 190f., 194f., 236, 253.

8:19ff SCHWEIZER, E. Erniedrigung und Erhöhung bei Jesus und seinen Nachfolgern (1962) §§ 1g, 11b. SCHüRMANN, H., "Beobachtungen zum Menschensohn-Titel in der Redenquelle" in: R. Pesch/R. Schnackenburg (eds.) Jesus und der Menschensohn (Freiburg 1975) 132f. WILLIAMS, J. A., A Conceptual History of Deuteronomism in the Old Testament, Judaism, and the New Testament (Louisville 1976) 309.

8:19-22 STONEHOUSE, N. B. The Witness of Matthew and Mark to Christ (1944) 139, 140. TAYLOR, V. The Formation of the Gospel Tradition (1949) 72f. SCHULZ, A. Nachfolge und Nachnahmen (1962) 105ff. BULTMANN, R. The History of the Synoptic Tradition (1963) 28f. HAHN, F. Christologische Hoheitstitel (1963) 83f. BORNKAMM-BARTH-HELD. Ueberlieferung und Auslegung im Matthäus-Evangelium (1961) 50f., 99, 158, 190ff., 194, 234. LüHRMANN, D. Die Redaktion der Logienquelle (1969) 58. OTOMO, Y. Nachfolge Jesu und Anfänge der Kirche im Neuen Testament (1970) 42-44. ERNST, J., Anfänge der Christologie (Stuttgart 1972) 130-33. HOFFMANN, P. Studien zur Theologie der Logienquelle (1972) 5, 72f., 90f., 149f., 182-87. SCHULZ, S. Q Die Spruchquelle der Evangelisten (1972) 434-42. GOULDER, M. D., Midrash and Lection in Matthew (London 1974) 322f. BORSCH, F. M., "Jesus the Wandering Preacher?" in: M. Hooker/G. Hickling (eds.) What about the New Testament. In honour of Christopher Evans (London 1975) 50-52. POLAG, A., Die Christologie der Logienquelle (Neukirchen-Vluyn 1977) 84f.

8:19f HAHN, F. Christologische Hoheitstitel (1963) 44, 45f.

8:19-20 SANFORD, J. A., The Kingdom Within (New York 1970) 88f.

8:19 LURIA, S., "Zur Quelle von Mt 8:19" ZNW 25 (1926) 282. BLAIR, E. P. Jesus in the Gospel of Matthew (1960) 100. HUMMEL, R. Die Auseinandersetzung zwischen Kirche und Judentum im Matthäusevangelium (1963) 27. METZGER, B. M., The Early Versions of the New Testament (Oxford 1977) 243.

8:20 STONEHOUSE, N. B. The Witness of Matthew and Mark to Christ (1944) 251. MANSON, W. Jesus the Messiah (1948) 116-18. BLAIR, E. P. Jesus in the Gospel of Matthew (1960) 77.

BORNKAMM-BARTH-HELD, Ueberlieferung und Auslegung im Matthäus-Evangelium (1961) 254f. SCHWEIZER, E. Erniedrigung und Erhöhung bei Jesus und seinen Nachfolgern (1962) § 31. HAHN, F. Christologische Hoheitstitel (1963) 25, 44. STROBEL, A. "Textgeschichtliches zum Thomas-Logion 86 (Mt 8, 20/Luk 9, 58)," VigChr 17 (4, '63) 211-24. GäRTNER, B. The Temple and the Community in Qumran and the New Testament (1965) 125. BRAUN, H. Qumran und NT II (1966) 98. McNAMARA, M. The New Testament and the Palestinian Targum to the Pentateuch (1966) 220,n.92. JEREMIAS, J. Neutestamentliche Theologie I (1971) 25, 33, 35, 248, 250, 252, 269. HAMERTON-KELLY, R. G., Pre-Existence, Wisdom, and the Son of Man (London 1973) 29, 35, 43, 95, 211. STANTON, G. N., Jesus of Nazareth in New Testament Preaching (Cambridge 1974) 132f, 156, 158f. KINGSBURY, J. D., Matthew: Structure, Christology, Kingdom (Philadelphia 1975) 113-15. DUNN, J. D. G., Unity and Diversity in the New Testament (London 1977) 38-40. GRUNDMANN, W., 'Weisheit im Horizont des Reiches Gottes" in: R. Schnackenburg et al. (eds.) Die Kirche des Anfangs. Festschrift für Heinz Schürmann (Leipzig 1977) 181. POLAG, A., Die Christologie der Logienquelle (Neukirchen-Vluyn 1977) 74. THEISSEN, G., Soziologie der Jesusbewegung (München 1977) 16. KELBER, W. H., "Mark and Oral Tradition" in: N. R. Peterson (ed.) Perspectives on Mark's Gospel (Missoula 1980) 25-27.

8:21f   HENGEL, M. Nachfolge und Charisma (1968) 2-18. HASEL, G. F. BiblOr (3-4, '69) 262-64. SASS, G. Ungereimtes bei Matthäus (1968) 14-15. HARRISVILLE, R. A. "Jesus and the Family," Interpretation 23 (1969) 425-38. SCHEDL, C. Targum, Evangelium, Synagoge (1969) 300f. OTOMO, Y. Nachfolge Jesu und Anfänge der Kirche im Neuen Testament (1970) 25-28.

8:21-22   HENGEL, M., Nachfolge und Charisma, Beiheft ZNW 34 (1968) 7-116. DAUTZENBERG, G. ThRv 66 (1, '70) 19-20. GRäSSER, E. ThLZ 95 (4, '70) 275-77.

8:21   BARRETT, C. K. The New Testament Background: Selected Documents (1956) 222. HAHN, F. Christologische Hoheitstitel (1963) 86. LANGE, J., Das Erscheinen des Auferstandenen im Evangelium nach Matthäus (Würzburg 1973) 46f, 219-21, 372. POLAG, A., Die Christologie der Logienquelle (Neukirchen-Vluyn 1977) 85.

8:22   PERLES, F., "Zwei Übersetzungsfehler im Text der Evangelien" ZNW 19 (1919-1920) 96. PERLES, F., "Noch einmal Mt 8:22" ZNW 25 (1926) 286. HENNECKE, E. & SCHNEEMELCHER, W. Neutestamentliche Apokryphen (1964) II 221. JüNGEL, E. Paulus und Jesus (1966) 182. BLACK, M. An Aramaic Approach to the Gospels and Acts (1967) 207f. KLEMM, H. G. "Das Wort von der Selbstbestattung der Toten. Beobachtungen zur Auslegungsgeschichte von Mt. viii. 22 Par.," NTS 16(1, '69) 60-75. SANFORD, J. A., The Kingdom Within (New York 1970) 87f. JEREMIAS, J. Neutestamentliche Theologie I (1971) 32, 43, 133, 156, 175. THEISSEN, G., Soziologie der Jesusbewegung (München 1977) 17. KELBER, W. H., "Mark and Oral Tradition" in: N. R. Peterson (ed.) Perspectives on Mark's Gospel (Missoula 1980) 25-27. McDONALD, J. I. H., Kerygma and Didache (Cambridge 1980) 81.

8:23ff STRECKER, G. Der Weg der Gerechtigkeit (1962) 1075, 176, 2304.

8:23-28 STONEHOUSE, N. B. The Witness of Matthew and Mark to Christ (1944) 138.

8:23-27 WILKENS, J. Einführung in das Evangelium nach Matthäus I (1934) 127-28. GOLDAMMER, K. "Navis Ecclesiae," ZNW 40 (1941) 76ff. LOEWENICH, W. von, Luther als Ausleger der Synoptiker (1954) 111f. BARTSCH, H. W. "Predigt über Matthäus 8, 23-27," Pastoralblätter 96 (1956) 166-69. EICHHOLZ, G. (ed.) Herr, tue meine Lippen auf (1957) 63-67. "Zu Suchen Seine Herrlichkeit" in: Predigtgedanken aus Vergangenheit und Gegenwart Bd. 2 (1960) 109-37. BORNKAMM, G. "Die Sturmstillung im Matthäus-evangelium," in: Wort und Dienst 1 (1948) 49-54· also in BORNKAMM-BARTH-HELD, Ueberlieferung und Auslegung im Matthäus-Evangelium (1961) 48-53. DOERNE, M. Er kommt auch noch heute (1961) 40-43. GNILKA, J. Die Verstockung Israels (1961) 34f. *DUPLACY, J. "Et il y eut un grand calme. . . . La tempête apaisée (Matthieu 8, 23-27)," BVieC 74 ('67) 15-28. MESSERSCHMIDT, L. "Jesu stiller stormen pa søen. Myte eller frelsehistorisk virkelighed?" (Jesus Stills the Storm on the Lake. Myth or a Reality of Salvation-History?), Catholica 24 (1-2), '67) 45-54. KAMPHAUS, F. Von der Exegese zur Predigt (1968) 129-31, 189-91. SCHEDL, C. Talmud, Evangelium, Synagoge (1969) 301-303. ITTEL, G. W. Jesus und die Jünger (1970) 43-45. OTOMO, Y. Nachfolge Jesu und Anfänge der Kirche im Neuen Testament (1970) 128f. SCHRAMM, T. Der Markus-Stoff bei Lukas (1971) 124f. BUTENUTH, A. & ALDRUP, P. "Vierter Sonntag nach Epiphanias: Matthäus 8, 23-27," in: Predigtstudien (1972/73) LANGE, E. (ed.) 99-103. STECK, K. G. GPM 27/1 (1972/73)

86-94. KRATZ, R., Auferweckung als Befreiung (Stuttgart 1973) 50-56. COPE, O. L., Matthew: A Scribe Trained for the Kingdom of Heaven (Washington D. C. 1976) 96-98. KLAUCK, H. J., Allegorie und Allegorese in Synoptischen Gleichnistexten (Münster 1978) 340-48. RIST, J. M., On the Independence of Matthew and Mark (Cambridge 1978) 56f.

8:23.24.25 BORNKAMM-BARTH-HELD, Ueberlieferung und Auslegung im Matthäus-Evangelium (1961) 50f., 190f., 195, 208, 219, 254f.

8:24 *MAGASS, W., " 'Er aber schlief' (Mt 8, 24). Ein Versuch über die Kleinigkeit (meloč)" LiBi 29-30 (1973) 55-59. METZGER, B. M., The Early Versions of the New Testament (Oxford 1977) 178.

8:25f. BORNKAMM-BARTH-HELD, Ueberlieferung und Auslegung im Matthäus-Evangelium (1961) 111, 192, 194f., 219, 223, 253f., 256, 280ff.

8:25 BLAIR, E. P. Jesus in the Gospel of Matthew (1960) 100. STRECKER, G. Der Weg der Gerechtigkeit (1962) 673121 13, 2131. HAHN, F. Christologische Hoheitstitel (1963) 86.

8:26 STRECKER, G. Der Weg der Gerechtigkeit (1962) 2337, 234. BRAUN, H. Qumran und NT II (1966) 92, 107, 269.

8:27 BLAIR, E. P. Jesus in the Gospel of Matthew (1960) 65. BORNKAMM-BARTH-HELD, Ueberlieferung und Auslegung im Matthäus-Evangelium (1961) 100, 189. STRECKER, G. Der Weg der Gerchtigkeit (1962) 1938. HAHN, F. Christologische Hoheitstitel (1963) 86.

8:28-34 WILKENS, J. Einführung in das Evangelium nach Matthäus I (1934) 128-30. STONEHOUSE, N. B. The Witness of Matthew and Mark to Christ (1944) 138. McNEILE, A. H. The Gospel According to St Matthew (1955) 114f. TRILLING, W. Das wahre Israel (1959) 110f. BORNKAMM-BARTH-HELD, Ueberlieferung und Auslegung im Matthäus-Evangelium (1961) 157, 162ff., 168, 200, 219, 221, 232f., 235, 256. STRECKER, G. Der Weg der Gerechtigkeit (1962) 392, 195. LAMARCHE, P. "Le Possédé de Gérasa (Mt 8, 28-34; Mc 5, 1-20; Lc 8, 26-39)," NRTh 90 (6, '68) 581-97. SCHEDL, C. Talmud, Evangelium, Synagoge (1961) 303-306. VENCOVSKY, J. "Der gadarenische Exorzismus. Mt 8, 28-34 und Parallelen," CommViat 14 (1, '71) 13-29. PESCH, R., Der Besessene von Gerasa (Stuttgart 1972). GOULDER, M. D., Midrash and Lection in Matthew (London 1974) 45, 316f, 324. HULL, J. M., Hellenistic Magic and the Synoptic Tradition (London 1974) 128, 131f, 138. BARTLETT, D. L., Fact and Faith (Valley Forge 1975) 52. TRITES, A. A., The New

Testament Concept of Witness (Cambridge 1977) 178. SWIDLER, L., Biblical Affirmations of Woman (Philadelphia 1979) 228.

8:28-32 METZGER, B. M. "Explicit references in the works of Origen to variant readings in N. T. manuscripts," in: Historical and Literary Studies (1968) 91f.

8:28 FARRER, A. St Matthew and St Mark (1954) 124. KNOX, W. L. The Sources of the Synoptic Gospels II (1957) 124. WALKER, N. "The Alleged Matthaean Errata," NTS 9 (1962-63) 394. BAARDA, Tj. "Gadarenes, Gerasenes, Gergesenes and the 'Diatessaron' Traditions," in: Neotestamentica et Semitica (1969) Ellis, E. E. & Wilcox, M. (eds.) 181-97.

8:29-32 BUTLER, B. C. The Originality of St Matthew (1951) 124ff.

8:29 VOLZ, P. Die Eschatologie der jüdischen Gemeinde (1934) 174. BLAIR, E. P. Jesus in the Gospel of Matthew (1960) 61. BORNKAMM-BARTH-HELD, Ueberlieferung und Auslegung im Matthäus-Evangelium (1961) 198, 232, 256f. DE KRUIJF, T., Der Sohn Des Lebendigen Gottes (Rome 1962) 41, 58f, 62, 69, 97, 144. STRECKER, G. Der Weg der Gerechtigkeit (1962) 67₃, 88, 89₁, 121₉, 123₁, 126, 176. HUMMEL, R. Die Auseinandersetzung zwischen Kirche und Judentum im Matthäusevangelium (1963) 1, 15. BRAUN, H. Qumran und NT II (1966) 97, 271. KINGSBURY, J. D., Matthew: Structure, Christology, Kingdom (Philadelphia 1975) 53-55. ARENS, E., The HΛΘON - Sayings in the Synoptic Tradition (Fribourg 1976) 212-15, 216-21.

9-10 KäSEMANN, E. Exegetische Versuche und Besinnungen (1964) I 197.

9 FEINE, D. P. & BEHM, D. J. Einleitung in das Neue Testament (1950) 49f.

9:1-17 EWALD,H. Die drei ersten Evangelien (1850) 196ff. PARKER, P. The Gospel Before Mark (1953) 178-79. IWAND, H. J. Predigt-Meditationen (1964) 463-69.

9:1-8 WILKENS, J. Einführung in das Evangelium nach Matthäus I (1934) 130-32. KäSEMANN, E. GPM 4 (1949/50) 266ff. IWAND, GPM 9 (1954/55) 235ff. GREEVEN, H. "Die Heilung des Gelähmten nach Matthäus," in: Wort und Dienst 4

(1955) 65-78. *DUPONT, J. "Le paralytique de Capharnaüm (dix-huitième dimanche après la Pentecôte)," LumVieSupp 35 ('57) 12-19. SCHLINK, E. in: Herr, tue meine Lippen auf (1957) Eichholz, G. (ed.) 293-98. BOSCH, D. Die Heidenmission in der Zukunftsschau Jesu (1959) 60-64. BLAIR, E. P. Jesus in the Gospel of Matthew (1960) 78, 79. DUPONT, J. "Le paralytique pardonné (Mt 9, 1-8)," NRTh 82 (9, '60) 940-58. KIIVIT, GPM 15 (1960/61) 283ff. DOERNE, M. Er kommt auch noch heute (1961) 143-45. FULLER, R. H. Interpreting the Miracles (1963) 50ff. HUMMEL, R. Die Auseinandersetzung zwischen Kirche und Judentum im Matthäusevangelium (1963) 36-38, 53-56, 139. BECKER, U./WIBBING, S., Wundergeschichten (Gütersloh 1965) 12ff. EULER, K. F. "Das Wunder der Heilung," in: Kleine Predigt-Typologie III (1965) Schmidt, L. (ed.) 164-70. Wir wissen weder Tag noch Stunde in: Predigtgedanken aus Vergangenheit und Gegenwart Bd. 6 (1966) 80-102. KAMPHAUS, F. Von Exegese zur Predigt (1968) 124-25, 178-80. SCHEDL, C. Talmud, Evangelium, Synagoge (1969) 306-309. VARGAS-MACHUCA, A. "El paralitico perdonado, en la redaccion de Mateo (Mt 9, 1-8) EstEc 44 (168, '69) 15-43. OTTO, G. Denken - um zu glauben (1970) 82-86. THYEN, H. Studien zur Sündenvergebung (1970) 242ff. SCHRAMMA, T. Der Markus-Stoff bei Lukas (1971) 99-103. EISINGER, W. GPM 27/4 (1973) 444-51. FRANKEMöLLE, H., Jahwebund und Kirche Christi (Münster 1974) 216f, 278, 294. GOULDER, M. D., Midrash and Lection in Matthew (London 1974) 316f, 324. LEROY, H., Zur Vergebung der Sünden (Stuttgart 1974) 53-60. *NEIRYNCK, F., "Les accords mineurs et la rédaction des évangiles. L'épisode du paralytique (Mt, IX, 1-8/Lc., V, 17-26, par. Mc, II, 1-12)" EphT 50 (1974) 215-30. SAND, A., Das Gesetz und die Propheten (Regensburg 1974) 64-68. CONZELMANN, H./LINDEMANN, A., Arbeitsbuch zum Neuen Testament (Tübingen 1975) 54f. REICKE, B., "The Synoptic Reports of the Healing of the Paralytic. Matthew 9:1-8 with parallels" in: J. K. Elliott (ed.) Studies in New Testament Language and Text: In honour of George D. Kilpatrick (Leiden 1976) 319-29. RIST, J. M., On the Independence of Matthew and Mark (Cambridge 1978) 30. HEIL, J. P., "Significant Aspects of the Healing Miracles in Matthew" CBQ 41 (1979) 274-87.

9:1 STONEHOUSE, N. B. The Witness of Matthew and Mark to Christ (1944) 138, 140, 141, 160. STRECKER, G. Der Weg der Gerechtigkeit (1962) 94, 96.

9:2ff STONEHOUSE, N. B. The Witness of Matthew and Mark to

Christ (1944) 153. HENNECKE, E & SCHNEEMELCHER, W. Neutestamentliche Apokryphen (1964) I 128.

9:2-17 BORNKAMM-BARTH-HELD, Ueberlieferung und Auslegung im Matthäus-Evangelium (1961) 167, 236f., 254.

9:2-8 BORNKAMM-BARTH-HELD, Ueberlieferung und Auslegung im Matthäus-Evangelium (1961) 165ff., 200, 219, 221, 224, 227, 232f., 237, 260f. STRECKER, G. Der Weg der Gerechtigkeit (1962) 220ff. LUTHER, M. Predigten über die Christus-Botschaft (1966) 80-83.

9:2 VOLZ, P. Die Eschatologie der jüdischen Gemeinde (1934) 217. STONEHOUSE, N. B. The Witness of Matthew and Mark to Christ (1944) 141, 160. FARRER, A. St Matthew and St Mark (1954) 124. KNOX, W. L. The Sources of the Synoptic Gospels II (1957) 125. BORNKAMM-BARTH-HELD, Ueberlieferung und Auslegung im Matthäus-Evangelium (1961) 105, 165f., 218, 253, 265, 267ff. "Beichte" in: TRE 5 (1980) 434.

9:3-12 ZIMMERMANN, H. Neutestamentliche Methodenlehre (1967) 234-37.

9:3f BORNKAMM-BARTH-HELD, Ueberlieferung und Auslegung im Matthäus-Evangelium (1961) 156, 167. NICKELS, P. Targum and New Testament (1967) 18.

9:4f HUMMEL, R. Die Auseinandersetzung zwishcen Kirche und Judentum im Matthäusevangelium (1963) 128.

9:4 BLAIR, E. P. Jesus in the Gospel of Matthew (1960) 87. EPP, E. J., The Theological Tendency of Codex Bezae Cantabrigiensis in Acts (Cambridge 1966) 44f. NICKELS, P. Targum and New Testament (1967) 128.

9:5-7 FARRER, A. St Matthew and St Mark (1954) 27.

9:6 STONEHOUSE, N. B. The Witness of Matthew and Mark to Christ (1944) 143, 251. BLAIR, E. P. Jesus in the Gospel of Matthew (1960) 46, 77. BORNKAMM-BARTH-HELD, Ueberlieferung und Auslegung im Matthäus-Evangelium (1961) 166, 257, 260ff. STRECKER, G. Der Weg der Gerechtigkeit (1962) 127, 175. LANGE, J., Das Erscheinen des Auferstandenen im Evangelium nach Matthäus (Würzburg 1973) 55, 61-65, 72, 90, 94-96, 106, 122, 146f, 151, 183, 494. METZGER, B. M., The Early Versions of the New Testament (Oxford 1977) 391.

9:8 STONEHOUSE, N. B. The Witness of Matthew and Mark to Christ (1944) 106, 143. BORNKAMM-BARTH-HELD, Ueberlieferung und Auslegung im Matthäus-Evangelium (1961) 165f., 236f., 257, 260f. STRECKER, G. Der Weg der

Gerechtigkeit (1962) 176, 221. HUMMEL, R. Die Auseinandersetzung zwischen Kirche und Judentum im Matthäusevangelium (1963) 102. *SCHENK, W. " 'Den Menschen' Mt 9:8," ZNW 54 (3-4, '63) 272-75. LEAL, J. " 'Qui dedit potestatem talem hominibus' (Mt 9, 8)," VerbDom 44 (1, '66) 53-59. LEIVESTAD, R. Exit of the Apocalyptic Son of Man NTS 18 (1971-72) 258f. LANGE, J., Das Erscheinen des Auferstandenen im Evangelium nach Matthäus (Würzburg 1973) 55, 61-65, 72, 93-95, 371, 410, 472, 474.

9:8b   LEAL, J. "Valor eclesiologico y sacramental de Mt 9, 8b: 'Qui dedit potestatem talem hominibus'," Est Bi (3, '65) 245-53.

9:9-10:3   PESCH, R., "Ein Beitrag zur Lösung eines alten Problems" ZNW 59 (1968) 40-56.

9:9ff   STONEHOUSE, N. B. The Witness of Matthew and Mark to Christ (1944) 141, 142. STRECKER, G. Der Weg der Gerechtigkeit (1962) 174.

9:9-17   PIROT, J. Paraboles et Allégories Evangeliques (1949) 16-34.

9:9-13   WILKENS, J. Einführung in das Evangelium nach Matthäus I (1934) 122-27. BORNKAMM-BARTH-HELD, Ueberlieferung und Auslegung im Matthäus-Evangelium (1961) 77, 245. RöSSLER, GPM 17 (1962/63) 239ff. HUMMEL, R. Die Auseinandersetzung zwischen Kirche und Judentum im Matthäus-Evangelium (1963) 38-40, 53-56, 139. Also in: Predigtgedanken aus Vergangenheit und Gegenwart Bd. 3-4 (1963) 33-49. BüCKMANN, O. in: Herr, tue meine Lippen auf (1964) Eichholz, G. (ed.) 301ff. IWAND, H. J. Predigt-Meditationen (1964) 32-35. ZIMMERMANN, H. Neutestamentliche Methodenlehre (1967) 90-92. SCHRAGE, W. GPM 23/3 (1968/69) 248-256. SCHEDL, C. Talmud, Evangelium, Synagoge (1969) 309-311. MOLNAR, M., GPM 29 (1975) 298-303. LAMARCHE, P., "L'appel de Levi. Marc 2, 13-17" Christus 23 (1976) 107-18. *LEWIS, J. J., "The Wilderness Controversy and Peirasmos" Colloquium 7 (1974) 42-44. BOYENS, A./LöFFLER, P., in: P. Krusche et al. (eds.) Predigtstudien für das Kirchenjahr 1975 III/2. Halbband (Stuttgart 1975) 107-14. *MAGASS, W., "Die Kirche und ihre Legitimation (Mt 9, 9-13)" LiBi 41-42 (1977) 5-20. RIST, J. M., On the Independence of Matthew and Mark (Cambridge 1978) 30-32. *THEOBALD, M., "Der Primat der Synchronie der Diachronie als Grundaxiom der Literarkritik. Methodische Erwägungen an Hand von Mk 2, 13-17/Mt 9, 9-13" BZ 22 (1978) 161-86. WALKER, W. O., "Jesus and the Tax Collectors" JBL 97 (1978) 221-38.

9:9-12   RAYAN, S., The Holy Spirit: Heart of the Gospel and

Christian Hope (New York 1978) 53f.

9:9-10 SCHALIT, A., König Herodes (1969) 296.

9:9 STONEHOUSE, N. B. The Witness of Matthew and Mark to Christ (1944) 142, 160. STAEHELIN, E. Die Verkündigung des Reiches Gottes in der Kirche Jesu Christi I (1951) 55. LINDARS, B. Matthew, Levi, Lebbaeus and the Value of the Western Text NTS 4 (1957-58) 220ff. STRECKER, G. Der Weg der Gerechtigkeit (1962) 231. PESCH, R. "Levi-Matthäus (Mc 2, 14/Mt 9, 9; 10, 3). Ein Beitrag zur Lösung eines alten Problems," ZNW 59 (1968) 40-56. ERNST, J., Anfänge der Christologie (Stuttgart 1972) 128-30. SANDMEL, S., We Jews and Jesus (New York 1977) 58.

9:10-34 COPE, O. L., Matthew. A Scribe Trained for the Kingdom of Heaven (Washington D. C. 1976) 65-73.

9:10-13 BAUMBACH, G. Das Verständnis des Bösen in den synoptischen Evangelien (1963) 94ff. BRAUN, H. Qumran und NT II (1966) 288, 295. SAND, A., Das Gesetz und die Propheten (Regensburg 1974) 57-59. ARENS, E., The HΛΘON - Sayings in the Synoptic Tradition (Fribourg 1976) 28-63. MEYER, B. F., The Aims of Jesus (London 1979) 158-62, 166.

9:10 STONEHOUSE, N. B. The Witness of Matthew and Mark to Christ (1944) 142. STRECKER, G. Der Weg der Gerechtigkeit (1962) 95, 96s. METZGER, B. M., The Early Versions of the New Testament (Oxford 1977) 439.

9:11 BLAIR, E. P. Jesus in the Gospel of Matthew (1960) 100. HAHN, F. Christologische Hoheitstitel (1963) 77, 84. SUMMERS, R. The Secret Sayings of the Living Jesus (1968) 69. WESTERHOLM, S., Jesus and Scribal Authority (Lund 1978) 70f.

9:12f JüLICHER, D. A. Die Gleichnisreden Jesu (1910) 174-77. STRECKER, G. Der Weg der Gerechtigkeit (1962) 138. SASS, G. Ungereimtes bei Matthäus (1968) 16-17.

9:12 BONHöFFER, A. Epiktet und das Neue Testament (1911) 93, 303. KLAUCK, H.-J., Allegorie und Allegorese in Synoptischen Gleichnistexten (Münster 1978) 148-60.

9:13 STONEHOUSE, N. B. The Witness of Matthew and Mark to Christ (1944) 143, 200. MOORE, G. F. Judaism (1946) I 503n. MASSAUX, E. Influence de l'Evangile de saint Matthieu sur la littérature chrétienne avant saint Irénée (1950) 75-76, 139-42, 239, 354-55. KUSCHKE, ZNW 43 (1950/51) 263. SCHWEIZER, E. Gemeinde und Gemeinde-Ordnung im Neuen Testament (1959) § 4 b. BLAIR, E. P. Jesus in the Gospel of Matthew (1960) 93, 123. BORNKAMM-BARTH-

HELD, Ueberlieferung und Auslegung im Matthäus-Evangelium (1961) 34, 77f., 130, 187, 245f., 250f. STRECKER, G. Der Weg der Gerechtigkeit (1962) 25, 324, 135, 136, 147, 174, 177. HUMMEL, R. Die Auseinandersetzung zwischen Kirche und Judentum im Matthäusevangelium (1963) 97-99, 99-103, 138-40. ZUROWSKA, F., "Barmherzigkeit will ich, nicht Opfer" RBL XVI (1963) 298-306. KäSEMANN, E. Exegetische Versuch und Besinnungen (1964) II 96. GäRTNER, B. The Temple and the Community in Qumran and the New Testament (1965) 116. STROBEL, A. Erkenntnis und Bekenntnis der Sünde in neutestamentlicher Zeit (1968) 45, 61. KäSEMANN, E. New Testament Questions of Today (1969) 97. ZIESLER, J. A. The Meaning of Righteousness in Paul (1972) 140f., 144f. *HILL, D., "On the Use and Meaning of Hosea vi. 6 in Matthew's Gospel" NTS 24 (1977) 107-19. METZGER, B. M., The Early Versions of the New Testament (Oxford 1977) 250. SWIDLER, L., Biblical Affirmations of Woman (Philadelphia 1979) 285. "Barmherzigkeit" in: TRE 5 (1980) 225.

9:14-17 WILKENS, J. Einführung in das Evangelium nach Matthäus I (1934) 138-41. SCHLATTER, A. Johannes der Täufer (1956) 87ff. FERNANDEZ, J. "La cuestion de ayuno (Mt 9, 14-17; Mc 2, 18-22; Lc 5, 33-39), " CultBib 19 (184, '62) 162-69. CREMER, F. G. "Christian von Stablo als Exeget. Beobachtungen zur Auslegung von Mt 9, 14-17," RBén 77 (3-4, '67) 328-41. SCHEDL, C. Talmud, Evangelium, Synagoge (1969) 311-13. OTOMO, Y. Nachfolge Jesu und Anfänge der Kirche im Neuen Testament (1970) 179-81. SCHRAMM, T. Der Markus-Stoff bei Lukas (1971) 105-111. PATSCH, H. Abendmahl und historischer Jesus (1972) 199f. BRAUN, H. GPM 6/4 (1951/52) 212-16. RIST, J. M., On the Independence of Matthew and Mark (Cambridge 1978) 32f. WESTERHOLM, S., Jesus and Scribal Authority (Lund 1978) 96-100.

9:14f JüLICHER, D. A. Die Gleichnisreden Jesu (1910) 178-88. BISER, E. Die Gleichnisse Jesu (1965) 126f., 131ff.

9:14-15 SAND, A., Das Gesetz und die Propheten (Regensburg 1974) 133-35.

9:14 STONEHOUSE, N. B. The Witness of Matthew and Mark to Christ (1944) 153.

9:15-17 STONEHOUSE, N. B. The Witness of Matthew and Mark to Christ (1944) 143.

9:15 STRECKER, G. Der Weg der Gerechtigkeit (1962) 189. HENNECKE, E. & SCHNEEMELCHER, W. Neutestamentliche Apokryphen (1964) I 156. SCHRAGE, W.

Das Verhältnis des Thomas-Evangeliums zur Synoptischen Tradition und zu den Koptischen Evangelienübersetzung (1964) 103. CREMER, F. G. Die Fastenansage Jesu Mk 2, 20 und Parallelen (1965). SCHREIBER, J. Theologie de Vertrauens (1967) 121, 155-57. STROBEL, A. Erkenntnis und Bekenntnis der Sünde in neutestamentlicher Zeit (1968) 41. ERNST, J., Anfänge der Christologie (Stuttgart 1972) 154-58.

9:16f JüLICHER, D. A. Die Gleichnisreden Jesu (1910) 188-202. SCHRAGE, W. Das Verhältnis des Thomas-Evangeliums zur Synoptischen Tradition und zu den Koptischen Evangelienübersetzungen (1964) 113.

9:16-17 SANFORD, J. A., The Kingdom Within (New York 1970) 74f. KLAUCK, H.-J., Allegorie und Allegorese in Synoptischen Gleichnistexten (Münster 1978) 169-74.

9:16 MERCURIO, R., " 'and then they will fast'," Worship 35 (3, '61) 150-54. SUMMERS, R. The Secret Sayings of the Living Jesus (1968) 39. *STEINHAUSER, M. G., "The Patch of Unshrunk Cloth (Mt 9:16)" ET 87 (1976) 312f.

9:17 NAGEL, W. "Neuer Wein in alten Schläuchen (Mt 9, 17), " VigChr 14 (1, '60) 1-8.

9:18-13:58 RIST, J. M., On the Independence of Matthew and Mark (Cambridge 1978) 34-55.

9:18ff STRECKER, G. Der Weg der Gerechtigkeit (1962) 195. NöTSCHER, F., Altorientalischer und alttestamentlicher Auferstehungsglaube (Darmstadt 1970⁻1926) 303.

9:18-34 STONEHOUSE, N. B. The Witness of Matthew and Mark to Christ (1944) 141.

9:18-31 BORNKAMM-BARTH-HELD, Ueberlieferung und Auslegung im Matthäus-Evangelium (1961) 170, 236, 240f.

9:18-26 EWALD, H. Die drei ersten Evangelien (1850) 237ff. WILKENS, J. Einführung in das Evangelium nach Matthäus I (1934) 135-37. BRAUN, GPM 4 (1949/50) 296ff. LOEWENICH, W. von, Luther als Ausleger der Synoptiker (1954) 21f. WEBER, GPM 9 (1954/55) 254ff. DEHN, G. in: Herr, tue meine Lippen auf (1957) Eichholz, G. (ed.) 320-25. NIEBERGALL, GPM 15 (1960/61) 311ff. BORNKAMM-BARTH-HELD, Ueberlieferung und Auslegung im Matthäus-Evangelium (1961) 157, 168ff., 200, 219, 221, 223ff., 241, 272, 286. FULLER, R. H. Interpreting the Miracles (1963) 55ff. GALBIATI, E., "Gesù guarisce l'emorroissa e risuscita la figlia di Giairo (Matt. 9, 18-26)," BiOr 6 (4-5, '64) 225-30. DOERNE, M. Er kommt auch noch heute (1961) 154-56. Wir wissen weder Tag noch Stunde in: Predigtgedanken aus Vergangenheit und

Gegenwart Bd. 6 (1966) 220-34. WEBER, O. Predigtmeditationen (1967) 227-30. LOHSE, E. Das Aergernis des Kreuzes (1969) 60-65. SCHEDL, C. Talmud, Evangelium, Synagoge (1969) 313-16. SCHRAMM, T. Der Markus-Stoff bei Lukas (1971) 126f. TRITES, A. A., The New Testament Concept of Witness (Cambridge 1977) 179. RIST, J. M., On the Independence of Matthew and Mark (Cambridge 1978) 58-60. SWIDLER, L., Biblical Affirmations of Woman (Philadelphia 1979) 181, 215, 228, 237, 259.

9:18-22 GOULDER, M. D., Midrash and Lection in Matthew (London 1974) 316f, 325f.

9:18 STONEHOUSE, N. B. The Witness of Matthew and Mark to Christ (1944) 179. BORNKAMM-BARTH-HELD, Ueberlieferung und Auslegung im Matthäus-Evangelium (1961) 169f., 203, 214, 216f., 222f., 286f. HAHN, F. Christologische Hoheitstitel (1963) 86. LANGE, J., Das Erscheinen des Auferstandenen im Evangelium nach Matthäus (Würzburg 1973) 370, 372-74, 479f.

9:20ff HENNECKE, E. & SCHNEEMELCHER, W. Neutestamentliche Apokryphen (1964) I 129.

9:20-22 BORNKAMM-BARTH-HELD, Ueberlieferung und Auslegung im Matthäus-Evangelium (1961) 157, 168f., 202, 204ff., 223ff., 227, 267f., 274f., 286.

9:20 STONEHOUSE, N. B. The Witness of Matthew and Mark to Christ (1944) 141. FARRER, A. St Matthew and St Mark (1954) 124. VATTIONI, F., "Et tetigit fimbriam vestimenti eius" Augustinianum 5 (1965) 533-38. BOUSSET, W. Die Religion des Judentums im Späthellenistischer Zeitalter (1966⁻1926) 179.

9:22 KNOX, W. L. The Sources of the Synoptic Gospels II (1957) 87. BLAIR, E. P. Jesus in the Gospel of Matthew (1960) 86. BORNKAMM-BARTH-HELD, Ueberlieferung und Auslegung im Matthäus-Evangelium (1961) 169, 183, 198, 200, 205f., 218, 230, 236, 253, 256, 262, 273f. STRECKER, G. Der Weg der Gerechtigkeit (1962) 12l9, 15.

9:23-26 GOULDER, M. D., Midrash and Lection in Matthew (London 1974) 316f, 325f. WESTERHOLM, S., Jesus and Scribal Authority (Lund 1978) 68.

9:23f BORNKAMM-BARTH-HELD, Ueberlieferung und Auslegung im Matthäus-Evangelium (1961) 219, 223, 252.

9:23 STONEHOUSE, N. B. The Witness of Matthew and Mark to Christ (1944) 141. FARRER, A. St Matthew and St Mark (1954) 124.

9:24 METZGER, B. M., The Early Versions of the New Testament (Oxford 1977) 250.

9:25 STONEHOUSE, N. B. The Witness of Matthew and Mark to Christ (1944) 78.

9:26 KNOX, W. L. The Sources of the Synoptic Gospels II (1957) 47.

9:27ff PARKER, P. The Gospel Before Mark (1953) 183-84.

9:27-34 SMITH, M., Clement of Alexandria and a secret Gospel of Mark (Cambridge 1973) 140f, 145, 200, 224, 229, 376f.

9:27-33 M'NEILE, A. H. The Gospel According to St Matthew (1955) 128f.

9:27-31 WILKENS, J. Einführung in das Evangelium nach Matthäus I (1934) 137-38. HIRSCH, E. Frühgeschichte des Evangeliums (1941) 294-96. BORNKAMM-BARTH-HELD, Ueberlieferung und Auslegung im Matthäus-Evangelium (1961) 168, 170, 202, 208ff., 211ff., 219, 221ff. STRECKER, G. Der Weg der Gerechtigkeit (1962) 392, 174, 1994. BULTMANN, R. The History of the Synoptic Tradition (1963) 213f. HUMMEL, R. Die Auseinandersetzung zwischen Kirche und Judentum im Matthäusevangelium (1963) 118, 120. GIBBS, J. M. Purpose and Pattern in Matthew's use of the Title "Son of David". NTS 10 (1963-64) 446f., 453f. BURGER, C. Jesus als Davidssohn (1970) 74-77. ROLOFF, J. Das Kerygma und der irdische Jesus (1970) 131-55. FUCHS, A. Sprachliche Untersuchungen zu Matthäus und Lukas (1971) 18-37, 45-170. MERKEL, H. ThLZ 97 (3, '72) 190-92. GOULDER, M. D. Midrash and Lection in Matthew (London 1974) 37, 45, 316f, 326f.

9:27-30 SCHEDL, C. Talmud, Evangelium, Synagogue (1969) 316f.

9:27 STONEHOUSE, N. B. The Witness of Matthew and Mark to Christ (1944) 141, 142, 143. MOORE, G. F. Judaism (1946) II 329n. FARRER, A. St Matthew and St Mark (1954) 124. BLAIR, E. P. Jesus in the Gospel of Matthew (1960) 56. STRECKER, G. Der Weg der Gerechtigkeit (1962) 118. HAHN, F. Christologische Hoheitstitel (1963) 245, 263. HUMMEL, R. Die Auseinandersetzung zwischen Kirche und Judentum im Matthäusevangelium (1963) 116, 117, 120. GIBBS, J. M. Purpose and Pattern in Matthew's use of the Title "Son of David". NTS 10 (1963-64) 454f. KINGSBURY, J. D., Matthew: Structure, Christology, Kingdom (Philadelphia 1975) 99-101. KüNZI, M., Das Naherwartungslogion Markus 9, 1 par (Tübingen 1977). "Barmherzigkeit" in: TRE 5 (1980) 225.

9:28f JEREMIAS, J. Neutestamentliche Theologie I (1971) 22, 157f., 160. HAHN, F. Christologische Hoheitstitel (1963) 86.

9:28 METZGER, B. M., The Early Versions of the New Testament (Oxford 1977) 253.

9:29 BORNKAMM-BARTH-HELD, Ueberlieferung und Auslegung im Matthäus-Evangelium (1961) 170, 183, 212, 227f., 230, 236, 256, 262, 273f. HAHN, F. Christologische Hoheitstitel (1963) 402. GOPPELT, L., Theologie des Neuen Testaments I (Göttingen 1975) 199ff.

9:30 STRECKER, G. Der Weg der Gerechtigkeit (1962) 120.

9:31-34 SCHEDL, C. Talmud, Evangelium, Synagoge (1969) 317-19.

9:31 STONEHOUSE, N. B. The Witness of Matthew and Mark to Christ (1944) 141. BORNKAMM-BARTH-HELD, Ueberlieferung und Auslegung im Matthäus-Evangelium (1961) 235, 244.

9:32-34 WILKENS, J. Einführung in das Evangelium nach Matthäus I (1934) 138-39. KNOX, W. L. The Sources of the Synoptic Gospels II (1957) 47. BORNKAMM-BARTH-HELD, Ueberlieferung und Auslegung im Matthäus-Evangelium (1961) 219, 234ff. HUMMEL, R. Die Auseinandersetzung zwischen Kirche und Judentum im Matthäusevangelium (1963) 155. GOULDER, M. D., Midrash and Lection in Matthew (London 1974) 316f, 327, 336, 345, 381.

9:32f STRECKER, G. Der Weg der Gerechtigkeit (1962) 96, 101, 118, 195. HUMMEL, R. Die Auseinandersetzung zwischen Kirche und Judentum im Matthäusevangelium (1963) 118, 124.

9:32 FARRER, A. St Matthew and St Mark (1954) 55, 124. KNOX, W. L. The Sources of the Synoptic Gospels II (1957) 63, 125.

9:33-41 SCHRAMM, T. Der Markus-Stoff bei Lukas (1971) 140f.

9:33-34 BLAIR, E. P. Jesus in the Gospel of Matthew (1960) 99. STRECKER, G. Der Weg der Gerechtigkeit (1962) 101, 109, 118.

9:33 BLAIR, E. P. Jesus in the Gospel of Matthew (1960) 101. STRECKER, G. Der Weg der Gerechtigkeit (1962) 673, 1761. HUMMEL, R. Die Auseinandersetzung zwischen Kirche und Judentum im Matthäusevangelium (1963) 144.

9:34 STONEHOUSE, N. B. The Witness of Matthew and Mark to Christ (1944) 134, 153. PARKER, P. The Gospel Before Mark (1953) 72-73. STRECKER, G. Der Weg der Gerechtigkeit (1962) 1013, 1762. METZGER, B. M., The Early Versions of the New Testament (Oxford 1977) 134.

9:35-16:12 STONEHOUSE, N. B. The Witness of Matthew and Mark to

Christ (1944) 143ff., 146, 153.

9:35-13:53 RIDDERBOS, H. Matthew's Witness to Jesus Christ (1958) 40-48.

9:35-11:1 *GRASSI, J. A., "The Last Testament-Succession Literary Background of Matthew 9:35-11:1 and Its Significance" BThB 7 (1977) 172-76. *BROWN, S., "The Mission to Israel in Matthew's Central Section (Mt 9:35-11:1)" ZNW 69 (1978) 73-90.

9:35-10:42 HIRSCH, E. Frühgeschichte des Evangeliums (1941) 48-50. FARRER, A. St Matthew and St Mark (1954) 195.

9:35-10:18 BUTLER, B. C. The Originality of St Matthew (1951) 102ff.

9:35-10:16 STRECKER, G. Der Weg der Gerechtigkeit (1962) 194ff.

9:35-10:8 *HAUG, M., "Mission: Was ist das? Wie geschieht das? Eine Befragung von Matthäus 9, 35-10, 8" Theologische Beiträge 6 (1975) 185-191.

9:35-10:5 STONEHOUSE, N. B. The Witness of Matthew and Mark to Christ (1944) 147. FARRER, A. St Matthew and St Mark (1954) 181. VARGA, S. J. GPM 13/3 (1958-59) 214-18. SEITZ, GPM 19 (1964/65) 305ff. SCHMITZ, E. D. in : Hören und Fragen (1967) Eichholz, G. & Falkenroth, A., (eds.) 436ff. HAAR, J. GPM 25 (1971) 352-58. GOULDER, M. D., Midrash and Lection in Matthew (London 1974) 327f. HASSELMANN, N./HIRSCHLER, H., Predigtstudien V/2. Halbband (Stuttgart 1977) 169-75.

9:35-10:1 STRECKER, G. Der Weg der Gerechtigkeit (1962) 175.

9:35ff BONHOEFFER, D. Nachfolge (1950) 133ff.

9:35-38 WILKENS, J. Einführung in das Evangelium nach Matthäus I (1934) 145-46. IWAND, H. J. in: Herr, tue meine Lippen auf (1957) Eichholz, G. (ed.) 238-41. IWAND, H. J. Predigt-Meditationen (1964) 90-94. HEPHATA in: Predigtgedanken aus Vergangenheit und Gegenwart Bd. 5 (1966) 149-66. LANGE, E. (ed.) Predigtstudien für das Kirchenjahr 1970/71 (1970/71) 182-86.

9:35-37 FREYNE, S. The Twelve: Disciples and Apostels (1968) 74ff.

9:35-36 PETZKE, G. Die Traditionen über Apollonius von Tyana und das Neue Testament (1970) 91, 143, 170-71.

9:35 STONEHOUSE, N. B. The Witness of Matthew and Mark to Christ (1944) 145, 153, 160, 227. MASSAUX, E. Influence de l'Evangile de saint Matthieu sur la littérature chrétienne avant saint Irénée (1950) 66-69. FARRER, A. St Matthew and St Mark (1954) 126. KNOX, W. L. The Sources of the Synoptic Gospels II (1957) 56. BORNKAMM-BARTH-HELD,

Ueberlieferung und Auslegung im Matthäus-Evangelium (1961) 49, 161, 234, 237, 247, 258. STRECKER, G. Der Weg der Gerechtigkeit (1962) 95, 12117, 128f., 175. HAHN, F. Das Verständnis der Mission im Neuen Testament (1965) 104, 105, 106. MARXSEN, W. Mark the Evangelist (1969) 123f., 138, 142, 145. SANFORD, J. A., The Kingdom Within (New York 1970) 56. KüMMEL, W. G. Einleitung in das Neue Testament (1973) 78f. FRANKEMöLLE, H., Jahwebund und Kirche Christi (Münster 1974) 100, 102, 111, 203, 225, 253, 266f., 342, 378, 380. GOULDER, M. D., Midrash and Lection in Matthew (London 1974) 37, 41, 90, 345f. KINGSBURY, J. D., Matthew: Structure, Christology, Kingdom (Philadelphia 1975) 20-25, 128-30, 152-54, 163-65. EGGER, W., Frohbotschaft und Lehre (Frankfurt 1976) 34f, 77, 154. SWIDLER, L., Biblical Affirmations of Woman (Philadelphia 1979) 236.

9:36ff STONEHOUSE, N. B. The Witness of Matthew and Mark to Christ (1944) 147. HAHN, F. Das Verständnis der Mission im Neuen Testament (1965) 102.

9:36 STONEHOUSE, N. B. The Witness of Matthew and Mark to Christ (1944) 220. BLAIR, E. P. Jesus in the Gospel of Matthew (1960) 79. STRECKER, G. Der Weg der Gerechtigkeit (1962) 1083. HUMMEL, R. Die Auseinandersetzung zwischen Kirche und Judentum im Matthäusevangelium (1963) 139. GOULDER, M. D., Midrash and Lection in Matthew (London 1974) 100, 327, 344, 392. METZGER, B. M., The Early Versions of the New Testament (Oxford 1977) 248. "Barmherzigkeit" in: TRE 5 (1980) 227.

9:37-10:42 HOFFMANN, P. Studien zur Theologie der Logienquelle (1972) 254-61.

9:37-10:40 POLAG, A., Die Christologie der Logienquelle (Neukirchen-Vluyn 1977) 67-72.

9:37-10:16 LüHRMANN, D. Die Redaktion der Logienquelle (1969) 59f. "Apostel" in: TRE 3 (1978) 435.

9:37ff KNOX, W. L. The Sources of the Synoptic Gospels II (1957) 48. STRECKER, G. Der Weg der Gerechtigkeit (1962) 158. HAHN, F. Christologische Hoheitstitel (1963) 88.

9:37f KNOX, W. L. The Sources of the Synoptic Gospels II (1957) 51. SCHRAGE, W. Das Verhältnis des Thomas-Evangeliums zur Synoptischen Tradition und zu den Koptischen Evangelienübersetzungen (1964) 153. HAHN, F. Das Verständnis der Mission im Neuen Testament (1965) 32f., 33f. OTOMO, Y. Nachfolge Jesu und Anfänge der Kirche im Neuen Testament (1970) 68-70. HOFFMANN, P. Studien zur Theologie der Logienquelle (1972) 256, 263, 287f., 289-93, 301,

304f., 313. SCHULZ, S. Q Die Spruchquelle der Evangelisten (1972) 404-19.

9:37-38 PETERS, G. W., A Biblical Theology of Missions (Chicago 1972) 223, 279, 289, 329. TALBERT, C. H., Literary Patterns, Theological Themes, and the Genre of Luke-Acts (Missoula 1974) 20. EDWARDS, R. A., A Theology of Q (Philadelphia 1976) 101-104. POLAG, A., Die Christologie der Logienquelle (Neukirchen-Vluyn 1977) 71.

9:37 STONEHOUSE, N. B. The Witness of Matthew and Mark to Christ (1944) 176. KNOX, W. L. The Sources of the Synoptic Gospels II (1957) 56. LEGRAND, L. "The Harvest is Plentiful (Mt 9:37)," Scripture 17 (37, '65) 1-9.

10-11 ARVEDSON, T. Das Mysterium Christi (1937) 129f.

10 SCHOTT, E., "Die Aussendungsrede" ZNW 7 (1906) 140-150. SCHLATTER, A. Die Theologie des Neuen Testaments (1909) I 141-47. BONHOEFFER, D. Nachfolge (1950) 135ff. FEINE, D. P. & BEHM, D. J. Einleitung in das Neue Testament (1950) 33f. STREETER, B. H. The Four Gospels (1951) 261f. FARRER, A. St Matthew and St Mark (1954) 49, 50. NEPPER-CHRISTENSEN, P. Das Matthäusevangelium. Ein Judenchristliches Evangelium? (1958) 20, 180, 190. BORNKAMM-BARTH-HELD, Ueberlieferung und Auslegung im Matthäus-Evangelium (1961) 15f., 93f., 237ff. STRECKER, G. Der Weg der Gerechtigkeit (1962) 12. GEORGI, D. Die Gegner des Paulus im 2. Korinther-Brief (1964) 206ff. KäSEMANN, E. Exegetische Versuche und Besinnungen (1964) II 115. HAHN, F. Das Verständnis der Mission im Neuen Testament (1965) 10, 108, 109, 111. GAECHTER, P. Die literarische Kunst im Matthäus-Evangelium (1968) 40-43. KäSEMANN, E. New Testament Questions of Today (1969) 105, 120. BEARE, F. W. "The Mission of the Disciples and the Mission Charge: Matthew 10 and Parallels," JBL 89 (1, '70) 1-13. KüNZI, M., Das Naherwartungslogion Matthäus 10, 23 (1970) 58, 73, 125ff., 129, 131ff., 135, 137, 139ff., 177. SCHILLE, G. Das vorsynoptische Judenchristentum (1970) 85ff. RADERMAKERS, J. "La Mission, engagement radical. Une lecture de Mt 10," NRTh 93 (10, '71) 1072-85. SELBY, D. J.,

Introduction to the New Testament (New York 1971) 112f.,
115, 134, 130f. HIERS, R. H., The Historical Jesus and the
Kingdom of God (Gainesville 1973) 61f. MUSSNER, F., "Gab
es eine 'galiläische Krisez'?" in: P. Hoffmann (ed.) Orientierung
an Jesus: Für Josef Schmid (Freiburg 1973) 244-48. ELLIS, P.
F., Matthew: His Mind and His Message (Collegeville 1974) 46-
53. GOULDER, M. D., Midrash and Lection in Matthew
(London 1974) 314, 318, 338ff. CONZELMANN,
H./LINDEMANN, A., Arbeitsbuch zum Neuen Testament
(Tübingen 1975) 64. "Amt" in: TRE 2 (1978) 515. "Bergpredigt"
in: TRE 5 (1980) 612.

10:1-5:23 BORSCH, F. H., "Jesus the Wandering Preacher?" in: M.
Hooker/C. Hickling (eds.) What about the New Testament?:
Essays in Honour of Christopher Evans (London 1975) 48f.

10:1-42 BARRETT, C. K. The Holy Spirit and the Gospel Tradition
(1947) 127-30.

10:1-18 BAUMBACH, G. Das Verständnis des Bösen in den
synoptischen Evangelien (1963) 102ff.

10:1-16 PARKER, P. The Gospel Before Mark (1953) 81-82.
DUNGAN, D. L. The Sayings of Jesus in the Churches of Paul
(1971) 51-63, 69-70. McDONALD, J. I. H., Kerygma and
Didache (Cambridge 1980) 118.

10:1-15 ITTEL, G. W. Jesus und die Jünger (1970) 56-59.

10:1-14 KERTELGE, K., "Offene Fragen zum Thema 'Geistliches Amt
und das neutestamentliche Verständnis von der repraesentatio
Christi' " in: R. Schnackenburg et al. (eds.) Die Kirche des
Anfangs: Für Heinz Schürmann (Freiburg 1978) 588-90.

10:1-7:11 EDWARDS, R. A., A Theology of Q (Philadelphia 1976) 99f.

10:1-5ff FREYNE, S. The Twelve: Disciples and Apostles (1968) 99ff.

10:1-4 HAHN, F. Das Verständnis der Mission im Neuen Testament
(1965) 33, 34. ITTEL, G. W. Jesus und die Jünger (1970) 28-41.
TRILLING, W., "Amt und Amtsverständnis bei Matthäus" in:
A. Descamps/ A. de Halleux (eds.) Mélanges Bibliques en
hommage au R. P. Béda Rigaux (Gembloux 1970) 40f.
SCHRAMM, T. Der Markus-Stoff bei Lukas (1971) 113f.
GOULDER, M. D., Midrash and Lection in Matthew
(London 1974) 338f. STAGG, E. and F., Woman in the World
of Jesus (Philadelphia 1978) 123-25.

10:1 STONEHOUSE, N. B. The Witness of Matthew and Mark to
Christ (1944) 145, 176. FARRER, A. St Matthew and St Mark
(1954) 195. TILLICH, P. Das Neue Sein (1959) 41-48. BLAIR,
E. P. Jesus in the Gospel of Matthew (1960) 46. BORN-
KAMM-BARTH-HELD, Ueberlieferung und Auslegung im

Matthäus-Evangelium (1961) 161, 237f., 240f., 247, 258.
HAHN, F. Das Verständnis der Mission im Neuen Testament
(1965) 106. METZGER, B. M., The Early Versions of the New
Testament (Oxford 1977) 178.

10:2ff STAEHELIN, E. Die Verkündigung des Reiches Gottes in der
Kirche Jesu Christi I (1951) 55. FARRER, A. St Matthew and
St Mark (1954) 51, 183. BORNKAMM, G. Jesus von Nazareth
(1956) 138ff.

10:2-16 "Apostel" in: TRE 3 (1978) 434.

10:2-4 EWALD, H. Die drei ersten Evangelien (1850) 205ff. OTOMO,
Y. Nachfolge Jesu und Anfänge der Kirche im Neuen
Testament (1970) 62-68. RIST, J. M., On the Independence of
Matthew and Mark (Cambridge 1978) 47.

10:2 STONEHOUSE, N. B. The Witness of Matthew and Mark to
Christ (1944) 176. BLAIR, E. P. Jesus in the Gospel of
Matthew (1960) 55. STRECKER, G. Der Weg der
Gerechtigkeit (1962) 21, 198, 204l, 206⁴. HUMMEL, R. Die
Auseinandersetzung zwischen Kirche und Judentum im
Matthäusevangelium (1963) 112f. "Amt" in: TRE 2 (1978) 516.
"Apostel" in: TRE 3 (1978) 430, 442. FITZMYER, J. A.,
"Aramaic Kepha' and Peter's Name in the New Testament" in:
E. Best/R. McL. Wilson (eds.) Text and Interpretation: For
Matthew Black (Cambridge 1979) 122-24.

10:3 LINDARS, B. "Matthew, Levi, Lebbaeus and the Value of the
Western Text" NTS 4 (1957-58) 220ff. PESCH, R. "Levi-
Matthäus (Mc 2, 14/Mt 9, 9; 10,3). Ein Beitrag zur Lösung
eines alten Problems," ZNW 59 (1968) 40-56.

10:4 CULLMANN, O. "Le douzième apôtre," RHPR 42 (2-3, '62)
133-40. HAHN, F. Christologische Hoheitstitel (1963) 62, 164.
LOHSE, E. and others (eds.) Der Ruf Jesu und die Antwort der
Gemeinde (1970) 204-12. METZGER, B. M., The Early
Versions of the New Testament (Oxford 1977) 172.

10:5-11:1 LUND, N. W. Chiasmus in the New Testament (1942) 263f.

10:5ff STAEHELIN, E. Die Verkündigung des Reiches Gottes in der
Kirche Jesu Christi I (1951) 57. STRECKER, G. Der Weg der
Gerechtigkeit (1962) 158. NEPPER-CHRISTENSEN, P. Das
Matthäusevangelium. Ein Judenchristliches Evangelium?
(1958) 17, 90, 180. KüNZI, M. Das Naherwartungslogion
Matthäus 10, 23 (1970) 5, 7, 140. THEISSEN, G., Soziologie
der Jesusbewegung (München 1977) 17. RIST, J. M., On the
Independence of Matthew and Mark (Cambridge 1978) 47-49.

10:5-42 STONEHOUSE, N. B. The Witness of Matthew and Mark to
Christ (1944) 130. SMITH, M., Tannaitic Parallels to the

Gospels (Philadelphia 1968) 4 D+.

10:5-23 FLEW, R. N. Jesus and His Church (1956) 126n.

10:5-6. HASLER, V. "Judenmission und Judenschuld," ThZ 24 (1968)
15.24. 173-90.

10:5b-42 GAECHTER, P. Die literarische Kunst im Matthäus-
Evangelium (1968) 41-42, 75-76.

10:5b-23 WILKENS, J. Einführung in das Evangelium nach Matthäus I
(1934) 147-52.

10:5-16 STRECKER, G. Der Weg der Gerechtigkeit (1962) 194f., 212ɜ.
GEORGI, D. Die Gegner des Paulus im 2. Korinther-Brief
(1964) 206f. HAHN, F. Das Verständnis der Mission im Neuen
Testament (1965) 32, 33-36. OTOMO, Y. Nachfolge Jesu und
Anfänge der Kirche im Neuen Testament (1970) 68-70.
"Apostel" in: TRE 3 (1978) 433. "Aramäisch" in: TRE 3 (1978)
604.

10:5-10 *WILKINSON, J., "The Mission Charge to the Twelve and
Modern Medical Missions" SJTh 27 (1974) 313-28.

10:5-8 GOULDER, M. D., Midrash and Lection in Matthew
(London 1974) 339-45.

10:5f STONEHOUSE, N. B. The Witness of Matthew and Mark to
Christ (1944) 146. KNOX, W. L. The Sources of the Synoptic
Gospels II (1957) 34, 49-51. TRILLING, W. Das wahre Israel
(1959) 78ff. BORNKAMM-BARTH-HELD, Ueberlieferung
und Auslegung im Matthäus-Evangelium (1961) 16, 94, 240.
STRECKER, G., Der Weg der Gerechtigkeit (1962) 41, 195,
239ɥ. HUMMEL, R. Die Auseinandersetzung zwischen Kirche
und Judentum im Matthäusevangelium (1963) 137f., 141.
SCHMITHALS, W. Paulus und Jakobus (1963) 93f.
KäSEMANN, E. Exegetische Versuche und Besinnungen
(1964) II 87f. WALKER, R. Die Heilsgeschichte im ersten
Evangelium (1967) 128. WREGE, H.-T. Die
UEberlieferungsgeschichte der Bergpredigt (1968) 173ff.
KäSEMANN, E. New Testament Questions of Today (1969)
87. KASTING, H. Die Anfänge der Urchristlichen Mission
(1969)37, 110-14. TAGAWA, K. People and Community in the
Gospel of Matthew NTS 16 (1969-70) 155f. KüNZI, M. Das
Naherwartungslogion Matthäus 10, 23 (1970) 29, 36, 69, 92,
118f., 121, 123f., 141, 145, 158, 160, 162. HOOKER, M. D.
"Uncomfortable Words: X. The Prohibition of Foreign
Missions (Mt 10:5-6)," ET 82 (12, '71) 361-65. JEREMIAS, J.
Neutestamentliche Theologie I (1971) 16, 26, 134, 225, 235, 291.
PATSCH, H. Abendmahl und historisher Jesus (1972) 109f.
KüMMEL, W. G. Einleitung in das Neue Testament (1973) 86f.

10:5-6 SCHüRMANN, H., "Mt 10:5b-6 und die Vorgeschichte des synoptischen Aussendungsberichtes" in: Neutestamentliche Aufsätze: Festschrift für J. Schmidt (1963) 270-82. SHIMADA, K., The Formulary Material in First Peter: A Study According to the Method of Traditionsgeschichte: Th.D. Dessertation (Ann Arbor 1966) 215f. EHRHARDT, A., The Acts of the Apostles (Manchester 1969) 5, 15, 40f. LANGE, J., Das Erscheinen des Aufestandenen im Evangelium nach Matthäus (Würzburg 1973) 49, 73, 87, 162, 165f., 249, 251-55, 257f, 260, 291, 322f, 361, 365, 398. MUSSNER, F., "Gab es eine 'galiläische Krisez'?" in: P. Hoffmann (ed.) Orientierung and Jesus: Für Josef Schmid (Freiburg 1973) 244-48. WILSON, S. G., The Gentiles and the Gentile Mission in Luke-Acts (Cambridge 1973) 5, 9, 12, 14-16, 21, 49f. FRANKEMöLLE, H., Jahwebund und Kirche Christi (Münster 1974) 41, 105, 109, 120, 123-30, 133, 135, 137, 261. BORSCH, F. H., "Jesus the Wandering Preacher?" in: M. Hooker/C. Hickling (eds.) What about the New Testament?: Essays in Honour of Christopher Evans (London 1975) 49. *BROWN, S., "The Two-fold Representation of the Mission in Matthew's Gospel" StTh 31 (1977) 21-32. POLAG, A., Die Christologie der Logienquelle (Neukirchen-Vluyn 1977) 44f, 71. GOULDER, M. D., Midrash and Lection in Matthew (London 1974) 80, 161, 342, 348.

10:5b-6 HAHN, F. Das Verständnis der Mission im Neuen Testament (1965) 22, 32f., 44f., 54, 107. HOFFMANN, P. Studien zur Theologie der Logienquelle (1972) 258-61, 275, 293.

10:5 STONEHOUSE, N. B. The Witness of Matthew and Mark to Christ (1944) 176. NEPPER-CHRISTENSEN, P. Das Matthäusevangelium. Ein Judenchristliches Evangelium? (1958) 14, 17, 20, 22, 25, 180-84, 196. STRECKER, G. Der Weg der Gerechtigkeit (1962) 422. HAHN, F. Christologische Hoheitstitel (1963) 45. KäSEMANN, E. New Testament Questions of Today (1969) 88. KüNZI, M. Das Naherwartungslogion Matthäus 10, 23 (1970) 65, 68, 73, 92, 94, 97f., 123, 128f., 131.

10:6 STONEHOUSE, N. B. The Witness of Matthew and Mark to Christ (1944) 147. 177. 184. NEPPER, CHRISTENSEN, P. Das Matthausevangelium. Ein Judenchristliches Evangelium? (1958) 181-82, 190-92. MINEAR, P. S. Images of the Church in the New Testament (1960) 85f. STRECKER, G. Der Weg der Gerechtigkeit (1962) 107, 212. HUMMEL, R. Die Auseinandersetzung zwischen Kirche und Judentum im Matthäusevangelium (1963) 144f., 146. KüNZI, M. Das Naherwartungslogion Matthäus 10, 23 (1970) 65, 82, 93. KLIJN, A. F. J./REININK, G. J., Patristic Evidence for

Jewish-Christian Sects (Leiden 1973) 23. LADD, G. E., A Theology of the New Testament (Grand Rapids 1974) 56, 74, 108, 200.

10:7-16 HOFFMANN, P. Studien zur Theologie der Logienquelle (1972) passim. SCHULZ, S. Q Die Spruchquelle der Evangelisten (1972) 404-19. TALBERT, C. H., Literary Patterns, Theological Themes and the Genre of Luke-Acts (Missoula 1974) 20. EDWARDS, R. A., A Theology of Q (Philadelphia 1976) 101-104.

10:7-15 IWAND, H. J. Predigt-Meditationen (1964) 647-54. STECK, K. G. GPM 19 (1964/65) 240ff. LINZ, M. in: Hören und Fragen (1967) Eichholz, G. & Falkenroth, A. (eds.) 360ff. LANGE, E (ed.) Predigtstudien für das Kirchenjahr 1970/71 (1971) 117-22. KLEIN, G. GPM 25 (1971) 375-85. FüRST, W., GPM 31/3 (1976/77) 277-81. GRAWIT, V./HEUE, R., in: Predigtstudien V/2. Halbband (Stuttgart 1977) 100-107. POLAG, A., Die Christologie der Logienquelle (Neukirchen-Vluyn 1977) 68-70.

10:7, 11-16 FRIEDRICH, G. GPM 11/3 (1956/57) 173-76.

10:7-8, 11-15 CONTI, M. "Il mandato di Cristo alla Chiesa (Mt. 10, 7-8. 11-15)," Antonianum 47 (1, '72) 17-68.

10:7f RICHARDSON, A. The Miracle—Stories of the Gospels (1948) 42f. BORNKAMM-BARTH-HELD, Ueberlieferung und Auslegung im Matthäus-Evangelium (1961) 15f., 109f., 237f., 239. STRECKER, G. Der Weg der Gerechtigkeit (1962) 175. JEREMIAS, J. Neutestamentliche Theologie I (1971) 40f., 100, 103, 105, 110, 132, 227, 254. HOFFMANN, P. Studien zur Theologie der Logienquelle (1972) 191, 274-76.

10:7 STONEHOUSE, N. B. The Witness of Matthew and Mark to Christ (1944) 234. CASALIS, G. "Sie Werden Euch Ueberantworten," in: Vom Herrengeheimnis der Wahrheit (1962) Scharf, K. (ed.) 305-14. HUMMEL, R. Die Auseinandersetzung zwischen Kirche und Judentum im Matthäusevangelium (1963) 124. HAHN, F. Das Verständnis der Mission im Neuen Testament (1965) 10, 38, 54, 106. BEYSCHLAG, K. Clemens Romanus und der Frühkatholizismus (1966) 276, 278. JüNGEL, E. Paulus und Jesus (1966) 174. KüNZI, M. Das Naherwartungslogion Matthäus 10, 23 (1970) 82, 122, 128, 146. SCHULZ, S., " 'Die Gottesherrschaft ist nahe herbeigekommen' (Mt 10, 7/Lk 10, 9). Der kerygmatische Entwurf der Q-Gemeinde Syriens "in: H. Balz/S. Schulz (eds.) Das Wort und die Wörter (Stuttgart 1973) 57-67. CONZELMANN, H./LINDEMANN, A., Arbeitsbuch zum Neuen Testament (Tübingen 1975) 18f.

KINGSBURY, J. D., Matthew: Structure, Christology, Kingdom (Philadelphia 1975) 138-40. EGGER, W., Frohbotschaft und Lehre (Frankfurt 1976) 59.

10:8b-10 HOFFMANN, P. Studien zur Theologie der Logienquelle (1972) 264-67.

10:8f BORNHäUSSER, D. K. Die Bergpredigt (1927) 169f.

10:8 STONEHOUSE, N. B. The Witness of Matthew and Mark to Christ (1944) 145. BETZ, H. D. Lukian von Samosata und das Neue Testament (1961) 113, 146, 156. STRECKER, G. Der Weg der Gerechtigleit (1962) 1374. TILLICH, P. Das Ewige im Jetzt (1964) 51-57. FENTON, J. "Raise the Dead," ET 80 (2, '68) 50-51. SUMMERS, R. The Secret Sayings of the Living Jesus (1968) 31. PESCH, R. Jesu ureigene Taten? Ein Beitrag zur Wunderfrage in: Quaestiones Disputatae Bd. 52 (1970) Rahner, K. & Schlier, H. (eds.) 44-45. GOULDER, M. D., Midrash and Lection in Matthew (London 1974) 75, 85f, 345f. "Abgaben" in: TRE 1 (1977) 329. "Amt" in: TRE 2 (1978) 515. CLARK, K. W., "The Making of the Twentieth Century New Testament" in: The Gentile Bias and other Essays (Leiden 1980) 151.

10:9ff STRECKER, G. Der Weg der Gerechtigkeit (1962) 196s.

10:9-15 BUTLER, B. C. The Originality of St Matthew (1951) 14ff.

10:9-13 BRAUN, H. Qumran und NT II (1966) 98, 288, 291, 299. POLAG, A., Die Christologie der Logienquelle (Neukirchen-Vluyn 1977) 67.

10:9-11 FARRER, A. St Matthew and St Mark (1954) 183.

10:9f KNOX, W. L. The Sources of the Synoptic Gospels II (1957) 50. JEREMIAS, J. Neutestamentliche Theologie I (1971) 226f.

10:9-10 CONTI, M. "Fondmanti biblici della povertà nel ministero apostolico (Mt. 10, 9-10)," Antonianum 46 (4, '71) 393-426. DERRETT, J. D. M., Jesus' Audience (London 1973) 181ff.

10:10 ELLIS, E. E. Paul's Use of the Old Testament (1957) 29, 36, 152, 185f. KNOX, W. L. The Sources of the Synoptic Gospels II (1957) 48. STRECKER, G. Der Weg der Gerechtigkeit (1962) 162. HENNECKE, E.& SCHNEEMELCHER, W. Neutestamentliche Apokryphen (1964) I 174. NICKELS, P. Targum and New Testament (1967) 18. GOULDER, M. D., Midrash and Lection in Matthew (London 1974) 79, 145, 148, 161, 293, 345f. THEISSEN, G., Soziologie der Jesusbewegung (München 1977) 18. *LEGRAND, L., "Bare-foot Apostles? The Shoes of St Mark (Mk 6:8-9 and parallels)" IndTheolStud 16 (1979) 201-19.

10:11-15 GOULDER, M. D., Midrash and Lection in Matthew

(London 1974) 332, 346f.

10:11-13 HOFFMANN, P. Studien zur Theologie der Logienquelle (1972) 272-74.

10:12-15 MEYER, B. F., The Aims of Jesus (London 1979) 214.

10:12f SCHENK, W. Der Segen im Neuen Testament (1967) 92-96. JEREMIAS, J. Neutestamentliche Theologie I (1971) 25-27, 29, 134, 211.

10:12-13 WESTERMANN, C., Blessing. In the Bible and the Life of the Church (Philadelphia 1978) 91, 93-98, 98-101.

10:12 METZGER, B. M., The Early Versions of the New Testament (Oxford 1977) 118.

10:13ff KäSEMANN, E. Exegetische Versuche und Besinnungen (1964) II 93f., 101. KäSEMANN, E. New Testament Questions of Today (1969) 94, 95, 103.

10:14f BROX, N. Zeuge und Märtyrer (1961) 27f. STRECKER, G. Der Weg der Gerechtigkeit (1962) 190з. KäSEMANN, E Exegetische Versuche und Besinnungen (1964) I 170.

10:14-15 SANFORD, J. A., The Kingdom Within (New York 1970) 72f.

10:14 TRILLING, W. Das wahre Israel (1959) 105f. JEREMIAS, J. Neutestamentliche Theologie I (1971) 228f. HOFFMANN, P. Studien zur Theologie der Logienquelle (1972) 268-72.

10:15-23 BUTLER, B. C. The Originality of St Matthew (1951) 80ff.

10:15f KNOX, W. L. The Sources of the Synoptic Gospels II (1957) 53-54.

10:15 BORNKAMM-BARTH-HELD, Ueberlieferung und Auslegung im Matthäus-Evangelium (1961) 56, 240. STRECKER, G. Der Weg der Gerechtigkeit (1962) 1022. WILLIAMSON, H. R. "Sodom and Homosexuality," ClR 48 (8, '63) 507-14. KäSEMANN, E. Exegetische Versuche und Besinnungen (1964) II 94. HAHN, F. Das Verständnis der Mission im Neuen Testament (1965) 26f. HASLER, V. Amen (1969) 62. KäSEMANN, E. New Testament Questions of Today (1969) 96. FURNISH, V. P., The Moral Teaching of Paul (Nashville 1979) 56.

10:16ff BEYSCHLAG, K. Clemens Romanus und der Frühkatholizismus (1966) 223.

10:16-25 GOULDER, M. D., Midrash and Lection in Matthew (London 1974) 347ff.

10:16-22 IWAND, H. J. Predigt-Meditationen (1964) 306-12.

10:16-21 HENNECKE, E. & SCHNEEMELCHER, W. Neutestamentliche Apokryphen (1964) I 95, 113, 116, 118; II 436.

10:16-20 HAMEL, GPM 17 (1962/63) 233ff. Also in: Predigtgedanken
aus Vergangenheit und Gegenwart Bd. 3-4 (1963) 21ff. STECK,
K. G. GPM 23/3 (1968/69) 240-48. COX, H./ GEORGI, D.,
in: GPM 29 (1975) 290-97. SCHWEINGEL,
U./DANNOWSKI, H.-W., in: P. Krusche et al. (eds.)
Predigtstudien für das Kirchenjahr 1975 III/2. Halbband
(1975) 102-107.

10:16 STONEHOUSE, N. B. The Witness of Matthew and Mark to
Christ (1944) 177. MASSAUX, E. Influence de l'Evangile de
saint Matthieu sur la littérature chrétienne avant saint Irénée
(1950) 150-52. SCHRAGE, W. Die konkreten Einzelgebote in
der paulinischen Paränese (1961) 243. STRECKER, G. Der
Weg der Gerechtigkeit (1962) 363. SCHRAGE, W. Das
Verhältnis des Thomas-Evangeliums zur Synoptischen
Tradition und zu den Koptischen Evangelienübersetzungen
(1964) 94. SUMMERS, R. The Secret Sayings of the Living
Jesus (1968) 30. KüNZI, M. Das Naherwartungslogion
Matthäus 10, 23 (1970) 40, 69, 115, 123, 153. SANFORD, J. A.,
The Kingdom Within (New York 1970) 128f. JEREMIAS, J.
Neutestamentliche Theologie I (1971) 33f., 166, 229, 242.
GOULDER, M. D., Midrash and Lection in Matthew
(London 1974) 72, 148, 160, 307, 347f. HOWARD, V. P., Das
Ego in den Synoptischen Evangelien (Marburg 1975) 149-52.
POLAG, A., Die Christologie der Logienquelle (Neukirchen-
Vluyn 1977) 99. McDONALD, J. I. H., Kerygma and Didache
(Cambridge 1980) 81.

10:17ff KNOX, W. L. The Sources of the Synoptic Gospels II (1957)
50f. STRECKER, G. Der Weg der Gerechtigkeit (1962) 134,
190 239₇. KüNZI, M. Das Naherwartungslogion Matthäus 10,
23, (1970) 90, 96, 98, 102, 118, 121f., 128, 132f., 142, 146, 156,
158, 178. THEISSEN, G., Soziologie der Jesusbewegung
(München 1977) 20.

10:17-25 HAHN, F. Das Verständnis der Mission im Neuen Testament
(1965) 33.

10:17-22 BUTLER, B. C. The Originality of St Matthew (1951) 79ff.
TRITES, A. A., The New Testament Concept of Witness
(Cambridge 1977) 183-85.

10:17-21 STRECKER, G. Der Weg der Gerechtigkeit (1962) 44.

10:17-20 DUPONT, J., "La persécution comme situation missionaire
(Marc 13: 9-11)" in: R. Schnackenburg et al. (eds.) Die Kirche
des Anfangs: Festschrift für Heinz Schürmann (Leipzig 1977)
101f, 105-107.

10:17f STRECKER, G. Der Weg der Gerechtigkeit (1962) 30.

10:17-18 GILS, F. Jésus Prophète D'Après Les Evangiles Synoptiques
(1957) 114-17.

10:17   STONEHOUSE, N. B. The Witness of Matthew and Mark to Christ (1944) 153. STRECKER, G. Der Weg der Gerechtigkeit (1962) 41, 422, 43, 190, 1965, 2394. CHRIST, F. Jesus Sophia (1970) 123, 133.

10:18   GILS, F. Jésus Prophète D'Après Les Evangiles Synoptiques (1957) 114-18. TRILLING, W. Das wahre Israel (1959) 105. BROX, N. Zeuge und Märtyrer (1961) 28f. STRECKER, G. Der Weg der Gerechtigkeit (1962) 34, 41, 2395. HAHN, F. Das Verständnis der Mission im Neuen Testament (1965) 109. BEYSCHLAG, K. Clemens Romanus und der Frühkatholizismus (1966) 270, 279. MARXSEN, W. Mark the Evangelist (1969) 122, 201f. KüNZI, M. Das Naherwartungslogion Matthäus 10, 23 (1970) 141f., 157. LANGE, J., Das Erscheinen des Auferstandenen im Evangelium nach Matthäus (Würzburg 1973) 257-60, 293f., 297, 299, 488. WILSON, S. G., The Gentiles and the Gentile Mission in Luke—Acts (Cambridge 1973) 15, 23f.

10:19ff   KNOX, W. L. The Sources of the Synoptic Gospels II (1957) 72.

10:19f   BARRETT, C. K. The Holy Spirit and the Gospel Tradition (1947) 130-32. HAHN, F. Christologische Hoheitstitel (1963) 107. HAHN, F. Das Verständnis der Mission im Neuen Testament (1965) 44. KäSEMANN, E. New Testament Questions of Today (1969) 91. KüNZI, M. Das Naherwartungslogion Matthäus 10, 23 (1970) 150, 159f. SCHULZ, S. Q Die Spruchquelle der Evangelisten (1972) 442-44.

10:19-20   TALBERT, C. H., Literary Patterns, Theological Themes, and the Genre of Luke-Acts (Missoula 1974) 55. KREMER, J., "Jesu Verheissung der Geistes. Zur Verankerung der Aussage von Joh 16:13 im Leben Jesu" in: R. Schnackenburg et al. (eds.) Die Kirche des Anfangs. Festschrift für Heinz Schürmann (Freiburg 1978) 262-67.

10:19   KäSEMANN, E. Exegetische Versuche und Besinnungen (1964) II 91. KüNZI, M. Das Naherwartungslogion Matthäus 10, 23 (1970) 22, 133, 158. METZGER, B. M., The Early Versions of the New Testament (Oxford 1977) 438. POLAG, A., Die Christologie der Logienquelle (Neukirchen-Vluyn 1977) 98.

10:20   HAHN, F. Christologie Hoheitstitel (1963) 107. THEISSEN, G., Soziologie der Jesusbewegung (München 1977) 18.

10:21f   KäSEMANN, E. Exegetische Versuche und Besinnungen (1964) II 103f. KäSEMANN, E. New Testament Questions of Today (1969) 105. JEREMIAS, J. Neutestamentliche

Theologie I (1971) 47, 137, 199, 232.

10:21 DELLING, G. Die Taufe im Neuen Testament (1963) 74.

10:22f KäSEMANN, E. New Testament Questions of Today (1969) 106.

10:22 DELLING, G. Die Zueignung des Heils in der Taufe (1961) 83. STROBEL, A. Untersuchungen zum Eschatologischen Verzögerungsproblem (1961) 278-80. STRECKER, G. Der Weg der Gerechtigkeit (1962) 239₄. HAHN, F. Christologische Hoheitstitel (1963) 45. KäSEMANN, E. Exegetische Versuche und Besinnungen (1964) II 102. KüNZI, M. Das Naherwartungslogion Matthäus 10, 23 (1970) 40, 47, 50, 54, 65, 79, 92f., 100, 112, 131, 148, 150.

10:23 STONEHOUSE, N. B. The Witness of Matthew and Mark to Christ (1944) 147, 184, 238ff. STAEHELIN, E. Die Verkündigung des Reiches Gottes in der Kirche Jesu Christi I (1951) 57. MANSON, T. W. The Teaching of Jesus (1945) 220ff. KüMMEL, W. G. Verheissung und Erfüllung (1953) 55-60. PARKER, P. The Gospel Before Mark (1953) 11-12, 80-81. FARRER, A. St Matthew and St Mark (1954) 120. KNOX, W. L. The Sources of the Synoptic Gospels II (1957) 34, 49, 50-54. DUPONT, J. " 'Vous n'aurez pas achevé les villes d'Israel avant que le fils de l'homme ne vienne (Mat. x 23)," NovTest 2 (3-4, '58) 228-44. BERKHOF, H. Der Sinn der Geschichte: Christus (1959) 82f., 141. SCHüRMANN, H. "Zur Traditions- und Redaktionsgeschichte von Mt 10, 23," BZ 3 (1, '59) 82-88. BAMMEL, E. "Matthäus 10, 23," StTh 15 (1, '61) 79-92. STRECKER, G. Der Weg der Gerechtigkeit (1962) 41f., 44₂, ₃, 125, 151₄. ESSAME, W. G. "Matthew x. 23," ET 72 (8, '61) 248. FEUILLET, A. "Les Origines et la Signification de Mt 10, 23," CBQ 23 (2, '61) 182-98. SCHWEIZER, E. Erniedrigung und Erhöhung bei Jesus und seinen Nachfolgern (1962) § 3h. CLARK, R. "Eschatology and Matthew 10:23 (Part I)," RestQ 7 (1-2, '63) 73-81. HAHN, F. Christologische Hoheitstitel (1963) 38. HUMMEL, R. Die Auseinandersetzung zwischen Kirche und Judentum im Matthäusevangelium (1963) 144. SCHMITHALS, W. Paulus und Jakobus (1963) 93f. CLARK, R. "Matthew 10:23 and Eschatology (II)," RestQ 8 (1, '65) 53-68. HAHN, F. Das Verständnis der Mission im Neuen Testament (1965) 22, 32f., 44f., 46, 59, 107. JüNGEL, E. Paulus und Jesus (1966) 237ff. GIBLIN, C. H. "Theological Perspective and Matthew 10:23b," ThSt 29 (4, '68) 637-61. HASLER, V. Amen (1969) 84. PESCH, R. Naherwartungen (1969) 131, 205. CHRIST, F. Jesus Sophia (1970) 123, 133. GASTON, L. No Stone on Another (1970) 18, 38, 409, 414, 451-55, 486. KüNZI, M. Das Naherwartungslogion Matthäus

10:23. Geschichte seiner Auslegung (1970) SCHILLE, G. Das vorsynoptischen Judenchristentum (1970) 85. JEREMIAS, J. Neutestamentliche Theologie I (1971) 26, 44, 134, 136f., 225, 229f., 235, 248f., 251f., 254, 261f. VöGTLE, A. Das Evangelium und die Evangelien (1971) 298-302, 319-21, 328-32. PATSCH, H. Abendmahl und historischer Jesus (1972) 124ff. PERRIN, N., The Kingdom of God in the Teaching of Jesus (Philadelphia 1963) 31, 33, 83, 85, 137, 146. BERKOUWER, G. C., The Return of Christ (Grand Rapids 1972) 68, 86, 89, 116. HIERS, R. H., The Historical Jesus and the Kingdom of God (Gainesville 1973) 29, 39, 53, 61, 66-68, 70f, 110. KüMMEL, W. G. Einleitung in das Neue Testament (1973) 86f. WILSON, S. G., The Gentiles and the Gentile Mission in Luke-Acts (Cambridge 1973) 16-18, 21-23, 25, 50f. FRANKEMöLLE, H., Jahwebund und Kirche Christi (Münster 1974) 41, 121, 123, 125, 127, 130-35, 170. GOULDER, M. D., Midrash and Lection in Matthew (London 1974) 339, 341f., 348, 380, 428. SCHüRMANN, H., "Beobachtungen zum Menschensohn-Titel in der Redenquelle" in: R. Pesch/ R. Schnackenburg (eds.) Jesus und der Menschensohn (Freiburg 1975) 137f. BORING, M. E., "Christian Prophecy and Matthew 10:23—A Test Exegesis" in: G. MacRae (ed.) Society of Biblical Literature 1976 Seminar Papers (Missoula 1976) 127-33. POLAG, A., Die Christologie der Logienquelle (Neukirchen-Vluyn 1977) 98, 133. *SABOURIN, L., "'You will not have gone through all the towns of Israel, before the Son of Man comes' (Mat. 10:23b)" BThB 7 (1977) 5-11. THEISSEN, G., Soziologie der Jesusbewegung (München 1977) 17. SCHILDENBERGER, J., "Die Vertauschung der Aussagen über Zeichen und Bezeichnetes. Eine hermeneutisch bedeutsame Redeweise" in: Kirche und Bibel. Festschrift für Bischof Eduard Schick (Paderborn 1979) 404. HARRINGTON, D. J., God's People in Christ (Philadelphia 1980) 25.

10:24-42 BLAIR, E. P. Jesus in the Gospel of Matthew (1960) 107.

10:24-33 HEIM, K. Der unerschütterliche Grund (1946) 68. SURKAU, H. W. GPM 6/4 (1951/52) 249-52. GOLLWITZER, GPM 17 (1962/63) 345ff. Also in: Predigtgedanken aus Vergangenheit und Gegenwart Bd. 3-4 (1963) 335ff. BüCKMANN, O., in: Herr, tue meine Lippen auf (1964) Eichholz, G. (ed.) 449ff. IWAND, H. J. Predigt-Meditationen (1964) 44-47. HARDER, G. GPM 23/4 (1968/69) 382-89. BRAUER, K./DANNOWSKI, H.-W., in: P. Krusche et al. (eds.) Predigtstudien für das Kirchenjahr 1975 III/2. Halbband (Stuttgart 1975) 256-62. RUHBACH, G., in: GPM 29 (1975) 449-56. POLAG, A., Die Christologie der Logienquelle (Neukirchen-Vluyn 1977) 82.

10:24f.38f.   LOHSE, E. and others (eds.) Der Ruf Jesu und die Antwort der Gemeinde (1970) 262-67.

10:24f   JüLICHER, D. A. Die Gleichnisreden Jesu (1910) 44-50. DODD, C. H. Some Johannine 'Herrworte' with Parallels in the Synoptic Gospels NTS 2 (1955-56) 76f. TRILLING, W. Das wahre Israel (1959) 64f. BORNKAMM-BARTH-HELD, Ueberlieferung und Auslegung im Matthäus-Evangelium (1961) 38, 94f., 255. STRECKER, G. Der Weg der Gerechtigkeit (1962) 42, 191. HAHN, F. Christologische Hoheitstitel (1963) 77, 78f., 81, 87. HENGEL, M. Nachfolge und Charisma (1968) 87f. KüNZI, M. Das Naherwartungslogion Matthäus 10, 23 (1970) 118, 136, 144. SCHULZ, S. Q Die Spruchquelle der Evangelisten (1972) 449-51.

10:24-25   WILKENS, J. Einführung in das Evangelium nach Matthäus I (1934) 156-57.

10:24   BEST, E. One Body in Christ (1955) 146. KNOX, W. L. The Sources of the Synoptic Gospels II (1957) 10. GOULDER, M. D., Type and History in Acts (London 1964) 127f. HENNECKE, E. & SCHNEEMELCHER, W. Neutestamentliche Apokryphen (1964) I 174. KüNZI, M. Das Naherwartungslogion Matthäus 10, 23 (1970) 40, 118, 143. JEREMIAS, J. Neutestamentliche Theologie I (1971) 26, 33, 209, 229, 239. KLIJN, A. F. J./REININK, G. J., Patristic Evidence for Jewish-Christian Sects (Leiden 1973) 16, 23f., 73, 76.

10:25   STONEHOUSE, N. B. The Witness of Matthew and Mark to Christ (1944) 153. KNOX, W. L. The Sources of the Synoptic Gospels II (1957) 10, 63. GASTON, L. "Beelzebul," ThZ 18 (1962) 247-55. BULTMANN, R. The History of the Synoptic Tradition (1963) 90f. HAHN, F. Christologische Hoheitstitel (1963) 92. HUMMEL, R. Die Auseinandersetzung zwischen Kirche und Judentum im Matthäusevangelium (1963) 124, 155. YATES, J. E. The Spirit and the Kingdom (1963) 94-98. BLACK, M. An Aramaic Approach to the Gospels and Acts (1967) 129f. SMITH, M., Tannaitic Parallels to the Gospels (Philadelphia 1968) 8 b n 5+. JEREMIAS, J. Neutestamentliche Theologie I (1971) 16, 19, 26, 95, 97, 166, 177, 209, 229, 231, 239, 269. KLIJN, A. F. J./REININK, G. J., Patristic Evidence for Jewish-Christian Sects (Leiden 1973) 16, 23, 76, 83. THEISSEN, G., Soziologie der Jesusbewegung (München 1977) 18. *MACLAURIN, E. C. B., "Beelzeboul" NovTest 20 (1978) 156-60.

10:26ff   KNOX, W. L. The Sources of the Synoptic Gospels II (1957) 54, 72.

10:26-42 WILKENS, J. Einführung in das Evangelium nach Matthäus I (1934) 152-56.

10:26-41 HAHN, F. Das Verständnis der Mission im Neuen Testament (1965) 33.

10:26-39 HOFFMANN, P. Studien zur Theologie der Logienquelle (1972) passim. BORNKAMM, G. GPM 6/4 (1951/52) 236-40.

10:26-33 BRAUN, H. Qumran und NT II (1966) 95. LüHRMANN, D. Die Redaktion der Logienquelle (1969) 49-52. GOULDER, M. D., Midrash and Lection in Matthew (London 1974) 349ff. TALBERT, C. H., Literary Patterns, Theological Themes, and the Genre of Luke-Acts (Missoula 1974) 55. EDWARDS, R. A., A Theology of Q (Philadelphia 1976) 120f. TRITES, A. A., The New Testament Concept of Witness (Cambridge 1977) 181-83.

10:26-31 GAECHTER, P. Die Literarische Kunst im Matthäus-Evangelium (1968) 42-43, 75-76.

10:26f JüLICHER, D. A. Die Gleichnisreden Jesu (1910) 91-97. KäSEMANN, E. Exegetische Versuche und Besinnungen (1964) I 209 II 97. SCHULZ, S. Q Die Spruchquelle der Evangelisten (1972) 461-65.

10:26-27 HAHN, F., "Die Worte vom Licht Lk 11, 33-36" in: P. Hoffmann (ed.) Orientierung an Jesus. Für Josef Schmid (Freiburg 1973) 113, 120f. POLAG, A., Die Christologie der Logienquelle (Neukirchen-Vluyn 1977) 96.

10:26 SCHRAGE, W. Das Verhältnis des Thomas-Evangeliums zur Synoptischen Tradition und zu den Koptischen Evangelienübersetzungen (1964) 34. SUMMERS, R. The Secret Sayings of the Living Jesus (1968) 56. KäSEMANN, E. New Testament Questions of Today (1969) 99. LINTON, O., "Le parallelismus membrorum dans le Nouveau Testament grec" in: A. Descamps/A. de Halleux (eds.) Mélanges Bibliques en hommage au R. P. Béda Rigaux (Gembloux 1970) 497f. RIST, J. M., On the Independence of Matthew and Mark (Cambridge 1978) 49f.

10:27 STRECKER, G. Der Weg der Gerechtigkeit (1962) 190. SCHRAGE, W. Das Verhältnis des Thomas-Evangeliums zur Synoptischen Tradition und zu den Koptischen Evangelienübersetzungen (1964) 79. DALTON, W. J., Christ's Proclamation to the Spirits (Rome 1965) 152f. SUMMERS, R. The Secret Sayings of the Living Jesus (1968) 29. KäSEMANN, E. New Testament Questions of Today (1969) 99.

10:28ff DEISSMANN, A. Licht vom Osten (1923) 232ff.

10:28-31 SCHULZ, S. Q Die Spruchquelle der Evangelisten (1972) 157-61.

10:28 BONHöFFER, A. Epiktet und das Neue Testament (1911) 176, 286. STONEHOUSE, N. B. The Witness of Matthew and Mark to Christ (1944) 107. MASSAUX, E. Influence de l'Evangile de saint Matthieu sur la littérature chrétienne avant saint Irénée (1950) 150-52, 281-82. BEST, E. One Body in Christ (1955) 216. STRECKER, G. Der Weg der Gerechtigkeit (1962) 162, 234. MARSHALL, I. H. "Uncomfortable Words VI. 'Fear him who can destroy both soul and body in hell' (Mt 10:28 R. S. V.)," ET 81 (9, '70) 276-80. NöTSCHER, F., Altorientalischer und alttestamentlicher Auferstehungsglaube (Darmstadt 1970⁻1926) 306. O'NEILL, J. C., The Theology of Acts in its Historical Setting (London 1970) 37f. SANFORD, J. A., The Kingdom Within (New York 1970) 161. JEREMIAS, J. Neutestamentliche Theologie I (1971) 17, 25-27, 137, 175, 230, 269. LADD, G. E., A Theology of the New Testament (Grand Rapids 1974) 55, 74, 196, 460. METZGER, B. M., The Early Versions of the New Testament (Oxford 1977) 439. GNILKA, J., "Martyriumsparänese und Sühnetod in synoptischen und jüdischen Traditionen" in: Die Kirche des Anfangs. Für H. Schürmann (Freiburg 1978) 232. "Auferstehung" in: TRE 4 (1979) 451.

10:29-31 DVORACEK, J. A., "Fürchtet euch nicht" Theologická príloha Krest 'anská revue 4 (1968) 73-76. SANFORD, J. A., The Kingdom Within (New York 1970) 90f.

10:29f MOORE, G. F. Judaism (1946) I 385. JEREMIAS, J. Neutestamentliche Theologie I (1971) 21f., 178f.

10:29 BRUNNER, E. Dogmatik I (1946) 270. BLAIR, E. P. Jesus in the Gospel of Matthew (1960) 91. LINTON, O., "Le parallelismus membrorum dans le Nouveau Testament grec" in: A. Descamps/A. de Halleux (eds.) Mélanges Bibliques en hommage au R. P. Béda Rigaux (Gembloux 1970) 506f.

10:30 BRUNNER, E. Dogmatik II (1950) 23, 181.

10:32f KNOX, W. L. The Sources of the Synoptic Gospels II (1957) 142. BLAIR, E. P. Jesus in the Gospel of Matthew (1960) 91. WAINWRIGHT, A. W. The Trinity in the New Testament (1962) 118-19. HAHN, F. Christologische Hoheitstitel (1963) 33, 34, 321. HENNECKE, E. & SCHNEEMELCHER, W. Neutestamentliche Apokryphen (1964) I 113, 258 II 109. McNAMARA, M. The New Testament and the Palestinian Targum to the Pentateuch (1966) 136. BORNKAMM, G. "Das Wort Jesu vom Bekennen," Geschichte und Glaube I (1968) 25-36. KäSEMANN, E. New Testament Questions of Today (1969) 77. BORSCH, F. H. The Christian & Gnostic Son of Man (1970) 16-20. KüNZI, M. Das Naherwartungslogion Matthäus 10, 23 (1970) 128f. JEREMIAS, J.

Neutestamentliche Theologie I (1971) 18, 25, 29, 152, 242, 262. SCHULZ, S. Q Die Spruchquelle der Evangelisten (1972) 66-76.

10:32-33   LOHSE, E., Die Einheit des Neuen Testaments (Göttingen 1973) 42-44. GOULDER, M. D., Midrash and Lection in Matthew (London 1974) 75, 350, 384f. LOHSE, E., Grundriss der neutestamentlichen Theologie (Stuttgart 1974) 47-49, 115. HIGGINS, A. J. B., " 'Menschensohn' oder 'ich' in Q: Lk 12: 8-9/Mt 10:32-33?" in: R. Pesch/R. Schnackenburg (eds.) Jesus und der Menschensohn (Freiburg 1975) 117-23. HOWARD, V. P., Das Ego in den Synoptischen Evangelien (Marburg 1975) 152-56. KüMMEL, W. G., "Das Verhalten Jesus gegenüber und das Verhalten des Menschensohns. Markus 8, 38 par und Lukas 12,3f par Matthäus 10, 32f" in: R. Pesch/R. Schnackenburg (eds.) Jesus und der Menschensohn. (Freiburg 1975) 210-24. PESCH, R. "Uber die Autorität Jesu. Eine Rückfrage anhand des Bekenner- und Verleugnerspruchs Lk 12:8f par." in: R. Schnackenburg et al. (eds.) Die Kirche des Anfangs. Festschrift für H. Schürmann (Leipzig 1977) 25-55. POLAG, A., Die Christologie der Logienquelle (Neukirchen-Vluyn 1977) 98, 114, 133. *PAGANI, S., "Le versioni latine africane del Nuovo Testamento: considerazioni su Mt 10, 32-33 in Tertulliano e Cipriano" BiOr 20 (1978) 255-70.

10:32   NESTLE, E., "Zu Mt 10:32" ZNW 9 (1908) 253. DENNEY, J. The Death of Christ (1956) 25. STRECKER, G. Der Weg der Gerechtigkeit (1962) 231. JüNGEL, E. Paulus und Jesus (1966) 242, 244, 258ff. KäSEMANN, E. New Testament Questions of Today (1969) 104. SANFORD, J. A., The Kingdom Within (New York 1970) 91f. LADD, G. E., A Theology of the New Testament (Grand Rapids 1974) 132f, 271. "Apokalyptik" in: TRE 3 (1978) 253. SCHILLEBEECKX, E., Die Auferstehung Jesu als Grund der Erlösung (Basel 1979) 80.

10:34ff   KNOX, W. L. The Sources of the Synoptic Gospels II (1957) 54.

10:34-42   GOULDER, M. D., Midrash and Lection in Matthew (London 1974) 351ff.

10:34-39   BENCKERT, GPM 17 (1962/63) 351ff. Also in: L. Liebe Gottes, Predigtgedanken aus Vergangenheit und Gegenwart Bd. 3-4 (1963) 296ff. BRAUN, H. Qumran und NT II (1966) 86, 97, 104, 107, 269, 289, 294. STECK, K. G. GPM 23/4 (1968/69) 375-82. VIDAL, M. "Seguimiento de Cristo y evangelizacion. Variacion sobre un tema de moral neotestamentaria (Mt. 10, 34-39)," Salmanticensis 18 (2-3, '71) 289-312. LOHSE, E., GPM 29 (1975) 438-43. SCHULZ, H./TILMANN, R., in: P.

Krusche et al. (eds.) Predigtstudien für das Kirchenjahr 1975 III/2. Halbband (Stuttgart 1975) 240-48. COPE, O. L., Matthew. A Scribe Trained for the Kingdom of Heaven (Washington D. C. 1976) 77-81.

10:34-37 SWIDLER, L., Biblical Affirmations of Woman (Philadelphia 1979) 179, 242, 257, 283.

10:34-36 HIRSCH, E. Frühgeschichte des Evangeliums (1941) 122-24. ROBERTS, T. A. "Some Comments on Matthew x. 34-36 and Luke xii. 51-53," ET 69 (10, '58) 304-306. BULTMANN, R. The History of the Synoptic Tradition (1963) 152-54. SCHULZ, S. Q Die Spruchquelle der Evangelisten (1972) 258-60. TALBERT, C. H., Literary Patterns, Theological Themes, and the Genre of Luke-Acts (Missoula 1974) 55. TANNEHILL, R. C., The Sword of His Mouth (Philadelphia 1975) 140-44. ARENS, E., The HΛΘΟΝ - Sayings in the Synoptic Tradition (Fribourg 1976) 63-90. EDWARDS, R. A., A Theology of Q (Philadelphia 1976) 127f. SCHENKE, H. M., "Die Tendenz der Weisheit zur Gnosis" in: B. Aland et al. (eds.) Gnosis. Festschrift für H. Jonas (Göttingen 1978) 363.

10:34f SCHRAGE, W. Das Verhältnis des Thomas-Evangeliums zur Synoptischen Tradition und zu den Koptischen Evangelienübersetzungen (1964) 57.

10:34 KNOX, W. L. The Sources of the Synoptic Gospels II (1957) 73. TRILLING, W. Das wahre Israel (1959) 143. STRECKER, G. Der Weg der Gerechtigkeit (1962) 1374, 144. HAHN, F. Christologische Hoheitstitel (1963) 166f. KäSEMANN, E. Exegetische Versuche und Besinnungen (1964) II 96. HENGEL, M. Nachfolge und Charisma (1968) 14f. MUSSNER, F. "Wege zum Selbstbewusstsein Jesus. Ein Versuch," BZ 12 (1968) 161-72. KäSEMANN, E. New Testament Questions of Today (1969) 97. BLACK, M. "Uncomfortable Words.III. The Violent Word," ET 81 (4, '70) 115-18. SANFORD, J. A., The Kingdom Within (New York 1970) 80f. HENGEL, M., Was Jesus a Revolutionist? (Philadelphia 1971) 23. JEREMIAS, J. Neutestamentliche Theologie I (1971) 25f., 29, 39, 128f., 137, 200, 231, 269. BANKS, R., Jesus and the Law in the Synoptic Tradition (London 1975) 204f. POLAG, A., Die Christologie der Logienquelle (Neukirchen-Vluyn 1977) 164.

10:35-39 SWIDLER, L., Biblical Affirmations of Woman (Philadelphia 1979) 259, 279, 354.

10:35f MOORE, G. F. Judaism (1946) II 357. DELLING, G. Die Taufe im Neuen Testament (1963) 74. HAHN, F. Christologische Hoheitstitel (1963) 167.

SANFORD, J. A. The Kingdom Within (New York 1970) 82f.
POLAG, A., Die Christologie der Logienquelle (Neukirchen-
Vluyn 1977) 165.

10:35   STRECKER, G. Der Weg der Gerechtigkeit (1962) 243.
WILLIAMS, J. A., A Conceptual History of Deuteronomism
in the Old Testament, Judaism and the New Testament. Ph.D.
Diss. (Louisville 1976) 309. LINTON, O., "Le parallelismus
membrorum dans le Nouveau Testament grec" in: A.
Descamps/A. de Halleux (eds.) Mélanges Bibliques en
hommage au R. P. Béda Rigaux (Gembloux 1970) 498-501.

10:36   HUMMEL, R. Die Auseinandersetzung zwischen Kirche und
Judentum im Matthäusevangelium (1963) 155.

10:37-42   KNOX, W. L. The Sources of the Synoptic Gospels II (1957)
54.

10:37-38   KöHLER, K., "Zu Mt 10:37f" ZNW 17 (1916) 270-72. FLEW,
R. N. Jesus and His Church (1956) 56-57. KNOX, W. L. The
Sources of the Synoptic Gospels II (1957) 86. SCHRAGE, W.
Das Verhältnis des Thomas-Evangeliums zur Synoptischen
Tradition und zu den Koptischen Evangelienübersetzungen
(1964) 120. ERNST, J., Anfänge der Christologie (Stuttgart
1972) 136-41. TALBERT, C. H., Literary Patterns,
Theological Themes, and the Genre of Luke-Acts (Missoula
1974) 55. POLAG, A., Die Christologie der Logienquelle
(Neukirchen-Vluyn 1977) 85. GNILKA, J.,
"Martyriumsparänese und Sühnetod in synoptischen und
jüdischen Traditionen" in: Die Kirche des Anfangs. Für Heinz
Schürmann (Freiburg 1978) 232-34. RIST, J. M., On the
Independence of Matthew and Mark (Cambridge 1978) 50-53.
SWIDLER, L., Biblical Affirmations of Woman (Philadelphia
1979) 179. McDONALD, J. I. H., Kerygma and Didache
(Cambridge 1980) 86.

10:37   SCHULZ, A. Nachfolge und Nachnahmen (1962) 80ff.
GREEVES, H. Ehe Nach dem Neuen Testament NTS 15 (1968-
69) 374f. JEREMIAS, J. Neutestamentliche Theologie I (1971)
152, 215f., 242. SCHULZ, S. Q Die Spruchquelle der
Evangelisten (1972) 446-49. FRIEDRICH, G., "Das Problem
der Autorität im Neuen Testament" in: Auf das Wort kommt es
an (Göttingen 1978) 288, 383-85. KELBER, W. H., "Mark and
Oral Tradition" Semeia 16 (1980) 25-27.

10:38f   STRECKER, G. Der Weg der Gerechtigkeit (1962) 2313.4.

10:38   STAEHELIN, E. Die Verkündigung des Reiches Gottes in der
Kirche Jesu Christi I (1951) 155. KNOX, W. L. The Sources of
the Synoptic Gospels II (1957) 54. SCHULZ, A. Nachfolge und
Nachnahmen (1962) 82-90.163f., 171f., 265ff. STRECKER, G.

Der Weg der Gerechtigkeit (1962) 192, 230⁴. SCHüTZ, F. Der
leidende Christus (1969) 16ff. SCHULZ, S. Q Die Spruchquelle
der Evangelisten (1972) 430-33.

10:39 STAEHELIN, E. Die Verkündigung des Reiches Gottes in der
Kirche Jesu Christi I (1951) 174. KNOX, W. L. The Sources of
the Synoptic Gospels II (1957) 86, 107. ROBINSON, J. M.
Kerygma und historischer Jesus (1960) 165. KäSEMANN, E.
Exegetische Versuche und Besinnungen (1964) II 98.
KäSEMANN, E. New Testament Questions of Today (1969)
99. OTOMO, Y. Nachfolge Jesu and Anfänge der Kirche im
Neuen Testament (1970) 44-52. SANFORD, J. A., The
Kingdom Within (New York 1970) 66-68, 188f. JEREMIAS, J.
Neutestamentliche Theologie I (1971) 25-27, 30, 36. SCHULZ,
S. Q Die Spruchquelle der Evangelisten (1972) 444-46.
ZMIJEWSKI, J., Die Eschatologiereden des Lukas-
Evangeliums (Bonn 1972) 479-82. CAVALLIN, H. C. C., Life
After Death I (Lund 1974) 4, 3nII. LADD, G. E., A Theology
of the New Testament (Grand Rapids 1974) 74, 133, 257.
HOFFMANN, P./EID, V., Jesus von Nazareth und eine
christliche Moral (Freiburg 1975) 212-14. *SATAKE, A., "Das
Leiden der Jünger 'um Meinetwillen' " ZNW 67 (1976) 4-19.
THEUNISSEN, M., "ὁ αἰτῶν λαμβάνει. Der Gebetsglaube
Jesu und die Zeitlichkeit des Christseins" in: Jesus, Ort der
Erfahrung Gottes. Für Bernhard Welte (Freiburg 1976) 30.
GNILKA, J., "Martyriumsparänese und Sühnetod in
synoptischen und jüdischen Traditionen" in: Die Kirche des
Anfangs. Für H. Schürmann (Freiburg 1978) 235. LEROY, H.,
"Wer sein Leben gewinnen will . . . 'Erlöste Existenz heute"
FZPhTh 25 (1978) 171-86. MEYER, B. F., The Aims of Jesus
(London 1979) 213.

10:40ff DODD, C. H. Some Johannine 'Herrworte' with Parallels in
the Synoptic Gospels NTS 2 (1955-56) 81ff. BORNKAMM-
BARTH-HELD, Ueberlieferung und Auslegung im Matthäus-
Evangelium (1961) 90, 114, 240, 258. KLEIN, G. Die Zwölf
Apostel (1961) 30f.

10:40-42 KNOX, W. L. The Sources of the Synoptic Gospels II (1957)
53f. BULTMANN, R. The History of the Synoptic Tradition
(1963) 142f. KIVIT, J. GPM 21/4 (1966/67) 350-54. SMITH,
M., Tannaitic Parallels to the Gospels (Philadelphia 1968) 8 b n
5+; A+. *VIDAL, M., "La 'Recompensa' como motivación del
comportamiento moral cristiano. Estudio exegético-teológico
de Mt. 10, 40-42" Salmanticensis 19 (1972) 261-78. SAND, A.,
Das Gesetz und die Propheten (Regensburg 1974) 171f.

10:40f KäSEMANN, E. Exegetische Versuche und Besinnungen
(1964) I 170.

10:40-41   FLEW, R. N. Jesus and His Church (1956) 83-84.

10:40   HANSON, S. The Unity of the Church in the New Testament (1946) 33f., 35f. STREETER, B. H. The Four Gospels (1951) 263f. BUTLER, B. C. "M. Vaganay and the 'Community Discourse'," NTS 1 (1954-55) 283ff. GEORGI, D. Die Gegner des Paulus im 2. Korinther-Brief (1964) 208f. LAMBRECHT, J. "Die Logia-Quellen von Markus 13," Biblica 47 (1966) 331-33. NICKELS, P. Targum and New Testament (1967) 18. HOFFMANN, P. Studien zur Theologie der Logienquelle (1972) 138, 183f., 257, 285f., 288, 304f. KERTELGE, K., Gemeinde und Amt im Neuen Testament (München 1972) 159f. SCHULZ, S. Q Die Spruchquelle der Evangelisten (1972) 457-59. GOULDER, M. D., Midrash and Lection in Matthew (London 1974) 75, 85, 157, 398. LADD, G. E., A Theology of the New Testament (Grand Rapids 1974) 118, 206, 381. EDWARDS, R. A., A Theology of Q (Philadelphia 1976) 105f. POLAG, A., Die Christologie der Logienquelle (Neukirchen-Vluyn 1977) 70. KERTELGE, K., "Offene Fragen zum Thema 'Geistliches Amt' und das neutestamentliche Verständnis von der 'repraesentation Christi' " in: R. Schnackenburg et al. (eds.) Die Kirche des Anfangs. Für H. Schürmann (Freiburg 1978) 589f. HEDRICK, C. W., "Resurrection: Radical Theology in the Gospel of Matthew" LexTheolQuart 14 (1979) 40-45.

10:41f   DELLING, G. Die Zueignung des Heils in der Taufe (1961) 83. STRECKER, G. Der Weg der Gerechtigkeit (1962) 162, 164, 209s. KäSEMANN, E. Exegetische Versuche und Besinnungen (1964) II 90, 93.

10:41-42   TRILLING, W., "Amt und Amtsverständnis bei Matthäus" in: A. Descamps/ A. de Halleux (eds.) Mélanges Bibliques en hommage au R. P. Béda Rigaux (Gembloux 1970) 38f. GOULDER, M. D., Midrash and Lection in Matthew (London 1974) 83f, 428.

10:41   STRECKER, G. Der Weg der Gerechtigkeit (1962) 1374. BULTMANN, R. The History of the Synoptic Tradition (1963) 147f. KäSEMANN, E. Exegetische Versuche und Besinnungen (1964) 11 89f. SATAKE, A. Die Gemeindeordnung in der Johannesapokalypse (1966) 175-77. KäSEMANN, E. New Testament Questions of Today (1969) 90, 94. BERGER, K. Zu den Sogenannten Sätzen Heiligen Rechts NTS 17 (1970-71) 25f. GOULDER, M. D., Midrash and Lection in Matthew (London 1974) 150, 367, 427, 444. MüLLER, U. B., Zur frühchristlichen Theologiegeschichte (Gütersloh 1976) 37.

10:42   BUTLER, B. C. "M. Vaganay and the 'Community Discourse'," NTS 1 (1954-55) 285ff. FLEW, R. N. Jesus and

His Church (1956) 147. KNOX, W. L. The Sources of the Synoptic Gospels II (1957) 101. SCHULZ, A. Nachfolge und Nachnahmen (1962) 158-161. STRECKER, G. Der Weg der Gerechtigkeit (1962) 191. HAHN, F. Christologische Hoheitstitel (1963) 224. BOUSSET, W. Die Religion des Judentums im Späthellenistischen Zeitalter (1966=1926) 187. NICKELS, P. Targum and New Testament (1967) 18. HASLER, V. Amen (1969) 36. KäSEMANN, E. New Testament Questions of Today (1969) 94. SCHWEIZER, E. Observance of the Law and Charismatic Activity in Matthew NTS 16 (1969-70) 222f. JEREMIAS, J., Neutestamentliche Theologie I (1971) 21, 113, 209, 247. KLIJN, A. F. J., "Die syrische Baruch-Apokalypse" in: W. G. Kümmel (ed.) Jüdische Schriften aus hellenistisch-römischer Zeit V/2 (Gütersloh 1976) 152. METZGER, B. M., The Early Versions of the New Testament (Oxford 1977) 39. THEISSEN, G., Soziologie der Jesusbewegung (München 1977) 19.

10:44   THEISSEN, G., Soziologie der Jesusbewegung (München 1977) 17.

11-12   SELBY, D. J., Introduction to the New Testament (New York 1971) 115, 134, 137, 139, 131-33. ELLIS, P. F., Matthew: His Mind and His Message (Collegeville 1974) 53-59.

11   EWALD, H. Die drei ersten Evangelien (1850) 251ff. BRANDT, W., "Matthäus 11" ZNW 11 (1910) 246. FARRER, A. St. Matthew and St. Mark (1954) 49. DE KRUIJF, T., Der Sohn Des Lebendigen Gottes (Rome 1962) 66, 70f, 78, 84, 90, 137. KäSEMANN, E. Exegetische Versuche und Besinnungen (1964) I 205. HOFFMANN, P. Studien zur Theologie der Logienquelle (1972) 22-25, 30. GOULDER, M. D., Midrash and Lection in Matthew (London 1974) 199, 314, 318, 338. FRIEDRICH, G., "Beobachtungen zur messianischen Hohepriestererwartung in den Synoptikern" in: Auf das Wort kommt es an (Göttingen 1978) 97. RIST, J. M., On the Independence of Matthew and Mark (Cambridge 1978) 53f.

11:1-24   FARRER, A. St. Matthew and St. Mark (1954) 50.

11:1-19   LENTZEN-DEIS, F. Die Taufe Jesu nach den Synoptikern (1970) 82ff.

11:1-15 TALBERT, C. H., Literary Patterns, Theological Themes and the Genre of Luke-Acts (Missoula 1974) 41.

11:1-5 RUDOLPH, K. Die Mandäer I (1960) 69, 77, 105, 246.

11:1 STONEHOUSE, N. B. The Witness of Matthew and Mark to Chrit (1944) 130, 147, 151, 160, 176. FARRER, A. St. Matthew and St. Mark (1954) 179. KNOX, W. L. The Sources of the Synoptic Gospels II (1957) 54. BLAIR, E. P. Jesus in the Gospel of Matthew (1960) 132. STRECKER, G. Der Weg der Gerechtigkeit (1962) 388, 130, 191. HAHN, F. Christologische Hoheitstitel (1963) 400. HAHN, F. Das Verständnis der Mission im Neuen Testament (1965) 104. FRANKEMöLLE, H., Jahwebund und Kirche Christi (Münster 1974) 92, 102, 133, 146, 269, 334, 342. KINGSBURY, J. D., Matthew: Structure, Christology, Kingdom (Philadelphia 1975) 20-25. EGGER, W., Frohbotschaft und Lehre (Frankfurt 1976) 34f.

11:2-13:53 *FRANSEN, I. "Cahier de Bible: Le Discours en Paraboles (Matthieu 11, 2-13, 53)," BVieC 18 ('57) 82-84.

11:2-12:50 KINGSBURY, J. D., Matthew: Structure, Christology, Kingdom (Philadelphia 1975) 18-20.

11:2-12:21 GAECHTER, P. Die literarische Kunst im Matthäus-Evangelium (1968) 28-29.

11:2-12:8 GOULDER, M. D., Midrash and Lection in Matthew (London 1974) 187, 189, 353-63.

11:2ff STONEHOUSE, N. B. The Witness of Matthew and Mark to Christ (1944) 145, 148. KNOX, W. L. The Sources of the Synoptic Gospels II (1957) 8, 54, 145.

11:2-27 ELLIS, P. F., Matthew: His Mind and His Message (Collegeville 1974) 55-57.

11:2-24 WILKENS, J. Einführung in das Evangelium nach Matthäus I (1934) 157-60. *BRUNEC, M. "De Legatione Ioannis Baptistae (Mt 11:2-24)," VerbDom 35 (4, '57) 193-203; (5, '57) 262-70; (6, '57) 321-31. BLAIR, E. P. Jesus in the Gospel of Matthew (1960) 88.

11:2-19 HIRSCH, E. Frühgeschichte des Evangeliums (1941) 90-94. STROBEL, A. Untersuchungen zum Eschatologischen Verzögerungsproblem (1961) 267-73. DELLING, G. Die Taufe im Neuen Testament (1963) 47. LüHRMANN, D. Die Redaktion der Logienquelle (1969) 24-31. SUGGS, M. J. Wisdom, Christology, and Law in Matthew's Gospel (1970) 36ff. DRURY, J., Tradition and Design in Luke's Gospel (Atlanta 1976) 166.

11:2-13 HAHN, F. Christologische Hoheitstitel (1963) 400.

11:2-11 FRIEDRICH, GPM 4 (1949/50) 16ff. STECK, GPM 9
(1954/55) 10ff. SCHLIER, H. in: Herr, tue meine Lippen auf
(1957) Eichholz, G. (ed.) 12-15. DOERNE, M. Er kommt auch
noch heute (1961) 15-17. BORNKAMM, G. GPM 15 (1960/61)
13ff. HOFFMANN, P. Studien zur Theologie der Logienquelle
(1972) passim.

11:2-10 LOHSE, E. Das Aergernis des Kreuzes (1969) 12-18.

11:2-9 SCHLATTER, D. A. Die Theologie des Neuen Testaments
(1909) I 393-97. *KRIEGER, N. "Ein Mensch in weichen
Kleidern." NovTest 1 ('56) 228-30.

11:2-6 LOEWENICH, W. von, Luther als Ausleger der Synoptiker
(1954) 263f. BLAIR, E. P. Jesus in the Gospel of Matthew
(1960) 52. BORNKAMM-BARTH-HELD, Ueberlieferung
und Auslegung im Matthäus-Evangelium (1961) 238f.
DUPONT, J. "L'Ambassade de Jean-Baptiste," NRTh 83
(1961) 805-21, 943-59. STRECKER, G. Der Weg der
Gerechtigkeit (1962) 175, 177. HAHN, F. Christologische
Hoheitstitel (1963) 221f., 393f. STUHLMACHER, P. Das
Paulinische Evangelium (1968) 218. WINK, W. John the
Baptist in the Gospel Tradition (1968) 23-24. BLANK, J.
Schriftauslegung in Theorie und Praxis (1969) 121, 124-28.
SCHULZ, S. Q Die Spruchquelle der Evangelisten (1972) 190-
203. KRAUS, H.-J. GPM 27/1 (1972/73) 21-27. *SABUGAL,
S., "La embajada mesiánica del Bautista (Mt 11, 2-6=Lc 7, 18-
23). Análisis histórico-tradicional" Augustinianum 13 (1973)
215-78. STANTON, G. N., "On the Christology of Q" in: B.
Lindars/ S. S. Smalley (eds.) Christ and the Spirit in the New
Testament. In Honour of Charles F. D. Moule (Cambridge
1973) 29, 33f. GOULDER, M. D., Midrash and Lection in
Matthew (London 1974) 354f, 387. LADD, G. E., A Theology
of the New Testament (Grand Rapids 1974) 65, 71, 142.
*SCHLIER, H., Der Herr ist nahe. Adventsbetrachtungen
(Freiburg 1974). DUNN, J. D. G., Jesus and the Spirit (London
1975) 54-62, 402. EDWARDS, R. A., A Theology of Q
(Philadelphia 1976) 64, 94-96. POLAG, A., Die Christologie
der Logienquelle (Neukirchen-Vluyn 1977) 35-38.
*SABUGAL, S., "La embajada mesiánica del Bautista, IV: La
fuente (Q) et Mt y Lc" Augustinianum 17 (1977) 395-424.
*SABUGAL, S., "La embajada mesiánica del Bautista (Mt 11,
2-6 par.). V: Hacia el evento histórico" Augustinianum 17
(1977) 511-39. TRITES, A. A., The New Testament Concept of
Witness (Cambridge 1977) 179. BöCHER, O., "Johannes der
Täufer in der neutestamentlichen Überlieferung" in: G.
Müller (ed.) Rechtfertigung Realismus Universalismus in
Biblischer Sicht. Festschrift für Adolf Köberle (Darmstadt

1978) 46-52. KOEPPEN, W./WIMMER, U., in: Predigtstudien für das Kirchenjahr 1978/79 I/2. (Stuttgart 1978) 37-48. MARXSEN, W., Christologie-praktisch (Gütersloh 1978) 40f.

11:2-5   VöGTLE, A. Das Evangelium und die Evangelien (1971) 219-42.

11:2f   HAHN, F. Christologische Hoheitstitel (1963) 88, 174.

11:2-3   BEUTLER, J., Martyria (Frankfurt 1972) 273, 286, 294.

11:2   KNOX, W. L. The Sources of the Synoptic Gospels II (1957) 4. BLAIR, E. P. Jesus in the Gospel of Matthew (1960) 55. STRECKER, G. Der Weg der Gerechtigkeit (1962) 1023.5. HAHN, F. Christologische Hoheitstitel (1963) 224. HUMMEL, R. Die Auseinandersetzung zwischen Kirche und Judentum im Matthäusevangelium (1963) 113ff. CHRIST, F. Jesus Sophia (1970) 76, 94.

11:3-6   DELLING, G. Die Taufe im Neuen Testament (1963) 48.

11:3-5   COPE, O. L., Matthew. A Scribe Trained for the Kingdom of Heaven (Washington D. C. 1976) 90-94.

11:3   LOEWENICH, W. von, Luther als Ausleger der Synoptiker (1954) 263f. STROBEL, A. Untersuchungen zum Eschatologischen Verzögerungsproblem (1961) 265-77. VöGTLE, A. Das Evangelium und die Evangelien (1971) 223-30.

11:4ff   STONEHOUSE, N. B. The Witness of Matthew and Mark to Christ (1944) 194.

11:4-6   JEREMIAS, J. Neutestamentliche Theologie I (1971) 31, 33, 39, 89, 106f., 199, 235, 262. VöGTLE, A. Das Evangelium und die Evangelien (1971) 231-36. GOPPELT, L., Theologie des Neuen Testaments I (Göttingen 1975) 112f. PERRIN, N., Jesus and the Language of the Kingdom (London 1976) 37.

11:4-5   STONEHOUSE, N. B., The Witness of Luke to Christ (Grand Rapids 1951) 121f. FARRER, A. St Matthew and St Mark (1954) 44. FLEW, R. N. Jesus and His Church (1956) 60. BORNKAMM-BARTH-HELD, Ueberlieferung und Auslegung im Matthäus-Evangelium (1961) 120, 238, 240. BOUSSET, W. Die Religion des Judentums im Späthellenistischen Zeitalter (1966=1926) 217. LADD, G. E., A Theology of the New Testament (Grand Rapids 1974) 76f, 144.

11:4   HAHN, F. Das Verständnis der Mission im Neuen Testament (1965) 54. BAMMEL, E. The Baptist in Early Christian Tradition NTS 18 (1971-72) 100f.

11:5f   HAHN, F. Christologische Hoheitstitel (1963) 395. KäSEMANN, E. Exegetische Versuche und Besinnungen

(1964) I 197, 228. JüNGEL, E. Paulus und Jesus (1966) 190.

11:5-6 GOULDER, M. D., Midrash and Lection in Matthew (London 1974) 85f, 278, 381. SEYBOLD, K./MüLLER, U., Krankheit und Heilung (Stuttgart 1978) 99-101. MEYER, B. F., The Aims of Jesus (London 1979) 140. SCHILLEBEECKX, E., Die Auferstehung Jesu als Grund der Erlösung (Basel 1979) 32.

11:5 FARRER, A. St Matthew and St Mark (1954) 27. KNOX, W. L. The Sources of the Synoptic Gospels II (1957) 8. ROBINSON, J. M. Kerygma und historischer Jesus (1960) 143. DE KRUIJF, T., Der Sohn Des Lebendigen Gottes (Rome 1962) 49, 63, 127, 134. STRECKER, G. Der Weg der Gerechtigkeit (1962) 243, 195. HAHN, F. Christologische Hoheitstitel (1963) 220. BRAUN, H. Qumran und NT II (1966) 318. NICKELS, P. Targum and New Testament (1967) 18. MARXSEN, W. Mark the Evangelist (1969) 119, 136, 144. CHRIST, F. Jesus Sophia (1970) 76, 144. NöTSCHER, F., Altorientalischer und alttestamentlicher Auferstehungsglaube (Darmstadt 1970=1926) 298. PESCH, R. Jesu ureigene Taten? Ein Beitrag zur Wunderfrage in: Quaestiones Disputatae Bd. 52 (1970) Rahner, K. & Schlier, H. (eds.) 36-44. JEREMIAS, J. Neutestamentliche Theologie I (1971) 83, 111, 114, 118, 134, 198. VöGTLE, A. Das Evangelium und die Evangelien (1971) 236-38. HEROLD, G., Zorn und Gerechtigkeit Gottes bei Paulus (Bern 1973) 221f. KERTELGE, K., "Die Vollmacht des Menschensohnes zur Sündenvergebung (Mk 2, 10)" in: P. Hoffmann (ed.) Orientierung an Jesus. Für Josef Schmid (Freiburg 1973) 207f. GOULDER, M. D., Midrash and Lection in Matthew (London 1974) 313, 316, 327, 357. FRIEDRICH, G., "Beobachtungen zur messianischen Hohepriestererwartung in den Synoptikern" in: Auf das Wort kommt es an (Göttingen 1978) 69. "Armut" in: TRE 4 (1979) 112. MEYER, B. F., The Aims of Jesus (London 1979) 157f.

11:6 HEINZELMANN, D. G. Das Ja Gottes (1924) 66. FLEW, R. N. Jesus and His Church (1956) 66. ROBINSON, J. M. Kerygma und historischer Jesus (1960) 34, 148. JüNGEL, E. Paulus und Jesus (1966) 193. MITTON, C. L. "Uncomfortable Words: IX. Stumbling-block Characteristics in Jesus," ET 82 (6, '71) 168-72. VöGTLE, A. Das Evangelium und die Evangelien (1971) 234-36. SCHILLEBEECKX, E., Die Auferstehung Jesu als Grund der Erlösung (Basel 1979) 80.

11:7ff STONEHOUSE, N. B. The Witness of Matthew and Mark to Christ (1944) 245.

11:7-19 BULTMANN, R. The History of the Synoptic Tradition (1963)

164f. HAHN, F. Christologische Hoheitstitel (1963) 374-77. SCHNIDER, F., Jesus der Prophet (Freiburg 1973) 40f, 50. GOULDER, M. D., Midrash and Lection in Matthew (London 1974) 355-59. EDWARDS, R. A., A Theology of Q (Philadelphia 1976) 96-99.

11:7-15 COPE, O. L., Matthew. A Scribe Trained for the Kingdom of Heaven (Washington D. C. 1976) 73-77.

11:7-11 FLEW, R. N. Jesus and His Church (1956) 22. ROBINSON, J. M. Kerygma und historischer Jesus (1960) 144. SCHULZ, S. Q Die Spruchquelle der Evangelisten (1972) 229-36.

11:7-10 MEYER, B. F., The Aims of Jesus (London 1979) 125f.

11:7-8 HAHN, F. Christologische Hoheitstitel (1963) 378. SCHRAGE, W. Das Verhältnis des Thomas-Evangeliums zur Synoptischen Tradition und zu den Koptischen Evangelienübersetzungen (1964) 160. DANIEL, C. "Les Esséniens et 'Ceux qui sont dans les maisons des rois'(Matthieu 11, 7-8 et Luc 7, 24-25)," RevQ 6 (2, '67) 261-77.

11:7 STRECKER, G. Der Weg der Gerechtigkeit (1962) 20.

11:8 HENNECKE, E. & SCHNEEMELCHER, W. Neutestamentliche Apokryphen (1964) II 324.

11:9f DELLING, G. Die Taufe im Neuen Testament (1963) 55.

11:9 STRECKER, G. Der Weg der Gerechtigkeit (1962) 186. HASLER, V. Amen (1969) 64. JEREMIAS, J. Neutestamentliche Theologie I (1971) 25, 53f., 86, 280.

11:10-19 BOUSSET, W. Die Religion des Judentums im Späthellenistischen Zeitalter (1966=1926) 87, 144, 217, 232, 346.

11:10-13 SCHREINER, J. Gestalt und Anspruch des Neuen Testaments (1969) 142f.

11:10-12 BRAUN, H. Qumran und NT II (1966) 92, 97, 107, 267f.

11:10-11 POLAG, A., Die Christologie der Logienquelle (Neukirchen-Vluyn 1977) 158.

11:10.14 MOORE, G. F. Judaism (1946) II 326.

11:10 STONEHOUSE, N. B. The Witness of Matthew and Mark to Christ (1944) 194. STRECKER, G. Der Weg der Gerechtigkeit (1962) 24, 631. DELLING, G. Die Taufe im Neuen Testament (1963) 47. HAHN, F. Christologische Hoheitstitel (1963) 118.

11:11ff STONEHOUSE, N. B. The Witness of Matthew and Mark to Christ (1944) 133.

11:11-14 ROBINSON, J. M. Kerygma und historischer Jesus (1960) 143-45. SANDMEL, S., We Jews and Jesus (New York 1977) 120.

11:11-13   LADD, G. E., The Presence of the Future (Grand Rapids 1974) 199ff.

11:11f   EHRHARDT, A. "The Disciples of Emmaus" NTS 10 (1963-64) 191f.

11:11   DIBEUUS, F., "Zwei Worte Jesu" ZNW 11 (1910) 190-92. BRUNNER, E. Dogmatik I (1946) 220. BRUNNER, E. Dogmatik II (1950) 240, 394. STAEHELIN, E. Die Verkündigung des Reiches Gottes in der Kirche Jesu Christi (1951) 57, 382. FLEW, R. N. Jesus and His Church (1956) 26. HULL, B. "Saint Joseph and Saint John the Baptist," ClR 41 ('56) 275-84. SCHNACKENBURG, R. Gottes Herrschaft und Reich (1959) 90-92, 111, 153. RUDOLPH, K. Die Mandäer I (1960) 72, 73, 78. STRECKER, G. Der Weg der Gerechtigkeit (1962) 162. SCHRAGE, W. Das Verhältnis des Thomas-Evangeliums zur Synoptischen Tradition und zu den Koptischen Evangelienübersetzungen (1964) 107. BIEDER, W., Die Verheissung der Taufe im Neuen Testament (Zürich 1966) 279. JüNGEL, E. Paulus und Jesus (1966) 176. NICKELS, P. Targum and New Testament (1967) 18. WINK, W. John the Baptist in the Gospel Tradition (1968) 24-25. HASLER, V. Amen (1969) 64. BERGER, K. Die Amen-Worte Jesus (1970) 80-82. FEUILLET, A. Morale Ancienne et Morale Chrétienne NTS 17 (1970-71) 127f. JEREMIAS, J. Neutestamentliche Theologie I (1971) 25f., 39f., 42, 44, 53, 56, 87, 100. METZGER, B. M., The Early Versions of the New Testament (Oxford 1977) 243. "Aramäisch" in: TRE 3 (1978) 609.

11:12ff   STAEHELIN, E. Die Verkündigung des Reiches Gottes in der Kirche Jesu Christi I (1951) 58.

11:12-19   SAND, A., Das Gesetz und die Propheten (Regensburg 1974) 135-37.

11:12f   KNOX, W. L. The Sources of the Synoptic Gospels II (1957) 99. ROBINSON, J. M. Kerygma und historischer Jesus (1960) 19, 144-47. BORNKAMM-BARTH-HELD, Ueberlieferung und Auslegung im Matthäus-Evangelium (1961) 58ff., 149. HUMMEL, R. Die Auseinandersetzung zwischen Kirche und Judentum im Matthäusevangelium (1963) 65. KäSEMANN, E. Exegetische Versuche und Besinnungen (1964) I 210. JüNGEL, E. Paulus und Jesus (1966) 175, 190-93. LENTZEN-DEIS, F. Die Taufe Jesu nach den Synoptikern (1970) 90. JEREMIAS, J. Neutestamentliche Theologie I (1971) 39-41, 43, 53f., 100, 113f., 119. HOFFMANN, P. Studien zur Theologie der Logienquelle (1972) 51-53, 56-60, 50-79, 121f. SCHULZ, S. Q Die Spruchquelle der Evangelisten (1972) 261-67.

11:12-13 PERRIN, N., The Kingdom of God in the Teaching of Jesus (Philadelphia 1963) 43, 171-74. WINK, W. John the Baptist in the Gospel Tradition (1968) 20-22, 29-30, 112. MENOUD, P.-H., "Le sens du verbe βιάζεται dans Lc 16, 16" in: A. Descamps/A. de Halleux (eds.) Mélanges Bibliques en hommage au R. P. Béda Rigaux (Gembloux 1970) 207-209. SCHNIDER, F., Jesus der Prophet (Freiburg 1973) 39, 45, 179ff. SAND, A., Das Gesetz und die Propheten (Regensburg 1974) 178-82. TALBERT, C. H., Literary Patterns, Theological Themes, and the Genre of Luke-Acts (Missoula 1974) 55. SCHULZ, S., Die Mitte der Schrift (Stuttgart 1976) 170-72. *BARNETT, P. W., "Who Were The 'Biastai' (Mt 11: 12-13)?" RThR 36 (1977) 65-70. POLAG, A., Die Christologie der Logienquelle (Neukirchen-Vluyn 1977) 48, 79.

11:12 BRANDT, W., "Matthäus c. 11, 12" ZNW 11 (1910) 247f. SCHOLANDER, H., "Zu Mt 11, 12" ZNW 13 (1912) 172-75. STONEHOUSE, N. B. The Witness of Matthew and Mark to Christ (1944) 245ff. STAEHELIN, E. Die Verkündigung Gottes in der Kirche Jesu Christi I (1951) 175, 328. PARKER, P. The Gospel Before Mark (1953) 77-78. STRATTON, C. "Pressure for the Kingdom. An Exposition," Interp 8 (1954) 414-21. SCHLATTER, A. Johannes der Täufer (1956) 66-71. ROBINSON, J. M. Kerygma und historischer Jesus (1960) 87. BRAUMANN, G. " 'Dem Himmelreich wird Gewalt angetan' (Mt 11:12 par.)," ZNW 52 (1-2, '61) 104-109. STRECKER, G. Der Weg der Gerechtigkeit (1962) 1021, 167, 171, 173, 187, 1961. PERRIN, N., The Kingdom of God in the Teaching of Jesus (Philadelphia 1963) 59f, 87, 121f, 152, 170, 186. HAHN, F. Christologische Hoheitstitel (1963) 165. KäSEMANN, E. Exegetische Versuche und Besinnungen (1964) II 118. HAHN, F. Das Verständnis der Mission im Neuen Testament (1965) 106. BEYSCHLAG, K. Clemens Romanus und der Frühkatholizismus (1966) 216. KäSEMANN, E. New Testament Questions of Today (1969) 122. SANFORD, J. A., The Kingdom Within (New York 1970) 66f, 68. LADD, G. E., The Presence of the Future (Grand Rapids 1974) 123, 159ff, 183, 190, 193. PERRIN, N., Jesus and the Language of the Kingdom (London 1976) 37, 41, 46, 52f, 83, 204. SWIDLER, L., Biblical Affirmations of Woman (Philadelphia 1979) 283. *THIERING, B. E., "Are the 'Violent Men' False Teachers?" NovT 21 (1979) 293-97. HARRINGTON, D. J., God's People in Christ (Philadelphia 1980) 24f.

11:13 BERGER, K. Die Gesetzesauslegung Jesu (1940) 209-27. TRILLING, W. Das wahre Israel (1959) 145f. RUDOLPH, K. Die Mandäer I (1960) 78. STRECKER, G. Der Weg der

Gerechtigkeit (1962) 607, 89, 144, 167, 1872. HUMMEL, R. Die Auseinandersetzung zwischen Kirche und Judentum im Matthäusevangelium (1963) 132, 133, 135. "Bergpredigt" in: TRE 5 (1980) 609.

11:14f FAHY, T. "St. John and Elias (Mt. 11, 14.15)," IThQ XXIII/3 (1956) 285-86. WINK, W. John the Baptist in the Gospel Tradition (1968) 30-32.

11:14 STAEHELIN, E. Die Verkündigung des Reiches Gottes in der Kirche Jesu Christi I (1951) 318. FAHY, T., "St. John and Elias," IThQ 23 ('56) 285-86. STRECKER, G. Der Weg der Gerechtigkeit (1962) 1863. NöTSCHER, F., Altorientalischer und alttestamentlicher Auferstehungsglaube (Darmstadt 1970=1926) 127. BöCHER, O., "Johannes der Täufer in der neutestamentlichen Überlieferung" in: G. Müller (ed.) Rechtfertigung Realismus Universalismus in Biblischer Sicht. Festschrift für A. Köberle (Darmstadt 1978) 47-52, 53.

11:15 KNOX, W. L. The Sources of the Synoptic Gospels II (1957) 88. STRECKER, G. Der Weg der Gerechtigkeit (1962) 1981. SCHRAGE, W. Das Verhältnis des Thomas-Evangeliums zur Synoptischen Tradition und zu den Koptischen Evangelienübersetzungen (1964) 42. METZGER, B. M., The Early Versions of the New Testament (Oxford 1977) 246.

11:16ff SCHWEIZER, E. Erniedrigung und Erhöhung bei Jesus und seinen Nachfolgern (1962) § 30. TESTA, E., "Un ostrakon sull'elogio funsbre e Mt 11,16ff e paralle" RivB 16 (1968) 539-46.

11:16-24 KRECK, W. GPM 11/4 (1956/57) 273-77. GOLLWITZER, H. GPM 13/4 (1958/59) 282-87. STRECKER, G. Der Weg der Gerechtigkeit (1962) 102, 1115, 168. SCHLINK, E. in: Herr, tue meine Lippen auf (1964) Eichholz, G. (ed.) 488ff. KLEIN, GPM 19 (1964/65) 370ff. BRUNNER, P. in: Hören und Fragen Bd. 5 (1967) Eichholz, G. & Falkenroth, A. (eds.) 583ff. GEENSE, A. GPM 25 (3, '71) 443-51. LANGE, E. (ed.) Predigtstudien für das Kirchenjahr 1970/71 (1971) 253-58. RANNENBERG, W./MüLLER, H. M., in: P. Krusche (ed.) Predigtstudien V/2. Halbband (Stuttgart 1977) 255-59.

11:16-19 JüLICHER, D. A. Die Gleichnisreden Jesu (1910) 23-36. PIROT, J. Paraboles et Allégories Evangeliques (1949) 63-70. MUSSNER, F. "Der nicht erkannte Kairos (Mt 11, 16-19=Lk 7, 31-35)," Biblica 40 3/4 (1959) 599-612. ROBINSON, J. M. Kerygma und historischer Jesus (1960) 144. JEREMIAS, J. Die Gleichnisse Jesu (1962) 160-62. WINK, W. John the Baptist in the Gospel Tradition (1968) 22-23. CHRIST, F. Jesus Sophia (1970) 63-80. HOFFMANN, P. Studien zur

Theologie der Logienquelle (1972) 56f., 196-98, 224-31 et al.
SCHULZ, S. Q Die Spruchquelle der Evangelisten (1972) 379-88. FRANKEMöLLE, H., Jahwebund und Kirche Christi
(Münster 1974) 115, 203, 262, 290. GOPPELT, L., Theologie
des Neuen Testaments. I (Göttingen 1975) 91f. ARENS, E.,
The HΛΘON- Sayings in the Synoptic Tradition (Fribourg
1976) 221-43. BETZ, O., "Rechtfertigung im Qumran" in: J.
Friedrich et al. (eds.) Rechtfertigung. Festschrift für E.
Käsemann (Tübingen 1976) 23. GRUNDMANN, W.,
"Weisheit im Horizont des Reiches Gottes. Eine Studie zur
Verkündigung Jesu nach der Spruchüberlieferung Q" in: R.
Schnackenburg et al. (eds.) Die Kirche des Anfangs. Festschrift
für H. Schürmann (Leipzig 1977) 180f. MANEK, J., . . . und
brachte Frucht. Die Gleichnisse Jesu (Berlin 1977) 39-41.
POLAG, A., Die Christologie der Logienquelle (Neukirchen-
Vluyn 1977) 47-89. *MAGASS, W., "Zum Verständnis des
Gleichnisses von den spielenden Kindern (Mt 11, 16-19)" LiBi
45 (1979) 59-70. MEYER, B. F., The Aims of Jesus (London
1979) 124.

11:16-17 SUMMERS, R. The Secret Sayings of the Living Jesus (1968)
75, 81. TESTA, E. "Un ostrakon sull'elogio funebre e Mt. 11, 16
ss. e paralleli," RivBi 16 (5, '68) 539-46. *ZELLER, D., "Die
Bildlogik des Gleichnisses Mt 11:16f/Lk 7:31f" ZNW 68 (1977)
252-57.

11:16 STRECKER, G. Der Weg der Gerechtigkeit (1962) 173.
JüNGEL, E. Paulus und Jesus (1966) 104. POLAG, A., Die
Christologie der Logienquelle (Neukirchen-Vluyn 1977) 45, 62.

11:17 EHRHARDT, A. "Greek Proverbs in the Gospel", The
Framework of the New Testament Stories (1964) 44-63, esp. 51.
NICKELS, P. Targum and New Testament (1967) 19.

11:18f HAHN, F. Christologische Hoheitstitel (1963) 44.
JEREMIAS, J. Neutestamentliche Theologie I (1971) 25f., 29,
56. FERGUSON, E. "Wine as a Table-Drink in the Ancient
World," RestQ 13 (3, '70) 141-53.

11:18-19 LJUNGMAN, H. "En Sifre-text till Matt. 11:18 f. par." (A
Text from the Siphr for Mt 11:18f. par.), SEA 22-23 ('57-'58)
238-42. SCHüRMANN, H., "Beobachtungen zum
Menschensohn-Titel in der Redenquelle" in: R. Pesch/R.
Schnackenburg (eds.) Jesus und der Menschensohn (Freiburg
1975) 131f. SCHENKE, H. M., "Die Tendenz der Weisheit zur
Gnosis" in: B. Aland et al. (eds.) Gnosis. Festschrift für H.
Jonas (Göttingen 1978) 359-65. SWIDLER, L., Biblical
Affirmations of Woman (Philadelphia 1979) 48.

11:19 KLEIN, G. ZNW 2 (1901) 346f. STONEHOUSE, N. B. The

Witness of Matthew and Mark to Christ (1944) 251.
MANSON, W. Jesus the Messiah (1948) 116-18. KNOX, W. L.
The Sources of the Synoptic Gospels II (1957) 33, 115. BLAIR,
E. P. Jesus in the Gospel of Matthew (1960) 77. ROBINSON, J.
M. Kerygma und historischer Jesus (1960) 19, 34. ASHBY, E.
"The Coming of the Son of Man," ET 72 (12, '61) 360-63.
SCHWEIZER, E. Erniedrigung und Erhöhung bei Jesus und
seinen Nachfolgern (1962) § 31. STRECKER, G. Der Weg der
Gerechtigkeit (1962) 60, 175, 1772. HAHN, F. Christologische
Hoheitstitel (1963) 25. LONGENECKER, R. N. Paul Apostle
of Liberty (1964) 140f. BRAUN, H. Qumran und NT II (1966)
87ff., 93f., 95, 112. JüNGEL, E. Paulus und Jesus (1966) 211.
STROBEL, A. Erkenntnis und Bekenntnis der Sünde in
neutestamentlicher Zeit (1968) 60. WREGE, H.-T. Die
Ueberlieferungsgeschichte der Bergpredigt (1968) 43f.
PETZKE, G. Die Traditionen über Apollonius von Tyana und
das Neue Testament (1970) 170, 229. JEREMIAS, J.
Neutestamentliche Theologie I (1971) 21, 25, 87, 111, 117, 120,
123, 142, 248f., 265. HAMERTON-KELLY, R. G., Pre-
Existence, Wisdom, and the Son of Man (Cambridge 1973) 11,
29f., 35, 42, 95, 211. LADD, G. E., A Theology of the New
Testament (Grand Rapids 1974) 54, 84, 154, 349. STANTON,
G. N., Jesus of Nazareth in New Testament Preaching
(Cambridge 1974) 142, 156, 158f. BECKER, J., "Das
Gottesbild Jesu und die älteste Auslegung von Ostern" in: G.
Strecker (ed.) Jesus Christus in Historie und Theologie.
Festschrift für H. Conzelmann (Tübingen 1975) 112-14, 117.
GRäSSER, E., "Jesus und das Heil Gottes" in: G. Strecker (ed.)
Jesus Christus in Historie und Theologie (Tübingen 1975) 178.
"Abstinenz" in: TRE 1 (1977) 394. METZGER, B. M., The
Early Versions of the New Testament (Oxford 1977) 118, 421.
*ORBE, A., "El Hijo del hombre come y bebe (Mt 11, 19; Lc 7,
34)" Gregorianum 58 (1977) 523-55. MEYER, B. F., The Aims
of Jesus (London 1979) 158-62. METZGER, B. M., "St.
Jerome's explicit references to variant readings in manuscripts
of the New Testament" in: E. Best et al. (eds.) Text and
Interpretation. Studies for Matthew Black (Cambridge 1979)
180.

11:20-19-1 VACCARI, A. "Gesù alla svolta della sua predicazione in
Galilea," Divinitas 7 (2, '63) 223-35.

11:20ff STONEHOUSE, N. B. The Witness of Matthew and Mark to
Christ (1944) 145, 153, 185. KNOX, W. L. The Sources of the
Synoptic Gospels II (1957) 53. "Apokalyptik" in: TRE 3 (1978)
254.

11:20-30 HIRSCH, E. Frühgeschichte des Evangeliums (1941) 97-100.

11:20-24 ADINOLFI, M. "La condanna a tre città orgogliose (Matt. 11, 20-24)," BiOr 2 (2, '60) 58-62. STRECKER, G. Der Weg der Gerechtigkeit (1962) 162, 168, 173, 176, 1903. KäSEMANN, E. Exegetische Versuche und Besinnungen (1964) II 98. KäSEMANN, E. New Testament Questions of Today (1969) 100. MUSSNER, F. Die Wunder Jesu (1967) 25-28. CHRIST, F. Jesus Sophia (1970) 64, 75, 76, 82, 84, 93, 94. DAVIES, W. D., The Gospel and the Land (London 1974) 240. GOULDER, M. D., Midrash and Lection in Matthew (London 1974) 359f. EDWARDS, R. A., A Theology of Q (Philadelphia 1976) 68f, 104f. *COMBER, J. A., "The Composition and Literary Characteristics of Matt 11:20-24" CBQ 39 (1977) 497-504.

11:20f STRECKER, G. Der Weg der Gerechtigkeit (1962) 227f. STROBEL, A. Erkenntnis und Bekenntnis der Sünde in neutestamentlicher Zeit (1968) 44.

11:20 STONEHOUSE, N. B. The Witness of Matthew and Mark to Christ (1944) 148. STRECKER, G. Der Weg der Gerechtigkeit (1962) 20. NICKELS, P. Targum and New Testament (1967) 19.

11:21ff MANSON, T. W. The Teaching of Jesus (1945) 28 n.2, 55, 272 n.2.

11:21-27 LüHRMANN, D. Die Redaktion der Logienquelle (1969) 60-68.

11:21-24 SCHULZ, S. Q Die Spruchquelle der Evangelisten (1972) 360-66. TANNEHILL, R. C., The Sword of His Mouth (Philadelphia 1975) 122-28. MCDONALD, J. I. H., Kerygma and Didache (Cambridge 1980) 21.

11:21-23 PARKER, P. The Gospel Before Mark (1953) 7-8. KNOX, W. L. The Sources of the Synoptic Gospels II (1957) 53, 56. HOFFMANN, P. Studien zur Theologie der Logienquelle (1972) 64, 73, 185, 208, 281, 284f., 288f., 293, 307f. BORSCH, F. H., "Jesus the Wandering Preacher?" in: M. Hooker/C. Hickling (eds.) What about the New Testament? In Honour of Christopher Evans (London 1975) 52. POLAG, A., Die Christologie der Logienquelle (Neukirchen-Vluyn 1977) 67-72, 74, 89.

11:21f HAHN, F. Das Verständnis der Mission im Neuen Testament (1965) 27, 28.

11:21 STONEHOUSE, N. B. The Witness of Matthew and Mark to Christ (1944) 148. KNOX, W. L. The Sources of the Synoptic Gospels II (1957) 12. ROBINSON, J. M. Kerygma und historischer Jesus (1960) 137. DALMAN, G. Orte und Wege Jesu (1967) 163f. DORMEYER, D., Die Passion Jesu als Verhaltensmodell (Münster 1974) 98A, 234. SAND, A., Das

Gesetz und die Propheten (Regensburg 1974) 86f. DUNN, J. D.
G., Jesus and the Spirit (London 1975) 70f, 72. METZGER, B.
M., The Early Versions of the New Testament (Oxford 1977)
35. "Aramäisch" in: TRE 3 (1978) 604.

11:22ff KäSEMANN, E. New Testament Questions of Today (1969)
95, 96.

11:22-24 HASLER, V. Amen (1969) 62.

11:22f KäSEMANN, E. Exegetische Versuche und Besinnungen
(1964) II 94.

11:22 KNOX, W. L. The Sources of the Synoptic Gospels II (1957)
54. BERGER, K. Die Amen-Worte Jesus, (1970) 79-80.

11:23-24 FURNISH, V. P., The Moral Teaching of Paul (Nashville
1979) 56.

11:23 STRECKER, G. Der Weg der Gerechtigkeit (1962) 24. HAHN,
F. Das Verständnis der Mission im Neuen Testament (1965) 27.
JEREMIAS, J. Neutestamentliche Theologie I (1971) 16, 21,
22, 25f., 29. DUNN, J. D. G., Jesus and the Spirit (London
1975) 70f, 85. MüLLER, U. B., "Die griechische Esra-
Apokalypse" in: W. G. Kümmel (ed.) Jüdische Schriften aus
hellenistisch-römischer Zeit. V. (Gütersloh 1976) 96.
METZGER, B. M., The Early Versions of the New Testament
(Oxford 1977) 391. METZGER, B. M., "St. Jerome's explicit
references to variant readings in manuscripts of the New
Testament" in: E. Best/R. McL. Wilson (eds.) Text and
Interpretation. Studies for Matthew Black (Cambridge 1979)
181.

11:24 PARKER, P. The Gospel Before Mark (1953) 73-74.
KäSEMANN, E. New Testament Questions of Today (1969)
95.

11:25ff ARVEDSON, T. Das Mysterium Christi (1937) 105f. KNOX,
W. L. The Sources of the Synoptic Gospels II (1957) 27, 55, 140.
BLAIR, E. P. Jesus in the Gospel of Matthew (1960) 65, 66, 67.
KäSEMANN, E. Exegetische Versuche und Besinnungen
(1964) II 139. *MUSSNER, F. "Wege zum Selbstbewusstsein
Jesu. Ein Versuch," BZ 12 (1968) 161-72.

11:25-30 HEINRICI, G. Neutestamentliche Studien (1914) 120-29.
WILKENS, J. Einführung in das Evangelium nach Matthäus I
(1934) 164-66. KRECK, W. GPM 6/1 (1951/52) 44-47.
DAVIES, W. D., " 'Knowledge' in the Dead Sea Scrolls and
Matthew xi. 25-30," HThR XLVI (1953) 113-39. CERFAUX,
L. Les Sources Scriptuaires de Mt., XI, 25-30, EphT 31 (1955)
331-42. FEUILLET, A. "Jésus et la sagesse divine d'après les
évangiles synoptiques. Le "logion johannique' et l'ancien
Testament," RB 62/2 (1955) 161-96. STECK, K. G. 'Ueber

Matthäus 11, 25-30," EvTh 15 (1955) 343-49. GILS, F. Jésus
Prophète D'Après Evangiles Synoptiques (1957) 78-82.
MERTENS, H. L'Hymne de Jubilation chez les Synoptiques
(1957) 5-78. WILCKENS, U. Weisheit und Torheit: Eine
exegetisch-religionsgeschichtliche Untersuchung zu 1 Kor. 1
und 2 (1959) 198ff. BLAIR, E. P. Jesus in the Gospel of
Matthew (1960) 153. LEGASSE, S. "La Révélation aus
NEPIOI," RivBi 67 (3, '60) 321-48. HUNTER, A. M. Crux
Criticorum - Matt. XI. 25-30 - A Reappraisal NTS 8 (1961-62)
241f. DE KRUIJF, T., Der Sohn Des Lebendigen Gottes
(Rome 1962) 66, 68f, 70f. Verkündigt das angenehme Jahr des
Herrn in: Predigtgedanken, Reiche C Bd. 1 (1962) 154-88.
SCHöNHERR, GPM 17 (1962/63) 72ff. STRECKER, G. Der
Weg der Gerechtigkeit (1962) 172. WAINWRIGHT, A. W. The
Trinity in the New Testament (1962) 137-39, 139-41, 177-78,
211-12. BULTMANN, R. The History of the Synoptic
Tradition (1963) 159f. HAHN, F. Christologische Hoheitstitel
(1963) 321f. OBENDIEK, H. in: Herr, tue meine Lippen auf
(1964) Eichholz, G. (ed.) 406ff. BRAUN, H. Qumran und NT II
(1966) 95, 102, 104f., 252, 295, 300. RINALDI, G. "Onus meum
leve. Osservazioni su Ecclesiastico 51 (v. 26, Volg. 34) e Matteo
11, 25-30," BiOr 9 (1, '67) 13-23. HENNECKE, E. &
SCHNEEMELCHER, W. Neutestamentliche Apokryphen
(1964) II 97, 340f. KRUSE, M. GPM 23/1 (1968/69) 71-77.
TöDT, H. E. "Sanftmut und Gewalt," in: Zuwendung und
Gerechtigkeit (1969) 16-23. HAMERTON-KELLY, R. G.,
Pre-Existence, Wisdom, and the Son of Man (Cambridge 1973)
68-70, 74. MACK, B. L., Logos und Sophia (Göttingen 1973)
114. *BEAUVERY, R., "La sagesse se rend justice . . . Mt 11,
25-30" AssS 45 (1974) 17-24. JOSUTTIS, M., GPM 29 (1974)
101-106. *RANDELLINI, L., "L'inno di giubilo: Mt 11, 25-30;
Lc 10, 20-24" RivB 22 (1974) 183-235. HUNTER, A. M.,
Gospel and Apostle (London 1975) 60-67. LUCK, U.,
"Weisheit und Christologie in Mt 11, 25-30" Wort und Dienst
13 (1975) 35-51. MARTIN, R. P., New Testament
Foundations. I (Grand Rapids 1975) 291-98. GRUNDMANN,
W., "Weisheit im Horizont des Reiches Gottes. Eine Studie zur
Verkündigung Jesu nach der Spruchüberlieferung Q" in: R.
Schnackenburg et al. (eds.) Die Kirche des Anfangs. Festschrift
für H. Schürmann (Leipzig 1977) 182-87. SCHRöER, H.,
GPM 33 (1979) 216-22.

11:25-27 ARVEDSON, T. Das Mysterium Christi (1937) 107ff.
STONEHOUSE, N. B. The Witness of Matthew and Mark to
Christ (1944) 17, 212ff. GOLLWITZER, H. GPM 11/3
(1956/57) 167-72. BLAIR, E. P. Jesus in the Gospel of
Matthew (1960) 46. DE KRUIJF, T., Der Sohn Des

Lebendigen Gottes (Rome 1962) 65f, 69, 82, 84, 133. CHRIST, F. Jesus Sophia (1970) 81-99. SUGGS, M. J. Wisdom, Christology, and Law in Matthew's Gospel (1970) 77ff. JEREMIAS, J. Neutestamentliche Theologie I (1971) 33, 35, 63, 68, 70, 118f., 175, 178, 182, 185, 244. HOFFMANN, P. Studien zur Theologie der Logienquelle (1972) 36, 38, 73, 97-101f., 104-42, 145, 153f., 176, 183, 187, 212, 229, 236, 262, 286f., 288, 294, 305-307, 325f. SCHULZ, S. Q Die Spruchquelle der Evangelisten (1972) 213-28. *GRIMM, W., "Der Dank für die empfangene Offenbarung bei Jesus und Josephus. Parallelen zu Mt 11, 25-27" BZ 17 (1973) 249-56. LANGE, J., Das Erscheinen des Auferstandenen im Evangelium nach Matthäus (Würzburg 1973) 123, 160, 163-65, 261. KERTELGE, K., "Apokalypsis Jesou Christou (Gal 1, 12)" in: J. Gnilka (ed.) Neues Testament und Kirche. Für R. Schnackenburg (Freiburg 1974) 276-79. TALBERT, C. H., Literary Patterns, Theological Themes and the Genre of Luke-Acts (Missoula 1974) 53. KINGSBURY, J. D., Matthew: Structure, Christology, Kingdom (Philadelphia 1975) 63-65. EDWARDS, R. A., A Theology of Q (Philadelpia 1976) 106f. POLAG, A., Die Christologie der Logienquelle (Neukirchen-Vluyn 1977) 160-62. *KLOPPENBORG, J. S., "Wisdom Christology in Q" LThPh 34 (1978) 129-47. SCHENKE, H. M., "Die Tendenz der Weisheit zur Gnosis" in: B. Aland et al. (eds.) Gnosis. Festschrift für H. Jonas (Göttingen 1978) 360-65.

11:25-26 DE KRUIJF, T., Der Sohn Des Lebendigen Gottes (Rome 1962) 66, 68, 72f, 124. MARCHEL, W. Abba, Père! La Prière du Christ et des Chrétiens (1963) 149-65. GOPPELT, L., Theologie des Neuen Testaments. I (Göttingen 1975) 224f, 250, 252.

11:25 STONEHOUSE, N. B. The Witness of Matthew and Mark to Christ (1944) 148, 151, 153. FLEW, R. N. Jesus and His Church (1956) 62-65. SCHRAGE, W. Die konkreten Einzelgebote in der paulinischen Paränese (1961) 243. DE KRUIJF, T., Der Sohn Des Lebendigen Gottes (Rome 1962) 62, 66f., 78, 83f, 133. STRECKER, G. Der Weg der Gerechtigkeit (1962) 173. HAHN, F. Christologische Hoheitstitel (1963) 319. BOUSSET, W. Die Religion des Judentums im Späthellenistischen Zeitalter (1966-1926) 65, 187, 377. JEREMIAS, J. Abba; Studien zur neutestamentlichen Theologie und Zeitgeschichte (1966) 51-54, 56-58. JEREMIAS, J. Neutestamentliche Theologie I (1971) 21, 25, 65, 67, 69, 70, 113, 166, 183-85. MEYER, B. F., The Aims of Jesus (London 1979) 169f.

11:26 JEREMIAS, J. Abba; Studien zur neutestamentlichen

Theologie und Zeitgeschichte (1966) 56-58. JEREMIAS, J. Neutestamentliche Theologie I (1971) 21, 31, 70, 185.

11:27-30   BLAIR, E. P. Jesus in the Gospel of Matthew (1960) 108, 136. DAVIES, W. D., The Sermon on the Mount (Cambridge 1966) 75f.

11:27   ARVEDSON, T. Das Mysterium Christi (1937) 154f. WINDISCH, H. The Meaning of the Sermon on the Mount (1937) 136f. HANSON, S. The Unity of the Church in the New Testament (1946) 34f. GUY, H. A. New Testament Prophecy. Its Origin and Significance (1947) 75ff. MANSON, W. Jesus the Messiah (1948) 103f. 107-109. KOEHLER, L. "Eine Handvoll Neues Testament," in: Ehrfurcht vor dem Leben. Festschrift für A. Schweitzer (1954) 80. HOUSSIAU, A. "L'Exégèse de Matthieu XI, 27B selon Saint Irénée," EphT XXIX (1953) 328-54. M'NEILE, A. H. The Gospel According to St Matthew (1955) 163-66. BARRETT, C. K. The New Testament Background: Selected Documents (1956) 90. *WINTER, P. "Matthieu xi 27 and Luke x 22 from the First to the Fifth Century," NovTest 1 ('56) 112-48. CULLMANN, O. Die Christologie des Neuen Testaments (1957) 292ff. TRILLING, W. Das wahre Israel (1959) 7f. BLAIR, E. P. Jesus in the Gospel of Matthew (1960) 47, 60, 67, 94, 97, 139, 140. DELLING, G. Die Zueignung des Heils in der Taufe (1961) 95. Van Iersel, B. M. F., 'Der Sohn' in den Synoptischen Jesusworten (1961) 146-61. DE KRUIJF, T., Der Sohn Des Lebendigen Gottes (Rome 1962) 8, 41, 65, 68f, 72-75, 83, 90, 93, 112, 114, 136-39, 142, 144, 148, 156, 166. STRECKER, G. Der Weg der Gerechtigkeit (1962) 127₃, 209₂, 210f. WAINWRIGHT, A. W. The Trinity in the New Testament (1962) 177-78. HAHN, F. Christologische Hoheitstitel (1963) 321-26. HUMMEL, R. Die Auseinandersetzung zwischen Kirche und Judentum im Matthäusevangelium (1963) 115. MARCHAL, W. Abba, Père! La Prière du Christ et des Chrétiens (1963) 165-71. SCHRAGE, W. Das Verhältnis des Thomas-Evangeliums zur Synoptischen Tradition und zu den Koptischen Evangelienübersetzungen (1964) 128. GRUNDMANN, W. "Matth. xi. 27 und die Johanneischen 'Der Vater - Der Sohn' Stellen," NTS 12 (1, '65) 42-49. HAHN, F. Das Verständnis der Mission im Neuen Testament (1965) 54f., 56. JEREMIAS, J. Abba; Studien zur neutestamentlichen Theologie und Zeitgeschichte (1966) 47-54. BRAUN, H. Jesus (1969) 34f. FRIEDLANDER, G. The Jewish Sources of the Sermon on the Mount (1969) 5, 79, 82. HOFFMANN, P. "Die Offenbarung des Sohnes. Die apokalyptischen Voraussetzungen und ihre Verarbeitung im Q-Logion Mt 11,

27 par Lk 10, 22," Kairos 12 (4, '70) 270-88. O'NEILL, J. C., The Theology of Acts in its Historical Setting (London 1970) 34-36. ORBE, A. "La revelacion del Hijo por el Padre segun san Ireneo (Adv. hear, IV 6). (Para la exegesis prenicena de Mt. 11, 27)," Gregorianum 51 ('70) 5-86. JEREMIAS, J. Neutestamentliche Theologie I (1971) 62-67, 73, 244, 246. English transl. New Testament Theology I (1971). VöGTLE, A. Das Evangelium und die Evangelien (1971) 333-36. LANGE, J., Das Erscheinen des Auferstandenen im Evangelium nach Matthäus (Würzburg 1973) 32, 123, 151-53, 155-59, 161, 164-67, 169-72, 175f, 200f, 205, 208-13, 215, 230-32, 242-46, 314f, 326, 342, 431, 436, 488, 491, 495-97, 499f. ROBINSON, J. A. T., "The Use of the Fourth Gospel for Christology Today" in: B. Lindars/S. S. Smalley (eds.) Christ and the Spirit in the New Testament. In Honour of C. F. D. Moule (Cambridge 1973) 69f, 73. GOULDER, M. D., Midrash and Lection in Matthew (London 1974) 156, 308, 330, 362, 385. DUNN, J. D. G., Jesus and the Spirit (London 1975) 14, 26, 27-34, 37-39, 41, 66, 90ff, 368. GOPPELT, L., Theologie des Neuen Testaments. I (Göttingen 1975) 251ff; II (1976) 554f. MEYER, B. F., The Aims of Jesus (London 1979) 152.

11:28ff ARVEDSON, T. Das Mysterium Christi (1937) 225f. "Apokalyptik" in: TRE 3 (1978) 254.

11:28-31 SWIDLER, L., Biblical Affirmations of Woman (Philadelphia 1979) 64, 284.

11:28-30 MANSON, W. Jesus the Messiah (1948) 73-75. BAUER, J. B. "Das milde Joch und die Ruhe, Matth. 11, 28-30," ThZ 17 (2, '61) 99-106. BORNKAMM-BARTH-HELD, Ueberlieferung und Auslegung im Matthäus-Evangelium (1961) 96f., 122, 139, 148. STRECKER, G. Der Weg der Gerechtigkeit (1962) 127, 166, 172ff., 177, 213, 231, 235. WAINWRIGHT, A. W. The Trinity in the New Testament (1962) 137-39. FEUILLET, A., "Le Nouveau Testament et le Coeur du Christ. Etude des principaux textes évangéliques utilisés par la liturgie du Sacré-Coeur," AmiCler 74 (May 21, '64) 321-33. SCHRAGE, W. Das Verhältnis des Thomas-Evangeliums zur Synopischen Tradition und zu den Koptischen Evangelienübersetzungen (1964) 172. BETZ, H. D. "The Logion of the Easy Yoke and of Rest (Matt 11:28-30)," JBL 86 (1, '67) 10-24. SUMMERS, R. The Secret Sayings of the Living Jesus (1968) 27. OTOMO, Y. Nachfolge Jesu und Anfänge der Kirche im Neuen Testament (1970) 127f. CHRIST, F. Jesus Sophia (1970) 100-19. SUGGS, M. J. Wisdom, Christology, and Law in Matthew's Gospel (1970) 31ff., 77ff. BAUER, J. B., Scholia Biblica et Patristica (Graz 1972) 53-60. BONHOEFFER, D., Gesammelte

Schriften. V (München 1972) 527ff. STANTON, G. N., "On the Christology of Q" in: B. Lindars/ S. S. Smalley (eds.) Christ and the Spirit in the New Testament. In Honour of C. F. D. Moule (Cambridge 1973) 37f. DUNN, J. D. G., Jesus and the Spirit (London 1975) 29ff, 172. HOWARD, V. P., Das Ego in den Synoptischen Evangelien (Marburg 1975) 198-204. DUNN, J. D. G., Unity and Diversity in the New Testament (London 1977) 259. SCHENKE, H. M., "Die Tendenz der Weisheit zur Gnosis" in: B. Aland et al. (eds.) Gnosis. Festschrift für H. Jonas (Göttingen 1978) 359-65. "Armut" in: TRE 4 (1979) 78.

11:28 COX, J. J. C. " 'Bearers of Heavy Burdens,' A Significant Textual Variant," AUSS 9 (1, '71) 1-15. JEREMIAS, J. Neutestamentliche Theologie I (1971) 114f., 157. LANG, B., Frau Weisheit (Düsseldorf 1975) 46f. EGGER, W., Frohbotschaft und Lehre (Frankfurt 1976) 126. "Berufung" in: TRE 5 (1980) 697.

11:29-30 DENNEY, J. The Death of Christ (1956) 32f. TRILLING, W. Das wahre Israel (1959) 128. SANFORD, J. A., The Kingdom Within (New York 1970) 93f.

11:29 BORNHäUSSER, D. K. Die Bergpredigt (1927) 37f. BLAIR, E. P. Jesus in the Gospel of Matthew (1960) 96, 135, 165. STRECKER, G. Der Weg der Gerechtigkeit (1962) 232, 74. *MAHER, M., " 'Take my yoke upon you' (Mt 11, 29)" NTS 22 (1975) 97-103. SWIDLER, L., Biblical Affirmations of Woman (Philadelphia 1979) 288.

11:30 LAMBERT, G. Mon Joug est Aisé et mon Fardeau Léger, NRTh 87 (1955) 963-69. BLAIR, E. P. Jesus in the Gospel of Matthew (1960) 79. THEUNISSEN, M., "ὁ αἰτῶν λαμβάνει. Der Gebetsglaube Jesu und die Zeitlichkeit des Christseins" in: Jesus, Ort der Erfahrung Gottes (Basel 1976) 32.

12 FARRER, A. St Matthew and St Mark (1954) 4. COPE, O. L., Matthew, A Scribe Trained for the Kingdom of Heaven (Washington D. C. 1976) 32-52. MIRANDA, J. P., Marx and the Bible (London 1977) 222f. COMBER, J. A., "The Verb Therapeuo in Matthew's Gospel" JBL 97 (1978) 431-34.

12:1ff STONEHOUSE, N. B. The Witness of Matthew and Mark to Christ (1944) 153.

12:1-14 EWALD, H. Die drei ersten Evangelien (1850) 196ff.

12:1-8 WILKENS, J. Einführung in das Evangelium nach Matthäus I (1934) 167-69. MOORE, G. F. Judaism (1946) I 503n, II 29. BORNKAMM-BARTH-HELD, Ueberlieferung und Auslegung im Matthäus-Evangelium (1961) 29, 33, 75ff., 85f., 148, 187. BENOIT, P. "Les épis arrachés (Mt 12, 1-8 et par.)," SBFLA 13 ('62-'63) 76-92. STRECKER, G. Der Weg der Gerechtigkeit (1962) 32f. HUMMEL, R. Die Auseinandersetzung zwischen Kirche und Judentum im Matthäusevangelium (1963) 40-44, 53-56, 90-92. BüCKMANN, O. in: Herr, tue meine Lippen auf (1964) Eichholz, G. (ed.) 416ff. GRASSI, J., "The Five Loaves of the High Priest" NovT 7 (1964) 119-22. IWAND, H.-J. Predigt-Meditationen (1964) 41-44. SUHL, A. Die Funktion der alttestamentlichen Zitate und Anspielungen im Markusevangelium (1965) 82ff. WREGE, H.-T. Die Ueberlieferungsgeschichte der Bergpredigt (1968) 50-51. HERRANZ MARCO, M. "Las espigas arrancadas en sabado (Mt 12, 1-8 par.) Tradicion y elaboracion literaria," EstBi 28 (3-4, '69) 313-48. CATCHPOLE, D. R. The Answer of Jesus to Caiaphas Mt. 26:64 NTS 17 (1970-71) 224f. SCHRAMM, T. Der Markus-Stoff bei Lukas (1971) 111f. GOULDER, M. D., Midrash and Lection in Matthew (London 1974) 17f, 187, 189, 328. SAND, A., Das Gesetz und die Propheten (Regensburg 1974) 59-61. AICHINGER, H., "Quellenkritische Untersuchung der Perikope vom Aehrenraufen am Sabbat Mk 2:23-28 par Mt 12:1-8 par Lk 6:1-5" in: A. Fuchs (ed.) Jesus in der Verkündigung der Kirche (Linz 1976) 110-53. *COHEN, M., "La controverse de Jésus et des Pharisiens à propos de la cueillette des épis, selon l'évangile de saint Matthieu" MSR 34 (1977) 3-12. SANDMEL, S., We Jews and Jesus (New York 1977) 136. *O'CONNELL, L. J., "Boismard's Synoptic theory: exposition and response" Theology Digest 26 (1978) 325-42. *COHN-SHERBOK, D. M., "An Analysis of Jesus' Arguments Concerning the Plucking of Grain on the Sabbath" Journal for the Study of the New Testament 2 (1979) 31-41. MCDONALD, J. I. H., Kerygma and Didache (Cambridge 1980) 50.

12:1-2 SUMMERS, The Secret Sayings of the Living Jesus (1968) 69.

12:1 STONEHOUSE, N. B. The Witness of Matthew and Mark to Christ (1944) 148, 149, 151.

12:2ff STRECKER, G. Der Weg der Gerechtigkeit (1962) 173.

12:4-5 TRITES, A. A., The New Testament Concept of Witness (Cambridge 1977) 192.

12:4   *MORGAN, C. S., " 'When Abiatar was High Priest' (Mk 2:26)" JBL 98 (1979) 409f.

12:5ff   GäRTNER, B. The Temple and the Community in Qumran and the New Testament (1965) 115.

12:5-10   KNOX, W. L. The Sources of the Synoptic Gospels II (1957) 78.

12:5   SAND, A., Das Gesetz und die Propheten (Regensburg 1974) 43-45. *LEVINE, E., "The Sabbath Controversy according to Matthew" NTS 22 (1976) 480-83.

12:6ff   DAVIES, W. D., The Sermon on the Mount (Cambridge 1966) 88.

12:6   BLAIR, E. P. Jesus in the Gospel of Matthew (1960) 148. STRECKER, G. Der Weg der Gerechtigkeit (1962) 146₂. HAHN, F. Christologische Hoheitstitel (1963) 239. HUMMEL, R. Die Auseinandersetzung zwischen Kirche und Judentum im Matthäusevangelium (1963) 90-92, 94, 107. GäRTNER, B. The Temple and the Community in Qumran and the New Testament (1965) 116f. HASLER, V. Amen (1969) 86. FRIEDRICH, G., "Beobachtungen zur messianischen Hohepriestererwartung in den Synoptikern" in: Auf das Wort kommt es an (Göttingen 1978) 80-82.

12:7, 11   "Barmherzigkeit" in: TRE 5 (1980) 235.

12:7   STONEHOUSE, N. B. The Witness of Matthew and Mark to Christ (1944) 200. SCHWEIZER, E. Gemeinde und Gemeinde-Ordnung im Neuen Testament (1959) § 4b. BLAIR, E. P. Jesus in the Gospel of Matthew (1960) 93, 123, BORNKAMM-BARTH-HELD, Ueberlieferung und Auslegung im Matthäus-Evangelium (1961) 34, 77f., 245, 251. STRECKER, G. Der Weg der Gerechtigkeit (1962) 25, 135, 136, 147, 174, 177. HUMMEL, R. Die Auseinandersetzung zwischen Kirche und Judentum im Matthäusevangelium (1963) 97-99, 99-103. GäRTNER, B. The Temple and the Community in Qumran and the New Testament (1965) 109, 116. STROBEL, A. Erkenntnis und Bekenntnis der Sünde in neutestamentlicher Zeit (1968) 45, 61.

12:8   STONEHOUSE, N. B. The Witness of Matthew and Mark to Christ (1944) 251, 255. KNOX, W. L. The Sources of the Synoptic Gospels II (1957) 142. BLAIR, E. P. Jesus in the Gospel of Matthew (1960) 77. JüNGEL, E. Paulus und Jesus (1966) 209. SANFORD, J. A., The Kingdom Within (New York 1970) 93. ERNST, J., Anfänge der Christologie (Stuttgart 1972) 152f.

12:9ff   STONEHOUSE, N. B. The Witness of Matthew and Mark to

Christ (1944) 153. KNOX, W. L. The Sources of the Synoptic Gospels II (1957) 84.

12:9-21 WILKENS, J. Einführung in das Evangelium nach Matthäus I (1934) 169-70.

12:9-16 FARRER, A. St Matthew and St Mark (1954) 194.

12:9-14 STONEHOUSE, N. B. The Witness of Matthew and Mark to Christ (1944) 145. FARRER, A. St Matthew and St Mark (1954) 50. MUNCK, J. Paul and the Salvation of Mankind (1959) 251f. BORNKAMM-BARTH-HELD, Ueberlieferung und Auslegung im Matthäus-Evangelium (1961) 73f., 85f., 224, 231f. STRECKER, G. Der Weg der Gerechtigkeit (1962) 32f. HUMMEL, R. Die Auseinandersetzung zwischen Kirche und Judentum im Matthäusevangelium (1963) 44-45, 53-56. CRIBBS, F. L., in: G. MacRae (ed.) SBL Seminar Papers 2 (1973) 13f. GOULDER, M. D., Midrash and Lection in Matthew (London 1974) 18, 187, 189, 317, 328f. SAND, A., Das Gesetz und die Propheten (Regensburg 1974) 61-63. WESTERHOLM, S., Jesus and Scribal Authority (Lund 1978) 100f. HEIL, J. P., "Significant Aspects of the Healing Miracles in Matthew" CBQ 41 (1979) 274-87. MEYER, B. F., The Aims of Jesus (London 1979) 162-68. SWIDLER, L., Biblical Affirmations of Woman (Philadelphia 1979) 181.

12:9-13 McDONALD, J. I. H., Kerygma and Didache (Cambridge 1980) 50.

12:9 STONEHOUSE, N. B. The Witness of Matthew and Mark to Christ (1944) 149, 160.

12:10ff KNOX, W. L. The Sources of the Synoptic Gospels II (1957) 78. STRECKER, G. Der Weg der Gerechtigkeit (1962) 722.

12:10 FARRER, A. St Matthew and St Mark (1954) 124. STRECKER, G. Der Weg der Gerechtigkeit (1962) 19. LOUIS, F. & DELTOMBE, F. "Pourquoi leur parles-tu en paraboles? Ceux qui voient sans apercevoir et entendent sans compredre," BibTerreSainte 76 ('65) 6-7.

12:11-30 TALBERT, C. H., Literary Patterns, Theological Themes, and the Genre of Luke-Acts (Missoula 1974) 54.

12:11f BORNKAMM-BARTH-HELD, Ueberlieferung und Auslegung im Matthäus-Evangelium (1961) 73f., 83, 89, 187, 227.

12:11-12 SANFORD, J. A., The Kingdom Within (New York 1970) 92f. LOHSE, E., Die Einheit des Neuen Testaments (Göttingen 1973) 40, 69-72.

12:11 STONEHOUSE, N. B. The Witness of Matthew and Mark to

Christ (1944) 248. BLAIR, E. P. Jesus in the Gospel of Matthew (1960) 113. STRECKER, G. Der Weg der Gerechtigkeit (1962) 19. BRAUN, H. Qumran und NT II (1966) 99, 289, 296. GOULDER, M. D., Midrash and Lection in Matthew (London 1974) 21f, 437. BANKS, R., Jesus and the Law in the Synoptic Tradition (London 1975) 129f. POLAG, A., Die Christologie der Logienquelle (Neukirchen-Vluyn 1977) 43, 80.

12:12 PARKER, P. The Gospel Before Mark (1953) 136-37. JüNGEL, E. Paulus und Jesus (1966) 209. GOULDER, M. D., Midrash and Lection in Matthew (London 1974) 18, 24, 120, 178, 303. BANKS, R., Jesus and the Law in the Synoptic Tradition (London 1975) 126f. METZGER, B. M., The Early Versions of the New Testament (Oxford 1977) 178.

12:13-17 FRIEDRICH, G., "Das Problem der Autorität im Neuen Testament" in: Auf das Wort kommt es an (Göttingen 1978) 409f.

12:14ff STRECKER, G. Der Weg der Gerechtigkeit (1962) 70.

12:14 STONEHOUSE, N. B. The Witness of Matthew and Mark to Christ (1944) 153. FARRER, A. St. Matthew and St Mark (1954) 55. STRECKER, G. Der Weg der Gerechtigkeit (1962) 176₂.

12:15ff VOLZ, P. Die Eschatologie der jüdischen Gemeinde (1934) 187.

12:15-21 STONEHOUSE, N. B. The Witness of Matthew and Mark to Christ (1944) 145. BORNKAMM-BARTH-HELD, Ueberlieferung und Auslegung im Matthäus-Evangelium (1961) 34, 116ff., 122, 132f., 141, 249. EGGER, W. Frohbotschaft und Lehre (Frankfurt 1976) 34f, 99.

12:15-16 LANGE, J., Das Erscheinen des Auferstandenen im Evangelium nach Matthäus (Würzburg 1973) 150, 261, 263-65, 359.

12:15 STONEHOUSE, N. B. The Witness of Matthew and Mark to Christ (1944) 145, 149, 160. BLAIR, E. P. Jesus in the Gospel of Matthew (1960) 87. STRECKER, G. Der Weg der Gerechtigkeit (1962) 121₁₇.

12:16 BLAIR, E. P. Jesus in the Gospel of Matthew (1960) 79. STRECKER, G. Der Weg der Gerechtigkeit (1962) 69. FRIEDRICH, G., "Beobachtungen zur messianischen Hohepriestererwartung in den Synoptikern" in: Auf das Wort kommt es an (Göttingen 1978) 101.

12:17ff STONEHOUSE, N. B. The Witness of Matthew and Mark to Christ (1944) 191. KNOX, W. L. The Sources of the Synoptic .

Gospels II (1957) 126. STRECKER, G. Der Weg der Gerechtigkeit (1962) 665, 176. WREGE, H.-T. Die Ueberlieferungsgeschichte der Bergpredigt (1968) 47-49.

12:17-21 ROTHFUCHS, W. Die Erfüllungszitate des Matthäus-Evangeliums (1969) 72-77.

12:17 STRECKER, G. Der Weg der Gerechtigkeit (1962) 712. HUMMEL, R. Die Auseinandersetzung zwischen Kirche und Judentum im Matthäus-Evangelium (1963) 132.

12:18ff SAND, A., Das Gesetz und die Propheten (Regensburg 1974) 154-56.

12:18-21 LOHMEYER, E. Gottesknecht und Davidsohn (1954) 8-14. TRILLING, W. Das wahre Israel (1959) 103f. BLAIR, E. P. Jesus in the Gospel of Matthew (1960) 39. LINDARS, B. New Testament (1961) 144-52. STRECKER, G. Der Weg der Gerechtigkeit (1962) 492, 67ff., 704, 83f., 1202. HAHN, F. Das Verständnis der Mission im Neuen Testament (1965) 109f. BRAUN, H. Qumran und NT II (1966) 304, 308, 324, 380. GRINDEL, J. "Matthew 12, 18-21," CBQ 29 (1, '67) 110-15. LANGE, J., Das Erscheinen des Auferstandenen im Evangelium nach Matthäus (Würzburg 1973) 261, 264-66, 268, 270, 272. GOULDER, M. D., Midrash and Lection in Matthew (London 1974) 126, 128f, 133, 320, 329f.

12:18 GILS, F. Jésus Prophète D'Après Les Evangiles Synoptiques (1957) 54-57. BLAIR, E. P. Jesus in the Gospel of Matthew (1960) 78, 79. LöVESTAM, E., Son and Savior (Lund 1961) 95f. DE KRUIJF, T., Der Sohn Des Lebendigen Gottes (Rome 1962) 30f, 47f, 50, 63f, 70, 114, 124, 127, 139, 142. STRECKER, G. Der Weg der Gerechtigkeit (1962) 1803. SCHWEIZER, E. Erniedrigung und Erhöhung bei Jesus und seinen Nachfolgern (1962) § 6a, b. DELLING, G. Die Taufe im Neuen Testament (1963) 56. GäRTNER, B. The Temple and the Community in Qumran and the New Testament (1965) 117. JEREMIAS, J. Abba; Studien zur neutestamentlichen Theologie und Zeitgeschichte (1966) 191-94. MARSHALL, I. H. Son of God or Servant or Yahweh? NTS 11 (1968-69) 331-35. JEREMIAS, J. Neutestamentliche Theologie I (1971) 60f. KINGSBURY, J. D., Matthew: Structure, Christology, Kingdom (Philadelphia 1975) 93-95. WENZ, H., Theologie des Reiches Gottes (Hamburg 1975) 54-56.

12:19 NICKELS, P. Targum and New Testament (1967) 19.

12:20 BLAIR, E. P. Jesus in the Gospel of Matthew (1960) 79. BORNKAMM-BARTH-HELD, Ueberlieferung und Auslegung im Matthäus-Evangelium (1961) 119, 132f., 139,

142, 251. STROBEL, A. Untersuchungen zum Eschatologischen Verzögerungsproblem (1961) 281. LANGE, J., Das Erscheinen des Auferstandenen im Evangelium nach Matthäus (Würzburg 1973) 262-64, 266.

12:20c GIAVINI, G. " 'Donec eiciat ad victoriam iudicium': Mt. 12, 20c ne suo contesto," RivBi 16 (2, '68) 201-205.

12:21 STRECKER, G. Der Weg der Gerechtigkeit (1962) 83.

12:22ff STRECKER, G. Der Weg der Gereechtigkeit (1962) 96 ι, 1686. HUMMEL, R. Die Auseinandersetzung zwischen Kirche und Judentum im Matthäusevangelium (1963) 120, 122ff.

12:22-50 EWALD, H. Die drei ersten Evangelien (1850) 226ff.

12:22-45 LUND, N. W. Chiasmus in the New Testament (1942) 272f. HUMMEL, R. Die Auseinandersetzung zwischen Kirche und Judentum im Matthäusevangelium (1963) 122-28. DOWNING, F. G. Towards the Rehabilitation of Q NTS 11 (1964-65) 170f. GAECHTER, P. Die literarische Kunst im Matthäus-Evangelium (1968) 26-28.

12:22-37 BULTMANN, R. The History of the Synoptic Tradition (1963) 13-14, 209. KüMMEL, W. G. Einführung in die exegetische Methoden (1963) 57-67. GOULDER, M. D., Midrash and Lection in Matthew (London 1974) 37, 45, 187, 330-33.

12:22-32 BARRETT, C. K. The Holy Spirit and the Gospel Tradition (1947) 59-63. HAHN, F. Christologische Hoheitstitel (1963) 298 ι. TRITES, A. A., The New Testament Concept of Witness (Cambridge 1977) 191f.

12:22-30 JüLICHER, D. A. Die Gleichnisreden Jesu (1910) 214-40. HIRSCH, E. Frühgeschichte des Evangeliums (1941) 60-64, 327-29. MOORE, G. F. Judaism (1946) II 309n. BAUMBACH, G. Das Verständnis des Bösen in den synoptischen Evangelien (1963) 111ff, 184f. LüHRMANN, D. Die Redaktion der Logienquelle (1969) 32-43. HOFFMANN, P. Studien zur Theologie der Logienquelle (1972) passim. SCHULZ, S. Q Die Spruchquelle der Evangelisten (1972) 203-13.

12:22-29 WILKENS, J. Einführung in das Evangelium nach Matthäus I (1934) 170-72.

12:22-28 POLAG, A., Die Christologie der Logienquelle (Neukirchen-Vluyn 1977) 39-41.

12:22-24 FARRER, A. St Matthew and St Mark (1954) 50. BURGER, C. Jesus als Davidssohn (1970) 77-79.

12:22-23 STONEHOUSE, N. B. The Witness of Matthew and Mark to Christ (1944) 145, 148, 153. DOWNING, F. G. Towards the

Rehabilitation of Q NTS 11 (1964-65) 172f. BLANK, J. Schriftauslegung in Theorie und Praxis (1969) 107, 110-112.

12:22 FARRER, A. St Matthew and St Mark (1954) 124.

12:23-24 BLAIR, E. P. Jesus in the Gospel of Matthew (1960) 99.

12:23 STONEHOUSE, N. B. The Witness of Matthew and Mark to Christ (1944) 106, 223. BLAIR, E. P. Jesus in the Gospel of Matthew (1960) 56, 101. STRECKER, G. Der Weg der Gerechtigkeit (1962) 118, 176l. HAHN, F. Christologische Hoheitstitel (1963) 245. HUMMEL, R. Die Auseinandersetzung zwischen Kirche und Judentum im Matthäusevangelium (1963) 116, 118, 120, 124. GIBBS, J. M. Purpose and Pattern in Matthew's use of the title "Son of David". NTS 10 (1963-64) 446f, 449f.

12:24ff STONEHOUSE, N. B. The Witness of Matthew and Mark to Christ (1944) 145. HUMMEL, R. Die Auseinandersetzung zwischen Kirche und Judentum im Matthäusevangelium (1963) 155.

12:24-30 GOPPELT, L., Theologie des Neuen Testaments. I (Göttingen 1975) 126.

12:24 PARKER, P. The Gospel Before Mark (1953) 72ff. STRECKER, G. Der Weg der Gerechtigkeit (1962) 1013, 1762. GOULDER, M. D., Midrash and Lection in Matthew (London 1974) 13, 120, 327, 330ff. HABICHT, C., "2. Makkabäerbuch" in: W. G. Kummel (ed.) Jüdische Schriften aus hellenistisch-römischer Zeit. I (Gütersloh 1976) 265.

12:25ff STONEHOUSE, N. B. The Witness of Matthew and Mark to Christ (1944) 145. HUMMEL, R. Die Auseinandersetzung zwischen Kirche und Judentum im Matthäusevangelium (1963) 118f.

12:25-45 FARRER, A. St Matthew and St Mark (1954) 49. GIBBS, J. M. Purpose and Pattern in Matthew's use of the title "Son of David". NTS 10 (1963-64) 461f.

12:25-37 LEIVESTAD, R. Christ the Conqueror (1954) 44ff.

12:25-32 BUTLER, B. C. The Originality of St Matthew (1951) 9ff.

12:25-30 HUMMEL, R. Die Auseinandersetzung zwischen Kirche und Judentum im Matthäusevangelium (1963) 125.

12:25-29 HAHN, F. Christologische Hoheitstitel (1963) 166.

12:25 KNOX, W. L. The Sources of the Synoptic Gospels II (1957) 62. BLAIR, E. P. Jesus in the Gospel of Matthew (1960) 87. SANFORD, J. A., The Kingdom Within (New York 1970) 109. KLAUCK, H. J., Allegorie und Allegorese in Synoptischen Gleichnistexten (Münster 1978) 174-79.

12:26 SANFORD, J. A., The Kingdom Within (New York 1970) 57.

12:27ff DAVIES, W. D., The Sermon on the Mount (Cambridge 1966) 19f.

12:27-28 BOUSSET, W. Die Religion des Judentums im Späthellenistischen Zeitalter (1966⁻1926) 217, 253, 337, 340f, 398. BLANK, J. Schriftauslegung in Theorie und Praxis (1969) 121-23. JEREMIAS, J. Neutestamentliche Theologie I (1971) 16, 25f, 29. HOWARD, V. P., Das Ego in den Synoptischen Evangelien (Marburg 1975) 156-163. MEYER, B. P., The Aims of Jesus (London 1979) 155f.

12:27 BARRETT, C. K. The New Testament Background: Selected Documents (1956) 31. HENGEL, M., Judentum und Hellenismus (Tübingen 1969) 442; ET: Judaism and Hellenism. I (London 1974) 241. GOULDER, M. D., Midrash and Lection in Matthew (London 1974) 120, 332f. DUNN, J. D. G., Jesus and the Spirit (London 1975) 48. HOWARD, V. P., Das Ego in den Synoptischen Evangelien (Marburg 1975) 162f. "Aramäisch" in: TRE 3 (1978) 604.

12:28-34 FULLER, R. H., "The Double Commandment of Love: A Test Case for the Criteria of Authenticity" in: L. Schottroff et al. (eds.) Essays in the Love Commandment (Philadelphia 1978) 41-56.

12:28f STAEHELIN, E. Die Verkündigung des Reiches Gottes in der Kirche Jesu Christi I (1951) 165. BRAUN, H. Qumran und NT II (1966) 87, 90, 92, 97, 107, 127, 267.

12:28 STONEHOUSE, N. B. The Witness of Matthew and Mark to Christ (1944) 244, 248. HANSON, S. The Unity of the Church in the New Testament (1946) 38f. DODD, C. H. The Parables of the Kingdom (1948) 43-45. RICHARDSON, A. The Miracle-Stories of the Gospels (1948) 39f. FLEW, R. N. Jesus and His Church (1956) 50, 51. KüMMEL, W. G. Verheissung und Erfüllung (1958) 17f, 98-101. TRILLING, W. Das wahre Israel (1959) 41. ROBINSON, J. M. Kerygma und historischer Jesus (1960) 95, 143, 163. RODD, C. S. "Spirit or Finger," ET 72 (5, '61) 157-58. DE KRUIJF, T., Der Sohn Des Lebendigen Gottes (Rome 1962) 114, 128, 130, 134, 157. STRECKER, G. Der Weg der Gerechtigkeit (1962) 89₁, 150₃, 168f, 171, 176, 177₂, 180₃, 190₃. WAINWRIGHT, A. W. The Trinity in the New Testament (1962) 211-212. BERKEY, R. F. "EGGIZEIN, PHTHANEIN, and Realized Eschatology," JBL 82 (2, '63) 177-87. HAHN, F. Christologische Hoheitstitel (1963) 299. HUMMEL, R. Die Auseinandersetzung zwischen Kirche und Judentum im Matthäusevangelium (1963) 123f. PERRIN, N., The Kingdom of God in the Teaching of Jesus (Philadelphia

1963) 20, 42, 48, 59f, 76, 87, 89, 114, 139, 170f, 173, 186. TöDT, H. E. Der Menschensohn in der synoptischen Ueberlieferung (1963) 237ff. YATES, J. E. The Spirit and the Kingdom (1963) 90ff, 181f. KäSEMANN, E. Exegetische Versuche und Besinnungen (1964) I 208f. GäRTNER, B. The Temple and the Community in Qumran and the New Testament (1965) 117. HAHN, F. Das Verständnis der Mission im Neuen Testament (1965) 106. HAMERTON-KELLY, R. G. "A Note on Matthew xii. 28 par. Luke xi. 20," NTS 11 (2, '65) 167-69. JüNGEL, E. Paulus und Jesus (1966) 112, 185. KüNG, H., Die Kirche (Freiburg 1967) 97f; ET: The Church (London 1967) 78. LENTZEN-DEIS, F. Die Taufe Jesu nach den Synoptikern (1970) 264f. BEASLEY-MURRAY, G. R., "Jesus and the Spirit" in: A Descamps/A. de Halleux (eds.) Mélanges Bibliques en hommage au R. P. Béda Rigaux (Gembloux 1970) 468-70. SANFORD, J. A., The Kingdom Within (New York 1970) 57. JEREMIAS, J. Neutestamentliche Theologie I (1971) 25, 40, 42, 83f, 98, 100, 105, 228. LORENZMEIER, T., "Zum Logion Mt 12, 28; Lk 11, 20" in: H. D. Betz/L. Schottroff (eds.) Neues Testament und Christliche Existenz. Festschrift für Herbert Braun (Tübingen 1973) 289-304. GOULDER, M. D., Midrash and Lection in Matthew (London 1974) 63, 332f. LADD, G. E., A Theology of the New Testament (Grand Rapids 1974) 64, 77, 103, 144. CONZELMANN, H./LINDEMANN, A., Arbeitsbuch zum Neuen Testament (Tübingen 1975) 353, 355. DUNN, J. D. G., Jesus and the Spirit (London 1975) 44-49, 52, 60, 78, 90f, 111. GOPPELT, L., Theologie des Neuen Testaments. I (Göttingen 1975) 196f, 203, 223, 298. HOFFMANN, P./EID, V., Jesus von Nazareth und eine christliche Moral (Freiburg 1975) 36-38. HOWARD, V. P., Das Ego in den Synoptischen Evangelien (Marburg 1975) 158-62. BEISSER, F., Das Reich Gottes (Göttingen 1976) 36-43. PERRIN, N., Jesus and the Language of the Kingdom (London 1976) 37. GERSTENBERGER, G./SCHRAGE, W., Leiden (Stuttgart 1977) 230; ET: Suffering (Nashville 1980) 265. POLAG, A., Die Christologie der Logienquelle (Neukirchen-Vluyn 1977) 45, 62. CLARK, K. W., "Realized Eschatology" in: The Gentile Bias and other Essays (Leiden 1980) 48, 55-62. HARRINGTON, D. J., God's People in Christ (Philadelphia 1980) 24. McDONALD, J. I. H., Kerygma and Didache (Cambridge 1980) 22.

12:29 HOENNICHE, G. in: Neutestamentliche Studien Georg Heinrici zu seinem 70. Geburtstag (1914) Deissmann, A. & Windisch, H. (eds.) 209ff. VOLZ, P. Die Eschatologie der jüdischen Gemeinde (1934) 392. BIEDER, W. Die Vorstellung von der Höllenfahrt Jesu Christi (1949) 33f. BRUNNER, E. Dogmatik II (1950) 322. STAEHELIN, E. Die Verkündigung des Reiches Gottes in der Kirche Jesu Christi I (1951) 166. SCHRAGE, W. Das Verhältnis des Thomas-Evangeliums zur Synoptischen Tradition und zu den Koptischen Evangelienübersetzungen (1964) 88. DUNN, J. D. G., Jesus and the Spirit (London 1975) 44, 48. KLAUCK, H.-J., Allegorie und Allegorese in Synoptischen Gleichnistexten (Münster 1978) 179-84. MEYER, B. F., The Aims of Jesus (London 1979) 156f.

12:30ff MADDOX, R. "The Function of the Son of Man According to the Synoptic Gospels." NTS 15 (1968-69) 58ff.

12:30-37 WILKENS, J. Einführung in das Evangelium nach Matthäus I (1934) 172-73. Also in Predigtgedanken aus Vergangenheit und Gegenwart Bd. 3-4 (1963) 391ff. BART, G., GPM 29 (1975) 478-83. KREYSSIG, P./STAMMLER, E., in: P. Krusche et al. (eds.) Predigtstudien für das Kirchenjahr 1975 III/2. Halbband (Stuttgart 1975) 274-79.

12:30.33-37 HAAR, J. GPM 17 (1962/3) 366-69. LOHSE, E. GPM 23/4 (1968/69) 409-16.

12:30-31 WILLIAMS, J. G. "A Note on the 'unforgivable Sin' Logion." NTS 12 (1965-66) 75f.

12:30 KLEIN, G. ZNW 2 (1901) 344f. STAEHELIN, E. Die Verkündigung des Reiches Gottes in der Kirche Jesu Christi I (1951) 166. SMITH, M., Tannaitic Parallels to the Gospels (Philadelphia 1968) 7 end +. JEREMIAS, J. Neutestamentliche Theologie I (1971) 35f, 166. POLAG, A., Die Christologie der Logienquelle (Neukirchen-Vluyn 1977) 44. FRIEDRICH, G., "Das Problem der Autorität im Neuen Testament" in: Auf das Wort kommt es an (Göttingen 1978) 288. *HOULDEN, J. L., "The Development of Meaning" Theology 82 (1979) 251-59.

12:31-37 IWAND, H.-J. Predigt-Meditationen (1964) 320-26. GAECHTER, P. Die literarische Kunst im Matthäus-Evangelium (1968) 26-28. HOLST, R., "Reexamining Mk 3:28f and its Parallels" in: ZNW 63 (1972) 122-24.

12:31f BARRETT, C. K. The Holy Spirit and the Gospel Tradition (1947) 103-107. STRECKER, G. Der Weg der Gerechtigkeit (1962) 190, 233. BAUMBACH, G. Das Verständnis des Bösen in den synoptischen Evangelien (1963) 100ff. BULTMANN, R. The History of the Synoptic Tradition (1963) 149f. HAHN, F. Christologische Hoheitstitel (1963) 107. HUMMEL, R. Die Auseinandersetzung zwischen Kirche und Judentum im Matthäusevangelium (1963) 124, 125. LöVESTAM, E. Spiritus

Blasphemia (1968). LOHSE, E. and others (eds.), Der Ruf Jesu
und die Antwort der Gemeinde (1970) 63-79. BELLET, M.
"L'Irrémissible ou le péché sans pardon," Christus 19 (74, '72)
261-68.

12:31-32 LöVESTAM, E., "Logiet om hädelse mot den helige Ande"
SEA 33 (1968) 101-17. DUNN, J. D. G., Jesus and the Spirit
(London 1975) 44, 49-53. BORING, M. E., "The Unforgivable
Sin Logion Mark III 28-29/ Matt XII 31-32/ Luke XII 10:
Formal Analysis and History of Tradition" NovT 18 (1976)
258-79. EDWARDS, R. A., A Theology of Q (Philadelphia
1976) 121f. MANEK, J., . . . und brachte Frucht. Die
Gleichnisse Jesu (Berlin 1977) 27-29. POLAG, A., Die
Christologie der Logienquelle (Neukirchen-Vluyn 1977) 162.

12:31 BRUNNER, E. Dogmatik I (1946) 227. FARRER, A. St
Matthew and St Mark (1954) 43. HUMMEL, R. Die
Auseinandersetzung zwischen Kirche und Judentum im
Matthäusevangelium (1963) 102. HENNECKE, E. &
SCHNEEMELCHER, W. Neutestamentliche Apokryphen
(1964) I 372. SATAKE, A. Die Gemeindeordnung in der
Johannesapokalypse (1966) 172-75. HASLER, V. Amen (1969)
27.

12:32-37 WREGE, H.-T. Die Ueberlieferungsgeschichte der Bergpredigt
(1968) 137-46, 157, 164, 172, 175.

12:32 MANSON, T. W. The Teaching of Jesus (1945) 215ff. KNOX,
W. L. The Sources of the Synoptic Gospels II (1957) 73.
SCHWEIZER, E. Erniedrigung und Erhöhung bei Jesus und
seinen Nachfolgern (1962) § 30. HAHN, F. Christologische
Hoheitstitel (1963) 43. KäSEMANN, E. Exegetische Versuche
und Besinnungen (1964) II 100. SCHRAGE, W. Das
Verhältnis des Thomas-Evangeliums zur Synoptischen
Tradition und zu den Koptischen Evangelienübersetzungen
(1964) 98. GäRTNER, B. The Temple and the Community in
Qumran and the New Testament (1965) 117. SATAKE, A. Die
Gemeindeordnung in der Johannesapokalypse (1966) 172-75.
WREGE, H.-T., Die Ueberlieferungsgeschichte der
Bergpredigt (1968) 156, 167, 168-80. KäSEMANN, E. New
Testament Questions of Today (1969) 102. JEREMIAS, J.
Neutestamentliche Theologie I (1971) 21-23, 25f, 175, 248f.
HOFFMANN, P. Studien zur Theologie der Logienquelle
(1972) 70f. SCHULZ, S. Q Die Spruchquelle der Evangelisten
(1972) 246-50. TALBERT, C. H., Literary Patterns,
Theological Themes, and the Genre of Luke-Acts (Missoula
1974) 55. METZGER, B. M., The Early Versions of the New
Testament (Oxford 1977) 179. THEISSEN, G., Soziologie der

Jesusbewegung (München 1977) 30.

12:33ff KNOX, W. L. The Sources of the Synoptic Gospels II (1957) 14, 16.

12:33-37 JüLICHER, D. A. Die Gleichnisreden Jesu (1910) 116-28. HIRSCH, E. Frühgeschichte des Evangeliums (1941) 327-29. STRECKER, G. Der Weg der Gerechtigkeit (1962) 138. KRAMER, M., "Hütet euch vor den falschen Propheten. Eine Überlieferungsgeschichtliche Untersuchung zu Mt 7, 15-23/Lk 6, 43-46/Mt 12, 33-37" Biblica 57 (1976) 349-77.

12:33-35 DUPONT, D. J. Les Béatitudes (1958) 44-49, 169s. BAUMBACH, G. Das Verständnis des Bösen in den synoptischen Evangelien (1963) 83ff. HUMMEL, R. Die Auseinandersetzung zwischen Kirche und Judentum im Matthäusevangelium (1963) 123, 126. SCHULZ, S. Q Die Spruchquelle der Evangelisten (1972) 316-20.

12:33f MONTEFIORE, H. "A comparison of the Parables of the Gospel according to Thomas and of the Synoptic Gospels." NTS 7 (1960-61) 238f.

12:33 KNOX, W. L. The Sources of the Synoptic Gospels II (1957) 11. HUTTON, W. R. "Make a Tree Good?" ET 75 (12, '64) 366-67. BLACK, M. An Aramaic Approach to the Gospels and Acts (1967) 202f. NICKELS, P. Targum and New Testament (1967) 19. SANFORD, J. A., The Kingdom Within (New York 1970) 110f. GOULDER, M. D., Midrash and Lection in Matthew (London 1974) 37, 40, 75, 99, 243.

12:34f RUDOLPH, K., Die Gnosis (Göttingen 1978) 280.

12:34-35 SUMMERS, R. The Secret Sayings of the Living Jesus (1968) 37.

12:34 STROBEL, A. Erkenntnis und Bekenntnis der Sünde in neutestamentlicher Zeit (1968) 44. GOULDER, M. D., Midrash and Lection in Matthew (London 1974) 79, 102, 243, 295. THEISSEN, G., Soziologie der Jesusbewegung (München 1977) 75. McDONALD, J. I. H., Kerygma and Didache (Cambridge 1980) 81.

12:35-37 MUSSNER, F. Die Wunder Jesu (1967) 28-31.

12:35.34b SCHRAGE, W. Das Verhältnis des Thomas-Evangeliums zur Synoptischen Tradition und zu den Koptischen Evangelienübersetzungen (1964) 100.

12:35 KNOX, W. L. The Sources of the Synoptic Gospels II (1957) 125.

12:36f BORNKAMM-BARTH-HELD, Ueberlieferung und Auslegung im Matthäus-Evangelium (1961) 98. STRECKER,

G. Der Weg der Gerechtigkeit (1962) 134s. HUMMEL, R. Die Auseinandersetzung zwischen Kirche und Judentum im Mätthausevangelium (1963) 126.

12:36-37 PARKER, P. The Gospel Before Mark (1953) 12-13. TRITES, A. A., The New Testament Concept of Witness (Cambridge 1977) 191.

12:36 DEWAILLY, L.-M. "La parole sans oeuvre (Mt 12, 36)," Mélanges offerts à M.-D. Chenu, Bibliothèque Thomiste XXXVII (1967) 203-19. HASLER, V. Amen (1969) 88. METZGER, B. M., The Early Versions of the New Testament (Oxford 1977) 81.

12:37 KNOX, W. L. The Sources of the Synoptic Gospels II (1957) 115. GOULDER, M. D., Midrash and Lection in Matthew (London 1974) 75, 158, 332, 358.

12:38ff STONEHOUSE, N. B. The Witness of Matthew and Mark to Christ (1944) 153.

12:38-45 WILKENS, J. Einführung in das Evangelium nach Matthäus I (1934) 173-75. FARRER, A. St Matthew and St Mark (1954) 120. STRECKER, G. Der Weg der Gerechtigkeit (1962) 102ff, 111l, 117, 176. HOFFMANN, P. Studien zur Theologie der Logienquelle (1972) passim. BRAUN, H. GPM 11/1 (1956/57) 75-77.

12:38-42 HIRSCH, E. Frühgeschichte des Evangeliums (1941) 102-104. GOLMBITZA, O. "Das Zeichen des Jona." NTS 8 (1961-62) 359f. HOWTON, J. "The Sign of Jonah," SJTh 15 (3, '62) 288-304. HUMMEL, R. Die Auseinandersetzung zwischen Kirche und Judentum im Matthäusevangelium (1963) 123, 126. HAAR, GPM 19 (1964-65) 359ff. FALKENROTH, A. in: Hören und Fragen (1967) Eichholz, G. & Falkenroth, A. (eds.) 549ff. NICKELS, P. Targum and New Testament (1967) 19. LANGE, E. (ed.) Predigtstudien für das Kirchenjahr 1970/71 (1970/71) 241-45. BORNKAMM, G. GPM 13/4 (1958/59) 276-79. STECK, K. G. GPM 25 (3, '71) 433-43. EDWARDS, R. A. The Sign of Jonah in the Theology of the Evangelists and Q, Studies in Biblical Theology, Second Series 18 (1971). SCHULZ, S. Q Die Spruchquelle der Evangelisten (1972) 250-57. HAHN, F., "Die Worte vom Licht Lk 11, 33-36" in: P. Hoffmann (ed.) Orientierung an Jesus. Für J. Schmid (Freiburg 1973) 131-33. GOULDER, M. D., Midrash and Lection in Matthew (London 1974) 37, 98, 162, 187, 189. TALBERT, C. H., Literary Patterns, Theological Themes, and the Genre of Luke-Acts (Missoula 1974) 54. EDWARDS, R. A., A Theology of Q (Philadelphia 1976) 113-15. SWIDLER, L., Biblical Affirmations of Woman (Philadelphia 1979) 168,

243, 253f, 257. RAISS, H./BRILL, S., "Zweiter Sonntag der Passionzeit (Reminiscere) Matthäus 12:38-42: Zeichenforderung" in: P. Krusche et al. (eds.) Predigtstudien 1980/1981 (Stuttgart 1980) 142-48.

12:38-41 SCOTT, R. B. Y. "The Sign of Jonah. An Interpretation," Interpretation 19 (1, '65) 16-25. HANSON, A. T., The New Testament Interpretation of Scripture (London 1980) 146-50.

12:38-40 GOODSPEED, E. J. A Life of Jesus (1950) 182-84. HAHN, F. Christologische Hoheitstitel (1963) 166. GOPPELT, L., Theologie des Neuen Testaments. I (Göttingen 1975) 196f. POLAG, A., Die Christologie der Logienquelle (Neukirchen-Vluyn 1977) 42f, 45, 74, 89f.

12:38 STONEHOUSE, N. B. The Witness of Matthew and Mark to Christ (1944) 149. KNOX, W. L. The Sources of the Synoptic Gospels II (1957) 8. BLAIR, E. P. Jesus in the Gospel of Matthew (1960) 100. HAHN, F. Christologische Hoheitstitel (1963) 75, 76, 84.

12:39f McNAMARA, M. The New Testament and the Palestinian Targum to the Pentateuch (1966) 77, n.21. JEREMIAS, J. Neutestamentliche Theologie I (1971) 25, 30, 135, 248, 251. PATSCH, H. Abendmahl und historischer Jesus (1972) 202ff.

12:39 BAUMBACH, G. Das Verständnis des Bösen in den synoptischen Evangelien (1963) 85ff. BRAUN, H. Qumran und NT II (1966) 268. EDWARDS, R. A. The Sign of Jonah (1971). VöGTLE, A. Das Evangelium und die Evangelien (1971) 103-105, 111-15. SCHüRMANN, H., "Beobachtungen zum Menschensohn-Titel in der Redenquelle" in: R. Pesch/R. Schnackenburg (eds.) Jesus und der Menschensohn (Freiburg 1975) 133f. PERRIN, N., Jesus and the Language of the Kingdom (London 1976) 45f. POLAG, A., Die Christologie der Logienquelle (Neukirchen-Vluyn 1977) 42f.

12:40-42 HENNECKE, E. & SCHNEEMELCHER, W. Neutestamentliche Apokryphen (1964) I 96, II 80.

12:40 STONEHOUSE, N. B. The Witness of Matthew and Mark to Christ (1944) 251. BIEDER, W. Die Vorstellung von der Höllenfahrt Jesu Christi (1949) 36ff. STAEHELIN, E. Die Verkündigung des Reiches Gottes in der Kirche Jesu Christi I (1951) 154. DENNEY, J. The Death of Christ (1956) 24. KNOX, W. L. The Sources of the Synoptic Gospels II (1957) 64. BLAIR, E. P. Jesus in the Gospel of Matthew (1960) 77. STRECKER, G. Der Weg der Gerechtigkeit (1962) 25, 103ff, 117. WALKER, N. "The Alleged Matthaean Errata," NTS 9 (1962-63) 392. HAHN, F. Christologische Hoheitstitel (1963)

46, 205. GäRTNER, B. The Temple and the Community in Qumran and the New Testament (1965) 112. JüNGEL, E. Paulus und Jesus (1966) 175, 202. NICKELS, P. Targum and New Testament (1967) 19. LEHMANN, K. Auferweckt am Dritten Tag nach der Schrift (1968) 169, 175, 183, 184, 228, 260, 277A, 278, 303, 305, 309, 310. GRASS, H. Ostergeschehen und Osterberichte (1970) 24n2, 87, 136nl, 137, 138, 296n6, 304n7. NöTSCHER, F., Altorientalischer und alttestamentlicher Auferstehungsglaube (Darmstadt 1970-1926) 143. VöGTLE, A. Das Evangelium und die Evangelien (1971) 119-27. COPE, L. "Matthew 12:40 and the Synoptic Source Question," JBL 92 (1, '73) 115. DRURY, J., Tradition and Design in Luke's Gospel (Atlanta 1976) 151f. POLAG, A., Die Christologie der Logienquelle (Neukirchen-Vluyn 1977) 90, 95, 133.

12:41ff MUSSNER, F. "Wege zum Selbstbewusstsein Jesu. Ein Versuch," BZ 12 (1968) 161-72.

12:41f KäSEMANN, E. Exegetische Versuche und Besinnungen (1964) II 94. HAHN, F. Das Verständnis der Mission im Neuen Testament (1965) 28. JüNGEL, E. Paulus und Jesus (1966) 189. LUZ, U. Das Geschichtsverständnis des Paulus (1968) 57. KäSEMANN, E. New Testament Questions of Today (1969) 95.

12:41-42 SCHNIDER, F., Jesus der Prophet (Freiburg 1973) 52, 174ff, 259. KINGSBURY, J. D., Matthew: Structure, Christology, Kingdom (Philadelphia 1975) 140-42. CAIRD, G. B., "Eschatology and Politics: Some Misconceptions" in: J. R. McKay/J. F. Miller (eds.) Biblical Studies. Essays in Honor of William Barclay (London 1976) 74, 77-79. POLAG, A., Die Christologie der Logienquelle (Neukirchen-Vluyn 1977) 90. CORRENS, D., "Jona und Salomo" in: W. Haubeck/M. Bachmann (eds.) Wort in der Zeit. Festgabe für Karl Heinrich Rengstorf (Leiden 1980) 85-94.

12:41 VOLZ, P. Die Eschatologie der jüdischen Gemeinde (1934) 269. BORNKAMM-BARTH-HELD, Ueberlieferung und Auslegung im Matthäus-Evangelium (1961) 110. STRECKER, G. Der Weg der Gerechtigkeit (1962) 2272. VöGTLE, A. Das Evangelium und die Evangelien (1971) 117-19. CAVALLIN, H. C. C., Life After Death. I (Lund 1974) 4, 4, nl4.

12:43-45 JüLICHER, D. A. Die Gleichnisreden Jesu (1910) 214-40. HUMMEL, R. Die Auseinandersetzung zwischen Kirche und Judentum im Matthäusevangelium (1963) 123, 126f, 142. LüHRMANN, D. Die Redaktion der Logienquelle (1969) 32-43. BARCLAY, W. And Jesus Said (1970) 193-97. JEREMIAS, J. New Testament Theology I (1971).

GOULDER, M. D., Midrash and Lection in Matthew (London 1974) 332, 335f. 395, 468. TALBERT, C. H., Literary Patterns, Theological Themes, and the Genre of Luke-Acts (Missoula 1974) 54. EDWARDS, R. A., A Theology of Q (Philadelphia 1976) 112. MANEK, J., . . . und brachte Frucht. Die Gleichnisse Jesu (Berlin 1977) 42f. POLAG, A., Die Christologie der Logienquelle (Neukirchen-Vluyn 1977) 76.

12:43.45   BOUSSET, W. Die Religion des Judentums im Späthellenistischen Zeitalter (1966⁻1926) 338f.

12:43   SCHULZ, S. Q Die Spruchquelle der Evangelisten (1972) 476-80.

12:44f   NYBERG, H. S. in: Coniectanae Neotestamentica XIII (1949) Riesenfeld, H. (ed.), 1-11. JEREMIAS, J. Neutestamentliche Theologie I (1971) 135, 152f.

12:45   STRECKER, G. Der Weg der Gerechtigkeit (1962) 392, 103, 105₅. DALTON, W. J., Christ's Proclamation to the Spirits (Rome 1965) 147f.

12:46-13:58   WILKENS, J. Einführung in das Evangelium nach Matthäus I (1934) 176-94.

12:46-50   WILKENS, J. Einführung in das Evangelium nach Matthäus I (1934) 193-94. STREETER, B. H. The Four Gospels (1951) 278f. FARRER, A. St Matthew and St Mark (1954) 184. *GERUTTI, A. "L'interpretazione del testo di S. Matteo XII, 46-50 nei Padri," Marianum 19 (2, '57) 185-221. TRILLING, W. Das wahre Israel (1959) 15f. BORNKAMM-BARTH-HELD, Ueberlieferung und Auslegung im Matthäus-Evangelium (1961) 49, 95, 98, 239. GNILKA, J. Die Verstockung Israels (1961) 94f. WEATHERHEAD, B. "Our Lady in Scripture-II: Oral Tradition," LifeSpir 16 (181, '61) 10-16. STRECKER, G. Der Weg der Gerechtigkeit (1962) 232. JENSEN, H. W. in: Herr, tue meine Lippen auf (1964) Eichholz, G. (ed.) 344ff. SCHRAGE, W. Das Verhältnis des Thomas-Evangeliums zur Synoptischen Tradition und zu den Koptischen Evangelienübersetzungen (1964) 185. GAECHTER, P. Die literarische Kunst im Matthäus-Evangelium (1968) 55-56, 76-77. NEIRYNCK, F. "Les Femmes au Tommbeau: Etude de la Rédaction Matthéenne. Matt. XXVIII 1-10." NTS 15 (1968-69) 183ff. SANFORD, J. A., The Kingdom Within (New York 1970) 86f. SCHRAMM, T. Der Markus-Stoff bei Lukas (1971) 123f. FRANKEMöLLE, H., Jahwebund und Kirche Christi (Münster 1974) 112, 150, 179f, 182, 277, 343, 346. DRURY, J., Tradition and Design in Luke's Gospel (Atlanta 1976) 151. STAGG, E. and F., Woman in the World of Jesus (Philadelphia 1978) 138f. RUETHER, R. R.,

Mary — The Feminine Face of the Church (London 1979) 31-35. SWIDLER, L., Biblical Affirmations of Woman (Philadelphia 1979) 178, 193, 225, 237, 258, 278.

12:46f STONEHOUSE, N. B. The Witness of Matthew and Mark to Christ (1944) 175.

12:46 STONEHOUSE, N. B. The Witness of Matthew and Mark to Christ (1944) 150.

12:47-50 HENNECKE, E. & SCHNEEMELCHER, W. Neutestamentliche Apokryphen (1964) I 103.

12:47 CONZELMANN, H./LINDEMANN, A., Arbeitsbuch zum Neuen Testament (Tübingen 1975) 27. METZGER, B. M., The Early Versions of the New Testament (Oxford 1977) 39, 118.

12:48ff *BENASSI, V. M. " 'Chi è mia madre, chi sono i miei fratelli?' (Mt. 12,48ss)," Marianum 18 (3-4, '57) 347-54.

12:49f STONEHOUSE, N. B. The Witness of Matthew and Mark to Christ (1944) 175. STRECKER, G. Der Weg der Gerechtigkeit (1962) 193₁₃.

12:50 KNOX, W. L. The Sources of the Synoptic Gospels II (1957) 16. BLAIR, E. P. Jesus in the Gospel of Matthew (1960) 58. HAHN, F. Christologische Hoheitstitel (1963) 321. McNAMARA, M. The New Testament and the Palestinian Targum to the Pentateuch (1966) 136. SAND, A., Das Gesetz und die Propheten (Regensburg 1974) 122f. METZGER, B. M., The Early Versions of the New Testament (Oxford 1977) 438.

13 STONEHOUSE, N. B. The Witness of Matthew and Mark to Christ (1944) 149ff. FEINE, D. P. & BEHM, D. J. Einleitung in das Neue Testament (1950) 17f. BUTLER, B. C. The Originality of St Matthew (1951) 85ff. STREETER, B. H. The Four Gospels (1951) 261f. DENIS, A. "De parabels van het koninkrijk (Mt. 13)" / The Parables of the Kingdom (Mt. 13)/, TvTh 1, (4, '61) 273-88. SONGER, H. "Jesus' Use of Parables: Matthew 13," RevEx 59 (4, '62) 492-500. STRECKER, G. Der Weg der Gerechtigkeit (1962) 38. LADD, G. E. "The Life-Setting of the Parables of the Kingdom," JournBibRel 31 (3, '63) 193-99. LADD, G. E. "The Sitz im Leben of the Parables of Mt. 13: the Soils," in: Studia Evangelica II (1964) Cross, F. L.

(ed.) 203-210. WILKENS, W. "Die Redaktion des Gleichniskapitels Mark 4 durch Matth.," ThZ 20 (5, '64) 305-27. BIEDER, W., Die Verheissung der Taufe im Neuen Testament (Zürich 1966) 279-81. DENIS, A.-M. "Las paraboles du royaume, révélation de mystére (Matt., 13)," Communio 1 (3, '68) 327-46. GAECHTER, P. Die literarische Kunst im Matthäus-Evangelium (1968) 14-15. REUMANN, J. Jesus in the Church's Gospels: Modern Scholarship and the Earliest Sources (1968) 185-88. GERHARDSSON, B. "De sju liknelserna i Matteus 13" (The Seven Parables in Matthew 13), SEA 34 ('69) 77-106. KINGSBURY, J. D. The Parables of Jesus in Matthew 13 (1969). GOULDER, M. D. JThS 21 (1, '70) 164-66. DANKER, F. W. "Fresh Perspectives on Matthean Theology. A Review Article," CThM 41 (8, '70) 478-90. OTOMO, Y. Nachfolge Jesu und Anfänge der Kirche im Neuen Testament (1970) 89-92. DANKER, F. W. CThM 42 (4, '71) 241-42. JEREMIAS, J. ThLZ 96 (4,'71) 270-71. SELBY, D. J., Introduction to the New Testament (New York 1971) 112, 116f, 133f. *GERHARDSSON, B., "The Seven Parables in Matthew xiii" NTS 19 (1972) 16-37. KüMMEL, W. G. Einleitung in das Neue Testament (1973) 77f. *MELLON, C., "La Parabole. Manière de parler, manière d'entendre" RechSR 61 (1973) 49-63. *LAMBRECHT, J., "Parabels in Mt. 13" TTh 17 (1977) 25-47. *CHARPENTIER, E., "Le chapitre des paraboles chez Matthieu (Mt 13)" Foi et Vie 78 (1979) 101-106. *WENHAM, D., "The Structure of Matthew XIII" NTS 25 (1979) 516-22.

13:1ff LOEWNICH, W. von, Luther als Ausleger der Synoptiker (1954) 31ff.

13:1-52 EWALD, H. Die drei ersten Evangelien (1850) 230ff. SCHLATTER, D. A. Die Theologie des Neuen Testaments (1909) Vol. I 399-405. FARRER, A. St Matthew and St Mark (1954) 175. DUPONT J. "Le chapitre des paraboles," NRTh 89 (8, '67) 800-20. GERHARDSSON, B. "The Parable of the Sower and its interpretation," NTS 14 (1968) 165-93. GüTTGEMANNS, E. Offene Fragen zur Formgeschichte des Evangeliums (1970) 89, 90. ELLIS, P. F., Matthew: His Mind and His Message (Collegeville 1974) 59-62. COPE, O. L., Matthew. A Scribe Trained for the Kingdom of Heaven (Washington D. C. 1976) 11-31. *SABOURIN, L., "The Parables of the Kindom" BThB 6 (1976) 115-60. WEDER, H., Die Gleichnisse Jesu als Metaphern (Göttingen 1980) 99-108.

13:1-35 KINGSBURY, J. D. The Parables of Jesus in Matthew 13 (1969) 22-91.

13:1-23 PIROT, J. Paraboles et Allégories Evangeliques (1949) 91-103. GERHARDSSON, B. "Liknelsen om fyrahanda sädesakrar och dess uttydning" (The Parable of the Four Types of Grain Field and its Explanation), SEA 31 ('66) 80-113. GERHARDSSON, B. "The Parable of the Sower and its Interpretation," NTS 14 (2, '68) 165-93. MARIN, L. 'Essai d'analyse structurale d'un récit-parabole: Matthieu 13/1-23," EThR 46 (1, '71) 35-74. SCHRAMM, T. Der Markus-Stoff bei Lukas (1971) 114-23. *DUPONT, J., "Le semeur est sorti pour semer. Mt 13, 1-23" AssS 46 (1974) 18-27. GOULDER, M. D., Midrash and Lection in Matthew (London 1974) 366f. ZINGG, P., Das Wachsen der Kirche. Beiträge zur Frage der lukanischen Redaktion und Theologie (Freiburg/(CH) 1974) 76, 97-100.

13:1-9 WILKENS, J. Einführung in das Evangelium nach Matthäus I (1934) 177-79. MICHAELIS, D. W. Die Gleichnisse Jesu (1956) 17-35. BARCLAY, W. And Jesus Said (1970) 18-24. CONZELMANN, H./LINDEMANN, A., Arbeitsbuch zum Neuen Testament (Tübingen 1975) 96f. SWIDLER, L., Biblical Affirmations of Woman (Philadelphia 1979) 226.

13:1-3 FARRER, A. St Matthew and St Mark (1954) 181. GOMA CIVIT, I. "Y les hablo en paraboles," CultBib 19 (184, '62) 131-37. KLAUCK, H.-J., Allegorie und Allegorese in Synoptischen Gleichnistexten (Münster 1978) 240f.

13:1-3a KINGSBURY, J. D. The Parables of Jesus in Matthew 13 (1969) 22-32.

13:1f LIGHTFOOT, R. H. History and Interpretation in the Gospels (1934) 39f. STONEHOUSE, N. B. The Witness of Matthew and Mark to Christ (1944) 149.

13:1-2 EGGER, W., Frohbotschaft und Lehre (Frankfurt 1976) 112.

13:1 STONEHOUSE, N. B. The Witness of Matthew and Mark to Christ (1944) 176. STRECKER, G. Der Weg der Gerechtigkeit (1962) 96. METZGER, B. M., The Early Versions of the New Testament (Oxford 1977) 433.

13:2 METZGER, B. M., The Early Versions of the New Testament (Oxford 1977) 178.

13:3ff STONEHOUSE, N. B. The Witness of Matthew and Mark to Christ (1944) 146.

13:3-52 STONEHOUSE, N. B. The Witness of Matthew and Mark to Christ (1944) 130.

13:3-34 PARKER, P. The Gospel Before Mark (1953) 52ff.

13:3-23 LOCKYER, H. All the Parables of the Bible (1963) 174ff.

MANEK, J., . . . und brachte Frucht. Die Gleichnisse Jesu (Berlin 1977) 20-25.

13:3-9.18-23   LINNEMANN, E. Gleichnisse Jesu (1969) 17, 18, 19, 24, 52, 120ff, 179ff.

13:3-8.18-23.   DILLON, R. J. "Towards a Tradition-History of the Parables of the True Israel," Biblica 47 (1966) 25-26.

13:3-9   JüLICHER, D. A. Die Gleichnisreden Jesu (1910) 514-38. GOMA CIVIT, I. "La parabola del sembrador," CultBib 20 (188, '63) 33-36. SCHRAGE, W. Das Verhältnis des Thomas-Evangeliums zur Synoptischen Tradition und zu den Koptischen Evangelienübersetzungen (1964) 42. TOUSSAINT, S. D. "The Introductory and Concluding Parables of Matthew Thirteen," BiblSa 121 (484, '64) 351-55. BISER, E. Die Gleichnisse Jesu (1965) 51ff, 129. GOULDER, M .D., Midrash and Lection in Matthew (London 1974) 54f, 59, 65, 188. LADD, G. E., A Theology of the New Testament (Grand Rapids 1974) 94f. GOPPELT, L., Theologie des Neuen Testaments. I (Göttingen 1975) 115f. *HORMAN, J., "The Source of the Version of the Parable of the Sower in the Gospel of Thomas" NovT 21 (1979) 326-43. WEDER, H., Die Gleichnisse Jesu als Metaphern (Göttingen 1980) 108-17.

13:3b-9   KINGSBURY, J. D. The Parables of Jesus in Matthew 13 (1969) 32-37.

13:3-8   SUMMERS, R. The Secret Sayings of the Living Jesus (1968) 42. PERRIN, N., Jesus and the Language of the Kingdom (London 1976) 8, 39, 96, 101, 129f, 143, 160, 162, 203. "Apologetik" in: TRE 3 (1978) 378. KLAUCK, H.-J., Allegorie und Allegorese in Synoptischen Gleichnistexten (Münster 1978) 186-200.

13:3-4   HENNECKE, E. & SCHNEEMELCHER, W. Neutestamentliche Apokryphen (1964) I 189. JEREMIAS, J. Palastinakundliches zum Gleichnis vom Säemann. NTS 13 (1966-67) 48f.

13:3   STAEHELIN, E. Die Verkündigung des Reiches Gottes in der Kirche Jesu Christi I (1951) 195.

13:4-9   SWIDLER, L., Biblical Affirmations of Woman (Philadelphia 1979) 166.

13:4   HARTMANN, L., Testimonium Linguae (Lund 1963) 28ff. METZGER, B. M., The Early Versions of the New Testament (Oxford 1977) 249, 439.

13:7   MASSAUX, E. Influence de l'Evangile de saint Matthieu sur la littérature chrétienne avant saint Irénée (1950) 267-71.

BRAUN, H. Qumran und NT II (1966) 105. DALMAN, G. Orte und Wege Jesu (1967) 264f. KLIJN, A. F. J., "Die syrische Baruch-Apokalypse" in: W. G. Kümmel (ed.) Jüdische Schriften aus hellenistisch-römischer Zeit. V (Gütersloh 1976) 182.

13:8ff   STAEHELIN, E. Die Verkündigung des Reiches Gottes in der Kirche Jesu Christi I (1951) 197.

13:8   STAEHELIN, E. Die Verkündigung des Reiches Gottes in der Kirche Jesu Christi I (1951) 142. SAND, A., Das Gesetz und die Propheten (Regensburg 1974) 114.

13:9-17   VIA, D. O. "Matthew on the Understandability of the Parables," JBL 84 (4, '65) 430-32.

13:9.43   SCHRAGE, W. Das Verhältnis des Thomas-Evangeliums zur Synoptischen Tradition und zu den Koptischen Evangelienübersetzungen (1964) 42.

13:9   STRECKER, G. Der Weg der Gerechtigkeit (1962) 198 l. KLAUCK, H.-J., Allegorie und Allegorese in Synoptischen Gleichnistexten (Münster 1978) 241f.

13:10ff   BORNKAMM-BARTH-HELD, Ueberlieferung und Auslegung im Matthäus-Evangelium (1961) 16f, 99ff, 216, 239. RUDOLPH, K. Die Mandäer II (1961) 257, 3. STRECKER, G. Der Weg der Gerechtigkeit (1962) 197 l. HAHN, F. Das Verständnis der Mission im Neuen Testament (1965) 107. WREGE, H.-T., Die Ueberlieferungsgeschichte der Bergpredigt (1968) 49-50.

13:10-18   FARRER, A. St Matthew and St Mark (1954) 181.

13:10-17   WILKENS, J. Einführung in das Evangelium nach Matthäus I (1934) 179-81. Verkündigt das angenehme Jahr des Hern in: Predigtgedanken aus Vergangenheit und Gegenwart Bd. I (1962) 283ff. MERKEL/GEORGI/BALTZER, GPM (1962/63) 110ff. GOMA CIVIT, I. "La gracia de conocer y entender," CultBib 21 (197, '64) 195, 204. HARDER, G. GPM 23/1 (1968/69) 94-102. KINGSBURY, J. D. The Parables of Jesus in Matthew 13 (1969) 37-52. KRAUS, H. J. GPM 11/4 227-30. KRAUSE, O., GPM 29 (1974) 132-37. EGGER, W., Frohbotschaft und Lehre (Frankfurt 1976) 114.

13:10-15   GILS, F. Jésus Prophète D'Après Les Evangiles Synoptiques (1957) 92-98. BROWN, R. E. "The Semitic Background of the New Testament Mysterion (I)," Biblica 39 (1958) 427-31. TRILLING, W. Das wahre Israel (1959) 58ff. SUHL, A. Die Funktion der alttestamentlichen Zitate und Anspielungen im Markusevangelium (1965) 145ff.

13:10-13   STRECKER, G. Der Weg der Gerechtigkeit (1962) 101 4, 106.

13:10   STONEHOUSE, N. B. The Witness of Matthew and Mark to Christ (1944) 149, 150, 176. BLAIR, E. P. Jesus in the Gospel of Matthew (1960) 103. STRECKER, G. Der Weg der Gerechtigkeit (1962) 193₁₂. KLAUCK, H.-J., Allegorie und Allegorese in Synoptischen Gleichnistexten (Münster 1978) 242-45.

13:11-17   STONEHOUSE, N. B. The Witness of Matthew and Mark to Christ (1944) 216.

13:11-12   KLAUCK, H.-J., Allegorie und Allegorese in Synoptischen Gleichnistexten (Münster 1978) 245-53.

13:11   GUY, H. A. New Testament Prophecy Its Origin and Significance (1947) 79ff. CERFAUX, L. "La Connaissance des Secrets du Royaume d'après Matt. XIII 11 et par." NTS 2 ('56) 238-49. BLAIR, E. P. Jesus in the Gospel of Matthew (1960) 102, 103, 105. GNILKA, J. Die Verstockung Israels (1961) 91f. STRECKER, G. Der Weg der Gerechtigkeit (1962) 230₃. BRAUN, H. Qumran und NT II (1966) 40, 95, 105. CHRIST, F. Jesus Sophia (1970) 81, 82, 99. SANFORD, J. A., The Kingdom Within (New York 1970) 43f. FRANKEMöLLE, H., Jahwebund und Kirche Christi (Münster 1974) 151, 202, 237, 253, 266, 269.

13:12f   HARRISVILLE, R. A. "Jesus and the Family," Interpretation 23 (4, '69) 425-38.

13:12   KNOX, W. L. The Sources of the Synoptic Gospels II (1957) 30. BLAIR, E. P. Jesus in the Gospel of Matthew (1960) 102, 103, HUMMEL, R. Die Auseinandersetzung zwischen Kirche und Judentum im Matthäusevangelium (1963) 148. KäSEMANN, E. Exegetische Versuche und Besinnungen (1964) II 96. SCHRAGE, W. Das Verhältnis des Thomas-Evangeliums zur Synoptischen Tradition und zu den Koptischen Evangelienübersetzungen (1964) 96. KäSEMANN, E. New Testament Questions of Today (1969) 98. KLAUCK, H.-J., Allegorie und Allegorese in Synoptischen Gleichnistexten (Münster 1978) 239-40.

13:13ff   HAHN, F. Das Verständnis der Mission im Neuen Testament (1965) 109.

13:13-18   GAECHTER, P. Die literarische Kunst im Matthäus-Evangelium (1968) 51-53.

13:13-17   SUHL, A. Die Funktion der alttestamentlichen Zitate und Anspielungen im Markusevangelium (1965) 97ff.

13:13-15   HESSE, F. Das Verstockungsproblem im Alten Testament (1955) 3, 4, 5, 23, 39, 64-66. GNILKA, J. "Das Verstockungsproblem nach Matthäus 13, 13-15," in:

Antijudaismus im Neuen Testament (1967) Eckert, Levinson, Stöhr (eds.) 119-28.

13:13   LOEWENICH, W. von, Luther als Ausleger der Synoptiker (1954) 31ff. STRECKER, G. Der Weg der Gerechtigkeit (1962) 703, 197, 229, 2301. HUMMEL, R. Die Auseinandersetzung zwischen Kirche und Judentum im Matthäusevangelium (1963) 128. BRAUN, H. Qumran und NT II (1966) 40, 95, 105. BLACK, M. An Aramaic Approach to the Gospels and Acts (1967) 215f. "Aramäisch" in: TRE 3 (1978) 609.

13:14-16   EHRHARDT, A. "The Disciples of Emmaus." NTS 10 (1963-64) 184f. WANKE, J., Die Emmauserzählung (Leipzig 1973) 15.

13:14f   MOORE, G. F. Judaism (1946) I 526n. GNILKA, J. Die Verstockung Israels (1961) 103-105. STRECKER, G. Der Weg der Gerechtigkeit (1962) 492, 703, 2303. HUMMEL, R. Die Auseinandersetzung zwischen Kirche und Judentum im Matthäusevangelium (1963) 129 n.4. WREGE, H.-T. Die Ueberlieferungsgeschichte der Bergpredigt (1968) 49f, 179.

13:14-15   BLOCH, R., "Midrash" in: W. S. Green (ed.) Approaches to Ancient Judaism (Missoula 1978) 49.

13:14   ODEBERG, H., " 'Sie haben Augen und sehen nichts' (schwed)" Eranos 14 (1957) 62-64. BLAIR, E. P. Jesus in the Gospel of Matthew (1960) 56, 119. STRECKER, G. Der Weg der Gerechtigkeit (1962) 712.

13:15f   KNACKSTEDT, J. K. Die beiden Brotvermehrungen im Evangelium NTS 10 (1963-64) 310f.

13:15   M'NEILE, A. H. The Gospel According to St Matthew (1955) 191f. BLAIR, E. P. Jesus in the Gospel of Matthew (1960) 102. HUMMEL, R. Die Auseinandersetzung zwischen Kirche und Judentum im Matthäusevangelium (1963) 145f. FRANKEMöLLE, H., Jahwebund und Kirche Christi (Münster 1974) 195, 201f.

13:16ff   STRECKER, G. Der Weg der Gerechtigkeit (1962) 230.

13:16f   McNAMARA, M. The New Testament and the Palestinian Targum to the Pentateuch (1966) 145, 240. WREGE, H.-T. Die Ueberlieferungsgeschichte der Bergpredigt (1968) 11f, 94. VöGTLE, A. Das Evangelium und die Evangelien (1971) 240-42. HOFFMANN, P. Studien zur Theologie der Logienquelle (1972) 5, 38, 63, 70f, 105, 203, 208, 210-12, 288, 297, 299, 308. SCHULZ, S. Q Die Spruchquelle der Evangelisten (1972) 419-21. KüMMEL, W. G. Einleitung in das Neue Testament (1973) 46f.

13:16-17   STONEHOUSE, N. B. The Witness of Matthew and Mark to

Christ (1944) 217. FLEW, R. N. Jesus and His Church (1956) 65-66. BLAIR, E. P. Jesus in the Gospel of Matthew (1960) 103. BORNKAMM-BARTH-HELD, Ueberlieferung und Auslegung im Matthäus-Evangelium (1961) 100ff, 279. STRECKER, G. Der Weg der Gerechtigkeit (1962) 722, 197. KäSEMANN, E. Exegetische Versuche und Besinnungen (1964) II 90. JüNGEL, E. Paulus und Jesus (1966) 112. JEREMIAS, J. Neutestamentliche Theologie I (1971) 25f, 36, 44, 67, 110, 244. SCHNIDER, F., Jesus der Prophet (Freiburg 1973) 60, 75, 137, 176ff, 259. TALBERT, C. H., Literary Patterns, Theological Themes, and the Genre of Luke-Acts (Missoula 1974) 53. HOFFMANN, P./EID, V., Jesus von Nazareth und eine christliche Moral (Freiburg 1975) 35f. EDWARDS, R. A., A Theology of Q (Philadelphia 1976) 64f, 106f.

13:16   BLAIR, E. P. Jesus in the Gospel of Matthew (1960) 102, 105. STRECKER, G. Der Weg der Gerechtigkeit (1962) 193 11. BRAUN, H. Qumran und NT II (1966) 40, 95, 105. CHRIST, F. Jesus Sophia (1970) 81, 99.

13:17f   STONEHOUSE, N. B. The Witness of Matthew and Mark to Christ (1944) 217.

13:17   KNOX, W. L. The Sources of the Synoptic Gospels II (1957) 56. McNAMARA, M. The New Testament and the Palestinian Targum to the Pentateuch (1966) 240, 244, 242, 245. SATAKE, A. Die Gemeindeordnung in der Johannesapokalypse (1966) 177. NICKELS, P. Targum and New Testament (1967) 19. SMITH, M., Tannaitic Parallels to the Gospels (Philadelphia 1968) 8 b n 5+. HASLER, V. Amen (1969) 66. ZIESLER, J. A., The Meaning of Righteousness in Paul (1972) 138f, 145. GOULDER, M. D., Midrash and Lection in Matthew (London 1974) 81, 352, 367, 427. KLIJN, A. F. J., "Die syrische Baruch-Apokalypse" in: W. G. Kümmel (ed.) Jüdische Schriften aus hellenistisch-römischer Zeit. V (Gütersloh 1976) 182.

13:18ff   BLAIR, E. P. Jesus in the Gospel of Matthew (1960) 106.

13:18-23   JüLICHER, D. A. Die Gleichnisreden Jesu (1910) 514-38. WILKENS, J. Einführung in das Evangelium nach Matthäus I (1934) 181-82. M'NEILE, A. H. The Gospel According to St Matthew (1955) 195f. STRECKER, G. Der Weg der Gerechtigkeit (1962) 722, 229. GOMA CIVIT, I. "El que oye la Palabra. . .," CultBib 20 (192, '63) 263-73. GERHARDSSON, B. "The Parable of the Sower and its Interpretation," NTS 14 (1968) 165-93; 175-79. KINGSBURY, J. D. The Parables of Jesus in Matthew 13 (1969) 52-63.

13:18   MICHAELIS, D. W. Die Gleichnisse Jesu (1956) 29-38. BLAIR, E. P. Jesus in the Gospel of Matthew (1960) 103. KLAUCK, H.-J., Allegorie und Allegorese in Synoptischen Gleichnistexten (Münster 1978) 253-55.

13:19-23   KLAUCK, H.-J., Allegorie und Allegorese in Synoptischen Gleichnistexten (Münster 1978) 200-209.

13:19   STAEHELIN, E. Die Verkündigung des Reiches Gottes in der Kirche Jesu Christi I (1951) 166. BAUMBACH, G. Das Verständnis des Bösen in den synoptischen Evangelien (1963) 56ff, 96f. JEREMIAS, J. Neutestamentliche Theologie I (1971) 40, 42f. HAHN, F. Das Verständnis der Mission im Neuen Testament (1965) 106-107. KINGSBURY, J. D., Matthew: Structure, Christology, Kingdom (Philadelphia 1975) 163-66.

13:21   STONEHOUSE, N. B. The Witness of Matthew and Mark to Christ (1944) 217.

13:22   FARRER, A. St Matthew and St Mark (1954) 175. HARTMAN, L., Testimonium Linguae (Lund 1963) 15ff. BOUSSET, W. Die Religion des Judentums im Späthellenistichen Zeitalter (1966-1926) 245.

13:23   STONEHOUSE, N. B. The Witness of Matthew and Mark to Christ (1944) 149. BLAIR, E. P. Jesus in the Gospel of Matthew (1960) 107. SAND, A., Das Gesetz und die Propheten (Regensburg 1974) 114.

13:24ff   STAEHELIN, E. Die Verkündigung des Reiches Gottes in der Kirche Jesu Christi I (1951) 58, 348. KNOX, W. L. The Sources of the Synoptic Gospels II (1957) 130. BERKHOF, H. Der Sinn der Geschichte: Christus (1959) 126f. BLAIR, E. P. Jesus in the Gospel of Matthew (1960) 99. HUMMEL, R. Die Auseinandersetzung zwischen Kirche und Judentum im Matthäusevangelium (1963) 156. "Apologetik" in: TRE 3 (1978) 254.

13:24-52   RIST, J. M., On the Independence of Matthew and Mark (Cambridge 1978) 54f.

13:24-33   *BERGMANN, W., Die zehn Gleichnisse vom Reich der Himmel (Lahr-Dinglingen 1976).

13:24-31   LADD, G. E., A Theology of the New Testament (Grand Rapids 1974) 95ff.

13:24-30.   MOORE, G. F. Judaism (1946) II 310.
36-43.
47-49.

13:24-30. MORGAN, G. C. The Parables and Metaphors of Our Lord
36-43.   (1943) 49ff. BRUNNER, E. Saat und Frucht (1946) 101-13.
MOUSON, J. "Explicatur parabola de zizaniis in agro (Mt
XIII, 24-30, 36-43)," CollMech 44 (2, '59) 171-75. SMITH, Ch.
W. F. "The Mixed State of the Church in Matthew's Gospel,"
JBL 82 (1963) 149-68, esp. 149-53. HAHN, F. Das Verständnis
der Mission im Neuen Testament (1965) 109. DIGNATH, W.
Die Botschaft von der Endzeit (1966) 43-62. SUMMERS, R.
The Secret Sayings of the Living Jesus (1968) 28, 43.

13:24-30 JüLICHER, D. A. Die Gleichnisreden Jesu (1910) 546-63, 566-
69. WILKENS, J. Einführung in das Evangelium nach
Matthäus I (1934) 182-84. STONEHOUSE, N. B. The Witness
of Matthew and Mark to Christ (1944) 150, 238. DODD, C. H.
The Parables of the Kingdom (1948) 183ff. STECK, GPM 4,
(1949/50) 59ff. M'NEILLE, A. H. The Gospel According to St
Matthew (1955) 202f. MICHAELIS, D. W. Die Gleichnisse
Jesu (1956) 42-53. OBENDIEK, H. in: Herr, tue meine Lippen
auf (1957) Eichholz, G. (ed.) 68-73. GILS, F. Jésus Prophète
D'Apres Les Evangiles Synoptiques (1957) 100-103.
BORNKAMM-BARTH-HELD, Ueberlieferung und
Auslegung im Matthäus-Evangelium (1961) 17, 68, 149, 255.
DOERNE, M. Er kommt auch noch heute (1961) 43-45.
JEREMIAS, J. Die Gleichnisse Jesu (1962) 19, 78, 84-89, 97f,
152, 222. MOWRY, L. "Parable," IDB III (1962) 653a.
STRECKER, G. Der Weg der Gerechtigkeit (1962) 16l3⁴2008,
215. LOCKYER, H. All the Parables of the Bible (1963) 180ff.
SCHRAGE, W. Das Verhältnis des Thomas-Evangeliums zur
Synoptischen Tradition und zu den Koptischen
Evangelienübersetzungen (1964) 123. BRAUN, H. Qumran
und NT II (1966) 269, 276. DAVIES, W. D., The Sermon on the
Mount (Cambridge 1966) 93. JüNGEL, E. Paulus und Jesus
(1966) 145, 147f. KINGSBURY, J. D. The Parables of Jesus in
Matthew 13 (1969) 63-76. BARCLAY, W. And Jesus Said
(1970) 38-44. LEHMANN, M. Synoptische Quellenanalyse
und die Frage nach dem historischen Jesus (1970) 73-74.
SCHWEIZER, E. "Zur Sondertradition der Gleichnisse bei
Matthäus," in: Tradition und Glaube (1971) Jeremias, G. (ed.)
278-79. CORELL, J. "La parabola de la cizana y su
explicacion," EsVe 2 ('72) 3-51. HAAR, J. GPM 4/1 (1972) 95-
100. PATSCH, H. Abendmahl und historischer Jesus (1972)
111ff. RANNENBERG, W. & RATSCHOW, E.-M. "Fünfter
Sonntag nach Epiphanias: Matthäus 13, 24-30," in:
Predigtstudien (1972/73) Lange, E. (ed.) 104-109. GOULDER,
M. D., Midrash and Lection in Matthew (London 1974) 4, 52,
54, 58ff, 65, 188, 301, 367ff, 379. WOJCIK, J., "The Two

Kingdoms in Matthew's Gospel" in: K. R. R. Gros Louis et al.
(eds.) Literary Interpretations of Biblical Narratives (Nashville
1974) 287. CONZELMANN, H./LINDEMANN, A.,
Arbeitsbuch zum Neuen Testament (Tübingen 1975) 87.
GOPPELT, L., Theologie des Neuen Testaments I (Göttingen
1975) 116f, 259. THEISOHN, J., Der auserwählte Richter.
(Göttingen 1975) 186ff. MANEK, J., . . .und brachte Frucht.
Die Gleichnisse Jesu (Berlin 1977) 43-46. *CATCHPOLE, D.
R., "John the Baptist, Jesus and the Parable of the Tares" SJTh
31 (1978) 557-70. WEDER, H., Die Gleichnisse Jesu als
Metaphern (Göttingen 1980) 120-28.

13:24   STONEHOUSE, N. B. The Witness of Matthew and Mark to
Christ (1944) 149. MASSAUX, E. Influence de l'Evangile de
saint Matthieu sur la littérature chrétienne avant saint Irénée
(1950) 267-71. STRECKER, G. Der Weg der Gerechtigkeit
(1962) 214f. BLACK, M. An Aramaic Approach to the Gospels
and Acts (1967) 129f.

13:26   PERRIN, N. Mark XIV.62: The end product of a Christian
Pesher Tradition? NTS 12 (1965-66) 153f.

13:27   HAHN, F. Christologische Hoheitstitel (1963) 92. HUMMEL,
R. Die Auseinandersetzung zwischen Kirche und Judentum im
Matthäusevangelium (1963) 155.

13:28   BLACK, M. An Aramaic Approach to the Gospels and Acts
(1967) 106f.

13:29   BLAIR, E. P. Jesus in the Gospel of Matthew (1960) 115.

13:31ff STAEHELIN, E. Die Verkündigung des Reiches Gottes in der
Kirche Jesu Christi I (1951) 392. GOULDER, M. D., Midrash
and Lection in Matthew (London 1974) 369ff.

13:31-35 DEHN, G. in: Herr, tue meine Lippen auf (1964) Eichholz, G.
(ed.) 295ff. IWAND, H. J. Predigt-Meditationen (1964) 30-32.
WILKENS, J. Einführung in das Evangelium nach Matthäus I
(1934) 184-85.

13:31-33 JüLICHER, D. A. Die Gleichnisreden Jesu (1910) 569-81.
BUTLER, B. C. The Originality of St Matthew (1951) 2ff.
MICHAELIS, D. W. Die Gleichnisse Jesu (1956) 54-60.
KUSS, O. "Zum Sinngehalt des Doppelgleichnisses vom
Senfkorn und Sauerteig," Biblica 40 3/4 (1959) 641-53.
KüNKEL, K. GPM 21/4 (1966/67) 383-89. DUPONT, J. "Les
paraboles du sénevé et du levain," NRTh 89 (9, '67) 897-913.
ZIMMERMANN, H. Neutestamentliche Methodenlehre
(1967) 123-25. GOLLWITZER, H., Veränderung im Diesseits
(München 1973) 121. TALBERT, C. H., Literary Patterns,
Theological Themes and the Genre of Luke-Acts (Missoula

1974) 56. ZINGG, P., Das Wachsen der Kirche (Freiburg/(CH) 1974) 100-109, 114f. GOPPELT, L., Theologie des Neuen Testaments. I (Göttingen 1975) 117. DUPONT, J., "Le Couple Parabolique du sénevé et du Cerain; Mt 13, 31-33; Lc 13, 18-21" in: G. Strecker (ed.) Jesus Christus in Historie und Theologie. Festschrift für Hans Conzelmann (Tübingen 1975) 331-45. SWIDLER, L., Biblical Affirmations of Woman (Philadelphia 1979) 170.

13:31f JEREMIAS, J. Die Gleichnisse Jesu (1962) 145-47. SCHRAGE, W. Das Verhältnis des Thomas-Evangeliums zur Synoptischen Tradition und zu den Koptischen Evangelienübersetzungen (1964) 61. BISER, E. Die Gleichnisse Jesu (1965) 79ff. HAHN, F. Das Verständnis der Mission im Neuen Testament (1965) 109. JüNGEL, E. Paulus und Jesus (1966) 151-54. SUMMERS, R. The Secret Sayings of the Living Jesus (1968) 43. KINGSBURY, J. D. The Parables of Jesus in Matthew 13 (1969) 76-84. BARCLAY, W. And Jesus Said (1970) 52-59. SCHULZ, S. Q Die Spruchquelle der Evangelisten (1972) 298-307.

13:31-32 DODD, C. H. The Parables of the Kingdom (1948) 189ff. LOCKYER, H. All the Parables of the Bible (1963) 184ff. MORGAN, G. C. The Parables and Metaphors of Our Lord (1943) 54ff. PIROT, J. Paraboles et Allégories Evangeliques (1949) 125-31. SANFORD, J. A., The Kingdom Within (New York 1970) 44f. GOULDER, M. D., Midrash and Lection in Matthew (London 1974) 52, 55, 59, 61, 65, 98, 357. LADD, G. E., A Theology of the New Testament (Grand Rapids 1974) 97-100. WOJCIK, J., "The Two Kingdoms in Matthew's Gospel" in: K. R. R. Gros Louis et al. (eds.) Literary Interpretations of Biblical Narratives (Nashville 1974) 285-87. CONZELMANN, H./LINDEMANN, A., Arbeitsbuch zum Neuen Testament (Tübingen 1975) 55f. PERRIN, N., Jesus and the Language of the Kingdom (London 1976) 39, 111, 119, 126, 129, 160. KLAUCK, H.-J., Allegorie und Allegorese in Synoptischen Gleichnistexten (Münster 1978) 210-18. RUDOLPH, K., Die Gnosis (Göttingen 1978) 247. MEYER, B. F., The Aims of Jesus (London 1979) 163f. HARRINGTON, D. J., God's People in Christ (Phildelphia 1980) 23. LAUFEN, R., "ΒΑΣΙΛΕΙΑ und ΕΚΚΛΗΣΙΑ. Eine traditions- und redaktionsgeschichtliche Untersuchung des Gleichnisses vom Senfkorn" in: J. Zmijewski/E. Nellessen (eds.) Begegnung mit dem Wort. Festschrift für H. Zimmermann (Bonn 1980) 105-40. WEDER, H., Die Gleichnisse Jesu als Metaphern (Göttingen 1980) 128-38.

13:32.36 BROCK, S. P. "An Additional Fragment of 0106?" JThS 20 (1, '69) 226-28.

13:32 STRECKER, G. Der Weg der Gerechtigkeit (1962) 24. BRAUN, H. Qumran und NT II (1966) 105, 242.

13:33-37 STROBEL, A. Untersuchungen zum Eschatologischen Verzögerungsproblem (1961) 222-33.

13:33-35 LOCKYER, H. All the Parables of the Bible (1963) 190ff. SUMMERS, R. The Secret Sayings of the Living Jesus (1968) 26, 43, 44.

13:33 MORGAN, G. C. The Parables and Metaphors of Our Lord (1943) 59ff. DODD, C. H. The Parables of the Kingdom (1948) 191ff. PIROT, J. Paraboles et Allégories Evangeliques (1949) 139-43. STAEHELIN, E. Die Verkündigung des Reiches Gottes in der Kirche Jesu Christi I (1951) 58. MOWRY, L. "Parable," IDB III (1962) 653a. SCHRAGE, W. Das Verhältnis des Thomas-Evangeliums zur Synoptischen Tradition und zu den Koptischen Evangelienübersetzungen (1964) 183. BISER, E. Die Gleichnisse Jesu (1965) 79ff. KINGSBURY, J. D. The Parables of Jesus in Matthew 13 (1969) 84-88. BARCLAY, W. And Jesus Said (1970) 60-66. SANFORD, J. A., The Kingdom Within (New York 1970) 44f. FUNK, R. W. "Beyond Criticism in Quest of Literacy: The Parable of the Leaven," Interpretation 25 (2, '71) 149-70. SCHULZ, S. Q Die Spruchquelle der Evangelisten (1972) 307-309. GOULDER, M. D., Midrash and Lection in Matthew (London 1974) 55, 59, 65, 98, 372, 437. WOJCIK, J., "The Two Kingdoms in Matthew's Gospel" in: K. R. R. Gros Louis et al. (eds.) Literary Interpretations of Biblical Narratives (Nashville 1974) 285-87. FUNK, R. W., Jesus as Precursor (Philadelphia and Missoula 1975) 51-72. PERRIN, N., Jesus and the Language of the Kingdom (London 1976) 39, 111, 129, 160. MANEK, J., . . . and brachte Frucht. Die Gleichnisse Jesu (Berlin 1977) 46-48 METZGER, B. M., The Early Versions of the New Testament (Oxford 1977) 42. SWIDLER, L., Biblical Affirmations of Woman (Philadelphia 1979) 242, 253, 257. HARRINGTON, D. J., God's People in Christ (Philadelphia 1980) 23. WEDER, H., Die Gleichnisse Jesu als Metaphern (Göttingen 1980) 128-38.

13:34-36 FARRER, A. St Matthew and St Mark (1954) 181.

13:34-35 KINGSBURY, J. D. The Parables of Jesus in Matthew 13 (1969) 88-91. KLAUCK, H.-J., Allegorie und Allegorese in Synoptischen Gleichnistexten (Münster 1978) 255f.

13:34 BORNKAMM-BARTH-HELD, Ueberlieferung und

Auslegung im Matthäus-Evangelium (1961) 100, 103. STRECKER, G. Der Weg der Gerechtigkeit (1962) 71.

13:35-52 PARKER, P. The Gospel Before Mark (1953) 13-14.

13:35 STONEHOUSE, N. B. The Witness of Matthew and Mark to Christ (1944) 191. FINDLAY, J. A. Jesus and His Parables (1951) 3ff. BLAIR, E. P. Jesus in the Gospel of Matthew (1960) 39, 56. GNILKA, J. Die Verstockung Israels (1961) 106f. LINDARS, B. New Testament Apologetic (1961) 156-58, 168, 262, 270. STRECKER, G. Der Weg der Gerechtigkeit (1962) 49, 70f. SEGBROECK, F. Van, "Le scandale de l'incroyance. La signification de Mt., XIII, 35," EphT 41 (3, '65) 344-72. BRAUN, H. Qumran und NT II (1966) 267, 305f. NELLESSEN, E. Das Kind und seine Mutter (1969) 38f. ROTHFUCHS, W. Die Erfüllungszitate des Matthäus-Evangeliums (1969) 78-80. HAMERTON-KELLY, R. G. Pre-Existence , Wisdom, and the Son of Man (1973) 72-76. GOULDER, M. D., Midrash and Lection in Matthew (London 1974) 366f, 372. METZGER, B. M., "St. Jerome's explicit references to variant readings in manuscripts of the New Testament" in: E. Best/ R. McL. Wilson (eds.) Text and Interpretation. Studies for Matthew Black (Cambridge 1979) 181.

13:36ff HUMMEL, R. Die Auseinandersetzung zwischen Kirche und Judentum im Matthäusevangelium (1963) 156. STAEHELIN, E. Die Verkündigung des Reiches Gottes in der Kirche Jesu Christi I (1951) 58.

13:36-52 KINGSBURY, J. D. The Parables of Jesus in Matthew 13 (1969) 92-129.

13:36-43 JüLICHER, D. A. Die Gleichnisreden Jesu (1910) 546-63. WILKENS, J. Einführung in das Evangelium nach Matthäus I (1934) 185-87. STONEHOUSE, N. B. The Witness of Matthew and Mark to Christ (1944) 238. MICHAELIS, D. W. Die Gleichnisse Jesu (1956) 49-52. GILS, F. Jésus Prophète D'Après Les Evangiles Synoptiques (1957) 100-103. DE GOEDT, M. "L'explication de la parabole de l'ivraie (Mt. XIII, 36-43). Création mattéenne ou aboutissement d'une histoire littéraire?" RevBi 66 (1, '59) 32-54. BLAIR, E. P. Jesus in the Gospel of Matthew (1960) 92, 102, 165. BORNKAMM-BARTH—HELD, Ueberlieferung und Auslegung im Matthäus-Evangelium (1961) 40, 55, 101f, 125, 153, 279. JEREMIAS, J. "Die Deutung des Gleichnisses vom Unkraut unter dem Weizen" in: Neotestamentica et Patristica, Festschrift für Oscar Cullmann (1962) 59-63. JEREMIAS, J. Die Gleichnisse Jesu (1962) 78-84, 91, 97, 105, 223.

STRECKER, G. Der Weg der Gerechtigkeit (1962) 72₂, 158, 160, 215, 218f, 242. BAUMBACH, G. Das Verständnis des Bösen in den synoptischen Evangelien (1963) 58ff, 70ff. JEREMIAS, J. Abba; Studien zur neutestamentlichen Theologie und Zeitgeschichte (1966) 261-65. GIROD, R. Commentaire sur L'Evangile selon Matthieu (1970) 141-53. VöGTLE, A. Das Evangelium und die Evangelien (1971) 267-71. SAND, A., Das Gesetz und die Propheten (Regensburg 1974) 165-67. CONZELMANN, H./LINDEMANN, A., Arbeitsbuch zum Neuen Testament (Tübingen 1975) 87. THEISOHN, J., Der auserwählte Richter (Göttingen 1975) 183ff. GOPPELT, L., Theologie des Neuen Testaments. II (Göttingen 1976) 565ff. MANEK, J.,... und brachte Frucht. Die Gleichnisse Jesu (Berlin 1977) 43-46. *MARGUERAT, D., "L'église et le monde en Matthieu 13, 36-4" RThPh 28 (1978) 111-29. WEDER, H., Die Gleichnisse Jesu als Metaphern (Göttingen 1980) 120-28.

13:36b-43 KINGSBURY, J. D. The Parables of Jesus in Matthew 13 (1969) 93-110.

13:36-42 PIROT, J. Paraboles et Allégories Evangeliques (1949) 108-19.

13:36f MEURER, S. Das Recht im Dienst der Versöhnung und des Friedens (1972) 76-79.

13:36 STONEHOUSE, N. B. The Witness of Matthew and Mark to Christ (1944) 149, 150, 176. STRECKER, G. Der Weg der Gerechtigkeit (1962) 96, 193₁₂.

13:36a KINGSBURY, J. D. The Parables of Jesus in Matthew 13 (1969) 92-93.

13:37ff BEST, E. One Body in Christ (1955) 99. HAHN, F. Das Verständnis der Mission im Neuen Testament (1965) 32.

13:37-50 STROBEL, A. Untersuchungen zum Eschatologischen Verzögerungsproblem (1961) 282-84.

13:37-43 BLAIR, E. P. Jesus in the Gospel of Matthew (1960) 107. BRAUN, H. Qumran und NT II (1966) 276.

13:37 STONEHOUSE, N. B. The Witness of Matthew and Mark to Christ (1944) 238. HAHN, F. Christologische Hoheitstitel (1963) 45. JüNGEL, E. Paulus und Jesus (1966) 238. JEREMIAS, J. Neutestamentliche Theologie I (1971) 248, 250f, 253.

13:38-41 HUMMEL, R. Die Auseinandersetzung zwischen Kirche und Judentum im Matthäusevangelium (1963) 147. HAHN, F. Das Verständnis der Mission im Neuen Testament (1965) 106.

13:38 VOLZ, P. Die Eschatologie der jüdischen Gemeinde (1934)

167. STONEHOUSE, N. B. The Witness of Matthew and Mark to Christ (1944) 232. STAEHELIN, E. Die Verkündigung des Reiches Gottes in der Kirche Jesu Christi I (1951) 140. TRILLING, W. Das wahre Israel (1959) 102f. HUMMEL, R. Die Auseinandersetzung zwischen Kirche und Judentum im Matthäusevangelium (1963) 147-57. SUMMERS, R. The Secret Sayings of the Living Jesus (1968) 59. LADD, G. E., A Theology of the New Testament (Grand Rapids 1974) 51, 65, 96, 112.

13:39ff   STAEHELIN, E. Die Verkündigung des Reiches Gottes in der Kirche Jesu Christi I (1951) 369.

13:39-50   VöGTLE, A. Das Neue Testament und die Zukunft des Kosmos (1970) 151-53, 155, 163.

13:39   METZGER, B. M., The Early Versions of the New Testament (Oxford 1977) 88.

13:40-43   KAHLEFELD, H. Parables and Instructions in the Gospels (1966) 62ff. THEISOHN, J., Der auserwählte Richter (Göttingen 1975) 184ff, 190f, 193ff, 198ff, 205, 259.

13:40   KNOX, W. L. The Sources of the Synoptic Gospels II (1957) 125.

13:41-43   SWIDLER, L., Biblical Affirmations of Woman (Philadelphia 1979) 285.

13:41f   STONEHOUSE, N. B. The Witness of Matthew and Mark to Christ (1944) 238.

13:41   HUMBERT, A. "Essai d'une Théologie du Scandale dans les Synoptiques," Biblica 35 (1954) 6-9. FLEW, R. N. Jesus and His Church (1956) 67n. TRILLING, W. Das wahre Israel (1959) 128f. BLAIR, E. P. Jesus in the Gospel of Matthew (1960) 81, 107, 108. BORNKAMM-BARTH-HELD, Ueberlieferung und Auslegung im Matthäus-Evangelium (1961) 41, 70, 112, 117, 125. STRECKER, G. Der Weg der Gerechtigkeit (1962) 166⁊, 211ₛ, 236. BAUMBACH, G. Das Verständnis des Bösen in den synoptischen Evangelien (1963) 103ff. HAHN, F. Christologische Hoheitstitel (1963) 39. HUMMEL, R. Die Auseinandersetzung zwischen Kirche und Judentum im Matthäusevangelium (1963) 155. JüNGEL, E. Paulus und Jesus (1966) 238. DAVIES, W. D., The Sermon on the Mount (Cambridge 1966) 72f. HIERS, R. H., The Historical Jesus and the Kingdom of God (Gainesville 1973) 30f. LANGE, J., Das Erscheinen des Auferstandenen im Evangelium nach Matthäus (Würzburg 1973) 104, 113, 122, 124, 150, 181f, 185-87, 207f, 213-15, 243, 296, 321f. LADD, G. E., A Theology of the New Testament (Grand Rapids 1974) 96,

112, 205. THEISOHN, J., Der auserwählte Richter (Göttingen 1975) 178, 188ff. MüLLER, U. B., Zur frühchristlichen Theologiegeschichte (Gütersloh 1976) 44f.

13:42.50 KäSEMANN, E. New Testament Questions of Today (1969) 95.

13:42 BLAIR, E. P. Jesus in the Gospel of Matthew (1960) 108. KäSEMANN, E. Exegetische Versuche und Besinnungen (1964) II 94. SMITH, M., Tannaitic Parallels to the Gospels (Philadelphia 1968) 3.9+. THEISOHN, J., Der auserwählte Richter (Göttingen 1975) 194, 198ff.

13:43 STAEHELIN, E. Die Verkündigung des Reiches Gottes in der Kirche Jesu Christi I (1951) 230, 369. BLAIR, E. P. Jesus in the Gospel of Matthew (1960) 81. STRECKER, G. Der Weg der Gerechtigkeit (1962) 198l. HUMMEL, R. Die Auseinandersetzung zwischen Kirche und Judentum im Matthäusevangelium (1963) 147. BOUSSET, W. Die Religion des Judentums im Späthellenistischen Zeitalter (1966-1926) 511. SUMMERS, R. The Secret Sayings of the Living Jesus (1968) 70. CAVALLIN, H. C. C., Life After Death. I (Lund 1974) 3n14, 7, 2, n9. FRANKEMöLLE, H., Jahwebund und Kirche Christi (Münster 1974) 160, 173, 266, 271, 283, 295. THEISOHN, J., Der auserwählte Richter (Göttingen 1975) 190, 195ff, 200. KLIJN, A. F. J., "Die syrische Baruch-Apokalypse" in: W. G. Kümmel (ed.) Jüdische Schriften aus hellenistisch-römischer Zeit. V (Gütersloh 1976) 156.

13:44ff KNOX, W. L. The Sources of the Synoptic Gospels II (1957) 27, 124, 129, 131.

13:44-52 "Anna" in: TRE 2 (1978) 753.

13:44-51 WILKENS, J. Einführung in das Evangelium nach Matthäus I (1934) 188-91.

13:44-50 *BERGMANN, W., Die zehn Gleichnisse vom Reich der Himmel (Lahr-Dinglingen 1976).

13:44-47 DODD, C. H. The Parables of the Kingdom (1948) 112ff. MONTEFIORE, H. A comparison of the Parables of the Gospel According to Thomas and the Synoptic Gospels. NTS 7 (1960-61) 239f.

13:44-46 JüLICHER, D. A. Die Gleichnisreden Jesu (1910) 581-85. RICHARDSON, A. The Miracle-Stories of the Gospels (1949) 11f. MICHAELIS, D. W. Die Gleichnisse Jesu (1956) 61-66. BRUNNER, P. in: Herr, tue meine Lippen auf (1964) Eichholz, G. (ed.) 348ff. IWAND, H.J. Predigt-Meditationen (1964) 654-58. HARDER, GPM (1964)/65) 281ff. EBERT, A. "Der Schatz im Acker und die kostbare Perle," in: Kleine Predigt-

Typologie III (1965) Schmidt, L. (ed.) 137-42. FENTON, J. C. "Expounding the Parables. IV. The Parables of the Treasure and the Pearl (Mt 13:44-46)," ET 77 (6, '66) 178-80. JüNGEL, E. Paulus und Jesus (1966) 142-45. KAHLEFELD, H. Parables and Instructions in the Gospels (1966) 150f. EICHHOLZ, G. in: Hören und Fragen (1967) Eichholz, G. & Falkenroth, A. (eds.) 410ff. DUPONT, J. Les Paraboles du Trésor et de la Perle. NTS 14 (1967-68) 408ff. SUMMERS, R. The Secret Sayings of the Living Jesus (1968) 44, 45. LEHMANN, M. Synoptische Quellenanalyse und die Frage nach dem historischen Jesus (1970) 155-56. LANGE, E. (ed.) Predigtstudien für das Kirchenjahr 1970/71 (1970/71) 164-68. FüRST, W. GPM 11/3 201-207. HARDER, GPM 19/3 281-90. EICHHOLZ, G. Gleichnisse der Evangelien (1971) 109-25. FISCHER, K. M. GPM 25 (2/1971) 327-34. GOULDER, M. D., Midrash and Lection in Matthew (London 1974) 366, 372f. GOPPELT, L., Theologie des Neuen Testaments. I (Göttingen 1975) 117. *HARRINGTON, W., "Hidden Treasure" Furrow 26 (1975) 523-29. HAHN, F., GPM 31 (1976/77) 328, 334. KRüGER, U./DOMAY, E., in: P. Krusche (ed.) Predigtstudien V/2. Halbband (Stuttgart 1977) 148-55. MANEK, J., . . . und brachte Frucht. Die Gleichnisse Jesu (Berlin 1977) 48f. WAELKENS, R., "L'analyse structurale des paraboles. Deux essais: Luc 15, 1-32 et Matthieu 13, 44-46" RThL 8 (1977) 160-78. "Agrapha" in: TRE 2 (1978) 108. WEDER, H., Die Gleichnisse Jesu als Metaphern (Göttingen 1980) 138-42.

13:44-45 FARRER, A. St Matthew and St Mark (1954) 175. BLAIR, E. P. Jesus in the Gospel of Matthew (1960) 107.

13:44 MORGAN, G. C. The Parables and Metaphors of Our Lord (1943) 66ff. PIROT, J. Paraboles et Allégories Evangeliques (1949) 144-48. STAEHELIN, E. Die Verkündigung des Reiches Gottes in der Kirche Jesu Christi.I (1951) 59. KULP, H. EvTh 13 (1953) 145-49. KNOX, W. L. The Sources of the Synoptic Gospels II (1957) 97, 124. GLOMBITZA, O. Der Perlenkaufmann. NTS 7 (1960-61) 153f. JEREMIAS, J. Die Gleichnisse Jesu (1962) 78, 100f, 104, 197-99. MOWRY, L. "Parable," IDB III (1962) 653a. DERRETT, J. D. M. "Law in the New Testament: The Treasure in the Field (Mt. XIII, 44)," ZNW 54 (1-2, '63) 31-42. LOCKYER, H. All the Parables of the Bible (1963) 196ff. NOACK, B. "En konstrueret lignelse refereret og kritiseret" (An Invented Parable Reported and Criticized), DTT 26 (4, '63) 238-43. SCHRAGE, W. Das Verhältnis des Thomas-Evangeliums zur Synoptischen Tradition und zu den Koptischen Evangelienübersetzungen

(1964) 196. LINNEMANN, E. Die Gleichnisse Jesu (1969) 13, 25, 26, 47, 50, 53, 103ff, 169ff. BARCLAY, W. And Jesus Said (1970) 67-72. DERRETT, J. D. M. Law in the New Testament (1970) 1-6. GIROD, R. Commentaire sur L'Evangile selon Matthieu (1970) 153-61. SANFORD, J. A., The Kingdom Within (New York 1970) 39-43. MAGASS, W. "'Der Schatz im Acker' (Mt 13, 44): Von der Kirche als einem Tauschphänomen-Paradigmatik und Transformation," LiBi 21-22 ('73) 2-18. GOULDER, M. D., Midrash and Lection in Matthew (London 1974) 55, 59, 61, 65, 375, 437. PERRIN, N., Jesus and the Language of the Kingdom (London 1976) 38, 100, 106, 112, 116, 118, 129, 160f. CROSSAN, J., Finding is the First Act (Philadelphia 1979). HARRINGTON, D. J., God's People in Christ (Philadelphia 1980) 23.

13:45f JEREMIAS, J. Die Gleichnisse Jesu (1962) 78, 104, 197-99. LINNEMANN, E. Gleichnisse Jesu (1969) 13, 25, 26, 47, 50, 53, 103ff, 169ff.

13:45-46 MORGAN, G. C. The Parables and Metaphors of Our Lord (1943) 72ff. BRUNNER, E. Saat und Frucht (1946) 34-47. FUCHS, E. "Bemerkungen zur Gleichnisauslegung," Zur Frage nach dem Historischen Jesus (1960) 136-42. GLOMBITZA, O. Der Perlenkaufmann. NTS 7 (1960-61) 153f. LOCKYER, H. All the Parables of the Bible (1963) 200ff. SCHIPPERS, R. "The Mashal-character of the Parable of the Pearl," in: Studia Evangelica II (1964) Cross, F. L. (ed.) 236-41. SCHRAGE, W. Das Verhältnis des Thomas-Evangeliums zur Synoptischen Tradition und zu den Koptischen Evangelienübersetzungen (1964) 155. JüNGEL, E. Paulus und Jesus (1966) 131. KINGSBURY, J. D. The Parables of Jesus in Matthew 13 (1969) 110-17. BARCLAY, W. And Jesus Said (1970) 73-78. GIROD, R. Commentaire sur L'Evangile selon Matthieu (1970) 161-77. BRUNNER, E. Saat und Frucht, Zwei Gleichnisse vom Gottesreich, Predigt 34. SANFORD, J. A., The Kingdom Within (New York 1970) 40-43. HARRINGTON, D. J., God's People in Christ (Philadelphia 1980) 23.

13:45 RUDOLPH, K. Die Mandäer II (1961) 23, 7. PERRIN, N., Jesus and the Language of the Kingdom (London 1976) 38, 100, 106, 116f, 129, 160f.

13:46 METZGER, B. M., The Early Versions of the New Testament (Oxford 1977) 436.

13:47ff STAEHELIN, E. Die Verkündigung des Reiches Gottes in der Kirche Jesu Christi I (1951) 59, 356, 366. "Apologetik" in: TRE 3 (1978) 254.

13:47-50 JüLICHER, D. A. Die Gleichnisreden Jesu (1910) 563-69. MORGAN, G. C. The Parables and Metaphors of Our Lord (1943) 77ff. STONEHOUSE, N. B. The Witness of Matthew and Mark to Christ (1944) 238. PIROT, J. Paraboles et Allégories Evangeliques (1949) 120-25. MICHAELIS, D. W. Die Gleichnisse Jesu (1956) 67-70. BORNKAMM-BARTH-HELD, Ueberlieferung und Auslegung im Matthäus-Evangelium (1961) 17, 55, 255. STRECKER, G. Der Weg der Gerechtigkeit (1962) 158, 218. BAUMBACH, G. Das Verständnis des Bösen in den synoptischen Evangelien (1963) 63ff, 70ff. LOCKYER, H. All the Parables of the Bible (1963) 204ff. SMITH, Ch. W. F. "The Mixed State of the Church in Matthew's Gospel," JBL 82 (1963) 149-68, esp. 153-56. HAHN, F. Das Verständnis der Mission im Neuen Testament (1965) 31, 109. BRAUN, H. Qumran und NT II (1966) 269. FISCHER, M. GPM 21/4 (1966/67) 409-14. HAMEL, J. in: Hören und Fragen (1967) Eichholz, G. & Falkenroth, A. (eds.) 148ff. SUMMERS, R. The Secret Sayings of the Living Jesus (1968) 45. KINGSBURY, J. D. The Parables of Jesus in Matthew 13 (1969) 117-25. GIROD, R. Commentaire sur L'Evangile selon Matthieu (1970) 177-95. PATSCH, H. Abendmahl und historischer Jesus (1972) 111ff. LADD, G. E., A Theology of the New Testament (Grand Rapids 1974) 100f. WOJCIK, J., "The Two Kingdoms in Matthew's Gospel" in: K. R. R. Gros Louis et al. (eds.) Literary Interpretations of Biblical Narratives (Nashville 1974) 287. PERRIN, N., Jesus and the Language of the Kingdom (London 1976) 39, 119. MANEK, J., . . . und brachte Frucht. Die Gleichnisse Jesu (Berlin 1977) 50f. HARRINGTON, D. J., God's People in Christ (Philadelphia 1980) 23. WEDER, H., Die Gleichnisse Jesu als Metaphern (Göttingen 1980) 142-47.

13:47f SCHRAGE, W. Das Verhältnis des Thomas-Evangeliums zur Synoptischen Tradition und zu den Koptischen Evangelienübersetzungen (1964) 37. JüNGEL, E. Paulus und Jesus (1966) 145-48.

13:47-48 DODD, Ch. H. The Parables of the Kingdom (1948) 187ff. STRECKER, G. Der Weg der Gerechtigkeit (1962) 161. BARCLAY, W. And Jesus Said (1970) 45-51. GOPPELT, L., Theologie des Neuen Testaments. I (Göttingen 1975) 116f. "Agrapha" in TRE 2 (1978) 108.

13:48 BLAIR, E. P. Jesus in the Gospel of Matthew (1960) 119. METZGER, B. M., The Early Versions of the New Testament (Oxford 1977) 423.

13:49f STAEHELIN, E. Die Verkündigung des Reiches Gottes in der

Kirche Jesu Christi I (1951) 289. STRECKER, G. Der Weg der
Gerechtigkeit (1962) 160f, 236.

13:49-50 THEISOHN, J., Der auserwählte Richter (Göttingen 1975)
184ff, 190, 193, 200, 263. WILCKENS, U., "Gottes geringste
Brüder—zu Mt 25: 31-46" in: E. E. Ellis/ E. Grässer (eds.) Jesus
und Paulus. Festschrift für W. G. Kümmel (Göttingen 1975)
367-72. SWIDLER, L., Biblical Affirmations of Woman
(Philadelphia 1979) 285.

13:50 KäSEMANN, E. Exegetische versuche und Besinnungen
(1964) II 94. SMITH, M., Tannaitic Parallels to the Gospels
(Philadelphia 1968) 3.9+.

13:51-52 MORGAN, G. C. The Parables and Metaphors of Our Lord
(1943) 83ff. LOCKYER, H. All the Parables of the Bible (1963)
208ff. TOUSSAINT, "The Introductory and Concluding
Parables of Matthew Thirteen," BiblSa 121 (484, '64) 351-55.
KINGSBURY, J. D. The Parables of Jesus in Matthew 13
(1969) 125-29. GIROD, R. Commentaire sur L'Evangile selon
Matthieu (1970) 195-211. GOULDER, M. D., Midrash and
Lection in Matthew (London 1974) 375f.

13:51 BLAIR, E. P. Jesus in the Gospel of Matthew (1960) 103, 104.
BORNKAMM-BARTH-HELD, Ueberlieferung und
Auslegung im Matthäus-Evangelium (1961) 99ff, 280.
STRECKER, G. Der Weg der Gerechtigkeit (1962) 193₁₁.₁₂.

13:52 JüLICHER, D. A. Die Gleichnisreden Jesu (1910) 128-33.
WILKENS, J. Einführung in das Evangelium nach Matthäus I
(1934) 191-92. STAEHELIN, E. Die Verkündigung des
Reiches Gottes in der Kirche Jesu Christi I (1951) 59, 368.
FLEW, R. N. Jesus and His Church (1956) 22. KNOX, W. L.
The Sources of the Synoptic Gospels II (1957) 20, 33, 124.
TRILLING, W. Das wahre Israel (1959) 121f. BLAIR, E. P.
Jesus in the Gospel of Matthew (1960) 28, 114, 158.
HARRISVILLE, R. A. The Concept o f Newness in the New
Testament (1960) 26ff. BORNKAMM-BARTH-HELD,
Ueberlieferung und Auslegung im Matthäus-Evangelium
(1961) 191. STRECKER, G. Der Weg der Gerechtigkeit (1962)
30, 37, 192, 216s. HAHN, F. Christologische Hoheitstitel
(1963) 123. HUMMEL, R. Die Auseinandersetzung zwischen
Kirche und Judentum im Matthäusevangelium (1963) 27.
HAHN, F. Das Verständnis der Mission im Neuen Testament
(1965) 105. BECKER, J. "Erwägungen zu Fragen der
neutestamentlichen Exegese," BZ 13 (1, '69) 99-102.
TRILLING, W., "Amt und Amtsverständnis bei Matthäus" in:
A. Descamps/A. de Halleux (eds.) Mélanges Bibliques en
hommage au R. P. Béda Rigaux (Gembloux 1970) 32-34.

BROER, I. Die Urgemeinde und das Grab Jesu (1972) 184f. LANGE, J., Das Erscheinen des Auferstandenen im Evangelium nach Matthäus (Würzburg 1973) 36, 40, 137, 150, 308-310, 313, 319, 321. *ZELLER, D., "Zu einer jüdischen Vorlage von Mt 13, 52" BZ 20 (1976) 223-26. DUNN, J. D. G., Unity and Diversity in the New Testament (London 1977) 117. METZGER, B. M., The Early Versions of the New Testament (Oxford 1977) 433. "Amt" in: TRE 2 (1978) 516. RIVKIN, E., A Hidden Revolution (Nashville 1978) 112f.

13:53-18:35   *GOODING, W. D., "Structure littéraire de Matthieu, XIII, 53 à XVIII, 35" RB 85 (1978) 227-52.

13:53-17:27   *MURPHY-O'CONNOR, J., "The Structure of Matthew XIV-XVII" RB 82 (1975) 360-84.

13:53-16:12   RIDDERBOS, H. Matthew's Witness to Jesus Christ (1958) 49-55.

13:53-58   EWALD, H. Die drei ersten Evangelien (1850) 243ff. WILKENS, J. Einführung in das Evangelium nach Matthäus I (1934) 192-94. FARRER, A. St Matthew and St Mark (1954) 184. GAECHTER, P. Die literarische Kunst im Matthäus-Evangelium (1968) 56-59, 73-74. GIROD, R. Commentaire sur L'Evangile selon Matthieu (1970) 211-37. RIST, J. M., On the Independence of Matthew and Mark (Cambridge 1978) 60f. SWIDLER, L., Biblical Affirmations of Woman (Philadelphia 1979) 178, 228, 237.

13:53-57   CHRIST, F. Jesus Sophia (1970) 68, 77.

13:53f   STRECKER, G. Der Weg der Gerechtigkeit (1962) 964.

13:53   STONEHOUSE, N. B. The Witness of Matthew and Mark to Christ (1944) 131, 149, 151. FARRER, A. St Matthew and St Mark (1954) 179. BLAIR, E. P. Jesus in the Gospel of Matthew (1960) 132. STRECKER, G. Der Weg der Gerechtigkeit (1962) 38₈, 130.

13:54-19:1   HAHN, F. Christologischen Hoheitstitel (1963) 400.

13:54-17:27   ELLIS, P. F., Matthew: His Mind and His Message (Collegeville 1974) 63-67.

13:54-16:12   STONEHOUSE, N. B. The Witness of Matthew and Mark to Christ (1944) 151f.

13:54ff   STONEHOUSE, N. B. The Witness of Matthew and Mark to Christ (1944) 153, 185.

13:54-58   STONEHOUSE, N. B. The Witness of Matthew and Mark to Christ (1944) 151. GOODSPEED, E. J. A Life of Jesus (1950) 95-99. SEGBROECK, F. Van, "Jésus rejeté par sa patrie (Mt 13, 54-58)," Biblica 49 (2, '68) 167-98. SCHNIDER, F., Jesus der Prophet (Freiburg 1973) 160f. CONZELMANN, H./LINDEMANN, A., Arbeitsbuch zum Neuen Testament (Tübingen 1975) 41. GLöCKNER, R., Die Verkündigung des Heils beim Evangelisten Lukas (Mainz 1975) 127f.

13:54-56   HAHN, F. Christologische Hoheitstitel (1963) 322.

13:54   STONEHOUSE, N. B. The Witness of Matthew and Mark to Christ (1944) 145, 160. BLAIR, E. P. Jesus in the Gospel of Matthew (1960) 94. HAHN, F. Das Verständnis der Mission im Neuen Testament (1965) 104.

13:55   BLINZLER, J., Die Brüder und Schwestern Jesu (Stuttgart 1967) 75-82. GRäSSER, E. Jesus in Nazareth (Notes on the Redaction and Theology of Mark). NTS 16 (1969-70) 14f. SWIDLER, L., Biblical Affirmations of Woman (Philadelphia 1979) 278.

13:57-26:10   *VööBUS, A., "Découverte du commentaire de Mose- bar Kephà sur l'évangile de Matthieu" RB 80 (1973) 359-62.

13:57   SCHRAGE, W. Das Verhältnis des Thomas-Evangeliums zur Synoptischen Tradition und zu den Koptischen Evangelienübersetzungen (1964) 75. SUMMERS, R. The Secret Sayings of the Living Jesus (1968) 36.

13:58   STONEHOUSE, N. B. The Witness of Matthew and Mark to Christ (1944) 145. BORNKAMM-BARTH-HELD, Ueberlieferung und Auslegung im Matthäus-Evangelium (1961) 265. STRECKER, G. Der Weg der Gerechtigkeit (1962) 121?. THEYSSEN, G. W. "Unbelief" in the New Testament (Rüschlikon 1965) 25f. GOULDER, M. D., Midrash and Lection in Matthew (London 1974) 41, 376, 378, 445.

14-20   PERRIN, N., The New Testament (New York 1974) 183-87.

14-17   SELBY, D. J., Introduction to the New Testament (New York 1971) 134-37, 139.

14:1-16:12   GOULDER, M. D., Midrash and Lection in Matthew (London 1974) 376-82.

14-16:8   TAYLOR, V. The Formation of the Gospel Tradition (1949) 57-59.

14:1-15:28   RIST, J. M., On the Independence of Matthew and Mark (Cambridge 1978) 63-67.

14 STONEHOUSE, N. B. The Witness of Matthew and Mark to Christ (1944) 146. RUDOLPH, K. Die Mandäer I (1960) 73, 74. WOJCIK, J., "The Two Kingdoms in Matthew's Gospel" in: K. R. R. Gros Louis et al. (eds.) Literary Interpretations of Biblical Narratives (Nashville 1974) 283-85.

14:1ff STONEHOUSE, N. B. The Witness of Matthew and Mark to Christ (1944) 151.

14:1-16.20 GAECHTER, P. Die literarische Kunst im Matthäus-Evangelium (1968) 29-30.

14:1-15 GIROD, R. Commentaire sur L'Evangile selon Matthieu (1970) 237-65.

14:1-13 WILKENS, J. Einführung in das Evangelium nach Matthäus I (1934) 195-96.

14:1-12 EWALD, H. Die drei ersten Evangelien (1850) 257ff. BöCHER, O., "Johannes der Täufer in der neutestamentlichen Überlieferung" in: G. Müller (ed.) Rechtfertigung Realismus Universalismus in Biblischer Sicht. FS für Adolf Köberle (Darmstadt 1978) 46-52. SCHRECKENBERG, H., "Flavius Josephus und die lukanischen Schriften" in: W. Haubeck/ W. Bachmann (eds.) Wort in der Zeit. Festgabe für K. H. Rengstorf (Leiden 1980) 187-90.

14:1-2 SCHRAMM, T. Der Markus-Stoff bei Lukas (1971) 128f. SAND, A., Das Gesetz und die Propheten (Regensburg 1974) 135-37.

14:1 STONEHOUSE, N. B. The Witness of Matthew and Mark to Christ (1944) 148, 151.

14:2 STONEHOUSE, N. B. The Witness of Matthew and Mark to Christ (1944) 145. TYSON, J. B., "Source Criticism of the Gospel of Luke" in: C. H. TALBERT, (ed.) Perspectives on Luke-Acts (Edinburgh 1978) 31.

14:3ff STONEHOUSE, N. B. The Witness of Matthew and Mark to Christ (1944) 132f.

14:3-12 WINK, W. John the Baptist in the Gospel Tradition (1968) 27-28. SWIDLER, L., Biblical Affirmations of Woman (Philadephia 1979) 229, 238.

14:4 McNAMARA, M. The New Testament and the Palestinian Targum to the Pentateuch (1966) 77 fn. 21.

14:7ff HENNECKE, E. & SCHNEEMELCHER, W. Neutestamentliche Apokryphen (1964) I 129.

14:8 METZGER, B. M., The Early Versions of the New Testament (Oxford 1977) 178.

14:9 METZGER, B. M., The Early Versions of the New Testament

(Oxford 1977) 440.

14:11   METZGER, B. M., The Early Versions of the New Testament (Oxford 1977) 178, 440.

14:12-13 BLAIR, E. P. Jesus in the Gospel of Matthew (1960) 86, 90. SMITH, M., Tannaitic Parallels to the Gospels (Philadelphia 1968) 7 end+.

14:12   BEST, E. One Body in Christ (1955) 53, 216. M'NEILE, A. H. The Gospel According to St Matthew (1955) 211-13. DAVIES, W. D., The Sermon on the Mount (Cambridge 1966) 72f. JANSSEN, E., "Testament Abrahams" in: W. G. Kümmel (ed.) Jüdische Schriften aus hellenistisch-römischer Zeit III (Gütersloh 1975) 216.

14:13-16:12 FARRER, A. St Matthew and St Mark (1954) 119, 190. M'NEILE, A. H. The Gospel According to St Matthew (1955) 237f. GILS, F. Jésus Prophéte D'Après Les Evangiles Synoptiques (1957) 16-23. SCHNEIDER, F. & STENGER, W. Johannes und die Synoptiker (1971) 89-178.

14:13-36 EWALD, H. Die drei ersten Evangelien (1850) 259ff.

14:13-21 STONEHOUSE, N. B. The Witness of Matthew and Mark to Christ (1944) 145. REICKE, B. Diakonie, Festfreude und Zelos (1951) 21f. FARRER, A. St Matthew and St Mark (1954) 175. M'NEILE, A. H. The Gospel According to St Matthew (1955) 215-17. KNACKSTEDT, J. "De duplici miraculo multiplicationis panum,' VerbDom 41 (1-2, '63) 140-53. HEISING, A. "Exegese und Theologie der alt- und neutestamentlichen Speisewunder," ZKTh 86 (1, '64) 80-96. KNACKSTEDT, J. "Die beiden Brotvermehrungen im Evangelium," NTS 10 (3, '64) 309-35. HEISING, A. Die Botschaft der Brotvermehrung (1967). KAMPHAUS, F. Von der Exegese zur Predigt (1968) 140-42. ROLOFF, J. Das Kerygma und der irdische Jesus (1970) 251ff. SCHRAMM, T. Der Markus-Stoff bei Lukas (1971) 129f. VAN CANGH, J.-V., La multiplication des pains et l'Eucharistie (Paris 1975). SWIDLER, L., Biblical Affirmations of Woman (Philadelphia 1979) 249, 279.

14:13b-21 WILKENS, J. Einführung in das Evangelium nach Matthäus I (1934) 196-98.

14:13f   DALMAN, G. Orte und Wege Jesu (1967) 185f.

14:13-14 EGGER, W., Frohbotschaft und Lehre (Frankfurt 1976) 34f, 124, 132.

14:13   STONEHOUSE, N. B. The Witness of Matthew and Mark to Christ (1944) 152. STRECKER, G. Der Weg der Gerechtigkeit (1962) 231². KüNZI, M. Das Naherwartungslogion Matthäus

10, 23 (1970) 19, 81, 155. COPE, L., "The Death of John the Baptist in the Gospel of Matthew; or, the Case of the Confusing Conjunction" CBQ 38 (1976) 515-19.

14:14-21 BECKER, U./WIBBING, S., Wundergeschichten (Gütersloh 1965) 55ff. FRIEDRICH, G., "Die beiden Erzählungen von der Speisung in Markus 6, 31-44; 8, 1-9" in: Auf das Wort kommt es an (Göttingen 1978) 25.

14:14 KNOX, W. L. The Sources of the Synoptic Gospels II (1957) 52. STRECKER, G. Der Weg der Gerechtigkeit (1962) 195₄. COMBER, J. A., "The Verb Therapeuo in Matthew's Gospel" JBL 97 (1978) 431-34. "Barmherzigkeit" in: TRE 5 (1980) 227.

14:15-21 BORNKAMM-BARTH-HELD, Ueberlieferung und Auslegung im Matthäus-Evangelium (1961) 171ff, 196, 221, 233. GILL, W. "The Historic Jesus and Ecumenical Endeavour," LondQuart HolRev 34 (4, '65) 279-84. GIROD, R. Commentaire sur L'Evangile selon Matthieu (1970) 267-81.

14:15 STONEHOUSE, N. B. The Witness of Matthew and Mark to Christ (1944) 138. NICKELS, P. Targum and New Testament (1967) 19.

14:16f STRECKER, G. Der Weg der Gerechtigkeit (1962) 193₉.

14:16 BORNKAMM-BARTH-HELD, Ueberlieferung und Auslegung im Matthäus-Evangelium (1961) 171ff, 175, 233. GRASSI, J. A., " 'You yourselves give them to eat.' An easily forgotten command of Jesus (Mk 6:37; Mt 14:16; Lk 9:13)" Bible Today 97 (1978) 1704-1709.

14:17 BLAIR, E. P. Jesus in the Gospel of Matthew (1960) 86. STRECKER, G. Der Weg der Gerechtigkeit (1962) 121₉, 13.

14:18-19 *STEHLY, R., "Bouddhisme et Nouveau Testament à propos de la marche de Pierre sur l'eau (Matthieu 14.28 s)" RHPR 57 (1977) 433-37.

14:19 BOUSSET, W. Die Religion des Judentums im Späthellenistischen Zeitalter (1966⁻1926) 178. DALMAN, G. Wege und Orte Jesu (1967) 187f. METZGER, B. M., The Early Versions of the New Testament (Oxford 1977) 176.

14:20 STRECKER, G. Der Weg der Gerechtigkeit (1962) 121₁₈.

14:21 GARRIDO, J. "Hallazgo de un papiro del Nuevo Testamento en copto sahidico," EstBi 17 (1, '58) 107-108. STRECKER, G. Der Weg der Gerechtigkeit (1962) 121₁₉.

14:22ff HANSON, S. The Unity of the Church in the New Testament (1946) 32f.

14:22-36 GIROD, R. Commentaire sur L'Evangile selon Matthieu (1970) 281-305. GOULDER, M. D., Midrash and Lection in

Matthew (London 1974) 377f.

14:22-34 Verkündigt das angenehme Jahr des Herrn in: Predigtgedanken aus Vergangenheit und Gegenwart Bd. I (1962) 215ff. HELD, H. J. GPM 17/1 87-94.

14:22-33 WILKENS, J. Einführung in das Evangelium nach Matthäus I (1934) 198-200. STONEHOUSE, N. B. The Witness of Matthew and Mark to Christ (1944) 145. M'NEILE, A. H. The Gospel According to St Matthew (1955) 219. VOLK, H. "Petrus steigt aus dem Boot," Catholica 14 (1, '60) 49-55. DENIS, A.-M. "Jesus' walking on the waters. A contribution to the history of the pericope in the Gospel Tradition," LSt 1 (3, '67) 284-97. ITTEL, G. W. Jesus und die Jünger (1970) 64-67. KLOPPENBURG, H. GPM 6/1 54-56. *GAIDE, G., "Jésus et Pierre marchent sur les eaux. Mt 14, 22-33" AssS 50 (1974) 23-31. BARTLETT, D. L., Fact and Faith (Valley Forge 1975) 50f. HOWARD, V. P., Das Ego Jesu in den Synoptischen Evangelien (Marburg 1975) 78-85.

14:22 STONEHOUSE, N. B. The Witness of Matthew and Mark to Christ (1944) 171. STRECKER, G. Der Weg der Gerechtigkeit (1962) 97.

14:23 METZGER, B. M., The Early Versions of the New Testament (Oxford 1977) 247. LIVIO, J.-B., "La significance théologique de la 'montagne' dans le premier evangile" Bulletin du Centre Protestant d'Études 30 (Geneve 1978) 13-20.

14:24-32 STONEHOUSE, N. B. The Witness of Matthew and Mark to Christ (1944) 218.

14:24 BORNKAMM-BARTH-HELD, Ueberlieferung und Auslegung im Matthäus-Evangelium (1961) 195, 219, 253f.

14:25 STRECKER, G. Der Weg der Gerechtigkeit (1962) 127₇.

14:26 STONEHOUSE, N. B. The Witness of Matthew and Mark to Christ (1944) 219. STRECKER, G. Der Weg der Gerechtigkeit (1962) 234₃.

14:27 STRECKER, G. Der Weg der Gerechtigkeit (1962) 193₈.

14:28-28:20 PAPYRUS BODMER XIX, published by Rodolphe Kasser (1962).

14:28ff STAEHELIN, E. Die Verkündigung des Reiches Gottes in der Kirche Jesu Christi I (1951) 291.

14:28-33 *GISPERT-SAUCH, G., "St Peter Walking on the Ganges?" Vidyajyoti 42 (1978) 468-72.

14:28-32 HIRSCH, E. Frühgeschichte des Evangelium (1941) 182-86. FARRER, A. St Matthew and St Mark (1954) 122.

14:28-31 STONEHOUSE, N. B. The Witness of Matthew and Mark to

Christ (1944) 80, 219. BORNKAMM-BARTH-HELD, Ueberlieferung und Auslegung im Matthäus-Evangelium (1961) 158, 193ff, 223, 227, 233f, 258f, 277. LöVESTAM, E. "Wunder und Symbolhandlung. Eine Studie über Matthäus 14, 28-31," KuD 8 (2, '62) 124-35. STRECKER, G. Der Weg der Gerechtigkeit (1962) 198f, 200$_8$, 202$_4$, 203f. HAHN, F. Christologische Hoheitstitel (1963) 86. HUMMEL, R. Die Auseinandersetzung zwischen Kirche und Judentum im Matthäusevangelium (1963) 115. BRAUMANN, G. "Der sinkende Petrus. Matth. 14, 28-31," ThZ 22 (6, '66) 403-14. LEE, G. M. "St. Peter on the Water (Matthew, xiv, 28-31)," MCh 9 (2, '66) 163-65. BROWN, R. E. et al. (eds.) Peter in the New Testament (Minneapolis 1973) 80-83. *KRATZ, R., "Der Seewandel des Petrus (Mt 14, 28-31)" BiLe 15 (1974) 86-101. DUNN, J. D. G., Unity and Diversity in the New Testament (London 1977) 117. RIST, J. M., On the Independence of Matthew and Mark (Cambridge 1978) 68f.

14:28f BORNKAMM-BARTH-HELD, Ueberlieferung und Auslegung im Matthäus-Evangelium (1961) 225, 260, 262, 266.

14:28.30 BLAIR, E. P. Jesus in the Gospel of Matthew (1960) 100.

14:28 HAHN, F., Christologischen Hoheitstitel (1963) 86.

14:30 STRECKER, G. Der Weg der Gerechtigkeit (1962) 20, 193$_8$, 213$_1$.

14:31ff BORNKAMM-BARTH-HELD, Ueberlieferung und Auslegung im Matthäus-Evangelium (1961) 105f, 254, 256, 260, 271, 280ff. GOULDER, M. D., Midrash and Lection in Matthew (London 1974) 343f.

14:31 STONEHOUSE, N. B. The Witness of Matthew and Mark to Christ (1944) 179. STRECKER, G. Der Weg der Gerechtigkeit (1962) 20, 194$_2$, 233$_4$, 234ff. BLACK, M. An Aramaic Approach to the Gospels and Acts (1967) 129f.

14:32 TILLICH, P. Das Ewige Jetzt (Sermon) (1964) 13-21.

14:33 STONEHOUSE, N. B. The Witness of Matthew and Mark to Christ (1944) 179, 180, 211, 214f, 217f. BLAIR, E. P. Jesus in the Gospel of Matthew (1960) 61, 65, 66, 102, 103, 104, 107, 125, 176$_2$, 193$_{7.14}$, 206. LöVESTAM, E., Son and Savior (Lund 1961) 104, 106f. DE KRUIJF, T., Der Sohn des Lebendigen Gottes (Rome 1962) 41, 76-80, 82, 89f, 97, 100, 104, 140f, 153. HAHN, F. Christologische Hoheitstitel (1963) 86, 314. HUMMEL, R. Die Auseinandersetzung zwischen Kirche und Judentum im Matthäusevangelium (1963) 115. VöGTLE, A., "Zum Problem der Herkunft von 'Mt 16, 17-19' " in: P. Hoffmann (ed.) Orientierung an Jesus. Für Josef Schmid

(Freiburg 1973) 384f. FRANKEMöLLE, H., Jahwebund und Kirche Christi (Münster 1974) 93, 151f, 165f. DUNN, J. D. G., Unity and Diversity in the New Testament (London 1977) 47. SWIDLER, L., Biblical Affirmations of Woman (Philadelphia 1979) 217.

14:34-15:20 WILKENS, J. Einführung in das Evangelium nach Matthäus I (1934) 200-205.

14:34-36 EGGER, W., Frohbotschaft und Lehre (Frankfurt 1976) 34, 135.

14:34 STRECKER, G. Der Weg der Gerechtigkeit (1962) 97.

14:35f STONEHOUSE, N. B. The Witness of Matthew and Mark to Christ (1944) 145.

14:35 KNOX, W. L. The Sources of the Synoptic Gospels II (1957) 125. STRECKER, G. Der Weg der Gerechtigkeit (1962) 121 17. EGGER, W., Frohbotschaft und Lehre (Frankfurt 1976) 36.

14:36 BOUSSET, W. Die Religion des Judentums im Späthellenistischen Zeitalter (1966⁻1926) 179.

14:47-50 GILS, F. Jésus Prophète D'Après Les Evangiles Synoptiques (1957) 100-103.

15:1-16:12 EWALD, H. Die drei ersten Evangelien (1850) 262ff.

15:1ff STONEHOUSE, N. B. The Witness of Matthew and Mark to Christ (1944) 146, 153, 196. BLAIR, E. P. Jesus in the Gospel of Matthew (1960) 112. SCHRAGE, W. Die konkreten Einzelgebote in der paulinischen Paränese (1961) 52. STRECKER, G. Der Weg der Gerechtigkeit (1962) 17, 142 3. STROBEL, A. Erkenntnis und Bekenntnis der Sünde in neutestamentlicher Zeit (1968) 44. WREGE, H.-T. Die Ueberlieferungsgeschichte der Bergpredigt (1968) 51-52.

15:1-20 BERGER, K. Die Gesetzesauslegung Jesu (1940) 497-505, 506-507. LUND, N. W. Chiasmus in the New Testament (1942) 277f. KNOX, W. L. The Sources of the Synoptic Gospels II (1957) 1-20. BORNKAMM-BARTH-HELD, Ueberlieferung und Auslegung im Matthäus-Evangelium (1961) 29, 80, 84, 148, 188, 196, 227. STRECKER, G. Der Weg der Gerechtigkeit (1962) 30f. BAUMBACH, G. Das Verständnis des Bösen in den synoptischen Evangelien (1963) 89ff. HUMMEL, R. Die

Auseinandersetzung zwischen Kirche und Judentum im Matthäusevangelium (1963) 46-49, 53-56. SUHL, A. Die Funktion der alttestamentlichen Zitate und Anspielungen im Markusevangelium (1965) 79ff. BRAUN, H. Qumran und NT II (1966) 100, 112, 115, 288, 295. GIROD, R. Commentaire sur L'Evangile selon Matthieu (1970) 305-55. ERNST, J., Anfänge der Christologie (Stuttgart 1972) 154-58. HüBNER, H., Das Gesetz in der synoptischen Tradition (Witten 1973) 142ff. GOULDER, M. D., Midrash and Lection in Matthew (London 1974) 19, 272, 378f, 382, 422. SAND, A., Das Gesetz u und die Propheten (Regensburg 1974) 68-72. HAHN, F., GPM 29 (1975) 405-13. STECK, W./HERRMANN, W., in: P. Krusche et al. (eds.) Predigtstudien für das Kirchenjahr 1975 III/2. Halbband (Stuttgart 1975) 212-220. COPE, O. L., Matthew. A Scribe Trained for the Kingdom of Heaven (Washington D. C. 1976) 52-65. SANDMEL, S., We Jews and Jesus (New York 1977) 136. WESTERHOLM, S., Jesus and Scribal Authority (Lund 1978) 71-85. McDONALD, J. I. H., Kerygma and Didache (Cambridge 1980) 104f.

15:1-11a.
18-20   MERKEL, GPM (1962/63) 316ff. Also in Predigtgedanken aus Vergangenheit und Gegenwart, Reihe C. Bd. 3-4 (1963) 255-62. SCHRöER, H. GPM 23/4 (1968/69) 346-54.

15:1-14   KäSEMANN, E. Exegetische Versuche und Besinnungen (1964) I 237-41.

15:1-12   GARLAND, D. E., The Intention of Matthew 23 (Leiden 1979) 122.

15:1-7   SWIDLER, L., Biblical Affirmations of Woman (Philadelphia 1979) 177, 230, 238.

15:1-6   M'NEILE, A. H. The Gospel According To St Matthew (1955) 224f. LIGHTSTONE, J. N., "Sadoq the Yavnean" in: W. S. Green (ed.) Persons and Institutions in Early Rabbinic Judaism (Missoula 1977) 68.

15:1   STONEHOUSE, N. B. The Witness of Matthew and Mark to Christ (1944) 152.

15:2   RUDOLPH, K. Die Mandäer II (1961) 404.

15:3ff   BLAIR, E. P. Jesus in the Gospel of Matthew (1960) 113.

15:3   STRECKER, G. Der Weg der Gerechtigkeit (1962) 139. BANKS, R., Jesus and the Law in the Synoptic Tradition (London 1975) 137f.

15:4-6   DERRETT, J. D M. KOPBAN, OΣE TIN ΔωPON. NTS 16 (1969-70) 364-68.

15:4a   STRECKER, G. Der Weg der Gerechtigkeit (1962) 222.

15:4b   STRECKER, G. Der Weg der Gerechtigkeit (1962) 22.

15:5f   BORNKAMM-BARTH-HELD, Ueberlieferung und Auslegung im Matthäus-Evangelium (1961) 58, 75.

15:5   *MOLITOR, J. "Mt 15, 5 in einer altgeorgische Fassung," BZ 1 (1, '57) 130-32. STRECKER, G. Der Weg der Gerechtigkeit (1962) 21. HUMMEL, R. Die Auseinandersetzung zwischen Kirche und Judentum im Matthäusevangelium (1963) 94. HENNECKE, E. & SCHNEEMELCHER, W. Neutestamentliche Apokryphen (1964) I 96. BUCHANAN, G. W. "Some Vow and Oath Formulas in the New Testament," HThR 58 (3, '65) 319-26. FALK, Z. W. "On Talmudic Vows," HThR 59 (3, '66) 309-12. FITZMYER, J. A. Essays on the Semitic Background of the New Testament (1971) 93-100.

15:6   SMITH, M., Tannaitic Parallels to the Gospels (Philadelphia 1968) 2 b n 92+.

15:7ff HENNECKE, E. & SCHNEEMELCHER, W. Neutestamentliche Apokryphen (1964) I 60.

15:7   FARRER, A. St Matthew and St Mark (1954) 175.

15:8f   STRECKER, G. Der Weg der Gerechtigkeit (1962) 22.

15:8   STAEHELIN, E. Die Verkündigung des Reiches Gottes in der Kirche Jesu Christi I (1951) 251. HUMMEL, R. Die Auseinandersetzung zwischen Kirche und Judentum im Matthäusevangelium (1963) 145f. FRANKEMöLLE, H., Jahwebund und Kirche Christi (Münster 1974) 195, 201f.

15:9   STRECKER, G. Der Weg der Gerechtigkeit (1962) 40l.

15:10-20 JüLICHER, D. A. Die Gleichnisreden Jesu (1910) 50-54, 54-67. BLAIR, E. P. Jesus in the Gospel of Matthew (1960) 114, 115.

15:10f BORNKAMM-BARTH-HELD, Ueberlieferung und Auslegung im Matthäus-Evangelium (1961) 82ff, 103, 153.

15:10   STRECKER, G. Der Weg der Gerechtigkeit (1962) 229s, 230. PASCHEN, W., Rein und Unrein (München 1970) 162f.

15:11   STAEHELIN, E. Die Verkündigung des Reiches Gottes in der Kirche Jesu Christi I (1951) 278. BLAIR, E. P. Jesus in the Gospel of Matthew (1960) 115. SCHRAGE, W. Die konkreten Einzelgebote in der paulinischen Paränese (1961) 243. SCHRAGE, W. Das Verhältnis des Thomas-Evangeliums zur Synoptischen Tradition und zu den Koptischen Evangelienübersetzungen (1964) 55. JüNGEL, E. Paulus und Jesus (1966) 209ff. SUMMERS, R. The Secret Sayings of the Living Jesus (1968) 31, 34. LIGHTSTONE, J. N., "Sadoq the Yavnean" in: W. S. Green (ed.) Persons and Institutions in

Early Rabbinic Judaism (Missoula 1977) 63. KLAUCK, H.-J., Allegorie und Allegorese in Synoptischen Gleichnistexten (Münster 1978) 260-72. MEYER, B. F., The Aims of Jesus (London 1979) 149.

15:12ff BORNKAMM-BARTH-HELD, Ueberlieferung und Auslegung im Matthäus-Evangelium (1961) 81f, 216.

15:12-15 SCHWEIZER, E., Matthäus und seine Gemeinde (Stuttgart 1974) I.3.4, I.4.3, I.5.3, X.4.2, Note 41.

15:12-14 STRECKER, G. Der Weg der Gerechtigkeit (1962) 139. HUMMEL, R. Die Auseinandersetzung zwischen Kirche und Judentum im Matthäusevangelium (1963) 128, 152. BANKS, R., Jesus and the Law in the Synoptic Tradition (London 1975) 142f.

15:12-13 BLAIR, E. P. Jesus in the Gospel of Matthew (1960) 115.

15:12 BLAIR, E. P. Jesus in the Gospel of Matthew (1960) 86, 90, 99.

15:13-14 BLAIR, E. P. Jesus in the Gospel of Matthew (1960) 112.

15:13 BLAIR, E. P. Jesus in the Gospel of Matthew (1960) 113. RUDOLPH, K. Die Mandäer II (1961) 23, 1. HAHN, F., Christologische Hoheitstitel (1963) 321. SCHRAGE, W. Das Verhältnis des Thomas-Evangeliums zur Synoptischen Tradition und zu den Koptischen Evangelienübersetzungen (1964) 95. BRAUN, H. Qumran und NT II (1966) 104.

15:14 FARRER, A. St Matthew and St Mark (1954) 175. DUPONT, D. J. Les Béatitudes (1958) 53-58. BLAIR, E. P. Jesus in the Gospel of Matthew (1960) 115. HENNECKE, E. & SCHNEEMELCHER, W. Neutestamentliche Apokryphen (1964) I 153. SCHRAGE, W. Das Verhältnis des Thomas-Evangeliums zur Synoptischen Tradition und zu den Koptischen Evangelienübersetzungen (1964) 85. SCHULZ, S. Q Die Spruchquelle der Evangelisten (1972) 472-74.

15:15-20 BORNKAMM-BARTH-HELD, Ueberlieferung und Auslegung im Matthäus-Evangelium (1961) 75, 82, 101f, 194, 197, 279.

15:15 STRECKER, G. Der Weg der Gerechtigkeit (1962) 198, 203, 2042, 205. RIST, J. M., On the Independence of Matthew and Mark (Cambridge 1978) 69.

15:16 STRECKER, G. Der Weg der Gerechtigkeit (1962) 19312.

15:17-20 SANFORD, J. A., The Kingdom Within (New York 1970) 110f.

15:18-20 BRUNNER, E. Dogmatik II (1950) 109. SCHRöER, H. GPM 23/4 (1968/69) 346-54.

15:19 BERGER, K. Die Gesetzeauslegung Jesus (1940) 390-92, et al.

MASSAUX, E. Influence de l'Evangile de saint Matthieu sur la littérature chrétienne avant saint Irénée (1950) 81-82, 620-24. STRECKER, G. Der Weg der Gerechtigkeit (1962) 134₄, 233₂. PASCHEN, W., Rein und Unrein (München 1970) 189-92f. PETZKE, G. Die Traditionen über Apollonius von Tyana und das Neue Testament (1970) 225, 227. BANKS, R., Jesus and the Law in the Synoptic Tradition (London 1975) 243f.

15:20   BLAIR, E. P. Jesus in the Gospel of Matthew (1960) 115. BORNKAMM-BARTH-HELD, Ueberlieferung und Auslegung im Matthäus-Evangelium (1961) 81ff, 227. STRECKER, G. Der Weg der Gerechtigkeit (1962) 311, 139.

15:21ff   KNOX, W. L. The Sources of the Synoptic Gospels II (1957) 34.

15:21-38   SWIDLER, L., Biblical Affirmations of Woman (Philadelphia 1979) 238.

15:21-28   JüLICHER, D. A. Die Gleichnisreden Jesu (1910) 254-59. HEINZELMANN, D. G. Das Ja Gottes (1924) 42. WILKENS, J. Einführung in das Evangelium nach Matthäus I (1934) 207-209. HIRSCH, E. Frühgeschichte des Evangeliums (1941) 304-306. STONEHOUSE, N. B. The Witness of Matthew and Mark to Christ (1944) 145. BRAUN, GPM 4 (1949/50) 93ff. LOEWENICH, W. von, Luther als Ausleger der Synoptiker (1954) 161f. FARRER, A. St Matthew and St Mark (1954) 123. STECK, K. G. GPM 9 (1954/55) 78ff. EICHHOLZ, G. (ed.) Herr, tue meine Lippen auf Bd. I (1957) 97-101. TRILLING, W. Das wahre Israel (1959) 80, 82, 110. FUCHS, E. GPM 15 (1960/61) 89-91. BORNKAMM-BARTH-HELD, Ueberlieferung und Auslegung im Matthäus-Evangelium (1961) 182, 184, 186ff, 199, 221ff, 227f, 231, 254, 265, 267f, 286. DOERNE, M. Er kommt auch noch heute (1961) 58-59. STRECKER, G. Der Weg der Gerechtigkeit (1962) 107f, 117, 176₇. MORILLON, M. "Jésus et la Cananéenne: un dialogue (Matth., 15, 21-28; Marc, 7, 24-30)," BibTerreSainte 69 ('64) 19-20. HAHN, F. Das Verständnis der Mission im Neuen Testament (1965) 24, 45, 109. HARRISVILLE, R. A. "The Woman of Canaan. A Chapter in the History of Exegesis," Interpretation 20 (3, '66) 274-87. SCHERER, P. E., "A Gauntlet with a Gift in it. From Text to Sermon on Matthew 15, 21-28 and Mark 7, 24-30" Interpretation 20 (1966) 387-99. SMART, J. D. The Quiet Revolution (1969) 71-84. BURGER, C. Jesus als Davidssohn (1970) 79-81. GIROD, R. Commentaire sur L'Evangile selon Matthieu (1970) 355-87. LOVISON, T. "La pericopa della Cananea Mt. 15, 21-28," RivBi 19 (3, '71) 273-305. LEGASSE, S. "L'épisode de la

Cananéenne d'après Mt 15, 21-28," BLE 73 (1-3, '72) 21-40.
HEINRICH, G. & ROSENBOOM, E. "Reminiscere:
Matthäus 15, 21-28," in: Predigtstudien (1972/73) Lange, E.
(ed.) 149-55. FRANKEMöLLE, H., Jahwebund und Kirche
Christi (Münster 1974) 114f, 118, 135-37, 261. GOULDER, M.
D., Midrash and Lection in Matthew (London 1974) 160, 318,
339, 379f. SWIDLER, L., Biblical Affirmations of Woman
(Philadelphia 1979) 183, 197, 231. WEINRICH, M., GPM 33
(1979) 381-89.

15:21f STONEHOUSE, N. B. The Witness of Matthew and Mark to
Christ (1944) 141.

15:21   STONEHOUSE, N. B. The Witness of Matthew and Mark to
Christ (1944) 152.

15:22   STONEHOUSE, N. B. The Witness of Matthew and Mark to
Christ (1944) 160, 223. MOORE, G. F. Judaism (1946) II 329n.
FARRER, A. St Matthew and St Mark (1954) 124. BLAIR, E.
P. Jesus in the Gospel of Matthew (1960) 65. BORNKAMM-
BARTH-HELD, Ueberlieferung und Auslegung im Matthäus-
Evangelium (1961) 208, 214, 222f, 253. STRECKER, G. Der
Weg der Gerechtigkeit (1962) 118f, 1203, 1246. HAHN, F.
Christologische Hoheitstitel (1963) 86, 245, 263f. HUMMEL,
R. Die Auseinandersetzung zwischen Kirche und Judentum im
Matthäus-evangelium (1963) 116, 118, 120. KINGSBURY, J.
D., Matthew: Structure, Christology, Kingdom (Philadelphia
1975) 99-101. "Barmherzigkeit" in: TRE 5 (1980) 225.

15:22b HAHN, F. Christologische Hoheitstitel (1963) 275.

15:24   STONEHOUSE, N. B. The Witness of Matthew and Mark to
Christ (1944) 146, 177, 184. FLEW, R. N. Jesus and His Church
(1956) 126. NEPPER-CHRISTENSEN, P. Das
Matthäusevangelium. Ein Judenchristliches Evangelium?
(1958) 9, 14, 19, 22, 25, 180, 190-93. TRILLING, W. Das wahre
Israel (1959) 78ff. BORNKAMM-BARTH-HELD,
Ueberlieferung und Auslegung im Matthäus-Evangelium
(1961) 94, 189. STRECKER, G. Der Weg der Gerechtigkeit
(1962) 117, 119, 194ff, 2399. HAHN, F. Christologische
Hoheitstitel (1963) 45, 275. HUMMEL, R. Die
Auseinandersetzung zwischen Kirche und Judentum im
Matthäusevangelium (1963) 137f, 141, 144-46. HAHN, F. Das
Verständnis der Mission im Neuen Testament (1965) 24, 44, 45,
107. BRAUN, H. Qumran und NT II (1966) 93, 96. NICKELS,
P. Targum und New Testament (1967) 19. WALKER, R. Die
Heilsgeschichte im ersten Evangelium (1967) 128. WREGE,
H.-T. Die ueberlieferungsgeschichte der Bergpredit (1968)
173ff. KASTING. H. Die Anfänge der Urchristlichen Mission

(1969) 37, 110-14. TAGAWA, K. "People and Community in the Gospel of Matthew." NTS 16 (1969-70) 153f. WILSON, S. G., The Gentiles and the Gentile Mission in Luke-Acts (Cambridge 1973) 10-12, 14-16, 21, 49f. FRANKEMöLLE, H., Jahwebund und Kirche Christi (Münster 1974) 41, 109, 114, 117, 120, 123f, 126, 128f, 135-38, 261. GOULDER, M. D., Midrash and Lection in Matthew (London 1974) 344, 379f. LADD, G. E., A Theology of the New Testament (Grand Rapids 1974) 56, 74, 106, 108. ZINGG, P., Das Wachsen der Kirche (Freiburg/(CH) 1974) 248. GRäSSER, E., "Jesus und das Heil Gottes" in: G. Strecker (ed.) Jesus Christus in Historie und Theologie. Festschrift für H. Conzelmann (Tübingen 1975) 8, 176-78. LINNEMANN, E., "Zeitansage und Zeitvorstellung in der Verkündigung Jesu" in: G. Strecker (ed.) Jesus Christus in Historie und Theologie. Festschrift für H. Conzelmann (Tübingen 1975) 244. MEYER, B. F., The Aims of Jesus (London 1979) 167f.

15:25   STONEHOUSE, N. B. The Witness of Matthew and Mark to Christ (1944) 179. HAHN, F. Christologische Hoheitstitel (1963) 86.

15:26-27   KLAUCK, H.-J., Allegorie und Allegorese in Synoptischen Gleichnistexten (Münster 1978) 273-80.

15:26   NICKELS, P. Targum and New Testament (1967) 19. METZGER, B. M., The Early Versions of the New Testament (Oxford 1977) 247.

15:27   TRILLING, W. Das wahre Israel (1959) 82f. BRAUN, H. Jesus (1969) 169.

15:28   STONEHOUSE, N. B. The Witness of Matthew and Mark to Christ (1944) 146. ROBINSON, J. M. Kerygma und historischer Jesus (1960) 30. BORNKAMM-BARTH-HELD, Ueberlieferung und Auslegung im Matthäus-Evangelium (1961) 105, 107, 182ff, 186, 188, 200, 205f, 209, 212, 218, 222, 227f, 230, 256, 262, 268f, 273f. STRECKER, G. Der Weg der Gerechtigkeit (1962) 121 15. HAHN, F. Christologische Hoheitstitel (1963) 402. HUMMEL, R. Die Auseinandersetzung zwischen Kirche und Judentum im Matthäusevangelium (1963) 140. GOPPELT, L., Theologie des Neuen Testaments. I (Göttingen 1975) 199ff.

15:29-39   SCHOTT, E. GPM 11/2 95-97.

15:29-38   WILKENS, J. Einführung in das Evangelium nach Matthäus I (1934) 209-211. SWIDLER, L., Biblical Affirmations of Woman (Philadelphia 1979) 250, 279.

15:29-31   TRILLING, W. Das wahre Israel (1959) 109f. STRECKER, G.

Der Weg der Gerechtigkeit (1962) 175. GOULDER, M. D., Midrash and Lection in Matthew (London 1974) 380ff. CONZELMANN, H./LINDEMANN, A., Arbeitsbuch zum Neuen Testament (Tübingen 1975) 95. EGGER, W., Frohbotschaft und Lehre (Frankfurt 1976) 34-36. *RYAN, T. J., "Matthew 15:29-31: An Overlooked Summary" Horizons 5 (1978) 31-42.

15:29 STONEHOUSE, N. B. The Witness of Matthew and Mark to Christ (1944) 134, 160. STRECKER, G. Der Weg der Gerechtigkeit (1962) 98, 147₂. SCHREIBER, J. Theologie des Vertrauens (1967) 214-16. LIVIO, J.-B., "La signification théologique de la 'montagne' dans le premier evangile" Bulletin du Centre Protestant d'Études 30 (Geneve 1978) 13-20.

15:30f STONEHOUSE, N. B. The Witness of Matthew and Mark to Christ (1944) 145. FARRER, A. St Matthew and St Mark (1954) 44.

15:30 STRECKER, G. Der Weg der Gerechtigkeit (1962) 121₁₇. LANGE, J., Das Erscheinen des Auferstandenen im Evangelium nach Matthäus (Würzburg 1973) 373, 379, 407-409, 411, 479. COMBER, J. A., "The Verb Therapeuo in Matthew's Gospel" JBL 97 (1978) 431-34.

15:31 BLAIR, E. P. Jesus in the Gospel of Matthew (1960) 101. STRECKER, G. Der Weg der Gerechtigkeit (1962) 176₁, 177₂. HUMMEL, R. Die Auseinandersetzung zwischen Kirche und Judentum im Matthäusevangelium (1963) 144.

15:32-16:1, 4 GOULDER, M. D., Midrash and Lection in Matthew (London 1974) 380ff.

15:32-39 STONEHOUSE, N. B. The Witness of Matthew and Mark to Christ (1944) 145. REICKE, B. Diakonie, Festfreude und Zelos (1951) 21f. KNACKSTEDT, J. K. "Die beiden Brotvermehrungen im Evangelium," NTS 10 (3, '64) 309-35. KAMPHAUS, F. Von der Exegese zur Predigt (1968) 140-42. SCHRAMM, T. Der Markus-Stoff bei Lukas (1971) 129f. VAN CANGH. J.-V., La multiplication des pains et l'Eucharistie (Paris 1975). FRIEDRICH, G., "Die beiden Erzählungen von der Speisung in Markus, 6, 31-44; 8, 1-9" in: Auf das Wort kommt es an (Göttingen 1978) 25.

15:32-38 BORNKAMM-BARTH-HELD, Ueberlieferung und Auslegung im Matthäus-Evangelium (1961) 171, 174ff.

15:32 FARRER, A. St Matthew and St Mark (1954) 120. "Barmherzigkeit" in: TRE 5 (1980) 227.

15:33 STRECKER, G. Der Weg der Gerechtigkeit (1962) 121₇, 193₉.

15:34 BORNKAMM-BARTH-HELD, Ueberlieferung und

Auslegung im Matthäus-Evangelium (1961) 176.

15:36 BOUSSET, W. Die Religion des Judentums im Späthellenistischen Zeitalter (1966⁻1926) 178.

15:37 STRECKER, G. Der Weg der Gerechtigkeit (1962) 121 18.

15:38 STRECKER, G. Der Weg der Gerechtigkeit (1962) 121 19. YATES, J. E. The Spirit and the Kingdom (1963) 232-37.

15:39-16:12 WILKENS, J. Einführung in das Evangelium nach Matthäus I (1934) 211, 215.

15:39 STONEHOUSE, N. B. The Witness of Matthew and Mark to Christ (1944) 160.

16-18f VöGTLE, A. Das Evangelium und die Evangelien (1971) 158-61, 167-70.

16 SASS, G. Der Fels der Kirche (1957).

16:1ff STONEHOUSE, N. B. The Witness of Matthew and Mark to Christ (1944) 153. STRECKER, G. Der Weg der Gerechtigkeit (1962) 140.

16:1-4 BUTLER, B. C. The Originality of St Matthew (1951) 141ff. BORNKAMM-BARTH-HELD, Ueberlieferung und Auslegung im Matthäus-Evangelium (1961) 264. BRüCKMANN, O. in: Herr, tue meine Lippen auf Bd. 3 (1964) Eichholz, G. (ed.) 68ff. JEWETT, R., Jesus against the Rapture (Philadelphia 1979) 66-83. SWIDLER, L., Biblical Affirmations of Woman (Philadelphia 1979) 242f, 254.

16:1 STONEHOUSE, N. B. The Witness of Matthew and Mark to Christ (1944) 141, 152, 160. FARRER, A. St Matthew and St Mark (1954) 181. STRECKER, G. Der Weg der Gerechtigkeit (1962) 103, 105.

16:2f KNOX, W. L. The Sources of the Synoptic Gospels II (1957) 75. HENNECKE, E. & SCHNEEMELCHER, W. Neutestamentliche Apokryphen (1964) 196. JüNGEL, E. Paulus und Jesus (1966) 188.

16:2-3 TALBERT, C. H., Literary Patterns, Theological Themes and the Genre of Luke-Acts (Missoula 1974) 55. METZGER, B. M., The Early Versions of the New Testament (Oxford 1977) 39f, 118. METZGER, B. M., "St. Jerome's explicit references to variant readings in manuscripts of the New Testament" in: E.

Best/R. McL. Wilson (eds.) Text and Interpretation. Studies for Matthew Black (Cambridge 1979) 181.

16:3   STONEHOUSE, N. B. The Witness of Matthew and Mark to Christ (1944) 161. BLAIR, E. P. Jesus in the Gospel of Matthew (1960) 100. SCHRAGE, W. Das Verhältnis des Thomas-Evangeliums zur Synoptischen Tradition und zu den Koptischen Evangelienübersetzungen (1964) 175.

16:4   BLAIR, E. P. Jesus in the Gospel of Matthew (1960) 86. NöTSCHER, F., Altorientalischer und alttestamentlicher Auferstehungsglaube (Darmstadt 1970⁻1926) 167. EDWARDS, R. A. The Sign of Jonah (1971). GOULDER, M. D., Midrash and Lection in Matthew (London 1974) 40, 162, 334, 382. PERRIN, N., Jesus and the Language of the Kingdom (London 1976) 45f.

16:5-17   ROLOFF, J. Das Kerygma und der irdische Jesus (1970) 254ff.

16:5-12   BORNKAMM-BARTH-HELD, Ueberlieferung und Auslegung im Matthäus-Evangelium (1961) 99, 101ff, 106ff, 198, 279. MASSON, C. Vers les Sources D'eau Vive (1961) 70ff. SUHL, A. Die Funktion der alttestamentlichen Zitate und Anspielungen im Markusevangelium (1965) 145ff. TRITES, A. A., The New Testament Concept of Witness (Cambridge 1977) 178f.

16:5   STRECKER, G. Der Weg der Gerechtigkeit (1962) 200₈.

16:6   BLAIR, E. P. Jesus in the Gospel of Matthew (1960) 30. GOULDER, M. D., Midrash and Lection in Matthew (London 1974) 14, 38, 370, 420.

16:7ff   STRECKER, G. Der Weg der Gerechtigkeit (1962) 193₁₂.

16:7   BLAIR, E. P. Jesus in the Gospel of Matthew (1960) 87, 104, 105.

16:8f   STRECKER, G. Der Weg der Gerechtigkeit (1962) 193₇.

16:11f   STRECKER, G. Der Weg der Gerechtigkeit (1962) 16, 138, 140.

16:12-23   VöGTLE, A. "Messiasbekenntnis und Petrusverheissung. Zur Komposition Mt, 16, 12-23 Par." BZ 1 (1957) 252-72.

16:12   STONEHOUSE, N. B. The Witness of Matthew and Mark to Christ (1944) 131, 153. FARRER, A. St Matthew and St Mark (1954) 175. BLAIR, E. P. Jesus in the Gospel of Matthew (1960) 86, 105, 112, 113. STRECKER, G. Der Weg der Gerechtigkeit (1962) 40₁, 193₁₁, ₁₂. HUMMEL, R. Die Auseinandersetzung zwischen Kirche und Judentum im Matthäusevangelium (1963) 19f.

16:13-ch. 18   EWALD, H. Die drei ersten Evangelien (1850) 269ff.

16:13-17:27 RIDDERBOS, H. Matthew's Witness to Jesus Christ (1958) 56-60. GAECHTER, P. Die literarische Kunst im Matthäus-Evangelium (1968) 12-13, 30-31.

16:13ff STONEHOUSE, N. B. The Witness of Matthew and Mark to Christ (1944) 216. STAEHELIN, E. Die Verkündigung des Reiches Gottes in der Kirche Jesu Christi I (1951) 59, 393. THYEN, H. Studien zur Sündenvergebung (1970) 224ff. VöGTLE, A. Das Evangelium und die Evangelien (1971) 142-55, 164-68.

16:13-28 SCHLATTER, D. A. Die Theologie des Neuen Testaments (1909) I, 150-55. HAENCHEN, E. "Die Komposition von Mk vii 27 - ix 1 und Par.", Festschrift Karl H. Rengstorf (1964) 81-109. HAENCHEN, E. "Leidensnachfolge," Die Bibel und Wir (1968) 102-34. PERRIN, N. What is Redaction Criticism? (1969) 57-62. HOFFMANN, P., "Der Petrus-Primat im Matthäus-evangelium" in: J. Gnilka (ed.) Neues Testament und Kirche. Für R. Schnackenburg (Freiburg 1974) 106-108.

16:13-26 LEHMANN, H. "Du bist Petrus. . ." Zum Problem von Matthäus 16, 13-26 EvTh (1953) 44-67.

16:13-23 BUTLER, B. C. The Originality of St Matthew (1951) 131ff. *VöGTLE, A. "Messiasbekenntnis und Petrusverheissung. Zur Komposition Mt 16:13-23 Par. (1. Teil)," BZ 1 (2, '57) 252-72. VöGTLE, A. "Messiasbekenntnis und Petrusverheissung. Zur Komposition Mt 16, 13-23 Par. (2. Teil)," BZ 2 (1, '58) 85-103. BONNARDIERE, A.-M. LA, "Tu es Petrus. La péricope 'Matthieu 16, 13-23' dans l'oeuvre de saint Augustin," Irénikon 34 (4, '61) 451-99. BORNKAMM-BARTH-HELD, Ueberlieferung und Auslegung im Matthäus-Evangelium (1961) 17, 42ff. STRECKER, G. Der Weg der Gerechtigkeit (1962) 206₂. ITTEL, G. W. Jesus und die Jünger (1970) 72-75. CATCHPOLE, D. R. The Answer of Jesus to Caiaphas. Mt. 26:64. NTS 17 (1970-71) 222f. VöGTLE, A. Das Evangelium und die Evangelien (1971) 137-70. *DALBERG, B. T., "The Typological Use of Jeremiah 1:4-19 in Matthew 16:13-23" JBL 94 (1975) 73-80. MEYER, B. F., The Aims of Jesus (London 1979) 215f.

16:13-21 SCHRAMM, T. Der Markus-Stoff bei Lukas (1971) 130-36.

16:13-20 WILKENS, J. Einführung in das Evangelium nach Matthäus I (1934) 215-19. MOORE, G. F. Judaism (1946) I 538n, II 309n, 326n. MARXSEN, W. Der 'Frühkatholizismus' im Neuen Testament (1958-64) 39-54. SWALLOW, F. R. "The Keys of God's Household," Scripture 11 (16, '59) 118-23. HAHN, F. Christologische Hoheitstitel (1963) 229. IWAND, H. J. Predigt-Meditationen (1964) 561-72. FRöR, GPM (1964/65)

217ff. DA SPINETOLI, O., "I problemi letterari" Atti della XIX settimana Biblica Italina (1967) 79-92. STECK, K. G. in: Hören und Fragen Bd. 5 (1967) Eichholz, G. & Falkenroth, A. (eds.) 324ff. GAECHTER, P. Die literarischen Kunst im Matthäus-Evangelium (1968) 58-59. KARRER, O. "Simon Petrus, Jünger, Apostel, Felsenfundament," BuK 23 (1968) 37-43. SUMMERS, R. The Secret Sayings of the Living Jesus (1968) 20, 31. LOHSE, E. Das Aergernis des Kreuzes (1969) 42-47. SPINETOLI, O. Da, Il Vangelo del primato, Esegesi biblica 4 (1969). SANFORD, J. A., The Kingdom Within (New York 1970) 77-79. LANGE, E. (ed.) Predigtstudien für das Kirchenjahr 1970/71 (1971) 95-100. FRöR, K. GPM 19/3 217-25. STECK, K. G. GPM 13/2 144-52. HOLTZ, T. GPM 25 (1971) 243-49. VöGTLE, A. Das Evangelium und die Evangelien (1971) 159-68. LEIVESTAD, R. Exit the Apocalyptic Son of Man. NTS 18 (1971-72) 257f. *TESTA, E., "Carisma e gerarchia nella Chiesa 'ex circumcisione'" EuD 24 (1971) 3-34. PAGNOTTA, U., "Tu sei Pietro. Considerazioni della Filologia del testo del Vangelo di Matteo (16, 13-20), considerato titolo giuridico del Primato Pontificio: sua autenticità et legittimità" RBR 8 (1973) 71-77. VöGTLE, A., "Zum Problem der Herkunft von 'Mt 16, 17-19'" in: P. Hoffmann (ed.) Orientierung an Jesus. Für Josef Schmid (Freiburg 1973) 374f, 380, 384. FRANKEMöLLE, H., Jahwebund und Kirche Christi (Münster 1974) 168, 232-43, 360. *GAIDE, G., "'Tu es le Christ'... 'Tu es Pierre'" AssS 52 (1974) 16-26. HEIN, K., Eucharist and Excommunication (Bern/Frankfurt 1975) 71-76. STOEVESANDT, H., GPM 31 (1976/77) 251-59. ALBRECHT, H. et al. in: P. Krusche (ed.) Predigtstudien V/2. Halbband (Stuttgart 1977) 72-79.

16:13-19 KARRER, O. "Simon Petrus, Jünger, Apostel, Felsenfundament," BuK 23 (2, '68) 37-43. JEUB, M., GPM 33 (1979) 253-60. *SELL, J., "Simon Peter's 'Confession' and the Acts of Peter and the Twelve Apostles" NovT 21 (1979) 344-56.

16:13-18 GALLUS, T. De primatu infallibilitatis ex Mt 16, 13-18 eruendo VD 33 (1955) 209-14.

16:13-17 VöGTLE, A. Das Evangelium und die Evangelien (1971) 165-67.

16:13-16 *SHARMA, A., "Matthew 16:13-16—An Exegetical Study" Jeevadhara 3 (1973) 187-94.

16:13-14 BULTMANN, R., "Die Frage nach dem Messianischen Bewusstsein Jesu und das Petrus-Bekenntnis" ZNW 19 (1919-1920) 165-74. STRECKER, G. Der Weg der Gerechtigkeit (1962) 200s.

16:13   STONEHOUSE, N. B. The Witness of Matthew and Mark to Christ (1944) 152, 251. BLAIR, E. P. Jesus in the Gospel of Matthew (1960) 124. ROBINSON, J. M. Kerygma und historischer Jesus (1960) 123. DE KRUIJF, T., Der Sohn des Lebendigen Gottes (Rome 1962) 72, 77f, 81, 84f, 97. STRECKER, G. Der Weg der Gerechtigkeit (1962) 125. HAHN, F. Christologische Hoheitstitel (1963) 45. LEIVESTAD, R. Exit the Apocalyptic Son of Man. NTS 18 (1971-72) 256-58. VöGTLE, A., "Zum Problem der Herkunft von 'Mt 16, 17-19," in: P. Hoffmann (ed.) Orientierung an Jesus. Für Josef Schmid (Freiburg 1973) 384, 386-88.

16:14   VOLZ, P. Die Eschatologie der jüdischen Gemeinde (1934) 193. GILS, F. Jésus Prophète D'Après Les Evangiles Synoptiques (1957) 20-23. BOUSSET, W. Die Religion des Judentums im Späthellenistischen Zeitalter (1966⁻1926) 233. NöTSCHER, F., Altorientalischer und alttestamentlicher Auferstehungsglaube (Darmstadt 1970⁻1926) 127. CARMIGNAC, J. "Pourquoi Jérémie est-il mentionné en Matthieu 16, 14?" in: Tradition und Glaube (1971) Jeremias, G. (ed.) 283-98.

16:15   SUDBRACK, J. " 'Und ihr - für wen haltet ihr mich?' (Mt 16, 15)," GuL 38 (4, '65) 246-59.

16:16ff   LöVESTAM, E., Son and Savior (Lund 1961) 103, 110f.

16:16-23   VöGTLE, A., "Zum Problem der Herkunft von 'Mt 16, 17-19' " in: P. Hoffmann (ed.) Orientierung an Jesus. Für Josef Schmid (1973) 373f.

16:16-19   WILLAERT, B. "La Connexion Littéraire entre la Première Prédiction de la Passion et la Confession de Pierre chez Synoptics,' ETL 32 ('56) 24-35. CULLMANN, O. "L'apôtre Pierre instrument du diable et instrument de Dieu: la place de Mt. 16:16-19 dans la tradition primitive," in: New Testament Essays, Studies in Memory of T. W. Manson (1959) Higgings, A. J. B. (ed.) 94-105. STRECKER, G. Der Weg der Gerechtigkeit (1962) 198. SUTCLIFFE, E. F. "St Peter's Double Confession in Mt 16:16-19," HeyJ 3 (1962) 31-41. TOBIN, W. J. "The Petrine Primacy Evidence of the Gospels," LuVit 23 (1, '68) 27-70. *RUIJS, R. C. M., "Exegese 'kerygmática' de algumas passagens sinóticas" RCB 9 (1972) 66-80. BROWN, R. E. et al. (eds.) Peter in the New Testament (Minneapolis 1973) 83-101. LEROY, H., Zur Vergebung der Sünden (Stuttgart 1974) 37-45. ECHTERNACH, H., "Das Papsttum - evangelisch gesehen" Catholica 30 (1976) 320-55.

16:16-18   MASSINGBERD, J. " 'Thou Art "Abraham" and Upon This

Rock. . .'," HeyJ 6 (3, '65) 289-301. BARBAGLI, P. "La promessa fatta a Pietro in Mt. XVI, 16-18," EphC 19 (2, '68) 323-53. FRANKEMöLLE, H., Jahwebund und Kirche Christi (Münster 1974) 155f, 232-47.

16:16-17   HENNECKE, E. & SCHNEEMELCHER, W. Neutestamentliche Apokryphen (1964) I 96, II 77, 313. VöGTLE, A. Das Evangelium und die Evangelien (1971) 165-67.

16:16   STONEHOUSE, N. B. The Witness of Matthew and Mark to Christ (1944) 211, 214f, 217. PARKER, P. The Gospel Before Mark (1953) 82-83. STANLEY, M. "La Confession de Pierre à Césarée," Sciences Ecclesiastiques VI ('54) 51-61. BLAIR, E. P. Jesus in the Gospel of Matthew (1960) 55, 61, 62, 65, 66, 67, 94, 102, 104, 107. DE KRUIJF, T., Der Sohn des Lebendigen Gottes (Rome 1962) VI, 41, 77-80, 82, 87, 97, 100, 104, 140, 144, 149, 152-54, 168. DE KRUIJF, T., " 'Filius Dei Viventis' (Mt 16, 16). Collationes ad christologiam evangelii secundum Matthaeum," VerbDom 39 (1, '61) 39-43. STRECKER, G. Der Weg der Gerechtigkeit (1962) 107, 125, 202, 2042, 206. HAHN, F. Christologische Hoheitstitel (1963) 113, 115. SEEBERG, A. Der Katechismus der Urchristenheit (1966) 175, 208. NICKELS, P. Targum and New Testament (1967) 19. DE VILLIERS, J. L. "Die Lewende God" (The Living God), NGTT 9 (2, '68) 82-94. BRUNNER, E. Dogmatik II, 23, 218. BROWN, R. E. et al. (eds.) Peter in the New Testament (Minneapolis 1973) 86f. VöGTLE, A., "Zum Problem der Herkunft von 'Mt 16, 17-19' " in: P. Hoffmann (ed.) Orientierung an Jesus. Für Josef Schmid (Freiburg 1973) 384-86. KLIJN, A. F. J., "Die syrische Baruch-Apokalypse" in: W. G. Kümmel (ed.) Jüdische Schriften aus hellenistisch-römischer Zeit. V (Gütersloh 1976) 157. MEYER, B. F., The Aims of Jesus (London 1979) 175-80. SWIDLER, L., Biblical Affirmations of Woman (Philadelphia 1979) 216f.

16:17ff   DIECKMANN, H. Biblica 4 (1923) 189-200. BETZ, J. "Christus-Petra-Petrus," in: Kirche und Ueberlieferung (1960) Betz, J. & Fries, H. (eds.) 1-21. BLAIR, E. P. Jesus in the Gospel of Matthew (1960) 104, 136. HAHN, F. Christologische Hoheitstitel (1963) 402. FRIEDRICH, G., "Beobachtungen zur messianischen Hohepriestererwartung in den Synoptikern" in: Auf das Wort kommt es an (Göttingen 1978) 83f. VIELHAUER, P., "Oikodome. Das Bild vom Bau in der christlichen Literatur vom Neuen Testament bis Clemens Alexandrinus" in: Oikodome (München 1979) 66-71.

16:17-23   SUTCLIFFE, E. F. "St Peter's Double Confession. An Additional Note," HeyJ 3 (3, '62) 275-76.

16:17-19 DELL, A., "Matthäus 16:17-19" ZNW 15 (1914) 1-49. DELL, A., "Zur Erklärung von Mt 16:17-19" ZNW 17 (1916) 27-32. HIRSCH, E. Frühgeschichte des Evangeliums (1941) 306-308. STONEHOUSE, N. B. The Witness of Matthew and Mark to Christ (1944) 80, 157. RICHARDSON, A. The Miracle-Stories of the Gospels (1948) 105f. FARRER, A. St Matthew and St Mark (1954) 122. LEIVESTAD, R. Christ the Conqueror (1954) 79ff. FLEW, R. N. Jesus and His Church (1956) 89-97. WILLAERT, B. " 'Tu es Petrus', Mt XVI 17-19" ColBG 2 ('56) 452-65. BETZ, O. "Felsenmann und Felsengemeinde. (Eine Parallele zu Mt 16, 17-19 in den Qumranpsalmen)," ZNW 48 (1-2, '57) 49-77. *FOSTER, K. "Tu es Petrus: the conclusions of the Dean of Christ Church," Tablet 209 ('57) 354. FLOOD, E. "One of the Promises to Peter," ClR 43 (10, '58) 584-94. BLAIR, E. P. Jesus in the Gospel of Matthew (1960) 32. CULLMANN, O. Petrus (1960). KESICH, V. "The Problem of Peter's Primacy in the New Testament and the Early Christian Exegesis," SVThQ 4 (2-3, '60) 2-25. BORNKAMM-BARTH-HELD, Ueberlieferung und Auslegung im Matthäus-Evangelium (1961) 41f, 45, 194, 257. MILWARD, P. "The Prophetic Perspective and the Primacy of Peter," AER 144 (2, '61) 122-29. DE KRUIJF, T., Der Sohn des Lebendigen Gottes (Rome 1962) 80-82, 151, 153. STRECKER, G. Der Weg der Gerechtigkeit (1962) 18, 201f, 203, 205, 206. BULTMANN, R. The History of the Synoptic Tradition (1963) 258f. CAVERO, I. "Tu es Petrus. Notas biblicas para el enriquecimiento de un texto dogmatico," EstBi 22 (2-3, '63) 351-62. HUMMEL, R. Die Auseinandersetzung zwischen Kirche und Judentum im Matthäusevangelium (1963) 59-64. LE GUILLOU, M.-J. "La Primauté de Pierre," Istina 10 (1, '64) 93-102. GUNDRY, R. H. "The Narrative Framework of Matthew xvi 17-19. A Critique of Professor Cullmann's Hypothesis," NovTest 7 (1, '64) 1-9. ROLOFF, J. Apostolat-Verkündigung-Kirche (1965) 163-65. SASSE, H. "Peter and Paul. Observations on the origin of the Roman Primacy," RThR 24 (1, '65) 1-11. SCHATTENMANN, J. "Das Logion Jesu, Mt. 16:17-19, das Vaterunser und der Missionsbefehl," in: Studien zum Neutestamentlichen Prosahymnus (1965) 40-48. BRAUN, H. Qumran und NT II (1966) 93, 94, 108, 145, 271, 326-28. BULTMANN, R. "Die Frage nach der Echtheit von Mt. 16:17-19," in: Exegetica (1967) Dinkler, E. (ed.) 255-78. FULLER, R. H. "The 'Thou Art Peter' Pericope and the Easter Appearances," McCormQuart 20 (4, '67) 309-15. ERNST, C. "The Primacy of Peter: Theology and Ideology-I," New Blackfriars 50 (587, '69) 347-55; ". . .-II," 51 (588, '69) 399-404. KASTING, H. Die Anfänge der Urchristlichen Mission (1969)

87f. OTOMO, Y. Nachfolge Jesu und Anfänge der Kirche im Neuen Testament (1970) 149-69. TRILLING, W., "Amt und Amtsverständnis bei Matthäus" in: A. Descamps/A. de Halleux (eds.) Mélanges Bibliques en hommage au R. P. Béda Rigaux (Gembloux 1970) 42-44. THYEN, H. Studien zur Sündenvergebung (1970) 218, 225ff, 245. VöGTLE, A. Das Evangelium und die Evangelien (1971) 149-57, 159-64. *BETTENCOURT, E., "Confissão de fé e primado em Mt 16, 17-19" RCB 9 (1972) 52-65. KERTELGE, K., Gemeinde und Amt im Neuen Testament (München 1972) 40f, 135f. *PACIOREK, A., "Mt 16, 17-19 przedredakcyjną jednostką literacką (De influxu traditionis primitivae in Mt 16, 17-19)" RTK 20 (1973) 59-67. VöGTLE, A., "Zum Problem der Herkunft von 'Mt 16, 17-19' " in: P. Hoffmann (ed.) Orientierung an Jesus. Für Josef Schmid (Freiburg 1973) 372-93. ELLIS, P. F., Matthew: His Mind and His Message (Collegeville 1974) 129-32. GOULDER, M. D., Midrash and Lection in Matthew (London 1974) 163, 378, 383-95. HOFFMANN, P., "Der Petrus-Primat im Matthäusevangelium" in: J. Gnilka (ed.) Neues Testament und Kirche. Für R. Schnackenburg (Freiburg 1974) 94-114. HOWARD, V. P., Das Ego in den Synoptischen Evangelien (Marburg 1975) 204-12. SCHMITHALS, W., "Jesus und die Apokalyptik" in: G. Strecker (ed.) Jesus Christus in Historie und Theologie. Festschrift für H. Conzelmann (Tübingen 1975) 77. THYEN, H., "Der irdische Jesus und die Kirche" in: G. Strecker (ed.) Jesus Christus in Historie und Theologie. Festschrift für H. Conzelmann (Tübingen 1975) 77, 127-30. *WILCOX, M., "Peter and the Rock: A Fresh Look at Matthew xvi. 17-19" NTS 22 (1975) 73-88. *BURGESS, J. A., A History of the Exegesis of Matthew 16: 17-19 from 1781 to 1965 (Ann Arbor 1976). GOPPELT, L., Theologie des Neuen Testaments. II (Göttingen 1976) 564. KäHLER, C., "Zur Form- und Traditionsgeschichte von Matth. xvi. 17-19" NTS 23 (1976) 36-58. "Amt" in: TRE 2 (1978) 511. "Apostel" in: TRE 3 (1978) 435, 463. RIST, J. M., On the Independence of Matthew and Mark (Cambridge 1978) 69. MEYER, B. F., The Aims of Jesus (London 1979) 185-97.

16:17.18f BULTMANN, R. Theologie des Neuen Testaments (1965) 40, 48, 51, 65.

16:17-18 DAVIES, W. D., The Sermon on the Mount (Cambridge 1966) 93f.

16:17 STONEHOUSE, N. B. The Witness of Matthew and Mark to Christ (1944) 215. ALGER, B., "Simon Barjona" Scripture XII (1960) 89-92. ROTH, C. "Simon-Peter," HThR 54 (1961) 91-

97. DE KRUIJF, T., Der Sohn des Lebendigen Gottes (Rome 1962) 77f, 84, 142, 163. FITZMYER, J. "The Name Simon," HThR 56 (1963) 1-5. HAHN, F. Christologische Hoheitstitel (1963) 321. DUPONT, J. "La Révélation du Fils de Dieu en faveur de Pierre (Mt. 16, 17) et de Paul (Gal. 1, 16)," RechSR 52 (3, '64) 411-20. ROMANIUK, K. " 'Cialo i Krew nie objawily Tobie, tylko Ojciec moj, ktory jest w niebiesiech' (Mt 16, 17) ('Caro et sanguis non revelavit tibi, sed Pater meus, qui in caelis est' (Mt 16, 17))," RBL 17 (6, '64) 346-54. ROTH, C. & FITZMYER, J. A. "The Name Simon - A Further Discussion," HThR 57 (1, '64) 60-61. McNAMARA, M. The New Testament and the Palestinian Targum to the Pentateuch (1966) 136. NICKELS, P. Targum and New Testament (1967) 20. VöGTLE, A. Das Evangelium und die Evangelien (1971) 148-50, 155-58, 160-67. BRUNNER, E. Dogmatik I 34, II 296. BROWN, R. E. et al. (eds.) Peter in the New Testament (Minneapolis 1973) 88f. KERTELGE, K., "Apokalypsis Jesou Christou (Gal 1, 12)" in: J. Gnilka (ed.) Neues Testament und **Kirche. Für R. Schnackenburg** (Freiburg 1974) 276-79. METZGER, B. M., The Early Versions of the New Testament (Oxford 1977) 117. "Aramäisch" in: TRE 3 (1978) 603.

16:18ff STONEHOUSE, N. B. The Witness of Matthew and Mark to Christ (1944) 255. HAHN, F. Christologische Hoheitstitel (1963) 239.

16:18-20 LORIA, R. " 'Legare e sciogliere' nella Chiesa primitiva alla luce della dottrina del Corpo Mistico," PaCl 46 (15-16, '67) 978-96.

16:18f HANSON, S. The Unity of the Church in the New Testament (1946) 36f. SCHWEIZER, E. Gemeinde und Gemeinde-Ordnung im Neuen Testament (1959) §§ 2b, 4e, f. BULTMANN, R. The History of the Synoptic Tradition (1963) 138-40. BORNKAMM, G. Geschichte und Glaube II (1971) 45-49.

16:18-19 GRILL, J., Untersuchungen über die Entstehung des vierten Evangeliums. II (Leipzig 1923) 36, 253f, 324, 373. STONEHOUSE, N. B. The Witness of Matthew and Mark to Christ (1944) 235ff, 256. STAEHELIN, E. Die Verkündigung des Reiches Gottes in der Kirche Jesu Christi I (1951) 198. LUDWIG, J. Die Primatworte Mt 16, 18.19 in der Altkirchlichen Exegese (1952). HAENDLER, G. "Die drei grossen nordafrik. Kirchenväter über Mt. 16, 18-19," ThLZ 81 (1956) 361-64. SCHMID, J. Das Evangelium nach Matthäus (1956) 251-54. TRILLING, W. Das wahre Israel (1959) 131ff. OBRIST, F. Echtheitsfragen und Deutung der Primatsstelle

Mt 16, 18f. in der deutschen protestantischen Theologie der letzten driessig Jahre (1961). BRäNDLE, M. "Neue Diskussion um das Felsenwort: Matthäus 16, 18.19," Orientierung 27 (Aug. 31, '63) 172-76. HUMMEL, R. Die Auseinandersetzung zwischen Kirche und Judentum im Matthäusevangelium (1963) 62-64. CARROL, K. L. Thou art Peter, NT vi (1963), 4, 268-76. HAHN, F. Das Verständnis der Mission im Neuen Testament (1965) 38, 40, 41, 43, 69, 108. GANDER, G., "La notion primitive d'Eglise d'après l'Evangile selon Matthieu, chapitre 16, versets 18 et 19" ÉΩtudes évangéliques 26 (1966) 1-143. KüNG, H., Die Kirche (Freiburg 1967) 135, 306, 394, 536-38, 541f, 544, 533, 556; ET: The Church (London 1967) 110, 256, 333, 457f, 461f, 464, 472, 475. SPINETOLI, O. Da, "La portata ecclesiologica di Mt. 16, 18-19,' Antonianum 42 (3-4, '67) 357-75. LANDUCCI, P. C. "La promessa del primato," PaCl 47 (4, '68) 212-22. CONZELMANN, H. Grundriss der Theologie des Neuen Testaments (1968) 49f.; Engl. edit. pp. 32-34. BORNKAMM, G., "Die Binde- und Lösegewalt der Kirche" in: Die Zeit Jesus. Festschrift für H. Schlier (Freiburg 1970) 93-107. DIDIER, M., L'évangile selon Matthieu (Gembloux 1971) 261-308.LANGE, J., Das Erscheinen des Auferstandenen im Evangelium nach Matthäus (Würzburg 1973) 115, 118-20, 122, 124f, 128, 130, 134, 137, 151, 170, 202, 206, 209, 230, 423, 432. SCHNACKENBURG, R., Aufsätze und Studien zum Neuen Testament (Leipzig 1973) 290ff, 317. LADD, G. E., The Presence of the Future (Grand Rapids 1974) 244ff, 258ff. CONZELMANN, H./LINDEMANN, A., Arbeitsbuch zum Neuen Testament (Tübingen 1975) 356, 388. MUSSNER, F., Petrus und Paulus - Pole der Einheit (Freiburg 1976) 14-22. "Amt" in: TRE 11 (1978) 511, 554. "Apostel" in: TRE 3 (1978) 453, 457, 458.

16:18b-19 LODS, M. "Le 'Tu es Petrus' dans l'exégèse patristique," ETh 21 (62, '58) 15-34.

16:18 SULZBACH, A. "Die Schlüssel des Himmelreichs", ZNW 4 (1903) 190-92. IMMISCH, O., "Matthäus 16, 18" ZNW 17 (1916) 18-26. FONCK, K. Biblica 1 (1920) 240-64. STONEHOUSE, N. B. The Witness of Matthew and Mark to Christ (1944) 210. BIEDER, W. Die Vorstellung von der Höllenfahrt Jesu Christi (1949) 43ff. EPPEL, R. "L'interprétation de Mt 16, 18b," in: Aux Sources de la Tradition Chrétienne (1950) Goguel, M. M. (ed.) 71-73. STAEHELIN, E. Die Verkündigung des Reiches Gottes in der Kirche Jesu Christi I (1951) 338. BAUER, J. B. "Ostiarii inferorum", Biblica 34 (1953) 430-31. CLAVIER, H. in: Neutestamentliche Studien für R. Bultmann zu seinem 70.

Geburtstag (1954) 94-109. FARRER, A. St Matthew and St
Mark (1954) 175. BEST, E. One Body in Christ (1955) 160,
162n. GROSCHE, R. Successio Petri, Catholica 10 (1955) 143-
47. CORTI, G. Pietro, fondamento e pastore perenne della
chiesa ScuC LXXXIV/5 (1956) 321-35. DELLAGIACOMA,
V. "Fragmenta Porphyrii super N. T.," VD 34 ('56) 211-16.
FLEW, R. N. Jesus and His Church (1956) 157n. *VOOGHT,
P. "L'argument patristique dans l'interprétation de matth.
XVI, 18 de Jean Huss," RechSR 45 (4, '57) 558-66. KLIJN, A.
F. J. "Die Wörter 'Stein' und 'Felsen' in der syrischen
Uebersetzung des Neuen Testaments," ZNW 50 (1-2, '59) 99-
105. KöBERT, R. "Zwei Fassungen von Mt. 16, 18 bei den
Syrern," Biblica 40 (4, '59) 1018-20. MUNCK, J. Paul and the
Salvation of Mankind (1959) 62f., 142. RINGGER, J. Das
Felsenwort. Zur Sinndeutung von Mt 16, 18 in: Begegnung der
Christen (1959) Roesle, M. & Cullmann, O. (eds.) 271-347.
SCHMID, J. Petrus "der Fels" und die Petrusgestalt der
Urgemeinde in: Begegnung der Christen (1959) Roesle, M. &
Cullmann, O. (eds.) 347-59. A. B., "Umfrage über Mt 16, 18
und 28, 18," Catholica 14 (2, '60) 157-59. KNIGHT, G. A. F. "
'Thou Art Peter'," ThT 17 (2, '60) 168-80. RENGSTORF, K. H.
Die Auferstehung Jesu (1960) 111, 156f. DE KRUIJF, T., Der
Sohn des Lebendigen Gottes (Rome 1962) 85, 150-52, 154, 158.
STRECKER, G. Der Weg der Gerechtigkeit (1962) 1667, 2064,
2073, 214. CARROLL, K. L. " 'Thou art Peter'," NovTest 6 (4,
'63) 268-76. HUMMEL, R. Die Auseinandersetzung zwischen
Kirche und Judentum im Matthäusevangelium (1963) 154ff.
ROLOFF, J. ApostolatVerkündigung-Kirche (1965) 106-111.
HOWARD, G. "The Meaning of Petros-Petra," RestQ 10 (4,
'67) 217-21. KüNG, H., Die Kirche (Freiburg 1967) 57, 92, 96f,
103, 204, 405, 419, 489, 542, 558; ET: The Church (London
1967) 8, 43, 73, 77, 83, 169, 342, 353f, 415, 462f, 476. ANON,
"Die Deutung des 'Felsen' und der 'Schlüssel' des
Himmelreiches.' Matth. 16, 18/19," Bausteine 8 (31, '68) 11-12.
BIEDERMANN, H. "Das Primatswort Mt 16, 18 im
römischen, orthodoxen und protestantischem Verständnis,"
BuK 23 (2, '68) 55-58. KNOCH, O. "Die Deutung der
Primatstelle Mt 16, 18 im Lichte der neueren Diskussion. Eine
Uebersicht," BuK 23 (2, '68) 44-46. GLOEGE, G. Reich Gottes
und Kirche im Neuen Testament (1968, reprint) 261-76.
REUMANN, J. Jesus in the Church's Gospels: Modern
Scholarship and the Earliest Sources (1968) 18-19. SMITH,
M., Tannaitic Parallels to the Gospels (Philadelphia 1968) 2 b n
103+. TESTA, E. "Le communità orientali dei primi secoli e il
primato di Pietro," RivB 16 (5, '68) 547-55. BLANK, J.

Schriftauslegung in Theorie und Praxis (1969) 86.
FITZMYER, J. A. Essays on the Semitic Background of the
New Testament (1971) 105-12. JEREMIAS, J.
Neutestamentliche Theologie I (1971) 165f., 235, 239, 247.
KLINZING, G. Die Umdeutung des Kultus in der
Qumrangemeinde und im Neuen Testament (1971) 205-207.
VöGTLE, A. Das Evangelium und die Evangelien (1971) 162-
64. *RINCON, A., Tú eres Pedro. Interpretación de 'piedra' en
Mat. 16,18 y sus relaciones con el tema bíblico de la edificación,
Colección Teológica (Pamplona 1972). BROWN, R. E. et al.
(eds.) Peter in the New Testament (Minneapolis 1973) 89-95,
114. DORMEYER, D., Die Passion Jesu als Verhaltensmodell
(Münster 1974) 162. FRANKEMöLLE, H., Jahwebund und
Kirche Christi (Münster 1974) 70f, 218, 220-47. GOULDER,
M. D., Midrash and Lection in Matthew (London 1974) 105,
162f, 169, 190, 391. LADD, G. E., A Theology of the New
Testament (Grand Rapids 1974) 116, 194, 281. METZGER, B.
M., The Early Versions of the New Testament (Oxford 1977)
80, 178. "Amt" in: TRE 2 (1978) 517. *SUBILIA, V., Tu sei
Pietro. L'enigma del fondamento biblico del papato, Collana
della Facoltà valdese di teologia, Brevi studi 2 (Turin 1978).
*LAMPE, P., "Das Spiel mit dem Petrusnamen—Matt. xvi.
18" NTS 25 (1979) 227-45. HARRINGTON, D. J., God's
People in Christ (Philadelphia 1980) 29.

16:18b VATTIONI, F. "Porte o portieri dell'inferno in Mt. 16:18b?"
RivB 8 (3, '60) 251-55.

16:19 STAEHELIN, E. Die Verkündigung des Reiches Gottes in der
Kirche Jesu Christi I (1951) 284, 291, 326, 399. FARRER, A. St
Matthew and St Mark (1954) 164. FLEW, R. N. Jesus and His
Church (1956) 25. KNOX, W. L. The Sources of the Synoptic
Gospels II (1957) 27, 133. McMASLAND , S. V. "Matthew
Twists the Scriptures," JBL 80 (1961) 148. EMERTON, J. A.
"Binding and Loosing-Forgiving and Retaining," JThS 13 (2,
'62) 325-31. STRECKER, G. Der Weg der Gerechtigkeit (1962)
2064, 2236. HAHN, F. Christologische Hoheitstitel (1963) 250.
HUMMEL, R. Die Auseinandersetzung zwischen Kirche und
Judentum im Matthäusevangelium (1963) 61f.
VORGRIMLER, H. "Das 'Binden und Lösen' in der Exegese
nach dem Tridentinum bis zu Beginnn des 20. Jahrhunderts,"
ZKTh 85 (4, '63) 460-77. KäSEMANN, E. Exegetische
Versuche und Besinnungen (1964) II 104. TURNER, N.
Grammatical Insights into the New Testament (1965) 80ff.
KüNG, H., Die Kirche (Freiburg 1967) 393f, 541; ET: The
Church (London 1967) 331, 333. NICKELS, P. Targum and
New Testament (1967) 20. STROBEL, A. Erkenntnis und

Bekenntnis der Sünde in neutestamentlicher Zeit (1968) 58.
KäSEMANN, E. New Testament Questions of Today (1969)
106. THYEN, H. Studien zur Sündenvergebung (1970) 218,
237, 247f., 252. JEREMIAS, J. Neutestamentliche Theologie I
(1971) 20, 22, 26, 29, 32, 40, 42, 109, 228. BROWN, R. E. et al.
(eds.) Peter in the New Testament (Minneapolis 1973) 95-101,
144. LANGE, J., Das Erscheinen des Auferstandenen im
Evangelium nach Matthäus (Würzburg 1973) 60, 63, 95f, 105,
113, 115f, 119f, 122, 130-34, 136f, 146f, 166, 172, 180, 342, 431,
436, 462, 491, 494. MANTEY, J. R., "Evidence that the Perfect
Tense in John 20:23 and Matthew 16:19 is Mistranslated"
JEThS 16 (1973) 129-38. MICHL, J., "Sündenbekenntnis und
Sündenvergebung in der Kirche des Neuen Testaments" MThZ
24 (1973) 189-207. *ELBERT, P. "The Perfect Tense in
Matthew 16:19 and Three Charismata" JEThS 17 (1974) 149-
55. GOULDER, M. D., Midrash and Lection in Matthew
(London 1974) 37, 75, 105, 286, 384. *RIGAUX, B., " 'Lier et
délier'. Les ministères de réconciliation dans l'église des Temps
apostoliques" Maison-Dieu 117 (1974) 86-135. GOPPELT, L.,
Theologie des Neuen Testaments. I (Göttingen 1975) 260.
THEISSEN, G., Soziologie der Jesusbewegung (München
(1977) 23. "Autorität" in: TRE 5 (1980) 32. "Bann" in: TRE 5
(1980) 165.

16:20   BLAIR, E. P. Jesus in the Gospel of Matthew (1960) 55.
STRECKER, G. Der Weg der Gerechtigkeit (1962) 206₃.
HAHN, F. Christologische Hoheitstitel (1963) 224.
HUMMEL, R. Die Auseindandersetzung zwischen Kirche und
Judentum im Matthäusevangelium (1963) 113. METZGER, B.
M. "Explicit references in the works of Origen to variant
readings in New Testament manuscripts", Historical and
Literary Studies (1968) 92f.

16:21-28:20 KINGSBURY, J. D., Matthew: Structure, Christology,
Kingdom (Philadelphia 1975) 21-25.

16:21-28 SCHLATTER, D. A. Die Theologie des Neuen Testaments
(1909) 484-90. WILKENS, J. Einführung in das Evangelium
nach Matthäus II (1937) 16-25. STRECKER, G. Der Weg der
Gerechtigkeit (1962) 182f. BRAUN, H. Qumran und NT II
(1966) 72. MUCKE, K.-P. "Vom Kreuztragen", in: Die
Passionstexte (1967) Frey, F. (ed.) 135-40.

16:21-27 Glaubet an den Gottgesandten in: Predigtgedanken aus
Vergangenheit und Gegenwart, Reihe C, BD. 2 (1962) 6-34.
JETTER, GPM (1962/63) 115ff. HAAR, H. GPM 23/1
(1968/69) 110-15. STECK, K. G. GPM 6/2 74-76. STECK, K.
G., GPM 29 (1974) 145-52.

16:21-26   KRECK, W. in: Herr, tue meine Lippen auf Bd. 3 (1964) Eichholz, G. (ed.) 133ff.

16:21   STONEHOUSE, N. B. The Witness of Matthew and Mark to Christ (1944) 66, 130, 131, 172, 237. VISCHER, W. Die evangelische Gemeindeordnung. Matthäus 16, 13 - 20, 28 (1946) 28-29. FARRER, A. St Matthew and St Mark (1954) 120, 181, 185. DENNEY, J. The Death of Christ (1956) 24f., 28. GILS, F. Jésus Prophète D'Après Les Evangiles Synoptiques (1957) 135-49. HOOKER, M. D. Jesus and the Servant (1959) 92-97. BLAIR, E. P. Jesus in the Gospel of Matthew (1960) 54, 55. STRECKER, G. Der Weg der Gerechtigkeit (1962) 612, 88, 91f., 973, 1044, 125, 1813. HAHN, F. Christologische Hoheitstitel (1963) 208. HUMMEL, R. Die Auseinandersetzung zwischen Kirche und Judentum im Matthäusevangelium (1963) 112ff. GüTTGEMANNS, E. Offene Fragen zur Formgeschichte des Evangeliums (1970) 218, 222. PATSCH, H. Abendmahl und historischer Jesus (1972) 185ff. KINGSBURY, J. D., Matthew: Structure, Christology, Kingdom (Philadlephia 1975) 21-25. GOPPELT, L., Theologie des Neuen Testaments. II (Göttingen 1976) 555. WILLIAMS, J. A., A Conceptual History of Deuteronomism in the Old Testament, Judaism, and the New Testament: Ph.D. Diss (Louisville 1976) 300.

16:22f   BORNKAMM-BARTH-HELD, Ueberlieferung und Auslegung im Matthäus-Evangelium (1961) 44, 112. STRECKER, G. Der Weg der Gerechtigkeit (1962) 198, 202, 204.

16:22.23   VISCHER, W. Die evangelische Gemeindeordnung. Matthäus 16, 13 - 20, 28 (1946) 30-31.

16:22   BLAIR, E. P. Jesus in the Gospel of Matthew (1960) 100. HAHN, F. Christologische Hoheitstitel (1963) 86. HAENCHEN, E. "Die Komposition von Mk vii 27 - ix 1 und Par.", in: ΧΑΡΙΣ ΚΑΙ ΣΟΦΙΑ. Festschrift Karl Heinrich Rengstorf (1964) 81-109, esp. 108 n.1.

16:23-24   KNOX, W. L. The Sources of the Synoptic Gospels II (1957) 87.

16:23   FLEW, R. N. Jesus and His Church (1956) 67n. STRECKER, G. Der Weg der Gerechtigkeit (1962) 205, 2063. BAUMBACH, G. Das Verständnis des Bösen in den synoptischen Evangelien (1963) 113ff. BROWN, R. E. et al. (eds.) Peter in the New Testament (Minneapolis 1973) 93-95. GOULDER, M. D., Midrash and Lection in Matthew (London 1974) 105, 169, 244, 391, 394. METZGER, B. M., The Early Versions of the New Testament (Oxford 1977) 277. "Antichrist" in: TRE 3 (1978) 22.

16:24ff BLAIR, E. P. Jesus in the Gospel of Matthew (1960) 107, 165. STRECKER, G. Der Weg der Gerechtigkeit (1962) 158.

16:24-28 VISCHER, W. Die evangelische Gemeindeordnung. Matthäus 16, 13 - 20, 28 (1946) 33-37. BORNKAMM-BARTH-HELD, Ueberlieferung und Auslegung im Matthäus-Evangelium (1961) 42f., 44f., 75, 89, 93, 95, 98, 255, 262.

16:24f STRECKER, G. Der Weg der Gerechtigkeit (1962) 2314. KäSEMANN, E. Exegetische Versuche und Besinnungen (1964) II 98. LOHSE, E. and others (eds.) Der Ruf Jesu und die Antwort der Gemeinde (1970) 262-67. PETERS, G. W. A Biblical Theology of Missions (1972) 185-86.

16:24 STONEHOUSE, N. B. The Witness of Matthew and Mark to Christ (1944) 172. STAEHELIN, E. Die Verkündigung des Reiches Gottes in der Kirche Jesu Christi I (1951) 155. STRECKER, G. Der Weg der Gerechtigkeit (1962) 43, 182. KäSEMANN, E. New Testament Questions of Today (1969) 100.

16:25 KNOX, W. L. The Sources of the Synoptic Gospels II (1957) 107. GEORGES, A. "Qui veut sauver sa vie, la perdra; qui perd sa vie, la sauvera," BVieC 83 ('68) 11-24. KäSEMANN, E. New Testament Questions of Today (1969) 99. MARXSEN, W. Mark the Evangelist (1969) 120, 124, 138, 142. ZMIJEWSKI, J., Die Eschatologiereden des Lukas-Evangeliums (Bonn 1972) 479-82. CAVALLIN, H. C. C., Life After Death. I (Lund 1974) 4, 3, nII. HOFFMANN,P./EID, V., Jesus von Nazareth und eine christliche Moral (Freiburg 1975) 212-14. THEUNISSEN, M., " ὁ αἰτῶν λαμβάνει. Der Gebetsglaube Jesu und die Zeitlichkeit des Christseins" in: Jesus, Ort der Erfahrung Gottes (Basel 1976) 30. GNILKA, J., "Martyriumsparänese und Sühnetod in synoptischen und jüdischen Traditionen" in: R. Schnackenburg et al. (eds.) Die Kirche des Anfangs. Für H. Schürmann (Freiburg 1978) 235. LEROY, S., "Wer sein Leben gewinnen will. . ." FZPhTh 25 (1978) 171-86.

16:26f HENNECKE, E. & SCHNEEMELCHER, W. Neutestmamentliche Apokryphen (1964) I 113; II 320, 472, 475.

16:26 BONHöFFER, A. Epiktet und das Neue Testament (1911) 176, 287. BEA, A. Biblica 14 (1933) 435-47. KNOX, W. L. The Sources of the Synoptic Gospels II (1957) 17. FASCHER, E. " 'Der unendliche Wert der Menschenseele'. Zur Auslegung von Mark 8, 36 und Mt 16, 26", in: Forschung und Erfahrung im Dienst der Seelsorge. Festgabe für Otto Haendler (1961) 44-57. SANFORD, J. A., The Kingdom Within (New York 1970) 160f. KLIJN, A. F. J., "Die syrische Baruch-Apokalypse" in: W. G. Kümmel (ed.) Jüdische Schriften aus hellenistisch-römischer Zeit. V (Gütersloh 1976) 157.

16:27f MOORE, G. F. Judaism (1946) II 336n. JEREMIAS, J. Neutestamentliche Theologie I (1971) 101, 137, 248, 250, 252, 260.

16:27 STONEHOUSE, N. B. The Witness of Matthew and Mark to Christ (1944) 234. STAEHELIN, E. Die Verkündigung des Reiches Gottes in der Kirche Jesu Christi I (1951) 338, 383. SCHOONHEIM, P. L. Een Semasiologisch Onderzoek van Parousia (1953) 121-22. LOEWENICH, W. von, Luther als Ausleger der Synoptiker (1954) 196ff. BLAIR, E. P. Jesus in the Gospel of Matthew (1960) 77, 81, 94. BORNKAMM-BARTH-HELD, Ueberlieferung und Auslegung im Matthäus-Evangelium (1961) 43, 55, 58, 89, 98, 117, 153. STRECKER, G. Der Weg der Gerechtigkeit (1962) 27f., 42f., 161 1, 163 6, 166 7, 236. HAHN, F. Christologische Hoheitstitel (1963) 33, 39. Studiorum Paulinorum Congressus Internationalis Catholicus 1961 (1963) I 227-28. JüNGEL, E. Paulus und Jesus (1966) 244, 258ff. KäSEMANN, E. New Testament Questions of Today (1969) 77. LANGE, J., Das Erscheinen des Auferstandenen im Evangelium nach Matthäus (Würzburg 1973) 104, 185, 207f, 215, 277, 299, 422-24, 499. GOULDER, M. D., Midrash and Lection in Matthew (London 1974) 121, 167f, 443. KINGSBURY, J. D., Matthew: Structure, Christology, Kingdom (Philadelphia 1975) 117-19. SANDERS, J. T., Ethics in the New Testament (Philadelphia 1975) 43. THEISOHN, J., Der auserwählte Richter (Göttingen 1975) 155, 178f, 183, 187f, 252, 259, 260. TRITES, A. A., The New Testament Concept of Witness (Cambridge 1977) 181.

16:28 STONEHOUSE, N. B. The Witness of Matthew and Mark to Christ (1944) 238ff. BLAIR, E. P. Jesus in the Gospel of Matthew (1960) 77, 81, 94. BORNKAMM-BARTH-HELD, Ueberlieferung und Auslegung im Matthäus-Evangelium (1961) 125, 255. STRECKER, G. Der Weg der Gerechtigkeit (1962) 42f., 44 3, 125, 166 7, 211 5. HAHN, F. Christologische Hoheitstitel (1963) 39. HUMMEL, R. Die Auseinandersetzung zwischen Kirche und Judentum im Matthäusevangelium (1963) 155. KäSEMANN, E. Exegetische Versuche und Besinnungen (1964) II 88. HAHN, F. Das Verständnis der Mission im Neuen Testament (1965) 107. JüNGEL, E. Paulus und Jesus (1966) 238ff. SASS, G. Ungereimtes bei Matthäus (1968) 20-21. MADDOX, R. The Function of the Son of Man According to the Synoptic Gospels. NTS 15 (1968-69) 54-55. HASLER, V. Amen (1969) 32. KäSEMANN, E. New Testament Questions of Today (1969) 88. KüNZI, M. Das Naherwartungslogion Matthäus 10, 23 (1970) 54, 58f., 93, 100, 102, 107, 123, 148, 158,

179. DE KRUIJF, T., Der Sohn des Lebendigen Gottes (Rome 1962) 72, 88, 90, 92, 99, 134, 157. LANGE, J., Das Erscheinen des Auferstandenen im Evangelium nach Matthäus (Würzburg 1973) 185-87, 213f, 422. THEISOHN, J. Der auserwählte Richter (Göttingen 1975) 178, 183, 188f, 262. KüNZI, M., Das Naherwartungslogion Markus 9, 1 par. (Tübingen 1977). SCHILDENBERGER, J., "Die Vertauschung der Aussagen über Zeichen und Bezeichnetes. Eine hermeneutisch bedeutsame Redeweise" in: Kirche und Bibel. Festgabe für E. Schick (Paderborn 1979) 402f. HARRINGTON, D. J., God's People in Christ (Philadelphia 1980) 25.

16:31 STONEHOUSE, N. B. The Witness of Matthew and Mark to Christ (1944) 129.

17 BOUSSET, W. Die Religion des Judentums im Späthellenistischen Zeitalter (1966⁻1926) 122.

17:1ff STAEHELIN, E. Die Verkündigung des Reiches Gottes in der Kirche Jesu Christi I (1951) 400.

17:1-13 WILKENS, J. Einführung in das Evangelium nach Matthäus II (1937) 26-34. VISCHER, W. Die evangelische Gemeindeordnung Matthäus 16, 13 - 20, 28 (1946) 38-43. GOODSPEED, E. J. A Life of Jesus (1950) 127-29. BALTENSWEILER, H. Die Verklärung Jesu (1959). ITTEL, G. W. Jesus und die Jünger (1970) 85-88. GOULDER, M. D., Midrash and Lection in Matthew (London 1974) 189, 393ff. *PEDERSEN, S., "Die Proklamation Jesu als des eschatologischen Offenbarungsträgers (Mt xvii 1-13)" NovT 17 (1975) 241-64. FRIEDRICH, G., "Beobachtungen zur messianischen Hohepriestererwartung in den Synoptikern" in: Auf das Wort kommt es an (Göttingen 1978) 98-101.

17:1-9.22.23. BRAUNEWELL, W. "Die Zukunft hat längst begonnen", in: Schriftauslegung. . . Die Passionstexte (1967) Frey, F. (ed.) 141ff.

17:1-9 RIESENFELD, H., Jésus Transfiguré (Copenhagen 1947). EICHHOLZ, G. (ed.) Herr, tue meine Lippen auf Bd. I (1957) 73-77. GILS, F. Jésus Prophète D'Après Les Evangiles Synoptiques (1957) 35-37, 73-78. FEUILLET, A. "Les Perspectives Propes à Chaque Evangèliste dans les Rècits de la

Transfiguration", Biblica 39 (1958) 292-99. HAAR, GPM (1960-61) 63ff. DOERNE, M. Er kommt auch noch heute (1961) 45-47. RIVERA, L. F. "El relato de la Transfiguracion en Mateo. Estudio de critica literaria," RevBi 26 (111-12, '64) 31-40. JOHNSON, S. L. "The Transfiguration of Christ," BiblSa 124 (494, '67) 133-48. OTTO, G. Denken - um zu glauben (1970) 73-77. LöWE, H. & HAARBECK, A. "Letzter Sonntag nach Epiphanias: Matthäus 17, 1-9" in: Predigtstudien (1972/73) Lange, E. (ed.) 110-17. SCHMUTZLER, S. GPM 27/1 (1972/73) 100-106. *COUNE, M., "Radieuse Transfiguration. Mt 17, 1-9; Mc 9, 2-10; Lc 9, 28-36" AssS 15 (1973) 44-84. KRATZ, R., Auferweckung als Befreiung (Stuttgart 1973) 22-24. NüTZEL, J. M., Die Verklärungserzählung im Markusevangelium (Würzburg 1973) 275-88. COPE, O. L., Matthew. A Scribe Trained for the Kingdom of Heaven (Washington D.C. 1976) 99-102. LIVIO, J.-B., "La signification théologique de la 'montagne' dans le premier evangile" Bulletin du Centre Protestant d'Etudes 30 (Geneve 1978) 13-20.

17:1-8   M'NEILE, A. H. The Gospel According to St Matthew (1955) 251f. BLAIR, E. P. Jesus in the Gospel of Matthew (1960) 131. STRECKER, G. Der Weg der Gerechtigkeit (1962) 198. ROEHRS, W. R. "God's Tabernacles Among Men. A Study of the Transfiguration," CThM 15 (1, '64) 18-25. WAGNER, W. H. "The Transfiguration and the Church," LQ 16 (4, '64) 343-48. SUHL, A. Die Funktion der alttestamentlichen Zitate und Anspielungen im Matthäusevangelium (1965) 104ff. BRAUN, H. Qumran und NT II (1966) 81, 106, 272, 309, 311. DAVIES, W. D., The Sermon on the Mount (Cambridge 1966) 20-26. SCHRAMM, T. Der Markus-Stoff bei Lukas (1971) 136-39. SAITO, T., Die Mosevorstellungen im Neuen Testament (Bern 1977) 53f. TRITES, A. A., The New Testament Concept of Witness (Cambridge 1977) 180f. RUDOLPH, K., Die Gnosis (Göttingen 1978) 165, 172.

17:1-2   SCHEP, J. A., The Nature of the Resurrection Body (Grand Rapids 1976) 165f.

17:1   STAEHELIN, E. Die Verkündigung des Reiches Gottes in der Kirche Jesu Christi I (1951) 95. FARRER, A. St Matthew and St Mark (1954) 121. KNOX, W. L. The Sources of the Synoptic Gospels II (1957) 12. BLAIR, E. P. Jesus in the Gospel of Matthew (1960) 134.

17:2-9   FUCHS, E. Programm der Entmythologisierung (1967) 33-39.

17:2   McNAMARA, M. The New Testament and the Palestinian Targum to the Pentateuch (1966) 224. NEIRYNCK, F.,

"Minor Agreements Matthew-Luke in the Transfiguration Story" in: P. Hoffmann (ed.) Orientierung an Jesus. Für Josef Schmid (Freiburg 1973) 256-60. CAVALLIN, H. C. C., Life After Death. I (Lund 1974) 7, 2, I, I. KLIJN, A. F. J., "Die syrische Baruch-Apokalypse" in: W. G. Kümmel (ed.) Jüdische Schriften aus hellenistisch-römischer Zeit. V (Gütersloh 1976) 156.

17:3ff VOLZ, P. Die Eschatologie der jüdischen Gemeinde (1934) 197.

17:3 DABECK, P. "Siehe, es erschienen Moses und Elia" (Mt 17, 3), Biblica 23 (1942) 175-89. STRECKER, G. Der Weg der Gerechtigkeit (1962) 208. HAHN, F. Christologische Hoheitstitel (1963) 402 Anm. 4.

17:4.9.13-23. BORNKAMM-BARTH-HELD, Ueberlieferung und Auslegung im Matthäus-Evangelium (²1961) 99ff.

17:4f HENNECKE, E. & SCHNEEMELCHER, W. Neutestamentliche Apokryphen (1964) II 482.

17:4 BLAIR, E. P. Jesus in the Gospel of Matthew (1960) 100. STRECKER, G. Der Weg der Gerechtigkeit (1962) 1938, 2042, 205. HAHN, F. Christologische Hoheitstitel (1963) 81, 86. LE DéAUT, R. "Acts 7, 48 et Mt 17, 4 (Par.) a la lumière du targum palestinien", RechSR 52 (1, '64) 85-90. McNAMARA, M. The New Testament and the Palestinian Targum to the Pentateuch (1966) 32 fn. 158. NICKELS, P. Targum and New Testament (1967) 20. SASS, G. Ungereimtes bei Matthäus (1968) 22-23.

17:5 GILS, F. Jésus Prophète D'Après Les Evangiles Synoptiques (1957) 35-37. HOOKER, M. D. Jesus and the Servant (1959) 68-73. BLAIR, E. P. Jesus in the Gospel of Matthew (1960) 134. BORNKAMM-BARTH-HELD, Ueberlieferung und Auslegung im Matthäus-Evangelium (1961) 118. DE KRUIJF, T., Der Sohn des Lebendigen Gottes (Rome 1962) 41, 57, 88f, 97, 132, 139. STRECKER, G. Der Weg der Gerechtigkeit (1962) 1784. DELLING, G. Die Taufe im Neuen Testament (1963) 56. HUMMEL, R. Die Auseinandersetzung zwischen Kirche und Judentum im Matthäusevangelium (1963) 115. JEREMIAS, J. Abba; Studien zur neutestamentlichen Theologie und Zeitgeschichte (1966) 192-94. NEIRYNCK, F., "Minor Agreements Matthew-Luke in the Transfiguration Story" in: P. Hoffmann (ed.) Orientierung an Jesus. Für Josef Schmid (Freiburg 1973) 260-69. KLIJN, A. F. J., "Die syrische Baruch-Apokalypse" in: W. G. Kümmel (ed.) Jüdische Schriften aus hellenistisch-römischer Zeit. V (Gütersloh 1976) 138.

17:6f STRECKER, G. Der Weg der Gerechtigkeit (1962) 1938, 2343.

17:6   STONEHOUSE, N. B. The Witness of Matthew and Mark to Christ (1944) 177.

17:7   LANGE, J., Das Erscheinen des Auferstandenen im Evangelium nach Matthäus (Würzburg 1973) 371, 425, 431, 479-81.

17:9-13   FARRER, A. St Matthew and St Mark (1954) 6. SUHL, A. Die Funktion der alttestamentlichen Zitate und Anspielungen im Markusevangelium (1965) 133ff. WINK, W. John the Baptist in the Gospel Tradition (1968) 30-31.

17:9   STONEHOUSE, N. B. The Witness of Matthew and Mark to Christ (1944) 237. BLAIR, E. P. Jesus in the Gospel of Matthew (1960) 77. O'NEILL, J. C., The Theology of Acts in its Historical Setting (London 1970) 43-4n.

17:10ff   NöTSCHER, F., Altorientalischer und alttestamentlicher Auferstehungsglaube (Darmstadt 1970⁻1926) 127.

17:10-13   BLAIR, E. P. Jesus in the Gospel of Matthew (1960) 105. ARENS, E., The HΛΘON - Sayings in the Synoptic Tradition (Fribourg 1976) 243-48. DRURY, J., Tradition and Design in Luke's Gospel (Atlanta 1976) 166f. BöCHER, O., "Johannes der Täufer in der neutestamentlichen Überlieferung" in: G. Müller (ed.) Rechtfertigung Realismus Universalismus in Biblischer Sicht. Für A. Köberle (Darmstadt 1978) 47-53. MEYER, B. F., The Aims of Jesus (London 1979) 126f.

17:10-11   VOLZ, P. Die Eschatologie der jüdischen Gemeinde (1934) 196, 200.

17:10   STONEHOUSE, N. B. The Witness of Matthew and Mark to Christ (1944) 177. STAEHELIN, E. Die Verkündigung des Reiches Gottes in der Kirche Jesu Christi I (1951) 318.

17:11ff.   STONEHOUSE, N. B. The Witness of Matthew and Mark to Christ (1944) 245.

17:11   BLAIR, E. P. Jesus in the Gospel of Matthew (1960) 86.

17:12f   STRECKER, G. Der Weg der Gerechtigkeit (1962) 186₃.₄.

17:12   STONEHOUSE, N. B. The Witness of Matthew and Mark to Christ (1944) 237, 251. HOOKER, M. D. Jesus and the Servant (1959) 93-97. BLAIR, E. P. Jesus in the Gospel of Matthew (1960) 77. BRAUN, H. Qumran und NT II (1966) 91, 296. BöHLIG, A., "Griechische und orientalische Einflüsse im Urchristentum" in: Mysterion und Wahrheit (Leiden 1968) 56. HASLER, V. Amen (1969) 33. WILLIAMS, J. A., A Conceptual History of Deuteronomism in the Old Testament, Judaism, and the New Testament: Ph.D. Diss. (Louisville 1976) 303f.

17:13   STONEHOUSE, N. B. The Witness of Matthew and Mark to

Christ (1944) 177. BLAIR, E. P. Jesus in the Gospel of Matthew (1960) 88, 105. STRECKER, G. Der Weg der Gerechtigkeit (1962) 193₁₁. HAHN, F. Christologische Hoheitstitel (1963) 377. TöDT, H. E. Der Menschensohn in der synoptischen Ueberlieferung (1963) 180.

17:14-21 BORNKAMM-BARTH-HELD, Ueberlieferung und Auslegung im Matthäus-Evangelium (₂1961) 112f., 171, 176ff., 219, 221, 226, 232f., 255, 258f., 262, 265. HOWARD, V. P., Das Ego in den Synoptischen Evangelien (Marburg 1975) 86-97.

17:14-20 WILKENS, J. Einführung in das Evangelium nach Matthäus II (1937) 35-38. STONEHOUSE, N. B. The Witness of Matthew and Mark to Christ (1944) 157. VISCHER, W. Die evangelische Gemeindeordnung. Matthäus 16, 13 - 20, 28 (1946) 43-46. WILKINSON, J. "The Case of the Epileptic Boy," ET 79 (2, '67) 39-42. RIST, J. M., On the Independence of Matthew and Mark (Cambridge 1978) 61f.

17:14 STONEHOUSE, N. B. The Witness of Matthew and Mark to Christ (1944) 78. FARRER, A. St Matthew and St Mark (1954) 124. BLAIR, E. P. Jesus in the Gospel of Matthew (1960) 86. BORNKAMM-BARTH-HELD, Ueberlieferung und Auslegung im Matthäus-Evangelium (1961) 214, 216.

17:15 HAHN, F. Christologische Hoheitstitel (1963) 81, 263f. "Barmherzigkeit" in: TRE 5 (1980) 225.

17:16 STONEHOUSE, N. B. The Witness of Matthew and Mark to Christ (1944) 177. KNOX, W. L. The Sources of the Synoptic Gospels II (1957) 125.

17:17 LOEWENICH, W. von, Luther als Ausleger der Synoptiker (1954) 135f. BORNKAMM-BARTH-HELD, Ueberlieferung und Auslegung im Matthäus-Evangelium (1961) 108, 179ff., 220. STRECKER, G. Der Weg der Gerechtigkeit (1962) 233₇. THEYSSEN, G. W. "Unbelief" in the New Testament (1965) 27ff. LANGE, J., Das Erscheinen des Auferstandenen im Evangelium nach Matthäus (Würzburg 1973) 328, 331-333, 340. FRANKEMöLLE, H., Jahwebund und Kirche Christi (Münster 1974) 11, 21-27, 152, 203. METZGER, B. M., The Early Versions of the New Testament (Oxford 1977) 250.

17:18 BLAIR, E. P. Jesus in the Gospel of Matthew (1960) 86. BORNKAMM-BARTH-HELD, Ueberlieferung und Auslegung im Matthäus-Evangelium (1961) 178, 181, 183, 206, 218. STRECKER, G. Der Weg der Gerechtigkeit (1962) 121₁₅.

17:19f STRECKER, G. Der Weg der Gerechtigkeit (1962) 176.

17:19 STONEHOUSE, N. B. The Witness of Matthew and Mark to Christ (1944) 177.

17:20   KNOX, W. L. The Sources of the Synoptic Gospels II (1957) 100, 102, 104. BORNKAMM-BARTH-HELD, Ueberlieferung und Auslegung im Matthäus-Evangelium (1961) 105, 108, 179ff., 200, 212, 232, 254, 258, 264, 276f., 278ff. SCHRAGE, W. Die konkreten Einzelgebote in der paulinischen Paränese (1961) 243. STRECKER, G. Der Weg der Gerechtigkeit (1962) 233. SCHRAGE, W. Das Verhältnis des Thomas-Evangeliums zur Synoptischen Tradition und zu den Koptischen Evangelienübersetzungen (1964) 116. THEYSSEN, G. W. "Unbelief" in the New Testament (1965) 19ff. JüNGEL, E. Paulus und Jesus (1966) 276. HASLER, V. Amen (1969) 67. SANFORD, J. A., The Kingdom Within (New York 1970) 157f. JEREMIAS, J. Neutestamentliche Theologie I (1971) 158f., 163, 187. SCHULZ, S. Q Die Spruchquelle der Evangelisten (1972) 465-68. GOULDER, M. D., Midrash and Lection in Matthew (London 1974) 37, 378, 395, 397. TALBERT, C. H., Literary Patterns, Theological Themes and the Genre of Luke-Acts (Missoula 1974) 54. DUNN, J. D. G., Jesus and the Spirit (London 1975) 72, 74f, 211. LANG, F. G., "Sola gratia im Markus-evangelium" in: J. Friedrich et al. (eds.) Rechtfertigung. Festschrift für Ernst Käsemann (Göttingen 1976) 324f. THEUNISSEN, M., "ὁ αίτην λαμβάnei. Der Gebetsglaube Jesu und die Zeitlichkeit des Christseins" in: Jesus, Ort der Erfahrung Gottes (Basel 1976) 26, 59f. ZMIJEWSKI, J., "Der Glaube und seine Macht. Eine traditionsgeschichtliche Untersuchung zu Mt 17, 20; 21,21; Mk 11,23; Lk 17,6" in: J. Zmijewski/E. Nellessen (eds.) Begegnung mit dem Wort. Festschrift für H. Zimmermann (Bonn 1980) 81-103.

17:20b   SASS, G. Ungereimtes bei Matthäus (1968) 24-25.

17:21f   MOORE, G. F. Judaism II (1946) 336n.

17:21   BORNKAMM-BARTH-HELD, Ueberlieferung und Auslegung im Matthäus-Evangelium (1961) 179. BOUSSET, W. Die Religion des Judentums im Späthellenistischen Zeitalter (1966⁻1926) 180, 340. SASS, G. Ungereimtes bei Matthäus (1968) 26-27. METZGER, B. M., The Early Versions of the New Testament (Oxford 1977) 40, 118.

17:22-   THOMPSON, W. G. "Sermo ecclesiasticus (Mt 17, 22-18, 35)
18:35   reconsideratus," VerbDom 47 (4, '69) 225-31. THOMPSON, W. G. Matthew's Advice to a Divided Community. Mt. 17, 22-18, 35, Analecta Biblica 44 (1970). KINGSBURY, J. D. Biblica 53 (1, '72) 152-56. ROLOFF, J. THLZ 97 (5, '72) 356-58.

17:22ff   KNOX, W. L. The Sources of the Synoptic Gospels II (1957) 100-101.

17:22-27 WILKENS, J. Einführung in das Evangelium nach Matthäus II (1937) 42-45. DAVIES, W. D., The Sermon on the Mount (Cambridge 1966) 111f.

17:22-23 STONEHOUSE, N. B. The Witness of Matthew and Mark to Christ (1944) 237. GILS, F. Jésus Prophète D'Après Les Evangiles Synoptiques (1957) 135-40. HOOKER, M. D. Jesus and the Servant (1959) 92-97. STRECKER, G. Der Weg der Gerechtigkeit (1962) 181з. DAVIES, W. D., The Sermon on the Mount (Cambridge 1966) 24. THOMPSON, W. G. Matthew's Advice to a Divided Community. Mt. 17,22-18, 35 (1970) 24-49. SCHRAMM, T. Der Markus-Stoff bei Lukas (1971) 130-36. PATSCH, H. Abendmahl und historischer Jesus (1972) 185ff. KINGSBURY, J. D., Matthew: Structure, Christology, Kingdom (Philadelphia 1975) 22-25.

17:22 STONEHOUSE, N. B. The Witness of Matthew and Mark to Christ (1944) 172, 251. BLAIR, E. P. Jesus in the Gospel of Matthew (1960) 77. STRECKER, G. Der Weg der Gerechtigkeit (1962) 97, 121₇, 186₄. POPKES, W. Christus Traditus (1967) 56, 153ff., 269, 280.

17:23 BLAIR, E. P. Jesus in the Gospel of Matthew (1960) 105. STRECKER, G. Der Weg der Gerechtigkeit (1962) 97з, 104₄, 193₈. GüTTGEMANNS, E. Offene Fragen zur Formgeschichte des Evangeliums (1970) 218, 222. O'NEILL, J. C., The Theology of Acts in its Historical Setting (London 1970) 43-4n.

17:24ff SEIDENSTICKER, Ph. Lebendiges Opfer (1954) 122ff.

17:24-27 STONEHOUSE, N. B. The Witness of Matthew and Mark to Christ (1944) 157. VISCHER, W. Die evangelische Gemeindeordnung Matthäus 16, 13 - 20, 28 (1946) 47-55. RICHARDSON, A. The Miracle-Stories of the Gospels (1948) 105ff. TAYLOR, V. The Formation of the Gospel Tradition (1949) 73f., 138. FARRER, A. St Matthew and St Mark (1954) 122. HUMBERT, A. "Essai d'une théologie du scandale dans les Synoptiques", Biblica 35 (1954) 26-28. BARRETT, C. K. The New Testament Background: Selected Documents (1956) 133. ENSLIN, M. S. The Literature of the Christian Movement (1956) 392f. BLAIR, E. P. Jesus in the Gospel of Matthew (1960) 148. BORNKAMM-BARTH-HELD, Ueberlieferung und Auslegung im Matthäus-Evangelium (1961) 17, 79, 84, 86, 194. BULTMANN, R. The History of the Synoptic Tradition (1963) 34f. DERRETT, J. D. M. "Peter's Penny: Fresh Light on Matthew xvii 24-7," NovTest 6 (1, '63) 1-15. HUMMEL, R. Die Auseinandersetzung zwischen Kirche und Judentum im Matthäusevangelium (1963) 103-106. LIVER, J. "The Half-

Shekel Offering in Biblical and Post-Biblical Literature," HThR 56 (3, '63) 173-98. SCHMITHALS, W. Paulus und Jakobus (1963) 91 n.2. MONTEFIORE, H. "Jesus and the Temple Tax," NTS 11 (1, '64) 60-71. LEE, G. M. "Studies in Texts: Matthew 17.24-27," Theology 68 (542, '65) 380-81. LOOS, H. van der, The Miracles of Jesus (1965) 185, 664, 680-84, 686, 687, 694. NICKLE, K. F. The Collection (1966) 86f. DERRETT, J. D. M. Law in the New Testament (1970) 247-65. ROLOFF, J. Das Kerygma und der irdische Jesus (1970) 117-19. THOMPSON, W. G. Matthew's Advice to a Divided Community. Mt. 17, 22-18, 35 (1970) 50-68. JEREMIAS, J. Neutestamentliche Theologie I (1971) 91f. LéGASSE, S. "Jèsus et l'impôt du Temple (Matthieu 17, 24-27)," SciE 24 (3, '72) 361-77. BROWN, R. E. et al. (eds.) Peter in the New Testament (Minneapolis 1973) 101-105. FRANKEMöLLE,H., Jahwebund und Kirche Christi (Münster 1974) 155f, 174-76. GOULDER, M. D., Midrash and Lection in Matthew (London 1974) 142, 152, 159, 190, 378, 395ff, 406. *MCELENEY, N.J., "Mt 17:24-27 —Who Paid the Temple Tax? A Lesson in Avoidance of Scandal" CBQ 38 (1976) 178-92. RIST, J. M., On the Independence of Matthew and Mark (Cambridge 1978) 70. *CASSIDY, R. J.,"Matthew 17:24-27— A Word on Civil Taxes" CBQ 41 (1979) 571-80.

17:24   BARRETT, C. K. The New Testament Background: Selected Documents (1956) 133. HAHN, F. Christologische Hoheitstitel (1963) 77. BLACK, M., " 'ΕΦΦΑΘΑ (Mk 7.34), [TA] ΠΑΣΧΑ (Mt 26.18 W), [TA] ΣΑΒΒΑΤΑ (Passim), [TA] ΔΙΔΡΑΧΜΑ (Mt 17.24 bis)" in: A. Descamps/ A. de Halleux (eds.) Mélanges Bibliques en hommage au R. P. Béda Rigaux (Gembloux 1970) 60-62.

17:25-   FARRER, A. St Matthew and St Mark (1954) 118.
18:1

17:25-27   BEST, E. I Peter and the Gospel Tradition NTS 16 (1969/70) 110f.

17:25-26   BöHLIG, A., "Vom 'Knecht' zum 'Sohn' " in: Mysterion und Wahrheit (Leiden 1968) 62. FRANKEMöLLE, H., Jahwebund und Kirche Christi (Münster 1974) 174-76.

17:25   STRECKER, G. Der Weg der Gerechtigkeit (1962) 2064. SMITH, M., Tannaitic Parallels to the Gospels (Philadelphia 1968) 2.22+.

17:26f   HUMMEL, R. Die Auseinandersetzung zwischen Kirche und Judentum im Matthäusevangelium (1963) 139.

17:26   DELLING, G., "Die 'Söhne (Kinder) Gottes' im Neuen Testament" in: R. Schnackenburg et al. (eds.) Die Kirche des

Anfangs. Für H. Schürmann (Freiburg 1978) 621.

17:27 STRECKER, G. Der Weg der Gerechtigkeit (1962) 374. HUMMEL, R. Die Auseinandersetzung zwischen Kirche und Judentum im Matthäusevangelium (1963) 159. PETZKE, G. Die Traditionen über Apollonius von Tyana und das Neue Testament (1970) 173f. *HOMEAU, H. A., "On Fishing for Staters: Matthew 17:27" ET 85 (1974) 340-42.

18 FEINE, D. P. & BEHM, D. J. Einleitung in das Neue Testament (1950) 33f. STREETER, B. H. The Four Gospels (1951) 261f. TRILLING, W. Das wahre Israel (1959) 85ff., 129ff. TRILLING, W. Hausordnung Gottes (1960) 19-65. BORNKAMM-BARTH-HELD, Ueberlieferung und Auslegung im Matthäus-Evangelium (1961) 17f., 36, 45, 113ff. MARTINEZ, E. R. "The Interpretation of 'Oi Mathētai' in Matthew 18," CBQ 23 (3, '61) 281-92. PESCH, W. Die sogenannte Gemeindeordnung Mt. 18, BZ NF 7 (1963) 220-35. BOUSSET, W. Die Religion des Judentums im Späthellenistischen Zeitalter (1966-1926) 424. BRAUN, H. Qumran und NT II (1966) 337. PESCH, W. Matthäus der Seelsorger (1966) 49-65. BONNARD, P. "Composition et signification historique de Matthieu XVIII", in: De Jésus aux Evangiles (1967) Potterie, I. de las (ed.) 130-40. GAECHTER, P. Die literarische Kunst im Matthäus-Evangelium (1968) 45-48. STROBEL, A. Erkenntnis und Bekenntnis der Sünde in neutestamentlicher Zeit (1968) 44. BORNKAMM, G. "The Authority to 'Bind' and 'Loose' in the Church in Matthew's Gospel: The Problem of Sources in Matthew's Gospel," Perspective 11 (1-2, '70) 37-50. BORNKAMM, G. Geschichte und Glaube II (1971) 37-50. SELBY, D. J., Introduction to the New Testament (New York 1971) 112, 120, 135-39. *SCHWEIZER, E., "Matthew's View of the Church in his 18th Chapter" AusBR 21 (1973) 7-14. ELLIS, P. F., Matthew: His Mind and His Message (Collegeville 1974) 67-74. FRANKEMöLLE, H., Jahwebund und Kirche Christi (Münster 1974) 180, 185-88, 226. SCHWEIZER, E., Matthäus und seine Gemeinde (Stuttgart 1974) 106-15. HOFFMANN, P. und EID,V., Jesus von Nazareth und eine christliche Moral (Freiburg 1975) 221-23. *ADDLEY, W. P., "Matthew 18 and the Church as the Body of Christ" BTh 26 (1976) 12-18.

GOPPELT, L., Theologie des Neuen Testaments II (Göttingen 1976) 566. NEILL, S., Jesus Through Many Eyes (Philadelphia 1976) 94-102. *ZIMMERMANN, H., "Die innere Struktur der Kirche und das Petrusamt nach Mt 18" Catholica 30 (1976) 168-83. "Bann" in: TRE 5 (1980) 165.

18:1-20:28 RIDDERBOS, H. Matthew's Witness to Jesus Christ (1958) 61-66.

18:1ff STONEHOUSE, N. B. The Witness of Matthew and Mark to Christ (1944) 130.

18:1-35 STRECKER, G. Der Weg der Gerechtigkeit (1962) 40, 43, 134, 158, 223. BULTMANN, R. The History of the Synoptic Tradition (1963) 149f.

18:1-20 DUNN, J. D. G., Unity and Diversity in the New Testament (London 1977) 117.

18:1-14 BUTLER, B. C. The Originality of St Matthew (1951) 93ff. OTOMO, Y. Nachfolge Jesu und Anfänge der Kirche im Neuen Testament (1970) 170-74. BOHREN, R. Wiedergeburt des Wunders (1972) 97-100. SANDERS, J. T., Ethics in the New Testament (Philadelphia 1975) 45f.

18:1-10 WILKENS, J. Einführung in das Evangelium nach Matthäus II (1937) 46-52.

18:1-6 CAVALLETTI, S., "Il bambino come parabola" EuD 25 (1972) 509-14.

18:1-5 VISCHER, W. Die evangelische Gemeindeordnung. Matthäus 16, 13 - 20, 28 (1946) 56-61. TRILLING, W. Das wahre Israel (1959) 85ff. STRECKER, G. Der Weg der Gerechtigkeit (1962) 232. PESCH, W. Matthäus der Seelsorger (1966) 18-21. HOFFMANN, P. und EID, V., Jesus von Nazareth und eine christliche Moral (Freiburg 1975) 187f, 190-200, 211f.

18:1-4 KNOX, W. L. The Sources of the Synoptic Gospels II (1957) 100. BORNKAMM-BARTH-HELD, Ueberlieferung und Auslegung im Matthäus-Evangelium (1961) 17, 110, 113f., 223f., 227, 229. STRECKER, G. Der Weg der Gerechtigkeit (1962) 162s, 163. HAHN, F. Das Verständnis der Mission im Neuen Testament (1965) 106. THOMPSON, W. G. Matthew's Advice to a Divided Community. Mt. 17, 22-18, 35 (1970) 69-84. SANFORD, J. A., The Kingdom Within (New York 1970) 191f. SCHRAMM, T. Der Markus-Stoff bei Lukas (1971) 140f. BERGER, K., Exegese des Neuen Testaments (Heidelberg 1977) 23.

18:1-3 SCHLATTER, D. A. Die Theologie des Neuen Testaments (1909) I 159-61.

18:1 VOLZ, P. Die Eschatologie der jüdischen Gemeinde (1934)

405. BLAIR, E. P. Jesus in the Gospel of Matthew (1960) 86. BORNKAMM-BARTH-HELD, Ueberlieferung und Auslegung im Matthäus-Evangelium (1961) 216. STRECKER, G. Der Weg der Gerechtigkeit (1962) 1219, 223. SCHRAGE, W. Das Verhältnis des Thomas-Evangeliums zur Synoptischen Tradition und zu den Koptischen Evangelienübersetzungen (1964) 51. METZGER, B.M. "Explicit references in the works of Origen to variant readings in New Testament manuscripts", Historical and Literary Studies (1968) 93. THYEN, H. Studien zur Sündenvergebung (1970) 237, 241ff. CLARK, K. W., "The Meaning of APA" in: The Gentile Bias and other Essays (Leiden 1980) 196.

18:2 STROBEL, A. Erkenntnis und Bekenntnis der Sünde in neutestamentlicher Zeit (1968) 44.

18:3ff ELLIS, E. E. & WILCOX, M. (eds.) Neotestamentica et Semitica (1969) 50-60.

18:3-35 STONEHOUSE, N. B. The Witness of Matthew and Mark to Christ (1944) 130.

18:3-5 STRECKER, G. Der Weg der Gerechtigkeit (1962) 134s.

18:3-4 SANFORD, J. A., The Kingdom Within (New York 1970) 54.

18:3 STONEHOUSE, N. B. The Witness of Matthew and Mark to Christ (1944) 228. KNOX, W. L. The Sources of the Synoptic Gospels II (1957) 16. ROBINSON, J. M. Kerygma und historischer Jesus (1960) 157, 161, 165, 168. BORNKAMM-BARTH-HELD, Ueberlieferung und Auslegung im Matthäus-Evangelium (1961) 110, 113ff. STRECKER, G. Der Weg der Gerechtigkeit (1962) 166s. DELLING, G. Die Taufe im Neuen Testament (1963) 89. BRAUN, H. Qumran und NT II (1966) 28. SUMMERS, R. The Secret Sayings of the Living Jesus (1968) 59. DUPONT, J. in: Neotestamentica et Semitica (1969) Ellis, E. E. & Wilcox, M. (eds.) 50-60. HASLER, V. Amen (1969) 38. FRANK, H. "Wenn ihr nicht werdet wie die Kinder" in: Weihnachten heute gesagt (1970) Nitschke, H. (ed.) 32-37. JEREMIAS, J. Neutestamentliche Theologie I (1971) 40f., 118, 153f., 177, 219. JEREMIAS, J. New Testament Theology I (1971) 31, 33, 116, 155f., 181, 227. THEUNISSEN, M., "δαίτϊν λαμβάνει. Der Gebetsglaube Jesu und die Zeitlichkeit des Christseins" in: Jesus, Ort der Erfahrung Gottes (Basel 1976) 32.

18:4 ROBINSON, J. M. Kerygma und historischer Jesus (1960) 165. LILLIE, W. Studies in New Testament Ethics (1961) 130f. STRECKER, G. Der Weg der Gerechtigkeit (1962) 174. KäSEMANN,E. Exegetische Versuche und Besinnungen (1964) I 78. STROBEL, A. Erkenntnis und Bekenntnis der

Sünde in neutestamentlicher Zeit (1968) 44. BERGER, K. Zu den Sogenannten Sätzen Heiligen Rechts. NTS 17 (1970-71) 28f.

18:5-9 THOMPSON, W. G. Matthew's Advice to a Divided Community. Mt. 17,22-18, 35, (1970) 100-51.

18:5 FLEW, R. N. Jesus and His Church (1956) 120. BULTMANN, R. The History of the Synoptic Tradition (1963) 142f. KäSEMANN, E. Exegetische Versuche und Besinnungen (1964) I 170. HEDRICK, C. W., "Resurrection: Radical Theology in the Gospel of Matthew" LThQ 14 (1979) 40-45.

18:6ff BLAIR, E. P. Jesus in the Gospel of Matthew (1960) 108. STROBEL, A. Erkenntnis und Bekenntnis der Sünde in neutestamentlicher Zeit (1968) 44.

18:6-14 TRILLING, W. Das wahre Israel (1959) 89ff.

18:6-9 VISCHER, W. Die evangelische Gemeindeordnung. Matthäus 16, 13 - 20, 28 (1946) 61-67. PESCH, W. Matthäus der Seelsorger (1966) 21-28. BLACK, M. An Aramaic Approach to the Gospels and Acts (1967) 169f. MEURER, S. Das Recht im Dienst der Versöhnung und des Friedens (1972) 45-58. RIST, J. M., On the Independence of Matthew and Mark (Cambridge 1978) 75f.

18:6-8 HAHN, F. Christologische Hoheitstitel (1963) 99.

18:6-7 BUTLER, B. C. The Originality of St Matthew (1951) 7ff. KNOX, W. L. The Sources of the Synoptic Gospels II (1957) 100f. SCHRAGE, W. Die konkreten Einzelgebote in der paulinischen Paränese (1961) 243. TALBERT, C. H., Literary Patterns, Theological Themes, and the Genre of Luke-Acts (Missoula 1974) 54. EDWARDS, R. A., A Theology of Q (Philadelphia 1976) 71.

18:6 MASSAUX, E. Influence de l'Evangile de saint Matthieu sur la littérature chrètienne avant saint Irénée (1950) 23-25. BOUSSET, W. Die Religion des Judentums im Späthellenistischen Zeitalter (1966⁻1926) 187. JüNGEL, E. Paulus und Jesus (1966) 276. LADD, G. E., A Theology of the New Testament (Grand Rapids 1974) 88, 229, 270f. KLIJN, A. F. J., "Die syrische Baruch-Apokalypse" in: W. G. Kümmel (ed.) Jüdische Schriften aus hellenistisch-römischer Zeit V (Gütersloh 1976) 152.

18:7 HUMBERT, A. "Essai d'une théologie du scandale dans les Synoptiques", Biblica 35 (1954) 9-10. FLEW, R. N. Jesus and His Church (1956) 67n. SASS, G. Ungereimtes bei Matthäus (1968) 28-29. DORMEYER, D., Die Passion Jesu als Verhaltensmodell (Münster 1974) 98A, 234. POLAG, A., Die Christologie der Logienquelle (Neukirchen-Vluyn 1977) 99.

18:8ff STROBEL, A. Erkenntnis und Bekenntnis der Sünde in neutestamentlicher Zeit (1968) 44.

18:8-10 STAUDINGER, J. Die Bergpredigt (1957) 92, 93, 94, 261.

18:8f KNOX, W.L. The Sources of the Synoptic Gospels II (1957) 21. DUPONT, D. J. Les Béatitudes (1958) 121-23.

18:8 M'NEILE, A. H. The Gospel According to St. Matthew (1955) 262f.

18:9-20 MEURER, S. Das Recht im Dienst der Versöhnung und des Friedens (1972) 59-62.

18:9 STONEHOUSE, N. B. The Witness of Matthew and Mark to Christ (1944) 227. NICKELS, P. Targum und New Testament (1967) 20.

18:10-14 JüLICHER, D. A. Die Gleichnisreden Jesu (1910) 314-33. BISHOP, E. F. F. "The Parable of the Lost or Wandering Sheep. Matthew 18.10-14; Luke 15.3-7," AThR 44 (1, '62) 44-57. GAECHTER, P. Die literarische Kunst im Matthäus-Evangelium (1968) 50-51. THOMPSON, W. G. Matthew's Advice to a Divided Community. Mt. 17, 22-18, 35 (1970) 152-74.

18:10-13 PIROT, J. Paraboles et Allégories Evangeliques (1949) 250-72. PESCH, W. Matthäus der Seelsorger (1966) 28-30.

18:10.18.19. HASLER, V. Amen (1969) 88.

18:10.19 McNAMARA, M. The New Testament and the Palestinian Targum to the Pentateuch (1966) 136.

18:10 MOORE, G. F. Judaism (1946) I 404. VISCHER, W. Die evangelische Gemeindeordnung. Matthäus 16, 13 - 20, 28 (1946) 67-68. HERING, J. "Un texte oublié: Mt 18, 10. A propos des controverses récentes sur le pédobaptisme," in: Aux Sources de la Tradition Chrétienne (1950) Goguel, M. M. (ed.) 95-102. STRECKER, G. Der Weg der Gerechtigkeit (1962) 149₂. BULTMANN, R. The History of the Synoptic Tradition (1963) 147f. HAHN, F. Christologische Hoheitstitel (1963) 321. BOUSSET, W. Die Religion des Judentums im Späthellenistischen Zeitalter (1966⁻1926) 187, 324. SASS, G. Ungereimtes bei Matthäus (1968) 30-31. NöTSCHER, F. "Das Angesicht Gottes schauen" nach biblischer und babylonischer Auffassung (1969). JEREMIAS, J. Neutestamentliche Theologie I (1971) 113, 177f. KLIJN, A. F. J., "Die syrische Baruch-Apokalypse" in: W. G. Kümmel (ed.) Jüdische Schriften aus hellenistisch-römischer Zeit V (Gütersloh 1976) 152.

18:11 KäSEMANN, E. Exegetische Versuche und Besinnungen (1964) II 96. KäSEMANN, E. New Testament Questions of

Today (1969) 97. BRUNNER, E. Dogmatik II, 414. ARENS, E., The HΔΘON-Sayings in the Synoptic Tradition (Fribourg 1976) 191-93. METZGER, B. M., The Early Versions of the New Testament (Oxford 1977) 41, 118.

18:12ff KNOX, W. L. The Sources of the Synoptic Gospels II (1957) 89, 100. BISER, E. Die Gleichnisse Jesu (1965) 109ff., 139. STROBEL, A. Erkenntnis und Bekenntnis der Sünde in neutestamentlicher Zeit (1968) 44. BEYSCHLAG, K., Simon Magnus und die Christliche Gnosis (Tübingen 1974) 129f, 133, 176, 179, 183f.

18:12-35 STONEHOUSE, N. B. The Witness of Matthew and Mark to Christ (1944) 157. BORNKAMM-BARTH-HELD, Ueberlieferung und Auslegung im Matthäus-Evangelium (1961) 78f. STRECKER, G. Der Weg der Gerechtigkeit (1962) 149₂, 232.

18:12-20 WILKENS, J. Einführung in das Evangelium nach Matthäus II (1937) 53-61.

18:12-18 BRAUN, H. Qumran und NT II (1966) 93, 102, 152, 287, 290, 328, 337.

18:12-14 VISCHER, W. Die evangelische Gemeindeordnung. Matthäus 16, 13 - 20, 28 (1946) 68-69. MICHAELIS, D. W. Die Gleichnisse Jesu (1956) 130-35. TRILLING, W. Das wahre Israel (1959) 91f. BORNKAMM-BARTH-HELD, Ueberlieferung und Auslegung im Matthäus-Evangelium (1961) 78f., 114f., 137, 139. JEREMIAS, J. Die Gleichnisse Jesu (1962) 35-37, 38, 67, 90, 96, 102, 132-35, 214. DUPONT, J. "La parabole de la Brebis perdue (Matthieu 18, 12-14; Luc 15, 4-7)," Gregorianum 49 (2, '68) 265-87. SUMMERS, R. The Secret Sayings of the Living Jesus (1968) 25. LINNEMANN, E. Gleichnisse Jesu (1969) 13, 15, 23, 24, 26, 34, 47, 50, 70ff., 150ff. SANFORD, J. A., The Kingdom Within (New York 1970) 178f. MEURER, S. Das Recht im Dienst der Versöhnung und des Friedens (1972) 45-58. SCHULZ, S. Q Die Spruchquelle der Evangelisten (1972) 387-91. GOULDER, M. D., Midrash and Lection in Matthew (London 1974) 50, 54, 59ff, 102, 163, 190, 266, 286, 307, 392, 398-400. SAND, A., Das Gesetz und die Propheten (Regensburg 1974) 122. TALBERT, C.H., Literary Patterns, Theological Themes, and the Genre of Luke-Acts (Missoula 1974) 55. "Abendmahl" in: TRE 1 (1977) 217. MANEK, J., . . .und brachte Frucht. Die Gleichnisse Jesu (Berlin 1977) 51-53. POLAG, A., Die Christologie der Logienquelle (Neukirchen-Vluyn 1977) 43. SWIDLER, L., Biblical Affirmations of Woman (Philadelphia 1979) 171, 274. "Bann" in: TRE 5 (1980) 165, 167. WEDER, H., Die Gleichnisse Jesu als Metaphern (Göttingen 1980 (2)) 168-77.

18:12-13   MOORE, G. F. Judaism (1946) I 344. JüNGEL, E. Paulus und
Jesus (1966) 131. TOLBERT, M. A., Perspectives on the
Parables (Philadelphia 1979) 55-57.

18:12   STRECKER, G. Der Weg der Gerechtigkeit (1962) 239₂.
BUSSBY, F. "Did a Shepherd Leave Sheep upon the
Mountains or in the Desert? A Note on Matthew 18.12 and
Luke 15.4," AThR 45 (1, '63) 93-94. SCHRAGE, W. Das
Verhältnis des Thomas-Evangeliums zur Synoptischen
Tradition und zu den Koptischen Evangelienübersetzungen
(1964) 193. BRUNNER, E. Dogmatik I, 202.

18:13   JüNGEL, E. Paulus und Jesus (1966) 175. HASLER, V. Amen
(1969) 68.

18:14   TRILLING, W. Das wahre Israel (1959) 165. BOUSSET, W.
Die Religion des Judentums im Späthellenistischen Zeitalter
(1966⁻1926) 187.316. PESCH, W. Matthäus der Seelsorger
(1966) 30-33. STROBEL, A. Erkenntnis und Bekenntnis der
Sünde in neutestamentlicher Zeit (1968) 44. TALBERT, C. H.,
Literary Patterns, Theological Themes, and the Genre of Luke-
Acts (Missoula 1974) 55.

18:15ff   CLEMEN, C. Primitive Christianity and Its Non-Jewish
Sources (1912) 208f. FARRER, A. St Matthew and St Mark
(1954) 188. KNOX, W. L. The Sources of the Synoptic Gospels
II (1957) 35, 121, 133. STRECKER, G. Der Weg der
Gerechtigkeit (1962) 134₆, 190₃, 203, 235. BULTMANN, R.
Theologie des Neuen Testaments (1965) 51, 65. THYEN, H.
Studien zur Sündenvergebung (1970) 56, 218, 237f. KüMMEL,
W. G. Einleitung in das Neue Testament (1973) 89f.
FRANKEMöLLE, H., Jahwebund und Kirche Christi
(Münster 1974) 180-83. THEISSEN, G., Soziologie der
Jesusbewegung (München 1977) 25. "Bahn" in TRE 5 (1980)
165-67, 188

18:15-35   HAHN, F. Christologische Hoheitstitel (1963) 83. OTOMO, Y.
Nachfolge Jesu und Anfänge der Kirche in Neuen Testament
(1970) 175-79. BORNKAMM, G. Geschichte und Glaube II
(1971) 42f.

18:15-22   STRECKER, G. Der Weg der Gerechtigkeit (1962) 122, 222ff.

18:15-20   HUMMEL, R. Die Auseinandersetzung zwischen Kirche und
Judentum im Matthäusevangelium (1963) 57f. DAVIES, W.
D., The Sermon on the Mount (Cambridge 1966) 78-81, 112-
114. PESCH, W. Matthäus der Seelsorger (1966) 36-45.
DIETZFELBINGEN, W. in: Hören und Fragen Bd. 5 (1967)
Eichholz, G. & Falkenroth, A. (eds.) 378ff. THOMPSON, W.
G. Matthew's Advice to a Divided Community. Mt. 17, 22-18,
35 (1970) 175-202. LANGE, E. (ed.) Predigstudien für das

Kirchenjahr 1970/71 (1970/71) 129-34. BORNKAMM, G. Geschichte und Glauben II (1971) 38-40, 42-44. FüRST, W. GPM 25 (1971) 291-98. FRICK, R. GPM 13/3 177-81. GEENSE, A. GPM 19/3 255-61. SURKAU, H. W. GPM 11/3 181-84. FRANKEMöLLE, H., Jahwebund und Kirche Christi (Münster 1974) 226-30. GOULDER, M. D., Midrash and Lection in Matthew (London 1974) 163, 257, 286, 346, 400-402. KOCH, E., in: GPM 31 (1976/77) 296-301. DUNN, J. D. G., Unity and Diversity in the New Testament (London 1977) 131. KöSTER, R./WIEDEMANN, H.-G., in: P. Krusche (ed.) Predigtstudien V/2 (Stuttgart 1977) 114-21. MARXSEN, W., Christologie - praktisch (Gütersloh 1978) 150-59.

18:15-18   VISCHER, W. Die evangelische Gemeindeordnung. Matthäus 16, 13 - 20, 28 (1946) 69-71. GALTIER, P. Aux Origines du Sacrement de Pénitence (1951) 43-50. SCHWEIZER, E. Gemeinde und Gemeinde-Ordnung im Neuen Testament (1959) §§ 2b, 4e-g, 6f. BRAUN, H. Jesus (1969) 49. BORNKAMM, G., "Die Binde- und Lösegewalt in der Kirche", in: Die Zeit Jesu. Für H. Schlier (Freiburg 1970) 93-107. *GALOT, J., " 'Qu'il soit pour toi comme le paien et le publicain' " NRTh 96 (1974) 1009-30. *CENTI, T. S., "A proposito di riconciliazione: dalla correzione fraterna alla tolleranza. (Riflessioni su un articolo confusionario del P. J. Galot)" RAM 26 (1975) 177-85. HEIN, K., Eucharist and Excommunication (Bern/Frankfurt 1975) 69-71. "Bann" in: TRE 5 (1980) 165.

18:15-17   MOORE, G. F. Judaism (1946) II 153. TRILLING, W. Das wahre Israel (1959) 92ff. BORNKAMM-BARTH-HELD, Ueberlieferung und Auslegung im Matthäus-Evangelium (1961) 78, 113, 127, 194, 257. DERRETT, J. D. M. Law in the New Testament: The Story of the Woman taken in Adultery. NTS 10 (1963-64) 6f. LANGE, J., Das Erscheinen des Auferstandenen im Evangelium nach Matthäus (Würzburg 1973) 131, 134-36, 143f. "Abendmahl" in: TRE 1 (1977) 217, 223. TRITES, A. A., The New Testament Concept of Witness (Cambridge 1977) 193. TALBERT, C. H., Literary Patterns, Theological Themes, and the Genre of Luke-Acts (Missoula 1974) 54.

18:15.21f   SCHULZ, S. Q Die Spruchquelle der Evangelisten (1972) 320-22.

18:15   STONEHOUSE, N. B. The Witness of Matthew and Mark to Christ (1944) 175. KNOX, W. L. The Sources of the Synoptic Gospels II (1957) 100, 133. SCHRAGE, W. Die konkreten Einzelgebote in der paulinishcen Paränese (1961) 243. STROBEL, A. Erkenntnis und Bekenntnis der Sünde in neutestamentlicher Zeit (1968) 44.

18:16ff MAURER, C. Ignatius von Antiochien und das Johannesevangelium (1949) 24, 37.

18:16b-17 GAECHTER, P. Die literarische Kunst im Matthäus-Evangelium (1968) 45-46.

18:16 STRECKER, G. Der Weg der Gerechtigkeit (1962) 24. BEUTLER, J. Martyria (1972) 192f.

18:17f STRECKER, G. Der Weg der Gerechtigkeit (1962) 201.

18:17 STONEHOUSE, N. B. The Witness of Matthew and Mark to Christ (1944) 256. KNOX, W. L. The Sources of the Synoptic Gospels II (1957) 33-34. TRILLING, W. Das wahre Israel (1959) 12. DE KRUIJF, Th., Der Sohn des lebendigen Gottes (Rome 1962) 82, 85, 150f, 153, 158. STRECKER, G. Der Weg der Gerechtigkeit (1962) 166₇, 207₃, 214, 217. HUMMEL, R. Die Auseinandersetzung zwischen Kirche und Judentum im Matthäusevangelium (1963) 23, 154ff. KüNG, H., Die Kirche (Freiburg 1967) 57, 92, 103, 393f.; ET: The Church (London 1967) 43, 74, 83, 332. STROBEL, A. Erkenntnis und Bekenntnis der Sünde in neutestamentlicher Zeit (1968) 44. TAGAWA, K. People and Community in the Gospel of Matthew NTS 16 (1969-70) 153f. FRANKEMöLLE, H., Jahwebund und Kirche Christi (Münster 1974) 121, 220-47. GOULDER, M. D., Midrash and Lection in Matthew (London 1974) 152, 154, 161, 295, 400f. "Amt"in: TRE 2 (1978) 555. "Bann" in: TRE 5 (1980) 165f.

18:18-19 KNOX, W. L. The Sources of the Synoptic Gospels II (1957) 27, 133.

18:18 STAEHELIN, E. Die Verkündigung des Reiches Gottes in der Kirche Jesu Christi I (1951) 326, 370. FARRER, A. St Matthew and St Mark (1954) 164. DODD, C. H. Some Johanine 'Herrworte' with Parallels in the Synoptic Gospels. NTS 2 (1955-56) 85ff. FLEW, R. N. Jesus and His Church (1956) 96-97. TRILLING, W. Das wahre Israel (1959) 95. DE KRUIJF, Th., Der Sohn des lebendigen Gottes (Rome 1962) 77, 82, 151, 153, 156. STRECKER, G. Der Weg der Gerechtigkeit (1962) 18₃, 206₄, 213₃, 223₆. KäSEMANN, E. Exegetische Versuche und Besinnungen (1964) II 104. HAHN, F. Das Verständnis der Mission im Neuen Testament (1965) 41. KüNG, H., Die Kirche (Freiburg 1967) 393f, 398, 449, 541, 544; ET: The Church (London 1967) 331, 336, 380, 458, 462, 464. NICKELS, P. Targum and New Testament (1967) 20. SASS, G. Ungereimtes bei Matthäus (1968) 32-33. STROBEL, A. Erkenntnis und Bekenntnis der Sünde in neutestamentlicher Zeit (1968) 45, 58. KäSEMANN, E. New Testament Questions of Today (1969) 107. BORNKAMM, G. "Die Binde- und Lösegewalt in der Kirche des Matthäus" in: Die Zeit Jesu. Festschrift für H. Schlier (1970) 93-107. THYEN, H. Studien zur Sündenvergebung (1970) 39, 151, 218, 227, 236ff., 241ff., 247. JEREMIAS, J. Neutestamentliche Theologie I (1971) 20, 22, 26, 29, 109, 228. VöGTLE, A. Das Evangelium und die Evangelien (1971) 246-48, 250-52. KERTELGE, K., Gemeinde und Amt im Neuen Testament (München 1972) 136f. LANGE, J., Das Erscheinen des Auferstandenen im Evangelium nach Matthäus (Würzburg 1973) 60, 63, 97, 105, 115, 119, 130-37, 140, 144-47, 151, 166, 170, 172, 180, 186, 202, 206, 209, 230, 326, 342, 423, 431, 436, 462f, 491, 494. MICHL, J., "Sündenbekenntnis und Sündenvergebung in der Kirche des Neuen Testaments" MThZ 24 (1973) 189-207. GOULDER, M. D., Midrash and Lection in Matthew (London 1974) 37, 75, 190, 286, 384, 389f, 392. LEROY, H., Zur Vergebung der Sünden (Stuttgart 1974) 45-53. RIGAUX, B., " 'Lier et délier'. Les ministères de réconciliation dans l'Eglise des Temps apostoliques" Maison-Dieu 117 (1974) 86-135. THEISSEN, G., Soziologie der Jesusbewegung (München 1977) 23. "Amt" in: TRE 2 (1978) 554.

18:19f TRILLING, W. Das wahre Israel (1959) 99. STROBEL, A. Erkenntnis und Bekenntnis der Sünde in neutestamentlicher Zeit (1968) 44. BORNKAMM, G. Geschichte und Glaube II (1971) 42-45.

18:19-20 VISCHER, W. Die evangelische Gemeindeordnung. Matthäus 16, 13-20, 28 (1946) 71-73. HENNECKE, E. & SCHNEEMELCHER, W. Neutestamentliche Apokryphen (1964) I 69, 110, 218. *CABA, J., "El poder de la petición communitaria (Mt. 18, 19-20)" Gregorianum 54 (1973) 609-54. *DERRETT, J. D. M., " 'Where two or three are convened in my name. . .': a sad misunderstanding" ET 91 (1979) 83-86.

18:19 FLEW, R. N. Jesus and His Church (1956) 47.BLAIR, E. P. Jesus in the Gospel of Matthew (1960) 91. HAHN, F.Christologische Hoheitstitel (1963) 321. SCHRAGE, W. Das Verhältnis des Thomas-Evangeliums zur Synoptischen Tradition und zu den Koptischen Evangelienübersetzungen (1964) 116. LANGE, J., Das Erscheinen des Auferstandenen im Evangelium nach Matthäus (Würzburg 1973) 97, 110, 132, 138, 140, 142f, 145-147, 150, 166, 170, 180.

18:20 KNOX, W. L. The Sources of the Synoptic Gospels II (1957) 100, 151, 154. TRILLING, W. Das wahre Israel (1959) 27f. BLAIR, E. P. Jesus in the Gospel of Matthew (1960) 46. McGOVERN, J. J. "There I Am in the Midst of Them," Worship 34 (8, '60) 450-53. BORNKAMM-BARTH-HELD,

Ueberlieferung und Auslegung im Matthäus-Evangelium (1961) 32f., 78, 96, 104, 126f. DELLING, G. Die Taufe im Neuen Testament (1961) 40, 43. STRECKER, G. Der Weg der Gerechtigkeit (1962) 1143,209f., 213. BULTMANN, R. The History of the Synoptic Tradition (1963) 147f., 149, 150f. HAHN, F. Christologische Hoheitstitel (1963) 119. SCHRAGE, W. Das Verhältnis des Thomas-Evangeliums zur Synoptischen Tradition und zu den Koptischen Evangelienübersetzungen (1964) 74. GäRTNER, B. The Temple and the Community in Qumran and the New Testament (1965) 114. BOUSSET, W. Die Religion des Judentums im Späthellenistischen Zeitalter (1966⁻1926) 346. BRUNNER, E. Dogmatik I, 276. SMITH, M., Tannaitic Parallels to the Gospels (Philadelphia 1968) 8bn3+; 8.2. LANGE, J., Das Erscheinen des Auferstandenen im Evangelium nach Matthäus (Würzburg 1973) 95, 140-43, 145, 171f, 185, 231, 314, 342, 346-49. WANKE, J., Die Emmauserzählung (Leipzig 1973) 35. GOULDER, M. D., Midrash and Lection in Matthew (London 1974) 78, 148, 154, 164, 352, 443. DUNN, J. D. G., Unity and Diversity in the New Testament (London 1977) 74. HEDRICK, C. W., "Resurrection: Radical Theology in the Gospel of Matthew", LThQ 14 (1979) 40-45.

18:21-35   JüLICHER, D. A. Die Gleichnisreden Jesu (1910) 302-14. WILKENS, J. Einführung in das Evangelium nach Matthäus II (1937) 62-66. VISCHER, W. Die evangelische Gemeindeordnung. Matthäus 16, 13 - 20, 28 (1946) 73-76. PIROT, J. Paraboles et Alégories Evangeliques (1949) 221-42. STECK, GPM 4 (1949/50) 284ff. MICHAELIS, D. W. Die Gleichnisse Jesu (1956) 189-95. DEHN, G. in: Herr, tue meine Lippen auf Bd. I (1957) Eichholz, G. (ed.) 311-15. FüRST, GPM (1960/61) 298ff. BIEDER, W., Die Verheissung der Taufe im Neuen Testament (Zürich 1966) 281f. DAVIES, W. D., The Sermon on the Mount (Cambridge 1966) 112-14. DOERNE, M. Er kommt auch noch heute (1966) 152-73. LINNEMANN, E. Gleichnisse Jesu (1969) 111ff., 173ff. BARCLAY, W. And Jesus Said (1970) 86-91. OTTO, G. Denken - um zu glauben (1970) 124-28. MEURER, S. Das Recht im Dienst der Versöhnung und des Friedens (1972) 59-62. *DEISS, L., "Le pardon entre frères. Mt 18, 21-35" AssS 55 (1974) 16-24. MANEK, J., . . . und brachte Frucht. Die Gleichnisse Jesu (Berlin 1977) 53-55.

18:21-22   MOORE, G. F. Judaism (1946) II 153n, 154. STAEHELIN, E. Die Verkündigung des Reiches Gottes in der Kirche Jesu Christi I (1951) 59. KNOX, W. L. The Sources of the Synoptic

Gospels II (1957) 100. STRECKER, G. Der Weg der Gerechtigkeit (1962) 392, 226l. HAHN, F. Christologische Hoheitstitel (1963) 83. PESCH, W. Matthäus der Seelsorger (1966) 45-46. STROBEL, A. Erkenntnis und Bekenntnis der Sünde in neutestamentlicher Zeit (1968) 44. DAVIES, W. D., The Sermon on the Mount (Cambridge 1966) 113. TALBERT, C. H., Literary Patterns, Theological Themes, and the Genre of Luke-Acts (Missoula 1974) 54. "Amt" in: TRE 2 (1978) 107. RIST, J. M., On the Independence of Matthew and Mark (Cambridge 1978) 70. SWIDLER, L., Biblical Affirmations of Woman (Philadelphia 1979) 286.

18:21 STONEHOUSE, N. B. The Witness of Matthew and Mark to Christ (1944) 175. FARRER, A. St Matthew and St Mark (1954) 122. KNOX, W. L. The Sources of the Synoptic Gospels II (1957) 133. BLAIR, E. P. Jesus in the Gospel of Matthew (1960) 100. STRECKER, G. Der Weg der Gerechtigkeit (1962) 198, 203, 2042. HAHN, F. Christologische Hoheitstitel (1963) 86. HUMMEl, R. Die Auseinandersetzung zwischen Kirche und Judentum im Matthäusevangelium (1963) 102. STROBLE, A. Erkenntnis und Bekenntnis der Sünde in neutestamentlicher Zeit (1968) 60.

18:22-35 "Barmherzigkeit" in: TRE 5 (1980) 227f.

18:22 BAUER, J. B. "Sermo Peccati. Hieronymus und das Nazaräerevangelium," BZ 4 (1, '60) 122-28. NICKELS, P. Targum and New Testament (1967) 20.

18:23ff STAEHELIN, E. Die Verkündigung des Reiches Gottes in der Kirche Jesu Christi I (1951) 60. KNOX, W. L. The Sources of the Synoptic Gospels II (1957) 135. HAHN, F. Das Verständnis der Mission im Neuen Testament (1965) 106. JüNGEL, E. Paulus und Jesus (1966) 102.

18:23-35 BRUNNER, E. Saat und Frucht (1946) 87-100. LOEWENICH, W. von, Luther als Ausleger der Synoptiker (1954) 165f. BLAIR, E. P. Jesus in the Gospel of Matthew (1960) 92. JEREMIAS, J. Die Gleichnisse Jesu (1962) 24, 26, 78, 136, 207-11. STRECKER, G. Der Weg der Gerechtigkeit (1962) 215. DEISS, L., "La parabole du débiteur impitoyable" AssS 76 (1964) 29-41. BISER, E. Die Gleichnisse Jesu (1965) 100ff. SCHNEIDER, G. Der Herr unser Gott (1965) 151-55. STUHLMACHER, P. Gerechtigkeit Gottes bei Paulus (1965) 246f. BREUKELMAN, F. H. "Eine Erklärung des Gleichnisses vom Schalksknecht," in: Parrhesia, Karl Barth-Festschrift (1966) 261-87. DAVIES, W. D., The Sermon on the Mount (Cambridge 1966) 113. WEISER, A. Die Knechtgleichnisse der synoptischen Evangelien (1971) in: Studien zum Alten und Neuen Testament Bd. XXIX, Hamp, P. & Schmid, J. (eds.) 75-

104. DIETZFELBINGER, C. "Das Gleichnis von der erlassenen Schuld. Eine theologische Untersuchung von Matthäus 18, 23-35," EvTh 32 (5, '72) 437-51. CROSSAN, J. D., in: G. MacRae (ed.) SBL Seminar Papers 2 (Montana 1973) 99f. GOLLWITZER, H., Veränderung im Diesseits (München 1973) 79. GOULDER, M. D., Midrash and Lection in Matthew (London 1974) 50, 54, 59-62, 65, 110, 402ff. WOJCIK, J., "The Two Kingdoms in Matthew's Gospel" in: Gros Louis et al. (eds.) Literary Interpretations of Biblical Narratives (Nashville 1974) 285-87. BERGMANN, W., Die zehn Gleichnisse vom Reich der Himmel (Lahr-Dinglingen 1976). *DEIDUN, T., "The Parable of the Unmerciful Servant (Mt 18:23-35)" BThB 6 (1976) 203-24. *KIPPER, J. B., "Quanto Valem os. 10.000 Talentos da Parábola (Mt 18, 23-35)" RCB 1 (1977) 83-89. "Autorität" in: TRE 5 (1980) 42. WEDER, H., Die Gleichnisse Jesu als Metaphern (Göttingen 1980 *(2)*) 210-18.

18:23-34   BRAUN, H. Jesus (1969) 139. DERRETT, J. D. M. Law in the New Testament (1970) 32-47. SCHüRMANN, H. Ursprung und Gestalt (1970) 281, 285, 286, 289, 290.

18:23-25   PERRIN, N., Jesus and the Language of the Kingdom (London 1976) 106, 150, 161.

18:23   STONEHOUSE, N. B. The Witness of Matthew and Mark to Christ (1944) 130. KNOX, W. L. The Sources of the Synoptic Gospels II (1957) 93. STRECKER, G. Der Weg der Gerechtigkeit (1962) 214. BLACK, M. An Aramaic Approach to the Gospels and Acts (1967) 129f.

18:24-28   SCHALIT, A. König Herodes (1969) 255.

18:24   STRECKER, G. Der Weg der Gerechtigkeit (1962) 20.

18:26   STONEHOUSE, N. B. The Witness of Matthew and Mark to Christ (1944) 179. BORNKAMM-BARTH-HELD, Ueberlieferung und Auslegung im Matthäus-Evangelium (1961) 217. HAHN, F. Christologische Hoheitstitel (1963) 86. METZGER, B. M., The Early Versions of the New Testament (Oxford 1977) 440.

18:27   HUMMEL, R. Die Auseinandersetzung zwischen Kirche und Judentum im Matthäusevangelium (1963) 102. "Barmherzigkeit" in: TRE 5 (1980) 227.

18:28   SMITH, M., Tannaitic Parallels to the Gospels (Philadelphia 1968) 6bn7+.

18:30   SIMPSON, R. T. Agreements of Matthew and Luke against Mark. NTS 12 (1965-66) 281f.

18:32-34   PESCH, W. Matthäus der Seelsorger (1966) 46-47.

18:32 HUMMEL, R. Die Auseinandersetzung zwischen Kirche und Judentum im Matthäusevangelium (1963) 102.

18:33-34 "Barmherzigkeit" in: TRE 5 (1980) 225.

18:33 FARRER, A. St Matthew and St Mark (1954) 168.

18:34 JANSSEN, E., "Testament Abrahams"in: W. G. Kümmel(ed.) Jüdische Schriften aus hellenistisch-römischer Zeit III (Gütersloh 1975) 233.

18:35 STONEHOUSE, N. B. The Witness of Matthew and Mark to Christ (1944) 175. STRECKER, G. Der Weg der Gerechtigkeit (1962) 149, 159, 215. HAHN, F. Christologische Hoheitstitel (1963) 321. PESCH, W. Matthäus der Seelsorger (1966) 47. STROBEL, A. Erkenntnis und Bekenntnis der Sünde in neutestamentlicher Zeit (1968) 45.

19-22 SELBY, D. J., Introduction to the New Testament (New York 1971) 139-43. ELLIS, P. F., Matthew: His Mind and His Message (Collegeville 1974) 72-77.

19 LEGRAND, L. "Matthew, Chapter 19, and the Three Vows," Review for Religious 23 (6, '64) 705-14. HILL, D., "A Note on Mt 19" ET 76 (1965) 133f. "Askese" in: TRE 4 (1979) 205.

19:1-25 FRANSE, I. "L'Avènement du Fils de l'Homme (Matthieu 19, 1-25, 46)," BVieC 48 ('62) 27-38.

19:1-20 SCHLATTER, D. A. Die Theologie des Neuen Testaments (1909) I 169-74.

19:1-15 GOULDER, M. D., Midrash and Lection in Matthew (London 1974) 18, 404f.

19:1-12 BORNKAMM-BARTH-HELD, Ueberlieferung und Auslegung im Matthäus-Evangelium (1961) 23, 88f., 147f., 224, 229f. SUHL, A. Die Funktion der alttestamentlichen Zitate und Anspielungen im Markusevangelium (1965). BRAUN, H. Qumran und NT II (1966) 103f., 162, 213, 225, 288, 292, 310. DAVIES, W. D., The Sermon on the Mount (Cambridge 1966) 109f. BALTENSWEILER, H. Die Ehe im Neuen Testament (1967) 82-112. HARRINGTON, W. J. "The New Testament and Divorce," IThQ 39 (2, '72) 178-87. McCAUGHEY, J. D. "Marriage and Divorce. A Response to Dr. Powers' Comments," Colloquium 5 (1, '72) 42-43. POWERS, B. W.

"Marriage and Divorce. The Dispute of Jesus with the Pharisees, and Its Inception," Colloquium 5 (1, '72) 34-41. SANDMEL, S., We Jews and Jesus (New York 1977) 136. RIST, J. M., On the Independence of Matthew and Mark (Cambridge 1978) 72-75. STAGG, E./F., Woman in the World of Jesus (Philadelphia 1978) 133-35, 216. McDONALD, J. I. H., Kerygma and Didache (Cambridge 1980) 50.

19:1-9   TRILLING, W. Das wahre Israel (1959) 178. HUMMEL, R. Die Auseinandersetzunge zwischen Kirche und Judentum im Matthäusevangelium (1963) 49-51, 53-56. SHANER, D. W. A Christian View of Divorce (1969) 46-50, 50ff. *DíEZ MACHO, A., "Cristo instituyó el matrimonio indisoluble" Sefarad 37 (1977) 261-91. SWIDLER, L., Biblical Affirmations of Woman (Philadelphia 1979) 231.

19:1-8   WAMBACQ, B. De libello repudii VD 33 (1955) 331-35.

19:1-2   STONEHOUSE, N. B. The Witness of Matthew and Mark to Christ (1944) 160. VISCHER, W. Die evangelische Gemeindeordnung. Matthäus 16, 13 - 20, 28 (1946) 77-78. EGGER, W., Frohbotschaft und Lehre (Frankfurt 1976) 34f. SANDMEL, S., We Jews and Jesus (New York 1977) 25.

19:1   TRILLING, W. Das wahre Israel (1959) 112. STONEHOUSE, N. B. The Witness of Matthew and Mark to Christ (1944) 131. HAHN, F. Christologische Hoheitstitel (1963) 400. BLAIR, E. P. Jesus in the Gospel of Matthew (1960) 132. FARRER, A. St Matthew and St Mark (1954) 179. STRECKER, G. Der Weg der Gerechtigkeit (1962) 29, 38₈, 92₁, 97, 130. BANKS, R., Jesus and the Law in the Synoptic Tradition (London 1975) 230f. KINGSBURY, J. D., Matthew: Structure, Christology, Kingdom (Philadelphia 1975) 23-25.

19:2-26:2 HAHN, F. Christologische Hoheitstitel (1963) 400.

19:2   COMBER, J. A., "The Verb Therapeuo in Matthew's Gospel", JBL 97 (1978) 431-34.

19:3-20:16 GAECHTER, P. Die literarische Kunst im Matthäus-Evangelium (1968) 12-13, 71-72.

19:3ff   STONEHOUSE, N. B. The Witness of Matthew and Mark to Christ (1944) 196, 203. MOORE, G. F. Judaism (1946) II 124. WREGE, H.-T. Die Ueberlieferungsgeschichte der Bergpredigt (1968) 52-53.

19:3-15   WILKENS, J. Einführung in das Evangelium nach Matthäus II (1937) 70-75.

19:3-12   BERGER, K. Die Gesetzesauslegung Jesu. Ihr historischer Hintergrund im Judentum und im Alten Testament I (1940) 570-74. VISCHER, W. Die evangelische Gemeindeordnung.

Matthäus 16, 13 - 20, 28 (1946) 78-88. DUPONT, J. Marriage et divorce dans l'Evangile. Matthieu 19, 3-12 et parallèles (1959). *BOISMARD, M.-E. RevBi 67 (3, '60) 463-64. *O'DOHERTY, E. CBQ 22 (3, '60) 343-45. ZIMMERMANN, H. "mē epi porneia (Mt 19, 9) ein literarisches Problem. Zur Komposition von Mt 19, 3-12," Catholica 16 (4, '62) 293-99. ISAKSSON, A. Marriage and Ministry in the New Temple. A Study with Special Reference to Mt. 19.3-12 and 1. Cor. 11.3-16 (Acta Seminarii Neotestamentici Upsaliensis XXIV 1965). FITZMYER, J. A. ThSt 27 (3, '66) 451-54. DELLING, G. ThLZ 92 (4, '67) 276-77. MASSINGBERD FORD J. JThS 18 (1, '67) 197-200. BALTENSWEILER, H. ThZ 23 (5, '67) 356-58. ZIMMERMANN, H. Neutestamentliche Methodenlehre (1967) 105-11, 231-34. FJäRSTEDT, B. "Fraga och svar i Matt. 19, 3-12" (Question and Answer in Matt. 19, 3-12), SEA 33 ('68) 118-40. FJäRSTEDT, B., "Frage och svar i Matt 19:3-12" SEA 33 (1968) 118-40. PHIPPS, W. E. Was Jesus Married? (1970) 79-91, 130, 133, 149, 165. *MOLONEY, F. J., "Matthew 19, 3-12 and Celibacy. A Redactional and Form Critical Study" Journal for the Study of the New Testament 2 (1979) 42-60.

19:3-10   SWIDLER, L., Biblical Affirmations of Woman (Philadelphia 1979) 174.

19:3-9   BLAIR, E. P. Jesus in the Gospel of Matthew (1960) 116. LEHMANN, M. R. "Gen 2:24 as the Basis for Divorce in Halakhah and New Testament," ZAW 72 (3, '60) 263-67. STRECKER, G. Der Weg der Gerechtigkeit (1962) 131f., 146. VACCARI, A. "O Divorcio nos Evangelhos," RCB 7 (25-26, '63) 60-79. BAUER, J. B., "De coniugali foedere quid edixerit Matthaeus?" VD 44 (1966) 74-78. BORNKAMM, G. "Ehescheidung und Wiederverheiratung im Neuen Testament," Geschichte und Glauben I (1968) 56-59. SAND, A. "Die Unzuchtsklausel in Mt. 31, 32 und 19, 3-9", MThZ 20 ('69) 118-29. DUNGAN, D. L. The Sayings of Jesus in the Churches of Paul (1971) 102-31. SAND, A., Das Gesetz und die Propheten (Regensburg 1974) 72-76. HOFFMANN, P./EID, V., Jesus von Nazareth und eine christliche Moral (Freiburg 1975) 111-13, 123-27. WESTERHOLM, S., Jesus and Scribal Authority (Lund 1978) 120-25. MEYER, B. F., The Aims of Jesus (London 1979) 139f.

19:3-8   SCHüRMANN, H., "Neutestamentliche Marginalien zur Frage nach der Institutionalität, Unauflösbarkeit und Sakramentalität der Ehe" in: Kirche und Bibel. Für Bischof E. Schick (Paderborn 1979) 412-15.

19:3-6   PLASTARAS, J. C. "Marriage in Sacred Scripture. Helps for a Nuptial Homily," HPR 67 (4, '67) 313-19.

19:3 STONEHOUSE, N. B. The Witness of Matthew and Mark to Christ (1944) 141, 160. BLAIR, E. P. Jesus in the Gospel of Matthew (1960) 100.

19:4 BLAIR, E. P. Jesus in the Gospel of Matthew (1960) 86. STRECKER, G. Der Weg der Gerechtigkeit (1962) 23, 614. GANSEWINKEL, A. van, "Ursprüngliche oder grundsäztliche Unauflösbarkeit der Ehe?" Diakonia 3 (2, '72) 88-93.

19:5 ELLIS, E. E. Paul's Use of the Old Testament (1957) 88, 97, 175, 185, 187. CONSIDINE, T. P. "Two in One Flesh. The Meaning in Sacred Scripture," ACR 39 (2, '62) 111-23. STRECKER, G. Der Weg der Gerechtigkeit (1962) 22. METZGER, B. M., The Early Versions of the New Testament (Oxford 1977) 34

19:6 BOHREN, R., Predigtlehre (München 1971) 322ff. "Agende" in: TRE 2 (1978) 9.

19:8f STONEHOUSE, N. B. The Witness of Matthew and Mark to Christ (1944) 205.

19:8 DAUBE, D. "Concessions to Sinfulness in Jewish Law," JJS 10 (1-2, '59) 1-13. STRECKER, G. Der Weg der Gerechtigkeit (1962) 1001, 146. BANKS, R., Jesus and the Law in the Synoptic Tradition (Cambridge 1975) 182f. "Bergpredigt" in: TRE 5 (1980) 622f.

19:9 VACCARI, A. "De matrimonio et divortio apud Matthaeum", Biblica 36 (1955) 149-51. *FAHY, T. "St Matthew, 19:9-Divorce or Separation?" IThQ 24 (3, '57) 173-74. STAUDINGER, J. Die Bergpredigt (1957) 284-88. FEGHALI, J., "A propos de l'incie de St Matthieu (V,32; XIX, 9)" L'Année Canonique VI (1958) 117-19. ZIMMERMANN, H. "me epi porneia (Mt 19,9) ein literarisches Problem. Zur Komposition von Mt. 19, 3-12", Catholica 16 (1962) 293-99. BYRON, B. "The Meaning of 'Except it be for Fornication'," ACR 40 (2, '63) 90-95. BAUER, J. B. "Die matthäische Ehescheidungsklausel (Mt 5, 32 und 19, 9)," BuLit 38 (2, '64-'65) 101-106. NOBER, P. VerbDom 45 (1, '67) 52-57. COINER, H. G. "Those 'Divorce and Remarriage' Passages (Mt 5, 32; 19,9; 1 Cor 7, 10-16), With Brief References to the Mark and Luke Passages", CThM 39 (1968) 367-84. MAHONEY, A., "A New Look at the Divorce Clauses in MT 5, 32 and 19, 9" CBQ 30 (1968) 29-38. MOINGT, J. "Le divorce 'pour motif d'impudicité' (Matthieu 5,32; 19,9)," RechSR 56 (3, '68) 337-84. GREEVEN, H. Ehe Nach dem Neuen Testament. NTS 15 (1968-69) 382ff. THOMPSON, T. L. "A Catholic View on Divorce," JES 6 (1, '69) 53-67. DERRETT, J. D. M. Law in the

New Testament (1970) 85 n.1, 367-88. OLSEN, N. V. The New Testament on Divorce (1971). BAUER, J. B., Scholia Biblica et Patristica (Graz 1972) 231. CROUZEL, H. "Le texte patristique de Matthieu v. 32 et xix. 9," NTS 18 (1, '72) 98-119. ERNST, J., Anfänge der Christologie (Stuttgart 1972) 150-52. NAUTIN, P., "Divorce et remarriage dans la tradition de l'église latine" RechSR 62 (1974) 7-54. DA SILVA, A. P., "Ainda uma teoria sobre Mt 5,32 e 19,9?" RCB 11 (1974) 112-19. BANKS, R., Jesus and the Law in the Synoptic Tradition (Cambridge 1975) 153f. VARGAS-MACHUCA, A., "Los casos de 'divorcio' admitidos por S.Mateo (5,32 y 19,9). Consecuencias para la teologia actual" EstEc 50 (1975) 5-54. METZGER, B. M., The Early Versions of the New Testament (Oxford 1977) 170. ZALESKI, J., "Elementy egzegezy patryszcnej we wspolczesnych interpretacjach tekstu Mt 5,32 czy 19:9" CoTh 47 (1977) 43-63. GELDARD, M., "Jesus' Teaching on Divorce: Thoughts on the Meaning of 'porneia' in Matthew 5:32 and 19:9" Churchman 92 (1978) 134-43. MANRIQUE, A., "Jesús de Nazaret ante el divorcio" Biblia y Fe 4 (1978) 33-46. WESTERHOLM, S., Jesus and Scribal Authority (Lund 1978) 117-20, 123-25. FURNISH, V. P., The Moral Teaching of Paul (Nashville 1979) 40. SCHüRMANN, H., "Neutestamentliche Marginalien zur Frage nach der Institutionalität, Unauflösbarkeit und Sakramentalität der Ehe" in: Kirche und Bibel. Für Bischof E. Schick (Paderborn 1979) 415-23. SWIDLER, L., Biblical Affirmations of Woman (Philadelphia 1979) 174f, 239, 259. BAUER, J. B., "Bemerkungen zu den matthäischen Unzuchtsklauseln (Mt 5,32; 19,9)" in: J. Zmijewski/E. Nellessen (eds.) Begegnung mit dem Wort. Für H. Zimmermann (Bonn 1980) 23-33.

19:10ff   BORNKAMM-BARTH-HELD, Ueberlieferung und Auslegung im Matthäus-Evangelium (^{2}1961) 90, 112.

19:10-12   HIRSCH, E. Frühgeschichte des Evangeliums (1941) 309-11. *WOLNIEWICZ, M. "Bezzenstwo dla Krolestwa Bozego"(De caelibatu pro regno Dei observando (Matth. 19:10-12), RBL 10 (1, '57) 23-34. CAUBET, J. "Superioridad de la virginidad sobre el matrimonio a la luz de los Evanglios. Renovacion de la doctrina del Tridentino," CultBib 18 (181, '61) 347-57. DAVIES, W. D., The Sermon on the Mount (Cambridge 1966) 109f. DANIEL, C. "Esséniens et Enunuques (Matthieu 19, 10-12)," RevQ 6 (3, '68) 353-90. ERNST, J., Anfänge der Christologie (Stuttgart 1972) 142-45. GALOT, J. "La motivation évangélique de célibat," Gregorianum 53 (4, '72) 731-58. *VAN CANGH, J.-M., "Fondement évangelique de la vie religieuse" NRTh 95 (1973) 635-47. NICOLAU, M.,

"Virginidad y continencia en la Sagrada Escritura" Manresa 47 (1975) 19-40. *STAGG, F., "Biblical Perspectives on the Single Person" RevEx 74 (!977) 5-19.

19:10-11 SANDMEL, S., We Jews and Jesus (New York 1977) 113.

19:10 GREEVEN, H. Ehe Nach dem Neuen Testament. NTS 15 (1968-69) 369ff. SWIDLER, L., Biblical Affirmations of Woman (Philadelphia 1979) 173.

19:11f OTOMO, Y. Nachfolge Jesu und Anfänge der Kirche im Neuen Testament (1970) 55f.

19:11-12 SASS, G. Ungereimtes bei Matthäus (1968) 34-36. BLINZLER, J., "Il testo più antico sul celibato" StPa 17 (1970) 121-37. BLINZLER, J., "Justinus Apol. I 15, 4 und Matthäus 19, 11-12" in: A. Descamps/A. de Halleux (eds.) Mélanges Bibliques en hommage au R. P. Béda Rigaux (Gembloux 1970) 45-55. SANFORD, J. A., The Kingdom Within (New York 1970) 170. SEGALLA, G. "Il testo più antico sul celebato: Mt. 19, 11-12," StPa 178 (1, '70) 121-37. RUDOLPH, K., Die Gnosis (Göttingen 1978) 264. STAGG, E./F., Woman in the World of Jesus (Philadelphia 1978) 135-37, 216.

19:11 HENNECKE, E. & SCHNEEMELCHER, W. Neutestamentliche Apokryphen (1964) I 258.

19:12ff STONEHOUSE, N. B. The Witness of Matthew and Mark to Christ (1944) 130. BAUER, W. "Matth. 19, 12 und die alten Schriften"in: Neutestamentliche Studien Georg Heinrici zu seinem 70. Geburtstag (1914) Deissmann, A. & Windisch, H. (eds.) 235-44. STAEHELIN, E. Die Verkündigung des Reiches Gottes in der Kirche Jesu Christi I (1951) 60, 203, 326. *BLINZLER, J. "Eisin eunouchoi. Zur Auslegung von Mt 19, 12," ZNW 28 (3-4, '57) 254-70. BETZ, H. D. Lukian von Samosata und das Neue Testament (1961) 75, 78. SCHRAGE, W. Die konkreten Einzelgebote in der paulinischen Paränese (1961) 242. STRECKER, G. Der Weg der Gerechtigkeit (1962) 363. BAUER, W. "Mt 19, 12 und die alten Christen," in: Aufsätze und Kleine Schriften (1967) Strecker, G. (ed.) 253-62. QUESNELL, Q. " 'Made Themselves Eunuchs for the Kingdom of Heaven' (Mt 19, 12)," CBQ 30 (3, '68) 335-58. GREEVEN, H. Ehe Nach dem Neuen Testament. NTS 15 (1968-1969) 372ff. BLINZLER, J. "Zur Ehe unfähig. . . Auslegung von Mt 19, 12", Aus der Welt und Umwelt des Neuen Testaments, Gesammelte Aufsätze I (1969) 20-40. JEREMIAS, J. Neutestamentliche Theologie I (1971) 40, 42, 100, 215.

19:12 TANNEHILL, R. C., The Sword of His Mouth (Missoula 1975) 134-40. *MARIN, F., "Un recurso obligado a la tradición presinóptica" EstBi 36 (1977) 205-16. *KODELL, J., "The Celibacy Logion in Matthew 19:12" BThB 8 (1978) 19-23. "Askese" in: TRE 4 (1979) 205. SWIDLER, L., Biblical Affirmations of Woman (Philadelphia 1979) 342. GERSTENBERGER, E. S.,/SCHRAGE, W., Frau und Mann (Stuttgart 1980) 143f.

19:13ff   STONEHOUSE, N. B. The Witness of Matthew and Mark to Christ (1944) 177.

19:13-22   BRAUN, H. Qumran und NT II (1966) 65, 71, 86, 94, 98, 110f., 288, 291.

19:13-15   VISCHER, W. Die evangelische Gemeindeordnung. Matthäus 16, 13 - 20, 28 (1946) 88-92. DAVIES, W. D., The Sermon on the Mount (Cambridge 1966) 111. BLINZLER, J. "Kind und Königreich Gottes (Mk 10, 14f)", Aus der Welt und Umwelt des Neuen Testaments, Gesammelte Aufsätze I (1969) 41-53. SCHRAMM, T. Der Markus-Stoff bei Lukas (1971) 141f. *CAVALLETTI, S., "Il bambino come parabola" EuD 25 (1972) 509-14. CRIBBS, F. L. in: G. MacRae (ed.) SBL Seminar Papers 2 (Montana 1973) 14f. WESTERMANN, C., Blessing. In the Bible and the Life of the Church (Philadelphia 1978) 83-85, 98-101.

19:14   SANFORD, J. A., The Kingdom Within (New York 1970) 107f.

19:16ff   SCHRAGE, W. Die konkreten Einzelgebote in der paulinischen Paränese (1961) 36. "Agrapha" in: TRE 2 (1978) 107.

19:16-30   WILKENS, J. Einführung in das Evangelium nach Matthäus II (1937) 76-85. VISCHER, W. Die evangelische Gemeindeordnung. Matthäus 16, 13 - 20, 28 (1946) 92-106. LOEWENICH, W. von, Luther als Ausleger der Synoptiker (1954) 224ff., 70f. BORNKAMM-BARTH-HELD, Ueberlieferung und Auslegung im Matthäus-Evangelium (1961) 26, 98ff., 224. ZIMMERLI, W. Gottes Offenbarung (1963) 316-24. CELADA, B., "Mateo 19:16-30 y la perfección cristiana" PaCl 50 (1971) 14-27. DRESCHER, H.-G., Nachfolge und Begegnung (Gütersloh 1972) 59-93. GOULDER, M. D., Midrash and Lection in Matthew (London 1974) 271-77, 405f. RIST, J. M., On the Independence of Matthew and Mark (Cambridge 1978) 57f.

19:16-29   FRANKEMöLLE, H., Jahwebund und Kirche Christi (Münster 1974) 292f.

19:16-26   KIIVIT, GPM (1964/65) 323ff. KLIJN, A. F. J. "The Question of the Rich Young Man in a Jewish-Christian Gospel," NovTest 8 (2-4, '66) 149-55. SCHMITZ, E. D. in: Hören und

Fragen Bd. 5 (1967) Eichholz, G. & Falkenroth, A. (eds.) 457ff.
SMART, J. D. The Quiet Revolution (1969) 85ff. LANGE, E.
(ed.) Predigtstudien für das Kirchenjahr 1970/71 (1970/71)
197-201. NIEBERGALL, A. GPM 3 (1971) 25, 379-89.
TRAUB, H. GPM 13/4 225-28. BRILL, S./CASPARY, H.-N.
in: P. Krusche (ed.) Predigtstudien V/2 (Stuttgart 1977) 189-96.

19:16-24 HENNECKE, E. & SCHNEEMELCHER, W.
Neutestamentliche Apokryphen (1964) I 77. *MACKRELL,
G. F., "The Rich Young Man" NB1 60 (1979) 84-89.

19:16-22 BERGER, K. Die Gesetzesauslegung Jesu (1940) 444-53.
DAVIES, W. D., The Sermon on the Mount (London 1966)
110f. LEGASSE, S. "L'Appel du riche", EFr 17 (41, '67) 30-37.
GAECHTER, P. Die literarische Kunst im Matthäus-
Evangelium (1968) 71-72. OTOMO, Y. Nachfolge Jesu und
Anfänge der Kirche im Neuen Testament (1970) 37-42, 126.
SANFORD, J. A., The Kingdom Within (New York 1970) 102-
105. CRIBBS, F. L. in: G. MacRae (ed.) SBL Seminar Papers 2
(Montana 1973) 15-20. BANKS, R., Jesus and the Law in the
Synoptic Tradition (Cambridge 1975) 243-45. COPE, O. L.,
Matthew. A Scribe Trained for the Kingdom of Heaven
(Washington 1976) 111-19. *BURCHILL, J. P., "Biblical Basis
of Religious life" Review of Religion 36 (1977) 900-17.

19:16-17 MOORE, G. F. Judaism (1946) I 395n, II 321. MASSAUX, E.
Influence de L'Evangile de saint Matthieu sur la littérature
chrétienne avant saint Irénée (1950) 485-87. SMITH, M.,
Tannaitic Parallels to the Gospels (Philadelphia 1968)
2bn113+. METZGER, B. M., The Early Versions of the New
Testament (Oxford 1977) 135f.

19:16 STONEHOUSE, N. B. The Witness of Matthew and Mark to
Christ (1944) 141. HAHN, F. Christologische Hoheitstitel
(1963) 76. NöTSCHER, F., Altorientalischer und
alttestamentlicher Auferstehungsglauben (Darmstadt
1970⁻1926) 221. METZGER, B. M., The Early Versions of the
New Testament (Oxford 1977) 437.

19:17-21 "Bergpredigt" in: TRE 5 (1980) 620.

19:17 STRECKER, G. Der Weg der Gerechtigkeit (1962) 164.
BRUNNER, A. " 'Einer nur ist der Gute' (Mt 19, 17)," GuL 38
(6, '65) 411-16. METZGER, B. M., The Early Versions of the
New Testament (Oxford 1977) 143, 178.

19:18f STRECKER, G. Der Weg der Gerechtigkeit (1962) 22, 1344.

19:19 SCHWEIZER, E. Gemeinde und Gemeinde-Ordnung im
Neuen Testament (1959) § 4b. BLAIR, E. P. Jesus in the Gospel
of Matthew (1960) 93. STRECKER, G. Der Weg der
Gerechtigkeit (1962) 222, 245, 137. SCHRAGE, W. Das

Verhältnis des Thomas-Evangeliums zur Synoptischen Tradition und zu den Koptischen Evangelienübersetzungen (1964) 70. LOHSE, E. and Others (eds.) Der Ruf Jesu und die Antwort der Gemeinde (1970) 61, 100f. BLOCH, R., "Midrash" in: W. S. Green (ed.) Approaches to Ancient Judaism (Missoula 1978) 49.

19:20ff SMITH, M., Clement of Alexandria and a secret Gospel of Mark (Cambridge 1973) 109, 137, 172f, 182, 274.

19:20 SCHALIT, A. König Herodes (1969) 592. WILLIAMS, J. A., A Conceptual History of Deuteronomism in the Old Testament, Judaism, and the New Testament (Ph.D.Diss. Southern Baptist Theological Seminary, Louisville 1976) 303f.

19:21 SACCHI, A. "'Se vuoi essere perfetto'(Mt. 19, 21): perfexione e vita cristiana," RivB 17 (3, '69) 313-25. STAEHELIN;, E. Die Verkündigung des Reiches Gottes in der Kirche Jesu Christi I (1951) 209, 326. TRILLING, W. Das wahre Israel(1959) 165ff. STRECKER, G. Der Weg der Gerechtigkeit (1962) 1412, 1421, 231. HUMMEL, R. Die Auseinandersetzung zwischen Kirche und Judentum im Matthäusevangelium (1963) 152, 156. ERNST, J., Anfänge der Christologie (Stuttgart 1972) 135f. THEISSEN, G., Soziologie der Jesusbewegung (München 1977) 23. "Basilius" in: TRE 5 (1980) 620.

19:22-23 HARTMAN, L., Testimonium Linguae (Lund 1963) 24ff.

19:22 KNOX, W. L. The Sources of the Synoptic Gospels II (1957) 57.

19:23ff STONEHOUSE, N. B. The Witness of Matthew and Mark to Christ (1944) 130. BORNKAMM-BARTH-HELD, Ueberlieferung und Auslegung im Matthäus-Evangelium (1961) 111.

19:23 DENK, J., "Camelus: 1.Kamel, 2. Schiffstau. (Matth 19, 23.)" ZNW 5 (1904) 256f. KNOX, W. L. The Sources of the Synoptic Gospels II (1957) 16. JüNGEL, E. Paulus und Jesus (1966) 238. METZGER, B. M., The Early Versions of the New Testament (Oxford 1977) 143.

19:24 CELADA, B., "Más acerca del camello y la aguja" Cultura Biblica 26 (1926) 157f. KNOX, W. L. The Sources of the Synoptic Gospels II (1957) 13. DELL'OCCA, E. C. "Camello por el ojo de una aguja," RevBi 25 (107-108, '63) 43-46. SANFORD, J. A., The Kingdom Within (New York 1970) 54f. BOERMA, C., Rich Man, Poor Man - and the Bible (London 1979) 82. KELBER, W. H., "Mark and Oral Tradition" Semeia 16 (1980) 25-27.

19:26 BRUNNER, E. Dogmatik I (1946) 269. JüNGEL, E. Paulus und Jesus (1966) 184.

19:27ff BORNKAMM-BARTH-HELD, Ueberlieferung und Auslegung im Matthäus-Evangelium (1961) 112, 224.

19:27-30 JüNGEL, E. Paulus und Jesus (1966) 164. BARCLAY, W. And Jesus Said (1970) 162-68. OTOMO, Y. Nachfolge Jesu und Anfänge der Kirche im Neuen Testament (1970) 57-60. SWIDLER, L., Biblical Affirmations of Woman (Philadelphia 1979) 232, 239, 259

19:27-29 SMITH, M., Tannaitic Parallels to the Gospels (Philadelphia 1968) 2bn65; 3bn24+,43. ERNST, J., Anfänge der Christologie (Stuttgart 1972) 134f.

19:27f STRECKER, G. Der Weg der Gerechtigkeit (1962) 230₄.

19:27 STRECKER, G. Der Weg der Gerechtigkeit (1962) 164₃, 198, 204₂. CLARK, K. W., "The Meaning of APA", The Gentile Bias and other Essays (Leiden 1980) 196.

19:28f KäSEMANN, E. Exegetische Versuche und Besinnungen (1964) II 92. KäSEMANN, E. New Testament Questions of Today (1969) 93.

19:28 VOLZ, P. Die Eschatologie der jüdischen Gemeinde (1934) 380, 405. STONEHOUSE, N. B. The Witness of Matthew and Mark to Christ (1944) 147, 176, 234. MOORE, G. F. Judaism (1946) II 307. STAEHELIN, E. Die Verkündigung des Reiches Gottes in der Kirche Jesu Christi I (1951) 60, 177, 237, 377. PARKER, P. The Gospel Before Mark (1953) 125-26. FARRER, A. St Matthew and St Mark (1954) 21. FLEW, R. N. Jesus and His Church (1956) 86. KNOX, W. L. The Sources of the Synoptic Gospels II (1957) 142. BORNKAMM-BARTH-HELD, Ueberlieferung und Auslegung im Matthäus-Evangelium (1961) 26, 262. SCHNEIDER, G., Neuschöpfung oder Wiederkehr (1961) 68-70. SCHULZ, A. Nachfolgen und Nachnahmen (1962) 119-23. SCHWEIZER, E. Erniedrigung und Erhöhung bei Jesus und seinen Nachfolgern (1962) § 3g. STRECKER, G. Der Weg der Gerechtigkeit (1962) 109, 162, 236, 238₃. CHARBEL, A. 'O conceito de 'palingenesia' ou regenraçáo em Mt. 19, 28," RCB 7 (23, '63) 13-17. DELLING, G. Die Taufe im Neuen Testament (1963) 98. HAHN, F. Christologische Hoheitstitel (1963) 38, 39. HUMMEL, R. Die Auseinandersetzung zwischen Kirche und Judentum im Matthäusevangelium (1963) 144. DUPONT, J. "Le logion des douze trônes (Mt 19, 28; Lc 22, 28-30)," Biblica 45 (3, '64) 355-92. HAHN, F. Das Verständnis der Mission im Neuen Testament (1965) 108. ROLOFF, J. Apostolat-Verkündigung-Kirche (1965) 148-50, 185f. BOUSSET, W. Die Religion des Judentums im Späthellenistischen Zeitalter (1966⁻1926) 234. BRAUN, H. Qumran und NT II (1966) 91, 94, 155, 270, 277, 327f. JüNGEL, E. Paulus und Jesus (1966) 239ff. KüNG, H.,

Die Kirche (Freiburg 1967) 74f, 413-15; ET: The Church (London 1967) 57, 59, 348-50. NICKELS, P. Targum and New Testament (1967) 20. HASLER, V. Amen (1969) 40. BORSCH, F. H. The Christian & Gnostic Son of Man (1970) 26-27. VöGTLE, A. Das Neue Testament und die Zukunft des Kosmos (1970) 29, 31, 34, 151-66, 188. JEREMIAS, J. Neutestamentliche Theologie I (1971) 199, 223, 225, 228, 248, 252f, 259, 261. BERKOUWER, G. C., The Return of Christ (Grand Rapids 1972) 223f., 304, 405. HOFFMANN, P. Studien zur Theologie der Logienquelle (1972) 5, 42, 150, 304. SCHULZ, S. Q Die Spruchquelle der Evangelisten (1972) 330-36. HAMERTON-KELLEY, R. G. Pre-Existence, Wisdom, and The Son of Man (1973) 42, 45, 46, 71, 81, 93. CAVALLIN, H. C. C., Life After Death I (Lund 1974) 4.6 n21; 4.4 nn8, 14. DAVIES, W. D., The Gospel and the Land (London 1974) 363-65. GOULDER, M. D., Midrash and Lection in Matthew (London 1974) 167, 185, 391, 405, 443f. LADD, G. E., A Theology of the New Testament (Grand Rapids 1974) 48, 109, 205, 628, 631. SCHMAHL, G., Die Zwölf im Markusevangelium (Trier 1974) 29-36. TALBERT, C. H., Literary Patterns, Theological Themes, and the Genre of Luke-Acts (Missoula 1974) 28. BROER, J., "Das Ringen der Gemeinde um Israel" in: R. Pesch/R. Schnackenburg (eds.) Jesus und der Menschensohn (Freiburg 1975) 148-65. CONZELMANN, H./LINDEMANN, A., Arbeitsbuch zum Neuen Testament (Tübingen 1975) 356. DUNN, J. D. G., Jesus and the Spirit (London 1975) 26, 36, 81, 160, 181. HOWARD V. P., Das Ego in den Synoptischen Evangelien (Marburg 1975) 176-83. THEISOHN, J., Der auserwählte Richter (Göttingen 1975) 79, 153ff, 156ff, 159ff, 162ff, 165f, 168ff, 173f, 178, 180, 182f, 199, 204, 210, 252-54. POLAG, A., Die Christologie der Logienquelle (Neukirchen-Vluyn 1977) 46, 49, 97. THEISSEN, G., Soziologie der Jesusbewegung (München 1977) 29. TRITES, A. A., The New Testament Concept of Witness (Cambridge 1977) 192f. "Amt" in: TRE 2 (1978) 512. TRILLING, W., "Die Entstehung des Zwölferkreises. Eine geschichtskritische Ueberlegung" in: R. Schnackenburg (ed.) Die Kirche des Anfangs. Für H. Schürmann (Freiburg 1978) 213-20.

19:29f   STAEHELIN, E. Die Verkündigung des Reiches Gottes in der Kirche Jesu Christi I (1951) 333.

19:29   STONEHOUSE, N. B. The Witness of Matthew and Mark to Christ (1944) 229. STAEHELIN, E. Die Verkündigung des Reiches Gottes in der Kirche Jesu Christi I (1951) 139. DELLIN, G. Die Zueignung des Heils in der Taufe (1961) 40,

43. STRECKER, G. Der Weg der Gerechtigkeit (1962) 151l, 162, 165₄. SCHREIBER, J. Theologie des Vertrauens (1967) 53, 68, 70, 85, 165-67, 216. MARXSEN, W. Mark the Evangelist (1969) 120, 124, 138, 142. NöTSCHER, F., Altorientalischer und alttestamentlicher Auferstehungsglaube (Darmstadt 1970⁻1926) 221. SANFORD, J. A., The Kingdom Within (New York 1970) 58f. VöGTLE, A. Das Neue Testament und die Zukunft des Kosmos (1970) 159, 163f. SWIDLER, L., Biblical Affirmations of Woman (Philadelphia 1979) 179, 257, 259, 279.

19:30-20:16 STOCKUM, T. C. Van, "Idiota cum euangelista Matthaeo luctans," NedThT 19 (1, '64) 15-21.

19:30 JüLICHER, D. A. Die Gleichnisreden Jesu (1910) 469-71. KNOX, W. L. The Sources of the Synoptic Gospels II (1957) 81. SCHRAGE, W. Das Verhältnis des Thomas-Evangeliums zur Synoptischen Tradition und zu den Koptischen Evangelienübersetzungen (1964) 32. JüNGEL, E. Paulus und Jesus (1966) 164. HOFFMANN, P./EID, V., Jesus von Nazareth und eine christliche Moral (Freiburg 1975) 201-208. EDWARDS, R. A., A Theology of Q (Philadelphia 1976) 130-32. METZGER, B. M., The Early Versions of the New Testament (Oxford 1977) 434.

19:32 HENNECKE, E. & SCHNEEMELCHER, W. Neutestamentliche Apokryphen (1964) II 323.

19:36 BONHOEFFER, D. Nachfolge (1950) 25ff.

19:46 FRANSEN, I. "L'Avénement du Fils de L'Homme (Matthieu 19, 1-25, 46)," BVieC 48 ('62) 27-38.

20:1ff STONEHOUSE, N. B. The Witness of Matthew and Mark to Christ (1944) 130. FINDLAY, J. A. Jesus and His Parables (1951) 51ff. ARVEDSON, T. "Nagra notiser till tva nytestamentliga perikoper" (Some Notes on Two NT Pericopes), SEA 21 ('56) 27-29. *GRYGLEWICZ, F. "The Gospel of the Overworked Workers," CBQ 19 (2, '57) 190-98. KNOX, W. L. The Sources of the Synoptic Gospels II (1957) 134-35. HAHN, F. Das Verständnis der Mission in Neuen Testament (1965) 106.

20:1-17 PIROT, J. Paraboles et Allégories Evangeliques (1949) 341-53.

20:1-16 JüLICHER, D. A. Die Gleichnisreden Jesu (1910) 459-71.
WILKENS, J. Einführung in das Evangelium nach Matthäus
II (1937) 88-89. MORGAN, G. C. The Parables and Metaphors
of Our Lord (1943) 112ff. STONEHOUSE, N. B. The Witness
of Matthew and Mark to Christ (1944) 157. VISCHER, W. Die
evangelishe Gemeindeordnung. Matthäus 16, 13 - 20, 28 (1946)
106-110. DODD, C. H. The Parables of the Kingdom (1948)
122f. NYGREN, A. Agape and Eros (1953) 86ff.
LOEWENICH, W. von, Luther als Ausleger der Synoptiker
(1954) 40ff. MICHAELIS, D. W. Die Gleichnisse Jesu (1956)
171-81. *DUPONT, J. "La parabole des ouvriers de la vigne
(Matthieu, XX, 1-16)," NRTh 79 (8, '57) 785-97. STECK, K. G.
in: Herr, tue meine Lippen auf Bd. I (1957) Eichholz, G. (ed.)
77-82. *MOUSON, J. "Explicatur parabola de operariis in
vineam missis (Mt. XX, 1-16)," CollMech 27 (6, '57) 611-15.
FUCHS, E. "Die der Theologie durch die historisch-kritische
Methode auferlegte Besinnung" EvTh 18/6 (1958) 256-61.
HUNTER, A. M. Interpreting the Parables (1960) 55ff.
BORNKAMM-BARTH-HELD, Ueberlieferung und
Auslegung im Matthäus-Evangelium (1961) 27, 112.
DUPLACY, J. "Le maître généreux et les ouvriers égoistes
(Matthieu 20, 1-16)," BVieC 44 ('62) 16-30. JEREMIAS, J. Die
Gleichnisse Jesu (1962) 29, 34, 37f., 78, 136-39. GALBIATI, E.
"Gli operai nella vigna (Matt. 20, 1-16)," BiOr 5 (1, '63) 22-29.
STRECKER, G. Der Weg der Gerechtigkeit (1963) 1653.
BLINZLER, J., "Gottes schenkende Güte" BuL 37 (1964) 229-
39. WENKER, W., "Alcane de Mt 20:1-16" RevBi 45 (1964)
355-92. BISER, E. Die Gleichnisse Jesu (1965) 83ff., 117.
DUPONT, J., "Les ouvriers de la vigne" AssS 22 (1965) 28-51.
FUCHS, D. E. "Das Wunder der Güte, Predigt über Mt. 20:1-
16" in Glaube und Erfahrung (1965) 471-79. ROLOFF, J.
Apostolat-Verkündigung-Kirche (1965) 111f.
STUHLMACHER, P. Gerechtigkeit Gottes bei Paulus (1965)
247f. BIEDER, W., Die Verheissung der Taufe (Zürich 1966)
282. JüNGEL, E. Paulus und Jesus (1966) 131, 160. MITTON,
C. L. "Expounding the Parables: VII. The Workers in the
Vineyard (Matthew 20:1-16)," ET 77 (10, '66) 307-11. WEBER,
O. Predigtmeditationen (1967) 130-33. LINNEMANN, E.
Gleichnisse Jesu (1969) 87ff., 157ff. BARCLAY, W. And Jesus
Said (1970) 162-68. LEHMANN, M. Synoptische
Quellenanalyse und die Frage nach dem historischen Jesus
(1970) 153. LOHSE, E. and Others (eds.) Der Ruf Jesu und die
Antwort der Gemeinde (1970) 89, 91, 157-78. ORBE, A. "San
Ireneo y la parabola de los obreros de la vina: Mt. 20, 1-16,"
EstEc 46 (1976, '71) 35-62. ORBE, A. "San Ireneo y la parabola
de los obreros de la vina: Mt. 20, 1-16. Parte segunda," EstEc 46

(177, '71) 183-206. MEURER, S. Das Recht im Dienst der Versöhnung und des Friedens (1972) 29-41. GEENSE, A. GPM 27/1 (1972/73) 107-15. *DERRETT, J. D. M., "Workers in the Vineyard: A Parable of Jesus" JJS 25 (1974) 64-91. *DUPONT, J., "Les ouvriers de la onzième heure. Mt 20, 1-16" AssS 56 (1974) 16-27. GOULDER, M. D., Midrash and Lection in Matthew (London 1974) 50, 54, 59f, 65, 99, 145, 407-11, 414. BERGMANN, W., Die zehn Gleichnisse vom Reich der Himmel (Lahr-Dinglingen 1976). *GLASSWELL, M. E., "The Parable of the Labourers in the Vineyard (Matthew 20, 1-16)" CV 19 (1976) 61-64. PERRIN, N., Jesus and the Language of the Kingdom (London 1976) 38, 96, 100, 116, 119, 129, 150-52, 154, 161, 163. FUNK, R. W., "The Narrative Parables: The Birth of a Language Tradition" in: J. Jervell/ W. A. Meeks (eds.) God's Christ and His People. Studies in Honor of N. A. Dahl (Oslo/New York 1977) 43-50. MANEK, J., . . . und brachte Frucht. Die Gleichnisse Jesu (Berlin 1977) 56-58. *RUSTON, R., "A Christian View of Justice" NB1 59 (1978) 344-58. *FEUILLET, A., "Les ouvriers envoyés à la vigne (Mt. XX, 1-16). Le service désintéressé et la gratuité de l'alliance" RThom 79 (1979) 5-24. TOLBERT, M. A., Perspectives on the Parables (Philadelphia 1979) 60. WEDER, H., Die Gleichnisse Jesu als Metaphern (Göttingen 1980 *(2)*) 218-30.

20:1-16a   WEBER, GPM 4 (1949/50) 69ff. BRAUN, GPM 9 (1954/55) 59ff. BENCKERT, GPM 15 (1960/61) 67ff. DOERNE, M. Er kommt auch noch heute (1961) 47-49. "Zu Suchen Seine Herrlichkeit" in Predigtgedanken aus Vergangenheit und Gegenwart Bd. 2 (1960) 171-205. EICHHOLZ, G. Gleichnisse der Evangelien (1971) 85-108. EICHHOLZ, G. Die Theologie des Paulus im Umriss (1972) 101f. HERMANN, W. & DOMAY, E. "Septuagesimae: Matthäus 20. 1-16a" in: Predigtstudien (1972/73) Lange, E. (ed.) 118-24.

20:1-15   PARKER, P. The Gospel Before Mark (1953) 17-18. BLAIR, E. P. Jesus in the Gospel of Matthew (1960) 92. FUCHS, E. "Bemerkungen zur Gleichnisauslegung", Zur Frage nach dem Historischen Jesus, Gesammelte Aufsätze II (1960) 136-42. SCHNEIDER, G. Der Herr unser Gott (1965) 142-46. BRAUN, H. Qumran und NT II (1966) 87, 93, 101, 153, 287. JüNGEL, E. Paulus und Jesus (1966) 164-69, 214. SMITH, M., Tannaitic Parallels to the Gospels (Philadelphia 1968) 3bn13+; 6bn2. BRAUN, H. Jesus (1969) 70f., 136. VON RAD, G. Predigten (1972) 71-76. GOLLWITZER,H., Veränderung im Diesseits (München 1973) 104. SCHUBERT, K., Jesus im Lichte der Religionsgeschichte des Judentums (Wien/München 1973) 125. SAND, A., Das Gesetz und die

Propheten (Regensburg 1974) 119f. GOPPELT, L., Theologie des Neuen Testaments I (Göttingen 1975) 174. *SPIES, O., "Die Arbeiter im Weinberg (Mt 20:1-15) in islamischer Ueberlieferung" ZNW 66 (1975) 279-83. "Amt" in: TRE 2 (1978) 512. HAUBECK, W., "Zum Verständnis der Parabel von den Arbeitern im Weinberg" in: W. Haubeck/M. Bachmann (eds.) Wort in der Zeit. Für K. H. Rengstorf (Leiden 1980) 95-107.

20:1-13 CROSSAN, J. D. in: G. MacRae (ed.) SBL Seminar Papers 2 (Montana 1973) 103f.

20:1-10 BOUSSET, W. Die Religion des Judentums im Späthellenistischen Zeitalter (1966⁻1926) 387.

20:1-6 MEYER, B. F., The Aims of Jesus (London 1979) 158-62.

20:1 STONEHOUSE, N. B. The Witness of Matthew and Mark to Christ (1944) 161. HAHN, F. Christologische Hoheitstitel (1963) 92. HUMMEL, R. Die Auseinandersetzung zwischen Kirche und Judentum im Matthäusevangelium (1963) 155.

20:3-5.7b MESSINA, G. "Parallelismi semitismi lezioni tendenziose nell'armonia Persiana", Biblica 30 (1949) 359.

20:4 *GLOVER, F. C., "Workers for the Vineyard" ET 86 (1975) 310-311.

20:6 STAEHELIN, E. Die Verkündigung des Reiches Gottes in der Kirche Jesu Christi I (1951) 277.

20:8-16 BAUER, J. B. "Gnadenlohn oder Tageslohn (Mt 20, 8-16)?" Biblica 42 (2, '61) 224-28. BAUER, J. B., Scholia Biblica et Patristica (Graz 1972) 62-66.

20:8 JEREMIAS, J. Die Gleichnisse Jesu (1962) 30-32.

20:9-13 PARKER, P. The Gospel Before Mark (1953) 136-37.

20:11ff STAEHELIN, E. Die Verkündigung des Reiches Gottes in der Kirche Jesu Christi I (1951) 238.

20:11 HAHN, F. Christologische Hoheitstitel (1963) 92. HUMMEl, R. Die Auseinandersetzung zwischen Kirche und Judentum im Matthäusevangelium (1963) 155.

20:12 HENNECKE, E. & SCHNEEMELCHER, W. Neutestamentliche Apokryphen (1964) II 333. NICKELS, P. Targum and New Testament (1967) 20.

20:13 BLACK, M., "Some Greek Words with 'Hebrew' Meanings in the Epistles and Apocalypse" in: J. R. McKay/J. F. Miller (eds.) Biblical Studies - Essays in Honor of W. Barclay (London 1976) 142.

20:15 KNOX, W. L. The Sources of the Synoptic Gospels II (1957) 28.

20:16-34 FARRER, A. St Matthew and St Mark (1954) 122.

20:16 ROBINSON, J. M. Kerygma und historischer Jesus (1960) 166. SUTCLIFFE, E. F. "Many Are Called But Few Are Chosen," IThQ 28 (2, '61) 126-31. JEREMIAS, J. Die Gleichnisse Jesu (1962) 30-33, 105, 109f., 137. SCHRAGE, W. Das Verhältnis des Thomas-Evangeliums zur Synoptischen Tradition und zu den Koptischen Evangelienübersetzungen (1964) 32. JüNGEL, E. Paulus und Jesus (1966) 164. SMITH, M., Tannaitic Parallels to the Gospels (Philadelphia 1968) 3bn18+. JEREMIAS, J. Neutestamentliche Theologie I (1971) 25f., 28, 30, 36. HOFFMANN, P./EID, V., Jesus von Nazareth und eine christliche Moral (Freiburg 1975) 201-208. METZGER, B. M., The Early Versions of the New Testament (Oxford 1977) 118. POLAG, A., Die Christologie der Logienquelle (Neukirchen/Vluyn 1977) 96. "Berufung" in: TRE 5 (1980) 687.

16a 118SASS, G. Ungereimtes bei Matthäus (1968) 37-38.

20:17-21:27 GAECHTER, P. Die literarische Kunst im Matthäus-Evangelium (1968) 31-32.

20:17-34 EWALD, H. Die drei ersten Evangelien (1850) 309ff. WILKENS, J. Einführung in das Evangelium nach Matthäus II (1937) 90-98.

20:17-28 VISCHER, W. Die evangelische Gemeindeordnung. Matthäus 16, 13 - 20, 28 (1946) 111-27. RUHTENBERG, R. *Durch Leiden zur Herrlichkeit," in: Die Passionstexte (1967) Freyd, F. (ed.) 146-54.

20:17-19 JüNGEL, E. Paulus und Jesus (1966) 164. SCHRAMM, T. Der Markus-Stoff bei Lukas (1971) 130-36. KINGSBURY, J. D., Matthew: Structure, Christology, Kingdom (Philadelphia 1975) 22-25.

20:17 STONEHOUSE, N. B. The Witness of Matthew and Mark to Christ (1944) 176, 177.

20:18-19 STONEHOUSE, N. B. The Witness of Matthew and Mark to Christ (1944) 172, 237. GILS, F. Jésus Prophète D'Aprè Les Evangiles Synoptiques (1957) 135-49. HOOKER, M. D. Jesus and the Servant (1959) 92-97. STRECKER, G. Der Weg der Gerechtigkeit (1962)181ᴣ. PATSCH, H. Abendmahl und historischer Jesus (1972) 185ff.

20:18 STONEHOUSE, N. B. The Witness of Matthew and Mark to Christ (1944) 251.

20:19 WILKENS, U. Die Missionsreden der Apostelgeschichte (1961) 131, 137-38, 143. STRECKER, G. Der Weg der Gerechtigkeit (1962) 30₆, 97ᴣ, 1044, 182. GüTTGEMANNS, E. Offene Frage zur Formgeschichte des Evangeliums (1970) 218, 222. O'NEILL, J. C., The Theology of Acts in its Historical

Setting (London 1970) 43f.n. WILCKENS, U., Die Missionsreden der Apostelgeschichte (Neukirchen 1974 *(3)*) 131, 137f, 143.

20:20-28   GOODSPEED, E. J. A Life of Jesus (1950) 158-60. CZEGLEDY, GPM (1964/65) 125ff. OKULI: Mt. 20, 20-28. CZEGLEDY, I. GPM (1965/1) 125-28. HAMEL, J. in Hören und Fragen Bd. 5 (1967) Eichholz, G. & Falkenroth, A. (eds.) 200ff. ITTEL, G. W. Jesus und die Jünger (1970) 94-95. LANGE, E. (ed.) Predigtstudien für das Kirchenjahr 1970/71 (1970/71) 153-58. GRöSSER, E. Göttinger Predigtmeditationen 25 (1/1971) 143-50. OKULI: Mt. 20:20-28. BRAUN, H. GPM 13/2, 75-80. OKULI: Mt. 20.20-28. WENDLAND, H. D. GPM 11/2, 91-95. HOWARD, V. P., Das Ego in den Synoptischen Evangelien (Marburg 1975) 97-107. GäRTNER, B./BARTELS, Chr. in: P. Krusche et al. (eds.) Predigtstudien V/1 (Stuttgart 1976/77) 148-54. HERBERT, K., in: GPM 31 (1976/77) 139-46. RIST, J. M., On the Independence of Matthew and Mark (Cambridge 1978) 76. STAGG, E./F., Woman in the World of Jesus (Philadelphia 1978) 216.

20:20-23   MOORE, G. F. Judaism (1946) II 309n. SWIDLER, L., Biblical Affirmations of Woman (Philadelphia 1979) 248.

20:20   STONEHOUSE, N. B. The Witness of Matthew and Mark to Christ (1944) 179. BORNKAMM-BARTH-HELD, Ueberlieferung und Auslegung im Matthäus-Evangelium (1961) 111, 113, 217. STRECKER, G. Der Weg der Gerechtigkeit (1962) 193₉. HAHN, F. Christologische Hoheitstitel (1963) 86.

20:21   VOLZ, P. Die Eschatologie der jüdischen Gemeinde (1934) 405. STONEHOUSE, N. B. The Witness of Matthew and Mark to Christ (1944) 228, 234. STRECKER, G. Der Weg der Gerechtigkeit (1962) 166₇, 211₅. NICKELS, P. Targum and New Testament (1967) 20. LANGE, J., Das Erscheinen des Auferstandenen im Evangelium nach Matthäus (Würzburg 1973) 185-87, 213f.

20:22-23   TRILLING, W. Das wahre Israel (1959) 19f. STRECKER, G. Der Weg der Gerechtigkeit (1962) 216. NICKELS, P. Targum and New Testament (1967) 21. METZGER, B. M., The Early Versions of the New Testament (Oxford 1977) 40.

20:23   STONEHOUSE, N. B. The Witness of Matthew and Mark to Christ (1944) 234. BLAIR, E. P. Jesus in the Gospel of Matthew (1960) 58. STRECKER, G. Der Weg der Gerechtigkeit (1962) 162. HAHN, F. Christologische Hoheitstitel (1963) 81, 86, 321.

20:24   STRECKER, G. Der Weg der Gerechtigkeit (1962) 194₃.

20:25-28   JEREMIAS, J. Abba; Studien zur neutestamentlichen Theologie und Zeitgeschichte (1966) 224-27. HOFFMANN, P./EID, V., Jesus von Nazareth und eine christliche Moral: (Freiburg 1975) 188, 190-200. ARENS, E., The HΔΘON-Sayings in the Synoptic Tradition (Fribourg 1976) 117-61.

20:25-26   KäSEMANN, E. Exegetische Versuche und Besinnungen (1964) I 109. SCHILLEBEECKX, E., Die Auferstehung Jesu als Grund der Erlösung (Basel 1979) 71.

20:25   CLARK, K. W., "The Meaning of (KATA) KYPIEYEIN", The Gentile Bias and Other Essays (Leiden 1980) 207-12.

20:27   SCHRAGE, W. Die konkreten Einzelgebote in der paulinischen Paränese (1961) 243.

20:28   NESTLE, E. Einführung in das Griechische Neue Testament (1909) 236f. VOLZ, P. Die Eschatologie der jüdischen Gemeinde (1934) 14. WINDISCH, H. The Meaning of the Sermon on the Mount (1937) 128ff., 170. STONEHOUSE, N. B. The Witness of Matthew and Mark to Christ (1944) 237, 251. MORRIS, L. The Apostolic Preaching of the Cross (1955) 26ff. STRECKER, G. Der Weg der Gerechtigkeit (1962) 134₆, 181, 183. HOOKER, M.D. Jesus and the Servant (1959) 74-79. HAHN, F. Christologische Hoheitstitel (1963) 45. HUMMEL, R. Die Auseinandersetzung zwischen Kirche und Judentum im Matthäusevangelium (1963) 101. DUNKERLEY, R. "The Etiquette of the Kingdom," LondQuart HolRev 33 (2, '64) 151-53. KäSEMANN, E. Exegetische Versuche und Besinnungen (1964) II 96. BOUSSET, W. Die Religion des Judentums in Späthellenistischen Zeitalter (1966⁻1926) 198. JEREMIAS, J. Abba; Studien zur neutestamentlichen Theologie und Zeitgeschichte (1966) 216-29. KäSEMANN, E. New Testament Questions of Today (1969) 97. JEREMIAS, J. New Testament Theology I (1971) 292. JEREMIAS, J. Neutestamentliche Theologie I (1971) 177f. PATSCH, H. Abendmahl und historischer Jesus (1972) 170ff. BRUNNER, E. Dogmatik I, 196, 220, 305; II 330, 335, 414. CAVALLIN, H. C. C., Life After Death I (Lund 1974) 4.3 n.11.METZGER, B. M., The Early Versions of the New Testament (Oxford 1977) 457. "Agrapha" in: TRE 2 (1978) 104.

20:29-28:28   DAVIS, W. H. Davis' notes on Matthew (1962) 80-108.

20:29-23:39   RIDDERBOS, H. Matthew's Witness to Jesus Christ (1958) 67-72.

20:29-34   BORNKAMM-BARTH-HELD, Ueberlieferung und Auslegung im Matthäus-Evangelium (1961) 156, 168, 198, 202, 207ff., 212ff., 219, 221ff., 227, 267ff., 286. STRECKER, G. Der

Weg der Gerechtigkeit (1962) 392, 1994. GIBBS, J. M. Purpose and Pattern in Matthew's use of the title "Son of David." NTS 10 (1963-64) 459f. HODGES, Z. C. "The Blind Men at Jericho," BiblSa 122 (488, '65) 319-30. BURGER, C. Jesus als Davidssohn (1970) 72-74. FUCHS, A. Sprachliche Untersuchungen zu Matthäus und Lukas (1971) 45-170. SCHRAMM, T. Der Markus-Stoff bei Lukas (1971) 143-45. RIST, J. M., On the Independence of Matthew and Mark (Cambridge 1978) 76f.

20:29   STONEHOUSE, N. B. The Witness of Matthew and Mark to Christ (1944) 160, 163, 177. FARRER, A. St Matthew and St Mark (1954) 185.

20:30-31   MOORE, G. F. Judaism (1946) II 329n. BLAIR, E. P. Jesus in the Gospel of Matthew (1960) 56. STRECKER, G. Der Weg der Gerechtigkeit (1962) 1203, 1246. HAHN, F. Christologische Hoheitstitel (1963) 86, 245, 263. "Barmherzigkeit" in: TRE 5 (1980) 225.

20:30   STONEHOUSE, N. B. The Witness of Matthew and Mark to Christ (1944) 223. FARRER, A. St Matthew and St Mark (1954) 121, 124. WALKER, N. "The Alleged Matthaean Errata", NTS 9 (1962/63) 394. HUMMEL, R. Die Auseinandersetzung zwischen Kirche und Judentum im Matthäusevangelium (1963) 116.

20:31f   HUMMEL, R. Die Auseinandersetzung zwischen Kirche und Judentum im Matthäusevangelium (1963) 116, 118, 120.

20:34   STONEHOUSE, N. B. The Witness of Matthew and Mark to Christ (1944) 220. BORNKAMM-BARTH-HELD, Ueberlieferung und Auslegung im Matthäus-Evangelium (1961) 198, 209f., 211, 226, 246, 251. PETZKE, G. Die Traditionen über Apollonius von Tyana und das Neue Testament (1970) 171, 179. "Barmherzigkeit" in: TRE 5 (1980) 227.

21:1-28:20   KüMMEL, W. G. Einleitung in das Neue Testament (1973) 77f.

21-25   SCHWEIZER, E., "Matthäus 21-25" in: P. Hoffmann (ed.) Orientierung an Jesus. Für J. Schmid (Freiburg 1973) 364-71. SCHWEIZER, E., Matthäus und seine Gemeinde (Stuttgart 1974) I.3.1, I.3.6, VII. GARLAND, D. E., The Intention of

Matthew 23 (Leiden 1979) 30-32. CLARK, K. W., "The Gentile Bias in Matthew", in: The Gentile Bias and other Essays (Leiden 1980) 2f.

21 RENDALL, R. "Quotation in Scripture as an Index of Wider Reference," EQ 36 (4, '64) 214-21.

21:1-46 WILKENS, J. Einführung in das Evangelium nach Matthäus II (1937) 191-94.

21:1-23.39. WREGE, H.-T. Die Ueberlieferungsgeschichte der Bergpredigt (1968) 54-57.

21:1-22 EWALD,H. Die drei ersten Evangelien (1850) 312ff. STONEHOUSE, N. B. The Witness of Matthew and Mark to Christ (1944) 158ff.

21:1-17 DUPONT, J. "L'entrée de Jésus à Jérusalem dans le rècit de saint Matthieu (XXI, 1-17)," LumVieSupp 48 ('60) 1-8. TRILLING, W. "Der Einzug in Jerusalem Mt 21, 1-17" in: Neutestamentliche Aufsätze (1963) Blinzler, Kuss, Mussner (eds.) 303ff. DUPONT, J., "L'entrée messianique in Scripture" EQ 36 (1964) 214-21. ZARRELLA, P. "L'entrata di Gesu in Gerusalemme nella redazione di Matteo (21, 1-17)," ScuC 98 (2, '70) 89-112. CASALIS, G. GPM 27/1 (1972/73) 8-16. WEISS, R. & BARTH, F. K. "Erster Advent: Matthäus 21, 1-17", in: Predigtstudien (1972/73) Lange, E. (ed.) 16-22.

21:1-16 BURGER, C. Jesus als Davidssohn (1970) 81-87.

21:1-13 MOORE,G. F. Judaism (1946) II 337.

21:1-11 WILKENS, J. Einführung in das Evangelium nach Matthäus II (1937) 99-102. M'NEILE, A. H. The Gospel According to St Matthew (1955) 297f. HUMMEL, R. Die Auseinandersetzung zwischen Kirche und Judentum im Matthäusevangelium (1963) 138f. JOHNSON, S. L., "The Triumphal Entry of Christ" BiblSa 495 (1967) 218-29. KRATZ, R., Auferweckung als Befreiung (Stuttgart 1973) 47-50. SCHNIDER, F., Jesus der Prophet (Freiburg 1973) 102ff, 236. *BARTNICKI, R., "Das Zitat von Zach IX, 9-10 und die Tiere im Bericht von Matthäus über den Einzug Jesu in Jerusalem (Mt XXI, 1-11)" NovT 18 (1976) 161-66. *BARTNICKI, R., "Tekst Za 9, 9-10 w perykopach Mt 21, 1-11 i J 12, 12-19" SThV 14 (1976) 47-66.

22:1-10 KINGSBURY, J. D., Matthew: Structure, Christology, Kingdom (Philadelphia 1975) 70-72.

21:1-9 IWAND, GPM 4 (1949/50) 6ff. LEIVESTAD, R. Christ the Conqueror (1954) 34ff. LOEWENICH, W. von, Luther als Ausleger der Synoptiker (1954) 17f. FRIEDRICH, GPM 9 (1954/55) 2ff. EICHHOLZ, G. (ed.) Herr, tue meine Lippen auf Bd. 1 (1957) 1-7, 115-21. SOUCEK, GPM (1960/61) 3ff.

BLENKINSOPP, J. "The Hidden Messiah and His Entry into Jerusalem," Scripture 13 (22, '61) 51-56; (23, '61) 81-88. BLENKINSOPP, J. "The Oracle of Judah and the Messianic Entry," JBL 80 (1, '61) 55-64. BORNKAMM-BARTH-HELD, Ueberlieferung und Auslegung im Matthäus-Evangelium (1961) 30f., 121f., 220. DOERNE, M. Er kommt auch noch heute (1961) 10-12. "Sehet, welch ein Mensch" Predigtgedanken aus Vergangenheit und Gegenwart Bd. 3 (1961) 116-23. STRECKER, G. Der Weg der Gerechtigkeit (1962) 72ff. 794. IWAND,H. J. Predigt-Meditationen (1964) 197-202. SCHILDENBERGER, J., "Der Einzug des Königs in seine Stadt" Am Tisch des Wortes 9 (1965) 19-26. LUTHER, M. Predigten über die Christus-Botschaft 1966) 49-54. MASTIN, B. A. "The Date of the Triumphal Entry," NTS 16 (1, '69) 76-82. SCHRAMM, T. Der Markus-Stoff bei Lukas (1971) 145-49. GOPPELT, L., Theologie des Neuen Testaments II (Göttingen 1976) 549. *BARTNICKI, R., "Il carattere messianico delle pericopi di Marco e Matteo sull'ingresso di Gesù in Gerusaleme" RivBi 25 (1977) 5-27. KLEIN, G./Sperl, A. in: P. Krusche (ed.) Predigtstudien für das Kirchenjahr 1978/79 I/2 (Stuttgart 1978) 23-29. RIST, J. M., On the Independence of Matthew and Mark (Cambridge 1978) 77-81. MEYER, B. F., The Aims of Jesus (London 1979) 168-70.

21:1-7 WALKER, N. "The Alleged Matthaean Errata," NTS 9 (1962/63) 394.

21:1-3 GOODSPEED, E. J. A Life of Jesus (1950) 160-64.

21:1 STONEHOUSE, N. B. The Witness of Matthew and Mark to Christ (1944) 141, 160.

21:2-7 BLOCH, R., "Midrash" in: W. S. Green (ed.) Approaches to Ancient Judaism (Missoula 1978) 48.

21:3 STONEHOUSE, N. B. The Witness of Matthew and Mark to Christ (1944) 255. HAHN, F. Christologische Hoheitstitel (1963) 85.

21:4f STONEHOUSE, N. B. The Witness of Matthew and Mark to Christ (1944) 185, 191. KNOX, W. L. The Sources of the Synoptic Gospels II (1957) 126f. BLAIR, E. P. Jesus in the Gospel of Matthew (1960) 90. HAHN, F. Christologische Hoheitstitel (1963) 274. HUMMEL, R. Die Auseindersetzung zwischen Kirche und Judentum im Matthäusevangelium (1963) 131, 134.

21:4 BLAIR, E. P. Jesus in the Gospel of Matthew (1960) 56. STRECKER, G. Der Weg der Gerechtigkeit (1962) 50, 56, 71␣. METZGER, B.M., The Early Versions of the New Testament

(Oxford 1977) 457

21:5ff "Apokalyptik" in: TRE 3 (1978) 254.

21:5.7 FRENZ, A. "Mt XXI 5.7," NovTest 13 (4, '71) 259-60.

21:5 BLAIR, E. P. Jesus in the Gospel of Matthew (1960) 39. STRECKER, G. Der Weg der Gerechtigkeit (1962) 18, 49₂, 55₇, 72, 83, 174. HAHN, F. Christologische Hoheitstitel (1963) 173, 187, 226. HUMMEL, R. Die Auseinandersetzung zwischen Kirche und Judentum im Matthäusevangelium (1963) 114. BRAUN, H. Qumran und NT II (1966) 267, 304. METZGER, B. M. "Explicit references in the works of Origen to variant readings in New Testament manuscripts", Historical and Literary Studies (1966) 93. ROTHFUCHS, W. Die Erfüllungszitate des Matthäus-Evangeliums (1969) 80-83. KüMMEL, W. G. Einleitung in das Neue Testament (1973) 81f. FRANKEMöLLE, H., Jahwebund und Kirche Christi (Münster 1974) 167, 170, 187, 245, 313. GOULDER, M. D., Midrash and Lection in Matthew (London 1974) 15, 22f, 128. METZGER, B. M., The Early Versions of the New Testament (Oxford 1977) 97. STAGG, E./F., Woman in the World of Jesus (Philadelphia 1978) 217.

21:7ff STAEHELIN, E. Die Verkündigung des Reiches Gottes in der Kirche Jesu Christi I (1951) 328.

21:7 PARKER, P. The Gospel Before Mark (1953) 182-83.

21:8-10 SWIDLER, L., Biblical Affirmations of Woman (Philadelphia 1979) 287.

21:8f STONEHOUSE, N. B. The Witness of Matthew and Mark to Christ (1944) 177. HUMMEL, R. Die Auseinandersetzung zwischen Kirche und Judentum im Matthäusevangelium (1963) 138.

21:9ff HUMMEL, R. Die Auseinandersetzung zwischen Kirche und Judentum im Matthäusevangelium (1963) 118.

21:9f GIBBS, J. M. Purpose and Pattern in Matthew's use of the title "Son of David." NTS 10 (1963/64) 446f.

21:9 STONEHOUSE, N. B. The Witness of Matthew and Mark to Christ (1944) 171, 224, 229. STAEHELIN, E. Die Verkündigung des Reiches Gottes in der Kirche Jesu Christi I (1951) 245, 328. BLAIR, E. P. Jesus in the Gospel of Matthew (1960) 56. DELLING, D. Die Zueignung des Heils in der Taufe (1961) 45. STRECKER, G. Der Weg der Gerechtigkeit (1962) 21₃, 23, 75, 114, 119. HAHN, F. Christologische Hoheitstitel (1963) 245, 402. HUMMEL, R. Die Auseinandersetzung zwischen Kirche und Judentum im Matthäusevangelium (1963) 116, 119, 120. GIBBS, J. M. Purpose and Pattern in Matthew's

use of the title "Son of David." NTS 10 (1963-64) 449f.
NICKELS, P. Targum and New Testament (1967) 21. LOHSE,
E., Die Einheit des Neuen Testaments (Göttingen 1973) 104,
108f. GOPPELT, L., Theologie des Neuen Testaments I
(Göttingen 1975) 215f. KINGSBURY, J. D., Matthew:
Structure, Christology, Kingdom (Philadelphia 1975) 99-102.

21:10-46 HAHN, F. Das Verständnis der Mission im Neuen Testament
(1965) 111.

21:10-17 HUMMEL, R. Die Auseinandersetzung zwischen Kirche und
Judentum im Matthäusevangelium (1963) 119. GOULDER,
M. D., Midrash and Lection in Matthew (London 1974) 412f.

21:10-11 BLAIR, E. P. Jesus in the Gospel of Matthew (1960) 101.

21:10 KRATZ, R., Auferweckung als Befreiung (Stuttgart 1973) 38,
47, 50, 52, 55f.

21:11 STRECKER, G. Der Weg der Gerechtigkeit (1962) 623, 651,2,
107. HAHN, F. Christologische Hoheitstitel (1963) 401.
BRUNNER, E. Dogmatik II, 381.

12:12ff HUMMEL, R. Die Auseinandersetzung zwischen Kirche und
Judentum im Matthäusevangelium (1963) 139. "Apokalyptik"
in: TRE 3 (1978) 254.

21:12-22 WILKENS, J. Einführung in das Evangelium nach Matthäus
II (1937) 103-11.

21:12-17 EPPSTEIN, V. "The Historicity of the Gospel Account of the
Cleansing of the Temple," ZNW 55 (1-2, '64) 42-58.
HAMILTON, N. Q. "Temple Cleansing and Temple Bank,"
JBL 83 (4, '64) 365-72. TROCME, E. "L'expulsion des
marchands du Temple," NTS 15 (1, '68) 1-22.

21:12-16 STRECKER, G. Der Weg der Gerechtigkeit (1962) 109f.
BRAUN, H. GPM 11/2, 134-36. TROCME, E. "Jésus-Christ
et le Temple: éloge d'un naif," RSPhTh 44 (3, '64) 245-51.
BRAUN, H. Qumran und NT II (1966) 16, 101f., 106, 157, 183,
221, 262, 271, 288, 293, 295. MEYER, B. F., The Aims of Jesus
(London 1979) 168-70.

21:12-13. SCHIDER, F. & STENGER, W. Johannes und die Synoptiker
23-27 (1971) 26-53.

21:12-13 MEYER, B. F., The Aims of Jesus (London 1979) 197-202.

21:12f MASSAUX, E. Influence de l'Evangile de saint Matthieu sur la
littérature chrétienne avant saint Irénée (1950) 510-12.
LEIVESTAD, R. Christ the Conqueror (1954) 34ff. M'NEILE,
A. H. The Gospel According to St Matthew (1955) 299f.
STRECKER, G. Der Weg der Gerechtigkeit (1962) 93.
PATSCH, H. Abendmahl und historischer Jesus (1972) 43f.

21:12 WALKER, N. "The Alleged Matthaean Errata," NTS 9 (1962/63) 393f. COLELLA, P. "Cambiamonete," RivB 19 (4, '71) 429-30.

21:13 STRECKER, G. Der Weg der Gerechtigkeit (1962) 22. HUMMEL, R. Die Auseinandersetzung zwischen Kirche und Judentum im Matthäusevangelium (1963) 95f., 107.

21:14-17 HUMMEL, R. Die Auseinandersetzung zwischen Kirche und Judentum im Matthäusevangelium (1963) 96f., 139. DOBIAS, F. M. GPM 19 (1965) 193-200. HARDER, G. in: Hören und Fragen Bd. 5 (1967) Eichholz, G. & Falkenroth, A. (eds.) 291ff. LANGE, E. (ed.) Predigtstudien für das Kirchenjahr 1970/71 (1970) 72-77. SCHWEIZER, E. GPM 25 (1971) 217-21. STECK, K. G. GPM 13/2, 122-27. SCHWEIZER, E., Matthäus und seine Gemeinde (Stuttgart 1974) IX, IX.1.1. LOHSE, E. in: GPM 31 (1976-77) 211-17. TONKS, H. and HOLLENWEGER, W. J., in: P. Krusche et al. (eds.) Predigtstudien V/2 (Stuttgart 1977) 47-51.

21:14-16 PARKER, P. The Gospel Before Mark (1953) 18-19. BORNKAMM-BARTH-HELD, Ueberlieferung und Auslegung im Matthäus-Evangelium (1961) 122, 235, 269. HUMMEL, R. Die Auseinandersetzung zwischen Kirche und Judentum im Matthäusevangelium (1963) 119f.

21:14f STRECKER, G. Der Weg der Gerechtigkeit (1962) 191.

21:14 GäRTNER, B. The Temple and the Community in Qumran and the New Testament (1965) 32, 111. KLINZING, G. Die Umdeutung des Kultus in der Qumrangemeinde und im Neuen Testament (1971) 209-10. EGGER, W., Frohbotschaft und Lehre (Frankfurt 1976) 34-36. COMBER, J. A., "The Verb Therapeuo in Matthew's Gospel" JBL 97 (1978) 431-34.

21:15f BOUSSET, W. Die Religion des Judentums im Späthellenistischen Zeitalter (1966⁻1926) 187.

21:15 STONEHOUSE, N. B. The Witness of Matthew and Mark to Christ (1944) 177, 224. BLAIR, E. P. Jesus in the Gospel of Matthew (1960) 56. RUDOLPH, K. Die Mandäer II (1961) 210, 3. STRECKER, G. Der Weg der Gerechtigkeit (1962) 213, 119, 175, 176l. HAHN, F. Christologische Hoheitstitel (1963) 245. HUMMEL, R. Die Auseinandersetzung zwischen Kirche und Judentum im Matthäusevangelium (1963) 116, 124. GOPPELT, L., Theologie des Neuen Testaments I (Göttingen 1975) 195, 215f.

21:16 LINDARS, B. New Testament Apologetic (1961) 50, 167-69, 172, 257, 264. STRECKER, G. Der Weg der Gerechtigkeit (1962) 25, 713. MOLONEY, F. J., "The Targum on Ps. 8 and the New Testament" Salesianum 37 (1975) 326-36.

21:18ff   "Apokalyptik" in: TRE 3 (1978) 254.

21:18-22   JüLICHER, D. A. Die Gleichnisreden Jesu (1910) 444-48. MORGAN, G. C. The Parables and Metaphors of Our Lord (1943) 116ff. STONEHOUSE, N. B. The Witness of Matthew and Mark to Christ (1944) 157. BORNKAMM-BARTH-HELD, Ueberlieferung und Auslegung im Matthäus-Evangelium (1961) 105, 232, 276ff. BARTSCH, H.-W. "Die 'Verfluchung' des Feigenbaums," ZNW 53 (3-4, '62) 256-60. STRECKER, G. Der Weg der Gerechtigkeit (1962) 93, 176.

21:18-20   DERRETT, J. D. M., "Figtrees in the New Testament" HeyJ 14 (1973) 249-65.

21:18-19   SAND, A., Das Gesetz und die Propheten (Regensburg 1974) 112-14.

21:19f   KNOX, W. L. The Sources of the Synoptic Gospels II (1957) 115. SASS, G. Ungereimtes bei Matthäus (1968) 39-41.

21:19   STRECKER, G. Der Weg der Gerechtigkeit (1962) 1217.16.

21:20   STRECKER, G. Der Weg der Gerechtigkeit (1962) 205.

21:21-22   BLAIR, E. P. Jesus in the Gospel of Matthew (1960) 91.

21:21   KNOX, W. L. The Sources of the Synoptic Gospels II (1957) 103. SCHRAGE, W. Die konkreten Einzelgebote in der paulinischen Paränese (1961) 243. STRECKER, G. Der Weg der Gerechtigkeit (1962) 234. SCHRAGE, W. Das Verhältnis des Thomas-Evangelium zur Synoptischen Tradition und zu den Koptischen Evangelienübersetzungen (1964) 116. THEYSSEN, G. W. "Unbelief" in the New Testament (1965) 18f. HASLER, V. Amen (1969) 41. DORMEYER, D., Die Passion Jesu als Verhaltensmodell (Münster 1974) 87. A.158. ZMIJEWSKI, J., "Der Glaube und seine Macht. Eine traditionsgeschichtliche Untersuchung zu Mt 17, 20: 21, 21; Mk 11, 23; Lk 17, 6" in J. Zmijewski/ E. Nellessen (eds.) Begegnung mit dem Wort. Für H. Zimmermann (Bonn 1980) 81-103.

21:22   BORNKAMM-BARTH-HELD, Ueberlieferung und Auslegung und Auslegung im Matthäus-Evangelium (1961) 272. STRECKER, G. Der Weg der Gerechtigkeit (1962) 182. Sanford, J. A., The Kingdom Within (New York 1970) 157f.

21:23-ch. 23   EWALD, H. Die drei ersten Evangelien (1850) 317ff.

21:23-22:14   SCHWEIZER, E., "Matthäus 21-25" in: P. Hoffmann (ed.) Orientierung an Jesus. Für J. Schmid (Freiburg 1973) 365-67.

21:23ff   "Autorität" in: TRE 5 (1980) 44.

21:23-46   BAMMEL, E. The Baptist in Early Christian Tradition. NTS 18 (1971-72) 102-104.

21:23-44   IWAND, H.-J. Predigt-Meditationen (1964) 572-75.

21:23-32   WILKENS, J. Einführung in das Evangelium nach Matthäus
            II (1937) 112-15. DRURY, J., Tradition and Design in Luke's
            Gospel (Atlanta 1976) 167.

21:23,31-32 SWIDLER, L., Biblical Affirmations of Woman (Philadelphia
            1979) 188, 250f.

21:23-27   GOODSPEED, E. J. A Life of Jesus (1950) 168-72.
            HOWARD, V. P., Das Ego in den Synoptischen Evangelien
            (Marburg 1975) 107-16. MEYER, B. F., The Aims of Jesus
            (London 1979) 168-70. FRICKEL, J., "Die Zöllner, Vorbild
            der Demut und wahrer Gottesverehrung" in: E. Dassmann/ K.
            S. Frank (eds.) Pietas. Für B. Kötting (JAC Erg.Bd.8)
            (Münster 1980) 369. LANGE, J., Das Erscheinen des
            Auferstandenen im Evangelium nach Matthäus (Würzburg
            1973) 25, 74, 88, 94, 145, 151, 166, 170, 180, 183, 431, 494.

21:23.24.27. Blair, E. P. Jesus in the Gospel of Matthew (1960) 46.

21:23f   STRECKER, G. Der Weg der Gerechtigkeit (1962) 175.

21:23   STONEHOUSE, N. B. The Witness of Matthew and Mark to
            Christ (1944) 160. STRECKER, G. Der Weg der Gerechtigkeit
            (1962) 127. HUMMEL, R. Die Auseinandersetzung zwischen
            Kirche und Judentum im Matthäusevangelium (1963) 145.
            BOUSSET, W. Die Religion des Judentums im
            Späthellenistischen Zeitalter (1966⁻1926) 167. LANGE, J., Das
            Erscheinen des Auferstandenen im Evangelium nach Matthäus
            (Würzburg 1973) 83-86, 88, 273f, 317, 479, 494.
            FRANKEMöLLE, H., Jahwebund und Kirche Christi
            (Münster 1974) 195, 202-204.

21:24-32   PIROT, J. Parabloes et Allégories Evangeliques (1949) 370-75.

21:25-27   BRAUN, H. Qumran und NT II (1966) 91f.

21:24-25   MEYER, B. F., The Aims of Jesus (London 1979) 125.

21:25   KNOX, W. L. The Sources of the Synoptic Gospels II (1957)
            91. HENGEL, M., Judentum und Hellenismus (Tübingen
            1969) 544; ET: Judaism and Hellenism II (London 1974) 199.

21:26   STONEHOUSE, N. B. The Witness of Matthew and Mark to
            Christ (1944) 106.

21:28-22:46 GAECHTER, P. Die literarische Kunst im Matthäus-
            Evangelium (1968) 15-16.

21:28-22:14 TILBORG, S. van, The Jewish Leaders in Matthew (Leiden
            1972) 47-63. FRANKEMöLLE, H., Jahwebund und Kirche
            Christi (Münster 1974) 26, 211, 219, 248f, 252, 254, 264.
            STANTON, G. N., "5 Ezra and Matthean Christianity in the
            Second Century" JThS 28 (1977) 67-83. *OGAWA, A.,
            "Paraboles de l'Israël véritable? Reconsidération critique de
            Mt. xxi 28 - xxii 14" NovT 21 (1979) 121-49.

21:28ff   KNOX, W. L. The Sources of the Synoptic Gospels II (1957) 97, 136.

21:28-44   MORGAN, G. C. The Parables and Metaphors of Our Lord (1943) 122ff.

21:28-43   SCHNIDER, F., Jesus der Prophet (Freiburg 1973) 107.

21:28-41   MINEAR, P. S. Images of the Church in the New Testament (1960) 43f.

21:28-32.43   PETERS, G. W. A Biblical Theology of Missions (1972) 49-50.

21:28-32   JüLICHER, D. A. Die Gleichnisreden Jesu (1910) 365-85. SCHLATTER, A., "Jesu Gleichnis von den beiden Söhnen" Jahrbuch der Theologischen Schule Bethel 2 (1931) 35-63. WILKENS, J. Einführung in das Evangelium nach Matthäus II (1937) 116-18. HIRSCH, E. Frühgeschichte des Evangeliums (1941) 316-18. STONEHOUSE, N. B. The Witness of Matthew and Mark to Christ (1944) 157. FINDLAY, J. A. Jesus and His Parables (1951) 53ff. SCHMID, J. "Das textgeschichtliche Problem der Parabel von den zwei Söhnen," in: Vom Wort des Lebens (1951) Meinertz, M. (ed.) 68-84. MICHAELIS, D. W. Die Gleichnisse Jesu (1956) 126-29. SCHMID, J. "Zwei unbekannte Gleichnisse Jesu," GuL 33 (6, '60) 428-33. BORNKAMM-BARTH-HELD, Ueberlieferung und Auslegung im Matthäus-Evangelium (1961) 56, 71. "Glaubet an den Gottgesandten" in Predigtgedanken aus Vergangenheit und Gegenwart Bd. 2 (1962) 35ff. SURKAU, GPM (1962/63) 127ff. HUMMEL, R. Die Auseinandersetzung zwischen Kirche und Judentum im Matthäusevangelium (1963) 23f. LOCKYER, H. All the Parables of the Bible (1963) 222ff. DEHN, G. in: Herr, tue meine Lippen auf Bd. 3 (1964) Eichholz, G. (ed.) 327ff. SILVA, R., "La parábola de los dos hijos" Cultura Biblica 22 (1965) 98-105. MICHAELIS, J. R. "The Parable of the Regretful Son," HThR 61 (1, '68) 15-26. KRAUSE, G. GPM 23/2 (1968/69) 121-26. BARCLAY, W. And Jesus Said (1970) 198-203. LEHMANN, M. Synoptische Quellenanalyse und die Frage nach dem historischen Jesus (1970) 154-55. DERRETT, J. D. M. "The Parable of the Two Sons," StTh 25 (2, '71) 109-16. KRECK, W. GPM 6/2, 76-79. GOLLWITZER, H., Veränderung im Diesseits (München 1973) 112. GOULDER, M. D., Midrash and Lection in Matthew (London 1974) 50, 54, 59f, 65, 99, 322, 357, 413ff. *MERKEL, H., "Das Gleichnis von den 'ungleichen Söhnen' (Matth. xxi. 28-32)" NTS 20 (1974) 254-61. KLEIN, G., in: GPM 29 (1975) 155-63. *LEGASSE, S., "Jésus et les prostituées" RThL 7 (1976) 137-54. SCHULZ, S., Die Mitte der Schrift (Stuttgart 1976) 169f. MANEK,J., . . . und brachte Frucht. Die Gleichnisse Jesu (Berlin 1977) 59f. *RICHARDS,

W. L., "Another Look at the Parable of the Two Sons" BR 23 (1978) 5-14. MEYER, B. F., The Aims of Jesus (London 1979) 158-62. WEDER, H., Die Gleichnisse Jesu als Metaphern (Göttingen 1980 *(2)*) 230-38.

21:28-31 STAEHELIN, E. Die Verkündigung des Reiches Gottes in der Kirche Jesu Christi I (1951) 61. TRILLING, W. Das wahre Israel (1959) 163. STRECKER, G. Der Weg der Gerechtigkeit (1962) 153ı. TOLBERT, M. A., Perspectives on the Parables (Philadelphia 1979) 75-78.

21:28b-31 MESSINA, G. "Parallelismi semitismi leziono tendenziose nell'armonia Persiana," Biblica 30 (1949) 357-59.

21:30 HAHN, F. Christologische Hoheitstitel (1963) 82.

21:31-43 HASLER, V. Amen (1969) 93.

21:31-32 PIROT, J. Paraboles et Allégories Evangeliques (1949) 63-70. SMITH, M., Tannaitic Parallels to the Gospels (Philadelphia 1968) 3bn27+. STRECKER, G. Der Weg der Gerechtigkeit (1962) 190ȝ. CHRIST, F. Jesus Sophia (1970) 75, 77. JEREMIAS, J. Neutestamentliche Theologie I (1971) 40, 42, 44, 100, 112, 118, 150. FRICKEL, J., "Die Zöllner, Vorbild der Demut und wahrer Gottesverehrung" in: E. Dassmann/K. S. Frank (eds.) Pietas. Für B. Kötting (JAC Erg.Bd.8) Münster 1980) 369.

21:31 STONEHOUSE, N. B. The Witness of Matthew and Mark to Christ (1944) 171, 228. FLEW, R. N. Jesus and His Church (1956) 25. KNOX, W. L. The Sources of the Synoptic Gospels II (1957) 16, 33, 97. TRILLING, W. Das wahre Israel (1959) 41. STROBEL, A. Erkenntnis und Bekenntnis der Sünde in neutestamentlicher Zeit (1968) 60. BRUNNER, E. Dogmatik II, 331. PRETE, B., "Il senso del 'Logion' di Gesù" BibOr 12 (1970) 49-58. SANFORD, J. A., The Kingdom Within (New York 1970) 51f. METZGER, B. M., "St Jerome's explicit references to variant readings in manuscripts of the New Testament" in: E. Best/R. McL. Wilson (eds.) Text and Interpretation. Studies in the New Testament presented to Matthew Black (Cambridge 1979) 181. SCHLOSSER, J., "Le règne de Dieu dans les dits de Jésus" RevSR 53 (1979) 164-76.

21:31b ROBINSON, J. M. Kerygma und historischer Jesus (1960) 34, 161, 162, 164.

21:32 BLAIR, E. P. Jesus in the Gospel of Matthew (1960) 120. ROBINSON, J. M. Kerygma und historischer Jesus (1960) 144f. BORNKAMM-BARTH-HELD, Ueberlieferung und Auslegung im Matthäus-Evangelium (1961) 25, 107, 130. STRECKER, G. Der Weg der Gerechtigkeit (1962) 153, 179, 187, 227ₔ 228ₔ. BULTMANN, R. The History of the Synoptic

Tradition (1963) 164f. THEYSSEN, G. W. "Unbelief" in the New Testament (1965) 63f. BRAUN, H. Qumran und NT II (1966) 18, 189. JüNGEL, E. Paulus und Jesus (1966) 175. JEREMIAS, J. Neutestamentliche Theologie I (1971) 26, 53, 55, 111, 159. ZIESLER, J. A. The Meaning of Righteousness in Paul (1972) 131f., 146. GOULDER, M.D., Midrash and Lection in Matthew (London 1974) 158, 262, 357, 413. SAND, A., Das Gesetz und die Propheten (Regensburg 1974) 199-201.

21:33-22:1f   DILLON, R. J. "Towards a Tradition-History of the Parables of the True Israel (Matthew 21, 33-22, 14)," Biblica 47 (1, '66) 1-42.

21:33-22:14   GOPPELT, L., Theologie des Neuen Testaments II (Göttingen 1976) 563.

21:33ff   BRUNNER, E. Dogmatik II (1950) 107, 323. "Autorität" in: TRE 5 (1980) 44.

21:33-46   JüLICHER, D. A. Die Gleichnisreden Jesu (1910) 385-406. WILKENS, J. Einführung in das Evangelium nach Matthäus II (1937) 119-23. PIROT,J. Paraboles et Allégories Evangeliques (1949) 376-90. GOODSPEED, E. J. A Life of Jesus (1950) 172-74. MICHAELIS, D. W. Die Gleichnisse Jesu (1956) 113-25. McCAUGHEY, J. D. "Two Synoptic Parables in the Gospel of Thomas," AusBR 8 (1-4, '60) 24-28. BORNKAMM-BARTH-HELD, Ueberlieferung und Auslegung im Matthäus-Evangelium (1961) 18, 40, 71, 224. STRECKER, G. Der Weg der Gerechtigkeit (1962) 33, 110f., 112₇, 215. LOCKYER, H. All the Parables of the Bible (1963) 225ff. HAAR, GPM (1964/65) 290ff. SCHRAGE, W. Das Verhältnis des Thomas-Evangeliums zur Synoptischen Tradition und zu den Koptischen Evangelienübersetzungen (1964) 137. LEON-DUFOUR, X. "La parabole des vignerons homicides," SciEccl 17 (3, '65) 365-96. PEDERSEN, S. "Zum Problem der vaticinia ex eventu. (Eine Analyse von Mt. 21, 33-46 par.; 22, 1-10 par.)," StTh 19 (1-2, '65) 167-88. SUHL, A. Die Funktion der alttestamentlichen Zitate und Anspielungen im Markusevangelium (1965) 138ff. SWAELES, R., "La parabole des vignerons homicides" AssS 29 (1966) 36-51. HELD, H. J. in Hören und Fragen Bd. 5 (1967) Eichholz, G. & Falkenroth, A. (eds.) 416ff. MUSSNER, F. "Die Bösen Winzer nach Mt 21, 33-46", Antijudaismus in N.T.? (1967) Eckert, Levinson, Stöhr (eds.) 129-34. SUMMERS, R. The Secret Sayings of the Living Jesus (1968) 49. TRILLING, W. "Gericht über das falsche Israel" in Christusverkündigung in den Synoptischen Evangelien (1969) 165. DASSONVILLE, A. E. The Parable of the Wicked Husbandmen in Luke (B.D. thesis, Rüschlikon 1970). DERRETT, J. D. N. Law in the New Testament (1970)

286-312. KLAUCK, H. J., "Das Gleichnis vom Mord im Weinberg" BiLe 11 (1970) 118-45. LANGE, E. (ed.) Predigtstudien für das Kirchenjahr 1970/71 (1970) 169-75.MüLLER, H. P. GPM 25 (2, '71) 334-43. SCHRAMM, T. Der Markus-Stoff bei Lukas (1971) 150-57. PATSCH, H. Abendmahl und historischer Jesus (1972) 200ff. HAAR, J. GPM 19/3, 290-96. STECK, K. G. GPM 13/3, 202-208. FRANKEMöLLE, H., Jahwebund und Kirche Christi (Münster 1974) 117f, 247-56, 279. GOULDER, M. D., Midrash and Lection in Matthew (London 1974) 50, 54, 56, 58f, 61, 65, 99, 322, 339, 420. SAND, A., Das Gesetz und die Propheten (Regensburg 1974) 112-114. *HUBAUT, M., "La parabole des vignerons homicides: son authenticitè, sa visée première" RThL 6 (1975) 51-61. *ROBINSON, J. A. T., "The Parable of the Wicked Husbandmen: A Test of Synoptic Relationships" NTS 21 (1975) 443-61. *ORCHARD, J. B., "J. A. T. Robinson and The Synoptic Problem" NTS 22 (1976) 346-52. PERRIN, N., Jesus and the Language of the Kingdom (London 1976) 8, 150, 161. SCHULZ, S., Die Mitte der Schrift (Stuttgart 1976) 163-65. WILLIAMS, J. A., A Conceptual History of Deuteronomism in the Old Testament, Judaism, and the New Testament (Ph.D.Diss. Southern Baptist Theological Seminary, Louisville 1976) 284-89. SCHEIDACKER, W., in: GPM 31 (1976-77) 335-40. TRITES, A. A., The New Testament Concept of Witness (Cambridge 1977) 193. WIMMER, U. und LOEWENICH, R. von, in: P. Krusche (ed.) Predigtstudien V/2 (Stuttgart 1977) 155-61. KLAUCK, H.-J., Allegorie und Allegorese in Synoptischen Gleichnistexten (Münster 1978) 286-316. VIELHAUER, Ph., "Oikodome, Das Bild vom Bau in der christlichen Literatur vom Neuen Testament bis Clemens Alexandrinus" in: Oikodome (München 1979) 56-58. WEDER, H., Die Gleichnisse Jesu als Metaphern (Göttingen 1980 *(2)*) 147-62.

21:33-45 TRILLING, W. Das wahre Israel (1959) 37ff. HUBAUT, M., La parabole des vignerons homicides (Paris 1976).

21:33-44 JEREMIAS, J. Die Gleichnisse Jesu (1962) 66, 67-75, 88. BöHLIG, A., "Vom 'Knecht' zum 'Sohn' " in: Mysterion und Wahrheit (Leiden 1968) 60f. BARCLAY, W. And Jesus Said (1970) 139-45. MANEK, J., . . . und brachte Frucht. Die Gleichnisse Jesu (Berlin 1977) 29-33.

21:33-43 BLAIR, E. P. Jesus in the Gospel of Matthew (1960) 60. BIEDER, W., Die Verheissung der Taufe im Neuen Testament (Zürich 1966) 282f. SCHNIDER, F., Jesus der Prophet (Freiburg 1973) 161ff. *TRILLING, W., "Les vignerons homicides. Mt 21, 33-43" AssS 58 (1974) 16-23.

HARRINGTON, D. J., God's People in Christ (Philadelphia 1980) 99f.

21:33-42 MASSAUX, E. Influence de l'Evangile de saint Matthieu sur la littérature chrétienne avant saint Irénée (1950) 267-71.

21:33-41 BISER, E. Die Gleichnisse Jesu (1965) 137ff. WEISER, A. Die Knechtsgleichnisse der synoptischen Evangelien (1971) 49-57. TOLBERT, M. A., Perspectives on the Parables (Philadelphia 1979) 75, 83-89.

21:33f MONTEFIORE, H. A Comparison of the Parables of the Gospel according to Thomas and of the Synoptic Gospels. NTS 7 (1960/61) 236f.

21:33 STRECKER, G. Der Weg der Gerechtigkeit (1962) 23, 363. HAHN, F. Christologische Hoheitstitel (1963) 92. HUMMEL, R. Die Auseinandersetzung zwischen Kirche und Judentum im Matthäusevangelium (1963) 155. SCHRAMM, T. Der Markus-Stoff bei Lukas (1971) 154-56.

21:34a HUMMEL, R. Die Auseinandersetzung zwischen Kirche und Judentum im Matthäusevangelium (1963) 148.

21:35ff BEYSCHLAG, K. Clemens Romanus und der Frühkatholizismus (1966) 223.

21:35 HAHN, F. Christologische Hoheitstitel (1963) 382.

21:37 BRUNNER, E. Dogmatik I (1946) 221.

21:39 STRECKER, G. Der Weg der Gerechtigkeit (1962) 113, 114l, 116f.

21:40f STRECKER, G. Der Weg der Gerechtigkeit (1962) 112l.

21:41-45 COPE, O. L., Matthew: A Scribe Trained for the Kingdom of Heaven (Washington 1976) 85f.

21:41 BLAIR, E. P. Jesus in the Gospel of Matthew (1960) 92. HUMMEL, R. Die Auseinandersetzung zwischen Kirche und Judentum im Matthäusevangelium (1963) 90, 148. LANGE, J., Das Erscheinen des Auferstandenen im Evangelium nach Matthäus (Würzburg 1973) 82f, 87, 215, 275-80, 282, 285, 306.

21:41b HUMMEL, R. Die Auseinandersetzung zwischen Kirche und Judentum im Matthäusevangelium (1963) 148.

21:42ff STONEHOUSE, N. B. The Witness of Matthew and Mark to Christ (1944) 193.

21:42 STONEHOUSE, N. B. The Witness of Matthew and Mark to Christ (1944) 196. ELLIS, E. E. Paul's Use of the Old Testament (1957) 88f., 165. HOOKER, M. D. Jesus and the Servant (1959) 97f. STRECKER, G. Der Weg der Gerechtigkeit (1962) 21, 713. HUMMEL, R. Die Auseinandersetzung zwischen Kirche und Judentum im

Matthäusevangelium (1963) 132. SCHRAGE, W. Das Verhältnis des Thomas-Evangelium zur Synoptischen Tradition und zu den Koptischen Evangelienübersetzungen (1964) 145. BRAUN, H. Qumran und NT II (1966) 210, 304f. BLOCH, R., "Midrash" in: W. S. Green (ed.) Approaches to Ancient Judaism (Missoula 1978) 49.

21:43f   SWAELES, R. "L'arrière-fond scripturaire de Matt. xxi. 43 et son lien avec Matt. xxi. 44," NTS 6 (4, '60) 310-13. STRECKER, G. Der Weg der Gerechtigkeit (1962) 218₃.

21:43   STONEHOUSE, N. B. The Witness of Matthew and Mark to Christ (1944) 230, 232, 240. PARKER, P. The Gospel Before Mark (1953) 82-83. NEPPER-CHRISTENSEN, P. Das Matthäusevangelium. Ein Judenchristliches Evangelium? (1958) 9, 17, 21, 22, 52, 198. TRILLING, W. Das wahre Israel (1959) 40ff. BLAIR, E. P. Jesus in the Gospel of Matthew (1960) 30, 31, 113, 159. BORNKAMM-BARTH-HELD, Ueberlieferung und Auslegung im Matthäus-Evangelium (1961) 40, 56, 104, 227. DE KRUIJF, Th., Der Sohn des lebendigen Gottes (Rome 1962) 128, 140, 157, 162. STRECKER, G. Der Weg der Gerechtigkeit (1962) 33, 35, 110f., 111₇, 115, 117, 169f., 190, 215₄. HUMMEL, R. Die Auseinandersetzung zwischen Kirche und Judentum im Matthäusevangelium (1963) 148-53, 154, 156. HAHN, F. Das Verständnis der Mission im Neuen Testament (1965) 107, 108, 109. SCHNACKENBURG, R., Present and Future (Notre Dame 1966). BORIG, R. Der Wahre Weinstock (1967) 131-34, 194, 250. KüMMEL, W. G. Einleitung in das Neue Testament (1973) 84-88. LANGE, J., Das Erscheinen des Auferstandenen im Evangelium nach Matthäus (Würzburg 1973) 83, 86f, 113, 164, 273, 275-77, 282, 284-86, 306, 312f, 322, 423, 489. GOULDER, M. D., Midrash and Lection in Matthew (London 1974) 63, 321, 332, 397, 414. LADD, G. E., A Theology of the New Testament (Grand Rapids 1974) 64, 103, 114.

21:44   STRECKER, G. Der Weg der Gerechtigkeit (1962) 110f. METZGER, B. M., The Early Versions of the New Testament (Oxford 1977) 134.

21:45   STONEHOUSE, N. B. The Witness of Matthew and Mark to Christ (1944) 106, 177. BRUNNER, E. Dogmatik I (1946) 391. BLAIR, E. P. Jesus in the Gospel of Matthew (1960) 95, 101. BLAIR, E. P. Jesus in the Gospel of Matthew (1960) 113. STRECKER, G. Der Weg der Gerechtigkeit (1962) 113₂, 116. HAHN, F. Christologische Hoheitstitel (1963) 401. HUMMEL, R. Die Auseinandersetzung zwischen Kirche und Judentum im Matthäusevangelium (1963) 148, 153. BROER, I.

Die Urgemeinde und das Grab Jesu (1972) 71f.

21:51f KNOX, W. L. The Sources of the Synoptic Gospels II (1957) 97.

22 VOLZ, P. Die Eschatologie der jüdischen Gemeinde (1934) 234.

22:1ff HAHN, F. Das Verständnis der Mission im Neuen Testament (1965) 28, 106. HUMMEL, R. Die Auseindersetzung zwischen Kirche und Judentum im Matthäusevangelium (1963) 85.

22:1-36 STREETER, B. H. The Four Gospels (1951) 585ff.

22:1-14 JüLICHER, D. A. Die Gleichnisreden Jesu (1910) 407-33. WILKENS, J. Einführung in das Evangelium nach Matthäus II (1937) 124-30. HIRSCH, E. Frühgeschichte des Evangeliums (1941) 138-42. MORGAN, G. C. The Parables and Metaphors of Our Lord (1943) 127ff. STONEHOUSE, N. B. The Witness of Matthew and Mark to Christ (1944) 157. MANSON, T. W. The Teaching of Jesus (1945) 83-86, 276 n.4. PIROT, J. Paraboles et Allégories Evangeliques (1949) 400-11. DINKLER, GPM 4 (1949/50) 269ff. PARKER, P. The Gospel Before Mark (1953) 65ff., 126-27. LOEWENICH, W. von, Luther als Ausleger der Synoptiker (1954) 42f. MERRIMAN, E. H. "Mt 22, 1-14." ET 66 (2, '54) 61. STECK, GPM 9 (1954/55) 241ff. BEST, E. One Body in Christ (1955) 107n., 170, 175n. SCHLIER, H. "Der Ruf Gottes", GuL 28/4 (1955) 241-47. EICHHOLZ, G. (ed.) Herr, tue meine Lippen auf Bd. I (1957) 299-305. MOUSON, J. "Explicatur parabola de magno convivio (Mt. XXII, 1-14; Lc. XIV, 16-24)," Coll Mech 43 (6, '58) 610-13. SQUILLACI, D. "Parabola delle nozze del figlio del re (Mt. 22, 1-14)," PaCl 38 (18, '59) 972-76. BLAIR, E. P. Jesus in the Gospel of Matthew (1960) 60. CASTELLINO, G. R. "L'abito di nozze nella parabola del convito e una lettera di Mari (Matteo 22, 1-14)," EstEc 34 (134-35, '60) 819-24. MINEAR, P. S. Images of the Church in the New Testament (1960) 56f. TRILLING, W. "Zur Ueberlieferungsgeschichte des Gleichnisses vom Hochzeitsmahl Mt 22, 1-14," BZ 4 (2, '60) 251-65. VAN BERGEN, P. "La parabole des invités qui se dérobent," LuVieSupp 49 ('60) 1-9. MERKEL, GPM 15 (1960/61) 290ff. BORNKAMM-BARTH-HELD, Ueberlieferung und Auslegung im Matthäus-Evangelium

(1961)18. DOERNE, M. Er Kommt auch noch heute (1961) 145-47. GNILKA, J. Die Verstockung Israels (1961) 99f., 112f. HASLER, V. "Die königliche Hochzeit, Mt. 22, 1-14", ThZ 18 (1962) 25-35. JEREMIAS, J. Die Gleichnisse Jesu (1962) 34, 61-63, 65-67, 93, 98, 125. MOWRY, L. "Parable", IDB III (1962) 652a. STRECKER, G. Der Weg der Gerechtigkeit (1962) 33f., 111, 215, 219l. LOCKYER, H. All the Parables of the Bible (1963) 227ff. SWAELES, R., "La parabole du festin nuptial" AssS 74 (1963) 33-49. SCHLIER, H. "Der Ruf Gottes Mt 22, 1.14", Besinnung auf das Neue Testament, Exegetische Aufsätze und Vorträge II (1964) 218-26. STREEFKERK, N. "Waardig en onwaardig" (Worthy and Unworthy), HomBib 24 (11, '65) 272-75. BIEDER, W., Die Verheissung der Taufe im Neuen Testament (Zürich 1966) 283. "Wir wissen weder Tag noch Stunde", Predigtgedanken aus Vergangenheit und Gegenwart Bd. 6 (1966) 119-34. SUMMERS, R. The Secret Sayings of the Living Jesus (1968) 47. LINNEMANN, E. Gleichnisse Jesu (1969) 94ff., 160ff. DERRETT, J. D. M. Law in the New Testament (1970) 126-55. HAHN, F. "Das Gleichnis von der Einladung zum Festmahl", Verborum Veritas, Festschrift G. Stählin (1970) 51-82. BATEY, R. A. New Testament Nuptial Imagery (1971) 41-44. EICHHOLZ, G. Gleichnisse der Evangelien (1971) 126-47. JEREMIAS, J.Neutestamentliche Theologie I (1971) 118, 121, 135, 238. SCHULZ, S. Q Die Spruchquelle der Evangelisten (1972) 391-403. GOULDER, M. D., Midrash and Lection in Matthew (London 1974) 50, 54, 59, 61, 65, 108, 168, 190, 199, 321, 374, 415-18. *MATURA, T., "Les invités à la noce royale. Mt 22, 1-14" AssS 59 (1974) 16-27. *PALMER, H., "Just Married, Cannot Come" NovT 18 (1976) 241-57. SCHULZ, S., Die Mitte der Schrift (Stuttgart 1976) 165-68. DUPONT, J. et al., La parabola degli invitati al banchetto (Brescia 1978). STAGG, E./F., Woman in the World of Jesus (Philadelphia 1978) 218. SWIDLER, L., Biblical Affirmations of Woman (Philadelphia 1979) 244.

22:1-13   DODD, C. H. The Parables of the Kingdom (1948) 121ff. MAERTENS, T. "L'Ecriture éclaire le problème foi-sacrement," ParLit 46 (5-6, '64) 530-33. HELBICH, H.-M. "Gottes Einladung und ihre Folgen", in: Kleine Predigt-Typologie, III (1965) Schmidt, L. (ed.) 404-11.

22:1-11   MONTEFIORE, H. A comparison of the Parables of the Gospel according to Thomas and of the Synoptic Gospels. NTS 7 (1960-61) 235f.

22:1-10   PARKER, P. The Gospel Before Mark (1953) 66-67. MICHAELIS, D. W. Die Gleichnisse Jesu (1956) 145-63.

GLOMBITZA, O. "Das Grosse Abendmahl, Luk. xiv 12-24", NovTest 5 (1962) 10-16. JEREMIAS, J. Die Gleichnisse Jesu (1962) 88, 93, 105, 128, 171, 174-79. SCHRAGE, W. Das Verhältnis des Thomas-Evangeliums zur Synoptischen Tradition und zu den Koptischen Evangelienübersetzungen (1964) 133. PEDERSEN,S., "Zum Problem der vaticinia ex eventu" StTh 19 (1965) 167-88. GRABNER-HAIDER, A. Verkündigung als Einladung (1969) 79-81. BARCLAY, W. And Jesus Said (1970) 151-57. VIA, D. A. "The Relationship of Form to Content in the Parables: The Wedding Feast," Interpretation 25 (2, '71) 171-84. WEISER, A. Die Knechtsgleichnisse der synoptischen Evangelien; Stud. z. Alten und Neuen Testament Bd. XXIX (1971) 58-63. CROSSAN, J. D. Parable and Example in the Teaching of Jesus NTS 18 (1971-72) 302f. TALBERT, C. H., Literary Patterns, Theological Themes, and the Genre of Luke-Acts (Missoula 1974) 56. CONZELMANN, H. und LINDEMANN, A., Arbeitsbuch zum Neuen Testament (Tübingen 1975) 87f. MANEK, J., . . . und brachte Frucht. Die Gleichnisse Jesu (Berlin 1977) 60-64. POLAG, A., Die Christologie der Logienquelle (Neukirchen-Vluyn 1977) 75, 92. WEDER, H., Die Gleichnisse Jesu als Metaphern (Göttingen 1980 *(2)*) 117-93.

22:1-4   SWAELES, R. "L'orientation ecclésiastique de la parabole du festin nuptial en Mt., XXII, 1-4," EphT 36 (3-4, '60) 655-84. PERRIN, N., Jesus and the Language of the Kingdom (London 1976) 96, 102, 116, 138, 161, 189.

22:2ff   STONEHOUSE, N. B. The Witness of Matthew and Mark to Christ (1944) 130. STAEHELIN, E. Die Verkündigung des Reiches Gottes in der Kirche Jesu Christi I (1951) 62. KNOX, W. L. The Sources of the Synoptic Gospels II (1957) 85.

22:2-14   BULTMANN, R. The History of the Synoptic Tradition (1963) 195f., 201f. BISER, E. Die Gleichnisse Jesu (1965) 87ff., 126. HAENCHEN, E. "Das Gleichnis vom grossen Mahl," Die Bibel und Wir (1968) 135-55. SANFORD, J. A., The Kingdom Within (New York 1970) 193f. VöGTLE, A. Das Evangelium und die Evangelien (1971) 171-218. BERGMANN, W., Die zehn Gleichnisse vom Reich der Himmel (Lahr-Dinglingen 1976). SHERWIN-WHITE, A. N., Roman Society and Roman Law in the New Testament (Grand Rapids 1978) 134.

22:2-10   VöGTLE, A. Das Evangelium und die Evangelien (1971) 212-14. GOPPELT, L., Theologie des Neuen Testaments I (Göttingen 1975) 187f. SWIDLER, L., Biblical Affirmations of Woman (Philadelphia 1979) 279. RESENHöFFT, W., "Jesu Gleichnis von den Talenten, ergänzt durch die Lukas-Fassung" NTS 26 (1979-80) 318-31.

22:2f STRECKER, G. Der Weg der Gerechtigkeit (1962) 170.

22:2 STRECKER, G. Der Weg der Gerechtigkeit (1962) 214f. BLACK, M. An Aramaic Approach to the Gospels and Acts (1967) 129f.

22:3f VöGTLE, A. Das Evangelium und die Evangelien (1971) 208-11.

22:4-7 VöGTLE, A. Das Evangelium und die Evangelien (1971) 178-80.

22:4 BLACK, M. An Aramaic Approach to the Gospels and Acts (1967) 129f.

22:6 HAHN, F. Christologische Hoheitstitel (1963) 382.

22:7 NEPPER-CHRISTENSEN, P. Das Matthäusevangelium. Ein Judenchristliches Evangelium? (1958) 15, 22, 26, 27. TRILLING, W. Das wahre Israel (1959) 66f. BLAIR, E. P. Jesus in the Gospel of Matthew (1960) 43, 89, 92, 161. RENGSTORF, K. H. "Die Stadt der Mörder (Mt 22:7)," Judentum, Urchristentum, Kirche (1960) 106-29. STRECKER, G. Der Weg der Gerechtigkeit (1962) 35, 110, 112f., 115, 117, 2402. HUMMEL, R. Die Auseinandersetzung zwischen Kirche und Judentum im Matthäusevangelium (1963) 90. ROBINSON, J. A. T., Redating the New Testament (London 1976) 19-21.

22:8-9 SANFORD, J. A., The Kingdom Within (New York 1970) 69-71.

22:9ff STRECKER, G. Der Weg der Gerechtigkeit (1962) 2183.

22:9-14 HUMMEL, R. Die Auseinandersetzung zwischen Kirche und Judentum im Matthäusevangelium (1963) 142.

22:9f STRECKER, G. Der Weg der Gerechtigkeit (1962) 117. VöGTLE, A. Das Evangelium und die Evangelien (1971) 183-88, 214-16.

22:9 SANFORD, J. A., The Kingdom Within (New York 1970) 49f.

22:10-14 BAUMBACH, G. Das Verständnis des Bösen in den synoptischen Evangelien (1963) 72ff.

22:10-13 SCHWEIZER, E. Gemeinde und Gemeinde-Ordnung im Neuen Testament (1959) § 4d,e.

22:10 "Bergpredigt" in: TRE 5 (1980) 609. JANSSEN, E., "Testament Abrahams" in: W. G. Kümmel (ed.) Jüdische Schriften aus hellenistisch-römischer Zeit III (Gütersloh 1975) 207.

22:11ff STAEHELIN, E. Die Verkündigung des Reiches Gottes in der Kirche Jesu Christi I (1951) 62. STRECKER, G. Der Weg der Gerechtigkeit (1962) 158.

22:11-14   BRUNNER, E. Saat und Frucht (1946) 61-72. MICHAELIS, D. W. Die Gleichnisse Jesu (1956) 160-63. BORNKAMM-BARTH-HELD, Ueberlieferung und Auslegung im Matthäus-Evangelium (1961) 18, 40, 55. JEREMIAS, J. Die Gleichnisse Jesu (1962) 61-63, 186-89. SMITH, Ch. W. F. "The Mixed State of the Church in Matthew's Gospel", JBL 82 (1963) 149-68, esp. 156-58. BARCLAY, W. And Jesus Said (1970) 158-61. WEISER, A. Die Knechtsgleichnisse der synoptischen Evangelien, Stud. z. Alten und Neuen Testament Bd. XXIX (1971) 58-64. MANEK, J., . . . und brachte Frucht. Die Gleichnisse Jesu (Berlin 1977) 64f.

22:11-13   BLAIR, E. P. Jesus in the Gospel of Matthew (1960) 92, 108, 165. BAUER, J. B. "De veste nuptiali (Matth. 22, 11-13)," VerbDom 43 (1, '65) 15-18. HAACKER, K. "Das hochzeitliche Kleid von Mt. 22, 11-13 und ein palästinisches Märchen," ZDPV 87 (1, '71) 95-97. BAUER, J. B., Scholia Biblica et Patristica (Graz 1972) 69-72.

22:11-12   SASS, G. Ungereimtes bei Matthäus (1968) 42-43. BETZ, H. D. Lukian von Samosata und das Neue Testament (1961) 81, 88, 115.

   22:12   LOEWENICH, W. von, Luther als Ausleger der Synoptiker (1954) 42f. CRIPS, K. "A Note on Matthew 22:12," ET 69 (1, '57) 30. BAUER, J. B., Scholia Biblica et Patristica (Graz 1972) 30f.

   22:13   HUMMEL, R. Die Auseinandersetzung zwischen Kirche und Judentum im Matthäusevangelium (1963) 147. KäSEMANN, E. Exegetische Versuche und Besinnungen (1964) II 94. NICKELS, P. Targum and New Testament (1967) 21. SMITH, M., Tannaitic Parallels to the Gospels (Philadelphia 1968) 3.9+.

22:14-18   HENNECKE, E. & SCHNEEMELCHER, W. Neutestamentliche Apokryphen (1964) I 60, II 394.

   22:14   VOLZ, P. Die Eschatologie der jüdischen Gemeinde (1934) 113. MOORE, G. F. Judaism (1946) II 322n. FLEW, R. N. Jesus and His Church (1956) 25, 159n. KNOX, W. L. The Sources of the Synoptic Gospels II (1957) 135. SQUILLACI, D. "La riprovazione del popolo ebraico," PaCl 38 (19, '59) 1043-49. HAHN, F. Das Verständnis der Mission im Neuen Testament (1965) 107. PESCH, W., "Berufene und Auserwählte" BuK 20 (1965) 16-18. SANFORD, J. A., The Kingdom Within (New York 1970) 63f. JEREMIAS, J. Neutestamentliche Theologie I (1971) 26, 34, 131f., 174. PERRIN, N., Jesus and the Language of the Kingdom (London 1976) 48. "Bergpredigt" in: TRE 5 (1980) 609. "Berufung" in: TRE 5 (1980) 687, 707.

22:15-22   WILKENS, J. Einführung in das Evangelium nach Matthäus II (1937) 137-39. BARTH, GPM 4 (1949/50) 290ff. EICHHOLZ, G. (ed.) Herr, tue meine Lippen auf Bd. I (1957) 316-20. VAN BERGEN, P. "L'mpôt dû à César," LuVieSupp 50 ('60) 12-18. TIBBE, GPM (1960/61) 309ff. DOERNE, M. Er kommt auch noch heute (1961) 151-54. SUHL, A. Die Funktion der alttestamentlichen Zitate und Anspielungen im Markusevangelium (1965) 110ff. "Wir wissen weder Tag noch Stunde", Predigtgedanken aus Vergangenheit und Gegenwart Bd. 6 (1966) 174-89. DERRETT, J. D. M. Law in the New Testament (1970) 313-37. SCHRAMM, T. Der Markus-Stoff bei Lukas (1971) 168-70. SAND, A., Das Gesetz und die Propheten (Regensburg 1974) 63f.

22:15-21   *DE SURGY, P., "Rendez à César ce qui est à César, et à Dieu ce qui est à Dieu. Mt 22, 15-21" AssS 60 (1975) 16-25.

22:15   METZGER, B. M., The Early Versions of the New Testament (Oxford 1977) 173.

22:16-22   SCHALIT, A., König Herodes (1969) 272.

22:16-21   SUMMERS, R. The Secret Sayings of the Living Jesus (1968) 26.

22:16   BLAIR, E. P. Jesus in the Gospel of Matthew (1960) 100. HAHN, F. Christologische Hoheitstitel (1963) 76. SCHALIT, A. König Herodes (1969) 479. CAVALLIN, H. C. C., Life After Death I (Lund 1974) 6.15.

22:17-21   SCHRAGE, W. Das Verhältnis des Thomas-Evangeliums zur Synoptischen Tradition und zu den Koptischen Evangelienübersetzungen (1964) 189.

22:17-19   SHERWIN-WHITE, A. N., Roman Society and Roman Law in the New Testament (Grand Rapids 1978) 33.

22:17   VOLZ, P. Die Eschatologie der jüdischen Gemeinde (1934) 165.

22:18   BLAIR, E. P. Jesus in the Gospel of Matthew (1960) 87. HUMMEL, R. Die Auseinandersetzung zwischen Kirche und Judentum im Matthäusevangelium (1963) 128.

22:19f   KNOX, W. L. The Sources of the Synoptic Gospels II (1957) 125.

22:19   SHERWIN-WHITE, A. N., Roman Society and Roman Law in the New Testament (Grand Rapids 1978) 34.

22:21   MOORE, G. P. Judaism (1946) II 118. SCHRAGE, W. Die konkreten Einzelgebote in der paulinischen Paränese (1961) 243. BRAUN, H. Qumran und NT II (1966) 289, 293.

22:22   KNOX, W. L., The Sources of the Synoptic Gospels II (1957) 12.

22:23ff STONEHOUSE, N. B. The Witness of Matthew and Mark to Christ (1944) 196.

22:23-40 FARRER, A. St Matthew and St Mark (1954) 190. RIVKIN, E., A Hidden Revolution (Nashville 1978) 95f.

22:23-33 WILKENS, J. Einführung in das Evangelium nach Matthäus II (1937) 140-45. BEST, E. One Body in Christ (1955) 203n. M'NEILE, A. H. The Gospel According to St Matthew (1955) 323f. *BARTINA, S. "Jesus y los saduceos. El Dios de Abraham, de Isac y de Jacob es 'El que hace existir' ". (Mt. 22, 23-33; Mc. 12, 18-27; Lc. 20, 27-40; Hebr. 11, 13-16), EstBi 21 (1962) 151-60. SUHL, A. Die Funktion der alttestamentlichen Zitate und Anspielungen im Markusevangelium (1965) 67ff. SCHRAMM, T. Der Markus-Stoff bei Lukas (1971) 170f. DINKLER, E. GPM 11/2, 130-33. STAGG, E./F., Woman in the World of Jesus (Philadelphia 1978) 137f. SWIDLER, L., Biblical Affirmations of Woman (Philadelphia 1979) 232, 239, 260.

22:23-30 SWIDLER, L., Biblical Affirmations of Woman (Philadelphia 1979) 176.

22:23-24 NöTSCHER, F., Altorientalischer und alttestamentlicher Auferstehungsglauben (Darmstadt 1970⁻1926) 189, 271.

22:23 STONEHOUSE, N. B. The Witness of Matthew and Mark to Christ (1944) 150. STRECKER, G. Der Weg der Gerechtigkeit (1962) 140. HUMMEL, R. Die Auseinandersetzung zwischen Kirche und Judentum im Matthäusevangelium (1963) 19f.

22:24 BLAIR, E. P. Jesus in the Gospel of Matthew (1960) 100. STRECKER, G. Der Weg der Gerechtigkeit (1962) 22, 28, 592, 134s. HAHN, F. Christologische Hoheitstitel (1963) 76.

22:25 KLIJN, A. F. J. and REININK, G. J., Patristic Evidence for Jewish-Christian Sects (Leiden 1973) 35. SHERWIN-WHITE, A. N., Roman Society and Roman Law in the New Testament (Grand Rapids 1978) 143.

22:29-32 VOLZ, P. Die Eschatologie der jüdischen Gemeinde (1934) 234-36, 267, 269, 401.

22:29-30 SANFORD, J. A., The Kingdom Within (New York 1970) 209f.

22:29 HUMMEL, R. Die Auseinandersetzung zwischen Kirche und Judentum im Matthäusevangelium (1963) 132.

22:30 MOORE, G. F., Judaism (1946) I 406, II 304, 392, 393n. BRUNNER, E. Dogmatik II (1950) 77, 265. STAEHELIN, E. Die Verkündigung des Reiches Gottes in der Kirche Jesu Christi I (1951) 213, 269, 278, 295, 332, 360. SUMMERS, R. The Secret Sayings of the Living Jesus (1968) 62. EDWARDS,

R. A., A Theology of Q (Philadelphia 1976) 110-12. SCHEP, J. A., The Nature of the Resurrection Body (Grand Rapids 1976) 25, 204, 210ff.

22:31ff JANSSEN, E., "Testament Abrahams" in: W. G. Kümmel (ed.) Jüdische Schriften aus hellenistisch-römischer Zeit III (Gütersloh 1975) 233.

22:31-32 NöTSCHER, F., Altorientalischer und alttestamentlicher Auferstehungsglauben (Darmstadt 1970⁻1926) 299, 306.

22:31 STONEHOUSE, N. B. The Witness of Matthew and Mark to Christ (1944) 201. KNOX, W. L. The Sources of the Synoptic Gospels II (1957) 125.

22:32 MOORE, G. F. Judaism (1946) II 383. STRECKER, G. Der Weg der Gerechtigkeit (1962) 22. CAVALLIN, H. C. C., Life After Death I (Lund 1974) 4.3.1.

22:33 BLAIR, E. P. Jesus in the Gospel of Matthew (1960) 101. HAHN, F. Das Verständnis der Mission im Neuen Testament (1965) 104.

22:34ff BORNKAMM, G. Jesus von Nazareth (1956) 101ff. KNOX, W. L. The Sources of the Synoptic Gospels II (1957) 58.

22:34-46 EICHHOLZ, G. (ed.) Herr, tue meine Lippen auf Bd. I (1957) 288-93. TRILLING, W., "Weisung und Anspruch" Am Tisch des Wortes 5 (1965) 26-37. BLANK, J. Schriftauslegung in Theorie und Praxis (1969) 221-36. KRAUS, H. J. GPM 9/4, 231-34.

22:34-40 WILKENS, J. Einführung in das Evangelium nach Matthäus II (1937) 146-49. BERGER, K. Die Gesetzesauslegung Jesu (1940) 181 (vs. 37), 202-208, 209-32 (vs. 40), 257. FRICK, GPM 4 (1949/50) 260ff. BUTLER, B. C. The Originality of St Matthew (1951) 19ff. KRAUS, H. J. GPM 9 (1954/55) 231ff. M'NEILE, A. H. The Gospel According to St Matthew (1955) 326. TRAUB, GPM 15 (1960/61) 277ff. BORNKAMM-BARTH-HELD, Ueberlieferung und Auslegung im Matthäus-Evangelium (1961) 140-43. RIDDERBOS, S. J. "Liefde als gebod" (Love as a Commandant), NedThT 16 (4, '62) 276-90. STRECKER, G. Der Weg der Gerechtigkeit (1962) 135f. HUMMEL, R. Die Auseinandersetzung zwischen Kirche und Judentum im Matthäusevangelium (1963) 51-53, 53-56. COPPENS, J. "La doctrine biblique sur l'amour de Dieu et du prochaun," EphT 40 (3, '64) 252-99. PESCH, W. "Das Höchste aber ist die Liebe. Das Liebesgebot in der Verkündigung Jesu," BuK 19 (3, '64) 85-89. SUHL, A. Die Funktion der alttestamentlichen Zitate und Anspielungen im Markusevangelium (1965) 87ff. DAVIES, W. D., The Sermon on the Mount (Cambridge 1966) 146f. STERN, J. B. "Jesus'

Citation of Dt 6, 5 and Lv 19, 18 in the Light of Jewish Tradition," CBQ 28 (3, '66) 312-16. "Wir wissen weder Tag noch Stunde", Predigtgedanken aus Vergangenheit und Gegenwart, Bd. 6 (1966) 66-79. BORNKAMM, G. "Das Doppelgebot der Liebe", in: Geschichte und Glaube I (1968) 37-45. BLANK, J. Schriftauslegung in Theorie und Praxis (1969) 221, 222-27. LOHSE, E. and Others (eds.) Der Ruf Jesu und die Antwort der Gemeinde (1970) 39-62, 102. REICKE, B. "Der barmherzige Samariter", Verborum Veritas, Festschrift G. Stählin (1970), Böcher, O. & Haacker, K. (eds.) 103-109. BORNKAMM, G. Geschichte und Glaube II (1971) 92-94. CROSSMAN, J. D. Parable and Example in the Teaching of Jesus. NTS 18 (1971-72) 287-89. FURNISH, V. P. The Love Command in the New Testament (1972) 30-34. VAN DEN ENDE, T. "La Loi et les Prophètes. Mt 22, 34-40," AssS 61 ('72) 18-27. STOEVESANDT, GPM 3/4 (1973) 431-43. FRANKEMÓLLE, H. Jahwebund und Kirche Christi (Münster 1974) 278, 283, 294, 297f, 301. *HULTGREN, A. J., "The Double Commandment of Love in Mt 22:34-40. Its Sources and Compositions" CBQ 36 (1974) 373-78. NISSEN, A., Gott und der Nächste im antiken Judentum. Untersuchungen zum Doppelgebot der Liebe (Tübingen 1974). FULLER, R. H., "Das Doppelgebot der Liebe" in: G. Strecker (ed.) Jesus Christus in Historie und Theologie. Für H. Conzelmann (Tübingen 1975) 317-29. FULLER, R. H., "The Double Commandment of Love. A Test Case for the Criteria of Authenticity" in: L. Schottroff et al., Essays in the Love Commandment (Philadelphia 1978) 41-56. HüBNER, H., Das Gesetz bei Paulus (Göttingen 1978) 78f.

22:34f   HUMMEL, R. Die Auseinandersetzung zwischen Kirche und Judentum im Matthäusevangelium (1963) 19f.

22:35-40 TRAUB, GPM (1960/61) 277ff. DAVIES, W. D., The Sermon on the Mount (Cambridge 1966) 116f. JüNGEL, E. Paulus und Jesus (1966) 169ff.

22:35   BLAIR, E. P. Jesus in the Gospel of Matthew (1960) 100. BOUSSET, W. Die Religion des Judentums im Späthellenistischen Zeitalter (1966-1926) 166.

22:36ff   VOLZ, P. Die Eschatologie der jüdischen Gemeinde (1934) 79.

22:36-37 SAND, A., Das Gesetz und die Propheten (Regensburg 1974) 41-43.

22:36   MOORE, G. F. Judaism (1946) II 85. BLAIR, E. P. Jesus in the Gospel of Matthew (1960) 100. HAHN, F. Christologische Hoheitstitel (1963) 76f.

22:37ff   STONEHOUSE, N. B. The Witness of Matthew and Mark to

Christ (1944) 200. SCHRAGE, W. Die konkreten Einzelgebote in der paulinischen Paränese (1961) 243.

22:37-40 *GERHARDSSON, B., "Det hermeneutiska programmet i Matt. 22-37-40" SEA 40 (1975) 66-89.

22:37-39 SANFORD, J. A., The Kingdom Within (New York 1970) 126f.

22:37 STRECKER, G. Der Weg der Gerechtigkeit (1962) 25f. DEQUEKER, L. "Moraal als godsdienstige levenshouding in de Bijbel" (Morals as a Religious Attitude in the Bibel), CollMech 49 (6, '64) 564-72. BLACK, M. An Aramaic Approach to the Gospels and Acts (1967) 57f. *HUFTIER, M., "Tu aimeras de tout ton coeur. . ." EsVie 89 (1979) 225-32.

22:38 SMITH, M., Tannaitic Parallels to the Gospels (Philadelphia 1968) 6bn5+.

22:39f STRECKER, G. Der Weg der Gerechtigkeit (1962) 22.

22:39 SCHWEIZER, E. Gemeinde und Gemeinde-Ordnung im Neuen Testament (1959) § 4b. STRECKER, G. Der Weg der Gerechtigkeit (1962) 21. CRIPPS, K. R. J. " 'Love your neighbour as yourself' Matthew xxii. 39 et par," ET 76 (1, '64) 26. FREEDMAN, D. N. "The Hebrew Old Testament and the Ministry Today. An Exegetical Study of Leviticus 19:18b," Pittsburgh Perspective 5 (1, '64) 9-14, 30. SCHRAGE, W. Das Verhältnis des Thomas-Evangeliums zur Synoptischen Tradition und zu den Koptischen Evangelienübersetzungen (1964) 70.

22:40 FARRER, A. St Matthew and St Mark (1954) 179. TRILLING, W. Das wahre Israel (1959) 146, 179f. BLAIR, E. P. Jesus in the Gospel of Matthew (1960) 93, 121, 123. BORNKAMM-BARTH-HELD, Ueberlieferung und Auslegung im Matthäus-Evangelium (1961) 23, 58, 60, 71, 74, 92, 148. SCHRAGE, W. Die konkreten Einzelgebote in der paulinischen Paränese (1961) 237. STRECKER, G. Der Weg der Gerechtigkeit (1962) 60₇, 135f., 144, 146. HUMMEL, R. Die Auseinandersetzung zwischen Kirche und Judentum im Matthäusevangelium (1963) 132, 133. BOUSSET, W. Die Religion des Judentums im Späthellenistischen Zeitalter (1966⁻1926) 144. BRUNNER, Mensch i. W., 97. FRANKEMöLLE, H., Jahwebund und Kirche Christi (Münster 1974) 295, 299, 302-304, 390. LADD, G. E., A Theology of the New Testament (Grand Rapids 1974) 132f, 514. SAND, A., Das Gesetz und die Propheten (Regensburg 1974) 189-93. SANDERS, J. T., Ethics in the New Testament (Philadelphia 1975) 42. "Bergpredigt" in: TRE 5 (1980) 610.

22:41ff STONEHOUSE, N. B. The Witness of Matthew and Mark to

Christ (1944) 196. GREER, R. A., The Captain of Our Salvation (Tübingen 1973) 160-62.

22:41-46 WILKENS, J. Einführung in das Evangelium nach Matthäus II (1937) 150-52. BORNKAMM-BARTH-HELD, Ueberlieferung und Auslegung im Matthäus-Evangelium (1961) 30, 224. LöVESTAM, E. "Die Davidssohnfrage," SEA 27 ('62) 72-82. SUHL, A. Die Funktion der alttestamentlichen Zitate und Anspielungen im Markusevangelium (1965) 98ff. FITZMYER, J. "Die Davidssohn-Ueberlieferung und Mt 22:41 (und die Parallelstellen)" Concilium 2 (1966) 780-86. SUHL, A. "Der Devaidssohn im Matthäus-Evangelium," ZNW 59 (1-2, '68) 57-81. BLANK, J. Schriftauslegung in Theorie und Praxis (1969) 221, 227-31. BURGER, C. Jesus als Davidssohn (1970) 87-90. FITZMYER, J. A. Essays on the Semitic Background of the New Testament (1971) 113-26. *FITZMYER, J. "The Son of David Tradition and Matthew 22, 41-46 and Parallels," The Dynamism of Biblical Tradition, 75-87. SAND, A., Das Gesetz und die Propheten (Regensburg 1974) 147-49. RIVKIN, E., A Hidden Revolution (Nashville 1978) 113. GARLAND, D. E., The Intention of Matthew 23 (Leiden 1979) 23-26.

22:41-45 STRECKER, G. Der Weg der Gerechtigkeit (1962) 119f, 123₂. HAHN, F. Christologische Hoheitstitel (1963) 86. GIBBS, J. M. Purpose and Pattern in Matthew's use of the title "Son of David." NTS 10 (1963/64) 448f. FRANKEMöLLE, H., Jahwebund und Kirche Christi (Münster 1974) 114, 137, 168f, 210, 319.

22:41 METZGER, B. M., The Early Versions of the New Testament (Oxford 1977) 151.

22:42 BLAIR, E. P. Jesus in the Gospel of Matthew (1960) 55. STRECKER, G. Der Weg der Gerechtigkeit (1962) 126₂. HAHN, F. Christologische Hoheitstitel (1963) 224, 245. HUMMEL, R. Die Auseinandersetzung zwischen Kirche und Judentum im Matthäusevangelium (1963) 113, 116. SASS, G. Ungereimtes bei Matthäus (1968) 44-46. KINGSBURY, J. D., Matthew: Structure, Christology, Kingdom (Philadelphia 1975) 100-102. FRIEDRICH, G., "Beobachtungen zur messianischen Hohepriestererwartung in den Synoptikern" in: Auf das Wort kommt es an (Göttingen 1978) 77-80.

22:43ff STONEHOUSE, N. B. The Witness of Matthew and Mark to Christ (1944) 194, 242.

22:43f SWAELE, R. L'Arrière-fond Scripturaire de Matt. XXI. 43 et son lien avec. Matt. XXI. 44 NTS 6 (1959/60) 310f. STRECKER, G. Der Weg der Gerechtigkeit (1962) 71₃.

22:43 BARRETT, C. K. The Holy Spirit and the Gospel Tradition (1947) 107-12. LANGE, J., Das Erscheinen des Auferstandenen im Evangelium nach Matthäus (Würzburg 1973) 227-29.

22:44 STRECKER, G. Der Weg der Gerechtigkeit (1962) 22. HORTON, F. L., The Melchizedek Tradition (Cambridge 1976) 23f.

22:45ff STONEHOUSE, N. B. The Witness of Matthew and Mark to Christ (1944) 223.

22:45 SEEBURG, A. Der Katechismus des Urchristenheit (1966) 72f., 78, 137.

22:46 STONEHOUSE, N. B. The Witness of Matthew and Mark to Christ (1944) 150. STRECKER, G. Der Weg der Gerechtigkeit (1962) 92, 119. METZGER, B. M., The Early Versions of the New Testament (Oxford 1977) 440.

23-25 SELBY, D. J., Introduction to the New Testament (New York 1971) 112, 143f. ELLIS, P. F., Matthew: His Mind and His Message (Collegeville 1974) 77-94.

23:37-24:2 GARLAND, D. E., The Intention of Matthew 23 (Leiden 1979) 26-30.

23 WINDISCH, H. The Meaning of the Sermon on the Mount (1937) 103, 119, 140, 150f. MOORE, G. F. Judaism (1946) II 192n. FEINE, D. P. & BEHM, D. J. Einleitung in das Neue Testament (1950) 33f. BUTLER, B. C. The Originality of St Matthew (1951) 73ff. HAENCHEN, E. "Mt 23", ZThK 48 (1951) 38-63. STREETER, B. H. The Four Gospels (1951) 253f. FARRER, A. St Matthew and St Mark (1954) 127. MUNCK, J. Paul and the Salvation of Mankind (1959) 254f., 257, 265. BLAIR, E. P. Jesus in the Gospel fo Matthew (1960) 30, 114. BORNKAMM-BARTH-HELD, Ueberlieferung und Auslegung im Matthäus-Evangelium (1961) 18f., 57, 71, 149. SCHRAGE, W. Die konkreten Einzelgebote in der paulinischen Paränese (1961) 52. STRECKER, G. Der Weg der Gerechtigkeit (1962) 12, 38. HAHN, F. Christologische Hoheitstitel (1963) 79, 400. RUBENSTEIN, R. L. "Scribes, Pharisees and Hypocrites. A Study in Rabbinic Psychology," Judaism 12 (4, '63) 456-68. KäSEMANN, E. Exegetische

Versuche und Besinnungen (1964) I 205, 219. HAENCHEN, E.
Mt 23 in: Gott und Mensch (1965) 29-55. BRAUN, H. Qumran
und NT II (1966) 17. GREENLEE, J. H. Nine Uncial
Palimpsests of the Greek New Testament (1968) 26-27.
LATEGAN, B. C. "Die Botsing tussen Jesus en die Fariseers
volgens Matt. 23" (The Conflict between Jesus and the
Pharisees according to Mt 23), NGTT 10 (4, '69) 217-30.
RICHARDSON, P. Israel in the Apostolic Church (1969)
104n, 109n, 163n, 164n. JEREMIAS, J. New Testament
Theology I (1971). KüMMEL, W. G. Einleitung in das Neue
Testament (1973) 77f. PESCH, W., "Theologische Aussagen
der Redaktion von Matthäus 23" in: P. Hoffmann (ed.)
Orientierung an Jesus. Für J. Schmid (Freiburg 1973) 286-99,
302-304. ELLIS, P. F., Matthew: His Mind and His Message
(Collegeville 1974) 80-82. SAND, A., Das Gesetz und die
Propheten (Regensburg 1974) 88-95. *GIRARD, R., "Les
malédictions contre les Pharisiens et la révélation évangélique"
Bulletin du Centre Protestant d'Etudes 27 (1975) 5-29.
*KELLY, M. "The Woes against the Scribes and Pharisees"
SIDIC 10 (1977) 17-22. SANDMEL, S., We Jews and Jesus
(New York 1977) 109, 125. FRIEDRICH, G., "Das Problem
der Autorität im Neuen Testament" in: Auf das Wort kommt es
an (Göttingen 1978) 285-87. *MOTTU, H. and VOUGA, F.,
"La Passion de la Parole. Jésus, prophète invectivant et
souffrant" Bulletin du Centre Protestant d'Etudes 30 (1978) 38-
46. GARLAND, D. E., The Intention of Matthew 23 (Leiden
1979). *MITTON, C. L., "Matthew's Disservice to Jesus"
Epworth Review 6 (1979) 47-54. HARRINGTON, D. J., God's
People in Christ (Philadelphia 1980) 100f.

23:1ff   MOORE, G.F. Judaism (1946) I 262n. KNOX, W. L. The
Sources of the Synoptic Gospels II (1957) 95ff. STRECKER,
G. Der Weg der Gerechtigkeit (1962) 138. STROBEL, A.
Erkenntnis und Bekenntnis der Sünde in neutestamentlicher
Zeit (1968) 45.

23:1-39 WILKENS, J. Einführung in das Evangelium nach Matthäus
II (1937) 153-64. LUND, N. W. Chiasmus in the New
Testament (1942) 283f.

23:1-36 GIBBS, J. M. Purpose and Patterns in Matthew's use of the
title "Son of David." NTS 10 (1963-64) 461f.

23:1-13 JEREMIAS, J. Neutestamentliche Theologie I (1971) 144f.
JEREMIAS, J. New Testament Theology I (1971) 45f.

23:1-12 GOODSPEED, E. J. A Life of Jesus (1950) 182-84.
BRANDENBURGER / MERKEL / BALTZER, GPM
(1964/65) 296ff. HELD, H. J. in: Hören und Fragen Bd. 5
(1967) Eichholz, G. & Falkenroth, A. (eds.) 424ff. OTOMO, Y.

Nachfolge Jesu und Anfänge der Kirche im Neuen Testament (1970) 106-110. LANGE, E. (ed.) Predigtstudien für das Kirchenjahr 1970/71 (1970) 176-81. STOEVESANDT, H. GPM 25 (1971) 343-52. STECK, K. G. GPM 13/3, 208-14. HERTZBER, A. und SEILER, A., in: P. Krusche (ed.) Predigtstudien V/2 (Stuttgart 1977) 162-68. GARLAND, D. E., The Intention of Matthew 23 (Leiden 1979) 34-63.

23:1-4 GOULDER, D. M., Midrash and Lection in Matthew (London 1974) 422f.

23:1-3 BORNKAMM-BARTH-HELD, Ueberlieferung und Auslegung im Matthäus-Evangelium (1961) 18, 22, 66, 80.

23:1f STRECKER, G. Der Weg der Gerchtigkeit (1962) 118.

23:1 STONEHOUSE, N. B. The Witness of Matthew and Mark to Christ (1944) 176, 177. STRECKER, G. Der Weg der Gerechtigkeit (1962) 92, 106, 114ı.

23:2-39 SMITH, M., Tannaitic Parallels to the Gospels (Philadelphia 1968) 4 F+.

23:2-29 RIVKIN, E., A Hidden Revelation (Nashville 1978) 81-87, 113f, 269f.

23:2-5 BOUSSET, W. Die Religion des Judentums im Späthellenistischen Zeitalter (1966⁻1926) 162, 179, 410. RIVKIN, E., A Hidden Revelation (Nashville 1978) 121f.

23:2-3 STONEHOUSE, N. B. The Witness of Matthew and Mark to Christ (1944) 196f. MOORE, G. F. Judaism (1946) II 9n. BLAIR, E. P. Jesus in the Gospel of Matthew (1960) 32. STRECKER, G. Der Weg der Gerechtigkeit (1962) 131, 16. HUMMEL, R. Die Auseinandersetzung zwischen Kirche und Judentum im Matthäusevangelium (1963) 31, 157. HENNECKE, E. & SCHNEEMELCHER, W. Neutestamentliche Apokryphen (1964) II 75, 389. GOULDER, M. D., Midrash and Lection in Matthew (London 1974) 151, 163, 178, 284, 421.

23:2 HAHN, F. Christologische Hoheitstitel (1963) 402. SAITO, T., Die Mosevorstellungen im Neuen Testament (Bern 1977) 71f.

23:3ff BANKS, R., Jesus and the Law in the Synoptic Tradition (Cambridge 1975) 175-77.

23:3 BLAIR, E. P. Jesus in the Gospel of Matthew (1960) 111, 112ff. STRECKER, G. Der Weg der Gerechtigkeit (1962) 138f.

23:4.13. LüHRMANN, D. Die Redaktion der Logienquelle (1969) 43-
23. 48.
25-27.
29-32.
34-36.

23:4, 5 MOORE, G. F. Judaism (1946) II 194, 194n.

23:4 STONEHOUSE, N. B. The Witness of Matthew and Mark to Christ (1944) 196. STRECKER, G. Der Weg der Gerechtigkeit (1962) 173. CHRIST, F. Jesus Sophia (1970) 107, 110, 111. JEREMIAS, J. Neutestamentliche Theologie I (1971) 25f. TALBERT, C. H., Literary Patterns, Theological Themes, and the Genre of Luke-Acts (Missoula 1974) 54. METZGER, B. M., The Early Versions of the New Testament (Oxford 1977) 422. POLAG, A., Die Christologie der Logienquelle (Neukirchen-Vluyn 1977) 82.

23:5-12 STRECKER, G. Der Weg der Gerechtigkeit (1962) 174.

23:5 MILIK, J.-T. "Les phylactères au temps de Jésus," Bib TerreSainte 36 ('61) 14-15. STRECKER, G. Der Weg der Gerechtigkeit (1962) 165z. CLARK, K. W., "The Gentile Bias in Matthew" in: The Gentile Bias and other Essays (Leiden 1980) 6.

23:6-7 TALBERT, C. H., Literary Patterns, Theological Themes, and the Genre of Luke-Acts (Missoula 1974) 54.

23:6 BRAUN, H. Qumran und NT II (1966) 287, 295. RIVKIN, E., A Hidden Revolution (Nashville 1978) 114.

23:7-11 BOVER, J. M. "Der 'Lehrer und Meister' in der Geschichte des Rabbinismus" (span), Sefarad XIV/2 (1954) 366-68.

23:7-10 PARKER, P. The Gospel Before Mark (1953) 19-20. FRANKEMöLLE, H., Jahwebund und Kirche Christi (Münster 1974) 99-101, 178f, 189.

23:7f STRECKER, G. Der Weg der Gerechtigkeit (1962) 33. HAHN, F. Christologische Hoheitstitel (1963) 75. JEREMIAS, J. Neutestamentliche Theologie I (1971) 17, 82, 166, 211, 247.

23:7 STRECKER, G. Der Weg der Gerechtigkeit (1962) 140.

23:8ff THEISSEN, G., Soziologie der Jesusbewegung (München 1977) 24. "Bergpredigt" in: TRE 5 (1980) 609.

23:8-12 BORNKAMM-BARTH-HELD, Ueberlieferung und Auslegung im Matthäus-Evangelium (1961) 19, 36f., 40, 90, 97. STRECKER, G. Der Weg der Gerechtigkeit (1962) 41, 217f. MICHAELS, J. R., "Christian Prophecy and Matthew 23:8-12 - A Test Exegesis" in: G. MacRae (ed.) Society of Biblical Literature 1976 Seminar Papers (Missoula 1976) 305-12.

23:8-11 HOFFMANN, P., und EID, V., Jesus von Nazareth und eine christliche Moral (Freiburg 1975) 223-25.

23:8-10 SPICQ, C. Dieu et L'Homme (1961) 51-52. STRECKER, G. Der Weg der Gerechtigkeit (1962) 37. HAHN, F. Christologische Hoheitstitel (1963) 402. HUMMEL, R. Die

Auseinandersetzung zwischen Kirche und Judentum im Matthäusevangelium (1963) 27f. KäSEMANN, E. Exegetische Versuche und Besinnungen (1964) II 84f. KäSEMANN, E. New Testament Questions of Today (1969) 84. TRILLING. W., "Amt und Amtsverständnis bei Matthäus" in: A. Descamps and A. Halleux (eds.) Mélanges Bibliques en hommage au R. P. Bëda Rigaux (Gembloux 1970) 30-32. GOPPELT, L., Theologie des Neuen Testaments II (Göttingen 1976) 564. DUNN, J. D. G., Unity and Diversity in the New Testament (London 1977) 117.

23:8-9   BARBOUR, R. S. "Uncomfortable Words: VIII. Status and Titles," ET 82 (5, '71) 137-42.

23:8   STONEHOUSE, N. B. The Witness of Matthew and Mark to Christ (1944) 175. HAHN, F. Christologische Hoheitstitel (1963) 77, 78f., 80f. BRAUN, H. Qumran und NT II (1966) 96, 287, 290. DAVIES, W. D., The Sermon on the Mount (Cambridge 1966) 89. GOPPELT, L., Theologie des Neuen Testaments I (Göttingen 1975) 212f. "Amt" in: TRE 2 (1978) 511. FRIEDRICH, G., "Das Problem der Autorität im Neuen Testament" in: Auf das Wort kommt es an (Göttingen 1978) 391-92.

23:9f   HAHN, F. Christologische Hoheitstitel (1963) 78.

23:9-10   BOUSSET, W. Die Religion des Judentums im Späthellenistischen Zeitalter (1966⁻1926) 169.

23:9   COLUNGA, A. "A nadie 'laméis padre sobre la tierra, porque uno solo es vuestro padre, el que esta en los cielos" (Mt 23, 9), Misc. bibl. B. Ubach. Montserrat (1953) 333-47. KNOX, W. L. The Sources of the Synoptic Gospels II (1957) 27. TOWNSEND, J. T. "Matthew xxiii. 9," JThS 12 (1, '61) 56-59. WAINWRIGHT, A. W. The Trinity in the New Testament (1962) 41-42. JEREMIAS, J. Neutestamentliche Theologie I (1971) 73, 166, 176.

23:10   SPICQ, C. "Une allusion au Docteur de Justice dans Matthieu, XXIII, 10?" RevBi 66 (3, '59) 387-96. BULTMANN, R. The History of the Synoptic Tradition (1963) 148f., 151. HAHN, F. Christologische Hoheitstitel (1963) 224. HUMMEL, R. Die Auseinandersetzung zwischen Kirche und Judentum im Matthäusevangelium (1963) 113ff. BRAUN, H. Qumran und NT II (1966) 287-95. JEREMIAS,J. Neutestamentliche Theologie I (1971) 166, 246f.

23:11f   SCHRAGE, W. Die konkreten Einzelgebote in der paulinischen Paränese (1961) 243. STRECKER, G. Der Weg der Gerechtigkeit (1962) 140.

23:11   ROBINSON, J. M. Kerygma und historischer Jesus (1960) 166.
KäSEMANN, E. Exegetische Versuche und Besinnungen
(1964) I 109.

23:12   MOORE, G. F. Judaism (1946) II 274. ROBINSON, J. M.
Kerygma und historischer Jesus (1960) 165. STRECKER, G.
Der Weg der Gerechtigkeit (1962) 174. KäSEMANN, E.
Exegetische Versuche und Besinnungen (1964) I 78, II 97.
CARLSTON, C. The Things that Defile (Mark VII. 14) and the
Law in Matthew and Mark. NTS 15 (1968-69) 78-80.
KäSEMANN, E. New Testament Questions of Today (1969)
98. SANFORD, J. A., The Kingdom Within (New York 1970)
188f. JEREMIAS, J. Neutestamentliche Theologie I (1971) 22,
25f., 28f., 35. SCHULZ, S. Q Die Spruchquelle der
Evangelisten (1972) 451-52. HOFFMANN, P. und EID, V.,
Jesus von Nazareth und eine christliche Moral (Freiburg 1975)
208-11. POLAG, A., Die Christologie der Logienquelle
(Neukirchen-Vluyn 1977) 163.

23:13ff   STONEHOUSE, N. B. The Witness of Matthew and Mark to
Christ (1944) 130. HAHN, F. Christologische Hoheitstitel
(1963) 402. DORMEYER, D., Die Passion Jesu als
Verhaltensmodell (Münster 1974) 98A, 234.

23:13-36 KüMMEL, W. G. "Die Weherufe über die Schriftgelehrten und
Pharisäer (Matthäus 23, 13-36)", in: Antijudaismus im Neuen
Testament? (1967) Eckert/Levinson/Stöhr (eds.) 135-47.
GOPPELT, L., Theologie des Neuen Testaments I (Göttingen
1975) 135-38.

23:13-35 SCHUBERT, K., Jesus im Lichte der Religionsgeschichte des
Judentums (Wien 1973) 47-52, 77f.

23:13-28 GARLAND, D. E., The Intention of Matthew 23 (Leiden 1979)
64-162.

23:13-19 McDONALD, J. I. H., Kerygma and Didache (Cambridge
1980) 21-22.

23:13-14 TALBERT, C. H., Literary Patterns, Theological Themes, and
the Genre of Luke-Acts (Missoula 1974) 54.

23:13   STAEHELIN, E. Die Verkündigung des Reiches Gottes in der
Kirche Jesu Christi I (1951) 62. FLEW, R. N. Jesus and His
Church (1956) 25, 95. STRECKER, G. Der Weg der
Gerechtigkeit (1962) 168, 1746. KäSEMANN, E. Exegetische
Versuche und Besinnungen (1964) II 103. SCHRAGE, W. Das
Verhältnis des Thomas-Evangeliums zur Synoptischen
Tradition und zu den Koptischen Evangelienübersetzungen
(1964) 91. BRAUN, H. Qumran und NT II (1966) 89f.
NICKELS, P. Targum and New Testament (1967) 21.
SUMMERS, R. The Secret Sayings of the Living Jesus (1968)

30. HENGEL, M., Judentum und Hellenismus (Tübingen 1969) 313+; ET: Judaism and Hellenism II (London 1974) 113. HOFFMAN, P. Studien zur Theologie der Logienquelle (1972) 70f. GOULDER, M. D., Midrash and Lection in Matthew (London 1974) 163, 165, 390, 421, 424. LADD, G. E., A Theology of the New Testament (Grand Rapids 1974) 70, 88, 103, 117. EDWARDS, R. A., A Theology of Q (Philadelphia 1976) 70. "Agrapha" in: TRE 2 (1978) 106. GARLAND, D. E., The Intention of Matthew 23 (Leiden 1979) 124-29.

23:14-36   STONEHOUSE, N. B. The Witness of Matthew and Mark to Christ (1944) 157.

23:14   METZGER, B. M., The Early Versions of the New Testament (Oxford 1977) 118

23:15   VOLZ, P. Die Eschatologie der jüdischen Gemeinde (1934) 78. BARRETT, C. K. The New Testament Background: Selected Documents (1956) 164. FLOWERS, H. J. "Matthew xxiii.15," ET 73 (3, '61) 67-69. HOAD, J. "On Matthew xxiii.15: a Rejoinder," ET 73 (7, '62) 211-12. HAHN, F. Das Verständnis der Mission im Neuen Testament (1965) 18, 43. BOUSSET, W. Die Religion des Judentums im Späthellenistischen Zeitalter (1966⁻1926) 84. NICKELS, P. Targum and New Testament (1967) 21. KASTING, H. Die Anfänge der Urchristlichen Mission (1969) 20f. JEREMIAS, J. Neutestamentliche Theologie I (1971) 17, 144, 146. GARLAND, D. E., The Intention of Matthew 23 (Leiden 1979) 129-31. *NOLAND, J., "Proselytism or Politics in Horace Satires I, 4, 138-43?" VigChr 33 (1979) 347-55.

23:16ff   STONEHOUSE, N. B. The Witness of Matthew and Mark to Christ (1944) 196, 207. KNOX, W. L. The Sources of the Synoptic Gospels II (1957) 23. GäRTNER, B. The Temple and the Community in Qumran and the New Testament (1965) 110.

23:16-24   BRAUN, H. Qumran und NT II (1966) 99, 101, 289, 293, 295.

23:16-22   BORNKAMM-BARTH-HELD, Ueberlieferung und Auslegung im Matthäus-Evangelium (1961) 136. STRECKER, G. Der Weg der Gerechtigkeit (1962) 16, 133. BULTMANN, R. The History of the Synoptic Tradition (1963) 133f. HUMMEL, R. Die Auseinandersetzung zwischen Kirche und Judentum im Matthäusevangelium (1963) 79-80. JEREMIAS, J. New Testament Theology I (1971) 145f., 174, 179, 207, 220. JEREMIAS, J. Neutestamentliche Theologie I (1971) 144f., 171, 175, 200, 202. GOULDER, M. D., Midrash and Lection in Matthew (London 1974) 293, 421, 424f. WESTERHOLM, S., Jesus and Scribal Authority (Lund 1978) 108-12. GARLAND, D. E., The Intention of Matthew 23 (Leiden 1979) 132-36.

23:16 KNOX, W. L. The Sources of the Synoptic Gospels II (1957) 10. NICKELS, P. Targum and New Testament (1967) 21.

23:18f HUMMEL, R. Die Auseinandersetzung zwischen Kirche und Judentum im Matthäusevangelium (1963) 94.

23:20 KNOX, W. L. The Sources of the Synoptic Gospels II (1957) 22.

23:33ff STONEHOUSE, N. B. The Witness of Matthew and Mark to Christ (1944) 197, 200.

23:23-33 SWIDLER, L., Biblical Affirmations of Woman (Philadelphia 1979) 284.

23:23-32 HOFFMANN, P. Studien zur Theologie der Logienquelle (1972) passim.

23:23-29 GARLAND, D. E., The Intention of Matthew 23 (Leiden 1979) 136-41.

23:23-28 TRILLING, W. Das wahre Israel (1959) 173f.

23:23-26 SANDMEL, S., We Jews and Jesus (New York 1977) 137.

23:23-24 MASSAUX, E. Influence de l'Evangile de saint Matthieu sur la littérature chrétienne avant saint Irénée (1950) 512-14, 540-41.

HUMMEL, R. Die Auseinandersetzung zwischen Kirche und Judentum im Matthäusevangelium (1963) 75. JEREMIAS, J. Neutestamentlichen Theologie I (1971) 25f., 29, 146, 158.

23:23 MOORE, G. F. Judaism (1946) II 9. KNOX, W. L. The Sources of the Synoptic Gospels II (1957) 114. BLAIR, E. P. Jesus in the Gospel of Matthew (1960) 93, 111, 113, 123. BORNKAMM-BARTH-HELD, Ueberlieferung und Auslegung im Matthäus-Evangelium (1961) 23f., 26, 58, 74f., 82ff., 107. STRECKER, G. Der Weg der Gerechtigkeit (1962) 322, 392, 1364, 139, 173, 232. BAUMBACH, G. Das Verständnis des Bösen in den synoptischen Evangelien (1963) 215ff. KINNIBURGH, E. "Hard Sayings-III. Matthew 23.23," Theology 66 (520, '63) 414-16. BOUSSET, W. Die Religion des Judentums im Späthellenistischen Zeitalter (1966⁻1926) 110. O'NEILL, J. C., The Theology of Acts in its Historical Setting (London 1970) 36f. LANGE, J., Das Erscheinen des Auferstandenen im Evangelium nach Matthäus (Würzburg 1973) 30f., 52, 250, 263, 266, 270, 276, 321-23, 333. FRANKEMöLLE, H., Jahwebund und Kirche Christi (Münster 1974) 294, 300-303. SAND, A., Das Gesetz und die Propheten (Regensburg 1974) 39-41. EDWARDS, R. A., A Theology of Q (Philadelphia 1976) 69. POLAG, A., Die Christologie der Logienquelle (Neukirchen-Vluyn 1977) 80f. WESTERHOLM, S., Jesus and Scribal Authority (Lund 1978) 57-61. "Barmherzigkeit" in: TRE 5 (1980) 225.

23:24.26 BLAIR, E. P. Jesus in the Gospel of Matthew (1960) 100.

23:24 KNOX, W. L. The Sources of the Synoptic Gospels II (1957) 10.

23:25ff KNOX, W. L. The Sources of the Synoptic Gospels II (1957) 12.

23:25-26 TRILLING, W. Das wahre Israel (1959) 173f. STRECKER, G. Der Weg der Gerechtigkeit (1962) 31f., 140. HAHN, F. Christologische Hoheitstitel (1963) 88. HENNECKE, E. & SCHNEEMELCHER, W. Neutestamentliche Apokryphen (1964) II 79. SANFORD, J. A., The Kingdom Within (New York 1970) 97f. GOULDER, M. D., Midrash and Lection in Matthew (London 1974) 164, 425f, 468. TALBERT, C. H., Literary Patterns, Theological Themes, and the Genre of Luke-Acts (Missoula 1974) 54. *NEUSNER, J., " 'First Cleanse the Inside.' The 'Halakhic' Background of a Controversy-Saying" NTS 22 (1976) 486-95. POLAG, A., Die Christologie der Logienquelle (Neukirchen-Vluyn 1977) 81. WESTERHOLM, S., Jesus and Scribal Authority (Lund 1978) 85-90. GARLAND, D. E., The Intention of Matthew 23 (Leiden 1979) 141-50.

23:25 KLEIN, G., "Rein und unrein Mt 23, 25. Lc 11, 37.42" ZNW 7 (1906) 252-54. STRECKER, G. Der Weg der Gerechtigkeit (1962) 387. SCHRAGE, W. Das Verhältnis des Thomas-Evangeliums zur Synoptischen Tradition und zu den Koptischen Evangelienübersetzungen (1964) 170. BOUSSET, W. Die Religion des Judentums im Späthellenistischen Zeitalter (1966⁻1926) 127. SCHULZ, S. Q Die Spruchquelle der Evangelisten (1972) 94-114. QUISPEL, G., "An Apocryphal Variant in Marcaius" Orientalia Lovaniensia Periodica 6-7 (1975-76) 487-92. HOLM-NIELSEN, S., "Die Psalmen Salomos" in: W. G. Kümmel (ed.) Jüdische Schriften aus hellenistisch-römischer Zeit IV (Gütersloh 1977) 70. METZGER, B. M., The Early Versions of the New Testament (Oxford 1977) 147.

23:26 STRECKER, G. Der Weg der Gerechtigkeit (1962) 139, 141. JEREMIAS, J. Neutestamentliche Theologie I (1971) 144, 157f.

23:27f TRILLING, W. Das wahre Israel (1959) 174. STRECKER, G. Der Weg der Gerechtigkeit (1962) 140. JEREMIAS, J. Neutestamentliche Theologie I (1971) 25, 146.

23:27-28 TALBERT, C. H., Literary Patterns, Theological Themes, and the Genre of Luke—Acts (Missoula 1974) 54. *LACHS, S. T., "On Matthew 23:27-28" HThR 68 (1975) 385-88. EDWARDS, R. A., A Theology of Q (Philadelphia 1976) 69f. POLAG, A.,

Die Christologie der Logienquelle (Neukirchen-Vluyn 1977) 82. GARLAND, D. E., The Intention of Matthew 23 (Leiden 1979) 150-59.

23:27   RUDOLPH, K., Die Gnosis (Göttingen 1978) 207.

23:28ff   STONEHOUSE, N. B. The Witness of Matthew and Mark to Christ (1944) 130.

23:28   BLAIR, E. P. Jesus in the Gospel of Matthew (1960) 111. STRECKER, G. Der Weg der Gerechtigkeit (1962) 141f. BAUMBACH, G. Das Verständnis des Bösen in den synoptischen Evangelien (1963) 103ff. DAVIES, W. D., The Sermon on the Mount (Cambridge 1966) 72f.

23:29ff   STRECKER, G. Der Weg der Gerechtigkeit (1962) 113f. HAHN, F. Das Verständnis der Mission im Neuen Testament (1965) 109. CHRIST, F. Jesus Sophia (1970) 120, 132. PATSCH, H. Abendmahl und historischer Jesus (1972) 204f. "Autorität" in TRE 5 (1980) 44.

23:29-39   HUMMEL, R. Die Auseinandersetzung zwischen Kirche und Judentum im Matthäusevangelium (1963) 158. TILBORG, S. van, The Jewish Leaders in Matthew (Leiden 1972) 63-72. MINEAR, P. S., "False Prophecy and Hypocrisy in the Gospel of Matthew" in: J. Gnilka (ed.) Neues Testament und Kirche. Für R. Schnackenburg (Freiburg 1974) 86-93. SCHULZ, S., Die Mitte der Schrift (Stuttgart 1976) 168f. GARLAND, D. E., The Intention of Matthew 23 (Leiden 1979) 163-209. JEWETT, R., Jesus against the Rapture (Philadelphia 1979) 84-104.

23:29-36   JEREMIAS, J. Neutestamentliche Theologie I (1971) 144f., 269. GOULDER, M. D., Midrash and Lection in Matthew (London 1974) 281, 332, 422, 427ff. WILLIAMS, J. A., A Conceptual History of Deuteronomism in the Old Testament, Judaism, and the New Testament (Ph.D. Diss. Southern Baptist Theological Seminary, Louisville 1976) 289-93, 310. TRITES, A. A., The New Testament Concept of Witness (Cambridge 1977) 194.

23:29-32   TALBERT, C. H., Literary Patterns, Theological Themes, and the Genre of Luke-Acts (Missoula 1974) 54.

23:29-31   TRILLING, W. Das wahre Israel (1959) 174. SATAKE, A. Die Gemeindeordnung in der Johannesapokalypse (1966) 179f. SCHNIDER, F., Jesus der Prophet (Freiburg 1973) 60, 136ff, 159, 177. EDWARDS, R. A., A Theology of Q (Philadelphia 1976) 70. GARLAND, D. E., The Intention of Matthew 23 (Leiden 1979) 163-66.

23:29.34f   BOUSSET, W. Die Religion des Judentums im Späthellenistischen Zeitalter (1966⁻1926) 190.

23:29f JEREMIAS, J. Neutestamentliche Theologie I (1971) 26, 35, 267.

23:29 REICKE, B. Diakonie, Festfreude und Zelos (1951) 261f. HAHN, F. Christologische Hoheitstitel (1963) 382. CHRIST, F. Jesus Sophia (1970) 122, 130. ZIESLER, J. A. The Meaning of Righteousness in Paul (1972) 138f., 145. VIELHAUER, Ph., "Oikodome. Das Bild vom Bau in der christlichen Literatur vom Neuen Testament bis Clemens Alexandrinus" in: Oikodome (München 1979) 54.

23:30-32 HUMMEL, R. Die Auseinandersetzung zwischen Kirche und Judentum im Matthäusevangelium (1963) 158.

23:30 STRECKER, G. Der Weg der Gerechtigkeit (1962) 89. WILLIAMS, J. A., A Conceptual History of Deuteronomism in the Old Testament, Judaism, and the New Testament (Ph.D. Diss. Southern Baptist Theological Seminary, Louisville 1976) 315.

23:31f JEREMIAS, J. Neutestamentliche Theologie I (1971) 26, 83, 89, 128.

23:31 HAHN, F. Christologische Hoheitstitel (1963) 382. BRAUN, H. Qumran und NT II (1966) 58, 104. BEUTLER, J. Martyria (1972) 172, 192, 216, 221.

23:32ff HUMMEL, R. Die Auseinandersetzung zwischen Kirche und Judentum im Matthäusevangelium (1963) 87f.

23:32-39 GNILKA, J. Die Verstockung Israels (1961) 100-102. BROWN, S., "The Matthean Apocalypse" Journal for the Study of the New Testament 4 (1979) 2-27.

23:32 BLAIR, E. P. Jesus in the Gospel of Matthew (1960) 119. HUMMEL, R. Die Auseinandersetzung zwischen Kirche und Judentum im Matthäusevangelium (1963) 158. WREGE, H.-T. Die Ueberlieferungsgeschichte der Bergpredigt (1968) 54f., 167. GARLAND, D. E., The Intention of Matthew 23 (Leiden 1979) 166-68.

23:33ff STONEHOUSE, N. B. The Witness of Matthew and Mark to Christ (1944) 130.

23:33-36 WELLS, G. The Jesus of the Early Christians (1971) 116-17. MEYER, B. F., The Aims of Jesus (London 1979) 207.

23:33 PARKER, P. The Gospel Before Mark (1953) 82-83. KNOX, W. L. The Sources of the Synoptic Gospels II (1957) 50. STRECKER, G. Der Weg der Gerechtigkeit (1962) 159. KINNIBURGH, E., "Hard Sayings" Th 66 (1963) 414-16. JEREMIAS, J. Neutestamentliche Theologie I (1971) 17, 130, 150. GARLAND, D. E., The Intention of Matthew 23 (Leiden 1979) 170f.

23:34ff BEYSCHLAG, K. Clemens Romanus und der Frühkatholizismus (1966) 223.

23:34-39 KLAAS, W. in: Herr, tue meine Lippen auf Bd. 3 (1964) Eichholz, G. (ed.) 356ff. WEBER, O. Predigtmeditationen (1967) 46-50. WEBER, GPM I, 33ff. EHRENBERG, GPM 6, 186ff. KRECK, GPM 9/1, 31-34. GRUNDMANN, W., "Weisheit im Horizont des Reiches Gottes. Eine Studie zur Verkündigung Jesu nach der Spruchüberlieferung Q" in: R. Schnackenburg (ed.) Die Kirche des Anfangs. Für H. Schürmann (Leipzig 1977) 180.

23:34-37 SCHENKE, H. M., "Die Tendenz der Weisheit zur Gnosis"in: B. Aland (ed.) Gnosis. Für H. Jonas (Göttingen 1978) 359-65.

23:34-36 TRILLING, W. Das wahre Israel (1959) 63f. HAHN, F. Christologische Hoheitstitel (1963) 382. SATAKE, A. Die Gemeindeordnung in der Johannesapokalypse (1960) 180-85. CHRIST, F. Jesus Sophia (1970) 120-35. SUGGS, M. J. Wisdom, Christology, and Law in Matthew's Gospel (1970) 13ff. JEREMIAS, J. Neutestamentliche Theologie I (1971) 83, 136, 235, 269. HOFFMANN, P. Studien zur Theologie der Logienquelle (1972) 164-66. SCHULZ, S. Q Die Spruchquelle der Evangelisten (1972) 336-45. SCHNIDER, F., Jesus der Prophet (Freiburg 1973) 74, 139ff, 159. LANG, B., Frau Weisheit (Düsseldorf 1975) 180. POLAG, A., Die Christologie der Logienquelle (Neukirchen-Vluyn 1977). GARLAND, D. E., The Intention of Matthew 23 (Leiden 1979) 171-87.

23:34-35 JEREMIAS, J. Neutestamentliche Theologie I (1971) 22, 129, 267. WILLIAMS, J. A., A Conceptual History of Deuteronomism in the Old Testament, Judaism, and the New Testament (Ph.D. Diss. Southern Baptist Theological Seminary, Louisville 1976) 315.

23:34 BORNKAMM-BARTH-HELD, Ueberlieferung und Auslegung im Matthäus-Evangelium (1961) 94, 104, 192. STRECKER, G. Der Weg der Gerechtigkeit (1962) 30, 37f., 39, 41, 154, 182, 2397. HUMMEL, R. Die Auseinandersetzung zwischen Kirche und Judentum im Matthäusevangelium (1963) 27. LAMBRECHT, J. "Die Logia-Quellen von Markus 13," Biblica 47 (1966) 357. SEITZ, O. J. F., "The Commission of Prophets and Apostles"in: Studia Evangelica IV (1968) 236-40. MINEAR, P. S., "False Prophecy and Hypocrisy in the Gospel of Matthew" in: J. Gnilka (ed.) Neues Testament und Kirche. Für R. Schnackenburg (Freiburg 1974) 76-78. HOWARD, V. P., Das Ego in den Synoptischen Evangelien (Marburg 1975) 163-67. MüLLER, U. B., Zur frühchristlichen Theologiegeschichte (Gütersloh 1976) 37. THEISSEN, G., Soziologie der Jesusbewegung (München 1977) 17, 24. "Amt" in: TRE 2 (1978) 517. SWIDLER, L., Biblical Affirmations of Woman (Philadelphia 1979) 64.

23:35f McNAMARA, M. The New Testament and the Palestinian Targum to the Pentateuch (1966) 160.

23:35 M'NEILE, A. H. The Gospel According to St Matthew (1955) 340f. RUDOLPH, K. Die Mandäer I (1960) 106,9. STRECKER, G. Der Weg der Gerechtigkeit (1962) 116. HUMMEL, R. Die Auseinandersetzung zwischen Kirche und Judentum im Matthäusevangelium (1963) 89f. BRAUN, H. Qumran und NT II (1966) 104. McNAMARA, M. The New Testament and the Palestinian Targum to the Pentateuch (1966) 160-63. NICKELS, P. Targum and New Testament (1967) 21. METZGER, B.M., The Early Versions of the New Testament (Oxford 1977) 172.

23:36 McNAMARA, M. The New Testament and the Palestinian Targum to the Pentateuch (1966) 163. HASLER, V. Amen (1969) 69. JEREMIAS, J. Neutestamentliche Theologie I (1971) 22, 44, 135.

23:37ff GOULDER, M. D., Midrash and Lection in Matthew (London 1974) 162, 268, 429f, 469. "Autorität"in: TRE 5 (1980) 44.

23:37-39 HIRSCH, E. Frühgeschichte des Evangeliums (1941) 132-34. STONEHOUSE, N. B. The Witness of Matthew and Mark to Christ (1944) 157. KNOX, W. L. The Sources of the Synoptic Gospels II (1957) 83, 150. STRECKER, G. Der Weg der Gerechtigkeit (1962) 113ff., 2402. BULTMANN, R. The History of the Synoptic Tradition (1963) 114f. SATAKE, A. Die Gemeindeordnung in der Johannesapokalypse (1966) 185-87. VAN DER KWAAK, H., "Die Klage über Jerusalem" NovT 8 (1966) 156-70. CHRIST, F. Jesus Sophia (1970) 136-52. SUGGS, M. J. Wisdom, Christology, and Law in Matthew's Gospel (1970) 31ff. JEREMIAS, J. Neutestamentliche Theologie I (1971) 36, 83, 269. HOFFMANN, P. Studien zur Theologie der Logienquelle (1972) 5, 40, 50, 73, 98, 117, 132, 137, 158, 171-80, 188-90, 199f., 290f., 304. SCHULZ, S. Q Die Spruchquelle der Evangelisten (1972) 346-60. SCHNIDER, F., Jesus der Prophet (Freiburg 1973) 74ff., 142ff. FRANKEMöLLE, H., Jahwebund und Kirche Christi (Münster 1974) 115, 250, 262, 286, 290. TALBERT, C. H., Literary Patterns, Theological Themes, and the Genre of Luke-Acts (Missola 1974) 56. WILCKENS, U., Die Missionsreden der Apostelgeschichte (Neukirchen 1974 *(3)*, 120, 202, 204, 218. NEUSNER, J., First Century Judais m in Crisis (Nashville 1975) 24f. EDWARDS, R. A., A Theology of Q (Philadelphia 1976) 66-68, 132f. GARLAND, D. E., The Intention of Matthew 23 (Leiden 1979) 187-209.

23:37-38   WILLIAMS, J. A., A Conceptual History of Deuteronomism in the Old Testament, Judaism, and the New Testament (Ph.D.Diss. Southern Baptist Theological Seminary, Louisville 1976) 294-97. MEYER, B. F., The Aims of Jesus (London 1979) 207f.

23:37.38   BRAUN, H. Qumran und NT II (1966) 89f., 269.

23:37   STONEHOUSE, N. B. The Witness of Matthew and Mark to Christ (1944) 185f. HAHN, F. Christologische Hoheitstitel (1963) 49, 382. HUMMEL, R. Die Auseinandersetzung zwischen Kirche und Judentum im Matthäusevangelium (1963) 158. JEREMIAS, J. Neutestamentliche Theologie I (1971) 22, 150, 174, 266, 270. MACK, B. L., Logos und Sophia (Göttingen 1973) 120. WILLIAMS, J. A., A Conceptual History of Deuteronomism in the Old Testament, Judaism and the New Testament (Ph.D.Diss. Southern Baptist Theological Seminary, Louisville 1976) 306, 310. MEYER, B. F., The Aims of Jesus (London 1979) 210f. SWIDLER, L., Biblical Affirmations of Woman (Philadelphia 1979) 64, 173, 242, 257.

23:38f   TRILLING, W. Das wahre Israel (1959) 67f. KüNZI, M. Das Naherwartungslogion Matthäus 10, 23 (1970) 120, 126, 155.

23:38   HUMMEL, R. Die Auseinandersetzung zwischen Kirche und Judentum im Matthäusevangelium (1963) 88f. GäRTNER, B. The Temple and the Community in Qumran and the New Testament (1965) 110.

23:39   STONEHOUSE, N. B. The Witness of Matthew and Mark to Christ (1944) 185. KüMMEL, W. G., Verheissung und Erfüllung (1953) 73-75. KNOX, W. L. The Sources of the Synoptic Gospels II (1957) 82. DELLING, G. Die Zueignung des Heils in der Taufe (1961) 42. STRECKER, G. Der Weg der Gerechtigkeit (1962) 117. HUMMEL, R. Die Auseinandersetzung zwischen Kirche und Judentum im Matthäusevangelium (1963) 141f., 143 n.5. KWAAK, H. VAN DER, "Die Klage über Jerusalem," NovTest 8 (2-4, '66) 156-70. SCHENK, W. Der Segen im Neuen Testament (1967) 107-110. HASLER, V. Amen (1969) 71. GASTON, L. No Stone on Another (1970) 451-55. LANGE, J., Das Erscheinen des Auferstandenen im Evangelium nach Matthäus (Würzburg 1973) 141, 235, 286, 298, 333, 336-39.

24-25 EWALD, H. Die drei ersten Evangelien (1850) 330ff.
BUTLER, B. C. The Originality of St Matthew (1951) 76ff.
FARRER, A. St Matthew and St Mark (1954) 127, 128. GILS,
F. Jésus Prophète D'Après Les Evangiles Synoptiques (1957)
126-33. BORNKAMM-BARTH-HELD, Ueberlieferung und
Auslegung im Matthäus-Evangelium (1961) 19ff., 56f., 70.
SUMMERS, R. "Matthew 24-25: An Exposition," RevEx 59
(4, '62) 501-11. KUPFERSCHMID, A. Das Kommen Christi
und unsere Zukunft. Eine Auslegung von Matthäus 24 und 25
(1963). FULLER, G. C. "The Olivet Discourse: An
Apocalyptic Timetable," WThJ 28 (2, '66) 157-63.
GAECHTER, P. Die literarische Kunst im Matthäus-
Evangelium (1968) 36-40. KüNZI, M. Das
Naherwartungslogion Matthäus 10, 23 (1970) 90, 98, 104, 107.
DIDIER, M., L'évangile selon Matthieu (Gembloux 1971) 309-
42. WALVOORD, J.F. "Christ's Olivet Discourse on the End
of the Age," BiblaSa 128 (510, '71) 109-16. *MARZOTTO, D.,
"Quando verrà il Figlio dell'uomo. . . Analisi strutturale di Mt
24-25" RivBi 20 (suppl. 1972) 547-70. CHRISTE, Y., La vision
de Matthieu (Matth. XXIV-XXV). Origines et dèveloppment
d'une image de la Seconde Parousie (Paris 1973). GOULDER,
M. D., Midrash and Lection in Matthew (London 1974) 191,
228, 231, 243, 314, 399, 427, 442. *KNOX, D. B., "The Five
Comings of Jesus" RThR 34 (1975)44-54. *SIBINGA, J. S.,
"The Structure of the Apocalyptic Discourse, Matthew 24 and
25" StTh 29 (1975) 71-79. *MONSARRAT, V., "Matthieu 24-
25. Du Temple aux dèmunis" Foi et Vie 76 (1977) 67-80.
*SABOURIN, L., "Il discorso sulla parousia e le parabole della
vigilanza (Matteo 24-25)" BiOr 20 (1978) 193-211.

24:1-25:46 RIDDERBOS, H. Matthew's Witness to Jesus Christ (1958)
73-79.

24 VOLZ, P. Die Eschatologie der jüdischen Gemeinde (1934)
148, 162. MOORE, G. F. Judaism (1946) II 360f.
SCHOONHEIM, P. L. Een Semasiologisch Onderzoek van
Parousia (1953) passim. SANT, C. "The Commentary of St.
Thomas on Mt 24: the Destruction of Jerusalem," MTh VII
(1954) 1-16. BEST, E. One Body in Christ (1955) 132.
FEUILLET, A. "Le sens du mot Parousie dans l'Evangile de
Mattheiu. Comparison entre Matth. XXIV et Jac. V, 1-11," in:
The Background of the New Testament and Its Eschatology,
Dodd-Festschrift, (1956) 261ff. BARCLAY, W. "Great
Themes of the New Testament¯VI. Matthew xxiv," ET 70 (11,
'59) 326-30; (12, '59) 376-79. BERKHOF, H. Der Sinn der
Geschichte: Christus (1959) 70, 78, 116, 127, 182f., 204. HAHN,
F. Christologische Hoheitstitel (1963) 107. ROARK, D. M.,

"The Great Eschatological Discourse" NovT 7 (1964) 123-27. BRAUN, H. Qumran und NT II (1966) 267. MIZZI, J. "The African Element in the Latin Text of Mt. XXIV of Cod. Cantabrigiensis," Rbèn 78 (1-2, '68) 33-66. TREVIJANO ETCHEVARRIA, R. M. "La escatologia del Evangelio de San Mateo," Burgense 9 ('68) 9-23. SCHREINER, J. Gestalt und Anspruch des Neuen Testaments (1969) 322f. KüNZI, M. Das Naherwartungslogion Matthäus 10, 23 (1970) 44, 81, 89, 93f., 99, 104, 141. LADD, G. E., The Presence of the Future (Grand Rapids 1974) 307ff. ROBINSON, J. A. T., Redating the New Testament (London 1976) 21-26. "Adventisten" in: TRE 1 (1977) 461. COURT, J. M., Myth and History in the Book of Revelation (London 1979) 49-54. CLARK, K. W., "The Gentile Bias in Matthew" in: The Gentile Bias and other Essays (Leiden 1980) 3.

24:1ff STAEHELIN, E. Die Verkündigung des Reiches Gottes in der Kirche Jesu Christi I (1951) 358. STRECKER, G. Der Weg der Gerechtigkeit (1962) 924.

24:1-39 WILKENS, J. Einführung in das Evangelium nach Matthäus II (1937) 165-67.

24:1-36 PESCH, R. "Eschatologie und Ethik. Auslegung von Mt 24, 1-36," BuL 11 (4, '70) 223-38. GOULDER, M. D., Midrash and Lection in Matthew (London 1974) 433f.

24:1-31 MESSERSCHMIDT, L. "Dommedagstalen his Matthaeus. De teologiske hovedtanker i Matthaeusevangeliet kap. 24, 1-31" (Judgment Day in Matthew. The Principal Theological Ideas in Mt 24:1-31), Catholica 25 (1-2, '68) 47-59. ELLIS, P. F., Matthew: His Mind and His Message (Collegeville 1974) 82-91.

24:1-14 MERKEL/GEORGI/BALTZER, GPM 19 (1964) 10-14. IWAND, H. J. Predigt-Meditationen (1964) 284-89. MERKEL/GEORGI/BALTZER, GPM (1964/65) 10ff. MOLTMANN, J. in: Hören und Fragen, Bd. 5 (1967) Eichholz, G. & Falkenroth, A. (eds.) 10ff. LANGE, E. (ed.) Predigtstudien für das Kirchenjahr 1970/71 (1970) 26-34. TRöGER, K. W. Göttinger Predigtmeditationen 25 (1, '70) 13-21. ROESSLER, R., in: P. Krusche (ed.) Predigtstudien. Für das Kirchenjahr 1976/77 V/1 (Stuttgart 1976) 17-25. FRIES, Z., und OEFFNER, E., "Zweiter Advent: Matthäus 24, 1-14: Jeder durchlebt sein Weltende" in: P. Krusche (ed.) Predigtstudien 1980/81 III/1 (Stuttgart 1980) 16-22.

24:1-4 ELLINGER, H., in: GPM 31 (1976/77) 7-15.

24:1-3 STRECKER, G. Der Weg der Gerechtigkeit (1962) 240₂. "Apokalyptik" in: TRE 3 (1978) 269.

24: -2 STRECKER, G. Der Weg der Gerechtigkeit (1962) 110, 113. HUMMEL, R. Die Auseinandersetzung zwischen Kirche und Judentum im Matthäusevangelium (1963) 85-90. KUPFERSCHMID, A. Das kommen Christi und unsere Zukunft (1963) 11-20.

24:1 STONEHOUSE, N. B. The Witness of Matthew and Mark to Christ (1944) 176. HARTMAN, L., Testimonium Linguae (Lund 1963) 21f. VIELHAUER, Ph., "Oikodome. Das Bild vom Bau in der christlichen Literatur vom Neuen Testament bis Clemens Alexandrinus" in: Oikodome (München 1979) 54, 59, 64-66.

24:2 BLAIR, E. P. Jesus in the Gospel of Matthew (1960) 148. JüNGEL, E. Paulus und Jesus (1966) 238.

24:3ff STAEHELIN, E. Die Verkündigung des Reiches Gottes in der Kirche Jesus Christi I (1951) 235. STRECKER, G. Der Weg der Gerechtigkeit (1962) 44.

24:3-51 GOODSPEED, E. J. A Life of Jesus (1950) 186-88.

24:3-36 WALVOORD, J. F. "Christ's Olivet Discourse on the Time of the End: Prophecies Fulfilled in the Present Age," BiblSa 128 (511, '71) 206-14.

24:3-8 KUPFERSCHMID, A. Das kommen Christi und unsere Zukunft (1963) 21-34.

24:3-5 HENNECKE, E. & SCHNEEMELCHER, W. Neutestamentliche Apokryphen (1964) II 472f.

24:3-4 LIVIO, J.-B., 'La signification théologique de la 'montagne' dans le premier evangile", Bulletin du Centre Protestant d'Etudes 30 (1978) 13-20.

24:3 VOLZ, P. Die Eschatologie der jüdischen Gemeinde (1934) 135. STONEHOUSE, N. B. The Witness of Matthew and Mark to Christ (1944) 176. STAEHELIN, E. Die Verkündigung des Reiches Gottes in der Kirche Jesu Christi I (1951) 161. FARRER, A. St Matthew and St Mark (1954) 181. BLAIR, E. P. Jesus in the Gospel of Matthew (1960) 77, 89, 134. STRECKER, G. Der Weg der Gerechtigkeit (1962) 193, 205, 237f., 240 HARTMAN, L., Testimonium Linguae (Lund 1963) 34ff. JüNGEL, E. Paulus und Jesus (1966) 253. MARXSEN, W. Mark the Evangelist (1969) 169, 199, 203. VöGTLE, A. Das Neue Testament und die Zukunft des Kosmos (1970) 151, 153-56. LADD, G. E., A Theology of the New Testament (Grand Rapids 1974) 47, 197f., 201.

24:4-25:46 MOORE, G. F. Judaism (1946) II 310. SMITH, M., Tannaitic Parallels to the Gospels (Philadelphia 1968) 4 G+.

24:4ff STRECKER, G. Der Weg der Gerechtigkeit (1962) 158.

24:4-14   *THOMPSON, W. G., "An Historical Perspective in the Gospel of Matthew" JBL 93 (1974) 243-62.

24:4   STONEHOUSE, N. B. The Witness of Matthew and Mark to Chrsit (1944) 130.

24:4b-8   HARTMAN, L. Prophecy interpreted (1966) 147-50, 159-62.

24:5-28   STRECKER, G. Der Weg der Gerechtigkeit (1962) 238ff.

24:5 (23)   HAHN, F. Christologische Hoheitstitel (1963) 224.

24:5   BLAIR, E. P. Jesus in the Gospel of Matthew (1960) 55. HUMMEL, R. Die Auseinandersetzung zwischen Kirche und Judentum im Matthäusevangelium (1963) 113. DAVIES, W. D., The Sermon on the Mount (Cambridge 1966) 70f. HOWARD, V. P., Das Ego in den Synoptischen Evangelien (Marburg 1975) 116-23. "Antichrist" in: TRE 3 (1978) 22.

24:6   KLIJN, A. F. J. "Die syrische Baruch-Apokalypse" in: W. G. Kümmel (ed.) Jüdische Schriften aus hellenistisch-römischer Zeit V (Gütersloh 1976) 153. METZGER, B. M., The Early Versions of the New Testamemt (Oxford 1977) 438.

24:7-9   KLIJN, A. F. J., "Die syrische Baruch-Apokalypse" in: W. G. Kümmel (ed.) Jüdische Schriften aus hellenistisch-römischer Zeit V (Gütersloh 1976) 139.

24:7f   STAEHELIN, E. Die Verkündigung des Reiches Gottes in der Kirche Jesu Christi I (1951) 162.

24:7   STAEHELIN, E. Die Verkündigung des Reiches Gottes in der Kirche Jesu Christi I (1951) 359. KLIJN, A. F. J., "Die syrische Baruch-Apokalypse" in: W. G. Kümmel (ed.) Jüdische Schriften aus hellenistisch-römischer Zeit V (Gütersloh 1976) 140. MüLLER, U. B., "Die griechische Esra-Apokalypse" in: W. G. Kümmel (ed.) Jüdische Schriften aus hellenistisch-römischer Zeit V (Gütersloh 1976) 94.

24:8-14   HARTMAN, L. Prophecy interpreted (1966) 150-51.

24:8   VOLZ, P. Die Eschatologie der jüdischen Gemeinde (1934) 147. MOORE, G. F. Judaism (1946) II 361f. KNOX, W. L. The Sources of the Synoptic Gospels II (1957) 51. KLIJN, A. F. J., "Die syrische Baruch-Apokalypse" in: W. G. Kümmel (ed.) Jüdische Schriften aus hellenistisch-römischer Zeit V (Gütersloh 1976) 140.

24:9ff   STRECKER, G. Der Weg Gerechtigkeit (1962) 42.

24:9-14   HIRSCH, E. Frühgeschichte des Evangeliums (1941) 311-14. KUPFERSCHMID, A. Das kommen Christi und unsere Zukunft (1963) 35-46. DUPONT, J., "La persésecution comme situation missionaire (Marc 13:9-11)" in: R. Schnackenburg (ed.) Die Kirche des Anfangs. Für H. Schürmann (Leipzig 1977) 99.

24:9-13   GILS, F. Jésus Prophète D'Après Les Evangiles Synoptiques (1957) 128-30.

24:9   TRILLING, W. Das wahre Israel (1959) 13. STRECKER, G. Der Weg der Gerechtigkeit (1962) 34, 55ₙ. HAHN, F. Christologische Hoheitstitel (1963) 109, 110. LANGE, J., Das erscheinen des Auferstandenen im Evangelium nach Matthäus (Würzburg 1973) 257f, 272, 286f, 292, 294, 297-99, 301f, 379, 488.

24:10ff   STAEHELIN, E. Die Verkündigung des Reiches Gottes in der Kirche Jesu Christi I (1951) 12. BORNKAMM-BARTH-HELD, Ueberlieferung und Auslegung im Matthäus-Evangelium (1961) 56, 70, 112, 149, 153. STRECKER, G. Der Weg der Gerechtigkeit (1962) 1374.

24:10-13   HUMMEL, R. Die Auseinandersetzung zwischen Kirche und Judentum im Matthäusevangelium (1963) 65.

24:10-12   SATAKE, A. Die Gemeindeordnung in der Johannesapokalypse (1966) 190f.

24:10   HUMBERT, A. "Essai d'une théologie du scandale dans les Synoptiques," Biblica 35 (1954) 6-9.

24:11-24   BOUSSET, W. Die Religion des Judentums im Späthellenistischen Zeitalter (1966⁻1926) 113, 224, 248, 254, 256.

24:11, 24   DAVIES, W. D., The Sermon on the Mount (Cambridge 1966) 70. "Antichrist" in: TRE 3 (1978) 22. "Bergpredigt" in: TRE 5 (1980) 607.

24:11   BLAIR, E. P. Jesus in the Gospel of Matthew (1960) 108. REILING, J., Hermas and Christian Prophecy (Leiden 1973) 59f. KLIJN, A. F. J., "Die syrische Baruch-Apokalypse" in: W. G. Kümmel (ed.) Jüdische Schriften aus hellenistisch-römischer Zeit V (Gütersloh 1976) 153.

24:12   BERGER, K. Die Gesetzeauslegung Jesu, (1940) 243-51. AUBINEAU, M. "Exégèse patristique de Mt. 24, 12: Quoniam abundavit iniquitas, refrigescet charitas multorum," in: Studia Patristica IV (1961) Cross, F. L. (ed.) 3-19. STRECKER, G. Der Weg der Gerechtigkeit (1962) 233. BAUMBACH, G. Das Verständnis des Bösen in den synoptischen Evangelien (1963) 99ff., 103ff. DAVIES, W. D., The Sermon on the Mount (Cambridge 1966) 72.

24:13   KäSEMANN, E. New Testament Questions of Today (1969) 106.

24:14   STONEHOUSE, N. B. The Witness of Matthew and Mark to Christ (1944) 130, 227, 228, 233. STAEHELIN, E. Die Verkündigung des Reiches Gottes in der Kirche Jesu Christi I

(1951) 12, 62, 162, 298, 387. FARRER, A. St Matthew and St Mark (1954) 120. GILS, F. Jésus Prophète D'Après Evangiles Synoptiques (1957) 115-17. NEPPER-CHRISTENSEN, P. Das Matthäusevangelium. Ein Judenchristliches Evangelium? (1958) 9, 19, 21, 186, 188, 198. MEINERTZ, M. "Zum Ursprung der Heidenmission," Biblica 40 (3-4, '59) 770-71. MUNCK, J. Paul and the Salvation of Mankind (1959) 38f., 49, 256, 264. TRILLING, W. Das wahre Israel (1959) 13f., 104f. BLAIR, E. P. Jesus in the Gospel of Matthew (1960) 31. STRECKER, G. Der Weg der Gerechtigkeit (1962) 34, 128ff., 212, 239. HAHN, F. Das Verständnis der Mission im Neuen Testament (1965) 59, 60, 104-106, 107f., 110. MARXSEN, W. Mark the Evangelist (1969) 124, 134f., 141f., 201f. BONNARD, P., "Matthieu, éducateur du peuple chrétien" in: A. Descamps and A. deHalleux (eds.) Mélanges Bibliques en hommage au R. P. Béda Rigaux (Gembloux 1970) 2f. KüNZI, M. Das Naherwartungslogion Matthäus 10, 23 (1970) 71, 99, 101, 140f., 155f., 160. JEREMIAS, J. Neutestamentliche Theologie I (1971) 40, 42f., 134. BERKOUWER, G. C., The Return of Christ (Grand Rapids 1972) 130, 137, 251, 409. KüMMEL, W. G. Einleitung in das Neue Testament (1973) 86f. WILSON, S. G., The Gentiles and the Gentile Mission in Luke-Acts (Cambridge 1973) 5, 24-26. FRANKEMöLLE, H., Jahwebund und Kirche Christi (Münster 1974) 120-23, 253, 266f., 270, 378. GOULDER, M. D., Midrash and Lection in Matthew (London 1974) 161, 339, 343, 449. LADD, G. E., A Theology of the New Testament (Grand Rapids 1974) 114, 200, 606, 623. KINGSBURY, J. D., Matthew: Structure, Christology, Kingdom (Philadelphia 1975) 128-30. WILCKENS, U., "Gottes geringste Brüder zu Mt 25, 31-46" in: E. E. Ellis und E. Grässer (eds.) Jesus und Paulus. Für W. G. Kümmel (Göttingen 1975) 365ff, 383.

24:15ff HUMMEL, R. Die Auseinandersetzung zwischen Kirche und Judentum im Matthäusevangelium (1963) 160 n. 85.

24:15-31 MOORE, G. F. Judaism (1946) II 336n.

24:15-28 Kupferschmid, A. Das Kommen Christi und unsere Zukunft (1963) 47-58. SCHLIER, H. in: Herr, tue meine Lippen auf, Bd. 1 (1957) Eichholz, G. (ed.) 325-329. BARTSCH, H. W. "Ich stehe vor der Tür!", in: Kleine Predigt-Typologie III (1965) 103-11. DOERNE, M. Er kommt auch noch heute (1966) 235-50.

24:15-25 GILS, F. Jésus Prophète D'Après Les Evangiles Synoptiques (1957) 128-30. HARTMAN, L. Prophecy interpreted (1966) 162-64. SWIDLER, L., Biblical Affirmations of Woman (Philadelphia 1979) 233, 240, 260.

24:15-22 SCHLATTER, D. A. Die Theologie des Neuen Testament (1909) I 530-31. HARTMAN, L. Prophecy interpreted (1966) 151-54. RIST, J. M., On the Independence of Matthew and Mark (Cambridge 1978) 81f.

24:15 CLEMEN, C. Primitive Christianity and Its Non-Jewish Sources (1912) 127f. STONEHOUSE, N. B. The Witness of Matthew and Mark to Christ (1944) 201. STAEHELIN, E. Die Verkündigung des Reiches Gottes in der Kirche Jesu Christi I (1951) 162. LOEWENICH, W. Von, Luther als Ausleger der Synoptiker (1954) 66f. RIGAUX, B. Biblica 40 (3-4, '59) 675-83. AALDERS, G. C. "De 'gruwel der verwoesting' " (The "Abomination of Desolation"), GThT 60 (1-2, '60) 1-5. COLUNGA, A. "La abominacion de la desolacion (Mt. 24, 15)," Cult Bib 17 (1972, '60) 183-85. STRECKER, G. Der Weg der Gerechtigkeit (1962) 23, 239s. SASS, G. Ungereimtes bei Matthäus (1968) 47-49. MARXSEN, W. Mark the Evangelist (1969) 163, 181, 203. KLIJN, A. F. J. ,"Die syrische Baruch-Apokalypse" in: W. G. Kümmel (ed.) Jüdische Schriften aus hellenistisch-römischer Zeit V (Gütersloh 1976) 141. "Apokalyptik" in: TRE 3 (1978) 269.

24:16 REICKE, B. The Disobedient Spirits and Christian Baptism (1946) 179f.

24:17-18 POLAG, A., Die Christologie der Logienquelle (Neukirchen-Vluyn 1977) 99f.

24:19 STAEHELIN, E. Die Verkündigung des Reiches Gottes in der Kirche Jesu Christi I (1951) 340. METZGER, B. M. "Explicit references in the works of Origen to variant readings in New Testament manuscripts," Historical and Literary Studies (1968) 93f. SAND, A., Das Gesetz und die Propheten (Regensburg 1974) 84-86. KLIJN, A. F. J., "Die syrische Baruch-Apokalypse" in: W. G. Kümmel (ed.) Jüdische Schriften aus hellenistisch-römischer Zeit V (Gütersloh 1976) 129.

24:20 NEPPER-CHRISTENSEN, P. Das Matthäusevangelium. Ein Judenchristliches Evangelium? (1958) 20, 22, 33. BORNKAMM-BARTH-HELD, Ueberlieferung und Auslegung im Matthäus-Evangelium (1961) 85ff. STRECKER, G. Der Weg der Gerechtigkeit (1962) 182, 32.

24:21 STAEHELIN, E. Die Verkündigung des Reiches Gottes in der Kirche Jesu Christi I (1951) 137, 189. STRECKER, G. Der Weg der Gerechtigkeit (1962) 23. HUMMEL, R. Die Auseinandersetzung zwischen Kirche und Judentum im Matthäusevangelium (1963) 160. BRANDENBURGER, E., "Himmelfahrt Moses" in: W. G. Kümmel (ed.) Jüdische

Schriften aus hellenistisch-römischer Zeit V (Gütersloh 1976)
75. KLIJN, A. F. J., "Die syrische Baruch-Apokalypse" in: W.
G. Kümmel (ed.) Jüdische Schriften aus hellenistisch-
römischer Zeit V (Gütersloh 1976) 139.

24:22ff STRECKER, G. Der Weg der Gerechtigkeit (1962) 2191.

24:22 "Apokalyptik" in: TRE 3 (1978) 282.

24:33ff STAEHELIN, E. Die Verkündigung des Reiches Gottes in der
Kirche Jesu Christi I (1951) 162.

24:23-26 BRAUN, H. Qumran und NT II (1966) 97, 112, 269, 276.

24:23-25 HARTMAN, L. Prophecy interpreted (1966) 154-55.
JüNGEL, E. Paulus und Jesus (1966) 252.

24:23-24 "Antichrist" in: TRE 3 (1978) 22.

24:23 MASSAUX, E. Influence de l'Evangile de saint Matthieu sur la
littérature chrétienne avant saint Irénée (1950) 515-16, 633-35.
BLAIR, E. P. Jesus in the Gospel of Matthew (1960) 55.
HUMMEL, R. Die Auseinandersetzung zwischen Kirche und
Judentum im Matthäusevangelium (1963) 113.

24:24 STRECKER, G. Der Weg der Gerechtigkeit (1962) 232.
KäSEMANN, E. Exegetische Versuche und Besinnungen
(1964) 112. DAVIES, W. D., The Sermon on the Mount
(Cambridge 1966) 70. MADDOX, R. The Function of the Son
of Man According to the Synoptic Gospels. NTS 15 (1968-69)
52-53. KLIJN, A. F. J., "Die syrische Baruch-Apokalypse" in:
W. G. Kümmel (ed.) Jüdische Schriften aus hellenistisch-
römischer Zeit V (Gütersloh 1976) 128, 153. "Antichrist" in:
TRE 3 (1978) 21, 22.

24:26-28 SCHULZ, S. Q Die Spruchquelle der Evangelisten (1972) 277-
37-41 87.

24:26-28 JüLICHER, D. A. Die Gleichnisreden Jesu (1910) 133-37.
GILS, F. Jésus Prophète D'Après Les Evangiles Synoptiques
(1957) 130-32. GOULDER, M. D., Type and History in Acts
(London 1964) 140f. HOFFMANN, P. Studien zur Theologie
der Logienquelle (1972) 37-41. TALBERT, C. H., Literary
Patterns, Theological Themes, and the Genre of Luke-Acts
(Missoula 1974) 54.

24:26-27 SANFORD, J. A., The Kingdom Within (New York 1970)
203f.

24:26.30 HENNECKE, E. & SCHNEEMELCHER, W.
Neutestamentliche Apokryphen (1964) II 472, 475.

24:26 STAEHELIN, E. Die Verkündigung des Reiches Gottes in der
Kirche Jesu Christi I (1951) 296. LAMBRECHT, J. "Die
Logia-Quellen von Markus 13," Biblica 47 (1966) 341-42.

DAVIES, W. D., The Gospel and the Land (London 1974) 84f.
JANSSEN, E., "Testament Abrahams" in: W. G. Kümmel (ed.)
Jüdische Schriften aus hellenistisch-römischer Zeit III
(Gütersloh 1975) 215. POLAG, A., Die Christologie der
Logienquelle (Neukirchen-Vluyn 1977) 99.

24:27-51   MOORE, G. F. Judaism (1946) II 337.

24:27.37   SCHWEIZER, E. Erniedrigung und Erhöhung bei Jesus und
39.44.   seinen Nachfolgern (1962) § 3g.

24:27f.   LüHRMANN, D. Die Redaktion der Logienquelle (1969) 71-
37-41   75.

24:27f   JüNGEL, E. Paulus und Jesus (1966) 254.

24:27   STAEHELIN, E. Die Verkündigung des Reiches Gottes in der
           Kirche Jesu Christi I (1951) 62, 296. HAHN, F. Christologische
           Hoheitstitel (1963) 36f., 38. KäSEMANN, E. Exegetische
           Versuche und Besinnungen (1964) I 295. BULTMANN, R.
           Theologie des Neuen Testaments (1965) 30f. JüNGEL, E.
           Paulus und Jesus (1966) 240-42, 244, 252-54. JEREMIAS, J.
           Neutestamentliche Theologie I (1971) 248, 251f., 259f., 262.
           KINGSBURY, J. D., Matthew: Structure, Christology,
           Kingdom (Philadelphia 1975) 158-60. KLIJN, A. F. J., "Die
           syrische Baruch-Apokalypse" in: W. G. Kümmel (ed.) Jüdische
           Schriften aus hellenistisch-römischer Zeit V (Gütersloh 1976)
           158. POLAG, A., Die Christologie der Logienquelle
           (Neukirchen-Vluyn 1977) 96.

24:28   EHRHARDT, A. "Greek Proverbs in the Gospel", The
           Framework of the New Testament Stories (1964) 44-63, esp. 53.
           JüNGEL, E. Paulus und Jesus (1966) 252. POLAG, A., Die
           Christologie der Logienquelle (Neukirchen-Vluyn 1977) 95.

24:29ff   STRECKER, G. Der Weg der Gerechtigkeit (1962) 236.

24:29-35   GOLLWITZER, H. GPM 6/4, 256-59.

24:29-31   KUPFERSCHMID, A. Das Kommen Christi und unsere
           Zukunft (1963) 59-71. HARTMAN, L. Prophecy interpreted
           (1966) 156-59, 165-67. SANFORD, J. A., The Kingdom Within
           (New York 1970) 206f.

24:29   STAEHELIN, E. Die Verkündigung des Reiches Gottes in der
           Kirche Jesu Christi I (1951) 239. STRECKER, G. Der Weg der
           Gerechtigkeit (1962) 20, 23. HUMMEL, R. Die
           Auseinandersetzung zwischen Kirche und Judentum im
           Matthäusevangelium (1963) 160. VöGTLE, A. Das Neue
           Testament und die Zukunft des Kosmos (1970) 71, 154-58.
           KLIJN, A. F. J., "Die syrische Baruch-Apokalypse" in: W. G.
           Kümmel (ed.) Jüdische Schriften aus hellenistisch-römischer
           Zeit V (Gütersloh 1976) 139.

24:30f STONEHOUSE, N. B. The Witness of Matthew and Mark to Christ (1944) 233. HAHN, F. Das Verständnis der Mission im Neuen Testament (1965) 110. JüNGEL, E. Paulus und Jesus (1966) 243.

24:30-31 KLOPPENBORG, J. S., "Didache 16:6-8 and Special Matthaean Tradition" ZNW 70 (1979) 54-67.

24:30, 31 BOUSSET, W. Die Religion des Judentums im Späthellenistischen Zeitalter (1966⁻1926) 264, 237.

24:30 STONEHOUSE, N. B. The Witness of Matthew and Mark to Christ (1944) 240, 252. STAEHELIN, E. Die Verkündigung des Reiches Gottes in der Kirche Jesu Christi I (1951) 246. BLAIR, E.P. Jesus in the Gospel of Matthew (1960) 77, 81, 82. LINDARS, B. New Testament Apologetic, (1961) 122-27, 257. STRECKER, G. Der Weg der Gerechtigkeit (1962) 23, 424, 115, 125, 241. HIGGINS, A. B. J. The Sign of the Son of Man (Matt. XXIV. 30) NTS 9 (1962-63) 380f. GLASSON, T. F. The ensign of the Son of Man (Mt. 24, 30) JThS NS 15 (1964) 299-300. PERRIN, N. Mark XIV. 62: The End Product of a Christian Pesher Tradition? NTS 12 (1965-66) 152f. BRAUN, H. Qumran und NT II (1966) 61, 272. SCHALIT, A. König Herodes (1969) 527. KüNZI, M. Das Naherwartungslogion Matthäus 10, 23 (1970) 115, 148, 158, 179. VöGTLE, A. Das Neue Testament und die Zukunft des Kosmos (1970) 154f. JEREMIAS, J. Neutestamentliche Theologie I (1971) 248, 251f., 262. BERKOUWER, G. C., The Return of Christ (Grand Rapids 1972) 153, 158, 165, 239. SCHüSSLER-FIORENZA, E. Priester für Gott (1972) 188f. THEISOHN, J., Der auserwählte Richter (Göttingen 1975) 183, 259, 260. KLIJN, A. F. J., "Die syrische Baruch-Apokalypse" in: W. G. Kümmel (ed.) Jüdische Schriften aus hellenistisch-römischer Zeit V (Gütersloh 1976) 139.

24:31-46 ROBINSON, J. A. T. The 'Parable' of the Sheep and the Goats. NTS 2 (1955-56) 225f.

24:31 MASSAUX, E. Influence de l'Evangile de saint Matthieu sur la littérature chrétienne avant saint Irénée (1950) 230-31, 624-26. KNOX, W. L. The Sources of the Synoptic Gospels II (1957) 27. BLAIR, E. P. Jesus in the Gospel of Matthew (1960) 81, 82. STRECKER, G. Der Weg der Gerechtigkeit (1962) 232, 115, 161l, 236. STUDIORUM PAULINORUM CONGRESSUS INTERNATIONALIS CATHOLICUS 1961 (1963) I 227-28. NöTSCHER, F., Altorientalischer und alttestamentlicher Auferstehungsglauben (Darmstadt 1970) 306. CAVALLIN, H. C. C., Life After Death I (Lund 1974) 5,8 n10. THEISOHN, J., Der auserwählte Richter (Göttingen 1975) 178, 187f, 260.

WILCKENS, U., "Gottes geringste Brüder - zu Mt 25, 31-46" in: E. E. Ellis und E. Grässer (eds.) Jesus und Paulus. Für W. G. Kümmel (Göttingen 1975) 365, 367ff.

24:32-25:46 FARRER, A. St Matthew and St Mark (1954) 188. ELLIS, P., Matthew: His Mind and His Message (Collegeville 1974) 91-94.

24:32-44 KUPFERSCHMID, A. Das Kommen Christi und unsere Zukunft (1963) 75-87.

24:32-33 JüLICHER, D. A. Die Gleichnisreden Jesu (1910) 3-11. MASSAUX, E. Influence de l'Evangile de saint Matthieu sur la littérature chrétienne avant saint Irénée (1950) 29-31, 251-52. STRECKER, G. Der Weg der Gerechtigkeit (1962) 240f. MANEK, J., . . .und brachte Frucht. Die Gleichnisse Jesu (Berlin 1977) 33f. KLAUCK, H.-J., Allegorie und Allegorese in Synoptischen Gleichnistexten (Münster 1978) 316-25.

24:32 STAEHELIN, E. Die Verkündigung des Reiches Gottes in der Kirche Jesu Christi I (1951) 86. PATSCH, H. Abendmahl und historischer Jesus (1972) 116f.

24:33 STONEHOUSE, N. B. The Witness of Matthew and Mark to Christ (1944) 229.

24:34-25:46 RIST, J. M., On the Independence of Matthew and Mark (Cambridge 1978) 82f.

24:34f TRILLING, W. Das wahre Israel (1959) 139f. LOHSE, E. and Others (eds.) Der Ruf Jesu und die Antwort der Gemeinde (1970) 105-107.

24:34 BLAIR, E. P. Jesus in the Gospel of Matthew (1960) 121. STRECKER, G. Der Weg der Gerechtigkeit (1962) 43, 143, 240₂. KäSEMANN, E. Exegetische Versuche und Besinnungen (1964) II 88. BRAUN, H. Qumran und NT II (1966) 268. HASLER, V. Amen (1969) 47. KäSEMANN, E. New Testament Questions of Today (1969) 88. KüNZI, M., Das Naherwartungslogion Markus 9,1 par. (Tübingen 1977) 213-24. SCHILDENBERGER, J., "Die Vertauschung der Aussagen über Zeichen und Bezeichnetes. Eine hermeneutisch bedeutsame Redeweise" in: Kirche und Bibel. Für Bischof E. Schick (Paderborn 1979) 404f. HARRINGTON, D. J., God's People in Christ (Philadelphia 1980) 25.

24:35 STAEHELIN, E. Die Verkündigung des Reiches Gottes in der Kirche Jesu Christi I (1951) 213. KNOX, W. L. The Sources of the Synoptic Gospels II (1957) 27. RUDOLPH, K. Die Mandäer I (1960) 106,9. STRECKER, G. Der Weg der Gerechtigkeit (1962) 143, 144₁. HENNECKE, E. & SCHNEEMELCHER, W. Neutestamentliche Apokryphen (1964) II 70, 75. VöGTLE, A. Das Neue Testament und die

Zukunft des Kosmos (1970) 71, 99, 101, 105, 106, 156, 158, 166. BRUNNER, E. Dogmatik I, 269.

24:36ff FRIEDRICH, G., "I Thessalonicher 5,1-11, der apologetische Einschub eines Späteren" in: Auf das Wort kommt es an (Göttingen 1978) 265.

24:36-25:30 GILS, F. Jésus Prophète D'Après Les Evangiles Synoptiques (1957) 130-32.

24:36-42 DEHN, G. in: Herr, tue meine Lippen auf, Bd. 3 (1964) Eichholz, G. (ed.) 468ff. TRAUB, H. GPM 11/4, 277-81.

24:36 MOORE, G. F. Judaism (1946) I 408. BLAIR, E. P. Jesus in the Gospel of Matthew (1960) 90, 98. DELLING, G. Die Zueignung des Heils in der Taufe (1961) 95. DeKRUIJF, T., Der Sohn Des Lebendigen Gottes (Rome 1962) 41, 72f, 91-93, 139, 167. STRECKER, G. Der Weg der Gerechtigkeit (1962) 241. HUMMEL, R. Die Auseinandersetzung zwischen Kirche und Judentum im Matthäusevangelium (1963) 115. SCHREIBER, J. Theologie des Vertrauens (1967) 130, 155-57. WINANDY, J. "Le logion de l'ignorance" (Mc XIII,32; Mt XXIV,36), RevBi 75 (1968) 63-79. "Apokalyptik" in: TRE 3 (1978) 283. "Astrologie" in: TRE 4 (1979) 308. METZGER, B. M., "St. Jerome's explicit references to variant readings in manuscripts of the New Testament" in: E. Best/R. Wilson (eds.) Text and Interpretation. For M. Black (Cambridge 1979) 182. SWIDLER, L., Biblical Affirmations of Woman (Philadelphia 1979) 167.

24:37ff STAEHELIN, E. Die Verkündigung des Reiches Gottes in der Kirche Jesu Christi I (1951) 62. STRECKER, G. Der Weg der Gerechtigkeit (1962) 242.

24:37-51 GOLLINGER, H. " 'Ihr wisst nicht, an welchem Tag euer Herr kommt.' Auslegung von Mt 24, 37-51," BuL 11 (4, '70) 238-47. GOULDER, M. D., Midrash and Lection in Matthew (London 1974) 434f.

24:37-42 BLOCH, R., "Midrash" in: W. S. Green (ed.) Approaches to Ancient Judaism (Missoula 1978) 49.

24:37-41 SANFORD, J. A., The Kingdom Within (New York 1970) 205f. TALBERT, C. H., Literary Patterns, Theological Themes, and the Genre of Luke-Acts (Missoula 1974) 54.

24:37-39 SCHOONHEIM, P. L. Een Semasiologisch Onderzoek van Parousia (1953) 30-31. HAHN, F. Christologische Hoheitstitel (1963) 36, 37f. JüNGEL, E. Paulus und Jesus (1966) 240-42, 244, 254-56. JEREMIAS, J. Neutestamentliche Theologie I (1971) 248, 259f., 262. HOFFMANN, P. Studien zur Theologie der Logienquelle (1972) 43, 64, 284, 308. GEIGER, R., Die

Lukanischen Endzeitreden (Bern 1973) 87-108. POLAG, A. Die Christologie der Logienquelle (Neukirchen-Vluyn 1977) 95.

24:37   VOLZ, P. Die Eschatologie der jüdischen Gemeinde (1934) 337. KäSEMANN, E. Exegetische Versuche und Besinnungen (1964) II 94. JüNGEL, E. Paulus und Jesus (1966) 252ff. KäSEMANN, E. New Testament Questions of Today (1969) 96.

24:38   KNOX, W. L. The Sources of the Synoptic Gospels II (1957) 109. STRECKER, G. Der Weg der Gerechtigkeit (1962) 24.

24:39-41   SWIDLER, L., Biblical Affirmations of Woman (Philadelphia 1979) 167, 242, 253.

24:39   STONEHOUSE, N. B. The Witness of Matthew and Mark to Christ (1944) 254. STRECKER, G. Der Weg der Gerechtigkeit (1962) 241. JüNGEL, E. Paulus und Jesus (1966) 252ff. POLAG, A., Die Christologie der Logienquelle (Neukirchen-Vluyn 1977) 95, 133.

24:40-25:30   WILKENS, J. Einführung in das Evangelium nach Matthäus II (1937) 179-80.

24:40-41   STAEHELIN, E. Die Verkündigung des Reiches Gottes in der Kirche Jesu Christi I (1951) 62. GOULDER, M. D., Type and History in Acts (London 1964) 140f. POLAG, A., Die Christologie der Logienquelle (Neukirchen-Vluyn 1977) 95f. SWIDLER, L., Biblical Affirmations of Woman (Philadelphia 1979) 257.

24:41   RIESENFELD, H. (ed.) "Zum Partizip Matth. 24,41" in: Coniectanea Neotestamentica XIII (1949) 12-16.

24:42-25:30   LAMBRECHT, J. "Die Logia-Quellen von Markus 13", Biblica 47 (1966) 350-54.

24:42ff   STAEHELIN, E. Die Verkündigung des Reiches Gottes in der Kirche Jesu Christi I (1951) 62. KNOX, W. L. The Sources of the Synoptic Gospels II (1957) 73, 135. BLAIR, E. P. Jesus in the Gospel of Matthew (1960) 80.

24:42-51   HIRSCH, E. Frühgeschichte des Evangeliums (1941) 120-22. BLAIR, E. P. Jesus in the Gospel of Matthew (1960) 108. EDWARDS, R. A., A Theology of Q (Philadelphia 1976) 125-27.

24:42-44   STRECKER, G. Der Weg der Gerechtigkeit (1962) 241f. SCHREIBER, J. Theologie des Vertrauens (1967) 154-57. SANFORD, J. A., The Kingdom Within (New York 1970) 206. KLAPPERT, B., "Arbeit Gottes und Mitarbeit des Menschen (Phil 2,6-11)" in: J. Moltmann (ed.) Recht auf Arbeit - Sinn der Arbeit (München 1979) 107.

24:42   STONEHOUSE, N. B. The Witness of Matthew and Mark to Christ (1944) 254. BORNKAMM-BARTH-HELD, Ueberlieferung und Auslegung im Matthäus-Evangelium (1961) 39. JEREMIAS, J. Die Gleichnisse Jesu (1962) 45, 49, 50-52. STRECKER, G. Der Weg der Gerechtigkeit (1962) 44, 123, 1583, 1592, 242. HAHN, F. Christologische Hoheitstitel (1963) 111. LöVESTAM, E. Spiritual Wakefulness in the New Testament (1963) 106f. BRAUN, H. Qumran und NT II (1966) 202. HARNISCH, W., Eschatologische Existenz (Göttingen 1973) 43A, 84A, 85, 85A, 97. "Allegorese"in: TRE 2 (1978) 280.

24:43ff   STONEHOUSE, N. B. The Witness of Matthew and Mark to Christ (1944) 256.

24:43-51   QUESNELL, Q. This Good News (1964) 94f. HOFFMANN, P. Studien zur Theologie der Logienquelle (1972) 43, 47f., 95, 97, 177, 200, 308.

24:43f. - 45-51   LüHRMANN, D. Die Redaktion der Logienquelle (1969) 69f.

24:43-44   JüLICHER, D. A. Die Gleichnisreden Jesu (1910) 1937-45. DODD, C. H. The Parables of the Kingdom (1948) 167ff. STROBEL, A. Untersuchungen zum Eschatologischen Verzögerungsproblem (1961) 207-15. JEREMIAS, J. Die Gleichnisse Jesu (1962) 19, 38, 45-48. PATSCH, H. Abendmahl und historischer Jesus (1972) 114f. SCHULZ, S.Q Die Spruchquelle der Evangelisten (1972) 268-71. HARNISCH, W., Eschatologische Existenz (Göttingen 1973) 72, 76, 84f, 87A, 94A, 95A. GOULDER, M. D., Midrash and Lection in Matthew (London 1974) 4, 55, 59f, 65, 154, 166. TALBERT, C. H., Literary Patterns, Theological Themes, and the Genre of Luke-Acts (Missoula 1974) 55. MANEK, J., . . . und brachte Frucht. Die Gleichnisse Jesu (Berlin 1977) 66f. POLAG, A., Die Christologie der Logienquelle (Neukirchen-Vluyn 1977) 95. LOSADA, D. A., "La venida imprevista del Senor" RivB 40 (1978) 201-16.

24:43   STAEHELIN, E. Die Verkündigung des Reiches Gottes in der Kirche Jesu Christi I (1951) 10. HAHN, F. Christologische Hoheitstitel (1963) 92. HUMMEL, R. Die Auseinandersetzung zwischen Kirche und Judentum im Matthäusevangelium (1963) 155. SCHRAGE, W. Das Verhältnis der Thomas-Evangeliums zur Synoptischen Tradition und zu den Koptischen Evangelienübersetzungen (1964) 67, 193. SUMMERS, R. The Secret Sayings of the Living Jesus (1968) 35. DUPONT,J., "La parabole du maï qui rentre dans la nuit (Mc 13, 34-36)" in: A. Descamps and A. de Halleux (eds.) Mélanges Bibliques en hommage au R. P. Béda Rigaux (Gembloux 1970) 108-15. KLAUCK, H. J. Allegorie und Allegorese in Synoptischen

Gleichnistexten (Münster 1978) 331-33. RUDOLPH, K., Die Gnosis (Göttingen 1978) 278.

24:44f STRECKER, G. Der Weg der Gerechtigkeit (1962) 1983.

24:44 MOORE, G. F. Judaism (1946) II 336. BLAIR, E. P. Jesus in the Gospel of Matthew (1960) 77. STRECKER, G. Der Weg der Gerechtigkeit (1962) 242. HAHN, F. Christologische Hoheitstitel (1963) 38. JüNGEL, E. Paulus und Jesus (1966) 240-42. HARNISCH, W., Eschatologische Existenz (Göttingen 1973) 43A, 85, 85A, 87A, 88f, 92A, 93A.

24:45ff STAEHELIN, E. Die Verkündigung des Reiches Gottes in der Kirche Jesu Christi I (1951) 63. HARNISCH, W., Eschatologische Existenz (Göttingen 1973) 85, 95, 95A, 115A.

24:45-57 STROBEL, A. Untersuchungen zum Eschatologischen Verzögerungsproblem (1961) 215-22. MANEK, J., . . .und brachte Frucht. Die Gleichnisse Jesu (Berlin 1977) 67-69.

24:45-51 JüLICHER, D. A. Die Gleichnisreden Jesu (1910) 145-61. WILKENS, J. Einführung in das Evangelium nach Matthäus II (1937) 179-80. STONEHOUSE, N. B. The Witness of Matthew and Mark to Christ (1944) 157. DODD, C. H. The Parables of the Kingdom (1948) 158ff. PIROT, J. Paraboles et Allégories Evangeliques (1949) 422-28. MICHAELIS, D. W. Die Gleichnisse Jesu (1956) 71-80. KNOX, W. L. The Sources of the Synoptic Gospels II (1957) 70f. JEREMIAS, J. Die Gleichnisse Jesu (1962) 53-55, 64f., 89. STRECKER, G. Der Weg der Gerechtigkeit (1962) 123. KUPFERSCHMID, A. Das Kommen Christi und unsere Zukunft (1963) 89-101. KAHLEFELD, H. Parables and Introduction in the Gospels (1966) 108f. WEISER, A. Die Knechtsgleichnisse der synoptischen Evangelien, SANT, Bd. XXIX (1971) 178-225. SCHULZ, S. Q Die Spruchquelle der Evangelisten (1972) 271-77. GOULDER, M. D., Midrash and Lection in Matthew (London 1974) 4, 54, 59f, 61, 65, 98, 167, 436f. TALBERT, C. H., Literary Patterns, Theological Themes, and the Genre of Luke-Acts (Missoula 1974) 55. POLAG, A., Die Christologie der Logienquelle (Neukirchen-Vluyn 1977) 81, 100. GARLAND, D. E., The Intention of Matthew 23 (Leiden 1979) 122f. SWIDLER, L., Biblical Affirmations of Woman (Philadelphia 1979) 169. "Autorität" in: TRE 5 (1980) 42.

24:45-48 HENNECKE, E. & SCHNEEMELCHER, W. Neutestamentliche Apokryphen (1964) II 387. EDWARDS, R. A., A Theology of Q (Philadelphia 1976) 65f.

24:46 STAEHELIN, E. Die Verkündigung des Reiches Gottes in der Kirche Jesu Christi I (1951) 327.

24:47   HASLER, V. Amen (1969) 72.

24:48   TRILLING, W. Das wahre Israel (1959) 30. STRECKER, G. Der Weg der Gerechtigkeit (1962) 44. JEREMIAS, J. Neutestamentliche Theologie I (1971) 138f.

24:50   STRECKER, G. Der Weg der Gerechtigkeit (1962) 241. HARNISCH, W., Eschatologische Existenz (Göttingen 1973) 114A.

24:51   BETZ, O. "The Dichotomized Servant and the End of Judas Iscariot (Light on the Dark Passages: Matthew 24, 51 and parallel; Acts 1,18)," RevQ 5 (1, '64) 43-58. KäSEMANN, E. Exegetische Versuche und Besinnungen (1964) II 94. NICKELS, P. Targum and New Testament (1967) 21. KäSEMANN, E. New Testament Questions of Today (1969) 95. SMITH, M., Tannaitic Parallels to the Gospels (Philadelphia 1968) 3.9+.

24:57ff STONEHOUSE, N. B. The Witness of Matthew and Mark to Christ (1944) 255.

25   VOLZ, P. Die Eschatologie der jüdischen Gemeinde (1934) 91, 302, 308. STONEHOUSE, N. B. The Witness of Matthew and Mark to Christ (1944) 157. BRUNNER, E. Dogmatik I (1946) 358. BUTLER, B. C. The Originality of St Matthew (1951) 76ff. STREETER, B. H. The Four Gospels (1951) 585ff. GREENLEE, J. H. Nine Uncial Palimpsests of the Greek New Testament (1968) 54-55. SCHREINER, J. Gestalt und Anspruch des Neuen Testaments (1969) 322f. STAATS, R. "Die Törichten Jungfrauen von Mt 25 in gnostischer und antignostischer Literatur", in: Christentum und Gnosis (1969) Eltester, W. (ed.) 98-115. KüNZI, M. Das Naherwartungslogion Matthäus 10, 23 (1970) 90, 93, 98, 104, 107. PAGELS, E. H., The Johannine Gospel in Gnostic Exegesis (Nashville 1973) 92f. "Aethiopien" in: TRE 1 (1977) 575. *DIAZ, J. A., "Sentido del 'Juicio Final' de Yahvé en la Apocalíptica y en Mt 25" Studium Ovetense 5 (1977) 77-98. GEIGER, M., "Theologie, Kirche und Todesstrafe" in: M. Geiger et al (eds.) Nein zur Todesstrafe (Basel 1978) 18f. RAYAN, S., The Holy Spirit (Maryknoll 1978) 62.

25:1ff STONEHOUSE, N. B. The Witness of Matthew and Mark to Christ (1944) 130. FINDLAY, J. A. Jesus and His Parables

(1951) 111ff. STAEHELIN, E. Die Verkündigung des Reiches Gottes in der Kirche Jesu Christi I (1951) 63, 114, 386. BLAIR, E. P. Jesus in the Gospel of Matthew (1960) 80. KNOX, W. L. The Sources of the Synoptic Gospels II (1957) 134f. BOUSSET, W. Die Religion des Judentums im Späthellenistischen Zeitalter (1966⁻1926) 390. "Apokalyptik" in: TRE 3 (1978) 254.

25:1-46 GOODSPEED, E. J. A Life of Jesus (1950) 189-91.

25:1-13 JüLICHER, D. A. Die Gleichnisreden Jesu (1910) 448-59. WILKENS, J. Einführung in das Evangelium nach Matthäus II (1937) 181-185. MORGAN, G. C. The Parables and Metaphors of Our Lord (1943) 147ff. PIROT, J. Paraboles et Allégories Evangeliques (1949) 429-48. TRILLHAAS, GPM 4, 308 (1949/50) KüMMEL, W. G. Verheissung und Erfüllung (1952) 50-52. GOLLWITZER, GPM 9 (1954/55) 265ff. BEST, E. One Body in Christ (1955) 169n, 170, 175n. MICHAELIS, D. W. Die Gleichnisse Jesu (1956) 87-94. KLAAS, W. in: Herr, tue meine Lippen auf, Bd. 1 (1957) Eichholz, G. (ed.) 334-41. STROBEL, F. A. "Zum Verständnis von Mat. XXV 1-13," NovTest 2 (3-4, '58) 199-27. SABBE, M. 'De parabel van de maagden" (The Parable of the Virgins), CollBrugGand 5 (3, '59) 369-78. BLAIR, E. P. Jesus in the Gospel of Matthew (1960) 94, 108. HUNTER, A. M. Interpreting the Parables (1960) 85ff. BORNKAMM, G. GPM 15 (1960/61) 325ff. DOERNE, M. Er kommt auch noch heute (1961) 161-63. STROBEL, A. Untersuchungen zum Eschatologischen Verzögerungsproblem (1961) 233-54. JEREMIAS, J. Die Gleichnisse Jesu (1962) 38, 48-50, 78, 171-75. HUMMEL, R. Die Auseinandersetzung zwischen Kirche und Judentum im Matthäusevangelium (1963) 160. KUPFERSCHMID, A. Das Kommen Christi und unsere Zukunft (1963) 103-113. LOCKYER, H. All the Parables of the Bible (1963) 237ff. PERRIN, N., The Kingdom of God in the Teaching of Jesus (Philadelphia 1963) 80, 114, 137, 144, 146. SMITH, Ch. W. F. "The Mixed State of the Church in Matthew's Gospel," JBL 82 (1963) 149-68, esp. 158. BLINZLER, J. "Bereitschaft für das Kommen des Herrn" BuL 37 (1963/1964) 89-100. ARMERDING, C. "Asleep in the Dust," BiblSa 121 (482, '64) 153-58. BIEDER, W., Die Verheissung der Taufe im Neuen Testament (Zürich 1966) 283f. BRAUN, H. Qumran und NT II (1966) 78, 318. DEISS, L., "La parabole des dix vierges" AssS 95 (1966) 33-57. KAHLEFELD, H. Parables and Instructions in the Gospels (1966) 117f. Wir wissen weder Tag noch Stunde, Predigtgedanken aus Vergangenheit und Gegenwart, Bd. 6 (1966) 289-320. MASSINGBERD, J. "The Parable of the Foolish Scholars (Matt. xxv, 1-13)," NovTest 9 (2, '67) 107-23.

OTTO, G. Handbuch des Religions-Unterrichts (1967) 303-25. BORNKAMM, G. Geschichte und Glaube I (1968) 49ff. LINNEMANN, E. Gleichnisse Jesu (1969) 130ff., 178ff. BARCLAY, W. And Jesus Said (1970) 133-38. MAISCH, I. "Das Gleichnis von den klugen und törichten Jungfrauen. Auslegung von Mt 25, 1-13," BuL 11 (4,'70) 247-59. SANFORD, J. A., The Kingdom Within (New York 1970) 194-96. BATEY, R. A. New Testament Nuptial Imagery (1971) 45-47. HERBERT, K. GPM 3/4 (1973) 488-96. *DONFRIED, K. P., "The Allegory of the Ten Virgins (Matt 25:1-13) as a summary of Matthaean Theology" JBL 93 (1974) 415-28. GOULDER, M. D., Midrash and Lection in Matthew (London 1974) 4, 54, 59, 65, 98, 108, 167, 192, 416, 438ff. TALBERT, C. H., Literary Patterns, Theological Themes, and the Genre of Luke-Acts (Missoula 1974) 55. *ARGYLE, A. W., "Wedding Customs at the Time of Jesus" ET 86 (1975) 214-15. *ASHBY, G., "The Parable of the Ten Virgins" Journal of Theology for Southern Africa 10 (1975) 62-64. CONZELMANN, H. und LINDEMANN, A., Arbeitsbuch zum Neuen Testament (Tübingen 1975) 89. BERGMANN, W., Die zehn Gleichnisse vom Reich der Himmel (Lahr-Dinglingen 1976). *WENTHE, D. O., "The Parable of the Ten Bridesmaids (Matthew 25:1-13)" Springfield 40 (1976) 9-16. FUNK, R. W., "The Narrative Parables: The Birth of a Language Tradition" in: J. Jervell and W. A. Meeks (eds.) God's Christ and His People. For N. A. Dahl (New York 1977) 43-50. *HAMANN, H. P., "The Ten Virgins: An Exegetical-Homiletical Study" Lutheran Theological Journal 11 (1977) 68-72. MANEK, J., . . . und brachte Frucht. Die Gleichnisse Jesu (Berlin 1977) 69-71. *LOSADA, D. A., "La venida imprevista del Senor" RivB 40 (1978) 201-16. *SCHENK, W., "Auferweckung der Toten oder Gericht nach den Werken. Tradition und Redaktion in Matthäus xxv 1-13" NovT 20 (1978) 278-99. STAGG, E. and F., Woman in the World of Jesus (Philadelphia 1978) 142f, 218. STOEVESANDT, H., GPM 33 (1979) 439-47. SWIDLER, L., Biblical Affirmations of Woman (Philadelphia 1979) 169, 253, 279. WEDER, H., Die Gleichnisse Jesu als Metaphern (Göttingen 1980 (2)) 239-49.

25:1-12 WEGENAST, K. Glaube-Schule-Wirklichkeit. Beiträge zur Theorie und Praxis des Religionsunterrichts (1970) 172-77. STRECKER, G. Der Weg der Gerechtigkeit (1962) 44, 1584. HAHN, F. Christologische Hoheitstitel (1963) 98-100.

25:1 STRECKER, G. Der Weg der Gerechtigkeit (1962) 214. HAHN, F. Das Verständnis der Mission im Neuen Testament (1965) 106. JEREMIAS, J. "LAMPADES Mt 25:1.3f.7f.," ZNW 56 (3-4, '65) 196-201.

25:2-12 PERRIN, N., Jesus and the Language of the Kingdom (London 1976) 38, 150, 154, 196. "Amen" in: TRE 2 (1978) 389.

25:5 KNOX, W. L. The Sources of the Synoptic Gospels II (1957) 71. TRILLING, W. Das wahre Israel (1959) 30. STRECKER, G. Der Weg der Gerechtigkeit (1962) 44.

25:6 VOLZ, P. Die Eschatologie der jüdischen Gemeinde (1934) 211. STAEHELIN, E. Die Verkündigung des Reiches Gottes in der Kirche Jesu Christi I (1951) 334. STRECKER, G. Der Weg der Gerechtigkeit (1962) 241. BRAUN, H. Qumran und NT II (1966) 202.

25:10ff HAHN, F. Christologische Hoheitstitel (1963) 99.

25:11ff RUDOLPH, K Die Mandäer II (1961) 318,3.

25:11f KNOX, W. L. The Sources of the Synoptic Gospels II (1957) 71, 80. HAHN, F. Christologische Hoheitstitel (1963) 96, 98. WREGE, H.-T. Die Ueberlieferungsgeschichte der Bergpredigt (1968) 148ff.

25:11 HAHN, F. Christologische Hoheitstitel (1963) 85.

25:12.40, 45 HASLER, V. Amen (1969) 93.

25:12 BRUNNER, E. Dogmatik I (1946) 283. STAEHELIN, E. Die Verkündigung des Reiches Gottes in der Kirche Jesu Christi I (1951) 238. BORNKAMM-BARTH-HELD, Ueberlieferung und Auslegung im Matthäus-Evangelium (1961) 130, 134f. HAHN, F. Christologische Hoheistitel (1963) 400, 402. JEREMIAS, J. Neutestamentliche Theologie I (1971) 17, 248, 250, 265.

25:13-30 *ELLUL, J., "Du texte au sermon (18). Les talents. Matthieu 25/13-30" EThR 48 (1973) 125-38.

25:13-14 PARKER, P. The Gospel Before Mark (1953) 68-69.

25:13 KNOX, W. L. The Sources of the Synoptic Gospels II (1957) 135. STRECKER, G. Der Weg der Gerechtigkeit (1962) 44, 159, 241f. HAHN, F. Christologische Hoheitstitel (1963) 99. HARNISCH, W., Eschatologische Existenz (Göttingen 1973) 85A, 86, 90, 90A.

25:14ff STONEHOUSE, N. B. The Witness of Matthew and Mark to Christ (1944) 255. FINDLAY, J. A. Jesus and His Parables (1951) 56ff. STAEHELIN, E. Die Verkündigung des Reiches Gottes in der Kirche Jesu Christi I (1951) 64. KNOX, W. L. The Sources of the Synoptic Gospels II (1957) 136. KAMLAH, E. "Kritik und Interpretation der Parabel von den anvertrauten Geldern. Mt. 25, 14ff.; Lk. 19, 12ff.," KuD 14 (1, '68) 28-38. KüMMEL, W. G. Einleitung in das Neue Testament (1973) 41f.

25:14-46　WALVOORD, J. F. "Christ's Olivet Discourse on the End of the Age. Signs of the End of the Age," BiblSa 128 (512, '71) 316-26.

25:14-31　MASSAUX, E.Influence de l'Evangile de saint Matthieu sur la littérature chrétienne avant saint Irénée (1950) 267-71.

25:14-30　JüLICHER, D. A. Die Gleichnisreden Jesu (1910) 472-95. WILKENS, J. Einführung in das Evangelium nach Matthäus II (1937) 186-91. HIRSCH, E. Frühgeschichte des Evangeliums (1941) 161-70. MORGAN, G. C. The Parables and Metaphors of Our Lord (1943) 152ff. DODD, C.H. The Parables of the Kingdom (1948) 146ff. PIROT, J. Paraboles et Allégories Evangeliques (1949) 391-99. MICHAELIS, D. W. Die Gleichnisse Jesu (1956) 100-12. KöSTER/BALTZER/MERKEL, GPM 13/4 (1959) 280-82. HUNTER, A. M. Interpreting the Parables (1960) 106ff. STRECKER, G. Der Weg der Gerechtigkeit (1962) 163, 165⁴. HAHN, F. Christologische Hoheitstitel (1963) 110. KUPFERSCHMID, A. Das Kommen Christi und unser Zukunft (1963) 115-25.LOCKYER, H. All the Parables of the Bible (1963) 241ff. LOHSE, E. GPM (1964/65) 364ff. BISER, E. Die Gleichnisse Jesu (1965) 65ff., 163ff. DERRETT, J. D. M. "Law in the New Testament: The Parable of the Talents and Two Logia," ZNW 56 (3-4, '65) 184-95. DIDIER, M., "La parabole des talents" AssS 93 (1965) 32-44. BIEDER, W., Die Verheissung der Taufe im Neuen Testament (Zürich 1966) 284. KAHLEFELD, H. Parables and Instructions in the Gospels (1966) 132ff. DIDIER, M. "La parabole des talents et des mines"in De Jésus aux Evangiles (1967) 248-71. LöWE, R. in: Hören und Fragen Bd. 5 (1967) Eichholz, G. & Falkenroth, A. (eds.) 558ff. DUPONT, J. "La parabole des talents (Mat. 25:14-30) ou des mines (Luc 19:12-27))," RThPh 19 (6, '69) 376-91. LüHRMANN, D. Die Redaktion der Logienquelle (1969) 70f. BARCLAY, W. And Jesus Said (1970) 169-73. FIEDLER, P. "Die übergebenen Talente. Auslegung von Mt 25, 14-30," BuL 11 (4, '70) 259-73. HAAR, J. GPM 25 (1971) 451-56. LANGE, E. (ed.) Predigtstudien für das Kirchenjahr 1970/71 (1971) 246-52. WEISER, A. Die Knechtsgleichnisse der synoptischen Evangelien (1971) 226-75. HOFFMANN, P. Studien zur Theologie der Logienquelle (1972) 5, 42f., 48-50. SCHULZ, S. Q Die Spruchquelle der Evangelisten (1972) 288-98. DINKLER, E. GPM 6/4, 260-63. CROSSAN, J. D., in: G. MacRae (ed.) SBL Seminar Papers II (Missoula 1973) 96-98. DAVIES, W. D., The Gospel and the Land (London 1974) 357. GOULDER, M. D., Midrash and Lection in Matthew (London 1974) 4, 54, 59, 61, 65, 366, 416, 440ff. LOHSE, E.,

Grundriss der neutestamentlichen Theologie (Stuttgart 1974) 34f, 121. *McGAUGHY, L. C., "The Fear of Yahweh and the Mission of Judaism: A Postexilic Maxim and Its Early Christian Expansion in the Parable of the Talents" JBL 94 (1975) 235-45. PERRIN, N., Jesus in and the Language of the Kingdom (London 1976) 149-51, 154, 161, 196. FUNK, R. W, "The Narrative Parables: The Birth of a Language Tradition" in: J. Jervell and W. A.Meeks (eds.) God's Christ and His People. For N. A. Dahl (New York 1977) 43-50. MANEK, J.,.. .und brachte Frucht. Die Gleichnisse Jesu (Berlin 1977) 71-74. PFITZNER, K. und LäPPLE, V., in: P. Krusche (ed.) Predigtstudien V/2 (Stuttgart 1977) 248-54. POLAG, A., Die Christologie der Logienquelle (Neukirchen-Vluyn 1977) 165f. KRUSE, M. in: GPM 33 (1979) 332-36. RESENHöFFT, W., "Jesu Gleichnis von den Talenten, ergänzt durch die Lukas-Fassung" NTS 26 (1979/1980) 318-31. WEDER, H., Die Gleichnisse Jesu als Metaphern (Göttingen 1980) 193-210.

25:14-28   PARKER, P. The Gospel Before Mark (1953) 67ff. DERRETT, J. D. M. Law in the New Testament (1970) 17-31. SAND, A., Das Gesetz und die Propheten (Regensburg 1974) 117f.

25:14   BLACK, M. An Aramaic Approach to the Gospels and Acts (1967) 58f.

25:16   STRECKER, G. Der Weg der Gerechtigkeit (1962) 20.

25:19   PARKER, P. The Gospel Before Mark (1953) 68-69. STRECKER, G. Der Weg der Gerechtigkeit (1962) 44, 106, 241. TRILLING, W. Das wahre Israel (1959) 30.

25:20ff   STAEHELIN, E. Die Verkündigung des Reiches Gottes in der Kirche Jesu Christi I (1951) 238.

25:20   KNOX, W. L. The Sources of the Synoptic Gospels II (1957) 125.

25:21, 23   LADD, G. E., A Theology of the New Testament (Grand Rapids 1974) 73f, 133f.

25:21   STAEHELIN, E. Die Verkündigung des Reiches Gottes in der Kirche Jesu Christi I (1951) 347. HENNECKE, E. & SCHNEEMELCHER, W. Neutestamentliche Apokryphen (1964) II 380.

25:22ff   HAHN, F. Christologische Hoheitstitel (1963) 82.

25:25   STRECKER, G. Der Weg der Gerechtigkeit (1962) 234.

25:26f   HENNECKE, E. & SCHNEEMELCHER, W. Neutestamentliche Apokryphen (1964) II 387.

25:26   BRAUN, H. Jesus (1969) 88, 89.

25:28f   KNOX, W. L. The Sources of the Synoptic Gospels II (1957) 117. HUMMEL, R. Die Auseinandersetzung zwischen Kirche und Judentum im Matthäusevangelium (1963) 148.

25:29   KNOX, W. L. The Sources of the Synoptic Gospels II (1957) 30. KäSEMANN, E. Exegetische Versuche und Besinnungen (1964) II 96f. SCHRAGE, W. Das Verhältnis des Thomas-Evangelium zur Synoptischen Tradition und zu den Koptischen Evangelienübersetzungen (1964) 96. KäSEMANN, E. New Testament Questions of Today (1969) 98. NEUHäUSLER, E. "Mit welchem Masstab misst Gott die Menschen? Deutung zweier Jesussprüche," BuL 11 (2, '70) 104-113. JEREMIAS, J. Neutestamentliche Theologie I (1971) 25f., 30. KLAUCK, H.-J., Allegorie und Allegorese in Synoptischen Gleichnistexten (Münster 1978) 239f.

25:30ff   KNOX, W. L. The Sources of the Synoptic Gospels II (1957) 136.

25:30-46   HENNECKE, E. & SCHNEEMELCHER, W. Neutestamentliche Apokryphen (1964) I 261, II 107, 387. BRAUN, H. Qumran und NT II (1966) 91, 269f.

25:30   BETZ, H. D. Lukian von Samosata und das Neue Testament (1961) 81, 88. HUMMEL, R. Die Auseinandersetzung zwischen Kirche und Judentum im Matthäusevangelium (1963) 147. SMITH, M., Tannaitic Parallels to the Gospels (Philadelphia 1968) 3.9+.

25:31-26:5   GOULDER, M. D., Midrash and Lection in Matthew (London 1974) 442-44.

25:31-26:1   PARKER, P. The Gospel Before Mark (1953) 21-22.

25:31ff   VOLZ, P. Die Eschatologie der jüdischen Gemeinde (1934) 80. MOORE, G. F. Judaism (1946) II 336n. FINDLAY, J. A. Jesus and His Parables (1959) 111ff. STAEHELIN, E. Die Verkündigung des Reiches Gottes in der Kirche Jesu Christi I (1951) 65, 230, 282, 355, 389, 394. *ROBINSON, J. A. T. "The 'Parable' of the Sheep and the Goats," NTS 2 ('56) 225-37. SCHWEIZER, E. Gemeinde und Gemeinde-Ordnung im Neuen Testament (1959) § 4d. BLAIR, E. P. Jesus in the Gospel of Matthew (1960) 67, 81, 89, 94, 165. STRECKER, G. Der Weg der Gerechtigkeit (1962) 109, 158f, 208, 235f., 237₂, 240, 242. KAMLAH, E. Die Form der katalogischen Paränese im Neuen Testament (1964) 25f, 27, 150, 1;160. WREGE, H.-T. Die Ueberlieferungsgeschichte der Bergpredigt (1968) 175f. NöTSCHER, F., Altorientalischer und alttestamentlicher Auferstehungsglauben (Darmstadt 1970) 192. JEREMIAS, J. Neutestamentliche Theologie I (1971) 35f., 115, 147, 205, 262. GRäSSER, E., "Der Mensch Jesus als Thema der Theologie" in: E. E. Ellis/ E. Grässer (eds.) Jesus und Paulus. Für W. G. Kümmel (Göttingen 1975) 142-45. THEISOHN, J., Der auserwählte Richter (Göttingen 1975) 168, 174f, 180f. "Apokalyptik"in: TRE 3 (1978) 254. "Barmherzigkeit"in: TRE 5 (1980) 227.

25:31-48 MINEAR, P. S. Images of the Church in the New Testament (1960) 85f.

25:31-46 BRANDT, W., "Die geringsten Brüder. Aus dem Gespräch der Kirche mit Matthäus 25:31-46" Jahrbuch der Theologischen Schule Bethel 8 (1937) 1-28. MORGAN, G. C. The Parables and Metaphors of Our Lord (1943) 157ff. IWAND, H. J. GPM 4 (1949/50) 305ff. HUNTER, A.M. Design for Life (1953) 34, 39. PARKER, P. The Gospel Before Mark (1953) 113-14. BORNKAMM, G. GPM 9 (1954/55) 257ff. FLEW, R. N. Jesus and His Church (1956) 147n. SCHLINK, E. in: Herr, tue meine Lippen auf, Bd. 1 (1957) Eichholz G. (ed.) 329-34. BLAIR, E. P. Jesus in the Gospel of Matthew (1960) 46, 79, 107, 108, 136. HUNTER, A. M. Interpreting the Parables (1960) 88ff. IWAND, H. J. GPM 15 (1960/61) 317ff. BORNKAMM-BARTH-HELD, Ueberlieferung und Auslegung im Matthäus-Evangelium (1961) 21, 34, 37, 40, 55, 89, 98, 153. CRANFIELD, C. E. B. "Diakonia. Matthew 25, 31-46," LondQuartHolRev 30 (4, '61) 275-81. DOERNE, M. Er kommt auch noch heute (1961) 159-61. BULTMANN, R. "Sermon (Mat 25:31-46)", in: Hören und Handeln, Festschrift für E. Wolf (1962) 47-51. JEREMIAS, J. Die Gleichnisse Jesu (1962) 78, 204-207, 210. ROBINSON, J. A. T. "The 'Parable' of the Sheep and the Goats", Twelve New Testament Studies (1962) 76-93. BULTMANN, R. The History of the Synoptic Tradition (1963) 123f., 125. HAHN, F. Christologische Hoheitstitel (1963) 100, 186-88. KUPFERSCHMID, A. Das Kommen Christi und unsere Zukunft (1963) 127-38. LOCKYER, H. All the Parables of the Bible (1963) 246ff. SMITH, Ch. W. F. "The Mixed State of the Church in Matthew's Gospel." JBL 82 (1963) 149-68, esp. 158-60. Studiorum Paulinorum Congressus Internationalis Catholicus 1961 (1963) I 227-28. TöDT, H. E. Der Menschensohn in der synoptischen Ueberlieferung (1963) 68f., 70-74. HAUFE, G., "Soviel ihr getan habt einem dieser meiner geringsten Brüder. . ." in: Ruf und Antwort. Für E. Fuchs (Leipzig 1964) 484-93. IWAND, H.-J. Predigt-Meditationen (1964) 224-47. DE LETTER, P. "The Day of Judgment," ClM 28 (10, '64) 369-79. MARCEL, P. " 'Frères et soeurs' du Christ," RevR 15 (4, '64) 18-30. BISER, E. Die Gleichnisse Jesu (1965) 58, 145ff. MADDOX, R. "Who are the 'Sheep' and the 'Goats'? A Study of the Purpose and Meaning of Matthew xxv: 31-46,' AusBR 13 (1-4, '65) 19-28. HAHN, F. Das Verständnis der Mission im Neuen Testament (1965) 30, 47, 109. MARCEL, P. " 'Frères et soeurs' du Christ (suite)," RevR 16 (1, '65) 12-26. MICHAELS, J. R. "Apostolic Hardships and Righteous Gentiles. A Study of Matthew 25:31-46," JBL 84 (1, '65) 27-37. BIEDER, W., Die Verheissung der Taufe im Neuen Testament (Zürich 1966) 284f. JEREMIAS, J. Abba; Studien zur neutestamentlichen Theologie und Zeitgeschichte (1966) 112-14. TURNER, H. E. W. "Expounding the Parables. VI. The Parable of the Sheep and the Goats (Matthew 25:31-46)," ET 77 (8, '66) 243-46. WINANDY, J. "La scène du Jugment Dernier (Mt., 25, 31-46)," SciEccl 18 (2, '66) 169-86. Wir wissen weder Tag noch Stunde, Predigtgedanken aus Vergangenheit und Gegenwart, Bd. 6 (1966) 251-66. SOLKOLOVSKIJ, P., "Hoffnung im Tun" Journal of the Moscow Partriarchate 5 (1967) 44-45. LAGO TOIMIL, M. " 'Allora il re dirà...' Cristo Re, in Mt. 25, 31-46," PaCl 47 (20, '68) 1318-321. CARLSTON, C. The Things that Defile (Mark VII. 14) and the Law in Matthew and Mark; NTS 15 (1968-69) 84-85. COPE, L., "Matthew xxv 31-46. 'The Sheep and the Goats' Reinterpreted," NovTest 11 (1-2, '69) 32-44. KNOCH, O. "Gott als Anwalt des Menschen. Mitmenschlichkeit als Aufgabe der Christen nach Mt 25, 31-46," BuK 24 (3, '69) 82-84. RENNES, J. "A propos de Matthieu 25/31-46," EThR 44 (3, '69) 233-34. BARCLAY, W. And Jesus Said (1970) 106-12. BROER, I. "Das Gericht des Menschensohnes über die Völker. Auslegung von Mt 25, 31-46," BuL 11 (4, '70) 273-95. INGELAERE, J.-C. "La 'Parabole' du Jugement Dernier (Matthieu 25/31-46)," RHPhR 50 (1, '70) 23-60. MATTILL, A. J. "What the world owes the church," HPR 71 (7, '71) 8-17. PETERS, G. W. A Biblical Theology of Missions (1972) 47, 333-34. THEBEAU, D.H. "On Separating Sheep from Goats," ChrTo 16 (22, '72) 1040-041. WALVOORD, J. F. "Christ's Olivet Discourse on the End of the Age. The Judgment of the Nations," BiblSa 129 (516, '72) 307-15. *AVANZO, M., "El Compromiso con el Necesitado en el Judaísmo y en el Evangelio" RivB 35 (1973) 23-41. *DUPREZ, A., "Le Jugement dernier. Mt. 25, 31-46" AssS 65 (1973) 17-28. *GEWALT, D., "Matthäus 25, 31-46 im Erwartungshorizont heutiger Exegese" LiBi 25-26 (1973) 9-21. GOLLWITZER, H., Veränderung im Diesseits (München 1973) 157. HAMEL, GPM 3/4 (1973) 474-81. MANEK, J., "Mit wem identifiziert sich Jesus (Matt. 25:31-46)?" in: B. Lindars/S. S. Smalley (eds.) Christ and the Spirit in the New Testament. For C. F. D. Moule (Cambridge 1973) 15-25. *OBERMüLLER, R., " ' ?Donde estuviste?' " RivB 35 (1973)

14-21. FRANKEMöLLE, H., Jahwebund und Kirche Christi (Münster 1974) 118, 139, 271, 281, 293, 295. GOULDER, M. D., Midrash and Lection in Matthew (London 1974) 52f, 161, 168, 192, 268, 339. *MATTILL, A. J., "Matthew 25:31-46 Relocated" RestQ 17 (1974) 107-14. SAND, A., Das Gesetz und die Propheten (Regensburg 1974) 165. *CHRISTIAN, P., Jesus und seine geringsten Brüder (Leipzig 1975). GOPPELT, L., Theologie des Neuen Testaments I (Göttingen 1975) 176f. WILCKENS, U., "Gottes geringste Brüder - zu Mt 25: 31-46" in: E. E. Ellis/E. Grässer (eds.) Jesus und Paulus. Für W. G. Kümmel (Göttingen 1975) 363-83. DIAZ, A. J., "Las 'Buenas obras' (o la 'justicia') dentro de la estructura de los principales temas de Teología Bílica" EstEc 52 (1977) 445-86. *BONNARD, P., "Matthieu 25, 31-46. Questions de lecture et d'interprétation" Foi et Vie 76 (1977) 81-87. *FRIEDRICH, J., Gott im Bruder? (Stuttgart 1977). MANEK, J.,...und brachte Frucht. Die Gleichnisse Jesu (Berlin 1977) 74-80. MIRANDA, J. P., Marx and the Bible (London 1977) 19, 117f. TRITES, A. A., The New Testament Concept of Witness (Cambridge 1977) 194f. "Armenfürsorge" in: TRE 4 (1979) 16f. "Armut" in: TRE 4 (1979) 80. BRäNDLE, R., Matt. 25, 31-46 im Werk des Johannes Chrysostomos (Tübingen 1979). *CATCHPOLE, D. R., "The Poor on Earth and the Son of Man in Heaven. A Re-Appraisal of Matthew xxv. 31-46" BJRL 61 (1979) 355-97. HEDRICK, C. W., "Resurrection: Radical Theology in the Gospel of Matthew" LThQ 14 (1979) 40-45. LAUFF, W. in: GPM 33 (1979) 427-32. *PIKAZA, X., "Dios, hombre y Cristo en el mensaje de Jesús (Introducción al tema de la autenticidad jesuánica de Mt 25, 31-46)" Salmanticensis 26 (1979) 5-50. "Barmherzigkeit" in: TRE 5 (1980) 227.

25:31-40 TILLICH, P. Das Neue Sein (1959) 33-36.

25:31-33, 46 SWIDLER, L., Biblical Affirmations of Woman (Philadelphia 1979) 285.

25:31-32 STONEHOUSE, N. B. The Witness of Matthew and Mark to Christ (1944) 233. DUPONT, J. L'Union Avec Le Christ Suivant Saint Paul (1952) 46-47.

25:31 STONEHOUSE, N. B. The Witness of Matthew and Mark to Christ (1944) 240. BLAIR, E. P. Jesus in the Gospel of Matthew (1960) 77. STRECKER, G. Der Weg der Gerechtigkeit (1962) 125, 1262, 1611, 1667. HAHN, F. Christologische Hoheitstitel (1963) 39. SCHNACKENBURG, R. Der Menschensohn im Johannesevangelium. NTS 11 (1964/65) 129f. JüNGEL, E. Paulus und Jesus (1966) 239. KüNZI, M. Das Naherwartungslogion Matthäus 10, 23 (1970) 115, 148, 179. JEREMIAS, J. Neutestamentliche Theologie I

(1971) 248, 251f., 254, 261. MANEK, J., "Mit wem identifiziert sich Jesus (Matt. 25:31-46)" in: B. Lindars/ S. S. Smalley (eds.) Christ and the Spirit in the New Testament. For C. F. D. Moule (Cambridge 1973) 15f, 25. THEISOHN, J., Der auserwählte Richter (Göttingen 1975) 79, 153, 155f, 158, 160f, 175ff, 182f, 199, 204, 252f, 258. KLOPPENBORG, J. S., "Didache 16:6-8 and Special Matthaean Tradition" ZNW 70 (1979) 54-67.

25:32   TRILLING, W. Das wahre Israel (1959) 12f. STRECKER, G. Der Weg der Gerechtigkeit (1962) 34. LANGE, J., Das Erscheinen des Auferstandenen im Evangelium nach Matthäus (Würzburg 1973) 150, 295, 297-302, 379, 488.

25:33   STAEHELIN, E. Die Verkündigung des Reiches Gottes in der Kirche Jesu Christi I (1951) 337.

25:34ff   CAVALLIN, H. C. C., Life After Death I (Lund 1974) 4.11.1.

25:34, 41   *PIKAZA, X., "La bendición y maldición del Hijo del Hombre (Transfondo veterotestamentario del 'Benditos-Malditos' de Mt 25, 34.41)" Salmanticensis 26 (1979) 277-86.

25:34   VOLZ, P. Die Eschatologie der jüdischen Gemeinde (1934) 167. STONEHOUSE, N. B. The Witness of Matthew and Mark to Christ (1944) 233. BRUNNER, E. Dogmatik I (1946) 329, 354. MASSAUX, E. Influence de l'Evangile de saint Matthieu sur la littérature chrétienne avant saint Irénée (1950) 624-26. STAEHELIN, E. Die Verkündigung des Reiches Gottes in der Kirche Jesu Christi I (1951) 200, 248, 356, 368, 378, 383, 390, 391. DUPONT, J. L'Union Avec Le Christ Suivant Saint Paul (1952) 82-83. LIETZMANN, H. "Matthäus 25:34 in den Freisinger Denkmälern", Kleine Schriften II (1958) 189-90. BLAIR, E. P. Jesus in the Gospel of Matthew (1960) 78, 81, 94, 108, 165. STRECKER, G. Der Weg der Gerechtigkeit (1962) 711. HAHN, F. Christologische Hoheitstitel (1963) 321. HUMMEL, R. Die Auseinandersetzung zwischen Kirche und Judentum im Matthäusevangelium (1963) 114. KAMLAH, E. Die Form der katalogischen Paränese im Neuen Testament (1964) 26, 27, 161, 162. SCHENK, W. Der Segen im Neuen Testament (1967) 59f. JEREMIAS, J. Neutestamentliche Theologie I (1971) 22, 42, 208, 236, 252, 254. CAVALLIN, H. C. C., Life After Death I (Lund 1974) 4.11.1; 4.11 n4. FRANKEMÖLLE, H., Jahwebund und Kirche Christi (Münster 1974) 160, 167, 170, 245, 265, 266, 313. LADD, G. E., A Theology of the New Testament (Grand Rapids 1974) 72, 74, 85, 103, 133, 171. WESTERMANN, C., Blessing In the Bible and the Life of the Church (Philadelphia 1978) 70, 98-101.

25:35ff   BOUSSET, W. Die Religion des Judentums im Späthellenistischen Zeitalter (1966⁻1926) 417.

25:35-45   SCHWEIZER, E. Erniedrigung und Erhöhung bei Jesus und seinen Nachfolgern (1962) § 14e.

25:35-40   SMITH, M., Tannaitic Parallels to the Gospels (Philadelphia 1968) 8b n5+. "Barmherzigkeit" in: TRE 5 (1980) 233.

25:35-39.   BERGER, K. Die Gesetzesauslegung Jesu (1940) 381-84.
42-45

25:35f, 40   SANFORD, J. A., The Kingdom Within (New York 1970) 183.

25:35-36   THEISSEN, G., Soziologie der Jesusbewegung (München 1977) 30.

25:35   STAEHELIN, E. Die Verkündigung des Reiches Gottes in der Kirche Jesu Christi I (1951) 390. KNOX, W. L. The Sources of the Synoptic Gospels II (1957) 125. RUDOLPH, K. Die Mandäer I (1960) 106.

25:36   WILLCOCK, J., "St. Matt. XXV. 36; 2 Tim. I. 16-18" ET 34 (1922-1923) 43. STEIDLE, B. " 'Ich war krank, und ihr habt mich besucht' (Mt 25, 36). I. Der Kranke im alten Heidentum, Judentum und Christentum," EuA 40 (6, '64) 443-58.

25:37-41   JEREMIAS, J. Neutestamentliche Theologie I (1971) 125, 128, 135, 142, 251.

25:37-39, 44   MESSINA, G. "Parallelismi semitismi lezioni tendenziose nell'armonia Persiana", Biblica 30 (1949) 359-61.

25:37   HAHN, F. Christologische Hoheitstitel (1963) 85.

25:38   KNOX, W. L. The Sources of the Synoptic Gospels II (1957) 125.

25:40   STONEHOUSE, N. B. The Witness of Matthew and Mark to Christ (1944) 176. MOORE, G. F. Judaism (1946) II 169n. BLAIR, E. P. Jesus in the Gospel of Matthew (1960) 78. HUMMEL, R. Die Auseinandersetzung zwischen Kirche und Judentum im Matthäusevangelium (1963) 114. GROSS, G. "Die 'geringsten Brüder' Jesu in Mt 25, 40 in Auseinandersetzung mit der neueren Exegese," BuL 5 (3, '64) 172-80. HAUFE, G. "Soviel ihr getan habt einem dieser meiner geringsten Brüder." in: Ruf und Antwort, Festgabe für Emil Fuchs (1964) 484-93. SASS, G. Ungereimtes bei Matthäus (1968) 50-52. JEREMIAS, J. Neutestamentliche Theologie I (1971) 44, 113, 167, 205, 252. LANGE, J., Das Erscheinen des Auferstandenen im Evangelium nach Matthäus (Würzburg 1973) 297, 299, 301, 375-79. MANEK, J., "Mit wem identifiziert sich Jesus (Matt. 25:31-46)" in: B. Lindars/S. S. Smalley (eds.) Christ and the Spirit in the New Testament. For C. F. D. Moule (Cambridge 1973) 16, 21ff, 25. BANKS, R., Jesus and the Law in the Synoptic Tradition (London 1975) 222f. THEUNISSEN, M., "ὁ αἰτῶν λαμβάνει. Der

Gebetsglaube Jesus und die Zeitlichkeit des Christseins" in: Jesus, Ort der Erfahrung Gottes (Basel 1976) 52f.

25:41-42 SMITH, M., Tannaitic Parallels to the Gospels (Philadelphia 1968) 3b n9+.

25:41.46 BLIGH, P. H. "Eternal Fire, Eternal Punishment, Eternal Life (Mt 25:41, 46)," ET 83 (1, '71) 9-11.

25:41 KAUPEL, H. Die Dämonen im Alten Testament (1930) 128f. BRUNNER, E. Dogmatik I (1946) 249, 354. MOORE, G. F. Judaism (1946) II 316n. BRUNNER, E. Dogmatik II (1950) 159. STAEHELIN, E. Die Verkündigung des Reiches Gottes in der Kirche Jesu Christi I (1951) 290, 383. KNOX, W. L. The Sources of the Synoptic Gospels II (1957) 125. HAHN, F. Christologische Hoheitstitel (1963) 85. NICKELS, P. Targum and New Testament (1967) 22. BOUSSET, W. Die Religion des Judentums im Späthellenistischen Zeitalter (1966⁻1926) 341. LADD, G. E., A Theology of the New Testament (Grand Rapids 1974) 64, 74, 88, 196, 205, 255. METZGER, B. M., The Early Versions of the New Testament (Oxford 1977) 118.

25:45 BANKS, R., Jesus and the Law in the Synoptic Tradition (London 1975) 222f.

25:46 STONEHOUSE, N. B. The Witness of Matthew and Mark to Christ (1944) 130. STAEHELIN, E. Die Verkündigung des Reiches Gottes in der Kirche Jesu Christi I (1951) 254. NöTSCHER, F., Altorientalischer und alttestamentlicher Auferstehungsglauben (Darmstadt 1970) 221. LADD, G. E., A Theology of the New Testament (Grand Rapids 1974) 73f, 206, 216, 255f.

26-28 KILPATRICK, G. D. The Origins of the Gospel According to St. Matthew (1950) 11, 37, 44-47, 67, 95f. LEIVESTAD, R. Christ the Conqueror (1954) 67ff. *DAHL, N. A. Die Passiongeschichte bei Matthaus, NTS 2 (1955) 17-32. LEON-DUFOUR, X. "Mt et Mc dans le récit de la Passion," Biblica 40 (3, '59) 684-96. BARTSCH, H.-W. "Die Passions und Ostergeschichten bei Matthäus. Ein Beitrag zur Redaktionsgeschichte des Evangeliums", in: Basileia, Festschrift für Walter Freytag (1961) Hermelink, J. & Margull, J. (eds.) 27-41. BORNKAMM-BARTH-HELD,

Ueberlieferung und Auslegung im Matthäus-Evangelium (1961) 134ff. BARTSCH, H. W. in: Entmythologisierende Auslegung, Aufsätze aus den Jahren 1940 bis 1960 (1962) 80-92. WALKER, N. "Yet another Look at the Passion Chronology," NovTest 6 (4, '63) 286-89. DAVIES, W. D., The Sermon on the Mount (Cambridge 1966) 16-18. ELLIS, P., Matthew: His Mind and His Message (Collegeville 1974) 94-98.

26:1-28:20   HIRSCH, E. Frühgeschichte des Evangeliums (1941) 236-49.

26-27   DAHL, N. A. "Die Passionsgeschichte bei Matthäus," ThLZ 79 (1954) 762-64. SELBY, D. J., Introduction to the New Testament (New York 1971) 145-47. *MINEAR, P. S., "Matthew, Evangelist, and Johann, Composer" ThT 30 (1973) 243-55. *SENIOR, D. P., The Passion Narrative According to Matthew (Gembloux 1975). GERSTENBERGER, G., und SCHRAGE, W., Leiden (Stuttgart 1977) 123-25, 146; ET: Suffering (Nashville 1980) 143-46, 170. *PUNNAKOTTIL, G., "The Passion Narrative According to Matthew. A Redaction critical study" Biblehashyam 3 (1977) 20-47. TOWNSEND, J. T., A Liturgical Interpretation of Our Lord's Passion in Narrative Form (New York 1977). TRITES, A. A., The New Testament Concept of Witness (Cambridge 1977) 185-90.

26:1-27:65   RIDDERBOS, H. Matthew's Witness to Jesus Christ (1958) 80-88.

26:1-27:61   EWALD, H. Die drei ersten Evangelien (1850) 341ff.

26:1-27:26   WILSON, W. R. The Execution of Jesus (1970) 47-50.

26   WOJCIK, J., "The Two Kingdoms in Matthew's Gospel"in: K. R. R. Gros Louis et al. (eds.) Literary Interpretations of Biblical Narratives (Nashville 1974) 287-89.

26:1-35   GAECHTER, P. Die literarische Kunst im Matthäus-Evangelium (1968) 33-34.

26:1-13   WILKENS, J. Einführung in das Evangelium nach Matthäus II (1937) 200-203.

26:1-5   SCHELKLE, K. H. Die Passion Jesu in der Verkündigung des Neuen Testament (1949) 64f. WENZEL, H.-G. "Der Weg des Menschensohnes," in: Die Passionstexte (1967) Frey, F. (ed.) 155-57. SCHRAMM, T. Der Markus-Stoff bei Lukas (1971) 182-84. SENIOR, D. P., The Passion Narrative According to Matthew (Leuven 1975) 9-27.

26:1   STONEHOUSE, N. B. The Witness of Matthew and Mark to Christ (1944) 131, 176. BLAIR, E. P. Jesus in the Gospel of Matthew (1960) 132. STRECKER, G. Der Weg der Gerechtigkeit (1962) 38s, 130, 158.

26:2   STONEHOUSE, N. B. The Witness of Matthew and Mark to Christ (1944) 237, 251. BLAIR, E. P. Jesus in the Gospel of Matthew (1960) 89, 97. SCHWEIZER, E. Erniedrigung und Erhöhung bei Jesus und seinen Nachfolgern (1962) § 3k. STRECKER, G. Der Weg der Gerechtigkeit (1962) 125, 126₂, 181₃, 182. HAHN, F. Christologische Hoheitstitel (1963) 46. JAUBERT, M. A. Le mercredi où Jésus fut livré, NTS 14 (1967/68) 146f. LOHSE, E. and Others (eds.) Der Ruf Jesu und die Antwort der Gemeinde (1970) 204-12. O'NEILL, J. C., The Theology of Acts in its historical setting (London 1970) 43fn. WILLIAMS, J. A., A Conceptual History of Deuteronomism in the Old Testament, Judaism, and the New Testament (Ph.D.Diss. Southern Baptist Theological Seminary, Louisville 1976) 303f. METZGER, B. M., The Early Versions of the New Testament (Oxford 1977) 439.

26:3f   STRECKER, G. Der Weg der Gerechtigkeit (1962) 181.

26:3   HUMMEL, R. Die Auseinandersetzung zwischen Kirche und Judentum im Matthäusevangelium (1963) 145. BROER, I. Die Urgemeinde und das Grab Jesu (1972) 72f. FRANKEMöLLE, H., Jahwebund und Kirche Christi (Münster 1974) 195, 202-204.

26:5   HUMMEL, R. Die Auseinandersetzung zwischen Kirche und Judentum im Matthäusevangelium (1963) 145.

26:6ff   STRECKER, G. Der Weg der Gerechtigkeit (1962) 87.

26:6-13   GOODSPEED, E. J. A Life of Jesus (1950) 192-94. M'NEILE, A.H. The Gospel According to St. Matthew (1955) 376. WULF, H. "Die Salbung in Bethania,' in: Die Passionstexte (1967) Frey, F. (ed.) 158-62. BLINZLER, J. Der Prozess Jesu (1969) 404-410. DERRETT, J. D. M. Law in the New Testament (1970) 266-75. LOHSE, E. and Others (eds.) Der Ruf Jesu und die Antwort der Gemeinde (1970) 247-58. ROLOFF, J. Das Kerygma und der irdische Jesus (1970) 220-23. SENIOR, D. P., The Passion Narrative According to Matthew (Leuven 1975) 28-40. RIST, J. M., On the Independence of Matthew and Mark (Cambridge 1978) 83f. STAGG, E./F., Woman in the World of Jesus (Philadelphia 1978) 117, 120f. SWIDLER, L., Biblical Affirmations of Woman (Philadelphia 1979) 196f, 220, 233, 240.

26:6   WESTERHOLM, S., Jesus and Scribal Authority (Lund 1978) 68f.

26:7   KöBERT, R. "Nardos pistike - kostnarde," Biblica 29 (1948) 279-81.

26:8   STONEHOUSE, N. B. The Witness of Matthew and Mark to Christ (1944) 176. BORNKAMM-BARTH-HELD,

Ueberlieferung und Auslegung im Matthäus-Evangelium (1961) 101, 112. STRECKER, G. Der Weg der Gerechtigkeit (1962) 193₁₅, 194₃.

26:10   BLAIR, E. P. Jesus in the Gospel of Matthew (1960) 87. NICKELS, P. Targum and New Testament (1967) 22.

26:11   "Abendmahl" in: TRE 1 (1977) 124.

26:13   NEPPER-CHRISTENSEN, P. Das Matthäusevangelium. Ein Judenchristliches Evangelium? (1958) 19, 21, 198. STRECKER, G. Der Weg der Gerechtigkeit (1962) 128f. HAHN, F. Das Verständnis der Mission im Neuen Testament (1965) 105, 106, 108. BRAUN, H. Qumran und NT II (1966) 242. HASLER, V. Amen (1969) 44. MARXSEN, W. Mark the Evangelist (1969) 122, 124, 138, 141f. JEREMIAS, J. Neutestamentliche Theologie I (1971 134f. KINGSBURY, J. D., Matthew: Structure, Christology, Kingdom (Philadelphia 1975) 128-30.

26:14-29   WILKENS, J. Einführung in das Evangelium nach Matthäus II (1937) 204-210.

26:14-16, 20-25   MISSFELDT, P. "Einer unter euch wird mich verraten," in: Die Passionstexte (1967) Frey, F. (ed.) 163-68.

26:14-19   SCHRAMM, T. Der Markus-Stoff bei Lukas (1971) 182-84.

26:14-16   JAUBERT, M. A. Le mercredi où Jésus fut livré. NTS 14 (1967/68) 145f. SENIOR, D. P., The Passion Narrative According to Matthew (Leuven 1975) 41-50.

26:14   STONEHOUSE, N. B. The Witness of Matthew and Mark to Christ (1944) 176.

26:15   STRECKER, G. Der Weg der Gerechtigkeit (1962) 25, 79. COLELLA, P., "Trenta denari" RivB 21 (1973) 325-27. DORMEYER, D., Die Passion Jesu als Verhaltensmodell (Münster 1974) 84.

26:16-28   SCHLATTER, D. A. Die Theologie des Neuen Testaments (1909) I 538-44.

26:16   STRECKER, G. Der Weg der Gerechtigkeit (1962) 91, 92₃.

26:17ff   ANDERSEN, A., "Zu Mt 26, 17ff und Lc 22, 15ff" ZNW 7 (1906) 87-90.

26:17-35   GOODSPEED, E. J. A Life of Jesus (1950) 195-202.

26:17-29   MAHONEY, J. "The Last Supper and the Qumran Calendar," CIR 48 (4, '63) 216-32. CARMIGNAC, J. "Comment Jésus et ses contemporains pouvaient-ils célébrer la Pâque à une date non officielle?" RevQ 5 (1, '64) 59-79. MENDOZA RUIZ, F. "El jueves, dia de la Ultima Cena," EstBi 23 (1, '64) 5-40; (2, '64) 151-71; (3-4, '64) 259-94; EstBi 24 (1-2, '65) 85-106. POWER, J.

"Pasch and Easter," Furrow 16 (4, '65) 195-204. DACQUINO, P. "Il gesto di Gesù Lall'ultima cena," BiOr 8 (4-5, '66) 173-84. IRWIN, K. W. "The Supper Text in the Gospel of Saint Matthew," DuRev 11 (2, '71) 170-84.

26:17-19   BATTENBERG, F. "Er lässt sich von uns nehmen," in: Die
26-29   Passionstexte (1967) Frey, F. (ed.) 169-75.

26:17-19   STONEHOUSE, N. B. The Witness of Matthew and Mark to Christ (1944) 157. BORNKAMM-BARTH-HELD, Ueberlieferung und Auslegung im Matthäus-Evangelium (1961) 134f., 156, 220. GIGLIOLI, A. "Il giorno dell'ultima cena e l'anno della morte di Gesú," RivB 10 (2, '62) 156-81. STRECKER, G. Der Weg der Gerechtigkeit (1962) 182. SENIOR, D., The Passion Narrative According to Matthew (Leuven 1975) 51-65. RIST, M., In the Independence of Matthew and Mark (Cambridge 1978) 84f.

26:17f   STONEHOUSE, N. B. The Witness of Matthew and Mark to Christ (1944) 176.

26:17   RUDOLPH, K. Die Mandäer II (1961) 133, 4. STRECKER, G. Der Weg der Gerechtigkeit (1962) 87.

26:18   BLAIR, E. P. Jesus in the Gospel of Matthew (1960) 86. STRECKER, G. Der Weg der Gerechtigkeit (1962) 87f., 182. HAHN, F. Christologische Hoheitstitel (1963) 81. BLACK, M., " 'ΕΦΦΑΘΑ (Mk 7.34), (ΤΑ) ΠΑΣΧΑ (Mt 26.18 W), (ΤΑ) ΣΑΒΒΑΤΑ (passim), (ΤΑ) ΔΙΔΡΑΧΜΑ (Mt 17, 24 b i s)"in: A. Descamps and A. deHalleux (eds.) Mélanges Bibliques en hommage au R. P. Béda Rigaux (Gembloux 1970) 60-62.

26:20-40   MEES, M. "Die Bezeugung von Mt. 26, 20-40 auf Papyrus (P64, P53, P45, P37) und ihre Bedeutung," Augustinianum 11 (2, '71) 409-31.

26:20-35   GAECHTER, P. Die literarische Kunst im Matthäus-Evangelium (1968) 33-34. *OGG, G. "The Chronology of the Last Supper," Historicity and Chronology in the New Testament, 75-96.

26:20-29   LE DéAUT, R. "De nocte Paschatis," VerbDom 41 (3-4, '63) 189-95.

26:20-25   STRECKER, G. Der Weg der Gerechtigkeit (1962) 124. SENIOR, D. P., The Passion Narrative According to Matthew (Leuven 1975) 66-75.

26:20   STONEHOUSE, N. B. The Witness of Matthew and Mark to Christ (1944) 138, 176, 177. JEREMIAS, J. Die Abendmahlsworte Jesu (1960) 38, 40, 42f.

26:21   HASLER, V. Amen (1969) 49.

26:22   HAHN, F. Christologische Hoheitstitel (1963) 86. NICKELS, P. Targum and New Testament (1967) 22.

26:23   FENSHAM, F. C. "Judas' Hand in the Bowl and Qumran," RevQ 5 (2, '65) 259-61. BRAUN, H. Qumran und NT II (1966) 31, 42.

26:24f STONEHOUSE, N. B. The Witness of Matthew and Mark to Christ (1944) 251.

26:24   STONEHOUSE, N. B. The Witness of Matthew and Mark to Christ (1944) 237. HOOKER, M. D. Jesus and the Servant (1959) 79f., 98f. BLAIR, E. P. Jesus in the Gospel of Matthew (1960) 56. SASS, G. Ungereimtes bei Matthäus (1968) 53-55. SANFORD, J. A., The Kingdom Within (New York 1970) 134-36. KINGSBURY, J. D., Matthew: Structure, Christology, Kingdom (Philadelphia 1975) 114-16. KLIJN, A. F. J., "Die syrische Baruch-Apokalypse" in: W. G. Kümmel (ed.) Jüdische Schriften aus hellenistisch-römischer Zeit V (Gütersloh 1976) 128.

26:25   STRECKER, G. Der Weg der Gerechtigkeit (1962) 182. HAHN, F. Christologische Hoheitstitel (1963) 75. NICKELS, P. Targum and the New Testament (1967) 22. CATCHPOLE, D. R. The Answer of Jesus to Caiaphas. Mt. 26:64, NTS 17 (1970/71) 214-19. DAUER, A. Die Passionsgeschichte im Johannesevangelium (1972) 25, 50f.

26:26-30 SENIOR, D. P., The Passion Narrative According to Matthew (Leuven 1975) 76-88.

26:26-29 GAUGLER, E., Das Abendmahl im Neuen Testament (Basel 1943) 11-13. M'NEILE, A. H. The Gospel According to St. Matthew (1955) 383-86. DENNEY, J. The Death of Christ (1956) 35ff. KNOCH, G. "Ursprüngliche Gestalt und wesentlicher Gehalt der neutestamentlichen Abendmahlsberichte", BuK 15 (2, '60) 37-40. TIERNEY, C. "The Eucharistic Sacrifice and the Narratives of Institution," ACR 39 (1, '62) 5-23. ROBINSON, D. W. B. "The Eucharistic Sacrifice in the Sacrament of the Body and Blood of Christ," RThR 23 (3, '64) 65-74. RODGERS, J. "Eucharistic Sacrifice: Blessing or Blasphemy?" Churchman 78 (4, '64) 248-54. CAVALLETTI, S. "Le fonti del 'seder' pasquale," BiOr 7 (4-5, '65) 153-60. CROW, P. A. "The Lord's Supper in Ecumenical Dialogue," ThT 22 (1, '65) 39-58. DU TOIT, A. B. Der Aspekt der Freude im urchristlichen Abendmahl (1965) 76-102. SASS, G. Ungereimtes bei Matthäus (1968) 56-58. SLIFER, M. D. "Christ's Mystical Presence and the Communion of Saints," TheolLife 8 (2, '65) 145-53. SUHL, A. Die Funktion der alttestamentlichen Zitate und Anspielungen im

Markusevangelium (1965) 110ff. EMERY, P.-Y. "L'Eucharistie: sacrifice du Christ et de l'Eglise (note conjointe)," VerbCar 20 (77, '66) 65-72. GERRISH, B. A. "The Lord's Supper in the Reformed Confessions," ThT 23 (2, '66) 224-43. CAIRD, G. B. "The Last Supper," ET 78 (2, '66) 58. HUNTER, A. M., SJTh 19 (3, '66) 362-64. KILMARTIN, E. J. ThSt 27 (4, '66) 674-77. KüHNE, G. "Die Abendmahlsfrage im Gespräch. C. Die Substanzfrage beim Abendmahl," PastBlät 106 (3, '66) 141-45. SEEMANN, M. "La catéchèse sur l'eucharistie dans une perspective biblique et oecuménique," VerbCaro 20 (77, '66) 50-64. DAW MYAT YIN, "The Doctrine of the Lord's Supper," SEAJTh 7 (4, '66) 37-48. KüNG, H., Die Kirche (Freiburg 1967) 254-59; ET: The Church (London 1967) 212-15. LEANEY, A. R. C. "What was the Lord's Supper?" Theology 70 (560, '67) 51-62. MACRAE, G. W. JBL 86 (1, '67) 107-108. *MARXSEN, W. "Das Mahl - Vorstellungen und Wandlungen," Kontexte, Bd. 3, 91-97. WILLIAMS, S. K., Jesus' Death as Saving Event (Missoula 1975) 204-211. SCHELKLE, K. H., "Das Herrenmahl" in: J. Friedrich et al. (eds.) Rechtfertigung. Für E. Käsemann (Göttingen 1976) 388-90. PESCH, R., Das Markusevangelium II (Freiburg 1977) 364-77. "Abendmahl" in: TRE 1 (1977) 47. PESCH, R., Wie Jesus das Abendmahl hielt (Freiburg 1977). FRIEDRICH, G., "Ursprung, Urform und Urbedeutung des Abendmahls" in: Auf das Wort kommt es an (Göttingen 1978) 309-14, 316. RIST, J. M., On the Independence of Matthew and Mark (Cambridge 1978) 85.

26:26-28   SCHüRMANN, H., Der Einsetzungsbericht (Münster 1955) 2ff. STRECKER, G. Der Weg der Gerechtigkeit (1962) 221f. MORETON, M. J. "The Sacrifice of Praise," ChurchQuartRev 165 (357, '64) 481-94. ALLIS, O. T. "The Communion of the Blood of Christ," ChrTo 9 (Mar. 12, '65) 606-608. LASH, N. "The Eucharist: Sacrifice or Meal?" ClR 50 (12, '65) 907-22. LYS, D. "Mon corps, c'est ceci (Notule sur Mt 26/26-28 et par.)," EThR 45 (4, '70) 389. SCHüRMANN, H. Ursprung und Gestalt (1970) 85, 86, 90, 99, 100, 103, 192.

26:26-27   RUDOLPH, K. Die Mandäer II (1961) 399, 1. DEQUEKER, L. "Het genre van de Joodse zegen in de Christelijke Eucharistie" (The Genre of the Jewish Blessing in the Christian Eucharist), CollMech 48 (6, '63) 529-48. SCHMID, R. Das Bundesopfer in Israel (1964) 125f. DAVIES, W. D., The Sermon on the Mount (Cambridge 1966) 16. "Abendmahl" in: TRE 1 (1977) 50.

26:26   ANDERSEN, A., "Mt 26:26 flg. und Parallelstellen im Lichte der Abendmahlslehre Justins" ZNW 7 (1906) 172-75.

STONEHOUSE, N. B. The Witness of Matthew and Mark to Christ (1944) 176. STAEHELIN, E. Die Verkündigung des Reiches Gottes in der Kirche Jesu Christi I (1951) 335. BOUSSET, W. Die Religion des Judentums im Späthellenistischen Zeitalter (1966⁻1926) 178. NICKELS, P. Targum and New Testament (1967) 22. WANKE, J., Die Emmauserzählung (Leipzig 1973) 104.

26:27ff STAEHELIN, E. Die Verkündigung des Reiches Gottes in der Kirche Jesu Christi I (1951) 139, 335.

26:27 METZGER, B. M., The Early Versions of the New Testament (Oxford 1977) 434. CLARK, K. W., "The Making of the Twentieth Century New Testament" in: The Gentile Bias and other Essays (Leiden 1980) 151f.

26:28-29 FRANKEMöLLE, H., Jahwebund und Kirche Christi (Münster 1974) 37-40, 65, 95, 213, 217.

26:28 WINDISCH, H. The Meaning of the Sermon on the Mount (1937) 64, 128ff., 170, 174. BRUNNER, E. Dogmatik II (1950) 335. MASSAUX, E. Influence de l'Evangile de saint Matthieu sur la littérature chrétienne avant saint Irénée (1950) 18-21. HOOKER, M. D. Jesus and the Servant (1959) 80-83. BLAIR, E. P. Jesus in the Gospel of Matthew (1960) 57, 79, 94, 107, 135. KUGELMANN, R. " 'This I My Blood of the New Covenant," Worship 35 (7, '61) 421-24. EMERTON, J. A. "to haima mou tes diathekes: The Evidence of the Syriac Versions," JThS 13 (1, '62) 111-17. STRECKER, G. Der Weg der Gerechtigkeit (1962) 181s, 184₂. HAHN, F. Christologische Hoheitstitel (1963) 208, 239. HUMMEL, R. Die Auseinandersetzung zwischen Kirche und Judentum im Matthäusevangelium (1963) 101. KäSEMANN, E. Exegetische Versuche und Besinnungen (1964) I 45. QUESNELL, Q. This Good News (1964) 180f. DAVID, J.-E. "To haima mou tes diathekes Mt 26:28: Un faux problème," Biblica 48 (2, '67) 291-92. MOST, W. G. "A Biblical Theology of Redemption in a Covenant Framework," CBQ 29 (1, '67) 1-19. SCHüRMANN, H. Ursprung und Gestalt (1970) 120, 121, 122, 153, 156, 194, 195, 312. NICKELS, P. Targum and New Testament (1967) 22. DELLING, G. Der Kreuzestod Jesu in der urchristlichen Verkündigung (1972) 11f. 30-32. LEROY, H., Zur Vergebung der Sünden (Stuttgart 1974) 30, 37. WILLIAMS, J. A., A Conceptual History of Deuteronomism in the Old Testament, Judaism, and the New Testament (Ph.D. Diss. Southern Baptist Theological Seminary, Louisville 1976) 310-18. "Abendmahl" in: TRE 1 (1977) 52, 54, 223.

26:29 GRILL, J. Untersuchungen über die Entstehung des vierten Evangeliums II (Leipzig 1923) 80, 201, 267, 274, 287. VOLZ, P.

Die Eschatologie der jüdischen Gemeinde (1934) 368. MANSON, T. W. The Teaching of Jesus (1945) 96ff. MOORE, G. F. Judaism (1946) II 365. STAEHELIN, E. Die Verkündigung des Reiches Gottes in der Kirche Jesu Christi I (1951) 299, 335. TRILLING, W. Das wahre Israel (1959) 68. BLAIR, E. P. Jesus in the Gospel of Matthew (1960) 58. HAHN, F. Christologische Hoheitstitel (1963) 321. HUMMEL, R. Die Auseinandersetzung zwischen Kirche und Judentum im Matthäusevangelium (1963) 141f. BRAUMANN, G. "Mit euch, Matth. 26, 29," ThZ 21 (3, '65) 161-69. LEBEAU, S. J. Le vin nouveau du royaume. Etude exégétique et patristique sur la Parole eschatologique de Jésus à le Cène (1966). BROWN, R. E. ThSt 29 (4, '68) 765-66. SWETNAM, J. Biblica 50 (4, '69) 585-87. HASLER, V. Amen (1969) 49. *LEBEAU, P. "La parole eschatologique de Jésus à la Cène (Mt. 26, 29) dans l'exégèse patristique," Studia Patristica VII, 516-23. SAND, A., Das Gesetz und die Propheten (Regensburg 1974) 86. JANSSEN, E., "Testament Abrahams" in: W. G. Kümmel (ed.) Jüdische Schriften aus hellenistisch-römischer Zeit III (Gütersloh 1975) 210.

26:30-56 WILKENS, J. Einführung in das Evangelium nach Matthäus II (1937) 211-20.

26:30-35 SCHART, D. "Das Leiden der Gemeinde an ihrem Herrn", in: Schriftauslegung. . .Die Passionstexte (1967) Frey, F. (ed.) 176ff.

26:30 SQUILLACI, D. "L'inno dell'Eucharistia," PaCl 43 (Mar. 15, '64) 287-92.

26:31ff STONEHOUSE, N. B. The Witness of Matthew and Mark to Christ (1944) 165, 177, 194. MINEAR, P. S. Images of the Church in the New Testament (1960) 85f.

26:31-46 HIERS, R. H., The Historical Jesus and the Kingdom of God (Gainesville 1973) 20, 38f, 43.

26:31-35 SENIOR, D. P., The Passion Narrative According to Matthew (Leuven 1975) 89-99.

26:31 BLAIR, E. P. Jesus in the Gospel of Matthew (1960) 56. STRECKER, G. Der Weg der Gerechtigkeit (1962) 22f., 221l. BRAUN, H. Qumran und NT II (1966) 93, 267, 306, 322f. ROTHFUCHS, W. Die Erfüllungszitate des Matthäus-Evangeliums (1969) 83f. BAMMEL, E., "P64(67) and the Last Supper" JThS 24 (1973) 189.

26:32 STONEHOUSE, N. B. The Witness of Matthew and Mark to Christ (1944) 91, 170ff., 172, 175. STRECKER, G. Der Weg der Gerechtigkeit (1962) 2084. ODENKIRCHEN, P. C. " 'Praecedam vos in Galileam' (Mt 26, 32 cf. 28, 7, 10; Mc 14, 28;

16, 7 cf. Lc 24, 6)," VerbDom 46 (4-5, '68) 193-223. SASS, G. Ungereimtes bei Matthäus (1968) 59-61. METZGER, B. M., The Early Versions of the New Testament (Oxford 1977) 249.

26:33-35 STRECKER, G. Der Weg der Gerechtigkeit (1962) 198.

26:33 STRECKER, G. Der Weg der Gerechtigkeit (1962) 204. DASSMAN, E., "Die Szene Christus-Petrus mit dem Hahn" in: E. Dassmann/K. S. Frank (eds.) Pietas. Für B. Kötting (JAC Erg.Bd.8) (Münster 1980) 510f.

26:34 HASLER, V. Amen (1969) 49. WILCOX, M. The Denial-Sequence in Mark 14:26-31, 66-72. NTS 17 (1970/71) 431f.

26:35 STONEHOUSE, N. B. The Witness of Matthew and Mark to Christ (1944) 176.

26:36-56 ROBINSON, B. P. "Gethsemane: The Synoptic and the Johannine Viewpoints," ChurchQuartRev 167 (362, '66) 4-11.

26:36-47 HOWARD, V. P., Das Ego in den Synoptischen Evangelien (Marburg 1975) 123-32.

26:36-46 DENNEY, J. The Death of Christ (1956) 41ff. STRECKER, G. Der Weg der Gerechtigkeit (1962) 183. BOMAN, T. Der Gebetskampf Jesu. NTS 10 (1963/64) 261f. AMBRUSTER, C. J. "The Messianic Significance of the Agony in the Garden," Scripture 16 (36, '64) 111-19. SCHRöRER/SCHLOSSER, GPM (1964) 146ff. BENOIT, P. Passion et Réssurrection du Seigneur (1966) 22-24. FREY, F. "Gethsemane" in: Schriftauslegung. . .Die Passionstexte (1967) Frey, F (ed.) 1182ff. JOHNSON, S. L. "The Agony of Christ," BiblSa 124 (496, '67) 303-13. TRAUB, H. in: Hören und Fragen, Bd. 5, 3 (1967) Eichholz, G. & Falkenroth, A. (eds.) 229ff. LANGE, E. (ed.) Predigtstudien für das Kirchenjahr (1970) 180-85. LINNEMANN, E. Studien zur Passionsgeschichte (1970) 11-40. FISCHER, K.M. GPM 25 (1, '71) 167-76. HOLLERAN, J. W., The Synoptic Gethsemane (Rome 1973). SENIOR, D. P., The Passion Narrative According to Matthew (Leuven 1975) 100-19. KABITZ, U./Kugler, G., in: P. Krusche (ed.) Predigtstudien. Für das Kirchenjahr 1976/77 V/1 (Stuttgart 1976) 177-83. JöRNS, K.-P., in: GPM 31 (1976/77) 163-70. FEUILLET, A., L'agonie de Gethsémani (Paris 1977).

26:36-40 BOMAN T. Die Jesus-Ueberlieferung im Lichte der neueren Volkskunde (1967) 208-21.

28:36 HENNECKE E. & SCHNEEMELCHER, W. Neutestamentliche Apokryphen (1964) I 156. METZGER, B. M., The Early Versions of the New Testament (Oxford 1977) 172.

26:37-46 STRECKER, G. Der Weg der Gerechtigkeit (1962) 198.

26:37 DALMAN, G. Orte und Wege Jesu (1967) 341f. METZGER, B. M., The Early Versions of the New Testament (Oxford 1977) 253.

26:38-40 FRANKEMöLLE, H., Jahwebund und Kirche Christi (Münster 1974) 11, 40-42.

26:38.40 BIRDSALL, J. N. "ĒGREGOREŌ," JThS 14 (2, '63) 390-91.

26:38 STRECKER, G. Der Weg der Gerechtigkeit (1962) 23, 43. HENNECKE, E. & SCHNEEMELCHER, W. Neutestamentliche Apokryphen (1964) I 350.

26:39-42 SAND, A., Das Gesetz und die Propheten (Regensburg 1974) 121f.

26:39.42 SUMMERALL, H. "What Was the Cup That Jesus Had to Drink?" ChrTo 14 (21, '70) 937-40.

26:39 STRECKER, G. Der Weg der Gerechtigkeit (1962) 21. HAHN, F. Christologische Hoheitstitel (1963) 321. NICKELS, P. Targum and New Testament (1967) 22. O'NEILL, J. C., The Theology of Acts in its Historical Setting (London 1970) 42f. DAUER, A. Die Passionsgeschichte im Johannesevangelium (1972) 48, 52f., 283. WILLIAMS, J. A., A Conceptual History of Deuteronomism in the Old Testament, Judaism, and the New Testament (Ph.D. Diss. Southern Baptist Theological Seminary, Louisville 1976) 317.

26:40 STRECKER, G. Der Weg der Gerechtigkeit (1962) 43, 205.

26:41 FARRER, A. St Matthew and St Mark (1954) 170. HENNECKE, E. & SCHNEEMELCHER, W. Neutestamentliche Apokryphen (1964) I 156. BRAUN, H. Qumran und NT II (1966) 120, 123, 180, 188, 251f., 256, 298, 312. SASS, G. Ungereimtes bei Matthäus (1968) 62-64. METZGER, B. M., The Early Versions of the New Testament (Oxford 1977) 177.

26:42 TRILLING, W. Das wahre Israel (1959) 163f. HAHN, F. Christologische Hoheitstitel (1963) 321. DAUER, A. Die Passionsgeschichte im Johannesevangelium (1972) 48, 52f.

26:45-50 RIST, J. M., On the Independence of Matthew and Mark (Cambridge 1978) 85f.

26:45-46 STAPLES, P. "The Kingdom of God Has Come," ET 71 (3, '59) 87-88.

26:45 HENNECKE, E. & SCHNEEMELCHER, W. Neutestamentliche Apokryphen (1964) I 156.

26:47-28:8 SCHNEIDER, G., Die Passion Jesu nach den drei älteren Evangelien (München 1973).

26:47-27:10 GAECHTER, P. Die literarische Kunst im Matthäus-Evangelium (1968) 66-67.

26:47-56 GOODSPEED, E. J. A Life of Jesus (1950) 205-207. BENOIT, P. Passion et Réssurrection du Seigneur (1966) 50-53. BASTIAN, H. "Die Gefangennahme Jesu" in: Schriftauslegung . . .Die Passionstexte (1967) Frey, F. (ed.) 189ff. BLINZLER, J. Der Prozess Jesu (1969) 73-101. SENIOR, D. P., The Passion Narrative According to Matthew (Leuven 1975) 120-56.

26:47 STONEHOUSE, N, B. The Witness of Matthew and Mark to Christ (1944) 176. HUMMEL, R. Die Auseinandersetzung zwischen Kirche und Judentum im Matthäusevangelium (1963) 145. FRANKEMöLLE, H. Jahwebund und Kirche Christi (Münster 1974) 195, 202-204.

26:49 HAHN, F. Christologische Hoheitstitel (1963) 75. METZGER, B. M., The Early Versions of the New Testament (Oxford 1977) 151.

26:50 DEISSMANN, A. Licht vom Osten (1923) 100ff. SPIEGELBERG, W., "Der Sinn von Mt 26:50" ZNW 28 (1929) 341ff. KLOSTERMANN, E., "Zu Spiegelbergs Aufsatz: Der Sinn von Mt 26:50" ZNW 29 (1930) 311. KLOSTERMANN, E. ZNW 29 (1930) 311. TAYLOR, V. The Life and Ministry of Jesus (1954) 188f. REHKOPF, F. "Mt 26:50: HETAIRE, EPH' HO PAREI," ZNW 52 (1-2, '61) 109-15. ELTESTER, W. "Freund, wozu du gekommen bist (Mt. xxvi 50)", in: Neotestamentica et Patristica, Festschrift für Oscar Cullmann (1962) 70-91. STRECKER, G. Der Weg der Gerechtigkeit (1962) 182. LEE, G. M. "Matthew xxvi. 50: Hetaire, eph' ho parei," ET 81 (2, '69) 55. METZGER, B. M., The Early Versions of the New Testament (Oxford 1977) 151.

26:51 DE JONGE, M. "De berichten over het scheuren van het voorhangel bij Jezus' dood in de synoptische evangelien" (The Accounts of the Rending of the Veil at Jesus' Death in the Synoptic Gospels), NedThT 21 (2, '66) 90-114.

26:52-54 STRECKER, G. Der Weg der Gerechtigkeit (1962) 183. DAUER, A. Die Passionsgeschichte im Johannesevangelium (1972) 51f.

26:52-53 BRAUN, H. Qumran und NT II (1966) 90, 92, 112, 289, 296.

26:52 LOEWENICH, W. von. Luther als Ausleger der Synoptiker (1954) 230f. MAADLAND, J. "Das Wort über das Schwert, Mt 26, 52" (Norw.) NTT 55 (3-4, '54) 162-73. KOSMALA, H., "Matthew xxvi 52-A Quotation from the Targum," NovTest 4 (1, 60) 3-5. HENNECKE, E. & SCHNEEMELCHER, W., Neutestamentliche Apokryphen (1964) II 42. NICKELS, P. Targum and New Testament (1967) 22. DAUER, A. Die

Passionsgeschichte im Johnnesevangelium (1972) 47, 51f. GOULDER, M. D., Midrash and Lection in Matthew (London 1974) 71, 74f, 126f, 244, 445.

26:53 HAHN, F. Christologische Hoheitstitel (1963) 321. METZGER, B. M., The Early Versions of the New Testament (Oxford 1977) 171, 373.

26:54 NEPPER-CHRISTENSEN, P. Das Matthäusevangelium. Ein Judenchristliches Evangelium ? (1958) 139-42. BLAIR, E. P. Jesus in the Gospel of Matthew (1960) 56, 57. STRECKER, G. Der Weg der Gerechtigkeit (1962) 612.4, 624. HUMMEL, R. Die Auseinandersetzung zwischen Kirche und Judentum im Matthäusevangelium (1963) 132, 134f. BANKS, R., Jesus and the Law in the Synoptic Tradition (London 1975) 211f.

26:55 STRECKER, G. Der Weg der Gerechtigkeit (1962) 127. BOUSSET, W. Die Religion des Judentum im Späthellenistischen Zeitalter (1966⁻1926) 167. SCHALIT, A. König Herodes (1969) 721.

26:56 NEPPER-CHRISTENSEN, P. Das Matthäusevangelium. Ein Judenchristliches Evangelium? (1958) 139, 140, 141. BLAIR, E. P. Jesus in the Gospel of Matthew (1960) 56, 121. STRECKER, G. Der Weg der Gerechtigkeit (1962) 50, 61, 624, 1944. HUMMEL, R. Die Auseinandersetzung zwischen Kirche und Judentum im Matthäusevangelium (1963) 131, 132, 134f. TILLICH, P. Das Ewige im Jetzt (1964) 100-109. GERHARDSSON, B. "Jésus livré et abandonné d'après la Passion selon Saint Matthieu," RevBi 76 (2 '69) 206-27. SWIDLER, L., Biblical Affirmations of Woman (Philadelphia 1979) 199.

26:57-27:26 *SHERWIN-WHITE, A. N., "The Trial of Christ," Historicity and Chronology in the New Testament, 97-116.

26:57-27:1 JAUBERT, A. "Les séances du sanhédrin et les récits de la passion," RHR 166 (2, '64) 143-69. JAUBERT, A. "Les séances du sanhédrin et les récits de la passion (suite)," RHR 167 (1, '65) 1-33.

26:57-75 GOODSPEED, E. J. A Life of Jesus (1950) 207-12.

26:57-68 WILKENS, J. Einführung in das Evangelium nach Matthäus II (1937) 221-24. OHLY, M. "Jesus vor dem Hohen Rat" in: Schriftauslegung . . . Die Passionstexte (1967) Frey, F. (ed.) 196ff. HOWARD, V. P., Das Ego in den Synoptischen Evangelien (Marburg 1975) 132-48. SENIOR, D. P., The Passion Narrative According to Matthew (Leuven 1975) 157-91.

26:57-58 BENOIT, P. Passion et Résurrection du Seigneur (1966) 74-77.
69-75

26:57f   STRECKER, G. Der Weg der Gerechtigkeit (1962) 204₃.

26:57   SCHNEIDER, G., Verleugnung, Verspottung und Verhör
         Jesu nach Lukas 22, 54-71 (München 1969) 47, 55, 65, 74, 107-
         109, 111, 147, 159. TALBERT, Ch. H., Literary Patterns,
         Theological Themes, and the Genre of Luke-Acts (Missoula
         1974) 21.

26:58   STRECKER, G. Der Weg der Gerechtigkeit (1962) 198.
         DAUER, A. Die Passionsgeschichte im Johannesevangelium
         (1972) 73, 77, 78, 96.

26:59-66 CRIBBS, F. L., in: G. MacRae (ed.) SBL Seminars Papers 2
          (Montana 1973) 62-65.

26:59-64 BENOIT, P. Passion et Résurrection du Seigneur (1966) 115-
          27. CATHCHPOLE, D. R. The Answer of Jesus to Caiaphas:
          Mt. 26:64. NTS 17 (1970/71) 223f.

26:59f   BEUTLER, J. Martyria (1972) 93, 197, 321.

26:60-61 FLEW, R. N. Jesus and His Church (1956) 40-42.

26:60   STRECKER, G. Der Weg der Gerechtigkeit (1962) 392.

26:61   HOFFMANN, R. A. "Das Wort Jesu von der Zerstörung und
         dem Wiederaufbau des Tempels", in: Neutestamentliche
         Studien Georg Heinrici zu seinem 70. Geburtstag (1914)
         Deissmann, A. & Windisch, H. (eds.) 130-39. BLAIR, E. P.
         Jesus in the Gospel of Matthew (1960) 148. RUDOLPH, K. Die
         Mandäer I (1960) 205. STRECKER, G. Der Weg der
         Gerechtigkeit (1962) 121₈. HUMMEL, R. Die
         Auseinandersetzung zwischen Kirche und Judentum im
         Matthäusevangelium (1963) 92-94, 106-108. HENNECKE, E.
         & SCHNEEMELCHER, W. Neutestamentliche Apokryphen
         (1964) I 337. GäRTNER, B. The Temple and the Community in
         Qumran and the New Testament (1965) 111, 113, 140. HAHN,
         F. Das Verständnis der Mission im Neuen Testament (1965)
         29f., 100, 111. SASS, G. Ungereimtes bei Matthäus (1968) 65-
         67. PESCH, R. Naherwartungen (1969) 88, 89, 90. MEYER, B.
         F., The Aims of Jesus (London 1979) 181-85. VIELHAUER,
         Ph., "Oikodome. das Bild vom Bau in der christlichen Literatur
         vom Neuen Testament bis Clemens Alexandrinus" in:
         Oikodome (München 1979) 59, 61, 64-66.

26:62-64 HUMMEL, R. Die Auseinandersetzung zwischen Kirche und
          Judentum im Matthäusevangelium (1963) 93f., 116.

26:63-65 LAMARCHE, P. "Le 'blasphème' de Jésus devant le
          sanhédrin," RechSR 50 (1, '62) 74-85. LAMARCHE, P. "La
          'blasfemia' de Jesus ante el Sanhedrin," Selecciones de Teologia
          2 (7, '63) 197-99.

26:63f MOORE, G. F. Judaism (1946) II 335. MASSAUX, E. Influence de l'Evangile de saint Matthieu sur la littérature chrétienne avant saint Irénée (1950) 71-73. BORNKAMM-BARTH-HELD, Ueberlieferung und Auslegung im Matthäus-Evangelium (1961) 30, 135ff. HAHN, F. Christologische Hoheitstitel (1963) 182.

26:63 STONEHOUSE, N. B. The Witness of Matthew and Mark to Christ (1944) 207. HOOKER, M. D., Jesus and the Servant (1959) 87-89. BLAIR, E. P. Jesus in the Gospel of Matthew (1960) 55, 61. LöVESTAM, E. "Die Frage des Hohenpriesters (Mark. 14:61 par. Mt. 26:63." SEA (1961) 93-107. De KRUIJF, Th., Der Sohn des Lebendigen Gottes (Rome 1962) 41, 78, 82, 95, 97, 101, 141, 144. HAHN, F. Christologische Hoheitstitel (1963) 224. HUMMEL, R. Die Auseinandersetzung zwischen Kirche und Judentum im Matthäusevangelium (1963) 113, 115. NICKELS, P. Targum and New Testament (1967) 22. SCHNEIDER, G., Verleugnung, Verspottung und Verhör Jesu nach Lukas 22, 54-71 (München 1969) 33, 47, 56f, 59, 113, 123.

26:64 VOLZ, P. Die Eschatologie der jüdischen Gemeinde (1934) 269. STONEHOUSE, N. B. The Witness of Matthew and Mark to Christ (1944) 238, 240f. NORDEN, E. Agnostos Theos (1956⁻1912) 272f. TRILLING, W. Das wahre Israel (1959) 67f. GLASSON, T. F. The Reply to Caiaphas (Mark XIV. 62). NTS 7 (1960/61) 89f. STRECKER, G. Der Weg der Gerechtigkeit (1962) 23, 42₄, 115, 236. WAINWRIGHT, A. W. The Trinity in the New Testament (1962) 176-77. HAHN, F. Christologische Hoheitstitel (1963) 182, 289. HUMMEl, R. Die Auseinandersetzung zwischen Kirche und Judentum im Matthäusevangelium (1963) 141f. HENNECKE, E. & SCHNEEMELCHER, W. Neutestamentliche Apokryphen (1964) II 475. TURNER, N. Grammatical Insights into the New Testament (1965) 72ff. JüNGEL, E. Paulus und Jesus (1966) 243. SCHNEIDER, G., Verleugnung, Verspottung und Verhör Jesu nach Lukas 22, 54-71 (München 1969) 33, 35, 47, 57, 59, 113, 123. KüNZI, M. Das Naherwartungslogion Matthäus 10, 23 (1970) 99, 158, 179. CATCHPOLE, D. R. "The Answer of Jesus to Caiaphas (Matt. XXVI. 64)," NTS 17 (2, '71) 213-26. LANGE, J., Das Erscheinen des Auferstandenen im Evangelium nach Matthäus (Würzburg 1973) 206, 214f, 230, 232, 234-36, 239, 242f, 298, 307, 333, 337-39. *VANNI, U., "La Passione come rivelazione di condanna e di salvezza in Matteo 26, 64 e 27, 54" EuD 27 (1974) 65-91. KINGSBURY, J. D., Matthew: Structure, Christology, Kingdom (Philadelphia 1975) 73-75. CAIRD, G. B., "Eschatology and Politics: Some

Misconceptions" in: J. R. McKay/J. F. Miller (eds.) Biblical Studies. In honour of W. Barclay (London 1976) 74. KLIJN, A. F. J., "Die syrische Baruch-Apokalypse" in: W. G. Kümmel (ed.) Jüdische Schriften aus hellenistisch-römischer Zeit V (Gütersloh 1976) 136.

26:65 BETZ, H. D. Lukian von Samosata und das Neue Testament (1961) 72, 140. METZGER, B. M., The Early Versions of the New Testament (Oxford 1977) 178.

26:67f HOOKER, M. D. Jesus and the Servant (1959) 89-91. BENOIT, P. Passion et Résurrection du Seigneur (1966) 93-95. PETERS, G. W. A Biblical Theology of Missions (1972) 287.

26:66-67 SHERWIN-WHITE, A. N., Roman Society and Roman Law in the New Testament (Grand Rapids 1978) 33. CRIBBS, F. L., in: G. MacRae (ed.) SBL Seminar Papers[2] (Montana 1973) 61f.

26:67 STONEHOUSE, N. B. The Witness of Matthew and Mark to Christ (1944) 180f. SCHNEIDER, G., Verleugnung, Verspottung und Verhör Jesu nach Lukas 22, 54-71 (München 1969) 39, 47, 55, 98, 99, 101.

26:68 STRECKER, G. Der Weg der Gerechtigkeit (1962) 126[2]. HUMMEL, R. Die Auseinandersetzung zwischen Kirche und Judentum im Matthäusevangelium (1963) 113. SCHNEIDER, G., Verleugnung, Verspottung und Verhör Jesu nach Lukas 22, 54-71 (München 1969) 39, 47, 55, 102f, 112. FRIEDRICH, G., "Beobachtungen zur messianischen Hohepriestererwartung in den Synoptikern" in: Auf das Wort kommt es an (Göttingen 1978) 82f.

26:69-75 WILKENS, J. Einführung in das Evangelium nach Matthäus II (1937) 225. RIBEIRO DE SANTANA, A. "St. Peter's Denial According to Origen," IES 6 (1, '67) 13-23. SCHMELING, J. "Verleugnung", in: Schriftauslegung...Die Passionstexte (1967) Frey, F. (ed.) 202ff. SENIOR, D. P., The Passion Narrative According to Matthew (Leuven 1975) 192-209.

26:69-72 STRECKER, G. Der Weg der Gerechtigkeit (1962) 204[3.4].

26:69 RUDOLPH, K. Die Mandäer I (1960) 115, 4. SCHNEIDER, G., Verleugnung, Verspottung und Verhör Jesu nach Lukas 22, 54-71 (München 1969) 47, 50, 52, 80, 83, 88.

26:70f BORNKAMM-BARTH-HELD, Ueberlieferung und Auslegung im Matthäus-Evangelium (1961) 112.

26:70 SMITH, M., Tannaitic Parallels to the Gospels (Philadelphia 1968) 2bn117+.

26:71 STRECKER, G. Der Weg der Gerechtigkeit (1962) 62[1]. SCHNEIDER, G., Verleugnung, Verspottung und Verhör

Jesu nach Lukas 22, 54-71 (München 1969) 47, 50, 52f, 83f, 88.
METZGER, B. M., The Early Versions of the New Testament
(Oxford 1977) 391.

26:72   DAUER, A. Die Passionsgeschichte im Johannesevangelium
(1972) 89, 90, 96.

26:73   PARKER, P. The Gospel Before Mark (1953) 80-90.
SCHNEIDER, G., Verleugnung, Verspottung und Verhör
Jesu nach Lukas 22, 54-71 (München 1969) 47, 52, 83f, 88.
DAUER, A. Die Passionsgschichte im Johannesevangelium
(1972) 77, 88, 89.

26:74   HENNECKE, E. & SCHNEEMELCHER, W.
Neutestamentliche Apokryphen (1964) I 97.

26:75   STREETER, B. H. The Four Gospels (1951) 322f.
SCHNEIDER, G., Verleugnung, Verspottung und Verhör
Jesu nach Lukas 22, 54-71 (München 1969) 43, 45, 47, 53f, 82,
95f, 169.

27-28   FARRER, A. St Matthew and St Mark (1954). NEIRYNCK,
F. Les Femmes au Tombeau Etude de La Rédaction
Matthéenne (Matt. XXVII. 1-10), 169ff.

27   GREENLEE, J. H. Nine Uncial Palimpsests of the Greek New
Testament (1968) 56-57.

27:1-31   GOODSPEED, E. J. A Life of Jesus (1950) 213-15.
*ESCANDE, J., "Judas et Pilate prisonniers d'une même
structure (Mt 27, 1-26)" Foi et Vie 78 (1979) 92-100.

27:1-10   WILKENS, J. Einführung in das Evangelium nach Matthäus
II (1937) 226.

27:1-2.   BENOIT, P. Passion et Résurrection du Seigneur (1966)
11-14   160-63.

27: -2   STRECKER, G. Der Weg der Gerechtigkeit (1962) 76.
SENIOR, D. P., The Passion Narrative According to Matthew
(Leuven 1975) 210-18.

27:1   HUMMEL, R. Die Auseinandersetzung zwischen Kirche und
Judentum im Matthäusevangelium (1963) 145. SCHNEIDER,
G., Verleugnung, Verspottung und Verhör Jesu nach Lukas 22,
54-71 (München 1969) 31, 47, 55f, 107f, 111.
FRANKEMöLLE, H., Jahwebund und Kirche Christi.

Studien zur Form- und Traditionsgeschichte des "Evangeliums" nach Matthäus (Münster 1974) 195, 202-204. METZGER, B. M., The Early Versions of the New Testament (Oxford 1977) 390. SHERWIN-WHITE, A. N., Roman Society and Roman Law in the New Testament (Grand Rapids 1978) 33.

27:2   METZGER, B. M., The Early Versions of the New Testament (Oxford 1977) 457f.

27:3ff   NEPPER-CHRISTENSEN, P. Das Matthäusevangelium. Ein Judenchristliches Evangelium? (1958) 139, 154, 155, 161. STRECKER, G. Der Weg der Gerechtigkeit (1962) 14, 84. GOULDER, M. D., Midrash and Lection in Matthew (London 1974) 127, 192, 445-47. 450.

27:3-16   BLOCH, R., "Midrash" in: W. S. Green (ed.) Approaches to Ancient Judaism: Theory and Practice (Missoula 1978) 48.

27:3-11   PARKER, P. The Gospel Before Mark (1953) 22-23.

27:3-10   BENOIT, P. La Mort de Judas, Synoptische Studien (1953) 1-19. M'NEILE, A. H. The Gospel According to St. Matthew (1955) 408f. BLAIR, E. P. Jesus in the Gospel of Matthew (1960) 158. LINDARS, B. New Testament Apologetic (1961) 98, 116-22. STRECKER, G. Der Weg der Gerechtigkeit (1962) 76ff., 181₂, 208₃. FLAMMERSFELD, H. "Das Ende des Judas", in: Schriftauslegung . . . Die Passionstexte (1967) Frey, F. (ed.) 207ff. JERVELL, J. "Jesu blods aker. Matt. 27, 3-10" (The Field of Jesus' Blood. Mt 27:3-10), NTT 69 (3, '68) 158-62. *SENIOR, D., "The Fate of the Betrayer. A Redactional Study of Matthew 27, 3-10" EphT 48 (1972) 372-426. SENIOR, D., "A Case Study of Matthean Creativity. Matthew 27:3-10" BR 19 (1974) 23-36. *van UNNIK, W. C., "The Death of Judas in St Matthew's Gospel" AThR supp.ser.3 (1974) 44-57. SENIOR, D. P., The Passion Narrative According to Matthew (Leuven 1975) 343-97.

27:3-5   STRECKER, G. Der Weg der Gerechtigkeit (1962) 182.

27:3   STRECKER, G. Der Weg der Gerechtigkeit (1962) 227₄.

27:4.19.24.   ZIESLER, J. A. The Meaning of Righteousness in Paul (1972) 137f., 145.

27:4   BEYSCHLAG, K. Clemens Romanus und der Frükatholizismus (1966) 102. STROBEL, A. Erkenntnis und Bekenntnis der Sünde in neutestamentlicher Zeit (1968) 45.

27:5-10   BRAUN, H. Qumran und NT II (1966) 267, 305f., 308, 324.

27:5   STRECKER, G. Der Weg der Gerechtigkeit (1962) 191. HUMMEL, R. Die Auseinandersetzung zwischen Kirche und Judentum im Matthäusevangelium (1963) 145. SILVA, R.

"Como murio Judas, el traidor?" CultBib 23 (212, '67) 35-40. METZGER, B. M., The Early Versions of the New Testament (Oxford 1977) 246.

27:6 STRECKER, G. Der Weg der Gerechtigkeit (1962) 211. "Aramäisch" in: TRE 3 (1978) 607.

27:9ff KNOX, W. L. The Sources of the Synoptic Gospels II (1957) 127.

27:9-10 STONEHOUSE, N. B. The Witness of Matthew and Mark to Christ (1944) 191. BLAIR, E. P. Jesus in the Gospel of Matthew (1960) 39. STRECKER, G. Der Weg der Gerechtigkeit (1962) 492, 557, 76ff., 83. PESCH, A. Agrapha, Aussercanonische Schrift-Fragmente (1967) 23f. ROTHFUCHS, W. Die Erfüllungszitate des Matthäus-Evangeliums (1969) 84-88. DUNN, J. D. G., Unity and Diversity in the New Testament (London 1977) 92f, 95f.

27:9 KNOX, W. L. The Sources of the Synoptic Gospels II (1957) 126f. NEPPER-CHRISTENSEN, P. Das Matthäusevangelium. Ein Judenchristliches Evangelium? (1958) 21, 140, 149, 150, 152, 155, 157, 159. BLAIR, E. P. Jesus in the Gospel of Matthew (1960) 56, 90. STRECKER, G. Der Weg der Gerechtigkeit (1962) 595, 1062. HUMMEL, R. Die Auseinandersetzung zwischen Kirche und Judentum im Matthäusevangelium (1963) 131, 132, 144.

27:10 HAHN, F. Christologische Hoheitstitel (1963) 73.

27:11-31a GAECHTER, P. Die literarische Kunst im Matthäus-Evangelium (1968) 67-68.

27:11-26 WILKENS, J. Einführung in das Evangelium nach Matthäus II (1937) 227-32. LOEWENICH, W. von. Luther als Ausleger der Synoptiker (1954) 266f. SANDERS, F. "Jesus vor Pilatus," in: Die Passionstexte (1967) Frey, F. (ed.) 213-18. QUINN, J. F. "The Pilate Sequence in the Gospel of Matthew," DuRev 10 (2, '70) 154-77. SENIOR, D. P., The Passion Narrative According to Matthew (Leuven 1975) 219-62.

27:11 HUMMEL, R. Die Auseinandersetzung zwischen Kirche und Judentum im Matthäusevangelium (1963) 114, 146. LEISTNER, R., Antijudaismus im Johannesevangelium? (Bern 1974) 118f. SANDMEL, S., We Jews and Jesus (New York 1977) 35.

27:12.14 HOOKER, M. D. Jesus and the Servant (1959) 87-89.

27:15-26 TRILLING, W. Das wahre Israel (1959) 48ff. BENOIT, P. Passion et Résurrection du Seigneur (1966) 160-63. BLINZLER, J. Der Prozess Jesu (1969) 301-17. FRANKEMöLLE, H., Jahwebund und Kirche Christi.

Studien zur Form- und Traditionsgeschichte des "Evangeliums" nach Matthäus (Münster 1974) 204-206, 237.

27:15-23 MACCOBY, H. Z. "Jesus and Barabbas," NTS 16 (1, '69) 55-60.

27:15-19 HENNECKE, E. & SCHNEEMELCHER, W. Neutestamentliche Apokryphen (1964) I 92, 336, 339.

27:16-17 DUNKERLEY, R. "Was Barabbas also Called Jesus?" ET 74 (4, '63) 126-27. NEVIUS, R. C. "A Reply to Dr. Dunkerley," ET 74 (8, '63) 255. METZGER, B. M. "Explicit references in the works of Origen to variant readings in the New Testament manuscripts", Historical and Literary Studies (1968) 94. METZGER, B. M., The Early Versions of the New Testament (Oxford 1977) 41.

27:16 TWOMEY, J. J. "Barabbas was a Robber", Scripture VIII (4, '56) 115-19.

27:17-22 HAHN, F. Christologische Hoheitstitel (1963) 178.

27:17.22 BLAIR, E. P. Jesus in the Gospel of Matthew (1960) 55.

27:17 HAHN, F. Christologische Hoheitstitel (1963) 208. HUMMEL, R. Die Auseinandersetzung zwischen Kirche und Judentum im Matthäusevangelium (1963) 112ff., 114.

27:19 OEPKE, A. "Noch einmal das Weib des Pilatus", ThLZ 73 (1948) 743. SCHELKLE, K. H. Die Passion Jesu in der Verkündigung des Neuen Testaments (1949) 115f. TRILLING, W. Das wahre Israel (1959) 48ff. STRECKER, G. Der Weg der Gerechtigkeit (1962) 116, 177s. DAUER, A. Die Passionsgeschichte im Johannesevangelium (1972) 115, 129, 154, 155, 233, 273. RUPPERT, L., Jesus als der leidende Gerechte? (Stuttgart 1972) 13, 47, 56f. STAGG, E./F., Woman in the World of Jesus (Philadelphia 1978) 217. DERRETT, J. D. M., " 'Have nothing to do with that just man!'(Matt 27, 19). Haggadah and the Account of the Passion" DRev 97 (1979) 308-15. SWIDLER, L., Biblical Affirmations of Woman (Philadelphia 1979) 198, 251.

27:20ff STRECKER, G. Der Weg der Gerechtigkeit (1962) 115f.

27:20-22 GIBBS, J. M. Purpose and Pattern in Matthew's use of the title "Son of David." NTS 10 (1963/64) 450f.

27:21 SCHALIT, A. König Abraham (1969) 701.

27:22 HAHN, F. Christologische Hoheitstitel (1963) 208. HUMMEL, R. Die Auseinandersetzung zwischen Kirche und Judentum im Matthäusevangelium (1963) 112ff. METZGER, B. M., The Early Versions of the New Testament (Oxford 1977) 246.

27:23-25 SCHELKLE, K. H., "Die 'Selbstverfluchung' Israels nach Matthäus 27:23-25" FrR 18 (1966) 51-54. SCHELKLE, K. H. "Die 'Selbstverfluchung' Israels nach Matthäus 27, 23-25", Antijudaismus im Neuen Testament? (1967) Eckert/Levinson/Stöhr (eds.) 148-56.

27:24ff HENNECKE, E. & SCHNEEMELCHER, W. Neutestamentliche Apokryphen (1964) I 337, 339, 341.

27:24f SCHELKLE, K. H. Die Passion Jesu in der Verkündigung des Neuen Testaments (1949) 25f. TRILLING, W. Das wahre Israel (1959) 50ff. STRECKER, G. Der Weg der Gerechtigkeit (1962) 115f. HUMMEL, R. Die Auseinandersetzung zwischen Kirche und Judentum im Matthäusevangelium (1963) 83. WREGE, H.-T. Die Ueberlieferungsgeschichte der Bergpredigt (1968) 48f., 173. KOSMALA, H. " 'His Blood on Us and Our Children' (The Background of Mat. 27, 24-25)," ASThI 7 ('68-'69) 94-126.

27:24-25 FRANKEMöLLE, H., Jahwebund und Kirche Christi. Studien zur Form- und Traditionsgeschichte des "Evangeliums" nach Matthäus (Münster 1974) 195, 204-11, 255, 326, 354.

27:24 STRECKER, G. Der Weg der Gerechtigkeit (1962) 177₅. STROBEL, A. Erkenntnis und Bekenntnis der Sünde in neutestamentlicher Zeit (1968) 45.

27:25 STAEHELIN, E. Die Verkündigung des Reiches Gottes in der Kirche Jesu Christi I (1951) 282. CAPRILE, G. "La responsabilità del popolo ebreo nella morte di Gesù," PaCl 39 (18, '60) 969-76. BAUM, G. The Jews and the Gospel (1961) 66-73. FESTORAZZI, F. "Populus Israel estne maledictus et repudiatus a Deo?" VerbDom 39 (5-6, '61) 255-71. STRECKER, G. Der Weg der Gerechtigkeit (1962) 107₁, 117, 231₁. HUMMEL, R. Die Auseinandersetzung zwischen Kirche und Judentum im Matthäusevangelium (1963) 89. NOBER, P. " 'Que o seu sangue caia sôbre nossos filhos' (Mt. 27, 25)," RCB 7 (24, '63) 17-28. STEVENS, G. H. "The Jews and the Crucifixion," ChrTo 9 (Dec. 18, '64) 290-92. VANDONE, L. M. "Responsabilità giudaica," PaCl 43 (Dec. 1, '64) 1276-81. FITZMEYER, J. "Anti-Semitism and the Cry of 'All the People' (Mt 27:25)," ThSt 26 (4, '65) 667-71. TOULAT, J., "O mistério de Israel" Vozes 1 (1966) 60-63. SASS, G. Ungereimtes bei Matthäus (1968) 68-70. SANDERS, W. "Das Blut Jesu und die Juden. Gedanken zu Matth. 27, 25," US 27 (3-4, '72) 168-71. *BOWMAN, J., "The Significance of Mt. 27:25" Milla wa-Milla 14 (1974) 26-31. "Antisemitismus" in: TRE 3 (1978) 123.

27:26-46 COPE, O. L., Matthew: A Scribe Trained for the Kingdom of Heaven (Washington 1976) 102-110.

27:26   SHERWIN-WHITE, A. N., Roman Society and Roman Law in the New Testament (Grand Rapids 1978) 26.

27:27-56   SCHEIFLER, J. R. "El Salmo 22 y la Crucifixion del Senor," EstBi 24 (1-2, '65) 5-83. KOSLOWSKY, G. "Mein Gott, mein Gott, warum hast du mich verlassen?," in: Die passionstexte (1967) Frey, F. 225-31.

27:27-37   WILKENS, J. Einführung in das Evangelium nach Matthäus II (1937) 233-34.

27:27-31   BENOIT, P. Passion et Résurrection du Siegneur (1966) 160-63. PETERS, G. W. A Biblical Theology of Missions (1972) 287. SENIOR, D. P., The Passion Narrative According to Matthew (Leuven 1975) 263-71.

27:27-29   DAUER, A. Die Passionsgeschichte im Johannesevangelium (1972) 154f.

27:27   REVUELTA SANUDO, M. "La localizacion del Pretorio," EstBi 20 (3, '61) 261-317. REYERO, S. "Los textos de Flavio Josefo y de Filon sobre la residencia de los procurados romanos en Jerusalén," Studium 1-2 (3, '62) 527-55. SANDMEL, S., We Jews and Jesus (New York 1977) 49.

27:28-31   MASSAUX, E. Influence de l'Evangile de saint Matthieu sur la littérature avant saint Irénée (1950) 71-73.

27:29   STRECKER, G. Der Weg der Gerechtigkeit (1962) 1816. HUMMEL, R. Die Auseinandersetzung zwischen Kirche und Judentum im Matthäusevangelium (1963) 114, 146. DALMAN, G. Orte und Wege Jesu (1967) 264f. SANDMEL, S., We Jews and Jesus (New York 1977) 35.

27:30   HAHN, F. Christologische Hoheitstitel (1963) 86.

27:31ff.   "Autorität" in: TRE 5 (1980) 44.

27:31b-61   GAECHTER, P. Die literarische Kunst im Matthäus-Evangelium (1968) 34-35.

27:31-56   COUSIN, H., Le Prophète assassiné. Histoire des textes évangéliques de la Passion (Paris 1976).

27:32-56   GOODSPEED, E. J. A Life of Jesus (1950) 216-22. BLINZLER, J. Der Prozess Jesu (1969) 357-74. SCHENK, W., Der Passionbericht nach Markus (Gütersloh 1974) 64ff.

27:32-44   SENIOR, D. P., The Passion Narrative According to Matthew (Leuven 1975) 272-91. RUPPERT, L., "Das Skandalon eines gekreuzigten Messias und seine Ueberwindung mit Hilfe der geprägten Vorstellung vom leidenden Gerechten" in: Kirche und Bibel. Für E. Schick (Paderborn 1979) 322-27.

27:32   "Afrika" in: TRE 1 (1977) 700.

27:33   NEPPER-CHRISTENSEN, P. Das Matthäusevangelium. Ein Judenchristliches Evangelium? (1958) 21, 87, 95.

27:34f SCHELKLE, K. H. Die Passion Jesu in der Verkündigung des Neuen Testaments (1949) 86f.

27:34 STRECKER, G. Der Weg der Gerechtigkeit (1962) 23. BRAUN, H. Qumran und NT II (1966) 312. METZGER, B. M., The Early Versions of the New Testament (Oxford 1977) 35, 440.

27:35 STRECKER, G. Der Weg der Gerechtigkeit (1962) 23, 281, 703, 713.

27:37 HUMMEL, R. Die Auseinandersetzung zwischen Kirche und Judentum im Matthäusevangelium (1963) 114, 146. SANDMEL, S., We Jews and Jesus (New York 1977) 35

27:38-54 WILKENS, J. Einführung in das Evangelium nach Matthäus II (1937) 235-39.

27:38 METZGER, B. M., The Early Versions of the New Testament (Oxford 1977) 326.

27:39-43 HUMMEL, R. Die Auseinandersetzung zwischen Kirche und Judentum im Matthäusevangelium (1963) 115.

27:39 STRECKER, G. Der Weg der Gerechtigkeit (1962) 23, 281.

27:40 MASSAUX, E. Influence de l'Evangile de saint Matthieu sur la littérature chrétienne avant saint Irénée (1950) 71-73. BLAIR, E. P. Jesus in the Gospel of Matthew (1960) 61, 148. De KRUIJF, Th., Der Sohn des Lebendigen Gottes (Rome 1962) 41, 97, 100f, 104, 122. HUMMEL, R. Die Auseinandersetzung zwischen Kirche und Judentum im Matthäusevangelium (1963) 115, 116. GäRTNER, B. The Temple and the Community in Qumran and the New Testament (1965) 113. PESCH, R. Naherwartungen (1969) 88, 89, 90. KINGSBURY, J. D., Matthew: Structure, Christology, Kingdom, (Philadelphia 1975) 74-76. METZGER, B. M., The Early Versions of the New Testament (Oxford 1977) 390. MEYER, B. F., The Aims of Jesus (London 1979) 181-85. VIELHAUER, Ph., "Oikodome. Das Bild vom Bau in der christlichen Literatur vom Neuen Testament bis Clemens Alexandrinus" in: Oikodome (München 1979) 59, 61f, 64-66.

27:40a HAHN, F. Das Verständnis der Mission im Neuen Testament (1965) 29f.

27:41 BOUSSET, W. Die Religion des Judentums im Späthellenistischen Zeitalter (1966⁻1926) 167.

27:42 HUMMEL, R. Die Auseinandersetzung zwischen Kirche und Judentum im Matthäusevangelium (1963) 114, 144f. METZGER, B. M., The Early Versions of the New Testament (Oxford 1977) 392. SANDMEL, S., We Jews and Jesus (New York 1977) 35.

27:43 MASSAUX, E. Influence de l'Evangile de saint Matthieu sur la littérature chrétienne avant saint Irénée (1950) 71-73. BLAIR, E. P. Jesus in the Gospel of Matthew (1960) 61. De KRUIJF, Th., Der Sohn des Lebendigen Gottes (Rome 1962) 97, 100f, 104. STRECKER, G. Der Weg der Gerechtigkeit (1962) 28f. HUMMEL, R. Die Auseinandersetzung zwischen Kirche und Judentum im Matthäusevangelium (1963) 115, 116.

27:45-56 SENIOR, D. P., The Passion Narrative According to Matthew (Leuven 1975) 292-334.

27:45-46 TILLICH, P. Das Neue Sein (1959) 159-62.
50-54

27:45-54 SCHNEIDER, G., "Die theologische Sicht des Todes Jesu in den Kreuzigungsberichten der Evangelien" Theologisch-praktische Quartalschrift 126 (1978) 14-22.

27:45-53 LINDIJER, C. H. "De tekenen bij Jezus' dood" (The Signs at Jesus' Death), HomBib 25 (3, '66) 55-59.

27:45-46 FLORIS, E. "L'abandon de Jésus et la mort de Dieu," EThR 42 (4, '67) 277-298. JOHNSON, S. L. "The Death of Christ," BiblSa 25 (497, '68) 10-19.

27:45 NICKELS, P. Targum and New Testament (1967) 22.

27:46 PARKER, P. The Gospel Before Mark (1953) 182-83. BAKER, N. "The Cry of Dereliction," ET 70 (2, '58) 54-55. NEPPER-CHRISTENSEN, P. Das Matthäusevangelium. Ein Judenchristliches Evangelium? (1958) 21, 25, 87. REHM, M. "Eli, Eli lamma sabachthani," BZ 2 (2, '58) 275-78. STRECKER, G. Der Weg der Gerechtigkeit (1962) 26f., 281. BOMAN, T. "Das letzte Wort Jesu," StTh 17 (2, '63) 103-19. LACAN, M.-F. " 'Mon Dieu, mon Dieu, pourquoi?' (Matthieu, 27, 46)," LuVie 13 (66, '64) 33-53. SOGGIN, J. A., "Appunti per l'esegesi crisitana della prima Parte del salmo 22," BiOr 7 (3, '65) 105-16. GUIRAU, J. M. "Mt. 27, 46 y la interpretacion del Ps. 21 en el Nuevo Testamento," CiDi 179 (3, '66) 383-430. JEREMIAS, J. Neutestamentliche Theologie I (1971) 16, 17, 60, 68, 71. HOLST, R. "The 'Cry of Dereliction'-Another Point Of View," Springfielder 35 (4, '72) 286-89. GREER, R. A., The Captain of Our Salvation (Tübingen 1973) 340f. *TRUDINGER, L. P., " 'Eli, Eli, Lama Sabachthani/': A Cry of Dereliction? or Victory?" JEThS 17 (1974) 235-38. "Aramäisch" in: TRE 3 (1978) 606. FRIEDRICH, G., "Beobachtungen zur messianischen Hohepriestererwartung in den Synoptikern" in: Auf das Wort kommt es an (Göttingen 1978) 83. RIST, J. M., On the Independence of Matthew and Mark (Cambridge 1978) 87. *SABOURIN, L., "As Sete Palavras de Jesus na Cruz" RCB 2 (1978) 299-303.

27:47 VOLZ, P. Die Eschatologie der jüdischen Gemeinde (1934) 195. STRECKER, G. Der Weg der Gerechtigkeit (1962) 27.

27:48 STRECKER, G. Der Weg der Gerechtigkeit (1962) 20, 232. BRAUN, H. Qumran und NT II (1966) 312. DAUER, A. Die Passionsgeschichte im Johannesevangelium (1972) 174, 204, 208. MüLLER, U. B., "Die griechische Esra-Apokalypse" in: W. G. Kümmel (ed.) Jüdische Schriften aus hellenistisch-römischer Zeit V (Gütersloh 1976) 93.

27:50 DAUER, A. Die Passionsgeschichte im Johannesevangelium (1972) 210, 214, 222.

27:51ff STAEHELIN, E. Die Verkündigung des Reiches Gottes in der Kirche Jesu Christi I (1951) 65, 309.

27:51-61 STONEHOUSE, N. B. The Witness of Matthew and Mark to Christ (1944) 157. BENOIT, P. Passion et Résurrection du Seigneur (1966) 245-47. POSSELT, H. "Die Grablegung Jesu," in: Schriftauslegung ... Die Passionstexte (1967) Frey, F. (ed.) 238-42. BLINZLER, J. Der Prozess Jesu (1969) 384-404.

27:51-54 ESSAME, W. G. "Matthew xxvii. 51-54 and John V. 25-29," ET 76 (3, '64) 103. HAHN, F. Das Verständnis der Mission im Neuen Testament (1965) 111. KRATZ, R., Auferweckung als Befreiung (Stuttgart 1973) 9, 10, 12, 14, 38-47, 50.

27:51-53 FASCHER, E. Das Weib des Pilatus (Matth. 27, 19). Die Auferweckung der Heiligen (Matth. 27, 51-53), (1951). JEREMIAS, J. Neutestamentliche Theologie I (1971) 293f. CAVALLIN, H. C. C., Life After Death I (Lund 1974) 4.1.n30. KINGSBURY, J. D., Matthew: Structure, Christology, Kingdom (Philadelphia 1975) 75-77. *SENIOR, D. P., "The Death of Jesus and the Resurrection of the Holy Ones (Mt 27: 51-53)" CBQ 38 (1976) 312-29. *RIEBL, M., Auferstehung Jesu in der Stunde seines Todes? Zur Botschaft von Mt 27, 51b-53 (Stuttgart 1978). *AGUIRRE, R., "El Reino de Dios y la muerte de Jesús en el evangelio de Mateo" EstEc 54 (1979) 363-82.

27:51f.54 BETZ, H. D. Lukian von Samosata und das Neue Testament (1961) 82, 123, 162, 165.

27:51.54 HENNECKE, E. & SCHNEEMELCHER, W. Neutestamentliche Apokryphen (1964) 122, 377.

27:51 NESTLE, E. "Matth 27, 51 und Parallelen", ZNW 3 (1902) 167f. DE JONGE, M. "Het motief van het gescheurde voorhangsel van de tempel in een aantal vroegchristlijke geschriften" (The Motif of the Torn Temple Veil in Some Early Christian Writings), NedThT 21 (4, '67) 257-76. HOFIUS, O., Der Vorhang vor dem Thron Gottes (Tübingen 1972) 34ff. 58.

KRATZ, R., Auferweckung als Befreiung (Stuttgart 1973) 9,
12-15, 38, 43, 56. SCHRECKENBERG, H., "Flavius Josephus
und die lukanischen Schriften" in: W. Haubeck/ M. Bachmann
(eds.) Wort in der Zeit. Für K. H. Rengstorf (Leiden 1980) 192f.

27:51b-53 BIEDER, W. Die Vorstellung von der Höllenfahrt Jesu Christi
(1949) 49ff.

27:52-53 STAEHELIN, E. Die Verkündigung des Reiches Gottes in der
Kirche Jesu Christi I (1951) 292. VITTONATTO, G. "La
Risurrezione dei Morti in Mt 27, 52-53," RivB III/3 (1955) 193-
219. NöTSCHER, F., Altorientalischer und alttestamentlicher
Auferstehungsglauben (Darmstadt 1970⁻1926) 303f. DUNN,
J. D. G., Jesus and the Spirit (London 1975) 118, 129. KLIJN,
A. F. J., "Die syrische Baruch-Apokalypse" in: W. G. Kümmel
(ed.) Jüdische Schriften aus hellenistisch-römischer Zeit V
(Gütersloh 1976) 155. MüLLER, U. B., "Die griechische Esra-
Apokalypse" in: W. G. Kümmel., Jüdische Schriften aus
hellenistich-römischer Zeit V (Gütersloh 1976) 99.

27:52 MASSAUX, E. Influence de l'Evangile de saint Matthieu sur la
littérature chrétienne avant saint Irénée (1950) 101-103.
STAEHELIN, E. Die Verkündigung des Reiches Gottes in der
Kirche Jesu Christi I (1951) 177. VITTONATO, H. "La
resurrezione dei morti," Sapienza 9 ('56) 131-50. KNOX, W. L.
The Sources of the Synoptic Gospels II (1957) 124.
STRECKER, G. Der Weg der Gerechtigkeit (1962) 217n.
NICKELS, P. Targum and New Testament (1967) 22.

27:53 STONEHOUSE, N. B. The Witnesses of Matthew and Mark to
Christ (1944) 195. MOORE, G. F. Judaism (1946) II 310n.
STAEHELIN, E. Die Verkündigung des Reiches Gottes in der
Kirche Jesu Christi I (1951) 292.

27:54 MASSAUX, E. Influence de l'Evangile de saint Matthieu sur la
littérature chrétienne avant saint Irénée (1950) 71-73.
STEMPVOORT, P. A. "Gods Zoon" of "een zoon Gods" in
Matth. 27, 54? NedThT (1954/55) 79-89. BLAIR, E. P. Jesus in
the Gospel of Matthew (1960) 61. De KRUIJF, Th., Der Sohn
des Lebendigen Gottes (Rome 1962) 41, 55, 78, 97, 103.
STRECKER, G. Der Weg der Gerechtigkeit (1962) 116, 234₃.
KRATZ, R., Auferweckung als Befreiung (Stuttgart 1973) 14,
38, 47, 50-52, 55f, 61, 70. VANNI, U., "La Passione come
rivelazione di condanna e di salvezza in Matteo 26, 64 e 27, 54"
EuD 27 (1974) 65-91. SWIDLER, L., Biblical Affirmations of
Woman (Philadelphia 1979) 197.

27:55ff STONEHOUSE, N. B. The Witness of Matthew and Mark to
Christ (1944) 177.

27:55-28:20   PERRIN, N., The Resurrection According to Matthew, Mark and Luke (Philadelphia 1977).

27:55-61   WILKENS, J. Einführung in das Evangelium nach Matthäus II (1937) 243-44.

27:55-56   SWIDLER, L., Biblical Affirmations of Woman (Philadelphia 1979) 194, 199, 208, 221, 233, 248, 279.

27:56-57   METZGER, B. M., The Early Versions of the New Testament (Oxford 1977) 11.

27:57-28:20   *LAI, P. H., "Production du sens par la foi. Autorités religieuses contestées/fondées. Analyse structural de Matthieu 27, 57-28, 20" RechSR 61 (1973) 65-96; *ibid:* GT: in: LiBi 32 (1974) 1-37. *GIBLIN, C. H., "Structural and Thematic Correlations in the Matthaean Burial-Resurrection Narrative (Matt 27:57-28:20)" NTS 21 (1975) 406-20.

27:57-28:10   CURTIS, K. P. G. "Three Points of Contact Between Matthew and John in the Burial and Resurrection Narratives," JThS 23 (2, '72) 440-44.

27:57-61   POSSELT, H. 'Die Grablegung Jesu", in: Die Passionstexte (1967) Frey, F. (ed.) 238ff. BROER, I. Die Urgemeinde und das Grab Jesu (1972) 44-59. CRIBBS, F. L., in: G. MacRae (ed.) SBL Seminar Papers 2 (Montana 1973) 79-81. MAHONEY, R., Two Disciples at the Tomb (Bern 1974) 118-21. RIST, J. M., On the Independence of Matthew and Mark (Cambridge 1978) 87. SWIDLER, L., Biblical Affirmations of Woman (Philadelphia 1979) 200.

27:57-60   *BARRICK, W. B., "The Rich Man from Arimathea (Matt 27:57-60) and 1QIsaa" JBL 96 (1977) 235-39.

27:57-58   HARTMAN, L., Testimonium Linguae (Lund 1963) 15ff, 27. GOULDER, M. D., Midrash and Lection in Matthew (London 1974) 192, 228, 447-49.

27:57   STONEHOUSE, N. B. The Witness of Matthew and Mark to Christ (1944) 229. TRILLING, W. Das wahre Israel (1959) 15. STRECKER, G. Der Weg der Gerechtigkeit (1962) 192. HAHN, F. Das Verständnis der Mission im Neuen Testament (1965) 105. SCHREIBER, J. Theologie des Vertrauens (1967) 56, 105, 152-54, 181.

27:59ff   STONEHOUSE, N. B. The Witness of Matthew and Mark to Christ (1944) 177.

27:59-61   SWIDLER, L., Biblical Affirmations of Woman (Philadelphia 1979) 208.

27:59-60   *CHARBEL, A., "A Sepultura de Jesus como Resulta dos Evangelhos" RCB 2 (1978) 351-62.

27:60 MASSAUX, E. Influence de l'Evangile de Matthieu sur la littérature chrétienne avant saint Irénée (1950) 360-62.

27:61 BLINZLER, J., Die Brüder und Schwestern Jesu (Stuttgart 1967) 73-86. SWIDLER, L., Biblical Affirmations of Woman (Philadelphia 1979) 234, 261.

27:62-28:20 *TISON, J.-M., "Le mystère pascal dans l'évangile de S Matthieu (Mt 27, 62-28, 20)" Telema 2 (1976) 14-20. KREMER, J., Die Osterevangelien - Geschichten um Geschichte (Stuttgart 1977).

27:62-28:15 WILKENS, J. Einführung in das Evangelium nach Matthäus II (1937) 245-48. GAECHTER, P. Die literarische Kunst im Matthäus-Evangelium (1968) 68-69. KRATZ, R., Auferweckung als Befreiung (Stuttgart 1973). LEON-DUFOUR, X., The Resurrection and the Message of Easter (London 1974) 141-46.

27:62ff DAVIES, W. D., The Sermon on the Mount (Cambridge 1966) 86.

27:62-66 STONEHOUSE, N. B. The Witness of Matthew and Mark to Christ (1944) 157. PARKER, P. The Gospel Before Mark (1953) 23-24. BARRETT, C. K. The New Testament Background: Selected Documents (1956) 14. BLAIR, E. P. Jesus in the Gospel of Matthew (1960) 163. STRECKER, G. Der Weg der Gerechtigkeit (1962) 1044. HUMMEL, R. Die Auseinandersetzung zwischen Kirche und Judentum im Matthäusevangelium (1963) 111f. BODE, E. L. The First Easter Morning (1970) 172-73. MARXSEN, W. The Resurrection of Jesus of Nazareth (1970) 43-46. BROER, I. Die Urgemeinde und das Grab Jesu (1972) 60-78. LEE, G. M. "The Guard at the Tomb," Theology 72 (586, '69) 169-75. KRATZ, R., Auferweckung als Befreiung (Stuttgart 1973) 9, 15, 57-62, 69f, 72. RIVKIN, E., A Hidden Revolution (Nashville 1978) 115. "Auferstehung" in: TRE 4 (1979) 502.

27:62 PARKER, P. The Gospel Before Mark (1953) 89-90. STRECKER, G. Der Weg der Gerechtigkeit (1962) 93, 113₂.

27:63ff STONEHOUSE, N. B. The Witness of Matthew and Mark to Christ (1944) 182.

27:63-64 KNOX, W. L. The Sources of the Synoptic Gospels II (1957) 124. HAHN, F. Christologische Hoheitstitel (1963) 205. NöTSCHER, F., Altorientalischer und alttestamentlicher Auferstehungsglauben (Darmstadt 1970) 299.

27:63 BLAIR, E. P. Jesus in the Gospel of Matthew (1960) 100. WALKER, N. "After Three Days," NovTest 4 (1960) 261-62. HAHN, F. Christologische Hoheitstitel (1963) 82.

27:64 SMYTH, K. "The Guard on the Tomb," HeyJ 2 (2, '61) 157-59. STRECKER, G. Der Weg der Gerechtigkeit (1962) 115. HUMMEL, R. Die Auseinandersetzung zwischen Kirche und Judentum im Matthäusevangelium (1963) 145.

27:65 HENNECKE, E. & SCHNEEMELCHER, W. Neutestamentliche Apokryphen (1964) I 98.

27:66 RUDOLPH, K. Die Mandäer II (1961) 168, 6. KRATZ, R., Auferweckung als Befreiung (Stuttgart 1973) 26, 60-62, 70.

27:69ff STRECKER, G. Der Weg der Gerechtigkeit (1962) 652.

28 KILPATRICK, G. D. The Origin of the Gospel According to St. Matthew (1950) 37, 40f., 43, 47-50, 95f. BLAIR, E. P. Jesus in the Gospel of Matthew (1960) 58. STRECKER, G. Der Weg der Gerechtigkeit (1962) 13. DRINKWATER, F. H. "How Far Was the Resurrection 'Historical'?" Continuum 4 (1, '66) 157-61. DRINKWATER, F. H. "The Resurrection Appearances: IN the Documents," Continuum 4 (3, '66) 464-68. *LILLIE, W. "The Empty Tomb and the Resurrection," Historicity and Chronology in the New Testament, 117-34. SELBY, D. J., Introduction to the New Testament (New York 1971) 147-49, 369. *WENHAM, D., "The Resurrection Narratives in Matthew's Gospel" TB 24 (1973) 21-54. *SMYTH, K., "Matthew 28: Resurrection as Theophany" IThQ 42(1975) 259-71. DRURY, J., Tradition and Design in Luke's Gospel (Atlanta 1976) 127f. "Auferstehung" in: TRE 4 (1979) 502.

28:1ff RENGSTORF, K. H. Die Auferstehung Jesu (1960) Passim. GRASS, H. Ostergeschehen und Osterberichte (1970) 23ff.

28:1-20 LIGHTFOOT, R. H. Locality and Doctrine in the Gospels (1938) 66ff. RIDDERBOS, H. Matthew's Witness to Jesus Christ (1958) 89-91. CRIBBS, F. L., in: G. MacRae (ed.) SBL Seminary Papers 2 (Montana 1973) 81f.

28:1-15 KREMER, J. Die Osterbotschaft der vier Evangelien (1968) 32-45.

28:1-10 M'NEILE, A. H. The Gospel According to St Matthew (1955) 437-39. DESCAMPS, A. "La Structure des Récits Evangeliques de la Résurrection", Biblica 40 (3-4, '59) 728-31. Glaubet an den Gottgesandten, Predigtgedanken aus Vergangenheit und Gegenwart, Bd. 2 (1962) 149-62. FüRST,

GPM (1962/63) 167ff. IWAND, H. J. in: Herr, tue meine Lippen auf, Bd. 3 (1964) Eichholz, G. (ed.) 192ff. LAMPARTNER, H. "Sehet, was hat Gott getan", in: Kleine Predigt-Typologie, III (1965) Schmidt, L. (ed.) 309-13. HODGES, Z. C. "The Women and the Empty Tomb," BiblSa 123 (492, '66) 301-309. KAMPHAUS, F. Von der Exegese zur Predigt (1968) 33-35. VOIGT, M. GPM 23/2 (1968/69) 163-68. KLASS, W. GPM 6/2 (1968/69) 102-108. GUTBROD, K. Die Auferstehung Jesu im Neuen Testament (1969) 55-59. NEIRYNCK, F. "Les Femmes au Tombeau: Etude de la rédaction Matthéenne (Matt. xxviii. 1-10)," NTS 15 (2, '69) 169-90. HUBBARD, B. J., The Matthean Redaction of a Primitive Apostolic Commissioning: An Exegesis of Matthew 28:16-20 (Missoula 1974) 177-79. BARTLETT, D. L., Fact and Faith (Valley Forge 1975) 107-109. BAUER, K. A., in: GPM 29 (1975) 196-203. MüLLER, H. M. und LINDNER, W. V., in: P. Krusche et al (eds.) Predigtstudien für das Kirchenjahr 1975 III/2. Halbband (Stuttgart 1975) 13-19. GOULDER, M. D., "Mark 16, 1-8 and Parallels" NTS 24 (1977-1978) 235-40. SCHILLEBEECKX, E., Jesus. An Experiment in Christology (London 1979) 338f.

28:1-8 TRILLING, W. "Die Auferstehung Jesu, Anfang der neuen Weltzeit" in: Christusverkündigung in den Synoptischen Evangelien (1969) 212. BODE, E. L. The First Easter Morning (1970) 7-10, 50-58, 139-40, 183-84. MARXSEN, W. The Resurrection of Jesus of Nazareth (1970) 44-46. KRATZ, R., Auferweckung als Befreiung (Stuttgart 1973) 9, 62-69. WANKE, J., Die Emmauserzählung. Eine redaktionsgeschichtliche Untersuchung zu Lk 24, 13-35. MAHONEY, R., Two Disciples at the Tomb (Bern 1974) 161-65, 194-202, 304f. COUSIN, H., Le prophète assassiné. Histoire des textes évangéliques de la Passion (Paris 1976). STAGG, E./F., Woman in the World of Jesus (Philadelphia 1978) 144-60. SWIDLER, L., Biblical Affirmations of Woman (Philadelphia 1979) 201, 221, 234.

28:1-7 STONEHOUSE, N. B. The Witness of Matthew and Mark to Christ (1944) 165. JOHNSON, B. A. "Empty Tomb Tradition in the Gospel of Peter" (Summary of a Dissertation), HThR 59 (4, '66) 447-48. TRILLING, W. Vierfalt und Einheit im Neuen Testament (1968), 112-24.

28:1-4 SCHNIDER, F. & STENGER, W., Die Ostergeschichten der Evangelien (1969) 30-33.

28:1 STONEHOUSE, N. B. The Witness of Matthew and Mark to Christ (1944) 89. DRIVER, G. R. "Two Problems in the New Testament," JThS 16 (2, '65) 327-37. BLINZLER, J., Die

Brüder und Schwestern Jesu (Stuttgart 1967) 73-86. BLACK, M. An Aramaic Approach to the Gospels and Acts (1967) 136f. BODE, E. L. The First Easter Morning (1970) 14-16. BROER, I. Die Urgemeinde und das Grab Jesu (1972) 87-137. MAHONEY, R., Two Disciples at the Tomb (Bern 1974) 202-12. SWIDLER, L., Biblical Affirmations of Woman (Philadelphia 1979) 208.

28:2-7 HENNECKE, E. & SCHNEEMELCHER, W. Neutestamentliche Apokryphen (1964) I 342.

28:2-4 BARTSCH, H.-W. Das Auferstehungszeugnis (1965) 11-15. MOULE, C. F. D. (ed.) The Significance of the Message of the Resurrection for Faith in Jesus Christ (1968) 72. BROER, I. Die Urgemeinde und das Grab Jesu (1972) 60ff. *WALTER, N., "Eine vormatthäische Schilderung der Auferstehung Jesu" NTS 19 (1973) 415-29.

28:2.4.5 BETZ, H. D. Lukian von Samosata und das Neue Testament (1961) 55, 143, 170.

28:2 KNOX, W. L. The Sources of the Synoptic Gospels II (1957) 125. DALMAN, G. Orte und Wege Jesu (1967) 395f. BODE, E. L. The First Easter Morning (1970) 50-51, 165-71. KRATZ, R., Auferweckung als Befreiung (Stuttgart 1973) 9-11, 13-15, 26, 36, 38, 51, 54, 56, 64f. CAVALLIN, H. C. C., Life After Death I (Lund 1974) 4.1.n.30.

28:3-4 BODE, E. L. The First Easter Morning (1970) 172-73.

28:4-7a OUTTIER, B. "Un feuillet du lectionnaire géorgien hanmeti à Paris," Muséon 85 (3-4, '72) 399-402, plates I-II.

28:4 STONEHOUSE, N. B. The Witness of Matthew and Mark to Christ (1944) 166, 182. MOULE, C. F. D. (ed.) The Significance of the Message of the Resurrection for Faith in Jesus Christ (1968) 87. KRATZ, R., Auferweckung als Befreiung (Stuttgart 1973) 9f, 26, 32, 38, 56, 61, 65, 68, 70f.

28:5-8 SCHNIDER, F. & STENGER, W. Die Ostergeschichten der Evangelien (1969) 34-43. SCHEP, J. A., The Nature of the Resurrection Body (Grand Rapids 1976) 127-29.

28:5-7 BODE, E. L. The First Easter Morning (1970) 53-54.

28:6f MOULE, C. F. D. (ed.) The Significance of the Message of the Resurrection for Faith in Jesus Christ (1968) 87.

28:6 STONEHOUSE, N. B. The Witness of Matthew and Mark to Christ (1944) 255. STRECKER, G. Der Weg der Gerechtigkeit (1962) 97.

28:7f STRECKER, G. Der Weg der Gerechtigkeit (1962) 205.

28:7.10 ODENKIRCHEN, P. C. " 'Praecedam vos in Galilaeam' (Mt 26, 32 cf. 28, 7.10; Mc 14, 28; 16, 7 cf. Lc 24, 6)," VerbDom 46 (1968) 193-223.

28:7 STONEHOUSE, N. B. The Witness of Matthew and Mark to Christ (1944) 91, 170ff., 173ff., 177. STRECKER, G. Der Weg der Gerechtigkeit (1962) 98, 2084. MOULE, C. F. D. The Significance of the Message of the Resurrection for Faith in Jesus Christ (1968) 79, 84. MARXSEN, W. Mark the Evangelist (1969) 83f., 87, 92. MAHONEY, R., Two Disciples at the Tomb (Bern 1974) 162-64.

28:8-20 WOJCIK, J., "The Two Kingdoms in Matthew's Gospel" in: K. R. R. Gros Louis et al. (eds.) Literary Interpretations of Biblical Narratives (Nashville 1974) 291f.

28:8-10 DODD, C. H. "The Appearances of the Risen Christ: a study in form-criticism of the Gospels," in More New Testament Studies (1968) 102-33. WANKE, J., Die Emmauserzählung. Eine redaktionsgeschichtliche Untersuchung zu Lk 24, 13-35 (Leipzig 1973) 6, 81. DUNN, J. D. G., Jesus and the Spirit (London 1975) 123, 126ff. SWIDLER, L., Biblical Affirmations of Woman (Philadelphia 1979) 204, 223, 234, 279.

28:8 STONEHOUSE, N. B. The Witness of Matthew and Mark to Christ (1944) 104, 107, 138, 165, 74.

28:9-20 PARKER, P. The Gospel Before Mark (1953) 118ff. RIST, J. M., On the Independence of Matthew and Mark (Cambridge 1978) 91.

28:9-11 STONEHOUSE, N. B. The Witness of Matthew and Mark to Christ (1944) 166.

28:9-10 SCHNIDER, F. & STENGER, W. Die Ostergeschichten der Evangelien (1969) 43-45. BODE, E. L. The First Easter Morning (1970) 54-56. TROMPF, G. W. The First Resurrection Appearance and the ending of Mark's Gospel. NTS 18 (1971-72) 313-22. KRATZ, R., Auferweckung als Befreiung (Stuttgart 1973) 9,69f, 76. ALSUP, J. E., The Post-Resurrection Appearance Stories of the Gospel-Tradition (Stuttgart 1975) 108ff, 114ff, 267f. "Auferstehung" in: TRE 4 (1979) 498. SCHILLEBEECKX, E., Die Auferstehung Jesu als Grund der Erlösung (Basel 1979) 104f.

28:9 STONEHOUSE, N. B. The Witness of Matthew and Mark to Christ (1944) 179-81. MOULE, C. F. D. (ed.) The Significance of the Message of the Resurrection for Faith in Jesus Christ (1968) 4. KüMMEL, W. G. (ed.) Jüdische Schriften aus hellenistisch-römischer Zeit I/1 (1973) 40.

28:10   STONEHOUSE, N. B. The Witness of Matthew and Mark to Christ (1944) 170, 175ff. STRECKER, G. Der Weg der Gerechtigkeit (1962) 98, 208, 234₃. HENNECKE, E. & SCHNEEMELCHER, W. Neutestamentliche Apokryphen (1964) I 130f. MOULE, C. F. D. (ed.) The Significance of the Message of the Resurrection for Faith in Jesus Christ (1968) 79, 84. GOULDER, M. D., Midrash and Lection in Matthew (London 1974) 242, 343, 381, 443. FRIEDRICH, G., "Die Bedeutung der Auferweckung Jesu nach Aussagen des Neuen Testaments" in: Auf das Wort kommt es an (Göttingen 1978) 336.

28:11-15:17   BULTMANN, R. The History of the Synoptic Tradition (1963) 286f., 288f.

28:11ff   STONEHOUSE, N. B. The Witness of Matthew and Mark to Christ (1944) 182.

28:11-15   STONEHOUSE, N. B. The Witness of Matthew and Mark to Christ (1944) 166. BARRETT, C. K. The New Testament Background: Selected Documents (1956) 14. SCHMID, J. Das Evangelium nach Matthäus (1956) 383-89. BLAIR, E. P. Jesus in the Gospel of Matthew (1960) 163. STRECKER, G. Der Weg der Gerechtigkeit (1962) 105. MOULE, C. F. D. (ed.) The Significance of the Message of the Resurrection for Faith in Jesus Christ (1968) 72. BROER, I. Die Urgemeinde und das Grab Jesu (1972) 60-78. KRATZ, R., Auferweckung als Befreiung (Stuttgart 1973) 9, 57, 70-72.

28:12-14   HENNECKE, E. & SCHNEEMELCHER, W. Neutestamentliche Apokryphen (1964) I 342.

28:13   RUDOLPH, K. Die Mandäer II (1961) 201. MOULE, C. F. D. (ed.) The Significance of the Message of the Resurrection for Faith in Jesus Christ (1968) 25. "Auferstehung" in: TRE 4 (1979) 522.

28:15   FEINE, D. P. & BEHM, D. J. Einleitung in das Neue Testament (1950) 53f. NEPPER-CHRISTENSEN, P. Das Matthäusevangelium. Ein Judenchristliches Evangelium? (1958) 14, 22, 87. STRECKER, G. Der Weg der Gerechtigkeit (1962) 107₂, 116f. HUMMEL, R. Die Auseinandersetzung zwischen Kirche und Judentum im Matthäusevangelium (1963) 146. DAVIES, W. D., The Sermon on the Mount (Cambridge 1966) 86. KUMMEL, W. G. Einleitung in das Neue Testament (1973) 85f.

28:16ff   STONEHOUSE, N. B. The Witness of Matthew and Mark to Christ (1944) 91, 182. STRECKER, G. Der Weg der Gerechtigkeit (1962) 98, 202₄, 206₄, 235₂. PETZKE, G. Die Traditionen über Apollonius von Tyana und das Neue

Testament (1970) 141, 187. JEREMIAS, J. Neutestamentliche
Theologie I (1971) 224, 287.

28:16-20 WILKENS, J. Einführung in das Evangelium nach Matthäus
II (1937) 249-52. MICHEL, O. "Der Abschluss des
Matthäusevangeliums. Ein Beitrag zur Geschichte der
Osterbotschaft," EvTh 10 (1950/51) 16-26. KNAK, S.
"Neutestamentliche Missionstexte nach neuerer Exegese."
Theologia Viatorum V (1953/54) 27-50. FLEW, R. N. Jesus
and His Church (1956) 138. BLAIR, E. P. Jesus in the Gospel of
Matthew (1960) 163. BARTH, K. "An Exegetical Study of
Matthew 28:16-20," in: The Theology of the Christian Mission
(1961) Anderson, G.H. (ed.) 55-71, (303). BORNKAMM-
BARTH-HELD, Ueberlieferung und Auslegung im Matthäus-
Evangelium (1961) 122ff., 133f., 139. STRECKER, G. Der
Weg der Gerechtigkeit (1962) 208ff. WENDLAND, H.-D.
GPM 17 (1962/63) 229-33. HAHN, F. Christologische
Hoheitstitel (1963) 130f. BORNKAMM, G. "Der
Auferstandene und der Irdische", in: Zeit und Geschichte
(1964) 171-91. IWAND, H.-J. Predigt-Meditationen (1964) 27-
30. KOSMALA, H. "The Conclusion of Matthew" in the
Annual of the Swedish Theological Institute (1965) Kosmala,
H. (ed.) 132-47. RANDELLINI, L., "La conclusione del
Vangelo di Matteo 28:16-20 nella luce della storia della
redazione" DiThom 68 (1965) 426. SQUILLACI, D.
"L'apparizione di Gesù sopra un monte della Galilea. Missione
degli Apostoli. Matt. 28, 16-20," PaCl 44 (June 15, '65) 641-45.
DAVIES, W. D., The Sermon on the Mount (Cambridge 1966)
16, 33f, 74f. TUCK, R. C. "The Lord Who Said Go: Some
Reflections on Matthew 28:16-20," ANQ 7 (2, '66) 85-92.
BAUMBACH, G. "Die Mission im Matthäus-Evangelium,"
(1967) 889-93. CULVER, R. D. "What is the Church's
Commission? Some Exegetical Issues in Matthew 28:16-20,"
BullEvang TheolSoc 10 (2, '67) 115-26. FLUSSER, D. "The
Conclusion of Matthew in a New Jewish Christian Source," in
the Annual of the Theological Institute (1967) Kosmala, H.
(ed.) 110. LUCK, U. "Herrenwort und Geschichte in Matth. 28,
16-20," EvTh 27 (8-9, '67) 494-508. WEBER, O.
Predigtmeditationen (1967) 185-87. DODD, C. H. "The
Appearance of the Risen Christ: a study in form-criticism of the
Gospels," More New Testament Studies (1968) 102-33.
GAECHTER, P. Die literarische Kunst im Matthäus-
Evangelium (1968) 78-79. GNILKA, J. "Der Missionsauftrag
des Herrn nach Mt 28 und Apg 1," BuL 9 (1, '68) 1-9. CULVER,
R. D. "What is the Church's Commission? Some Exegetical
Issues in Matthew 28:16-20," BiblSa 125 (499, '68) 239-53.
STOTT, J. R. W. "The Great Commission," ChrTo 12 (15, '68)

723-25; (16, '68) 778-82; (17, '68) 826-29. KAMPHAUS, F. Von der Exegese zur Predigt (1968) 43-45. KREMER, J. Die Osterbotschaft der vier Evangelien (1968) 142f. MOULE, C. F. D. (ed.) The Significance of the Message of the Resurrection for Faith in Jesus Christ (1968) 35, 92. SEIDENSTICKER, Ph. Die Auferstehung Jesu in der Botschaft der Evangelisten (1968) 90ff. STUHLMACHER, P. Das Paulinische Evangelium (1968) 254. FüRST, W. GPM 23/3 (1968/69) 235-40. KASTING, H. Die Anfänge der Urchristlichen Mission (1969) 34-38, 43, 84. SCHNIDER, F. & STENGER. W. Die Ostergeschichten der Evangelien (1969) 45-55. BURCHARD, C., Der dreizehnte Zeuge (Göttingen 1970) 131f, 178. MALINA, B. J. "The Literary Structure and Form of Matt. XXVIII. 16-20," NTS 17 (1, '70) 87-103. MARXSEN, W. The Resurrection of Jesus of Nazareth (1970) 47-48. OTTO, G. Denken-um zu glauben (1970) 21-26. WILCKENS, U. Auferstehung (1970) 69-71. ROBINSON, J. M. (ed.) The Future of Our Religious Past (1971) 203-29. ZUMSTEIN, J. "Matthieu 28:16-20," RThPh 22 (1, '72) 14-33. *LANGE, J., Das Erscheinen des Auferstandenen im Evangelium nach Matthäus (Würzburg 1973). MICHEL, H.-J., Die Abschiedsrede des Paulus an die Kirche Apg 20:17-38 (München 1973) 57ff. NEIRYNCK, F., "Minor Agreements Matthew-Luke in the Transfiguration Story" in: P. Hoffmann (ed.) Orientierung an Jesus. Für J. Schmid (Freiburg 1973) 257f. WANKE, J., Die Emmauserzählung. Eine redaktionsgeschichtliche Untersuchung zu Lk 24, 13-35 (Leipzig 1973) 5, 12. BARTSCH, H. W., "Der Ursprüngliche Schluss der Leidensgeschichte. Ueberlieferungsgeschichtliche Studien zum Markus-Schluss" in: M. Sabbe (ed.) L'Evangile selon Marc (Gembloux 1974) 411-33. DAVIES, W. D. The Gospel and the Land (London 1974) 240, 242, 342n.20, 413n.15. FRANKEMöLLE, H., Jahwebund und Kirche Christi (Münster 1974) 42-72, 118, 243, 321-25, 336, 370. *HUBBARD, B. J., The Matthean Redaction of a Primitive Apostolic Commissioning: An Exegesis of Matthew 28: 16-20 (Missoula 1974). *KINGSBURY, J. D., "The Composition and Christology of Matt 28: 16-20" JBL 93 (1974) 573-84. LEON-DUFOUR, X., The Resurrection and the Message of Easter (London 1974) 94-104, 146-48. BARTLETT, D. L., Fact and Faith (Valley Forge 1975) 109-112. BLAUERT, H., in: GPM 29 (1975) 280-86. DUNN, J. D. G., Jesus and the Spirit (London 1975) 115, 123ff, 128, 137, 153. *GIBLIN, C. H., "A Note on Doubt and Reassurance in Mt 28: 16-20" CBQ 37 (1975) 68-75. KRUSCHE, P. und BäUMLER, C., in: P. Krusche et al. (eds.) Predigtstudien für das Kirchenjahr 1975

III/2.Halbband (Stuttgart 1975) 92-102. MURPHY-O'CONNOR, J., in: RB 83 (1976) 97-102. *OSBORNE, G. R., "Redaction Criticism and the Great Commission: A Case Study Toward a Biblical Understanding of Inerrancy" JEThS 19 (1976) 73-85. *VöGTLE, A., Was Ostern Bedeutet.Meditation zu Matthäus 28, 16-20 (Freiburg 1976). MEIER, J. P., "Two Disputed Questions in Matt 28:16-20" JBL 96 (1977) 407-24. SAITO, T., Die Mosevorstellungen im Neuen Testament (Bern 1977) 54f. *SCHIEBER, H., "Konzentrik im Matthäusschluss. Ein form- und gattungskritischer Versuch zu Mt 28, 16-20" Kairos 19 (1977) 286-307. "Apostel" in: TRE 3 (1978) 434. *HENDRICKX, H., The Resurrection Narratives of the Synoptic Gospels (Manila 1978). LIVIO, J.-B., "La signification théologique de la 'montagne' dans le premièr évangile" Bulletin du Centre Protestant d'Etudes 30 (Genéve 1978) 13-20. *PARKHURST, L. G., "Matthew 28:16-20 Reconsidered" ET 90 (1979) 179-80. STECK, K. G., in: GPM 33 (1979) 310-17. SWIDLER, L., Biblical Affirmations of Woman (Philadelphia 1979) 222.

28:16-17   ELLIS, I. P. 'But Some Doubted', NTS 14 (1967/68) 574ff.

28:16   BLAIR, E. P. Jesus in the Gospel of Matthew (1960) 134. SCHREIBER, J. Theologie des Vertrauens (1967) 214-16. MOULE, C. F. D. (ed.) The Significance of the Message of the Resurrection for Faith in Jesus Christ (1968) 122. STROBEL, A. "Der Berg der Offenbarung (Mt 28, 16; Apg 1, 12)", Verborum Veritas (1970) 133-46. CHAVASSE, C. "Not the Mountain Appointed. Studies in Texts: Matthew 28:16," Theology 74 (616, '71) 478. LANGE, J., Das Erscheinen des Auferstandenen im Evangelium nach Matthäus (Würzburg 1973) 44, 308, 356, 358, 375, 385, 392f, 398, 403, 434, 436f, 439-41, 445, 447-51, 462, 470, 474f.

28:17   STONEHOUSE, N. B. The Witness of Matthew and Mark to Christ (1944) 167, 169, 170, 172, 175. BLAIR, E. P. Jesus in the Gospel of Matthew (1960) 68. STRECKER, G. Der Weg der Gerechtigkeit (1962) 194₂, 234. KWIK, R. J. "Some Doubted," ET 77 (6, '66) 181. ELLIS, I. P. " 'But Some Doubted'," NTS 14 (4, '68) 574-80. MOULE, C. F. D. (ed.) The Significance of the Message of the Resurrection for Faith in Jesus Christ (1968) 79. LOHFINK, G. Die Himmelfahrt Jesu (1971) 173f. LANGE, J., Das Erscheinen des Auferstandenen im Evangelium nach Matthäus (Würzburg 1973) 332, 339f, 353, 370, 472-75, 478, 483f.

28:18-20   FEINE, P. Der Apostel Paulus (1927) 359f. STONEHOUSE, N. B. The Witness of Matthew and Mark to Christ (1944) 168ff., 236, 255. DENNEY, J. The Death of Christ (1956) 45f.

SCHMID, J. Das Evangelium nach Matthäus (1956) 392-97.
NEPPER-CHRISTENSEN, P. Das Matthäusevangelium. Ein
Judenchristliches Evangelium? (1958) 9, 52, 182, 183, 185, 186,
195, 197, 198, 200. GILMORE, A. Christian Baptism (1959)
112f., 292. TRILLING, W. Das wahre Israel (1959) 6ff.
BLAIR, E. P. Jesus in the Gospel of Matthew (1960) 31, 45ff.,
58, 65, 66, 67, 108, 134, 155. BEASLEY-MURRAY, G. R.
Baptism in the New Testament (1962) 77ff. BRINKTRINE, J.
"An et quomodo existentia Hierarchiae Ecclesiasticae e Sacris
Scripturis erui possit," Divinitas 6 (1, '62) 134-37.
STRECKER, G. Der Weg der Gerechtigkeit (1962) 43, 158.
HAHN, F. Christologische Hoheitstitel (1963) 243, 331f., 402.
EICHHOLZ, G. (ed.) Herr, tue meine Lippen auf Bd. 3 (1964)
282ff. KäSEMANN, E. Exegetische Versuche und
Besinnungen (1964) II 87. VöGTLE, A. "Das christologische
und ekklesiologische Anliegen von Mt. 28, 18-20", in: Studia
Evangelica II (1964) Cross, F. L. (ed.) 266-94. CRETER, F.
"Allein Gott in der Höh' sei Ehr!" in: Kleine Predigt-Typologie
III (1965) 398-404. HAHN, F. Das Verständnis der Mission im
Neuen Testament (1965) 20, 22, 50, 52f., 54-57, 60, 62, 103, 106.
TRILLING, W. Vielfalt und Einheit im Neuen Testament
(1968) 125-39. WREGE, H.-T. Die Ueberlieferungsgeschichte
der Bergpredigt (1968) 173ff. CARLSTON, C. The Things that
Defile (Mark VII. 14) and the Law in Matthew and Mark. NTS
15 (1968/69) 83ff. KASTING, H. Die Anfänge der
Urchristlichen Mission (1969) 34-38, 40, 111-13, 134-36, 142f.
KäSEMANN, E. New Testament Questions of Today (1969)
87. TAGAWA, K. People and Community in the Gospel of
Matthew. NTS 16 (1969/70) 153ff. EVANS, C. F. Resurrection
and the New Testament (1970) 88ff. LOHSE, E. and Others
(eds.) Der Ruf Jesu und die Antwort der Gemeinde (1970) 94-
98, 109-111. DE RIDDER, R. R. The dispersion of the people
of God. The Covenant Basis of Matthew 28:18-20 against the
Background of Jewish, Pre-Christian Proselytizing and
Diaspora, and the Apostleship of Jesus Christ (1971).
VöGTLE, A. Das Evangelium und die Evangelien (1971) 253-
72. PETERS, G. W. A Biblical Theology of Missions (1972)
137, 176, 178, 195, 251-52, 261, 266, 271, 309. *KOSMALA, H.
"The Conclusion of Matthew," ASThI IV, 132-47.
*HARRISON, E. F., "Did Christ Command World
Evangelism?" ChrTo 18 (1973) 210-14. LANGE, J., Das
Erscheinen des Auferstandenen im Evangelium nach Matthäus
(Würzburg 1973) 17f, 20, 22, 40, 51, 64, 73, 88, 109, 114, 119,
148-50, 152, 166-68, 170-73, 175-80, 186, 188, 202, 205f, 208-13,
215-18, 237f, 242-46, 267, 291, 307, 321, 341f, 349-54, 356, 362,
379, 388, 414f, 430f, 438, 450, 480, 491, 494f. GOULDER, M.

D., Midrash and Lection in Matthew (London 1974) 186, 339, 341, 449. SAND, A., Das Gesetz und die Propheten (Regensburg 1974) 162-65, 168-71. TALBERT, C. H., Literary Patterns, Theological Themes and the Genre of Luke-Acts (Missoula 1974) 62. DUNN, J. D. G., Jesus and the Spirit (London 1975) 124, 129, 173. *O'BRIEN, P. T., "The Great Commission of Matthew 28:18-20. A Missionary Mandate or Not?" RThR 35 (1976) 66-78. "Amt" in: TRE 2 (1978) 516. BEST, E., From Text to Sermon (Atlanta 1978) 23. *LOEWEN, H., "The Great Commission" Direction 7 (1978) 33-35. TREVIJANO ETCHEVERRIA, R., "La mission de la Iglesia primitiva y los mandatos del Señor en los Evangelios" Salmanticensis 25 (1978) 5-36. "Auferstehung" in: TRE 4 (1979) 502. HEDRICK, C. W., "Resurrection: Radical Theology in the Gospel of Matthew" LThQ 14 (1979) 40-45.

28:18-19 NESTLE, E., "Ein arabisches Zitat von Mt 28, 18, 19" ZNW 9 (1908) 250. HAHN, F. Christologische Hoheitstitel (1963) 324. HAMERTON-KELLY, R. G. Pre-Existence, Wisdom, and The Son of Man (1973) 68-70, 166, 220.

28:18 NESTLE, E. ZNW 4 (1903) 246f. NESTLE, E., "Eine Variante in Matt 28:18" ZNW 7 (1906) 183. BRUNNER, E. Dogmatik II (1950) 335. BARRETT, C. K. The New Testament Background: Selected Documents (1956) 90. BERKHOF, H. Der Sinn der Geschichte: Christus (1959) 72, 76f., 147. BLAIR, E. P. Jesus in the Gospel of Matthew (1960) 54, 67, 98, 139, 140. A. B. "Umfrage über Mt 16, 18 und 28, 18," Catholica 14 (2, '60) 157-59. BORNKAMM-BARTH-HELD, Ueberlieferung und Auslegung im Matthäus-Evangelium (1961) 257, 287. De KRUIJF, Th., Der Sohn des Lebendigen Gottes (Rome 1962) 74, 112, 155. RENGSTORF, K. H. "Old and New Testament Traces of a Formula of the Judaean Royal Ritual," NovTest 5 (4, '62) 229-44. STRECKER, G. Der Weg der Gerechtigkeit (1962) 127₂, 166₇. HAHN, F. Das Verständnis der Mission im Neuen Testament (1965) 108. SCHELBERT, G., "Mir ist alle Gewalt gegeben" BuK 20 (1965) 37-39. MOULE, C. F. D. (ed.). The Significance of the Message of the Resurrection for Faith in Jesus Christ (1968) 93. CHRIST, F. Jesus Sophia (1970) 61, 86, 87. VöGTLE, A. Das Evangelium und die Evangelien (1971) 255-58. LANGE, J., Das Erscheinen des Auferstandenen im Evangelium nach Matthäus (Würzburg 1973) 18, 23, 61, 64, 84, 86, 88, 92-97, 105, 112, 119, 132, 145-48, 150-52, 166f, 169-75, 177, 214, 242, 284, 293, 303, 315, 326, 342, 348-50, 431, 434, 438, 474, 491, 494. FRANKEMöLLE, H., Jahwebund und Kirche Christi (Münster 1974) 61-72, 170. FRIEDRICH, G., "Die Auferweckung Jesu, eine Tat Gottes oder ein Interpretament der Jünger" in: Auf das Wort kommt es an (Göttingen 1978) 349f. FRIEDRICH, G., "Die Bedeutung der Auferweckung Jesu nach Aussagen des Neuen Testaments" in: Auf das Wort kommt es an (Göttingen 1978) 369f.

28:18b   TRILLING, W. Das wahre Israel (1959) 6f.

28:19-20   STONEHOUSE, N. B. The Witness of Matthew and Mark to Christ (1944) 240. SCHWEIZER, E. Gemeinde und Gemeindeordnung im Neuen Testament (1959) § 26c. STRECKER, G. Der Weg der Gerechtigkeit (1962) 128, 196, 227. DELLING, G. Die Taufe im Neuen Testament (1963) 80. GAERTNER, C. A. "New Testament Teachings and 20th-Century Church Practice with Special Reference to Relations with Missions and Sister Churches," CThM 36 (4, '65) 239-42. KASPER, W. (ed.) Christsein ohne Entscheidung oder Soll die Kirche Kinder taufen? (1970) 62-65. MARXSEN, W. The Resurrection of Jesus of Nazareth (1970) 165-68. THYEN, H. Studien zur Sündenvergebung (1970) 146f., 235. TROMPF, G. W. The First Resurrection Appearance and the ending of Mark's Gospel. NTS 18 (1971/72) 326f. ROGERS, C. "The Great Commission," BiblSa 130 (519, '73) 258-67. *ROGERS, C., "The Great Commission" BiblSa 130 (1973) 258-67. FENEBERG, W., Der Markusprolog (München 1974) 20f, 23, 25f, 37, 53, 117, 149. GOPPELT, L., Theologie des Neuen Testaments II (Göttingen 1976) 332, 547. MARTIN, R. P., Worship in the Early Church (Grand Rapids 1976⁻1974) 94-97. DUNN, J. D. G., Unity and Diversity in the New Testament (London 1977) 145, 155f. "Bergpredigt" in: TRE 5 (1980) 608.

28:19.20a   TRILLING, W. Das wahre Israel (1959) 12ff.

28:19   CONYBEARE, F. C. ZNW 2 (1901) 275-88. STONEHOUSE, N. B. The Witness of Matthew and Mark to Christ (1944) 186. BRUNNER, E. Dogmatik I (1946) 96, 216, 228. BARRETT, C. K. The Holy Spirit and the Gospel Tradition (1947) 102f., 132f. BARTH, M., Die Taufe - ein Sakrament? (Zürich 1951) 525-54. KNOX, W. L. The Sources of the Synoptic Gospels II (1957) 33. BLAIR, E. P. Jesus in the Gospel of Matthew (1960) 60, 94. DELLING, G. Die Zueignung des Heils in der Taufe (1961) 39, 83, 87, 94-96. ANON., "New Testament Studies: 2. The threefold name," HibJour 61 (1, '62) 43-44. DE KRUIJF, Th., Der Sohn des lebendigen Gottes (Rome 1962) 41, 72, 74, 112f, 115, 146f, 150. STRECKER, G. Der Weg der Gerechtigkeit (1962) 33, 118, 192s, 212ı, 216, 239. WAINWRIGHT, A. W. The Trinity in the New Testament (1962) 237-41, 251-52. DELLING, G. Die Taufe im Neuen Testament (1963) 75f. HAHN, F. Christologische Hoheitstitel (1963) 79, 320.

HUMMEL, R. Die Auseinandersetzung zwischen Kirche und Judentum im Matthäusevangelium (1963) 140-42. GAMBA, G., "In Margine all 'autenticità" Salmanticensis 26 (1964) 463-74. HENNECKE, E. & SCHNEEMELCHER, W. Neutestamentliche Apokryphen (1964) I 249. HAHN, F. Das Verständnis der Mission im Neuen Testament (1965) 10, 56, 60, 105, 107f., 109. BEYSCHLAG, K. Clemens Romanus und der Frühkatholizismus (1966) 276f. BIEDER, W., Die Verheissung der Taufe im Neuen Testament (Zürich 1966) 107-18. SEEBERG, A. Der Katechismus der Urchristenheit (1966) 65, 66, 208, 236-38, 250. MOULE, C. F. D. (ed.) The Significance of the Message of the Resurrection of Faith in Jesus Christ (1968) 92, 93. KüNZI, M. Das Naherwartungslogion Matthäus 10, 23 (1970) 27, 40, 120, 151, 153. JEREMIAS, J. Neutestamentliche Theologie I (1971) 63, 246, 287. AUD DER MAUR, H. & KLEINHEYER, B. Zeichen des Glaubens (1972) 19-40. GERHARDSSON, B., "Monoteism och högkristologi i Matteusevangeliet" SEA 37-38 (1972-73) 125-44. LANGE, J., Das Erscheinen des Auferstandenen im Evangelium nach Matthäus (Würzburg 1973) 23, 86, 150f, 169-71, 176f, 240, 248, 266, 292f, 299-303, 305-308, 310, 313-15, 342, 379, 404, 413f, 462, 488, 494. FRANKEMöLLE, H., Jahwebund und Kirche Christi (Münster 1974) 93, 107, 109, 121, 135, 144, 165, 261, 306, 319, 322f, 326. HARE, D. R. A., and HARRINGTON, D. J., "Make Disciples of All the Gentiles (Mt 28:19)" CBQ 37 (1975) 359-69. *MEIER, J. P., "Nations or Gentiles in Matthew 28:19?" CBQ 39 (1977) 94-102. SANDMEL, S., We Jews and Jesus (New York 1977) 44.

28:19a TRILLING, W. Das wahre Israel (1959) 12ff., 118.

28:19b TRILLING, W. Das wahre Israel (1959) 18ff.

28:20 HEINZELMANN, D. G. "Siehe, ich bin bei euch alle Tage bis an der Welt Ende." Jesus ist da (Predigt) Das Ja Gottes (1924) 91. BRUNNER, E. Dogmatik I (1946) 30, 276. STAEHELIN, E. Die Verkündigung des Reiches Gottes in der Kirche Jesu Christi I (1951) 266, 368. FLEW, R. N. Jesus and His Church (1956) 112. BLAIR, E. P. Jesus in the Gospel of Matthew (1960) 32, 43, 67, 165. EAGER, B. "The Lord is With You," Scripture 12 (18, '60) 48-54. BORNKAMM-BARTH-HELD, Ueberlieferung und Auslegung im Matthäus-Evangelium (1961) 37, 66, 97, 104, 126f., 220, 251, 255, 257, 287. DELLING, G. Die Zueignung des Heils in der Taufe (1961) 95, 96. SCHRAGE, W. Die konkreten Einzelgebote in der Paulinischen Paränese (1961) 87. STRECKER, G. Der Weg der Gerechtigkeit (1962) 40, 44, 114, 129f., 142, 198, 212, 213$_3$, 214, 238. HAHN, F. Christologische Hoheitstitel (1963) 119,

402. HUMMEL, R. Die Auseinanderstezung zwischen Kirche und Judentum im Matthäusevangelium (1963) 142. BRAUN, H. Qumran und NT II (1966) 299. DAVIES, W. D., The Sermon on the Mount (Cambridge 1966) 17. MARXSEN, W. Mark the Evangelist (1969) 202, 205. BERKOUWER, G. C., The Return of Christ (Grand Rapids 1972) 132, 142-45, 235. *McKENZIE, J. L., "God with us" The Way 12 (1972) 14-19. WANKE, J., Die Emmauserzählung (Leipzig 1973) 35. FRANKEMOLLE, H., Jahwebund und Kirche Christi (Münster 1974) 12, 60f, 207, 284, 288, 301, 335. KINGSBURY, J. D., Matthew: Structure, Christology, Kingdom (Philadelphia 1975) 77-79. "Amt" in: TRE 2 (1978) 517.

28:20a TRILLING, W. Das wahre Israel (1959) 21ff. HUMMEL, R. Die Auseinandersetzung zwischen Kirche und Judentum im Matthäusevangelium (1963) 60. LANGE, J., Das Erscheinen des Auferstandenen im Evangelium nach Matthäus (Würzburg 1973) 18, 114, 240, 284, 310, 316, 318, 320f, 323-25, 342, 349, 379, 404, 423, 445, 449, 462, 489, 494. FRANKEMöLLE, H., Jahwebund und Kirche Christi (Münster 1974) 95-98, 101, 135, 307, 338.

28:20b TRILLING, W. Das wahre Israel (1959) 26ff. SASS, G. Ungereimtes bei Matthäus (1968) 71-73. LANGE, J., Das Erscheinen des Auferstandenen im Evangelium nach Matthäus (Würzburg 1973) 23, 95, 119, 170-72, 210, 328-31, 339-50, 353, 379, 405, 415, 438, 482, 495.

Mark

1-16:8 FARMER, W. R., The Twelve Last Verses of Mark (London 1974) 47, 85, 90, 92, 94, 98.

1-13 BONHOURS, J. F., "Une étude de l'ordonnance de la triple tradition" RechSR 60 (1972) 595-614. DORMEYER, D., Die Passion Jesu als Verhaltensmodell (Münster 1974) 58-65. KELBER, W. H., The Kingdom in Mark (Philadelphia 1974).

1-12 *BUTTERWORTH, R., "The Composition of Mark 1-12" HeyJ 13 (1, '72) 5-26.

1-9 SANDMEL, S., We Jews and Jesus (New York 1977) 19.

1-8:26 VIA, D. O., Kerygma and Comedy in the New Testament (Philadelphia 1975) 75, 117, 124, 154. EGGER, W., Frohbotschaft und Lehre (Frankfurt 1976) 87, 167. TANNEHILL, R. C., "The Gospel of Mark as Narrative Christology" Semeia 16 (1980) 60-71.

1-6 FARRER, A. A Study in St. Mark (1951) 146ff, 152ff. *DENIS, A.-M. "Les richesses du Fils de Dieu selon saint Marc (I-VI, 30)" VieS 41 (448, '59) 229-39. PESCH, R. Naherwartungen (1969) 68f.

1-4 GROS LOUIS, K. R. R., "The Gospel of Mark" in: Gros Louis et al. (eds.) Literary Interpretations of Biblical Narratives (Nashville 1974) 296-309.

1-3 WEEDEN, Th, J., in: G. MacRae (ed.) SBL Seminar Papers 2 (Montana 1973) 206-207.

1:1-3:6 PESCH, R. Naherwartungen (1969) 57f. EGGER, W., Frohbotschaft und Lehre (Frankfurt 1976) 42. SCHWEIZER, E., "Die Theologische Leistung des Markus" EvTh 24 (1964) 337-55; and in: R. Pesch (ed.) Das Markus-Evangelium (Darmstadt 1979) 168-71.

1-2 GNILKA, J. Die Verstockung Israels (1961) 57f.

1 LIGHTFOOT, R. H. The Gospel Message of St. Mark (1950) 15-30. STREETER, B. H. The Four Gospels (1951) 90f, 576f. GREENLEE, J. H., Nine Uncial Palimpsests of the Greek New Testament (Salt Lake City 1968) 28-29, 58-59. LEHMANN, M. Synoptische Quellenanalyse und die Frage nach dem historischen Jesus (1970) 44-46, 61-81. BJORCK, S. et al. (eds.) Valda Texter ur Nya Testamentet (Stockholm 1972) 10-13. EGGER, W. Frohbotschaft und Lehre (Frankfurt 1976) 39-43, 103.

1:1-39 *ZEHRER, F. Synoptischer Kommentar zu den drei ersten Evangelien, I (1962).

1:1-20 CONZELMANN, H. and LINDEMANN, A., Arbeitsbuch zum Neuen Testament (Tübingen 1975) 57, 67f.

1:1-15 EWALD, H., Die drei ersten Evangelien (Göttingen 1850) 154ff. *SEITZ, J. F. "Praeparatio Evangelica in the Markan Prologue," JBL 82 (2, '63) 201-206. *KECK, L. E. "The Introduction to Mark's Gospel" NTS 12 (4, '66) 352-70. WINK, W. John the Baptist in the Gospel Tradition (1968) 1-8. IERSEL, B. M. F., "Anfang der Verkündigung über Jesus Christus" Vox Theol (1969) 169-79. PESCH, R. "Anfang des Evangeliums Jesu Christi. Eine Studie zum Prolog des Markusevangeliums (Mk 1, 1-15)" in: Die Zeit Jesu (1970) Bornkamm, G. & Rahner, K. (eds.). ETCHEVERRIA, R. T., Comienzo del Evangelio. Estudio sobre el prólogo de San Marcos (Burgos 1971). *Recensions:* S. Legasse, BLE 73 (1972) 282-83; G. Testa, DiThom 75 (1972) 206-207; J. J. O'Rourke, CBQ 35 (1973) 121. LANGKAMMER, H., "Tradycja i redakcja w prologu Ewangelii Marka" RTK 20 (1973) 37-57. EGGER, W., Frohbotschaft und Lehre (Frankfurt 1976) 39f, 55. PESCH, R., Das Markusevangelium I (Freiburg 1976) 73 (lit!). DAUTZENBERG, G., "Die Zeit des Evangeliums. Mk. 1:1-15 und die Konzeption des Markusevangeliums" BZ 21 (1977) 219-34, BZ 22 (1978) 76-91. WILLIAMSON, L., "Translations and Interpretation: New Testament" Interp 32 (1978) 158-70. GNILKA, J., Das Evangelium nach Markus I (Einsiedeln/Neukirchen 1978) 39 (lit!). PESCH, R., "Anfang des Evangeliums Jesu Christi" in: Das Markus-Evangelium (Darmstadt 1979) 311-55.

1:1-13 STONEHOUSE, N. B. The Witness of Matthew and Mark to Christ (1944) 5ff, 96. ROBINSON, J. M. Das Geschichtsverständnis des Markus-Evangeliums (1956) 11ff. GRUNDMANN, W. Das Evangelium nach Markus (1959) 29f. MAUSER, U. Christ in the Wilderness (1963) 77ff, 130. SIMPSON, R. T., "The major agreements of Matthew and Luke against Mark" NTS 12 (1965-1966) 275f. KECK, L. E., "The Introduction to Mark's Gospel" NTS 12 (1965-1966) 352f. CONZELMANN, H. and LINDEMANN, A., Arbeitsbuch zum Neuen Testament (Tübingen 1975) 67f. POPPI, A., L'inizio del Vangelo. Predicazione del Battista.Battesima e tentazione di Gesù (Padua 1976).

1:1-11 FENEBERG, W., Der Markusprolog. Studien zur Formbestimung des Evangeliums (München 1974).

1:1-8 ROBINSON, J. M. Das Geschichtsverständnis des Markus-Evangeliums (1956) 15ff. *BUSE, I. "St. John and 'The First Synoptic Pericope'" NovTest 3 (1-2, '59) 57-61. HAHN, F. Christologische Hoheitstitel (1963) 118, 378f, 380. BULTMANN, R., The History of the Synoptic Tradition (Oxford 1963) 245-47. VIELHAUER, P. Aufsätze zum Neuen

Testament (München 1965) 47-54. *RUDDICK, C. T. "Behold, I Send My Messenger" JBL 88 (4, '69) 381-417. ZIMMERMANN, W-D. Markus über Jesus (1970) 11-16. RENKEMA, J., "Een verkennend onderzoek naar de leesbaarheid van bijbelvertalingen" NedThT 29 (1975) 305-21. PESCH, R., Das Markusevangelium I (Freiburg 1976) 86f. (lit!). GNILKA, J., Das Evangelium nach Markus I (Einsiedeln/Neukirchen 1978) 40 (lit!). Pesch, R., "Anfang des Evangeliums Jesu Christi" in: G. Bornkamm/K. Rahner (eds.) Die Zeit Jesu (1970) 108-44; and in: R. Pesch (ed.) Das Markus-Evangelium (Darmstadt 1979) 315-16. SCHMITHALS, W. Das Evangelium nach Markus (Gütersloh/Würzburg 1979) 73 (lit!). FUCHS, A., "Die Überschneidungen von Mk und "Q" nach B. H. Streeter und E. P. Sanders and ihre wahre Bedeutung" in W. Haubeck/M. Bachmann (eds.) Wort in der Zeit. Für K. H. Rengstorf (Leiden 1980) 57-81. SCHRECKENBERG, H., "Flavius Josephus und die lukanischen Schriften" in: W. Haubeck/M. Bachmann (eds.) Wort in der Zeit. Für K. H. Rengstorf (Leiden 1980) 187-90.

1:1-5   DELLING, G. Die Taufe im Neuen Testament (1963) 42f, 47. NICKELS, P. Targum and New Testament (1967) 23.

1:1-4   RAWLINSON, A. E. J. St Mark (1925, repr. 1956) 250f.

1:1-3   FARRER, A. A Study in St Mark (1951) 54ff, 66f.

1:1-2   SCHWEIZER, E., "Mark's contribution to the Quest of the Historical Jesus" NTS 10 (1963-1964) 424f.

1:1   NESTLE, E., Einführung in das Griechische Neue Testament (Göttingen 1909) 247f. HAUCK, D. F. Exc. "euangelion" Das Evangelium des Markus (1931) 12f. STONEHOUSE, N. B. The Witness of Matthew and Mark to Christ (1944) 7ff, 97, 99. KLOSTERMANN, E. Das Markusevangelium (1950) 3f. FARRER, A. A Study in St. Mark (1951) 53f. SCHMID, J. Das Evangelium nach Markus (1958) 15-17. ROBINSON, J. M. Kerygma und Historischer Jesus (1960) 146. STRECKER, G. Der Weg der Gerechtigkeit (1962) 48, 126. HAHN, F. Christologische Hoheitstitel (1963) 208, 380. HAHN, F. Das Verständnis der Mission im Neuen Testament (1965) 61, 105. MINETTE DE TILLESSE, G. Le Secret Messianique dans L'Evangile de Marc (1968) 353-54, 395-6, 403-8. KASTING, H. Die Anfänge der Urchristlichen Mission (1969) 82f. PESCH, R. Naherwartungen (1969) 54, 114, 124, 194, 209. MARXSEN, W. Mark the Evangelist (1969) 40ff, 131ff, 148ff. LAMARCHE, P. "Commencement de l'évangile de Jésus, Christ, Fils de Dieu (Mc 1, 1)" NRTh 92 (10, '70) 1024-36. STRECKER, G. "Literarische Ueberlegungen zum εὐαγγέλιον-Begriff im Markusevangelium", Neues Testament und Geschichte (1972) Baltensweiler, H. & Reicke, B. (eds). 91-104. SCHNACKENBURG, R., " 'Das Evangelium' im Verständnis des ältesten Evangelisten" in: P. Hoffmann (ed.) Orientierung an Jesus. Für J. Schmid (Freiburg 1973) 310, 321-23. LADD, G. E., A Theology of the New Testament (Grand Rapids 1974) 140, 142, 162, 221. CONZELMANN, H. and LINDEMANN, A., Arbeitsbuch zum Neuen Testament (Tübingen 1975) 30. *BOUTTIER, M., "Commencement, force et fin de l'evangile" EThR 51 (1976) 465-93. EGGER, W., Frohbotschaft und Lehre (Frankfurt 1976) 39, 43, 48, 54-56, 90, 98, 106, 165. *ARNOLD, G., "Mk. 1:1 und Eröffnungswendungen in griechischen und lateinischen Schriften" ZNW 68 (1977) 123-27. *SLOMP, J., "Are the words 'Son of God' in Mark 1:1 Original?" BTr 28 (1977) 143-50. *FEUILLET, A., "Le 'Commencement' de l'Économie Chrétienne d'après He. 2:3-4 Mc. 1:1 et Ac. 1:1-2" NTS 24 (1978) 163-74. PESCH, R., "Anfang des Evangeliums Jesu Christi" in: G. Bornkamm/K. Rahner (eds.) Die Zeit Jesu (1970) 108-44; and in: R. Pesch (ed.) Das Markus-Evangelium (Darmstadt 1979) 336, 338. KELBER, W. H., "Mark and Oral Tradition" Semeia 16 (1980) 44-45. MALBON, E. S., "Mythic Structure and Meaning in Mark" Semeia 16 (1980) 109-13.

1:2-15 CLÉVENOT, M., So kennen wir die Bibel nicht (München 1978) 84-89. PESCH, R., "Anfang des Evangeliums Jesu Christi" in: G. Bornkamm/K. Rahner (eds.) Die Zeit Jesu (1970) 108-44; and in: R. Pesch (ed.) Das Markus-Evangelium (Darmstadt 1979) 317.

1:2-13 YATES, J. E., The Spirit and the Kingdom (London 1963) 22-46.

1:2-11 KONINGS, J., "The Pre-Markan Sequence in Jn.6" in: M. Sabbe (ed.) L'Evangile selon Marc (Gembloux 1974) 172. BÖCHER, O., "Johannes der Täufer in der neutestamentlichen Überlieferung" in: G. Müller (ed.) Rechtfertigung Realismus Universalismus in Biblischer Sicht. Für A. Köberle (Darmstadt 1978) 45-52.

1:2-8 BIEDER, W., Die Verheissung der Taufe im Neuen Testament (Zürich 1966) 34-41. *MARCONCINI, B., "La predicazione del Battista in Marco e Luca confrontata con la redazione di Matteo" RivB 20 (1972) 451-66. VIA, D. O., Kerygma and Comedy in the New Testament (Philadelphia 1975) 118, 121, 126, 144. PESCH, R., "Anfang des Evangeliums Jesu Christi" in: G. Bornkamm/K. Rahner (eds.) Die Zeit Jesu (1970) 108-44; and in: R. Pesch (ed.) Das Markus-Evangelium (Darmstadt 1979) 317-24.

1:2-6 SUHL, A. Die Funktion der alttestamentlichen Zitate und Anspielungen im Markusevangelium (1965) 133ff. *BOISMARD, M.-E. "Evangile des Ebionites et problème synoptique (Mc, I, 2-6 et par.)" RB 73 (3, '66) 321-52. *NEIRYNCK, F. "Une nouvelle théorie synoptique (Apropos de Mc., I,2-6 et par). Notes critiques," EphT 44 (1, '68) 141-53.

1:2-3 STONEHOUSE, N. B. The Witness of Matthew and Mark to Christ (1944) 8f, 15. HOOKER, M. D., Jesus and the Servant (London 1959) 65-67. STRECKER, G. Der Weg der Gerechtigkeit (1962) 63. HAHN, F. Christologische Hoheitstitel (1963) 73. MAUSER, U. Christ in the Wilderness (1963) 80ff. YATES, J. E., The Spirit and the Kingdom (London 1963) 45f, 235f. SCHREIBER J. Theologie des Vertrauens (1967) 42, 193f, 195. NEIRYNCK, F., "Urmarcus Redivivus?" in: M. Sabbe (ed.) L'Evangile selon Marc (Gembloux 1974) 105-18. REIM, G., Studien zum Alttestamentlichen Hintergrund des Johannesevangeliums (Cambridge 1974) 4-6. MEYER, B. F., The Aims of Jesus (London 1979) 117. PESCH, R., "Anfang des Evangeliums Jesu Christi" in: G. Bornkamm/K. Rahner (eds.) Die Zeit Jesu (1970) 108-44; and in: R. Pesch (ed.) Das Markus-Evangelium (Darmstadt 1979) 318-20, 338f.

1:2 BOUSSET, W., Die Religion des Judentums im Späthellenistischen Zeitalter (Berlin 1966=1926) 232. SIMPSON, R. T., "The Major Agreements of Matthew and Luke against Mark" NTS 12 (1965-1966) 276f. PESCH, R. Naherwartungen (1969) 54, 57, 58, 60, 68, 70, 86, 110, 173. SCHILLEBEECKX, E., Die Auferstehung Jesu als Grund der Erlösung (Basel 1979) 79. BACHMANN, M., "Johannes der Täufer bei Lukas: Nachzügler oder Vorläufer?" in: W. Haubeck/M. Bachmann (eds.) Wort in der Zeit. Für K. H. Rengstorf (Leiden 1980) 128f.

1:3-4 PARKER, P. The Gospel Before Mark (1953) 175-76. *ORTEGA, A. "Nueva vision de Marcos I, 3-4" Salmanticensis 9 (3, '62) 599-607.

1:3 *GAROFALO, S. " 'Preparare la strada al Signore' " RevBi 6 (2, '58) 131-34. BRAUN, H., Qumran und NT II (Tübingen 1966) 314.

1:4-8 KLOSTERMANN, E. Das Markusevangelium (1950) 5f. SCHMID, J. Das Evangelium nach Markus (1958) 23f. MAUSER, U. Christ in the Wilderness (1963) 82ff. MASSAUX, E. Influence de l'Evangile de saint Matthieu sur la littérature chrétienne avant saint Irénée (1950) 348-50. TALBERT, C. H., Literary Patterns, Theological Themes, and the Genre of Luke-Acts (Missoula 1974) 117.

1:4-5 RUDOLPH, K., Die Mandäer I (Göttingen 1960) 62, 73, 230.
BRAUMANN, G., Vorpaulinische christliche
Taufverkündigung bei Paulus (Stuttgart 1962) 30f, 39f, 49.
EGGER, W., Frohbotschaft und Lehre (Frankfurt 1976) 42f,
103. PESCH, R., "Anfang des Evangeliums Jesu Christi" in: G.
Bornkamm/K. Rahner (eds.) Die Zeit Jesu (1970) 108-44; and
in: R. Pesch (ed.) Das Markus-Evangelium (Darmstadt 1979)
320-21. *TREVIJANO ETCHEVERRIA, R. "La tradicion
sobre el Bautista en Mc. 1, 4-5 y par" Burgense 12 ('71) 9-39.

1:4 DELLING, G. Die Zueignung des Heils in der Taufe (1961) 71.
RUDOLPH, D., Die Mandäer II (Göttingen 1961) 406².
WAGNER, G., Das Religionsgeschichtliche Problem von
Römer 6:1-11 (Zürich 1962) 65f. STRECKER, G. Der Weg der
Gerechtigkeit (1962) 227f. KAESEMANN, E. Exegetische
Versuche und Besinnungen (1964) I 45. HAHN, F. Das
Verständnis der Mission im Neuen Testament (1965) 35, 114.
Jüngel, E. Paulus und Jesus (1966) 175. SCHüTZ, R. Johannes
der Täufer (1967). MARXSEN, W. Mark the Evangelist (1969)
35ff, 45ff, 48ff, 59f. DUNN, J. D. G. Baptism in the Holy Spirit
(1970) 9, 15-17. O'NEILL, J. C., The Theology of Acts in its
Historical Setting (London 1970) 151-52. CONZELMANN, H.
and LINDEMANN, A., Arbeitsbuch zum Neuen Testament
(Tübingen 1975) 28f. *ELLIOTT, J. K., "*Ho baptizon* and
Mark 1:4" ThZ 31 (1975) 14-15. GOPPELT, L., Theologie des
Neuen Testaments I (Göttingen 1975) 87f, 128. "Abendmahl"
in: TRE 1 (1977) 52. METZGER, B. M., The Early Versions of
the New Testament (Oxford 1977) 434. MEYER, B. F., The
Aims of Jesus (London 1979) 119. MUELLER, T., "An
Application of Case Grammar to two New Testament
Passages" Concordia Theology Quarterly 43 (1979) 320-25.
CLARK, K. W., "The Making of the Twentieth Century New
Testament" in: The Gentile Bias and other Essays (Leiden 1980)
149.

1:5 KNOX, W. L. The Sources of the Synoptic Gospels. Vol. 2: St.
Luke & St. Matthew (1957) 5. DELLING, G. Die Zueignung
des Heils in der Taufe (1961) 75. DELLING, G. Die Taufe im
Neuen Testament (1963) 43, 45. LEHMANN, E. "Communal
Worship in the New Testament and Contemporary Rabbinic
Literature" Studia Evangelica III, ed. F. L. Cross (1964) 246-
49. HAHN, F. Das Verständnis der Mission im Neuen
Testament (1965) 96. KONINGS, J., "The Pre-Markan
Sequence in Jn.6" in: M. Sabbe (ed.) L'Evangile selon Marc
(Gembloux 1974) 172. EGGER, W., Frohbotschaft und Lehre
(Frankfurt 1976) 82. HARRINGTON, D. J., God's People in
Christ (Philadelphia 1980) 22-23.

1:6-8 BRAUN, H. Qumran und NT II (Tübingen 1966) 3, 9, 14, 17, 70.

1:6 DELLING, G. Die Taufe im Neuen Testament (1963) 47. HAHN, F. Christologische Hoheitstitel (1963) 371. VIELHAUER, Ph. "Tracht und Speise Johannes des Täufers" Aufsätze zum Neuen Testament (1965) 47-54. MEYER, B. F., The Aims of Jesus (London 1979) 115. PESCH, R., "Anfang des Evangeliums Jesu Christi" in: G. Bornkamm/ K. Rahner (eds.) Die Zeit Jesu (1970) 108-44; and in: R. Pesch (ed.) Das Markus-Evangelium (Darmstadt 1979) 321-22. BACHMANN, M., "Johannes der Täufer bei Lukas: Nachzügler oder Vorläufer?" in W. Haubeck/ M. Bachmann (eds.) Wort in der Zeit. Für K. H. Rengstorf (Leiden 1980) 129-30.

1:7-8 ROBINSON, J. M. Das Geschichtsverständnis des Markus-Evangeliums (1956) 18ff. KNOX, W. L. The Sources of the Synoptic Gospels Vol. 2: St. Luke & St. Matthew (1957) 5. LENTZEN-DEIS, F. Die Taufe Jesu nach den Synoptikern (1970) 89. BEUTLER, J., Martyria (Frankfurt 1972) 285f. HOFFMANN, P., Studien zur Theologie der Logienquelle (Münster 1972) 19-22. LANG, F., "Erwägungen zur eschatologische Verkündigung Johannes des Täfers" in: G. Strecker (ed.) Jesus Christus in Historie und Theologie. Für H. Conzelmann (Tübingen 1975) 461, 466. EDWARDS, R. A., A Theology of Q (Philadelphia 1976) 81-82. SANDMEL, S., We Jews and Jesus (New York 1977) 120. RAYAN, S., The Holy Spirit: Heart of the Gospel and Christian Hope (New York 1978) 1f. PESCH, R., "Anfang des Evangeliums Jesu Christi" in: G. Bornkamm/K. Rahner (eds.) Die Zeit Jesu (1970) 108-44; and in: R. Pesch (ed.) Das Markus-Evangelium (Darmstadt 1979) 322-23. McDONALD, J. I. H., Kerygma and Didache (Cambridge 1980) 17.

1:7 SCHLATTER, A. Johannes der Täufer (1956) 103ff. *WEEKS, W. R. "Mark i.7" ET 73 (2, '61) 54. HAHN, F. Christologische Hoheitstitel (1963) 393. YATES, J. E., The Spirit and the Kingdom (London 1963) 31ff. CULLMANN, O. "He who comes after me" in Vorträge und Aufsätze e. K. Fröhlich (1966) 169-75. GOPPELT, L., Theologie des Neuen Testaments I (Göttingen 1975) 90f. PESCH, R., "Anfang des Evangeliums Jesu Christi" in: G. Bornkamm/K. Rahner (eds.) Die Zeit Jesu (1970) 108-44; and in: R. Pesch (ed.) Das Markus-Evangelium (Darmstadt 1979) 340.

1:8 BARTH, M., Die Taufe -ein Sakrament? (Zürich 1951) 20-37, 98-100. *BOTHA, F. J. "ἐβάπτισα in Mark I, 8" ET 69/9 (1953) 286. TAYLOR, V. The Gospel according to St. Mark (1953)

157f. *YATES, J. E. "The Form of Mark i.8b 'I baptized you with water; he will baptize you with the Holy Spirit'" NTS 4 (4, '58) 334-38. DELLING, G. Die Taufe im Neuen Testament (1963) 46. YATES, J. E., The Spirit and the Kingdom (London 1963) 9f, 20ff, 129f, 219f. SIMPSON, R. T., "The Major Agreements of Matthew and Luke against Mark" NTS 12 (1965-1966) 277f. DUNN, J. D. G. Baptism in the Holy Spirit (1970) 8-14.18-21). *DUNN, J. D. G. "Spirit-and-Fire Baptism" Nov Test 14 (2, '72) 81-92. LADD, G. E., A Theology of the New Testament (Grand Rapids 1974) 36, 287, 344. LOHSE, E., Grundriss der neutestamentlichen Theologie (Stuttgart 1974) 22f. METZGER, B. M., The Early Versions of the New Testament (Oxford 1977) 178, 245.

1:9-15 TRAUB, H. GPM 11/1 43-47. FUCHS, E. GPM 19 (1964) 63-68. FUCHS, E. GPM (1964/5) 63ff. NAUCK, W. Hören und Fragen, eds. G. Eichholz & A. Falkenroth. Bd. 5. Evangelienreihe 3 (1967) 99ff. ESSER, H. H. GPM 25 (1970) 81-89. ADLOFF, K., in: GPM 31 (1976-1977) 70-80. PESCH, R., "Anfang des Evangeliums Jesu Christi" in: G. Bornkamm/K. Rahner (eds.) Die Zeit Jesu (1970) 108-44; and in R. Pesch (ed.) Das Markus-Evangelium (Darmstadt 1979) 316-17, 324.

-13 ZIMMERMANN, W. D. Markus über Jesus (1970) 16-20. PESCH, R., Das Markusevangelium I (Freiburg 1976) 98-100 (lit!)

1:9-11 BÜCHSEL, D. F., Der Geist im Neuen Testament (Gütersloh 1926) 161-65. SCHNIEWIND, J. Das Evangelium nach Markus (1949) 46. KLOSTERMANN, E. Das Markusevangelium (1950) 7f. MASSAUX, E. Influence de l'Evangile de saint Matthieu sur la littérature chrétienne avant saint Irénée (1950) 350-52. FARRER, A. A. Study in St. Mark (1951) 155ff, 321ff. BARTH, M., Die Taufe - ein Sakrament? (Zürich 1951) 59-101. TAYLOR, V. The Gospel According to St. Mark (1953) 617-19. FARRER, A. St. Matthew and St. Mark (1954) 8. *CRANFIELD, C. E. B. "The Baptism of our Lord - A Study of St. Mark 1, 9-11" SJTh 8 ('55) 53-63. DENNEY, J. The Death of Christ (1956) 18f. *BUSE, I. "The Markan Account of the Baptism of Jesus and Isaiah LXIII" JThS 7 ('56) 74-75. ROBINSON, J. M. Das Geschichtsverständnis des Markus-Evangeliums (1956) 20ff. RAWLINSON, A. E. J. St. Mark (1956=1925) 251-56. *FEUILLET, A. "Le Baptême de Jésus d'après l'Evangile selon Saint Marc (1, 9-11)" CBQ 21 (4, '59) 468-90. GRUNDMANN, W. Das Evangelium nach Markus (1959) 32-34. *LEGAULT, A. "Le baptême de Jésus et la doctrine du Serviteur souffrant"

SciEccl 13 (2, '61) 147-66. MAUSER, U. Christ in the Wilderness (1963) 90ff, 143. WREDE, W. Das Messiasgeheimnis in den Evangelien (1963) 71-73. DELLING, G. Die Taufe im Neuen Testament (1963) 150. HAHN, F. Christologische Hoheitstitel (1963) 301f, 340-46, 396. BULTMANN, R., The History of the Synoptic Tradition (Oxford 1963) 247-53. *FEUILLET, A. "Le Baptême de Jésus" RB 71 (3, '64) 321-52. SUHL, A. Die Funktion der alttestamentlichen Zitate und Anspielungen im Markusevangelium (1965) 97ff. DIGNATH, W./WIBBING, S. Taufe-Versuchung-Verklärung (1966) 12-32. BIEDER, W., Die Verheissung der Taufe im Neuen Testament (Zürich 1966) 81-84. BAUHAUER, O. (ed.) Entmythologisierung des Evangeliums (1968) 9-21. BEST, E. "The Commentators and the Gospels" ET 79 ('68) 260-64. *ZELLER, D. "Jesu Taufe - ein literarischer Zugang zu Markus 1, 9-11" BuK 23 (3, '68) 90-94. MARXSEN, W. Mark the Evangelist (1969) 31, 33, 38. LINDSEY, R. L. A Hebrew Translation of the Gospel of Mark (1970) 61. DUNN, J. D. G. Baptism in the Holy Spirit (1970) 26f, 29f, 34f. VOEGTLE, A. Das Evangelium und die Evangelien (1971) 314-17. JEREMIAS, J. Neutestamentliche Theologie I. (1971) 58f. WEINACHT, H. Die Menschwerdung des Sohnes Gottes im Markusevangelium (1972) 46-53. *LENTZEN-DEIS, Die Taufe Jesu nach den Synoptikern CBQ 34 (2, '72) 227-29. (Review). *Reviews ad:* LENTZEN-DEIS, F., Die Taufe Jesu: C. J. A. Hickling, HeyJ 13 (1972) 459-62; B. Piepiorka, ZKTh 94 ('72) 320-23. VÖGTLE, A., "Die sogenannte Taufperikope Mk. 1:9-11" in: Evangelisch-Katholischer Kommentar zum N. T. Vorarbeiten Heft 4 (Zürich 1972). HARTMAN, L., "Dop, ande och barnaskap. Några traditionshistoriska överväganden till Mk 1:9-11 par" SEA 37-38 (1972- 1973) 88-106. *RICHTER, G., "Zu den Tauferzählungen Mk 1:9-11 und Jn 1:32-34" ZNW 65 (1974) 43-56. *RIQUELME, J., 'Significación del Bautismo de Jesús" Teología y Vida 15 (1974) 115-39. TALBERT, C. H., Literary Patterns, Theological Themes, and the Genre of Luke-Acts (Missoula 1974) 18, 116, 117. *WENTHE, D. O., "The Historical-Critical Interpretation of the Baptism of Jesus from the Perspective of Traditional Lutheran Exegesis" Springfielder 37 (1974) 230-40. ACHTEMEIER, P. J., Mark (Philadelphia 1975) 35-44. DUNN, J. D. G., Jesus and the Spirit (London 1975) 27, 62-66. GOPPELT, L., Theologie des Neuen Testaments I (Göttingen 1975) 92f. HARTMAN, L., "Taufe, Geist und Sohnschaft. Traditionsgeschichtliche Erwägungen zu Mk 1: 9-11 par." in: A. Fuchs (ed.) Jesus in der Verkündigung der Kirche (Freistadt 1976) 89-109.

*LÉGASSE, S., "Le Baptême de Jésus et le Baptême chrétien" SBFLA 27 (1977) 51-68. *POPPI, A., L'inizio del Vangelo. Predicazione del Battista (Padua 1976). *Recension:* G. Giavini, ScuolCatt 105 (1977) 478-86. GNILKA, J., Das Evangelium nach Markus I (Einsiedeln/Neukirchen 1978) 49 (lit!). *FEUILLET, A., "Vocation et mission des prophètes, Baptême et mission de Je½sus. Etude de christologie biblique" NV 54 (1979) 22-40. SCHMITHALS, W., Das Evangelium nach Markus (Gütersloh/Würzburg 1979) 82 (lit!). "Berufung" in: TRE 5 (1980) 684.

1:9   SCHMID, J. Das Evangelium nach Markus (1958) 28-31. STRECKER G. Der Weg der Gerechtigkeit (1962) 90. SCHREIBER, J. Theologie des Vertrauens (1967) 120f, 125f, 150, 155, 159, 175. LINTON, O., "Evidence of a Revised Edition of St. Mark's Gospel" NTS 14 (1967-1968) 322f. MARXSEN, W. Mark the Evangelist (1969) 50f, 58, 62. PETZKE, G., Die Traditionen über Apollonius von Tyana und das Neue Testament (Leiden 1970) 91, 164. CONZELMANN, H. and LINDEMANN, A., Arbeitsbuch zum Neuen Testament (Tübingen 1975) 17. MALBON, E. S., "Mythic Structure and Meaning in Mark" Semeia 16 (1980) 103-107.

1:10-11   DELLING, G. Die Taufe im Neuen Testament (1963) 55f. VOEGTLE, A. Das Evangelium und die Evangelien (1971) 335-436). BERTRAND, D. A., Le Baptême de Jésus (Tübingen 1973) 7, 8, 13, 45, 111, 112, 125.

0   GILMORE, A., Christian Baptism (London 1959) 88f. YATES, J. E., The Spirit and the Kingdom (London 1963) 33f, 59f, 98f, 162f. KOEHLER, L. "Eine Handvoll Neues Testament" in: Schweitzer, A. Ehrfurcht vor dem Leben (1964) 71-81. *DE COCK, J. "Het symbolisme van de duif bij het doopsel van Christus" Bijdragen 21 (4, '60) 363-76. *LENTZEN-DEIS, F. "Das Motiv der 'Himmelsöffnung' in verschiedenen Gattungen der Umweltliteratur des Neuen Testaments" Biblica 50 (3, '69) 301-27. LENTZEN-DEIS, F. Die Taufe Jesu nach den Synoptikern (1970) 102f, 108, 127, 131, 280, 281. *KECK, L. E. "The Spirit and the Dove" NTS 17 (1, '70) 41-67. KLIJN, A. F. J. and REININK, G. J., Patristic Evidence for Jewish-Christian Sects (Leiden 1973) 9. *TOSATO, A., "Il battesimo di Gesù e alcuni passi trascurati dello Pseudo-Filone" Biblica 56 (1975) 405-409. *GERO, S., "The Spirit as a dove at the Baptism of Jesus" NovT 18 (1976) 17-35. METZGER, B. M., The Early Versions of the New

Testament (Oxford 1977) 173. SWIDLER, L., Biblical Affirmations of Woman (Philadelphia 1979) 60.

1:11 STONEHOUSE, N. B. The Witness of Matthew and Mark to Christ (1944) 13, 16ff. MANSON, W., Jesus the Messiah (Philadelphia 1948) 110. SCHNIEWIND, J. Das Evangelium nach Markus (1949) 46-48. KLOSTERMANN, E. Das Markusevangelium (1950) 9-11. CULLMANN, O. Die Christologie des Neuen Testaments (1957) 65ff. TAYLOR, V., "The Origin of the Markan Passion-Sayings" NTS 1 (1954-1955) 163ff. HOOKER, M. D., Jesus and the Servant (London 1959) 68-73. SCHMID, J., Das Evangelium nach Markus (1958) 17-20. BLAIR, E. P. Jesus in the Gospel of Matthew (1960) 60, 64. LINDARS, B. New Testament Apologetic (1961) 139. LÖVESTAM, E., Son and Saviour (Lund 1961) 91, 94ff, 104. KILPATRICK, G. D. "The Order of Some Noun and Adjective Phrases in the New Testament" in: Donum Gratulatorium, FS. E. Stauffer (1962) 111-14. SCHWEIZER, E. Erniedrigung und Erhöhung bei Jesus und seinen Nachfolgern (1962)§5c. HAHN, F. Christologische Hoheitstitel (1963) 281-307. *BONNARD, P. E. "Trois lectures du psaume 2" BVieC 53 ('63) 37-44. HENNECKE, E., and SCHNEEMELCHER, W., Neutestamentliche Apokryphen I (Tübingen 1964) 103. BRAUN, H., Qumran und NT II (Tübingen 1966) 10, 17, 25, 57, 189, 255, 315. JEREMIAS, J. Abba (1966) 192-94. NICKELS, P. Targum and New Testament (1967) 23. STROBEL, A. Erkenntnis und Bekenntnis der Sünde in neutestamentlicher Zeit (1968) 38. *BRETSCHER, P. G. "Exodus 4:22-23 and the Voice from Heaven" JBL 87 (3, '68) 301-311. GABOURY, A., "Deux fils uniques Isaac et Jésus" in: Studia Evangelica IV (1968) 198-204. *MARSHALL, I. H. "Son of God or Servant of Yahweh? -A Reconsideration of Mark 1.11" NTS 15 (3, '69) 326-36. JEREMIAS, J. Neutestamentliche Theologie I (1971) 59-61. KECK, L. E., "The Spirit and the Dove" NTS 17 (1970-1971) 58ff. DORMEYER, D., Die Passion Jesu als Verhaltensmodell (Münster 1974) 164, 606. KONINGS, J., "The Pre-Markan Sequence in Jn 6" in: M. Sabbe (ed.) L'Évangile selon Marc (Gembloux 1974) 173. DUNN, J. D. G., Jesus and the Spirit (London 1975) 27, 63, 366, 371, 378. MÜLLER, U. B., "Die griechische Esra-Apokalypse" in: W. G. Kümmel (ed.) Jüdische Schriften aus hellenistisch-römischer Zeit V (Gütersloh 1976) 96. MICHEL, O., "Das Licht des Messias" in: E. Bammel et al.

(eds.) Donum Gentilicium. In honour of D. Daube (Oxford 1978) 40-50. PESCH, R., "Anfang des Evangeliums Jesu Christi" in: G. Bornkamm/K. Rahner (eds.) Die Zeit Jesu (1970) 108-44; and in: R. Pesch (ed.) Das Markus-Evangelium (Darmstadt 1979) 340. MALBON, E. S., "Mythic Structure and Meaning in Mark" Semeia 16 (1980) 109-13.

1:12-13   LIGHTFOOT, R. H. History and Interpretation in the Gospels (1934) 65f. STONEHOUSE, N. B. The Witness of Matthew and Mark to Christ (1944) 21f. BARRETT, C. K., The Holy Spirit and the Gospel Tradition (New York 1947) 46-53. MASSAUX, E. Influence de l'Evangile de saint Matthieu sur la littérature chrétienne avant saint Irénée (1950) 543-45. FARRER, A. A Study in St. Mark (1951) 59ff, 66f, 155ff, 280ff. LEIVESTAD, R., Christ the Conqueror (London 1954) 54ff. ROBINSON, J. M. Das Geschichtsverständnis des Markus-Evangeliums (1956) 25ff. DENNEY, J. The Death of Christ (1956) 20. DUPONT, J., "L'Arriere-fond Biblique du Recit des Tentations de Je⅛sus" NTS 3 (1956-1957) 287f. GILS, F., Jésus Prophète D'Apres Les Evangiles Synoptiques (Louvain 1957) 83-85. *FEUILLET, A. "L'épisode de la Tentation d'après l'Evangile selon Saint Marc (I, 12-13)" EstBi 19 (1, '60) 49-73. SCHWEIZER, E. Erniedrigung und Erhöhung bei Jesus und seinen Nachfolgern (1962) §4d. BULTMANN, R., The History of the Synoptic Tradition (Oxford 1963) 253f. JEREMIAS, J. "Nachwort zum Artikel von H.-G. Leder" ZNW 54 (3-4, '63) 278-279. LEDER, H.-G. "Sündenfallerzählung und Versuchungsgeschichte. Zur Interpretation von Mc 1 12f" ZNW 54 (3-4, '63) 188-216. MAUSER, U. Christ in the Wilderness (1963) 96ff, 129f, 141. HAHN, F. Christologische Hoheitstitel (1963) 239, 345f. KELLY, H. A., "The Devil in the Desert' CBQ 26 (1964) 190-220. BEST, E. The Temptation and the Passion; The Markan Soteriology (1965) 3, 4, 6, 7, 15, 26, 158f. SIMPSON, R. T., "The Major Agreements of Matthew and Luke against Mark" NTS 12 (1965-1966) 277f. MINETTE DE TILLESSE, G. Le Secret Messianique dans L'Evangile de Marc (1968) 104-111. DUPONT, J. Les Tentations de Jésus au Désert (1968) 11, 14, 35, 45, 72, 75, 80, 85-87, 91. DUPONT, J. Die Versuchungen Jesu in der Wüste (1969). MARXSEN, W. Mark the Evangelist (1969) 31ff, 38. JEREMIAS, J. Neutestamentliche Theologie I (1971) 7ff, 78f, 99. SCHNACKENBURG, R. Schriften zum Neuen Testament (1971) 101-128. *KIRK, J. A. "The Messianic Role of Jesus and the Temptation Narrative: A Contemporary Perspective" EQ 44 (1, '72) 11-29. *GONZALEZ FAUS, J. I. "Las tentaciones de Jesus y la tentacion cristiana" EstEc 47 (181, '72) 155-88.

1:12-13 *BOMBO, C. "As Tentações de Jesus nos Sinóticos" RCB 10 (1973) 83-102. *VARGAS-MACHUCA, A., "La tentación de Jesús según Mc 1:12-13. Hecho real o relato de tipo haggádico" EstEc 48 (1973) 163-90. *COLLINS, R. F., "The Temptation of Jesus" MTh 26 (1974) 32-45. KONINGS, J., "The Pre-Markan Sequence in Jn 6" in: M. Sabbe (ed.) L'Evangile selon Marc (Gembloux 1974) 172. *POKORNY, P., "The Temptation Stories and their Intention" NTS 20 (1974) 115-27. TALBERT, C. H., Literary Patterns, Theological Themes, and the Genre of Luke-Acts (Missoula 1974) 117. SANDELIN, K.-G., Die Auseinandersetzung mit der Weisheit in I Korinther 15 (Abo 1976) 106-107. FRIEDRICH, G., "Beobachtungen zur messianischen Hohepriestererwartung in den Synoptikern" in: Auf das Wort kommt es an. Gesammelte Aufsätze (Göttingen 1978) 75, 76. GNILKA, J., Das Evangelium nach Markus I (Einsiedeln/Neukirchen 1978) 55f (lit!). RIST, J. M., On the Independence of Matthew and Mark (Cambridge 1978) 22-24. CARROLL, W. D., "The Jesus of Mark's Gospel" Bible Today 103 (1979) 2105-2112. PESCH, R., "Anfang des Evangeliums Jesu Christi" in: G. Bornkamm/ K. Rahner (eds.) Die Zeit Jesu (1970) 108-44; and in: R. Pesch (ed.) Das Markus-Evangelium (Darmstadt 1979) 329-31.

1:12 MARXSEN, W. Mark the Evangelist (1969) 42, 47f.

1:13 HOLZMEISTER, P. U. " 'Jesus lebte mit den wilden Tieren' Mk 1, 13" Vom Wort des Lebens, ed. N. Adler (1951) 85-92. FARRER, A. St. Matthew and St. Mark (1954) 106, 111. *SCHULZE, W. A. Der Heilige und die wilden Tiere: Mc 1, 13b ZNW 46 (3-4, '55) 280-83. HAHN, F. Christologische Hoheitstitel (1963) 303, 345f. FASCHER, E. "Jesus und die Tiere" ThLZ 90 (8, '65) 561-70. MARXSEN, W. Mark the Evangelist (1969) 31, 38, 47. "Adam" in: TRE 1 (1977) 416. "Anfechtung" in: TRE 2 (1978) 688. "Aramäisch" in: TRE 3 (1978) 608. PESCH, R., "Anfang des Evangeliums Jesu Christi" in: G. Bornkamm/K. Rahner (eds.) Die Zeit Jesu (1970) 108-44; and in: R. Pesch (ed.) Das Markus-Evangelium (Darmstadt 1979) 340f.

1:14-8:30 *HARRINGTON, W. J., "The Gospel of Mark: A Tract for our Times" DoLi 25 (1975) 482-99.

1:14-8:26 STONEHOUSE, N. B. The Witness of Matthew and Mark to Christ (1944) 27ff. HAHN, F. Das Verständnis der Mission im Neuen Testament (1965) 96-98.

1:14-3:6   SIMPSON, P., "Reconciliation in the Making: A Reading of Mk 1:14-3:6" AfrER 17 (1975) 194-203. EGGER, W., Frohbotschaft und Lehre (Frankfurt 1976) 22, 163.

1:14-45   DRURY, J., Tradition and Design in Luke's Gospel (Atlanta 1976) 85-89.

1:14-20   ZIMMERMANN, W.-D. Markus über Jesus (1970) 21-22. *BRIÈRE, J., "Jésus agit par ses disciples" AssS 34 (1973) 32-46.

1:14-15   MANSON, W., Jesus the Messiah (Philadelphia 1948) 97-98. *ROBINSON, J. M. Das geschichtsverständnis des Markus Evangeliums (1956) 13f, 29ff, 38. *MUSSNER, F. "Die Bedeutung von Mk 1, 14f, für die Reichsgottesverkündigung TTHZ 66 (5, '57) 257-75. GRUNDMANN, W. Das Evangelium nach Markus (1959) 38f. HAHN, F. Das Versta%ndnis der Mission im Neuen Testament (1965) 61, 96. BRAUN, H., Qumran und NT II (Tübingen 1966) 87-91, 104, 127. JUENGEL, E. Paulus und Jesus (1966) 112. MUSSNER, F. "Gottesherrschaft und Sendung Jesu nach Mk 1, 14f. Zugleich ein Beitrag über die innere Struktur des Markusevangeliums" Praesentia Salutis (1967) 81. STUHLMACHER, P. Das Paulinische Evangelium (1968) 234. MINETTE DE TILLESSE, G. Le Secret Messianique dans L'Evangile de Marc (1968) 403-408, 395-96. MARXSEN, W. Mark the Evangelist (1969) 65f, 118, 125, 127, 134, 138, 146, 187f. TRILLING, W. "Die Botschaft vom Reiche Gottes" Christusverkündigung in der Synoptischen Evangelien (1969) 40. AMBROZIC, A. M., St. Mark's Concept of the Kingdom of God (Würzburg 1970) 2-27. GUETTGEMANNS, E. Offene Fragen zur Formgeschichte des Evangeliums (1970) 202, 203, 209. BOHREN, R., Predigtlehre (München 1971) 196. KELBER, W. H. "The History of the Kingdom in Mark— Aspects of Markan Eschatology" Proceeding I ed. L. C. McGaughy (1972) 63-95. STRECKER, G. "Literarische Ueberlegungen zum εὐαγγέλιον-Begriff im Markusevangelium" Neues Testament und Geschichte, H. Baltensweiler, B. Reicke (eds.) (1972) 91-104, 93-97. GOLLWITZER, H., Veränderung im Diesseits (München 1973) 28. MUSSNER, F., "Gab es eine 'galiläische Krise'?" in: P. Hoffmann (ed.) Orientierung an Jesus (Freiburg 1973) 239f, 241, 242. KELBER, W. H., The Kingdom in Mark (Philadelphia 1974) 7-12, 31n, 41, 45, 74, 94, 107, 139. KONINGS, J., "The Pre-Markan Sequence in Jn 6" in: M. Sabbe (ed.) L'Evangile selon Marc (Gembloux 1974) 172. ACHTEMEIER, P. J., Mark (Philadelphia 1975) 52, 53. CONZELMANN, H. and LINDEMANN, A., Arbeitsbuch zum Neuen Testament (Tübingen 1975) 326. GLOCKNER, R., Die

Verkündigung des Heils beim Evangelisten Lukas (Mainz 1975) 129f. BEISSER, F., Das Reich Gottes (Göttingen 1976) 64-66. EGGER, W., Frohbotschaft und Lehre (Frankfurt 1976) 28, 39, 43-64, 73, 75, 77, 83. PESCH, R., Das Markusevangelium I (Freiburgn 1976) 107f (lit!) KAHMANN, J. J. A., "Marc 1:14-15 en hun plaats in het geheel van het Marcus-evangelie" Bijdragen 38 (1977) 84-98. MIRANDA, J. P., Marx and the Bible (London 1977) 211-13. BUSSE, U., Das Nazareth-Manifest Jesu (Stuttgart 1978) 62-67. BRUCE, F. F., The Time is Fulfilled (Exeter 1978) 15-32. GNILKA, J., Das Evangelium nach Markus I (Einsiedeln/Neukirchen 1978) 64 (lit!) MARXSEN, W., Christologie praktisch (Gütersloh 1978) 42-46, 97. PESCH, R., "Anfang des Evangeliums Jesu Christi" in: G. Bornkamm/K. Rahner (eds.) Die Zeit Jesu (1970) 108-44; and in: Das Markus-Evangelium (Darmstadt 1979) 332-34, 341-42. SCMITHALS, W., Das Evangelium nach Markus (Gütersloh/Würzburg 1979) 95 (lit!) KELBER, W. H., "Mark and Oral Tradition" Semeia 16 (1980) 36. TANNEHILL, R. C., "The Gospel of Mark as Narrative Christology" Semeia 16 (1980) 64.

1:14   STONEHOUSE, N. B. The Witness of Matthew and Mark to Christ (1944) 10, 11, 14, 26, 43, 48, 129. FEINE, D. P. and BEHM, D. J., Einleitung in das Neue Testament (Heidelberg 1950) 113f. BORNKAMM-BARTH-HELD, Ueberlieferung und Auslegung im Matthäus-Evangelium (1961) 256. HAHN, F. Christologische Hoheitstitel (1963) 377, 380. DELLING, G. Die Taufe im Neuen Testament (1963) 57. POPKES, W. Christus Traditus (1967) 143ff, 181, 210, 281. MARXSEN, W. Mark the Evangelist (1969) 38ff, 123f, 127f, 132f. FENEBERG, W., Der Markusprolog (München 1974) 96, 145ff. KONINGS, J., "The Pre-Markan Sequence in Jn6" in: M. Sabbe (ed.) L'Evangile selon Marc (Gembloux 1974) 172. TALBERT, C. H., Literary Patterns, Theological Themes, and the Genre of Luke-Acts (Missoula 1974) 104. PESCH, R., "Anfang des Evangeliums Jesu Christi" in: G. Bornkamm/ K. Rahner (eds.) Die Zeit Jesu (1970) 108-144; and in: R. Pesch (ed.) Das Markus-Evangelium (Darmstadt 1979) 341. MALBON, E. S., "Mythic Structure and Meaning in Mark" Semeia 16 (1980) 103-107.

1:15-20   YATES, J. E., The Spirit and the Kingdom (London 1963) 47-51.

1:15   GUY, H. A., New Testament Prophecy (London 1947) 86f. SCHNIEWIND, J. Das Evangelium nach Markus (1949) 49-51. *BLACK, M. and HUTTON, W. R. "The Kingdom of God has come" ET 63 (9, '52) 289-90; 64 ('52) 89-91. BARRETT, C. K., The New Testament Background: Selected Documents

(London 1956) 89. SCHMID, J. Das Evangelium nach Markus
(1958) 31-39. BOSCH, D. Die Heidenmission in der
Zukunftsschau Jesu (1959) 54-57. BLAIR, E. P. Jesus in the
Gospel of Matthew (1960) 89. STRECKER, G. Der Weg der
Gerechtigkeit (1962) 86f, 89, 94, 186. MOWRY, L. "Parable"
IDB III 653b (1962). PERRIN, N., The Kingdom of God in the
Teaching of Jesus (Philadelphia 1963) 20, 48, 60, 64, 65, 66, 80,
86, 91, 92, 114, 127, 170, 199. YATES, J. E., The Spirit and the
Kingdom (London 1963) 47ff. HAHN, F. Das Verständnis der
Mission im Neuen Testament (1965) 35, 105, 114. JUENGEL,
E. Paulus und Jesus (1966) 174ff. BLACK, M. An Aramaic
Approach to the Gospels and Acts (1967) 208f. MINETTE DE
TILLESSE, G. Le Secret Messianique dans l'Evangile de Marc
(1967) 390-94. STROBEL, A. Erkenntnis und Bekenntnis der
Sünde in neutestamentlicher Zeit (1968) 39. MOULE, C. F. D.,
"Fulfilment - Words in the New Testament: Use and Abuse"
NTS 14 (1967-1968) 317f. PESCH, R. Naherwartungen (1969)
54, 57, 61, 116, 118, 131, 151, 170. MARXSEN, W. Mark the
Evangelist (1969) 59, 120, 124, 130, 132, 146. JEREMIAS, J.
Neutestamentliche Theologie I (1971) 40f, 50, 89, 100, 103, 105,
128, 159. PATSCH, H., Abendmahl und historischer Jesus
(Stuttgart 1972) 108f. *GLASSWELL, M. E., "The New
Testament View of Time" Communio Viatorum 16 (1973) 249-
55. HIERS, R. H., The Historical Jesus and the Kingdom of
God (Gainesville 1973) 13, 17, 49, 53, 50f, 68.
SCHNACKENBURG, R., " 'Das Evangelium' im Verständnis
des ältesten Evangelisten" in: P. Hoffmann (ed.) Orientierung
an Jesus (Freiburg 1973) 310f, 320f. FENEBERG, W., Der
Markusprolog (München 1974) 145f, 149, 151. GOULDER,
M. D., Midrash and Lection in Matthew (London 1974) 37,
242, 277f, 344. KELBER, W. H., The Kingdom in Mark
(Philadelphia 1974) 3n, 7-12, 14, 38, 41, 74, 90, 100, 116, 124n.
KONINGS, J., "The Pre-Markan Sequence in Jn 6" in: M.
Sabbe (ed.) L'Evangile selon Marc (Gembloux 1974) 172.
PERRIN, N., The New Testament (New York 1974) 288-290.
ACHTEMEIER, P. J., Mark (Philadelphia 1975) 49-50.
BANKS, R., Jesus and the Law in the Synoptic Tradition
(London 1975) 211f. PERRIN, N., Jesus and the Language of
the Kingdom (London 1976) 37. THEUNISSEN, M., "ὁ αἰτῶν
λαμβάνει. Der Gebetsglaube Jesu und die Zeitlichkeit des
Christseins" in: Jesus, Ort der Erfahrung Gottes (Basel 1976)
19. "Amt" in: TRE 2 (1978) 510. "Anfechtung" in: TRE 2 (1978)
704. "Apokalyptik" in: TRE 3 (1978) 253. PESCH, R. "Anfang
des Evangeliums Jesu Christi" in: G. Bornkamm/K. Rahner
(eds.) Die Zeit Jesu (1970) 108-44; and in: R. Pesch (ed.) Das
Markus-Evangelium (Darmstadt 1979) 337. SCHLOSSER, J.,

"Le règne de Dieu dans les dits de Jésus" RevSR 53 (1979) 164-76. McDONALD, J. I. H., Kerygma and Didache (Cambridge 1980) 20-21. MALBON, E. S., "Mythic Structure and Meaning in Mark" Semeia 16 (1980) 109-13.

1:16-8:26 WEEDEN, T. J., "Die Häresie, die Markus zur Abfassung seines Evangeliums veranlasst hat" in: "The Heresy that necessitated Mark's Gospel" ZNW 59 (1968) 145-58; and in: R. Pesch (ed.) Das Markus-Evangelium (Darmstadt 1979) 238-39.

1:16-3:12 FARRER, A. A Study in St. Mark (1951) 144ff. KECK, L. E., "The Introduction to Mark's Gospel" NTS 12 (1965-1966) 362f. KELBER, W. H. "The History of the Kingdom in Mk— Aspects of Markan Eschatology" Proceedings ed. L. C. McGaughy Vol. I (1972) 63-95, 63-65.

1:16-3:6 GOULDER, M. D., Type and History in Acts (London 1964) 127ff.

1:16-2:12 FARRER, A. A Study in St. Mark (1951) 61ff.

1:16-20 EWALD, H., Die drei ersten Evangelien (Göttingen 1850) 191ff. GOODSPEED, E. J., A Life of Jesus (New York 1950) 47-49. FARRER, A. A Study in St. Mark (1951) 60ff, 307f, 314f. TAYLOR, V., The Life and Ministry of Jesus (London 1954) 75f. SCHULZ, A. Nachfolgen und Nachahmen (1962) 108ff. BULTMANN, R., The History of the Synoptic Tradition (Oxford 1963) 56-57. ROLOFF, J. Apostolat-Verkündigung-Kirche (1965) 153f. SCHILLE, G. Die urchristliche Kollegialmission (1967) 26ff, 79f, 125ff, 132f. *AGNEW, F. "Vocatio primorum discipulorum in traditione synoptica" VerbDom 46 (3, '58) 129-47. WUELLNER, W. H., The Meaning of 'Fishers of Men' (Philadelphia 1967) 170f, 232f. HAENCHEN, E., "Historie und Verkündigung bei Markus und Lukas" Die Bibel und Wir (1968) 156-81. MINETTE DE TILLESSE, G. Le Secret Messianique dans L'Evangile de Marc (1968) 258-61. MEYE, R. P. Jesus and the Twelve (1968) 99-106. REPLOH, K-G. Markus-Lehrer der Gemeinde (1969) 27-35. *PESCH, R. "Berufung und Sendung, Nachfolge und Mission. Eine Studie zu Mk 1, 16-20" ZKTh 91 (1, '69) 1-31. OTOMO, Y. Nachfolge Jesu und Anfänge der Kirche im Neuen Testament (1970) 29-34, 120-22. LEHMANN, M. Synoptische Quellenanalyse und die Frage nach dem historischen Jesus (1970) 59-61. GUETTGEMANNS, E. Offene Fragen zur Formgeschichte des Evangeliums (1970) 202, 229, 246f. ITTEL, G. W. Jesus und die Jünger (1970) 14. ERNST, J., Anfänge der Christologie (Stuttgart 1972) 127-28. BEST, E., "Mark's Preservation of the Tradition" in: M. Sabbe (ed.) L'Évangile selon Marc

(Gembloux 1974) 25f. KONINGs, J., "The Pre-Markan Sequence in Jn 6" in: M. Sabbe (ed.) L'Évangile selon Marc (Gembloux 1974) 172. SCHMAHL, G., Die Zwölf im Markus-evangelium (Trier 1974) 114-16. TALBERT, C. H., Literary Patterns, Theological Themes, and the Genre of Luke-Acts (Missoula 1974) 40, 41. CONZELMANN, H. and LINDEMANN, A., Arbeitsbuch zum Neuen Testament (Tübingen 1975) 77f. VIA, D. O., Kerygma and Comedy in the New Testament (Philadelphia 1975) 83, 116, 120, 144, 145. EGGER, W., Frohbotschaft und Lehre (Frankfurt 1976) 40, 152. PESCH, R., Das Markusevangelium I (Freiburg 1976) 116 (lit!). "Amt" in: TRE 2 (1978) 510. FRIEDRICH, G., "Das Problem der Autorität im Neuen Testament" in: Auf das Wort kommt es an (Göttingen 1978) 287-88. GNILKA, J., Das Evangelium nach Markus I (Einsiedeln/Neukirchen 1978) 71 (lit!). RIST, J. M., On the Independence of Matthew and Mark (Cambridge 1978) 25-26. BEST, E., "Markus als Bewahrer der Überlieferung" in: M. Sabbe (ed.) L'Évangile selon Marc (Gembloux 1974) 21-34; and in: R. Pesch (ed.) Das Markus-Evangelium (Darmstadt 1979) 394-95. SCHMITHALS, W., Das Evangelium nach Markus (Gütersloh/Würzburg 1979) 104 (lit!). ERNST, J., "Die Petrustradition im Markusevangelium - ein altes Problem neu angegangen" in: J. Zmijewski/E. Nellessen (eds.) Begegnung mit dem Wort. Für H. Zimmermann (Bonn 1980) 36-38. TANNEHILL, R. C., "The Gospel of Mark as Narrative Christology" Semeia 16 (1980) 64-65, 69.

1:16-18 SCHULZ, A. Nachfolgen und Nachahmen (1962) 98ff. SCHWEIZER E., Erniedrigung und Erhöhung bei Jesus und seinen Nachfolgern (1962) §1c. KLEIN, G. "Die Berufung des Petrus" Rekonstruktion und Interpretation (1969) 11-48.

1:16 FARRER, A. St. Matthew and St. Mark (1954) 110. BARTINA, "La red esparavel del Evangelio (Mt 4, 18; Mc 1, 16)" EstBi 19 (3, '60) 215-27. STRECKER, G. Der Weg der Gerechtigkeit (1962) 94, 206. MARXSEN, W. Mark the Evangelist (1969) 58, 62f. THEISSEN, G., Soziologie der Jesusbewegung (München 1977) 16. DERRETT, J. D. M., " 'ΗΣΑΝ ΓΑΡ ΑΛΙΕΙΣ'. Jesus's Fisherman and the Parable of the Net" NovT 22 (1980) 108-37.

1:17 SCHMID, J. Das Evangelium nach Lukas (1955) 178-82. *MANEK, J. "Fishers of Men" NovTest 2 (2, '57) 138-41. *SMITH, C. W. F. "Fishers of Men. Footnotes on a Gospel Figure" HThR 52 (3, '59) 187-203. *WUELLNER, H, The Meaning of "Fishers of Men" (1967). *WUELLNER, H, The Meaning of "Fishers of Men" Rev.: J. Roloff LW 15 (3, '68)

252; LW 18 (3, '68) 311-12. JEREMIAS, J, Neutestamentliche Theologie I (1971) 91, 133, 157, 166, 227. "Amt" in: TRE 2 (1978) 511. "Aramäisch" in: TRE 3 (1978) 609. *MacLAURIN, E. C. B., "The Divine Fisherman" St. Mark's Review 94 (1978) 26-28.

1:19-20 SCHULZ, A. Nachfolgen und Nachahmen (1962) 98ff, 100f.

1:20 FARRER, A. St. Matthew and St Mark (1954) 195, 197. SCHüRMANN, H. Ursprung und Gestalt (1970) 51, 52, 53, 133, 270. SMITH, M., Tannaitic Parallels to the Gospels (Philadelphia 1968) 3bn36+. THEISSEN, G., Soziologie der Jesusbewegung (München 1977) 17.

1:21ff PETZKE, G., Die Traditionen über Apollonius von Tyana und das Neue Testament (Leiden 1970) 77, 168, 170, 175, 180, 190. SMITH, M., Clement of Alexandria and a secret Gospel of Mark (Cambridge, Mass. 1973) 110, 219, 224f, 235.

1:21-3:6 KOCH, D-A., Die Bedeutung der Wundererzählungen für die Christologie des Markusevangeliums (Berlin/New York 1975) 53-55.

1:21-45 EWALD, H., Die drei ersten Evangelien (Göttingen 1850) 193ff. *DIDEBERG, D. and BEERNAERT, P. M., " 'Jésus vint en Galilée.' Essai sur la structure de Marc 1:21-45" NRTh 98 (1976) 306-23.

1:21-39 BORNKAMM-BARTH-HELD Ueberlieferung und Auslegung im Matthäus-Evangelium (1961) 161, 177, 234. *PESCH, R. "Ein Tag vollmächtigen Wirkens Jesu in Kapharnaum (Mk 1, 21-34.35-39) BuL 9 (2, '68) 114-28. (3, '68) 177-95. (4, '68) 261-77. SMITH, M., Tannaitic Parallels to the Gospels (Philadelphia 1968) 5bn38+. NEIRYNCK, F., "Urmarcus redivivus?" in: M. Sabbe (ed.) L'Evangile selon Marc (Gembloux 1974) 132. EGGER, W., Frohbotschaft und Lehre (Frankfurt 1976) 40-42. ERNST, J., "Die Petrustradition im Markusevangelium - ein altes Problem neu angegangen" in: J. Zmijewski/E. Nellessen (eds.) Begegnung mit dem Wort. Für H. Zimmermann (Bonn 1980) 38-44.

1:21-38 KONINGS, J., "The Pre-Markan Sequence in Jn 6" in: M. Sabbe (ed.) L'Evangile selon Marc (Gembloux 1974) 172.

1:21-34 GOODSPEED, E. J., A Life of Jesus (New York 1950) 51-53. SCHRAMM, T. Der Markus-Stoff bei Lukas (1971) 85-91. TALBERT, C. H., Literary Patterns, Theological Themes, and the Genre of Luke-Acts (Missoula 1974) 41. VIA, D. O., Kerygma and Comedy in the New Testament (Philadelphia 1975) 83, 116, 118, 119, 131, 133, 135, 144. PESCH, R., Das Markusevangelium I (Freiburg 1976) 117 (lit!).

1:21-31 EGGER, W., Frohbotschaft und Lehre (Frankfurt 1976) 65. SWIDLER, L., Biblical Affirmations of Woman (Philadelphia 1979) 225, 226.

1:21-29 WEISS, B., "Ein Tag in Kapernaum" in: A.Deissmann/H. Windisch (eds.) Neutestamentliche Studien. Georg Heinrici-zu seinem 70. Geburtstag (Leipzig 1914) 101-107. TAYLOR, V., The Life and Ministry of Jesus (London 1954) 84f.

1:21-28 LIGHTFOOT, R. H. History and Interpretation in the Gospels (1934) 68f, 186f. BAUERNFEIND, O. Die Worte der Dämonen im Markusevangelium (1927) 3-18, 29-34. KLOSTERMANN, E. Das Markusevangelium (1950) 14-17. FARRER, A. A Study in St. Mark (1951) 63ff, 84ff. BUTLER, B. C., The Originality of St. Matthew (Cambridge 1951) 124ff. GRUNDMANN, W. Das Evangelium nach Markus (1959) 44f. BORNKAMM-BARTH-HELD, Ueberlieferung und Auslegung im Matthäus-Evangelium (1961) 29, 85, 164. BULTMANN, R., The History of the Synoptic Tradition (Oxford 1963) 209f. YATES, J. E., The Spirit and the Kingdom (London 1963) 51-54. KEE, H. W., "The Terminology of Mark's Exorcism Stories" NTS 14 (1967-1968) 241f. *BRIÈRE, J., "Le cri et le secret. Signification d'un exorcisme" AssS 35 (1973) 34-46. *NIELSEN, H. K., "Et bidrag til vurderingen af traditionen om Jesu helbredelsesvirksomhed" DTT 36 (1973) 269-300. SCHENKE, L., Die Wundererzählungen des Markusevangeliums (Stuttgart 1974) 95-108. BARTLETT, D. L., Fact and Faith (Valley Forge 1975) 35-36, 42-43. CONZELMANN, H. and LINDEMANN, A., Arbeitsbuch zum Neuen Testament (Tübingen 1975) 42-48, 68, 75. KOCH, D-A., Die Bedeutung der Wundererzählungen für die Christologie des Markusevangeliums (Berlin/New York 1975) 43-46, 52-55. Von der OSTEN-SACKEN, P. "Streitgespräch und Parabel als Formen markinischer Christologie" in: G. Strecker (ed.) Jesus Christus in Historie und Theologie. Für H. Conzelmann (Tübingen 1975) 376-80. *de BURGOS NUNEZ, M., "La enseñanza liberadora de Jesús desde la Sinagoga. Ensayo de semiótica narrativa en Marcos 1:21-28" Communio 9 (1976) 201-19. PESCH, R., Das Markusevangelium I (Freiburg 1976) 128 (lit!). GNILKA, J., Das Evangelium nach Markus I (Einsiedeln/Neukirchen 1978) 76 (lit!). RIST, J. M., On the Independence of Matthew and Mark (Cambridge 1978) 26-28. RIVKIN, E., A Hidden Revolution (Nashville 1978) 105. SEYBOLD, K, and MÜLLER, U., Krankheit und Heilung (Stuttgart 1978) 111. MEYER, B. F., The Aims of Jesus (London 1979) 162-68. SCHMITHALS, W., Das Evangelium nach Markus

(Gütersloh/Würzburg 1979) 116 (lit!). STRECKER, G., "Zur Messiasgeheimnistheorie im Markusevangelium" Studia Evangelica 3 (1964) 87-104; and in: R. Pesch (ed.) Das Markus-Evangelium (Darmstadt 1979) 192-93. ERNST, J., "Die Petrustradition im Markusevangelium - ein altes Problem neu angegangen" in: J. Zmijewski/E. Nellessen (eds.) Begegnung mit dem Wort. Für H. Zimmermann (Bonn 1980) 38-39. GUILLEMETTE, P., "Un Enseignement Nouveau, Plein d'Autorité" NovT 22 (1980) 222-47. TANNEHILL, R. C., "The Gospel of Mark as Narrative Christology" Semeia 16 (1980) 65. KERTELGE, K. Die Wunder Jesu im Markus-Evangelium (1970) 50-60. ZIMMERMANN, W.-D. Markus über Jesus (1970) 23-24.

1:21-22   HARTMANN, L., Testimonium Linguae (Lund 1963) 26. KOCH, D-A., Die Bedeutung der Wundererzählungen für die Christologie des Markus-evangeliums (Berlin/New York 1975) 43f. EGGER, W., Frohbotschaft und Lehre (Frankfurt 1976) 28, 146-49.

1:21f   HAHN, F. Christologische Hoheitstitel (1963) 230. GüTTGEMANNS, E. Offene Fragen zur Formgeschichte des Evangeliums (1970) 202, 214, 207, 229. *STEIN, R. H. "The 'Redaktionsgeschichtlich' Investigation of a Markan Seam (Mc 1: 21f)" ZNW 61 (1-2, '70) 70-94.

1:21   HENDRIKS, W., "Zur Kollektionsgeschichte des Markusevangeliums" in: M. Sabbe (ed.) L'Evangile selon Marc (Gembloux 1974) 52-53, 55. KONINGS, J., "The Pre-Markan Sequence in Jn 6" in: M. Sabbe (ed.) L'Evangile selon Marc (Gembloux 1974) 173. "Aramäisch" in: TRE 3 (1978) 608. MALBON, E. S., "Mythic Structure and Meaning in Mark" Semeia 16 (1980) 103-107.

1:22-27   MINETTE DE TILLESSE, G. Le Secret Messianique dans L'Evangile de Marc (1968) 77-83, 98.

1:22-23   SCHWEIZER, E., "Mark's Contribution to the Quest of the Historical Jesus' NTS 10 (1963-1964) 423f. BARRETT, C. K., The Holy Spirit and the Gospel Tradition (New York 1947) 79-82. KLOSTERMANN, E. Das Markusevangelium (1950) 13f. *FLOWERS H. J. "ως ἐξουσίαν ἔχων (Mk 1, 22)" ET 66 (8, '55) 254. *HUDSON, D. F. "Zu Mk 1, 22" ET 67 (1, '55) 17. BLAIR, E. P. Jesus in the Gospel of Matthew (1960) 46, 47. KAHLEFELD, H. Parables and Instructions in the Gospels (1966) 21f. *ARGYLE, A. W. "The Meaning of exousia in Mark 1:22, 27-" ET 80 (11, '69) 343. PESCH, R. Naherwartungen (1969) 57 122, 150, 189, 198. BROER, I., Die Urgemeinde und das Grab Jesu (München 1972) 129f, 153.

LANGE, J., Das Erscheinen des Auferstandenen im Evangelium nach Matthäus (Würzburg 1973) 25-28, 33f, 37, 40, 70-72, 78, 89f, 94, 100, 317, 394f, 397, 431, 491.

1:22f. SCHWEIZER, E., "Mark's Contribution to the Quest of the Historical Jesus" NTS 10 (1963-1964) 423f.

1:23-28 TAYLOR, V. The Formation of the Gospel Tradition (1949) 77, 120f. BLAIR, E. P. Jesus in the Gospel of Matthew (1960) 46. STRECKER, G. Der Weg der Gerechtigkeit (1962) 23. HAHN, F. Christologische Hoheitstitel (1963) 295f, 297, 392. BAUMBACH, G. Das Verständnis des Bösen in den Synoptischen Evangelien (1963) 42ff. MUSSNER, F. Die Wunder Jesu (1967) 45f. LEHMANN, M. Synoptische Quellenanalyse und die Frage nach dem historischen Jesus (1970) 35ff. JEREMIAS, J. Neutestamentliche Theologie I (1971) 93-96, 98. EGGER, W., Frohbotschaft und Lehre (Frankfurt 1976) 66f, 147.

1:23-27 CAVE, C. H., "The Obedience of Unclean Spirits" NTS 11 (1964-1965) 95f.

1:23-24 SEYBOLD, K, and MÜLLER, U., Krankheit und Heilung (Stuttgart 1978) 128.

1:23 HAHN, F. Christologische Hoheitstitel (1963) 299. TALBERT, C. H., Literary Patterns, Theological Themes, and the Genre of Luke-Acts (Missoula 1974) 41.

1:24-25 *TREVIJANO, R., "El trasfondo apocaliptico de Mc 1, 24, 25; 5, 7.8 y par" Burgense 11 ('70) 117-33.

1:24 TAYLOR, V. The Gospel According to St. Mark (1953) 177f. BLAIR, E. P. Jesus in the Gospel of Matthew (1960) 66. *SCHWEIZER, E. "'Er wird Nazoräer heissen'(zu Mc 1:24 Mt 2:23" Judentum, Urchristentum, Kirche (1960) 90-93, (= Neotestamentica 1963, 51-55). MUSSNER, F. "Ein Wortspiel in Mk 1:24?" BZ 4 (2, '60) 285-86. BORNKAMM-BARTH-HELD, Ueberlieferung und Auslegung im Matthäus-Evangelium (1961) 163f, 256. STRECKER, G. Der Weg der Gerechtigkeit (1962) 62, 94. HAHN, F. Christologische Hoheitstitel (1963) 235-238, 386. BRAUN, H., Qumran und NT II (Tübingen 1966) 65, 76, 79, 90, 92, 105, 107, 269, 296, 336. STROBEL, A. Erkenntnis und Bekenntnis der Sünde in Neutestamentlicher Zeit (1968) 38. BEST, E., "Mark's Preservation of the Tradition" in: M. Sabbe (ed.) L'Evangile selon Marc (Gembloux 1974) 22f. KOCH, D.-A., Die Bedeutung der Wundererzählungen für die Christologie des Markusevangeliums (Berlin/New York 1975) 57-59. ARENS, E., The HΛΘON - Sayings in the Synoptic Tradition (Fribourg 1976) 210-12, 216-21. BÄCHLI, O., "'Was habe ich mit Dir zu schaffen?' Eine formelhafte Frage im AT und NT" ThZ 33 (1977) 69-80. TRITES, A. A., The New Testament Concept of Witness (Cambridge 1977) 177. FRIEDRICH, G., "Beobachtungen zur messianischen Hohepriesterwartung in den Synoptikern" in: Auf das Wort kommt es an (Göttingen 1978) 66-69. *GUILLEMETTE, P., "Mc 1:24 est-il une formule de défense magique?" SciE 30 (1978) 81-96. BEST, E., "Markus als Bewahrer der Überlieferung" in: M. Sabbe (ed.) L'Evangile selon Marc (Gembloux 1974) 21-34; and in: R. Pesch (ed.) Das Markus-Evangelium (Darmstadt 1979) 391-92. LUZ, U., "Das Geheimnismotiv und die markinische Christologie" ZNW 56 (1965) 9-30; and in: R. Pesch (ed.) Das Markus-Evangelium (Darmstadt 1979) 218f.

1:25   SCHMID, J. Das Evangelium nach Markus (1958) 43-47. BLAIR, E. P. Jesus in the Gospel of Matthew (1960) 52. BOUSSET, W., Die Religion des Judentums im Späthellenistischen Zeitalter (Berlin 1966 = 1926) 340. BARRETT, C. K., The New Testament Background: Selected Documents (London 1956) 34. MINETTE DE TILLESSE, G. Le Secret Messianique dans l'Evangile de Marc (1968) 249-51.

1:26   JEREMIAS, J. Neutestamentliche Theologie I (1971) 97f.

1:27-32 BETZ, H. D., Lukian von Samosata und das Neue Testament (Berlin 1961) 146f, 150, 157f.

1:27   BARRETT, C. K., The Holy Spirit and the Gospel Tradition (New York 1947) 78-82. DAVIES, W. D., Torah in the Messianic Age and/ or the Age to come (Philadelphia 1952) 71. HARRISVILLE, R. A., The Concept of Newness in the New Testament (Minneapolis 1960) 24ff. BLAIR, E. P. Jesus in the Gospel of Matthew (1960) 46. KILPATRICK, G. D. "Some Problems in New Testament Text and Language" Neotestamentica et Semitica ed E. E. Ellis and M. Wilcox (1969) 198-208. YATES, J. E., The Spirit and the Kingdom (London 1963) 34f, 51f. GRÄSSER, E., "Jesus in Nazareth" NTS 16 (1969-1970) 12ff. PESCH, R. Naherwartungen (1969) 57, 59, 101, 102, 198. LANGE, J., Das Erscheinen des Auferstandenen im Evangelium nach Matthäus (Würzburg 1973) 25-27, 34, 78, 100. AMBROZIC, A., in: J. Plevnik (ed.) Word and Spirit. In honour of D. M. Stanley (Willowdale 1975). KOCH, D.-A., Die Bedeutung der Wundererzählungen für die Christologie des Markusevangeliums (Berlin/ New York 1975) 19f, 23f, 39f, 44f. EGGER, W., Frohbotschaft und Lehre (Frankfurt 1976) 148f.

1:28   BOOBYER, G. H., "The Secrecy Motif in St. Mark's Gospel" NTS 6 (1959-1960) 231f. HAHN, F. Das Verständnis der

Mission im Neuen Testament (1965) 96. FREYNE, S. The Twelve; Disciples and Apostles (1968) 73, 116. MARXSEN, W. Mark the Evangelist (1969) 60, 62, 64, 67. MUSSNER, F., "Gab es eine 'galiläische Krise'?" in: P. Hoffmann (ed.) Orientierung an Jesus (Freiburg 1973) 239f. KOCH, D.-A., Die Bedeutung der Wundererzählungen für die Christologie des Markusevangeliums (Berlin/New York 1975) 45f. MALBON, E. S., "Mythic Structure and Meaning in Mark" Semeia 16 (1980) 103-107.

1:29-6:44   CRIBBS, F. L., in: G. MacRae (ed.) SBL Seminar Papers 2 (Montana 1973) 9-12.

1:29-44   PARKER, P. The Gospel Before Mark (1953) 176-77.

1:29-39   *GAIDE, G., "De l'admiration à la foi" AssS 36 (1974) 39-48. SCHENKE, L., Die Wundererzählungen des Markusevangeliums (Stuttgart 1974) 109-29.

1:29-34   ZIMMERMANN, W.-D. Markus über Jesus (1970) 24-26.

1:29-32   KOCH, D.-A., Die Bedeutung der Wundererzählungen für die Christologie des Markusevangeliums (Berlin/New York 1975) 134-36.

1:29-31   STRECKER, G. Der Weg der Gerechtigkeit (1962) 206. PESCH, R. Neuere Exegese - Verlust oder Gewinn? (1968) 145-62. *RIGATO, M. L. "Tradizione e redazione in Mc 1:29-31 (e paralleli). La guarigione della suocera di Simon Pietro" RevBi 17 (2, '69) 139-74. KERTELGE, K. Die Wunder Jesu im Markusevangelium (1970) 60-62. ROLOFF, J. Das Kerygma und der irdische Jesus (1970) 115-17. STANTON, G. N., Jesus of Nazareth in New Testament Preaching (Cambridge 1974) 58f. CONZELMANN, H. and LINDEMANN, A., Arbeitsbuch zum Neuen Testament (Tübingen 1975) 68. EGGER, W., Frohbotschaft und Lehre (Frankfurt 1976) 67f. PESCH, R., Das Markusevangelium I (Freiburg 1976) 132 (lit!). RIST, J. M., On the Independence of Matthew and Mark (Cambridge 1978) 29. SEYBOLD, K. and MÜLLER, U., Kranheit und Heilung (Stuttgart 1978) 107-108. SWIDLER, L., Biblical Affirmations of Woman (Philadelphia 1979) 180, 184, 226, 236, 258. TANNEHILL, R. C., "The Gospel of Mark as Narrative Christology" Semeia 16 (1980) 66f.

1:30-31   TAYLOR, V. The Formation of the Gospel Tradition (1949) 120f. RENGSTORF, K. H. Das Evangelium nach Lukas (1949) 77. SCHNIEWIND, J. Das Evangelium nach Markus (1949) 83f. SCHMID J. Das Evangelium nach Markus (1958) 52-55. ACHTEMEIER, P. J., Mark (Philadelphia 1975) 16. STAGG, E. F., Woman in the World of Jesus (Philadelphia 1978) 220.

1:31 TALBERT, C. H., Literary Patterns, Theological Themes, and the Genre of Luke-Acts (Missoula 1974) 41.

1:32ff. WREDE, W., "Rückblick auf Markus" in: Das Messiasgeheimnis in den Evangelien (1901) 115-49; and in: R. Pesch (ed.) Das Markus-Evangelium (Darmstadt 1979) 33-34.

1:32-39 FISCHER, K. M. GPM 23/4 (1968/69) 362-67. STECK, K. G. GPM 17 (1963) 330/337 Erhaltet euch in der Liebe Gottes (Predigtgedanken aus Vergangenheit und Gegenwart, Reihe C, Band 3-4) (1963) 273-78. CONZELMANN, H. and LINDEMANN, A., Arbeitsbuch zum Neuen Testament (Tübingen 1975) 68f. KOCH, D.-A., Die Bedeutung der Wundererzählungen für die Christologie des Markusevangeliums (Berlin/New York 1975) 135f, 161-66, 166f, 170f.

1:32-34 KERTELGE, K. Die Wunder Jesu im Markusevangelium (1970) 31-33. GUETTGEMANNS, E. Offene Fragen zur Formgeschichte des Evangeliums (1970) 160 n. 51, 206, 123, 229, 247. LEHMANN, M. Synoptische Quellenanalyse und die Frage nach dem historischen Jesus (1970) 35f. 44. *KOWALSKI, T. W., "Les sources pré-synoptiques de Marc 1, 32-34 at paralèles" RechSR 60 (1972) 541-73. NEIRYNCK, F., "Urmarcus redivivus?" in: M. Sabbe (ed.) L'Evangile selon Marc (Gembloux 1974) 130-44. EGGER, W., Frohbotschaft und Lehre (Frankfurt 1976) 28, 64-67, 75f, 85, 108, 139, 157. PESCH, R., Das Markusevangelium I (Freiburg 1976) 136 (lit!). GNILKA, J., Das Evangelium nach Markus I (Einsiedeln/Neukirchen 1978) 85 (lit!). DIBELIUS, M., "Sammlung" in: Die Formgeschichte des Evangeliums 1919, 1933², 219-34; and in: R. Pesch (ed.) Das Markus-Evangelium (Darmstadt 1979) 73-74. LUZ, U., "Das Geheimnismotiv und die markinische Christologie" ZNW 56 (1965) 9-30; and in: R. Pesch (ed.) Das Markus-Evangelium (Darmstadt 1979) 213f. ERNST, J., "Die Petrustradition im Markusevangelium - ein altes Problem neu angegangen" in: J. Zmijewski/E. Nellessen (eds.) Begegnung mit dem Wort. Für H. Zimmermann (Bonn 1980) 41-42. TANNEHILL, R. C., "The Gospel of Mark as Narrative Christology" Semeia 16 (1980) 66f.

1:32 KNOX, W. L. The Sources of the Synoptic Gospels II (1957) 125. HARTMAN, L., Testimonium Linguae (Lund 1963) 22f. SCHREIBER, J. Theologie des Vertrauens (1967) 84f, 95, 100-102, 149, 152, 154. METZGER, B. M., The Early Versions of the New Testament (Oxford 1977) 245.

1:33-34 MUSSNER, F., "Gab es eine 'galiläische Krise'?" in: P. Hoffmann (ed.) Orientierung an Jesus (Freiburg 1973) 239f.

1:33   BORNKAMM-BARTH-HELD, Ueberlieferung und
        Auslegung im Matthäus-Evangelium (1961) 161.
        SCHREINER, J. Gestalt und Anspruch des Neuen Testaments
        (1969) 166f.

1:34   BLAIR, E. P. Jesus in the Gospel of Matthew (1960) 52, 66.
        HAHN, F. Christologische Hoheitstitel (1963) 297. WREDE,
        W. Das Messiasgeheimnis in den Evangelien (1963) 23, 31-33,
        152. FREYNE, S. The Twelve: Disciples and Apostles (1968)
        73, 140. KÜMMEL, W. G., Einleitung in das Neue Testament
        (Heidelberg 1973¹⁷) 61-63. ACHTEMEIER, P. J., Mark
        (Philadelphia 1975) 79-81.

1:35-39 SCHREIBER, J. Theologie des Vertrauens (1967) 101-103,
        211. MINETTE DE TILLESSE, G. Le Secret Messianique
        dans L'Evangile de Marc (1968) 410-20. *WICHELHAUS, M.
        "Am ersten Tag der Woche. Mk i 35-39 und die didaktischen
        Absichten des Markus-Evangelisten" NovTest 11 (1-2, '69) 45-
        66. ZIMMERMANN, W. D. Markus über Jesus (1970) 26-27.
        PESCH, R., Das Markusevangelium I (Freiburg 1976) 140
        (lit!).

1:35-38 BORSCH, F. H., "Jesus the Wandering Preacher?" in: M.
        Hooker/O. Hickling (eds.) What about the New Testament? In
        honour of C. Evans (London 1975) 48. ARENS, E., The
        HΛΘΟΝ - Sayings in the Synoptic Tradition (Fribourg 1976)
        193-209. EGGER, W., Frohbotschaft und Lehre (Frankfurt
        1976) 74f. ERNST, J., "Die Petrustradition im
        Markusevangelium - ein altes Problem neu angegangen" in: J.
        Zmijewski/E. Nellessen (eds.) Begegnung mit dem Wort. Für
        H. Zimmermann (Bonn 1980) 42-43.

1:35   MAUSER, U. Christ in the Wilderness (1963) 103ff, 128, 144,
        146. BRAUN, H., Qumran und NT II (Tübingen 1966) 106.
        SCHREIBER, J. Theologie des Vertrauens (1967) 84, 99-101,
        148f. MARXSEN, W. Mark the Evangelist (1969) 32, 61, 120.
        PESCH, R. Naherwartungen (1969) 57, 58, 123, 150, 157. VIA,
        D. O., Kerygma and Comedy in the New Testament
        (Philadelphia 1975) 133, 144, 145. *KIRCHSCHLÄGER, W.,
        "Jesu Gebetsverhalten als Paradigma zu Mk 1:35" Kairos 20
        (1978) 303-310.

1:37   METZGER, B. M., The Early Versions of the New Testament
        (Oxford 1977) 245.

1:38-39 MUSSNER, F., "Gab es eine 'galiläische Krise'?" in: P.
        Hoffmann (ed.) Orientierung an Jesu (Freiburg 1973) 239f.

1:38   SCHREIBER, J. Theologie des Vertrauens (1967) 99-101.
        MARXSEN, W. Mark the Evangelist (1969) 61f, 144.
        ACHTEMEIER, P. J., Mark (Philadelphia 1975) 52-53.

METZGER, B. M., The Early Versions of the New Testament (Oxford 1977) 436. *WRETLIND, D. O., "Jesus' Philosophy of Ministry: A Study of a Figure of Speech in Mk 1:38"JEThS 20 (1977) 321-23.

1:39, 41   PETZKE, G., Die Traditionen über Apollonius von Tyana und das Neue Testament (Leiden 1970) 77f, 91, 136, 170ff, 179f.

1:39   BORNKAMM-BARTH-HELD Ueberlieferung und Auslegung im Matthäus- Evangelium (1961) 258. FREYNE, S. The Twelve: Disciples and Apostles (1968) 18, 73, 141f. MARXSEN, W. Mark the Evangelist (1969) 58, 61f. GUETTGEMANNS, E. Offene Fragen zur Formgeschichte des Evangeliums (1970) 202, 229. EGGER, W., Frohbotschaft und Lehre (Frankfurt 1976) 28, 40, 73-79, 83, 94. RIST, J. M., On the Independence of Matthew and Mark (Cambridge 1978) 29. MALBON, E. S., "Mythic Structure and Meaning in Mark" Semeia 16 (1980) 103-107.

1:40-3:19   DRURY, J., Tradition and Design in Luke's Gospel (Atlanta 1976) 89-91.

1:40-45   RAUCH, C. ZNW 3 (1902) 300-303. RAWLINSON, A. E. J. St. Mark (1925) 256. FARRER, A. A Study in St. Mark (1951) 63ff, 224ff. KNOX, W. L. The Sources of the Synoptic Gospels II (1957) 7, 26, 46, 153. GRUNDMANN, W. Das Evangelium nach Markus (1959) 52f. MASSON, C., Vers les Sources D'eau Vive (Lausanne 1961) 11ff. STRECKER, G. Der Weg der Gerechtigkeit (1962) 199n.4. HAHN, F. Christologische Hoheitstitel (1963) 239. WREDE, W. Das Messiasgeheimnis in den Evangelien (1963) 48-50. SUHL, A. Die Funktion der alttestamentlichen Zitate und Anspielungen im Markusevangelium (1965) STECK, K. GPM 21/3 (1966/67) 320. MUSSNER, F. Die Wunder Jesu (1967) 34-42. MINETTE DE TILLESSE, G. Le Secret Messianique dans l'Evangile de Marc (1968) 41-51, 64-69. *Paul, A. "La guérison d'un lépreux. Approche d'un récit de Marc (1, 40-45)" NThR 92 (6, '70) 592-604. LEHMANN, M. Synoptische Quellenanalyse und die Frage nach dem historischen Jesus (1970) 51-54. KERTELGE, K. Die Wunder Jesu im Markus-evangelium (1970) 62-75. ZIMMERMANN, W.-D. Markus über Jesus (1970) 27-29. PESCH, R. Jesu ureigene Taten? Ein Beitrag zur Wunderfrage. Quastiones Disputatae ed. K. Rahner und H. Schlier Bd. 52. (1970) 52-87. JEREMIAS, J. New Testament Theology, I: The Proclamation of Jesus (1971) 86, 89, 92. SCHRAMM, T. Der Markus-Stoff bei Lukas (1971) 91-99. *HERRANZ MARCO, M., "La curación de un leproso según San Marcos" EstBi 31 (1972) 399-433. SCHENKE, L., Die Wundererzählungen des Markusevangeliums (Stuttgart 1974)

130-45. CONZELMANN, H., and LINDEMANN, A., Arbeitsbuch zum Neuen Testament (Tübingen 1975) 69. KOCH, D.-A., Die Bedeutung der Wundererzählungen für die Christologie des Markusevangeliums (Berlin/New York 1975) 73-78. EGGER, W., Frohbotschaft und Lehre (Frankfurt 1976) 42f. PESCH, R., Das Markusevangelium I (Freiburg 1976) 149 (lit!). van LINDEN, P., Knowing Christ through Mark's Gospel (Chicago 1977). *ELLIOTT, J. K., "The Healing of the Leper in the Synoptic Parallels" ThZ 34 (1978) 175-76. FRIEDRICH, G., "Beobachtungen zur messianischen Hohepriestererwartung in den Synoptikern" in: Auf das Wort kommt es an (Göttingen 1978) 85. GNILKA, J., Das Evangelium nach Markus (Einsiedeln/Neukirchen 1978) 89 (lit!). RIST, J. M., On the Independence of Matthew and Mark (Cambridge 1978) 29-30. SEYBOLD, K. and MÜLLER, U., Krankheit und Heilung (Stuttgart 1978) 118-20. CARROLL, W. D., "The Jesus of Mark's Gospel" Bible Today 103 (1979) 2105-112. *CAVE, C. H., "The Leper: Mark 1:40-45" NTS 25 (1979) 245-50. LUZ, U., "Das Geheimnismotiv und die markinische Christologie" ZNW 56 (1965) 9-30; and in: R. Pesch (ed.) Das Markus-Evangelium (Darmstadt 1979) 215f. "Barmherzigkeit" in: TRE 5 (1980) 225. TANNEHILL, R. C., "The Gospel of Mark as Narrative Christology" Semeia 16 (1980) 66f.

1:40-44 HENNECKE, E. and SCHNEEMELCHER, W., Neutestamentliche Apokryphen I (Tübingen 1964) 60. CRIBBS, F. L., in: G. MacRae (ed.) SBL Seminar Papers 2 (Montana 1973) 12-13. EGGER, W., Frohbotschaft und Lehre (Frankfurt 1976) 80f.

1:40-41 BETZ, H. D., Lukian von Samosata und das Neue Testament (Berlin 1961) 150, 155f.

1:40 SCHMID, J. Das Evangelium nach Markus (1958) 51f. HAHN, F. Christologische Hoheitstitel (1963) 84f, 86. MUSSNER, F., "Gab es eine 'galiläische Krise'?" in: P. Hoffmann (ed.) Orientierung an Jesus. Für J. Schmid (Freiburg 1973) 239f.

1:41 RICHARDSON, A. The Miracle-Stories of the Gospels (1948) 33f. WESTERHOLM, S., Jesus and Scribal Authority (Lund 1978) 68. "Barmherzigkeit" in: TRE 5 (1980) 227.

1:43-44 MINETTE DE TILLESSE, G. Le Secret Messianique dans L'Evangile de Marc (1968) 45-47.

1:43 KOCH, D.-A., Die Bedeutung der Wundererzählungen für die Christologie des Markusevangeliums (Berlin/New York 1975) 76f.

1:44-45 BROX, N. Zeuge und Märtyrer (1961) 26f.

1:44 MINETTE DE TILLESSE, G. Le Secret Messianique dans L'Evangile de Marc (1968) 249-51. ACHTEMEIER, P. J., Mark (Philadelphia 1975) 79-81. KOCH, D.-A., Die Bedeutung der Wundererzählungen für die Christologie des Markusevangeliums (Berlin/New York 1975) 75f. TRITES, A. A., The New Testament Concept of Witness (Cambridge 1977) 178. FRIEDRICH, G., "Das Problem der Autorität im Neuen Testament" in: Auf das Wort kommt es an (Göttingen 1978) 287.

1:45 MAUSER, U. Christ in the Wilderness (1963) 103ff, 124, 143f. HAHN, F. Christologische Hoheitstitel (1963) 230. *DANKER, F. W. "Mark 1:45 and the Secrecy Motif" CThM 37 (8, '66) 492-99. PESCH, R. Naherwartungen (1969) 57, 58, 106, 121. GUETTGEMANNS, E. Offene Fragen zur Formgeschichte des Evangeliums (1970) 206 n. 123, 220 n. 246, 241 n. 61. *ELLIOTT, J. K. "The Conclusion of the Pericope of the Healing of the Leper and Mark i.45" JThS 22 (1, '71) 153-57. FARMER, W. R., The Twelve last verses of Mark (London 1974) 91, 100, 101, 102. ACHTEMEIER, P. J., Mark (Philadelphia 1975) 53. KOCH, D.-A., Die Bedeutung der Wundererzählungen für die Christologie des Markusevangeliums (Berlin/New York 1975) 74f. EGGER, W., Frohbotschaft und Lehre (Frankfurt 1976) 28, 33, 40, 42f, 79-84, 85, 101-103, 150f. *ELLIOTT, J. K., "Is *ho exelthōn* a title for Jesus in Mark 1:45?" JThS 27 (1976) 402-405.

2-3 MARTIN, R. P., New Testament Foundations I (Grand Rapids 1975) 129, 181-83, 208. CLEVENOT, M., So kennen wir die Bibel nicht (München 1978) 90-93.

2:1-3:6 EWALD, H., Die drei ersten Evangelien (Göttingen 1850) 196ff. STONEHOUSE, N. B. The Witness of Matthew and Mark to Christ (1944) 60. TAYLOR, V. The Formation of the Gospel Tradition (1949) 177f. KNOX, W. L. The Sources of the Synoptic Gospels (1953) 8ff. (v.I) GRANT, F. C. The Gospels (1957) 81f. BEST, E. The Temptation and the Passion: The Markan Soteriology (1965) 71-73, 116f. KUHN, H.-W. Aeltere Sammlungen im Markusevangelium (1971) 53-98. *MOURLON BEERNAERT, P., "Jésus controversé.

Structure et Théologie de Marc 2:1-3:6" NRTh 95 (1973) 129-49. *DEWEY, J., "The Literary Structure of the Controversy Stories in Mk 2:1-3:6" JBL 92 (1973) 394-401. *CLARK, D. J., "Criteria for Identifying Chiasm" LiBi 35 (1975) 63-72. KOCH, D.-A., Die Bedeutung der Wundererzählungen für die Christologie des Markusevangelium (Berlin/New York 1975) 32-34. Von der OSTEN-SACKEN, P., "Streitgespräch und Parabel als Formen markinischer Christologie" in: G. Strecker (ed.) Jesus Christus in Historie und Theologie. Für H. Conzelmann (Tübingen 1975) 375f, 379-81, 384. EGGER, W., Frohbotschaft und Lehre (Frankfurt 1976) 42, 151. *KOLENKOW, A. B., "Healing Controversy as a Tie Between Miracle and Passion Material for a Proto-Gospel" JBL 95 (1976) 623-38. PESCH, R., Das Markusevangelium I (Freiburg 1976) 151 (lit!). *THISSEN, W., Erzählung der Befreiung (Würzburg 1976).

2   CALLOUD, J., "Towards a Structural Analysis of the Gospel of Mark" Semeia 16 (1980) 133-65.

2:1-12   WREDE, W., "Zur Heilung des Gelähmten" ZNW 5 (1904) 354. RIESENFELD, H., Jésus Transfiguré (Copenhagen 1947) 326-30. MANSON, W., Jesus the Messiah (Philadelphia 1948) 40-42. FARRER, A. A Study in St. Mark (1951) 65ff, 73ff, 270ff. *CABANISS, A. "A Fresh Exegesis of Mark 2:1-13" Interpretation 11 ('57) 324-27. BOSCH, D. Die Heidenmission in der Zukunftsschau Jesu (1959) 60-64. GRUNDMANN, W. Das Evangelium nach Markus (1959) 59. *MEAD, R. T. "The Healing of the Paralytic - a Unit?" JBL 80 (4, '61) 348-54. FULLER, R. H. Interpreting the Miracles (1963) 50ff. MAUSER, U. Christ in the Wilderness (1963) 124f, 127. HAHN, F. Christologische Hoheitstitel (1963) 218, 228. BULTMANN, R., The History of the Synoptic Tradition (Oxford 1963) 14-16, 64-66, 212f. YATES, J. E., The Spirit and the Kingdom (London 1963) 54ff. HENNECKE, E. and SCHNEEMELCHER, W., Neutestamentliche Apokryphen I (Tübingen 1964) 128, 339. IERSEL, B. van "Der Gelähmte aus Kapharnaum" Heilig Land 17 (1964) 73-75. BECKER, U.-WIBBING, S. Wundergeschichten (1965) 12-33. GAMBA, G. G., "Considerazioni in margine alla poetica di Mc 2:1-12" Salesianum 28 (1966) 324-49. MINETTE DE TILLESSE, G. Le Secret Messianique dans l'Evangile de Marc (1968) 116-22. KAMPHAUS, F. Von der Exegese zur Predigt (1968) 120-23. STROBEL, A. Erkenntnis und Bekenntnis der Sünde in neutestamentlicher Zeit (1968) 58. SCHREINER, J. Gestalt und Anspruch des neuen Testaments (1969) 160f. KERTELGE, K. Die Wunder Jesu im Markusevangelium

(1970) 75-82. ZIMMERMANN, W.-D. Markus über Jesus
(1970) 30-33. GUETTGEMANNS, E. Offene Fragen zur
Formgeschichte des Evangeliums (1970) 83 n. 10, 229, 230.
JEREMIAS, J. Neutestamentliche Theologie I: Die
Verkündigung Jesu (1971) 90, 93f, 115. COLPE, C.
'Traditionsüberschreitende Argumentationen zu Aussagen
Jesu über sich selbst" Tradition und Glaube, ed. G. Jeremias,
K. G. Kuhn zum 65. Geburtstag (1971). 232-236. MAISCH, I.
Die Heilung des Gelähmten. (1971). KUHN, H.-W. Aeltere
Sammlungen im Markusevangelium (1971) 53-57.
SCHRAMM, T. Der Markus-Stoff bei Lukas (1971) 99-103.
KERTELGE, K., "Die Vollmacht des Menchensohnes zur
Sündenvergebung" in: P. Hoffmann (ed.) Orientierung an
Jesus. Für J. Schmid (Freiburg 1973) 206-208. *DORMEYER,
D., "Narrative Analyse von Mk 2:1-12" LiBi 31 (1974) 68-88.
KONINGS, J., "The Pre-Markan Sequence in Jn 6" in: M.
Sabbe (ed.) L'Evangile selon Marc (Gembloux 1974) 172.
LEROY, H., Zur Vergebung der Sünden (Stuttgart 1974) 53-
55. SCHENKE, L., Die Wundererzählungen des Markus-
evangeliums (Stuttgart 1974) 146-60. TALBERT, C. H.,
Literary Patterns, Theological Themes, and the Genre of Luke-
Acts (Missoula 1974) 19, 42. ACHTEMEIER, P. J., Mark
(Philadelphia 1975) 46, 75-76. CONZELMANN, H. and
LINDEMANN, A., Arbeitsbuch zum Neuen Testament
(Tübingen 1975) 54f, 73, 75. GNILKA, J., "Das Elend vor dem
Menschensohn" in: R. Pesch/R. Schnackenburg (eds.) Jesus
und der Menschensohn (Freiburg 1975) 196-209. GOPPELT,
L., Theologie des Neuen Testaments I (Göttingen 1975) 181ff.
KOCH, D.-A., Die Bedeutung der Wundererzählungen für die
Christologie des Markusevangeliums (Berlin/New York 1975)
46-50, 52-55. VIA, D. O., Kerygma and Comedy in the New
Testament (Philadelphia 1975) 83, 118, 135, 145. PESCH, R.,
Das Markusevangelium I (Freiburg 1976) 162 (lit!). REICKE,
B., "The Synoptic Reports of the Healing of the Paralytic" in: J.
K. Elliott (ed.) Studies in New Testament Language and Text.
In honour of G. D. Kilpatrick (Leiden 1976) 319-29. BERGER,
K., Exegese des Neuen Testaments (Heidelberg 1977) 29f.
GERSTENBERGER, G. and SCHRAGE, W., Leiden
(Stuttgart 1977) 229f; ET: J. E. Steely, Suffering (Nashville
1980) 264-65. MANEK, J., . . . und brachte Frucht. Die
Gleichnisse Jesu (Berlin 1977) 29-33. *MARCO, M. H., "El
proceso ante el Sanhedrín" EstBi 36 (1977) 35-55. GNILKA, J.,
Das Evangelium nach Markus I (Einsiedeln/Neukirchen 1978)
95 (lit!). *PETERSEN, N. R., " 'Point of View' in Mark's
Narrative" Semeia 12 (1978) 97-121. RIST, J. M., On the
Independence of Matthew and Mark (Cambridge 1978) 30.

SEYBOLD, K. and MULLER, U., Krankheit und Heilung (Stuttgart 1978) 125-26, 142f. LUZ, U., "Das Geheimnismotiv und die markinische Christologie" ZNW 56 (1965) 9-30; and in: R. Pesch (ed.) Das Markus-Evangelium (Darmstadt 1979) 212f. MERKEL, F., in: GPM 33 (1979) 396-401. CALLOUD, J., "Toward a Structural Analysis of the Gospel of Mark" Semeia 16 (1980) 141-51.

2:1-2   HAHN, F. Christologische Hoheitstitel (1963) 230. EGGER, W., Frohbotschaft und Lehre (Frankfurt 1976) 28, 43, 69, 77, 82, 149-51.

2:1   STRECKER, G. Der Weg der Gerechtigkeit (1962) 94f. NICKELS P. Targum and New Testament (1967) 23. MINETTE DE TILLESSE G. Le Secret Messianique dans L'Evangile de Marc (1968) 243-46. MUSSNER, F., "Gab es eine 'galiläische Krise'?" in: P. Hoffmann (ed.) Orientierung an Jesus. Für J. Schmid (Freiburg 1973) 239f. PERRIN, N., "Die Christologie des Markus-Evangeliums" in: "The Christology of Mark" JR 51 (1971) 173-87; and in: R. Pesch (ed.) Das Markus-Evangelium (Darmstadt 1979) 366. MALBON, E. S., "Mythic Structures and Meaning in Mark" Semeia 16 (1980) 103-107.

2:2   METZGER, B. M., The Early Versions of the New Testament (Oxford 1977) 439.

2:3-5   STROBEL, A. Erkenntnis und Bekenntnis der Sünde in neutestamentlicher Zeit (1968) 59. *RASCO, E. "Cuatro' y 'la fe': quiénes y de quién? (Mc 2,3b.5a)" Biblica 50 (1, '69) 59-67.

2:3-4   BORNKAMM-BARTH—HELD Ueberlieferung und Auslegung im Matthäus-Evangelium (1961) 165f, 267.

2:4   JAHNOW, H., "Das Abdecken des Daches" ZNW 24 (1925) 155-58. KRAUSS, S., "Das Abdecken des Daches" ZNW 25 (1926) 307-310.

2:5ff   FRIEDRICH, G. "Beobachtungen zur messianischen Hohepriestererwartung in den Synoptikern" in: Auf das Wort kommt es an (Göttingen 1978) 84f.

2:5-11   VIA, D. O., Kerygma and Comedy in the New Testament (Philadelphia 1975) 120, 131, 160. RIVKIN, E., A Hidden Revolution (Nashville 1978) 106.

2:5-10   BAUMBACH, G. Das Verständnis des Bösen in den synoptischen Evangelien (1963) 22ff. HAHN, F. Christologische Hoheitstitel (1963) 43, 239. STROBEL, A. Erkenntnis und Bekenntnis der Sünde in neutestamentlicher Zeit (1968) 39, 45, 58f.

2:5   BOUSSET, W., Die Religion des Judentums im Späthellenistischen Zeitalter (Berlin 1966=1926) 391.

JEREMIAS, J. Neutestamentliche Theologie I: Die Verkündigung Jesu (1971) 21f, 116, 160, 162, 166. BOHREN, R. Wiedergeburt des Wunders (1972) 71-77. LANGE, J., Das Erscheinen des Auferstandenen im Evangelium nach Matthäus (Würzburg 1973) 55-57. MIRANDA, J. P., Marx and the Bible (London 1977) 213. SCHMITHALS, W., Das Evangelium nach Markus (Gütersloh/Würzburg 1979) 158 (lit!).

2:6-7 VIA, D. O., Kerygma and Comedy in the New Testament (Philadelphia 1975) 131, 136, 150, 152.

2:6 SCHMID, J. Das Evangelium nach Markus (1958) 59-63.

2:7 NICKELS, P. Targum and New Testament (1967) 23. PESCH, R. Naherwartungen (1969) 102, 153, 179, 189, 194. "Beichte" in: TRE 5 (1980) 437.

2:8-11 FARRER, A. A Study in St. Mark (1951) 75ff.

2:8 KNOX, W. L. The Sources of the Synoptic Gospels II (1957) 62.

2:9-11 BETZ, H. D., Lukian von Samosata und das Neue Testament (Berlin 1961) 155, 158.

2:9 HOFFMANN, P. and EID, V., Jesus von Nazareth und eine christliche Moral (Freiburg 1975) 38f. PERRIN, N., "Die Christologie des Markus-Evangeliums" in: "The Christology of Mark" JR 51 (1971) 173-87; and in: R. Pesch (ed.) Das Markus-Evangelium (Darmstadt 1979) 366.

2:10-11 HAMMERTON-KELLY, R. G., Pre-Existence, Wisdom, and the Son of Man (London 1973) 49, 50, 57, 61, 63, 95, 240.

2:10 FARRER, A. A Study in St. Mark (1951) 270ff, 279ff. TAYLOR, V. The Gospel According to St. Mark (1953) 199f, 200f. *BOOBYER, G. H. "Mark II, 10a and the Interpretation of the Healing of the Paralytic" HThR XLVII ('54) 115-20. SCHMID, J. Das Evangelium nach Markus (1958) 160-62. BOOBYER, G. H., "The Secrecy Motif in St. Mark's Gospel" NTS 6 (1959-1960) 229f. *CEROKE, C. P. "Is Mk 2, 10 a Saying of Jesus?" CBQ 22 (4, '60) 369-90. BLAIR, E. P. Jesus in the Gospel of Matthew (1960) 46. SCHWEIZER, E. Erniedrigung und Erhöhung bei Jesus und seinen Nachfolgern (1962) §3 1. BULTMANN, R., The History of the Synoptic Tradition (Oxford 1963) 149f. WREDE, W. Das Messiasgeheimnis in den Evangelien (1963) 16-19, 222. HAHN, F. Christologische Hoheitstitel (1963) 25, 43. HOOKER, M. D. The Son of Man in Mark (1967) 81-93, 94, 174, 175f. MINETTE DE TILLESSE, G. Le Secret Messianique dans L'Evangile de Marc (1968) 390-94, 367-68. STROBEL, A. Erkenntnis und Bekenntnis der Sünde in neutestamentlicher

Zeit (1968) 58-59. *HAY, L. S. "The Son of Man in Mark 2:10 and 2:28" JBL 89 (1, '70) 69-75. JEREMIAS, J. Neutestamentliche Theologie I: Die Verkündigung Jesu (1971) 248-250, 255. KERTELGE, K., "Die Vollmacht des Menschensohnes zur Sündenvergebung" in: P. Hoffmann (ed.) Orientierung an Jesus. Für J. Schmid (Freiburg 1973) 205-13. COPPENS, J., "Les Logia du Fils de l'Homme dans l'évangile de Marc" in: M. Sabbe (ed.) L'Evangile selon Marc (Gembloux 1974) 500, 518-20. PERRIN, N., "The Christology of Mark" in: M. Sabbe (ed.) L'Evangile selon Marc (Gembloux 1974) 480-81. PERRIN, N., A Modern Pilgrimage in New Testament Christology (Philadelphia 1974) 115-21. DUNN, J. D. G., Jesus and the Spirit (London 1975) 40, 78. FRIEDRICH, G. "Beobachtungen zur messianischen Hohepriestererwartung in den Synoptikern" in: Auf das Wort kommt es an (Göttingen 1978) 96-97. MALBON, E. S., "Mythic Structure and Meaning in Mark" Semeia 16 (1980) 109-13.

2:11   HAHN, F. Christologische Hoheitstitel (1963) 43. STROBEL, A. Erkenntnis und Bekenntnis der Sünde in neutestamentlicher Zeit (1968) 58. BOHREN, R. Wiedergeburt des Wunders (1972) 78-85.

2:12-13   MUSSNER, F., "Gab es eine 'galiläische Krise'?" in: P. Hoffmann (ed.) Orientierung an Jesus. Für J. Schmid (Freiburg 1973) 239f.

2:12   DORMEYER, D., Die Passion Jesu als Verhaltensmodell (Münster 1974) 59. KOCH, D.-A., Die Bedeutung der Wundererzählungen für die Christologie des Markusevangeliums (Berlin/New York 1975) 19-21.

2:13-3:12   FARRER, A. A Study in St. Mark (1951) 69ff, 78f, 81ff.

2:13-28   PIROT, J. Paraboles et Allégories Evangeliques (1949) 16-34. TALBERT, C. H., Literary Patterns, Theological Themes, and the Genre of Luke-Acts (Missoula 1974) 42. ACHTEMEIER, P. J., Mark (Philadelphia 1975) 12-14.

2:13-17   ZIMMERMANN, H. Neutestamentliche Methodenlehre (1967) 177-181, 92-98. VAN IERSEL, B. M. F. "La vocation de Lévi (Mc. 11:13-17 par) Tradition et rédaction" De Jésus aux Evangiles (1967) 212-32. STOCK, H./WEGENAST, K./WIBBING, S. Streitgespräche (1968) 84-107. STROBEL, A. Erkenntnis und Bekenntnis der Sünde in neutestamentlicher Zeit (1968) 39. GRABNER-HIADER, A. Verkündigung als Einladung (1969) 81-83. *GAMBA, G. G. "Considerazioni in margine alla redazione di Mc 2, 13-17" DiThom 72 (2, '69) 201-26. *LAMARCHE, P. "The Call to Conversion and Faith. The Vocation of Levi (mk 2, 13-17)" LuVit 25 (2, '70) 301-12.

PETZKE, G., Die Traditionen über Apollonius von Tyana und das Neue Testament (Leiden 1970) 170, 228. ZIMMERMANN, W.-D. Markus über Jesus (1970) 33-36. VIA, D. O., Kerygma and Comedy in the New Testament (Philadelphia 1975) 81, 83, 102, 131, 133, 134, 136. *LAMARCHE, P., "L'appel de Levi" Christus 23 (1976) 107-18. PESCH, R., Das Markusevangelium I (Freiburg 1976) 169 (lit!). GNILKA, J., Das Evangelium nach Markus I (Einsiedeln/Neukirchen 1978) 103 (lit!). RIST, J. M., On the Independence of Matthew and Mark (Cambridge 1978) 30-32. *THEOBALD, M., "Der Primat der Synchronie vor der Diachronie als Grundaxiom derLiterarkritik." Bib Zeit 22 (1978) 161-86. SCHMITHALS, W., Das Evangelium nach Markus (Gütersloh/Würzburg 1979) 165 (lit!).

2:13-16 CALLOUD, J., Towards a Structural Analysis of the Gospel of Mark" in: Semeia 16 (1980) 141-51.

2:13-14 FLEW, R. N. Jesus and His Church (1956) 42-43.

2:13 HAHN, F. Christologische Hoheitstitel (1963) 230. MAUSER, U. Christ in the Wilderness (1963) 124f, 127f, 132, 139f, 141. MINETTE DE TILLESSE, G. Le Secret Messianique dans L'Evangile de Marc (1968) 258-61. GUETTGEMANNS, E. Offene Fragen zur Formgeschichte des Evangeliums (1970) 202, 214, n207, 229. EGGER, W., Frohbotschaft und Lehre (Frankfurt 1976) 28, 151-53.

2:14-17 SCHWEIZER, E. Erniedrigung und Erhöhung bei Jesus und seinen Nachfolgern (1962) §1d, 11b. SCHALIT, A. König Herodes (1969) 296. SCHWEIZER, E. Gott Versöhnt: 6 Reden in Nairobi (1971) 57-67.

2:14 LINDARS, B., "Matthew, Levi, Lebbaeus and the Value of the Western Text" NTS 4 (1957-1958) 220ff. ROBINSON, J. M. Kerygma und historischer Jesus (1960) 141. SCHULZ, A. Nachfolgen und Nachahmen (1962) 98ff. BULTMANN, R., The History of the Synoptic Tradition (Oxford 1963) 51f, 56f. GIBBS, J. M., "Purpose and Pattern in Matthew's use of the Title 'Son of David' " NTS 10 (1963-1964) 454f. MEYE, R. P. Jesus and the Twelve (1968) 140-42. METZGER, B. M. "Explicit references in the works of Origen to variant readings in New Testament manuscripts" Historical and Literary Studies (1968) 94f. *PESCH, R. "Levi-Matthäus (Mc 2: 14/Mt 9:9 10:3). Ein Beitrag zur Lösung eines alten Problems" ZNW 59 (1-2, '68) 40-56. OTOMO, Y. Nachfolge Jesu und Anfänge der Kirche im Neuen Testament (1970) 33f. JEREMIAS J. Neutestamentliche Theologie I: Verkündigung Jesu (1971) 164, 223. SCHNEIDER, G., Anfragen an das Neue Testament

(Essen 1971) 138f. ERNST, J., Anfänge der Christologie (Stuttgart 1972) 128-130. PATSCH, H., Abendmahl und historischer Jesus (Stuttgart 1972) 215f. SCHMAHL, G., Die Zwölf im Markusevangelium (Trier 1974) 114-16. GOPPELT, L., Theologie des Neuen Testaments I (Göttingen 1975) 80, 132, 178, 184, 256.

2:15-3:6 TALBERT, C. H., Literary Patterns, Theological Themes and the Genre of Luke-Acts (Missoula 1974) 19.

2:15-17 TAYLOR, V. The Formation of the Gospel Tradition (1949) 23, 64f. BAUMBACH, G. Das Verständnis des Bösen in den synoptischen Evangelien (1963) 19ff. MINETTE DE TILLESSE, G. Le Secret Messianique dans L'Evangile de Marc (1968) 122-24. OTOMO, Y. Nachfolge Jesu und Anfänge der Kirche im Neuen Testament (1970) 98-100. KUHN, H.-W. Aeltere Sammlungen im Markusevangelium (1971) 58-61. PESCH, R., "Das Zöllnergastmahl" in: A. Descamps/A. de Halleux (eds.) Mélanges Bibliques en hommage au R. P. Béda Rigaux (Gembloux 1970) 63-87. BRAUN, H., "Gott, die Eröffnung des Lebens für die Nonkonformisten, Erwägungen zu Markus 2:15-17" in: G. Ebeling et al. (eds.) Festschrift für Ernst Fuchs (Tübingen 1973) 97-101. GOPPELT, L., Theologie des Neuen Testaments I (Göttingen 1975) 178f. ARENS, E., The HΛΘΟΝ - Sayings in the Synoptic Tradition (Fribourg 1976) 28-63. "Abendmahl" in: TRE 1 (1977) 49. MEYER, B. F., The Aims of Jesus (London 1979) 158-162, 166.

2:15-16 MEYE, R. P. Jesus and the Twelve (1968) 142-45. GERSTENBERGER, G. and SCHRAGE, W., Leiden (Stuttgart 1977) 219f; ET: J. E. Steely, Suffering (Nashville 1980) 253.

2:15 STRECKER, G. Der Weg der Gerechtigkeit (1962) 95 n.2, 96 n.5. PESCH, R., "Das Zöllnergastmahl" in: A. Descamps/A. de Halleux (eds.) Mélanges Bibliques en hommage au R. P. Béda Rigaux (Gembloux 1970) 63-87. WANKE, J., Die Emmauserzählung (Leipzig 1973) 101. METZGER, B. M., The Early Versions of the New Testament (Oxford 1977) 439.

2:16-19 BOUSSET, W., Die Religion des Judentums im Späthellenistischen Zeitalter (Berlin 1966=1926) 132, 180.

2:16-17 *ALONSO, J. "La parabola del médico en Mc 2, 16-17" CultBib 16 (1964, '59) 10-12. BERGER, K. Die Gesetzesauslegung Jesu (1972) 577-82.

2:16 KLOSTERMANN, E. Das Markusevangelium (1950) 25f. HAHN, F. Christologische Hoheitstitel (1963) 77, 84. STROBEL, A. Erkenntnis und Bekenntnis der Sünde in neutestamentlicher Zeit (1968) 60. JEREMIAS, J.

Neutestamentliche Theologie I (1971) 55, 111, 120, 123.
DORMEYER, D., Die Passion Jesu als Verhaltensmodell
(Münster 1974) 308-309. TALBERT, C. H., Literary Patterns,
Theological Themes, and the Genre of Luke-Acts (Missoula
1974) 42. "Abendmahl" in: TRE 1 (1977) 49, 213.
FRIEDRICH, G., "Das Problem der Autorität im Neuen
Testament" in: Auf das Wort kommt es an (Göttingen 1978)
285-87. WESTERHOLM, S., Jesus and Scribal Authority
(Lund 1978) 70-71.

2:17   MASSAUX, E. Influence de l'Evangile de saint Matthieu sur la
littérature chrétienne saint Irénée (1950) 139-42. *MOUSON,
J. "Non veni vocare justos, sed peccatores (Mt. IX, 13 - Mc II,
17 - Lc V,32)" CollMech 43 (2, '58) 134-39. ROBINSON, J. M.
Kerygma und historischer Jesus (1960) 115. STRECKER, G.
Der Weg der Gerechtigkeit (1962) 33. HENNECKE, E. and
SCHNEEMELCHER, W., Neutestamentliche Apokryphen I
(Tübingen 1964) 113. *LEE, G. M. " 'They that are whole need
not a physician' " ET 76 (8, '65) 254. STROBEL, A. Erkenntnis
und Bekenntnis der Sünde in neutestamentlicher Zeit (1968) 39,
60. JEREMIAS, J. Neutestamentliche Theologie I (1971) 25,
111, 115, 117-21, 146. LADD, G. E., A Theology of the New
Testament (Grand Rapids 1974) 56, 75, 79, 101. PERRIN, N.,
Jesus and the Language of the Kingdom (London 1976) 38.
"Abendmahl" in: TRE 1 (1977) 49. KLAUCK, H.-J., Allegorie
und Allegorese in Synoptischen Gleichnistexten (Münster
1978) 148-60. "Berufung" in: TRE 5 (1980) 686. McDONALD,
J. I. H., Kerygma and Didache (Cambridge 1980) 81.

2:18ff.   RUDOLPH, K., Die Mandäer I (Göttingen 1960) 78. SMITH,
M., Clement of Alexandria and a secret Gospel of Mark
(Cambridge, Mass. 1973) 111, 211f, 250, 255.
CONZELMANN, H., Theologie als Schriftauslegung
(München 1974) 56f, 63.

2:18-28   MEYE, R. P. Jesus and the Twelve (1968) 145-46.

2:18-22   TAYLOR, V. The Formation of the Gospel Tradition (1949)
34-35. KLOSTERMANN, E. Das Markusevangelium (1950)
30f. KüMMEL, W. G. Verheissung und Erfüllung (1953) 68-70.
SCHLATTER, A. Johannes der Täufer (1956) 87ff. FüRST,
W. GPM 13 (1958) 50-54. FERNANDEZ "La cuestion del
ayuno (Mt. 9, 14-17; Mc 2, 18-22; Lc 5, 33-39), CultBib 19 (184,
'62) 162-69. BULTMANN, R., The History of the Synoptic
Tradition (Oxford 1963) 18f. HAMEL, J. GPM 19 (1964) 74-
80. IWAND, H.-J., Predigt-Meditationen (1964) 539-57.
BISER, E. Die Gleichnisse Jesu (1965) 126f, 131ff.
KAHLEFELD, H. Parables and Instructions in the Gospels
(1966) 45ff. BAUER, G. in *Hören und Fragen* eds. G. Eichholz

und A. Falkenroth (1967) 124ff. *CREMER, F. G. "Das Fastenstreitgespräch (Mk 2, 18-22 parr) bei Beda Venerabilis und Hrabanus Maurus. Zur Charakteristik mittelalterlicher Florilegien" RBén 77 (1-2, '67) 157-74. MERKEL, H., "Jesus und die Pharisäer" NTS 14 (1967-1968) 202f. *O'HARA, J. "Christian Fasting. Mk 2, 18-22" Scripture 19 (47, '67) 82-95. MINETTE DE TILLESSE, G. Le Secret Messianique dans L'Evangile de Marc (1968) 124-28. *KEE, A. "The Question about Fasting" NovTest 11 (3, '69) 161-73. LINDARS, B., NTS 16 (1969-1970) 324-29. OTOMO, Y. Nachfolge Jesu und Anfänge der Kirche im Neuen Testament (1970) 99-100, 179-81. LANGE, E. (ed.) Predigtstudien für das Kirchenjahr 1970/71. (1970) 107-112. WICHELHAUS, M. GPM 25 (1970) 95-101. ROLOFF, J. Das Kerygma und der irdische Jesus (1970) 223.237. ZIMMERMANN, W.-D. Markus über Jesus (1970) 36-39. KUHN, H.-W. Aeltere Sammlungen im Markusevangelium (1971) 61-72. SCHRAMM, T. Der Markus-Stoff bei Lukas (1971) 105-111. BERGER, K. Die Gesetzesauslegung Jesu (1972) 577-84. -- *GAIDE, G., "Question sur le jeûne" AssS 39 (1972) 44-54. PATSCH, H., Abendmahl und historischer Jesus (Stuttgart 1972) 199f. *ZIESLER, J. A., "The Removal of the Bridegroom" NTS 19 (1973) 190-94. KÜCHLER, E.-A. and BRAUN, F., in: P. Krusche et al. (eds.) Predigtstudien für das Kirchenjahr 1976/1977 I/1.Halbband (Stuttgart 1976) 90-97. PESCH, R., Das Markusevangelium I (Freiburg 1976) 178 (lit!). POKORNY, P., in: GPM 31/1 (1976-1977) 81-85. GNILKA, J., Das Evangelium nach Markus I (Einsiedeln/Neukirchen 1978) 110f. (lit!). RIST, J. M., On the Independence of Matthew and Mark (Cambridge 1978) 32-33. WAIBEL, M., "Die Auseiandersetzung mit der Fasten- und Sabbatpraxis Jesu in urchristlichen Gemeinden" in: G. Dautzenberg et al. (eds.) Zur Geschichte des Urchristentums (Freiburg 1979) 63-80. CALLOUD, J., "Toward a Structural Analysis of the Gospel of Mark" Semeia 16 (1980) 151-59. TANNEHILL, R. C., "The Gospel of Mark as Narrative Christology" Semeia 16 (1980) 70-71.

2:18-20   TAYLOR, V. The Formation of the Gospel Tradition (1949) 33f, 64f. SCHELKLE, K. H., Die Passion Jesu in der Verkündigung des Neuen Testaments (Heidelberg 1949) 22f. HAHN, F. Christologische Hoheitstitel (1963) 126. *FEUILLET, A., "La controverse sur la jeûne (Mc 2, 18-20; Mt 9, 14-15; Lc 5, 33-35)" NRTh 90 (2, '68) 113-36; (3, '68) 252-77. BATEY, R. A. New Testament Nuptial Imagery (1971) 38-41. BURKILL, T. A. New Light on the Earliest Gospel (1972) 39-

47. MARXSEN, W., Christologie-praktisch (Gütersloh 1978) 141-49. RIVKIN, E., A Hidden Revolution (Nashville 1978) 93.

2:18-19 SCHILLE, O., Offen für alle Menschen (Stuttgart 1974) 28ff. MARXSEN, W., Christologie-praktisch (Gütersloh 1978) 49f.

2:18 HAHN, F. Christologische Hoheitstitel (1963) 99. SUMMERS, R. The Secret Sayings of the Living Jesus (1968) 69. SCHüTZ, F. Der leidende Christus (1969) 49ff. BROER, I., Die Urgemeinde und das Grab Jesu (München 1972) 129f. TALBERT, C. H., Literary Patterns, Theological Themes, and the Genre of Luke-Acts (Missoula 1974) 42.

2:19-22 BERGER, K., Exegese des Neuen Testaments (Heidelberg 1977) 59-61.

2:19-20 TAYLOR, V., Jesus and His Sacrifice (London 1948) 82-85, 90. DENNEY, J. The Death of Christ (1956) 23f. GNILKA, J. Die Verstockung Israels (1961) 67f. HAHN, F. Christologische Hoheitstitel (1963). SCHRAGE, W. Das Verhältnis des Thomas-Evangeliums zur Synoptischen Tradition und zu den Koptischen Evangelienübersetzungen (1964) 104. JEREMIAS, J. Neutestamentliche Theologie I (1971) 25f, 28, 117, 166. DORMEYER, D., Die Passion Jesu als Verhaltensmodell (Münster 1974) 77, 254, 57. KLAUCK, H.-J., Allegorie und Allegorese in Synoptischen Gleichnistexten (Münster 1978) 160-69.

2:19 RAWLINSON, A. E. J. St Mark (1925) 256f. BRUNNER, E. Dogmatik II (1949) 296. STONEHOUSE, N. B. The Witness of Matthew and Mark to Christ (1944) 232. BRAUN, H., Qumran und NT II (Tübingen 1966) 78. *CREMER, F. G. "'Die Söhne des Brautgemachs' (Mk 2, 19 parr) in der griechischen und lateinischen Schrifterklärung" BZ 11 (2, '67) 246-53. PHIPPS, W. E. Was Jesus married? 71-72. (1970). ERNST, J., Anfänge der Christologie (Stuttgart 1972) 154-58. KÜMMEL, W. G., Einleitung in das Neue Testament (Heidelberg 1973 *(17)*) 61f.

2:20 TAYLOR, V., "The Origin of the Markan Passion-Sayings" NTS 1 (1954-1955) 163ff. *DUNKERLEY, R. "The Bridegroom Passage" ET 64 (10, '53) 303-304. KUEMMEL, W. G. Verheissung und Erfüllung (1953) 68-70. *SCHAEFER, K. Th. ". . . und dann werden sie fasten, an jenem Tage" (Mk 2, 20 und Parallelen) Synoptische Studien, ed. Wikenhauser (1953) 124-47. *BRAUMANN, G. " 'An jenem Tag' Mk 2, 20" NovTest 6 (4, '63) 264-67. HAHN, F. Christologische Hoheitstitel (1963) 99. *CREMER, F. G. Die Fastenansage Jesu. Mk 2, 20 und Parallelen in der Sicht der patristischen und scholastischen Exegese (1965). SCHREIBER, J. Theologie des Vertrauens (1967) 120f, 123-25, 150, 155f, 202. MINETTE DE

TILLESSE, G. Le Secret Messianique dans L'Evangile de Marc (1968) 414-20. STROBEL, A. Erkenntnis und Bekenntnis der Sünde in neutestamentlicher Zeit (1968) 41. PESCH, R. Naherwartungen (1969) 101, 108, 113, 114, 119, 149, 167.

2:21-22   JüLICHER, D. A. Die Gleichnisreden Jesu (1910) 188-212. HARRISVILLE, R. A., The Concept of Newness in the New Testament (Minneapolis 1960) 21ff. MOWRY L. "Parable" IDB III (1962) 653b. SCHRAGE, W. Das Verhältnis des Thomas-Evangeliums zur Synoptischen Tradition und zu den Koptischen Evangelienübersetzungen (1964) 113. KEE, A., "The Old Coat and the New Wine" NovT 12 (1970) 13-21. SANFORD, J. A., The Kingdom Within (New York 1970) 74-75. *TRUDINGER, P., "The Word on the Generation Gap. Reflections on a Gospel Metaphor" BThB 5 (1975) 311-15. KLAUCK, H.-J., Allegorie und Allegorese in Synoptischen Gleichnistexten (Münster 1978) 169-74. KONRAD, J.-F., "Das Neue an Jesus" in: H. H. Henrix/M. Stöhr (eds.) Exodus und Kreuz im ökumenischen Dialog zwischen Juden und Christen (Aachen 1978) 154-65. SCHMITHALS, W., Das Evangelium nach Markus (Gütersloh/Würzburg 1979) 175 (lit!).

2:21   SCHNEIDER, G., Neuschöpfung oder Wiederkehr (1961) 67. NICKELS, P. Targum and New Testament (1967) 23. SUMMERS, R. The Secret Sayings of the Living Jesus (1968) 39.

2:22   GROS LOUIS, K. R. R., "The Gospel of Mark" in: Gros Louis et al. (eds.) Literary Interpretations of Biblical Narratives (Nashville 1974) 320f.

2:23-6:13   RIST, J. M., On the Independence of Matthew and Mark (Cambridge 1978) 34-55.

2:23-3:6   FARRER, A. St Matthew and St Mark (1954) 138, 197. *TROADEC, H. "Le Fils de l'Homme est Maître même du sabbat (Marc 2, 23-3, 6)" BVieC 21 ('58) 73-83. JEREMIAS, J. Neutestamentliche Theologie I (1971) 265f. BOHREN, R., Predigtlehre (München 1971) 102, 196. *DUPREZ, A., "Deux affrontements un jour de sabbat" AssS 40 (1972) 43-53. Goulder, M. D., Midrash and Lection in Matthew (London 1974) 313f. KONINGS, J., "The Pre-Markan Sequence in Jn 6' in: M. Sabbe (ed.) L'Evangile selon Marc (Gembloux 1974) 172, 173. LOHSE, E., Grundriss der neutestamentlichen Theologie (Stuttgart 1974) 119f. CLEVENOT, M., So kennen wir die Bibel nicht (München 1978) 110-111.

2:23-28   RIESENFELD, H., Jésus Transfiguré (Copenhagen 1947) 319-23. STONEHOUSE, N. B. The Witness of Matthew and Mark to Christ (1944) 31f. FARRER, A. A Study in St Mark (1951) 72ff, 159f, 275ff. GRUNDMANN, W. Die Jüdische Sabbatordnung (1959) 67-69. *BEARE, F. W. " 'The Sabbath Was Made for Man?' " JBL 79 (2, '60) 130-36. BULTMANN, R., The History of the Synoptic Tradition (Oxford 1963) 15f. *GRASSI, J. A. "The Five Loaves of the High Priest (Mt xii, 1-8; Mk ii, 23-28; Lk vi, 1-5; i Sam. xxi, 1-6)" NovTest 7 (2, '64) 119-22. KAESEMANN, E. Exegetische Versuche und Besinnungen (1964) I 207. SUHL, A. Die Funktion der alttestamentlichen Zitate und Anspielungen im Markusevangelium (1965) 82ff. *LEITCH, J. W. "Lord Also of the Sabbath" SJTh 19 (4, '66) 426-33. JüNGEL, E. Paulus und Jesus (1966) 209. BOUSSET, W., Die Religion des Judentums im Späthellenistischen Zeitalter (Berlin 1966=1926) 126. BRAUN, H., Qumran und NT II (Tübingen 1966) 99f, 289, 296. DAVIES, W. D., The Sermon on the Mount (Cambridge 1966) 103. MERKEL, H., NTS 14 (1967-1968) 203f. STOCK/WEGENAST/WIBBING Streitgespräche (1968) 27-51. MINETTE DE TILLESSE, G. Le Secret Messianique dans L'Evangile de Marc (1968) 128-43. ZIMMERMANN, W.-D. Markus über Jesus (1970) 39-40. GASTON, L. No Stone on Another (1970) 79-81. ROLOFF, J. Das Kerygma und der irdische Jesus (1970) 52-62. OTOMO, Y. Nachfolge Jesu und Anfänge der Kirche im Neuen Testament (1970) 100f. CATCHPOLE, D. R., 'The Answer of Jesus to Caiaphas" NTS 17 (1970-1971) 224f. KUHN, H.-W. Aeltere Sammlungen im Markusevangelium (1971) 72-98. SCHRAMM, T. Der Markus-Stoff bei Lukas (1971) 111f. *HULTGREN, A. J. "The Formation of the Sabbath Pericope in Mark 2:23-28" JBL 91 (1, '72) 38-43. BERGER, K. Die Gesetzesauslegung Jesu (1972) 577-82. HÜBNER, H., Das Gesetz in der synoptischen Tradition (Witten 1973) 113ff. ACHTEMEIER, P. J., Mark (Philadelphia 1975) 16. CONZELMANN, H. and LINDEMANN, A., Arbeitsbuch zum Neuen Testament (Tübingen 1975) 72. GOPPELT, L., Theologie des Neuen Testaments I (Göttingen 1975) 144, 145ff. AICHINGER, H., "Quellenkritische Untersuchung der Perikope vom Ährenraufen am Sabbat" in: A. Fuchs (ed.) Jesus in der Verkündigung der Kirche (Freistadt 1976) 110-53. PESCH, R., Das Markusevangelium I (Freiburg 1976) 187 (lit!). GERSTENBERGER, G. and SCHRAGE, W., Leiden (Stuttgart 1977) 129; ET: J. E. Steely, Suffering (Nashville 1980) 150. SANDMEL, D., We Jews and Jesus (New York 1977) 136. FRIEDRICH, G., "Das Problem der Autorität im

Neuen Testament" in: Auf das Wort kommt es an (Göttingen 1978) 285-87. *GAMBA, G. G., "Struttura letteraria e significato dottrinale di Marco 2:23-28 e 3:1-6" Salesianum 40 (1978) 529-82. GNILKA, J., Das Evangelium nach Markus I (Einsiedeln/Neukirchen 1978) 118 (lit!). RIVKIN, E., A Hidden Revolution (Nashville 1978) 91-92. WESTERHOLM, S., Jesus and Scribal Authority (Lund 1978) 96-100. WAIBEL, M., "Die Auseinandersetzung mit der Fasten- und Sabbatpraxis Jesu in urchristlichen Gemeinden" in: G. Dautzenberg (ed.) Zur Geschichte des Urchristentums (Freiburg 1979) 80-95. TANNEHILL, R. C., "The Gospel of Mark as Narrative Christology" Semeia 16 (1980) 70-71.

2:23-24 KNOX, W. L. The Sources of the Synoptic Gospels II (1957) 78. SCHWEIZER, E. Erniedrigung und Erhöhung bei Jesus und seinen Nachfolgern (1962) §14e. "Aramäisch" in: TRE 3 (1978) 608.

2:23 MOORE, G. F., Judaism II (Cambridge, Mass. 1946) 29. TALBERT, C. H., Literary Patterns, Theological Themes, and the Genre of Luke-Acts (Missoula 1974) 42. *DELEBECQUE, E., "Les épis 'égrenés' dans les Synoptiques" Revue des Etudes Grecques 88 (1975) 133-42.

2:24 PRYKE, E. J., "IΔE and IΔOY" NTS 14 (1967-1968) 418f. METZGER, B. M., The Early Versions of the New Testament (Oxford 1977) 440.

2:25-28 SMITH, M., Clement of Alexandria and a Secret Gospel of Mark (Cambridge, Mass. 1973) 211f, 249.

2:26-28 *DEENICK, J. W. "The Fourth Commandment and its Fulfillment" RThR 28 (2, '69) 54-61.

2:26 FARRER, A. St Matthew and St Mark (1954) 76. DORMEYER, D., Die Passion Jesu als Verhaltensmodell (Münster 1974) 53, 69. METZGER, B. M., The Early Versions of the New Testament (Oxford 1977) 368. *MORGAN, C. S., "When Abiathar was High Priest" JBL 98 (1979) 409-410.

2:27-28 *GILS, F., " 'Le sabbat a été fait pour l'homme et non l'homme pour le sabbat' (Mc, II, 27) Réflexions à propos de Mc, II 27-28" RevBi 69 (4, '62) 506-23. KAESEMANN, E. Exegetische Versuche und Besinnungen (1964) I 219. BJöRNSTAD, E. J. Jesus and the Law in the Gospel of Mark (1966) 48-52. THYEN, H. Studien zur Sündenvergebung (1970) 255f. SANFORD, J. A., The Kingdom Within (New York 1970) 93. ERNST, J., Anfänge der Christologie (Stuttgart 1972) 152-53. ACHTEMIER, P. J., Mark (Philadelphia 1975) 28, 46.

2:27 MOORE, G. F., Judaism II (Cambridge, Mass. 1946) 31. MANSON, T. W. "Mark ii, 27f" Coniextanea Neotestamentica (in honorem Antonii Fridrichsen) (1947) 138-46. BORNKAMM-BARTH-HELD, Ueberlieferung und Auslegung im Matthäus-Evangelium (1961) 29, 85. *GILS, F., "Le sabbat a été fait pour l'homme et non l'homme pour le sabbat" RB 69 (1962) 506-23. HAHN, F. Christologische Hoheitstitel (1963) 43, 44, QUESNELL, Q., This Good News (Milwaukee 1964) 173f. SMITH, M., Tannaitic Parallels to the Gospels (Philadelphia 1968) 6bn5+. BAUMERT, N., Täglich Sterben und Auferstehen (München 1973) 101. HOOKER, M. D. The Son of God in Mark (1967) 94-98. BRAUN, H. Jesus (1969) 81, 82, 83, 128, 161f. JEREMIAS, J. Neutestamentliche Theologie I (1971) 21, 25-29, 175, 201f. LANGE, J., Das Erscheinen des Auferstandenen im Evangelium nach Matthäus (Würzburg 1973) 65-67. LOHSE, E., Die Einheit des Neuen Testaments (Göttingen 1973) 40, 67f. BANKS, R., Jesus and the Law in the Synoptic Tradition (London 1975) 120-22. GERSTENBERGER, G. and SCHRAGE, W., Leiden (Stuttgart 1977) 218f.; ET: J. E. Steely, Suffering (Nashville 1980) 252. SCHMITHALS, W., Das Evangelium nach Markus (Gütersloh/Würzburg 1979) 183 (lit!). TOLBERT, M. A., Perspectives on the Parables (Philadelphia 1979) 79.

2:28-30   YATES, J. E., The Spirit and the Kingdom (London 1963) 38f, 58f, 85ff.

2:28   FARRER, A. A Study in St Mark (1951) 275ff. BOOBYER, G. H., "The Secrecy Motif in St Mark's Gospel" NTS 6 (1959-1960) 229f. LANGE, J., Das Erscheinen des Auferstandenen im Evangelium nach Matthäus (Würzburg 1973) 38, 60, 65-67, 71f, 90, 94, 121, 206, 230. SCHWEIZER, E. Erniedrigung und Erhöhung bei Jesus und seine Nachfolgern (1962) §31, 14e. WREDE, W. Das Messiasgeheimnis in den Evangelien (1963) 16-19, 222. HAHN, F. Christologische Hoheitstitel (1963) 25, 43, 44, 73. HOOKER, M. D. The Son in Mark (1967) 93-102, 174, 175f., 178, 182, 193. NICKELS, P. Targum and New Testament (1967) 23. FLENDER, H. Die Botschaft Jesu von der Herrschaft Gottes (1968) 86ff.93. MINETTE DE TILLESSE, G. Le Secret Messianique dans L'Evangile de Marc (1968) 390-94, 395-96. HAY, L. S. "The Son of Man in Mark 2, 10 and 2, 28" JBL 89 (1970) 69-75. JEREMIAS, J. Neutestamentliche Theologie I (1971) 248f, 255. WEINACHT, H. Die Menschwerdung des Sohnes Gottes im Markusevangelium (1972) 133f. COPPENS, J., "Les Logia du Fils de l'Homme dans L'évangile de Marc" in: M. Sabbe (ed.) L'Evangile selon Marc (Gembloux 1974) 500, 520f. PERRIN, N., A Modern Pilgrimage in New Testament Christology (Philadelphia 1974) 115-21. ACHTEMEIER, P. J., Mark

(Philadelphia 1975) 45. MALBON, E. S., "Mythic Structure and Meaning in Mark" Semeia 16 (1980) 109-13.

3-4   LAMBRECHT, J., "Redaction and Theology in Mk 4" in: M. Sabbe (ed.) L'Evangile selon Marc (Gembloux 1974) 279-80.

3:1ff   LIGHTFOOT, R. H. History and Interpretation in the Gospels (1934) 45f.

3   GREENLEE, J. H., Nine Uncial Palimpsests of the Greek New Testament (Salt Lake City 1968) 45-46, 60-61. DORMEYER, D., Die Passion Jesu als Verhaltensmodell (Münster 1974) 282.

3:1-7   YATES, J. E., The Spirit and the Kingdom (London 1963) 55f.

3:1-6   STONEHOUSE, N. B. The Witness of Matthew and Mark to Christ (1944) 59, 60. MOORE, G. F., Judaism II (Cambridge, Mass. 1946) 31n. RIESENFELD, H., Jésus Transfiguré (Copenhagen 1947) 324ff. BOUSSET, W., Die Religion des Judentums im Späthellenistischen Zeitalter (Berlin 1966=1926) 126. RENGSTORF, K. H. Die Wunder Jesu im Markusevangelium (1949) 82-85. TAYLOR, V. The Formation of the Gospel Tradition (1949) 64f, 155. FARRER, A. A Study in St Mark (1951) 69ff, 79ff, 158ff, 308f, 317ff. FARRER, A. St Matthew and St Mark (1954) 77, 78, 128, 131. *MULDER, H. "Doden op de Sabbat?" HomBib 25 (5, '66) 116-18. BRAUN, H., Qumran und NT II (Tübingen 1966) 99, 289, 296. MINETTE DE TILLESSE, G. Le Secret Messianique dans L'Evangile de Marc (1967) 70-71, 128-43. SCHREINER, J. Gestalt und Anspruch des neuen Testaments (1969) 160f. ZIMMERMANN, W.-D. Markus über Jesus (1970) 41-44. KERTELGE, K. Die Wunder Jesu im Markusevangelium (1970) 82-85. ROLOFF, J. Das Kerygma und der irdische Jesus (1970) 63-66. JEREMIAS, J. Neutestamentliche Theologie (1971) 90, 93, 202, 265. CRIBBS, F. L., "A Study of the Contacts that Exist between St Luke and St John" in: G. MacRae (ed.) SBL Seminary Papers 2 (Montana 1973) 13-14. SCHENKE, L., Die Wundererzählungen des Markusevangeliums (Stuttgart 1974) 161-72. CONZELMANN, H. and LINDEMANN, A., Arbeitsbuch zum Neuen Testament (Tübingen 1975) 91. GOPPELT, L., Theologie des Neuen Testaments (Göttingen 1975) 144-47. KOCH, D.-A., Die Bedeutung der Wundererzählungen für die

Christologie des Markusevangeliums (Berlin/New York 1975)
50-52, 52-55. PESCH, R., Das Markusevangelium I (Freiburg
1976) 197 (lit!). SIBINGA, J. S., "Text and Literary Art in Mk
3;1-6" in: J. K. Elliott (ed.) Studies in New Testament Language
and Text. In honour of G. D. Kilpatrick (Leiden 1976) 357-65.
*DIETZFELBINGER, C., "Vom Sinn der Sabbatheilungen
Jesu" EvTh 38 (1978) 281-98. *GAMBA, G. G., "Struttura
letteraria e significato dottrinale di Marco 2:23-28 e 3:1-6"
Salesianum 40 (1978) 529-82. GNILKA, J., Das Evangelium
nach Markus I (Einsiedeln/Neukirchen 1978) 124 (lit!).
RIVKIN, E., A Hidden Revolution (Nashville 1978) 92-93.
SEYBOLD, K. and MÜLLER;, U., Krankheit und Heilung
(Stuttgart 1978) 101-105, 125-26. WESTERHOLM, S., Jesus
and Scribal Authority (Lund 1978) 100-101. LUZ, U., "Das
Geheimnismotiv und die markinische Christologie" ZNW 56
(1965) 9-30; and in: R. Pesch (ed.) Das Markus-Evangelium
(Darmstadt 1979) 212f. MEYER, B. F., The Aims of Jesus
(London 1979) 162-68. SWIDLER, L., Biblical Affirmations of
Woman (Philadelphia 1979) 181.

3:1-4 KNOX, W. L. The Sources of the Synoptic Gospels II (1957)
59, 78, 84. BERGER, K. Die Gesetzesauslegung Jesu (1972)
577-82.

3:1 METZGER, B. M., The Early Versions of the New Testament
(Oxford 1977) 434.

3:2-4 "Aramäisch" in: TRE 2 (1978) 608.

3:2 HABICH, Chr., "2. Makkabäerbuch" in: W. G. Kümmel (ed.)
Jüdische Schriften aus hellenistisch-römischer Zeit I
(Gütersloh 1976) 265. METZGER, B. M., The Early Versions
of the New Testment (Oxford 1977) 176.

3:4-5 BETZ, H. D., Lukian von Samosata und das Neue Testament
(Berlin 1961) 115, 135, 155. BAUMBACH, G. Das Verständnis
des Bösen in den synoptischen Evangelien (1963) 16ff.

3:4 JüNGEL, E. Paulus und Jesus (1966) 208ff.
DAUTZENBERG, G., Sein Leben bewahren (München 1966).
SANFORD, J. A., The Kingdom Within (New York 1970) 92f.
LOHSE, E., Die Einheit des Neuen Testaments (Göttingen
1973) 40, 68f. CAVALLIN, H. C. C., Life after Death I (Lund
1974) 4, 3, nII. GERSTENBERGER, G. and SCHRAGE, W.,
Leiden (Stuttgart 1977) 218f.; ET: J. E. Steely., Suffering
(Nashville 1980) 252.

3:5-6 STONEHOUSE, N. B. The Witness of Matthew and Mark to
Christ (1944) 44;, 71, 82.

3:5 HESSE, F., Das Verstockungsproblem im Alten Testament
(Berlin 1955) 3, 4. BORNKAMM-BARTH-HELD

Ueberlieferung und Auslegung im Matthäus-Evangelium (1961) 196. PETZKE, G., Die Traditionen über Apollonius von Tyana und das Neue Testament (Leiden 1970) 172, 180. "Affeckt" in: TRE 1 (1977) 597. METZGER, B. M., The Early Versions of the New Testament (Oxford 1977) 93.

3:6-7   MAUSER, U. Christ in the Wilderness (1963) 124f, 127f.

3:6   LIGHTFOOT, R. H. History and Interpretation in the Gospels (1934) 110f. FARRER, A. St Matthew and St Mark (1954) 48, 110, 134. ROBINSON, J. M. Kerygma und historischer Jesus (1960) 20. SCHREIBER, J. Theologie des Vertrauens (1967) 43, 47, 89, 109, 111, 181-83, 198f, 240. PESCH, R. Naherwartungen (1969) 58-60, 68 — 53, 54, 57. SCHALIT, A. König Herodes (1969) 479. LEHMANN, M. Synoptische Quellenanalyse und die Frage nach dem historischen Jesus (1970) 146-48. DORMEYER, D., Die Passion Jesu als Verhaltensmodell (Münster 1974) 174, 658. *BENNETT, W. J., "The Herodians of Mark's Gospel" NovT 17 (1975) 9-14. TANNEHILL, R. C., "The Gospel of Mark as Narrative Christology" Semeia 16 (1980) 68.

3:7-6:6   EGGER, W., Frohbotschaft und Lehre (Frankfurt 1976) 22, 110, 163.

3:7-6:4   SCHWEIZER, E., "Die Theologische Leistung des Markus" EvTh 24 (1964) 337-55; and in: R. Pesch (ed.) Das Markus-Evangelium (Darmstadt 1979) 171-73.

3:7ff   LIGHTFOOT, R. H. History and Interpretation in the Gospels (1934) 109ff. KNOX, W. L. The Sources of the Synoptic Gospels (1953) I, - 17ff, 22f. BORNKAMM-BARTH-HELD, Ueberlieferung und Auslegung im Matthäus-Evangelium (1961) 269. STRECKER, G. Der Weg der Gerechtigkeit (1962) 69.

3:7-19   BAUERNFEIND, O. Die Worte der Dämonen im Markusevangelium (1927) 18-23, 56-67. EWALD, H., Die drei ersten Evangelien (Göttingen 1850) 204ff. LIGHTFOOT, R. H., Locality and Doctrine in the Gospels (London 1938) 118ff. VAGANAY, L., "Existe-t-il chez March quelques Traces du Sermon sur la Montagne?" NTS 1 (1954-1955) 192ff.

3:7-13   KONINGS, J., "The Pre-Markan Sequence in Jn 6" in: M. Sabbe (ed.) L'Evangile selon Marc (Gembloux 1974) 173.

3:7-12   *KECK, L. E. "Mark 3;7-12 and Mark's Christology" JBL 84 (4, '65) 341-58. *BURKILL, T. A. "Mark 3:7-12 and the Alleged Dualism in the Evangelist's Miracle Material" JBL 87 (4, '68) 409-17. FEYNE, S. The Twelve: Disciples and Apostles (1968) 67, 73, 74, 79. *EGGER, W. "Die Verborgenheit in Mk

3, 7-12" Biblica 50 (4, '69) 466-90. SCHüTZ, F. Der leidende Christus (1969) 119ff. REPLOH, K-G. Markus - Lehrer der Gemeinde (1969) 36-43. KERTELGE, K. Die Wunder Jesu im Markusevangelium (1970) 34-35. ZIMMERMANN, W.-D. Markus über Jesus (1970) 34-46. SCHRAMM, T. Der Markus-Stoff bei Lukas (1971) 113f. PETZKE, G., Die Traditionen über Apollonius von Tyana und das Neue Testament (Leiden 1970) 78, 179. BROER, I., Die Urgemeinde und das Grab Jesu (München 1972) 120f, 124f. NEIRYNCK, F., "Urmarcus redivivus?" in: M. Sabbe (ed.) L'Evangile selon Marc (Gembloux 1974) 130-44. PERRIN, N., "The Christology of Mark" in: M. Sabbe (ed.) L'Evangile selon Marc (Gembloux 1974) 477-78. TALBERT, C. H., Literary Patterns, Theological Themes, and the Genre of Luke-Acts (Missoula 1974) 42. KOCH, D.-A. Die Bedeutung der Wundererzählungen für die Christologie des Markusevangeliums (Berlin/New York 1975) 166-68. EGGER, W., Frohbotschaft und Lehre (Frankfurt 1976) 28, 35, 77, 79, 91-111, 139. PESCH, R., Das Markusevangelium I (Freiburg 1976) 202 (lit!). GNILKA, J., Das Evangelium nach Markus I (Einsiedeln/Neukirchen 1978) 132 (lit!). LUZ, U., "Das Geheimnismotiv und die markinische Christologie" ZNW 56 (1965) 9-30; and in: R. Pesch (ed.) Das Markus-Evangelium (Darmstadt 1979) 213f.

3:7-11 MUSSNER, F., "Gab es eine 'galiläische Krise'?" in: P. Hoffmann (ed.) Orientierung an Jesus. Für J. Schmid (Freiburg 1973) 239f.

3:7-8 BOISMARD, M. E., "Influence matthéennes sur l'ultime rédaction de l'évangile de Marc" in: M. Sabbe (ed.) L'Evangile selon Marc (Gembloux 1974) 97-100. NIERYNCK, F., "Urmarcus redivivus?" in: M. Sabbe (ed.) L'Evangile selon Marc (Gembloux 1974) 132-38.

3:7 DAVIES, W. D., The Gospel and the Land (London 1974) 240, 351, n.46, 411, 418, 432.

3:7-8 HAHN, F. Das Verständnis der Mission im Neuen Testament (1965 2nd ed.) 96. STONEHOUSE, N. B. The Witness of Matthew and Mark to Christ (1944) 29, 42, 176.

3:8-13 FARRER, A. St Matthew and St Mark (1954) 196f.

3:8 MARXSEN, W. Mark the Evangelist (1969) 67, 70, 75. TALBERT, C. H., Literary Patterns, Theological Themes, and the Genre of Luke-Acts (Missoula 1974) 42.

3:9 LEHMANN, M. Synoptische Quellenanalyse und die Frage nach dem historischen Jesus (1970) 59f.

3:10-12   DIBELIUS, M., Aufsätze zur Apostelgeschichte (Göttingen 1951) 15f.; ET: Studies in the Acts of the Apostles (London 1956) 9f. DIBELIUS, M., "Sammlung" in: Die Formgeschichte des Evangeliums (1933=1919) 219-34; and in: R. Pesch (ed.) Das Markus-Evangelium (Darmstadt 1979) 73-74.

3:11-12   KÜMMEL, W. G., Einleitung in das Neue Testament (Heidelberg 1973 *(17)*) 61ff. ACHTEMEIER, P. J., Mark (Philadelphia 1975) 79-81. LUZ, U., "Das Geheimnismotiv und die markinische Christologie" ZNW 56 (1965) 9-30; and in: R. Pesch (ed.) Das Markus-Evangelium (Darmstadt 1979) 218f.

3:11   ROBINSON, J. M. Das Geschichtsverständnis der Markus-Evangeliums (1956) 45ff. HAHN, F. Christologische Hoheitstitel (1963) 297. STÄHLIN, G., "Tὸ πνεῦμα Ἰησοῦ (Apostelgeschichte 16:7)" in: B. Lindars/S. S. Smalley (eds.) Christ and the Spirit in the New Testament. In honour of C. F. D. Moule (Cambridge 1973) 243f. LOHSE, E., Grundriss der neutestamentlichen Theologie (Stuttgart 1974) 116f. ACHTEMEIER, P. J., Mark (Philadelphia 1975) 36, 44. DONAHUE, J. R., "Temple, Trial and Royal Christology" in: W. H. Kelber (ed.) The Passion in Mark (Philadelphia 1976) 73, 74, 75. PERRIN, N., "The High Priest's Question and Jesus' Answer" in: W. H. Kelber (ed.) The Passion in Mark (Philadelphia 1976) 86, 87, 88, 90. FRIEDRICH, G., "Beobachtungen zur messianischen Hohepriestererwartung in den Synoptikern" in: Auf das Wort kommt es an (Göttingen 1978) 70-71. MALBON, E. S., "Mythic Structure and Meaning in Mark" Semeia 16 (1980) 109-13.

3:12-19   FREYNE, S. The Twelve: Disciples and Apostles (1968) 81ff.

3:12   BLAIR, E. P. Jesus in the Gospel of Matthew (1960) 52. MINETTE DE TILLESSE, G. Le Secret Messianique dans L'Evangile de Marc (1968) 249-51. BOUSSET, W., Die Religion des Judentums im Späthellenistischen Zeitalter (Berlin 1966=1926) 340.

3:13-6:56   FARRER, A. A Study in St Mark (1951) 79ff, 144f.

3:13-5:43   FARRER, A. St Matthew and St Mark (1954) 99, 107.

3:13ff   SCHILLE, G. Die urchristliche Kollegialmission (1967) 91f, 123ff, 131ff. MEYE, R. P. Jesus and the Twelve (1968) 146-48. EGGER, W., Frohbotschaft und Lehre (Frankfurt 1976) 155.

3:13-19   STONEHOUSE, N. B., The Witness of Luke to Christ (Grand Rapids 1951) 98f. FARRER, A. A Study in St Mark (1951) 80f, 95f, 108ff, 310f. FARRER, A. St Matthew and St Mark (1954) 8, 21, 51, 90. GRUNDMANN, W. Das Evangelium nach Markus (1959) 79f. *BURGERS, W. "De instelling van de

Twaalf in het Evangelie van Marcus" EphT 36 (3-4, '60) 625-54.
ROLOFF, J. Apostolat-Verkündigung Kirche (1965) 145-48.
FARMER, W. R. et al., Christian History and Interpretation:
Studies presented to John Knox (1967) 209f. MEYE, R. P.
Jesus and the Twelve (1968). REPLOH, K. G. Markus-Lehrer
der Gemeinde (1969) 43-50. ITTEL, G. W. Jesus und die Jünger
(1970) 28-41. ZIMMERMANN, W. D. Markus über Jesus
(1970) 46-48. OTOMO, Y. Nachfolge Jesu und Anfänge der
Kirche im Neuen Testament (1970) 62-68. SCHRAMM, T. Der
Markus-Stoff bei Lukas (1971) 113f. *SCHMAHL, G., "Die
Berufung der Zwölf im Markusevangelium" TThZ 81 (1972)
203-13. KÜMMEL, W. G., Einleitung in das Neue Testament
(Heidelberg 1973 *(17)*) 31f. SCHMAHL, G., Die Zwölf im
Markusevangelium (Trier 1974) 44-67. TALBERT, C. H.,
Literary Patterns, Theological Themes, and the Genre of Luke-
Acts (Missoula 1974) 42. GOPPELT, L., Theologie des Neuen
Testaments I (Göttingen 1975) 257ff. PESCH, R., Das
Markusevangelium I (Freiburg 1976) 209 (lit!). GNILKA, J.,
Das Evangelium nach Markus I (Einsiedeln/Neukirchen 1978)
136 (lit!). STAGG, E./F., Woman in the World of Jesus
(Philadelphia 1978) 123-25. SCHMITHALS, W., Das
Evangelium nach Markus (Gütersloh/Würzburg 1979) 204
(lit!) 729. TANNEHILL, R. C., "The Gospel of Mark as
Narrative Christology" Semeia 16 (1980) 69.

3:13-14 STRECKER, G. Der Weg der Gerechtigkeit (1962) 192.
HENGEL M. Nachfolge und Charisma (1968) 90f.

3:13 MAUSER, U. Christ in the Wilderness (1963) 109, 118, 139ff.
*DESCAMPS, A. "Aux origines du ministère. La pensée de
Jésus" RThL 2 (1, '71) 3-45. LANGE, J., Das Ercheinen des
Auferstandenen im Evangelium nach Matthäus (Würzburg
1973) 339, 394-96, 399f, 402, 408, 410, 421.

3:14ff BORNKAMM, G. Jesus von Nazareth (1956) 137ff.

3:14-35 CARRINGTON, P. The Primitive Christian Calendar (1952)
136-38.

3:14-19 BUTLER, B. C., The Originality of St Matthew (Cambridge
1951) 102ff.

3:14-15 FLEW, R. N. Jesus and His Church (1956) 56, 77-85, 131 n.175.
HAHN, F. Das Verständnis der Mission im Neuen Testament
(1965) 32, 33. JEREMIAS, J. Neutestamentliche Theologie I
(1971) 74, 96, 98, 224, 226f. BORSCH, F. H., "Jesus the
Wandering Preacher?" in: M. Hooker/C. Hickling (eds.) What
about the New Testament? In honour of C. Evans (London
1975) 48f. KERTELGE, K., "Offene Fragen zum Thema

'Geistliches Amt' und das neutestamentliche Verständnis von der 'repraesentatio Christi' " in: R. Schnackenburg et al. (eds.) Die Kirche des Anfangs. Für H. Schürmann (Freiburg 1978) 588-90.

3:14 TRILLING, W., "Die Entstehung des Zwölferkreises. Eine geschichtskritische überlegung" in: R. Schnackenburg et al. (eds.) Die Kirche des Anfangs. Für H. Schürmann (Freiburg 1978) 205f.

3:15 BARRETT, C. K., The Holy Spirit and the Gospel Tradition (New York 1947) 78f, 127-30. HAHN, F. Christologische Hoheitstitel (1963) 297. LANGE, J., Das Erscheinen des Auferstandenen im Evangelium nach Matthäus (Würzburg 1973) 26, 69-73, 91.

3:16-19 KLOSTERMANN, E. Das Markusevangelium (1950) 34-36. TAYLOR, V. The Gospel According to St Mark (1953) 619-27. CULLMANN, O. "Der zwölfte Apostel" in Vorträge und Aufsätze, ed. Karlfried Frölich (1966) 214-22. FREYNE, S. The Twelve: Disciples and Apostles (1968) 36. DORMEYER, D., Die Passion Jesu als Verhaltensmodell (Münster 1974) 83. "Apostel" in: TRE 3 (1978) 430, 434. RIST, J. M., On the Independence of Matthew and Mark (Cambridge 1978) 47.

3:16 STRECKER, G. Der Weg der Gerechtigkeit (1962) 206. SCHREIBER, J. Theologie des Vertrauens (1967) 165-67. CAVALLIN, H. C. C., Life after Death I (Lund 1974) 6n15. ACHTEMEIER, P. J., Mark (Philadelphia 1975) 96. "Amt" in: TRE 2 (1978) 511. TRILLING, W., "Die Entstehung des Zwölferkreises. Eine geschichtskritische Überlegung" in: R. Schnackenburg et al. (eds.) Die Kirche des Anfangs. Für H. Schürmann (Freiburg 1978) 205f. FITZMYER, J. A., "Aramaic 'Kepha' and Peter's name in the New Testament" in: E. Best/R. McL. Wilson (eds.) Text and Interpretation. In honour of M. Black (Cambridge 1979) 122-24. ERNST, J., "Die Petrustradition im Markusevangelium - ein altes Problem neu angegangen" in: J. Zmijewski/E. Nellessen (eds.) Begegnung mit dem Wort. Für H. Zimmermann (Bonn 1980) 44-46.

3:17 GRILL, S. "Die Donnersöhne Mk 3, 17 nach dem syrischen Text" Bible und Liturgie 23/5 (1956) 137-38. FISCHER, ZNW 23 (1924) 310f. JEREMIAS, J. Neutestamentliche Theologie I (1971) 16f, 77, 223. PREUSCHEN, E., "Die Donnersöhne Mc 3:17" ZNW 18 (1917-1918) 141-44. "Aramäisch" in: TRE 3 (1978) 604.

3:18 HAHN, F. Christologische Hoheitstitel (1963) 164. *WAUTIER, A. "Thomas, jumeau de Thaddée ou de Jésus"

CahCER 18 (71, '71) 66-68. LINDARS, B., "Matthew, Levi, Lebbaeus and the Value of the Western Text" NTS 4 (1957-1958) 220ff. HENGEL, M., Judentum und Hellenismus (Tübingen 1969) 194; ET: Judaism and Hellenism (London 1974) I 105. "Aramäisch" in: TRE 3 (1978) 603, 606.

3:19b ff BEST, E. The Temptation and the Passion: The Markan Soteriology (1965). BJØRNSTAD, E. J. Jesus and the Law in the Gospel of Mark (1966) 56-60.

3:19-35 EWALD, H., Die drei ersten Evangelien (Göttingen 1850) 224ff.

3:19b-35 BARTLETT, D. L., Fact and Faith (Valley Forge 1975) 34. TRITES, A. A., The New Testament Concept of Witness (Cambridge 1977) 191-92. RIVKIN, E., A Hidden Revolution (Nashville 1978) 106-107.

3:20ff LIGHTFOOT, R. H. History and Interpretation in the Gospels (1934) 111f. KNOX, W. L. The Sources of the Synoptic Gospels II (1957) 63.

3:20-4:44 STONEHOUSE, N. B., The Witness of Luke to Christ (Grand Rapids 1951) 94, 102f.

3:20-4:34 LAMBRECHT, J. Marcus Interpretator. Stijl en boodschap in Mc. 3, 20-4, 34. (1969). Rev. J. Dupont Biblica 51 (4, '70) 584-86.

3:20-4:20 *ACHTEMEIER, P. J., "Mark as Interpreter of the Jesus Traditions" Interpretation 32 (1978) 339-52.

3:20-35 *LAMBRECHT, J. "Ware verwantschap en eeuwige zonde. Ontstaan en structuur van Mc. 3, 20-35" Bijdragen 29 (2, '68) 114-50. II: 29 (3, '68) 234-58. III: 29 (4, '68) 369-93. ZIMMERMANN, W.-D. Markus über Jesus (1970) 48-53. SMITH, M., Tannaitic Parallels to the Gospels (Philadelphia 1968) 5bn38+. KONINGS, J., "The Pre-Markan Sequence in Jn 6" in: M. Sabbe (ed.) L'Evangile selon Marc (Gembloux 1974) 152, 172, 173. *LAMBRECHT, J., "The Relatives of Jesus in Mark" NovT 16 (1974) 241-58. ACHTEMEIER, P. J., Mark (Philadelphia 1975) 32. KOCH, D.-A., Die Bedeutung der Wundererzählungen für die Christologie des Markusevangeliums (Berlin/New York 1975) 140-47. *DANIELI, G., "Maria e i fratelli di Gesù nel Vangelo di Marco" Marianum 40 (1978) 91-109. GNILKA, J., Das Evangelium nach Markus I (Einsiedeln/Neukirchen 1978) 143 (lit!).

3:20-30 *ROULIN, P. "Le péché contre l'Esprit-Saint" BVieC 29 ('59) 38-45. BAUMBACH, G. Das Verständnis des Bösen in den synoptischen Evangelien (1963) 32ff. BARRETT, C. K., The

Holy Spirit and the Gospel Tradition (New York 1947) 59-63, 103-107. PESCH, R., Das Markusevangelium I (Freiburg 1976) 220f. (lit!).

3:20-29   DOWNING, F. G., "Towards the Rehabilitation of Q" NTS 11 (1964-1965) 170f.

3:20-22   TALBERT, C. H., Literary Patterns, Theological Themes, and the Genre of Luke-Acts (Missoula 1974) 40.

3:20-21   TILLICH, P. Das Neue Sein (1959) 103-106. BULTMANN, R., The History of the Synoptic Tradition (Oxford 1963) 29f. SCHROEDER, H-H., Eltern und Kinder in der Verkündigung Jesu (Hamburg-Bergstedt 1972) 110-24. STANTON, G. N., Jesus of Nazareth in New Testament Preaching (Cambridge 1974) 154f. KOCH, D-A., Die Bedeutung der Wundererzählungen für die Christologie des Markusevangeliums (Berlin/New York 1975) 145-47. OBERLINNER, L., Historische überlieferung und christologische Aussage (Stuttgart 1975) 149-243. *BEST, E., "Mark 3:20, 21, 31-35" NTS 22 (1976) 309-19. SWIDLER, L., Biblical Affirmations of Woman (Philadelphia 1979) 178.

3:20   MINETTE DE TILLESSE, G. Le Secret Messianique dans L'Evangile de Marc (1968) 244-46. HENDRIKS, W., "Zur Kollektionsgeschichte des Markusevangeliums" in: M. Sabbe (ed.) L'Evangile selon Marc (Gembloux 1974) 55.

3:21-35   TANNEHILL, R. C., "The Gospel of Mark as Narrative Christology" in: Semeia 16 (1980) 69.

3:21-30   SMITH, M., Clement of Alexandria and a Secret Gospel of Mark (Cambridge, Mass. 1973) 219, 224f, 229.

3:21   ROBINSON, J. M., Kerygma und historischer Jesus (1960) 95. HAHN, F. Christologische Hoheitstitel (1963) 220. *WANSBROUGH, H. "Mark iii.21 -Was Jesus out of his mind?" NTS 18 (2, '72) 233-35. HENNECKE, E. and SCHNEEMELCHER, W., Neutestamentliche Apokryphen I (Tübingen 1964) 312. DUNN, J. D. G., Jesus and the Spirit (London 1975) 87. *WENHAM, D., "The Meaning of Mk 3:21" NTS 21 (1975) 295-300. SANDMEL, S., We Jews and Jesus (New York 1977) 87. THEISSEN, G., Soziologie der Jesusbewegung (München 1977) 17. GAIN, D. B., Evidence for Supposing that our Greek Text of the Gospel of St Mark is translated from Latin (Grahamstown 1978).

3:22-30   GRANT, F. C. The Gospels (1957) 81f. BULTMANN, R., The History of the Synoptic Tradition (Oxford 1963) 13f, 329f, 168f. HAHN, F. Christologische Hoheitstitel (1963) 297f, 298, 299f. HAHN, F. Das Verständnis der Mission im Neuen

Testament (1965) 96. MINETTE DE TILLESSE, G. Le Secret Messianique dans L'Evangile de Marc (1968) 99-104, 143, 217. FENEBERG, W., Der Markusprolog (München 1974) 92, 181f. GOULDER, M. D., Midrash and Lection in Matthew (London 1974) 313f, 327, 331, 348. KOCH, D.-A., Die Bedeutung der Wundererzählungen für die Christologie des Markusevangeliums (Berlin/New York 1975) 141-45.

3:22-29 DUNN, J. D. G., Unity and Diversity in the New Testament (London 1977) 188f.

3:22-27 JüLICHER, D. A. Die Gleichnisreden Jesu (1910) 214-40. ACHTEMEIER, P. J., Mark (Philadelphia 1975) 71-72. EDWARDS, R. A., A Theology of Q (Philadelphia 1976) 110-12.

3:22-26 TAYLOR, V. The Formation of the Gospel Tradition (1949) 38, 64f. TANNEHILL, R. C., The Sword of His Mouth (Philadelphia 1975) 177-85.

3:22 KLOSTERMANN, E. Das Markusevangelium (1950) 83. PARKER, P. The Gospel Before Mark (1953) 72-73. ROBINSON, J. M. Kerygma und historischer Jesus (1960) 95. DEVISCH, M., "La relation entre l'evangile de Marc et le document Q" in: M. Sabbe (ed.) L'Evangile selon Marc (Gembloux 1974) 84-85, 87. "Antichrist" in: TRE 3 (1978) 22. "Aramäisch" in: TRE 3 (1978) 604.

3:23ff Von der OSTEN-SACKEN, P., "Streitgespräch und Parabel als Formen markinischer Christologie" in: G. Strecker (ed.) Jesus Christus in Historie und Theologie. Für H. Conzelmann (Tübingen 1975) 385-87.

3:23-35 HAHN, P. Christologische Hoheitstitel (1963) 166.

3:23-30 MUSSNER, F. Die Wunder Jesu (1967) 28-31. BUTLER, B. C., The Originality of St Matthew (Cambridge 1951) 8ff. LEIVESTAD, R., Christ the Conqueror (London 1954) 45ff. TALBERT, C. H., Literary Patterns, Theological Themes, and the Genre of Luke-Acts (Missoula 1974) 40. DIBELIUS, M., "Sammlung" in: Die Formgeschichte des Evangeliums (1933=1919) 219-34; and in: R. Pesch (ed.) Das Markus-Evangelium (Darmstadt 1979) 70.

3:23-27 BEASLEY-MURRAY, G. R., "Jesus and the Spirit" in: A. Descamps/A. de Halleux (eds.) Mélanges Bibliques en hommage au R. P. Béda Rigaux (Gembloux 1970) 470-71.

3:23, 26 "Aramäisch" in: TRE 3 (1978) 608.

3:23 STONEHOUSE, N. B. The Witness of Matthew and Mark to Christ (1944) 56. SIMPSON, R. T., "The Major Agreements of

Matthew and Luke against Mark" NTS 12 (1965-1966) 280f. "Antichrist" in: TRE 3 (1978) 22.

3:24-26 PERRIN, N., Jesus and the Language of the Kingdom (London 1976) 41, 48, 53. MEYER, B. F., The Aims of Jesus (London 1979) 156.

3:24-25 SANFORD, J. A., The Kingdom Within (New York 1970) 109. KLAUCK, H.-J., Allegorie und Allegorese in Synoptischen Gleichnistexten (Münster 1978) 174-79.

3:24 BOUSSET, W., Die Religion des Judentums im Späthellenistischen Zeitalter (Berlin 1966=1926) 341.

3:26-27 KRUSE, H., "Das Reich Satans" Biblica 58 (1977) 29-61.

3:26 BORNKAMM-BARTH-HELD Ueberlieferung und Auslegung im Matthäus Evangelium (1961) 256.

3:27-33 BROWN, R. E. et al., Peter in the New Testament (Minneapolis 1973) 64-69.

3:27 BIEDER, W., Die Vorstellung von der Höllenfahrt Jesu Christi (Zürich 1949) 33ff. DODD, C. H. The Parables of the Kingdom (1948) 123ff. ROBINSON, J. M. Das Geschichtsverständnis des Markus-Evangeliums (1956) 30ff. ROBINSON, J. M. Kerygma und historischer Jesus (1960) 143. HAHN, F. Christologische Hoheitstitel (1963) 166. BARTSCH, H.-W., "Das Thomas-Evangelium und die Synoptischen Evangelien" NTS 6 (1959-1960) 255f. PERRIN, N., The Kingdom of God in the Teaching of Jesus (Philadelphia 1963) 76, 114, 115. DUNN, J. D. G., Jesus and the Spirit (London 1975) 44, 48f. PERRIN, N., Jesus and the Language of the Kingdom (London 1976) 41, 48, 53-54. FRIEDRICH, G., "Beobachtungen zur messianischen Hohepriestererwartung in den Synoptikern" in: Auf das Wort kommt es an (Göttingen 1978) 69. KLAUCK, H.-J., Allegorie und Allegorese in Synoptischen Gleichnistexten (Münster 1978) 179-84. SEYBOLD, K. and MÜLLER, U., Krankheit und Heilung (Stuttgart 1978) 97-98. MEYER, B. F., The Aims of Jesus (London 1979) 156-57. SCHRAGE, W. Das Verhältnis des Thomas-Evangeliums zur Synoptischen Tradition und zu den Koptischen Evangelienübersetzungen (1964) 88. KäSEMANN, E. Exegetische Versuche und Besinnungen (1964) 208. (I).

3:28-30 *EVANS, O. E. "The Unforgivable Sin" ET 68 (8, '57) 240-44. SATAKE, A. Die Gemeindeordnung in der Johannesapokalypse (1966) 172-75.

3:28-29 KNOX, W. L. The Sources of the Synoptic Gospels v. 2 (1957) 73. BORNKAMM-BARTH-HELD Ueberlieferung und Auslegung im Matthäus Evangelium (1961) 31. HAHN, F.

Christologische Hoheitstitel (1963) 107, 299f. BAUMBACH,
G. Das Verständnis des Bösen in den Synoptischen Evangelien
(1963) 24ff. TöDT, H. E. Der Menschensohn in der
synoptischen Ueberlieferung (1963) 282-88. *SCROGGS, R.
"The Exaltation of the Spirit by Some Early Christians" JBL 84
(4, '65) 359-73. *WILLIAMS, J. G. "A Note on the
'Unforgivable Sin' Logion" NTS 12 (1, '65) 75-77.
LöVESTAM, E. "Logiet om hädelse mot den helige Ande
(Mark 3:28f. par Matt. 12:31ff; Luk. 12:10)" SEA 33 ('68) 101-
17. LöVESTAM, E. Spiritus Blasphemia. Eine Studie zu Mk
3,28 par Mt 12, 31f, Lk 12, 10 (1966-67) Rev. J. Lähnemann
ThLZ 94 (10, '69) 759-61, F. Lentzen-Deis Biblica 51 (4, '70)
587-90, E. Bammel JThS 22 (1, '71) 192-94. STROBEL, A.
Erkenntnis und Bekenntnis der Sünde in neutestamentlicher
Zeit (1968) 39. WREGE, H.-T. Die Ueberlieferungsgeschichte
der Bergpredigt (1968) 164. HASLER, V. Amen (1969) 27.
THYEN, H. Studien zur Sündenvergebung (1970) 253ff.
LOHSE, E. et al. (eds.) Der Ruf Jesu und die Antwort der
Gemeinde (1970) 63-79. JEREMIAS, J., Neutestamentliche
Theologie I (1971) 22, 25-27, 44, 83. YATES, J. E., The Spirit
and the Kingdom (London 1963) 85-90.

3:28-29 WREGE, H.-T., Die Überlieferungsgeschichte der Bergpredigt
(Tübingen 1968) 11, 33, 108, 144ff, 164-67. *HOLST, R.,
"Reexamining Mk 3:28f. and its Parallels" ZNW 63 (1972) 122-
24. DUNN, J. D. G., Jesus and the Spirit (London 1975) 44, 49-
53, 60, 71, 90. *BORING, M. E., "The Unforgivable Sin Logion
Mk 3:28-29/Mt 12:31-32/Lk 12:10 Formal Analysis and
History of Tradition" NovT 18 (1976) 258-79. "Antichrist" in:
TRE 3 (1978) 22.

3:28 GRUNDMANN, W. Das Evangelium nach Markus (1959) 85f.
HAHN, F. Christologische Hoheitstitel (1963) 43.
JEREMIAS, J. New Testament Theology I (1971) 11, 15, 16,
17, 35.

3:29-30 EDWARDS, R. A., A Theology of Q (Philadelphia 1976) 121-
22.

3:29 TAYLOR, V. The Gospel According to St Mark (1953) 244.
FLEW, R. N., Jesus and His Church (1956) 48, 49.
ROBINSON, J. M. Kerygma und historischer Jesus (1960) 95.
YATES, J. E., The Spirit and the Kingdom (London 1963) 58f,
91. SCHRAGE, W. Das Verhältnis des Thomas-Evangeliums
zur Synoptischen Tradition und zu den Koptischen
Evangelienübersetzungen (1964) 98. KAESEMANN, E.
Exegetische Versuche und Besinnungen II (1964) II 97.
KAESEMANN, E. New Testament Questions of Today (1969)

99. BERGER, K. Die Amen-Worte Jesu (1970) 36-41. JEREMIAS, J. Neutestamentliche Theologie I (1971) 21, 25, 116. BERGER, K., "Zu den Sogenannten Sätzen Heiligen Rechts" NTS 17 (1970-1971) 37f. DORMEYER, D., Die Passion Jesu als Verhaltensmodell (Münster 1974) 77, 102. LADD, G. E., A Theology of the New Testament (Grand Rapids 1974) 46, 47, 88, 255.

3:30 DEVISCH, M., "La relation entre l'evangile de Marc et le document Q" in: M. Sabbe (ed.) L'Evangile selon Marc (Gembloux 1974) 85-87.

3:31ff JEREMIAS, J. Neutestamentliche Theologie I (1971) 48f, 166.

3:31-35 TAYLOR, V. The Gospel According to St Mark (1953) 247-49. TILLICH, P. Das Neue Sein (1959) 103-106. BULTMANN, R., The History of the Synoptic Tradition (Oxford 1963) 29-31, 56f. SCHRAGE, W. Das Verhältnis des Thomas-Evangeliums zur Synoptischen Tradition und zu den Koptischen Evangelienübersetzungen (1964) 185. BRAUN, H., Qumran und NT II (Tübingen 1966) 237. BLINZLER, J., Die Brüder und Schwestern Jesu (Stuttgart 1967) 73-86. SANFORD, J. A., The Kingdom Within (New York 1970) 86-87. SCHRAMM, T. Der Markus-Stoff bei Lukas (1971) 123f. SCHROEDER, H.-H., Eltern und Kinder in der Verkündigung Jesu (Hamburg-Bergstedt 1972) 110-24. TALBERT, C. H., Literary Patterns, Theological Themes, and the Genre of Luke-Acts (Missoula 1974) 43. KOCH, D.-A., Die Bedeutung der Wundererzählungen für die Christologie des Markusevangeliums (Berlin/New York 1975) 145-47. OBERLINNER, L., Historische Überlieferung und Christologische Aussage (Stuttgart 1975) 149-243. TANNEHILL, R. C., The Sword of His Mouth (Missoula 1975) 165-71. Von der OSTEN-SACKEN, P., "Streitgespräch und Parabel als Formen markinischer Christologie" in: G. Strecker (ed.) Jesus Christus in Historie und Theologie. Für H. Conzelmann (Tübingen 1975) 386-88, 392. *BEST, E., "Mark 3:20, 21, 31-35" NTS 22 (1976) 309-19. PESCH, R., Das Markusevangelium I (Freiburg 1976) 225 (lit!). STAGG, E./F., Woman in the World of Jesus (Philadelphia 1978) 138-39, 208-209. RUETHER, R. R., Mary - The Feminine Face of the Church (London 1979) 31-35. SWIDLER, L., Biblical Affirmations of Woman (Philadelphia 1979) 178, 193, 225, 237, 258, 278.

3:31 SCHMID, J. Das Evangelium nach Markus (1958) 85-87. BLINZLER, J. Aus der Welt und Umwelt des Neuen Testaments I (1969) 57-60.

3:32 DORMEYER, D., Die Passion Jesu als Verhaltensmodell (Münster 1974) 132, 424.

3:33-35 MEYE, R. P. Jesus and the Twelve (1968) 148-52.

3:34-35 FRIEDRICH, G., "Das Problem der Autorität im Neuen Testament" in: Auf das Wort kommt es an (Göttingen 1978) 383-85.

3:34 PRYKE, E. J., "IΔE and IΔOY" NTS 14 (1967-1968) 418f.

3:35 FLEW, R. N. Jesus and His Church (1956) 56, 59. BLAIR, E. P. Jesus in the Gospel of Matthew (1960) 58. MINEAR, P. S., Images of the Church in the New Testament (Philadelphia 1960) 170f. HAHN, F. Christologische Hoheitstitel (1963) 321. KAESEMANN, E. Exegetische Versuche und Besinnungen (1964) II 97. HENNECKE, E. und SCHNEEMELCHER, W., Neutestamentliche Apokryphen I (Tübingen 1964) 114. BERGER, K., "Zu den Sogenannten Sätzen Heilgen Rechts" NTS 17 (1970-1971) 28f. RAYAN, S., The Holy Spirit: Heart of the Gospel and Christian Hope (New York 1978) 6f. GERSTENBERGER, E. S. und SCHRAGE, W., Frau und Mann (Stuttgart 1980) 124, 162.

4-8 *HEGERMANN, H. "Bethsaida und Gennesar. Eine traditions- und redaktionsgeschichtliche Studie zu Mc 4-8" Judentum, Urchristentum, Kirche (1960) 130-40.

4:1-8:26 ACHTEMEIER, P. J., Mark (Philadelphia 1975) 92.

4:1-6:44 DRURY, J., Tradition and Design in Luke's Gospel (Atlanta 1976) 91-96.

4 DOBSCHUTZ, E. von, "Paarung und Dreiung in der evangelischen Überlieferung" in: A. Deissmann/H. Windisch (eds.) Neutestamentliche Studien G. Heinrici (Leipzig 1914) 96-99. SCHILLE, G., "Bemerkungen zur Formgeschichte des Evangeliums. Rahmen und Aufbau des Markus-Evangeliums" NTS 4 (1957-1958) 18ff. *MIGUENS, M. "La predicazione di Gesù in parabole (Mc. 4; Lc. 8, 4-18; Mt. 13)" BiblOr 1 (2, '59) 35-40. *WHITE, K. D., "The Parable of the Sower" JThS 15 (1964) 300-307. WILDER, A. N., The Language of the Gospel (New York 1964) 90ff. HAHN, F. Das Verständnis der Mission im Neuen Testament (1965) 96. *LAMBRECHT, J. "De vijf

parabels van Mc. 4, Struktuur en theologie van de parabelrede"
Bijdragen 29 (1, '68) 25-53. SCHREINER, J. Gestalt und
Anspruch des neuen Testaments (1969) 160f. *PEDERSEN, S.
"Er Mark 4 et 'lignelseskapitel'?" (Is Mark 4 a "Parable-
Chapter"?) DTT 33 (1, '70) 20-30. *BOERS, H. Theology Out
of the Ghetto. A New Testament Exegetical Study Concerning
Religious Exclusiveness (1971). WEINACHT, H. Die
Menschwerdung des Sohnes Gottes im Markus-evangelium
(1972) 89-98. KOLENKOW, A. B., "Beyond Miracles,
Suffering and Eschatology" in: G. MacRae (ed.) SBL Seminar
Papers 2 (Montana 1973) 171. RÄISÄNEN, H., Die
Parabeltheorie im Markusevangelium (Helsinki 1973) 114-27.
LAMBRECHT, J., "Redaction and Theology in Mk 4" in: M.
Sabbe (ed.) L'Evangile selon Marc (Gembloux 1974) 269-307.
ACHTEMEIER, P. J., Mark (Philadelphia 1975) 65-70. KEE,
H. C., "The Function of Scriptural Quotations and Allusions in
Mk 11-16" in: E. E. Ellis/E. Grässer (eds.) Jesus und Paulus.
Für W. G. Kümmel (Göttingen 1975) 180. MOULE, C. F. D.,
"On Defining the Messianic Secret in Mark" in: E. E. Ellis/E.
Grässer (eds.) Jesus und Paulus. Für W. G. Kümmel
(Göttingen 1975) 245-47. Von der OSTEN-SACKEN, P.,
"Streitgespräch und Parabel als Formen markinischer
Christologie" in: G. Strecker (ed.) Jesus Christus in Historie
und Theologie. Für H. Conzelmann (Tübingen 1975) 385, 387-
89. ROBINSON, J. M., "Gnosticism and the New Testament"
in: B. Aland et al. (eds.) Gnosis. Für H. Jonas (Göttingen 1978)
135-40. DIBELIUS, M., "Sammlung" [Die Formgeschichte
des Evangeliums (1933 *(2.aufl)*) 219-34], in: R. Pesch (ed.) Das
Markus-Evangelium (Darmstadt 1979) 76-77.

4:1-34   EWALD, H., Die drei ersten Evangelien (Göttingen 1850)
230ff. LIGHTFOOT, R. H. History and Interpretation in the
Gospels (1934) 74ff. FEINE, D. P. und BEHM, D. J.,
Einleitung in das Neue Testament (Heidelberg 1950) 28f.
BUTLER, B. C., The Originality of St Matthew (Cambridge
1951) 85ff. FINDLAY, J. A. Jesus and His Parables (1951)
19ff. KNOW, W. L. The Sources of the Synoptic Gospels
(1953) vol. 1. 35ff. TAYLOR, V. The Gospel According to St
Mark (1953) 249f. FARRER, A. St Matthew and St Mark
(1954) 197. *MARXSEN, W. "Redaktionsgeschichtliche
Erklärung der sogenannten Parabeltheorie des Markus ZThK
52/3 ('55) 255-72. GRANT, F. C. The Gospels (1957) 91f.
SCHMID, J. Das Evangelium nach Markus (1958) 88-91.
*BOOBYER, G. H. "The Redaction of Mark iv. 1-34" NTS 8
(1, '61) 59-70. MAUSER, U. Christ in the Wilderness (1963)
120ff. YATES, J. E., The Spirit and the Kingdom (London

1963) 65f. GERHARDSON, B. "the Parable of the Sower and its Interpretation" NTS 14 ('68) 165-93. PESCH, R. Naherwartungen (1969) 58, 59, 65, 97, 106, 107, 119. REPLOH, K.-G. Markus - Lehrer der Gemeinde (1969) 59-74. QUESNELL, Q. The Mind of Mark (1969) 72-88, 209-21. LEHMANN, M. Synoptische Quellenanalyse und die Frage nach dem historischen Jesus (1970) 56-90. KUHN, H.-W. Aeltere Sammlungen im Markusevangelium (1971) 99-146. WEEDEN, T. J. Mark-Traditions in Conflict (1971) 139-58. KELBER, W. H. "The History of the Kingdom in Mark - Aspects of Markan Eschatology" Proceedings I, ed. L. C. McGaughy (1972) 63-95. *PRYOR, J. W. "Markan Parable Theology. An Inquiry into Mark's Principles of Redaction" ET 83 (8, '72) 242-45. *WENHAM, D., "The Synoptic Problem Revisited: Some New Suggestions about the Composition of Mk 4: 1-34"TB 23 (1972) 3-38. RÄISÄNEN, H., Die Parabeltheorie im Markusevangelium (Helsinki 1973). WEEDEN, Th.J., "The Conflict between Mark and His Opponents over Kingdom Christology" in: G. MacRae (ed.) SBL Seminar Papers 2 (Montana 1973) 207-23. *ENGLEZAKIS, B., "Markan Parable: More than Word Modality, a Revelation of Contents" DBM 2 (1974) 349-57. *MERENDINO, P., "Gleichnisrede und Wortliturgie. Zu Mk 4:1-34" Archiv für Liturgiewissenschaft 16 (1974) 7-31. SCHENKE, L., Die Wundererzählungen des Markusevangeliums (Stuttgart 1974) 3-16. *LAMBRECHT, J., "Parables in Mc 4" TvTh (1975) 26-43. EGGER, W., Frohbotschaft und Lehre (Frankfurt 1976) 113f. *LOSADA, D. A., "Las para⅛bolas de crecimiento en el Evangelio de Marcos" RevBi 38 (1976) 113-25. PESCH, R., Das Markusevangelium I (Freiburg 1976) 227f. (lit!). *TROCME, E., "Why Parables? A study of Mk 4" BJRL 59 (1977) 458-71. *JONES, P. R., "The Seed Parables of Mark" RevEx 75 (1978) 519-38. KLAUCK, H.-J., Allegorie und Allegorese in Synoptischen Gleichnistexten (Münster 1978) 185-259. SCHMITHALS, W., Das Evangelium nach Markus (Gütersloh/Würzburg 1979) 228f. (lit!). KELBER, W. H., "Mark and Oral Tradition" Semeia 16 (1980) 43. WEDER, H., Die Gleichnisse Jesu als Metaphern (Göttingen 1980 *(2)*) 99-108.

4:1-22 GERTNER, M. "Midrashim in the New Testament" JSS 7 (1962) 267-92. NICKELS, P. Targum and New Testament (1967) 24.

4:1-20 BRUNNER, E. Saat und Frucht (1946) 7-21. PIROT, J. Paraboles et Allégories Evangeliques (1949) 91-103. MOWRY, L. "Parable" (Mk. 4:1-9, 13-20) IDB III (1962) 652b.

*SCHWEIZER, E. "Marc 4, 1-20" EThR 43 (4, '68) 256-64. LINNEMANN, E. Gleichnisse Jesu (1969) 17, 18, 19, 24, 52, 120ff, 179ff. MOULE, C. F. D. "Mark 4:1-20 Yet Once More" Neotestamentica et Semitica (eds.) E. E. Ellis and M. Wilcox (1969) 95-113. BARCLAY, W. And Jesus Said (1970) 18-24. EICHHOLZ, G. Gleichnisse der Evangelien (1971) 65-84. KUHN, H.-W. Aeltere Sammlungen im Markusevangelium (1971) 112-22. SCHRAMM, T. Der Markus-Stoff bei Lukas (1971) 114-23. *SEIM, T. K., "Apostolat og Forkynnelse. En studie til Mk 4:1-20" DTT 35 (1972) 206-22. *DRURY, J., "The Sower, the Vineyard, and the Place of Allegory in the Interpretation of Mark's Parables" JThS 24 (1973) 367-79. *BOWKER, J. W., "Mystery and Parable: Mk 4:1-20" JThS 25 (1974) 300-17. ZINGG, P., Das Wachsen der Kirche (Freiburg 1974) 76, 97-100. CONZELMANN, H. und LINDEMANN, A., Arbeitsbuch zum Neuen Testament (Tübingen 1975) 96f. *SCHWEIZER, E., "From the New Testament Text to the Sermon. Mk 4: 1-20" RevEx 72 (1975) 181-88. CLEVENOT, M., So kennen wir die Bibel nicht (München 1978) 111-12. *LEMCIO, E. E., "External Evidence for the Structure and Function of Mark iv. 1-20, vii. 14-23 and viii. 14-21" JThS 29 (1978) 323-38.

4:1-9   SCHNACKENBURG, R., Gottes Herrschaft und Reich (Freiburg 1959) 100-103, 111. TALBERT, C. H., Literary Patterns, Theological Themes, and the Genre of Luke-Acts (Missoula 1974) 43. CONZELMANN, H. und LINDEMANN, A., Arbeitsbuch zum Neuen Testament (Tübingen 1975) 86, 96. PESCH, R., Das Markusevangelium I (Freiburg 1976) 235 (lit!). GNILKA, J., Das Evangelium nach Markus I (Einsiedeln/Neukirchen 1978) 155f. (lit!). SWIDLER, L., Biblical Affirmations of Woman (Philadelphia 1979) 166.

4:1-5   SMITH, M., Tannaitic Parallels to the Gospels (Philadelphia 1968) 5bn38+.

4:1-2   SCHWEIZER, E., "Mark's Contribution to the Quest of the Historical Jesus" NTS 10 (1963-1964) 425f. GNILKA, J. Die Verstockung Israels (1961) 57f. HAHN, F. Christologische Hoheitstitel (1963) 230. ZIMMERMANN, W.-D. Markus über Jesus (1970) 53-54. RÄISÄNEN, H., Die Parabeltheorie im Markusevangelium (Helsinki 1973) 48-64. LAMBRECHT, J., "Redaction and Theology in Mark 4" in: M. Sabbe (ed.) L'Evangile selon Marc (Gembloux 1974) 272-73, 303-306. EGGER, W., Frohbotschaft und Lehre (Frankfurt 1976) 28, 33, 104, 110-119, 145. KLAUCK, H.-J., Allegorie und Allegorese in Synoptischen Gleichnistexten (Münster 1978) 240-41.

4:1   LEHMANN, M. Synoptische Quellenanalyse und die Frage nach dem historischen Jesus (1970) 57, 59f, 88, 101. KELBER, W. H., The Kingdom in Mark (Philadelphia 1974) 26, 27-28, 29, 34;, 52. TALBERT, C. H., Literary Patterns, Theological Themes, and the Genre of Luke-Acts (Missoula 1974) 43. MALBON, E. S., "Mythic Structure and Meaning in Mark" Semeia 16 (1980) 103-107.

4:2-20   MANSON, T. W., The Teaching of Jesus (Cambridge 1945) 75-80. MANEK, J., . . . und brachte Frucht. Die Gleichnisse Jesu (Berlin 1977) 20-25.

4:2-4   SWIDLER, L., Biblical Affirmations of Woman (Philadelphia 1979) 226.

4:2   PARKER, P. The Gospel Before Mark (1953) 52-53.

4:3ff   GOULDER, M. D., Midrash and Lection in Matthew (London 1974) 51, 54, 58, 60f. "Apokalyptik" in: TRE 3 (1978) 255.

4:3-8.14-20   LUCK, U., "Das Gleichnis vom Säemann und die Verkündigung Jesu" WuD NF 11 (1971) 73-92. HAHN, F., "Das Gleichnis von der ausgestreuten Saat und seine Deutung (Mk 4:3-8, 14-20)" in: E. Best/ R. McL. Wilson (eds.) Text and Interpretation. In honour of M. Black (Cambridge 1979) 133-42.

4:3-9   JüLICHER, D. A. Die Gleichnisreden Jesu (1910) 514-38. DODD, C. H. The Parables of the Kingdom (1948) 180ff. HAUCK, F. ThW V. S. 756, 20f. MICHAELIS, D. W. Die Gleichnisse Jesu (1956) 17-35. QUISPEL, G., "Some Remarks on the Gospel of Thomas" NTS 5 (1958-1959) 277ff. HUNTER, A. M. Interpreting the Parables (1960) 46ff, 10ff. GNILKA, J. Die Verstockung Israels (1961) 60f. *WHITE, K. D. "The Parable of the Sower" JTS 15 (2, '64) 300-307. SCHRAGE, W. Das Verhältnis des Thomas-Evangelium zur synoptischen Tradition und zu den Koptischen Evangelienübersetzungen (1964) 42. WILDER, A. N., The Language of the Gospel (New York 1964) 92f. BISER, E. Die Gleichnisse Jesu (1965) 51ff, 129. *NEIL, W. "Expounding the Parables: II. The Sower (Mk 4:3-8)" ET 77 (3, '65) 74-77. *JEREMIAS, J. "Palästinakundliches zum Gleichnis vom Säemann (Mark. IV. 3-8 Par.)" NTS 13 (1, '66) 48-53. KAHLEFELD, H. Parables and Instructions in the Gospels (1966) 15ff. JüNGEL, Paulus und Jesus (1966) 131, 151. GUTBROD, K. Ein Weg zu den Gleichnissen Jesu (1967) 38-50. GERHARDSSON, B. "The Parable of the Sower and its Interpretation" NTS 14 (1968) 165-93. LEHMANN, M. Synoptische Quellenanalyse und die Frage nach dem historischen Jesus (1970) 76f, 81, 85, 88.

LOHSE, E. et al., Der Ruf Jesu und die Antwort der Gemeinde (1970) 80-93. ZIMMERMANN, W.-D. Markus über Jesus (1970) 54-55. LOHSE, E., Die Einheit des Neuen Testaments (Göttingen 1973) 53f. LAMBRECHT, J., "Redaction and Theology in Mk 4" in: M. Sabbe (ed.) L'Evangile selon Marc (Gembloux 1974) 298-303. *WILDER, A. N., "The Parable of the Sower: Naiveté and Method in Interpretation" Semeia 2 (1974) 134-51. BULTMANN, R., "Die Interpretation von Mk 4:3-9 seit Jülicher" in: E. E. Ellis/E. Grässer (eds.) Jesus und Paulus. Für W. G. Kümmel (Göttingen 1975) 30-34. *GEISCHER, H,.-J., "Verschwenderische Güte. Versuch über Mk 4:3-9"EvTh 38 (1978) 418-27. *HORMAN, J., "The Source of the Version of the Parable of the Sower in the Gospel of Thomas" NovT 21 (1979) 326-43. *WEEDEN, T. J., "Recovering the Parabolic Intent in the Parable of the Sower" JAAR 47 (1979) 97-120. WEDER, H., Die Gleichnisse Jesu als Metaphern (Göttingen 1980 *(2)*) 108-17.

4:3-8 RÄISÄNEN, H., Die Parabeltheorie im Markusevangelium (Helsinki 1973) 83-87. PERRIN, N., Jesus and the Language of the Kingdom (London 1976) 8, 39, 96, 101, 129, 130, 143, 160, 162, 203. KLAUCK, H.-J., Allegorie und Allegorese in Synoptischen Gleichnistexten (Münster 1978) 186-200. *PAYNE, P. B., "The Order of Sowing and Ploughing in the Parable of the Sower" NTS 25 (1978) 123-29.

4:3 PASCHEN, W. Rein und Unrein (1970) 162ff. METZGER, B. M., The Early Versions of the New Testament (Oxford 1977) 245, 439. KLAUCK, H.-J., Allegorie und Allegorese in Synoptischen Gleichnistexten (Münster 1978) 241-42.

4:4 HARTMAN, L., Testimonium Linguae (Lund 1963) 28ff. METZGER, B. M., The Early Versions of the New Testament (Oxford 1977) 439.

4:7 MASSAUX, E. Influence de l'Evangile de saint Matthieu sur la littérature chrétienne avant saint Irénée (1950) 267-71.

4:9.23 *BISHOP, E. F. F. "Ακούειν ἀκουέτω Mark 4, 9.23" BTr 7/1 ('56) 38-40. SCHRAGE, W., Das Verhältnis des Thomas-Evangeliums zur Synoptischen Tradition und zu den Koptischen Evangelien-Uebersetzungen (1964) 42.

4:9 KLAUCK, H.-J., Allegorie und Allegorese in Synoptischen Gleichnistexten (Münster 1978) 241-42.

4:10ff GUY, H. A., New Testament Prophecy (London 1947) 79ff, 170ff. FINDLAY, J. A. Jesus and His Parables (1951) 4ff. CARRINGTON, P. The Primitive Christian Calendar (1952) 139-42. RUDOLPH, K., Die Mandäer II (Göttingen 1961) 257, n3. STRECKER, G. Der Weg der Gerechtigkeit (1962) 72, 106.

HAHN, F. Christologische Hoheitstitel (1963) 230.
GOPPELT, L. Christologie und Ethik (1968) 22f.
RICHARDSON, P., Israel in the Apostolic Church (London 1969) 57-58, 166-67. SMITH, M., Clement of Alexandria and a Secret Gospel of Mark (Cambridge, Mass. 1973) 117, 178, 183f, 197, 199, 212, 236, 250, 277.

4:10-20 STONEHOUSE, N. B. The Witness of Matthew and Mark to Christ (1944) 74ff.

4:10-13 MINETTE DE TILLESSE, G. Le Secret Messianique dans L'Evangile de Marc (1968) 168-80, 228-37. SCHWEIZER, E. Beiträge zur Theologie des Neuen Testaments (1970) 14-17. LAMBRECHT, J., "Redaction and Theology in Mk 4" in: M. Sabbe (ed.) L'Evangile selon Marc (Gembloux 1974) 277-85.

4:10-12 WAGENMANN, J., Die Stellung des Apostels Paulus neben den Zwölf (Giessen 1926) 58ff. STONEHOUSE, N. B. The Witness of Matthew and Mark to Christ (1944) 75. TAYLOR, V. The Formation of the Gospel Tradition (1949) 79f. *MANSON, W. "The Purpose of the Parables: A Re-Examination of St Mark iv. 10-12" ET 68 ('57) 132-35. ROBINSON, J. M. Kerygma und historischer Jesu (1960) 72. *SIEGMAN, E. "Teaching In Parables (Mk 4, 10-12); Lk 8, 9-10; Mt 13, 10-15)" CBQ 23 (2, '61) 161-81. MOWRY, L. "Parable" IDB III (1962) 652b. JEREMIAS, J. Die Gleichnisse Jesu (1962) 9-14, 64, 97. COUTTS, J. " 'Those Outside' (Mark 4, 10-12)" Studia Evangelica II, ed. F. L. Cross (1964) 155-57. SUHL, A. Die Funktion der alttestamentlichen Zitate und Anspielungen im Markusevangelium (1965) 145ff. JÜNGEL, E. Paulus und Jesus (1966) 132. MANSON, W. "The Purpose of the Parables: A Re-examination of Mark iv. 10-12" Jesus and the Christian (1967) 58-66. LEHMANN, M. Synoptische Quellenanalyse und die Frage nach dem historischen Jesus (1970) 86-88. ZIMMERMANN, W.-D. Markus über Jesus (1970) 55-57. AMBROZIC, A. M., St. Mark's Concept of the Kingdom of God (Würzburg 1970) 43-108. HAHN, F., "Die Worte vom Licht Lk 11:33-36" in: P. Hoffmann (ed.) Orientierung an Jesus. Für J. Schmid (Freiburg 1973) 119f. HOFFMANN, P., "Mk 8:31. Zur Herkunft und markinischen Rezeption einer alten Überlieferung" in: P. Hoffmann (ed.) Orienterung an Jesus. Für J. Schmid (Freiburg 1973) 192f. KONINGS, J., "The Pre-Markan Sequence in Jn 4" in: M. Sabbe (ed.) L'Evangile selon Marc (Gembloux 1974) 173. *LAMPE, P., "Die markinische Deutung des Gleichnisses vom Sämann Mk 4:10-12" ZNW 65 (1974) 140-50. SCHELKLE, K. H., "Der Zweck der Gleichnisreden (Mk 4:10-12)" in: J. Gnilka (ed.) Neues Testament und Kirche. Für R. Schnackenburg

(Freiburg 1974) 71-74. CONZELMANN, H. und LINDEMANN, A., Arbeitsbuch zum Neuen Testament (Tübingen 1975) 97. OBERLINNER, L., Historische Überlieferung und christologische Aussage (Stuttgart 1975) 215-33. EGGER, W., Frohbotschaft und Lehre (Frankfurt 1976) 109. PESCH, R., Das Markusevangelium I (Freiburg 1976) 241 (lit!). *KIRKLAND, J. R., "The Earliest Understanding of Jesus' Use of Parables: Mk 4:10-12 In Context" NovT 19 (1977) 1-21. GNILKA, J., Das Evangelium nach Markus I (Einsiedeln/Neukirchen 1978) 161f. (lit!). TANNEHILL, R. C., "The Gospel of Mark as Narrative Christology" Semeia 16 (1980) 70.

4:10-11 MOSLEY, A. W., "Jesus' Audience in the Gospels of St Mark and St Luke" NTS 10 (1963-1964) 140f. MEYE, R. P. Jesus and the Twelve (1968) 152-56.

4:10 *BURKILL, T. A. "The Cryptology of Parables in St Mark's Gospel" NovTest 1 (4, '56) 246-62. BLAIR, E. P. Jesus in the Gospel of Matthew (1960) 103. GNILKA, J. Die Verstockung Israels (1961) 58f. STRECKER, G. Der Weg der Gerechtigkeit (1962) 192. HAHN, F. Christologische Hoheitstitel (1963) 339. MEYE, R. P. "Mark 4:10: 'Those about Him with the Twelve'" in: Studia Evangelica II, ed. F. L. Cross (1964) 211-18. MEYE, R. P. Jesus and the Twelve (1968) 113. MINETTE DE TILLESSE, G. Le Secret Messianique dans L'Evangile de Marc (1968) 186-88, 238-42, 173-79. LEHMANN, M. Synoptische Quellenanalyse und die Frage nach dem historischen Jesus (1970) 57, 76. PASCHEN, W. Rein und Unrein (1970) 159f. *DOZZI, D. E., "Chi sono 'Quelli attorno a Lui' di Mc 4:10?" Marianum 36 (1974) 153-83. LAMBRECHT, J., "Redaction and Theology in Mk 4" in: M. Sabbe (ed.) L'Evangile selon Marc (Gembloux 1974) 277-81. ACHTEMEIER, P. J., Mark (Philadelphia 1975) 93.

4:11-13 LEHMANN, M. Synoptische Quellenanalyse und die Frage nach dem historischen Jesus (1970) 85f.

4:11-12 STONEHOUSE, N. B. The Witness of Matthew and Mark to Christ (1944) 108, 150. MANSON, T. W., The Teaching of Jesus (Cambridge 1945) 16, 18, 59, 64, 75-80. FEINE, D. P. und BEHM, D. J., Einleitung in das Neue Testament (Heidelberg 1950) 57f. VON LOEWENICH, W. "Luther und die Gleichnistheorie" ThLZ 77 (1952) 483-88. HAUCK, F. ThWV, ('54) 753, 35ff. *SUTCLIFFE, E. "Effect as Purpose: A Study in Hebrew Thought Patterns" Biblica 35 ('54) 320-327. TAYLOR, V., The Life and Ministry of Jesus (London 1954) 96f. *WIBERG, B. "Forherdelsestanken i evangelierne" (The

Idea of Obduracy in the Gospels) DTT 21 ('58) 16-32.
SCHNACKENBURG, R., Gottes Herrschaft und Reich
(Freiburg 1959) 126-30. BOOBYER, G. H., "The Secrecy Motif
in St Mark's Gospel" NTS 6 (1959-1960) 232f. GNILKA, J. Die
Verstockung Israels (1961) 23-28, 82f, 198-205. HAHN, F. Das
Verständnis der Mission im Neuen Testament (1965) 96.
BRAUN, H., Qumran und NT II (Tübingen 1966) 39.
JüNGEL, E. Paulus und Jesus (1966) 137. *AMBROZIC, A.
M. "Mark's Concept of the Parable" CBQ 29 (2, '67) 220-27.
MINETTE DE TILLESSE, G. Le Secret Messianique dans
L'Evangile de Marc (1968) 169-73. SMITH, M., Tannaitic
Parallels to the Gospels (Philadelphia 1968) 6bn2+, 8.7.
JEREMIAS, J. Neutestamentliche Theologie I (1971) 21f, 25,
27, 40, 42, 67, 100, 121f, 244. *HAUFE, G., "Erwägungen zum
Ursprung der sogenannten Parabeltheorie Mk 4: 11-12" EvTh
32 (1972) 413-21. *RÄISÄNEN, H., Die Parabeltheorie im
Markusevangelium (Helsinki 1973). *HUBAUT, M., "Le
'mystère' révélé dans les paraboles (Mc 4:11-12)" RThL 5 (1974)
454-61. LAMBRECHT, J., "Redaction and Theology in Mk 4"
in: M. Sabbe (ed.) L'Evangile selon Marc (Gembloux 1974)
281-85. EGGER, W., Frohbotschaft und Lehre (Frankfurt
1976) 115-18. KLAUCK, H.-J., Allegorie und Allegorese in
Synoptischen Gleichnistexten (Münster 1978) 245-53.
LAUFEN, R., "BAEIΛEIA und EKKΛHEIA. Eine traditions-
und redaktionsgeschichtliche Untersuchung des Gleichnisses
vom Senfkorn" in: J. Zmijewski/ E. Nellessen (eds.) Begegnung
mit dem Wort. Für H. Zimmermann (Bonn 1980) 132-34.
TANNEHILL, R. C., "The Gospel of Mark as Narrative
Christology" Semeia 16 (1980) 69.

4:11 CERFAUX, L., "La connaissance des secrets du Royaume
d'apres Matt 13:11 et Parallèles" NTS 2 (1955-1956) 238ff.
GREEVEN, D. H., "KAI Frequency in Greek Letters" NTS 15
(1968-1969) 370ff. FLEW, R. N. Jesus and His Church (1956)
62-64. BAIRD, J. A. "A Pragmatic Approach to Parable
Exegesis: Some New Evidence on Mark 4:11, 33-34" JBL 76 (3,
'57) 201-207. GNILKA, J. Die Verstockung Israels (1961) 45-
48. KAESEMANN, E. Exegetische Versuche und Besinnungen
(1964) II 98. = KAESEMANN, E. New Testament Questions of
Today (1969) 100. MINETTE DE TILLESSE, G. Le Secret
Messianique dans L'Evangile de Marc (1968) 194-201, 390-94.
SANFORD, J. A., The Kingdom Within (New York 1970) 43-
44. *HAACKER, K., "Erwägungen zu Mc 4:11" NovT (1972)
219-25. *BROWN, S., "The Secret of the Kingdom of God (Mk
4:11)" JBL 92 (1973) 60-74. ACHTEMEIER, P. J., Mark
(Philadelphia 1975) 57-59. GOPPELT, L., Theologie des

Neuen Testaments I (Göttingen 1975) 118, 219, 222f, 225.
*OBERMÜLLER, R., "Hablar de la revelación según el Nuevo
Testamento. Un estudio terminológico" RevBi 39 (1977) 117-
27. MEYER, B. F., The Aims of Jesus (London 1979) 169.
MALBON, E. S., "Mythic Structure and Meaning in Mark"
Semeia 16 (1980) 109-13.

4:12 WINDISCH, H., "Die Verstockungsidee in Mk 4:12" ZNW 26
(1927) 203-209. LOEWENICH, W. von., Luther als Ausleger
der Synoptiker (München 1954) 31ff. HESSE, F., Das
Verstockunqsproblem im Alten Testament (Berlin 1955) 3, 4, 5,
64. BLAIR, E. P. Jesus in the Gospel of Matthew (1960) 102.
KAESEMANN, E. Exegetische Versuche und Besinnungen
(1964) I 197. NICKELS, P. Targum and New Testament (1967)
24. BLACK, M. An Aramaic Approach to the Gospels and
Acts (1967) 77f. STROBEL, A. Erkenntnis und Bekenntnis der
Sünde in neutestamentlicher Zeit (1968) 39. MINETTE DE
TILLESSE, G. Le Secret Messianique dans L'Evangile de
Marc (1968) 189-94. *PEISKER, C. H. "Konsekutives hina in
Markus 4:12" ZNW 59 (1-2, '68) 126-27. BLOCH, R.,
"Midrash" in: W. S. Green (ed.) Approaches to Ancient
Judaism Theory and Practice (Missoula 1978) 49.

4:13-20 JüLICHER, D. A. Die Gleichnisreden Jesu (1910) 514-38.
JEREMIAS, J. Die Gleichnisse Jesu (1962) 10f, 75-78, 84, 97,
105. BAUMBACH, G. Das Verständnis des Bösen in den
synoptischen Evangelien (1963) 36ff. MINETTE DE
TILLESSE, G. Le Secret Messianique dans L'Evangile de
Marc (1968) 167-68, 415-20. GERHARDSSON, B. "The
Parable of the Sower and its Interpretation" NTS 14 (1968)
165-93. MOULE, C. F. D., "Mark 4:1-20 Yet Once More" in: E.
E. Ellis/ M. Wilcox (eds.) Neotestamentica et Semitica
(Edinburgh 1969) 106-109. LOHSE, E. et al., Der Ruf Jesu und
die Antwort der Gemeinde (1970) 80-85, 88. ZIMMERMANN,
W.-D. Markus über Jesus (1970) 57-58. *WENHAM, D., "The
Interpretation of the Parable of the Sower" NTS 20 (1974) 299-
319. CONZELMANN, H. und LINDEMANN, A.,
Arbeitsbuch zum Neuen Testament (Tübingen 1975) 86, 98.
PESCH, R., Das Markusevangelium I (Freiburg 1976) 247
(lit!).

4:13 LAMBRECHT, J., "Redaction and Theology in Mk 4" in: M.
Sabbe (ed.) L'Evangile selon Marc (Gembloux 1974) 280-82.
ACHTEMEIER, P. J., Mark (Philadelphia 1975) 93. EGGER,
W., Frohbotschaft und Lehre (Frankfurt 1976) 115, 117-19.
KLAUCK, H.-J., Allegorie und Allegorese in Synoptischen
Gleichnistexten (Münster 1978) 253-55.

4:14-20 LUCK, U. "Das Gleichnis vom Säemann und die Verkündigung Jesu" WuD NF 11 (1971) 73-92. RÄISÄNEN, H., Die Parabeltheorie im Markusevangelium (Helsinki 1973) 72-76. LAMBRECHT, J., "Redaction and Theology in Mk 4" in: M. Sabbe (ed.) L'Evangile selon Marc (Gembloux 1974) 298-303. KLAUCK, H.-J., Allegorie und Allegorese in Synoptischen Gleichnistexten (Münster 1978) 200-209. *O'MAHONY, G., "Mark's Gospel and the Parable of the Sower" Bible Today 98 (1978) 1764-68. HAHN, F., "Das Gleichnis von der ausgestreuten Saat und seine Deutung (Mk 4:3-8, 14-20)" in: E. Best/R.McL.Wilson (eds.) Text and Interpretation. In honour of M.Black (Cambridge 1979) 133-42. PAYNE, P. B., "The Seeming Inconsistency of the Interpretation of the Parable of the Sower" NTS 26 (1980) 564-68.

4:14 BARRETT, C. K., The New Testament Background: Selected Documents (London 1956) 89.

4:15 "Aramäisch" in: TRE 3 (1978) 608.

4:17 LAMBRECHT, J., "Redaction and Theology in Mk 4" in: M. Sabbe (ed.) L'Evangile selon Marc (Gembloux 1974) 300-302.

4:18 KLAUCK, H.-J., Allegorie und Allegorese in Synoptischen Gleichnistexten (Münster 1978) 242-45.

4:19 HARTMAN, L., Testimonium Linguae (Lund 1963) 15ff. BOUSSET, W., Die Religion des Judentums im Späthellenistischen Zeitalter (Berlin 1966=1926) 245. BRAUN, H., Qumran und NT II (Tübingen 1966) 288, 291. LAMBRECHT, J., "Redaction and Theology in Mk 4" in: M. Sabbe (ed.) L'Evangile selon Marc (Gembloux 1974) 300-302. "Armut" in: TRE 4 (1979) 77. CLARK, K. W., "The Making of the Twentieth Century New Testament" in: K. W. Clark (ed.) The Gentile Bias and Other Essays (Leiden 1980) 149-50. *KOSMALA, H. "The Three Nets of Belial (A Study in the Terminology of Qumran and the New Testament" ASThI vol. IV, 91-113.

4:20 SMITH, M., Tannaitic Parallels to the Gospels (Philadelphia (1968) 5bn38+.

4:21ff CONZELMANN, H. und LINDEMANN, A., Arbeitsbuch zum Neuen Testament (Tübingen 1975) 63, 96.

4:21-32 FARRER, A. St Matthew and St Mark (1954) 7, 9. *CRANFIELD, C. E. B. "Message of Hope (Mk 4, 21-32)" Interpretation 9 (2, '55) 150-64. STRECKER, G. Der Weg der Gerechtigkeit (1962) 186. *ESSAME, W. G. "kai elegen in Mark iv. 21, 24, 26, 30" ET 77 (4, '66) 121.

4:21-25   TAYLOR, V. The Formation of the Gospel Tradition (1949) 90-92. GNILKA, J. Die Verstockung Israels (1961) 39f, 61f. JEREMIAS, J. Die Gleichnisse Jesu (1962) 11, 89-91. McNAMARA, M. The New Testament and the Palestinian Targum to the Pentateuch (1966) 139, 142. ZIMMERMANN, H. Neutestamentliche Methodenlehre (1967) 181-89. MINETTE DE TILLESSE, G. Le Secret Messianique dans L'Evangile de Marc (1968) 280-81. ZIMMERMANN, W.-D. Markus über Jesus (1970) 58-59. LEHMANN, M. Synoptische Quellenanalyse und die Frage nach dem historischen Jesus (1970) 76f, 81, 86. RÄISÄNEN, H., Die Parabeltheorie im Markusevangelium (Helsinki 1973) 76-82. BEST, E., "Mark's Preservation of the Tradition"in: M.Sabbe (ed.) L'Evangile selon Marc(Gembloux 1974) 30-32; GT: "Markus als Bewahrer der Überlieferung" in: R. Pesch (ed.) Das Markus-Evangelium (Darmstadt 1979) 398-400. LAMBRECHT, J., "Redaction and Theology in Mk 4" in: M.Sabbe (ed.) L'Evangile selon Marc (Gembloux 1974) 285-90. TALBERT, C. H., Literary Patterns, Theological Themes, and the Genre of Luke-Acts (Missoula 1974) 43. ACHTEMEIER, P. J., Mark (Philadelphia 1975) 16-17. EGGER, W., Frohbotschaft und Lehre (Frankfurt 1976) 114, 118f. GNILKA, J., Das Evangelium nach Markus I (Einsiedeln/Neukirchen 1978) 178 (lit!).

4:21-23   PESCH, R., Das Markusevangelium I (Freiburg 1976) 251 (lit!). STRECKER, G., "Zur Messiasgeheimnistheorie im Markusevangelium" [orig: Studia Evangelica III (1964) 87-104]; in: R. Pesch (ed.) Das Markus-Evangelium (Darmstadt 1979) 202-203.

4:21-22   MOSLEY, A. W., "Jesus' Audiences in the Gospels of St Mark and St Luke"NTS 10 (1963-1964) 143f. HAHN, F.,"Die Worte vom Licht Lk 11:33-36" in: P. Hoffmann (ed.) Orientierung an Jesus. Für J. Schmid (Freiburg 1973) 120f. LAMBRECHT, J., "Redaction and Theology in Mk 4" in: M. Sabbe (ed.) L'Evangile selon Marc (Gembloux 1974) 286-89. SWIDLER, L., Biblical Affirmations of Woman (Philadelphia 1979) 166, 266, 253, 258.

4:21   JÜLICHER, D. A. Die Gleichnisreden Jesu (1910) 79-88. DODD, C. H. The Parables of the Kingdom (1948) 142ff. SCHRAGE, W. Das Verhältnis des Thomas-Evangeliums zur Synoptischen Tradition und zu den Koptischen Evangelienübersetzungen (1964) 81. JEREMIAS, J. Abba: Studien zur neutestamentlichen Theologie und Zeitgeschichte (1966) 99-102. DERRETT, J. D. M. Law in the New Testament (1970) 189-207. *SCHNEIDER, G. "Das Bildwort von der Lampe. Zur Traditionsgeschichte eines Jesus-Wortes" ZNW 61

(3-4, '70) 183-209. JEREMIAS, J. Neutestamentliche Theologie I (1971) 25-27, 108. HAHN, F., "Die Worte vom Licht Lk 11:33-36" in: P. Hoffmann (ed.) Orientierung an Jesus. Für J. Schmid (Freiburg 1973) 108, 109-14. GAIN, D. B., Evidence for Supposing that Our Greek Text of the Gospel of St Mark is Translated from Latin. . . (Grahamstown 1978). KLAUCK, H.-J., Allegorie und Allegorese in Synoptischen Gleichnistexten (Münster 1978) 227-35. TOLBERT, M. A., Perspectives on the Parables (Philadelphia 1979) 78f.

4:22   JüLICHER, D. A. Die Gleichnisreden Jesu (1910) 91-97. SCHRAGE, W. Das Verhältnis des Thomas-Evangeliums zur Synoptischen Tradition und zu den Koptischen Evangelienübersetzungen (1964) s.34. GOULDER, M. D., Midrash and Lection in Matthew (London 1974) 65, 72, 283, 349, 353, 366, 371f, 375. KLAUCK, H.-J., Allegorie und Allegorese in Synoptischen Gleichnistexten (Münster 1978) 235-38.

4:23-24   KLAUCK, H.-J., Allegorie und Allegorese in Synoptischen Gleichnistexten (Münster 1978) 241f.

4:24-29   WEDER, H., Die Gleichnisse Jesu als Metaphern (Göttingen 1980 *(2)*) 117-20.

4:24-25   *VAGANAY, L. "Existe-t-il chez Marc quelques Traces du Sermon sur la Montagne?" NTS 1 (3, '55) 192-200. KAESEMANN, E. Exegetische Versuche und Besinnungen II (1964) 79, 97. EDWARDS, R. A., A Theology of Q (Philadelphia 1976) 87-90. PESCH, R., Das Markusevangelium I (Freiburg 1976) 254 (lit!).

4:24   McNAMARA, M. The New Testament and the Palestinian Targum to the Pentateuch (1966) 138f, 142. NICKELS, P. Targum and New Testament (1967) 24. SMITH, M., Tannaitic Parallels to the Gospels (Philadelphia 1968) 6bn1+, bn5. "Aramäisch" in: TRE 3 (1978) 609. KLAUCK, H.-J., Allegorie und Allegorese in Synoptischen Gleichnistexten (Münster 1978) 238f.

4:25   SCHRAGE, W. Das Verhältnis des Thomas-Evangeliums zur Synoptischen Tradition und zu den Koptischen Evangelienübersetzungen (1964) 96. TILLICH, P. Das Ewige im Jetzt (1964) 31-40. SMITH, M., Tannaitic Parallels to the Gospels (Philadelphia 1968) 6bn2+. BERGER, K., "Zu den Sogenannten Sätzen Heiligen Rechts" NTS 17 (1970-1971) 19f. JEREMIAS, J. Neutestamentliche Theologie I (1971) 22, 25-27, 32. GOULDER, M. D., Midrash and Lection in Matthew (London 1974) 37, 65, 366, 407, 441. KLAUCK, H.-J., Allegorie und Allegorese in Synoptischen Gleichnistexten (Münster 1978) 239f.

4:26 BULTMANN, R., Theologie des Neuen Testaments (Tübingen 1965) 6f. ZIMMERMANN, W.-D. Markus über Jesus (1970) 59-61.

4:26-32 RÄISÄNEN, H., Die Parabeltheorie im Markusevangelium (Helsinki 1973) 87f. LAMBRECHT, J., "Redaction and Theology in Mk 4" in: M. Sabbe (ed.) L'Evangile selon Marc (Gembloux 1974) 291-97.

4:26-29 Jülicher, D. A. Die Gleichnisreden Jesu (1910) 538-46, 561-63. MORGAN, G. C. The Parables and Metaphors of Our Lord (1943) 163ff. BRUNNER, E. Saat und Frucht (1946) 34-47. DODD, C. H. The Parables of the Kingdom (1948) 176ff. PIROT, J. Paraboles et Allégories Evangeliques (1949) 132-38. HARDER, G. "Das Gleichnis von der selbstwachsenden Saat Mark 4, 26-29" Theologia Viatorum 1948/49, 51-70. FRICK, R. GPM 6 (1951) 224-28. HAUCK, F. ThW V (1954) 756, 19f. TAYLOR, V., The Life and Ministry of Jesus (London 1954) 68f. *MUSSNER, F. "Gleichnisauslegung und Heilsgeschichte. Dargetan am Gleichnis von der selbstwachsenden Saat" TThZ 5 ('55) 257-66. MICHAELIS, D. W. Die Gleichnisse Jesu (1956) 36-41. DINKLER, E. GPM 11 (1957) 198-200. SCHNACKENBURG, R., Gottes Herrschaft und Reich (Freiburg 1959) 104-106, 111. GNILKA, J. Die Verstockung Israels (1961) 74-78. JEREMIAS, J. Die Gleichnisse Jesu (1962) 92, 104, 151-53, 224. MOWRY, L. "Parable" IDB III 653 (1962). KLEIN, GPM (1962/63) 320ff. LOCKYER, H. All the Parables of the Bible (1963) 251ff. Ristow, H. (ed.) Predigtgedanken aus Vergangenheit und Gegenwart Reihe c, Band 3-4 (1963) 279-88. KLEIN, G. GPM 17 (1963) 320-26. BULTMANN, R., The History of the Synoptic Tradition (Oxford 1963) 172f. OBENDIEK, H. Herr, tue meine Lippen auf, ed. G. Eichholz (1964) 335ff. BISER, E. Die Gleichnisse Jesu (1965) 79ff. SUHL, A. Die Funktion de alttestamentlichen Zitate und Anspielungen im Markusevangelium (1965) 148, 152ff. JüNGEL, E. Paulus und Jesus (1966) 149-51. DIGNATH, W. Die Botschaft von der Endzeit (1966) 19-42. *BALTENSWEILER, H. "Das Gleichnis von der selbstwachsenden Saat (Markus 4, 26-29) und die theologische Konzeption des Markusevangelisten" Oikonomia, Festschrift für O. Cullmann (1967) 69-75. DUPONT, J. "La parabole de la semence qui pousse toute seule (Marc 4, 26-29)" RechSR 55 (3, '67) 367-92. MERKEL, F. GPM 23 (1968/69) 357-62. AMBROZIC, A. M., St Mark's Concept of the Kingdom of God (Würzburg 1970) 109-26. LEHMANN, M. Synoptische Quellenanalyse und die Frage nach dem historischen Jesus (1970) 62-64, 67f, 70f, 73f, 76f, 80-

83, 88. GUETTGEMANNS, E. Offene Fragen zur Formgeschichte des Evangeliums (1970) 65, 229. BARCLAY, W. And Jesus Said (1970) 32-37. KUHN, H.-W. Aeltere Sammlungen im Markusevangelium (1971) 104-12. *DOTY, W. G. "An Interpretation: Parable of the Weeds and Wheat" Interpretation 25 (2, '71) 185-93. — BONHOEFFER, D., Gesammelte Schriften V (München 1972) 576f. KERTELGE, K., Gemeinde und Amt im Neuen Testament (München 1972) 45f. KÜMMEL, W. G., "Hoch einmal: Das Gleichnis von der selbstwachsenden Saat" in: P. Hoffmann (ed.) Orientierung an Jesus. Für J. Schmid (Freiburg 1973) 220-37. LOHSE, E., Die Einheit des Neuen Testaments (Göttingen 1973) 51f. *STUHLMANN, R., "Beobachtungen und Überlegungen zu Mk 4:26-29" NTS 19 (1973) 153-62. TALBERT, C. H., Literary Patterns, Theological Themes, and the Genre of Luke-Acts (Missoula 1974) 40. ACHTEMEIER, P. J., Mark (Philadelphia 1975) 58. BRAUN, D., GPM 29 (1975) 419-29. CONZELMANN, H., und LINDEMANN, A., Arbeitsbuch zum Neuen Testament (Tübingen 1975) 58, 89, 96, 98f. DUPONT, J., "Encore la parabole de la Semence qui pousse toute seule (Mc 4:26-29)" in: E. E. Ellis/E. Grässer (eds.) Jesus und Paulus. Für W. G. Kümmel (Göttingen 1975) 96-108. ROESSLER, R., in: P. Krusche et al. (eds.) Predigtstudien für das Kirchenjahr 1975 III/2. Halbband (Stuttgart 1975) 226-34. PERRIN, N., Jesus and the Language of the Kingdom (London 1976) 39, 119, 129f. PESCH, R., Das Markusevangelium I (Freiburg 1976) 259 (lit!). MANEK, J.,.. . und brachte Frucht. Die Gleichnisse Jesu (Berlin 1977) 25-27. CLEVENOT, M., So kennen wir die Bibel nicht (München 1978) 113f. GNILKA, J., Das Evangelium nach Markus I (Einsiedeln/Neukirchen 1978) 182 (lit!). KLAUCK, H.-J., Allegorie und Allegorese in Synoptischen Gleichnistexten (Münster 1978) 218-27. TOLBERT, M. A., Perspectives on the Parables (Philadelphia 1979) 79-81. BÖHMIG, W./MEIER, C., in: P. Krusche et al. (eds.) Predigstudien für das Kirchenjahr 1980-1981 III/1. Halbband (Stuttgart 1980) 120-26.

4:26-27 WOLFF, H. W., Wegweisung (München 1965) 120f.

4:26 MINETTE DE TILLESSE, G. Le Secret Messianique dans L'Evangile de Marc (1968) 390-94. MALBON, E. S., "Mythic Structure and Meaning in Mark" Semeia 16 (1980) 109-13.

4:29 BLACK, M. An Aramaic Approach to the Gospels and Acts (1967) 163f. DORMEYER, D., Die Passion Jesu als Verhaltensmodell (Münster 1974) 141, 470. DUPONT, J., "Encore la parabole de la Semence qui pousse toute seule (Mc 4:26-29)" in: E. E. Ellis/E. Grässer (eds.) Jesus und Paulus. Für

W. G. Kümmel (Göttingen 1975) 101-104. JANSSEN, E., "Testament Abrahams" in: W. G. Kümmel (ed.) Jüdische Schriften aus hellenistisch-römischer Zeit III (Gütersloh 1975) 214.

4:30ff   BISER, E. Die Gleichnisse Jesu (1965) 79ff.

4:30-32   JüLICHER, D. A. Die Gleichnisreden Jesu (1910) 569-81. DODD, C. H., The Parables of the Kingdom (1948) 189ff. BUTLER, B. C., The Originality of St Matthew (Cambridge 1951) 2ff. MICHAELIS, D. W. Die Gleichnisse Jesu (1956) 54-60. FLEW, R. N. Jesus and His Church (1956) 27-28. *MUSSNER, F. "1QHodajoth und das Gleichnis vom Senfkorn (Mk 4, 30-32 par) BZ 4 (1, '60) 128-30. JEREMIAS, J. Die Gleichnisse Jesu (1962) 90, 92, 104, 145-48. KUSS, O. "Zur Senfkornparabel" Auslegung und Verkündigung I (1963) 78-84. SCHRAGE, W. Das Verhältnis des Thomas-Evangeliums zur Synoptischen Tradition und zu den Koptischen Evangelienübersetzungen (1964) 61. HAHN, F. Das Verständnis der Mission im Neuen Testament (1965) 31, 96. JüNGEL, E. Paulus und Jesus (1966) 151-54. ZIMMERMANN, H. Neutestamentliche Methodenlehre (1967) 123-25. BLACK, M. An Aramaic Approach to the Gospels and Acts (1967) 165f. GUETTGEMANNS, E. Offene Fragen zur Formgeschichte des Evangeliums (1970) 65, 229. BARCLAY, W. And Jesus Said (1970) 52-59. LEHMANN, M. Synoptische Quellenanalyse und die Frage nach dem historischen Jesus (1970) 62, 76f. AMBROZIC, A. M., St Mark's Concept of the Kingdom of God (Würzburg 1970) 127-42. SANFORD, J. A., THe Kingdom Within (New York 1970) 44f. KUHN, H.-W. Aeltere Sammlungen im Markusevangelium (1971) 99-104. MCARTHUR, H. K. "The Parable of the Mustard Seed" CBQ 33 (2, '71) 198-210. *FUNK, R. W., "The Looking-Glass Tree is for the Birds." Interpretation 27 (1973) 3-9. TALBERT, C. H., Literary Patterns, Theological Themes, and the Genre of Luke-Acts (Missoula 1974) 40. ZINGG, P., Das Wachsen der Kirche (Freiburg 1974) 100-107, 114f. CONZELMANN, H. und LINDEMANN, A., Arbeitsbuch zum Neuen Testament (Tübingen 1975) 55f, 96. FUNK, R. W., Jesus as Precursor (Missoula 1975) 19-26. PERRIN, N., Jesus and the Language of the Kingdom (London 1976) 39, 111, 119, 126, 129, 160. PESCH, R., Das Markusevangelium I (Freiburg 1976) 264 (lit!). MANEK, J., . . . und brachte Frucht. Die Gleichnisse Jesu (Berlin 1977) 27-29. *CASALEGNO, A., "La parabola del granello di senape (Mc 4:30-32)" RivB 26 (1978) 139-61. CLEVENOT, M., So kennen wir die Bibel nicht (München

1978) 114f. GNILKA, J., Das Evangelium nach Markus I
(Einsiedeln/Neukirchen 1978) 186 (lit!). KLAUCK, H.-J.,
Allegorie und Allegorese in Synoptischen Gleichnistexten
(Münster 1978) 210-18. MEYER, B. F., The Aims of Jesus
(London 1979) 163f. TOLBERT, M. A., Perspectives on the
Parables (Philadelphia 1979) 79-81. HARRINGTON, D. J.,
God's People in Christ (Philadelphia 1980) 23. LAUFEN, R.,
"ΒΑΣΙΛΕΙΑ und ΕΚΚΛΗΣΙΑ. Eine traditions- und
redaktionsgeschichtliche Untersuchung des Gleichnisses vom
Senfkorn" in: J. Zmijewski/E. Nellessen (eds.) Begegnung mit
dem Wort. Für H. Zimmermann (Bonn 1980) 105-40.
WEDER, H., Die Gleichnisse Jesu als Metaphern (Göttingen
1980 *(2)*) 128-38.

4:30   KNOX, W. L., The Sources of the Synoptic Gospels II (1957)
79, 130. *BARTSCH, H.-W. "Eine bisher übersehene Zitierung
der LXX in Mark 4, 30" ThZ 15 (2, '59) 126-28. MINETTE DE
TILLESSE, G. Le Secret Messianique dans L'Evangile de
Marc (1968) 390-94. KILPATRICK, G. D. "Some Problems in
New Testament Text and Language" Neotestamentica et
Semitica ed. E. Earle Ellis and Max Wilcox (1969) 201-203.
JEREMIAS, J. Neutestamentliche Theologie I (1971) 40, 42,
46, 89. LAMBRECHT, J., "Redaction and Theology in Mk 4"
in: M. Sabbe (ed.) L'Evangile selon Marc (Gembloux 1974)
294. MALBON, E. S., "Mythic Structure and Meaning in
Mark" Semeia 16 (1980) 109-13.

4:31-32   HAUCK, F. ThW V (1954) 756, 21f. LAMBRECHT, J.,
"Redaction and Theology in Mk 4" in: M. Sabbe (ed.)
L'Evangile selon Marc (Gembloux 1974) 293-95.

4:32   NICKELS, P. Targum and New Testament (1967) 24.

4:33-34   MANSON, T. W., The Teaching of Jesus (Cambridge 1945)
75ff. *BAIRD, J. A. " Pragmatic Approach to Parable
Exegesis: Some New Evidence on Mark 4:11.33-34" JBL 76 (3,
'57) 201-207. GNILKA, J. Die Verstockung Israels (1961) 50-
52, 59f. HAHN, F. Christologische Hoheitstitel (1963) 230.
MOSLEY, A. W., "Jesus' Audiences in the Gospels of St Mark
and St Luke" NTS 10(1963-1964) 140f. MINETTE DE
TILLESSE, G. Le Secret Messianique dans L'Evangile de
Marc (1968) 181-86. LEHMANN, M. Synoptische
Quellenanalyse und die Frage nach dem historischen Jesus
(1970) 58, 85, 87f. ZIMMERMANN, W.-D. Markus über
Jesus (1970) 61. RÄISÄNEN, H., Die Parabeltheorie im
Markusevangelium (Helsinki 1973) 48-64. LAMBRECHT, J.,
"Redaction and Theology in Mk 4" in: M. Sabbe (ed.)
L'Evangile selon Marc (Gembloux 1974) 273-77. TALBERT,

C. H., Literary Patterns, Theological Themes, and the Genre of Luke-Acts (Missoula 1974) 40. EGGER, W., Frohbotschaft und Lehre (Frankfurt 1976) 115-18. PESCH, R., Das Markusevangelium I (Freiburg 1976) 267 (lit!). GNILKA, J., Das Evangelium nach Markus I (Einsiedeln/Neukirchen 1978) 190 (lit!). KLAUCK, H.-J., Allegorie und Allegorese in Synoptischen Gleichnistexten (Münster 1978) 255f. TOLBERT, M. A., Perspectives on the Parables (Philadelphia 1979) 78.

4:33   MOLLAND, E. Opuscula Patristica (1970). JüNGEL, E. Paulus und Jesus (1966) 127, 137. STRECKER, G. Der Weg der Gerechtigkeit (1962) 71, 72. SMITH, M., Tannaitic Parallels to the Gospels (Philadelphia 1968) 8bn7+.

4:34   PARKER, P. The Gospels Before Mark (1953) 53-54. STRECKER G. Der Weg der Gerechtigkeit (1962) 192. MEYE, R. P. Jesus and the Twelve (1968) 152-56. MINETTE DE TILLESSE, G. Le Secret Messianique dans L'Evangile de Marc (1968) 238-42. PESCH, R. Naherwartungen (1969) 59, 68, 84, 97, 156. KÜMMEL, W. G., Einleitung in das Neue Testament (Heidelberg 1973 *(17)*) 62f. ACHTEMEIER, P. J., Mark (Philadelphia 1975) 93.

4:35-8:26   KNOX, W. L., The Sources of the Synoptic Gospels (1953) I 39ff. *ACHTEMEIER, P. J. "Towards the Isolation of Pre-Markan Miracle Catenae" JBL 89 (3, '70) 265-91. *ACHTEMEIER, P. J. "The Origin and Function of the Pre-Marcan Miracle Catenae" JBL 91 (2, '72) 198-221. KELBER, W. H. "The History of the Kingdom in Mk—Aspects of Markan Eschatology" Proceedings Vol. I (1972) ed. L. C. McGaughy, 63-95. ACHTEMEIER, P. J., Mark (Philadelphia 1975) 77-79. MEYE, R., "Ps 107 as 'Horizont' for Interpreting the Miracle stories of Mk 4:32-8:26" in: R. A. Guelich (ed.) Unity and Diversity in New Testament Theology (Grand Rapids 1978) 1-13.

4:35-6:52   KUHN, H.-W. Aeltere Sammlungen im Markusevangelium (1971) 191-213.

4:35-6:6a   SCHMITHALS, W. Wunder und Glaube. Eine Auslegung von Markus 4, 35-6, 6a (1970). Rev. G. Bassarak in THLZ 96 (8, '71) 588-90.

4:35-5:43   EWALD, H., Die drei ersten Evangelien (Göttingen 1850) 237ff. BORNKAMM-BARTH-HELD Ueberlieferung und Auslegung im Matthäus-Evangelium (1961) 177, 189, 234, 258. KUHN, H.-W. Aeltere Sammlungen im Markusevangelium (1971) 191-203.

4:35-41 FARRER, A., A Study in St Mark (1951) 85ff. *BAUER, J. B.
"Procellam cur sedarit Salvator" VerbDom 35 (2, '57) 89-96.
*ACHTEMEIER, P. "Person and Deed. Jesus and the Storm-
Tossed Sea" Interpretation 16 (2, '62) 169-76. HAHN, F.
Christologische Hoheitstitel (1963) 313. BECKER,
U./WIBBING, S. Wundergeschichten (1965) 33-45.
*SCHILLE, G. "Die Seesturmerzählung Markus 4:35-41 als
Beispeil neutestamentlicher Aktualisierung" ZNW 56 (1-2, '65)
30-40. KAMPHAUS, F. Von der Exegese zur Predigt (1968)
126-29. MEYE, R. P. Jesus and the Twelve (1968) 66-73.
*CONZELMANN, H. "Auslegung von Markus 4, 35-41 par;
Markus 8, 31-37 par; Römer 1, 3f" Evang Erzieher 20 (7, '68)
249-60. MINETTE DE TILLESSE, G. Le Secret Messianique
dans L'Evangile de Marc (1968) 411-20. SCHREINER, J.
Gestalt und Anspruch des neuen Testaments (1969) 180f.
SCHENKE, L. Herrlichkeit und Kreuz (1969) 11-16.
ZIMMERMANN, W.-D. Markus über Jesus (1970) 61-63.
LEHMANN, M. Synoptische Quellenanalyse und die Frage
nach dem historischen Jesus (1970) 44. KERTELGE, K. Die
Wunder Jesu im Markusevangelium (1970) 91-100. ITTEL, G.
W. Jesus und die Jünger (1970) 42-43. SCHMITHALS, W.
Wunder und Glaube (1970) 56-58. SCHRAMM, T. Der
Markus-Stoff bei Lukas (1971) 124f. JEREMIAS, J.
Neutestamentliche Theologie I (1971) 46, 49, 91-93. LANGE,
J., Das Erscheinen des Auferstandenen im Evangelium nach
Matthäus (Würzburg 1973) 340-42. SCHENKE, L., Die
Wundererzählungen des Markusevangeliums (Stuttgart 1974)
1-93. TALBERT, C. H., Literary Patterns, Theological
Themes, and the Genre of Luke-Acts (Missoula 1974) 42.
CONZELMANN, H. und LINDEMANN, A., Arbeitsbuch
zum Neuen Testament (Tübingen 1975) 70. KOCH, D.-A., Die
Bedeutung der Wundererzählungen für die Christologie des
Markusevangeliums (Berlin/New York 1975) 93-99.
*SURIANO, T. M., " 'Who Then is This?'...Jesus Masters the
Sea" Bible Today 79 (1975) 449-56. PESCH, R., Das
Markusevangelium I (Freiburg 1976) 277 (lit!). GNILKA, J.,
Das Evangelium nach Markus I (Einsiedeln/Neukirchen 1978)
192 (lit!). KLAUCK, H.-J., Allegorie und Allegorese in
Synoptischen Gleichnistexten (Münster 1978) 340-48. RIST, J.
M., On the Independence of Matthew and Mark (Cambridge
1978) 56f. TANNEHILL, R. C., "The Gospel of Mark as
Narrative Christology" Semeia 16 (1980) 68, 70.

4:35 SCHREIBER, J. Theologie des Vertrauens (1967) 12f, 84f, 95f,
120-22, 149f, 205f. BROER, I. Die Urgemeinde und das Grab
Jesu (1972) 142f, 145f. BETZ, H. D., Lukian von Samosata und

das Neue Testament (Berlin 1961) 166, 172. ACHTEMEIER, P. J., Mark (Philadelphia 1975) 14.

4:36-41 MALBON, E. S., "Mythic Structure and Meaning in Mark" Semeia 16 (1980) 103-107.

4:36 GAIN, D. B., Evidence for Supposing that Our Greek Text of the Gospel of St Mark is Translated from Latin. . . (Grahamsstown 1978).

4:37-41 BULTMANN, R., The History of the Synoptic Tradition (Oxford 1963) 215f.

4:37 METZGER, B. M., The Early Versions of the New Testament (Oxford 1977) 441.

4:38-39 LINTON, O., "Evidences of a Second Century Revised Edition of St Mark's Gospel" NTS 14 (1967-1968) 332f.

4:38 HAHN, F. Christologische Hoheitstitel (1963) 77, 86. DORMEYER, D., Die Passion Jesu als Verhaltensmodell (Münster 1974) 75A, 87.

4:39-40 KEE, H. C., "The Terminology of Mark's Exorcism Stories" NTS 14 (1967-1968) 243f.

4:39 BETZ, H. D., Lukian von Samosata und das Neue Testament (Berlin 1961) 115, 157. BOUSSET, W., Die Religion des Judentums im Späthellenistischen Zeitalter (Berlin 1966=1926)340. LINTON, O., "Le parallelismus membrorum dans le Nouveau Testament grec" in: A. Descamps/A. de Halleux (eds.) Mélanges Bibliques en hommage au R. P. Béda Rigaux (Gembloux 1970) 491f.

4:40-41 STONEHOUSE, N. B. The Witness of Matthew and Mark to Christ (1944) 70f, 106, 65.

4:40 BORNKAMM-BARTH-HELD, Ueberlieferung und Auslegung im Matthäus-Evangelium (1961) 201, 254. DORMEYER, D., Die Passion Jesu als Verhaltensmodell (Münster 1974) 60.

4:41 BOHREN, R. Wiedergeburt des Wunders (1972) 86-96. CLARK, K. W., "The Meaning of APA" in: The Gentile Bias and Other Essays (Leiden 1980) 195.

5 GREENLEE, J. H., Nine Uncial Palimpsests of the Greek New Testament (Salt Lake City 1968) 47f, 383-89. SCHENKE, L., Die Wundererzählungen des Markusevangeliums (Stuttgart 1974) 17-22.

5:1ff BOUSSET, W., Die Religion des Judentums im Späthellenistischen Zeitalter (Berlin 1966=1926) 338. PETZKE, G., Die Tradition über Apollonius von Tyana und das Neue Testament (Leiden 1970) 175, 180. EGGER, W., Frohbotschaft und Lehre (Frankfurt 1976) 98.

5:1-21 *AURELIO, T., "Mistero del regno e unione con Gesù: Mc 5:1-21" BiOr 19 (1977) 59-68.

5:1-20 BAUERNFEIND, O. Die Worte der Dämonen im Markusevangelium (1927) 23-28, 34-56. STONEHOUSE, N. B. The Witness of Matthew and Mark to Christ (1944) 28, 56. FARRER, A., A Study in St Mark (1951) 83ff, 325ff. KNOX, W. L. The Sources of the Synoptic Gospels (1953) I, 39ff. *HAWTHORN, T. "The Gerasene Demoniac. A Diagnois"ET 66/3 ('54) 79-80. *LOUW, J. "De bezetene en de kudde, Marc 5:1-20. Een hypothese" (The Demoniac and the Herd. Mk 5:1-20. An Hypothesis) NedThT 13 (1, '58) 59-61. BOOBYER, G. H., "The Secrecy Motif in St Mark's Gospel" NTS 6 (1959-1960) 229f. MASSON, C., Vers les Sources D'eau Vive (Lausanne 1961) 20ff. BAUMBACH, G. Das Verständnis des Bösen in den synoptischen Evangelien (1963) 45ff. HAHN, F. Christologische Hoheitstitel (1963) 296f. *CAVE, C. H. "The Obedience of Unclean Spirits" NTS 11 (1, '64) 93-97. *SAHLIN, H. "Die Perikope vom gerasenischen Besessenen und der Plan des Markusevangeliums" StTh 18 (2, '64) 159-72. HAHN, F. Das Verständnis der Mission im Neuen Testament (1965) 97. MUSSNER, F. Die Wunder Jesu (1967) 50f. LA-MARCHE, P. "Le Possédé de Gérase (Mt. 8, 28-34; Mc 5, 1-20; Lc 8, 26-39)" NRTh 90, (1968) 581-97. *CRAGHAN, J. F. "The Gerasene Demoniac" CBQ 30 (4, '68) 522-36. MINETTE DE TILLESSE, G. Le Secret Messianique dans L'Evangile de Marc (1968) 83-88, 98. Van IERSEL, B. M. F., "Jesus, Teufel und Dämonen" Annalen van het Thijmgenootschap 55 (1968) 5-22. *BLIGH, J. "The Gerasene Demoniac and the Resurrection of Christ" CBQ 31 (3, '69) 383-90. Van IERSEL, B. M. F., "Eine Legion erschlagen von einem Manne" Schrift 1 (1969) 8-12. ZIMMERMANN, W.-D. Markus über Jesus (1970) 63-66. SCHMITHALS, W. Wunder und Glaube (1970) 31-55. LEHMANN, M. Synoptische Quellenanalyse und die Frage nach dem historischen Jesus (1970) 36f, 44. KERTELGE, K. Die Wunder Jesu im Markus-Evangelium (1970) 101-110. *ARGENTI, C. "A Meditation on Mark 5:1-20" ER 23 (4, '71) 398-408. *DE MELLO, M. "The Gerasene Demoniac. The Power of Jesus Confronts the Power of Satan" ER 23 (4, '71) 409-18. *PESCH, R. "The Markan Version of the Healing of the Gerasene Demoniac" ER 23 (4, '71) 349-76. *STAROBINSKI, J. "An Essay in Literary Analysis - Mark

5:1-20" ER 23 (4, '71) 277-397. *PESCH, R., Der Bessessene von Gerasa. Enstehung und Uberlieferung einer Wundergeschichte (Stuttgart 1972). *BURGOS, M.de, "El poseso de Gerasa (Mc 5:1-20): Jesús portador de una existencia liberadora" Communio 6 (1973) 103-18. NIELSEN, H. K., "Et bidrag til vurderingen af traditionen om Jesu helbredelsesvirksomhed" DTT 36 (1973) 269-300. *PAUL, A., "Le récit (biblique) comme surface. Eléments théoriques pour une sémantique narrative" RSPhTh 58 (1974) 584-98. SCHENKE, L., Die Wundererzählungen des Markusevangeliums (Stuttgart 1974) 173-95. TALBERT, C. H., Literary Patterns, Theological Themes, and the Genre of Luke-Acts (Missoula 1974) 41. BARTLETT, D. L., Fact and Faith (Valley Forge 1975) 36f, 43. CONZELMANN, H. und LINDEMANN, A., Arbeitsbuch zum Neuen Testament (Tübingen 1975) 72. KOCH, D.-A., Die Bedeutung der Wundererzählungen für die Christologie des Markusevangeliums (Berlin/New York 1975) 62-64, 78-84. ANNEN, F., Heil für die Heiden (Frankfurt 1976). PESCH, R., Das Markusevangelium I (Freiburg 1976) 295 (lit!). *HARSCH, H., "Psychologische Interpretation biblischer Texte. Ein Versuch zu Mk 5:1-20: Die Heilung des Besessenen von Gerasa" US 32 (1977) 39-45. TRITES, A. A., The New Testament Concept of Witness (Cambridge 1977) 178. GNILKA, J., Das Evangelium nach Markus I (Einsiedeln/Neukirchen 1978) 199 (lit!). SEYBOLD, K. und MÜLLER, U., Krankheit und Heilung (Stuttgart 1978) 111-13. *DERRETT, J. D. M., "Contributions to the Study of the Gerasene Demoniac" Journal for the Study of the New Testament 3 (1979) 2-17. SCHMITHALS, W., Das Evangelium nach Markus (Gütersloh/Würzburg 1979) 265 (lit!).

5:1-16 SMITH, M., Clement of Alexandria and a Secret Gospel of Mark (Cambridge, Mass. 1973) 374ff.

5:1-13 BUTLER, B. C., The Originality of St Matthew (Cambridge 1951) 124ff.

5:1-5 CAVE, C. H., "The Obedience of Unclean Spirits" NTS 11 (1964-1965) 94f.

5:1-2 SWIDLER, L., Biblical Affirmations of Woman (Philadelphia 1979) 228.

5:1 KLOSTERMANN, E. Das Markusevangelium (1950) 47. BETZ, H. D., Lukian von Samosata und das Neue Testament (Berlin 1961) 37, 155. BAARDA, T. J. "Gadarenes, Gerasenes, Gergesenes and the 'Diatessaron' Traditions" Neotestamentica et Semitica, ed. E. E. Ellis and M. Wilcox (1969) 181-97. MALBON, E. S., "Mythic Structure and Meaning in Mark" Semeia 16 (1980) 103-107.

5:2 HAHN, F. Christologische Hoheitstitel (1963) 299. BROER, I. Die Urgemeinde und das Grab Jesu (1972) 118f.

5:5 DORMEYER, D., Die Passion Jesu als Verhaltensmodell (Münster 1974) 75A, 87. METZGER, B. M., The Early Versions of the New Testament (Oxford 1977) 171, 244.

5:6 HAHN, F. Christologische Hoheitstitel (1963) 86.

5:7, 9 BETZ, H. D., Lukian von Samosata und das Neue Testament (Berlin 1961) 153, 155ff, 163.

5:7 FLEW, R. N. Jesus and His Church (1956) 77-86. ROBINSON, J. M. Das Geschichtsverständnis des Markus-Evangeliums (1956) 37, 43, 44, 45f, 47, 98. *BURKILL, T. A. "Concerning Mk 5, 7 and 5, 18-20" StTh 11 ('57) 159-66. HAHN, F. Christologische Hoheitstitel (1963) 282, 301. HENNECKE, E. und SCHNEEMELCHER, W., Neutestamentliche Apokryphen II (Tübingen 1964) 327. HENGEL, M., Judentum und Hellenismus (Tübingen 1969) 546; ET: Judaism and Hellenism II (London 1974) 201. DORMEYER, D., Die Passion Jesu als Verhaltensmodell (Münster 1974) 164A, 606. ACHTEMEIER, P. J., Mark (Philadelphia 1975) 36. KOCH, D.-A., Die Bedeutung der Wundererzählungen für die Christologie des Markusevangeliums (Berlin/New York 1975) 57-59. ARENS, E., The HΛΘON - Sayings in the Synoptic Tradition (Fribourg 1976) 212-21. DONAHUE, J. R., "Temple, Trial, and Royal Christology" in: W. H. Kelber (ed.) The Passion in Mark (Philadelphia 1976) 73-75. BÄCHLI, O., " 'Was habe ich mit Dir zu schaffen?' Eine formelhafte Frage im AT und NT" ThZ 33 (1977) 69-80. FRIEDRICH, G., Beobachtungen zur messianischen Hohepriestererwartung in den Synoptikern" in: Auf das Wort kommt es an (Göttingen 1978) 70f. SEYBOLD, K. und MÜLLER, U., Krankheit und Heilung (Stuttgart 1978) 128f. MALBON, E. S., "Mythic Structure and Meaning in Mark" Semeia 16 (1980) 109-13.

5:8-9 BARRETT, C. K., The New Testament Background: Selected Documents (London 1956) 34.

5:8 NICKELS, P. Targum and New Testament (1967) 24. KOCH, D.-A., Die Bedeutung der Wundererzählungen für die Christologie des Markusevangeliums (Berlin/New York 1975) 63f.

5:9-14 CAVE, C. H., "The Obedience of Unclean Spirits" NTS 11 (1964-1965) 94f.

5:10   *SCHWARZ, G., " 'Aus der Gegend' (Mk 5:10b)" NTS 22 (1976) 214-15.

5:11-13 HARNACK, A., "Zu Mc 5:11-13" ZNW 8 (1907) 162.

5:11   DORMEYER, D., Die Passion Jesu als Verhaltensmodell (Münster 1974) 67A, 42.

5:12-13 JEREMIAS, J. Neutestamentliche Theologie I (1971) 90f.

5:16-20 LIGHTFOOT, R. H. History and Interpretation in the Gospels (1934) 88ff. BURKILL, T. A. "Concerning Mk 5,7 and 5, 18-20" StTh 11 (1957) 159-66. BORNKAMM-BARTH-HELD Ueberlieferung und Auslegung im Matthäus-Evangelium (1961) 93, 162. "Barmherzigkeit" in: TRE 5 (1980) 225.

5:18-20 KOCH, D.-A., Die Bedeutung der Wundererzählungen für die Christologie des Markusevangeliums (Berlin/New York 1975) 78-84.

5:19-20 STONEHOUSE, N. B. The Witness of Matthew and Mark to Christ (1944) 43, 58. HAHN, F. Christologische Hoheitstitel (1963) 73.

5:20   HARTMANN, L., Testimonium Linguae (Lund 1963) 37ff.

5:21-43 TAYLOR, V. The Formation of the Gospel Tradition (1949) 120, 122f. FARRER, A. A Study in St Mark (1951) 49ff, 83ff, 134f, 142ff, 167ff, 327ff, 337f. CARRINGTON, P. The Primitive Christian Calendar (1952) 144-46. TAYLOR, V., The Life and Ministry of Jesus (London 1954) 100f. BULTMANN, R., The History of the Synoptic Tradition (Oxford 1963) 214f. FULLER, R. H. Interpretating the Miracles (1963) 55ff. MINETTE DE TILLESSE, G. Le Secret Messianique dans L'Evangile de Marc (1968) 52-57. SMITH, M., Tannaitic Parallels to the Gospels (Philadelphia 1968) 5bn38+. KERTELGE, K. Die Wunder Jesu in Markusevangelium (1970) 110-20. ZIMMERMANN, W.-D. Markus über Jesus (1970) 66-68. SCHRAMM, T. Der Markus-Stoff bei Lukas (1971) 126f. DORMEYER, D., Die Passion Jesu als Verhaltensmodell (Münster 1974) 85A, 142. SCHENKE, L., Die Wundererzählungen des Markusevangeliums (Stuttgart 1974) 196-216. SCHMAHL, G., Die Zwölf im Markusevangelium (Trier 1974) 128f. ACHTEMEIER, P. J., Mark (Philadelphia 1975) 32, 77. BARTLETT, D. L., Fact and Faith (Valley Forge 1975) 43f. PESCH, R., Das Markusevangelium I (Freiburg 1976) 314 (lit!). TRITES, A. A., The New Testament Concept of Witness (Cambridge 1977) 179. GNILKA, J., Das Evangelium nach Markus I (Einsiedeln/Neukirchen 1978) 208 (lit!). RIST, J. M., On the Independence of Matthew and Mark (Cambridge 1978) 58-60.

SWIDLER, L., Biblical Affirmations of Woman (Philadelphia 1979) 215, 228, 237, 259.

5:21-24. LEHMANN, M. Synoptische Quellenanalyse und die Frage
35-43   nach dem historischen Jesus (1970) 39-41. SCHMITHALS, W.
         Wunder und Glaube (1970) 69-82.

5:21-34 EGGER, W., Frohbotschaft und Lehre (Frankfurt 1976) 95-97,
         137f.

5:21-24 TALBERT, C. H., Literary Patterns, Theological Themes, and
         the Genre of Luke-Acts (Missoula 1974) 43. KOCH, D.-A., Die
         Bedeutung der Wundererzählungen für die Christologie des
         Markusevangeliums (Berlin/New York 1975) 65-68.

5:21   ACHTEMEIER, P. J., Mark (Philadelphia 1975) 13-14.
         MALBON, E. S., "Mythic Structure and Meaning in Mark"
         Semeia 16 (1980) 103-107.

5:22ff   NÖTSCHER, F., Altorientalischer und altestamentlicher
         Auferstehungsglaube (Darmstadt 1970=1926) 303.

5:22   BARRETT, C. K., The New Testament Background: Selected
         Documents (London 1956) 51. HAHN, F. Christologische
         Hoheitstitel (1963) 86. *PESCH, R. "Jairus (Mk 5,22/Lk 8,
         41)" BZ 14 (2, '70) 252-56.

5:24-43 STAGG, E./F., Woman in the World of Jesus (Philadelphia
         1978) 209.

5:24-34 SWIDLER, L., Biblical Affirmations of Woman (Philadelphia
         1979) 181.

5:24b-34 *BAILEY, J. L. "Comparing the Contributions of the Synoptic
         Writers" BTh 18 (3, '68) 54-57. SCHMITHALS, W. Wunder
         und Glaube (1970) 83-91.

5:24-27 KONINGS, J., "The Pre-Markan Sequence in Jn 6" in: M.
         Sabbe (ed.) L'Evangile selon Marc (Gembloux 1974) 163.

5:25ff   HENNECKE, E. und SCHNEEMELCHER, W.,
         Neutestamentliche Apokryphen I (Tübingen 1964) 129.

5:25-34 FARRER, A. A Study in St Mark (1951) 83ff, 97f, 167f, 224f,
         328f. RICHARDSON, A. The Miracle-Stories of the Gospels
         (1948) 61f. HAHN, F. Christologische Hoheitstitel (1963) 312f,
         318. HAHN, F. Das Verständnis der Mission im Neuen
         Testament (1965) 95. NIELSEN, H. K., "Et bidrag til
         vurderingen af traditionen om Jesu helbredelsesvirksomhed"
         DTT 36 (1973) 269-300. GROS LOUIS, K. R. R., "The Gospel
         of Mark" in: Gros Louis et al. (eds.) Literary Interpretations of
         Biblical Narratives (Nashville 1974) 323f. TALBERT, C. H.,
         Literary Patterns, Theological Themes, and the Genre of Luke-
         Acts (Missoula 1974) 43. KOCH, D.-A., Die Bedeutung der

Wundererzählungen für die Christologie des Markusevangeliums (Berlin/New York 1975) 136-39. SEYBOLD, K. und MÜLLER, U., Krankheit und Heilung (Stuttgart 1978) 131f, 136f, 139f. LUZ, U., "Das Geheimnismotiv und die markinische Christologie" [orig: ZNW 56 (1965) 9-30]: in: R. Pesch (ed.) Das Markus-Evangelium (Darmstadt 1979) 212f.

5:27ff KAESEMANN, E. Exegetische Versuche und Besinnungen (1964) I 215.

5:27 METZGER, B. M., The Early Versions of the New Testament (Oxford 1977) 435.

5:29-33 BORNKAMM-BARTH-HELD Ueberlieferung und Auslegung im Matthäus-Evangelium (1961) 205f, 218, 243, 274.

5:30-33 *BROWN, R. E. Jesus—God and Man. Rev. F. Danker CBQ 30 (3, '68) 432-33.

5:31 HAHN, F. Christologische Hoheitstitel (1963) 77.

5:33-16:20 GRYGLEWICZ, F., "The St. Adalbert Codex of the Gospels" NTS 11 (1964-1965) 259f.

5:33 STONEHOUSE, N. B. The Witness of Matthew and Mark to Christ (1944) 103, 106f. LINTON, O., "Evidences of a Second Century Revised Edition of St Mark's Gospel" NTS 14 (1967-1968) 333f.

5:34-36 HENNECKE, E. und SCHNEEMELCHER, W., Neutestamentliche Apokryphen (Tübingen 1964) I 128, 155; II 317.

5:34 ROBINSON, J. M. Kerygma und historischer Jesus (1960) 30. BORNKAMM-BARTH-HELD, Ueberlieferung und Auslegung im Matthäus-Evangelium (1961) 201, 205. JEREMIAS, J. Neutestamentliche Theologie I (1971) 157, 160, 166, 210. GOPPELT, L., Theologie des Neuen Testaments I (Göttingen 1975) 199f, 203.

5:35-43 STONEHOUSE, N. B. The Witness of Matthew and Mark to Christ (1944) 49, 60, 62ff. TALBERT, C. H., Literary Patterns, Theological Themes, and the Genre of Luke-Acts (Missoula 1974) 43. KOCH, D.-A., Die Bedeutung der Wundererzählungen für die Christologie des Markusevangeliums (Berlin/New York 1975) 65-68.

5:35-37 HAHN, F. Christologische Hoheitstitel (1963) 77, 79.

5:35 BLACK, M. An Aramaic Approach to the Gospels and Acts (1967) 127f. DORMEYER, D., Die Passion Jesu als Verhaltensmodell (Münster 1974) 90A, 174.

5:36 BORNKAMM-BARTH-HELD Ueberlieferung und Auslegung im Matthäus-Evangelium (1961) 169, 201, 221.

5:37 PESCH, R. Naherwartungen (1969) 99, 100, 134, 153. SCHMAHL, G., Die Zwölf im Markusevangelium (Trier 1974) 129-31. ERNST, J., "Die Petrustradition im Markusevangelium - ein altes Problem neu angegangen" in: J. Zmijewski/E. Nellessen (eds.) Begegnung mit dem Wort. Für H. Zimmermann (Bonn 1980) 47.

5:38-43 WESTERHOLM, S., Jesus and Scribal Authority (Lund 1978) 68.

5:39-40 DIBELIUS, M., Aufsätze zur Apostelgeschichte (Göttingen 1951); ET: Studies in the Acts of the Apostles (London 1956) 18f.

5:39 *KER, R. E. and POWELL, W. "Zu Mk 5, 39" ET 65 (10, '54) 315-16; 66 (2, '54) 61; (4, '55) 125 (7, '55) 215. BORNKAMM-BARTH-HELD, Ueberlieferung und Auslegung im Matthäus-Evangelium (1961) 252. HOFFMANN, P. Die Toten in Christus (1966) 202-204.

5:41-43 BETZ, H. D., Lukian von Samosata und das Neue Testament (Berlin 1961) 150, 155, 157f.

5:41 *HINDLEY, J. C. "Our Lord's Aramaic - A Speculation" ET 72 (6, '61) 180-81. MCNAMARA, M. The New Testament and the Palestinian Targum to the Pentateuch (1966) 94, n.62. NEPPER-CHRISTENSEN, P., Das Matthäusevangelium (Aarhus 1958) 110-12. "Aramäisch" in: TRE 3 (1978) 609.

5:42 DORMEYER, D., Die Passion Jesu als Verhaltensmodell (Münster 1974) 67A, 42.

5:43 LIGHTFOOT, R. H. History and Interpretation in the Gospels (1934) 71f. WREDE, W. Das Messiasgeheimnis in den Evangelien (1963) 15, 33, 156, 254-58. MINETTE DE TILLESSE, G. Le Secret Messianique dans L'Evangile de Marc (1968) 249-51. EFIRD, J. M., "Note on Mark 5:43" in: J.M.Efird (ed.) The Use of the Old Testament in the New and other Essays (Durham 1972) 307-309. KÜMMEL, W. G., Einleitung in das Neue Testament (Heidelberg 1973 (17)) 62f. ACHTEMEIER, P. J., Mark (Philadelphia 1975) 79-81.

6-10 KLOSTERMANN, E. Das Markusevangelium (1950) 54.

6-8 LANGKAMMER, H., in: S. Lach et al. (eds.) Materialy pomocnicze do wykladów z biblistyki II (Lublin 1977).

6 SCHOTT, E., "Die Aussendungsrede Mt 10; Mc 6; Lc 9.10" ZNW 7 (1906) 140-50. RUDOLPH, K., Die Mandäer I (Göttingen 1960) 73, 74; II (1961) 234. KÜNZI, M., Das Naherwartungslogion Matthäus 10:23 (Tübingen 1970) 70, 127, 133, 137, 139, 144. KONINGS, J., "The Pre-Markan Sequence in Jn 6" in: M. Sabbe (ed.) L'Evangile selon Marc (Gembloux 1974) 147-77. SHERWIN-WHITE, A. N., Roman Society and Roman Law in the New Testament (Grand Rapids 1978) 21, 136.

6:1ff LIGHTFOOT, R. H. History and Interpretation in the Gospels (1934) 112f, 184ff. HAHN, F. Das Verständnis der Mission im Neuen Testament (1965) 102.

6:1-8:26 STONEHOUSE, N. B. The Witness of Matthew and Mark to Christ (1944) 151.

6:1-6 EWALD, H., Die drei ersten Evangelien (Göttingen 1850) 243ff. JüLICHER, D. A. Die Gleichnisreden Jesu (1910) 171-74. GOGUEL, M. ZNW 12, (1911) 321-24. GOODSPEED, E. J., A Life of Jesus (New York 1950) 95-99. KNOX, W. L. The Sources of the Synoptic Gospels (1953) I, 47ff. MASSON, C., Vers les Sources D'eav Vive (Lausanne 1961) 38ff. HAHN, F. Christologische Hoheitstitel (1963) 394f, 397. HAENCHEN, E. "Historie und Verkündigung bei Markus und Lukas" Die Bibel und Wir (1968) 156-81. *GRäSSER, E. "Jesus in Nazareth (Mark VI.1-6a) Notes on the Redaktion and Theology of St. Mark" NTS 16 (1, '69) 1-23. *SCHNACKENBURG, R. "The Primitive Church and its Traditions of Jesus" Perspective 10 (2, '69) 103-24. SCHüTZ, F. Der leidende Christus (1969) 42ff. ZIMMERMANN, W.-D. Markus über Jesus (1970) 68-71. SCHMITHALS, W. Wunder und Glaube (1970) 92-99. CHRIST, F. Jesus Sophia (1970) 61, 62, 66, 68, 92. SCHUERMANN, H., "Zur Traditionsgeschichte der Nazareth-Perikope Lk 4:16-30" in: A. Descamps/A. de Halleux (eds.) Mélanges Bibliques en hommage au R. P. Béda Rigaux (Gembloux 1970) 188-91, 199f, 205. GRAESSER, E. "Jesus in Nazareth (Mc 6:1-6a)" Jesus in Nazareth, eds. E. Grässer et al. (1972) 1-37. GRAESSER, E. "Jesus in Nazareth (Mk 6, 1-6a). Bemerkungen zur Redaktion und Theologie des Markus", Text und Situation (1973) 13-49. SCHNIDER, F., Jesus der Prophet (Freiburg 1973) 147ff. DAVIES, W. D., The Gospel and the Land (London 1974) 236-40, 434 n75. KONINGS, J., "The Pre-Markan Sequence in Jn 6" in: M.

Sabbe (ed.) L'Evangile selon Marc (Gembloux 1974) 172f.
NEIRYNCK, F., "Urmarcus redivivus?" in: M. Sabbe (ed.)
L'Evangile selon Marc (Gembloux 1974) 106. *PERROT, C.,
"Jésus à Nazareth. Mc 6:1-6" AssS 45 (1974) 40-49. TALBERT,
C. H., Literary Patterns, Theological Themes, and the Genre of
Luke-Acts (Missoula 1974) 18, 41. ACHTEMEIER, P. J.,
Mark (Philadelphia 1975) 28f. CONZELMANN, H. und
LINDEMANN, A., Arbeitsbuch zum Neuen Testament
(Tübingen 1975) 41. GLÖCKNER, R., Die Verkündigung des
Heils beim Evangelisten Lukas (Mainz 1975) 127f, 216f.
KOCH, D.-A., Die Bedeutung der Wundererzählungen für die
Christologie des Markusevangeliums (Berlin/New York 1975)
139f, 147-53, 154f. OBERLINNER, K., Historische
Überlieferung und christologische Aussage (Stuttgart 1975) 86-
88, 249-350. PESCH, R., Das Markusevangelium I (Freiburg
1976) 325 (lit!). BUSSE, U., Das Nazareth-Manifest Jesu. Eine
Einführung in das lukanische Jesusbild nach Lk 4:16-30
(Stuttgart 1978) 62-67. GNILKA, J., Das Evangelium nach
Markus I (Einsiedeln/Neukirchen 1978) 226f (lit!). *MAYER,
B., "Überlieferungs- und redaktionsgeschichtliche
Überlegungen zu Mk 6:1-6a" BZ 22 (1978) 187-98. RIST, J. M.,
On the Independence of Matthew and Mark (Cambridge 1978)
60f. SWIDLER, L., Biblical Affirmations of Woman
(Philadelphia 1979) 178, 228, 237.

6:1 HENDRIKS, W., "Zur Kollektionsgeschichte des
Markusevangeliums" in: M. Sabbe (ed.) L'Evangile selon Marc
(Gembloux 1974) 55. NEIRYNCK, F., "Urmarcus redivivus"
in: M. Sabbe (ed.) L'Evangile selon Marc (Gembloux 1974)
106.

6:2 PESCH, R. Naherwartungen (1969) 101, 102, 106, 189.
HAHN, F., Christologische Hoheitstitel (1963) 230.
BORNKAMM-BARTH-HELD Ueberlieferung und
Auslegung im Matthäus-Evangelium (1961) 189. PETZKE, G.,
Die Traditionen über Apollonius von Tyana und das Neue
Testament (Leiden 1970) 108, 170, 190. KONINGS, J., "The
Pre-Markan Sequence in Jn 6" in: M. Sabbe (ed.) L'Evangile
selon Marc (Gembloux 1974) 173. DUNN, J. D. G., Jesus and
the Spirit (London 1975) 16, 70, 76.

6:3 CLARKE, W. K. L., New Testament Problems (New York
1929) 31-34. VOLZ, P., Die Eschatologie der jüdischen
Gemeinde (Tübingen 1934) 208. KLOSTERMANN, E. Das
Markusevangelium (1950) 55. TAYLOR, V., The Text of the
New Testament (London 1961) 83f. HAHN, F. Das
Verständnis der Mission im Neuen Testament (1965) 39.

BLINZLER, J., Die Brüder und Schwestern Jesu (Stuttgart 1967) 28-30, 71f, 75-82. STAUFFER, E. "Jeschu Ben Mirjam (Mk 6:3)" Neotestamentica et Semitica, eds. E. E. Ellis and M. Wilcox (1969) 119-28. BLINZLER, J. Aus der Welt und Umwelt des Neuen Testaments. Gesammelte Aufsätze I (1969) 11, 37, 55, 58, 59. *McARTHUR, H. K., " 'Son of Mary' " NovT 15 (1973) 38-58. VAWTER, B., This Man Jesus (New York 1973) 186ff. DORMEYER, D., Die Passion Jesu als Verhaltensmodell (Münster 1974) 207A, 236A, 237. KONINGS, J., "The Pre-Markan Sequence in Jn 6" in: M. Sabbe (ed.) L'Evangile selon Marc (Gembloux 1974) 173. SWIDLER, L., Biblical Affirmations of Woman (Philadelphia 1979) 278.

6:4   HAHN, F. Christologische Hoheitstitel (1963) 390. SCHRAGE, W. Das Verhältnis des Thomas-Evangelium zur Synoptischen Tradition und zu den Koptischen Evangelienübersetzungen (1964) 75. BLINZLER, J., Die Brüder und Schwestern Jesu (Stuttgart 1967) 62f. KÜMMEL, W. G., Einleitung in das Neue Testament (Heidelberg 1973 *(17)*) 167f. KONINGS, J., "The Pre-Markan Sequence in Jn 6" in: M. Sabbe (ed.) L'Evangile selon Marc (Gembloux 1974) 172. DUNN, J. D. G., Jesus and the Spirit (London 1975) 82. WILLIAMS, J. A., A Conceptual History of Deuteronomism in the Old Testament (Louisville 1976) 310. THEISSEN, G., Soziologie der Jesusbewegung (München 1977) 17.

6:5-8:26   SCHWEIZER, E., "Die Theologische Leistung des Markus" [orig.: EvTh 24 (1964) 337-55] in R. Pesch (ed.) Das Markus-Evangelium (Darmstadt 1979) 174df.

6:5   BORNKAMM-BARTH-HELD, Ueberlieferung und Auslegung im Matthäus-Evangelium (1961) 265. GROS LOUIS, K. R. R., "The Gospel of Mark" in: Gros Louis et al. (eds.) Literary Interpretations of Biblical Narratives (Nashville 1974) 321. DUNN, J. D. G., Jesus and the Spirit (London 1975) 70. GOPPELT, L., Theologie des Neuen Testaments I (Göttingen 1975) 196f.

6:6-32   MINETTE DE TILLESSE, G. Le Secret Messianique dans L'Evangile de Marc (1968) 413-20.

6:6-13   EWALD, H., Die drei ersten Evangelien (Göttingen 1850) 246ff. MEYE, R. P. Jesus and the Twelve (1968) 106-110. FREYNE, S. The Twelve: Disciples and Apostles (1968) 94. REPLOH, K.-G. Markus-Lehrer der Gemeinde (1969) 50-58. ZIMMERMANN, W.-D. Markus über Jesus (1970) 71-74. HOFFMANN, P. Studien zur Theologie der Logienquelle (1972) 237-43, 261-63. SCHUBERT, K., Jesus im Lichte der

Religionsgeschichte des Judentums (München 1973) 126f.
EDWARDS, R. A., A Theology of Q (Philadelphia 1976) 99f.
PESCH, R., Das Markusevangelium I (Freiburg 1976) 331f.
(lit!). GNILKA, J., Das Evangelium nach Markus I
(Einsiedeln/Neukirchen 1978) 236 (lit!). KERTELGE, K.,
"Offene Fragen zum Thema 'Geistliches Amt' und das
neutestamentliche Verständnis von der 'repraesentatio Christi'
" in: R. Schnackenburg et al. (eds.) Die Kirche des Anfangs.
Für H. Schürmann (Freiburg 1978) 588-90.

6:6-11   BUTLER, B. C., The Originality of St Matthew (Cambridge 1951) 102ff.

6:6b-8:26   EGGER, W., Frohbotschaft und Lehre (Frankfurt 1976) 22, 154, 163.

6:6b   HAHN, F. Christologische Hoheitstitel (1963) 230. EGGER, W., Frohbotschaft und Lehre (Frankfurt 1976) 28, 77, 125, 153-55.

6:7ff   GOULDER, M. D., Midrash and Lection in Matthew (London 1974) 314, 338, 344f, 377.

6:7-56   FARRER, A. A Study in St Mark (1951) 88ff, 94ff, 190f, 312f.

6:7-32   DORMEYER, D., Die Passion Jesu als Verhaltensmodell (Münster 1974) 85A, 142.

6:7-31   ACHTEMEIER, P. J., Mark (Philadelphia 1975) 32.

6:7-13   BARRETT, C. K., The Holy Spirit and the Gospel Tradition (New York 1947) 127-30. FARRER, A. A Study in St Mark (1951) 90ff, 108ff. FARRER, A. St Matthew and St Mark (1954) 8, 21, 195, 197. ROLOFF, J. Apostolat-Verkündigung-Kirche (1965) 150-52. KASTING, H. Die Anfänge der Urchristlichen Mission (1969) 111, 125f. PESCH, R. Naherwartungen (1969) 42, 58, 59. OTOMO, Y. Nachfolge Jesu und Anfänge der Kirche im Neuen Testament (1970) 68-70. ITTEL, G. W. Jesus und die Jünger (1970) 49-53. MUSSNER, F., "Gab es eine 'galiläische Krise'?" in: P. Hoffmann (ed.) Orientierung an Jesus. Für J. Schmid (Freiburg 1973) 244-48. *DELORME, J., "La mission des Douze en Galileé" AssS 46 (1974) 43-50. SCHMAHL, G., Die Zwölf im Markusevangelium (Trier 1974) 67-81. TALBERT, C. H., Literary Patterns, Theological Themes, and the Genre of Luke-Acts (Missoula 1975) 27. CONZELMANN, H. und LINDEMANN, A., Arbeitsbuch zum Neuen Testament (Tübingen 1975) 64. EGGER, W., Frohbotschaft und Lehre (Frankfurt 1976) 51, 153f. SCHMITHALS, W., Das Evangelium nach Markus (Gütersloh/Würzburg 1979) 307 (lit!). McDONALD, J. I. H., Kerygma and Didache

(Cambridge 1980) 118. TANNEHILL, R. C., "The Gospel of Mark as Narrative Christology" Semeia 16 (1980) 69.

6:7-11 HAHN, F. Das Verständnis der Mission im Neuen Testament (1965) 32, 33-36, 102. SCHILLE, G. Die urchristliche Kollegialmission (1967) 30ff, 74ff, 78f, 86f. DUNGAN, D. L. The Sayings of Jesus in the Churches of Paul (1971) 63-66, 74-75. BORSCH, F. H., "Jesus the Wandering Preacher?" in: M. Hooker/C. Hickling (eds.) What about the New Testament. In honour of C. Evans (London 1975) 48f.

6:7 FARRER, A. St Matthew and St Mark (1954) 109-110. PESCH, R. Naherwartungen (1969) 106, 173, 198. JEREMIAS, J. Neutestamentliche Theologie I (1971) 83, 96, 98. LANGE, J., Das Erscheinen des Auferstandenen im Evangelium nach Matthäus (Würzburg 1973) 69-73, 91, 398. GOULDER, M. D., Midrash and Lection in Matthew (London 1974) 338f. TALBERT, C. H., Literary Patterns, Theological Themes, and the Genre of Luke-Acts (Missoula 1974) 62.

6:8-11 BUTLER, B. C., The Originality of St Matthew (Cambridge 1951) 14ff.

6:8-9 NICKELS, P. Targum and New Testament (1967) 24. HOFFMANN, P. Studien zur Theologie der Logienquelle (1972) 264-67. DERRETT, J. D. M., Jesus's Audience (London 1973) 181-86. *LEGRAND, L., "Bare foot Apostles? The Shoes of St Mark (Mk 6:8-9 and par.)" Indian Theological Studies 16 (1979) 201-19.

6:8 PESCH, R. Naherwartungen (1969) 97, 148, 153. TALBERT, C. H., Literary Patterns, Theological Themes, and the Genre of Luke-Acts (Missoula 1974) 27.

6:9ff KNOX, W. L. The Sources of the Synoptic Gospels II (1957) 49ff.

6:9-13 BUCHHEIM, K., Der historische Christus (München 1974) 205ff.

6:10-11 JEREMIAS, J. Neutestamentliche Theologie I (1971) 25f, 28f, 135, 228f.

6:10 SCHMAHL, G., Die Zwölf im Markusevangelium (Trier 1974) 82-87. *LEE, G. M., "Two Notes on St Mark" NovT 18 (1976) 36.

6:11 VOLZ, P., Die Eschatologie der jüdischen Gemeinde (Tübingen 1934) 303. BRAUN, H., Qumran und NT II (Tübingen 1966) 93, 299. *CAIRD, G. B. "Uncomfortable Words II. Shake off the Dust from Your Feet (Mk 6:11)" ET 81

(2, '69) 40-43. HOFFMANN, P. Studien zur Theologie der Logienquelle (1972) 268-72. KLIJN, A. F. J., "Die griechische Esra-Apokalypse" in: W. G. Kümmel (ed.) Jüdische Schriften aus hellenistisch-römischer Zeit V (Gütersloh 1976) 130. TRITES, A. A., The New Testament Concept of Witness (Cambridge 1977) 179f.

6:12ff SCHILLE, G., 'Bemerkungen zur Formgeschichte des Evangeliums. Rahmen und Aufbau des Markus-Evangeliums" NTS 4 (1957-1958) 13ff. HAHN, F. Das Verständnis der Mission im Neuen Testament (1965) 33, 35, 114.

6:12-13 EGGER, W., Frohbotschaft und Lehre (Frankfurt 1976) 31.

6:13 RUDOLPH, K., Die Mandäer II (Göttingen 1961) 170. A.6. "Amt" in: TRE 2 (1978) 511. HAHN, F. Christologische Hoheitstitel (1963) 297.

6:14-10:52 BEST, E. The Temptation and the Passion: The Markan Soteriology (1965) 119ff.

6:14-8:30 CLÉVENOT, M., So kennen wir die Bibel nicht (München 1978) 93.

6:14-7:30 RIST, J. M., On the Independence of Matthew and Mark (Cambridge 1978) 63-67.

6:14ff GOULDER, M. D., Midrash and Lection in Matthew (London 1974) 353, 355f, 363.

6:14-29 EWALD, H., Die drei ersten Evangelien (Göttingen 1850) 257ff. BARRETT, C. K., The New Testament Background: Selected Documents (London 1956) 197. CULLMANN, O. Die Christologie des Neuen Testaments (1957) 30ff. WINK, W. John the Baptist in the Gospel Tradition (1968) 8-13. ZIMMERMANN, W.-D. Markus über Jesus (1970) 74-77. BÖCHER, O., "Johannes der Täufer in der neutestamentlichen Überlieferung" in: G. Müller (ed.) Rechtfertigung Realismus. Für A. Köberle Darmstadt 1978) 46-52. GNILKA, J., Das Evangelium nach Markus I (Einsiedeln/Neukirchen 1978) 243 (lit!). SCHRECKENBERG, H., "Flavius Josephus und die lukanischen Schriften" in: W. Haubeck/M. Bachmann (eds.) Wort in der Zeit. Für K. H. Rengstorf (Leiden 1980) 187-90.

6:14-16 HAHN, Christologische Hoheitstitel (1963) 174, 222, 227, 397. SCHRAMM, T. Der Markus-Stoff bei Lukas (1971) 128f. HOEHNER, H. W. Herod Antipas (1972) 117-22. GNILKA, J., "Das Martyrium Johannes des Täufers (Mk 6:17-29)" in: P. Hoffmann (ed.) Orientierung an Jesus. Für J. Schmid (Freiburg 1973) 79-81. TALBERT, C. H., Literary Patterns, Theological Themes, and the Genre of Luke-Acts (Missoula

1974) 27. KOCH, D.-A., Die Bedeutung der Wundererzählungen für die Christologie des Markusevangeliums (Berlin/New York 1975) 154f. PESCH, R., Das Markusevangelium I (Freiburg 1976) 337 (lit!). TYSON, J. B., "Source Criticism of the Gospel of Luke" in: C. H. Talbert (ed.) Perspectives on Luke-Acts (Danville 1978) 31. SCHILLEBEECKX, E., Die Auferstehung Jesu als Grund der Erlösung (Basel 1979) 79.

6:14-15 BRAUN, H., Qumran und NT II (Tübingen 1966) 219, 272. SCHNIDER, F., Jesus der Prophet (Freiburg 1973) 52, 105, 181ff.

6:14 LJUNGVIK, H., "Zum Markusevangelium 6:14" ZNW 33 (1934) 90-92. KLOSTERMANN, E. Das Markusevangelium (1950) 58. DUNN, J. D. G., Jesus and the Spirit (London 1975) 70, 84. METZGER, B. M., The Early Versions of the New Testament (Oxford 1977) 434, 437.

6:15 RUDOLPH, K., Die Mandäer II (Göttingen 1961) 29. BOUSSET, W., Die Religion des Judentums im Späthellenistichen Zeitalter (Berlin 1966=1926) 232. SMITH, M., Clement of Alexandria and a Secret Gospel of Mark (Cambridge 1973) 136f. HAHN, F. Christologische Hoheitstitel (1963) 382.

6:16 PESCH, R. Naherwartungen (1969) 59, 110, 132, 133, 136. BACHMANN, M., "Johannes der Täufer bei Lukas: Nachzügler oder Vorläufer?" in: W. Haubeck/M. Bachmann (eds.) Wort in der Zeit. Für K. H. Rengstorf (Leiden 1980) 136f.

6:17ff RUDOLPH, K., Die Mandäer I (Göttingen 1960) 68.

6:17-29 GNILKA, J., "Das Martyrium Johannes des Täufers (Mk 6:17-29)" in: P. Hoffmann (ed.) Orientierung an Jesus. Für J. Schmid (Freiburg 1973) 78-92. DORMEYER, D., Die Passion Jesu als Verhaltensmodell (Münster 1974) 71A. KONINGS, J., "The Pre-Markan Sequence in Jn 6" in: M. Sabbe (ed.) L'Evangile selon Marc (Gembloux 1974) 173. PESCH, R., Das Markusevangelium I (Freiburg 1976) 344 (lit!). BERGER, K., Exegese des Neuen Testaments (Heidelberg 1977) 77-82, 220f. *LOSADA, D., "La muerte de Juan el Bautista. Mc 6:17-29" RevBi 39 (1977) 143-54. SWIDLER, L., Biblical Affirmations of Woman (Philadelphia 1979) 229, 238. BACHMANN, M., "Johannes der Täufer bei Lukas: Nachzügler oder Vorläufer?" in: W. Haubeck/M. Bachmann (eds.) Wort in der Zeit. Für K. H. Rengstorf (Leiden 1980) 135f. WILCH, J. R., "Jüdische Schuld am Tode Jesu -Antijudaismus in der Apostelgeschichte?" in: W. Haubeck/M. Bachmann (eds.) Wort in der Zeit. Für K. H. Rengstorf (Leiden 1980) 130f.

6:17-19 HAHN, F. Christologische Hoheitstitel (1963) 377. *DERRETT, J. D. M. "Herod's Oath and the Baptist's Head" BZ 9 (1, '65) 49-59. *DERRETT, J. D. M. "Herod's Oath and the Baptist's Head (Concl.) (With an Appendix on Mk IX. 12-13, Mal III. 24, Micah VII.6)" BZ 9 (2, '65) 233-46. *DE LA POTTERIE, I. "Mors Johannis Baptistae (Mc 6, 17-29)" VerbDom 44 (3, '66) 142-51. DERRETT, J. D. M. Law in the New Testament (1970) 339-58.

6:17-18 HAHN, F. Das Verständnis der Mission im Neuen Testament (1965) 75. TALBERT, C. H., Literary Patterns, Theological Themes, and the Genre of Luke-Acts (Missoula 1974) 48.

6:17 STAFF, E./F., Woman in the World of Jesus (Philadelphia 1978) 209f.

6:18 BRAUN, H., Qumran und NT II (Tübingen 1966) 18.

6:19 NICKELS, P. Targum and New Testament (1967) 24. SWIDLER, L., Biblical Affirmations of Woman (Philadelphia 1979) 228.

6:21-35 DORMEYER, D., Die Passion Jesu als Verhaltensmodell (Münster 1974) 85A, 142.

6:21-29 KLOSTERMANN, E. Das Markusevangelium (1950) 60f.

6:22 BLACK, M. An Aramaic Approach to the Gospels and Acts (1967) 99f. LINTON, O., "Evidence of a Second Century Revised Edition of St Mark's Gospel" NTS 14 (1967-1968) 335f. HOEHNER, H. W. Herod Antipas (1972) 151-57.

6:25 BROER, I. Die Urgemeinde und das Grab Jesu (1972) 48, 164f.

6:27 LINTON, O., "Evidence of a Second Century Revised Edition of St Mark's Gospel" NTS 14 (1967-1968) 336f. METZGER, B. M., The Early Versions of the New Testament (Oxford 1977) 177.

6:29-31a RAUCH, C. ZNW 3 (1902) 303-308.

6:29 PESCH, R. Naherwartungen (1969) 52, 53, 54, 58, 59, 68. JANSSEN, E., "Testament Abrahams" in: W. G. Kümmel (ed.) Jüdische Schriften aus hellenistisch-römischer Zeit III (Gütersloh 1975) 216.

6:30-10:52 PESCH, R. Naherwartungen (1969) 69.

6:30-8:30 RICHARDSON, A. The Miracle-Stories of the Gospels (1948) 88ff.

6:30-8:26 LIGHTFOOT, R. H. History and Interpretation in the Gospels (1934) 113ff. *CERFAUX, L. "La section des pains (Mc VI, 31-VIII, 26; Mt XIV, 13-XVI, 12) Synoptische Studien (Wikenhauser) 1953, 64-77. TAYLOR, V. The Gospel

According to St Mark (1953) 628-32. PESCH, R. Naherwartungen (1969) 60-62. DENIS, A. M., "La section des pains selon Marc 6:30-8:26 und Théologie de l'Eucharistie" in: Studia Evangelica 4 (1968) 171-79. *COMBET-GALLAND, C., "Analyse structurale de Marc 6:30-8:26" Foi et Vie 77 (1978) 34-36.

6:30-8:21 SCHNIDER, F./STENGER, W. Johannes und die Synoptiker (1971) 89-178. *SYNGE, F. C. "Common Bread. The Craftsmanship of a Theologian" Theology 75 (621-'72) 131-35.

6:30-7:30 *BONNARD, P., "La méthod historico-critique appliquée à Marc 6:30-8:26" Foi et Vie 77 (1978) 6-18.

6:30-56 EWALD, H., Die drei ersten Evangelien (Göttingen 1850) 259ff. KNOX, W. L. The Sources of the Synoptic Gospels (1953) I 43ff. KONINGS, J., "The Pre-Markan Sequence in Jn 6" in: M. Sabbe (ed.) L'Evangile selon Marc (Gembloux 1974) 147-76. EGGER, W., Frohbotschaft und Lehren (Frankfurt 1976) 123-26, 142. *DELORME, J., "L'intégration des petites unités littéraires dans l'évangile de Marc du point de vue de la sémiotique structurale" NTS 25 (1979) 469-91.

6:30-55 Groupe d'Entrevernes (ed.) Signes et paraboles. Sémiotique et texte évangélique (Paris 1977); ET: Signs and Parables: Semiotics and Gospel Texts (1978). *PACE, G., "La prima moltiplicazione dei pani. Topografia" BiOr 21 (1979) 85-91.

6:30-53 *O'HARA, J. "Two Bethsaidas or One?" Scripture 15 (29, '63) 24-27.

6:30-46 *TREVIJANO ETCHEVERRIA, R., "La multiplicación de los panes (Mc 6:30-46; 8:1-10 y par.—" Burgense 15 (1974) 435-65. *TREVIJANO ETCHEVERRIA, R., "Crisis mesiánica en la multiplicación de los panes (Mc 6:30-46 y Jn 6:1-15)" Burgense 16 (1975) 413-39.

0-44 FARRER, A. A Study in St Mark (1951) 93ff, 101ff. CARRINGTON, P. The Primitive Christian Calendar (1952) 153-55. LEE, E. K., "St Mark and the Fourth Gospel" NTS 3 (1956-1957) 51ff. *ZIENER, G. "Die Brotwunder im Markusevangelium" BZ 4 (2, '60) 282-85. *MONTEFIORE, H. "Revolt in the Desert? (Mark vi. 30ff.)" NTS 8 (2, '62) 135-41. *FRIEDRICH, G. "Die beiden Erzählungen von der Speisung in Mark. 6, 31-44; 8, 1-9" ThZ 20 (1, '64) 10-22. HERBERT, S. S. M. "History in the Feeding of the Five Thousand" Studia Evangelica II, ed. F. L. Cross (1964) 65-72. BECKER, U./WIBBING, S. Wundergeschichten (1965) 55-74. BEST, E. The Temptation and the Passion: The Markan Soteriology

(1965) 76-78. KAMPHAUS, D. Von der Exegese zur Predigt (1968) 134-40. RUDDICK, C. T. "Behold, I send My Messenger" JBL 88 ('69) 381-417. ZIMMERMANN, W.-D. Markus über Jesus (1970) 77-80. KONINGS, J., "The Pre-Markan Sequence in Jn 6" in: M. Sabbe (ed.) L'Evangile selon Marc (Gembloux 1974) 173. SCHENKE, L., Die Wundererzählungen des Markusevangeliums (Stuttgart 1974) 217-37. TALBERT, C. H., Literary Patterns, Theological Themes, and the Genre of Luke-Acts (Missoula 1974) 27. Van CANGH. J.-M., "La multiplication des pains dans l'évangile de Marc. Essai d'exégèse globale" in: M. Sabbe (ed.) L'Evangile selon Marc (Gembloux 1974) 309-46. KOCH, D.-A., Die Bedeutung der Wundererzählungen für die Christologie des Markusevangeliums (Berlin/New York 1975) 99-104, 107-112. Van CANGH, J.-M., La Multiplication des pains et l'Eucharistie (Paris 1975). *TREVIJANO ETCHEVERRIA, R., "Historia de milagro y cristologia en la multiplicación de los panes" Burgense 17 (1976) 9-38. GNILKA, J., Das Evangelium nach Markus I (Einsiedeln/Neukirchen 1978) 253f (lit!).

6:30-34 SCHRAMM, T. Der Markus-Stoff bei Lukas (1971) 129f. EGGER, W., Frohbotschaft und Lehre (Frankfurt 1976) 121-34, 142, 155, 157.

6:30-33 DOBSCHÜTZ, E. von, "Zur Erzählkunst des Markus" ZNW 27 (1928) 193-98. MAUSER, U. Christ in the Wilderness (1963) 104f, 143. Van CANGH, J.-M., "La multiplication des pains dans l'évangile de Marc" in: M. Sabbe (ed.) L'Evangile selon Marc (Gembloux 1974) 342.

6:30-32 KNOX, W. L. The Sources of the Synoptic Gospels I (1953) 21ff.

6:30-31 MONTEFIORE, H. W., "Revolt in the Desert?" NTS 8 (1961-1962) 135f. ROLOFF, J. Apostolat-Verkündigung-Kirche (1965) 140-43. EGGER, W., Frohbotschaft und Lehre (Frankfurt 1976) 28, 33, 75, 79, 98, 102f. PESCH, R., Das Markusevangelium I (Freiburg 1976) 346 (lit!).

6:30 NEPPER-CHRISTENSEN, P., Das Matthäusevangelium (Aarhus 1958) 182, 187, 189, 190. HAHN, F. Christologische Hoheitstitel (1963) 230. HAHN, F. Das Verständnis der Mission im Neuen Testament (1965) 32, 33. PESCH, R. Naherwartungen (1969) 53, 54, 60, 66, 69. HENDRIKS, W., "Zur Kollektionsgeschichte des Markusevangeliums" in: M. Sabbe (ed.) L'Evangile selon Marc (Gembloux 1974) 55. SCHMAHL, G., Die Zwölf im Markusevangelium (Trier 1974) 78f. "Apostel" in: TRE 3 (1978) 442. McDONALD, J. I. H., Kerygma and Didache (Cambridge 1980) 106.

6:31f   MAUSER, U. Christ in the Wilderness (1963) 103ff, 119, 144.

6:31-56 SMITH, M., Tannaitic Parallels to the Gospels (Philadelphia 1968) 5bn38+.

6:31-44 KONINGS, J., "The Pre-Markan Sequence in Jn 6" in: M. Sabbe (ed.) L'Evangile selon Marc (Gembloux 1974) 155. FRIEDRICH, G., "Die beiden Erzählungen von der Speisung in Mk 6:31-44; 8:1-9" [orig.: ThZ 20 (1964) 10-22] in: Auf das Wort kommt es an (Göttingen 1978) 13-25. SWIDLER, L., Biblical Affirmations of Woman (Philadelphia 1979) 249, 279.

6:31-33 EGGER, W., Frohbotschaft und Lehre (Frankfurt 1976) 101.

6:31   HAHN, F. Christologische Hoheitstitel (1963) 339. MINETTE DE TILLESSE, G. Le Secret Messianique dans L'Evangile de Marc (1968) 238-42. KÜMMEL, W. G., Römer 7 und das Bild des Menschen im Neuen Testament (München 1974) 66f. Van CANGH, J.-M., "La multiplication des pains dans l'évangile de Marc" in: M. Sabbe (ed.) L'Evangile selon Marc (Gembloux 1974) 344.

6:32ff HAHN, F. Das Verständnis der Mission im Neuen Testament (1965) 97.

6:32-16:8 SMITH, M., Clement of Alexandria and a Secret Gospel of Mark (Cambridge, Mass. 1973) 158-63, 192.

6:32-52 KUHN, H.-W. Aeltere Sammlungen im Markusevangelium (1971) 203-210.

6:32-44 *BUSE, I. "The Gospel Accounts of the Feeding of the Multitudes" ET 74 (6, '63) 167-70. KERTELGE, K. Die Wunder Jesu im Markusevangelium (1970) 129-39. SCHNIDER, F./STENGER, W. Johannes und die Synoptiker (1971) 94-103. *HIERS, R. H. and KENNEDY, C. A., "The Bread and Fish Eucharist in the Gospels and Early Christian Art" Perspectives in Religious Studies 3 (1976) 20-47. PESCH, R., Das Markusevangelium I (Freiburg 1976) 356f (lit!). SAITO, T., Die Mosevorstellungen im Neuen Testament (Bern 1977) 47-50. KONINGS, J., "The Pre-Markan Sequence in Jn 6" in: M. Sabbe (ed.) L'Evangile selon Marc (Gembloux 1974) 162f. EGGER, W., Frohbotschaft und Lehre (Frankfurt 1976) 28, 33-35, 104.

6:32   HAHN, F. Christologische Hoheitstitel (1963) 339. Van CANGH, J.-M., "La multiplication des pains dans l'e⅛vangile de Marc" in: M. Sabbe (ed.) L'Evangile selon Marc (Gembloux 1974) 327, 328. "Abendmahl" in: TRE 1 (1977) 49.

6:34-44 *RICHARDSON, A. "The Feeding of the Five Thousand" (Mk 6, 33-34). Interpretation 9/2 ('55) 223-26. *STAUFFER, E. "Zum apokalyptischen Festmahl in Mk 6, 34ff" ZNW 46

('55) 264-66. *SHAW, A. "The Marcan Feeding Narratives" Church QuartRev 162 (344, '61) 268-78. HEISING, A. Die Botschaft der Brotvermehrung (1967). *HEISING, A. "Das Kerygma der wunderbaren Fischvermehrung (Mk 6, 34-44 parr)" BuL 10 (1, '69) 52-57. ROLOFF, J. Das Kerygma und der irdische Jesus (1970) 241ff. JEREMIAS, J. Neutestamentliche Theologie I (1971) 90-93, 166.

6:34   RICHARDSON, A. The Miracle-Stories of the Gospels (1948) 33f.

y forgotten Command of Jesus" Bible Today 97 (1978) 1704-1709.

6:38   HENNECKE, E./SCHNEEMELCHER, W., Neutestamentliche Apokryphen I (Tübingen 1964) 129.

6:39-40   DALMAN, G. Orte und Wege Jesu (1967) 187f.

6:39   Van CANGH, J.-M., "La multiplication des pains dans l'évangile de Marc" in: M. Sabbe (ed.) L'Evangile selon Marc (Gembloux 1974) 344. METZGER, B. M., The Early Versions of the New Testament (Oxford 1977) 176.

6:40   *DERRETT, J. D. M., "Leek-beds and Methodology" BZ 19 (1975) 101-103.

6:41   JEREMIAS, J. Die Abendmahlsworte Jesu (1960) 166-68. WANKE, J., Die Emmauserzählung. Eine redaktionsgeschichtliche Untersuchung zu Lk 24:13-35 (Leipzig 1973) 98. Van CANGH, J.-M., "La multiplication des pains dans l'évangile de Marc" in: M. Sabbe (ed.) L'Evangile selon Marc (Gembloux 1974) 330-37, 340, 345.

6:42   Van CANGH, J.-M., "La multiplication des pains dans l'évangile de Marc" in: M. Sabbe (ed.) L'Evangile selon Marc (Gembloux 1974) 340.

6:43   Van CANGH, J.-M., "La multiplication des pains dans l'évangile de Marc" in: M. Sabbe (ed.) L'Evangile selon Marc (Gembloux 1974) 333-38, 340, 345.

6:44   Van CANGH, J.-M., "La multiplication des pains dans l'évangile de Marc" in: M. Sabbe (ed.) L'Evangile selon Marc (Gembloux 1974) 328. "Abendmahl" in: TRE 1 (1977) 49.

6:45-8:27   STREETER, B. H. The Four Gospels (1951) 172ff. CONZELMANN, H. Die Mitte der Zeit (1964) 45ff, 48.

6:45-8:26   TAYLOR, V., Behind the Third Gospel (Oxford 1926) 138ff. TALBERT, C. H., Literary Patterns, Theological Themes, and the Genre of Luke-Acts (Missoula 1974) 28, 33, 62, 66. CONZELMANN, H. und LINDEMANN, A., Arbeitsbuch zum Neuen Testament (Tübingen 1975) 57.

6:45ff.   STONEHOUSE, N. B., The Witness of Luke to Christ (Grand Rapids 1951) 107f.

6:45-56   ZIMMERMANN, W.-D. Markus über Jesus (1970) 80-83.

6:45-52   STONEHOUSE, N. B. The Witness of Matthew and Mark to Christ (1944) 28, 70, 71ff. STRECKER, G. Der Weg der Gerechtigkeit (1962) 199. MAUSER, U. Christ in the Wilderness (1963) 126f. DENIS, A.-M., "La marche de Jésus sur les eaux. Contribution al'histoire de la péricope dans la tradition évangelique." De Jésus aux Evangiles (1967) 233-47. *SNOY T. "La rédaction marcienne de la marche sur les eaux (Mc. VI 45-52)" EphT 44 (1, '68) 205-41; (3, '68) 433-81. MEYE, R. P. Jesus and the Twelve (1968) 66-73. MINETTE DE TILLESSE, G. Le Secret Messianique dans L'Evangile de Marc (1968) 410-20. *KREMER, J. "Jesu Wandel auf dem See nach Mk 6, 45-52. Auslegung und Meditation" BuL 10 (3, '69) 221-32. QUESNELL, Q. The Mind of Mark (1969) 60-67. KERTELGE, K. Die Wunder Jesu im Markusevangelium (1970) 145-50. ITTEL G. W. Jesus und die Jünger (1970) 60-64. SCHNIDER, F./STENGER, W. Johannes und die Synoptiker (1971) 103-34. JEREMIAS, J. Neutestamentliche Theologie I (1971) 91-93. BOHREN, R., Predigtlehre (München 1971) 195. KONINGS, J., "The Pre-Markan Sequence in Jn 6" in: M. Sabbe (ed.) L'Evangile selon Marc (Gembloux 1974) 150-55, 173. SCHENKE, L., Die Wundererzählungen des Markusevangeliums (Stuttgart 1974) 238-53. ALSUP, J. E., The Post-Resurrection Appearance Stories of the Gospel-Tradition (Stuttgart 1975) 140f, 168ff. HOWARD, V. P., Das Ego Jesu in den Synoptischen Evangelien (Marburg 1975) 78-85. KOCH, D.-A., Die Bedeutung der Wundererzählungen für die Christologie des Markusevangeliums (Berlin/New York 1975) 34-37, 104-108. *LOSADA, D., "Jesús camina sobre las aguas. Un relato apocalíptico" RevBi 38 (1976) 311-19. PESCH, R., Das Markusevangelium I (Freiburg 1976) 364 (lit!). GNILKA, J., Das Evangelium nach Markus I (Einsiedeln/Neukirchen 1978) 265 (lit!). *RITT, H., "Der 'Seewandel Jesu' (Mk 6:45-52 par.). Literarische und theologische Aspekte" BZ 23 (1979) 71-84. SCHMITHALS, W., Das Evangelium nach Markus (Gütersloh/Würzburg 1979) 331 (lit!). TANNEHILL, R. C., "The Gospel of Mark as Narrative Christology" Semeia 16 (1980) 68, 70.

6:45-46   BETZ, H. D., Lukian von Samosata und das Neue Testament (Berlin 1961) 64, 166f, 172. BROER, I. Die Urgemeinde und das Grab Jesu (1972) 147f.

6:45   STONEHOUSE, N. B., The Witness of Luke to Christ (Grand
        Rapids 1951) 104f. DALMAN, G. Orte und Wege Jesu (1967)
        178f. SCHREIBER, J. Theologie des Vertrauens (1967) 84, 95,
        96, 97, 159f, 164, 167, 170f, 176f, 205, 207. BROER, I. Die
        Urgemeinde und das Grab Jesu (1972) 147f. Van CANGH, J.-
        M., "La multiplication des pains dans l'évangile de Marc" in:
        M. Sabbe (ed.) L'Evangile selon Marc (Gembloux 1974) 328.
        ACHTEMEIER, P. J., Mark (Philadelphia 1975) 13. EGGER,
        W., Frohbotschaft und Lehre (Frankfurt 1976) 104.
        "Aramäisch" in: TRE 3 (1978) 604.

6:46   MAUSER, U. Christ in the Wilderness (1963) 107ff, 118, 128,
        139ff, 143. BROER, I. Die Urgemeinde und das Grab Jesu
        (1972) 147f.

6:47-56 MUSSNER, F. Die Wunder Jesu (1967) 61-68.

6:47-52 HAHN, F. Christologische Hoheitstitel (1963) 313f. HAHN, F.
        Das Verständnis der Mission im Neuen Testament (1965) 95.

6:47-51 "Auferstehung" in: TRE 4 (1979) 501.

6:47-48 KONINGS, J., "The Pre-Markan Sequence in Jn 6" in: M.
        Sabbe (ed.) L'Evangile selon Marc (Gembloux 1974) 168.

6:47   BROER, I. Die Urgemeinde und das Grab Jesu (1972) 142-49.

6:48-52 MALBON, E. S., "Mythic Structure and Meaning in Mark"
        Semeia 16 (1980) 103-107.

6:48   SNOY, T., "Marc 6:48 '. . .et il voulait les déspasser.'
        Proposition pour la solution d'une énigme" in: M. Sabbe (ed.)
        L'Evangile selon Marc (Gembloux 1974) 347-63.

6:49-50 BORNKAMM-BARTH-HELD, Ueberlieferung und
        Auslegung im Mattha⅛us Evangelium (1961) 193. LINTON,
        O., "Evidence of a Second Century Revised Edition of St
        Mark's Gospel" NTS 14 (1967-1968) 337f. NEIRYNCK, F.,
        "Urmarcus redivivus" in: M. Sabbe (ed.) L'Evangile selon Marc
        (Gembloux 1974) 114-15.

6:50   STONEHOUSE, N. B. The Witness of Matthew and Mark to
        Christ (1944) 80, 103, 106. HAHN, F. Christologische
        Hoheitstitel (1963) 182. SNOY, T., "Marc 6:48 '. . .et il voulait
        les dépasser.' Proposition pour la solution d'une énigme" in: M.
        Sabbe (ed.) L'Evangile selon Marc (Gembloux 1974) 358.

6:51   STONEHOUSE, N. B. The Witness of Matthew and Mark to
        Christ (1944) 71ff, 106, 218ff. *RENIE, J. "Une antilogie
        évangélique. Mc 6, 51-52; Mt 14, 32-33" Biblica 36 ('55) 223-26.
        BORNKAMM-BARTH-HELD Ueberlieferung und
        Auslegung im Matthäus Evangelium (1961) 102, 105, 172, 193,
        196, 208.

6:52-56 LEHMANN, M. Synoptische Quellenanalyse und die Frage nach dem historischen Jesus (1970) 35f, 44.

6:52-53 *O'CALLAGHAN, J. "Papiros neotestamentarios en la cueva 7 de Qumran?" Biblica 53 (1, '72) 91-100. *MARTINI, C. M. "Note sui papiri della grotta 7 di Qumran" Biblica 53 (1, '72) 101-104. *VOGT, E. "Entdeckung neutestamentlicher Texte beim Toten Meer?" Orientierung 36 (11, '72) 138-40. O'CALLAGHAN, J., "Les papyrus de la grotte 7 de Qumran" NRTh 95 (1973) 188-95.

6:52 RICHARDSON, A. The Miracle-Stories of the Gospels (1948) 93f. STRECKER, G. Der Weg der Gerechtigkeit (1962) 230. *QUESNELL, Q. The Mind of Mark. Interpretation and Method through the Exegesis of Mark 6, 52 (1962) Rev. G. Dautzenberg Bib Zeit 15 (1, '71) 151-53; U. Luz, ThLZ 96 (5, '71) 349-51. SNOY, T., "Marc 6:48 '. . .et il voulait les dépasser.' Proposition pour la solution d'une énigme" in: M. Sabbe (ed.) L'Evangile selon Marc (Gembloux 1974) 358. Van CANGH, J.-M., "La multiplication des pains dans l'évangile de Marc" in: M. Sabbe (ed.) L'Evangile selon Marc (Gembloux 1974) 342. ACHTEMEIER, P. J., Mark (Philadelphia 1975) 93. EGGER, W., Frohbotschaft und Lehre (Frankfurt 1976) 128, 141.

6:53-8:21 STREETER, B. H. The Four Gospels (1951) 173f.

6:53-56 KERTELGE, K. Die Wunder Jesu im Markusevangelium (1970) 35-36. KOCH, D.-A., Die Bedeutung der Wundererzählungen für die Christologie des Markusevangeliums (Berlin/New York 1975) 169-71. EGGER, W., Frohbotschaft und Lehre (Frankfurt 1976) 28, 69, 96, 123f, 134-42. PESCH, R., Das Markusevangelium I (Freiburg 1976) 367 (lit!). GNILKA, J., Das Evangelium nach Markus I (Einsiedeln/Neukirchen 1978) 271 (lit!). LUZ, U., "Das Geheimnismotiv und die markinische Christologie" [orig.: ZNW 56 (1965) 9-30] in: R. Pesch (ed.) Das Markus-Evangelium (Darmstadt 1979) 213.

6:53 SCHREIBER, J. Theologie des Vertrauens (1967) 97, 159f, 170f. KONINGS, J., "The Pre-Markan Sequence in Jn 6" in: M. Sabbe (ed.) L'Evangile selon Marc (Gembloux 1974) 155, 173. Van CANGH, J.-M., "La multiplication des pains dans l'évangile de Marc" in: M. Sabbe (ed.) L'Evangile selon Marc (Gembloux 1974) 328. *RINALDI, G., "Traversata del lago e sbarco e Genezaret in 'Marco' 6:53" BiOr 17 (1975) 43-46. GAIN, D. B., Evidence for Supposing that our Greek Text of the Gospel of St Mark is Translated from Latin. . . (Grahamstown 1978). MALBON, E. S., "Mythic Structure and Meaning in Mark" Semeia 16 (1980) 103-107.

6:54-56 KONINGS, J., "The Pre-Markan Sequence in Jn 6" in: M. Sabbe (ed.) L'Evangile selon Marc (Gembloux 1974) 155. DIBELIUS, M., "Sammlung" [orig.: Die Formgeschichte des Evangeliums (1933) *(2)* 219-34] in: R. Pesch (ed.) Das Markus-Evangelium (Darmstadt 1979) 73f.

6:56 HAHN, F. Christologische Hoheitstitel (1963) 313. BOUSSET, W., Die Religion des Judentums im Späthellenistischen Zeitalter (Berlin 1966=1926) 179. PESCH, R. Naherwartungen (1969) 137, 141, 148.

7:1-9:1 FARRER, A. A Study in St Mark (1951) 94ff, 148f.

7:1-8:26 EWALD, H., Die drei ersten Evangelien (Göttingen 1850) 262ff.

7 FARRER, A. A Study in Mark (1951) 94ff, 312f. BOUSSET, W., Die Religion des Judentums im Späthellenistischen Zeitalter (Berlin 1966=1926) 127. PETZKE, G., Die Traditionen über Apollonius von Tyana und das Neue Testament (Leiden 1970) 109, 209. HENGEL, M., Was Jesus a Revolutionist? (Philadelphia 1971) 7f. ROBINSON, J. M., "Gnosticism and the New Testament" in: B. Aland et al. (eds.) Gnosis. Für H. Jonas (Göttingen 1978) 135-36.

7:1-23 MANSON, T. W., The Teaching of Jesus (Cambridge 1945) 19f, 49f, 299f, 315-19. TAYLOR, V. The Formation of the Gospel Tradition (1949) 81f, 176. FARRER, A. St Matthew and St Mark (1954) 10, 188. KNOX, W. L. The Sources of the Synoptic Gospels (1953) I 52ff. GRANT, F. C. The Gospels (1957) 92f. GRUNDMANN, W. Das Evangelium nach Markus (1959) 147f. KNOX, W. L. The Sources of the Synoptic Gospels II (1957) 10, 46. SCHMID, J. Das Evangelium nach Markus (1958) 139-41. BAUMBACH, G. Das Verständnis des Bösen in den synoptischen Evangelien (1963) 14ff. BULTMANN, R., The History of the Synoptic Tradition (Oxford 1963) 17f. YATES, J. E., The Spirit and the Kingdom (London 1963) 61f. SUHL, A. Die Funktion der alttestamentlichen Zitate und Anspielungen im Markusevangelium (1965) 79ff. MERKEL, H., "Jesus und die Pharisäer" NTS 14 (1967-1968) 205f. CARLSTON, C. E., "The Things that Defile (Mk 7:14)" NTS 15 (1968-1969) 91ff. MINETTE DE TILLESSE, G. Le Secret Messianique dans L'Evangile de Marc (1968) 143-48. STOCK/WEGENAST/ WIBBING Streitgespräche (1968) 52-

84. QUESNELL, Q. The Mind of Mark (1969) 221-29. ZIMMERMANN, W.-D. Markus über Jesus (1970) 83-86. BERGER, K. Die Gesezesauslegung Jesu (1972) 577-82. ERNST, J., Anfänge der Christologie (Stuttgart 1972) 154-58. HÜBNER, H., Das Gesetz in der synoptischen Tradition (Witten 1973) 142ff. KONINGS, J., "The Pre-Markan Sequence in Jn 6" in: M. Sabbe (ed.) L'Evangile selon Marc (Gembloux 1974) 155. TALBERT, C. H., Literary Patterns, Theological Themes, and the Genre of Luke-Acts (Missoula 1974) 33. KOCH, D.-A., Die Bedeutung der Wundererzählungen für die Christologie des Markusevangeliums (Berlin/New York 1975) 34-36. HÜBNER, H., "Mark 7:1-23 und das 'Jüdisch-Hellenistische' Gesetzesverständnis" NTS 22 (1976) 319-45. PESCH, R., Das Markusevangelium I (Freiburg 1976) 368 (lit!). *LAMBRECHT, J., "Jesus and the Law. An Investigation of Mk 7:1-23" EphT 53 (1977) 24-82. SANDMEL, S., We Jews and Jesus (New York 1977) 136. GNILKA, J., Das Evangelium nach Markus I (Einsiedeln/Neukirchen 1978) 274 (lit!). RIVKIN, E., A Hidden Revolution (Nashville 1978) 88-90. WESTERHOLM, S., Jesus and Scribal Authority (Lund 1978) 71-85. SCHMITHALS, W., Das Evangelium nach Markus (Gütersloh/Würzburg 1979) 341 (lit!). McDONALD, J. I. H., Kerygma and Didache (Cambridge 1980) 104-105.

7:1-15 OTOMO, Y. Nachfolge Jesu und Anfänge der Kirche im Neuen Testament (1970) 101-104.

7:1-13 BLAIR, E. P. Jesus in the Gospel of Matthew (1960), 114. HAHN, F. Das Verständnis der Mission im Neuen Testament (1965) 97. PESCH, R., Das Markusevangelium I (Freiburg 1976) 377 (lit!). SWIDLER, L., Biblical Affirmations of Woman (Philadelphia 1979) 177, 238.

7:1-8 JEREMIAS, J. Neutestamentliche Theologie I (1971) 143, 202. GOPPELT, L., Theologie des Neuen Testaments I (Göttingen 1975) 140f.

7:2-5 DELLING, G. Die Taufe im Neuen Testament (1963) 25. BOUSSET, W., Die Religion des Judentums im Späthellenistischen Zeitalter (Berlin 1966=1926) 127. SMITH, M., Tannaitic Parallels to the Gospels (Philadelphia 1968) 2bn104.+.

7:2 KAESEMANN, E. Exegetische Versuche und Besinnungen (1964) I 237.

7:3-4 RUDOLPH, K., Die Mandäer II (Göttingen 1961) 404. STRECKER, G. Der Weg der Gerechtigkeit (1962) 17.

7:3   TAYLOR, V. The Gospel According to St Mark (1953) 338f. BARRETT, C. K., The New Testament Background: Selected Documents (London 1956) 215. *WEIS, P. R. "A Note on Pygmei" NTS 3 (3, '57) 233-36. *REYNOLDS, S. M. "PYGMHI (Mark 7:3) as 'Cupped Hand'" JBL 85 (1, '66) 87-88. *HENGEL, M. "Mc 7:3 pygme: Die Geschichte einer exegetischen Aporie und der Versuch ihrer Lösung" ZNW 60 (3-4, '69) 182-98. *REYNOLDS, S. M. "A Note on Dr. Hengel's Interpretation of pygme in Mark 7:3" ZNW 62 (3-4, '71) 295-96. *McHARDY, W. D., "Mark 7:3 - A Reference to the Old Testament?" ET 87 (1976) 119. *ROSS, J.M., " 'With the Fist' " ET 87 (1976) 374-75. METZGER, B. M., The Early Versions of the New Testament (Oxford 1977) 177. GAIN, D. B., Evidence for Supposing that our Greek Text of the Gospel of St Mark is Translated from Latin. . . (Grahamstown 1978).

7:5-23   DIBELIUS, M., "Sammlung" [orig: Die Formgeschichte des Evangeliums 1933*(2)* 219-34] in: R. Pesch (ed.) Das Markus-Evangelium (Darmstadt 1979) 70-80.

7:5-13   LIGHTSTONE, J. N., "Sadoq the Yavnean" in: W. S. Green (ed.) Persons and Institutions in Early Rabbinic Judaism (Missoula 1977) 68.

7:5-8   TAYLOR, V. The Formation of the Gospel Tradition (1949) 64f.

7:6ff   HENNECKE, E./SCHNEEMELCHER, W., Neutestamentliche ryphen I (Tübingen 1964) 60.

7:6-13   MANSON, T. W., The Teaching of Jesus (Cambridge 1945) 315-19. BERGER, K. Die Gesetzesauslegung Jesu (1972) 461-96, 506-507.

7:6.9   KAESEMANN, E. Exegetische Versuche und Besinnungen (1964) I 237.

7:6-7   JEREMIAS, J. Neutestamentliche Theologie I (1971) 25, 198.

7:6   MASSAUX, E. Influence de l'Evangile de saint Matthieu sur la littérature chrétienne avant saint Irénée (1950) 21-23. STROBEL, A. Erkenntnis und Bekenntnis der Sünde in neutestamentlicher Zeit (1968) 40.

7:8-13   SWIDLER, L., Biblical Affirmations of Woman (Philadelphia 1979) 230.

7:8-9   KAESEMANN, E. Exegetische Versuche und Besinnungen (1964) I 237.

7:8   BLAIR, E. P. Jesus in the Gospel of Matthew (1960) 112. JEREMIAS, J. Neutestamentliche Theologie I (1971) 25, 27, 29, 35, 203. FRIEDRICH, G., "Das Problem der Autorität im

Neuen Testament" in: Auf das Wort kommt es an (Göttingen 1978) 285-87.

7:9-13   BORNKAMM-BARTH-HELD Ueberlieferung und Auslegung im Matthäus-Evangelium (1961) 81. *BLIGH, J., "Qorban" HeyJ 5 (2, '64) 192-93. BRAUN, H., Qumran und NT II (Tübingen 1966) 99, 287, 291. *DERRETT, J. D. M. "Korban, ho estin doron" NTS 16 (4, '70) 364-68. SCHROEDER, H.-H., Eltern und Kinder in der Verkündigung Jesu (Hamburg-Bergstedt 1972) 157-65. GOPPELT, L., Theologie des Neuen Testaments I (Göttingen 1975) 140f, 159.

7:10ff   LIGHTFOOT, R. H. History and Interpretation in the Gospels (1934) 105f.

7:10-13   KASEMANN, E. Exegetische Versuche und Besinnungen (1964) I 237.

7:11   KLOSTERMANN, E. Das Markusevangelium (1950) 69. TAYLOR, V. The Gospel According to St Mark (1953) 341f. *ZEITLIN, S. "Korban: A Gift" JQR 59 (2, '68) 133-35. *FITZMYER, J. A. "The Aramaic Qorban Inscription from Jebel Hallet et Turi and Mark 7:11/Matt 15:5-" JBL 78 (1, '59) 60-65. *ZEITLIN, "Korbin" JQR 54 (2, '62) 160-63. NICKELS, P. Targum and New Testament (1967) 24. FITZMYER, J. A. Essays on the Semitic Background of the New Testament (1971) 93-100. "Aramäisch" in: TRE 3 (1978) 607.

7:13   BANKS, R., Jesus and the Law in the Synoptic Tradition (London 1975) 248-49. FRIEDRICH, G., "Das Problem der Autorität im Neuen Testament" in: Auf das Wort kommt es an (Göttingen 1978) 285-87.

7:14-23   JüLICHER, D. A. Die Gleichnisreden Jesu (1910) 54-67. *PASCHEN, W. Rein und Unrein. Untersuchung zur biblischen Wortgeschichte (1970), 223-79. GOPPELT, L., Theologie des Neuen Testaments I (Göttingen 1975) 142ff. PESCH, R., Das Markusevangelium I (Frieburg 1976) 384 (lit!). *LEMCIO, E. E., "External Evidence for the Structure and Function of Mk 4:1-20; 7:14-23 and 8:14-21" JThS 29 (1978) 323-38.

7:14-15   GNILKA, J. Die Verstockung Israels (1961) 41f. YATES, J. E., The Spirit and the Kingdom (London 1963) 61. PASCHEN, W. Rein und Unrein (1970) 155f.

7:14a   PASCHEN, W. Rein und Unrein (1970) 157ff.

7:14   DAVIES, W. D., Torah in the Messianic Age/or the Age to Come (Philadelphia 1952) 88. *CARLSTON, C. "The Things

that Defile (Mark vii.14) and the Law in Matthew and Mark"
NTS 15 (1, '68) 75-96. PASCHEN, W. Rein und Unrein (1970)
162ff. WREDE, W., "Rückblick auf Markus" [orig: Das
Messiasgeheimnis in den Evangelien (1901) 115-49] in: R.
Pesch (ed.) Das Markus-Evangelium (Darmstadt 1979) 35-36.

7:15ff BORNKAMM-BARTH-HELD Ueberlieferung und
Auslegung im Matthäus Evangelium (1961) 81, 83, 102, 153.
SCHWEIZER, E., "Mark's Contribution to the Quest of the
Historical Jesus" NTS 10 (1963-1964) 427f.

7:15-23 SCHWEIZER, E., in: GPM 27 (1973) 362-66.

7:15 SCHRAGE, W. Die konkreten Einzelgebote in der
paulinischen Paränese (1961) 243. SCHRAGE, W. Das
Verhältnis des Thomas Evangeliums zur Synoptischen
Tradition und zu den Koptischen Evangelienübersetzungen
(1964) 55. BULTMANN, R., Theologie des Neuen Testaments
(Tübingen 1965) 17f. KAESEMANN, E. Exegetische Versuche
und Besinnungen I (1964) 219. BJORNSTAD, E. J. Jesus and
the Law in the Gospel of Mark (1966) 35-39. JUENGEL, E.
Paulus und Jesus (1966) 209ff. *MERKEL, H. "Markus 7, 15-
das Jesuswort über die innere Verunreinigung" ZRGG 20 (4,
'68) 340-63. PASCHEN, W., Rein und Unrein (München 1970)
168, 171, 174, 176f, 179. JEREMIAS, J. Neutestamentliche
Theologie I (1971) 25-27, 148f, 200, 202f. SCHUBERT, K.,
Jesus im Lichte der Religionsgeschichte des Judentums
(München 1973) 130f. TANNEHILL, R. C., The Sword of His
Mouth (Missoula 1975) 88-95. PERRIN, N., Jesus and the
Language of the Kingdom (London 1976) 41, 48, 53-54.
LIGHTSTONE, J. N., "Sadoq the Yavnean" in: W. S. Green
(ed.) Persons and Institutions in Early Rabbinic Judaism
(Missoula 1977) 63. "Apokryphen" in: TRE 3 (1978) 323.
FRIEDRICH, G., "Das Problem der Autorität im Neuen
Testament" in: Auf das Wort kommt es an (Göttingen 1978)
285-87. HÜBNER, H., Das Gesetz bei Paulus (Göttingen 1978)
77. KLAUCK, H.-J., Allegorie und Allegorese in Synoptischen
Gleichnistexten (Münster 1978) 260-72. RUDOLPH, K., Die
Gnosis (Göttingen 1978) 280. MEYER, B. F., The Aims of
Jesus (London 1979) 149.

7:16 SCHRAGE, W. Das Verhaltnis des Thomas-Evangeliums zur
Synoptischen Tradition und zu den Koptischen
Evangelienübersetzungen (1964) 42.

7:17ff HAHN, F. Christologische Hoheitstitel (1963) 230.
KAESEMANN, E. Exegetische Versuche und Besinnungen
(1964) I 238.

7:17-19 PERRIN, N., Jesus and the Language of the Kingdom (London 1976) 54.

7:17-18 MOSLEY, A. W., "Jesus' Audiences in the Gospels of St Mark and St Luke" NTS 10 (1963-1964) 140f.

7:17 GNILKA, J. Die Verstockung Israels (1961) 58f. ACHTEMEIER, P. J., Mark (Philadelphia 1975) 93.

7:18 WREDE, W. Das Messiasgeheimnis in den Evangelien (1963) 102-104, 108, 169, 179. LAMBRECHT, J., "Redaction and Theology in Mk 4" in: M. Sabbe (ed.) L'Evangile selon Marc (Gembloux 1974) 281. ACHTEMEIER, P. J., Mark (Philadelphia 1975) 93.

7:19c PASCHEN, W. Rein und Unrein (1970) 168ff.

7:20 STROBEL, A. Erkenntnis und Bekenntnis der Sünde in neutestamentlicher Zeit (1968) 40.

7:21ff PASCHEN, W. Rein und Unrein (1970) 188f.

7:21-22 BETZ, H.D., Lukian von Samosata und das Neue Testament (Berlin 1961) 69, 190, 193. BAUMBACH, G. Das Verständnis des Bösen in den synoptischen Evangelien (1963) 14ff. PASCHEN, W. Rein und Unrein (1970) 191f. McDONALD, J. I. H., Kerygma and Didache (Cambridge 1980) 85.

7:21 MASSAUX, E. Influence de l'Evangile de saint Matthieu sur la littérature chrétienne avant saint Irénée (1950) 620-24. STROBEL, A. Erkenntnis und Bekenntnis der Sünde in neutestamentlicher Zeit (1968) 40. PASCHEN, W. Rein und Unrein (1970) 197, 190, 193f.

7:23 METZGER, B. M., The Early Versions of the New Testament (Oxford 1977) 435.

7:24ff HAHN, F. Christologische Hoheitstitel (1963) 96, 297. GOULDER, M. D., Midrash and Lection in Matthew (London 1974) 317, 319f.

7:24-8:26 TAYLOR, V. The Gospel According to St Mark (1953) 632-36. GRANT, F. C. The Gospels (1957) 93f.

7:23-37 FARRER, A. St Matthew and St Mark (1954) 23n. 29.

7:24-30 JüLICHER, D. A. Die Gleichnisreden Jesu (1910) 254-59. TAYLOR, V. The Formation of the Gospel Tradition (1949) 75f, 148. FARRER, A. A Study in St Mark (1951) 41f, 50f, 148f. 298f, 312f, 335f. FARRER, A. St Matthew and St Mark (1954) 63, 173. TAYLOR, V., The Life and Ministry of Jesus (London 1954) 129, 131, 134-38. BOSCH, D. Die Heidenmission in der Zukunftsschau Jesu (1959) 97-103. *DIAZ, J. ALONSO, "Cuestion sinoptica y universalidad del mensaje cristiano en el pasaje evangélico de la mujer cananea

(Mc 7, 24-30; Mt 15, 21-28)" Cult Bib 20 (192, '63) 274-79.
SCHMITHALS, W. Paulus und Jakobus (1963) 93. HAHN,
F. Das Verständnis der Mission im Neuen Testament (1965)
24f, 45, 50, 97f. *BURKILL, T. A. "The Syrophoenician
woman: The congruence of Mark 7:24-31" ZNW 57 (1-2, '66)
23-37. *BURKILL, T. A. "The historical development of the
story of the Syrophoenician woman (Mark vii: 24-31)" NovTest
9 (3, '67) 161-77. BURKILL, T. A., "The Syrophoenician
Woman" Studia Evangelica IV (1968) 166-70. *FLAMMER,
B. "Die Syrophoenizerin. Mk 7, 24-30" ThQ 148 (4, '68) 463-78.
LEHMANN, M. Synoptische Quellenanalyse und die Frage
nach dem historischen Jesus (1970) 38. KERTELGE, K. Die
Wunder Jesu Im Markusevangelium (1970) 151-56.
ZIMMERMANN, W.-D. Markus über Jesus (1971) 78-88.
JEREMIAS, J. Neutestamentliche Theologie I (1971) 90, 96,
109, 161, 164, 235. BURKILL, T. A. New Light on the Earliest
Gospel (1972) 48-95, 96-120. *DERRETT, J. D. M., "Law in
the New Testament: The Syro-Phoenician Woman and the
Centurion of Capernaum" NovT 15 (1973) 161-86.
SCHUBERT, K., Jesus im Lichte der Religionsgeschichte des
Judentums (München 1973) 132f. SCHENKE, L., Die
Wundererzählungen des Markusevangeliums (Stuttgart 1974)
254-67. SCHILLE, G., Offen für alle Menschen (Stuttgart
1974) 21ff. KOCH, D.-A., Die Bedeutung der
Wundererzählungen für die Christologie des
Markusevangeliums (Berlin/New York 1975) 85-92. PESCH,
R., Das Markusevangelium I (Freiburg 1976) 391 (lit!).
*DERMIENCE, A., "Tradition et rédaction dans la péricope
de la Syrophénicienne: Marc 7:24-30" RThL 8 (1977) 15-29.
GNILKA, J., Das Evangelium nach Markus I
(Einsiedeln/Neukirchen 1978) 289 (lit!). SCHMITHALS, W.,
"Zur Herkunft der gnostischen Elemente in der Sprache des
Paulus" in: B.Aland et al. (eds.) Gnosis. Für H. Jonas
(Göttingen 1978) 401. STAGG, E./F., Woman in the World of
Jesus (Philadelphia 1978) 210. SWIDLER, L., Biblical
Affirmations of Woman (Philadelphia 1979) 183, 230f, 238.
'Barmherzigkeit' in: TRE 5 (1980) 225.

7:24, 30 MUNCK, J., Paul and the Salvation of Mankind (London
1959) 260f.

7:24-25 WREDE, W., "Rückblick auf Markus" [orig: Das
Messiasgeheimnis in den Evangelien (1901), 115-49] in: R.
Pesch (ed.) Das Markus-Evangelium (Darmstadt 1979) 37f.

7:24 TAYLOR, V., The Life and Ministry of Jesus (London 1954)
54, 111, 129, 134-38. WREDE, W. Das Messiasgeheimnis in

den Evangelien (1963) 34, 36f, 53, 126f, 140, 146, 153, 173, 179, 254-56. HAHN, F. Das Verständnis der Mission im Neuen Testament (1965) 23, 97. MINETTE DE TILLESSE, G. Le Secret Messianique dans L'Evangile de Marc (1968) 248-51. KONINGS, J., "The Pre-Markan Sequence in Jn 6" in: M. Sabbe (ed.) L'Evangile selon Marc (Gembloux 1974) 155, 173. ACHTEMEIER, P. J., Mark (Philadelphia 1975) 27f. KOCH, D.-A., Die Bedeutung der Wundererzählungen für die Christologie des Markusevangeliums (Berlin/New York 1975) 89-92. MALBON, E. S., "Mythic Structure and Meaning in Mark" Semeia 16 (1980) 103-107.

7:25-30 KONINGS, J., "The Pre-Markan Sequence in Jn 6" in: M. Sabbe (ed.) L'Evangile selon Marc (Gembloux 1974) 155.

7:25 METZGER, B. M., The Early Versions of the New Testament (Oxford 1977) 162.

7:26-29 QUESNELL, Q., This Good News (Milwaukee 1964) 170f.

7:27-9:1 HAENCHEN, E., "Die Komposition von Mk 7:27-9:1" NovT 6 (1963) 81-109.

7:27-28 KLAUCK, H.-J., Allegorie und Allegorese in Synoptischen Gleichnistexten (Münster 1978) 273-80.

7:27 MUNCK, J., Paul and the Salvation of Mankind (London 1959) 261f. BORNKAMM-BARTH-HELD Ueberlieferung und Auslegung im Matthäus Evangelium (1961) 187-89. STRECKER, G. Der Weg der Gerechtigkeit (1962) 107. HAHN, F. Christologische Hoheitstitel (1963) 81. HAHN, F. Das Verständnis der Mission im Neuen Testament (1965) 24f, 62, 63f, 102f. SHIMADA, K., The Formulary Material in First Peter: A Study According to the Method of Traditionsgeschichte (Th.D. Diss. on Microfilm, Ann Arbor 1966) 214f. NICKELS, P. Targum and New Testament (1967) 24. SNOY, T., "Marc 6, 48: '. . . et il voulait le dépasser'" in: M. Sabbe (ed.) L'Evangile selon Marc (Gembloux 1974) 352. ZINGG, P., Das Wachsen der Kirche (Freiburg 1974) 271-78. METZGER, B. M., The Early Versions of the New Testament (Oxford 1977) 438.

7:28 *STORCH, W. "Zur Perikope von der Syrophönizierin. Mk 7, 28 und Ri 1, 7" BZ 14 (2, '70) 256-57. WEINACHT, H. Die Menschwerdung des Sohnes Gottes im Markusevangelium (1972) 136-38.

7:29 BORNKAMM-BARTH-HELD, Ueberlieferung und Auslegung im Matthäus Evangelium (1961) 186-88. PETZKE, G., Die Traditionen über Apollonius von Tyana und das Neue Testament (Leiden 1970) 136, 180.

7:30   BORNKAMM-BARTH-HELD Ueberlieferung und Auslegung im Matthäus-Evangelium (1961) 218, 222.

7:31   HAHN, F. Das Verständnis der Mission im Neuen Testament (1965) 97. SCHREIBER, J. Theologie des Vertrauens (1967) 158, 160, 170-72, 176-78, 209-212. MARXSEN, W. Mark the Evangelist (1969) 63, 69f, 72.

7:31-37   WEBER, O. GPM 4, (1949/50) 230ff. FARRER, A. A Study in St Mark (1951) 40ff, 104f, 224ff. FARRER, A. St Matthew and St Mark (1954) 28, 173. EICHHOLZ, G. Herr, tue meine Lippen auf. (1957) 261-65. FISCHER, GPM 15 (1960/61) 238ff. BORNKAMM-BARTH-HELD (1961) 195ff, 286. DOERNE, M. Er kommt auch noch heute (1961) 126-29. LELOIR, L., "Ephphatha" AssS 65 (1963) 31-42. HEPHATA Predigtgedanken aus Vergangenheit und Gegenwart (1966) 237-62. MINETTE DE TILLESSE G. Le Secret Messianique dans L'Evangile de Marc (1968) 57-62. ZIMMERMANN, W.-D. Markus über Jesus (1970) 88-89. KERTELGE K. Die Wunder Jesu im Markusevangelium (1970) 157-61. BOHREN, R., Predigtlehre (München 1971) 183, 194. JEREMIAS, J. Neutestamentliche Theologie I (1971) 90, 93f. MOLNAR, M., in: GPM 27 (1973) 383-89. GOULDER, M. D., Midrash and Lection in Matthew (London 1974) 317, 327, 354, 381. KONINGS, J., "The Pre-Markan Sequence in Jn 6" in: M. Sabbe (ed.) L'Evangile selon Marc (Gembloux 1974) 158, 159, 173. SCHENKE, L., Die Wundererzählungen des Markusevangeliums (Stuttgart 1974) 264-80. CONZELMANN, H. und LINDEMANN, A., Arbeitsbuch zum Neuen Testament (Tübingen 1975) 95. KOCH, D.-A., Die Bedeutung der Wundererzählungen für die Christologie des Markusevangeliums (Berlin/New York 1975) 34-36, 72f, 77f. PESCH, R., Das Markusevangelium I (Freiburg 1976) 400 (lit!). GNILKA, J., Das Evangelium nach Markus I (Einsiedeln/Neukirchen 1978) 295 (lit!). POKORNÝ, P., in: GPM 33 (1979) 345-50.

7:31   TAYLOR, V., The Life and Ministry of Jesus (London 1954) 131f. DAVIES, W. D., The Gospel and the Land (London 1974) 239, 419, 432f. GOULDER, M. D., Midrash and Lection in Matthew (London 1974) 380f. KONINGS, J., "The Pre-Markan Sequence in Jn 6" in: M. Sabbe (ed.) L'Evangile selon Marc (Gembloux 1974) 160, 161. ACHTEMEIER, P. J., Mark (Philadelphia 1975) 13, 27. KOCH, D.-A., Die Bedeutung der Wundererzälungen für die Christologie des Markusevangeliums (Berlin/New York 1975) 89-92. *LANG, F. G., " 'Über Sidon mitten ins Gebiet der Dekapolis.'

Geographie und Theologie in Markus 7, 31" Zeitschrift des deutschen Palästina-Vereins 94 (1978) 145-60. SWIDLER, L., Biblical Affirmations of Woman (Philadelphia 1979) 230. MALBON, E. S., "Mythic Structure and Meaning in Mark" Semeia 16 (1980) 103-107.

7:32ff   STREETER, B. H. The Four Gospels (1951) 169f.

7:32-37   TAYLOR, V., The Life and Ministry of Jesus (London 1954) 131f. HULL, J. M., Hellenistic Magic and the Synoptic Tradition (London 1974) 138-40.

7:33-34   PETZKE, G., Die Traditionen über Apollonius von Tyana und das Neue Testament (Leiden 1970) 136, 143, 179-80.

7:33   MINETTE DE TILLESSE, G. Le Secret Messianique dans L'Evangile de Marc (1968) 238-42. ACHTEMEIER, P. J., Mark (Philadelphia 1975) 79-81.

7:34   KLOSTERMANN, E. Das Markusevangelium (1950) 73. NEPPER-CHRISTENSEN, P., Das Matthäusevangelium (Aarhus 1958) 110-12. *RABINOWITZ, I. " 'Be Opened' = 'Ephphata' (Mark 7:34): Did Jesus Speak Hebrew?" ZNW 53 (3-4, '-62) 229-38. NICKELS, P. Targum and New Testament (1967) 25. BLACK, M., "ΕΦΦΑΘΑ (Mk 7:34), [TA] πΑΣΧΑ (Mt 26:18W), [TA] ΣΑΒΒΑΤΑ (passim), [TA] ΔΙΔΡΑΧΜΑ (Mt 17:24 bis)," in: A. Descamps/A. de HALLEUX (eds.) Mélanges Bibliques en hommage au R. P. Béda Rigaux (Gembloux 1970) 57-60. *RABINOWITZ, I. "Ephphatha (Mark 7:34): Certainly Hebrew, Not Aramaic" JSS 16 (2, '71) 151-56. METZGER, B. M., The Early Versions of the New Testament (Oxford 1977) 80. "Aramäisch" in: TRE 3 (1978) 606.

7:36-37   WREDE, W. Das Messiasgeheimnis in den Evangelien (1963) 15, 126f, 255-58. LUZ, U., "Das Geheimnismotiv und die markinische Christologie" [orig: ZNW 56 (1965) 9-30] in: R. Pesch (ed.) Das Markus-Evangelium (Darmstadt 1979) 216.

7:36   LIGHTFOOT, R. H. History and Interpretation in the Gospels (1934) 71f. MINETTE DE TILLESSE, G. Le Secret Messianique dans L'Evangile de Marc (1968) 249-51.

7:37   HERING, J. "Remarks sur Marc 7:37" Coniectanea Neotestamentica Festschrift Antoni Fridrichsen (1947) 91-96. ROBINSON, J. M. Kerygma und historischer Jesus (1960) 115. METZGER, B. M., The Early Versions of the New Testament (Oxford 1977) 374, 437.

7:38   COPPENS, J., "Les logia du Fils de l'Homme dans l'évangile de Marc" in: M. Sabbe (ed.) L'Evangile selon Marc (Gembloux 1974) 499.

8-10 ACHTEMEIER, P. J., Mark (Philadelphia 1975) 34f, 97-100.

8:1-9:1 FARRER, A. A Study in St Mark (1951) 99ff, 312f.

  8 NEIRYNCK, F., "Le discours anti-apocalyptique de Marc 8" EphT 45 (1969) 154-64. ROBINSON, J. M., "Gnosticism and the New Testament" in: B. Aland et al. (eds.) Gnosis. Für H. Jonas (Göttingen 1978) 141f.

  ff HAHN, F. Das Verständnis der Mission im Neuen Testament (1965) 97.

8:1-21 SCHENKE, L., Die Wundererzählungen des Markusevangeliums (Stuttgart 1974) 281-307.

8:1-10 HAHN, F. Christologische Hoheitstitel (1963) 391. KNACKSTEDT, J., "Die beiden Brotvermehrungen im Evangelium" NTS 10 (1963-1964) 309-35. *ENGLISH, E. S. "A Neglected Miracle" BiblSa 126 (504, '69) 300-305. KERTELGE, K. Die Wunder Jesu im Markusevangelium (1970) 139-45. LEHMANN, M. Synoptische Quellenanalyse und die Frage nach dem historischen Jesu (1970) 41-44. NICOL, W., The Semeia in the Fourth Gospel (Leiden 1972) 35, 57, 71f. SCHELLONG, D., in: GPM 27 (1973) 354-62. TREVIJANO ETCHEVERRIA, R., "La multiplicación de los panes (Mc. 6, 30-46; 8, 1-10 par.) Burgense 15 (1974) 435-65. Van CANGH, J.-M., "La multiplication des pains dans l'évangile de Marc. Essai d'exégèse globale" in: M. Sabbe (ed.) L'Evangile selon Marc (Gembloux 1974) 309-46. Van CANGH, J.-M., La multiplication des pains et l'Eucharistie (Paris 1975). EGGER, W., Frohbotschaft und Lehre (Frankfurt 1976) 123. "Abendmahl" in: TRE 1 (1977) 49. SCHMITHALS, W., Das Evangelium nach Markus (Gütersloh/Würzburg 1979) 363 (lit!). SWIDLER, L., Biblical Affirmations of Woman (Philadelphia 1979) 249f, 279.

8:1-9 STONEHOUSE, N. B. The Witness of Matthew and Mark to Christ (1944) 60. TAYLOR, V., The Life and Ministry of Jesus (London 1954) 129f. VÖÖBUS, A., The Gospels in Study and Preaching (Philadelphia 1966) 203-34. WEBER, O. Predigtmeditationen (1967) 224-27. KAMPHAUS, F. Von der Exegese zur Predigt (1968) 134-40, 206, 208. ROLOFF, J. Das

Kerygma und der irdische Jesus (1970) 241ff. ZIMMERMANN, W.-D. Markus über Jesus (1970) 90-91. SCHENKE, L., Studien zur Passionsgeschichte des Markus (Würzburg 1971) 170ff. SCHNIDER, F./STENGER, W. Johannes und die Synoptiker (1971) 94-98. DORMEYER, D., Die Passion Jesu als Verhaltensmodell (Münster 1974) 101ff. KONINGS, J., "The Pre-Markan Sequence in Jn 6" in: M. Sabbe (ed.) L'Evangile selon Marc (Gembloux 1974) 155, 173. KOCH, D.-A., Die Bedeutung der Wundererzählungen für die Christologie des Markusevangeliums (Berlin/New York 1975) 34-36, 109, 12. PESCH, R., Das Markusevangelium I (Freiburg 1976) 405 (lit!). SAITO, T., Die Mosevorstellungen im Neuen Testament (Bern 1977) 47-50. FRIEDRICH, G., "Die beiden Erzählungen von der Speisung in Markus 6, 31-44; 8, 1-9" in: Auf das Wort kommt es an Göttingen 1978) 13-25. GNILKA, J., Das Evangelium nach Markus I (Einsiedeln/Neukirchen 1978) 299f (lit!).

8:1-2 SCHWEIZER, E., "Mark's Contribution to the Quest of the Historical Jesus" NTS 10 (1963-1964) 427f. EGGER, W., Frohbotschaft und Lehre (Frankfurt 1976) 129f.

8:1 SCHREIBER, J. Theologie des Vertrauens (1967) 120f, 122f, 125, 155, 170f, 176. KONINGS, J., "The Pre-Markan Sequence in Jn 6" in: M. Sabbe (ed.) L'Evangile selon Marc (Gembloux 1974) 163.

8:2 RICHARDSON, A. The Miracle-Stories of the Gospels (1948) 33f. FARRER, A. St Matthew and St Mark (1954) 111, 112, 120. SCHREIBER, J. Theologie des Vertrauens (1967) 117-19. "Barmherzigkeit" in: TRE 5 (1980) 227.

8:3 *DANKER, F. W. "Mrk 8:3" JBL 82 (2, '63) 215-16. Van CANGH, J.-M., "La multiplication des pains dans l'évangile de Marc" in: M. Sabbe (ed.) L'Evangile selon Marc (Gembloux 1974) 338, 339.

8:4 MAUSER, U. Christ in the Wilderness (1963) 103ff, 78n. SCHREIBER, J. Theologie des Vertrauens (1967) 168-71, 205, 210.

8:5.8 STRECKER, G. Der Weg der Gerechtigkeit (1962) 39_2.

8:6-8 Van CANGH, J.-M., "La multiplication des pains dans l'évangile de Marc" in: M. Sabbe (ed.) L'Evangile selon Marc (Gembloux 1974) 333, 335-37, 340, 345.

8:6 JEREMIAS, J. Die Abendmahlsworte Jesu (1960) 166-68.

8:9 DORMEYER, D., Die Passion Jesu als Verhaltensmodell (Münster 1974) 67A, 42.

8:10-13 ZIMMERMANN, W.-D. Markus über Jesus (1970) 91-93. PESCH, R., Das Markusevangelium I (Freiburg 1976) 410 (lit!). GNILKA, J., Das Evangelium nach Markus I (Einsiedeln/Neukirchen 1978) 305 (lit!).

8:10 JEREMIAS, J. Abba (1966) 87-90. SCHREIBER, J. Theologie des Vertrauens (1967) 158-60, 169, 171, 176, 205. KONINGS, J., "The Pre-Markan Sequence in Jn 6" in: M. Sabbe (ed.) L'Evangile selon Marc (Gembloux 1974) 155, 173. MALBON, E. S., "Mythic Structure and Meaning in Mark" Semeia 16 (1980) 103-107.

8:11ff. GOPPELT, L., Theologie des Neuen Testaments I (Göttingen 1975) 196f.

8:11-21 STONEHOUSE, N. B., The Witness of Luke to Christ (Grand Rapids 1951) 108f. SCHMAHL, G., Die Zwölf im Markusevangelium (Trier 1974) 123.

8:11-15 RIVKIN, E., A Hidden Revolution (Nashville 1978) 94f.

8:11-13 TAYLOR, V., The Life and Ministry of Jesus (London 1954) 130f. GRANT, F. C. The Gospels (1957) 81f. KERTELGE, K. Die Wunder Jesu im Markusevangelium (1970) 23-27. KONINGS, J., "The Pre-Markan Sequence in Jn 6" in: M. Sabbe (ed.) L'Evangile selon Marc (Gembloux 1974) 173. KOCH, D.-A., Die Bedeutung der Wundererzählungen für die Christologie des Markusevangeliums (Berlin/New York 1975) 34-36, 155-59.

8:11-12 TAYLOR, V. The Formation of the Gospel Tradition (1949) 78f. *VOEGTLE, A. "Der Spruch vom Jonaszeichen (Mk 8, 11f)" Synoptische Studien, Wilkenhauser ('53) 230-77. HAHN, F. Christologische Hoheitstitel (1963) 390. *LINTON, O. "The Demand for a Sign from Heaven (Mk 8, 11-12 and Parallels)" StTh 19 (1-2, '65) 112-29. JEREMIAS, J. Neutestamentliche Theologie I (1971) 22, 25f, 29, 44, 77, 82, 135, 251. *MERLI, D., "Il segno di Giona" BiOr 14 (1972) 61-77. KONINGS, J., "The Pre-Markan Sequence in Jn 6" in: M. Sabbe (ed.) L'Evangile selon Marc (Gembloux 1974) 155. EDWARDS, R. A., A Theology of Q (Philadelphia 1976) 113-15. PERRIN, N., Jesus and the Language of the Kingdom (London 1976) 45f. SWIDLER, L., Biblical Affirmations of Woman (Philadelphia 1979) 242f, 254, 257. TANNEHILL, R. C., "The Gospel of Mark as Narrative Christology" Semeia 16 (1980) 69.

8:11 DEVISCH, M., "La relation entre l'évangile de Marc et la document Q" in: M. Sabbe (ed.) L'Evangile selon Marc (Gembloux 1974) 85.

8:12ff   RICHARDSON, A. The Miracle-Stories of the Gospels (1948) 46ff.

8:12   KNOX, W. L. The Sources of the Synoptic Gospels 2 (1957) 8, 65. SCHWEIZER, E., Erniedrigung und Erhöhung bei Jesus und seinen Nachfolgern (1962) §31. JUENGEL, E. Paulus und Jesus (1966) 257. PESCH, R. Naherwartungen (1969) 86, 87, 101, 183, 184. HASLER, V. Amen (1969) 30. BERGER, K. Die Amen-Worte Jesus (1970) 59-62. VOEGTLE, A. Das Evangelium und die Evanglien (1971) 103-105, 111-15. PATSCH, H., Abendmahl und historischer Jesus (Stuttgart 1972) 202ff. LAMBRECHT, J., "Redaction and Theology in Mk 4" in: M. Sabbe (ed.) L'Evangile selon Marc (Gembloux 1974) 284. 'Amen" in: TRE 2 (1978) 389.

8:13-21 MALBON, E. S., "Mythic Structure and Meaning in Mark" Semeia 16 (1980) 103-107.

8:13   KONINGS, J., "The Pre-Markan Sequence in Jn 6" in: M. Sabbe (ed.) L'Evangile selon Marc (Gembloux 1974) 155, 173.

8:14-30 LIGHTFOOT, R. H. History and Interpretation in the Gospels (19-34) 90ff.

8:14-21 FARRER, A. St Matthew and St Mark (1954) 57, 92. MASSON, C., Vers les Sources d'eau Vive (Lausanne 1961) 70ff. *MANEK, J. "Mark viii 14-21" NovTest 7 (1, '64) 10-14. SUHL, A. Die Funktion der altestamentlichen Zitate und Anspielungen im Markusevangelium (1965) 145ff. MINETTE DE TILLESSE, G. Le Secret Messianique dans L'Evangile de Marc (1968) 412-20. KONINGS, J., "The Pre-Markan Sequence in Jn 6" in: M. Sabbe (ed.) L'Evangile selon Marc (Gembloux 1974) 155, 173. Van CANGH, J.-M., "La multiplication des pains dans l'évangile de Marc "in: M. Sabbe (ed.) L'Evangile selon Marc (Gembloux 1974) 342. KOCH, D. A., Die Bedeutung der Wundererzählungen für die Christologie des Markusevangeliums (Berlin/New York 1975) 110-12. EGGER, W., Frohbotschaft und Lehre (Frankfurt 1976) 128, 134. *LAMBIASI, F., "L'Autenticità storica della controversie con i Farisei" BiOr 18 (1976) 3-27. PESCH, R., Das Markusevangelium I (Freiburg 1976) 415 (lit!). TRITES, A. A., The New Testament Concept of Witness (Cambridge 1977) 178f. GNILKA, J., Das Evangelium nach Markus I (Einsiedeln/Neukirchen 1978) 309 (lit!). *LEMCIO, E. E., "External Evidence for the Structure and Function of Mark iv 1-20" JThS 29 (1978) 323-38. *McCOMBIE, F., "Jesus and the Leaven of Salvation" New Blackfriars 59 (1978) 450-62. DIBELIUS, M., "Sammlung" [orig: Die Formgeschichte des Evangeliums 1933 (2) 219-34] in: R. Pesch (ed.) Das Markus-

Evangelium (Darmstadt 1979) 77f. TANNEHILL, R. C., "The Gospel of Mark as Narrative Christology" Semeia 16 (1980) 68, 70.

8:14-17 WILCOX, M., "The Denial Sequence in Mark 14:26-31, 66-72" NTS 17 (1970-1971) 434f.

8:15 *ZIEHNER, G. "Das Bildwort vom Sauerteig Mk 8.15" TThZ 67 (4, '58) 247-48. *NEGOITA, A. and DANIEL, C. "L'énigme du levain. Ad Mc. viii 15; Mt. xvi 6; et Lc. xii 1," NovTest 9 (4, '67) 306-14. HOEHNER, H. W. Herod Antipas (1972) 202-13.

8:16-18 HESSE, F., Das Verstockungsproblem im Alten Testament (Berlin 1955) 3-5, 23, 64, 66.

8:17-21 GNILKA, J. Die Verstockung Israels (1961) 32f. BORNKAMM-BARTH-HELD, Ueberlieferung und Auslegung im Matthäus-Evangelium (1961) 102, 105, 172, 196, 280. HAHN, F. Das Verständnis der Mission im Neuen Testament (1965) 97.

8:17-18 KONINGS, J., "The Pre-Markan Sequence in Jn 6" in: M. Sabbe (ed.) L'Evangile selon Marc (Gembloux 1974) 173.

8:17 STRECKER, G. Der Weg der Gerechtigkeit (1962) 230. LAMBRECHT, J., "Redaction and Theology in Mk 4" in: M. Sabbe (ed.) L'Evangile selon Marc (Gembloux 1974) 281. ACHTEMEIER, P. J., Mark (Philadelphia 1975) 93.

8:18 HENNECKE, E. und SCHNEEMELCHER, W., Neutestamentliche Apokryphen II (Tübingen 1964) 341. *JEWELL, A. J. "Did St Mark 'Remember'?" LondQuartHolRev 35 (2, '66) 117-20.

8:19-28 ACHTEMEIER, P. J., Mark (Philadelphia 1975) 29f.

8:22-10:52 *BEST, E. "Discipleship in Mark: Mark 8.22-10.52" SJTh 23 (3, '70) 323-37.

8:22-26 RICHARDSON, A. The Miracle-Stories of the Gospels (1948) 82ff. STREETER, B. H. The Four Gospels (1951) 169f, 173f. FARRER, A. A Study in St Mark (1951) 40ff, 104f, 120ff, 224ff, 341ff. PARKER, P. The Gospel Before Mark (1953) 183-84. TAYLOR, V., The Life and Ministry of Jesus (London 1954) 131f. BORNKAMM-BARTH-HELD, Ueberlieferung und Auslegung im Matthäus-Evangelium (1961) 195ff, 286. BEAUVERY, J., "La guérsion d'un aveugle à Bethsaida" NRTh 90 (1968) 1083-1091. PESCH, R. Naherwartungen (1969) 52, 54, 60, 61, 69. ROLOFF, J. Das Kerygma und der irdische Jesus (1970) 127-31. ZIMMERMANN, W.-D. Markus über Jesus (1970) 95-96. KERTELGE, K. Die Wunder Jesu im Markus-evangelium (1970) 161-65. JEREMIAS, J.

Neutestamentliche Theologie (1971) 90, 93f. NICOL, W., The Semeia in the Fourth Gospel (Leiden 1972) 15, 93f. KONINGS, J., "The Pre-Markan Sequence in Jn 6" in: M. Sabbe (ed.) L'Evangile selon Marc (Gembloux 1974) 153-56, 173. SCHENKE, L., Die Wundererzählungen des Markusevangeliums (Stuttgart 1974) 308-13. CONZELMANN, H. und LINDEMANN, A. Arbeitsbuch zum Neuen Testament (Tübingen 1975) 58. KOCH. D.-A., Die Bedeutung der Wundererzählungen für die Christologie des Markusevangeliums (Berlin/New York 1975) 34-37, 68-72. *WALKER, G., "The Blind Recover Their Sight" ET 87 (1975) 23. PESCH, R., Das Markusevangelium I (Freiburg 1976) 421 (lit!). GNILKA, J., Das Evangelium nach Markus I (Einsiedeln/Neukirchen 1978) 312 (lit!). KLAUCK, H.-J., Allegorie und Allegorese in Synoptischen Gleichnistexten (Münster 1978) 348-54. SEYBOLD, K. und MÜLLER, U., Krankheit und Heilung (Stuttgart 1978) 133f. *JOHNSON, E. S., "Mark viii. 22-26: The Blind Man from Bethsaida" NTS 25 (1979) 370-83. LUZ, U., "Das Geheimnismotiv und die markinische Christologie" [orig: ZNW 56 (1965) 9-30] in: R. Pesch (ed.) Das Markus-Evangelium (Darmstadt 1979) 215. SCHMITHALS, W., Das Evangelium nach Markus (Gütersloh/Würzburg 1979) 371 (lit!).

8:22   DALMAN, G. Orte und Wege Jesu (1967) 178f. LINTON, O., "Evidences of a Second Century Revised Edition of St Mark's Gospel" NTS 14 (1967-1968) 339f. "Aramäisch" in: TRE 3 (1978) 604. MALBON, E. S., "Mythic Structure and Meaning in Mark" Semeia 16 (1980) 103-107.

8:24   *LEE, G. M., "Mark viii 24" NovT 20 (1978) 74.

8:25   LINTON, O., "Evidences of a Second Century Revised Edition of St Mark's Gospel" NTS 14 (1967-1968) 340f.

8:26   LIGHTFOOT, R. H. History and Interpretation in the Gospels (1934) 71f. MANSON, T. W., The Teaching of Jesus (London 1945) 134, 214, 223, 225, 278-85. TAYLOR, V., The Text of the New Testament (London 1961) 84f. WREDE, W. Das Messiasgeheimnis in den Evangelien (1963) 256-58. PESCH, R. Naherwartungen (1969) 53, 54, 60, 61, 69, 173. KÜMMEL, W. G., Einleitung in das Neue Testament (Heidelberg 1973) *(17)*) 61-63.

8:27ff LIGHTFOOT, R. H. History and Interpretation in the Gospels (1934) 221f. CULLMANN, O. Die Christologie des Neuen Testaments (1957) 122ff. SCHWEIZER, E. Erniedrigung und Erhöhung bei Jesus und seinen Nachfolgern (1962) §11s. WREDE, W. Das Messiasgeheimnis inden Evangelien (1963)

9, 11f, 14, 21f, 115-124, 237-39. 252f. HAHN, F. Christologische Hoheitstitel (1963) 335. DINKLER, E. "Petrusbekenntnis und Satanswort, Das Problem der Messianität Jesu" Zeit und Geschichte (1964) 127-53. BULTMANN, R. Die Frage nach dem messianischen Bewusstsein Jesu und das Petrusbekenntnis" Exegetica (1967) 1-10. THYEN, H. Studien zur Sündenvergebung (1970) 218ff. GUETTGEMANNS, E. Offene Fragen zur Formgeschichte des Evangeliums (1970) 211, 259, 260. VOEGTLE, A. Das Evangelium und die Evangelien (1971) 146-49, 161-63.

8:27-14:9 WEEDEN, T. G., "Die Häresie, die Markus zur Abfassung seines Evangeliums veranlasst hat" [orig: "The Heresy that necessitated Mark's Gospel" ZNW 59 (1968) 145-58] in: R. Pesch (ed.) Das Markus-Evangelium (Darmstadt 1979) 239f.

8:27-10:52 WEISS, K. "Ekklesiologie, Tradition und Geschichte in der Jüngerunterweisung Mark 8, 27-10, 52" Der historische Jesus und der kerygmatische Christus, eds. H. Ristow und K. Matthiae (1961) 414-38. TOEDT, H. E. Der Menschensohn in der synoptischen Ueberlieferung (1963) 134-36. *SIMONSEN, H. "Mark. 8, 27-10, 52 i Markusevangeliets komposition" (Mark 8:27-10, 52 in the Composition of the Gospel of Mark DTT 27 (2, '64) 83-99. BEST, E. The Temptation and the Passion: The Markan Soteriology (1965) 121-24, 125. SCHREIBER, J. Theologie des Vertrauens (1967) 194-203. PESCH, R. Naherwartungen (1969) 62-64. MEYE, R. P. Jesus and the Twelve (1968) 73-80. GUETTGEMANNS, E. Offene Fragen zur Formgeschichte des Evangeliums (1970) 211, 212, 261. *VENETZ, H.-J. "Widerspruch und Nachfolge. Zur Frage des Glaubens an Jesus nach Mk 8, 27-10, 52" FZPhTh 19 (1, '72) 111-19. *DULING, D. C. "Interpreting the Markan 'Hodology:' Biblical Criticism in Preaching and Teaching" Nexus 17 (1974) 2-11. SCHMAHL, G., Die Zwölf im Markusevangelium (Trier 1974) 116-22. *VELLANICKAL, M., "Suffering in the Life and Teaching of Jesus" Jeevadhara 4 (1974) 144-61. KOCH, D.-A., Die Bedeutung der Wundererzählungen für die Christologie des Markusevangeliums (Berlin/New York 1975) 113f, 121f, 130-32. EGGER, W., Frohbotschaft und Lehre (Frankfurt 1976) 21, 85, 144, 166. *EGGER, W., Glaube und Nachfolge (Klosterneuburg 1978). TANNEHILL, R. C., "The Gospel of Mark as Narrative Christology" Semeia 16 (1980) 72-76.

8:27-10:45 LIGHTFOOT, R. H. History and Interpretation in the Gospels (1934) 77ff, 117ff. *FAW, C. E. "The Heart of the Gospel of Mark" JBR 24 ('56) 77-82. GRANT, F. C. The Gospels (1957)

96ff. HAHN, F. Das Verständnis der Mission im Neuen Testament (1965) 96, 98. OTOMO, Y. Nachfolge Jesu und Anfänge der Kirche im Neuen Testament (1970) 81-85. PERRIN, N., The New Testament: An Introduction (New York 1974) 155-58. ACHTEMEIER, P. J., Mark (Philadelphia 1975) 92.

8:27-10:31 SCHWEIZER, E., "Die Theologische Leistung des Markus" [orig: EvTh 24 (1964) 337-55] in: R. Pesch (ed.) Das Markus-Evangelium (Darmstadt 1979) 176-78.

8:27-9:50 EWALD, H., Die drei ersten Evangelien (Göttingen 1850) 269ff.

8:27-9:30 STONEHOUSE, N. B. The Witness of Matthew and Mark to Christ (1944) 34, 35, 66ff.

8:27-9:13 HORSTMANN, M. Studien zur markinischen Christologie. Mk 8, 27-9:13 als Zugang zum Christusbild des zweiten Evangeliums (1969). *LAFONTAINE, R. and MOURLON BEERNAERT, P. "Essai sur la structure de Marc 8, 27-9, 13" RechSR 57 (4, '69) 543-61. *LAMBRECHT, J., "The Christology of Mark" BThB 3 (1973) 256-73.

8:27-9:1 CARRINGTON, P. The Primitive Christian Calendar (1952) 165-68. *HAENCHEN, E. "Die Komposition von Mk viii 27-ix 1 und Par" NovTest 6 (2-3, '63) 81-109. HAENCHEN, E. "Leidensnachfolge" Die Bible und Wir (1968) 102-34. PERRIN, N. What is Redaction Criticism? (1969) 40-57. THYEN, H. Studien zur Sündenvergebung (1970) 218-36. ZIMMERMANN, W.-D. Markus über Jesus (1970) 97-101. PERRIN, N. "The Christology of Mark" in: M. Sabbe (ed.) L'Evangile selon Marc (Gembloux 1974) 475. KOCH, D.-A., "Zum Verhältnis von Christologie und Eschatologie im Markusevangelium" in: G. Strecker (ed.) Jesus Christus in Historie und Theologie. Für H. Conzelmann (Tübingen 1975) 395-408. PERRIN, N., "Die Christologie des Markus-Evangeliums" [orig: "The Christology of Mark" JR 51 (1971) 173-87] in: R. Pesch (ed.) Das Markus-Evangelium (Darmstadt 1979) 360-61.

8:27ff BULTMANN, R., Theologie des Neuen Testaments (Tübingen 1965) 27f, 48. WOLFF, H. W., Wegweisung (München 1965) 182. CONZELMANN, H., Theologie als Schriftauslegung (München 1974) 35, 38, 79f, 145, A14. CONZELMANN, H. und LINDEMANN, A., Arbeitsbuch zum Neuen Testament (Tübingen 1975) 345, 367.

8:27-38 KRECK, W. GPM 11/2 (1957) 79-83. Van LINDEN, P., Knowing Christ through Mark's Gospel (Chicago 1977).

WREDE, W., "Rückblick auf Markus" [orig: Das Messiasgeheimnis in den Evangelien (1901) 115-49] in: R. Pesch (ed.) Das Markus-Evangelium (Darmstadt 1979) 13-21.

8:27-35 *DENAUX, A., "La confession de Pierre et la première annonce de la Passion. Mc 8, 27-35" AssS 55 (1974) 31-39.

8:27-33 BUTLER, B. C., The Originality of St Matthew (Cambridge 1951) 131ff. *WILLAERT, B. Le Connexion littéraire entre la première prédiction de la Passion et la confession de Pierre chez les Synoptiques EphT (1, '56) 24-45. STRECKER, G. Der Weg der Gerechtigkeit (1962) 202. HAHN, F. Christologische Hoheitstitel (1963) 174f, 196f, 226-30. *MARTINI, C. M. "La confessione messianica di Pietro a Cesarea e l'inizic del nuovo popolo di Dio secondo il Vangelo di S. Marco (8, 27-33)" CiCa 118/2 (June 7 '67) 544-51. POTTERIE, I., "La confessione messianica di Pietro" in: Atti della XIX settimana Italiana (1967) 59-77. MINETTE DE TILLESSE, G. Le Secret Messianique dans L'Evangile de Marc (1968) 293-326. *DENAUX, A. "Petrusbelijdenis en eerste lijdensvoorspelling. Een exegese van Mc. 8, 27-33 par. Lc 9, 18-22" (Peter's Confession and the First Prediction of the Passion. An Exegesis of Mk 8:27-33. Lk 9:18-22) CollBrugGand 15 (2, '69) 188-220. HORSTMANN, M. Studien zur Markinischen Christologie (1969) 8-31. ITTEL, G. W. Jesus und die Jünger (1970) 70-72. VOEGTLE, A. Das Evangelium und die Evangelien (1971) 139-42, 155-59. SCHRAMM, T. Der Markus-Stoff bei Lukas (1971) 130-36. LANGE, J., Das Ercheinen des Auferstandenen im Evangelium nach Matthäus (Würzburg 1973) 122, 128-30. SCHUBERT, K., Jesus im Lichte der Religionsgeschichte des Judentums (München 1973) 133-35. KONINGS, J., "The Pre-Markuan Sequence in Jn 6" in:. M. Sabbe (ed.) L'Evangile selon Marc (Gembloux 1974) 155, 173. TALBERT, C. H., Literary Patterns, Theological Themes, and the Genre of Luke-Acts (Missoula 1974) 27. ACHTEMEIER, P. J., Mark (Philadelphia 1975) 42f.97. GOPPELT, L., Theologie des Neuen Testaments I (Göttingen 1975) 217-20. *ERNST, J., "Petrusbekenntnis - Leidensankündigung - Satanswort (Mk 8, 27-33). Tradition und Redaktion" Catholica 32 (1978) 46-73. GNILKA, J., Das Evangelium nach Markus II (Einsiedeln/Neukirchen 1979) 9f. (lit!). LUZ, U., "Das Geheimnismotiv und die markinische Christologie" [orig: ZNW 56 (1965) 9-30] in: R. Pesch (ed.) Das Markus-Evangelium (Darmstadt 1979) 220-25. MEYER, B. F., The Aims of Jesus (London 1979) 215f. ERNST, J., "Die Petrustradition im Markusevangelium - ein altes Problem neu angegangen" in: J. Zmijewski/E. Nellessen (eds.) Begegnung mit dem Wort. Für H. Zimmermann (Bonn 1980) 48-50.

8:27-30   BULTMANN, R., "Die Frage nach dem messianischen Bewusstsein Jesu und das Petrus-Bekenntnis" ZNW 19 (1919-1920) 165-74. MOORE, G. F., Judaism II (Cambridge, Mass. 1946) 309n. SCHMID, J. Das Evangelium nach Markus (1958) 155-59. BULTMANN, R., The History of the Synoptic Tradition (Oxford 1963) 257-59. *PESCH, R., "Das Messiasbekenntnis des Petrus (Mk 8, 27-30). Neuverhandlung einer alten Frage" BZ 17 (1973) 178-95; BZ 18 (1974) 20-31. SCHNIDER, F., Jesus der Prophet (Freiburg 1973) 181, 183ff, 235. DORMEYER, D., Die Passion Jesu als Verhältensmodell (Münster 1974) 113A.314. EGGER, W., Frohbotschaft und Lehre (Frankfurt 1976) 87-90. PESCH, R., Das Markusevangelium II (Freiburg 1977) 35f (lit!). SCHMITHALS, W., Das Evangelium nach Markus (Gütersloh/Würzburg 1979) 378 (lit!). SWIDLER, L., Biblical Affirmations of Woman (Philadelphia 1979) 217. "Bekenntnisschriften" in: TRE 5 (1980) 488.

8:27-29   HAHN, F. Christologische Hoheitstitel (1963) 175, 222f. MANSON, W., Jesus the Messiah (Philadelphia 1948) 108f.

8:27-28   MOORE, G. F., Judaism II (Cambridge, Mass. 1946) 326. GNILKA, J., "Das Martyrium Johannes des Täufers (Mk 6, 17-29)" in: P. Hoffmann (ed.) Orientierung an Jesus. Für J. Schmid (Freiburg 1973) 79-81.

8:27   STREETER, B. H. The Four Gospels (1951) 176f. ROBINSON, J. M. Kerygma und historischer Jesus (1960) 123. HAHN, F. Christologische Hoheitstitel (1963) 230. HAHN, F. Das Verständnis der Mission im Neuen Testament (1965) 23, 98. SCHREIBER, J. Theologie des Vertrauens (1967) 175-77, 207f, 212. PESCH, R. Naherwartungen (1969) 54, 62, 63, 69, 70, 84. QUESNELL Q. The Mind of Mark (1969) 129-38. KÜMMEL, W. G., Einleitung in das Neue Testament (Heidelberg 1973(17)) 63f. NEIRYNCK, F., "Urmarcus redivivus?" in: M. Sabbe (ed.) L'Evangile selon Marc (Gembloux 1974) 120-22. ACHTEMEIER, P. J., Mark (Philadelphia 1975) 36f. MALBON, E. S., "Mythic Structure and Meaning in Mark" Semeia 16 (1980) 103-107.

8:28-29   OBS, D. J., "La parabole du figuier qui bourgeonne' RB 75 (1968) 526-48. SMITH, M., Clement of Alexandria and a Secret Gospel of Mark (Cambridge, Mass. 1973) 136f, 154, 211.

8:28   SCHLATTER, A. Johannes der Taufer (1956) 50ff. HAHN, F. Christologische Hoheitstitel (1963), 174, 382, 398. BOUSSET,

W., Die Religion des Judentums im Späthellenistischen Zeitalter (Berlin 1966=1926) 232. SCHNIDER, F., Jesus der Prophet (Freiburg 1973) 52, 105, 110, 182.

8:29ff   STONEHOUSE, N. B. The Witness of Matthew and Mark to Christ (1944) 215ff, 11, 67, 79f. CULLMANN, O., The State in the New Testament (New York 1956) 26f.

8:29-33   GERSTENBERGER, G. und SCHRAGE, W., Leiden (Stuttgart 1977) 148-49; ET: J. E. Steely, Suffering (Nashville 1980) 172.

8:29-31   BURKILL, T. A., "St Mark's Philosophy of History" NTS 3 (1956-1957) 142-48. ACHTEMEIER, P. J., Mark (Philadelphia 1975) 46.

8:29-30   FRIEDRICH, G., "Beobachtungen zur messianischen Hohepriestererwartung in den Synoptikern" in: Auf das Wort kommt es an (Göttingen 1978) 83.

8:29   HAHN, F. Christologische Hoheitstitel (1963) 174f, 215. BRAUN, H., Qumran und NT II (Tübingen 1966) 65. JEREMIAS, J. Neutestamentliche Theologie I (1971) 245f. DESCAMPS, A., "Pour une histoire du titre 'Fils de Dieu'" in: M. Sabbe (ed.) L'Evangile selon Marc (Gembloux 1974) 552. BEST, E., From Text to Sermon (Atlanta 1978) 26. *FRANKEMÖLLE, H., "Jüdische Messiaswartung und christlicher Messiasglaube. Hermeneutische Anmerkungen im Kontext des Petrusbekenntnises Mk 8, 29" Kairos 20 (1978) 97-109. MEYER, B. F., The Aims of Jesus (London 1979) 175-80.

8:30-10:52 MINETTE DE TILLESSE, G. Le Secret Messianique dans L'Evangile de Marc (1968) 369-80.

8:30-32   WILLIAMS, J. A., A Conceptual History of Deuteronomism in the Old Testament, Judaism, and the New Testament (Louisville 1976) 298-310.

8:30-31   STRECKER, G. Der Weg der Gerechtigkeit (1962) 201.

8:30   YATES, J. E., The Spirit and the Kingdom (London 1963) 133f. WREDE, W. Das Messiasgeheimnis in den Evangelien (1963) 254-58. MINETTE DE TILLESSE, G. Le Secret Messianique dans L'Evangile de Marc (1968) 249-51. VOEGTLE, A. Das Evangelium und die Evangelien (1971) 139-43. KÜMMEL, W. G., Einleitung in das Neue Testament (Heidelbert 1973(17)) 62f. ACHTEMEIER, P. J., Mark (Philadelphia 1975) 79-81.

8:31-11:10 *REEDY, C. J. "Mk 8:31-11:10 and the Gospel Ending. A Redaction Study" CBQ 34 (2, '72) 188-97.

8:31-9:1   LAMBRECHT, J. Die Redaktion der Markus-Apokalypse (1967) 296-97.

8:31ff   *TAYLOR, V. "The Origin of the Markan Passion-Sayings" NTS 1/3 ('55) 159-67. SCHWEIZER, E. Erniedrigung und Erhöhung bei Jesus und seinen Nachfolgern (1962) §1 h-1 11 a d m. STRECKER, G. "Die Leidens-und Auferstehungsvoraussagen im Markusevangelium (Mk 8, 31; 9, 31; 10, 32-34)" ZThK 64 (1, '67) 16-39. STRECKER, G. "The Passion-and Resurrection Predictions in Mark's Gospel (Mark 8:31; 9:31; 10:32-34)" Interpretation 22 (4, '68) 421-42. CONZELMANN, H. "Auslegung von Markus 4, 35-41 par; Markus 8, 31-37 par; Römer 1, 3f" EvangErzieher 20, 1968, 249-60. KLAPPERT, B., "Arbeit Gottes und Mitarbeit des Menschen (Phil 2, 6-11)" in: J. Moltmann (ed.) Recht auf Arbeit - Sinn der Arbeit (München 1979) 99-101.

8:31-38   METZ, J. B., 'Messianische Geschichte als Leidensgeschichte" in: J. Gnilka (ed.) Neues Testament und Kirche. Für R. Schnackenburg (Freiburg 1974) 63-70. *METZ, J. B. und MOLTMANN, J., Leidensgeschichte. Zwei Meditationen zu Markus 8, 31-38 (Freiburg 1974). TRAUB, H., in: GPM 33 (1979) 124-30.

8:31-35   FRIEDRICH, G. GPM 6 (1951) 25-28.

8:31-33   TAYLOR, V. The Formation of the Gospel Tradition (1949) 149f. ROBINSON, J. M. Kerygma und historischer Jesus (1960) 72. REPLOH, K-G. Markus - Lehrer der Gemeinde (1969) 100-104. PESCH, R., Das Markusevangelium II (Freiburg 1977) 56 (lit!). FARICY, R., Praying for Inner Healing (London 1979) 34f. TANNEHILL, R. C., "The Gospel of Mark as Narrative Christology" Semeia 16 (1980) 73f.

8:31-32   SCHELKLE, K. H., Die Passion Jesu in der Verkündigung des Neuen Testaments (Heidelberg 1949) 64f. *FEUILLET, A. "Les trois grandes prophéties de la Passion et de la Résurrection des évangiles synoptiques" RThom 67 (4, '67) 533-60; 68 (1, '68) 41-74. HAMERTON-KELLY, R. G., Pre-Existence, Wisdom, and the Son of Man (Cambridge 1973) 53, 56-59, 231f. DIBELIUS, M., "Sammlung" [orig: Die Formgeschichte des Evangeliums 1933 *(2)*, 219-34] in: R. Pesch (ed.) Das Markus-Evangelium (Darmstadt 1979) 75f.

8:31   LIGHTFOOT, R. H. History and Interpretation in the Gospels (1934) 214f. STONEHOUSE, N. B. The Witness of Matthew and Mark to Christ (1944) 47, 48, 66, 110, 112, 129, 237. TAYLOR, V., Jesus and His Sacrifice (London 1948) 29, 47, 85-91, 97, 102, 113, 152, 169, 173f, 241, 255, 259.

BONHOEFFER D. Nachfolge (1950) 80-82. FARRER, A. St
Matthew and St Mark (1954) 96, 102, 111, 112, 120. TAYLOR,
V., The Life and Ministry of Jesus (London 1954) 50, 72, 75,
114f, 135, 140-45, 154. TAYLOR, V., "The Origin of the
Markan Passion Sayings" NTS 1 (1954-1955) 159-67.
DENNER, J. The Death of Christ (1956) 24f, 28. KNOX, W. L.
The Sources of the Synoptic Gospels 2 (1957) 43, 148.
GRUNDMANN, W. Das Evangelium nach Markus (1959)
171-73. HOOKER, M., Jesus and the Servant (London 1959)
92-97. WILCKENS, U., Die Missionsreden der
Apostelgeschichte (Neukirchen 1961) 112f, 138f, 142, 162, 196.
PERRIN, N., The Kingdom of God in the Teaching of Jesus
(Philadelphia 1963) 102f, 106, 142. YATES, J. E., The Spirit
and the Kingdom (London 1963) 107f, 132f, 138ff. HAHN, F.
Christologische Hoheitstitel (1963) 46f, 48, 50f, 52f, 174f, 205,
215. *MEYER, D. "POLLA PATHEIN" ZNW 55 (1-2, '64)
132. HAHN, F. Das Verständnis der Mission im Neuen
Testament (1965) 61, 103. POPKES, W. Christus Traditus
(1967) 154ff, 162, 165, 280. HOOKER, M. D. The Son of man
in Mark (1967) 103-16, 120, 129, 131-32, 134-36. SCHREIBER,
J. Theologie des Vertrauens (1967) 41f, 46, 70, 100, 103f, 107-
109, 113, 115, 129, 201. LEHMANN, K. Auferweckt am
Dritten Tag nach der Schrift (1968) 97, 99, 141, 163f, 167, 178.
MINETTE DE TILLESSE, G. Le Secret Messianique dans
l'Evangile de Marc (1968) 390-94. SMITH, M., Tannaitic
Parallels to the Gospels (Philadelphia 1968) 8bn7+.
SCHNEIDER, G., Verleugnung, Verspottung und Verhör
Jesu nach Lukas 22, 54-71 (München 1969) 25, 33, 36f, 174f.
PESCH, R. Naherwartungen (1969) 62, 63, 70, 106, 157, 169.
GRASS, H. Ostergeschehen und Osterberichte (1970) 24n2,
127n3, 130n4, 131, 136n1, 146, 267, 305n1.
GUETTGEMANNS, E. Offene Fragen zur Formsgeschichte
des Evangeliums (1970) 210-12, 214, 214n207, 215-17, 216n217,
217n228, 218, 219-20. LOHSE, E. et al. Der Ruf Jesu und die
Antwort der Gemeinde (1970) 204-12. GASTON, L. No Stone
on Another (1970) 398-400, 395, 469, 470, 472. JEREMIAS,J.
New Testament Theology I (1971) 13, 260, 263, 277, 281f.
MICHEL, O. "Der Umbruch: Messianität - Menschensohn"
(Fragen zu Markus 8, 31) Tradition und Glaube, ed. G.
Jeremias, (1971) 310-16. JEREMIAS, J. Neutestamentliche
Theologie I (1971) 267-70. VOEGTLE, A. Das Evangelium und
die Evangelien (1971) 139-41. O'NEILL, J. C., The Theology of
Acts in its Historical Setting (London 1970) 43f.n. PETZKE,
G., Die Traditionen über Apollonius von Tyana und das Neue
Testament (Leiden 1970) 171, 173, 206. DELLING, G., Der

Kreuzestod Jesu in der urchristlichen Verkündigung (Göttingen 1972) 59-61. PATSCH, H., Abendmahl und historischer Jesus (Stuttgart 1972) 185ff. RUPPERT, L., Jesus als der leidende Gerechte? (Stuttgart 1972) 47, 56, 60-63.65. ZMIJEWSKI, J., Die Eschatologiereden des Lukas-Evangeliums (Bonn 1972) 406f, 419, 519, 557. HOFFMANN, P., "Mk 8,31. Zur Herkunft und markinischen Rezeption einer alten Überlieferung" in: P. Hoffmann (ed.) Orientierung an Jesus. Für J. Schmid (Freiburg 1973) 170-84, 185, 195-202. LANGE, J., Das Erscheinen des Auferstandenen im Evangelium nach Matthäus (Würzburg 1973) 122, 128, 203-206, 317f, 420-24. WANKE, J., Die Emmauserzählung. Eine redaktionsgeschichtliche Untersuchung zu Lk 24, 13-25 (Leipzig 1973) 86, 88, 91f, A.665. BEST, E., "Mark's Preservation of the Tradition" in: M. Sabbe (ed.) L'Evangile selon Marc (Gembloux 1974) 26f.; GT: in: R. Pesch (ed.) Das Markus-Evangelium (Darmstadt 1979) 396. CAVALLIN, H. C. C., Life after Death I (Lund 1974) 5, 8, n17. DORMEYER, D., Die Passion Jesu als Verhaltensmodell (Münster 1974) 66, 70, 231. LADD, G. E., A Theology of the New Testament (Grand Rapids 1974) 182, 186, 319, 330. PERRIN, N., "The Christology of Mark" in: M. Sabbe (ed.) L'Evangile selon Marc (Gembloux 1974) 484. *BENNETT, W. J., " 'The Son of Man must. . .' " NovT 17 (1975) 113-29. GOPPELT, L., Theologie des Neuen Testaments I (Göttingen 1975) 227, 236, 282, 295. KOCH, D.-A., "Zum Verhältnis von Christologie und Eschatologie im Markusevangelium" in: G. Strecker (ed.) Jesus Christus in Historie und Theologie. Für H. Conzelmann (Tübingen 1975) 400-403. PESCH, R., "Die Passion des Menschensohnes" in: R. Pesch/R. Schnackenburg (eds.) Jesus und der Menschensohn (Freiburg 1975) 168-73. STRECKER, G., "Das Evangelium Jesu Christi" in: G. Strecker (ed.) Jesus Christus in Historie und Theologie. Für H. Conzelmann (Tübingen 1975) 518, 540. Von Der OSTEN-SACKEN, P., "Streitgespräch und Parabel als Formen markinischer Christologie" in: G. Strecker (ed.) Jesus Christus in Historie und Theologie. Für H. Conzelmann (Tübingen 1975) 377, 391. KELBER, W. H., "From Passion Narrative to Gospel" in: W. H. Kelber (ed.) The Passion in Mark (Philadelphia 1976) 154-56. *PEREZ GORDO, A., "Notas sobre los anuncios de la Passion" Burgense 17 (1976) 251-70. WEEDEN, Th.J., "The Cross as Power in Weakness" in: W. H. Kelber (ed.) The Passion in Mark (Philadelphia 1976) 115-17. WILLIAMS, J. A., A Conceptual History of Deuteronomism in the Old Testament, Judaism, and the New Testament (Louisville 1976)

301-303. GERSTENBERGER, G. und SCHRAGE, W., Leiden (Stuttgart 1977) 142; ET: J. E. Steely, Suffering (Nashville 1980) 164f. RIVKIN, E., A Hidden Revolution (Nashville 1978) 107-109. "Auferstehung" in: TRE 4 (1979) 489. PERRIN, N., "Die Christologie des Markus-Evangeliums" [orig: "The Christology of Mark" JR 51 (1971) 173-87] in: R. Pesch (ed.) Das Markus-Evangelium (Darmstadt 1979) 370. SCHMITHALS, W., Das Evangelium nach Markus (Gütersloh/Würzburg 1979) 383 (lit!). STRECKER, G., "Zur Messiasgeheimnistheorie im Markusevangelium" [orig: Studia Evangelica 3 (1964) 87-104] in: R. Pesch (ed.) Das Markus-Evangelium (Darmstadt 1979) 203-205. MALBON, E. S., "Mythic Structure and Meaning in Mark" Semeia 16 (1980) 109-13. TANNEHILL, R. C., "The Gospel of Mark as Narrative Christology" Semeia 16 (1980) 68, 71, 74, 77f, 86.

8:32-33 WREDE, W. Das Messiasgeheimnis in den Evangelien (1963) 98-101. SCHMITHALS, W., Das Evangelium nach Markus (Gütersloh/Würzburg 1979) 386 (lit!).

8:32 PARKER, P. The Gospel Before Mark (1953) 58-59. SMITH, M., Tannaitic Parallels to the Gospels (Philadelphia 1968) 2bn100.+. WINANDY, J., "Le logion de l'ignorance" RB 75 (1968) 63-79. DORMEYER, D., Die Passion Jesu als Verhaltensmodell (Münster 1974) 113A.314. GOULDER, M. D., Midrash and Lection in Matthew (London 1974) 377f. ACHTEMEIER, P. J., Mark (Philadelphia 1975) 93. EGGER, W., Frohbotschaft und Lehre (Frankfurt 1976) 88.

8:33ff YATES, J. E., The Spirit and the Kingdom (London 1963) 57f, 118f, 123ff.

8:33 ROBINSON, J. M. Das Geschichtsverständnis des Markus-Evangeliums (1956) 37, 38, 39, 40, 58, 70, 75, 77. BAUMBACH, G. Das Verständnis des Bösen in den synoptischen Evangelien (1963) 38ff. *ARVEDSON, T. "Lärjungaskapets 'demoni'. Nagra reflexioner till Mk 8, 33 par" (The Disciples and Satan. Reflections on Mk 8: 33 par) SEA 28-29 ('63-'64) 54-63. HAHN, F. Christologische Hoheitstitel (1963) 86, 230. KÄSEMANN, E. Exegetische Versuche und Besinnungen I (1964) 216. JEREMIAS, J. Neutestamentliche Theologie I (1971) 17, 77, 80, 245, 270. *OSBORNE, B. A. E., "Peter: Stumbling-Block and Satan" NovT 15 (1973) 187-90. LADD, G. E., A Theology of the New Testament (Grand Rapids 1974) 51, 66, 141, 186. ACHTEMEIER, P. J., Mark (Philadelphia 1975) 96. "Antichrist" in: TRE 3 (1978) 22. "Aramäisch" in: TRE 3 (1978) 608. FRIEDRICH, G., "Das Problem der Autorität im Neuen Testament" in: Auf das Wort kommt es an

(Göttingen 1978) 389. SWIDLER, L., Biblical Affirmations of Woman (Philadelphia 1979) 283.

8:34ff   *MERTENS, H. "De Noodzakelijkheid van de Christelijke Versterving volgens het Nieuw Testament" (The Necessity of Christian Mortification according to the NT) CollMech 44 (3, '59) 272-80. BURKILL, T. A., "St Mark's Philosophy of History" NTS 3 (1956-1957) 144ff. KAESEMANN, E. Exegetische Versuche und Besinnungen I (1964) 255.

8:34-9:1 PESCH, R. Naherwartungen (1969) 21, 22, 42, 43, 69. REPLOH, K-G. Markus - Lehrer der Gemeinde (1969) 123-40. KONINGS, J., "The Pre-Markan Sequence in Jn 6" in: M. Sabbe (ed.) L'Evangile selon Marc (Gembloux 1974) 155. TALBERT, C. H., Literary Patterns, Theological Themes, and the Genre of Luke-Acts (Missoula 1974) 28. CONZELMANN, H. und LINDEMANN, A., Arbeitsbuch zum Neuen Testament (Tübingen 1975) 79-81, 249, 349, 373. PESCH, R., Das Markusevangelium II (Freiburg 1977) 67f (lit!). GNILKA, J., Das Evangelium nach Markus II (Einsiedeln/Neukirchen 1979) 21 (lit!). SCHMITHALS, W., Das Evangelium nach Markus (Gütersloh/Würzburg 1979) 389 (lit!).

8:34-38 *KAHMANN, A. "Het volgen van Christus door zelfverloochening en kruisdragen volgens Mark. 8, 34-38 par" (The Following of Christ through Self-denial and Carrying the Cross according to Mk 8:34-38)" TvTh 1 (3, '61) 205-26. MINETTE DE TILLESSE G. Le Secret Messianique dans L'Evangile de Marc (1968) 263-64, 274, 415-20. MADDOX, R., "The Function of the Son of Man according to the Synoptic Gospels" NTS 15 (1968-1969) 68ff. PESCH, R. Naherwartungen (1969) 63, 138, 186. OTOMO, Y. Nachfolge Jesu und Anfänge der Kirche im Neuen Tesatment (1970) 44-54, 120-22. BERGER, K. Die Gesetzesauslegung Jesu (1972) 405-407, 437f. KOLENKOW, A. B., "Beyond Miracles, Suffering and Eschatology" in: G. MacRae (ed.) SBL Seminar Papers 2 (Montana 1973) 163f. TANNEHILL, R. C., "The Gospel of Mark as Narrative Christology" Semeia 16 (1980) 81f.

8:34-37 BULTMANN, R., The History of the Synoptic Tradition (Oxford 1963) 82f.

8:34-35 LOHSE, E. et al. Der Ruf Jesu und die Antwort der Gemeinde (1970) 262-67. GOULDER, M. D., Midrash and Lection in Matthew (London 1974) 36, 42 253, 351. KONINGS, J., "The Pre-Markan Sequence in Jn 6" in: M. Sabbe (ed.) L'Evangile selon Marc (Gembloux 1974) 173. WILLIAMS, J. A., A Conceptual History of Deuteronomism in the Old Testament

(Louisville SBThS 1976) 309. BEST, E., From Text to Sermon
(Atlanta 1978) 22.

8:34 DINKLER, E. "Jesu Wort vom Kreuztragen"
Neutestamentliche Studien für Rudolf Bultmann zu seinem
siebzigsten Geburtstag (1954) 110-29. GREEVEN, H.,
"Erwägungen zur Synoptischen Textkritik" NTS 6 (1959-1960)
290f. ROBINSON, J. M. Kerygma und historischer Jesus
(1960) 121. STRECKER, G. Der Weg der Gerechtigkeit (1962)
182. SCHULZ, A. Nachfolgen und Nachahmen (1962) 82-90,
162-65, 265ff. HAHN, F. Christologische Hoheitstiel (1963) 44.
WREDE, W. Das Messiasgeheimnis in den Evangelien (1963)
138ff. *FLETCHER, D. R. "Condemned to Die. The Logion
on Cross-Bearing: What Does It Mean?" Interpretation 18 (2,
'64) 156-64. DALMAN, G. Orte und Wege Jesu (1967) 215f.
HOOKER M. D. The Son of Man in Mark (1967) 116-20, 138.
SMITH, M., Tannaitic Parallels to the Gospels (Philadelphia
1968) 2bn102.+ WREGE, H.-T., Die Überlieferungsgeschichte
der Bergpredigt (Tübingen 1968) 30, 164, 169. MARXSEN, W.
Mark the Evangelist (1969) 158, 160, 183. *GRIFFITHS, J. G.
"The Disciple's Cross" NTS 16 (4, '70) 358-64. JEREMIAS, J.
Neutestamentliche Theologie I (1971) 32, 232, 255, 269.
SCHNACKENBURG, R., " 'Das Evangelium' im Verständnis
des ältesten Evangelisten" in: P. Hoffmann (ed.) Orientierung
an Jesus. Für J. Schmid (Freiburg 1973) 317f. SCHMAHL, G.,
Die Zwölf im Markusevangelium (Trier 1974) 117-19.
SANDERS, J. T., Ethics in the New Testament (Philadelphia
1975) 32. *SCHWARZ, G., " '. . . aparnēsastho heauton. . !?
(Markus viii 34 Parr.)" NovT 17 (1975) 109-12. FRIEDRICH,
G., "Das Problem der Autorität im Neuen Testament" in: Auf
das Wort kommt es an (Göttingen 1978) 289. "Askese" in: TRE
4 (1979) 205. FARICY, R., Praying for Inner Healing (London
1979) 48-50. WREDE, W., "Rückblick auf Markus" [orig: Das
Messiasgeheimnis in den Evangelien (1901) 115-49] in: R.
Pesch (ed.) Das Markus-Evangelium (Darmstadt 1979) 34f.
TANNEHILL, R. C., "The Gospel of Mark as Narrative
Christology" Semeia 16 (1980) 73, 76.

8:35ff WAINWRIGHT, A. W., The Trinity in the New Testament
(London 1962) 120f, 162f.

8:35-37 DUNN, J. D. G., Jesus and the Spirit (London 1975) 172.

8:35 KNOX, W. L. The Sources of the Synoptic Gospels 2 (1957)
107, 146. ROBINSON, J. M. Kerygma und historischer Jesus
(1960) 57, 165. BAUER, J. B. "Wer sein Leben retten will . . .
Mk. 8,35 parr" Neutestamentliche Aufsätze; Festschrift für
Joseph Schmid zum 70. Geburtstag (1963) 7-10. MAUSER, U.

Christ in the Wilderness (1963) 123f. KAESEMANN, E. Exegetische Versuche und Besinnungen II (1964) 97. HAHN, F. Das Verständnis der Mission im Neuen Testament (1965) 60, 105. *DAUTZENBERG, G. Sein Leben bewahren. Psyché in den Herrenworten der Evangelien (1966). *SUDBRACK, J. " 'Wer sein Leben um meinetwillen verliert . . .' (Mk 8, 35) Biblische Ueberlegungen zur Grundlegung christlicher Existenz" GuL 40 (3, '67) 161-70. Rev. M. D. Hooker ThLZ 93 (11, '68) 835-36. MINETTE DE TILLESSE, G. Le Secret Messianique dans L'Evangile de Marc (1968) 395-96, 405-409. PESCH, R. Naherwartungen (1969) 128, 136. MARYSEN, W. Mark the Evangelist (1969) 89, 121, 124f, 127, 136f. SANFORD, J. A., The Kingdom Within (New York 1970) 188f. BERGER, K., "Zu den Sogenannten Sätzen Heiligen Rechts" NTS 17 (1970-1971) 19f. JEREMIAS, J. Neutestamentliche Theologie I (1971) 25-27, 29, 36, 137, 234, 269. BAUER, J. B., Scholia Biblica et Patristica (Graz 1972) 43-46, 58. STRECKER, G. "Literarische Ueberlegungen zum εὐαγγέλιον-Begriff im Markusevangelium" Neues Testament und Geschichte, eds. H. Baltensweiler und B. Reicke (1972) 91-104, 97. ZMIJEWSKI, J., Die Eschaologiereden des Lukas-Evangeliums (Bonn 1972) 479-82. SCHNACKENBURG, R., " 'Das Evangelium' im Verständnis des ältesten Evangelisten" in: P. Hoffmann (ed.) Orientierung an Jesus. Für J. Schmid (Freiburg 1973) 310-12, 316-18. FENEBERG, W., Der Markusprolog (München 1974) 146ff. KÜMMEL, W. G., Römer 7 und das Bild des Menschen im Neuen Testament (München 1974) 169f. LADD, G. E., The Presence of the Future (Grand Rapids 1974) 207f. LADD, G. E., A Theology of the New Testament (Grand Rapids 1974) 73f, 257, 302. ACHTEMEIER, P. J., Mark (Philadelphia 1975) 49f. HOFFMANN, P., und EID, V., Jesus von Nazareth und eine christliche Moral (Freiburg 1975) 212-14. STRECKER, G., "Das Evangelium Jesu Christ" in: G. Strecker (ed.) Jesus Christus in Historie und Theologie. Für H. Conzelmann (Tübingen 1975) 538-40. TANNEHILL, R. C., The Sword of His Mouth (Missoula 1975) 95-101. EGGER, W., Frohbotschaft und Lehre (Frankfurt 1976) 50. PERRIN, N., Jesus and the Language of the Kingdom (London 1976) 41, 48, 50, 52. *SATAKE, A., "Das Leiden der Jünger 'um meinetwillen' " ZNW 67 (1976) 4-19. GNILKA, J., "Martyriumsparänese und Sühnetod in synoptischen und jüdischen Traditionen" in: R. Schnackenburg et al. (eds.) Die Kirche des Anfangs. Für H. Schürmann (Freiburg 1978) 235. LEROY, H., " 'Wer sein Leben gewinnen will. . .' Erlöste

Existenz heute" FZPhTh 25 (1978) 171-86. *BEARDSLEE,
A., "Saving One's Life by Losing It" JAAR 47 (1979) 57-72.
KELBER, W. H., "Mark and Oral Tradition" Semeia 16 (1980)
43f. TANNEHILL, R. C., "The Gospel of Mark as Narrative
Christology" Semeia 16 (1980) 75f.

8:36   PASCHER, E. "Der unendliche Wert der Menschenseele. Zur
Auslegung von Mark 8, 36 und Matth. 16, 26" Forschung und
Erfahrung Im Dienst der Seelsorge (1961) 44-57. NICKELS, P.
Targum and New Testament (1967) 25. SANFORD, J. A., The
Kingdom Within (New York 1970) 160f. KÜMMEL, W. G.,
Römer 7 und das Bild des Menschen im Neuen Testament
(München 1974) 169f, 174f.

8:38-39   LUZ, U., "Das Jesusbild der vormarkinischen Tradition" in: G.
Strecker (ed.) Jesus Christus in Historie und Theologie. Für H.
Conzelmann (Tübingen 1975) 359.

8:38   MANSON, T. W., The Teaching of Jesus (Cambridge 1945)
213ff. KUEMMEL, W. G. Verheissung und Erfüllung (1953)
38-40, 84f. TAYLOR, V. The Gospel According to St. Mark
(1953) 384. FARRER, A. St Matthew and St Mark (1954) 25,
102. BURKILL, T. A., "St Mark's Philosophy of History" NTS
3 (1956-1957) 143ff. KNOX, W. L. The Sources of the Synoptic
Gospels 2 (1957) 17, 66, 142. BOOBYER, G. H., "The Secrecy
Motif in St Mark's Gospel" NTS 6 (1959-1960) 229f. BLAIR,
E. P. Jesus in the Gospel of Matthew (1960) 74, 81.
ROBINSON, J. M. Kerygma und historischer Jesus (1960) 18,
143. SCHWEIZER, E. Erniedrigung und Erhöhung bei Jesus
und seinen Nachfolgern (1962) §3 fo. WAINWRIGHT, A. W.,
The Trinity in the New Testament (London 1962) 120f. HAHN,
F. Christologische Hoheitstitel (1963) 24, 33, 34, 36, 39f, 321,
328, 339. PERRIN, N., The Kingdom of God in the Teaching of
Jesus (Philadelphia 1963) 85, 102f, 109, 114, 137, 139.
KAESEMANN, E. Exegetische Versuche und Besinnungen
(1964) I 211; II 78, 97. SCHNACKENBURG, R., "Der
Menschensohn im Johannesevangelium" NTS 11 (1964-1965)
129f. BULTMANN, R., Theologie des Neuen Testaments
(Tübingen 1965) 20, 30f. FULLER, R. H. The Foundation of
New Testament Christology (1965) 121ff. JüNGEL, E. Paulus
und Jesus (1966) 225, 227, 230, 242-44, 258-62. HOOKER, M.
D. The Son of Man in Mark (1967) 116-22, 125-26, 156-58, 178-
79, 181-82, 192-93. SCHREIBER, J. Theologie des Vertrauens
(1967) 110f, 140-42. MINETTE DE TILLESSE, G. Le Secret
Messianique dans L'Evangile de Marc (1968) 390-94.
STROBEL, A. Erkenntnis und Bekenntnis der Sünde in
neutestamentlicher Zeit (1968) 39. FLENDER, H. Die

Botschaft Jesu von der Herrschaft Gottes (1968) 76ff, 83, 91, 93.
BORNKAMM, G. "Das Wort Jesu vom Bekennen"-
Geschichte und Glaube I (1968) 25-36. HORSTMANN, M.
Studien zur Markinischen Christologie (1969) 34-56. PESCH,
R. Naherwartungen (1969) 118-19, 170-74. KAESEMANN, E.
New Testament Questions of Today (1969) 77, 99, 111.
GASTON, L. No Stone on Another (1970) 33, 322, 403-405.
VOEGTLE, A. Das Neue Testament und die Zukunft des
Kosmos (1970) 100, 151, 161, 163. KUENZI, M. Das
Naherwartungslogion Matthäus 10, 23 (1970) 7, 100, 116, 148,
179. BORSCH, F. H. The Christian & Gnostic Son of Man
(1970) 18-20. BERGER, K., "Zu den Sogenannten Sätzen
Heiligen Rechts" NTS 17 (1970-1971) 25f. JEREMIAS, J.
Neutestamentliche Theologie I (1971) 251f, 254f, 261f.
HAMERTON-KELLY, R. G., Pre-Existence, Wisdom, and
the Son of Man (Cambridge 1973) 42, 55, 57, 60f, 81, 93f, 229.
HIERS, R. H., The Historical Jesus and the Kingdom of God
(Gainsville 1973) 29f, 72. HOFFMANN, P., "Mk 8, 31. Zur
Herkunft und markinischen Rezeption einer alten
Überlieferung" in: P. Hoffmann (ed.) Orientierung an Jesus.
Für J. Schmid (Freiburg 1973) 198-200. LANGE, J., Das
Erscheinen des Auferstandenen im Evangelium nach Matthäus
(Würzburg 1973) 189-91, 195, 200, 208, 296, 422f, 499. LOHSE,
E., in: Die Einheit des Neuen Testaments (Göttingen 1973) 15,
42-44, 136. BEST, E. "Mark's Preservation of the Tradition" in:
M. Sabbe (ed.) L'Evangile selon Marc (Gembloux 1974) 24;
GT: in: R. Pesch (ed.) Das Markus-Evangelium (Darmstadt
1979) 393. COPPENS, J., "Les logia du Fils de l'Homme dans
l'évangile de Marc" in: M. Sabbe (ed.) L'Evangile selon Marc
(Gembloux 1974) 501-504. DESCAMPS, A., "Pour une
histoire du titre 'Fils de Dieu' " in: M. Sabbe (ed.) L'Evangile
selon Marc (Gembloux 1974) 559. LADD, G. E., A Theology
of the New Testament (Grand Rapids 1974) 88, 205, 271, 275,
307. LOHSE, E., Grundriss der neutestamentlichen Theologie
(Stuttgart 1974) 47-49. PERRIN, N., "The Christology of
Mark" in: M. Sabbe (ed.) L'Evangile selon Marc (Gembloux
1974) 481f. ACHTEMEIER, P. J., Mark (Philadelphia 1975)
48, 56. GRÄSSER, E., "Jesus und das Heil Gottes" in: G.
Strecker (ed.) Jesus Christus in Historie und Theologie. Für H.
Conzelmann (Tübingen 1975) 177. KÜMMEL, W. G., "Das
Verhalten Jesus gegenüber und das Verhalten des
Menschensohnes" in: R. Pesch/R. Schnackenburg (eds.) Jesus
und der Menschensohn (Freiburg 1975) 210-24. LOHSE, E.,
"Christus als Weltenrichter" in: G. Strecker (ed.) Jesus Christus
in Historie und Theologie. Für H. Conzelmann (Tübingen

1975) 480f. LUZ, U., "Das Jesusbild der vormarkinischen Tradition" in: G. Strecker (ed.) Jesus Christus in Historie und Theologie. Für H. Conzelmann (Tübingen 1975) 354-56. STRECKER, G., "Das Evangelium Jesu Christi" in: G. Strecker (ed.) Jesus Christus in Historie und Theologie. Für H. Conzelmann (Tübingen 1975) 538. THEISOHN, J., Der auserwählte Richter (Göttingen 1975) 155f, 178f, 183. METZGER, B. M., The Early Versions of the New Testament (Oxford 1977) 251. PESCH, R., "Uber die Autorität Jesu. Eine Rückfrage anhand des Bekenner - und Verleugnerspruch Lk.12:8f par." in: R. Schnackenburg et al. (eds.) Die Kirche des Anfangs. Für H. Schürmann (Leipzig 1977) 25-55. TRITES, A. A., The New Testament Concept of Witness (Cambridge 1977) 181. HOOKER, M. D., "Is the Son of Man Problem Really Insoluble?" in: E. Best/R. McL. Wilson (eds.) Text and Interpretation. In honour of M. Black (Cambridge 1979) 162. MALBON, E. S., "Mythic Structure and Meaning in Mark" Semeia 16 (1980) 109-13.

9:1-10:11 *ELLINGWORTH, P., "How is Your Handbook Wearing?" BTr 30 (1979) 236-41.

9 BOUSSET, W., Die Religion des Judentums im Späthellenistischen Zeitalter (Berlin 1966=1926) 122, 233.

9:1-32 GRANT, F. C. The Gospels (1957) 94f.

9:1-13 *SYNGE, F. C. "The Transfiguration Story" ET 82 (3, '70) 82-83.

9:1-10 *SOUBIGOU, L., "A Transfiguração de Christo Segunda São Marcos (9, 1-10)" RCB 12 (1975) 59-72. RAYAN, S., The Holy Spirit: Heart of the Gospel and Christian Hope (New York 1978) 7, 33.

9:1-8 GILS, F., Jésus Prophète D'après Les Evangiles Synoptiques (Louvain 1957) 73-78. REPLOH, K.-G. Markus - Lehrer der Gemeinde (1969) 112-13. RUDOLPH, K., Die Gnosis (Göttingen 1978) 165.

9:1-6 GEORGI, D., Die Gegner des Paulus im 2.Korintherbrief (Neukirchen 1964) 206f.

9:1-5   SMITH, M., Clement of Alexandria and a Secret Gospel of Mark (Cambridge, Mass. 1973) 102, 115, 136f, 147, 163n.8, 167, 175, 212, 223, 225f.

9:1-4   HENNECKE, E. und SCHNEEMELCHER, W., Neutestamentliche Apokryphen II (Tübingen 1964) 363, 481f.

9:1-3   YATES, J. E., The Spirit and the Kingdom (London 1963) 116ff, 200ff.

9:1   VOLZ, P., Die Eschatologie der jüdischen Gemeinde (Tübingen 1934) 207. MANSON, T. W., The Teaching of Jesus (Cambridge 1945) 278-85. KUEMMEL, W. G. Verheissung und Erfüllung (1953) 18-22, 37f, 59f. BERKHOF, H., Der Sinn der Geschichte: Christus (Göttingen 1959) 82f. BOSCH, D. Die Heidenmission in der Zukunftsschau Jesu (1959) 144-48. HAHN, F. Christologie Hoheitstitel (1963) 254, 339. PERRIN, N., The Kingdom of God in the Teaching of Jesus (Philadelphia 1963) 61, 65, 67f, 80, 85f, 135, 137, 139, 146f, 188. TOEDT, H. E. Der Menschensohn in der synoptischen Ueberlieferung (1963) 189-83. YATES, J. E., The Spirit and the Kingdom (London 1963) 118-24. KAESEMANN, E. Exegetische Versuche und Besinnungen (1964) II 88. = New Testament Questions of Today (1969) 88. TROCME, E. "Marc 9, 1: prédiction ou réprimande?" Studia Evangelica II, ed. F. L. Cross (1964) 259-65. CULLMANN, O. Heil als Geschichte (1965) 179, 189ff, 194, 202f. SUHL, A. Die Funktion der alttestamentlichen Zitate und Anspielungen im Markusevangelium (1965) 22, 23, 24, 25, 55, 56, 109. JüNGEL, E. Paulus und Jesus (1966) 238. BORNKAMM, G. "Die Verzögerung der Parusie" Geschichte und Glaube I (1968) 46-55. MINETTE DE TILLESSE, G. Le Secret Messianique dans L'Evangile de Marc (1968) 390-94, 471. HASLER, V. Amen (1969) 32. HORSTMANN, M. Studien zur Markinischen Christologie (1969) 56-69. MARXSEN, W. Mark the Evangelist (1969) 84, 195, 205. *PERRIN, N. "The Composition of Mark ix, 1," NovTest 11 (1-2, '69) 67-70. PESCH, R. Naherwartungen (1969) 63, 92, 114, 134, 169, 170, 171, 182, 183, 184, 186, 195, 205, 206, 240. AMBROZIC, A. M., St Mark's Concept of the Kingdom of God (Würzburg 1970) 218-60. BERGER, K. Die Amen-Worte Jesu (1970) 62-67. GASTON, L. No Stone on Another (1970) 38, 86, 195, 349, 350, 409, 412, 451-55, 472. KUENZI, M. Das Naherwartungslogion Matthäus 10, 23 (1970) 100, 102, 134ff, 152. OTOMO, Y. Nachfolge Jesu und Anfänge der Kirche im Neuen Testament (1970) 54f. VOEGTLE, A. Das Neue Testament und die Zukunft des Kosmos (1970) 100, 130, 151, 161. JEREMIAS, J.

Neutestamentliche Theologie I (1971) 40f, 44, 100, 231f, 252f,
269. = New Testament Theology I (1971) 31, 33, 35, 96, 100,
136f, 267, 283. VOEGTLE, A. Das Evangelium und die
Evangelien (1971) 318-28, 330-32. BERKOUWER, G. C., The
Return of Christ (Grand Rapids 1972) 68, 86-88. PATSCH, H.,
Abendmahl und historischer Jesus (Stuttgart 1972) 119ff.
RAHNER, K. und THÜSING, W., Christologie-systematisch
und exegetisch (Freiburg 1972) 232f. ZMIJEWSKI, J., Die
Eschatologiereden des Lukas-Evangeliums (Bonn 1972) 149,
238, 276f, 297, 338. HIERS, R. H., The Historical Jesus and the
Kingdom of God (Gainsville 1973) 13f, 29, 62, 72. *MOIR, I.
A., "The Reading of Codex Bezae (D-05) at Mark ix. 1" NTS 20
(1973) 105. COPPENS, J., "Les logia du Fils de l'Homme dans
l'évangile de Marc" in: M. Sabbe (ed.) L'Evangile selon Marc
(Gembloux 1974) 502f. ACHTEMEIER, P. J., Mark
(Philadelphia 1975) 55. WENZ, H., Theologie des Reiches
Gottes (Hamburg 1975) 57-66. CAIRD, G. B., "Eschatology
and Politics: Some Misconceptions" in: J. R. McKay/J. F.
Miller (eds.) Biblical Studies. In honour of W. Barclay (London
1976) 74. NEIRYNCK, F., "Note on the Codex Bezae in the
Textual Apparatus of the Synopsis" EphT 52 (1976) 358-363.
PERRIN, N., Jesus and the Language of the Kingdom
(London 1976) 37f. *GREEVEN, H., "Nochmals Mk ix.1 in
Codex Bezae (D,05)" NTS 23 (1977) 305-308. *KUNZI, M.,
Das Naherwartungslogion Markus 9, 1 par (Tübingen 1977).
BRUCE, F. F., The Time is Fulfilled (Exeter 1978) 23.
SCHILDENBERGER, J., "Die Vertauschung der Aussagen
über Zeichen und Bezeichnetes. Eine hermeneutisch
bedeutsame Redeweise" in: Kirche und Bibel. Für E. Schick
(Paderborn 1979) 402f. SCHLOSSER, J., "Le règne de Dieu
dans les dits de Jésus" RevSR 53 (1979) 164-76. CLARK, K.
W., "Realized Eschatology" in: The Gentile Bias and other
Essays (Leiden 1980) 53-55. HARRINGTON, D. J., God's
People in Christ (Philadelphia 1980) 25. MALBON, E. S.,
"Mythic Structure and Meaning in Mark" Semeia 16 (1980)
109-13.

9:2ff   GLASSON, T. F., Moses in the Fourth Gospel (London 1963)
68ff. GEORGI, D., Die Gegner des Paulus im 2.Korintherbrief
(Neukirchen 1964) 215f. SCHENKE, L., Studien zur
Passiongeschichte des Markus (Würzburg 1971) 484f.
KÜMMEL, W. G., Einleitung in das Neue Testament
(Heidelberg 1973 *(17)*) 61f. HABICHT, Chr.,
"2.Makkabäerbuch" in: W. G. Kümmel (ed.) Jüdische
Schriften aus hellenistisch-römischer Zeit I (Gütersloh 1976)
206.

9:2-13:2 FARRER, A. A Study in St Mark (1951) 108ff, 229f.
9:2-10:31 FARRER, A. A Study in St Mark (1951) 108ff, 313f.
9:2-29 *DENIS, A.-M. "Une théologie de la Rédemption. La
Transfiguration chez saint Marc" VieS 41 (453, '59) 136-49.
SMITH, M., Tannaitic Parallels to the Gospels (Philadelphia
1968) 5bn38+.
9:2-27 CARRINGTON, P. The Primitive Christian Calendar (1952)
176-79.
9:2-13 GOODSPEED, E. J., A Life of Jesus (New York 1950) 127-29.
SCHMAUCH, W. GPM 11 (1956/57) 69-72. *MASSON, C.
"La transfiguration de Jésus (Marc 9:2.13)" RThPh 97 (1, '64)
1-14. DIGNATH, W./WIBBING, S. Taufe-Versuchung-
Verklärung (1966) 55-80. RIVERA, L. F., "El Misterio del hijo
del hombre eh la . . ." RevBi 28 (1966) 19-34. *BALAGUE, M.
"La Transfiguracion" RevBi 29 (1, '67) 51-58. ITTEL, G. W.
Jesus und die Jünger (1970) 79-85. ZIMMERMANN, W.-D.
Markus über Jesus (1970) 101-104. *NARDONI, E., La
Transfiguración de Jesús y el diálogo sobre Eliás según el
Evangelio de San Marcos (Buenos Aires 1977). PESCH, R.,
Das Markusevangelium II (Freiburg 1977) 82-84 (lit!).
9:2-10 RIESENFELD, H., Jésus Transfiguré (Copenhagen 1947).
*BALTENSWEILER, H. Die Verklärung Jesu. Historisches
Ereignis und synoptische Berichte (1959). Revs.: G. H. Boobyer
JThS 11 (1, '60) 133-35. F. J. Leenhardt ThZ 16 (5, '60) 417-19.
*RIVERA, L. F. "Interpretatio Transfigurationis Jesu in
redactione evangelii Marci" VerbDom 46 (2, '68) 99-104.
SEIDENSTICKER, Ph. Die Auferstehung Jesu in der
Botschaft der Evangelisten (1968) 48ff. *RIVERA, L. F. "El
relato de la Transfiguracion en la redaccion del evangelio de
Marcos" RevBi 31 (3, '69) 143-58; (4, '69) 229-43. *COUNE, M.
"L'évangile de la transfiguration" ParLiturg 52 (2, '70) 157-70.
*THRALL, M. E. "Elijah and Moses in Mark's account of the
Transfiguration" NTS 16 (4, '70) 305-17. *GENNARINI, S.,
"Le principali interpretazioni postliberali della pericope della
transfigurazione di Gesù" RSLR 8 (1972) 80-132. COUNE, M.,
"Radieuse Transfiguration. Mt 17:1-9; Mc 9:2-10; Lc 9:28-36"
AssS 15 (1973) 44-84. *NÜTZEL, J. M., Die
Verklärungserzählung im Markusevangelium (Würzburg
1973). SCHMAHL, G., Die Zwölf im Markusevangelium
(Trier 1974) 131f. *TREMEL, B., "Des récits apocalytiques:
Baptême et Transfiguration" LuVie 23 (1974) 70-83. *FUCHS,
A., "Die Verklärungserzählung des Markusevangeliums in der
Sicht moderner Exegese" Theologisch-praktische
Quartalschrift 125 (1977) 29-37. FRIEDRICH, G.,

"Beobachtungen zur messianischen Hohepriestererwartung in
den Synoptikern" in: Auf das Wort kommt es an (Göttingen
1978) 98-101. SCHMITHALS, W., Das Evangelium nach
Markus (Gütersloh/Würzburg 1979) 399, 721 (lit!). ERNST,
J., "Die Petrustradition im Markusevangelium - ein altes
Problem neu angegangen" in: J. Zmijewski/E. Nellessen (eds.)
Begegnung mit dem Wort. Für H. Zimmermann (Bonn 1980)
50-53.

9:2-9 BULTMANN, R., The History of the Synoptic Tradition
(Oxford 1963) 259-61.

9:2-8 FARRER, A. A Study in St Mark (1951) 108ff, 119f, 128f,
156f, 169, 313f. TAYLOR, V., The Life and Ministry of Jesus
(London 1954) 29, 146-49. *MUELLER, H.-P. "Die
Verklärung Jesu. Eine motivgeschichtliche Studie" ZNW 51 (1-
2, '60) 56-64. HAHN, F. Christologische Hoheitstitel (1963)
310-12, 334-40, 396. MAUSER, U. Christ in the Wilderness
(1963) 110ff, 143. HAHN, F. Das Verständnis der Mission im
Neuen Testament (1965) 95. SUHL, A. Die Funktion der
alttestamentliche Zitate und Anspielungen im
Markusevangelium (1965) 104ff. DAVIES, W. D., The Sermon
on the Mount (Cambridge 1966) 20-26. MARXSEN, W.
Predigten (1968) 97-103. HORSTMANN, M. Studien zur
Markinischen Christologie (1969) 71-103. LOHFINK, G. Die
Himmelfahrt Jesu (1971) 189-91. SCHRAMM, T. Der
Markus-Stoff bei Lukas (1971) 136-39. KELBER, W. H., "The
History of the Kingdom in Mark - Aspects of Markan
Eschatology" in: L. C. McGaughy (ed.) SBL Seminar Papers 1
(Montana 1972) 63-95. WEINACHT, H. Die Menschwerdung
des Sohnes Gottes im Markusevangelium (1972) 53-60.
LANGE, J., Das Erscheinen des Auferstandenen im
Evangelium nach Matthäus (Würzburg 1973) 415, 419-24, 432,
434-36. *MÜLLER, U. B., "Die christologische Absicht des
Markusevangeliums und die Verklärungsgeschichte" ZNW 64
(1973) 159-93. SCHNIDER, F., Jesus der Prophet (Freiburg
1973) 100ff. DORMEYER, D., Die Passion Jesu als
Verhaltensmodell (Münster 1974) 137A, 440. TALBERT, C.
H., Literary Patterns, Theological Themes, and the Genre of
Luke-Acts (Missoula 1974) 28, 61. ACHTEMEIER, P. J.,
Mark (Philadelphia 1975) 44. ALSUP, J. E., The Post-
Resurrection Appearance Stories of the Gospel Tradition
(Stuttgart 1975) 42f, 141ff. DUNN, J. D. G., Jesus and the
Spirit (London 1975) 27, 181. KOCH, D.-A., Die Bedeutung
der Wundererzählungen für die Christologie des
Markusevangeliums (Berlin/New York 1975) 123-26. *STEIN,
R. H., "Is the Transfiguration (Mark 9:2-8) a Misplaced

Resurrection-Account?" JBL 95 (1976) 79-96. SAITO, T., Die Mosevorstellungen im Neuen Testament (Bern 1977) 37-47, 141-43. TRITES, A. A., The New Testament Concept of Witness (Cambridge 1977) 180f. MARXSEN, W., Christologie-praktisch (Gütersloh 1978) 50f. GNILKA, J., Das Evangelium nach Markus II (Einsiedeln/Neukirchen 1979) 29f. (lit!). "Auferstehung" in: TRE 4 (1979) 501. KLAPPERT, B., "Arbeit Gottes und Mitarbeit des Menschen (Phil 2, 6-11)" in: J. Moltmann (ed.) Recht auf Arbeit - Sinn der Arbeit (München 1979) 98-100. *TRITES, A. A., "The Transfiguration of Jesus: The Gospel in Microcosm" EQ 51 (1979) 67-79.

9:2-3 BETZ, H. D., Lukian von Samosata und das Neue Testament (Berlin 1961) 132f, 143. YATES, J. E., The Spirit and the Kingdom (London 1963) 116-18. *RIVERA, L. F. "El misterio del Hijo del Hombre en la transfiguracion (Mr 9, 2-3)" RevBi 28 (1, '66) 19-34. *GERBER, W. "Die Metamorphose Jesu, Mark 9, 2f par" ThZ 23 (6, '67) 385-95. NEIRYNCK, F., "Minor Agreements Matthew-Luke in the Transfiguration Story" in: P. Hoffmann (ed.) Orientierung an Jesus. Für J. Schmid (Freiburg 1973) 254-65.

9:2 MAUSER, U. Christ in the Wilderness (1963) 119f, 141f. LANGE, J., Das Erscheinen des Auferstandenen im Evangelium nach Matthäus (Würzburg 1973) 418-29. DORMEYER, D., Die Passion Jesu als Verhaltensmodell (Münster 1974) 63, 66A.33, 113A.314. *McCURLEY, F. R., " 'And After Six Days' (Mark 9:2): A Semitic Literary Device" JBL 93 (1974) 67-81. SCHMAHL, G., Die Zwölf im Markusevangelium (Trier 1974) 132-37. TALBERT, C. H., Literary Patterns, Theological Themes, and the Genre of Luke-Acts (Missoula 1974) 62. SCHEP, J. A., The Nature of the Resurrection Body (Grand Rapids 1976) 165f.

9:3 STROBEL, A. Erekenntnis und Bekenntnis der Sünde in neutestamentlicher Zeit (1968) 39.

9:4 CLARKE, W. K. L., New Testament Problems (New York 1929) 34-36. HAHN, F. Christologische Hoheitstitel (1963) 185, 359, 370. DORMEYER, D., Die Passion Jesu als Verhaltensmodell (Münster 1974) 75A.87. TALBERT, C. H., Literary Patterns, Theological Themes, and the Genre of Luke-Acts (Missoula 1974) 62.

9:5 HAHN, F. Christologische Hoheitstitel (1963) 75, 77, 86. NICKELS, P. Targum and New Testament (1967) 25.

9:6 STONEHOUSE, N. B. The Witness of Matthew and Mark to Christ (1944) 69, 102, 107.

9:7-13   *RIVERA, L. F. "El misterio del Hijo del hombre en la Transfiguracion" RevBi 28 (2, '66) 79-89.

9:7   STONEHOUSE, N. B. The Witness of Matthew and Mark to Christ (1944) 13, 18, 19, 68. TAYLOR, V., "The Origin of the Markan Passion Sayings" NTS 1 (1954-1955) 163ff. HOOKER, M. D., Jesus and the Servant (London 1959) 68-73. DELLING, G. Die Taufe im Neuen Testament (1963) 56, 112. HAHN, F. Christologische Hoheitstitel (1963) 75, 281, 396. JEREMIAS, J. Abba (1966) 192-94. MINETTE DE TILLESSE, G. Le Secret Messianique dans L'Evangile de Marc (1968) 354-56. LANGE, J., Das Erscheinen des Auferstandenen im Evangelium nach Matthäus (Würzburg 1973) 263, 266, 416-18, 420. NEIRYNCK, F., "Minor Agreements Matthew-Luke in the Transfiguration Story"in: P. Hoffmann (ed.) Orientierung an Jesus. Für J. Schmid (Freiburg 1973) 254-65. DESCAMPS, A., "Pour une histoire du titre 'Fils de Dieu' " in: M. Sabbe (ed.) L'Evangile selon Marc (Gembloux 1974) 559. DORMEYER, D., Die Passion Jesu als Verhaltensmodell (Münster 1974) 164A.66. KONINGS, J., "The Pre-Markan Sequence in Jn 6" in: M. Sabbe (ed.) L'Evangile selon Marc (Gembloux 1974) 173. MÜLLER, U. B., "Die griechische Esra Apokalypse"in: W. G. Kümmel (ed.) Jüdische Schriften aus hellenistisch-römischer Zeit V (Gütersloh 1976) 96. MALBON, E. S., "Mythic Structure and Meaning in Mark" Semeia 16 (1980) 109-13.

9:9-13   FARRER, A. St Matthew and St Mark (1954) 4-7. GRUNDMANN, W. Das Evangelium nach Markus (1959) 185-87. HAHN, F. Christologische Hoheitstitel (1963) 52. SCHREIBER, J. Theologie des Vertrauens (1967) 28, 109-14. WINK, W. John the Baptist in the Gospel Tradition (1968) 13-17. HORSTMANN, M. Studien zur Markinischen Christologie (1969) 105-36. GASTON, L. No Stone on Another (1970) 402-403. WANKE, J., Die Emmauserzählung. Eine redaktionsgeschichtliche Untersuchung zu Lk 24, 13-35 (Leipzig 1973) A.676. GNILKA, J., Das Evangelium nach Markus II (Einsiedeln/Neukirchen 1979) 39 (lit!). KLAPPERT, B., "Arbeit Gottes und Mitarbeit des Menschen (Phil 2, 6-11)" in: J. Moltmann (ed.) Recht auf Arbeit - Sinn der Arbeit (München 1979) 99.

9:9, 12   PESCH, R., "Die Passion des Menschensohnes" in: R. Pesch/R. Schnackenburg (eds.) Jesus und der Menschensohn (Freiburg 1975) 174-75.

9:9-10   LIGHTFOOT, R. H., Locality and Doctrine in the Gospels (London 1938) 30ff. HAHN, F. Christologische Hoheitstitel

(1963) 205. HORSTMANN, M. Studien zur Markinischen Christologie (1969) 105-34. REPLOH, K.-G. Markus - Lehrer der Gemeinde (1969) 113-15. GOPPELT, L., Theologie des Neuen Testaments I (Göttingen 1975) 220f. STRECKER, G., "Zur Messiasgeheimnistheorie im Markusevangelium" [orig: Studia Evangelica III (1964) 87-104] in: R. Pesch (ed.) Das Markus-Evangelium (Darmstadt 1979) 200-202.

9:9   RAWLINSON, A. E. J. St Mark (1925=1956) 258-62. STONEHOUSE N. B. The Witness of Matthew and Mark to Christ (1944) 68, 108, 112, 237. STRECKER, G. Der Weg der Gerechtigkeit (1962) 186. HAHN, F. Christologische Hoheitstitel (1963) 46, 47, 339. WREDE, W. Das Messiasgeheimnis in den Evangelien (1963) 34-36, 40ff, 66ff. HENNECKE, E. und SCHNEEMELCHER, W., Neutestamentliche Apokryphen II (Tübingen 1964) 483. HOOKER, M. D. The Son of Man in Mark (1967) 122-34. SCHREIBER, J. Theologie des Vertrauens (1967) 41f, 45-47, 222f, 237. MINETTE DE TILLESSE, G. Le Secret Messianique dans L'Evangile de Marc (1968) 249-51, 281-83, 390-94. PESCH, R. Naherwartungen (1969) 84, 97, 101, 119, 148, 153, 169, 199. GUETTGEMANNS, E. Offene Fragen zur Formgeschichte des Evangeliums (1970) 211, 260. O'NEILL, J. C., The Theology of Acts in its Historical Setting (London 1970) 43-4n. KÜMMEL, W. G., Einleitung in das Neue Testament (Heidelberg 1973 *(17)*) 62f. COPPENS, J., "Les logia du Fils de L'Homme dans l'évangile de Marc" in: M. Sabbe (ed.) L'Evangile selon Marc (Gembloux 1974) 499. LOHSE, E., Grundriss der neutestamentlichen Theologie (Stuttgart 1974) 117f. PERRIN, N., "The Christology of Mark" in: M. Sabbe (ed.) L'Evangile selon Marc (Gembloux 1974) 480. PERRIN, N., A Modern Pilgrimage in New Testament Christology (Philadelphia 1974) 115-21. ACHTEMEIER, P. J., Mark (Philadelphia 1975) 46, 48, 79-81. EGGER, W., Frohbotschaft und Lehre (Frankfurt 1976) 88f. PERRIN, N., "Die Christologie des Markus-Evangeliums" [orig: "The Christology of Mark" JR 51 (1971) 173-87] in: R. Pesch (ed.) Das Markus-Evangelium (Darmstadt 1979) 366. MALBON, E. S., "Mythic Structure and Meaning in Mark" Semeia 16 (1980) 109-13.

9:10-13   HORSTMANN, M. Studien zur Markinischen Christologie (1969) 134-36.

9:11ff.   NÖTSCHER, F., Altorientalischer und alttestamentlicher Auferstehungsglauben (Darmstadt 1970=1926) 127.

9:11-13   STONEHOUSE, N. B. The Witness of Matthew and Mark to Christ (1944) 15, 245. TAYLOR, V., Jesus and His Sacrifice

(London 1948) 92-97. SCHELKLE, K. H., Die Passion Jesu in
der Verkündigung des Neuen Testament (Heidelberg 1949)
64ff. GRANT, F. C. The Gospels (1957) 81f. BLAIR, E. P.
Jesus in the Gospel of Matthew (1960) 105. HAHN, F.
Christologische Hoheitstitel (1963) 377, 380. REPLOH, K.-G.
Markus - Lehrer der Gemeinde (1969) 115-19. ARENS, E., The
HΛΘON-Sayings in the Synoptic Tradition (Fribourg 1976)
243-48. BÖCHER, O., "Johannes der Täufer in der
neutestamentlichen Überlieferung" in: Rechtfertigung
Realismus. Für A. Köberle (Darmstadt 1978) 47, 52, 53.
RIVKIN, E., A Hidden Revolution (Nashville 1978) 105f.
MEYER, B. F., The Aims of Jesus (London 1979) 126f.
SWIDLER, L., Biblical Affirmations of Woman (Philadelphia
1979) 228. BACHMANN, M., "Johannes der Täufer bei
Lukas: Nachzügler oder Vorläufer?" in: W. Haubeck/M.
Bachmann (eds.) Wort in der Zeit. Für K. H. Rengstorf (Leiden
1980) 131f.

9:11-12 MOSLEY, A. W., "Jesus' Audiences in the Gospels of St Mark
and St Luke" NTS 10 (1963-1964) 140f. BOUSSET, W., Die
Religion des Judentums im Späthellenistischen Zeitalter
(Berlin 1966=1926) 232.

9:11 HAHN, F. Das Verständnis der Mission im Neuen Testament
(1965) 61f, 63f. BLACK, M. An Aramaic Approach to the
Gospels and Acts (1967) 119f.

9:12.31 LOHSE, E. et al. (eds) Der Ruf Jesu und die Antwort der
Gemeinde (1970) 204-12.

9:12-13 BULTMANN, R., The History of the Synoptic Tradition
(Oxford 1963) 124f. LINTON, O., "Evidences of a Second-
Century Revised Edition of St Mark's Gospel" NTS 14 (1967-
1968) 341f. DORMEYER, D., Die Passion Jesu als
Verhaltensmodell (Münster 1974) 97.

9:12 TAYLOR, V. Jesus and His Sacrifice (London 1948) 29, 47, 87,
91-97, 113, 156, 173, 255, 259. TAYLOR, V., The Life and
Ministry of Jesus (London 1954) 141-45. TAYLOR, V., "The
Origin of the Markan Passion Sayings" NTS 1 (1954-1955)
159ff. HOOKER, M. D., Jesus and The Servant (London 1959)
93-97. WILCKENS, U., Die Missionsreden der
Apostelgeschichte (Neukirchen 1974=1961) 112, 116f, 153f.
SCHWEIZER, E. Erniedrigung und Erhöhung bei Jesus und
seinen Nachfolgern (1962) §3k. HAHN, F. Christologische
Hoheitstitel (1963) 46f, 51f, 53. SUHL, A. Die Funktion der
alttestamentlichen Zitate und Anspielungen im
Markusevangelium (1965) 125, 126, 127, 128, 130, 131.
BRAUN, H., Qumran und NT II (Tübingen 1966) 57f, 91f, 94,
160, 315. HOOKER, M. D. The Son of Man in Mark (1967) 30,

122-34. MINETTE DE TILLESSE, G. Le Secret Messianique dans L'Evangile de Marc (1968) 390-94. GUETTGEMANNS, E. Offene Fragen zur Formgeschichte des Evangeliums (1970) 215, 219, 219n244, 220, 248. JEREMIAS, J. Neutestamentliche Theologie I (1971) 199, 248, 267f, 272f, 280.=New Testament Theology (1971) 260, 281, 286, 295. SCHENKE, L., Studien zur Passionsgeschichte des Markus (Würzburg 1971) 252f. ZMIJEWSKI, J., Die Eschatologiereden des Lukas-Evangeliums (Bonn 1972) 407-409. HIERS, R. H., The Historical Jesus and the Kingdom of God (Gainsville 1973) 45, 49f, 99. HOFFMANN, P., "Mk 8, 31. Zur Herkunft und markinischen Rezeption einer alten Überlieferung" in: P. Hoffman (ed.) Orientierung an Jesus. Für J. Schmid (Freiburg 1973) 178f, 189f. COPPENS, J., "Les logia du Fils de l'Homme dans l'évangile de Marc" in: M. Sabbe (ed.) L'Evangile selon Marc (Gembloux 1974) 498. DESCAMPS, A., "Pour une histoire du titre 'Fils de Dieu" in: M. Sabbe (ed.) L'Evangile selon Marc (Gembloux 1974) 514-17. PERRIN, N., "The Christology of Mark" in: M. Sabbe (ed.) L'Evangile selon Marc (Gembloux 1974) 482. PERRIN, N., A Modern Pilgrimage in New Testament Christology (Philadelphia 1974) 115-21. ACHTEMEIER, P. J., Mark (Philadelphia 1975) 46-48. DIETZFELBINGER, Chr., "Pseudo-Philo: Antiquitates Biblicae" in: W. G. Kümmel (ed.) Jüdische Schriften aus hellenistisch-römischer Zeit II (Gütersloh 1975) 213n.1. WILLIAMS, J. A., A Conceptual History of Deuteronomism in the Old Testament (Louisville 1976) 301, 303. BRUCE;, F. F., The Time is Fulfilled (Exeter 1978) 26. PERRIN, N., "Die Christologie des Markus-Evangeliums" [orig: "The Christology of Mark" JR 51 (1971) 173-87] in: R. Pesch (ed.) Das Markus-Evangelium (Darmstadt 1979) 368. MALBON, E. S., "Mythic Structure and Meaning in Mark" Semeia 16 (1980) 109-13.

9:13 HAHN, F. Christologische Hoheitstitel (1963) 52. HASLER, V. Amen (1969) 33. DERRETT, J. D. M. Law in the New Testament (1970) 343, 344, 358-62, 395. JEREMIAS, J. Neutestamentliche Theologie I (1971) 133, 267, 269, 280. HOFFMANN, P., "Mk 8, 31. Zur Herkunft und markinischen Rezeption einer alten Überlieferung" in: P. Hoffmann (ed.) Orientierung an Jesus. Für J. Schmid (Freiburg 1973) 178f. WILLIAMS, J. A., A Conceptual History of Deuteronomism in the Old Testament (Louisville 1976) 310.

9:14-29 FARRER, A. A Study in St Mark (1951) 41f, 50ff, 110f, 120f, 224f. WEBER, O. GPM 19 (1956/57) 83-86. *RIESENFELD, H. "De fientlige andarna (Mk 9:14-29)" (The Enemy Spirits)

SEA 22-23 ('57-'58) 64-74. SOUCEK, J. B. GPM 13 (1958/59)
65-68. BAUMBACH, G. Das Verständnis des Bösen in den
synoptischen Evangelien (1963) 47ff. HAHN, F.
Christologische Hoheitstitel (1963) 297. FUERST, GPM 19
(1964/65) 115ff. SCHUBERT, B. "Ich glaube" Kleine Predigt-
Typologie III, ed. L. Schmidt (1965) 27-31. BARTH, G. in
Hören und Fragen, eds. G. Eichholz und A. Falkenroth (1967)
183ff. OTTO, G. Handbuch des Religions-Unterrichts (1967)
262-93. WEBER, O. Predigtmeditationen (1967) 249-52.
MINETTE DE TILLESSE, G. Le Secret Messianique dans
L'Evangile de Marc (1968) 89-99. REPLOH, K.-G. Markus -
Lehrer der Gemeinde (1969) 211-21. HAAR, J. GPM 25 (1970)
129-36. KERTELGE, K. Die Wunder Jesu im
Markusevangelium (1970) 174-79. LANGE, E. (ed.)
Predigtstudien für das Kirchenjahr 1970/71 (1970) 143-47.
ROLOFF, J. Das Kerygma und der irdische Jesus (1970) 143-
52, 205ff. ZIMMERMANN, W.-D. Markus über Jesus (1970)
104-106. BORNKAMM, G. Geschichte und Glaube 2.Teil
(1971) 21-36. JEREMIAS, J. Neutestamentliche Theologie I
(1971) 90, 93, 95f, 164 = New Testament Theology I (1971) 86,
89, 91f, 166. SCHRAMM, T. Der Markus-Stoff bei Lukas
(1971) 139f. SCHENK, W., "Tradition und Redaktion in der
Epileptiker-Perikope Mk 9: 14-29" ZNW 63 (1972) 76-94.
SCHENKE, L., Die Wundererzählungen des
Markusevangeliums (Stuttgart 1974) 314-49. TALBERT, C.
H., Literary Patterns, Theological Themes, and the Genre of
Luke-Acts (Missoula 1974) 28. ACHTEMEIER, P. J.,
"Miracles and the Historical Jesus: A Study of Mark 9:14-29"
CBQ 37 (1975) 471-91. BARTLETT, D. L., Fact and Faith
(Valley Forge 1975) 44f. CONZELMANN, H. und
LINDEMANN, A., Arbeitsbuch zum Neuen Testament
(Tübingen 1975) 58. HOWARD, V. P., Das Ego in den
Synoptischen Evangelien (Marburg 1975) 86-97. KOCH, D.-
A., Die Bedeutung der Wundererzählungen für die
Christologie des Markusevangeliums (Berlin/New York 1975)
114-26, 189f. KLEINERT, L./Ü. und KRUSE, M., in: P.
Krusche et al. (eds.) Predigtstudien für das Kirchenjahr 1976-
1977 V/1.Halbband (Stuttgart 1976) 133-42. LANG, F. G.,
"Sola gratia im Markusevangelium. Die Soteriologie des
Markus nach 9:14-29 und 10:17-31" in: J. Friedrich et al. (eds.)
Rechtfertigung. Für E. Käsemann (Göttingen 1976) 321-37.
PETZKE, G., "Die historische Frage nach den Wundertaten
Jesu. Dargestellt am Beispiel des Exorzismus Mark ix. 14-29
par" NTS 22 (1976) 180-204. GÁBRIS, K., in: GPM 31 (1976-
1977) 125-34. PESCH, R., Das Markusevangelium II

(Freiburg 1977) 97f (lit!). RIST, J. M., On the Independence of Matthew and Mark (Cambridge 1978) 61f. SEYBOLD, K. und MÜLLER, U., Krankheit und Heilung (Stuttgart 1978) 112-16, 139f, 159-61. GNILKA, J., Das Evangelium nach Markus II (Einsiedeln/Neukirchen 1979) 43 (lit!). SCHMITHALS, W., Das Evangelium nach Markus (Gütersloh/Würzburg 1979) 407 (lit!).

9:14-18 FUERST, W. GPM 19 (1965) 115-19.

9:15 SCHREIBER, J. Theologie des Vertrauens (1967) 155-57. METZGER, B. M., The Early Versions of the New Testament (Oxford 1977) 330. KLAUCK, H.-J., Allegorie und Allegorese in Synoptischen Gleichnistexten (Münster 1978) 160-69.

9:17 HAHN, F. Christologische Hoheitstitel (1963) 76, 77, 86, 264, 299.

9:19 MINETTE DE TILLESSE, G. Le Secret Messianique dans L'Evangile de Marc (1968) 413-20. STROBEL, A. Erkenntnis und Bekenntnis der Sünde in neutestamentlicher Zeit (1968) 39. SNOY, T., "Marc 6, 48: '. . .et il voulait les dépasser' " in: M. Sabbe (ed.) L'Evangile selon Marc (Gembloux 1974) 355f.

9:20 BETZ, H. D., Lukian von Samosata und das Neue Testament (Berlin 1961) 148.

9:22 "Barmherzigkeit" in: TRE 5 (1980) 227, 234.

9:23-24 BORNKAMM-BARTH-HELD, Ueberlieferung und Auslegung im Matthäus-Evangelium (1961) 179f, 268. JEREMIAS, J. Neutestamentliche Theologie I (1971) 160, 162-64, 196.

9:24 "Anfechtung" in: TRE 2 (1978) 705.

9:25 NESTLE, E., "Mk 9:25" ZNW 14 (1913) 267. BARRETT, C. K., The New Testament Background: Selected Documents (London 1956) 34. ROBINSON, J. M. Das Geschichtsverständnis der Markus-Evangeliums (1956) 43, 44, 49, 51, 69. BETZ, H. D., Lukian von Samosata und das Neue Testament (Berlin 1961) 156f. BOUSSET, W., Die Religion des Judentums im Späthellenistischen Zeitalter (Berlin 1966=1926) 340. METZGER, B. M., The Early Versions of the New Testament (Oxford 1977) 177.

9:28-29 MINETTE DE TILLESSE, G. Le Secret Messianique dans L'Evangile de Marc (1968) 228-37.

9:28 HAHN, F. Christologische Hoheitstitel (1963) 339. MOSLEY, A. W., "Jesus' Audiences in the Gospels of St Mark and St Luke" NTS 10 (1963-1964) 140f. BLACK, M. An Aramaic Approach to the Gospels and Acts (1967) 119f. MINETTE DE

TILLESSE, G. Le Secret Messianique dans L'Evangile de Marc (1968) 238-42. ACHTEMEIER, P. J., Mark (Philadelphia 1975) 93.

9:29ff PETZKE, G., Die Traditionen über Apollonius von Tyana und das Neue Testament (Leiden 1970) 136, 171, 173, 180.

9:29 MOORE, G. F., Judaism II (Cambridge, Mass. 1946) 206n. BORNKAMM-BARTH-HELD Ueberlieferung und Auslegung im Matthäus-Evangelium (1961) 178, 259. BOUSSET, W., Die Religion des Judentums im Späthellenistischen Zeitalter (Berlin 1966=1926) 180, 340.

9:30-10:52 SCHREIBER, J. Theologie des Vertrauens (1967) 196-201.

9:30-50 ZIMMERMANN, W.-D. Markus über Jesus (1970) 106-11.

9:30-37 BRIÈRE, J., "Le Fils de l'homme livré aux hommes. Mc 9, 30-37" AssS 56 (1974) 42-52.

9:30-32 TAYLOR, V. The Formation of the Gospel Tradition (1949) 149f. DAVIES, W. D., The Sermon on the Mount (Cambridge 1966) 24. REPLOH, K.-G. Markus - Lehrer der Gemeinde (1969) 104-107. SCHRAMM, T. Der Markus-Stoff bei Lukas (1971) 130-36. WANKE, J., Die Emmauserzählung. Eine redaktionsgeschichtliche Untersuchung zu Lk 24, 13-35 (Leipzig 1973) 88f. TALBERT, C. H., Literary Patterns, Theological Themes, and the Genre of Luke-Acts (Missoula 1974) 29. PESCH, R., Das Markusevangelium II (Freiburg 1977) 101 (lit!). GNILKA, J., Das Evangelium nach Markus II (Einsiedeln/Neukirchen 1979) 52 (lit!). DIBELIUS, M., "Sammlung" [orig: Formgeschichte des Evangeliums 1933 *(2)* 219-34] in: R. Pesch (ed.) Das Markus-Evangelium (Darmstadt 1979) 75f. STRECKER, G., "Zur Messiasgeheimnistheorie im Markusevangelium"[orig: Studia Evangelica III (1964) 87-104] in: R. Pesch (ed.) Das Markus-Evangelium (Darmstadt 1979) 203-205.

9:30-31 HAHN, F. Das Verständnis der Mission im Neuen Testament (1965) 97. KÜMMEL, W. G., Einleitung in das Neue Testament (Heidelberg 1973 *(17)*) 61f.

9:30 TAYLOR, V., The Life and Ministry of Jesus (London 1954) 153f. LEE, E. K., "St Mark and the Fourth Gospel" NTS 3 (1956-1957) 53ff. MINETTE DE TILLESSE, G. Le Secret Messianique dans L'Evangile de Marc (1968) 249-51. DAVIES, W. D., The Gospel and the Land (London 1974) 251, 411, 419, 419n.28, 433, 434n.76. KONINGS, J., "The Pre-Markan Sequence in Jn 6" in: M. Sabbe (ed.) L'Evangile selon Marc (Gembloux 1974) 155, 173. TALBERT, C. H., Literary Patterns, Theological Themes, and the Genre of Luke-Acts

(Missoula 1974) 114. MALBON, E. S., "Mythic Structure and Meaning in Mark" Semeia 16 (1980) 103-107.

9:31-34   TANNEHILL, R. C., "The Gospel of Mark as Narrative Christology" Semeia 16 (1980) 73f.

9:31-32   YATES, J. E., The Spirit and the Kingdom (London 1963) 125ff, 138ff.

9:31   STONEHOUSE, N. B. The Witness of Matthew and Mark to Christ (1944) 48, 110, 112, 237. FARRER, A. St Matthew and St Mark (1954) 93, 96, 111. TAYLOR, V., The Life and Ministry of Jesus (London 1954) 57n,75, 114, 136, 141-45, 154. TAYLOR, V., "The Origin of the Markan Passion Sayings" NTS 1 (1954-1955) 159ff. DENNEY, J. The Death of Christ (1956) 25. BURKILL, T. A., "St. Mark's Philosophy of History" NTS 3 (1956-1957) 143ff. HOOKER, M. D., Jesus and the Servant (London 1959) 92-97. HAHN, F. Christologische Hoheitstitel (1963) 46, 47, 48f, 50, 52, 205, 226, 230. YATES, J. E., The Spirit and the Kingdom (London 1963) 125-29. HAHN, F. Das Verständnis der Mission im Neuen Testament (1965) 103. HOOKER, M. D. The Son of Man in Mark (1967) 134-36, 139, 140, 160, 161, 181, 182. POPKES, W. Christus Traditus (1967) 153ff, 228f, 243f, 258ff, 271ff. SCHREIBER, J. Theologie des Vertrauens (1967) 41f, 103f, 107-109, 115f, 201. LEHMANN, K. Auferweckt am Dritten Tag nach der Schrift (1968) 163f, 183. MINETTE DE TILLESSE, G. Le Secret Messianique dans L'Evangile de Marc (1968) 390-94. STRECKER, G. "The Passion and Resurrection Predictions in Mark's Gospel (Mark 8:31; 9:31; 10:32-34)" Interpretation 22 ('68) 421-42. STROBEL, A. Erkenntnis und Bekenntnis der Sünde in neutestamentlicher Zeit (1968) 38. BAMMEL, E. The Trial of Jesus (1970) 56ff. GASTON, L. No Stone on Another (1970) 395, 398, 400, 470, 472. GRASS, H. Ostergeschehen und Osterb erichte (1970) 127n3, 130n4, 131, 136n1, 146, 267, 305n1. GUETTGEMANNS, E. Offene Fragen zur Formgeschichte des Evangeliums (1970) 210, 211, 212, 214, 214n207, 215 215n216, 217, 219, 221, 223, 227. O'NEILL, J. C., The Theology of Acts in its historical setting (London 1970) 43fn JEREMIAS, J. Neutestamentliche Theologie I (1971) 21f, 267 69, 272f, 280f. RUPPERT, L., Jesus als der leidende Gerechte (Stuttgart 1972) 56, 60f, 63, 71. PATSCH, H., Abendmahl und historischer Jesus (Stuttgart 1972) 185ff. HOFFMANN, P "Zur Herkunft und markinischen Rezeption einer alten Überlieferung" in: P. Hoffmann (ed.) Orientierung an Jesus Für J. Schmid (Freiburg 1973) 170-76, 185f, 188, 190f, 194-96 199. SCHÜRMANN, H., "Wie hat Jesus seinen Tod bestande und verstanden?" in: P. Hoffmann (ed.) Orientierung an Jesus. Für J. Schmid (Freiburg 1973) 328f. WANKE, J., Die Emmauserzählung (Leipzig 1973) 66, 73, 91A.665. BEST, E., "Mark's Preservation of the Tradition" in: M. Sabbe (ed.) L'Evangile selon Marc (Gembloux 1974) 26f; GT: in: R. Pesch (ed.) Das Markus-Evangelium (Darmstadt 1979) 396. DORMEYER, D., Die Passion Jesu als Verhaltensmodell (Münster 1974) 66. KONINGS, J., "The Pre-Markan Sequence in Jn VI" in: M. Sabbe (ed.) L'Evangile selon Marc (Gembloux 1974) 173. PERRIN, N., "The Christology of Mark" in: M. Sabbe (ed.) L'Evangile selon Marc (Gembloux 1974) 484. PERRIN, N., A Modern Pilgrimage in New Testament Christology (Philadelphia 1974) 115-21. WILCKENS, U., Die Missionsreden der Apostelgeschichte (Neukirchen 1961=1974) 112-15. ACHTEMEIER, P. J., Mark (Philadelphia 1975) 47f, 97. GOPPELT, L., Theologie des Neuen Testaments I (Göttingen 1975) 236f, 275, 282, 295. PESCH, R., "Die Passion des Menschensohnes" in: R. Pesch/R. Schnackenburg (eds.) Jesus und der Menschensohn (Freiburg 1975) 176-79. KELBER, W. H., "From Passion Narrative to Gospel" in: W. H. Kelber (ed.) The Passion in Mark (Philadelphia 1976) 154-56. WILLIAMS, J. A., A Conceptual History of Deuteronomism in the Old Testament, Judaism, and the New Testament (Ph.D.Diss. Southern Baptist Theological Seminary, Louisville 1976) 298-310. "Auferstehung" in: TRE 4 (1979) 489. PERRIN, N., "Die Christologie des Markus-Evangeliums" [orig: "The Christology of Mark" JR 51 (1971) 173-87] in: R. Pesch (ed.) Das Markus-Evangelium (Darmstadt 1979) 370. MALBON, E. S., "Mythic Structure and Meaning in Mark" Semeia 16 (1980) 109-13. TANNEHILL, R. C., "The Gospel of Mark as Narrative Christology" Semeia 16 (1980) 68.

9:32 WREDE, W. Das Messiasgeheimnis in den Evangelien (1963) 93-95. ACHTEMEIER, P. J., Mark (Philadelphia 1975) 93.

9:33-50 STONEHOUSE, N. B. The Witness of Matthew and Mark to Christ (1944) 27-34. CARRINGTON, P. The Primitive Christian Calendar (1952) 180-82. KNOX, W. L. The Sources of the Synoptic Gospels I (1953) 24ff. *SCHNACKENBURG, R. "Mk 9, 33-50" Synoptische Studien (Wikenhauser '53) 184-206. BUTLER, B. C., "M. Vaganay and the 'Community Discourse' " NTS 1 (1954-1955) 283ff. KNOX, W. L. The Sources of the Synoptic Gospels II (1957) 100-101. NEIRYNCK, F., "Die Überlieferung der Jesus-Worte" Concilium 2 (1966) 774-80. *NEIRYNCK, F. "The Tradition of the Sayings of Jesus: Mk 9, 33-50" The Dynamism of Biblical Tradition, ed. P. Benoit (1967) 62-74. PESCH, R., Das

Markusevangelium II (Freiburg 1977) 102 L'(lit!). SCHMITHALS, W., Das Evangelium nach Markus (Gütersloh/Würzburg 1979) 427 (lit!).

9:33-42 BUTLER, B. C., The Originality of St Matthew (Cambridge 1951) 93ff.

9:33-37 BLACK, M. An Aramaic Approach to the Gospels and Acts (1967) 218f. REPLOH, K.-G. Markus - Lehrer der Gemeinde (1969) 140-48. SANFORD, J. A., The Kingdom Within (New York 1970) 191f. SCHILLING, H. Grundlagen der Religionspädagogik (1970) 381-88, 388f. PARKER, T. H. L., Calvin's New Testament Commentaries (London 1971) 142, 145f. *STRUS, A., "Mc 9, 33-37. Problema dell'autenticità e dell'interpretazione" RivB 20 (1972) 589-619. TALBERT, C. H., Literary Patterns, Theological Themes, and the Genre of Luke-Acts (Missoula 1974) 29. GNILKA, J., Das Evangelium nach Markus II (Einsiedeln/Neukirchen 1979) 54 (lit!).

9:33-35 PESCH, R., Das Markusevangelium II (Freiburg 1977) 105 (lit!).

9:33, 35 BULTMANN, R., The History of the Synoptic Tradition (Oxford 1963) 65f, 143f.

9:33-34 HAHN, F. Christologische Hoheitstitel (1963) 227. HOFFMANN, P. und EID, V., Jesus von Nazareth und eine christliche Moral (Freiburg 1975) 186f, 190-200.

9:33 SCHREIBER, J. Theologie des Vertrauens (1967) 162, 176, 208, 210-12, 214, 216. MALBON, E. S., "Mythic Structure and Meaning in Mark" Semeia 16 (1980) 103-107.

9:34 BETZ, H. D., Lukian von Samosata und das Neue Testament (Berlin 1961) 112, 115, 137, 155. SCHRAGE, W. Das Verhältnis des Thomas-Evangeliums zur Synoptischen Tradition und zu den Koptischen Evangelienübersetzungen (1964) S.51. "Aramäisch" in: TRE 3 (1978) 605.

9:35-50 BEST, E., "Mark's Preservation of the Tradition" in: M. Sabbe (ed.) L'Evangile selon Marc (Gembloux 1974) 28f; GT: in: R. Pesch (ed.) Das Markus-Evangelium (Darmstadt 1979) 397f.

9:35-37 SANFORD, J. A., The Kingdom Within (New York 1970) 54. ACHTEMEIER, P. J., Mark (Philadelphia 1975) 98.

9:35 BLACK, M. An Aramiac Approach to the Gospels and Acts (1967) 220f. BEST, E., "Mark's Preservation of the Tradition" in: M. Sabbe (ed.) L'Evangile selon Marc (Gembloux 1974) 27f; GT: in: R. Pesch (ed.) Das Markus-Evangelium (Darmstadt 1979) 396f. SCHMAHL, G., Die Zwölf im Markusevangelium (Trier 1974) 87-90. HOFFMANN, P. und EID, V., Jesus von Nazareth und eine christliche Moral (Basel 1975) 201-208.

TANNEHILL, R. C., "The Gospel of Mark as Narrative Christology" Semeia 16 (1980) 75f.

9:36ff   BETZ, H. D., Lukian von Samosata und das Neue Testament (Berlin 1961) 112, 115, 137, 155.

9:36-37   PESCH, R., Das Markusevangelium II (Freiburg 1977) 107 (lit!).

9:37   DELLING, G. Die Zueignung des Heils in der Taufe (1961) 40, 43, 46, 51. BULTMANN, R., The History of the Synoptic Tradition (Oxford 1963) 142f, 147f, 150f. BLACK, M. An Aramaic Approach to the Gospels and Acts (1967) 219f. LINTON, O., "Evidences of a Second-Century Revised Edition of St Mark's Gospel" NTS 14 (1967-1968) 342f, 352f. BERGER, K., "Zu den Sogenannten Sätzen Heiligen Rechts" NTS 17 (1970-1971) 28f. GOULDER, M. D., Midrash and Lection in Matthew (London 1974) 351f. KONINGS, J., "The Pre-Markan Sequence in Jn 6" in: M. Sabbe (ed.) L'Evangile selon Marc (Gembloux 1974) 173.

9:38ff   KLEIN, G., Die Zwölf Apostel (Göttingen 1961) 28f. FENEBERG, W., Der Markusprolog (München 1974) 41, 81, 159, 181.

9:38-45   BLACK, M. An Aramaic Approach to the Gospels and Acts (1967) 170f.

9:38-42   REPLOH, K.-G. Markus - Lehrer der Gemeinde (1969) 148-53.

9:38-41   BLACK, M. An Aramaic Approach to the Gospels and Acts (1967) 169f. PESCH, R., Das Markusevangelium II (Freiburg 1977) 112 (lit!).

9:38-40   SCHWEIZER, E., Gemeinde und Gemeindeordnung im Neuen Testament (Zürich 1959) §2d. BULTMANN, R., The History of the Synoptic Tradition (Oxford 1963) 24f. JEREMIAS, J. Neutestamentliche Theologie I (1971) 95f. = New Testament Theology I (1971) 91, 92.

9:38   BOUSSET, W., Die Religion des Judentums im Späthellenistischen Zeitalter (Berlin 1966=1926) 340. STONEHOUSE, N. B. The Witness of Matthew and Mark to Christ (1944) 56, 77, 176. DELLING, G. Die Zueignung des Heils in der Taufe (1961) 40, 46. HAHN, F. Christologische Hoheitstitel (1963) 77. BLACK, M. An Aramaic Approach to the Gospels and Acts (1967) 169f. MEYE, R. P. Jesus and the Twelve (1968) 156f. SMITH, M., Tannaitic Parallels to the Gospels (Phildelphia 1968) 4.14+. METZGER, B. M., The Early Versions of the New Testament (Oxford 1977) 177.

9:39   DELLING, G. Die Zueignung des Heils in der Taufe (1961) 46, 51. HAHN, F. Christologische Hoheitstitel (1963) 224.

9:40　SMITH, M., Tannaitic Parallels to the Gospels (Philadelphia 1968) 7end+. *HORVATH, T., "Is hemon in Mk 9, 40 Authentic?" JES 8 (2, '71) 385-86.

9:41-42　BULTMANN, R., The History of the Synoptic Tradition (Oxford 1963) 142f, 147-49, 150f.

9:41　FLEW, R. N. Jesus and His Church (1956) 83, 120. DELLING, G. Die Zueignung des Heils in der Taufe (1961) 40, 43, 46, 58. KLEIN, G., Die Zwölf Apostel (Göttingen 1961) 30f. HAHN, F. Christologische Hoheitstitel (1963) 208, 223f. SMITH, M., Tannaitic Parallels to the Gospels (Philadelphia 1968) A+. HASLER, V. Amen (1969) 36. PESCH, R. Naherwartungen (1969) 92, 110, 114, 135, 141, 183. BERGER, K., "Zu den Sogenannten Sätzen Heiligen Rechts" NTS 17 (1970-1971) 25f. JEREMIAS, J. Neutestamentliche Theologie I (1971) 44m246f. ACHTEMEIER, P. J., Mark (Philadelphia 1975) 42f.

9:42-50　DERRETT, J. D. M., "Salted with Fire. Studies in Texts: Mark 9:42-50" Theology 76 (1973) 364-68. PESCH, R., Das Markusevangelium II (Freiburg 1977) 118f (lit!). GNILKA, J., Das Evangelium nach Markus II (Einsiedeln/Neukirchen 1979) 62 (lit!).

9:42-48　BEST, E. One Body in Christ (1955) 221f. RIST, J. M., On the Independence of Matthew and Mark (Cambridge 1978) 75f.

9:42-47　DORMEYER, D., Die Passion Jesu als Verhaltensmodell (Münster 1974) 98.

9:42　BOUSSET, W., Die Religion des Judentums im Späthellenistischen Zeitalter (Berlin 1966=1926) 187. BUTLER, B. C., The Originality of St Matthew (Cambridge 1951) 7ff. BEST, E. One Body in Christ (1955) 221. SCHRAGE, W. Die konkreten Einzelgebote in der paulinischen Paränese (1961) 243. JEREMIAS, J. Neutestamentliche Theologie I (1971) 113, 149, 160, 163, 247. EDWARDS, R. A., A Theology of Q (Philadelphia 1976) 71.

9:43ff　WREGE, H.-T., Die Überlieferungsgeschichte der Bergpredigt (Tübingen 1968) 64ff. GOULDER, M. D., Midrash and Lection in Matthew (London 1974) 36, 63, 81f, 259, 286, 290. ACHTEMEIER, P. J., Mark (Philadelphia 1975) 55f.

9:43-48　TRAUB, H. GPM 11/3 193-98. BENCKERT, H. GPM 13/3, 190-93. DUPONT, D. J. Les Béatitudes (1958) 121-23. BARTH, G. in Hören und Fragen, ed. G. Eichholz und A. Falkenroth, (1967) 398ff. REPLOH, K.-G. Markus - Lehrer der Gemeinde (1969) 153-54. FISCHER, K. M. GPM 25 (1971) 313-20. LANGE, E. (ed.) Predigtstudien für das Kirchenjahr

1970/1971 (1971) 145-51. STECK, K. G., in: GPM 31 (1976-1977) 315-22. BONHOEFFER, H., in: Predigtstudien für das Kirchenjahr 1977 V/2.Halbband (Stuttgart 1977) 135-41.

9:43-47   FRIEDRICH, G., "Das Problem der Autorität im Neuen Testament" in: Auf das Wort kommt es an (Göttingen 1978) 289. *KOESTER, H., "Mark 9:43-47 and Quintilian 8.3.75" HThR 71 (1978) 151-53.

9:43   LADD, G. E., A Theology of the New Testament (Grand Rapids 1974) 71, 73, 196, 216, 256.

9:44-46   METZGER, B. M., The Early Versions of the New Testament (Oxford 1977) 41.

9:47-50   FRIEDLANDER, G. The Jewish Sources of the Sermon on the Mount (1969) 29f.

9:47-48   NÖTSCHER, F., Altorientalischer und alttestamentlicher Auferstehungsglauben (Darmstadt 1970=1926) 306, 315.

9:47   MINETTE DE TILLESSE, G. Le Secret Messianique dans L'Evangile de Marc (1968) 390-94. AMBROZIC, A. M., St Mark's Concept of the Kingdom of God (Würzburg 1970) 184-89. JEREMIAS, J. Neutestamentliche Theologie I (1971) 17, 22, 40f, 100, 153. MALBON, E. S., "Mythic Structure and Meaning in Mark" Semeia 16 (1980) 109-13.

9:49-50   JüLICHER, D. A. Die Gleichnisreden Jesu (1910) 67-79. BORNKAMM-BARTH-HELD Ueberlieferung und Auslegung im Matthäus-Evangelium (1961) 209ff, 221, 267. CULLMANN, O. "Das Gleichnis vom Salz" Vorträge und Aufsätze, ed. K. Fröhlich (1966) 192-201. KARAVIDOPULOS, J., "Der Sinn des 'Salzes' in den Worten Jesu" Theology 39 (1968) 386-93. REPLOH, K.-G. Markus - Lehrer der Gemeinde (1969) 154-56.

9:49   *BAARDA, T. J. "Mark ix. 49" NTS 5 (4, '59) 318-21. *ZIMMERMANN, H. " 'Mit Feuer gesalzen werden' Eine Studie zu Mk 9:49" ThQ 139 (1, '59) 28-39. BAUER, J. B., Scholia Biblica et Patristica (Graz 1972) 119f. METZGER, B. M., The Early Versions of the New Testament (Oxford 1977) 41.

9:50   DODD, C. H. The Parables of the Kingdom (1948) 139ff. *CULLMANN, O. "Que signifie le sel dans la parabole de Jésus? - Les évangélistes, premiers commentateurs du Logion" RHPhR 37 (1, '57) 36-43. WREGE, H.-T., Die Überlieferungsgeschichte der Bergpredigt (Tübingen 1968) 28f. KLAUCK, H.-J., Allegorie und Allegorese in Synoptischen Gleichnistexten (Münster 1978) 280-86. JEREMIAS, J. Neutestamentliche Theologie I (1971) 32, 37f.

10-12 CLEVENOT, M., So kennen wir die Bibel nicht (München 1978) 93-95.

10-11 YATES, J. E., The Spirit and the Kingdom (London 1963) 169-75.

10 SIEDERS, A., "Het tiende gebod en" Vox Theologica 34 (1963-1964) 115-16. BRAUN, H., Qumran und NT II (Tübingen 1966) 104. VAN LINDEN, P., Knowing Christ through Mark's Gospel (Chicago 1977).

10:1-45 GRANT, F. C. The Gospels (1957) 95f. KUHN, H.-W. Aeltere Sammlungen im Markusevangelium (1971) 146-91.

10:1-34 SMITH, M., Clement of Alexandria and a Secret Gospel of Mark (Cambridge Mass. 1973) 149ff.

10:1-31 EWALD, H., Die drei ersten Evangelien (Göttingen 1850) 304ff. ZIMMERMANN, W.-D. Markus über Jesus (1970) 111-17. McDONALD, J. I. H., Kerygma and Didache (Cambridge 1980) 50, 119f.

10:1-16 CARRINGTON, P. The Primitive Christian Calendar (1952) 182-84.

10:1-12 BULTMANN, R.. The History of the Synoptic Tradition (Oxford 1963) 26f, 49f. BERGER, K. Die Gesetzesauslegung Jesu (1972) 533-38, 539-53, 553-57, 557-70, 574-75. HÜBNER, E., in: GPM 2 (1973) 451-61. HOFFMANN, P. und EID, V., Jesus von Nazareth und eine christliche Moral (Basel 1975) 111-13, 122f. PESCH, R., Das Markusevangelium II (Freiburg 1977) 126f (lit!). SANDMEL, S., We Jews and Jesus (New York 1977) 25, 136, *DESCAMPS, A.-L., "Les textes évangéliques sur le mariage" RThL 9 (1978) 259-86. RIST, J. M., On the Independence of Matthew and Mark (Cambridge 1978) 72-75. STAGG. E./F., Woman in the World of Jesus (Philadelphia 1978) 133-35, 210f, 220. GNILKA, J., Das Evangelium nach Markus II (Einsiedeln/Neukirchen 1979) 68f (lit!). SCHMITHALS, W., Das Evangelium nach Markus (Gütersloh/Würzburg 1979) 436 (lit!). SWIDLER, L., Biblical Affirmations of Woman (Philadelphia 1979) 174f, 231, 239, 259.

10:1 TAYLOR, V., The Life and Ministry of Jesus (London 1954) 156f. STRECKER, G. Der Weg der Gerechtigkeit (1962) 29. HAHN, F. Christologische Hoheitstitel (1963) 230. REPLOH, K.-G. Markus - Lehrer der Gemeinde (1969) 173-79. LEHMANN, M. Synoptische Quellenanalyse und die Frage nach dem historischen Jesus (1970) 143f. PETZKE, G., Die Traditionen über Apollonius von Tyana und das Neue Testament (Leiden 1970) 78, 91. HIERS, R. H., The Historical Jesus and the Kingdom of God (Gainsville 1973) 66, 72f. HENDRIKS, W., "Zur Kollektionsgeschichte des Markusevangeliums" in: M. Sabbe (ed.) L'Evangile selon Marc (Gembloux 1974) 55. KONINGS, J., "The Pre-Markan Sequence in Jn VI" in: M. Sabbe (ed.) L'Evangile selon Marc (Gembloux 1974) 155, 173. TALBERT, C. H., Literary Patterns, Theological Themes, and the Genre of Luke-Acts (Missoula 1974) 114. EGGER, W., Frohbotschaft und Lehre (Frankfurt 1976) 28, 35, 145, 155f. MALBON, E. S., "Mythic Structure and Meaning in Mark" Semeia 16 (1980) 103-107.

10:2ff MOORE, G. F., Judaism II (Cambridge, Mass. 1946) 124. GOULDER, M. D., Midrash and Lection in Matthew (London 1974) 259, 262, 290f. THEISSEN, G., Soziologie der Jesusbewegung (München 1977) 75.

10:2-16 *DELORME, J., "Le mariage, les enfants et les disciples de Jésus. Mc 10,2-16" AssS 58 (1974) 42-51.

10:2-12 SUHL, A. Die Funktion der alttestamentlichen Zitate und Anspielungen im Markusevangelium (1965) 72ff, 77, 95. BJØRNSTAD, E. J. Jesus and the Law in the Gospel of Mark (1966) 53-56.

10:2-12 STENDAHL, K., The Bible and the Role of Women (Philadelphia 1966) 26f. BALTENSWEILER, H. Die Ehe im Neuen Testament (1967) 43-78. ZIMMERMANN, H. Neutestamentliche Methodenlehre (1967) 105-11. MERKEL, H., "Jesus und die Pharisäer" NTS 14 (1967-1968) 206f. BORNKAMM, G. "Ehescheidung und Wiederverheiratung im Neuen Testament" Geschichte und Glaube I (1968) 56-59. GREEVEN, D. H., "Ehe nach dem Neuen Testament" NTS 15 (1968-1969) 376ff. FRIEDLANDER, G. The Jewish Sources of the Sermon on the Mount (1969) 55, 219, 263. REPLOH, K.-G. Markus - Lehrer der Gemeinde (1969) 179-85. SHANER, D. W. A Christian View of Divorce (1969) 38-43, 50ff. LOHSE, E. et al. (eds.) Der Ruf Jesu und die Antwort der Gemeinde (1970) 230, 238f. KUHN, H.-W. Aeltere Sammlungen im Markusevangelium (1971) 160-68. DUNGAN, D. L. The

Sayings of Jesus in the Churches of Paul (1971) 102-31. *CATCHPOLE, D. R., "The Synoptic Divorce Material As A Traditio-Historical Problem" BJRL 57 (1974) 92-127. PERRIN, N., The New Testament (New York 1974) 43-45. SCHMAHL, G., Die Zwölf im Markusevangelium (Trier 1974) 120f. *TREVIJANO ETCHEVERRÍA, R., "Matrimonio y divorcio en Mc 10, 2-12 y par." Burgense 18 (1977) 113-51. *LÖVESTAM, E., "De synoptiska Jesus-orden om skilsmässa och omgifte: referensramar och implikationer" SEA 43 (1978) 65-73. RIVKIN, E., A Hidden Revolution (Nashville 1978) 91. STENDAHL, K., "Die biblische Auffassung von Mann und Frau" in: E. Moltmann-Wendel (ed.) Frauenbefreiung (München 1978) 119-21. DIBELIUS, M., "Sammlung [orig: Formgeschichte des Evangeliums 1933 (2) 219-34] in: R. Pesch (ed.) Das Markus-Evangelium (Darmstadt 1979) 71. GRÄSSER, E. in: GPM 33 (1979) 402-410.

10:2, 10 *ELLINGWORTH, P., "Text and Context in Mark 10:2, 10" Journal for the Study of the New Testament 5 (1979) 63-66.

10:2-9 TAYLOR, V. The Formation of the Gospel Tradition (1949) 64f. STRECKER, G. Der Weg der Gerechtigkeit (1962) 131. DAVIES, W. D., The Sermon on the Mount (Cambridge 1966) 144. WESTERHOLM, S., Jesus and Scribal Authority (Lund 1978) 120-25. MEYER, B. F., The Aims of Jesus (London 1979) 139f. SCHÜRMANN, H., "Neutestamentliche Marginalien zur Frage nach der Institutionalität, Unauflösbarkeit und Sakramentalität der Ehe" in: Kirche und Bibel. Für Bischof E. Schick (Paderborn 1979) 412-15.

10:4 STRECKER, G. Der Weg der Gerechtigkeit (1962) 24. KELBER, W. H., "Mark and Oral Tradition" Semeia 16 (1980) 25-27.

10:5ff HENGEL, M., Judentum und Hellenismus (Tübingen 1969) 564; ET: Judaism and Hellenism I (London 1974) 309.

10:5-6 FRIEDRICH, G., "Das Problem der Autorität im Neuen Testament" in: Auf das Wort kommt es an (Göttingen 1978) 285-87.

10:5 *BERGER, K. "Hartherzigkeit und Gottes Gesetz. Die Vorgeschichte des antijüdischen Vorwurfs in Mc 10:5" ZNW 61 (1-2, '70) 1-47. MIRANDA, J. P., Marx and the Bible (London 1977) 158.

10:6-9 "Adam" in: TRE 1 (1977) 416.

10:6 SCHNEIDER, G., Neuschöpfung oder Wiederkehr (1961) 66f. *VATTIONI, F. "A propos de Marc 10, 6" SciE 20 (3, '68) 433-36. "Adam" in: TRE 1 (1977) 416.

10:7-9 GERSTENBERGER, E. S. und SCHRAGE, W., Frau und Mann (Stuttgart 1980) 150-52, 167-68.

10:8 BURKILL, T. A. "Two into One: The Notion of Carnal Union in Mark 10:8; 1 Cor. 6:16; Eph. 5:31" ZNW 62 (1-2, '71) 115-20.

10:9 STRECKER, G. Der Weg der Gerechtigkeit (1962) 132. HENSS, W., Das Verhältnis zwischen Diatessaron, Christlicher Gnosis und "Western Text" (Berlin 1967) 4f. BOHREN, R., Predigtlehre (München 1971) 322f. JEREMIAS, J. Neutestamentliche Theologie I (1971) 216f.

10:10-12 MINETTE DE TILLESSE, G. Le Secret Messianique dans L'Evangile de Marc (1968) 228-37. SCHÜRMANN, H., "Neutestamentliche Marginalien zur Frage nach der Institutionalität, Unauflösbarkeit und der Sakramentalität der Ehe" in: Kirche und Bibel. Für Bischof E. Schick (Paderborn 1979) 415-23. SWIDLER, L., Biblical Affirmations of Woman (Philadelphia 1979) 174f.

10:10-11 MOSLEY, A. W., "Jesus' Audiences in the Gospels of St. Mark and St. Luke" NTS 10 (1963-1964) 140f.

10:10 GNILKA, J. Die Verstockung Israels (1961) 58f. PASCHEN, W., Rein und Unrein (1970) 156f, 159. ACHTEMEIER, P. J., Mark (Philadelphia 1975) 93. KELBER, W. H., "Mark and Oral Tradition" Semeia 16 (1980) 25-27.

10:11-12 STRECKER, G. Der Weg der Gerechtigkeit (1962) 17, 131f. HAHN, F. Christologische Hoheitstitel (1963) 92. *BAMMEL, E. "Markus 10:11f und das jüdische Eherecht" ZNW 61 (1-2, '70) 95-101. DERRETT, J. D. M. Law in the New Testament (1970) 367-88. LOHSE, E. et al. (eds) Der Ruf Jesu und die Antwort der Gemeinde (1970). OLSEN, N. V. The New Testament Logia on Divorce (1971) BERGER, K., "Zu den sogenannten Sätzen heiligen Rechts" NTS 17 (1970-1971) 14f, 28f. ERNST, J., Anfänge der Christologie (Stuttgart 1972) 150-52. GOPPELT, L., Theologie des Neuen Testaments I (Göttingen 1975) 161f. WESTERHOLM, S., Jesus and Scribal Authority (Lund 1978) 117-20, 123-25. FURNISH, V. P., The Moral Teaching of Paul (Nashville 1979) 40.

10:11 *DELLING, G. "Das Logion Mark x 11 und seine Abwandlungen im Neuen Testament" NovTest 1 (4, '56) 263-74. *TURNER, N. The Translation of μοιχᾶται ἐπ' αὐτήν in Mark 10, 11. The Bible Translator 7/4 (1956) 151-52. STRECKER, G. Der Weg der Gerechtigkeit (1962) 24. DELLING, G. "Das Logion Markus 10, 11 und seine Abwandlungen im Neuen Testament" Studien zum Neuen Testament und zum hellenistischen Judentum (1970) 226-35.

*SCHALLER, B. " 'Commits adultery with her' not 'against her', Mk 10:11" ET 83 (4, '72) 107-108. DUNN, J. D. G., Unity and Diversity in the New Testament (London 1977) 74. *STEIN, R. H., " 'Is It Lawful for a Man to Divorce His Wife?' " JEThS 22 (1979) 115-21.

10:12 TAYLOR, V. The Gospel According to St. Mark (1953) 421. LILLIE, W., Studies in New Testament Ethics (Edinburgh 1961) 123f. BERGER, K., "Zu den sogenannten Sätzen heiligen Rechts" NTS 17 (1970-1971) 28f. BANKS, R., Jesus and the Law in the Synoptic Tradition (London 1975) 157f.

10:13-13:37 DRURY, J., Tradition and Design in Luke's Gospel (Atlanta 1976) 103-109.

10:13ff FRIEDRICH, G., "Beobachtungen zur messianischen Hohepriestererwartung in den Synoptikern" in: Auf das Wort kommt es an (Göttingen 1978) 85-88.

10:13-45 SMITH, M., Clement of Alexandria and a secret Gospel of Mark (Cambridge, Mass. 1973) 167-88, 192.

10:13-31 BERGER, K. Die Gesetzesauslegung Jesu (1972) 396-417, 421-39.

10:13-27 WEISS, J., " 'Zum reichen Jüngling' Mk 10, 13-27" ZNW 11 (1910) 79-83.

10:13-16 CLARKE, W. K. L., New Testament Problems (New York 1929) 36-39. JEREMIAS, J. "Mc 10, 13-16 Parr. und die Uebung der Kindertaufe in der Urkirche" ZNW 40 (1941) 243-45. TAYLOR, V. The Formation of the Gospel Tradition (1949) 72f, 148. *SIMSA, R. M. "Jesis krti nemluvatnka - duchem. (Jesus tauft die unmündigen Kinder - mit dem Geist) Krestanska Revue. XXII (1955) 293-94. SCHWEIZER, E., Gemeinde und Gemeindeordnung im Neuen Testament (Zürich 1959) §2d. ROBINSON, J. M. Kerygma und historischer Jesus (1960) 157. BRAUN, H. GPM 17 (1963) 258-62. BULTMANN, R., The History of the Synoptic Tradition (Oxford 1963) 56f. DELLING, G. Die Taufe im Neuen Testament (1963) 134f. Erhaltet euch in der Liebe Gottes (Predigtgedanken aus Vergangenheit und Gegenwart [1963]) 99-117. NIESEL, W., Herr, tue meine Lippen auf (1964) ed. G. Eichholz. 441ff. FISCHER, M. GPM 23 (1968/69) 275-83. REPLOH, K.-G. Markus - Lehrer der Gemeinde (1969) 186-91. THYEN, H. "Gottesherrschaft und Entfremdung" Zuwendung und Gerechtigkeit (1969) 24-28. KASPER, W. (ed.) Christsein ohne Entscheidung oder Soll die Kirche Kinder taufen? (1970) 60f. KLEIN, G. Aegernisse (1970) 58-81. OTTO, G., Denken - um zu glauben (Hamburg 1970) 113-17. SCHILLING, H.

Grundlagen der Religionspädagogik (1970) 371-81, 388f.
SCHRAMM, T. Der Markus-Stoff bei Lukas (1971) 141f.
CRIBBS, F. L., " A Study of the Contacts That Exist Between
St. Luke and St. John" in: G. MacRae (ed.) SBL Seminar
Papers II (Missoula 1973) 14f. KRAUSE, G. (ed.), Die Kinder
im Evangelium (Stuttgart 1973). TALBERT, C. H., Literary
Patterns, Theological Themes, and the Genre of Luke-Acts
(Missoula 1974) 52f. CONZELMANN, H. und
LINDEMANN, A., Arbeitsbuch zum Neuen Testament
(Tübingen 1975) 78, 91. HOLZE, H., und Riess, R. in: P.
Krusche et al. (eds.) Predigtstudien für das Kirchenjahr 1975
III/2. Halbband (Stuttgart 1975) 140-47. STECK, K. G., in:
GPM 29 (1975) 329-41. ALEXANDER, N., "The Epistle for
Today" in: J. R. McKay/J. F. Miller (eds.) Biblical Studies:
Essays in Honor of W. Barclay (London 1976) 119-34. PESCH,
R., Das Markusevangelium II (Freiburg 1977) 134 (lit!).
RAYAN, S., The Holy Spirit (Maryknoll/NY 1978) 57f.
GNILKA, J., Das Evangelium nach Markus II
(Einsiedeln/Neukirchen 1979) 79 (lit!). SCHMITHALS, W.,
Das Evangelium nach Markus (Gütersloh/Würzburg 1979)
442 (lit!). SWIDLER, L., Biblical Affirmations of Woman
(Philadelphia 1979) 290. WOLFF, H. W., "Kindertaufe?" in:..
. Wie eine Fackel (Neukirchen-Vluyn 1980) 163-71.

10:13-14 BLACK, M. An Aramaic Approach to the Gospels and Acts
(1967) 219f.

10:14-15 FLEW, R. N. Jesus and His Church (1956) 25. MINETTE DE
TILLESSE, G. Le Secret Messianique dans L'Evangile de
Marc (1968) 390-94. BLINZLER, J. "Kind und Königreich
Gottes (Mk 10, 14f)" Aus der Welt und Umwelt des Neuen
Testaments (1969) 41-53. AMBROZIC, A. M., St. Mark's
Concept of the Kingdom of God (Würzburg 1970) 144-67.
JEREMIAS, J. Neutestamentliche Theologie I (1971) 40, 100,
118, 219.

10:14 ROBINSON, J. M. Kerygma und historischer Jesus (1960) 161.
SANFORD, J. A., The Kingdom Within (New York 1970)
107f. "Abendmahl" in: TRE 1 (1977) 202. LEWIS, J. P., "Mark
10:14, *Koluein*, and *Baptizein*" RestQ 21 (1978) 129-34.
SCHLOSSER, J., "Le règne de Dieu dans les dits de Jésus"
RevSR 53 (1979) 164-76. MALBON, E. S., "Mythic Structure
and Meaning in Mark" Semeia 16 (1980) 109-13.

10:15 BOUSSET, W., Die Religion des Judentums im
Späthellenistischen Zeitalter (Berlin 1966=1926) 214.
ROBINSON, J. M. Kerygma und historischer Jesus (1960) 32,
157, 161. DELLING, G. Die Taufe im Neuen Testament (1963)

90. KAESEMANN, E. Exegetische Versuche und Besinnungen (1964) II 97. *SCHILLING, F. A. "What Means the Saying about Receiving the Kingdom of God as a Little Child (ten basileian tou theou hos paidion)? Mk x. 15; Lk xviii.17" ET 77 (2, '65) 56-58. JüNGEL, E. Paulus und Jesus (1966) 183f. BLACK, M. An Aramaic Approach to the Gospels and Acts (1967) 219f. HASLER, V. Amen (1969) 38. KAESEMANN, E. New Testament Questions of Today (1969) 99. JEREMIAS, J. Neutestamentliche Theologie I (1971) 40f, 153f, 219. *BARBAGLI, P., "Fondamenti biblici della dottrina dell' 'Infanzia spirituale'" EphC 24 (1973) 3-43. KONINGS, J., "The Pre-Markan Sequence in Jn VI" in: M. Sabbe (ed.) L'Evangile selon Marc (Gembloux 1974) 172. LADD, G. E., A Theology of the New Testament (Grand Rapids 1974) 65, 69, 72, 103, 216, 303, 591. HOFFMANN, P., und EID, V., Jesus von Nazareth und eine christliche Moral (Freiburg 1975) 211f. PERRIN, N., Jesus and the Language of the Kingdom (London 1976) 41, 48, 53f. McDONALD, J. I. H., Kerygma and Didache (Cambridge 1980) 81. MALBON, E. S., "Mythic Structure and Meaning in Mark" Semeia 16 (1980) 109-13.

10:16   SCHENK, W. Der Segen im Neuen Testament (1967) 66-73. JEREMIAS, J. Neutestamentliche Theologie I (1971) 184f. WESTERMANN, C., Blessing. In the Bible and the Life of the Church (Philadelphia 1978) 83-85, 98-101. KELBER, W. H., "Mark and Oral Tradition" Semeia 16 (1980) 26.

10:17ff   BOUSSET, W., Die Religion des Judentums im Späthellenistischen Zeitalter (1966=1926) 189. KNOX, W. L. The Sources of the Synoptic Gospels II (1957) 57-58. BEYSCHLAG, K., Clemens Romanus und der Frühkatholizismus (Tübingen 1966) 88. GOGARTEN, F. Christ the Crisis (1967) 256f. PETZKE, G., Die Traditionen über Apollonius von Tyana und das Neue Testament (Leiden 1970) 109, 223. SMITH, M., Clement of Alexandria and a secret Gospel of Mark (Cambridge/Mass. 1973) 114, 123, 170f, 279. GOULDER, M. D., Midrash and Lection in Matthew (London 1974) 271-79, 301, 306, 308. CONZELMANN, H., und LINDEMANN, A., Arbeitsbuch zum Neuen Testament (Tübingen 1975) 358f. THEISSEN, G., Soziologie der Jesusbewegung (München 1977) 18, 75.

10:17-45 CARRINGTON, P. The Primitive Christian Calendar (1952) 184-85, 187-89.

10:17-34 SMITH, M., Clement of Alexandria and a secret Gospel of Mark (Cambridge 1973) 79, 98, 170, 368f.

10:17-31 SCHMID, J. Das Evangelium nach Markus (1958) 194-98. *WALTER, N. "Zur Analyse von Mc 10:17-31" ZNW 53 (3-4, '62) 206-18. BULTMANN, R., The History of the Synoptic Tradition (Oxford 1963) 21f. ZIMMERLI, W., Gottes Offenbarung (München 1963) 316-24. LEGASSE, S. L'Appel du riche (Marc 10, 17-31 et parallèles) (1966). MINETTE DE TILLESSE, G. Le secret Messianique dans L'Evangile de Marc (1968) 149-52, 261-63, 415-20. CELADA, B., "Problemas acerca de la riqueza y seguimiento de Jesús" Cultura Biblica 26 (1969) 218-22. LEHMANN, M. Synoptische Quellenanalyse und die Frage nach dem historischen Jesus (1970) 90-102. KUHN, H.-W. Aeltere Sammlungen im Markusevangelium (1971) 146-51. DRESCHER, H.-G., Nachfolge und Begegnung (Gütersloh 1972) 59-93. *MEES, M., "Das Paradigma vom reichen Mann und seiner Berufung nach den Synoptikern und dem Nazaräerevangelium" VChr 9 (1972) 245-65. ACHTEMEIER, P. J., Mark (Philadelphia 1975) 56. LANG, F. G., "Sola gratia im Markusevangelium. Die Soteriologie des Markus nach 9:14-29 und 10:17-31" in: J. Friedrich et al. (eds.) Rechtfertigung. Für E. Käsemann (Tübingen/Göttingen 1976) 329-37. PESCH, R., Das Markusevangelium II (Freiburg 1977) 146f (lit!). RIST, J. M., On the Independence of Matthew and Mark (Cambridge 1978) 57f. *TILLARD, J. M. R., "Le propos de pauvreté et l'exigence évangélique" NRTh 100 (1978) 207-32. "Armut" in: TRE 4 (1979) 77. EGGER, W., Nachfolge als Weg zum Leben. Chancen neuerer exegetischer Methoden dargestellt an Mk 10, 17-31 (Klosterneuburg 1979). SCHMITHALS, W., Das Evangelium nach Markus (Gütersloh/Würzburg 1979) 449 (lit!).

10:17-30 *LÉGASSE, S., "Tout quitter pour suivre le Christ. Mc 10, 17-30" AssS 59 (1974) 43-54. TALBERT, C. H., Literary Patterns, Theological Themes, and the Genre of Luke-Acts (Missoula 1974) 52f.

10:17-27 OBENDIEK, H. in: Herr, tue meine Lippen auf, ed. G. Eichholz (1964) 419ff. SUHL, A. Die Funktion der alttestamentlichen Zitate und Anspielungen im Markusevangelium (1965) 77ff. REPLOH, K.-G. Markus - Lehrer der Gemeinde (1969) 191-201. SMART, J. D. The Quiet Revolution (1969) 85-96. LEHAMNN, M. Synoptische Quellenanalyse und die Frage nach dem historischen Jesus (1970) 90. BERGER, K. Die Gesetzesauslegung Jesu (1972) 268-74, 362f, 396-417, 417-21, 421-39, 439-49, 458-60. HARNISCH, W., "Die Berufung des Reichen" in: G. Ebeling et al. (eds.) Festschrift für Ernst Fuchs (Tübingen 1973) 161-76. GOPPELT, L., Theologie des Neuen Testaments I (Göttingen 1975) 132f. DIAZ, J. A., "Las —Buenas obras' (o la 'justicia') dentro de la estructura de los principales temas de Teología Biblica" EstEc 52 (1977) 445-86. GNILKA, J., Das Evangelium nach Markus II (Einsiedeln/Neukirchen 1979) 83 (lit!).

10:17-22   SCHULZ, A. Nachfolgen und Nachahmen (1962) 76ff. MEYE, R. P. Jesus and the Twelve (1968) 157-59. BRAUN, H. Jesus (1969) 106-108, 109, 122, 163. *TROADEC, H. "La vocation de l'homme riche" VieS 120 (557, '69) 138-48. LEHMANN, M. Synoptische Quellenanalyse und die Frage nach dem historischen Jesus (1970) 96f. OTOMO, Y. Nachfolge Jesu und Anfänge der Kirche im Neuen Testament (1970) 37-42. SANFORD, J. A., The Kingdom Within (New York 1970) 102-105. CRIBBS, F. L., "A Study of the Contacts That Exist Between St. Luke and St. John" in: G. MacRae (ed.) SBL Seminar Papers 2 (Montana 1973) 15-22. *RIGA, P. J., "Poverty as Counsel and as Precept" Bible Today 65 (1973) 1123-28. VAN CANGH, J. M., "Fondement évangélique de la vie religieuse" NRTh 95 (1973) 635-47. DORMEYER, D., Die Passion Jesu als Verhaltensmodell (Münster 1974) 309f. *GALOT, J., "Le fondement évangélique du voeu religieux de pauverté" Gregorianum 56 (1975) 441-67. LANG, F. G., "Sola gratia im Markusevangelium" in: J. Friedrich et al. (eds.) Rechtfertigung. Für E. Käsemann (Tübingen/Göttingen 1976) 330-32. *O'HARA, M. L., "Jesus' Reflections on a Psalm" Bible Today 90 (1977) 1237-240. BRUCE, F. F., The Time is Fulfilled (Exeter 1978) 63.

10:17-18   MASSAUX, E. Influence de L'Evangile de saint Matthieu sur la littérature chrétienne avant saint Irénée (1950) 485-87. DUNN, J. D. G., Unity and Diversity in the New Testament (London 1977) 74.

10:17   MOORE, G. F., Judaism II (Cambridge/Mass. 1946) 321. BURKILL, T. A., "St. Mark's Philosophy of History" NTS 3 (1956-1957) 144ff. SPICQ, C. Dieu et L'Homme (1961) 13-16. HAHN, F. Christologische Hoheitstitel (1963) 76f. TALBERT;, C. H., Literary Patterns, Theological Themes, and the Genre of Luke-Acts (Missoula 1974) 114. "Bekehrung" in: TRE 5 (1980) 449.

10:18   WAINWRIGHT, A. W., The Trinity in the New Testament (London 1962) 41f. BRAUN, H., Qumran und NT II (Tübingen 1966) 71. *LEE, G. M. "Studies in Texts: Mark 10:18" Theology 70 (562, '67) 167-68. BLACK, M. An Aramaic Approach to the Gospels and Acts (1967) 122f. CELADA, B.,

"Nadie es bueno sino sólo Dios" Cultura Bíblica 26 (1969) 106-108. JEREMIAS, J. Neutestamentliche Theologie I (1971) 25f, 29. SANDMEL, S., We Jews and Jesus (New York 1977) 87.

10:19-22   LEHMANN, M. Synoptische Quellenanalyse und die Frage nach dem historischen Jesus (1970) 92-96.

10:19   STRECKER, G. Der Weg der Gerechtigkeit (1962) 22.

10:20-34   SMITH, M., Clement of Alexandria and a secret Gospel of Mark (Cambridge/Mass. 1973) 165f., 175, 185, 192.

10:20   HAHN, F. Christologische Hoheitstitel (1963) 77.

10:21   BARRETT, C. K., The New Testament Background: Selected Documents (London 1956) 223. RUDOLPH, K., Die Mandäer I (Göttingen 1960) 128. SCHWEIZER, E. Erniedrigung und Erhöhung bei Jesus und seinen Nachfolgern (1962) §1e. KOCH, K. "Der Schatz im Himmel" in: Leben angesichts des Todes, eds. B. Lohse und H. P. Schmidt (1968) 47-60. LEHMANN, M. Synoptische Quellenanalyse und die Frage nach dem historischen Jesus (1970) 21, 93f. JEREMIAS, J., Neutestamentliche Theologie I (1971) 20, 157, 205, 213-15. ERNST, J., Anfänge der Christologie (Stuttgart 1972) 135f. "Armenfürsorge" in: TRE 4 (1979) 16.

10:22-23   HARTMAN, L., Testimonium Linguae (Lund 1963) 24ff.

10:22   LEHMANN, M. Synoptische Quellenanalyse und die Frage nach dem historischen Jesus (1970) 95f. DORMEYER, D., Die Passion Jesu als Verhaltensmodell (Münster 1974) 67 A.42, 75 A.87.

10:23-31   *MALONE, D., "Riches and Discipleship: Mark 10:23-31" BThB 9 (1979) 78-88.

10:23-27   *LEGASSE, S. "Jésus a-t-il announcé la Conversion Finale d'Israel? (A propos de Marc x.23-27)" NTS 10 (4, '64) 48P-487. LEHMANN, M. Synoptische Quellenanalyse und die Frage nach dem historischen Jesus (1970) 96f, 99f.

10:23-26   LILLIE, W., Studies in New Testament Ethics (Edinburgh 1961) 95f.

10:23-25   LINTON, O., "Evidences of a Second-Century Revised Edition of St. Mark's Gospel" NTS 14 (1967-1968) 343f. MINETTE DE TILLESSE, G. Le Secret Messianique dans l'Evangile de Marc (1968) 390-94. AMBROZIC, A. M., St. Mark's Concept of the Kingdom of God (Würzburg 1970) 168-83. PERRIN, N., Jesus and the Language of the Kingdom (London 1976) 41, 48, 56.

10:23-24   MANSON, W., Jesus the Messiah (Philadelphia 1948) 89-91.

10:23   ROBINSON, J. M. Kerygma und historischer Jesus (1960) 161, 164. JUENGEL, E. Paulus und Jesus (1966) 182, 238. JEREMIAS, J. Neutestamentliche Theologie I (1970) 40f, 100. MALBON, E. S., "Mythic Structure and Meaning in Mark" Semeia 16 (1980) 109-13.

10:24-25   "Amt" in: TRE 2 (1978) 511.

10:24   JEREMIAS, J. Neutestamentliche Theologie I (1971) 40f, 166. MALBON, E. S., "Mythic Structure and Meaning in Mark" Semeia 16 (1980) 109-13.

10:25   CELADA, B., "Más acerca de camello y la aguja" Cultura Bíblica 26 (1926) 157f. ROBINSON, J. M. Kerygma und historischer Jesus (1960) 161, 164. JUENGEL, E. Paulus und Jesus (1966) 183. *BEST, E. "Uncomfortable Words: VII. The Camel and the Needle's Eye (Mk 10:25)" ET 82 (3, '70) 83-89. SANFORD, J. A., The Kingdom Within (New York 1970) 54f. JEREMIAS, J. Neutestamentliche Theologie I (1971) 29, 40f, 100, 214. *KOBERT, R., "Kamel und Schiffstau: Zu Markus 10, 25 (Par.) und Koran 7, 40/38" Biblica 53 (1972) 229-33. THEISSEN, G., Soziologie der Jesusbewegung (München 1977) 18. "Armenfürsorge" in: TRE 4 (1979) 16. SCHLOSSER, J., "Le règne de Dieu dans les dits de Jésus" RevSR 53 (1979) 164-76. KELBER, W. H., "Mark and Oral Tradition" Semeia 16 (1980) 25-27. MALBON, E. S., "Mythic Structure and Meaning in Mark" Semeia 16 (1980) 109-13.

10:26   BLACK, M. An Aramaic Approach to the Gospels and Acts (1967) 103f.

10:27   MANSON, W., Jesus the Messiah (Philadelphia 1948) 89-91. JUENGEL, E., Paulus und Jesus (1966) 184. JEREMIAS, J. Neutestamentliche Theologie I (1971) 25-27, 214.

10:28ff   STAEHELIN, E. Die Verkündigung des Reiches Gottes in der Kirche Jesu Christi I (1951) 52, 207. THEISSEN, G., Soziologie der Jesusbewegung (München 1977) 16.

10:28-31   HAAR, J. GPM 19 (1964) 35-40. WUELLNER, W. H., The Meaning of "Fishers of Men" (Philadelphia 1967) 54f. REPLOH, K.-G. Markus - Lehrer der Gemeinde (1969) 201-210. OTOMO, Y. Nachfolge Jesu und Anfänge der Kirche im Neuen Testament (1970) 57-60, 120-22. LANGE, E. (ed.) Predigtstudien für das Kirchenjahr 1970/71, (1970) 73-78. LEHMANN, M. Synoptische Quellenanalyse und die Frage nach dem historischen Jesus (1970) 92, 94, 100f. KELBER, W. H., The Kingdom in Mark (Philadelphia 1974) 87-89. LANG, F. G., "Sola gratia im Markusevangelium" in: J. Friedrich et al.(eds.) Rechtfertigung. Für E. Käsemann (Göttingen 1976) 333-35. GNILKA, J., Das Evangelium nach Markus II

(Einsiedeln/Neukirchen 1979) 91 (lit). ERNST, J., "Die Petrustradition im Markusevangelium - ein altes Problem neu angegangen" in: J. Zmijewski/E.Nellessen (eds.) Begegnung mit dem Wort. Für H. Zimmermann (Bonn 1980) 53.

10:28f.32 SCHWEIZER, E. Erniedrigung und Erhöhung bei Jesus und seinen Nachfolgern (1962) §1f, 11b.

10:28-30 SCHULZ, A. Nachfolgen und Nachahmen (1962) 117ff. ERNST, J., Anfänge der Christologie (Stuttgart 1972) 134f. SCHROEDER, H.-H., Eltern und Kinder in der Verkündigung Jesu (Hamburg-Bergstedt 1972) 125-32. BORSCH, F.H., "Jesus the Wandering Preacher?" in: M. Hooker/O. Hickling (eds.) What about the New Testament? In honour of C. Evans (London 1975) 48. SWIDLER, L., Biblical Affirmations of Woman (Philadelphia 1979) 179, 232, 239, 259, 279.

10:28 BLACK, M. An Aramaic Approach to the Gospels and Acts (1967) 129f. BEST, E., "Mark's Preservation of the Tradition" in: M. Sabbe (ed.) L.'Evangile selon Marc (Gembloux 1974) 25; GT: in: R. Pesch (ed.) Das Markus-Evangelium (Darmstadt 1979) 394. DORMEYER, D., Die Passion Jesu als Verhaltensmodell (Münster 1974) 113A.314. *THEISSEN, G., "'Wir haben alles verlassen' (MC.X 28). Nachfolge und soziale Entwurzelung in der jüdisch-palästinischen Gesellschaft des I.Jahrhunderts n.Ch." NovT 19 (1977) 161-96.

10:29-30 BULTMANN, R., The History of the Synoptic Tradition (Oxford 1963) 110f. SANFORD, J. A., The Kingdom Within (New York 1970) 58f. VOEGTLE, A. Das Neue Testament und die Zukunft des Kosmos (1970) 147f. STRECKER, G. "Literarische Ueberlegungen zum εὐαγγέλιον -Begriff im Markusevangelium" Neues Testament und Gesschichte eds. H. Baltensweiler und B. Reicke (1972) 91-104, 98. ACHTEMEIER, P. J., Mark (Philadelphia 1975) 98. TANNEHILL, R. C., The Sword of His Mouth (Philadelphia 1975) 147-52. *SATAKE, A., "Das Leiden der Jünger 'um meinetwillen'" ZNW 67 (1976) 4-19. *GARCIA BURILLO, J., "El ciento por uno (Mc 10, 29-30 par). Historia de las interpretaciones y exégesis" EstBi 36 (1977) 173-203. SIDER, R. J., "Sharing the Wealth: The Church as the Biblical Model for Public Policy" ChrC 94 (1977) 560-65. McDONALD., J. I. H., Kerygma and Didache (Cambridge 1980) 86.

10:29 DELLING, G. Die Zueignung des Heils in der Taufe (1961) 43. HAHN, F. Das Verständnis der Mission im Neuen Testament (1965) 60, 105. BLACK, M. An Aramaic Approach to the Gospels and Acts (1967) 57f. MINETTE DE TILLESSE, G. Le

Secret Messianique dans L'Evangile de Marc (1968) 405-409, 395-96. MARXSEN, W. Mark the Evangelist (1969) 89, 120f, 124f, 136, 217f. PESCH, R. Naherwartungen (1969) 128, 134, 148, 183. HASLER, V. Amen (1969) 40. SCHNACKENBURG, R., " 'Das Evangelium' im Verständnis des ältesten Evangelisten" in: P. Hoffmann (ed.) Orientierung an Jesus. Für J. Schmid (Freiburg 1973) 310, 312, 316-18. DORMEYER, D., Die Passion Jesu als Verhaltensmodell (Münster 1974) 77. ACHTEMEIER, P. J., Mark (Philadelphia 1975) 49f. EGGER, W., Frohbotschaft und Lehre (Frankfurt 1976) 50. METZGER, B. M., The Early Versions of the New Testament (Oxford 1977) 421. THEISSEN, G., Soziologie und Jesusbewegung (München 1977) 17. KELBER, W. H., "Mark and Oral Tradition" Semeia 16 (1980) 43f.

10:30 STRECKER, G. Der Weg der Gerechtigkeit (1962) 86. BOUSSET, W., Die Religion des Judentums im Späthellenistischen Zeitalter (Berlin 1966=1926) 245. NICKELS, P. Targum and New Testament (1967) 25. VOEGTLE, A. Das Neue Testament und die Zukunft des Kosmos (1970) 27, 148, 163. DORMEYER, D., Die Passion Jesu als Verhaltensmodell (Münster 1974) 77. LADD, G. E., A Theology of the New Testament (Grand Rapids 1974) 46f, 72. BAUMGARTEN, J., Paulus und die Apokalyptik (Neukirchen-Vluyn 1975) 184f. THEISSEN, G., Soziologie der Jesusbewegung (München 1977) 18.

10:31 SCHRAGE, W. Das Verhältnis des Thomas-Evangelium zur Synoptischen Tradition und zu den Koptischen Evangelienübersetzungen (1964) 32. JUENGEL, E. Paulus und Jesus (1966) 164. JEREMIAS, J. Neutestamentliche Theologie I (1971) 25-28, 238. GOULDER, M. D., Midrash and Lection in Matthew (London 1974) 37, 73, 76, 409. HOFFMANN, P. und EID, V., Jesus von Nazareth und eine christliche Moral (Freiburg 1975) 201-208. PERRIN, N., Jesus and the Language of the Kingdom (London 1976) 41, 48, 52.

10:32ff PETZKE, G., Die Traditionen über Apollonius von Tyana und das Neue Testament (Leiden 1970) 171, 173. CONZELMANN, H. und LINDEMANN, A., Arbeitsbuch zum Neuen Testament (Tübingen 1975) 373.

10:32-13:2 FARRER, A. A Study in St. Mark (1951) 117ff.

10:32-52 EWALD, H., Die drei ersten Evangelien (Göttingen 1850) 309ff.

10:32-45 FREIDRICH, G. GPM 6 (1952) 69-73. BORSCH, F. The Son of Man in Myth and History (1967) 389f. WEBER, O. (GPM) Predigtmeditationen (1967) 28-31. ZIMMERMANN, W.-D.

Markus über Jesus (1970) 118-22. PATSCH, H., Abendmahl
und historischer Jesus (Stuttgart 1972) 171ff.

10:32-34 SCHELKLE, K. H., Die Passion Jesu in der Verkündigung des
Neuen Testaments (Heidelberg 1949) 62ff. TAYLOR, V. The
Formation of the Gospel Tradition (1949) 149f. DENNEY, J.
The Death of Christ (1956) 25, 30ff. HAHN, F. Christologische
Hoheitstitel (1963) 48. LAMBRECHT, J. Die Redaktion der
Markus-Apokalypse (1967) 21-25. STRECKER, G. "The
Passion- and Resurrection Predictions in Mark's Gospel (Mark
8:31; 9:31; 10:32-34)" Interpretation 22 ('68) 421-42. REPLOH,
K.-G. Markus - Lehrer der Gemeinde (1969) 107-111.
GASTON, L., No Stone on Another (Leiden 1970) 398-400.
SCHRAMM, T. Der Markus-Stoff bei Lukas (1971) 130-36
WANKE, J., Die Emmauserzählung. Eine
redaktionsge-
schichtliche Untersuchung zu Lk 24, 13-35 (Leipzig 1973) 89.
*McKINNIS, R., "An Analysis of Mark 10, 32-34" NovT 18
(1976) 81-100. PESCH, R., Das Markusevangelium II (Freiburg 1977) 150 (lit!). GNILKA, J., Das Evangelium nach Markus II (Einsiedeln/Neukirchen 1979) 95 (lit!). DIBELIUS, M.,
"Sammlung" [orig: Die Formgeschichte des Evangeliums 1933
(2) 219-34] in: R. Pesch (ed.) Das Markus-Evangelium (Darmstadt 1979) 75f. STRECKER, G., "Zur Messiasgeheimnistheorie im Markusevangelium" [orig: Studia Evangelica III (1964)
87-104] in: R. Pesch (ed.) Das Markus-Evangelium (Darmstadt
1979) 203-205. TANNEHILL, R. C., "The Gospel of Mark as
Narrative Christology" Semeia 16 (1980) 68.

10:32-33 SCHWEIZER, E., "Mark's Contribution to the Quest of the
Historical Jesus" NTS 10 (1963-1964) 428f. KAESEMANN,
E., Exegetische Versuche und Besinnungen (1964) II 78. MAL-
BON, E. S., "Mythic Structure and Meaning in Mark" Semeia
16 (1980) 103-107.

10:32 STONEHOUSE, N. B. The Witness of Matthew and Mark to
Christ (1944) 34, 77, 103, 105, 177. ROBINSON, J. M. Ker-
ygma und historischer Jesus (1960) 146. HAHN, F. Christolo-
gische Hoheitstitel (1963) 227. WREDE, W. Das
Messiasgeheimnis in den Evangelien (1963) 21, 96f, 11f, 275-77.
MINETTE DE TILLESSE, G. Le Secret Messianique dans
L'Evangile de Marc (1968) 238-42. MEYE, R. P. Jesus and the
Twelve (1968) 159-64. WREDE, W., The Messianic Secret
(Cambridge 1971) 276-78. SCHMAHL, G., Die Zwölf im Mar-
kusevangelium (Trier 1974) 90-93. TALBERT, C. H., Literary
Patterns, Theological Themes, and the Genre of Luke-Acts
(Missoula 1974) 20, 114. DUNN, J. D. G., Jesus and the Spirit
(London 1975) 76. WILLIAMS, J. A., A Conceptual History

of Deuteronomism in the Old Testament, Judaism, and the New Testament (Ph.D.Diss. Louisville 1976) 300.

10:33-41   TANNEHILL, R. C., "The Gospel of Mark as Narrative Christology" Semeia 16 (1980) 73f.

10:33-34   TAYLOR, V., Jesus and His Sacrifice (London 1948) 29, 47, 85-91, 113, 173f, 255. FARRER, A. St Matthew and St Mark (1954) 93, 96. TAYLOR, V., The Life and Ministry of Jesus (London 1954) 75, 114, 136, 141-45, 154f, 158. TAYLOR, V., "The Origin of the Markan Passion Sayings" NTS 1 (1954-1955) 159ff. HOOKER, M. D., Jesus and the Servant (London 1959) 92-97. WILCKENS, U., Die Missionsreden der Apostelgeschichte (Neukirchen 1961) 102, 112-14, 130f, 138, 158. HAHN, F. Christologische Hoheitstitel (1963) 46, 47f, 52, 205, 227. HAHN, F. Das Verständnis der Mission im Neuen Testament (1965) 103. HOOKER, M. D. The Son of Man in Mark (1967) 137-40. BAMMEL, E. The Trial of Jesus (1970) 56f. GUETTGEMANNS, E. Offene Fragen zur Formgeschichte des Evangeliums (1970) 210-13, 214, 217, 227. JEREMIAS, J. Neutestamentliche Theologie I (1971) 267-69. RUPPERT, L., Jesus als der leidende Gerechte (Stuttgart 1972) 56, 60f, 63. HOFFMANN, P., "Zur Herkunft und markinischen Rezeption einer alten Überlieferung" in: P. Hoffmann (ed.) Orientierung an Jesus. Für J. Schmid (Freiburg 1973) 171, 175f, 186-88, 191. LOHSE, E., Die Einheit des Neuen Testaments (Göttingen 1973) 37f, 88. BEST, E., "Mark's Preservation of the Tradition" in: M. Sabbe (ed.) L'Evangile selon Marc (Gembloux 1974) 26f; GT: in: R. Pesch (ed.) Das Markus-Evangelium (Darmstadt 1979) 396. PERRIN, N., "The Christology of Mark" in: M. Sabbe (ed.) L'Evangile selon Marc (Gembloux 1974) 484. ACHTEMEIER, P. J., Mark (Philadelphia 1975) 47f, 97. GOPPELT, L., Theologie des Neuen Testaments I (Göttingen 1975) 236, 273. PESCH, R., "Die Passion des Menschensohnes" in: R. Pesch/R. Schnackenburg (eds.) Jesus und der Menschensohn (Freiburg 1975) 179-81. VIA, D. O., Kerygma and Comedy in the New Testament (Philadelphia 1975) 77, 117, 131, 140, 150, 153. WILLIAMS, J. A., A Conceptual History of Deuteronomism in the Old Testament, Judaism, and the New Testament (Ph.D.Diss. Louisville 1976) 298-310. GERSTENBERGER, G. und SCHRAGE, W., Leiden (Stuttgart 1977) 142; ET: J. E. Steely, Suffering (Nashville 1980) 165. SHERWIN-WHITE, A. N., Roman Society and Roman Law in the New Testament (Grand Rapids 1978) 34. "Auferstehung" in: TRE 4 (1979) 489. PERRIN, N., "Die Christologie des Markus-Evangeliums" [orig: "The

Christology of Mark" JR 51, 1971, 173-87] in: R. Pesch (ed.) Das Markus-Evangelium (Darmstadt 1979) 370.

10:33 BOUSSET, W., Die Religion des Judentums im Späthellenistischen Zeitalter (Berlin 1966=1926) 167. POPKES, W. Christus Traditus (1967) 159, 165, 188f, 280. MINETTE DE TILLESSE, G. Le Secret Messianique dans L'Evangile de Marc (1968) 390-94. PESCH, R. Naherwartungen (1969) 64, 86, 123, 234. SCHNEIDER, G., Verleugnung, Verspottung und Verhör Jesu nach Lukas 22, 54-71 (München 1969) 36-38, 157, 213. LOHSE, E. et al. eds. Der Ruf Jesu und die Antwort der Gemeinde (1970) 204-12. HOFFMANN, P., "Zur Herkunft und markinischen Rezeption einer alten Überlieferung" in: P. Hoffmann (ed.) Orientierung an Jesus. Für J. Schmid (Freiburg 1973) 194f. WANKE, J., Die Emmauserzählung. Eine redaktionsgeschichtliche Untersuchung zu Lk 24, 13-35 (Leipzig 1973) 65f, 91. DORMEYER, D., Die Passion Jesu als Verhaltsmodell (Münster 1974) 70. PERRIN, N., A Modern Pilgrimage in New Testament Christology (Philadelphia 1974) 115-21. MALBON, E. S., "Mythic Structure and Meaning in Mark" Semeia 16 (1980) 109-13.

10:34 BURKILL, T. A., "St Mark's Philosophy of History" NTS 3 (1956-1957) 143ff. SCHREIBER, J. Theologie des Vertrauens (1967) 42, 100, 103, 107-109, 115f. O'NEILL, J. C., The Theology of Acts in its Historical Setting (London 1970) 43f.n. DORMEYER, D., Die Passion Jesu als Verhaltensmodell (Münster 1974) 66.

10:35ff GRILL, J., Untersuchungen über die Entstehung des vierten Evangeliums II (Leipzig 1923) 29, 305, 315, 318, 323. MOORE, G. F., Judaism II (Cambridge/Mass. 1946) 309n. SCHILLE, G. Die urchristliche Kollegialmission (1967) 125ff. HIERS, H., The Historical Jesus and the Kingdom of God (Gainsville 1973) 30, 42, 44, 74-76.

10:35-45 LIGHTFOOT, R. H. History and Interpretation in the Gospels (1934) 117ff. GOODSPEED, E. J., A Life of Jesus (New York 1950) 158-60. FARRER, A. A Study in St Mark (1951) 118ff. TAYLOR, V., The Life and Ministry of Jesus (London 1954) 159f. *URNER, H. "Der Dienst Jesu Christi. Markus 10, 35-45" CommViat 2 (2-3, '59) 287-90. KLAAS, W. Herr, tue meine Lippen auf, ed. G. Eichholz (1964) 124ff. BRAUN, H., Qumran und NT II (Tübingen 1966) 10, 92, 94, 101f, 287, 291, 335. LAMBRECHT, J. Die Redaktion der Markus-Apokalypse (1967) 25-29. ITTEL, G. W. Jesus und die Jünger (1970) 91-94. KUHN, H.-W. Aeltere Sammlungen im Markusevangelium (1971) 151-60. GOPPELT, L., Theologie des Neuen

Testaments I (Göttingen 1975) 274f. HOWARD, V. P., Das Ego in den Synoptischen Evangelien (Marburg 1975) 97-107. *RADERMAKERS, J., "Revendiquer ou servir? Mk 10, 35-45" AssS 60 (1975) 28-39. PESCH, R., Das Markusevangelium II (Freiburg 1977) 166f (lit!). RIST, J. M., On the Independence of Matthew and Mark (Cambridge 1978) 76. GNILKA, J., Das Evangelium nach Markus I (Einsiedeln/Neukirchen 1979) 98 (lit!). HÜBNER, E., in: GPM 33 (1979) 157-63. SCHMITHALS, W., Das Evangelium nach Markus (Gütersloh/Würzburg 1979) 463 (lit!).

10:35-40   ROLOFF, J. Apostolat-Verkündigung-Kirche (1965) 155f. *FEUILLET, A. "La coupe et le baptême de la Passion (Mc, x,35-40; cf. Mt, xx, 20-23; Lc, xii, 50)" RevBi 74 (3, '67) 356-91. REPLOH, K.-G. Markus - Lehrer der Gemeinde (1969) 156-63. KÜMMEL, W. G., Einleitung in das Neue Testament (Heidelberg 1973 *(17)*) 209f. DORMEYER, D., Die Passion Jesu als Verhaltensmodell (Münster 1974) 309f. *LÉGASSE, S., "Approche de l'Episode préévangélique des Fils de Zébédée (Marc 10, 35-40 par)" NTS 20 (1974) 161-77. SWIDLER, L., Biblical Affirmations of Woman (Philadelphia 1979) 248.

10:35   HAHN, F. Christologische Hoheitstitel (1963) 77, 78. BEST, E., "Mark's Preservation of the Tradition" in: M. Sabbe (ed.) L'Evangile selon Marc (Gembloux 1974) 26; GT: in: R. Pesch (ed.) Das Markus-Evangelium (Darmstadt 1979) 395.

10:36   METZGER, B. M., The Early Versions of the New Testament (Oxford 1977) 438.

10:37   HAHN, F. Christologische Hoheitstitel (1963) 164.

10:38-40   BARTH, M., Die Taufe - ein Sakrament? (Zollikon-Zürich 1951) 42-55.

10:38-39   ROBINSON, J. A. T. "The One Baptism" Twelve New Testaments Studies (1962) 158-75. DELLING, G. Die Taufe im Neuen Testament (1963) 81, 150. *BRAUMANN, G. "Leidenskelch und Todestaufe (Mc 10:38f)" ZNW 56 (3-4, '65) 178-83. *WEHRLI, E. "Jesus' Baptism and Ours" TheoLife 8 (1, '65) 24-34. HAHN, F. Das Verständnis der Mission im Neuen Testament (1965) 77. BEST, E. The Temptation and the Passion: The Markan Soteriology (1965) 152-57. BIEDER, W., Die Verheissung der Taufe im Neuen Testament (Zürich 1966) 101-103. DELLING, G. "βάπτισμα, βαπτισθῆναι" Studien zum Neuen Testament und zum hellenistischen Judentum (1970) 236-56. JEREMIAS, J. Neutestamentliche Theologie I (1971) 137, 231, 233f, 269f. FENEBERG, W., Der Markusprolog (München 1974) 20, 23, 26, 170. WILLIAMS, J. A., A Conceptual History of Deuteronomism in the Old

Testament, Judaism, and the New Testament (Ph.D.Diss. Louisville 1976) 309, 317. "Abendmahl" in: TRE 1 (1977) 51. GERSTENBERGER, G. und SCHRAGE, W., Leiden (Stuttgart 1977) 155f; ET: J. E. Steely, Suffering (Nashville 1980) 180. *HOWARD, V., "Did Jesus Speak about His Own Death?" CBQ 39 (1977) 515-27.

10:38 TAYLOR, V., Jesus and His Sacrifice (London 1948) 97-99, 150, 152, 165, 258, 263, 293. *DELLING, G. "baptisma baptisthenai" NovTest 2 (2, '57) 92-115. BEASLEY-MURRAY, G. R. Baptism in the New Testament (1962) 53f, 72ff. WAGNER, G., Das religionsgeschichtliche Problem von Römer 6, 1-11 (Zürich 1962) 301f; ET: Pauline Baptism and Pagan Mysteries (Edinburgh 1967) 288f. MAUSER, U. Christ in the Wilderness (1963) 91f. DELLING, G., Die Taufe im Neuen Testament (1963) 56. PATSCH, H., Abendmahl und historischer Jesus (Stuttgart 1972) 205ff. ACHTEMEIER, P. J., Mark (Philadelphia 1975) 93. GOPPELT, L., Theologie des Neuen Testaments I (Göttingen 1975) 107, 235, 237, 245, 275.

10:39 GRILL, J., Untersuchungen über die Entstehung des vierten Evangeliums II (Leipzig 1923) 303, 305, 313, 316, 319f. KNOX, W. L. The Sources of the Synoptic Gospels I (1953) 71ff. CONZELMANN, H. und LINDEMANN, A., Arbeitsbuch zum Neuen Testament (Tübingen 1975) 401f. GOPPELT, L., Theologie des Neuen Testaments I (Göttingen 1975) 275f. TANNEHILL, R. C., "The Gospel of Mark as Narrative Christology" Semeia 16 (1980) 83.

10:40 TAYLOR, V. The Gospel According to St Mark (1953) 442. CONZELMANN, H. und LINDEMANN, A., Arbeitsbuch zum Neuen Testament (Tübingen 1975) 26.

10:41-45 SCHULZ, A. Nachfolgen und Nachahmen (1962) 260-65. REPLOH, K.-G. Markus-Lehrer der Gemeinde (1969) 163-72.

10:41 SCHMAHL, G., Die Zwölf im Markusevangelium (Trier 1974) 93-95.

10:42ff MANSON, T. W., The Teaching of Jesus (Cambridge 1945) 313ff. STROBEL, A. Erkenntnis und Bekenntnis der Sünde in neutestamentlicher Zeit (1968) 40.

10:42-45 FLEW, R. N. Jesus and His Church (1956) 95, 137n., 164. BULTMANN, R., The History of the Synoptic Tradition (Oxford 1963) 143f, 147ff. JEREMIAS, J. Abba (1966) 224-27. ACHTEMEIER, P. J., Mark (Philadelphia 1975) 98. GOPPELT, L., Theologie des Neuen Testaments I (Göttingen 1975) 165, 241-47. VIA, D. O., Kerygma and Comedy in the New Testament (Philadelphia 1975) 82, 84, 129, 133, 140, 153.

ARENS, E., The HΛΘON-Sayings in the Synoptic Tradition (Fribourg 1976) 117-161. "Abendmahl" in: TRE 1 (1977) 215. "Amt" in: TRE 2 (1978) 512. BECKWITH, R., "The Bearing of the Holy Spirit" in: P. Moore (ed.) Man, Woman, and Priesthood (London 1979) 61. KLAPPERT, B., "Arbeit Gottes und Mitarbeit des Menschen (Phil 2, 6-11)" in: J. Moltmann (ed.) Recht auf Arbeit - Sinn der Arbeit (München 1979) 100f, 120. TANNEHILL, R. C., "The Gospel of Mark as Narrative Christology" Semeia 16 (1980) 75f.

10:42-44   TANNEHILL, R. C., The Sword of His Mouth (Philadelphia 1975) 102-107. FRIEDRICH, G., "Das Problem der Autorität im Neuen Testament" in: Auf das Wort kommt es an (Göttingen 1978) 391.

10:42   FRIEDRICH, G., "Das Problem der Autorität im Neuen Testament" in: Auf das Wort kommt es an (Göttingen 1978) 405. CLARK, K. W., "The Making of the Twentieth Century New Testament" in: The Gentile Bias and Other Essays (Leiden 1980) 150. CLARK, K. W., "The Meaning of (KATA)KYPIEYEIN" in: The Gentile Bias and Other Essays (Leiden 1980) 207-12.

10:42a   PASCHEN, W. Rein und Unrein (1970) 157f.

10:43-45   KOLENKOW, A. B., "Beyond Miracles, Suffering and Eschatology" in: G. MacRae (ed.) SBL Seminar Papers 2 (Montana 1973) 164f. SCHMAHL, G., Die Zwölf im Markusevangelium (Trier 1974) 119f.

10:43-44   ROBINSON, J. M. Kerygma und historischer Jesus (1960) 166. HOFFMANN, P. und EID, V., Jesus von Nazareth und eine christliche Moral (Freiburg 1975) 187, 190-200, 214.

10:43   METZGER, B. M., The Early Versions of the New Testament (Oxford 1977) 250.

10:45   MANSON, T. W., Jesus the Messiah (Philadelphia 1948) 131-34. TAYLOR, V., Jesus and His Sacrifice (London 1948) 29, 47, 74, 99-105, 113, 127, 202, 242, 245, 257-61, 280. SCHELKLE, K. H., Die Passion Jesu in der Verkündigung des Neuen Testaments (Heidelberg 1949) 63, 67, 72, 84, 129, 132, 135, 150, 187, 192. TAYLOR, V. The Gospel According to St Mark (1953) 445f. TAYLOR, V., The Life and Ministry of Jesus (London 1954) 141-45. TAYLOR, V., "The Origin of the Markan Passion Sayings" NTS 1 (1954-1955) 159ff. MORRIS, L., The Apostolic Preaching of the Cross (Grand Rapids 1955) 26ff, 58f. ROBINSON, J. M. Das Geschichtsverständnis des Markus-Evangeliums (1956) 46, 69, 76, 77, 79f, 83f. BARRETT, C. K. "The Background of Mark 10, 45" New Testament Essays, ed. A. J. B. Higgins (1959) 1-18. BOSCH, D.

Die Heidenmission in der Zukunftsschau Jesu (1959) 175-77. HOOKER, M. D., Jesus and the Servant (London 1959) 74-79. *LEVINSON, N. "Lutron" SJTh 12 (3, '59) 277-85. STRECKER, G. Der Weg der Gerechtigkeit (1962) 67. SCHWEIZER, E. Erniedrigung und Erhöhung bei Jesus und seinen Nachfolgern (1962) §6 ce. HAHN, F. Christologische Hoheitstitel (1963) 45, 52, 57-59, 62, 63, 66. DELLING, G. Die Taufe im Neuen Testament (1963) 58, 94, 117. HELDERMAN, J., "De vrijkoop in het Nieuwe Testament met name in" Vox Theologie 34 (1963-1964) 84-95. BEST, E. The Temptation and the Passion: The Markan Soteriology (1965) 140-44. HAHN, F. Das Verständnis der Mission im Neuen Testament (1965) 43, 98, 101. MORRIS, L. The Apostolic Preaching of the Cross (1965) 29ff. SUHL, A. Die Funktion der alttestamentlichen Zitate und Anspielungen im Markusevangelium (1965) 114ff, 126. BOUSSET, W., Die Religion des Judentums im Späthellenistischen Zeitalter (Berlin 1966=1926) 198. JEREMIAS, J. Abba (1966) 216-29. SHIMADA, K., The Formulary Material in First Peter: A Study According to the Method of Traditionsgeschichte (Th.D.Diss. Union Seminary, New York/Ann Arbor 1966) 249-52. HOOKER, M. D. The Son of Man in Mark (1967) 140-47, 181-82. *FEUILLET, A. "Le logion sur la rancon" RSPhTh 51 (3, '67) 365-402. POPKES, W. Christus Traditus (1967) 169ff, 199f, 221ff, 234f, 237f, 250ff, 258ff, 269f. NICKELS, P. Targum and New Testament (1967) 25. MAURER, C., "Das Messiasgeheimnis des Markus-evangeliums" NTS 14 (1967-1968) 521f. *COMBRINK, H. J. B. Die diens van Jesus, 'n Eksegetiese beskouing oor Markus 10:45 (1968). LEHMANN, K. Auferweckt am Dritten Tag nach der Schrift (1968) 124f, 129A, 138A. MINETTE DE TILLESSE, G. Le Secret Messianique dans L'Evangile de Marc (1968) 390-94, 416-20. REUMANN, J., Jesus in the Church's Gospels (Philadelphia 1968) 445-47. SMITH, M., Tannaitic Parallels to the Gospels (Philadelphia 1968) 3.5.+ STROBEL, A. Erkenntnis und Bekenntnis der Sünde in neutestamentlicher Zeit (1968) 39, 40. BORSCH, F. H. The Christian & Gnostic Son of Man (1970) 23-26. DELLING, G., Studien zum Neuen Testament und zum hellenistischen Judentum (Göttingen 1970) 194-96. DERRETT, J. D. M. Law in the New Testament (1970) 148, 448. GASTON, L. No Stone on Another (1970) 401-402, 471, 472. GRIMM, W., "Weil ich dich lieb habe. . . ." in: Das Institum Judaicum der Universität Tübingen (Tübingen 1970) 24-27. KESSLER, H. Die theologische Bedeutung des Todes Jesu (1970) 282-85. LOHSE, E. et al. (eds.) Der Ruf Jesu und die Antwort der Gemeinde (1970) 204-12, 263f. SCHILLE, G.

in: *ThLZ* 95 (1, '70) 34-35. SCHüRMANN, H. Ursprung und
Gestalt (1970) 119, 137, 138, 157, 165, 170. THYEN, H. Studien
zur Sündenvergebung (1970) 167, 224. JEREMIAS, J.
Neutestamentliche Theologie I (1971) 25, 272f, 277-79. = New
Testament Theology I (1971) 14, 265, 293f. BARRETT, C. K.
"Mark 10.45: A Ransom for Many" New Testament Essays
(1972) 20-26. DELLING, G., Der Kreuzestod Jesu in der
urchristlichen Verkündigung (Göttingen 1972) 64f, 68-70.
PATSCH, H., Abendmahl und historischer Jesu (Stuttgart
1972) 170ff, 213ff. *ROLOFF, J., "Anfänge der
soteriologischen Deutung des Todes Jesu (Mk 10, 45 und Lk
22, 27)" NTS 19 (1972) 38-64. SCHÜRMANN, H., "Wie hat
Jesus seinen Tod bestanden und verstanden?" in: P. Hoffmann
(ed.) Orientierung an Jesus (Freiburg 1973) 347, 350, 352f.
TROMCE, E., 'Is there a Markan Christology?" in:
B.Lindars/S. S. Smalley (eds.) Christ and the Spirit in the New
Testament. In honour of C. F. D. Moule (Cambridge 1973) 7f.
COPPENS, J., "Les logia du Fils de l'Hommes dans l'évangile
de Marc" in: M. Sabbe (ed.) L'Evangile selon Marc (Gembloux
1974) 499. DORMEYER, D., Die Passion Jesu als
Verhaltensmodell (Münster 1974) 110. KONINGS, J., "The
Pre-Markan Sequence in Jn 6" in: M. Sabbe (ed.) L'Evangile
selon Marc (Gembloux 1974) 173. LADD, G. E., A Theology
of the New Testament (Grand Rapids 1974) 156, 186, 187, 426,
433. PERRIN, N., "The Christology of Mark" in: M. Sabbe
(ed.) L'Evangile selon Marc (Gembloux 1974) 482f.
STANTON, G. N., Jesus of Nazareth in New Testament
Preaching (Cambridge 1974) 36, 101, 108, 157, 162.
ACHTEMEIER, P. J., Mark (Philadelphia 1975) 46f, 97f.
HOWARD, V. P., Das Ego in den Synoptischen Evangelien
(Marburg 1975) 234-38. KERTELGE, K., "Der dienende
Menschensohn (Mk 10, 45)" in: R. Pesch/R. Schnackenburg
(eds.) Jesus und der Menschensohn (Freiburg 1975) 225-39.
KOCH, D.-A., "Zum Verhältnis von Christologie und
Eschatologie im Markusevangelium" in: G. Strecker (ed.) Jesus
Christus in Historie und Theologie. Für H. Conzelmann
(Tübingen 1975) 402-405. STUHLMACHER, P., "Jesus als
Versöhner" in: G. Strecker (ed.) Jesus Christus in Historie und
Theologie. Für H. Conzelmann (Tübingen 1975) 101f.
WILLIAMS, S. K., Jesus' Death as Saving Event (Missoula
1975) 213-17. VIA, D. O., Kerygma and Comedy in the New
Testament (Philadelphia 1975) 73f, 81, 119, 128, 134, 155.
"Abendmahl" in: TRE 1 (1977) 50, 54. *MOULDER, W. J.,
"The Old Testament Background and the Interpretation of Mk
10, 45" NTS 24 (1977) 120-27. *ADINOLFI, M., "Gli omologhi
del sacrificio di espiazione nel giudaismo antico" BiOr 20 (1978)

113-22. "Amt" in: TRE 2 (1978) 512, 518. BEST, E., From Text to Sermon (Atlanta 1978) 22. BETZ, O., "Rechtfertigung und Heiligung" in: G. Müller (ed.) Rechtfertigung Realismus. Für A. Köberle (Darmstadt 1978) 43. FRIEDRICH, G., "Das Problem der Autorität im Neuen Testament" in: Auf das Wort kommt es an (Göttingen 1978) 390. GNILKA, J., "Martyriumsparänese und Sühnetod in synoptischen und jüdischen Traditionen" in: R. Schnackenburg (ed.) Die Kirche des Anfangs. Für H. Schürmann (Freiburg 1978) 241-44. *ADINOLFI. M., "Il servo di Jhwh nel logion servizio e del riscatto (Mc 10, 45)" Bi Or 21 (1979) 43-61. PERRIN, N., "Die Christologie des Markus-Evangeliums [orig: "The Christology of Mark" JR 51 (1971) 173-87] in: R. Pesch (ed.) Das Markus-Evangelium (Darmstadt 1979) 368f. MALBON, E. S., "Mythic Structure and Meaning in Mark" Semeia 16 (1980) 109-13.

10:46-13:37   Den HEYER, C. J., Exegetische methoden in discussie. Een analyse van Markus 10, 46-13, 37 (Kampen 1978).

10:46-12:40   FARLA, P. J., Jezus' oordeel over Israel. Een form- en redaktionsgeschichtliche analyse van Mc 10, 46-12, 40 (Kampen 1978).

10:46ff   HAHN, F. Christologische Hoheitstitel (1963) 75, 173. HENNECKE, E. und SCHNEEMELCHER, W., Neutestamentliche Apokryphen I (Tübingen 1964) 339. MARXSEN, W. Mark the Evangelist (1969) 66, 73, 75. GOULDER, M. D., Midrash and Lection in Matthew (London 1974) 316f, 326, 331.

10:46-16:18   HAHN, F. Das Verständnis der Mission im Neuen Testament (1965) 96, 98-101.

10:46-52   RICHARDSON, A. The Miracle-Stories of the Gospels (1948) 88f. FARRER, A. A Study in St Mark (1951) 41f, 117f, 120ff, 224f, 236f, 344f. FRICK, R. GPM 11 (1957) 219-23. STRECKER, G. Der Weg der Gerechtigkeit (1962) 199. HAHN, F. Christologische Hoheitstitel (1963) 262-64, 268, 270. GIBBS, J. M., "Purpose and Pattern in Matthew's Use of the Title 'Son of David'" NTS 10 (1963-1964) 453f. WILDER, A. N., The Language of the Gospel (New York 1964) 69ff. HENSS, W., Das Verhältnis zwischen Diatessaron, Christlicher Gnosis und "Western Text" (Berlin 1967) 14f. LAMBRECHT, J. Die Redaktion der Markus-Apokalypse (1967) 29-30. PESCH, R. Naherwartungen (1969) 52, 54, 62, 63, 69. TRILLING, W. "Die Zeichen der Messiaszeit" Christusverkündigung in den Synoptischen Evangelien (1969) 146. REPLOH, K.-G. Markus - Lehrer der Gemeinde (1969) 222-26. ROLOFF, J. Das Kerygma und der irdische Jesus

(1970) 121-26. ZIMMERMANN, W.-D. Markus über Jesus (1970) 122-24. KERTELGE, K. Die Wunder Jesu im Markusevangelium (1970) 179-82. BURGER, Chr. Jesus als Davidssohn (1970) 42-46, 59-63. JEREMIAS, J. Neutestamentliche Theologie I (1971) 90, 93f. SCHRAMM, T. Der Markus-Stoff bei Lukas (1971) 143-45. FUCHS, A. Sprachliche Untersuchungen zu Matthäus und Lukas (1971) 45-170. *PAUL, A., "Guérison de Bartimée. Mc 10, 46-52" AssS 61 (1972) 44-52. NIELSEN, H. K., "Et bidrag til vurderingen af traditionen om Jesu helbredelsevirksomhed" DTT 36 (1973) 269-300. *ROBBINS, V. K., "The Healing of Blind Bartimaeus (10:46-52) in the Marcan Theology" JBL 92 (1973) 224-43. SCHENKE, L., Die Wundererzählungen des Markusevangeliums (Stuttgart 1974) 350-69. SCHMAHL, G., Die Zwölf im Markusevangelium (Trier 1974) 122. STOCK, A., Umgang mit theologischen Texten (Zürich 1974) 88-93. KOCH, D.-A., Die Bedeutung der Wundererzählungen für die Christologie des Markusevangeliums (Berlin/New York 1975) 126-32. PESCH, R., Das Markusevangelium II Freiburg 1977) 175 (lit!). *ACHTEMEIER, P. J., " 'And he followed him!': Miracles and Discipleship in Mark 10:46-52" Semeia 11 (1978) 115-45. JOHNSON, E. S., "Mark 10:46-52: Blind Bartimaeus" CBQ 40 (1978) 191-204. RIST, J. M., On the Independence of Matthew and Mark (Cambridge 1978) 76f. SEYBOLD, K., und MÜLLER, U., Krankheit und Heilung (Stuttgart 1978) 108f. GNILKA, J., Das Evangelium nach Markus II (Einsiedeln/Neukirchen 1979) 108 (lit!). SCHMITHALS, W., Das Evangelium nach Markus (Gütersloh/Würzburg 1979) 471f. (lit!). "Barmherzigkeit" in: TRE 5 (1980) 225.

10:46   SMITH, M., Clement of Alexandria and a secret Gospel of Mark (Cambridge/Mass. 1973) 65, 188-92, 194. HENDRIKS, W., "Zur Kollektionsgeschichte des Markusevangeliums" in: M. Sabbe (ed.) L'Evangile selon Marc (Gembloux 1974) 52f, 55. TALBERT, C. H., Literary Patterns, Theological Themes, and the Genre of Luke-Acts (Missoula 1974) 114. "Aramäisch" in: TRE 3 (1978) 604. MALBON, E. S., "Mythic Structure and Meaning in Mark" Semeia 16 (1980) 103-107.

10:47-48   BOOBYER, G. H., "The Secrecy Motif in St Mark's Gospel" NTS 6 (1959-60) 229f. HAHN, F. Christologische Hoheitstitel (1963) 245, 263. GIBBS, J. M., "Purpose and Pattern in Matthew's Use of the Title 'Son of David' " NTS 10 (1963-64) 446f. WREDE, W., The Messianic Secret (Cambridge 1971) 279f. BEST, E., "Mark's Preservation of the Tradition" in: M. Sabbe (ed.) L'Evangile selon Marc (Gembloux 1974) 23. ACHTEMEIER, P. J., Mark (Philadelphia 1975) 44f. "Barmherzigkeit" in: TRE 5 (1980) 225.

10:47   STRECKER, G. Der Weg der Gerechtigkeit (1962) 62, 94.

10:48-49   MOORE, G. F., Judaism II (Cambridge/Mass. 1946) 309n. DORMEYER, D., Die Passion Jesu als Verhaltensmodell (Münster 1974) 64, 164A.606.

10:50   DORMEYER, D., Die Passion Jesu als Verhaltensmodell (Münster 1974) 64. METZGER, B. M., The Early Versions of the New Testament (Oxford 1977) 238.

10:51-52   HAHN, F. Christologische Hoheitstitel (1963) 75f, 81, 84, 86, 227. "Barmherzigkeit" in: TRE 5 (1980) 227.

10:51   NICKELS, P. Targum and New Testament (1967) 25. "Aramäisch" in: TRE 3 (1978) 608.

10:52   ROBINSON, J. M. Kerygma und historischer Jesus (1960) 30. BETZ, H. D., Lukian von Samosata und das Neue Testament (Berlin 1961) 155, 157, 159. MEYE, R. P. Jesus and the Twelve (1968) 164-66. PESCH, R. Naherwartungen (1969) 53, 54, 62, 63, 69, 132, 49, 231. GOPPELT, L., Theologie des Neuen Testaments I (Göttingen 1975) 199f.

11-16   ACHTEMEIER, P. J., Mark (Philadelphia 1975) 82-91. KEE, H. C., "The Function of Scriptural Quotations and Allusions in Mark 11-16" in: E. E. Ellis/E. Grässer (eds.) Jesus und Paulus. Für W. G. Kümmel (Göttingen 1975) 165-88. SCHWEIZER, E., "Die theologische Leistung des Markus" [orig. EvTh 24 (1964) 337-55] in: R. Pesch, Das Markus-Evangelium (Darmstadt 1979) 178-83.

11:1-16:8   PESCH, R. Naherwartungen (1969) 69f.

11:1-16:8   TANNEHILL, R. C., "The Gospel of Mark as Narrative Christology" Semeia 16 (1980) 76-88.

11:1-14:72   ACHTEMEIER, P. J., Mark (Philadelphia 1975) 92.

11:1-13:37   BURKILL, T. A. "Strain on the Secret: An Examination of Mark 11:1-13:37" ZNW 51 (1-2, '60) 31-46.

11-13   GUILDING, A., The Fourth Gospel and Jewish Worship (Oxford 1960) 197-206. DORMEYER, D., Die Passion Jesu als Verhaltensmodell (Münster 1974) 85ff.

11-12   MINETTE DE TILLESSE, G. Le Secret Messianique dans l'Evangile de Marc (1968) 255-58. REUMANN, J., Jesus in the Church's Gospels (Philadelphia 1968) 253-56, 258f. *STOCK,

K., "Gliederung und Zusammenhang in Mk 11-12" Biblica 59 (1978) 481-515.

11:1-12:44   PESCH, R. Naherwartungen (1969) 64f.

11:1-12:12   DOEVE, J. W., "Purification du Temple et Dessèchement du Figuier" NTS 1 (1954-55) 297ff. SMITH, C. W. F. "Tabernacles in the Fourth Gospel and Mark" NTS 9 (2, '63) 130-46. HAHN, F. Das Verständnis der Mission im Neuen Testament (1965) 98f.

11   *DE Q. ROBIN, A. "The Cursing of the Fig Tree in Mark xi. A Hypothesis" NTS 8 (3, '62) 276-81. BOUSSET, W., Die Religion des Judentums im Späthellenistischen Zeitalter (Berlin 1966=1926) 112. *CHRISTENSEN, J., "Indtog og tempeldom. En studie i Markus kap. 11" DTT 39 (1976) 1-9.

11:1ff   KNOX, W. L. The Sources of the Synoptic Gospels I (1953) 77ff.

11:1-27   DONAHUE, J. R., Are you the Christ? (Missoula 1973) 115-17, 120.

11:1-26   EWALD, H., Die drei ersten Evangelien (Göttingen 1850) 312ff. ZIMMERMANN, W.-D. Markus über Jesus (1970) 124-30. SCHMITHALS, W., Das Evangelium nach Markus (Gütersloh/Würzburg 1979) 482 (lit!).

11:1-25   STONEHOUSE, N. B. The Witness of Matthew and Mark to Christ (1944) 158f.

11:1-22   KELBER, W. H. "The History of the Kingdom in Mk— Aspects of Markan Eschatology" Proceedings (1972) I, 63-95.

11:1-18   DONAHUE, J. R., Are you the Christ? (Missoula 1973) 113-17.

11:1-16   CONZELMANN, H., und LINDEMANN, A., Arbeitsbuch zum Neuen Testament (Tübingen 1975) 374f.

11:1-11   MOORE, G. F., Judaism II (Cambridge/Mass. 1946) 337. FLEW, R. N. Jesus and His Church (1956) 39-40. VAN BERGEN, P. "L'Entrée messianique de Jésus à Jérusalem" QuestLitPar 38 (1, '57) 9-24. LAMBRECHT, J. Die Redaktion der Markus-Apokalypse (1967) 31. BURGER, C. Jesus als Davidssohn (1970) 46-52, 63-64. SCHENKE, L., Studien zur Passionsgeschichte des Markus (Würzburg 1971) 27f, 181ff. *BARTNICKI, R., "Mesjanski charakter perykopy Marka o wjeździe Jezusa do Jerozolimy (Mk 11, 1-11)" RTK 20 (1973) 5-16. SCHENK, W., Der Passionsbericht nach Markus (Gütersloh 1974) 166ff. PESCH, R., Das Markusevangelium II (Freiburg 1977) 189 (lit!). GNILKA, J., Das Evangelium nach Markus II (Einsiedeln/Neukirchen 1979) 113 (lit!).

11:1-10 LIGHTFOOT, R. H. The Gospel Message of St Mark (1950) 61f. LEIVESTAD, R., Christ the Conqueror (London 1954) 34ff. BULTMANN, R., The History of the Synoptic Tradition (Oxford 1963) 261f. HAHN, F. Christologische Hoheitstitel (1963) 87f, 170f, 264-67, 274, 276, 307. BRAUN, H., Qumran und NT II (Tübingen 1966) 45. GUARNA, Saverio, Tradition and Interpretation in Mark 11:1-10 (1969). *DERRETT, J. D. M. "Law in the New Testament: the Palm Sunday colt" NovTest 13 (4, '71) 241-58. *PATSCH, H. "Der Einzug Jesu in Jerusalem. Ein historischer Versuch" ZThK 68 (1, '71) 1-26. SCHRAMM, T. Der Markus-Stoff bei Lukas (1971) 145-49. HIERS, R. H., The Historical Jesus and the Kingdom of God (Gainesville/Florida 1973) 77-83. SCHNIDER, F., Jesus der Prophet (Freiburg 1973) 81, 102ff. DORMEYER, D., Die Passion Jesu als Verhaltensmodell (Münster 1974) 91ff, 190f. KONINGS, J., "The Pre-Markan Sequence in Jn VI" in: M. Sabbe (ed.) L'Evangile selon Marc (Gembloux 1974) 173. TALBERT, C. H., Literary Patterns, Theological Themes, and the Genre of Luke-Acts (Missoula 1974) 20. *BARTNICKI, R., "Il carattere messianico delle pericopi di Marco e Matteo sull'ingresso di Gesù in Gerusalemme (Mc. 11, 1-10; Mt 21, 1-9)" RivB 25 (1977) 5-27. *BARTNICKI, R., "Teologia ewangelistów w perykopach o wjeździe Jezusa do Jerozolimy" SThV 15 (1977) 55-76. RIST, J. M., On the Independence of Matthew and Mark (Cambridge 1978) 77-81. MEYER, B. F., The Aims of Jesus (London 1979) 168-70.

11:1-7 *BRUCE, F. F. "The Book of Zechariah and the Passion Narrative" BJRL 43 (1960/61) 339f, n.1.

11:1-6 LEHMANN, M. Synoptische Quellenanalyse und die Frage nach dem historischen Jesus (1970) 36f.

11:1-3 GOODSPEED, E., A Life of Jesus (New York 1950) 160-64.

11:1 ADLER, N., Das erste christliche Pfingstfest (Münster 1938) 33f. KLOSTERMANN, E. Das Markusevangelium (1950) 110-112, 113. SCHMAUCH, W. "Der Ölberg. Exegese zu einer Ortsangabe besonders bei Matthäus und Markus" (1952) 391-96 in ThLZ. PESCH, R. Naherwartungen (1969) 34, 53, 54, 69, 173. SCHENKE, L., Studien zur Passionsgeschichte des Markus (Würzburg 1971) 73ff. DORMEYER, D., Die Passion Jesu als Verhaltensmodell (Münster 1974) 111. TALBERT, C. H., Literary Patterns, Theological Themes, and the Genre of Luke-Acts (Missoula 1974) 114. WILLIAMS, J. A., A Conceptual History of Deuteronomism in the Old Testament, Judaism, and the New Testament (Ph.D.Diss. Southern Baptist Theological Seminary, Louisville 1976) 300.

MALBON, E. S., "Mythic Structure and Meaning in Mark" Semeia 16 (1980) 103-107.

11:2ff FRIEDRICH, G., "Das Problem der Autorität im Neuen Testament" in: Auf das Wort kommt es an (Göttingen 1978) 389.

11:2.5.7 *KUHN, H.-W. "Das Reittier Jesu in der Einzugsgeschichte des Markusevangeliums" ZNW 50 (1-2, '59) 82-91.

11:2-4 BUCHHEIM, K., Der Historische Christus (München 1974) 205ff.

11:2-3 MICHEL, O., "Eine Philologische Frage zur Einzugsgeschichte" NTS 6 (1959-60) 81f.

11:2 DORMEYER, D., Die Passion Jesu als Verhaltensmodell (Münster 1974) 89.

11:3 *BRATCHER, R. G. "A Note on Mark XI, 3" ET 64 (3, '52) 93. HAHN, F. Christologische Hoheitstitel (1963) 85, 87f, 90f, 94. BROER I. Die Urgemeinde und das Grab Jesu (1972) 55f.

11:4-5 TALBERT, C. H., Literary Patterns, Theological Themes, and the Genre of Luke-Acts (Missoula 1974) 41.

11:6 DORMEYER, D., Die Passion Jesu als Verhaltensmodell (Münster 1974) 91. TALBERT, C. H., Literary Patterns, Theological Themes, and the Genre of Luke-Acts (Missoula 1974) 41.

11:7 STRECKER, G. Der Weg der Gerechtigkeit (1962) 73. BAUER, W. "Der Palmesel (Neutestamentliche Exegese)" Aufsätze und Kleine Schriften, ed. G. Strecker (1967) 109-21. HENGEL, M., Was Jesus a Revolutionist? (Philadelphia 1971) 17.

11:8-10 SANDMEL, S., We Jews and Jesus (New York 1977) 138.

11:9-10:17 CROSSAN, J. D. "Redaction and Citation in Mark 11:9-10:17" Proceedings, ed. L. C. McGaughy (1972) 17-61.

11:9-10 LIGHTFOOT, R. H. History and Interpretation in the Gospels (19-34) 121f. HAHN, F. Christologische Hoheitstitel (1963) 72, 264f, 270, 273. LOHSE, E., "Hosianna" NovT 6 (1963) 113-19. LOHSE, E. "Hosianna", in: Χάρις καὶ σοφία Festschrift. K. H. Rengstorf (1964) 113-19. SUHL, A. Die Funktion de alttestamentlichen Zitate und Anspielungen im Markusevangelium (1965) 52ff. *CROSSAN, J. D., "Redaction and Citation in Mark 11:9-10 and 11:17" BR 17 (1972) 33-50. DORMEYER, D., Die Passion Jesu als Verhaltensmodell (Münster 1974) 164A.607.

11:9 KLEIN, G. ZNW 2 (1901) 345f. DELLING, G. Die Zueignung des Heils in der Taufe (1961) 42, 45f. KILPATRICK, G. D.,

"Κύριος again" in: P. Hoffmann (ed.) Orientierung and Jesus (Freiburg 1973) 216f.

11:10 DELLING, G. Die Zueignung des Heils in der Taufe (1961) 45f. SCHENK, W. Der Segen im Neuen Testament (1967) 110-13. AMBROZIC, A. M., St Mark's Concept of the Kingdom of God (Würzburg 1970) 28-41. KELBER, W. H., The Kingdom in Mark (Philadelphia 1974) 74, 92-94, 96. MALBON, E. S., "Mythic Structure and Meaning in Mark" Semeia 16 (1980) 109-13.

11:11-19 SCHNACKENBURG, R. "The Primitive Church and its Tradition of Jesus" Perspective 10, 1969, 103-24.

11:11-12 HAHN, F. Christologische Hoheitstitel (1963) 171.

11:11 KLOSTERMANN, E. Das Markusevangelium (1950) 115f. PESCH, R. Naherwartungen (1969) 71, 72, 83, 84, 86, 156, 178. DORMEYER, D., Die Passion Jesu als Verhaltensmodell (Münster 1974) 66A.36, 67A.39 SCHMAHL, G., Die Zwölf im Markusevangelium (Trier 1974) 96-98. TALBERT, C. H., Literary Patterns, Theological Themes, and the Genre of Luke-Acts (Missoula 1974) 20f, 114. WILLIAMS, J. A., A Conceptual History of Deuteronomism in the Old Testament, Judaism, and the New Testament (Ph.D. Diss. Southern Baptist Theological Seminary 1976) 300. MALBON, E. S., "Mythic Structure and Meaning in Mark" Semeia 16 (1980) 103-107.

11:12-12:44 Luz, U., "Das Jesusbild der vormarkinischen Tradition" in: G. Strecker (ed.) Jesus Christus in Historie und Theologie. Für H. Conzelmann (Tübingen 1975) 358. VON DER OSTEN-SACKEN, P., "Streitgespräch und Parabel als Formen markinischer Christologie" in: G. Strecker (ed.) Jesus Christus in Historie und Theologie. Für H. Conzelmann (Tübingen 1975) 383f.

11:12-33 SCHENKE, L., Studien zur Passionsgeschichte des Markus (Würzburg 1971) 28ff.

11:12-25 LAMBRECHT, J. Die Redaktion der Markus-Apokalypse (1967) 32-37. *HULL, R. "The Cursing of the Fig Tree. A Study in social change and the theology of hope" ChrC 84 (1967) 1429-31. ACHTEMEIER, P. J., Mark (Philadelphia 1975) 23-26. RADAELLI, A. et al., "Lettura 'di un' miracolo (Mc 11, 12-25) come introduzione all'intendimento 'del' miracolo" RBR 13 (1978) 115-85.

11:12ff FINDLAY, J. A. Jesus and His Parables (1951) 31ff.

11:12-21 PESCH, R., Das Markusevangelium II (Freiburg 1977) 201f (lit!).

11:12-14 KOCH. D.-A., Die Bedeutung der Wundererzählungen für die
:20-25 Christologie des Markusevangeliums (Berlin/New York 1975)
132-43.

11:12-14 SCHENK, W., Der Passionsbericht nach Markus (Güters-
:20-21 loh 1974) 158ff. *GIESEN, H., "Der verdorrte Feigenbaum -
Eine symbolische Aussage? Zu Mk 11, 12-14. 20f" BZ 20 (1976)
95-111.

11:12-14 JüLICHER, D. A. Die Gleichnisreden Jesu (1910) 444-48.
STONEHOUSE, N. B. The Witness of Matthew and Mark to
Christ (1944) 46, 60, 157. RICHARDSON, A. The Miracle-
Stories of the Gospels (1948) 55-57. FARRER, A. A Study in
St Mark (1951) 161ff. *ANZALONE, V. "Il fico maledetto
(Mc. XI, 12-14 e 20-25)" PaCl 37 (5, '58) 257-64. *BIRDSALL,
J. N. "The Withering of the Fig Tree (Mark xi.12-14, 20-22)"
ET 73 (6, '62) 191. BULTMANN, R., The History of the
Synoptic Tradition (Oxford 1963) 230f. HAHN, F.
Christologische Hoheitstitel (1963) 171. *MUENDERLEIN,
G. "Die Verfluchung des Feigenbaumes (Mk.xi.12-14)" NTS 10
(1, '63) 89-104. SCHREIBER, J. Theologie des Vertrauens
(1967) 134-40. LEHMANN, M. Synoptische Quellenanalyse
und die Frage nach dem historischen Jesus (1970) 37. *KAHN,
J. G. "La parabole du figuier stérile et les arbres récalcitrants de
la Genèse" NovTest 13 (1, '71) 38-45. DERRETT, J. D. M.,
"Figtrees in the New Testament" HeyJ 14 (1973) 249-65.
HIERS, R. H., The Historical Jesus and the Kingdom of God
(Gainsville/Florida 1973) 83-85. TALBERT, C. H., Literary
Patterns, Theological Themes, and the Genre of Luke-Acts
(Missoula 1974) 21. *ROMANIUK, K., " 'Car ce n'était pas la
saison des figues. . .' (Mk 11:12-14 parr)" ZNW 66 (1975) 275-
78. GNILKA, J., Das Evangelium nach Markus II
(Einsiedeln/Neukirchen 1979) 122 (lit!).

11:12 MALBON, E. S., "Mythic Structure and Meaning in Mark"
Semeia 16 (1980) 103-107.

11:13-14 LINTON, O., "Evidences of a Second-Century Revised Edition
of St. Mark's Gospel" NTS 14 (1967-68) 344f.

11:13 BLASS, F., Philosophy of the Gospels (1898) 196ff. *SMITH,
C. W. "No Time for Figs" JBL 79 (4, '60) 315-27. *HIERS, R.
H. " 'Not the Season for Figs' " JBL 87 (4, '68) 394-400. *DEN
HEYER, C. J., " 'Want het was de tijd niet voor vijgen' (Mk 11,
13)" GThT 76 (1976) 129-40. CLARK, K. W., "The Meaning of
ARA" in: The Gentile Bias and other Essays (Leiden 1980) 196.

11:14 JEREMIAS, J. Neutestamentliche Theologie I (1971) 91, 132f.

11:15ff GAERTNER, B. The Temple and the Community in Qumran
and the New Testament (1965) 106. GERSTENBERGER, G.,

und SCHRAGE, W., Leiden (Stuttgart 1977) 173; ET: Suffering (Nashville 1980) 200f.

11:15-12:40   TAYLOR, V. The Formation of the Gospel Tradition (1949) 38f.

11:15-19   LIGHTFOOT, R. H. "The Cleansing of the Temple in St Mark's Gospel" The Gospel Message of St Mark (1950) 60-69. TAYLOR, V. The Gospel According to St Mark (1953) 461f. *BUCHANAN, G. W. "Mark 11.15-19: Brigands in the Temple" HUCA 30 ('59) 169-77. GILL, W. A. The Cleansing of the Temple in the Gospel of Mark (1967). SCHWEIZER, E. Gott Versöhnt: 6 Reden in Nairobi (1971) 21-32. SCHENK, W., Der Passionsbericht nach Markus (Gütersloh 1974) 151ff. GOPPELT, L., Theologie des Neuen Testaments I (Göttingen 1975) 147f. *DERRETT, J. D. M., "The Zeal of the House and the Cleansing of the Temple" DRev 95 (1977) 79-94. FRIEDRICH, G., "Beobachtungen zur messianischen Hohepriestererwartung in den Synoptikern" in: Auf das Wort kommt es an (Göttingen 1978) 88-90. GNILKA, J., Das Evangelium nach Markus II (Einsiedeln/Neukirchen 1979) 126 (lit!). MEYER, B. F., The Aims of Jesus (London 1979) 168-70.

11:15-18   FARRER, A. A Study in St Mark (1951) 159ff, 216f. ROLOFF, J. Das Kerygma und der irdische Jesus (1970) 90-110. TALBERT, C. H., Literary Patterns, Theological Themes, and the Genre of Luke-Acts (Missoula 1974) 21.

11:15-17   BLAKEWAY, C. E. "The Cleansing of the Temple" ET 22 (1911) 279-82. EISLER, R. "Jesus and Blood Sacrifices" Quest 1921. CALDECOTT, A. "The Significance of the 'Cleansing of the Temple'" JTS XXIV (1923) 382-86. BURKITT, F. C. "The Cleansing of the Temple" JTS XXV (1924) 386-90. *BRAUN, F. M., "L'expulsion des vendeurs" RB 38 ('29) 178ff. PLOOIJ, D. "Jesus and the Temple" ET XLII ('30) 36-39. ROBERTS, E. J. "The Position of the Temple Cleansing in the Fourth Gospel" ET XLIV ('33) 427. DURABLE, A. M. "Le signe du temple" RB XLVIII ('39) 21-44. LOHMEYER, E. "Die Reinigung des Temples" ThB X ('41) 257-64. LIGHTFOOT, R. H. The Gospel Message of St Mark (1950) 60-69. MASSAUX, E. Influence de l'Evangile de saint Matthieu sur la littérature chrétienne avant saint Irénée (1950) 510-12. MANSON, T. W. "The Cleansing of the Temple" BJRL XXXIII (1951) 271-82. COOKE, F. A. "The Cleansing of the Temple" ET LXIII ('52) 321-22. LEIVESTAD, R., Christ the Conqueror (London 1954) 34ff. MENDERS, S. "Die Tempelreinigung" ZNW XLVII (-56) 92-112. MONTGOMERY, R. B. "The House of Prayer. Mark 11:17" College of the Bible Quarterly XXXVI ('59) 21-27.

ROTH, C. "The Cleansing of the Temple and Zechariah xiv 21" NovTest IV ('60) 174-81. WALKER, N. "The Alleged Matthaean Errata" NTS IX ('63/63) 393-94. VOGELS, H. "Die Tempelreinigung und Golgotha" BZ VI ('62) 102-107. HAHN, F. Christologische Hoheitstitel (1963) 171f. HAHN, F. Das Verständnis der Mission im Neuen Testament (1963) 28-30. HAMILTON, N. Q. "Temple Cleansing and Temple Bank" JBL LXXXIII ('64) 365-72. EPPSTEIN, V. "The Historicity of the Gospel Account of the Cleansing of the Templel" ZNW LV ('64) 42-58. *GILL, W. A., The Cleansing of the Temple in the Gospel of Mark (Th.M. thesis, Rüschlikon 1967). WAGNER, G., "The Cleansing of the Temple" Survey Bulletin (Rüschlikon 1967) 30-42. *BJERKELUND, C. J. "En tradisjons-og redaksjonshistorisk analyse av perikopene om tempelrenselsen" (A Tradition-historical and Redaction-historical Analysis of the Pericope on the Cleansing of the Temple NTT 69 (4, '68) 206-18. SCHILLE, G. Das vorsynoptische Judenchristentum (1970) 46f. GASTON, L. No Stone on Another (1970) 81-88, 94, 117. SCHNIDER F./STENGER, W. Johannes und die Synoptiker (1971) 26-53. *HIERS, R. H. "Purification of the Temple: Preparation for the Kingdom of God" JBL 90 (1, '71) 82-90. *FLANAGAN, N. M., "Mark and the Temple Cleansing" Bible Today 63 (1972) 980-84. HIERS, R. H., The Historical Jesus and the Kingdom of God (Gainsville/Florida 1973) 86-89. SCHNIDER, F., Jesus der Prophet (Freiburg 1973) 81, 83ff. KONINGS, J., "The Pre-Markan Sequence in Jn VI" in: M. Sabba (ed.) L'Evangile selon Marc (Gembloux 1974) 172. BARRETT, C. K., "The House of Prayer and the Den of Thieves" in: E. E. Ellis/E. Grässer (eds.) Jesus and Paulus. Für W. G. Kümmel (Göttingen 1975) 13-20. *JEREMIAS, J., "Zwei Miszellen: 1. Antik-Jüdische Münzdeutungen. 2.Zur Geschichtlichkeit der Tempelreinigung" NTS 23 (1977) 177-80. MEYER, B. F., The Aims of Jesus (London 1979) 197-202. SWIDLER, L., Biblical Affirmations of Woman (Philadelphia 1979) 284.

11:15-16 *ROTH, C. "The cleansing of the Temple and Zechariah xiv 21" NovTest 4 (3, '60) 174-81. HAHN, F. Christologische Hoheitstitel (1963) 172. SCHÜRMANN, H., "Wie hat Jesus seinen Tod verstanden und bestanden" in: P. Hoffmann (ed.) Orientierung an Jesus. Für J. Schmid (Freiburg 1973) 341f. DORMEYER, D., Die Passion Jesu als Verhaltensmodell (Münster 1974) 245, 247f.

11:15 PARKER, P. The Gospel Before Mark (1953) 56-57. BETZ, H. D., Lukian von Samosata und das Neue Testament (Berlin 1961) 33, 113. HENDRIKS, W., "Zur Kollektionsgeschichte des Markusevangeliums" in: M. Sabbe (ed.) L'Evangile selon Marc (Gembloux 1974) 52-55. WILLIAMS, J. A., A Conceptual History of Deuteronomism in the Old Testament, Judaism, and the New Testament (Ph.D. Diss. Southern Baptist Theological Seminary, Louisville 1976) 300. MALBON, E. S., "Mythic Structure and Meaning in Mark" Semeia 16 (1980) 103-107.

11:16-19 TALBERT, C. H., Literary Patterns, Theological Themes, and the Genre of Luke-Acts (Missoula 1974) 42.

11:16 YATES, J. E., The Spirit and the Kingdom (London 1963) 169-75. GAERTNER, B. The Temple and the Community in Qumran and the New Testament (1965) 109. BEST, E., "Mark's Preservation of the Tradition" in: M. Sabbe (ed.) L'Evangile selon Marc (Gembloux 1974) 26; GT: R. Pesch (ed.) Das Markus-Evangelium (Darmstadt 1979) 395. BARRETT, C. K., "The House of Prayer and the Den of Theives" in: E. E. Ellis/E. Grässer (eds.) Jesus und Paulus. Für W. G. Kümmel (Göttingen 1975) 14, 17-19. *FORD, J. M., "Money 'bags' in the Temple (Mk 11, 16)" Biblica 57 (1976) 249-53.

11:17-33 SCHRAMM, T. Der Markus-Stoff bei Lukas (1971) 149f.

11:17 MASSAUX, E. Influence de l'Evangile de saint Matthieu sur la littérature chrétienne avant saint Irénée (1950) 510-12. HAHN, F. Christologische Hoheitstitel (1963) 113, 171f, 230. *ZEITLIN, S., "There was No Court of Gentiles In the Temple Area" JQR 56 ('65) 88. DODD, C. H. According to the Scriptures (1965) 86f. HAHN, F. Das Verständnis der Mission im Neuen Testament (1965) 30, 60, 99, 103. TROCMÉ, E., "L'Expulsion des Marchands du Temple" NTS 15 (1968-69) 7ff. PETZKE, G., Die Traditionen über Apollonius von Tyana und das Neue Testament (Leiden 1970) 208, 227. JEREMIAS, J. Neutestamentliche Theologie I (1971) 25f, 145, 198, 199f, 236. CROSSAN, J. D., "Redaction and Citation in Mark 11, 9-10 and 11, 17" BR 17 (1972) 33-50. LANGE, J., Das Erscheinen des Auferstandenen im Evangelium nach Mattäus (Würzburg 1973) 75, 79-81, 83, 87, 91, 297, 301, 317. DORMEYER, D., Die Passion Jesu als Verhaltensmodell (Münster 1974) 141. BARRETT, C. K., "The House of Prayer and the Den of Thieves" in: E. E. Ellis/E. Grässer (eds.) Jesus und Paulus. Für W. G. Kümmel (Göttingen 1975) 15-19. DUNN, J. D. G., Jesus and the Spirit (London 1975) 16, 160. KEE, H. C., "The Function of Scriptural Quotations and Allusions in Mark 11-16" in: E. E. Ellis/E. Grässer (eds.) Jesus und Paulus. Für W. G. Kümmel (Göttingen 1975) 186. DUNN, J. D. G., Unity nd Diversity in the New Testament (London 1977) 125f.

11:18 HAHN, F. Christologische Hoheitstitel (1963) 47. BOUSSET, W., Die Religion des Judentums im Späthellenistischen Zeitalter (Berlin 1966=1926) 167. SCHENKE, L., Studien zur Passiongeschichte des Markus (Würzburg 1971) 56ff. DORMEYER, D., Die Passion Jesu als Verhaltensmodell (Münster 1974) 67f, 70, 72. KONINGS, J., "The Pre-Markan Sequence in Jn 6" in: M. Sabbe (ed.) L'Evangile selon Marc (Gembloux 1974) 173. Von der OSTEN-SACKEN, P., "Streitgespräch und Parabel als Formen markinischer Christologie" in: G. Strecker (ed.) Jesus Christus in Historie und Theologie. Für H. Conzelmann (Tübingen 1975) 379-81, 383. SANDMEL, S., We Jews and Jesus (New York 1977) 138. RIVKIN, E., A Hidden Revolution (Nashville 1978) 107-109. TANNEHILL, R. C., "The Gospel of Mark as Narrative Christology" Semeia 16 (1980) 77.

11:19-25 HAHN, F. Christologische Hoheitstitel (1963) 171.

11:19 DORMEYER, D., Die Passion Jesu als Verhaltensmodell (Münster 1974) 66A.36, 67A.39.

11:20-25 JüLICHER, D. A. Die Gleichnisreden Jesu (1910) 444-48. BULTMANN, R., The History of the Synoptic Tradition (Oxford 1963) 54f, 147f. SCHREIBER, J. Theologie des Vertrauens (1967) 134-40, 151. BOHREN, R., Predigtlehre (München 1971) 196. GNILKA, J., Das Evangelium nach Markus II (Einsiedeln/Neukirchen 1979) 132 (lit!).

11:20-22 BIRDSALL, J. N. "The Withering of the Fig-Tree (Mark xi 12-14, 20-22)" ET 73 (6, '62) 191.

11:20-21 HIERS, H., The Historical Jesus and the Kingdom of God (Gainsville 1973) 84f, 110.

11:20 JEREMIAS, J. Neutestamentliche Theologie I (1971) 91f.

11:21 HAHN, F. Christologische Hoheitstitel (1963) 75. PRYKE, E. J., "IΔE and IΔOY" NTS 14 (1967-1968) 418f. DORMEYER, D., Die Passion Jesu als Verhaltensmodell (Münster 1974) 113A.314. ERNST, J., "Die Petrustradtionen im Markusevangelium - ein altes Problem neu angegangen" in: J.Zmijewski/E. Nellessen (eds.) Begegnung mit dem Wort. Für H. Zimmermann (Bonn 1980) 53-54.

11:22-25 BEST, E., "Mark's Preservation of the Tradition"in: M. Sabbe (ed.) L'Evangile selon Marc (Gembloux 1974) 30; GT: in: R. Pesch (ed.) Das Markus-Evangelium (Darmstadt 1979) 398. PESCH, R., Das Markusevangelium II (Freiburg 1977) 208 (lit!).

11:22-23 KNOX, W. L. The Sources of the Synoptic Gospels II (1957) 103f.

11:22   GOGARTEN, F. Christ the Crisis (1967) 239f.

11:23-24   HASLER, V. Amen (1969) 41. DUNN, J. D. G., Jesus and the Spirit (London 1975) 72, 75, 211.

11:23   *BRUCE, F. F. "The Book of Zechariah and the Passion Narrative" BJRL 43 ('60, '61) 347f. SCHRAGE, W. Das Verhältnis des Thomas-Evangeliums zur Synoptischen Tradition und zu den Koptischen Evangelienübersetzungen (1964) 116. BERGER, K. Die Amen-Worte Jesu (1970) 46-48. SANFORD, J. A., The Kingdom Within (New York 1970) 157-58. JEREMIAS, J. Neutestamentliche Theologie I (1971) 44, 159, 163, 186. ZMIJEWSKI, J., "Der Glaube und seine Macht. Eine Traditionsgeschichtliche Untersuchung zu Mt 17, 20; 21, 21; Mk 11, 23; Lk 17, 6" in: J. Zmijewski/E. Nellessen (eds.) Begegnung mit dem Wort. Für H. Zimmermann (Bonn 1980) 81-103.

11:25   BUTLER, B. C., The Originality of St Matthew (Cambridge 1951) 134ff. STRECKER, G. Der Weg der Gerechtigkeit (1962) 18. STROBEL, A. Ekenntnis und Bekenntnis der Sünde in neutestamentlicher Zeit (1968) 60. GOULDER, M. D., Midrash and Lection in Matthew (London 1974) 41, 65, 110, 258, 286f, 298, 402f. MOULE, C. F. D., " '. . .As we forgive. . .'-A Note on the Distinction between Deserts and Capacity in the Understanding of Forgiveness" in: E. Bammel et al. (eds.) Donum Gentilicium. In honour of D. Daube (Oxford 1978) 75.

11:27-13:37   CONZELMANN, H. und LINDEMANN, A., Arbeitsbuch zum Neuen Testament (Tübingen 1975) 375.

11:27-12:44   EWALD, H., Die drei ersten Evangelien (Göttingen 1850) 317ff. VON DER OSTEN-SACKEN, P., "Streitgespräch und Parabel als Formen markinischer Christologie" in: G. Strecker (ed.) Jesus Christus in Historie und Theologie. Für H. Conzelmann (Tübingen 1975) 375f, 382-84.

11:27-12:40   BEST, E. The Temptation and the Passion: The Markan Soteriology (1965) 84ff. KONINGS, J., "The Pre-Markan Sequence in Jn 6" in: M. Sabbe (ed.) L'Evangile selon Marc (Gembloux 1974) 173.

11:27-12:37   KNOX, W. L. The Sources of the Synoptic Gospels I (1953) 85ff.

11:27-12:12   LAMBRECHT, J. Die Redaktion der Markus-Apokalypse (1967) 37-44.

11:27ff   ROBINSON, J. M. Das Geschichtsverständnis des Markus-Evangeliums (1956) 57, 72, 74f. STROBEL, A. Erkenntnis und Bekenntnis der Sünde in neutestamentlicher Zeit (1968) 61. FENEBERG, W., Der Markusprolog (München 1974) 92, 170f.

11:27-33　BARRETT, C. K., The Holy Spirit and the Gospel Tradition (New York 1947) 79-82. TAYLOR, V. The Formation of the Gospel Tradition (1949) 64f, 179. GOODSPEED, E. J., A Life of Jesus (New York 1950) 168-72. GRANT, F. C. The Gospels (1957) 81f. RUDOLPH, K., Die Mandäer I (Göttingen 1960) 235. HAHN, F. Christologische Hoheitstitel (1963) 113, 171, 375. BRAUN, H. Jesus (1969) 159-61. *KREMER, J. "Jesu Antwort auf die Frage nach seiner Vollmacht. Eine Auslegung von Mk 11, 27-33" BUL 9 (2, '68) 128-36. *SCHNACKENBURG, R. "Die Vollmacht Jesu. Zu Mk 11, 27-33" KG 27 (4, '71) 105-109. DONAHUE, J. R., Are You the Christ? (Missoula 1973) 115, 117, 118, 120, 121. *SHAE, G. S., "The Question on the Authority of Jesus" NovT 16 (1974) 1-29. DUNN, J. D. G., Jesus and the Spirit (London 1975) 64, 77. HOWARD, V. P., Das Ego in den Synoptischen Evangelien (Marburg 1975) 107-16. PESCH, R., Das Markusevangelium II (Freiburg 1977) 213 (lit!). SANDMEL, S., We Jews and Jesus (New York 1977) 137. RIVKIN, E., A Hidden Revolution (Nashville 1978) 107-109. GNILKA, J., Das Evangelium nach Markus II (Einsiedeln/Neukirchen 1979) 136 (lit!). MEYER, B. F., The Aims of Jesus (London 1979) 168-70. SCHMITHALS, W., Das Evangelium nach Markus (Gütersloh 1979) 505 (lit!).

11:27-32　ZIMMERMANN, W.-D. Markus über Jesus (1970) 130-32.

11:27-30　ROBINSON, J. M., Kerygma und historischer Jesus (1960) 144f.

11:27-28　KÜMMEL, W. G., Einleitung in das Neue Testament (Heidelberg 1973 *(17)*) 61f.

11:27　*BISHOP, E. F. F. "Jesus Walking or Teaching in the Temple (Mk XI, 27; JN X, 23)" ET LXIII ('52) 226-27. GREEVEN, H., "Erwägungen zur Synoptischen Textkritik" NTS 6 (1959-1960) 295f. BOUSSET, W., Die Religion des Judentums im Späthellenistischen Zeitalter (Berlin 1966=1926) 167. SCHREIBER, J. Theologie des Vertrauens (1967) 182, 185-88, 202. DORMEYER, D., Die Passion Jesu als Verhaltensmodell (Münster 1974) 70. HENDRIKS, W., "Zur Kollektionsgeschichte des Markusevangeliums" in: M. Sabbe (ed.) L'Evangile selon Marc (Gembloux 1974) 52-55. WILLIAMS, J. A., A Conceptual History of Deuteronomism in the Old Testament, Judaism, and the New Testament (Ph.D. Diss. Louisville 1976) 300, 302. MALBON, E. S., "Mythic Structure and Meaning in Mark" Semeia 16 (1980) 103-107.

11:28-31　DORMEYER, D., Die Passion Jesu als Verhaltensmodell (Münster 1974) 309f.

11:28-30   BARTH, M., Die Taufe - ein Sakrament? (Zürich 1951) 128.

11:28   PESCH, R. Naherwartungen (1969) 64, 102, 103, 198. DUNN, J. D. G., Jesus and the Spirit (London 1975) 77, 79.

11:29-33   DELLING, G. Die Taufe im Neuen Testament (1963) 42, 47, 55.

11:29-30   MEYER, B. F., The Aims of Jesus (London 1979) 125.

11:30   SMITH, M., Clement of Alexandria and a Secret Gospel of Mark (Cambridge/Mass. 1973) 207f.

11:33-12:40   KONINGS, J., "The Pre-Markan Sequence in Jn 6" in: M. Sabbe (ed.) L'Evangile selon Marc (Gembloux 1974) 172.

11:33   PESCH, R. Naherwartungen (1969) 101, 110, 192, 198. DORMEYER, D., Die Passion Jesu als Verhaltensmodell (Münster 1974) 309f.

12-13   DUNN, J. D. G. Baptism in the Holy Spirit (1970) 26, 30, 35. JEREMIAS, J. Die Abendmahlsworte Jesu (1960) 84-86.

12:1ff   "Apokalyptik" in: TRE 3 (1978) 255. ROBINSON, J. M. Das Geschichtsverständnis des Markus-Evangeliums (1956) 99f.

12:1-44   ZIMMERMANN, W.-D. Markus über Jesus (1970) 132-40.

12:1-37   DAUBE, D., "The Earliest Structure of the Gospels" NTS 5 (1958-1959) 180f.

12:1-12   JüLICHER, D. A. Die Gleichnisreden Jesu (1910) 385-406. LOHMEYER, E. "Das Gleichnis von den bösen Weingärtnern" ZsystTh 18 (1941) 242-59. TAYLOR, V., Jesus and His Sacrifice (London 1948) 106-108, 280. MASSAUX, E. Influence de l'Evangile de saint Matthieu sur la littérature chrétienne avant saint Irénée (1950) 267-71. MICHAELIS, D. W. Die Gleichnisse Jesu (1956) 113-25. GRANT, F. C. The Gospels (1957) 98f. BOSCH, D. Die Heidenmission in der Zukunftsschau Jesu (1959) 116-24, 131. SWAELES, R., "L'Arrière-fond Scripturaire de Matt 21, 43 et son lien avec Matt 21, 44" NTS 6 (1959-1960) 310f. VAN IERSEL, B. M. F. "Das Gleichnis von den Bösen Winzern" in: 'Der Sohn' in den Synoptischen Jesusworten (1961) 124. JEREMIAS, J. Die Gleichnisse Jesu (1962) 67-75, 78, 166, 202. SCHRAGE, W. Das Verhältnis des Thomas-Evangeliums zur Synoptischen Tradition und zu den Koptischen Evangelienübersetzungen

(1964) 137. SUHL, A. Die Funktion der alttestamentlichen Zitate und Anspielungen im Markusevangelium (1965) 138ff. SCHREIBER, J. Theologie des Vertrauens (1967) 42f, 88, 138, 202, 220, 232. *HENGEL, M. "Das Gleichnis von den Weingärtnern Mc 12:1-12 im Lichte der Zenonpapyri und der rabbinischen Gleichnisse" ZNW 59 (1-2, '68) 1-39. MINETTE DE TILLESSE, G. Le Secret Messianique dans L'Evangile de Marc (1968) 218-19, 287-92. DASSONVILLE, A. E. The Parable of the Wicked Husbandmen in Luke (1970). DERRETT, J. D. M. Law in the New Testament (1970) 286-312. *KLAUCK, H.-J. "Das Gleichnis vom Mord im Weinberg (Mk 12, 1-12; Mt 21, 33-46; Lk 20, 9-19)" BuL 11 (2, '70) 118-45. SANDVIK, Björn, Das Kommen des Herrn beim Abendmahl (1970) 53ff. SCHRAMM, T. Der Markus-Stoff bei Lukas (1971) 150-67. *CROSSAN, J. D. "The Parable of the Wicked Husbandmen" JBL 90 (4, '71) 451-65. *NEWELL, J. E./R. R., "The Parable of the Wicked Tenants" NovT (1972) 226-37. PATSCH, H., Abendmahl und historischer Jesus (Stuttgart 1972) 200ff. DONAHUE, J. R., Are You the Christ? (Missoula 1973) 112-28, 136. *MERLI, D., "La parabola dei vignaioli infedeli (Mc 12:1-12)" BiOr 15 (1973) 97-108. SCHNIDER, F., Jesus der Prophet (Freiburg 1973) 44, 130, 152ff, 161ff. BLANK, J., "Die Sendung des Sohnes" in: J. Gnilka (ed.) Neues Testaments und Kirche. Für R. Schnackenburg (Freiburg 1974) 11-141. DEHANDSCHUTTER, B., "La parabole des vignerons homicides (Mc 12, 1-2) et l'Evangile selon Thomas" in: M. Sabbe (ed.) L'Evangile selon Marc (Gembloux 1974) 203-19. *DERRETT, J. D. M., "Allegory and Wicked Vinedressers" JThS 25 (1974) 426-32. DESCAMPS, A., "Pour une histoire du titre 'Fils de Dieu' " in: M. Sabbe (ed.) L'Evangile selon Marc (Gembloux 1974) 549. GOULDER, M. D., Midrash and Lection in Matthew (London 1974) 51, 52, 54, 58, 61, 411, 420. *SNODGRASS, K. R., "The Parable of the Wicked Husbandmen: Is the Gospel of Thomas Version the Original?" NTS 21 (1974) 142-44. CONZELMANN, H. und LINDEMANN, A., Arbeitsbuch zum Neuen Testament (Tübingen 1975) 82, 88f, 369. HUBAUT, M., "La parabole des vignerons homicides: son authenticité, sa visée première" RThL 6 (1975) 51-61. MARTIN, R. P., New Testament Foundations I (Grand Rapids 1975) 194, 299-305. ROBINSON, J. A. T., "The Parable of the Wicked Husbandmen: A Test of Synoptic Relationships" NTS 21 (1975) 443-61. WILLIAMS, J. A., A Conceptual History of Deuteronomism in the Old Testament, Judaism, and the New Testament (Ph.D.Diss. Louisville 1976)

284-89, 293-94. PESCH, R., Das Markusevangelium II (Freiburg 1977) 223f (lit!). *STRUS, A., "Funkcja obrazu w przekazie biblijnym: obraz winnicy w Iz 5, 1-7 i w Ewangelii" SThV 15 (1977) 25-54. KLAUCK, H.-J., Allegorie und Allegorese in Synoptischen Gleichnistexten (Münster 1978) 286-316. GNILKA, J., Das Evangelium nach Markus II (Einsiedeln/Neukirchen 1979) 141 (lit!). SCHMITHALS, W., Das Evangelium nach Markus (Gütersloh/Würzburg 1979) 512 (lit!). STECK, K. G., in: GPM 33 (1979) 138-47. WEDER, H., Die Gleichnisse Jesu als Metaphern (Göttingen 1980) *(2)*) 147-62.

12:1-11 PIROT, J. Paraboles et Allégories Evangeliques (1949) 376-80. HAUCK, F. ThW (1954) 757, 34f. 749, 22. BÖHLIG, A., "Vom 'Knecht' zum 'Sohn' " in: Mysterion und Wahrheit (Leiden 1968) 60-61. BARCLAY, W. And Jesus Said (1970) 139-45. *HUBAUT, M., La parabole des vignerons homicides (Paris 1976). PERRIN, N., Jesus and the Language of the Kingdom (London 1976) 8, 150, 161. VIELHAUER, Ph., "Oikodome. Das Bild vom Bau in der christlichen Literatur vom Neuen Testament bis Clemens Alexandrinus" in: Oikodome: Aufsätze zum Neuen Testament II (München 1979) 56-58. HARRINGTON, D. J., God's People in Christ (Philadelphia 1980) 98-99.

12:1-9 KüMMEL, W. G. "Das Gleichnis von den Bösen Weingärtnern (Mark 12, 1-9) Aux Sources de la Tradition Chrétienne, ed. M. M. Goguel (1950) 120-31. BAMMEL, E., "Das Gleichnis von den bösen Winzern" Revue Internationale des Droits de l'Antiquité 3/6 (1959) 11-17. GNILKA, J. Die Verstockung Israels (1961) 69f, 73f. HAHN, F. Christologische Hoheitstitel (1963) 315f. BISER, E. Die Gleichnisse Jesu (1965) 137ff. HAHN, F. Das Verständnis der Mission im Neuen Testament (1965) 31, 95. KüMMEL, W. G. Heilsgeschehen und Geschichte (1965) 207-17. WEISER, A. Die Knechtsgleichnisse der synoptischen Evangelien (1971) 49-57. WILSON, S. G., The Gentiles and the Gentile Mission in Luke-Acts (Cambridge 1973) 7f, 23, 29-30. TOLBERT, M. A., Perspectives on the Parables (Philadelphia 1979) 75, 83-89.

12:1-8 DODD, C. H., The Parables of the Kingdom (1948) 124ff.

12:1-2 MONTEFIORE, H., "A Companion to the Parables of the Gospel according to Thomas and of the Synoptic Gospels" NTS 7 (1960-1961) 236f. KONINGS, J., "The Pre-Markan Sequence in Jn 6" in: M. Sabbe (ed.) L'Evangile selon Marc (Gembloux 1974) 172.

12:1   PARKER, P. The Gospel Before Mark (1953) 58-59. LINTON,
        O., "Evidences of a Second Century Revised Edition of St
        Mark's Gospel" NTS 14 (1967-1968) 346f. SCHRAMM, T.
        Der Markus-Stoff bei Lukas (1971) 154-56.

12:5   DERRETT, J. D. M. Law in the New Testament (1970) 287-88.
        VOEGTLE, A. Das Evangelium und die Evangelien (1971)
        209-211.

12:6-8 THRALL, M. E., "Elijah and Moses in Mark's Account of the
        Transfiguration" NTS 16 (1969-1970) 312f.

12:6   HAHN, F. Christologische Hoheitstitel (1963) 281. DUNN, J.
        D. G., Jesus and the Spirit (London 1975) 27, 35f, 38.

12:9-11 HAHN, F. Christologische Hoheitstitel (1963) 72f.

12:9   BLACK, M. An Aramaic Approach to the Gospels and Acts
        (1967) 58f. PESCH, R. Naherwartungen (1969) 39, 72, 93, 108,
        170, 200.

12:10-11 SUHL, A. Die Funktion der alttestamentlichen Zitate und
        Anspielungen im Markusevangelium (1965) 125, 129, 130, 159f.
        DONAHUE, J. R., Are You the Christ? (Missoula 1973) 122-
        25, 134. DORMEYER, D., Die Passion Jesu als
        Verhaltensmodell (Münster 1974) 98, 162. BERGER, K.,
        Exegese des Neuen Testaments (Heidelberg 1977) 61ff.

12:10   HENNECKE, E. und SCHNEEMELCHER, W.,
        Neutestamentliche Apokryphen II (Tübingen 1964) 211.
        SCHRAGE, W. Das Verhältnis des Thomas-Evangeliums zur
        synoptischen Tradition und zu den Koptischen
        Evangelienübersetzungen (1964) 145. GAERTNER, B. The
        Temple and the Community in Qumran and the New
        Testament (1965) 133. PESCH, R. Naherwartungen (1969) 86,
        136, 144, 145, 192. KLINZING, G. Die Umdeutung des Kultus
        in der Qumrangemeinde und im Neuen Testament (1971) 208-
        209. HOFFMANN, P., "Mk 8, 31. Zur Herkunft und
        markinischen Rezeption einer alten Überlieferung" in: P.
        Hoffmann (ed.) Orientierung and Jesus. Für J. Schmid
        (Freiburg 1973) 177f. BLOCH, R., "Midrash" in: W. S. Green
        (ed.) Approaches to Ancient Judaism: Theory and Practice
        (Missoula 1978) 49.

12:12-17 HENGEL, M., Was Jesus a Revolutionist? (Philadelphia 1971)
        33f.

12:12   LIGHTFOOT, R. H., Locality and Doctrine in the Gospels
        (London 1938) 16ff. SCHENKE, L., Studien zur
        Passionsgeschichte des Markus (Würzburg 1971) 56, 58ff.
        DORMEYER, D., Die Passion Jesu als Verhaltensmodell
        (Münster 1974) 68, 72.

12:13ff BORNKAMM, G. Jesus von Nazareth (1956) 110ff.

12:13-13:2 FARRER, A. A Study in St Mark (1951) 122ff.

12:13-44 LAMBRECHT, J. Die Redaktion der Markus-Apokalypse (1967) 44-55.

12:13-40 CARRINGTON, P. The Primitive Christian Calendar (1952) 197-201. GRANT, F. C. The Gospels (1957) 81f.

12:13-17 BAUMBACH, G. Das Verständnis des Bösen in den synoptischen Evangelien (1963) 40ff. HAHN, F. Christologische Hoheitstitel (1963) 164. DAVIES, W. D., The Sermon on the Mount (Cambridge 1966) 97f. SAUNDERS, E. W., Jesus in the Gospels (Englewood Cliffs/N.J. 1967) 226ff. SCHALIT, A. König Herodes (1969) 272. DERRETT, J. D. M. Law in the New Testament (1970) 313-37. *GEORGE, A. "Jésus devant le problème politique" LuVie 20 (105, '71) 5-17. JEREMIAS, J. Neutestamentliche Theologie I (1971) 77, 81, 219f. SCHRAMM, T. Der Markus-Stoff bei Lukas (1971) 168-70. *BREYMAYER, R. "Zur Pragmatik des Bildes. Semiotische Beobachtungen zum Streitgespräch Mk 12, 13-17 ('Der Zinsgroschen') unter Berücksichtigung der Spieltheorie" LiBi 13-14 (-72) 19-51. *STOCK, A., " 'Render to Caesar' " Bible Today 62 (1972) 929-34. FUNK, R. W., Jesus as Precursor (Philadelphia 1975) 82-92. GOPPELT, L., Theologie des Neuen Testaments I (Göttingen 1975) 158, 164. PETZKE, G., "Der historische Jesus in der sozialethischen Diskussion" in: G. Strecker (ed.) Jesus Christus in Historie und Theologie. Für H. Conzelmann (Tübingen 1975) 223-35. TANNEHILL, R. C., The Sword of His Mouth (Philadelphia 1975) 171-77. *GÜTTGEMANNS, E., "Narrative Analyse des Streitgesprächs über den 'Zinsgroschen' " LiBi 41-42 (1977) 88-105. *JASON, H., "Der Zinsgroschen: Analyse der Erzählstruktur" LiBi 41-42 (1977) 49-87. PESCH, R., Das Markusevangelium II (Freiburg 1977) 229 (lit!). *OGLE, A. B., "What is Left for Caesar? A Look at Mark 12:13-17 and Romans 13:1-7" ThT 35 (1978) 254-64. RIVKIN, E., A Hidden Revolution (Nashville 1978) 93f. GNILKA, J., Das Evangelium nach Markus II (Einsiedeln/Neukirchen 1979) 150 (lit!). SCHMITHALS, W., Das Evangelium nach Markus (Gütersloh/Würzburg 1979) 524 (lit!).

12:13-15 HENNECKE, E., und SCHNEEMELCHER, W., Neutestamentliche Apokryphen I (Tübingen 1964) 60.

12:13-14 KONINGS, J., "The Pre-Markan Sequence in Jn VI" in: M. Sabbe (ed.) L'Evangile selon Marc (Gembloux 1974) 172.

12:13　SCHALIT, A. König Herodes (1969) 479. CAVALLIN, H. C. C., Life After Death I (Lund 1974) 6 n.15. BENNETT, W. J., "The Herodians of Mark's Gospel" NovT 17 (1975) 9-14.

12:14-17　SCHRAGE, W. Das Verhältnis des Thomas-Evangeliums zur Synoptischen Tradition und zu den Koptischen Evangelienübersetzungen (1964) 189. DORMEYER, D., Die Passion Jesu als Verhaltensmodell (Münster 1974) 309f. RUDOLPH, K., Die Gnosis (Göttingen 1978) 284.

12:14, 19　BLAIR, E. P. Jesus in the Gospel of Matthew (1960) 100.

12:14　DELLING, G., Römer 13, 1-7 innerhalb der Briefe des Neuen Testaments (Berlin 1962) 13f. HAHN, F. Christologische Hoheitstitel (1963) 76f. BRAUN, H., Qumran und NT II (Tübingen 1966) 162, 213.

12:16-17　ROBINSON, J. M. Das Geschichtsverständnis des Markus-Evangeliums (1956) 65f.

12:16　METZGER, B. M., The Early Versions of the New Testament (Oxford 1977) 435.

12:17-27　NICKELS, P. Targum and New Testament (1967) 25.

12:17　*BEA, A. "'Date a Cesare quel che è di Cesare e a Dio quel che è di Dio'" CiCa 109 (3, '58) 572-83. GOPPELT, L. "Die Freiheit zur Kaisersteuer" Ecclesia und Res Publica (1961) 40-50. SCHRAGE, W. Die konkreten Einzelgebote in der paulinischen Paränese (1961) 225, 243. DELLING, G., Römer 13, 1-7 innerhalb der Briefe des Neuen Testaments (Berlin 1962) 12-17. *SEVENSTER, J. N. "Geeft den keizer wat des keizers is, en Gode wat Gods is" (Render to Caesar the things that are Caesar's and to God the things that are God's) NedThT 17 (1, '62) 21-31. GOPPELT, L., "The Freedom to Pay the Imperial Tax (Mark 12, 17)" in: Studia Evangelica II (1963) 183-94; GT in: G. Kretschmar/B. Lohse (eds.) Ecclesia und Res Publica (Göttingen 1961) 41-50. GOPPELT, L., Christologie und Ethik (1968) 208-19. GOPPELT, L., Theologie des Neuen Testaments I (Göttingen 1975) 157f. BERGER, K., Exegese des Neuen Testaments (Heidelberg 1977) 62f. FRIEDRICH, G., "Das Problem der Autorität im Neuen Testament" in: Auf das Wort kommt es an (Göttingen 1978) 406. Furnish, V. P., The Moral Teaching of Paul (Nashville 1979) 131, 133.

12:18-34　RIVKIN, E., A Hidden Revolution (Nashville 1978) 109-111.

12:18-27　TAYLOR, V. The Formation of the Gospel Tradition (1949) 64f, 179. SCHMID, J. Das Evangelium nach Markus (1958) 227f. *BARTINA, S. "Jesus y los saduceos. El Dios de Abraham, de Isaac y de Jacob's es 'El que hace existir' (Mt 22, 23-33; Mc 12, 18-27; Lc 20, 27-40; Hebr 11, 13-16)" EstBi 21 (2,

'62) 151-60. *ELLIS, E. E. "Jesus, the Sadducees and Qumran" NTS 10 (2, '64) 274-79. BOUSSET, W., Die Religion des Judentums im Späthellenistischen Zeitalter (Berlin 1966=1926) 193. MINETTE DE TILLESSE, G. Le Secret Messianique dans L'Evangile de Marc (1968) 154-56, 160. JEREMIAS, J. Neutestamentliche Theologie I (1971) 180, 217, 235, 237. SCHRAMM, T. Der Markus-Stoff bei Lukas (1971) 170f. *AMMASSARI, A., "Jesù ha veramente insegnato la risurrezione!" BiOr 15 (1973) 65-73. CAVALLIN, H. C. C., Life After Death I (Lund 1974) 1.1.2;3.6.3;5.4.4. GOPPELT, L., Theologie des Neuen Testaments I (Göttingen 1975) 78, 123f, 284. PESCH, R., Das Markusevangelium II (Freiburg 1977) 235f (lit!). STAGG, E. and F., Woman in the World of Jesus (Philadelphia 1978) 132-38, 217. GNILKA, J., Das Evangelium nach Markus II (Einsiedeln/Neukirchen 1979) 156 (lit!). "Auferstehung" in: TRE 4 (1979) 451. SWIDLER, L., Biblical Affirmations of Woman (Philadelphia 1979) 176, 232, 239, 260.

12:18 NÖTSCHER, F., Altorientalischer und alttestamentlicher Auferstehungsglauben (Darmstadt 1970=1926) 189, 271. CAVALLIN, H. C. C., Life After Death I (Lund 1974) 6.2.2.

12:19 HAHN, F. Christologische Hoheitstitel (1963) 76f.

12:20 STRECKER, G. Der Weg der Gerechtigkeit (1962) 39. BLACK, M., An Aramaic Approach to the Gospels and Acts (1967) 58f.

12:24-27 DAALEN, VAN D. H., "Some Observations on Mk 12:24-27" in: Studia Evangelica IV (Berlin 1968) 241-45.

12:24-25 SANFORD, J. A., The Kingdom Within (New York 1970) 209f.

12:24 BLACK, M. An Aramaic Approach to the Gospels and Acts (1967) 57f.

12:25 MOORE, G. F., Judaism II (Cambridge, Mass. 1946) 392. HENNECKE, E. und SCHNEEMELCHER, W., Neutestamentliche Apokryphen II (Tübingen 1964) 92, 100. BRAUN, H., Qumran und NT II (Tübingen 1966) 272. PESCH, R. Naherwartungen (1969) 87, 101, 132, 161, 192. JEREMIAS, J. Neutestamentliche Theologie I (1971) 20, 27, 180, 217. HIERS, R. H., The Historical Jesus and the Kingdom of God (Gainsville 1973) 33f. CAVALLIN, H. C. C., Life After Death I (Lund 1974) 3.2.3.6;7.2 n11. SCHEP, J. A., The Nature of the Resurrection Body (Grand Rapids 1976), 11, 210ff. GERSTENBERGER, E. S. und SCHRAGE, W., Frau und Mann (Stuttgart 1980) 143.

12:26ff BOUSSET, W., Die Religion des Judentums im Späthellenistischen Zeitalter (Berlin 1966=1926) 193, 274.

12:26-27 *DREYFUS, F., "L'argument scripturaire de Jésus en faveur de la résurrection des morts (Marc, XII, 26-27)" RevBi 66 (2, '59) 213-25. CAVALLIN, H. C. C., Life After Death I (Lund 1974) 4.3.1;7.2 n29.

12:26 PARKER, P. The Gospel Before Mark (1953) 90-91. NÖTSCHER, F., Altorientalischer und alttestamentlicher Auferstehungsglauben (Darmstadt 1970=1926) 299. JEREMIAS, J. Neutestamentliche Theologie I (1971) 69, 180, 183, 199. CAVALLIN, H. C. C., Life After Death I (Lund 1974) 7.2 n23.

12:27 JEREMIAS, J. Neutestamentliche Theologie I (1971) 179f.

12:28ff KNOX, W. L. The Sources of the Synoptic Gospels II (1957) 57-58. STROBEL, A. Erkenntnis und Bekenntnis der Sünde in neutestamentlicher Zeit (1968) 40.

12:28-34 MANSON, T. W., The Teaching of Jesus (Cambridge 1945) 260-63. TAYLOR, V. The Formation of the Gospel Tradition (1949) 64f. GOODSPEED, E. J., A Life of Jesus (New York 1950) 177-79. BUTLER, B. C., The Originality of St Matthew (Cambridge 1951) 19ff. BORNKAMM, G. "Das Doppelgebot der Liebe" Neutestamentliche Studien für Rudolf Bultmann zu seinem siebzigsten Geburtstag (1954) 85-93. FUCHS, E. "Was heisst: 'Du sollst deinen Nächsten lieben wie dich selbst'?" Zur Frage nach dem Historischen Jesus (1960) 1-20. BULTMANN, R., The History of the Synoptic Tradition (Oxford 1963) 54f. SCHNEIDER, G. Der Herr unser Gott (1965) 147-50. SUHL, A. Die Funktion der alttestamentlichen Zitate und Anspielungen im Markusevangelium (1965) 10, 87ff. DAVIES, W. D., The Sermon on the Mount (Cambridge 1966) 98f, 146f. JüNGEL, E. Paulus und Jesus (1966) 169. MERKEL, H., "Jesus und die Pharisäer" NTS 14 (1967-1968) 197f. BORNKAMM, G. "Das Doppelgebot der Liebe" Geschichte und Glaube I (1968) 37-45. MINETTE DE TILLESSE, G. Le Secret Messianique dans L'Evangile de Marc (1968) 149-52, 160. BLANK, J. Schriftauslegung in Theorie und Praxis (1969) 133, 221, 222-27. BURCHARD, C., "Das doppelte Liebesgebot" in: E. Lohse et al. (eds.) Der Ruf Jesu und die Antwort der Gemeinde. Für J. Jeremias (Göttingen 1970) 39-62. *ERNST, J. "Die Einheit von Gottes-und Nächstenliebe in der Verkündigung Jesu" ThG 60 (1, '70) 3-14. REICKE, B., "Der barmherzige Samariter" Verborum Veritas, Festschrift für Gustav Stählin zum 70. Geburtstag, eds. O. Böcher und K. Haacker (1970) 103-109. BORNKAMM, G. Geschichte und

Glaube II (1971) 92-94. KUHN, H.-W. "Zum Problem des Verhältnisses der markinischen Redaktion zur israelitisch-jüdischen Tradition" Tradition und Glaube, ed. G. Jeremias, Festschrift G. Kuhn (1971) 301-305. BERGER, K. Die Gesetzesauslegung Jesu (1972) 177-257, 396ff, 582f. FURNISH, V. P. The Love Command in the New Testament (1972) 25-30. McBRIDE, S. D., "The Yoke of the Kingdom. An Exposition of Deuteronomy 6:4-5" Interp 27 (1973) 273-306. *SCHNEIDER, G., "Die Neuheit der christlichen Nächstenliebe" TThZ 82 (1973) 257-75. *BERG, L., "Das neutestamentliche Liebesgebot - Prinzip der Sittlichkeit" TThZ 83 (1974) 129-45. KONINGS, J., "The Pre-Markan Sequence in Jn VI" in: M. Sabbe (ed.) L'Evangile selon Marc (Gembloux 1974) 172. NEIRYNCK, F., "Urmarcus redivivus?" in: M. Sabbe (ed.) L'Evangile selon Marc (Gembloux 1974) 106. NISSEN, A., Gott und der Nächste im antiken Judentum (Tübingen 1974). TALBERT, C. H., Literary Patterns, Theological Themes, and the Genre of Luke-Acts (Missoula 1974) 52, 53. ACHTEMEIER, P. J., Mark (Philadelphia 1975) 19. FULLER, R. H., "Das Doppelgebot der Liebe" in: G. Strecker (ed.) Jesus Christus in Historie und Theologie. Für H. Conzelmann (Tübingen 1975) 317-29; ET: in: Essays on the Love Commandment (Philadelphia 1978) 41-56. GOPPELT, L., Theologie des Neuen Testaments I (Göttingen 1975) 149, 153f. *LAMBIASI, F., "L'Autenticità storica della controversie con i Farisei" BiOr 18 (1976) 3-27. PESCH, R., Das Markusevangelium II (Freiburg 1977) 249 (lit!). *DIEZINGER, W., "Zum Liebesgebot Mk xii, 28-34 und Parr" NovT 20 (1978) 81-83. GNILKA, J., Das Evangelium nach Markus II (Einsiedeln/Neukirchen 1979) 162 (lit!). KLEIN, G. in: GPM 33 (1979) 389-96. SCHMITHALS, W., Das Evangelium nach Markus (Gütersloh/Würzburg 1979) 539 (lit!).

12:28-31 SIMPSON, R. T., "The Major Agreements of Matthew and Luke Against Mark" NTS 12 (1965-1966) 279f.

12:28 SCHRAGE, W. Die konkreten Einzelgebote in der paulinischen Paränese (1961) 255. *LOHFINK, N. "Das Hauptgebot im Alten Testament" GuL 36 (4, '63) 271-81. BOUSSET, W., Die Religion des Judentums im Späthellenistischen Zeitalter (Berlin 1966=1926) 138. DAVIES, W. D., The Sermon on the Mount (Cambridge 1966) 116f. KOCH, D.-A., Die Bedeutung der Wundererzählungen für die Christologie des Markusevangeliums (Berlin 1975) 173-75.

12:29-31 *NISSEN, A., Gott und der Nächste im antiken Judentum (Tübingen 1974).

12:29 HAHN, F. Christologische Hoheitstitel (1963) 72.

12:30-31 SCHRAGE, W. Die konkreten Einzelgebote in der paulinischen Paränese (1961) 49, 59, 243. JüNGEL, E. Paulus und Jesus (1966) 210f.

12:31 MONTEFIORE, H. "Thou Shalt Love the Neighbour as Thyself" Donum Gratulatorium (1962) 157-70. SCHRAGE, W. Das Verhältnis des Thomas-Evangeliums zu Synoptischen Tradition und zu den Koptischen Evangelienübersetzungen (1964) 70. BRAUN, H., Qumran und NT II (Tübingen 1966) 87, 96, 287, 290, 295.

12:32-34 DERRETT, J. D. M., "Law in the New Testament: Fresh Light on the Parable of the Good Samaritan" NTS 11 (1964-1965) 34f. MEYER, B. F., The Aims of Jesus (London 1979) 151. AMBROZIC, A. M., St Mark's Concept of the Kingdom of God (Würzburg 1970) 190-94. MALBON, E. S., "Mythic Structure and Meaning in Mark" Semeia 16 (1980) 109-13.

12:32 HAHN, F. Christologische Hoheitstitel (1963) 76, 77.

12:34 STRECKER, G. Der Weg der Gerechtigkeit (1962) 92. JüNGEL, E. Paulus und Jesus (1966) 211. MINETTE DE TILLESSE, G. Le Secret Messianique dans L'Evangile de Marc (1968) 390-94. BULTMANN, R., Theologie des Neuen Testaments (Tübingen 1965) 29f, 52.

12:35ff HAHN, F. Christologische Hoheitstitel (1963) 91, 106, 115, 117, 240, 291. BORSCH, F. H. The Son of Man in Myth and History (1967) 394-97.

12:35-37, 38-40 BULTMANN, R., The History of the Synoptic Tradition (Oxford 1963) 113f, 136f.

12:35-37 MOORE, G. F., Judaism II (Cambridge, Mass. 1946) 336. GRANT, F. C. The Gospels (1957) 99f. HAHN, F. Christologische Hoheitstitel (1963) 86, 88, 113-15, 191, 192, 259-62. FLENDER H. Heil und Geschichte in der Theologie des Lukas (1965) 41-42. SUHL, A. Die Funktion der alttestamentlichen Zitate und Anspielungen im Markusevangelium (1965) 53, 55, 89ff, 110. MINETTE DE TILLESSE, G. Le Secret Messianique dans L'Evangile de Marc (1968) 156-57, 331-33. BLANK, J. Schriftauslegung in Theorie und Praxis (1969) 221, 227-31. BURGER, C. Jesus als Davidssohn (1970) 52-59, 64-70. FITZMYER, J. A. Essays on the Semitic Background of the New Testament (1971) 113-26. WEINACHT, H. Die Menschwerdung die Sohnes Gottes im Markusevangelium (1972) 134f. SCHNEIDER, G. "Die Davidssohnfrage (Mk 12, 35-37)" Biblica 53 (1, '72) 65-90. *LÖVESTAM, E., "Die Davidssohnfrage" SEA 27 (1962) 72-82. BRAUN, H., Qumran und NT II (Tübingen 1966) 65, 76,

308, 313. LANGE, J., Das Erscheinen des Auferstandenen im Evangelium nach Matthäus (Würzburg 1973) 228, 230, 232, 236-38. SAND, A., Das Gesetz und die Propheten (Regensburg 1974) 147-49. ACHTEMEIER, P. J., Mark (Philadelphia 1975) 43. CONZELMANN, H. und LINDEMANN, A., Arbeitsbuch zum Neuen Testament (Tübingen 1975) 367. DUNN, J. D. G., Unity and Diversity in the New Testament (London 1977) 42, 51f. PESCH, R., Das Markusevangelium II (Freiburg 1977) 256f (lit!). FRIEDRICH, G., "Beobachtungen zur messianischen Hohepriestererwartung in den Synoptikern" in: Auf das Wort kommt es an (Göttingen 1978) 77-80. RIVKIN, E., A Hidden Revolution (Nashville 1978) 107. GNILKA, J., Das Evangelium nach Markus II (Einsiedeln/Neukirchen 1979) 168 (lit!). *MORICONI, B., "Chi è Gesù? Mc 12, 35-37 momento culminante di rivelazione" EphC 30 (1979) 23-51. SCHMITHALS, W., Das Evangelium nach Markus (Gütersloh/Würzburg 1979) 547 (lit!).

12:35   HAHN, F. Christologische Hoheitstitel (1963) 76, 230, 245. DORMEYER, D., Die Passion Jesu als Verhaltensmodell (Münster 1974) 142.

12:36   BARRETT, C. K., The Holy Spirit and the Gospel Tradition (New York 1947) 107-12. YATES, J. E., The Spirit and the Kingdom (London 1963) 85ff. HAHN, F. Christologische Hoheitstitel (1963) 114, 131. SHIMADA, K., The Formulary Material in First Peter (Th.D. Diss. Union Theological Seminary, New York, Ann Arbor 1966) 386-93. JEREMIAS, J. Neutestamentliche Theologie (1971) 20f, 85, 199. LINDEMANN, A., Die Aufhebung der Zeit (Gütersloh 1975) 82f, 207. LONGENECKER, R. N., Biblical Exegesis in the Apostolic Period (Grand Rapids 1975) 57, 61, 73, 167, 178-80. HORTON, F. L., The Melchizedek Tradition (London 1976) 23f.

12:37-40   BUTLER, B. C., The Originality of St Matthew (Cambridge 1951) 73ff.

12:37   SEEBERG, A. Der Katechismus der Urchristenheit (1966) 72f, 78.

12:38ff   STROBEL, A. Erkenntnis und Bekenntnis der Sünde in neutestamentlicher Zeit (1968) 40.

12:38-42   KOCH, D.-A., Die Bedeutung der Wundererzählungen für die Christologie des Markusevangeliums (Berlin/New York 1975) 155-57.

12:38-40   PESCH, R., Das Markusevangelium II (Freiburg 1977) 260 (lit!). RIVKIN, E., A Hidden Revolution (Nashville 1978) 107, 121f. GNILKA, J., Das Evangelium nach Markus

(Einsiedeln/Neukirchen 1979) 173 (lit!). SWIDLER, L., Biblical Affirmations of Woman (Philadelphia 1979) 184, 232, 256.

12:38 RENGSTORF, K. H. "Die ΣΤΟΛΑΙ der Schriftgelehrten. Eine Erläuterung zu Mark 12, 38" Abraham unser Vater (1963) 383-404. HAHN, F. Christologische Hoheitstitel (1963) 113.

12:40-44 STAGG, E./F., Woman in the World of Jesus (Philadelphia 1978) 211f.

12:40 *DERRETT, J. D. M. " 'Eating up the Houses of Widows': Jesus's Comment on Lawyers?" NovTest 14 (1, '72) 1-9.

12:41ff DALMAN, G. Orte und Wege Jesu (1967) 315f.

12:41-44 STAEMMLER, W. GPM 11, 223-227. FRIEDRICH, G. GPM 13, 218-21. TAYLOR, V. The Formation of the Gospel Tradition (1949) 72f. IWAND, H.-J.- Predigt-Meditationen (1964) 38-41. FISCHER GPM 1964/5 311ff. KLAAS, W. Herr, tue meine Lippen auf ed. G. Eichholz (1964) 387ff. SCHMITZ, E. D. Hören und Fragen, ed. G. Eicholz und A. Falkenroth (1967) 444ff. *SIMON, L. "Le sou de la veuve. Marc 12/41-44" EThR (2, '69) 115-26. SCHOENHERR, A. GPM 25 (1971) 360-66. LANGE, E. (ed.) Predigtstudien für das Kirchenjahr 1970/71 (1971) 187-91. *LEE, G. M. "The Story of the Widow's Mite" ET 82 (11, '71) 344. BULTMANN, R., The History of the Synoptic Tradition (Oxford 1963) 32f. WEST, H. P., "A Primitive Version of Luke in the Composition of Matthew" NTS 14 (1967-68) 80f. PESCH, R., "Die Salbung Jesu in Bethanien (Mk 14, 3-9)" in: P. Hoffmann (ed.) Orientierung and Jesus. Für J. Schmid (Freiburg 1973). 274f. HARTMANN, G. und RÜCK, H., in: P. Krusche (ed.) Predigtstudien V/2 (Stuttgart 1977) 175-82. PESCH, R., Das Markusevangelium II (Freiburg 1977) 264 (lit!). SANDMEL, S., We Jews and Jesus (New York 1977) 125. GNILKA, J., Das Evangelium nach Markus II (Einsiedeln/Neukirchen 1979) 175 (lit!). SWIDLER, L., Biblical Affirmations of Woman (Philadelphia 1979) 180, 183, 232, 256. CASPARI, H.-N. und KRAUS, M., in: P. Krusche (ed.) Predigtstudien III/1 (Stuttgart 1980) 148-57.

12:42 SPERBER, D. "Mark xii 42 and its metrological background. A Study in ancient Syriac versions" NovTest 9 (3, '67) 178-90.

12:43 HASLER, V. Amen (1969) 44.

12:44 PESCH, R. Naherwartungen (1969) 53, 54, 64, 65, 69, 71.

13 EWALD, H., Die drei ersten Evangelien (Göttingen 1850) 330ff. MANSON, T. W., The Teaching of Jesus (Cambridge 1945) 260-63. KLOSTERMANN, E. Das Markusevangelium (1950) 131f. LIGHTFOOT, R. H. The Gospel Message of St Mark (1950) 48-59. LIGHTFOOT, R. H. "The Connexion of Chapter Thirteen With the Passion Narrative" The Gospel Message of St Mark (1950) 48-59. STREETER, B. H. The Four Gospels (1951) 491ff. TAYLOR, V. The Gospel According to St Mark (1953) 636-44. *BEASLEY-MURRAY, G. R., "The Rise and Fall of the Little Apocalypse Theory" ET 64 (('11, '53) 346-49. BEASLEY-MURRAY, G. R. Jesus and the Future (1954). ++*SCHATTENMANN, J. "The Little Apocalypse of the Synoptics and the First Epistle of Peter" ThT XI 2 (1954) 193-98. *CRANFIELD, C. E. B. "St Mark 12" SJTh 7 (1954) 224-303. ++Rev. M. Scharlemann CTM 27 ('56) 64. BORNKAMM, G. Jesus von Nazareth (1956) 85ff. BEASLEY-MURRAY, G. R. A Commentary on Mark Thirteen (1957). GRANT, F. C. The Gospels (1957) 100f. GILS, F., Jésus Prophète D'Après Les Evangiles Synoptiques (Louvain 1957) 127-33. *MUSSNER, F. Was lehrt Jesus über das Ende der Welt? Eine Auslegung von Markus 13 (1958). BOSCH, D. Die Heidenmission in der Zukunftsschau Jesu (1959) 149-53. JEREMIAS, J. Die Abendmahlsworte Jesu (1960) 84-86. NEVILLE, G. The Advent Hope (1961). PERRIN, N., The Kingdom of God in the Teaching of Jesus (Philadelphia 1963) 130f, 133f, 199. YATES, J. E., The Spirit and the Kingdom (London 1963) 154-61. HENNECKE, E./SCHNEEMELCHER, W., Neutestamentliche Apokryphen II (Tübingen 1964) 434ff. *MUSSNER, F. Was lehrt Jesus über das Ende der Welt? 2nd ed. (1964). *LAMBRECHT, J. "Redactio Sermonis Eshatologici" VerbDom 43 (6, '65) 278-87. SUHL, A. Die Funktion der alttestamentlichen Zitate und Anspielungen im Markusevangelium (1965) 16ff, 152ff. MUSSNER, F., Christ and the End of the World (Notre Dame/Indiana 1965). BOUSSET, W., Die Religion des Judentums im Späthellenistischen Zeitalter (Berlin 1966=1926) 264. BRAUN, H., Qumran und NT II (Tübingen 1966) 90f, 238, 241, 270, 274. HERMANN, I., "Die Gefährdung der Welt und ihre Erneuerung" BiLe 7 (1966) 305-309. *HARTMAN, L. Prophecy Interpretated. The Formation of Some Jewish Apocalyptic Texts and of the Eschatological Discourse Mark 13 par (1966). *LAMBRECHT, J. "Die Logia-Quellen von Markus 13" Biblica 47 (3, '66) 321-60. *WALTER, N. "Tempelzerstörung und synoptische Apokalypse" ZNW 57 (1-

2, '66) 38-49. *HOWARD, J. K. "Our Lord's Teaching Concerning His Parousia: A Study in the Gospel of Mark" EQ 38 (3, '66) 150-57. JüNGEL, E. Paulus und Jesus (1966) 243. LAMBRECHT, J. "La structure de Marc XIII" De Jésus aux Evangiles, ed. I. de la Potterie (1, '67) 141-64. *LAMBRECHT, J. Die Redaktion der Markus-Apokalypse. Literarische Analyse und Struckturuntersuchung (1967). ERNST, J. Die Eschatologischen Gegenspieler in den Schriften des Neuen Testaments (1967) 3-23. HOOKER, M. D. The Son of Man in Mark (1967) 148-59, 166, 171. SCHREIBER, J. Theologie des Vertrauens (1967) 86, 91, 120-23, 126-29, 131f, 141, 154, 207. LAMBRECHT, J., Die Redaktion der Markus-Apokalypse (Rome 1967). LAMBRECHT, J., "La structure de Mk 13" in: I. de la Potterie (ed.) De Jesus aux Evangelium Tradition et Rédaction (Gembloux 1967) 141-64. GREENLEE, J. H., Nine Uncial Palimpsests of the Greek New Testament (Salt Lake City 1968) 30-32. REUMANN, J., Jesus in the Church's Gospel (Philadelphia 1968) 300-305. *PESCH, R. Naherwartungen (1968). MINETTE DE TILLESSE, G. Le Secret Messianique dans L'Evangile de Marc (1968) 372-73, 420-38. *NEIRYNCK, F. "Le discours anti-apocalyptique de Mc., XIII" EphT 45 (1, '69) 154-64. *GNILKA, J. "Markus 13 in der Diskussion" BZ 13 (1, '69) 129-34. *LEGASSE, S. "Le Discours eschatologique de Marc d'après trois ouvrages récents" BLE 71 (4, '70) 241-61. MARXSEN, W. Mark the Evangelist (1969) 151-206. SCHREINER, J. Gestalt und Anspruch des Neuen Testaments (1969) 15, 161, 320ff, 322ff. Reviews: Pesch, R. Naherwartungen, HARTMAN, L. Biblical 50 (4, '69) 576-80: SCHWEIZER, E., "Eschatology in Mark's Gospel" in: E. E. Ellis/M. Wilcox (eds.) Neotestamentica et Semitica. In Honour of M. Black (Edinburgh 1969) 114-17. STRECKER, G. ThLZ 95 (4, '70) 274-75; ELLIOTT, J. H. CBQ 31 (1, '69) 119-21; LAMBRECHT, J. ThRv 65 (6, '69) 457-59; *FLÜCKIGER, F. "Die Redaktion der Zukunftsrede in Mark 13" ThZ 26 (6, '70) 395-409. SNOY, T. RBen 80 (1-2, '70) 175-77. GUETTGEMANNS E. Offene Fragen zu Formsgeschichte des Evangeliums (1970) 101, 102, 102n, 124, 231. GASTON, L. No Stone on Another (1970) 6, 65, 357, 430, 433, 447, 448, 453, 477. WEEDEN, T. J., Mark - Traditions in Conflict (1971) 73-100. WEINACHT, H. Die Menschwerdung des Sohnes Gottes im Markusevangelium (1972) 98-110. *GLASSON, T. F. "Mark xiii and the Greek Old Testament" ET 69 (7, '58) 213-15. PERROT, C. 'Essai sur le Discours eschatologique (Mc. XIII, 1-37; Mt. XXIVml-36; Lk. XXI, 5-36)" RechSr 47 (4, '59) 481-514. HAHN, F. Christologische Hoheitstitel (1963) 39, 107,

181. CONZELMANN, H. "Geschichte und Eschaton nach Mc 13" ZNW 50 (3-4, '59) 210-21. *BEASLEY-MURRAY, "The Eschatological Discourse of Jesus" RevExp 57 (2, '60) 153-66. *BLIGH, J. "Eschatology and Social Doctrine" HeyJ 3 (3, '62) 262-67. HAHN, F. Das Verständnis der Mission im Neuen Testament (1965) 46, 58f, 96, 99f. KELBER, W. H., "The History of the Kingdom in Mark - Aspects of Markan Eschatology" in: L. C. McGaughy (ed.) Proceedings. SBL Meeting 1972. Vol. 1 (Montana) 63-95 (80-82). SCHROEDER, H.-H., Eltern und Kinder in der Verkündigung Jesu (Hamburg-Bergstedt 1972) 137-39. KOLENKOW, A. B., "Beyond Miracles, Suffering and Eschatology" in: G. MacRae (ed.) SBL 1973 Seminar Papers II (Cambridge/Mass. 1973) 172-83. KÜMMEL, W. G., Einleitung in das Neue Testament (Heidelberg 1973 *(17)*) 103f. CONZELMANN, H., Theologie als Schriftauslegung (München 1974) 44A. 1, 54A.1, 61-73, 76A.7, 81f. FENEBERG, W., Der Markusprolog (München 1974) 125, 133f. GRAYSTON, K., "The Study of Mark XIII" BJRL 56 (1974) 371-87. LADD, G. E., The Presence of the Future (Grand Rapids 1974) 307ff. LADD, G. E., A Theology of the New Testament (Grand Rapids 1974) 196, 201, 299. *LANGKAMMER, H., "Paruzja syna człowieczego (Mk 13)" RTK 21 (1974) 61-74. ACHTEMEIER, P. J., Mark (Philadelphia 1975) 55, 102-110, 115-17. GOPPELT, L., Theologie des Neuen Testaments I (Göttingen 1975) 108f. HAHN, F., "Die Rede von der Parusie des Menschensohnes. Markus 13" in: R. Pesch/R. Schnackenburg (eds.) Jesus und der Menschensohn (Freiburg 1975) 240-66. LAWS, S., "Can Apocalyptic be Relevant? in: M. Hooker/C. Hickling (eds.) What about the New Testament? Essays in Honour of C. F. Evans (London 1975) 96-101. RESENHÖFFT, W., Der Tag des Menschensohnes (Bern 1975). *ROUSSEAU, F., "La structure de Marc 13" Biblica 56 (1975) 157-72. SANDERS, J. T., Ethics in the New Testament (Philadelphia 1975) 33-36. VIA, D. A., Kerygma and Comedy in the New Testament (Philadelphia 1975) 82, 118f, 150f. *WENHAM, D., "Recent Study of Mark 13" TSFBulletin (London) 71 (1975) 6-15; 72 (1975) 1-9. PERRIN, N., Jesus and the Language of the Kingdom (London 1976) 59f. BERGER, K., Exegese des Neuen Testaments (Heidelberg 1977) 209f. *COMBET-GALLAND, C., "Marc 13. Les saisons du monde" Foi et Vie 76 (1977) 45-66. DUNN, J. D. G., Unity and Diversity in the New Testament (London 1977) 328-31. N. N., Apocalypses et théologie de l'espérance. Congrès de Toulouse 1975 (Paris 1977). PESCH, R., Das Markusevangelium II (Freiburg 1977)

267f (lit!). *TAGAWA, K., "Marc 13. La tâtonnement d'un homme réaliste éveillé face á la tradition apocalyptique" Foi et Vie 76 (1977) 11-44. "Apokalyptik" in: TRE 3 (1978) 253. CLEVENOT, M., So kennen wir die Bibel nicht (München 1978) 98f. COURT, J. M., Myth and History in the Book of Revelation (London 1979) 49-54. GNILKA, J., Das Evangelium nach Markus II (Einsiedeln/Neukirchen 1979) (lit!). ROBINSON, J. M., "Geschichte seit dem Jahr 30 n.Chr. im Markus-Evangelium" [orig. Das Geschichtsverständnis des Markus-Evangeliums, 1956, 82-102] in: R. Pesch (ed.) Das Markus-Evangelium (Darmstadt 1979) 123-27. SCHMITHALS, W., Das Evangelium nach Markus (Gütersloh/Würzburg 1979) 556f (lit!). WEEDEN, T. J., "Die Häresie, die Markus zur Abfassung seines Evangeliums veranlasst hat" [orig. "The Heresy that necessitated Mark's Gospel" ZNW 59, 1968, 145-58] in: R. Pesch (ed.) Das Markus-Evangelium (Darmstadt 1979) 244-53. KELBER, W. H., "Mark and Oral Tradition" Semeia 16 (1980) 40f. McDONALD, J. I. H., Kerygma and Didache (Cambridge 1980) 87, 116f. MALBON, E. S., "Mythic Structure and Meaning in Mark" Semeia 16 (1980) 113-16. NEIRYNCK, F., "Marc 13. Examen critique de l'interprétation de R. Pesch" in: J. Lambrecht (ed.) L'Apocalypse johannique et l'Apocalyptique dans le Nouveau Testament (Gembloux 1980) 369-401. PESCH, R., "Markus 13" in: J. Lambrecht (ed.) L'Apocalypse johannique et l'Apocalyptique dans le Nouveau Testament (Gembloux 1980) 355-68.

13:1ff   ROBINSON, J. M. Das Geschichtsverständnis des Markus-Evangeliums (1956) 91ff.

13:1-37   KNOX, W. L., The Sources of the Synoptic Gospels (1953) I, 103ff. *HARTMAN, L. Prophecy Interpreted (1966) -Reviews: FITZMYER, J. Interpretation 23 (2, '69) 249-51; HOLTZ, T. ThLZ 92 (12, '67) 910-12; HOOKER, M. D. JThS 19 (1, '68) 263-65. *LAMBRECHT, J. "Die'Midrasch-Quelle' von Mk 13" Biblica 49 (2, '68) 254-70; Rev. R. Pesch, ThRv 64 (1, '68) 25-27. *LAMBRECHT, J. Die Redaktion der Markus-Apokalypse (1967). Rev. E. Grässer ThLZ 94 (2, '69) 117-19; Elliott, J. H. CBQ 30 (2, '68) 267-69; Hartman, L. Biblica 49 (1, '68) 130-33; SNOY, T. RBen 78 (1-2, '68) 153-56. ZIMMERMANN, W.-D. Markus über Jesus (1970) 140-45. SCHRAMM, T. Der Markus-Stoff bei Lukas (1971) 171-82. JEREMIAS, J. New Testament Theology I (1971) 38, 123ff. KELBER, W. H. "The History of the Kingdom in Mark — Aspects of Markan Eschatology" Proceedings I (1972) ed. L. C. McGaughy, 63-95.

13:1-31 CARRINGTON, P. The Primitive Christian Calendar (1952) 202, 206-210.

13:1-27 LOHSE, E., Die Einheit des Neuen Testaments (Göttingen 1973) 138-40. LOHSE, E., Grundriss der neutestamentlichen Theologie (Stuttgart 1974) 60f, 118.

13:1-5 PESCH, R. Naherwartungen (1969) 83-107.

13:1-4 BRANDON, S. G. F., "The Date of the Markan Gospel" NTS 7 (1960-61) 133f. YATES, J. E., The Spirit and the Kingdom (London 1963) 154ff. ERNST, J. Die Eschatologischen Gegenspieler in den Schriften des Neuen Testaments (1967) 4-5. LAMBRECHT, J. Die Redaktion der Markus-Apokalypse (1967) 68-91. MARXSEN, W. Mark the Evangelist (1969) 170, 191. GASTON, L. No Stone on Another (1970) 10-13, 66. CONZELMANN, H., Theologie als Schriftauslegung (München 1974) 64-67. GNILKA, J., Das Evangelium nach Markus II (Einsiedeln/Neukirchen 1979) 181 (lit!).

13:1-2 BOUSSET, W., Die Religion des Judentums im Späthellenistischen Zeitalter (Berlin 1966=1926) 112. MARXSEN, W. Mark the Evangelist (1969) 162, 167, 169. GEIGER, R., Die Lukanischen Endzeitreden (Bern 1973) 161f. HIERS, R. H., The Historical Jesus and the Kingdom of God (Gainsville/Florida 1973) 91-94. PESCH, R., Das Markusevangelium II (Freiburg 1977) 273 (lit!). VIELHAUER, Ph., "Oikodome. Das Bild vom Bau in der christlichen Literatur vom Neuen Testament bis Clemens Alexandrinus" in: Oikodome. Neutestamentliche Aufsätze II (München 1979) 59, 64-66.

13:1 HAHN, F. Christologische Hoheitstitel (1963) 76, 77. HARTMAN, L., Testimonium Linguae (Lund 1963) 21f. CONZELMANN, H. Die Mitte der Zeit (1964) 70ff. PRYKE, E. J., "IΛΕ and IΛOY" NTS 14 (1967-68) 418f. PETZKE, G., Die Traditionen über Apollonius von Tyana und das Neue Testament (Leiden 1970) 117, 174. DORMEYER, D., Die Passion Jesu als Verhaltensmodell (Münster 1974) 66 A.36, 67 A.39, 72. VIELHAUER, Ph., "Oikodome. Das Bild vom Bau in der christlichen Literatur vom Neuen Testament bis Clemens Alexandrinus" in: Oikodome. Neutestamentliche Aufsätze II (München 1979) 54.

13:2-3 MARXSEN, W. Mark the Evangelist (1969) 154, 162f, 167, 194, 202.

13:2 KUEMMEL, W. G. Verheissung und Erfüllung (1953) 92-95. FLEW, R. N. Jesus and His Church (1956) 40-42. HAHN, F. Christologische Hoheitstitel (1963) 176. HAHN, F. Das Verständnis der Mission im Neuen Testament (1965) 29f, 95,

99f. BRAUN, H., Qumran und NT II (Tübingen 1966) 101, 133, 157f, 183, 221, 278, 288, 293, 295, 326. JUENGEL, E. Paulus und Jesus (1966) 238. MARXSEN, W. Mark the Evangelist (1969) 154, 158, 162, 166ff, 180f, 192. *GASTON, L. No Stone on Another (1970) 24, 46, 64, 65, 66, 72, 73, 242, 244, 365, 424, 479. DUPONT, J. "Il n'en sera pass laissé sur pierre (Marc 13, 2; Lc 19, 44), Biblica 52 (3, '71) 301-20. DORMEYER, D., Die Passion Jesu als Verhaltensmodell (Münster 1974) 159f. WILLIAMS, J. A., A Conceptual History of Deuteronomism in the Old Testament, Judaism, and the New Testament (Ph.D.Diss. Southern Baptist Theological Seminary, Louisville 1976) 294f, 297f.

13:3-37   LIGHTFOOT, R. H. History and Interpretation in the Gospels (1934) 80f, 94ff. GOODSPEED, E. J., A Life of Jesus (New York 1950) 186-88. FARRER, A. A Study in St Mark (1951) 127ff, 164ff, 284f, 360ff.

13:3-8   GEIGER, R., Die Lukanischen Endzeitreden (Bern 1973) 165-67.

13:3-4   MARXSEN, W. Mark the Evangelist (1969) 169, 172. PESCH, R., Das Markusevangelium II (Freiburg 1977) 277 (lit!)

13:3   HAHN, F. Christologische Hoheitstitel (1963) 339. HARTMAN, L., Testimonium Linguae (Lund 1963) 34ff. MAUSER, U. Christ in the Wilderness (1963) 108f, 124, 119f, 139, 141f. MINETTE DE TILLESSE, G. Le Secret Messianique dans L'Evangile de Marc (1968) 238-42. WILCOX, M., "The Denial-Sequence in Mark 14:26-31, 66-72" NTS 17 (1970-71) 430f. DORMEYER, D., Die Passion Jesu als Verhaltensmodell (Münster 1974) 66 A.36, 67 A.39, 72, 110, 113 A.314. ERNST, J., "Die Petrustradition im Markusevangelium - ein altes Problem neu angegangen" in: J.Zmijewski/E. Nellessen (eds.) Begegnung mit dem Wort. Für H. Zimmermann (Bonn 1980) 54f. MALBON, E. S., "Mythic Structure and Meaning in Mark" Semeia 16 (1980) 103-107.

13:4-37   MOORE, G. F., Judaism II (Cambridge/Mass. 1946) 310.

13:4   HAHN, F. Christologische Hoheitstitel (1963) 76. SCHREIBER J. Theologie des Vertrauens (1967) 128f. MARXSEN, W. Mark the Evangelist (1969) 162, 166, 168f, 179f, 186f. LADD, G. E., A Theology of the New Testament (Grand Rapids 1974) 196, 198, 201. KLIJN, A. F. J., "Die syrische Baruch-Apokalypse" in: W. G. Kümmel (ed.) Jüdische Schriften aus hellenistisch-römischer Zeit V (Gütersloh 1976) 139.

13:5-37   BUTLER, B. C., The Originality of the St Matthew (Cambridge 1951) 76ff. SMITH, M., Tannaitic Parallels to the

Gospels (Philadelphia 1968) 4 H+. KELBER, W. H., "Mark and Oral Tradition" Semeia 16 (1980) 43.

13:5-27 JUENGEL, E. Paulus und Jesus (1966) 24f.

13:5-22 DORMEYER, D., Die Passion Jesu als Verhaltensmodell (Münster 1974) 85 A. 142.

13:5-13 ERNST, J. Die Eschatologischen Gegenspieler in den Schriften des Neuen Testaments (1967) 5-8. MARXSEN, W. Mark the Evangelist (1969) 171, 178f, 184, 202.

13:5-8 HARTMAN, L. Prophecy interpreted (1966) 147-50, 159-62. LAMBRECHT, J. Die Redaktion der Markus-Apokalypse (1967) 91-114. GASTON, L. No Stone on Another (1970) 13-16, 37, 62. CONZELMANN, H., Theologie als Schriftauslegung (München 1974) 69f. PESCH, R., Das Markusevangelium II (Freiburg 1977) 282 (lit!).

13:5-6 KECK, L. E., "The Introduction to Mark's Gospel" NTS 12 (1965-66) 365f. MARXSEN, W. Mark the Evangelist (1969) 161f, 171f. KELBER, W. H., "Mark and Oral Tradition" Semeia 16 (1980) 40f.

13:5 MARXSEN, W. Mark the Evangelist (1969) 166, 170, 178.

13:6 MASSAUX, E. Influence de l'Evangile de saint Matthieu sur la littérature chrétienne avant saint Irénée (1950) 514-16. DELLING, G. Die Zueignung des Heils in der Taufe (1961) 40, 43, 51, 92. HAHN, F. Christologische Hoheitstitel (1963) 182. MARXSEN, W. Mark the Evangelist (1969) 158, 173, 185. HOWARD, V. P., Das Ego in den Synoptischen Evangelien (Marburg 1975) 116-23. "Antichrist" in: TRE 3 (1978) 22.

13:7-20 GOULDER, M. D., Type and History in Acts (London 1964) 112-17.

13:7-8 HAHN, F. Das Verständnis der Mission im Neuen Testament (1965) 61f, 95.

13:7 HAHN, F. Christologische Hoheitstitel (1963) 186. JÜNGEL E. Paulus und Jesus (1966) 244. MARXSEN, W. Mark the Evangelist (1969) 159, 161, 166, 172f, 176, 178, 191, 197. KEE, H. C., "The Function of Scriptural Quotations and Allusions in Mark 11-16" in: E. E. Ellis/E. Grässer (eds.) Jesus und Paulus. Für W. G. Kümmel (Göttingen 1975) 168, 173ff.

13:8-12 MARXSEN, W. Mark the Evangelist (1969) 173.

13:8 BOSCH, D. Die Heidenmission in der Zukunftsschau Jesu (19-59) 150-52. JUENGEL, E. Paulus und Jesus (1966) 244. MARXSEN, W. Mark the Evangelist (1969) 41, 159, 161, 166, 172f, 176, 191. KLIJN, A. F. J., "Die syrische Baruch-Apokalypse" in: W. G. Kümmel (ed.) Jüdische Schriften aus

hellenistisch-römischer Zeit V (Gütersloh 1976) 140.
MÜLLER, U. B., "Die griechische Esra-Apokalypse" in: W. G.
Kümmel (ed.) Jüdische Schriften aus hellenistisch-römischer
Zeit V (Gütersloh 1976) 94.

13:9ff HAHN, F. Christologische Hoheitstitel (1963) 107, 168.
YATES, J. E., The Spirit and the Kingdom (London 1963) 15f,
38ff, 96ff, 100f, 157ff, 184f. KUENZI, M. Das
Naherwartungslogion Matthäus 10, 23 (1970) 7, 96, 102, 122,
142, 158.

13:9-13 BULTMANN, R., The History of the Synoptic Tradition
(Oxford 1963) 122f. HAHN, F. Das Verständnis der Mission
im Neuen Testament (1965) 44, 63. HARTMAN, L. Prophecy
interpreted (1966) 150-51, 167-69. LAMBRECHT, J. Die
Redaktion der Markus-Apokalypse (1967) 114-44.
SCHREIBER, J. Theologie des Vertrauens (1967) 131f.
PESCH, R. Naherwartungen (1969) 125-38. GASTON, L. No
Stone on Another (1970) 16-23. DONAHU, J. R., Are you the
Christ? (Missoula 1973) 212-22. GEIGER, R., Die
Lukanischen Endzeitreden (Bern 1973) 172-79.
CONZELMANN, H., Theologie als Schriftauslegung
(München 1974) 63, A. 7, 70f. DORMEYER, D., Die Passion
Jesu als Verhaltsmodell (Münster 1974) 173A.651; 191;
254A.57. PESCH, R., Das Markusevangelium II (Freiburg
1977) 289 (lit!). TRITES, A. A., The New Testament Concept
of Witness (Cambridge 1977) 183-85.

13:9-11 *KILPATRICK, G. D. "The Gentile Mission in Mark and Mk
13:9-11" Studies in the Gospels (1955) 145-58. BEASLEY-
MURRAY, G. R. Jesus and the Future (1954) 197, 252-55.
RICHARDSON, P., Israel in the Apostolic Church (London
1969) 67f, 168ff. DUPONT, J., "La persécution comme
situation missionaire (Marc 13:9-11)" in: R. Schnackenburg et
al. (eds.) Die Kirche des Anfangs. Für H. Schürmann (Leipzig
1977) 97-114.

13:9-10 *KILPATRICK, G. D. "Mark XIII 9-10" JThS 9 (1, '58) 81-86.

13:9 BOSCH, D. Die Heidenmission in der Zukunfsschau Jesu
(1959) 155-57, 159-61. BROX, N. Zeuge und Märtyrer (1961)
28f. SCHREIBER, J. Theologie des Vertrauens (1967) 91, 173-
83. DANKER, F. W. "Double entendre in Mark XIII 9"
NovTest 10 (2-3, '68) 162-63. MARXSEN, W. Mark the
Evangelist (1969) 164ff, 174ff, 201f. GASTON, L. No Stone on
Another (1970) 13, 16, 30, 452, 472. BEUTLER, J., Martyria
(Frankfurt 1972) 198, 299, 303, 358. DONAHUE, J. R., Are
you the Christ? (Missoula 1973) 70, 97, 170, 212-15, 218, 242.
KLIJN, A. F. J., "Die syrische Baruch-Apokalypse" in: W. G.

Kümmel (ed.) Jüdische Schriften aus hellenistisch-römischer Zeit V (Gütersloh 1976) 130. *SATAKE, A., "Das Leiden der Jünger 'um meinetwillen' " ZNW 67 (1976) 4-19. WILLIAMS, J. A., A Conceptual History of Deuteronism in the Old Testament, Judaism, and the New Testament (Ph.D.Diss. Southern Baptist Theological Seminary, Louisville 1976) 309. GERSTENBERGER, G. und SCHRAGE, W., Leiden (Stuttgart 1977) 194; ET: Suffering (Nashville 1980) 224.

13:10 STONEHOUSE, N. B. The Witness of Matthew and Mark to Christ (1944) 10, 113, 228. *FARRER, A. "An Examination of Mark XIII.10" JTS 7 ('56) 75-79. GILS, F., Jésus Prophète D'Après Les Evangiles Synoptiques (Louvain 1957) 115-17. MUNCK, J., Paul and the Salvation of Mankind (London 1959) 38-40, 49. BOSCH, D. Die Heidenmission in der Zukunftsschau Jesu (1959) 143-48, 154-74. HAHN, F. Christologische Hoheitstitel (1963) 186. HAHN, F. Das Verständnis der Mission im Neuen Testament (1965) 20, 31, 32, 50, 53, 57-63, 102f, 113f. LINTON, O., "Evidences of a Second-Century Revised Edition of St. Mark's Gospel" NTS 14 (1967-68) 347f. MINETTE DE TILLESSE, G. Le Secret Messianique dans L'Evangile de Marc (1968) 395-96, 405-409. MARXSEN, W. Mark the Evangelist (1969) 89, 98, 120ff, 129, 174ff, 201f. KUENZI, M. Das Naherwartungslogion Matthäus 10, 23 (1970) 91, 96, 139f, 159f. JEREMIAS, J. New Testament Theology I (1971) 34, 125, 133f. JEREMIAS, J. Neutestamentliche Theologie (1971) 42, 126, 134f. *THOMPSON, J. W. "The Gentile Mission As an Eschatological Necessity" RestQ 14 (1, '71) 18-27. BOHREN, R., Predigtlehre (München 1971) 233. BERKOUWER, G. C., The Return of Christ (Grand Rapids 1972) 127, 130, 153, 251. STRECKER, G. "Literarische Ueberlegungen zum Ευαγγελιον Begriff im Markusevangelium" Neues Testament und Geschichte eds. H. Baltensweiler/B. Reicke (1972) 98-101, 94-104. LANGE, J., Das Erscheinen des Auferstandenen im Evangelium nach Mattäus (Würzburg 1973) 80, 258, 286-94, 297, 301, 342, 436, 439, 488. SCHNACKENBURG, R., " 'Das Evangelium' im Verständnis des ältesten Evangelisten" in: P. Hoffmann (ed.) Orientierung an Jesus. Für J. Schmid (Freiburg 1973) 310-13. WILSON, S. G., The Gentiles and the Gentile Mission in Luke-Acts (Cambridge 1973) 15, 18-27, 30, 47-48. DORMEYER, D., Die Passion Jesu als Verhaltensmodell (Münster 1974) 79A. 116. LADD, G. E., A Theology of the New Testament (Grand Rapids 1974) 114f, 200, 202, 207. ACHTEMEIER, P. J., Mark (Philadelphia 1975) 49f, 53. STRECKER, G., "Das Evangelium Jesu Christi" in: G. Strecker (ed.) Jesus Christus in Historie und Theologie. Für H. Conzelmann (Tübingen 1975) 538-40. "Apokalyptik" in: TRE 3 (1978) 253.

13:11-12   KNOX, W. L. The Sources of the Synoptic Gospels II (1957) 128.

13:11   ADLER, N., Das erste christliche Pfingstfest (Münster 1938) 70f. BARRETT, C. K., The Holy Spirit and the Gospel Tradition (New York 1947) 130ff. KNOX, W. L. The Sources of the Synoptic Gospels II (1957) 66. BOSCH, D. Die Heidenmission in der Zukunftsschau Jesu (1959) 159-61. WAINWRIGHT, A. W., The Trinity in the New Testament (London 1962) 209f. YATES, J. E., The Spirit and the Kingdom (London 1963) 94-98. HAHN, F. Christologische Hoheitstitel (1963) 107. MARXSEN, W. Mark the Evangelist (1969) 39, 129, 158. JEREMIAS, J. Neutestamentliche Theologie I (1971) 21f, 25f. BEASLEY-MURRAY, G. R., "Jesus and the Spirit" in: A. Descamps/A. deHalleux (eds.) Mélanges Bibliques en hommage au R. P. Béda Rigaux (Gembloux 1970) 473f. DORMEYER, D., Die Passion Jesu als Verhaltensmodell (Münster 1974) 126. NEIRYNCK, F., "Urmarcus redivivus?" in: M. Sabbe (ed.) L'Evangile selon Marc (Gembloux 1974) 118-20. HOWARD, V. P., Das Ego in den Synoptischen Evangelien (Marburg 1975) 223-30. KREMER, J., "Jesu Verheissung des Geistes. Zur Verankerung der Aussage von John 16:13 im Leben Jesu" in: R. Schnackenburg (ed.) Die Kirche des Anfangs. Für H. Schürmann (Freiburg 1978) 262-67. SCHWEIZER, E., Heiliger Geist (Stuttgart 1978) 82f, 144.

13:12   MASSAUX, E. Influence de l'Evangile de saint Matthieu sur la littérature chrétienne avant saint Irénée (1950) 633-35. JUENGEL, E. Paulus und Jesus (1966) 244. MARXSEN, W. Mark the Evangelist (1969) 39, 159, 161, 177, 201. JEREMIAS, J. Neutestamentliche Theologie I (1971) 126, 137, 199, 232. SCHROEDER, H.-H., Eltern und Kinder in der Verkündigung Jesu (Hamburg-Bergstedt 1972) 133-56. DONAHUE, J. R., Are you the Christ? (Missoula 1973) 57, 70, 170, 212, 213-15. MÜLLER, U. B., "Die griechische Esra-Apokalypse" in: W. G. Kümmel (ed.) Jüdische Schriften aus hellenistisch-römischer Zeit V (Gütersloh 1976) 94. WILLIAMS, J. A., A Conceptual History of Deuteronomism in the Old Testament, Judaism, and the New Testament (Ph.D.Diss. Southern Baptist Theological Seminary, Louisville 1976) 309.

13:13   HAHN, F. Christologische Hoheitstitel (1963) 45. MARXSEN, W. Mark the Evangelist (1969) 158, 161f, 176f.

JEREMIAS, J. Neutestamentliche Theologie I (1971) 22, 126, 130, 178, 232. CARLSTON, C. E., "The Things that Defile. (Mark VII:14) and the Law in Matthew and Mark" NTS 15 (1968-1969) 79f. *SATAKE, A., "Das Leiden der Jünger 'um meinetwillen' " ZNW 67 (1976) 4-19.

13:13b KAESEMANN, E. New Testament Questions of Today (1969) 99. KAESEMANN, E. Exegetische Versuche und Besinnungen II (1964) 97.

13:14-27 BOUSSET, W., Die Religion des Judentums im Späthellenistischen Zeitalter (Berlin 1966=1926) 113, 222, 224, 237, 255f, 264. ERNST, J. Die Eschatologischen Gegenspieler in den Schriften des Neuen Testaments (1967) 8-10. SCHILLE, O., Offen für all Menschen (Stuttgart 1974) 24ff.

13:14-23 GILS, F., Jésus Prophète D'Après Les Evangiles Synoptiques (Louvain 1957) 128-30. HARTMAN, L. Prophecy interpreted (1966) 162-64. JEREMIAS J. Neutestamentliche Theologie I (1971) 124-26, 130. CONZELMANN, H., Theologie als Schriftauslegung (München 1974) 71f. GNILKA, J., Das Evangelium nach Markus II (Einsiedeln/Neukirchen 1979) 193 (lit!).

13:14-20 *SCHOEPS, H.-J. "Ebionitische Apokalyptik im Neuen Testament" ZNW 51 (1-2, '60) 101-11. HARTMAN, L. Prophecy interpreted (1966) 151-54. JUENGEL, E. Paulus und Jesus (1966) 244. LAMBRECHT, J. Die Redaktion der Markus-Apokalypse (1967) 144-68. PESCH, R. Naherwartungen (1969) 138-54. GASTON, L. No Stone on Another (1970) 23-29. O'NEILL, J. C., The Theology of Acts in its Historical Setting (London 1970) 1-3. GEIGER, R., Die Lukanischen Endzeitreden (Bern 1973) 193-210. DORMEYER, D., Die Passion Jesu als Verhaltensmodell (Münster 1974) 160, 279. PESCH, R., Das Markusevangelium II (Freiburg 1977) 296 (lit!). RIST, J. M., On the Independence of Matthew and Mark (Cambridge 1978) 81f. SWIDLER, L., Biblical Affirmations of Woman (Philadelphia 1979) 233, 240, 260.

13:14 DODD, C. H., "The Fall of Jerusalem and the 'Abomination of Desolation' " JRS 37 (1947) 47ff. *GUY, H. A. "Mark XIII, 14" ET 65 (1, '53) 30. BEASLEY-MURRAY G. R. Jesus and the Future (1954) 8, 18, 38, 43, 90, 92, 202, 213, 255-58. *RIGAUX, B. "Bdelygma tes eremoseos (Mc 13, 14; Mt 24, 15)" Biblica (3, '59) 675-83. BRUCE, F. F. "The Book of Zechariah and the Passion Narrative" BJRL 43, 1960-61. HAHN, F. Christologische Hoheitstitel (1963) 186. *SHAW, R. H. "A Conjecture on the Signs of the End" AThR 47 (1, '65) 96-102.

SCHREIBER, J. Theologie des Vertrauens (1967) 76, 142-44, 189. MARXSEN, W. Mark the Evangelist (1969) 163f, 166, 168, 171, 179f, 182f, 185ff. JEREMIAS, J. Neutestamentliche Theologie I (1971) 97, 127, 129f, 234, 260. METZGER, B. M., The Early Versions of the New Testament (Oxford 1977) 248.

13:15-16   MARXSEN, W. Mark the Evangelist (1969) 165, 184, 192, 197.

13:16   HAHN, F. Christologische Hoheitstitel (1963) 170.

13:17   DORMEYER, D., Die Passion Jesu als Verhaltensmodell (Münster 1974) 98. SAND, A., Das Gesetz und die Propheten (Regensburg 1974) 84-86. STAGG, E./F., Woman in the World of Jesus (Philadelphia 1978) 212.

13:19-20   SCHREIBER, J. Theologie des Vertrauens (1967) 123, 144f, 157.

13:19   MASSAUX, E. Influence de l'Evangile de saint Matthieu sur la littérature chrétienne avant saint Irénée (1950) 633-35. MARXSEN, W. Mark the Evangelist (1969) 41, 184f, 192.

13:20, 22   BRAUN, H., Qumran und NT II (Tübingen 1966) 93, 147.

13:20   HAHN, F. Christologische Hoheitstitel (1963) 73. JEREMIAS, J. Neutestamentliche Theologie I (1971) 20, 23, 25, 27, 140f. HOLM-NIELSEN, S., "Die Psalmen Salomos" in: W. G. Kümmel (ed.) Jüdische Schriften aus hellenistisch-römischer Zeit IV (Gütersloh 1977) 106. HOOKER, M. D., "Is the Son of Man problem really insoluble?" in: E. Best/R. McL.Wilson (eds.) Text and Interpretation. In honour of M. Black (Cambridge 1979) 162f.

13:21ff   HAHN, F. Christologische Hoheitstitel (1963) 181. GEIGER, R., Die Lukanischen Endzeitreden (Bern 1973) 193-210.

13:21-23   HARTMAN, L. Prophecy interpreted (1966) 154-55. LAMBRECHT J. Die Redaktion der Markus-Apokalypse (1967) 168-73. MARXSEN, W. Mark the Evangelist (1969) 158, 184, 192, 197. PESCH, R. Naherwartungen (1969) 154-75. KERTELGE, K. Die Wunder Jesu im Markusevangelium (1970) 27-29. GASTON, L. No Stone on Another (1970) 29-30, 37, 49. PESCH, R., Das Markusevangelium II (Freiburg 1977) 301 (lit!).

13:21-22   MARXSEN, W. Mark the Evangelist (1969) 161f, 181, 185f. ACHTEMEIER, P. J., Mark (Philadelphia 1975) 42f. KELBER, W. H., "Mark and Oral Tradition" Semeia 16 (1980) 40f.

13:21   MASSAUX, E. Influence de l'Evangile de saint Matthieu sur la littérature chrétienne avant saint Irénée (1950) 633-35. HAHN, F. Christologische Hoheitstitel (1963) 182. PRYKE, E. J., "IΔE and ΙΔΟΥ" NTS 14 (1967-1968) 418f. CONZELMANN, H., Theologie als Schriftauslegung (München 1974) 68, 70.A40f.

13:22 MASSAUX, E. Influence de l'Evangile de saint Matthieu sur la littérature chrétienne avant saint Irénée (1950) 633-35. HAHN, F. Christologische Hoheitstitel (1963) 181. KAESEMANN, E. Exegetische Versuche und Besinnungen I (1964) 112. NICKELS, P. Targum and New Testament (1967) 25. JEREMIAS, J. Neutestamentliche Theologie I (1971) 77, 126. HENNECKE, E. und SCHNEEMELCHER, W., Neutestamentliche Apokryphen II (Tübingen 1964) 473. HARNISCH, W., Eschatalogische Existenz (Göttingen 1973) 9, 13, 161, 162A. KEE, H. C., "The Function of Scriptural Quotations and Allusions in Mark 11-16" in: E. E. Ellis/E. Grässer (eds.) Jesus and Paulus. Für W. G. Kümmel (Göttingen 1975) 169, 171ff, 183. VÖGTLE, A., "Der 'eschatalogische' Bezug der Wir-Bitten des Vaterunsers" in: E. E. Ellis/E. Grässer (eds.) Jesus und Paulus. Für W. G. Kümmel (Göttingen 1975) 357.

13:24ff HAHN, F. Christologische Hoheitstitel (1963) 181.

13:24-37 MOORE, G. F., Judaism II (Cambridge/Mass. 1946) 337, 365.

13:24-27 *MUSSNER, F. "Die Wiederkunft des Menschensohnes nach Markus 13, 24-27 und 14, 61-62" BuK 16 (4, '61) 105-107. HARTMAN, L. Prophecy interpreted (1966) 156-59, 165-67. LAMBRECHT, J. Die Redaktion der Markus-Apokalypse (1967) 173-93. SCHREIBER, J. Theologie des Vertrauens (1967) 82, 93, 216, 129, 132-34, 139-41. MARXSEN, W. Mark the Evangelist (1969) 159, 161, 184, 187, 194f. VOEGTLE, A. Das Neue Testament und die Zukunft des Kosmos (1970) 68-70, 104. GASTON, L. No Stone on Another (1970) 26, 30-35, 147. SANFORD, J. A., The Kingdom Within (New York 1970) 206f. JEREMIAS, J. Neutestamentliche Theologie I (1971) 125f. GEIGER, R., Die Lukanischen Endzeitreden (Bern 1973) 212-15. DORMEYER, D., Die Passion Jesu als Verhaltensmodell (Münster 1974) 214, 279. MINEAR, P. S., To Die and To Live. Christ's Resurrection and Christian Vocation (New York 1977) 123-49. PESCH, R., Das Markusevangelium II (Freiburg 1977) 305 (lit!) GNILKA, J., Das Evangelium nach Markus II (Einsiedeln/Neukirchen 1979) 199 (lit!).

13:24-25 VOEGTLE, A. Das Neue Testament und die Zunkunft des Kosmos (1970) 28-31, 34, 67-71, 72, 73, 151, 154. JEREMIAS, J. Neutestamentliche Theologie I (1971) 33, 35, 126, 128. BRANDENBURGER, E., "Himmelfahrt Moses" in: W. G.

Kümmel (ed.) Jüdische Schriften aus hellenistisch-römischer Zeit V (Gütersloh 1976) 77.

13:24   MARXSEN, W. Mark the Evangelist (1969) 167, 185, 194.

13:25   METZGER, B. M., The Early Versions of the New Testament (Oxford 1977) 14, 32.

13:26-27   HAHN, F. Christologische Hoheitstitel (1963) 39. JUENGEL E. Paulus und Jesus (1966) 243f.

13:26.28-29   HENNECKE, E. und SCHNEEMELCHER, W., Neutestamentliche Apokryphen II (Tübingen 1964) 211, 472.

13:26   STONEHOUSE, N. B. The Witness of Matthew and Mark to Christ (1944) 111-15. MANSON, T. W., The Teaching of Jesus (Cambridge 1945) 278-85. BEASLEY-MURRAY, G. R. Jesus and the Future (1954) 258-60. BURKILL, T. A., "St Mark's Philosophy of History" NTS 3 (1956-1957) 143ff. HAHN, F. Christologische Hoheitstitel (1963) 181f, 254. PERRIN, N., "Mark 14:62. The End Product of a Christian Pescher Tradition? NTS 12 (1965-1966) 153f. HOOKER, M. D. The Son of Man in Mark (1967) 113, 119, 148-59, 166, 167, 181, 192, 193. NICKELS, P. Targum and New Testament (1967) 25. MINETTE DE TILLESSE, G. Le Secret Messianique dans L'Evangile de Marc (1968) 368-70, 390. HIGGINS, A. J. B., "Is the Son of Man Problem Insoluble?" in: E. E. Ellis/ M. Wilcox (eds.) Neotestamentica et Semitica. In honour of M. Black (Edinburgh 1969) 76f, 80f. WEEDEN, T. J. Mark - Traditions in Conflict (1971) 126-37. JEREMIAS, J. Neutestamentliche Theologie I (1971) 126, 231, 248, 251f, 259, 260-62. DONAHUE, J. R., Are You the Christ? (Missoula 1973) 94, 137, 143, 149, 152, 155, 160, 165, 168-72, 183, 200. HAMERTON-KELLY, R. G., Pre-Existence, Wisdom and the Son of Man (Cambridge 1973) 55, 57f, 60f. HOFFMANN, P., "Mk 8, 31. Zur Herkunft und markinischen Rezeption einer alten Überlieferung" in: P. Hoffmann (ed.) Orientierung an Jesus. Für J. Schmid (Freiburg 1973) 198-200. COPPENS, J., "Les logia du Fils de l'Homme dans l'évangile de Marc" in: M. Sabbe (ed.) L'Evangile selon Marc (Gembloux 1974) 505-508. LOHSE, E., Grundriss der neutestamentlichen Theologie (Stuttgart 1974) 46f. PERRIN, N., "The Christology of Mark" in: M. Sabbe (ed.) L'Evangile selon Marc (Gembloux 1974) 481f. PERRIN, N., A Modern Pilgrimage in New Testament Christology (Philadelphia 1974) 115-21. ACHTEMEIER, P. J., Mark (Philadelphia 1975) 46. GOPPELT, L., Theologie des Neuen Testaments I (Göttingen 1975) 230ff. MALBON, E. S., "Mythic Structure and Meaning in Mark" Semeia 16 (1980) 109-13.

13:27 MASSAUX, E. Influence de l'Evangile de saint Matthieu sur la littérature chrétienne avant saint Irénée (1950) 624-26. HAHN, F. Das Verständnis der Mission im Neuen Testament (1965) 32. VOEGTLE, A. Das Neue Testament und die Zukunft des Kosmos (1970) 28, 44, 71, 154.

13:28-37 ERNST, J. Die Eschatologischen Gegenspieler in den Schriften des Neuen Testaments (1967) 10-13. MARXSEN, W. Mark the Evangelist (1969) 159, 161f. DUPONT, J., "La parabole du maître qui rentre dans la nuit (Mc 13, 34-36)" in: A. Descamps/A.de Halleux (eds.) Mélanges Bibliques en hommage au R. P. Béda Rigaux (Gembloux 1970) 90-92. GEIGER, R., Die Lukanischen Endzeitreden (Bern 1973) 223-48.

13:28-32 PESCH, R. Naherwartungen (1969) 175-95. PESCH, R., Das Markusevangelium II (Freiburg 1977) 312f (lit!). GNILKA, J., Das Evangelium nach Markus II (Einsiedeln/Neukirchen 1979) 203 (lit!).

13:28-31 LAMBRECHT, J. Die Redaktion der Markus-Apokalypse (1967) 193-227.

13:28-30 GASTON, L. No Stone on Another (1970) 35-38, 63.

13:28-29 HENNECKE, E. und SCHNEEMELCHER, W., Neutestamentliche Apokryphen II (Tübingen 1964) 211, 472. JüLICHER, D. A. Die Gleichnisreden Jesu 1910) 3-11. KUEMMEL, W. G. Verheissung und Erfüllung (1953) 14-16. SCHREIBER, J. Theologie des Vertrauens (1967) 128, 134-40, 141. *DUPONT, J. "La parabole du figuier qui bourgeonne (Mc, xiii, 28-29 et par)" RevBi 75 (4, '68) 526-48. PATSCH, H., Abendmahl und historischer Jesus (Stuttgart 1972) 116f. MANEK, J., . . .und brachte Frucht. Die Gleichnisse Jesu (Berlin 1977) 33f. KLAUCK, H.-J., Allegorie und Allegorese in Synoptischen Gleichnistexten (Münster 1978) 316-25.

13:28 MÜNDERLEIN, G., "Die Verfluchung des Feigenbaumes" NTS 10 (1963-1964) 92f. *PEREZ FERNANDEZ, M. "'prope est aestas' (Mc 13, 28; Mt 24, 32; Lc 21, 29)" VerbDom 46 (6, '68) 361-69.

13:29 MARXSEN, W. Mark the Evangelist (1969) 166, 187. HIERS, R. H., The Historical Jesus and the Kingdom of God (Gainsville 1973) 14, 29f.

13:30-37 HASLER, V. Amen (1969) 47.

13:30-31 SCHREIBER, J. Theologie des Vertrauens (1967) 140-42. MARXSEN, W. Mark the Evangelist (1969) 162, 164. LOHSE, E. and others eds. Der Ruf Jesu und die Antwort der Gemeinde (1970) 105f.

13:30 KUEMMEL, W. G. Verheissung und Erfüllung (1953) 14f, 21f, 53-55. BOSCH, D. Die Heidenmission in der Zukunfsschau Jesu (1959) 144-48. BERKHOF, H., Der Sinn der Geschichte: Christus (Göttingen 1959) 82f. *LöVESTAM, E. "En problematisk eskatologisk utsaga: Mark. 13:30 par." (An Obscure Eschatological Statement: Mk 13:30 par) SEA 28-29 ('63-'64) 64-80. CULLMANN, O. Heil als Geschichte (1965) 179, 189, 193ff, 202f. MARXSEN, W. Mark the Evangelist (1969) 161, 166, 187, 194, 205. BERGER, K. Die Amen-Worte Jesu (1970) 68-69. KUENZI, M. Das Naherwartungslogion Matthäus 10, 23 (1970) 88, 90, 134ff. VOEGTLE, A. Das Neue Testament und die Zukunft des Kosmos (1970) 100f, 104f, 130. GASTON, L. No Stone on Another (1970) 39, 322, 451-55. VOEGTLE, A. Das Evangelium und die Evangelien (1971) 317-28. PATSCH, H., Abendmahl und historischer Jesus (Stuttgart 1972) 123f. KÜNZI, M., Das Naherwartungslogion Markus 9, 1 par. (Tübingen 1977) 213-24. SCHILDENBERGER, J., "Die Vertauschung der Aussagen über Zeichen und Bezeichnetes. Eine hermeneutisch bedeutsame Redeweise" in: Kirche und Bibel. Für E. Schick (Paderborn 1979) 404f. HARRINGTON, D. J., God's People in Christ (Philadelphia 1980) 25. LÖVESTAM, E., "The ἡ γενεὰ αὕτη Eschatology in Mk 13, 30 parr." in: J. Lambrechts (ed.) L'Apocalypse johannique et l'Apocalyptique dans le Nouveau Testament (Gembloux 1980) 403-13.

13:31-33 BULTMANN, R. "Gottes Zukunft" Kleine Predigt-Typologie III (1965) 32ff.

13:31-32 GASTON, L. No Stone on Another (1970) 38-39, 63.

13:31 VOEGTLE, A. Das Neue Testament und die Zukunft des Kosmos (1970) 28, 42f, 99-102, 104f, 107, 151. JEREMIAS, J. Neutestamentliche Theologie I (1971) 25f, 235. DORMEYER, D., Die Passion Jesu als Verhaltensmodell (Münster 1974) 279A. 120.

13:32-37 LAMBRECHT, J. Die Redaktion der Markus-Apokalypse (1967) 228-56.

13:32-33 JEWETT, R., Jesus against the Rapture. Seven Unexpected Prophecies (Philadelphia 1979) 15-33.

13:32 KUEMMEL, W. G. Verheissung und Erfüllung (1953) 34-36, 142f. BEASLEY-MURRAY, G. R. Jesus and the Future (1954) 261-64. FLEW, R. N. Jesus and His Church (1956) 33-34. *PEZZELLA, S. "Marco 13, 32 e la scienza di Cristo" RivB 7 (2, '59) 147-52. VAN IERSEL, B. M. F. "Mk 13, 32 - Mt. 24, 36" in 'Der Sohn' in den Synoptischen Jesusworten (1961) 117. WAINWRIGHT, A. W., The Trinity in the New Testament

(London 1962) 178f. PERRIN, N., The Kingdom of God in the Teaching of Jesus (Philadelphia 1963) 86, 137, 145, 190. HAHN, F. Christologische Hoheitstitel (1963) 320, 327, 328. FASCHER, E. "Von dem Tage aber und von der Stunde weiss niemand" Ruf und Antwort (Festgabe für Emil Fuchs (1964) 475-83. GRUNDMANN, W., "Matt 11, 27 und die johanneischen 'Der Vater - der Sohn'-Stellen" NTS 12 (1965-1966) 42f. SCHREIBER, J. Theologie des Vertrauens (1967) 103, 120, 128-31. *WINANDY, J. "Le logion de l'ignorance (Mc, XIII, 32; Mt., XXIV, 36)" RevBi 75 (1, '68) 63-79. MARXSEN, W. Mark the Evangelist (1969) 161f, 164, 187. KÜNZI, M. Das Naherwartungslogion Matthäus 10, 23 (1970) 109, 181. JEREMIAS, J. Neutestamentliche Theologie I (1971) 20, 63, 132, 246. VOEGTLE, A. Das Evangelium und die Evangelien (1971) 318-23, 332-34. DORMEYER, D., Die Passion Jesu als Verhaltensmodell (Münster 1974) 126A.380, 280A. 125. ACHTEMEIER, P. J., Mark (Philadelphia 1975) 44. DUNN, J. D. G., Jesus and the Spirit (London 1975) 27-29, 34f. SANDMEL, S., We Jews and Jesus (New York 1977) 87. "Astrologie" in: TRE 4 (1979) 308.

13:33-37 JÜLICHER, D. A. Die Gleichnisreden Jesu (1910) 161-71. DODD, C. H. The Parables of the Kingdom (1948) 161ff. MICHAELIS, D. W. Die Gleichnisse Jesu (1956) 81-86. JEREMIAS, J. Die Gleichnisse Jesu (1962) 38, 50-52, 67, 78, 166. HAHN, F. Christologische Hoheitstitel (1963) 111. BULTMANN, R., The History of the Synoptic Tradition (Oxford 1963) 173f, 194, 205. LÖVESTAM, E., Spiritual Wakefulness in the New Testament (Lund 1963) 80f, 87f. SCHREIBER, J. Theologie des Vertrauens (1967) 134, 151f, 91-94, 129-131, 155. MINETTE DE TILLESSE, G. Le Secret Messianique dans L'Evangile de Marc (1968) 414-20. PESCH, R. Naherwartungen (1969) 195-202. MARXSEN, W. Mark the Evangelist (1969) 162, 187, 198, 202. GASTON, L. No Stone on Another (1970) 39-41, 59, 23, 63, 324. *WEISER, A. "Von der Predigt Jesu zur Erwartung der Parusie" BuL 12 (1, '71) 25-31. WEISER, A. Die Knechtsgleichnisse der synoptischen Evangelien (1971) 131-53. PESCH, R., Das Markusevangelium II (Freiburg 1977) 318 (lit!). MANEK, J.,.. .und brachte Frucht. Die Gleichnisse Jesu (Berlin 1977) 35f. KLAUCK, H.-J., Allegorie und Allegorese in Synoptischen Gleichnistexten (Münster 1978) 326-39. GNILKA, J., Das Evangelium nach Markus II (Einsiedeln/Neukirchen 1979) 207f (lit!). WEDER, H., Die Gleichnisse Jesu als Metaphern (Göttingen 1980 *(2)*) 162-68.

13:33 STRECKER, G. Der Weg der Gerechtigkeit (1962) 86f.

13:34-47   SWIDLER, L., Biblical Affirmations of Woman (Philadelphia 1979) 169.

13:34-37   CROSSAN, J. D., "The Servant Parables of Jesus" in: G.MacRae (ed.) SBL Seminar Papers 2 (Montana 1973) 95f.

13:34-36   DUPONT, J., "La parabole du maître qui rentre dans la nuit (Mc 13, 34-36)" in: A. Descamps/A.de Halleux (eds.) Mélanges Bibliques en hommage au R. P. Béda Rigaux (Gembloux 1970) 89-116. PERRIN, N., Jesus and the Language of the Kingdom (London 1976) 161, 196.

13:34   MASSAUX, E. Influence de l'Evangile de saint Matthieu sur la littérature chrétienne avant saint Irénée (1950) 267-71. DIDIER, M. "La parabole des talents et des mines" De Jésus aux Evangiles (1967) 248-71.

13:35-36   MONTEFIORE, H., "A Comparison of the Parables of the Gospel According to Thomas and of the Synoptic Gospels" NTS 7 (1960-1961) 243f.

13:35   STONEHOUSE, N. B. The Witness of Matthew and Mark to Christ (1944) 113, 161, 254. LÖVESTAM, E., Spiritual Wakefulness in the New Testament (Lund 1963) 82ff. WEINACHT, H,. Die Menschwerdung des Sohnes Gottes im Markusevangelium (1972) 133ff.

13:37   GASTON, L. No Stone on Another (1970) 30, 37, 52, 53, 63, 325.

14-16   TAYLOR, V. "The Construction of the Passion and Resurrection Narrative" The Gospel According to St Mark (1953) 653-64. KNOX, W. L. The Sources of the Synoptic Gospels I (1953) 115-47. LEIVESTAD, R., Christ the Conqueror (London 1954) 65ff. TAYLOR, V., "The Origin of the Markan Passion-Sayings" NTS 1, 1954-55, 159-67. PIPER, O. A. "God's Good News. The Passion Story According to Mark" Interpretation 9 (2, '55) 165-82. HAHN, F. Christologische Hoheitstitel (1963) 211. *KELBER, W. H., The Passion in Mark (Philadelphia 1976); Recension: L. E. Keck, Interpretation 31 (1977) 432-34. *OSWALD, J., "Die Beziehungen zwischen Psalm 22 und dem vormarkinischen Passionsbericht" ZKTh 101 (1979) 53-66. *ZELLER, D., "Die Handlungsstruktur der Markuspassion. Der Ertrag

strukturalistischer Literaturwissenschaft für die Exegese" ThQ
159 (1979) 213-27. MALBON, E. S., "Mythic Structure and
Meaning in Mark" Semeia 16 (1980) 113-16.

14:1-16:8   PESCH, R. Naherwartungen (1969) 66f. *SMITH, R. H.,
"Darkness at Noon: Mark's Passion Narrative" CThM 44
(1973) 325-38. *DORMEYER, D., Die Passion Jesu als
Verhaltensmodell (Münster 1974). PERRIN, N., The New
Testament. An Introduction. (New York 1974) 148, 159-61.
*SCHLIER, H., Die Markuspassion (Einsiedeln 1974).
DORMEYER, D., Der Sinn des Leidens Jesu. Historisch-
kritische und text-pragmatische Analysen zur Markuspassion
(Stuttgart 1979). GNILKA, J., Das Evangelium nach Markus
II (Einsiedeln/Neukirchen 1979) 216f (lit!).

14-15   EWALD, H., Die drei ersten Evangelien (Göttingen 1850)
341ff. RAWLINSON, A. E. J. "The Last Supper and the
Crucifixion in relation to the Passover" St Mark (1925) 262-
267. KLOSTERMANN, E. "Die Leidensgeschichte" Das
Markusevangelium (1950) 139. MAURER, Chr. "Knecht
Gottes und Sohn Gottes im Passionsbericht des
Markusevangeliums" ZThK 50, 1953, 1-38. DIBELIUS, M.
"Das historische Problem der Leidensgeschichte" Botschaft
und Geschichte (1953) 248-57. SCHMID, J. "Die Erfüllung der
Schrift in der Passion" Das Evangelium nach Markus (1958)
304-308. GRUNDMANN, W. Das Evangelium nach Markus
(1959) 280f. HAHN, F. Christologische Hoheitstitel (1963) 47,
66, 176, 195. *BARTSCH, H.-W. "Historische Erwägungen
zur Leidensgeschichte" EvTh 22 (9, '62) 449-59. MINETTE DE
TILLESSE, G. Le Secret Messianique dans L'Evangile de
Marc (1968) 376-80. *SCHREIBER, J. Die Markuspassion
(1969). *KREMER, J. Das Aergernis des Kreuzes (1969).
*LINNEMANN, E. Studien zur Passionsgeschichte (1970).
GUETTGEMANNS, E. Offene Fragen zur Formgeschichte
des Evangeliums (1970) 214, 217, 219, 222. RUPPERT, L.,
Jesus als der leidende Gerechte? (Stuttgart 1972) 10-13.
ACHTEMEIER, P. J., Mark (Philadelphia 1975) 86-90.
CONZELMANN, H. und LINDEMANN, A., Arbeitsbuch
zum Neuen Testament (Tübingen 1975) 375-78. *O'COLLINS,
G., "The Crucifixion" DoLi 26 (1976) 247-63. O'COLLINS, G.,
The Calvary Christ (Philadelphia 1977). GERSTENBERGER,
G. und SCHRAGE, W., Leiden (Stuttgart 1977) 123-25, 143-
46, 153, 166f, 169; ET: J. E. Steely, Suffering (Nashville 1980)
143-46, 166-70, 177, 192f, 196. *GOUDERS, K., Das Kreuz
und die Kreuze. Texte aus Dichtung und Theologie (Stuttgart
1977). TOWNSEND, J. T., A Liturgical Interpretation of our
Lord's Passion in Narrative Form (New York 1977). TRITES,

A. A., The New Testament Concept of Witness (Cambridge 1977) 185-90. *LAMARCHE, P., "L'humiliation du Christ" Christus (1979) 461-70.

14:1-15:15   WILSON, W. R. The Execution of Jesus (1970) 44-47.

14   TEMPLE, S., "The Two Traditions of the Last Supper, Betrayal and Arrest" NTS 7 (1960-1961) 77f. GREENLEE, J. H., Nine Uncial Palimpsests of the Greek New Testament (Salt Lake City 1968) 17-20. LEHMANN, M. Synoptische Quellenanalyse und die Frage nach dem historischen Jesus (1970) 103-12. HAY, D. M., Glory at the Right Hand: Psalm 110 in Early Christianity (Nashville 1973) 64f.

14:1ff   LIGHTFOOT, R. H. History and Interpretation in the Gospels (1934) 126ff, 130ff. KNOX, W. L. The Sources of the Synoptic Gospels I (1953) 116ff.

14:1-42   *SCHENKE, L., Studien zur Passionsgeschichte des Markus (Würzburg 1971) DORMEYER, D., Die Passion Jesu als Verhaltensmodell (Münster 1974) 302-17.

14:1-41   *Van RULER, A. A., Marcus 14, 1-41 (Kampen 1971).

14:1-25   *DANKER, F. W. "The Literary Unity of Mark 14:1-25" JBL 85 (4, '66) 467-72.

14:1-24   CLEVENOT, M., So kennen wir die Bibel nicht (München 1978) 95-96.

14:1-16   LAMBRECHT, J. Die Redaktion der Markus-Apokalypse (1967) 55-60.

14:1-11   JAUBERT, A., "Le mercredi où Jésus fut Livré" NTS 14 (1967-1968) 155ff. SCHENKE, L., Studien zur Passionsgeschichte des Markus (Würzburg 1971) 141-50. PESCH, R., "Die Salbung Jesu in Bethanien (Mk 14, 3-9)" in: P. Hoffmann (ed.) Orientierung and Jesus. Für J. Schmid (Freiburg 1973) 268-70, 278.

14:1-10   BRAUN, H., Qumran und NT II (Tübingen 1966) 45f, 49f.

14:1-9   *PLATT, E. E., "The Ministry of Mary of Bethany" ThT 34 (1977) 29-39.

14:1-2   JEREMIAS, J. Die Abendmahlsworte Jesu (1960) 86-88. BULTMANN, R., The History of the Synoptic Tradition (Oxford 1963) 262f, 277-79. VÖÖBUS, A. The Prelude to the Lukan Passion Narrative (1968) 57-60. KREMER, J. Das Aergernis des Kreuzes (1969) 11-12. ZIMMERMANN, W.-D. Markus über Jesus (1970) 145-46. SCHRAMM, T. Der Markus-Stoff bei Lukas (1971) 182-84. SCHENKE, L., Studien zur Passionsgeschichte des Markus (Würzburg 1971) 12-66. CONZELMANN, H., Theologie als Schriftauslegung

(München 1974) 77f. DORMEYER, D., Die Passion Jesu als Verhaltensmodell (Münster 1974) 66-72. KONINGS, J., "The Pre-Markan Sequence in Jn 6" in: M. Sabbe (ed.) L'Evangile selon Marc (Gembloux 1974) 173. SCHENK, W. Der Passionsbericht nach Markus (Gütersloh 1974) 143ff. VIA, D. O., Kerygma and Comedy in the New Testament (Philadelphia 1975) 129, 136, 144, 152, 155. PESCH, R., Das Markusevangelium II (Freiburg 1977) 322 (lit!). RIVKIN, E., A Hidden Revolution (Nashville 1978) 107-109. SCHMITHALS, W., Das Evangelium nach Markus (Gütersloh/Würzburg 1979) 587 (lit!).

14:1 KLOSTERMANN, E. Das Markusevangelium (1950) 140f. FARRER, A. St Matthew and St Mark (1954) 104, 142. BOUSSET, W., Die Religion des Judentums im Späthellenistischen Zeitalter (Berlin 1966=1926) 167. PESCH, R. Naherwartungen (1969) 49, 51, 53, 54, 157. PATSCH, H., Abendmahl und historischer Jesus (Stuttgart 1972) 61f. "Aramäisch" in: TRE 3 (1978) 608.

14:3ff WILCKENS, U., "Vergebung für die Sünderin (Lk 7, 36-50)" in: P. Hoffmann (ed.) Orientierung an Jesus. Für J. Schmid (Freiburg 1973) 398-400. GERSTENBERGER, E. S. und SCHRAGE, W., Frau und Mann (Stuttgart 1980) 117.

14:3-11 ZIMMERMANN, W.-D. Markus über Jesus (1970) 147-49.

14:3-10 STROBEL, A. Erkenntnis und Bekenntnis der Sünde in neutestamentlicher Zeit (1968) 59. DRURY, J., Tradition and Design in Luke's Gospel (Atlanta 1976) 91-96.

14:3-9 JEREMIAS, J., "Die Salbunggeschichte" ZNW 35 (1936) 75. GOODSPEED, E. J., A Life of Jesus (New York 1950) 192-94. BULTMANN, R., The History of the Synoptic Tradition (Oxford 1963) 36f, 64-68, 276f. DERRETT, J. and DUNCAN M. "The Anointing at Bethany" Studia Evangelica II, ed. F. L. Cross (1964) 174-82. PREUSCHEN, E. "Die Salbung in Bethanien" (1902) ZNW 3, 252f. VON SYBEL, L. "Die Salbungen (Mt 26, 6-13; Lk 7, 36-50; John 12, 1-8)" ZNW 23 (1924) 184-93. TAYLOR, V. The Formation of the Gospel Tradition (1949) 57f, 70, 74f. FARRER, A. A Study in St Mark (1951) 128ff, 134f, 167f, 219f. *LEGAULT, A "An Application of the Form-Critique Method to the Anointings in Galilee (Lk 7, 36-50) and Bethany (Mt 26, 6-13; Mk 14, 3-9; Jn 12, 1-8)" CBQ XVI (1954) 131-45. TILLICH, P. Das Neue Sein (1959) 52-55. HAHN, F. Das Verständnis der Mission im Neuen Testament (1965) 101f. JEREMIAS, J. Abba (1966) 107-15. HENSS, W., Das Verhältnis zwischen Diatessaron, Christlicher Gnosis und "Western Text" (Berlin 1967) 11f, 16-

223, 57. SCHNEIDER, G., Verleugnung, Verspottung und Verhör Jesu nach Lukas 22, 54-71 (München 1969) 20, 27, 50, 153, 156. KREMER, J. Das Aergernis des Kreuzes (1969) 13-15. DERRETT, J. D. M. Law in the New Testament (1970) 266-75. LOHSE, E. and others (eds.) Der Ruf und die Antwort der Gemeinde (1970) 247-58. ROLOFF, J. Das Kerygma und der irdische Jesus (1970) 210-15. SCHENKE, L., Studien zur Passionsgeschichte des Markus (Würzburg 1971) 67-118. PATSCH, H., Abendmahl und historischer Jesus (Stuttgart 1972) 198f. HIERS, R. H., The Historical Jesus and the Kingdom of God (Gainsville 1973) 94-96. PESCH, R., "Die Salbung Jesu in Bethanien (Mk 14, 3-9)" in: P. Hoffmann (ed.) Orientierung an Jesus. Für J. Schmid (Freiburg 1973) 267-85. DORMEYER, D., Die Passion Jesu als Verhaltensmodell (Münster 1974) 73-82. *ELLIOTT, J. K., "The Anointing of Jesus" ET 85 (1974) 105-107. KONINGS, J., "The Pre-Markan Sequence in Jn 6" in: M. Sabbe (ed.) L'Evangile selon Marc (Gembloux 1974) 173. SCHENK, W., Der Passionsbericht nach Markus (Gütersloh 1974) 175ff. TALBERT, C. H., Literary Patterns, Theological Themes, and the Genre of Luke-Acts (Missoula 1974) 20, 42. PESCH, R., Das Markusevangelium II (Freiburg 1977) 336 (lit!). RIST, J. M., On the Independence of Matthew and Mark (Cambridge 1978) 83f. STAGG, E./F., Woman in the World of Jesus (Philadelphia 1978) 117, 120f, 213. GNILKA, J., Das Evangelium nach Markus II (Einsiedeln/Neukirchen 1979) 221 (lit!). SCHMITHALS, W., Das Evangelium nach Markus (Gütersloh/Würzburg 1979) 589 (lit!). SWIDLER, L., Biblical Affirmations of Woman (Philadelphia 1979) 196, 220, 233, 240. ASKANI, T. und KREUSSIG, P., in: P. Krusche et al. (eds.) Predigtstudien für das Kirchenjahr 1980/1981 III/1.Halbband (Stuttgart 1980) 171-78.

14:3-8   "Abendmahl" in: TRE 1 (1977) 49.

14:3   NESTLE, E. "Die unverfälschte köstliche Narde" ZNW 3 (1902) 169-71. GRILL, J., Untersuchungen über die Entstehung des vierten Evangeliums II (Leipzig 1923) 135, 173, 188. NICKELS, P. Targum and New Testament (1967) 26. BLACK, M. An Aramaic Approach to the Gospels and Acts (1967) 223f. SCHILLE, G. Das vorsynoptische Judenchristentum (1970) 75f. WESTERHOLM, S., Jesus and Scribal Authority (Lund 1978) 68f. MALBON, E. S., "Mythic Structure and Meaning in Mark" Semeia 16 (1980) 103-107.

14:4-5   BAUER, J. "Ut Quid Perditio Ista? - zu Mk 14, 4f. und Parr" NovTest 3 (1-2, '59) 54-56. STORCH, R., "Was soll diese Verschwendung?" in: Der Ruf Jesu und die Antwort der

Gemeinde. Für J. Jeremias (Göttingen 1970) 247-58. BAUER, J. B., Scholia Biblica et Patristica (Graz 1972) 48-50.

14:4 BLACK, M. An Aramaic Approach to the Gospels and Acts (1967) 103f.

14:5ff BUSE, I., "St John and the Marcan Passion Narrative" NTS 4 (1957-1958) 215ff.

14:6-9 SWIDLER, L., Biblical Affirmations of Woman (Philadelphia 1979) 287.

14:6 NICKELS, P. Targum and New Testament (1967) 26. CLARK, K. W., "The Making of the Twentieth Century New Testament" in: The Gentile Bias and Other Essays (Leiden 1980) 150.

14:7 JEREMIAS, J. Neutestamentliche Theologie I (1971) 25-27, 269.

14:8-9 BERGER, K. Die Amen-Worte Jesu (1970) 50-54.

14:8 PREUSCHEN, E. "Die Salbung Jesu in Bethanien" ZNW 3 (1902) 252f. HOLTZMANN, O. "Zur Salbung Jesu in Bethanien ZNW 4 (1903) 181. PREUSCHEN, E. "Zur Salbung Jesu in Bethanien" ZNW 4 (1903) 88. GOETZ, K. G. "Zur Salbung Jesu in Bethanien" ZNW 4 (1903) 181-85. TAYLOR, V., Jesus and His Sacrifice (London 1948) 108-11, 235. JEREMIAS, J. Abba (1966) 209f, 212-14. NICKELS, P. Targum and New Testament (1967) 26. RIEDL, J., "Die Evangelische Leidengeschichte und ihre Theologische Aussage" BuL 41 (1968) 84-87. BLINZLER, J. Der Prozess Jesu (1969) 4th ed. 404-410, 423. JEREMIAS, J. Neutestamentliche Theologie I (1971) 269f, 272f. BROER, I. Die Urgemeinde und das Grab Jesu (1972) 34f, 165.

14:9-20 ALAND, K., "Der Schluss des Markusevangeliums" in: M. Sabbe (ed.) L'Evangile selon Marc (Gembloux 1974) 442-46.

14:9 LINDER, G. "Zur Salbung Jesu in Bethanien" ZNW 4 (1903) 179-81. JEREMIAS, J. "Mk 14, 9" ZNW 44 (1952/53) 103-107. *GREENLEE, J. H. "Eis mnemosynon autes, 'For her Memorial': Mt xxvi. 13 Mk xiv. 9" ET 71 (8, '60) 245. KAESEMANN, E. Exegetische Versuche und Besinnungen (1964) I 22. HAHN, F. Das Verständnis der Mission im Neuen Testament (1965) 101f. JEREMIAS, J. Abba (1966) 115-20. MINETTE DE TILLESSE, G. Le Secret Messianique dans L'Evangile de Marc (1968) 395-96, 405-408. HASLER, V. Amen (1969) 44. MARXSEN, W. Mark the Evangelist (1969) 120, 122, 125, 129, 135. PESCH, R. Naherwartungen (1969) 97, 129, 130, 141, 173, 174. ROLOFF, J. Das Kerygma und der irdische Jesus (1970) 215-20. JEREMIAS, J.

Neutestamentliche Theologie I (1971) 44, 134f. STRECKER, G. "Literarische Ueberlegungen zum εὐαγγέλιον - Begriff im Markusevangelium" Neues Testament und Geschichte eds. H. Baltensweiler, B. Reicke (1972) 91-104. SCHNACKENBURG, R., " 'Das Evangelium' im Verständnis des ältesten Evangelisten" in: P. Hoffmann (ed.) Orientierung and Jesus. Für J. Schmid (Freiburg 1973) 310f, 314-16. WILSON, S. G., The Gentiles and the Gentile Mission in Luke-Acts (Cambridge 1973) 18f, 21, 23-27, 30, 50. FENEBERG, W., Der Markusprolog (München 1974) 146f. NEIRYNCK, F., "Urmarcus redivivus?" in: M. Sabbe (ed.) L'Evangile selon Marc (Gembloux 1974) 108. ACHTEMEIER, P. J., Mark (Philadelphia 1975) 49f, 53.

14:10ff PATSCH, H., Abendmahl und historischer Jesus (Stuttgart 1972) 61f. WEEDEN, T. J., "Die Häresie, die Markus zur Abfassung seines Evangeliums veranlasst hat" [orig: "The Heresy that necessitated Mark's Gospel" ZNW 59 (1968) 145-58] in: R. Pesch (ed.) Das Markus-Evangelium (Darmstadt 1979) 240.

14:10-16 BULTMANN, R., The History of the Synoptic Tradition (Oxford 1963) 162f, 263f.

14:10-11 KNOX, W. L., The Sources of the Synoptic Gospels I (1953) 116ff. *BUCHHEIT, G. Judas Iskarioth, Legende - Geschichte -Deutung (1954). Rev. P. Benoit RB 63 ('56) 141-42. HAHN, F. Christologische Hoheitstitel (1963) 62. KREMER, J. Das Aergernis des Kreuzes (1969) 5-16. SCHENKE, L., Studien zur Passionsgeschichte des Markus (Würzburg 1971) 119-50. CONZELMANN, H., Theologie als Schriftauslegung (München 1974) 77f. DORMEYER, D., Die Passion Jesu als Verhaltensmodell (Münster 1974) 82-85. SCHENK, W., Der Passionsbericht nach Markus (Gütersloh 1974) 143ff. PESCH, R., Das Markusevangelium II (Freiburg 1977) 340 (lit!). GNILKA, J., Das Evangelium nach Markus II (Einsiedeln/Neukirchen 1979) 228 (lit!). SCHMITHALS, W., Das Evangelium nach Markus (Gütersloh/Würzburg 1979) 597. (lit!).

14:10 SCHMAHL, G., Die Zwölf im Markusevangelium (Trier 1974) 98-100. GOPPELT, L., Theologie des Neuen Testaments I (Göttingen 1975) 273f. "Amt" in: TRE 2 (1978) 511. TRILLING, W., "Die Entstehung des Zwölferkreises. Eine geschichtskritische Überlegung" in: R. Schnackenburg (ed.) Die Kirche des Anfangs. Für H. Schürmann (Freiburg 1978) 206f.

14:11 BAARDA, T., "Markus 14, 11: *epēggeilanto.* 'Bron' of 'Redaktie'?" GThT 73 (1973) 65-75.

14:12ff LIGHTFOOT, R. H. History and Interpretation in the Gospels (1934) 137ff. KNOX, W. L. The Sources of the Synoptic Gospels (1953) I 119ff.

14:12-31 GOODSPEED, E. J., A Life of Jesus (New York 1950) 195-202. DORMEYER, D., Die Passion Jesu als Verhaltensmodell (Münster 1974) 117-24.

14:12-26 BITTLINGER, A. Das Abendmahl im Neuen Testament und in der frühen Kirche (1969) 11-20.

14:12-25 ZIMMERMANN, W.-D. Markus über Jesus (1970) 149-55. SCHENKE, L., Studien zur Passionsgeschichte des Markus (Würzburg 1971) 152-347. ROBBINS, V. K., "Last Meal: Preparation, Betrayal, and Absence" in: W. H. .Kelber (ed.) The Passion in Mark (Philadelphia 1976) 21-40. *EDANAD, A., "Institution of the Eucharist according to the Synoptic Gospels" Biblebhashyam 4 (1978) 322-32.

14:12-18 SCHÜRMANN, H., Der Paschamahlbericht (Münster 1953) 75ff. BRAUN, H., Qumran und NT II (Tübingen 1966) 45, 49, 51.

14:12-18a SCHüRMANN, H. Ursprung und Gestalt (1970) 83, 122, 146, 274.

14:12-17 RAUCH, C. "Bermerkungen zum Markustexte" ZNW 3 (1902) 308-14.

14:12-16 KREMER, J. Das Aergernis des Kreuzes (1969) 17-19. SCHENKE, L., Studien zur Passionsgeschichte des Markus (Würzburg 1971) 152-98. PATSCH, H., Abendmahl und historischer Jesus (Stuttgart 1972) 62f. DORMEYER, D., Die Passion Jesu als Verhaltensmodell (Münster 1974) 88-94. SCHENK, W., Der Passionsbericht nach Markus (Gütersloh 1974) 182ff. "Abendmahl" in: TRE 1 (1977) 48. PESCH, R., Das Markusevangelium II (Freiburg 1977) 345 (lit!). RIST, J. M., On the Independence of Matthew and Mark (Cambridge 1978) 84f. GNILKA, J., Das Evangelium nach Markus II (Einsiedeln/Neukirchen 1979) 231 (lit!). SCHMITHALS, W., Das Evangelium nach Markus (Gütersloh/Würzburg 1979) 603 (lit!).

14:12 SCHMID, J. Das Evangelium nach Markus (1958) 252f, 268-73, 260-62. NICKELS, P. Targum and New Testament (1967) 26.

14:13 NEIRYNCK, F., "Urmarcus redivivus?" in: M. Sabbe (ed.) L'Evangile selon Marc (Gembloux 1974) 123f.

14:14 DIBELIUS, M. Botschaft und Geschichte I (1953) 272-77. HAHN, F. Christologische Hoheitstitel (1963) 77, 80f, 91f, 94. SCHNACKENBURG, R., " 'Das Evangelium' im Verständnis des ältesten Evangelisten" in: P. Hoffmann (ed.) Orientierung an Jesus. Für J. Schmid (Freiburg 1973) 310f, 318-20.

14:17ff BORNKAMM, G. Jesus von Nazareth (1956) 147ff. AALEN, S. "Das Abendmahl als Opfermahl im Neuen Testament" in: Χάρις καὶ σοφία (1964) (128-) 147-52.

14:17-52 BEERNAERT, P. M., "Structure littéraire et lecture théologique de Marc 14: 17-52" in: M. Sabbe (ed.) L'Evangile selon Marc (Gembloux 1974) 236, 241-67.

14:17-31 BEERNAERT, P. M., "Structure littéraire et lecture théologique de Marc 14: 17-52" in: M. Sabbe (ed.) L'Evangile selon Marc (Gembloux 1974) 244f, 249-52.

14:17-26 KLOSTERMANN, E. Das Markusevangelium (1950) 146f. *DOCKX, "Le récit du repas pascal. Marc 14, 17-26" Biblica 46 (4, '65) 445-53. GRÄSSER, E., in: GPM 27 (1973) 139-47. STIERLE, B., und ZIPPERT, C., in: P. Krusche (ed.) Predigtstudien III/1 (Stuttgart 1980) 178-85.

14:17-25 SCHLINK, E. "Gerechtigkeit und Rechtfertigung" Zuwendung und Gerechtigkeit (1969) 43-48. *HEIN, K. "Judas Iscariot: Key to the Last-Supper Narratives?" NTS 17 (2, '71) 227-32.

14:17-21 TAYLOR, V., Jesus and His Sacrifice (London 1948) 111-14, 235. BULTMANN, R., The History of the Synoptic Tradition (Oxford 1963)264f. ROLOFF, J. Apostolat-Verkündigung-Kirche (1965) 159-61. KREMER, J. Das Aergernis des Kreuzes (1969) 19-21. SCHENKE, L., Studien zur Passionsgeschichte des Markus (Würzburg 1971) 199-285. PATSCH, H., Abendmahl und historischer Jesus (Stuttgart 1972) 62f. HOFFMANN, P., "Mk 8, 31. Zur Herkunft und markinischen Rezeption einer alten Überlieferung" in: P. Hoffmann (ed.) Orientierung an Jesus. Für J. Schmid (Freiburg 1973) 188-91. DORMEYER, D., Die Passion Jesu als Verhaltensmodell (Münster 1974) 94-100. MAHONEY, R., Two Disciples at the Tomb (Bern/Frankfurt 1974) 83-85, 88-92. SCHENK, W., Der Passionsbericht nach Markus (Gütersloh 1974) 185ff. TALBERT, C. H., Literary Patterns, Theological Themes, and the Genre of Luke-Acts (Missoula 1974) 28. PESCH, R., Das Markusevangelium II (Freiburg 1977) 353 (lit!).

14:17 BROER, I. Die Urgemeinde und das Grab Jesu (1972) 141f, 149-52. HENDRIKS, W., "Zur Kollektionsgeschichte des Markusevangeliums" in: M. Sabbe (ed.) L'Evangile selon Marc (Gembloux 1974) 53, 55. SCHMAHL, G., Die Zwölf im Markusevangelium (Trier 1974) 100-101.

14:18-25 *SYNGE, F. C., "Mark 14:18-25. Supper and Rite" Journal of Theology for Southern Africa 4 (1973) 38-43.

14:18-21 SCHüRMANN, H. Ursprung und Gestalt (1970) 92, 93, 125, 131, 205. LINNEMANN, E. Studien zur Passionsgeschichte (1970) 82-93, 102-108.

14:18, 20 REHKOPF, F., Die lukanische Sonderquelle (Tübingen 1959) 8ff.

14:18 JEREMIAS, J. Die Abendmahlsworte Jesu (1960) 42-44. LINDARS, B. New Testament Apologetic (1961) 98f. HAHN, F. Christologische Hoheitstitel (1963) 62. HASLER, V. Amen (1969) 49. BERGER, K. Die Amen-Worte Jesu (1970) 49-50.

14:19 REHKOPF, F., Die lukanische Sonderquelle (Tübingen 1959) 22ff. HAHN, F. Christologische Hoheitstitel (1963) 86.

14:20 REHKOPF, F., Die lukanische Sonderquelle (Tübingen 1959) 8ff. SCHMAHL, G., Die Zwölf im Markusevangelium (Trier 1974) 101-102. "Amt" in: TRE 2 (1978) 511. TRILLING, W., "Die Entstehung des Zwölferkreises. Eine geschichtskritische Überlegung" in: R. Schnackenburg (ed.) Die Kirche des Anfangs. Für H. Schürmann (Freiburg 1978) 206f.

14:21-22 YATES, J. E., The Spirit and the Kingdom (London 1963) 126f, 138f, 142f, 147f.

14:21 LIGHTFOOT, R. H. History and Interpretation in the Gospels (1934) 154f. TAYLOR, V., Jesus and His Sacrifice (London 1948) 29, 47, 112-14, 156, 195, 256, 259. *CHRISTENSEN, J. "Der Menschensohn geht dahin, wie von ihm geschrieben Steht" DTT 19 (1956) 83-92. *CHRISTENSEN, J. "Le fils de l'homme s'en va, ainsi qu'il est écrit de lui" StTh 10 (1, '56) 28-39. GRANT, F. C. The Gospels (1957) 83f. REHKOPF, F., Die lukanische Sonderquelle (Tübingen 1959) 13ff. SCHWEIZER, E. Erniedrigung und Erhöhung bei Jesus und seinen Nachfolgern (1962) §3k. HAHN, F. Christologische Hoheitstitel (1963) 46, 47, 50, 52, 53, 205. HENNECKE, E. und SCHNEEMELCHER, W., Neutestamentliche Apokryphen II (Tübingen 1964) 473. HOOKER, M. D. The Son of Man in Mark (1967) 159-61, 181, 182. NICKELS, P. Targum and New Testament (1967) 26. POPKES, W. Christus Traditus (1967) 153, 161, 163, 245, 268, 280. LINTON, O., "Evidences of a Second-Century Revised Edition of St Mark's Gospel" NTS 14 (1967-1968) 348f. MINETTE DE TILLESSE, G. Le secret Messianique dans L'Evangile de Marc (1968) 390-94. STROBEL, A. Erkenntnis und Bekenntnis der Sünde in neutestamentlicher Zeit (1968) 39. WREGE, H.-T., Die Überlieferungsgeschichte der Bergpredigt (Tübingen 1968) 46, 173, 175, 180. WILCOX, M., "The Composition of John 13:21-30" in: E. E. Ellis/M. Wilcox (eds.) Neotestamentica et Semitica (Edinburgh 1969) 152-55. GUETTGEMANNS, E.

Offen Fragen zur Formgeschichte des Evangeliums (1970) 211, 215, 216. SANFORD, J. A., The Kingdom Within (New York 1970) 134-36. JEREMIAS, J. Neutestamentliche Theologie I (1971) 248, 264, 268f. HIERS, R. H., The Historical Jesus and the Kingdom of God (Gainsville 1973) 98f. HOFFMANN, P., "Mk 8:31. Zur Herkunft und markinischen Rezeption einer alten Überlieferung" in: P. Hoffmann (ed.) Orientierung an Jesus. Für J. Schmid (Freiburg 1973) 170f, 175f, 178, 179, 186, 194-96, 199. SCHÜRMANN, H., "Wie hat Jesus seinen Tod bestanden und verstanden?" in: P. Hoffmann (ed.) Orientierung an Jesus. Für J. Schmid (Freiburg 1973) 328f. WANKE, J., Die Emmauserzählung (Leipzig 1973) 91, 94. COPPENS, J., "Les Logia du Fils de l'Homme dans l'évangile de Marc" in: M. Sabbe (ed.) L'Evangile selon Marc (Gembloux 1974) 499, 501. DORMEYER, D., Die Passion Jesu als Verhaltensmodell (Münster 1974) 97-99. PERRIN, N., "The Christology of Mark" in: M. Sabbe (ed.) L'Evangile selon Marc (Gembloux 1974) 484. PERRIN, N., A Modern Pilgrimage in New Testament Christology (Philadelphia 1974) 115-21. SAND, A., Das Gesetz und die Propheten (Regensburg 1974) 86. ACHTEMEIER, P. J., Mark (Philadelphia 1975) 46. KOCH, D. A., "Zum Verhältnis von Christologie und Eschatologie im Markusevangelium" in: G. Strecker (ed.) Jesus Christus in Historie und Theologie. Für H. Conzelmann (Tübingen 1975) 403-405. PESCH, R., "Die Passion des Menschensohnes" in: R. Pesch/R. Schnackenburg (eds.) Jesus und der Menschensohn. Für A. Vögtle (Freiburg 1975) 181-83. VIA, D. O., Kerygma and Comedy in the New Testament (Philadelphia 1975) 129, 134, 144, 153. ROBBINS, V. K., "Last Meal: Preparation, Betrayal, and Absence" in: W. H. Kelber (ed.) The Passion in Mark (Philadelphia 1976) 31-34. GERSTENBERGER, G., und SCHRAGE, W., Leiden (Stuttgart 1977) 152f; ET: Suffering (Nashville 1980) 177. PERRIN, N., "Die Christologie des Markus-Evangeliums" [orig: "The Christology of Mark" JR 51 (1971) 173-87] in: R. Pesch (ed.) Das Markus-Evangelium (Darmstadt 1979) 369-70. MALBON, E. S., "Mythic Structure and Meaning in Mark" Semeia 16 (1980) 109-13. TANNEHILL, R. C., "The Gospel of Mark as Narrative Christology" Semeia 16 (1980) 84-85.

14:22ff   RUDOLPH, K., Die Mandäer II (Göttingen 1961) 399, 1. BULTMANN, R., Theologie des Neuen Testaments (Tübingen 1965) 148ff.

14:22-27   BRAUN, H., Qumran und NT (Tübingen 1966) 32, 35, 38f, 41-43, 51, 322.

14:22-26   BARTSCH, H. W., "Der ursprüngliche Schluss der Leidensgeschichte" in: M. Sabbe (ed.) L'Evangile selon Marc (Gembloux 1974) 416-17. GNILKA, J., Das Evangelium nach Markus II (Einsiedeln/Neukirchen 1979) 239 (lit!).

14:22-25   ANDERSON, A. "Das Abendmahl in den zwei ersten Jahrhunderten nach Christus" ZNW 3 (1903) 128-34. TAYLOR, V., Jesus and His Sacrifice (London 1948) 114-18, 215. TAYLOR, V. The Gospel According to St Mark (1953) 664-67. *TURNER, N. "The Style of St Mark's Eucharistic Words" JTS VIII/1 '57 108-111. SCHMID, J. Das Evangelium nach Markus (1958) 264-68. *DU ROY, J.-B. "Le dernier repas de Jésus BVieC 26 ('59) 44-52. *AHERN, B. M. "Gathering the Fragments: The Lord's Supper" Worship 35 (7, '61) 424-29. BULTMANN, R., The History of the Synoptic Tradition (Oxford 1963) 278f. BEST, E. The Temptation and the Passion: The Markan Soteriology (1965) 91, 144-47, 187. DU TOIT, A. B. Der Aspect der Freude im urchristlichen Abendmahl (1965) 76-102. SUHL, A. Die Funktion der alttestamentlichen Zitate und Anspielungen im Markusevangelium (1965) 110ff. KÜNG, H., Die Kirche (Freiburg 1967) 254-59; ET: The Church (London 1967) 212-15. *BECK, N. A. "The Last Supper as an Efficacious Symbolic Act" JBL 89 (2, '70) 192-98. TAYLOR, V. New Testament Essays (1970) 51-54. *FENEBERG, R., Christliche Passafeier und Abendmahl (München 1971); *Review*: H. K. McARTHUR, CBQ 34 (1972) 494-96. *NARDONI, E. "Por una comunidad libre. La ultima cena segun Mc 14,22-25 y el éxodo" RevBi 33 (1, '71) 27-42. SCHENKE, L., Studien zur Passionsgeschichte des Markus (Würzburg 1971) 286-341. BROER, I. Die Urgemeinde und das Grab Jesu (1972) 151f. KERTELGE, K., "Die soteriologischen Aussagen in der urchristlichen Abendmahlsüberlieferung und ihre Beziehung zum geschichtlichen Jesus" TThZ 81 (1972) 193-202. SCHÜRMANN, H., "Wie hat Jesus seinen Tod bestanden und verstanden?" in: P. Hoffmann (ed.) Orientierung an Jesus. Für J. Schmid (Freiburg 1973) 353-59. DORMEYER, D., Die Passion Jesu als Verhaltensmodell (Münster 1974) 100-110. KILPATRICK, G. D., "Eucharist as Sacrifice and Sacrament in the New Testament" in: J. Gnilka (ed.) Neues Testament und Kirche. Für R. Schnackenburg (Freiburg 1974) 429-33. SCHENK, W., Der Passionsbericht nach Markus (Gütersloh 1974) 189ff. GOPPELT, L., Theologie des Neuen Testaments I (Göttingen 1975) 261-67. WILLIAMS, S. K., Jesus' Death as Saving Event (Missoula 1975) 204-11, 217-20. SCHELKLE, K. H., "Das Herrenmahl" in: J. Friedrich et al. (eds.)

Rechtfertigung. Für E. Käsemann (Tübingen 1976) 388-90. "Abendmahlsfeier" in: TRE 1 (1977) 230. *MERKLEIN, H., "Erwägungen zur Überlieferungsgeschichte der neutestamentlichen Abendmahlstraditionen" BZ 21 (1977) 88-101, 235-24. *PESCH, R., "The Last Supper and Jesus' Understanding of His Death" Biblebhashyam³ (1977) 58-75. PESCH, R., Das Markusevangelium II (Freiburg 1977) 363f, 376f (lit!). PESCH, R., Wie Jesus das Abendmahl hielt (Freiburg 1977). PESCH, R., Das Abendmahl und Jesu Todesverständnis (Freiburg 1978). RIST, J. M., On the Independence of Matthew and Mark (Cambridge 1978) 85. SCHMITHALS, W., Das Evangelium nach Markus (Gütersloh/Würzburg 1979) 613 (lit!). KERTELGE, K., "Das Abendmahl Jesu im Markusevangelium" in: J. Zmijewski/E. Nellessen (eds.) Begegnung mit dem Wort. Für H. Zimmermann (Bonn 1980) 67-80.

14:22-24 SCHELKLE, K. H., Die Passion Jesu in der Verkündigung des Neuen Testament (Heidelberg 1949) 186f. HAHN, F. Christologische Hoheitstitel (1963) 48, 60. HAHN, F. Das Verständnis der Mission im Neuen Testament (1965) 43. KESSLER, H. Die theologische Bedeutung des Todes Jesu (1970) 275-78, 280f. SCHILLE, G. Das vorsynoptische Judenchristentum (1970) 32-33. SCHüRMANN, H. Ursprung und Gestalt (1970) 85, 86, 100, 103, 122, 204. *JEREMIAS, J. " 'This is My Body. . .' " ET 83 (7, '72) 196-203. "Abendmahl"in: TRE 1 (1977) 47. FRIEDRICH, G., "Ursprung, Urform und Urbedeutung des Abendmahls" in: Auf das Wort kommt es an (Göttingen 1978) 306-14.

14::22-23 SCHMID, R., Das Bundesopfer in Israel (München 1964) 125f.

14:22 WELLHAUSEN, J., "Kommentar zu Mk 14:22" ZNW 7 (1906). JEREMIAS, J., "Das Brotbrechen beim Passahmahl" ZNW 33 (1934) 203. TAYLOR, V., Jesus and His Sacrifice (London 1948) 80, 87, 118-25, 176f, 202, 236, 242f, 266. MAURER, Chr. Ignatius von Antiochien und das Johannesevangelium (1949) 78f. SCHÜRMANN, H., Der Einsetzungsbericht (Münster 1955) 43ff. *TORRES, M. "Un problema de traduccion. Est es mi cuerpo o esto es mi cuerpo"?" CultBib 15 (158, '58) 1-9. *GOLDBERG, A., "Sitzend zur Rechten der Kraft" BZ 8 (1964) 284-92. NICKELS, P. Targum and New Testament (1967) 26. KREMER, J. Das Aergernis des Kreuzes (1969) 22-26. BROER, I. Die Urgemeinde und das Grab Jesu (1972) 151f, 162. WANKE, J., Die Emmauserzählung (Leipzig 1973) 98, 104. DORMEYER, D., Die Passion Jesu als Verhaltensmodell (Münster 1974) 100-

102. TALBERT, C. H., Literary Patterns, Theological Themes, and the Genre of Luke-Acts (Missoula 1974) 21. VAN CANGH, J. M., "La multiplication des pains dans l'évangile de Marc" in: M. Sabbe (ed.) L'Evangile selon Marc (Gembloux 1974) 331. ROBBINS, V. K., "Last Meal: Preparation, Betrayal, and Absence" in: W. H. Kelber (ed.) The Passion in Mark (Philadelphia 1976) 34-37. *WINNETT, A. R., "The Breaking of the Bread: Does it Symbolize the Passion?" ET 88 (1977) 181-82.

14:23-24 SCHÜRMANN, H., Der Einsetzungsbericht (Münster 1955) 17ff.

14:24-25 FLEW, R. N. Jesus and His Church (1956) 65, 72-77.

14:24 DALMAN, G., Jesus-Jeschua (Leipzig 1922) 145ff, 155f. MANSON, W., Jesus the Messiah (Philadelphia 1948) 143f. TAYLOR, V., Jesus and His Sacrifice (London 1948) 74, 81, 123, 125-39, 182, 202-204, 236, 242f, 261, 266, 280. TAYLOR, V., "The Origin of the Markan Passion Sayings" NTS 1 (1954-1955) 159ff. *EMERTON, J. A. "The Aramaic underlying τὸ αἷμά μου τῆς διαθήκης in Mk 14,24" JThSt VI/2, 1955, 238ff. SCHÜRMANN, H., Der Einsetzungsbericht (Münster 1955) 64ff. ROBINSON, J. M. Das Geschichtsverständnis des Markus-Evangeliums (1956) 79f, 96, 99. BOSCH, D. Die Heidenmission in der Zukunftsschau Jesu (1959) 175-77. HOOKER, M. D., Jesus and the Servant (London 1959) 80-83. BRUCE, F. F. "The Book of Zechariah and the Passion Narrative" BJRL 43 (1960/61) 347. SCHWEIZER, E. Erniedrigung und Erhöhung bei Jesus und seinen Nachfolgern (1962) §6e. STRECKER, G. Der Weg der Gerechtigkeit (1962) 67. HAHN, F. Christologische Hoheitstitel (1963) 57, 61, 64, 66. TOEDT, H. E. Der Menschensohn in der synoptischen Ueberlieferung (1963) 186-89, 190f, 250f. *EMERTON, J. A. "Mark XIV.24 and the Targum to the Psalter" JThS 15 (1, '64) 58-59. KAESEMANN, E. Exegetische Versuche und Besinnungen (1964) I 99. HAHN, F. Das Verständnis der Mission im Neuen Testament (1965) 28, 101. SUHL, A. Die Funktion der alttestamentlichen Zitate und Anspielungen im Markusevangelium (1965) 114ff, 126. NICKELS, P. Targum and New Testament (1967) 26. POPKES, W. Christus Traditus (1967) 169, 171ff, 256, 260. SCHREIBER, J. Theologie des Vertrauens (1967) 19, 90f, 117, 123, 120-23. MAURER, C., "Das Messiasgeheimnis des Markusevangeliums" NTS 14 (1967-1968) 520f. SMITH, M., Tannaitic Parallels to the Gospels (Philadelphia 1968) 3.5+. STROBEL, A. Erkenntnis und Bekenntnis der Sünde in neutestamentlicher Zeit (1968) 39. KREMER, J. Das Aergernis des Kreuzes (1969) 26-27.

LOHSE, E. and others (eds.) Der Ruf Jesu und die Antwort der Gemeinde (1970) 204-12. THYEN, H. Studien zur Sündenvergebung (1970) 154-63. JEREMIAS, J. Neutestamentliche Theologie I (1971) 116, 272f. DELLING, G., Der Kreuzestod Jesu in der urchristlichen Verkündigung (Göttingen 1972) 30-33, 67f. WILSON, S. G., The Gentiles and the Gentile Mission in Luke-Acts (Cambridge 1973) 7-9, 30, 50. *HOOK, N., "The Dominical Cup Saying" Theology 77 (1974) 624-30. GOPPELT, L., Theologie des Neuen Testaments I (Göttingen 1975) 155, 235, 240f, 243. WILLIAMS, J. A., A Conceptual History of Deuteronomism in the Old Testament, Judaism, and the New Testament (Ph.D.Diss. Southern Baptist Theological Seminary, Louisville 1976) 310-18. "Abendmahl" in: TRE 1 (1977) 52, 54. KLAPPERT, B., "Arbeit Gottes und Mitarbeit des Menschen (Phil 2, 6-11)" in: J. Moltmann (ed.) Recht auf Arbeit - Sinn der Arbeit (München 1979) 102, 114. "Beschneidung" in: TRE 5 (1980) 721.

14:25   GRILL, J., Untersuchungen über die Entstehung des vierten Evangeliums II (Leipzig 1923) 201, 267, 274, 287. TAYLOR, V., Jesus and His Sacrifice (London 1948) 125, 139-42, 184, 259. VOGELS, H. "Mk 14, 25 und Parallelen" Vom Wort des Lebens, Festschrift Max Meinertz (1951) 93-104. ROBINSON, J. M. Kerygma und historischer Jesus (1960) 157, 162. STRECKER, G. Der Weg der Gerechtigkeit (1962) 87. HAHN, F. Christologische Hoheitstitel (1963) 105. PERRIN, N., The Kingdom of God in the Teaching of Jesus (Philadelphia 1963) 61, 68, 80, 85f, 183, 188. HAHN, F. Das Verständnis der Mission im Neuen Testament (1965) 28, NICKELS, P. Targum and New Testament (1967) 26. MINETTE DE TILLESSE, G. Le Secret Messianique dans L'Evangile de Marc (1968) 390-94. STROBEL, A. Erkenntnis und Bekenntnis der Sünde in neutestamentlicher Zeit (1968) 40. HASLER, V. Amen (1969) 49. KREMER, J. Das Aergernis des Kreuzes (1969) 29-30. PESCH, R. Naherwartungen (1969) 69, 92, 119, 152. AMBROZIC, A. M., St Mark's Concept of the Kingdom of God (Würzburg 1970) 196-216. BERGER, K. Die Amen-Worte Jesus (1970) 54-59. SCHüRMANN, H. Ursprung und Gestalt (1970) 80, 87, 118, 120, 203. JEREMIAS, J. Neutestamentliche Theologie I (1971) 40, 42, 44, 100ff, 138, 185. *ZIESLER, J. A., "The Vow of Abstinence. A Note on Mark 14:25 and Parallels" Colloquium 5 (1972) 12-14. *PALMER, D., "Defining a Vow of Abstinence" Colloquium 5 (1973) 38-41. SCHNACKENBURG, R., " 'Das Evangelium' im Verständnis des ältesten Evangelisten" in: P. Hoffmann (ed.)

Orientierung an Jesus. Für J. Schmid (Freiburg 1973) 319f. LADD, G. E., A Theology of the New Testament (Grand Rapids 1974) 74, 186, 190. "Abendmahl" in: TRE 1 (1977) 49, 52. "Amen" in: TRE 2 (1978) 389. SCHLOSSER, J., "Le règne de Dieu dans les dits de Jésus RevSR 53 (1979) 164-76. MALBON, E. S., "Mythic Structure and Meaning in Mark" Semeia 16 (1980) 109-13.

14:26-16:8   LIETZMANN, H. "Bemerkungen zum Prozess Jesu" I & II Kleine Schriften II (1958) 264-68, 269-76. LIETZMANN, H. "Der Prozess Jesu" Kleine Schriften II (1958) 251-63.

14:26-50   ZIMMERMANN, W.-D. Markus über Jesus (1970) 155-61.

14:26-42   KUHN, K. G. "Jesus in Gethsemane" EvTh 12 (1952/53) 260-85. SCHMID, J. "Jesu Leidenskampf in Gethsemane" Das Evangelium nach Markus (1958) 277f. MINETTE DE TILLESSE, G. Le Secret Messianique dans L'Evangile de Marc (1968) 410-20. SCHENKE, L., Studien zur Passionsgeschichte des Markus (Würzburg 1971) 348-564.

14:26-31   KLEIN, G. "Die Verleugnung des Petrus" Rekonstruktion und Interpretation (1969) 49-98. SCHENKE, L., Studien zur Passionsgeschichte des Markus (Würzburg 1971) 348-460. *WILCOX, M. "The Denial-Sequence in Mark xiv. 26-31, 66-72" NTS 17 (4, '71) 426-36. DORMEYER, D., Die Passion Jesu als Verhaltensmodell (Münster 1974) 110-17. PESCH, R., "Die Verleugnung des Petrus" in: J. Gnilka (ed.) Neues Testament und Kirche. Für R. Schnackenburg (Freiburg 1974) 42-62. SCHENK, W., Der Passionsbericht nach Markus (Gütersloh 1974) 223ff. TALBERT, C. H., Literary Patterns, Theological Themes, and the Genre of Luke-Acts (Missoula 1974) 28. PESCH, R., Das Markusevangelium II (Freiburg 1977) 384f. (lit!). SCHMITHALS, W., Das Evangelium nach Markus (Gütersloh 1979) 625f. (lit!).

14:26   KREMER, J. Das Aergernis des Kreuzes (1969) 31-32. PATSCH, H., Abendmahl und historischer Jesus (Stuttgart 1972) 62f. ACHTEMEIER, P. J., Mark (Philadelphia 1975) 46. MALBON, E. S., "Mythic Structure and Meaning in Mark" Semeia 16 (1980) 103-107.

14:27-16:5   SMITH, M., Clement of Alexandria and a secret Gospel of Mark (Cambridge/Mass. 1973) 165f, 175, 191f.

14:27-42   CARRINGTON, P. The Primitive Christian Calendar (1952) 216-18. *LINNEMANN, E. "Die Verleugnung des Petrus" ZThK 63 (1, '66) 1-32. HAHN, F. GPM 27 (1973) 147-56.

14:27-31   SCHELKLE, K. H., Die Passion Jesu in der Verkündigung des Neuen Testament (Heidelberg 1949) 17-21. GNILKA, J., Das

Evangelium nach Markus II (Einsiedeln/Neukirchen 1979) 250 (lit!). ERNST, J., "Die Petrustradition im Markusevangelium - ein altes Problem neu angegangen" in: J.Zmijewski/E. Nellessen (eds.) Begegnung mit dem Wort. Für H. Zimmermann (Bonn 1980) 56f.

14:27-28   BRUCE, F. F. "The Book of Zechariah and the Passion Narrative" BJRL 43 (1960-61), 342-45. NICKELS, P. Targum. and New Testament (1967) 26. KREMER, J. Das Aergernis des Kreuzes (1969) 32-34. JEREMIAS, J. Neutestamentliche Theologie I (1971) 165, 199, 231, 239, 270f, 281f. CROSSAN, J. D. "Redaction and Citation in Mk 11:9-10:17 and 14:27" Proceedings (1972) I, ed. L. C. McGaughy 17-61. DAVIES, W. D., The Gospel and the Land (London 1974) 228.

14:27   TAYLOR, V., Jesus and His Sacrifice (London 1948) 145-47, 255. FEINE, P. und BEHM, J., Einleitung in das Neue Testament (Heidelberg 1950) 112f. STRECKER, G. Der Weg der Gerechtigkeit (1962) 122. SUHL, A. Die Funktion der alttestamentlichen Zitate und Anspielungen im Markusevangelium (1965) 29, 62ff, 102, 132. JEREMIAS, J. New Testament Theology I (1971) 168, 205, 297f. CROSSAN, J. D., "Redaction and Citation in Mark 11:9-10, 17 and 14:27" in: L. C. Mc Gaugh (ed.) SBL Seminar Papers I (Montana 1972) 17-62. DAUER, A., Die Passionsgeschichte im Johannesevangelium (München 1972) 234, 295f. *SCHROEDER, R. P., "The 'Worthless' Shepherd. A Study of Mark 14:27" Currents in Theology and Mission 2 (1975) 342-44.

14:28   GRASS, K., "Zu Mk 14:28" ZNW 13 (1912) 176. LIGHTFOOT, R. H., Locality and Doctrine in the Gospels (London 1938) 52ff. STONEHOUSE, N. B. The Witness of Matthew and Mark to Christ (1944) 27, 39, 77, 91, 170ff. KUEMMEL, W. G. Verheissung und Erfüllung (1953) 70-72. STRECKER, G. Der Weg der Gerechtigkeit (1962) 48, 94, 97f. SCHREIBER, J. Theologie des Vertrauens (1967) 42, 96, 101, 107-109, 116. MEYE, R. P. Jesus and the Twelve (1968) 80-85. ODENKIRCHEN, P. C. "Praecedam vos in Galilaeam (Mt 26, 32 cf. 28, 7.10; Mc 14, 28; 16, 7 cfr. Lc 24, 6)" VerbDom 46 (1968) 192-223. KASTING, H. Die Anfänge der Urchristlichen Mission (1969) 82-84, 86, 93f. MARXSEN, W. Mark the Evangelist (1969) 75f, 80ff, 86ff, 111f, 115. PESCH, R. Naherwartungen (1969) 157, 168, 232, 242. GRASS, H. Ostergeschehen und Osterberichte (1970) 18n2, 19n1, 21, 33, 108, 113. KÜMMEL, W. G., Einleitung in das Neue Testament (Heidelberg 1973 *(17)*) 60f. LANGE, J., Das Erscheinen des Auferstandenen im Evangelium nach Mattäus (Würzburg

1973) 203, 358, 367-69, 386, 451f, 461-63. WANKE, J., Die Emmauserzählung (Leipzig 1973) 52 A.389. DAVIES, W. D., The Gospel and the Land (London 1974) 226-30 passim, 424-38 passim, 409-13 passim. MAHONEY, R., Two Disciples at the Tomb (Bern/Frankfurt 1974) 154-56. PERRIN, N., The New Testament (New York 1974) 148-51. *STEIN, R. H., "A Short Note on Mark xiv.28 and xvi.7" NTS 20 (1974) 445-52. MALBON, E. S., "Mythic Structure and Meaning in Mark" Semeia 16 (1980) 103-107. TANNEHILL, R. C., "The Gospel of Mark as Narrative Christology" Semeia 16 (1980) 83f.

14:29-31   TALBERT, C. H., Literary Patterns, Theological Themes, and the Genre of Luke-Acts (Missoula 1974) 33.

14:29-30   KREMER, J. Das Aergernis des Kreuzes (1969) 34-35.

14:29   HAHN, F. Christologische Hoheitstitel (1963) 84. SCHNEIDER, G., Verleugnung, Verspottung und Verhör Jesu nach Lukas 22, 54-71 (München 1969) 85, 122, 125, 150.

14:30   STREETER, B. H. The Four Gospels (1951) 404ff. *LATTEY, C. "A Note on Cockcrow" Scripture VI 2 (1953) 53-55. HASLER, V. Amen (1969) 49. SCHNEIDER, G., Verleugnung, Verspottung und Verhör Jesu nach Lukas 22, 54-71 (München 1969) 42, 51, 53f, 94. *BRADY, D., "The Alarm to Peter in Mark's Gospel" Journal for the Study of the New Testament 4 (1979) 42-57. *WENHAM, J. W., "How Many Cock-Crowings? The Problem of Harmonistic Text-Variants" NTS 25 (1979) 523-25.

14:32-16:8   FARRER, A. A Study in St Mark (1951) 133ff, 192f. CLEVENOT, M., So kennen wir die Bibel nicht (München 1978) 121-27.

14:32-15:47   SCHENKE, L., Der gekreuzigte Christus. Versuch einer literarkritischen und traditionsgeschichtlichen Bestimmung der vormarkinischen Passionsgeschichte (Stuttgart 1974).

14:32ff   *CURTIS, J. B. "An Investigation of the Mount of Olives in the Judaeo-Christian Tradition" HUCA 28 ('57) 137-80. STROBEL, A. Erkenntnis und Bekenntnis der Sünde in neutestamentlicher Zeit (1968) 39. HIERS, R. H., The Historical Jesus and the Kingdom of God (Gainsville/Florida 1973) 40, 70, 101f. GERSTENBERGER, G., und SCHRAGE, W., Leiden (Stuttgart 1977) 205, 235; ET: Suffering (Nashville 1980) 237f, 270f.

14:32-52   LINNEMANN, E. Studien zur Passionsgeschichte (1970) 41-69. SCHENKE, L., Der gekreuzigte Christus (Stuttgart 1974) 111-34.

14:32-42   DIBELIUS, M. "Gethsemane" The Crozer Quarterly 12, 1935, 254ff. SCHELKLE, K. H., Die Passion Jesu in der

Verkündigung des Neuen Testament (Heidelberg 1949) 33f, 39, 41, 50, 53, 76, 79. DENNEY, J. The Death of Christ (1956) 41ff. *HERING, J. "Simples remarques sur la prière à Gethsémané. Matthieu 26:36-46; Marc 14:32-42; Luc 22:40-46" RHPhR 39 (2, '59) 97-102. HERING, J. "Zwei exegetische Probleme in der Perikope von Jesus in Gethsemane (Markus xiv 32-42; Matthäus xxvi 36-46; Lukas xxii 40-46)" Neotestamentica et Patristica (Festschrift für O. Cullmann (1962) 64-69. BULTMANN, R., The History of the Synoptic Tradition (Oxford 1963) 267f. BOMAN, Th. "Der Gebetskampf Jesu" NTS 10, (1963) 261ff. MAUSER, U. Christ in the Wilderness (1963) 107f, 119, 128ff. BRAUN, H., Qumran und NT (Tübingen 1966) 188, 238, 312. BENOIT, P. Passion et Résurrection du Seigneur (1966) 17-22. *LESCOW, T. "Jesus in Gethsemane" EvTh 26 (3, '66) 141-59. BOMAN, T. Die Jesus-Ueberlieferung im Lichte der neueren Volkskunde (1967) 208-21. PESCH, R. Naherwartungen (1969) 66, 97, 118, 138, 201, 206. PESCH, W. Den Menschen helfen (1969) 20-28. *BARBOUR, R. S. "Gethsemane in the Tradition of the Passion" NTS 16 (3, '70) 231-51. LINNEMANN, E. Studien zur Passionsgeschichte (1970) 11-4. SCHENKE, L., Studien zur Passionsgeschichte des Markus (Würzburg 1971) 461-560. *KELBER, W. H., "Mark 14:32-42: Gethsemane. Passion Christology and Discipleship Failure" ZNW 63 (1972) 166-87. HOFFMANN, P., "Mark 8, 31. Zur Herkunft und markinischen Rezeption einer alten Überlieferung" in: P. Hoffmann (ed.) Orientierung an Jesus. Für J. Schmid (Freiburg 1973) 191f. *HOLLERAN, J. W., The Synoptic Gethsemane (Rome 1973) *MOHN, W., "Gethsemane (Mk 14:32-42)" ZNW 64 (1973) 194-208. DORMEYER, D., Die Passion Jesu als Verhaltensmodell (Münster 1974) 124-37. SCHENK, W., Der Passionsbericht nach Markus (Gütersloh 1974) 193ff. SCHENKE, L., Der gekreuzigte Christus (Stuttgart 1974) 124-34. SCHMAHL, G., Die Zwölf im Markusevangelium (Trier 1974) 134f. TALBERT, C. H., Literary Patterns, Theological Themes, and the Genre of Luke-Acts (Missoula 1974) 28. DUNN, J. D. G., Jesus and the Spirit (London 1975) 17-20. HOWARD, V. P., Das Ego in den Synoptischen Evangelien (Marburg 1975) 123-32. KELBER, W. H., "The Hour of the Son of Man and the Temptation of the Disciples" in: W. H. Kelber (ed.) The Passion in Mark (Philadelphia 1976) 41-60. SZAREK, G., "A Critique of Kelber's 'The Hour of the Son of Man and the Temptation of the Disciples: Mark 14:32-42" in: G. MacRae (ed.) SBL 1976 Seminar Papers (Missoula 1976) 111-18. DUNN, J. D. G.,

Unity and Diversity in the New Testament (London 1977) 100.
*FEUILLET, A., L'agonie de Gethsémani. Enquête exégétique
et théologique suivie d'un étude du "Mystère de Jésus" de
Pascal (Paris 1977); *Review:* CARLE, P.-L., Divinitas 21
(1977) 429-32. PESCH, R., Das Markusevangelium II
(Freiburg 1977) 396 (lit!). GNILKA, J., Das Evangelium nach
Markus II (Einsiedeln/Neukirchen 1979) 255 (lit!).
SCHMITHALS, W., Das Evangelium nach Markus
(Gütersloh/Würzburg 1979) 633 (lit!). ERNST, J., "Die
Petrustradition im Markusevangelium - ein altes Problem neu
angegangen" in: J. Zmijewski/E. Nellessen (eds.) Begegnung
mit dem Wort. Für H. Zimmermann (Bonn 1980) 55f.

14:32-35 KLAPPERT, B., "Arbeit Gottes und Mitarbeit des Menschen
(Phil 2, 6-11)" in: J. Moltmann (ed.) Recht auf Arbeit - Sinn der
Arbeit (München 1979) 106-108.

14:32-33 KREMER, J. Das Aergernis des Kreuzes (1969) 36-37.

14:32 TALBERT, C. H., Literary Patterns, Theological Themes, and
the Genre of Luke-Acts (Missoula 1974) 28. METZGER, B.
M., The Early Versions of the New Testament (Oxford 1977)
172. MALBON, E. S., "Mythic Structure and Meaning in
Mark" Semeia 16 (1980) 103-107.

14:33ff RIESENFELD, H., Jésus Transfiguré (Copenhagen 1947)
280ff, 289.

14:33-38 DIBELIUS, M. Botschaft und Geschichte I (1953) 258-71.

14:33 FEINE, P., und BEHM, J., Einleitung in das Neue Testament
(Heidelberg 1950) 58f. ROLOFF, J., Apostolat-
Verkündigung-Kirche (Gütersloh 1965) 152f. SCHMAHL, G.,
Die Zwölf im Markusevangelium (Trier 1974) 135-37.

14:34-36 KONINGS, J., "The Pre-Markan Sequence in Jn VI" in: M.
Sabbe (ed.) L'Evangile selon Marc (Gembloux 1974) 173.

14:34 KREMER, J. Das Aergernis des Kreuzes (1969) 37-38.
DAUER, A., Die Passionsgeschichte im Johannesevangelium
(München 1972) 232, 283, 295.

14:35-41 STRECKER, G. Der Weg der Gerechtigkeit (1962) 39.

14:35-36 KREMER, J. Das Aergernis des Kreuzes (1969) 38-39.
HOFFMANN, P., "Mk 8, 31. Zur Herkunft und markinischen
Rezeption einer alten Überlieferung" in: P. Hoffmann (ed.)
Orientierung an Jesus. Für J. Schmid (Freiburg 1973) 193f,
197. TANNEHILL, R. C., "The Gospel of Mark as Narrative
Christology" Semeia 16 (1980) 86.

14:35 PESCH, R. Naherwartungen (1969) 117, 133, 149, 184, 201.

14:36　TAYLOR, V., Jesus and His Sacrifice (London 1948) 37, 150-52, 256, 258, 263, 276. SPICQ, C. Dieu et L'Homme (1961) 68-69. *MARCHEL, W. "Abba, Pater! Oratio Christi et christianorum" VerbDom 39 (5-6, '61) 240-47. HAHN, F. Christologische Hoheitstitel (1963) 321f. MARCHEL, W., Abba, Père! La Prière du Christ et des Chrétiens (Rome 1963) 101-27. JEREMIAS, J. Abba (1966) 56-58. NICKELS, P. Targum and New Testament (1967) 27. PESCH, R. Naherwartungen (1969) 110, 117, 134, 156, 194. VAN UNNIK, W. C. "Alles ist dir möglich" (Mk 14, 36), Verborum Veritas, Festschrift für G. Stählin, eds. O. Böcher und K. Haacker (1970) 27-36. JEREMIAS, J. Neutestamentliche Theologie I (1971) 16, 68, 70, 138, 164, 182, 242, 269. DAUER, A., Die Passionsgeschichte im Johannesevangelium (München 1972) 48, 232, 283. CONZELMANN, H., und LINDEMANN, A., Arbeitsbuch zum Neuen Testament (Tübingen 1975) 352. DUNN, J. D. G., Jesus and the Spirit (London 1975) 18-23, 26, 34, 39, 41. HOWARD, V. P., Das Ego in den Synoptischen Evangelien (Marburg 1975) 123-32. JANSSEN, E., "Testament Abrahams" in: W. G. Kümmel (ed.) Jüdische Schriften aus hellenistisch-römischer Zeit III (Gütersloh 1975) 221. WILLIAMS, J. A., A Conceptual History of Deuteronomism in the Old Testament, Judaism, and the New Testament (Ph.D.Diss. Southern Baptist Theological Seminary, Louisville 1976) 317. DUNN, J. D. G., Unity and Diversity in the New Testament (London 1977) 187. "Aramäisch" in: TRE 3 (1978) 602. FRIEDRICH, G., "Das Problem der Autorität im Neuen Testament" in: Auf das Wort kommt es an (Göttingen 1978) 390.

14:37-46　KNOX, W. L. The Sources of the Synoptic Gospels I (1953) 128ff.

14:37-42　KREMER, J. Das Aergernis des Kreuzes (1969) 39-40.

14:37　STRECKER, G. Der Weg der Gerechtigkeit (1962) 206. PESCH, R. Naherwartungen (1969) 132, 133, 200, 201. ACHTEMEIER, P. J., Mark (Philadelphia 1975) 96.

14:38　STRECKER, G. Der Weg der Gerechtigkeit (1962) 183. WULF, F., "Der Geist ist willig aber das Fleisch schwach" GuL 37 (1964) 241-43. PESCH, R. Naherwartungen (1969) 149, 150, 200, 201. JEREMIAS, J. Neutestamentliche Theologie I (1971) 25, 138, 196, 234. KÜMMEL, W. G., Römer 7 und das Bild des Menschen im Neuen Testament (München 1974) 175f. SCHWEIZER, E., Heiliger Geist (Stuttgart 1978) 83-85.

14:40-41　SCHWEIZER, E., "Mark's Contribution to the Quest of the Historical Jesus" NTS 10 (1963-64) 430f.

14:40 KNOX, W. L. The Sources of the Synoptic Gospels II (1957) 55, 116. BROER, I. Die Urgemeinde und das Grab Jesu (1972) 129f. KELBER, W. H., "The Hour of the Son of Man and the Temptation of the Disciples" in: W. H. Kelber (ed.) The Passion in Mark (Philadelphia 1976) 47-49.

14:41ff YATES, J. E., The Spirit and the Kingdom (London 1963) 138ff.

14:41-46 RIST, J. M., On the Independence of Matthew and Mark (Cambridge 1978) 85f.

14:41-42 TAYLOR, V., Jesus and His Sacrifice (London 1948) 154-56, 169. POPKES, W. Christus Traditus (1967) 159, 180, 245, 268. WILCKENS, U., Die Missionsreden der Apostelgeschichte (Neukirchen 1974=1961) 112-16.

14:41 *BOOBYER, G. H. "APECHEI in Mark xiv 41, NTS 2 (1955) 44-48. HAHN, F. Christologische Hoheitstitel (1963) 205, 46f, 48, 53. MAUSER, U. Christ in the Wilderness (1963) 134f. BLACK, M. An Aramaic Approach to the Gospels and Acts (1967) 225f. HOOKER, M. D. The Son of Man in Mark (1967) 161-63, 181, 182. NICKELS, P. Targum and New Testament (1967) 27. POPKES, W. Christus Traditus (1967) 153ff, 184, 232. MINETTE DE TILLESSE, G. Le Secret Messianique dans L'Evangile de Marc (1968) 390-94. STROBEL, A. Erkenntnis und Bekenntnis der Sünde in neutestamentlicher Zeit (1968) 38. GUETTGEMANNS, E. Offen Fragen zur Formgeschichte des Evangeliums (1970) 215, 215n216, 216. JEREMIAS, J. Neutestamentliche Theologie I (1971) 22, 138, 248, 268. DELLING, G., Der Kreuzestod Jesu in der urchristlichen Verkündigung (Göttingen 1972) 68-70. HOFFMANN, P., "Mk 8, 31. Zur Herkunft und markinischen Rezeption einer alten Überlieferung" in: P. Hoffmann (ed.) Orientierung an Jesus. Für J. Schmid (Freiburg 1973) 170-76, 178, 192-96, 199. COPPENS, J., "Les logia du Fils de l'Homme dans l'évangile de Marc" in: M. Sabbe (ed.) L'Evangile selon Marc (Gembloux 1974) 499. PERRIN, N., "The Christology of Mark" in: M. Sabbe (ed.) L'Evangile selon Marc (Gembloux 1974) 484. PERRIN, N., A Modern Pilgrimage in New Testament Christology (Philadelphia 1974) 115-21, 131f. ACHTEMEIER, P. J., Mark (Philadelphia 1975) 46. PESCH, R., "Die Passion des Menschensohnes" in: R. Pesch/R. Schnackenburg (eds.) Jesus und der Menschensohn. Für A. Vögtle (Freiburg 1975) 183f. KELBER, W. H., "The Hour of the Son of Man and the Temptation of the Disciples" in: W. H. Kelber (ed.) The Passion in Mark (Philadelphia 1976) 49-56. PERRIN, N., "The High-Priest's Question and Jesus' Answer" in: W. H. Kelber (ed.) The Passion in Mark (Philadelphia 1976) 89-91. WILLIAMS, J. A., A Conceptual History of Deuteronomism in the Old Testament, Judaism, and the New Testament (Ph.D.Diss. Southern Baptist Theological Seminary, Louisville 1976) 306. GAIN, D. B., Evidence for Supposing That Our Greek Text of the Gospel of St. Mark Is Translated from Latin. . . (Grahamstown/S. Africa 1978). PERRIN, N., "Die Christologie des Markus-Evangeliums" [orig. "The Christology of Mark" JR 51 (1971) 173-87] in: R. Pesch (ed.) Das Markus-Evangelium (Darmstadt 1979) 369f. MALBON, E. S., "Mythic Structure and Meaning in Mark" Semeia 16 (1980) 109-13. TANNEHILL, R. C., "The Gospel of Mark as Narrative Christology" Semeia 16 (1980) 84f.

14:42   HAHN, F. Christologische Hoheitstitel (1963) 62.

14:43-16:8   SCHNEIDER, G., Die Passion Jesu nach den älteren Evangelien (München 1973). CZERSKI, J., "Die Passion Christi in den synoptischen Evangelien im Lichte der historisch-literarischen Kritik" CoTh 46 (special issue 1976) 81-96.

14:43ff   STROBEL, A. Erkenntnis und Bekenntnis der Sünde in neutestamentlicher Zeit (1968) 39.

14:43-53a   GNILKA, J., Das Evangelium nach Markus II (Einsiedeln/Neukirchen 1979) 266 (lit!).

14:43-52   GOODSPEED, E. J., A Life of Jesus (New York 1950) 205-207. CARRINGTON, P. The Primitive Christian Calendar (1952) 218-19. BULTMANN, R. The History of the Synoptic Tradition (Oxford 1963) 268f. BENOIT, P. Passion et Résurrection du Seigneur (1966) 43-50. BLINZLER, J. Der Prozess Jesu (1969) 4th ed. 69, 73-101. SCHENKE, L., Studien zur Passionsgeschichte des Markus (Würzburg 1971) 356ff, 398f, 469f. SCHNEIDER, G., "Die Verhaftung Jesu. Traditionsgeschichte von Mk 14:42-52" ZNW 63 (1972) 188-209. SCHRAGE, W. GPM 27 (1973) 157-66. DORMEYER, D., Die Passion Jesu als Verhaltensmodell (Münster 1974) 138-46. MOURLON BEERNAERT, P., "Structure littéraire et lecture théologique de Marc 14, 17-52" in: M. Sabbe (ed.) L'Evangile selon Marc (Gembloux 1974) 248, 256-59. SCHENK, W., Der Passionsbericht nach Markus (Gütersloh 1974) 206ff. SCHENKE, L., Der Gekreuzigte Christus (Stuttgart 1974) 111-24, 129-34. TALBERT, C. H., Literary Patterns, Theological Themes, and the Genre of Luke-Acts (Missoula 1974) 29. PESCH, R., Das Markusevangelium II (Freiburg 1977) 403f (lit!). SCHMITHALS, W., Das

Evangelium nach Markus (Gütersloh/Würzburg 1979) 644 (lit!).

14:43-45 KREMER, J. Das Aergernis des Kreuzes (1969) 41-43.

14:43 REHKOPF, F., Die lukanische Sonderquelle (Tübingen 1959) 31ff. BOUSSET, W., Die Religion des Judentums im späthellenistischen Zeitalter (Berlin 1966=1926) 167. HOFFMANN, P., "Mk 8, 31. Zur Herkunft und markinischen Rezeption einer alten Überlieferung" in: P. Hoffmann (ed.) Orientierung an Jesus. Für J. Schmid (Freiburg 1973) 191f. SCHMAHL, G., Die Zwölf im Markusevangelium (Trier 1974) 102-106. WILLIAMS, J. A., A Conceptual History of Deuteronomism in the Old Testament, Judaism, and the New Testament (Ph.D. Diss. Southern Baptist Theological Seminary, Louisville 1976) 302f. "Amt" in: TRE 2 (1978) 511. RIVKIN, E., A Hidden Revolution (Nashville 1978) 107-109. TRILLING, W., "Die Entstehung des Zwölferkreises. Eine geschichtskritische Überlegung" in: R. Schnackenburg (ed.) Die Kirche des Anfangs. Für H. Schürmann (Freiburg 1978) 206f.

14:46-49 KREMER, J. Das Aergernis des Kreuzes (1969) 43-44.

14:46 HAHN, F. Christologische Hoheitstitel (1963) 84. SCHNEIDER, G., Verleugnung, Verspottung und Verhör Jesu nach Lukas 22, 54-71 (München 1969) 49, 63, 73f, 146f, 156, 159.

14:47 REHKOPF, F., Die lukanische Sonderquelle (Tübingen 1959) 56ff. HAHN, F. Christologische Hoheitstitel (1963) 170.

14:48-49 REHKOPF, F., Die lukanische Sonderquelle (Tübingen 1959) 71ff. NEIRYNCK, "Urmarcus redivivus?" in: M. Sabbe (ed.) L'Evangile selon Marc (Gembloux 1974) 109-14.

14:48 HAHN, F. Christologische Hoheitstitel (1963) 172. SCHALIT, A. König Herodes (1969) 721. BLINZLER, J. Der Prozess Jesu (1969) 4th ed. 176f, 308.

14:49 STRECKER, G. Der Weg der Gerechtigkeit (1962) 186. HAHN, F. Christologische Hoheitstitel (1963) 113, 230. BOUSSET, W., Die Religion des Judentums im späthellenistischen Zeitalter (Berlin 1966=1926) 167. DAUER, A., Die Passsionsgeschichte im Johannesevangelium (München 1972) 80f, 295. SWIDLER, L., Biblical Affirmations of Woman (Philadelphia 1979) 199. TANNEHILL, R. C., "The Gospel of Mark as Narrative Christology" Semeia 16 (1980) 84f.

14:50-52 KREMER, J. Das Aergernis des Kreuzes (1969) 45.

14:50　　LANGE, J., Das Erscheinen des Auferstandenen im Evangelium nach Matthäus (Würzburg 1973) 452-54, 456, 460. WANKE, J., Die Emmauserzählung (Leipzig 1973) 73A.389.

14:51-52　KLINGER, J., "Die aufgegebene Exegese der zwei Versetten" Roczniki Teologiczne Chrześcijańskiej Akademii Teologicznej (Warszawa) 8 (1966) 126-49. *VANHOYE, A. "La fuite du jeune homme nu (Mc 14, 51-52)" Biblica 52 (3, '71) 401-406. *SCROGGS, R., and GROFF, K. I., "Baptism in Mark: Dying and Rising with Christ" JBL 92 (1973) 531-48. *FLEDDERMANN, H., "The Flight of a Naked Young Man (Mark 14:51-52)" CBQ 41 (1979) 412-18. *NEIRYNCK, F., "La Fuite du Jeune Homme en Mc 14, 51-52" EphT (1979) 43-66. SMITH, M., Clement of Alexandria and a secret Gospel of Mark (Cambridge, Mass. 1973) 109, 116, 176f., 193, 223, 237. MOURLON BEERNAERT, P., "Structure Littéraire et lecture théologique de Marc 14, 17-52" in: M. Sabbe, (ed.) L'Evangile selon Marc (Gembloux 1974) 256f.

14:53-15:47　GENEST, O., Le Christ de la Passion (Tournai 1978).

14:53-15:20　SCHENKE, L., Der gekreuzigte Christus (Stuttgart 1974) 15-76.

14:53-15:5　GNILKA, J., "Die Verhandlungen vor dem Synhedrion und vor Pilatus nach Markus 14, 53-15, 5" in: Evangelisch-Katholischer Kommentar zum Neuen Testament. Vorarbeiten Heft 2 (Zürich 1970) 5-21.

14:53-15:1　DRURY, J., Tradition and Design in Luke's Gospel (Atlanta 1976) 109-13. SCHMITHALS, W., Das Evangelium nach Markus (Gütersloh/Würzburg 1979) 651f (lit!). STROBEL, A., Die Stunde der Wahrheit (Tübingen 1980) 61-94.

14:53ff　KNOX, W. L. The Sources of the Synoptic Gospels I (1953) 131ff.

14:53-72　GOODSPEED, E. J., A Life of Jesus (New York 1950) 207-12. CARRINGTON, P. The Primitive Christian Calendar (1952) 219-21. *SCHNEIDER, G. "Jesus vor dem Synedrium" BuL 11 (1, '70) 1-15. ZIMMERMANN, W.-D. Markus über Jesus (1970) 161-65. LOHSE, E., Die Einheit des Neuen Testaments (Göttingen 1973) 89-91. SCHENKE, L., Der gekreuzigte Christus (Stuttgart 1974) 15-46. ACHTEMEIER, P. J., Mark (Philadelphia 1975) 88f. FORTNA, R. T., "Jesus and Peter at the High Priest's House: A Test Case for the Question of the Relation Between Mark's and John's Gospels" NTS 24 (1978) 371-83.

14:53-71　PERRIN, N., "The Christology of Mark" in: M. Sabbe (ed.) L'Evangile selon Marc (Gembloux 1974) 474f. PERRIN, N.,

"Die Christologie des Markus-Evangeliums" [orig: "The Christology of Mark" JR 51 (1971) 173-87] in: R. Pesch (ed.) Das Markus-Evangelium (Darmstadt 1979) 359f.

14:53-65 TAYLOR, V. The Gospel According to St Mark (1953) 644-46. SCHMID, J. Das Evangelium nach Markus (1958) 285f. BENOIT, P. Passion et Résurrection du Seigneur (1966) 69-74. O'NEILL, J. C., "The Silence of Jesus" NTS 15 (1968-1969) 157ff. *DONAHUE, J. R., Are You the Christ? (Cambridge, Mass. 1973). GEYER, H.-G. GPM 27/2 (1973) 167-75. SCHENK, W., Der Passionsbericht nach Markus (Gütersloh 1974) 229ff. SCHENKE, L., Der gekreuzigte Christus (Stuttgart 1974) 23-46, 55-60. HOWARD, V. P., Das Ego in den Synoptischen Evangelien (Marburg 1975) 132-48. DONAHUE, J. R, "Temple, Trial, and Royal Christology" in: W. H. Kelber (ed.) The Passion in Mark (Philadelphia 1976) 61-79. GNILKA, J., Das Evangelium nach Markus II (Einsiedeln/Neukirchen 1979) 273f (lit!). STROBEL, A., Die Stunde der Wahrheit (Tübingen 1980) passim.

14:53-64 SCHNIDER, F., Jesus der Prophet (Freiburg 1973) 156ff.

14:53-54 KREMER, J. Das Aergernis des Kreuzes (1969) 46-47. DORMEYER, D., Die Passion Jesu als Verhaltensmodell (Münster 1974) 149f. PESCH, R., Das Markusevangelium II (Freiburg 1977) 427 (lit!).

14:53 HAHN, F. Christologische Hoheitstitel (1963) 47. BOUSSET, W., Die Religion des Judentums im späthellenistischen Zeitalter (Berlin 1966=1926) 167. BLINZLER, J. Der Prozess Jesu (1969) 37, 59, 124, 131, 179, 180, 223. SCHNEIDER, G., Verleugnung, Verspottung und Verhör Jesu nach Lukas 22, 54-71 (München 1969) 16f, 27, 31, 55f, 73-75, 107-11, 122. DONAHUE, J. R., Are You the Christ? (Missoula 1973) 9, 55, 57, 63-66, 68, 87, 101, 117, 164, 172. TALBERT, C. H., Literary Patterns, Theological Themes, and the Genre of Luke-Acts (Missoula 1974) 21f. DONAHUE, J. R., "Temple, Trial, and Royal Christology" in: W. H. Kelber (ed.) The Passion in Mark (Philadelphia 1976) 61-65. WILLIAMS, J. A., A Conceptual History of Deuteronomism in the Old Testament, Judaism, and the New Testament (Ph.D. Diss. Southern Baptist Theological Seminary, Louisville 1976) 302f. RIVKIN, E., A Hidden Revolution (Nashville 1978) 107-109.

14:53b *WINTER, P. "Markus 15:53b.55-64 ein Gebilde des Evangelisten" ZNW 53 (3-4, '62) 260-63.

14:54, 66-72 SCHENK, W., Der Passionsbericht nach Markus (Gütersloh 1974) 215ff. SCHENKE, L., Der gekreuzigte Christus (Stuttgart 1974) 17-23. *ERNST, J., "Noch einmal: Die

Verleugnung Jesu durch Petrus (Mk 14, 54.66-72)" Catholica 30 (1976) 207-26. ERNST, J., "Die Petrustradition im Markusevangelium - ein altes Problem neu angegangen" in: J. Zmijewski/E. Nellessen (eds.) Begegnung mit dem Wort. Für H. Zimmermann (Bonn 1980) 56-57.

14:54 *BUCHANAN, G. W. "Mark XIV 54" ET 68 (1, '56) 27. BLINZLER, J. Der Prozess Jesu (1969) 124, 126, 166, 169, 212, 410. SCHNEIDER, G., Verleugnung, Verspottung und Verhör Jesu nach Lukas 22, 54-71 (München 1969) 16, 27, 65, 75-79, 98. LINNEMANN, E. Studien zur Passionsgeschichte (1970) 77-82, 96-101, cf. 102-108. WILCOX, M., "The Denial-Sequence in Mark 14:26-31, 66-72" NTS 17 (1970-1971) 433f. BROER, I. Die Urgemeinde und das Grab Jesu (1972) 107, 112, 119f, 129f. DAUER, A., Die Passionsgeschichte im Johannesevangelium (München 1972) 73, 77f. DONAHUE, J. R., Are you the Christ? (Missoula 1973) 9, 11, 42, 55-57, 67f, 87. NEIRYNCK, F., "Urmarcus redivivus" in: M. Sabbe (ed.) L'Evangile selon Marc (Gembloux 1974) 126-28. DEWEY, K. E., "Peter's Curse and Cursed Peter" in: W. H. Kelber (ed.) The Passion in Mark (Philadelphia 1976) 97-105.

14:55ff STROBEL, A. Erkenntnis und Bekenntnis der Sünde in neutestamentlicher Zeit (1968) 39. *SCHNEIDER, G. "Gab es eine vorsynoptische Szene 'Jesus vor dem Synedrium'?" NovTest 12 (1, '70) 22-39. BAMMEL, E. The Trial of Jesus (1970) 55f, 64f, 82.

14:55-65 LIGHTFOOT, R. H. History and Interpretation in the Gospels (1934) 142ff. JEREMIAS, J. "Zur Geschichtlichkeit des Verhörs Jesu vor dem Hohen Rat" ZNW 43 (1950/51) 145-50. JEREMIAS, J. Abba (1966) 139-44. MAURER, C., "Das Messiasgeheimnis des Markusevangeliums" NTS 14 (1967-1968) 515f. BLINZLER, J. Der Prozess Jesu (1969) 124, 159, 174, 176, 208, 212, 228. SCHNEIDER, G., Verleugnung, Verspottung und Verhör Jesu nach Lukas 22, 54-71 (München 1969) 16, 26f, 31, 78. LOHSE, E., Die Einheit des Neuen Testaments (Göttingen 1973) 92, 99-101. DORMEYER, D., Die Passion Jesu als Verhaltensmodell (Münster 1974) 157-74. PESCH, R., Das Markusevangelium II (Freiburg 1977) 444-46 (lit!). *JUEL, D., Messiah and Temple (Missoula 1977).

14:55-64 *BRAUMANN, G. "Markus 15, 2-5 und Markus 14, 55-64" ZNW 52 (3-4, '61) 273-78. WINTER, P. "Markus 14:53b. 55-64 ein Gebilde des Evangelisten" ZNW 53 (3-4, '62) 260-63. BULTMANN, R., The History of the Synoptic Tradition (Oxford 1963) 120f, 269-71. HAHN, F. Christologische Hoheitstitel (1963) 177. BENOIT, P. Passion et Résurrection du Seigneur (1966) 115-27. KREMER, J. Das Aergernis des Kreuzes (1969) 47-48. SCHNEIDER, G., Verleugnung, Verspottung und Verhör Jesu nach Lukas 22, 54-71 (München 1969) 16f, 20, 30, 32, 213. SCHREIBER, J. Die Markuspassion (1969) 54-58. LINNEMANN, E. Studien zur Passionsgeschichte (1970) 109-31. CRIBBS, F. L., "A Study of the Contacts That Exist Between St. Luke and St. John" in: G. MacRae (ed.) SBL Seminar Papers II (Missoula 1973) 62-65. SCHUBERT, K., Jesus im Lichte der Religionsgeschichte des Judentums (Wien/München 1973) 138-62. *LEGASSE, S., "Jésus devant le Sanhédrin. Recherche sur les traditions évangéliques" RThL 5 (1974) 170-97.

14:55-62   CATCHPOLE, D. R., "The Answer of Jesus to Caiaphas. Mt. 26:64" NTS 17 (1970-1971) 223f.

14:55-59   STROBEL, A., Die Stunde der Wahrheit (Tübingen 1980) 62-66.

14:55-56   NORDEN, E., Agnostos Theos (Stuttgart 1956=1912) 194ff. HAHN, F. Christologische Hoheitstitel (1963) 181.

14:55   BLINZLER, J. Der Prozess Jesu (1969) 59, 138, 145, 166, 176, 214. DONAHUE, J. R., Are you the Christ? (Missoula 1973) 3, 9, 23, 57, 64, 67-71, 75, 87, 97, 101, 113. DONAHUE, J. R., "Temple, Trial, and Royal Christology" in: W. H. Kelber (ed.) The Passion in Mark (Philadelphia 1976) 62-64.

14:56ff   HAHN, F. Christologische Hoheitstitel (1963) 177, 290.

14:56-59   DONAHUE, J. R., Are you the Christ? (Missoula 1973) 71-84.

14:56-57   BEUTLER, J., Martyria (Frankfurt 1972) 172, 197, 321.

14:56   SCHNEIDER, G., Verleugnung, Verspottung und Verhör Jesu nach Lukas 22, 54-71 (München 1969) 32, 42, 128f. DONAHUE, J. R., "Temple, Trial, and Royal Christology" in: W. H. Kelber (ed.) The Passion in Mark (Philadelphia 1976) 62-64.

14:57-58   HAHN, F. Das Verständnis der Mission im Neuen Testament (1965) 51. KONINGS, J., "The Pre-Markan Sequence of Jn VI" in: M. Sabbe (ed.) L'Evangile selon Marc (Gembloux 1974) 172.

14:57   DONAHUE, J. R., "Temple, Trial, and Royal Christology" in: W. H. Kelber (ed.) The Passion in Mark (Philadelphia 1976) 63-66. WEEDEN, T. J., "The Cross as Power in Weakness" in: W. H. Kelber (ed.) The Passion in Mark (Philadelphia 1976) 121-24.

14:58   HOFFMANN, R. A., "Das Wort Jesu von der Zerstörung und dem Wiederaufbau des Tempels" in: A. Deissmann/H.

Windisch (eds.) Neutestamentliche Studien. Für G. Heinrici (Leipzig 1914) 130-39. BERTRAM, G. Die Leidensgeschichte und der Christuskult (1922) 56f. CALDECOTT, A. "Zur Tempelreinigung" JThST 24 (1923) 382ff. BURKITT, F. C. "Zur Tempelreinigung" JThST 25 (1924) 386ff. GOGUEL, M. Congr. d'Hist. du Christ I (1928) 117-36. BRAUN, F. M. RevBi 38, 1929, 178-200. PLOOIJ, D. "Jesus and the Temple" ET 42 (1931) 36-39. *WENSCHKEWITZ, H. "Die Spiritualisierung der Kultusbegriffe Tempel, Priester und Opfer im NT" Angelos Beiheft 4 (1932) 71-230. DIBELIUS, M. Formgeschichte (1934) 182f. VOLZ, P. Die Eschatologie der jüdischen Gemeinde im ntl. Zeitalter (1934) 52, 172, 217, 376-78. VIELHAUER, Ph. Oikodome (1939) 62-70. LOHMEYER, E. Kultus und Evangelium (1942) 77ff. MICHEL, "ναός", ThWB IV (1942) 888f. SCHOEPS, H.-J. Die Tempelzerstörung (1942). GAVNER, H. "Christ and the temple sacrifices" ET 59 (1947/48) 223ff. SIMON, M. "Retour du Christ et reconstruction du Temple dans la pensée chrétienne primitive" Aux sources de la tradition chrétienne, (1950) 247-57. DUPONT, J., Σὺν Χριστῷ; L'Union Avec Le Christ Suivant Saint Paul (Bruges 1952) 147-50. HARDER, G. in: Theologia Viatroum (1952) 72-74. KüMMEL, W. G. Verheissung und Erfüllung (1953) 92-97. TAYLOR, V. The Gospel According to St. Mark (1953) 566f. FLEW, R. N. Jesus and His Church (1956) 40-42. FRIEDRICH, G. ZThK 53 (1956) 289ff. MENDNER, S. "Die Tempelreinigung" ZNW 47 (1956) 101f. BRANDON, S. G. F. The Fall of Jerusalem and the Christian Church (1957). BULTMANN, R. Tradition (1957) 126f. CULLMANN, O. "L'opposition contre le temple de Jérusalem" NTS 5 (1958/59) 158-72. *BIHLER, J. "Der Stephanusbericht (Apg 6, 8-15 und 7, 54-8, 2" BZ 3 (1959) 252-70. RUDOLPH, K. Die Mandäer I (Göttingen 1960) 105. LINDARS, B. New Testament Apologetics (1961) 66-72. JEREMIAS, J. Die Gleichnisse Jesu (1962) 121, 218-20. HAHN, F. Christologische Hoheitstitel (1963) 176f, 239, 398. *FASCHER, E. "Jerusalems Untergang in der urchristlichen und altkirchlichen Ueberlieferung" ThLZ 89 (2, '64) 81-98. BARTSCH, H.-W. "Tempelwort:urspr. entscheidender Anklagepunkt" ThZ 20 (1964) 99f. DODD, C. H. According to the Scriptures (1965) 86f. BEST, E. The Temptation and the Passion, the Markan Soteriology (1965) 94, 99, 132, 177. HAHN, F. Das Verständnis der Mission im Neuen Testament (1965) 29f, 50, 65, 100. GAERTNER, B. The Temple and the Community in Qumran and the New Testament (1965) 57, 111, 113. BRAUN, H., Qumran und NT II (Tübingen 1966) 133,

158, 183, 326. SCHREIBER, J. Theologie des Vertrauens (1967) 41-43, 114-116, 186f, 232, 242. GASTON, L. No Stone on Another (1970) 65, 67, 71, 154, 370, 480; SANDVIK, B. Das Kommen des Herrn beim Abendmahl (1970) 56, 64, 81, 139. Rev. J. R. DONAHUE ThSt 32 (2, '71) 306-309. JEREMIAS, J. "Die Drei-Tage-Worte der Evangelien" Tradition und Glaube (1971) 221-29. JEREMIAS, J. Neutestamentliche Theologie I (1971) 129f, 238f, 271. KLINZING, G., Die Umdeutung des Kultus in der Qumrangemeinde und im Neuen Testament (Göttingen 1971) 202-204. DONAHUE, J. R., Are you the Christ? (Missoula 1973) 104-13. DORMEYER, D., Die Passion Jesu als Verhaltensmodell (Münster 1974) 159-62. SCHENKE, L., Der gekreuzigte Christus (Stuttgart 1974) 33-37. CULLMANN, O., "Von Jesus zum Stephanuskreis und zum Johannesevangelium" in: E. E. Ellis/E. Grässer (eds.) Jesus und Paulus. Für W. G. Kümmel (Göttingen 1975) 47ff. DUNN, J. D. G., Jesus and the Spirit (London 1975) 160, 186. HOWARD, V. P., Das Ego in den Synoptischen Evangelien (Marburg 1975) 135-142. KEE, H. C., "The Function of Scriptural Quotations and Allusions in Mark 11-16" in: E. E. Ellis/E. Grässer (eds.) Jesus and Paulus. Für W. G. Kümmel (Göttingen 1975) 170f. DONAHUE, J. R., "Temple, Trial, and Royal Christology" in W. H. Kelber (ed.) The Passion in Mark (Philadelphia 1976) 66-71. KELBER, W. H., "From Passion Narrative to Gospel" in: W. H. Kelber (ed.) The Passion in Mark (Philadelphia 1976) 168-172. KLIJN, A. F. J., "Die syrische Baruch-Apokalypse" in: W. G. Kümmel (ed.) Jüdische Schriften aus hellenistisch-römischer Zeit V. (Gütersloh 1976) 125. *THEISSEN, G., "Die Tempelweissagung Jesu. Prophetie im Spannungsfeld von Stadt und Land" ThZ 32 (1976) 144-158. WEEDEN, T. J., "The Cross as Power in Weakness" in: W. H. Kelber (ed.) The Passion in Mark (Philadelphia 1976) 121-131 passim. WILLIAMS, J. A., A Conceptual History of Deuteronomism in the Old Testament, Judaism, and the New Testament (Ph.D. Diss. Southern Baptist Theological Seminary, Louisville 1976) 294-297. METZGER, B. M., The Early Versions of the New Testament (Oxford 1977) 69. *BIGUZZI, G. "Mc. 14, 58: un tempio *acheiropoïetos*" RivB 26 (1978) 225-240. FRIEDRICH, G., "Beobachtungen zur messianischen Hohepriestererwartung in den Synoptikern" in: Auf das Wort kommt es an (Göttingen 1978) 80-82. MEYER, B. F., The Aims of Jesus (London 1979) 181-185. VIELHAUER, P., "Oikodome. Das Bild vom Bau in der christlichen Literatur von Neuen Testament bis Clemens Alexandrinus" in: Oikodome. Neutestamentliche Aufsätze II (München 1979) 59-61, 64-66.

14:59   BEUTLER, J., Martyria (Frankfurt 1972) 172, 187, 212.

14:60ff   LIGHTFOOT, R. H. History and Interpretation in the Gospels (1934) 179ff. HAHN, F. Christologische Hoheitstitel (1963) 177, 181, 282.

14:60-65 STROBEL, A., Die Stunde der Wahrheit (Tübingen 1980) 66-73.

14:60-62 DONAHUE, J. R., Are you the Christ?(Missoula 1973) 21, 23, 84-95.

14:60-61 FARICY, R., Praying for Inner Healing (London 1979) 69f.

14:60   SCHNEIDER, G., Verleugnung, Verspottung und Verhör Jesu nach Lukas 22, 54-71. (München 1969) 32f, 56, 101, 173. GAIN, D. B., Evidence for Supposing That Our Greek Text of the Gospel of St Mark is Translated from Latin . . . (Grahamstown, S. Africa 1978).

14:61-65 KREMER, J. Das Aergernis des Kreuzes (1969) 48-50.

14:61-62 MOORE, G. F., Judaism II (Cambridge, Mass. 1946) 335. CULLMANN, O. Die Christologie des Neuen Testaments (1957) 118ff. HAHN, F. Christologische Hoheitstitel (1963) 128f, 177, 180, 181-83, 188, 288f. HAHN, F. Das Verständnis der Mission im Neuen Testament (1965) 55. MINETTE DE TILLESSE, G. Le Secret Messianique dans L'Evangile de Marc (1968) 333-37. DONAHUE, J. R., Are you the Christ? (Missoula 1973) 88-95, 138-42. DESCAMPS, A., "Pour une histoire de titre 'Fils de Dieu' " in: M. Sabbe (ed.) L'Evangile selon Marc (Gembloux 1974) 552, 559. ACHTEMEIER, P. J., Mark (Philadelphia 1975) 46-48. CONZELMANN, H. und LINDEMANN, A., Arbeitsbuch zum Neuen Testament (Tübingen 1975) 367f.377. VIA, D. O., Kerygma and Comedy in the New Testament (Philadelphia 1975) 81, 90, 131, 140f, 153, 167. PERRIN, N., "The High Priest's Question and Jesus' Answer" in: W. H. Kelber (ed.) The Passion in Mark (Philadelphia 1976) 80-95. STROBEL, A., Die Stunde der Wahrheit (Tübingen 1980) 73-76. TANNEHILL, R. C., "The Gospel of Mark as Narrative Christology" Semeia 16 (1980) 87f.

14:61   HOOKER, M. D., Jesus and the Servant (London 1959) 87-89. SCHOEPS, H.-J., Paulus (Tübingen 1959) 166f. LÖVESTAM, E. "Die Frage des Hohenpriesters (Mark 14, 61 par. Matth. 26, 63," SEA 26 ('61) 93-107. HAHN, F. Christologische Hoheitstitel (1963) 54, 194, 202, 239, 281, 287. SCHENK, W. Der Segen im Neuen (1967) 116. MINETTE DE TILLESSE, G. Le Secret Messianique dans L'Evangile de Marc (1968) 358-63. BLINZLER, J. Der Prozess Jesu (1969)

60, 148, 149, 150, 178, 189, 196. RIEDL, J., "Die Evangelische Leidensgeschichte und ihre Theologische Aussage" BuL 41 (1968) 87f. SCHNEIDER, G., Verleugnung, Verspottung und Verhör Jesu nach Lukas 22, 54-71 (München 1969) 33f, 57, 78, 101, 112f, 115, 121, 123f. FENEBERG, W., Der Markusprolog (München 1974) 35, 119, 152, 156. LADD, G. E., A Theology of the New Testament (Grand Rapids 1974) 142, 163, 168. ACHTEMEIER, P. J., Mark (Philadelphia 1975) 42. DONAHUE, J. R., "Temple, Trial, and Royal Christology" in: W. H. Kelber (ed.) The Passion in Mark (Philadelpia 1976) 63f, 66. PERRIN, N., "The High Priest's Question and Jesus' Answer" in: W. H. Kelber (ed.) The Passion in Mark (Philadelphia 1976) 86-88. MALBON, E. S., "Mythic Structure and Meaning in Mark" Semeia 16 (1980) 109-13.

14:62   STONEHOUSE, N. B. The Witness of Matthew and Mark to Christ (1944) 13, 111, 113, 114, 239. MANSON, T. W., The Teaching of Jesus (Cambridge 1945) 214f, 266ff, 278-85. KUEMMEL, W. G. Verheissung und Erfüllung (1953) 43-45. NORDEN, E., Agnostos Theos (Stuttgart 1956=1912) 272f. BURKILL, T. A., "St Mark's Philosophy of History" NTS 3 (1956-57) 143ff. *ROBINSON, J. A. T. The Second Coming - Mark XIV.62 ET 67 (11, '56) 336-40. *McARTHUR, H. K. "Mark XIV 62 NTS 4 (2, '58) 156-58. *GLASSON, T. F. "The Reply to Caiaphas (Mark xiv. 62)" NTS 7 (1, '60) 88-93. *LINTON, O. "The Trial of Jesus and the Interpretation of Psalm cx" NTS 7 (3, '61) 258-62. SCHWEIZER, E. Erniedrigung und Erhöhung bei Jesus und seinen Nachfolgern (1962) §3ef. STRECKER, G. Der Weg der Gerechtigkeit (1962) 87. DE KRUIJF, Th., Der Sohn des Lebendigen Gottes (Rome 1962) 32, 36, 96-98. WAINWRIGHT, A. W., The Trinity in the New Testament (London 1962) 175f. SCHWEIZER, E., "The Son of Man Again" NTS 9 (1962-63) 257f. PERRIN, N., The Kingdom of God in the Teaching of Jesus (Philadelphia 1963) 93, 101-103, 106, 135f, 142-44, 154, 188, 190. HAHN, F. Christologische Hoheitstitel (1963) 24, 39, 40, 290. *GOLDBERG, A. M. "Sitzend zur Rechten der Kraft." BZ 8 (2, '64) 284-93. SCHNACKENBURG, R., "Der Menschensohn im Johannesevangelium" NTS 11 (1964-65) 129f. MARSHALL, I. H., "The Synoptic Son of Man Sayings in Recent Discussion" NTS 12 (1965-66) 346f. SUHL, A. Die Funktion der alttestamentlichen Zitate und Anspielungen im Markus-evangelium (1965) 54ff, 66, 132, 133. *PERRIN, N. "Mark XIV. 62: The End Product of a Christian Pesher Tradition?" NTS 12 (2, '66) 150-55. BOUSSET, W., Die Religion des Judentums im späthellenistischen Zeitalter (Berlin

1966=1926) 316. SHIMADA, K., The Formulary Material in First Peter (Th.D. Diss. Union Theological Seminary New York, Ann Arbor 1966) 379-86, 391-93. JUENGEL, E. Paulus und Jesus (1966) 223, 243f. BORSCH, F. The Son of Man in Myth and History (1967) 391-94. HOOKER, M. D. The Son of Man in Mark (1967) 113, 157, 163-73, 178, 181, 182, 197. NICKELS, P. Targum and New Testament (1967) 27. *BORSCH, F. H. "Mark xiv 62 and I Enoch lxii.5" NTS 14 (4, '68) 565-67. MINETTE DE TILLESSE, G. Le Secret Messianique dans L'Evangile de Marc (1968) 368-73, 390-94. SCHALIT, A. König Herodes (1969) 527. PESCH, R. Naherwartungen (1969) 39, 43, 110, 111, 118, 161, 168, 169, 170, 171, 240. BAMMEL, E. The Trial of Jesus (1970) 75, 81f, 122ff. DERRETT, J. D. M. Law in the New Testament (1970) 223n.2, 389n.1, 424n.2, 425, n.2 452. GASTON, L. No Stone on Another (1970) 388-90, 403, 455, 480. WEEDEN, T. J. Mark - Traditions in Conflict (1971) 126-37. JEREMIAS, J. Neutestamentliche Theologie I (1971) 21, 199, 260-62. HIGGINS, A. J. B., "Is the Son of Man Problem Insoluble?" in: E. E. Ellis/M. Wilcox (eds.) Neotestamentica et Semitica (Edinburgh 1969) 76f, 80ff. SCHNEIDER, G., Verleugnung, Verspottung und Verhör Jesu nach Lukas 22, 54-71 (München 1969) 29, 33f, 37, 41, 57, 69, 114f, 118, 120f, 125f, 146, 148, 172f. BOHREN, R., Predigtlehre (München 1971) 283. DAUER, A., Die Passionsgeschichte im Johannesevangelium (München 1972) 88, 188, 295. ZMIJEWSKI, J., Die Eschatologiereden des Lukasevangeliums (Bonn 1972) 110, 237f, 244f, 248, 557. DONAHUE, J. R., Are you the Christ? (Missoula 1973) 172-77. HAMERTON-KELLY, R. G., Pre-Existence, Wisdom, and the Son of Man (Cambridge 1973) 55, 57f, 60f, 93f, 229, 232. HIERS, R. H., The Historical Jesus and the Kingdom of God (Gainsville/Florida 1973) 30, 41, 68, 102-105, 110. HOFFMANN, P., "Mk 8, 31. Zur Herkunft und markinischen Rezeption einer alten Überlieferung" in: P. Hoffmann (ed.) Orientierung an Jesus. Für J. Schmid (Freiburg 1973) 193, 198-200. LANGE, J., Das Erscheinen des Auferstandenen im Evangelium nach Mattäus (Würzburg 1973) 189, 214, 230, 232-34, 237f, 243, 422. WILSON, S. G., The Gentiles and the Gentile Mission in Luke-Acts (Cambridge 1973) 67f. BARTSCH, H.-W., "Der ursprüngliche Schluss der Leidensgeschichte" in: M. Sabbe (ed.) L'Evangile selon Marc (Gembloux 1974) 418. COPPENS, J., "Les logia du Fils de l'Homme dans l'évangile de Marc" in: M. Sabbe (ed.) L'Evangile selon Marc (Gembloux 1974) 508-12. DAVIES, W. D., The Gospel and the Land (London 1974) 230 n.25, 259, 411, 420 n.30, 434 n.75. DORMEYER, D., Die Passion Jesu als

Verhaltensmodell (Münster 1974) 164-67. LADD, G. E., A
Theology of the New Testament (Grand Rapids 1974) 157, 168,
205, 245. PERRIN, N., "The Christology of Mark" in: M.
Sabbe (ed.) L'Evangile selon Marc (Gembloux 1974) 481f.
PERRIN, N., A Modern Pilgrimage in New Testament
Christology (Philadelpia 1974) 10-21, 115-21, 127f.
SCHENKE, L., Der gekreuzigte Christus (Stuttgart 1974) 37-
44. GOPPELT, L., Theologie des Neuen Testaments I
(Göttingen 1975) 219, 230-32, 248. HOWARD, V. P., Das Ego
in den Synoptischen Evangelien (Marburg 1975) 142-48.
PESCH, R., "Die Passion des Menschensohnes" in: R.
Pesch/R. Schnackenburg (eds.) Jesus und der Menschensohn
(Freiburg 1975) 184-89. THEISOHN, J., Der auserwählte
Richter (Göttingen 1975) 154ff, 158. DONAHUE, J. R.,
"Temple, Trial, and Royal Christology" in: W. H. Kelber (ed.)
The Passion in Mark (Philadelphia 1976) 62-64. KLIJN, A. F.
J., "Die syrische Baruch-Apokalypse" in: W. G. Kümmel (ed.)
Jüdische Schriften aus hellnistisch-römischer Zeit V (Gütersloh
1976) 136. PERRIN, N., "The High-Priest's Question and
Jesus' Answer" in: W. H. Kelber (ed.) The Passion in Mark
(Philadelphia 1976) 89-92. *KEMPTHORNE, R., "The
Marcan Text of Jesus' Answer to the High Priest (Mark xiv
62)" NovT 19 (1977) 197-208. "Apokalyptik" in: TRE 3 (1978)
253. BRUCE, F. F., The Time is Fulfilled (Exeter 1978) 25.
FRIEDRICH, G., "Beobachtungen zur messianischen
Hohepriestererwartung in den Synoptikern" in: Auf das Wort
kommt es an (Göttingen 1978) 96f. GOURGUES, M., A la
droite de Dieu. Résurrection de Jésus et actualisation du
Psaume 110:1 dans le Nouveau Testament (1978). HOOKER,
M. D., "Is the Son of Man problem really insoluble?" in: E.
Best/R. McL.Wilson (eds.) Text and Interpretation. Studies in
the New Testament presented to Matthew Black (Cambridge
1979) 163. BEASLEY-MURRAY, G. R., "Jesus and
Apocalyptic: With Special Reference to Mark 14, 62" in: J.
Lambrecht (ed.) L'Apocalypse johannique et l'Apocalyptique
dans le Nouveau Testament (Gembloux 1980) 415-29.
MALBON, E. S., "Mythic Structure and Meaning in Mark"
Semeia 16 (1980) 109-13.

14:63-64 HAHN, F. Christologische Hoheitstitel (1963) 177.
DONAHUE, J. R., Are you the Christ? (Missoula 1973) 95-98.

14:63 BETZ, H. D., Lukian von Samosata und das Neue Testament
(Berlin 1961) 72, 140.

14:64 BRAUN, H., Qumran und NT II (Tübingen 1966) 65.
SCHNEIDER, G., Verleugnung, Verspottung und Verhör
Jesu nach Lukas 22, 54-71 (München 1969) 36f, 69, 103, 113,

122, 127, 130, 156-58, 171, 213. BROER, I. Die Urgemeinde und das Grab Jesu (1972) 175f. SHERWIN-WHITE, A. N., Roman Society and Roman Law in the New Testament (Grand Rapids 1978) 33. STROBEL, A., Die Stunde der Wahrheit (Tübingen 1980) 92-94.

14:65   VAN UNNIK, W. C., "Jesu Verhöhnung vor dem Synedrium (Mc 14, 65 par" ZNW 29 (1930) 310f. HOOKER, M. D., Jesus and the Servant (London 1959) 89-91. *GUNDRY, R. H. "LMTLYM: 1 Q Isaiah a 50, 6 and Mark 14, 65-" RevQum 2 (4, '60) 559-67. BENOIT, P. "Les outrages à Jesus Prophète (Mc xiv 65 par)" Neotestamentica et Patristica (Cullmann-Festschrift) 1962, 92-. HAHN, F. Christologische Hoheitstitel (1963) 47, 398. BENOIT, P. Passion et Résurrection du Seigneur (1966) 93-95. BLINZLER, J. Der Prozess Jesu (1969) 162-66, 212, 354, 427. SCHNEIDER, G., Verleugnung, Verspottung und Verhör Jesu nach Lukas 22, 54-71 (München 1969) 17, 26, 33, 39-41, 55, 67, 97-103, 146f, 152, 171. CRIBBS, F. L., "A Study of the Contacts That Exist Between St Luke and St John" in: G. MacRae (ed.) SBL Seminar Papers II (Montana 1973) 61f. DONAHUE, J. R., Are you the Christ? (Missoula 1973) 98. VAN UNNIK, W. C., "Jesu Verhöhnung vor dem Synhedrium (Mc xiv.65 par)" in: Sparsa Collecta. The Collected Essays of W. C. van Unnik I (Leiden 1973) 3-5. TALBERT, C. H., Literary Patterns, Theological Themes, and the Genre of Luke-Acts (Missoula 1974) 22. TANNEHILL, R. C., "The Gospel of Mark as Narrative Christology" Semeia 16 (1980) 79f.

14:66ff   GERSTENBERGER, G., und SCHRAGE, W., Leiden (Stuttgart 1977) 216f.; ET: Suffering (Nashville 1980) 249.

14:66-72 *HENSON, B. "St Peter's Denials of Christ" Listener 56 ('56) 267-68. *MASSON, C. "Le reniement de Pierre. Quelques aspects de la formation d'une tradition" RHPhR 37 (1, '57) 24-35. *KLEIN, G. "Die Verleugnung des Petrus, ZThk 58 (3, '61) 285-328. MASSON, C., Vers les Sources d'Eau Vive (Lausanne 1961) 87ff. STRECKER, G. Der Weg der Gerechtigkeit (1962) 39. SCHNEIDER, G., Verleugnung, Verspottung und Verhör Jesu nach Lukas 22, 54-71 (München 1969) 16f, 26f, 42, 146f, 152. WILCOX, M., "The Denial-Sequence in Mark 14:26-31, 66-72" NTS 17 (1970-71) 426-36. SCHENKE, L., Studien zur Passionsgeschichte des Markus (Würzburg 1971) 364ff, 427, 429. LAMPE, G. W. H., "St Peter's Denial" BJRL 55 (1973) 346-68. LANGE, J., Das Erscheinen des Auferstandenen im Evangelium nach Mattäus (Würzburg 1973) 452-54, 461. STECK, K. G. GPM 27 (1973) 175-83. DORMEYER, D., Die Passion Jesu als Verhaltensmodell (Münster 1974) 150-55.

PESCH, R., "Die Verleugnung des Petrus" in: J. Gnilka (ed.) Neues Testament und Kirche. Für R. Schnackenburg (Freiburg 1974) 42-62. PESCH, R., Das Markusevangelium II (Freiburg 1977) 453 (lit!). GEWALT, D., "Die Verleugnung des Petrus" LiBi 43 (1978) 113-44. STAGG, E./F., Woman in the World of Jesus (Philadelphia 1978) 213. GNILKA, J., Das Evangelium nach Markus II (Einsiedeln/Neukirchen 1979) 289 (lit!).

14:66-68 KREMER, J. Das Aergernis des Kreuzes (1969) 50-51.

14:67-71 WILDER, A. N., The Language of the Gospel (New York 1964) 55f.

14:67 STRECKER, G. Der Weg der Gerechtigkeit (1962) 94. SCHNEIDER, G., Verleugnung, Verspottung und Verhör Jesu nach Lukas 22, 54-71 (München 1969) 52f, 78-81, 84, 88, 93.

14:68 BOYD, W. J. P. "Peter's Denials - Mark xiv. 68, Luke xxii. 57" ET 67 ('56) 341. SMITH, M., Tannaitic Parallels to the Gospels (Philadelphia 1968) 2bn117.+ SCHNEIDER, G., Verleugnung, Verspottung und Verhör Jesu nach Lukas 22, 54-71 (München 1969) 43, 51, 54, 66, 81f, 84, 89f, 95. DEWEY, K. E., "Peter's Curse and Cursed Peter" in: W. H. Kelber (ed.) The Passion in Mark (Philaelphia 1976) 102-105. WENHAM, J. W., "How Many Cock-Crowings? The Problem of Harmonistic Text-Variants" NTS 25 (1979) 523-25.

14:69ff BAMMEL, E. The Trial of Jesus (1970) 66ff.

14:69-71 KREMER, J. Das Aergernis des Kreuzes (1969) 52-53.

14:70-72 NICKLE, K. F., The Collecuon (London 1966) 66.

14:70 MEYE, R. P. Jesus and the Twelve (1968) 166f. SCHNEIDER, G., Verleugnung, Verspottung und Verhör Jesu nach Lukas 22, 54-71 (München 1969) 52, 66, 82f, 85-89, 146f. BAUER, J. B., Scholia Biblica et Patristica (Graz 1972) 228.

14:71 SCHNEIDER, G., Verleugnung, Verspottung und Verhör Jesu nach Lukas 22, 54-71 (München 1969) 52, 81, 86, 89, 158, 192.

14:72-73. STREETER, B. H. The Four Gospels (1951) 322f.

14:72 *BIRDSALL, J. N. "To rhema hos eipen auto ho Iesous: Mk xiv. 72" NovTest 2 (3-4, '58) 272-75. HAHN, F. Christologische Hoheitstitel (1963) 88. SCHNEIDER, G., Verleugnung, Verspottung und Verhör Jesu nach Lukas 22, 54-71 (München 1969) 42f, 51, 53f, 90, 93-95, 105f. SCHENKE, L., Studien zur Passionsgeschichte des Markus (Würzburg 1971) 412ff. LEE, G. M., "Mark 14, 72: *epibalōn eklaien*" Biblica 53 (1972) 411f. DEWEY, K. E., "Peter's Curse and Cursed Peter" in: W. H. Kelber (ed.) The Passion in Mark (Philadelphia 1976) 102-104.

WENHAM, J. W., "How Many Cock-Crowings? The Problem of Harmonistic Text-Variants" NTS 25 (1979) 523-25.

15-16   PATTE, D./A., Structural Exegesis: From Theory to Practice. Exegesis of Mark 15 and 16. Hermeneutical Implications (Philadelphia 1978).

15   SCHILLE, G., "Bemerkungen zur Formgeschichte des Evangeliums. Rahmen und Aufbau des Markus-Evangeliums" NTS 4 (1957-58) 5ff. WEINACHT, H. Die Menschwerdung des Sohnes Gottes im Markus-evangelium (1972) 61-69.

15:1ff   KNOX, W. L. The Sources of the Synoptic Gospels (1953) I 135ff. HAHN, F. Christologische Hoheitstitel (1963) 177f., 215.

15:1-37   PATTE, D./A., Structural Exegesis (Philadelphia 1978) 50-52.

15:1-27   BULTMANN, R., The History of the Synoptic Tradition (Oxford 1963) 272f, 276f, 283f.

15:1-20   GOODSPEED, E. J., A Life of Jesus (New York 1950) 213-15. GRUNDMANN, W. Das Evangelium nach Markus (1959) 310f. HAHN, F. Christologische Hoheitstitel (1963) 179, 195f, 211. ZIMMERMANN, W. D. Markus über Jesus (1970) 165-70.

15:1-5, 16-20   SCHENKE, L., Der gekreuzigte Christus (Stuttgart 1974) 51-60.

15:1-15   DREWES, G. "Auf dass wir Frieden hätten" Kleine Predigt-Typologie III, ed. L. Schmidt (1965) 281-85. LOHSE, E., GPM 27 (1973) 183-89. PATTE, D./A., Structural Exegesis (Philadelphia 1978) 40. FÜRST, W., in: GPM 32 (1978/79) 135-40. GNILKA, J., Das Evangelium nach Markus II (Einsiedeln/Neukirchen 1979) 296 (lit!).

15:1-5   BENOIT, P. Passion et Résurrection du Seigneur (1966) 155-59. KREMER, J. Das Aergernis des Kreuzes (1969) 54-55. DORMEYER, D., Die Passion Jesu als Verhaltensmodell (Münster 1974) 174-79. PESCH, R., Das Markusevangelium II (Freiburg 1977) 459 (lit!).

15:1   KLOSTERMANN, E. Das Markusevangelium (1950) 158. HAHN, F. Christologische Hoheitstitel (1963) 47, 62. BOUSSET, W., Die Religion des Judentums im Späthellenistischen Zeitalter (Berlin 1966=1926) 167.

SCHREIBER, J. Theologie des Vertrauens (1967) 99-101, 149,
154, 173, 182. BLINZLER, J. Der Prozess Jesu (1969) 59, 121,
124, 138, 210-15, 250, 255, 259, 416, 417. SCHNEIDER, G.,
Verleugnung, Verspottung und Verhör Jesu nach Lukas 22, 54-
71 (München 1969) 16, 18, 27, 30-32, 38, 56, 74f, 105-111, 192.
DAUER, A., Die Passionsgeschichte im Johannesevangelium
(München 1972) 67, 71, 121f, 145. SCHENK, W., Der
Passionsbericht nach Markus (Gütersloh 1974) 229ff.
SCHENKE, L., Der gekreuzigte Christus (Stuttgart 1974) 51f.
TALBERT, C. H., Literary Patterns, Theological Themes, and
the Genre of Luke-Acts (Missoula 1974) 22. GOPPELT, L.,
Theologie des Neuen Testaments I (Göttingen 1975) 272f.
WILLIAMS, J. A., A Conceptual History of Deuteronomism
in the Old Testament, Judaism, and the New Testament (Ph.D.
Diss. Southern Baptist Theological Seminary, Louisville 1976)
302f. RIVKIN, E., A Hidden Revolution (Nashville 1978) 107-
109. SHERWIN-WHITE, A. N., Roman Society and Roman
Law in the New Testament (Grand Rapids 1978) 33.
STROBEL, A., Die Stunde der Wahrheit (Tübingen 1980) 76f.

15:2ff BUSE, I., "St John and the Markan Passion Narrative" NTS 4
(1957-58) 217ff. STROBEL, A. Erkenntnis und Bekenntnis der
Sünde in neutestamentlicher Zeit (1968) 39. *BRAUMANN,
G. "Markus 15, 2-5 und Markus 14, 55-64" ZNW 52 (3-4, '61)
273-78. LIGHTFOOT, R. H. History and Interpretation in the
Gospels (1934) 148f.

15:2-20 NEIRYNCK, F., "Urmarcus redivivus?" in: M. Sabbe (ed.)
L'Evangile selon Marc (Gembloux 1974) 107.

15:2-15 SCHENK, W., Der Passionsbericht nach Markus (Gütersloh
1974) 243ff. SCHMITHALS, W., Das Evangeliums nach
Markus (Gütersloh/Würzburg 1979) 670 (lit!).

15:2-5 STROBEL, A., Die Stunde der Wahrheit (Tübingen 1980) 95-
99.

15:2 RIEDL, J., "Die evangelische Leidensgeschichte und ihre
theologische Aussage" BuL 41 (1968) 88-90. DAUER, A., Die
Passionsgeschichte im Johannesevangelium (München 1972)
122f, 162, 233. LEISTNER, R., Antijudaismus im
Johannesevangelium? (Bern 1974) 118f. SCHENKE, L., Der
gekreuzigte Christus (Stuttgart 1974) 52-54. TALBERT, C. H.,
Literary Patterns, Theological Themes, and the Genre of Luke-
Acts (Missoula 1974) 22. CLARK, K. W., "The Making of the
Twentieth Century New Testament" in: The Gentile Bias and
other Essays (Leiden 1980) 150f.

15:3-15 SCHELKLE, K. H., Die Passion Jesu in der Verkündigung des
Neuen Testament (Heidelberg 1949) 44f.

15:3-5   NEIRYNCK, F., "Urmarcus redivivus?" in: M. Sabbe (ed.) L'Evangile selon Marc (Gembloux 1974) 128f.

15:4-5   HAHN, F. Christologische Hoheitstitel (1963) 54, 194, 202.

15:4   PRYKE, E. J., "IΔE and IΔOY" NTS 14 (1967-68) 418f.

15:5   Hooker, M. D., Jesus and the Servant (London 1959) 87-89.

15:6-15   BENOIT, P. Passion et Résurrection du Seigneur (1966) 155-59. KREMER, J. Das Aergernis des Kreuzes (1969) 55-58. BLINZLER, J. Der Prozess Jesu (1969) 301-17. SCHUBERT, K., Jesus im Lichte der Religionsgeschichte des Judentums (Wien/München 1973) 163-69. DORMEYER, D., Die Passion Jesu als Verhaltensmodell (Münster 1974) 179-86. SCHENKE, L., Der gekreuzigte Christus (Stuttgart 1974) 47-51. PESCH, R., Das Markusevangelium II (Freiburg 1977) 468 (lit!).

15:6-14   STROBEL, A., Die Stunde der Wahrheit (Tübingen 1980) 118-31.

15:6   CHAVEL, C. B. "The Releasing of a Prisoner on the Eve of the Passover in Ancient Jerusalem" JBL 60, 1961, 273ff.

15:7ff   *SOLTERO, C., "Pilatus, Jesus et Barabbas" VerbDom 45 (5-6, '67) 326-30.

15:7   *TWOMEY, J. J. "Barabbas was a Robber," Scripture 8 ('56) 115-19. BARRETT, C. K., The New Testament Background (London 1956) 199. "Aramäisch" in: TRE 3 (1978) 603.

15:8   LEE, G. M., "Mark xv 8" NovT 20 (1978) 74.

15:9   TALBERT, C. H., Literary Patterns, Theological Themes, and the Genre of Luke-Acts (Missoula 1974) 22.

15:10.15-19 HOFFMANN, P., "Mk 8, 31. Zur Herkunft und markinischen Rezeption einer alten Überlieferung" in: P. Hoffmann (ed.) Orientierung an Jesus (Freiburg 1973) 187f.

15:10-11 LINTON, O., "Evidences of a Second-Century Revised Edition of St Mark's Gospel" NTS 14 (1967-68) 349f.

15:12   SANDMEL, S., We Jews and Jesus (New York 1977) 49.

15:13   DAUER, A., Die Passionsgeschichte im Johannesevangelium (München 1972) 103, 128, 160.

15:14   DAUER, A., Die Passionsgeschichte im Johannesevangelium (München 1972) 115, 122, 128, 130, 160, 233.

15:15   HAHN, F. Christologische Hoheitstitel (1963) 47, 62. SCHREIBER, J. Theologie des Vertrauens (1967) 66ff. BLINZLER, J. Der Prozess Jesu (1969) 177, 185, 249, 307, 310. DAUER, A., Die Passionsgeschichte im Johannesevangelium (München 1972) 126, 131, 233. "Apostel" in: TRE 3 (1978) 467. SHERWIN-WHITE, A. N., Roman Society and Roman Law in the New Testament (Grand Rapids 1978) 26. STROBEL, A., Die Stunde der Wahrheit (Tübingen 1980) 105f, 132-37.

15:16-20 KREYENBUEHL, J. Der Ort der Verurteilung Jesu ZNW 3 (1902) 15-22. KLOSTERMANN, E. Das Markusevangelium (1950) 161. TAYLOR, V. The Gospel According to St Mark (1953) 646-48. TOEDT, H. E. Der Menschensohn in der Synoptischen Ueberlieferung (1963) 159-62. BENOIT, P. Passion et Résurrection du Seigneur (1966) 155-59. KREMER, J. Das Aergernis des Kreuzes (1969) 58-59. SCHüTZ, F. Der leidende Christus (1969) 129ff. FUERST, W. GPM 27 (1973) 189-94. DAUER, A., Die Passionsgeschichte im Johannesevangelium (München 1972) 154f, 225. DORMEYER, D., Die Passion Jesu als Verhaltensmodell (Münster 1974) 187-91. SCHENK, W., Der Passionsbericht nach Markus (Gütersloh 1974) 250ff. SCHENKE, L., Der gekreuzigte Christus (Stuttgart 1974) 54f. PESCH, R., Das Markusevangelium II (Freiburg 1977) 474 (lit!). PATTE, D./A., Structural Exegesis (Philadelphia 1978) 40f. GNILKA, J., Das Evangelium nach Markus II (Einsiedeln/Neukirchen 1979) 305 (lit!). SCHMITHALS, W., Das Evangelium nach Markus (Gütersloh/Würzburg 1979) 677 (lit!). TANNEHILL, R. C., "The Gospel of Mark as Narrative Christology" Semeia 16 (1980) 79.

15:17-20 MASSAUX, E. Influence de L'Evangile de saint Matthieu sur la littérature chrétienne avant saint Irénée (1950) 71-73.

15:18   SANDMEL, S., We Jews and Jesus (New York 1977) 49.

15:19   HAHN, F. Christologische Hoheitstitel (1963) 47, 86.

15:20-47 SCHENKE, L., Der gekreuzigte Christus (Stuttgart 1974) 77-110.

15:20-41 ZIMMERMANN, W.-D. Markus über Jesus (1970) 170-74. SCHREIBER, J. Der Kreuzigungsbericht des Markusevangeliums (1961) SCHREIBER, J. Theologie des Vertrauens (1967) 22-82. ZIMMERMANN, W.-D. Markus über Jesus (1970) 170-74. ADLOFF, K. GPM 27 (1973) 195-204.

15:20-39 Herr, tue meine Lippen auf, ed. G. Eichholz (1957) 128-33.

15:20b-41 TAYLOR, V., "The Narrative of the Cruficixion" NTS 8 (1961-62) 333f. SCHENK, W., Der Passionsbericht nach Markus. Untersuchungen zur Überlieferungsgeschichte der Passionstraditionen (Gütersloh 1974). SCHENKE, L., Der gekreuzigte Christus (Stuttgart 1974) 83-102. COUSIN, H., Le prophète assassiné. Histoire des textes évangéliques de la Passion (Paris 1976). WEEDEN, Th.J., "The Cross as Power in

Weakness" in: W. H. Kelber (ed.) The Passion in Mark (Philadelphia 1976) 115-34. GNILKA, J., Das Evangelium nach Markus II (Einsiedeln/Neukirchen 1979) 309 (lit!). RUPPERT, L., "Das Skandalon eines gekreuzigten Messias und seine Überwindung mit Hilfe der geprägten Vorstellung vom leidenden Gerechten" in: Kirche und Bibel. Für Bischof E. Schick (Paderborn 1979) 322-27.

15:20b-24 PESCH, R., Das Markusevangelium II (Freiburg 1977) 481 (lit!).

15:20-22 SCHREIBER, J. Theologie des Vertrauens (1967) 32f, 62-66.

15:20-21 KREMER, J. Das Aergernis des Kreuzes (1969) 60-61.

15:20 HAHN, F. Christologische Hoheitstitel (1963) 47.

15:21ff KNOX, W. L. The Sources of the Synoptic Gospels (1953) I 142ff. BORNKAMM, G. Jesus von Nazareth (1956) 151ff.

15:21-41 GOODSPEED, E. J., A Life of Jesus (New York 1950) 216-22. TAYLOR, V. The Gospel According to St Mark (1953) 649-51. DORMEYER, D., Die Passion Jesu als Verhaltensmodell (Münster 1974) 191-215. REUMANN, J. H., "Psalm 22 at the Cross. Lament and Thanksgiving for Jesus Christ" Interp 28 (1974) 39-58.

15:21-33 PATTE, D./A., Structural Exegesis (Philadelphia 1978) 41f.

15:21-32 BLINZLER, J. Der Prozess Jesu (1969) 357-74. SCHMITHALS, W., Das Evangelium nach Markus (Gütersloh/Würzburg 1979) 680 (lit!).

15:21 HENGEL, M., Judentum und Hellenismus (Tübingen 1969) 180*; ET: Judaism and Hellenism II (London 1974) 67. *LEE, G. M., "Mark xv 21, 'The Father of Alexander and Rufus' " NovT 17 (1975) 303. KLAPPERT, B., "Der Verlust und die Wiedergewinnung der israelitischen Kontur der Leidensgeschichte Jesu" in: H. H. Henrix/M. Stöhr (eds.) Exodus und Kreuz im ökumenischen Dialog zwischen Juden und Christen (Aachen 1978) 121. RUDOLPH, K., Die Gnosis (Göttingen 1978) 178.

15:22ff LEE, E. K., "St Mark and the Fourth Gospel" NTS 3 (1956-57) 55ff.

15:22-41 DRURY, J., Tradition and Design in Luke's Gospel (Atlanta 1976) 113-19.

15:22-32 TAYLOR, V. "The Narrative of the Crucifixion" NTS 8 ('62) 333f. KREMER, J. Das Aergernis des Kreuzes (1969) 61-62.

15:22-23 CRIBBS, F. L., "A Study of the Contacts That Exist Between St Luke and St John" in: G. MacRae (ed.) SBL Seminar Papers II (Montana 1973) 76.

15:22 SCHMID, J. Das Evangelium nach Markus (1958) 297-301. "Aramäisch" in: TRE 3 (1978) 605. MALBON, E. S., "Mythic Structure and Meaning in Mark" Semeia 16 (1980) 103-107.

15:23 DAUER, A., Die Passionsgeschichte im Johannesevangelium (München 1972) 173f, 206, 223f. KLAPPERT, B., "Der Verlust und die Wiedergewinnung der Israelitischen Kontur der Leidensgeschichte Jesu" in: H. H. Henrix/M. Stöhr (eds.) Exodus und Kreuz im ökumenischen Dialog zwischen Juden und Christen (Aachen 1978) 121.

15:24-27 KREMER, J. Das Aergernis des Kreuzes (1969) 64-66.

15:24 KLOSTERMANN, E. Das Markusevangelium (1950) 163f. HAHN, F. Christologische Hoheitstitel (1963) 235. SUHL, A. Die Funktion der alttestamentlichen Zitate und Anspielungen im Markusevangelium (1965) 47ff, 65, 125. SCHREIBER, J. Theologie des Vertrauens (1967) 24, 28, 31f, 51, 58, 62-64, 71f, 239. KREMER, J. Das Aergernis des Kreuzes (1969) 62-64.

15:25-32 PESCH, R., Das Markusevangelium II (Freiburg 1977) 491 (lit!).

15:25 *LIPINSKI, E. "Godzina ukrzyzowania (De hora Crucifixionis)" RuchBibLit 12 (2, '59) 126-37. *MAHONEY, A. "A New Look at 'The Third Hour' of Mk 15, 25" CBQ 28 (3, '66) 292-99. BRAUN, H., Qumran und NT (Tübingen 1966) 45, 50. SCHREIBER, J. Theologie des Vertrauens (1967) 34-40, 66-82. BROER, I. Die Urgemeinde und das Grab Jesu (1972) 56f, 140, 152f, 166.

15:26-27 KLAPPERT, B., "Der Verlust und die Wiedergewinnung der israelitischen Kontur der Leidensgeschichte Jesu" in: H. H. Henrix/M. Stöhr (eds.) Exodus und Kreuz im ökumenischen Dialog zwischen Juden und Christen (Aachen 1978) 121f.

15:26 *LEE, G. M. "The Inscription on the Cross" PEQ 100 (2, '68) 144. *YADIN, Y., "Epigraphy and Crucifixion" IEJ 23 (1973) 18-22, plate 12. CONZELMANN, H., und LINDEMANN, A., Arbeitsbuch zum Neuen Testament (Tübingen 1975) 379.

15:27 HAHN, F. Christologische Hoheitstitel (1963) 172. SCHREIBER J. Theologie des Vertrauens (1967) 28, 44-58, 62-64, 71f. METZGER, B. M., The Early Versions of the New Testament (Oxford 1977) 326.

15:28 STROBEL, A. Erkenntnis und Bekenntnis der Sünde in neutestamentlicher Zeit (1968) 38. METZGER, B. M., The Early Versions of the New Testament (Oxford 1977) 41.

15:29-36 SCHREIBER, J., Theologie des Vertrauens (1967) 44-48, 101.

15:29-34 *DVORACEK, J. A. "Vom Leiden Gottes. Markus 15, 29-34" CommViat 14 (4, '71) 231-52.

15:29-32 TANNEHILL, R. C., "The Gospel of Mark as Narrative Christology" Semeia 16 (1980) 80.

15:29-31 KREMER, J. Das Aergernis des Kreuzes (1969) 66-68.

15:29 HAHN, F. Christologische Hoheitstitel (1963) 176. HAHN, F. Das Verständnis der Mission im Neuen Testament (1965) 29f, 100. GAERTNER, B. The Temple and the Community in Qumran and the New Testament (1965) 113. SCHREIBER, J. Theologie des Vertrauens (1967) 41f, 114-16. BAMMEL, E. The Trial of Jesus (1970) 92ff, 96. SANDVIK, B. Das Kommen des Herrn beim Abendmahl (1970) 56, 64, 144. WEEDEN, Th.J., "The Cross as Power in Weakness" in: W. H. Kelber (ed.) The Passion in Mark (Philadelphia 1976) 121-25, 129-31. WILLIAMS, J. A., A Conceptual History of Deuteronomism in the Old Testament, Judaism, and the New Testament (Ph.D.Diss. Southern Baptist Theological Seminary, Louisville, 1976) 294-97. MEYER, B. F., The Aims of Jesus (London 1979) 181-85. VIELHAUER, P., "Oikodome. Das Bild vom Bau in der christlichen Literatur vom Neuen Testament bis Clemens Alexandrinus" in: Oikodome. Neutestamentliche Aufsätze II (München 1979) 59, 61-62, 64-66.

15:30-32 SCHREIBER, J. Theologie des Vertrauens (1967) 31, 43f.

15:30 MASSAUX, E. Influence de l'Evangile de saint Matthieu sur la littérature chrétienne avant saint Irénée (1950) 71-73. WEEDEN, T. J., "The Cross as Power in Weakness" in: W. H. Kelber (ed.) The Passion in Mark (Philadelphia 1976) 116, 118f.

15:31-32 RIVKIN, E., A Hidden Revolution (Nashville 1978) 107-109.

15:31 BOUSSET, W., Die Religion des Judentums im späthellenistischen Zeitalter (Berlin 1966=1926) 367. SCHNEIDER, G., Verleugnung, Verspottung und Verhör Jesu nach Lukas 22, 54-71 (München 1969) 99, 112f. HAHN, F. Christologische Hoheitstitel (1963) 47. BAMMEL, E. The Trial of Jesus (1970) 93f, 98. SMITH, M., Clement of Alexandria and a secret Gospel of Mark (Cambridge, Mass. 1973) 154f. WEEDEN, T. J., "The Cross as Power in Weakness" in: W. H. Kelber (ed.) The Passion in Mark (Philadelphia 1976) 116, 118f.

15:32 HAHN, F. Christologische Hoheitstitel (1963) 178. PESCH, R. Naherwartungen (1969) 114, 115, 127, 148, 152. ACHTEMEIER, P. J., Mark (Philadelphia 1975) 43. SANDMEL, S., We Jews and Jesus (New York 1977) 49.

15:33ff STROBEL, A. Kerygma und Apokalyptik (1967) 139-45.

15:33-41   BEST, E. The Temptation and the Passion: The Markan Soteriology (1965) 97-102. TRILLING, W. "Der Tod Jesu, Ende der alten Weltzeit" Christusverkundigung in den Synoptischen Evangelien (1969) 191. SCHMITHALS, W., Das Evangelium nach Markus (Gütersloh/Würzburg 1979) 692 (lit!).

15:33-39   BULTMANN, R., The History of the Synoptic Tradition (Oxford 1963) 273f, 282-84. PESCH, R., Das Markusevangelium II (Freiburg 1977) 502f (lit!). *CULPEPPER, R. A., "The Passion and Resurrection in Mark" RevEx 75 (1978) 583-600. *SCHNEIDER, G., "Die theologische Sicht des Todes Jesu in den Kreuzigungsberichten der Evangelien" Theologisch-Praktische Quartalschrift 126 (1978) 14-22.

15:33-34   SCHREIBER, J. Theologie des Vertrauens (1967) 23f, 27, 49, 99-101, 103.

15:33   NESTLE, E. Die Sonnenfinsternis bei Jesu Tod (1902) 246f. HOLZMEISTER, U., "Die Finsternis beim Tode Jesu" Biblica 22 (1941) 404-411. HENNECKE, E. und SCHNEEMEL-CHER, W., Neutestamentliche Apokryphen I (Tübingen 1964) 122. NICKELS, P. Targum and New Testament (1967) 27. SCHREIBER, J. Theologie des Vertrauens (1967) 37-40, 69f, 76f, 242. KREMER, J. Das Aergernis des Kreuzes (1969) 69-70. KLAPPERT, B., "Der Verlust und die Wiedergewinnung der israelitischen Kontur der Leidensgeschichte Jesu" in: H. H. Henrix/M. Stöhr (eds.) Exodus und Kreuz im ökumenischen Dialog zwischen Juden und Christen (Aachen 1978) 115-18, 122. "Astrologie" in: TRE 4 (1979) 307.

15:34-46   PATTE, D. and A., Structural Exegesis (Philadelphia 1978) 42-43.

15:34-39   GESE, H., Vom Sinai zum Zion (München 1974) 194-96.

15:34, 37 KLAPPERT, B., "Der Verlust und die Wiedergewinnung der israelitischen Kontur der Leidensgeschichte Jesu" in: H. H. Henrix/M. Stöhr (eds.) Exodus und Kreuz im ökumenischen Dialog zwischen Juden und Christen (Aachen 1978) 118-20, 122.

15:34   LIGHTFOOT, R. H. History and Interpretation in the Gospels (1934) 157ff. ZIMMERMANN, F. "The Last Words of Jesus" JBL 66 ('47) 465ff. *READ, H. C. "The Cry of Dereliction" ET 68 (9, '57) 260-62. *BLIGHT, W. "The Cry of Dereliction" ET 68 (9, '57) 285. *GNILKA, J. " 'Mein Gott, mein Gott, warum hast du mich verlassen?' (Mk 15, 34 Par)" BZ 3 (2, '59) 294-97. HARNACK, A. VON, Studien zur Geschichte des Neuen

Testaments und der Alten Kirche (Berlin/Leipzig 1931) 98ff.
SCHELKLE, K. H., Die Passion Jesu in der Verkündigung des
Neues Testament (Heidelberg 1949) 91f. RUDOLPH, K., Die
Mandäer I (Göttingen 1960) 106. JOHNSON, H., The
Humanity of the Saviour (London 1962) 59-63. SCHWEIZER,
E., "Mark's Contribution to the Quest of the Historical Jesus"
NTS 10 (1963-1964) 431f. BRAUN, H., Qumran und NT II
(Tübingen 1966) 92, 107. BOMAN, T. Die Jesus-
Ueberlieferung im Lichte der neueren Volkskunde (1967) 221-
36. NICKELS, P. Targum and New Testament (1967) 27.
GESE, H. "Psalm 22 und das Neue Testament" ZThK 65 ('68)
1-22. KREMER, J. Das Aergernis des Kreuzes (1969) 70-71.
BAMMEL, E. The Trial of Jesus (1970) 91f, 100. *DANKER,
F. W. "The Demonic Secret in Mark: A Reexamination of the
Cry of Dereliction (15:34)" ZNW 61 (1-2, '70) 48-69.
JEREMIAS, J. Neutestamentliche Theologie I (1971) 16f, 60,
68, 182, 184, 198f. BROER, I. Die Urgemeinde und das Grab
Jesu (1972) 56f, 166. RUPPERT, L., Jesus als der leidende
Gerechte? (Stuttgart 1972) 46A.15, 50A.31, 52. DUNN, J. D.
G., Jesus and the Spirit (London 1975) 19, 21, 23.
GERSTENBERGER, G., und SCHRAGE, W., Leiden
(Stuttgart 1977) 150f; ET: Suffering (Nashville 1980) 174-76.
METZGER, B. M., The Early Versions of the New Testament
(Oxford 1977) 315, 316. "Aramäisch" in: TRE 3 (1978) 605.
FRIEDRICH, G., "Die Bedeutung der Auferweckung Jesu
nach Aussagen des Neuen Testaments" in: Auf das Wort
kommt es an (Göttingen 1978) 360. *LEON-DUFOUR, X.,
"Le dernier cri de Jésus" Etudes 348 (1978) 666-82. RIST, J. M.,
On the Independence of Matthew and Mark (Cambridge 1978)
87. *RUBINKIEWICZ, R., "Mk 15, 34 i Hbr 1, 8-9 w świetle
tradycji targumicznej" RTK 25 (1978) 59-67. *SABOURIN, L.,
"As Sete Palavras de Jesus na Cruz" RCB 2 (1978) 299-303.
FARICY, R., Praying for Inner Healing (London 1979) 37.
KLAPPERT, B., "Arbeit Gottes und Mitarbeit des Menschen
(Phil 2, 6-11)" in: J. Moltmann (ed.) Recht auf Arbeit - Sinn der
Arbeit (München 1979) 109f. SWIDLER, L., Biblical
Affirmations of Woman (Philadelphia 1979) 289. "Autonomie"
in: TRE 5 (1980) 8. TANNEHILL, R. C., "The Gospel of Mark
as Narrative Christology" Semeia 16 (1980) 79.

15:35-36 HAHN, F. Christologische Hoheitstitel (1963) 355. KREMER,
J. Das Aergernis des Kreuzes (1969) 72-73.

15:35 MASSAUX, E. Influence de l'Evangile de saint Matthieu sur la
littérature chrétienne avant saint Irénée (1950) 71-73. HAHN,
F. Christologische Hoheitstitel (1963) 239. SCHREIBER, J.
Theologie des Vertrauens (1967) 91-94, 97-100, 153, 139f.

15:36 DALMAN, G., Jesus-Jeschua (Leipzig 1922) 185-87.
DORMEYER, D., Die Passion Jesu als Verhaltensmodell
(Münster 1974) 201-204. MASSAUX, E. Influence de
L'Evangile de saint Matthieu sur la littérature chrétienne avant
saint Irénée (1950) 360-62. LEE, G. M., "Two Notes on St
Mark" NovT (1976) 36. MÜLLER, U. B., "Die griechische
Esra-Apokalypse" in: W. G. Kümmel (ed.) Jüdische Schriften
aus hellenistisch-römischer Zeit V (Gütersloh 1976) 93.
METZGER, B. M., The Early Versions of the New Testament
(Oxford 1977) 246. KLAPPERT, B., "Arbeit Gottes und
Mitarbeit des Menschen (Phil 2, 6-11)" in: J. Moltmann (ed.)
Recht auf Arbeit - Sinn der Arbeit (München 1979) 107.

15:37 HAHN, F. Christologische Hoheitstitel (1963) 166.
SCHREIBER, J. Theologie des Vertrauens (1967) 25, 27-29,
31-33, 38-41, 43-49, 51f. KREMER, J. Das Aergernis des
Kreuzes (1969) 73-74. GUETTGEMANNS, E. Offene Fragen
zur Formgeschichte des Evangeliums (1970) 101n120, 101n121,
101n122.

15:38-41 SCHREIBER, J. Theologie des Vertrauens (1967) 41f.

15:38-39 HENNECKE, E. und SCHNEEMELCHER, W.,
Neutestamentliche Apokryphen I (Tübingen 1964) 122f, 377.
HAHN, F. Das Verständnis der Mission im Neuen Testament
(1965) 101.

15:38 LINDESKOG, G. "The Veil of the Temple" Coniectanea
Neotestamentica (in honorem of Antonii Fridrichsen) (1947)
132-37. *CELADA, B. "El velo del templo" CultBib 15 (1959,
'58) 109-12. BRANDON, S. G. F., "The Date of the Markan
Gospel" NTS 7 (1960-1961) 131f. YATES, J. E., The Spirit and
the Kingdom (London 1963) 232ff. HAHN, F. Das Verständnis
der Mission im Neuen Testament (1965) 95. PELLETIER, A.
"La Tradition synoptique du 'Voile déchiré à la lumière des
réalités archéologiques" RechSR 46 (2, '58) 161-80. KREMER,
J. Das Aergernis des Kreuzes (1969) 74-75. LINNEMANN, E.
Studien zur Passionsgeschichte. DORMEYER, D., Die
Passion Jesu als Verhaltensmodell (Münster 1974) 204-206.
*LAMARCHE, P., "La mort du Christ et le voile du temple
selon Marc" NRTh 106 (1974) 583-99. WEEDEN, T. J., "The
Cross as Power in Weakness" in: W. H. Kelber (ed.) The
Passion in Mark (Philadelphia 1976) 121-24. "Astrologie" in:
TRE 4 (1979) 307. SCHRECKENBERG, H., "Flavius
Josephus und die lukanischen Schriften" in: W. Haubeck/ M.
Bachmann (eds.) Wort in der Zeit. Für K. H. Rengstorf (Leiden
1980) 192-93.

15:39 SCHNEIDER, C. "Der Hauptmann am Kreuz" ZNW 33 (1934) 1ff. MASSAUX, E. Influence de l'Evangile de saint Matthieu sur la littérature chrétienne avant saint Irénée (1950) 360-62. *BRATCHER, R. G. "A Note on huios theou (Mark xv.39)" ET 68 ('56) 27-28. HAHN, F. Christologische Hoheitstitel (1963) 318. *MICHAELIS, J. R. "The Centurion's Confession and the Spear Thrust," CBQ 29 (1, '67) 102-109. SCHREIBER, J. Theologie des Vertrauens (1967) 90f, 222f, 225f, 230f, 234f, 237-39. *BLIGH, P. H. "A Note on Huios Theou in Mark 15:39" ET 80 (2, '68) 51-53. STROBEL, A. Erkenntnis und Bekenntnis der Sünde in neutestamentlicher Zeit (1968) 39. RIEDL, J., "Die Evangelische Leidensgeschichte und ihre Theologische Aussage" BuL 41 (1968) 90-94. GRÄSSER, E., "Jesus in Nazareth (Mark VI.1-6a). Notes on the Redaction and Theology of St Mark" NTS 16 (1969-1970) 22f. PESCH, R. Naherwartungen (1969) 59, 93, 146, 170, 179, 194, 231, 235. *GLASSON, T. F. "Mark xv.39: the Son of God" ET 80 (9, '69) 286. *BRATCHER, R. G. "Mark xv. 39: the Son of God" ET 80 (9, '69) 286. KREMER, J. Das Aergernis des Kreuzes (1969) 76-78. *GUY, H. A. "Son of God in Mk 15:39" ET 81 (5, '70) 151. BAMMEL, E. The Trial of Jesus (1970) 91ff, 99ff. GÜTTGEMANNS, E. Offene Fragen zur Formgeschichte des Evangeliums (1970) 88, 101n122, 102, 260. *HARNER, P. B., "Qualitative Anarthrous Predicate Nouns: Mark 15:39 and John 1:1" JBL 92 (1973) 75-87. *SWAIN, L., "Preaching from the Lectionary in 1973: The Gospel According to St Mark" CIR 58 (1973) 342-49. BARTSCH, H. W., "Der ursprüngliche Schluss der Leidensgeschichte" in: M. Sabbe (ed.) L'Evangile selon Marc (Gembloux 1974) 419. DESCAMPS, A., "Pour une histoire du titre 'Fils de Dieu' " in: M. Sabbe (ed.) L'Evangile selon Marc (Gembloux 1974) 553. PERRIN, N., "The Christology of Mark" in: M. Sabbe (ed.) L'Evangile selon Marc (Gembloux 1974) 479. TALBERT, C. H., Literary Patterns, Theological Themes, and the Genre of Luke-Acts (Missoula 1974) 22. ACHTEMEIER, P. J., Mark (Philadelphia 1975) 44. EGGER, W., Frohbotschaft und Lehre (Frankfurt 1976) 88, 90, 98, 106f. *STOCK, K., "Das Bekenntnis des Centurio. Mk 15, 39 im Rahmen des Markusevangeliums" ZKTh 100 (1978) 289-301. KLAPPERT, B., "Arbeit Gottes und Mitarbeit des Menschen (Phil 2, 6-11)" in: J. Moltmann (ed.) Recht auf Arbeit - Sinn der Arbeit (München 1979) 107. TANNEHILL, R. C., "The Gospel of Mark as Narrative Christology" Semeia 16 (1980) 88.

15:40-16:8 *DHANIS, E. "L'ensevelissement de Jésus et la visite au tombeau dans l'évangile de saint Marc (Mc XV, 40-XVI, 8)"

Gregorianum 39 (2, '58) 367-410. PERRIN, N., The Resurrection According to Matthew, Mark, and Luke (Philadelphia 1977) 14-38. STAGG, E. and F., Woman in the World of Jesus (Philadelphia 1978) 214-15. GERSTENBERGER, E. S. und SCHRAGE, W., Frau und Mann (Stuttgart 1980) 129f.

15:40, 47 DORMEYER, D., Die Passion Jesu als Verhaltensmodell (Münster 1974) 235-37. OBERLINNER, L., Historische Überlieferung und christologische Aussage (Stuttgart 1975) 86-120.

15:40, 42 METZGER, B. M., The Early Versions of the New Testament (Oxford 1977) 11.

15:40-41 TAYLOR, V. The Gospel According to St Mark (1953) 651-53. HENGEL, M. "Maria Magdalena und die Frauen als Zeugen" in: Abraham unser Vater (Festschrift Otto Michel) 1963, 243-56. MEYE, R. P. Jesus and the Twelve (1968) 169-71. KREMER, J. Das Aergernis des Kreuzes (1969) 78-79. JEREMIAS, J. Neutestamentliche Theologie (1971) 164, 213, 215, 218. WANKE, J., Die Emmauserzählung (Leipzig 1973) 75. MAHONEY, R., Two Disciples at the Tomb (Bern 1974) 105-109. TALBERT, C. H., Literary Patterns, Theological Themes, and the Genre of Luke-Acts (Missoula 1974) 114. ACHTEMEIER, P J., Mark (Philadelphia 1975) 35f. PESCH, R., Das Markusevangelium II (Freiburg 1977) 509 (lit!). SWIDLER, L., Biblical Affirmations of Woman (Philadelphia 1979) 194, 199, 208, 221, 234, 248, 279, 305.

15:40 MEHLMANN, J., "Da origem e do significado de nome" RCB 7 (1963) 93-107. BLINZLER, J., Die Brüder und Schwestern Jesu (Stuttgart 1967) 73-86. BODE, E. L. The First Easter Morning (1970) 20-22. PESCH, R., "Der Schluss der vormarkinischen Passionsgeschichte und des Markusevangeliums" in: M. Sabbe (ed.) L'Evangile selon Marc (Gembloux 1974) 384-86.

15:41 NEIRYNCK, F., "Urmarcus redivivus?" in: M. Sabbe (ed.) L'Evangile selon Marc (Gembloux 1974) 129-30. WEEDEN, T. J., "The Cross as Power in Weakness" in: W. H. Kelber (ed.) The Passion in Mark (Philadelphia 1976) 130, 132f. WILLIAMS, J. A., A Conceptual History of Deuteronomism in the Old Testament, Judaism, and the New Testament (Ph.D.Diss. Southern Baptist Theological Seminary, Louisville 1976) 300.

15:42-16:8 PESCH, R., "Der Schluss der vormarkinischen Passionsgeschichte und des Markusevangeliums: Mk, 15:42 -

16:8" in: M. Sabbe (ed.) L'Evangile selon Marc (Gembloux 1974) 365-409.

15:42ff CLARKE, W. K. L., New Testament Problems (New York 1929) 104f.

15:42-47 KENNARD, J. S. The Burial of Jesus 74 (1955) 227-38. MASSON, C., Vers les Sources d'eau Vive (Lausanne 1961) 102ff. BENOIT, P. Passion et Résurrection du Seigneur (1966) 243-45. SEIDENSTICKER, Ph. Die Auferstehung Jesu in der Botschaft der Evangelisten (1968) 62f. SCHREIBER, J. Die Markuspassion (1969) 58-60. GRASS, H. Ostergeschehen und Osterberichte (1970) 173ff. ZIMMERMANN, W.-D. Markus über Jesus (1970) 175-76. CRIBBS, F. L., "A Study of the Contacts That Exist Between St Luke and St John" in: G. MacRae (ed.) SBL Seminar Papers II (Missoula 1973) 79-81. DORMEYER, D., Die Passion Jesu als Verhaltensmodell (Münster 1974) 216-21. MAHONEY, R., Two Disciples at the Tomb (Bern 1974) 105-18, 142f. SCHENK, W., Der Passionsbericht nach Markus (Gütersloh 1974) 254ff. PESCH, R., "Der Schluss der vormarkinischen Passionsgeschichte und des Markusevangeliums: Mk 15, 42-16, 8" in: M. Sabbe (ed.) L'Evangile selon Marc (Gembloux 1974) 368f, 375-77, 386-92, 403-405. SCHENKE, L., Der gekreuzigte Christus (Stuttgart 1974) 77-83. PESCH, R., Das Markusevangelium II (Freiburg 1977) 518f (lit!). RIST, J. M., On the Independence of Matthew and Mark (Cambridge 1978) 87. GNILKA, J., Das Evangelium nach Markus II (Einsiedeln/Neukirchen 1979) 330 (lit!). SCHMITHALS, W., Das Evangelium nach Markus (Gütersloh/Würzburg 1979) 702 (lit!). SWIDLER, L., Biblical Affirmations of Woman (Philadelphia 1979) 200.

15:42-46 PATTE, D., and A., Structural Exegesis (Philadelphia 1978) 48-50.

15:42-43 HARTMANN, L., Testimonium Linguae (Lund 1963) 27. KREMER, J. Das Aergernis des Kreuzes (1969) 80-82.

15:43-46 PATTE, D. and A., Structural Exegesis (Philadelphia 1978) 93.

15:43 BARRETT, C. K., The New Testament Background (London 1956) 241. HARTMAN, L., Testimonium Linguae (Lund 1963) 15ff. McNAMARA, M. The New Testament and the Palestinian Targum to the Pentateuch (1966) 241. MINETTE DE TILLESSE, G. Le Secret Messianique dans L'Evangile de Marc (1968) 390-94. MEYE, R. P. Jesus and the Twelve (1968) 167-69. AMBROZIC, A. M., St Mark's Concept of the Kingdom of God (Würzburg 1970) 261-63. METZGER, B. M., The Early Versions of the New Testament (Oxford 1977) 435.

MALBON, E. S., "Mythic Structure and Meaning in Mark" Semeia 16 (1980) 109-13.

15:44 MASSAUX, E. Influence de l'Evangile de saint Matthieu sur la littérature chrétienne avant saint Irénée (1950) 360-62. METZGER, B. M., The Early Versions of the New Testament (Oxford 1977) 254.

15:45-47 SWIDLER, L., Biblical Affirmations of Woman (Philadelphia 1979) 208.

15:45 MASSAUX, E. Influence de l'Evangile de saint Matthieu sur la littérature chrétienne avant saint Irénée (1950) 360-62.

15:46 RUDOLPH, K., Die Mandäer II (Göttingen 1961) 416, 6. KREMER, J. Das Aergernis des Kreuzes (1969) 82-83. MAHONEY, R., Two Disciples at the Tomb (Bern 1974) 114-16. CROSSAN, J. D., "Empty Tomb and Absent Lord" in: W. H. Kelber (ed.) The Passion in Mark (Philadelphia 1976) 146-48. *CHARBEL, A., "A Sepultura de Jesus como Resulta dos Evangelhos" RCB 2 (1978) 351-62.

15:47-16:8 PATTE, D. and A., Structural Exegesis (Philadelphia 1978) 44f, 55f.

15:47 RUDOLPH, K. Die Mandäer I (Göttingen 1960) 97. BLINZLER, J., Die Brüder und Schwestern Jesu (Stuttgart 1967) 73-86. KREMER, J. Das Aergernis des Kreuzes (1969) 83-84. HENGEL, M. "Maria Magdalena und die Frauen als Zeugen" Abraham unser Vater, Festschrift Otto Michel (1963) 243-56. BODE, E. L. The First Easter Morning (1970) 20-22. WANKE, J., Die Emmauserzählung (Leipzig 1973) 75. MAHONEY, R., Two Disciples at the Tomb (Bern 1974) 105-109, 115f. PESCH, R., "Der Schluss der vormarkinischen Passionsgeschichte und des Markusevangeliums" in: M. Sabbe (ed.) L'Evangile selon Marc (Gembloux 1974) 377-78, 384-86. TALBERT, C. H., Literary Patterns, Theological Themes, and the Genre of Luke-Acts (Missoula 1974) 113f. SWIDLER, L., Biblical Affirmations of Woman (Philadelphia 1979) 234, 261.

16 EWALD, H., Die drei ersten Evangelien (Göttingen 1850) 362ff. FARRER, A. St Matthew and St Mark (1954). *BOWMAN, D. J. "The Resurrection in Mark" Bible Today i

(11, '64) 709-13. NEIRYNCK, F., "Les Femmes ou Tombeau: Etude de la Rédaction Matthéenne (Matt. 28: 1-10)" NTS 15 (1968-69) 168ff. *BARTSCH, H. W. "Der Schluss des Markus-Evangeliums. Ein ueberlieferungsgeschichtliches Problem" ThZ 27 (4, '71) 241-54. WEEDEN, T. J. Mark - Traditions in Conflict (1971) 101-17. *SCHMITHALS, W., "Der Markusschluss, die Verklärungsgeschichte und die Aussendung der Zwölf" ZThK 69 (1972) 379-411. *BENITO, A., "Marcos 16. Redacción y Hermenéutica" Salmanticensis 24 (1977) 279-305. TRITES, A. A., The New Testament Concept of Witness (Cambridge 1977) 190.

16:1ff RENGSTORF, K. H., Die Auferstehung Jesu (Witten 1960). HAHN, F. Christologische Hoheitstitel (1963) 205. GRASS, H. Ostergeschehen und Osterberichte (1970) 15ff. LIGHTFOOT, R. H., Loyalty and Doctrine in the Gospels (1938) 10ff. SWIDLER, L., Biblical Affirmations of Woman (Philadelphia 1979) 201, 222, 234.

16:1-8 STONEHOUSE, N. B. The Witness of Matthew and Mark to Christ (1944) 109ff. KLOSTERMANN, E. Das Markusevangelium (1950) 168. FRIEDRICH, GPM 4 (1949/50) 123ff. DINKLER, GPM 9 (1954/55) 106ff. Herr, tue meine Lippen auf, ed. G. Eichholz (1957) 133-38. *CHEEK, J. L. "The Historicity of the Markan Resurrection Narrative" JBL 27 (3, '59) 191-200. *HEBERT, G. "The Resurrection-Narrative in St Mark's Gospel" ABR 8 (1-4, '59) 58-65. SCHWEIZER, GPM 15 (1960/61) 120ff. *WAETJEN, H. "The Ending of Mark and the Gospel's Shift in Eschatology" Annual of the Swedish Theological Institute, IV, 114-31. MASSON, C., Vers les Sources d'Eau Vive (Lausanne 1961) 114f. *HEBERT, G. "The Resurrection-Narrative in St Mark's Gospel" SJTh 15 (1, '62) 66-73. *GALBIATI, E. "E risorto, non è qui (Marco 16, 1-8)" BiblOr 5 (2, '63) 67-72. BULTMANN, R., The History of the Synoptic Tradition (Oxford 1963) 284f. ALAND, K., "Bemerkungen zum Schluss des Markusevangeliums" in: E. E. Ellis/ M. Wilcox (eds.) Neotestamentica et Semitica. In Honour of M.Black (Edinburgh 1969) 158-62, 164-68. BARTSCH, H.-W. Das Auferstehungszeugnis (1965) 9-11. LUTHER, M. Predigten über die Christus-Botschaft (1966) 170-81. OTTO, G. Handbuch des Religions-Unterrichts (1967) 190-217. SEIDENSTICKER, Ph. Die Auferstehung Jesu in der Botschaft der Evangelisten (1968) 83ff. KAMPHAUS, F. Von der Exegese zur Predigt (1968) 29-33, 75-86. KREMER, J. Die Osterbotschaft der vier Evangelien (1968) 13-31. MOULE, C. F. D. (ed.) The Significance of the Message of the Resurrection

for Faith in Jesus Christ (1968) 25, 58, 71, 92. DELORME, J.,
"Résurrection et tombeau de Jésus" Lectio divina 50 (1969)
105-51. HORSTMANN, M. Studien zur Markinischen
Christologie (1969) 128-34. SCHREINER, J. Gestalt und
Anspruch des neuen Testaments (1969) 169, 170f. GUTBROD,
K. Die Auferstehung Jesu im Neuen Testament (1969) 59f.
MARXSEN, W. Mark the Evangelist (1969) 76, 78f, 81, 86.
SCHWEIZER, GPM 1960/61 120ff. SCHENKE, L.
Auferstehungsverkündigung und leeres Grab (1968) Rev. J.
Murphy-O'Connor RevBib 76 (3, '69) 431-34. *GHIBERTI, G.
"Discussione sul sepolcro vuoto" RivB 17 (4, '69) 393-419.
SCHNIDER, F./Stenger, W. Die Ostergeschichten der
Evangelien (1969) 17-23. *BROER, I. "Zur heutigen
Discussion der Grabesgeschichte BuL 10 (1, '69) 40-52. BODE,
E. L. The First Easter Morning (1970) 7-10, 25-49, 127-29, 159-
60. WILCKENS, U. Auferstehung (1970) 43-58. EVANS, C. F.
Resurrection and the New Testament (1970) 75ff. BENOIT, P.
and MURPHY, R. (eds.) Immortality and Resurrection (1970)
61-63. ZIMMERMANN, W.-D. Markus über Jesus (1970)
177-79. *BODE, E. L. "A Liturgical Sitz im Leben for the
Gospel Tradition of the Women's Easter Visit to the Tomb of
Jesus?" CBQ 32 (2, '70) 237-42. *MEYE, R. P., "Mark's Special
Easter Emphasis" ChrTo 15 (13, '71) 584-86. *SCHLIER, H.
"Die Osterbotschaft aus dem Grab (Markus 16, 1-8) KG 27 (1,
'71) 1-6. BROER, I, Die Urgemeinde und das Grab Jesu (1972)
83, 86, 104, 132, 281ff. *GUETTGEMANNS, E. "Linguistische
Analyse von Mk 16, 1-8" LiBi 11-12 ('72) 13-53. BALTZER,
K./Brandenburger E./Merkel F. GPM 72 (1973) 205-209.
*SMITH, R. H., "New and Old in Mark 16:1-8" CThM 43
(1972) 518-27. CRIBBS, F. L., "A Study of the Contacts That
Exist Between St Luke and St John" in: G. MacRae (ed.) SBL
Seminar Papers II (Montana 1973) 81f. FRIEDRICH, G., "Lk
9, 51 und die Entrückungschristologie des Lukas" in: P.
Hoffmann (ed.) Orientierung an Jesus. Für J. Schmid
(Freiburg 1973) 50f. *HORVATH, T., "The Early Markan
Tradition on the Resurrection (Mk. 16, 1-8)" RUO 43 (1973)
445-48. WANKE, J., Die Emmauserzählung (Leipzig 1973) 69,
73, 116; notes 300, 525, 527. ALAND, K., "Der Schluss des
Markusevangeliums" in: M. Sabbe (ed.) L'Evangile selon Marc
(Gembloux 1974) 435-70; reprinted in: Aland K.,
Neutestamentliche Entwürfe (München 1979) 246-83.
*AMMASSARI, A., "Il racconto degli avvenimenti della
mattina di Pasqua secondo Marco 16, 1-8" BiOr 16 (1974) 49-
64. BROWN, R. E., The Virginal Conception and Bodily
Resurrection of Jesus (London 1974) 113-25. DORMEYER,

D., Die Passion Jesu als Verhaltensmodell (Münster 1974) 221-35. LEON-DUFOUR, X., The Resurrection and the Message of Easter (London 1974) 128-38. MAHONEY, R., Two Disciples at the Tomb (Bern 1974) 114-17, 141-62, 194-202. PESCH, R., "Der Schluss der vormarkinischen Passionsgeschichte und des Markusevangeliums: Mk 15, 42 - 16, 8" in: M. Sabbe (ed.) L'Evangile selon Marc (Gembloux 1974) 370-72, 377-84, 391-409. SCHENK, W., Der Passionsbericht nach Markus (Gütersloh 1974) 259ff. SCHENKE, L., Der gekreuzigte Christus (Stuttgart 1974) 77, TALBERT, C. H., Literary Patterns, Theological Themes, and the Genre of Luke-Acts (Missoula 1974) 22. ALSUP, J. E., The Post-Resurrection Appearance Stories of the Gospel-Tradition (Stuttgart 1975) 86ff. BARTLETT, D. L., Fact and Faith (Valley Forge 1975) 103-107. CONZELMANN, H., und LINDEMANN, A., Arbeitsbuch zum Neuen Testament (Tübingen 1975) 245. DUNN, J. D. G., Jesus and the Spirit (London 1975) 391. GOPPELT, L., Theologie des Neuen Testaments I (Göttingen 1975) 287f, 295f. *SYNGE, F. C., "Mark 16.1-8" Journal of Theology for Southern Africa II (1975) 71-73. COUSIN, H., Le prophète assassiné. Histoire des textes évangéliques de la Passion (Paris 1976). CROSSAN, J. D., "Empty Tomb and Absent Lord" in: W. H. Kelber (ed.) The Passion in Mark (Philadelphia 1976) 135-52. *GOULDER, M. D., "The Empty Tomb" Theology 79 (1976) 206-14. KELBER, W. H., "Conclusion: From Passion Narrative to Gospel" in: W. H. Kelber (ed.) The Passion in Mark (Philadelphia 1976) 162-64. KREMER, J., Die Osterevangelien - Geschichten um Geschichte (Stuttgart 1977). *MANGATT, G., "At the Tomb of Jesus" Biblebhashyam 3 (1977) 91-96. PESCH, R., Das Markusevangelium II (Freiburg 1977) 541-43 (lit!). *GOULDER, M. D., "Mark xvi. 1-8 and Parallels" NTS 24 (1978) 235-40. *NEIRYNCK, F., "*Anateilantos tou hēliou* (Mc 16, 2)" EphT 54 (1978) 70-103. STAGG, E./F., Woman in the World of Jesus (Philadelphia 1978) 144-60, 217. "Auferstehung" in: TRE 4 (1979) 497. GNILKA, J., Das Evangelium nach Markus II (Einsiedeln/Neukirchen 1979) 337 (lit!). *NIEMANN, F.-J., "Die Erzählung vom leeren Grab bei Markus" ZkTh 101 (1979) 188-99. SCHILLEBEECKX, E., Die Auferstehung Jesu als Grund der Erlösung (Basel 1979) 104f. SCHILLEBEECKX, E., Jesus. An Experiment in Christology (London 1979) 334-37. SCHMITHALS, W., Das Evangelium nach Markus (Gütersloh/Würzburg 1979) 706f (lit!). SCHÖNHERR, A., in: GPM 33 (1979) 184-90. LINDEMANN, A., "Die Osterbotschaft des Markus. Zur Theologischen Interpretation von Mark 16.1-8" NTS 26

(1979/80) 298-317. PAULSEN, H., "Mk XVI 1-8" NovT 22 (1980) 138-75.

16:1-7   DINKLER, E., GPM 9 (1955) 106-11.

16:1.2a.4   KOCH, D.-A., Die Bedeutung der Wundererzählungen für die Christologie des Markusevangeliums (Berlin/New York 1975) 155-57.

16:1   RUDOLPH, K., Die Mandäer I (Göttingen 1960) 97, II (1961) 416. HENGEL, M. "Maria Magdalena und die Frauen als Zeugen" Abraham unser Vater (1963) 243-56. BLINZLER, J. Der Prozess Jesu (1969) 123, 399, 403, 405, 413. BODE, E. L. The First Easter Morning (1970) 14-16, 20, 22. BROER, I. Die Urgemeinde und das Grab Jesu (1972) 87-137.

16:1-2   HAHN, F. Christologische Hoheitstitel (1963) 205. SWIDLER, L., Biblical Affirmations of Woman (Philadelphia 1979) 208, 221. D., Die Passion Jesu als Verhaltensmodell (Münster 1974) 235-37. MAHONEY, R., Two Disciples at the Tomb (Bern 1974) 105-109, 114-16, 143-45. PESCH, R., "Der Schluss der vormarkinischen Passionsgeschichte und des Markusevangeliums" in: M. Sabbe (ed.) L'Evangile selon Marc (Gembloux 1974) 384-86. OBERLINNER, L., Historische Überlieferung und christologische Aussage (Stuttgart 1975) 108-12. SWIDLER, L., Biblical Affirmations of Woman (Philadelphia 1979) 248.

16:2   SCHREIBER, J. Theologie des Vertrauens (1967) 84f, 100-102. BODE, E. L. The First Easter Morning (1970) 130-31. WANKE, J., Die Emmauserzählung (Leipzig 1973) 73. MAHONEY, R., Two Disciples at the Tomb (Bern 1974) 143-45.

16:3   LOHFINK, G. Die Himmelfahrt Jesu (1971) 128f. METZGER, B. M., The Early Versions of the New Testament (Oxford 1977) 326.

16:4   *PALMER, D. W., "The Origin, Form, and Purpose of Mark XVI.4 in Codex Bobbiensis" JThS 27 (1976) 113-22.

16:5-8   RIESENFELD, H., Jésus Transfiguré (Copenhagen 1947) 284ff.

16:5-7   SCHNIDER, F.,/Stenger, W. Die Ostergeschichten der Evangelien (1969) 23-30.

16:5   *MCINDOE, J. H. "The Young Man at the Tomb" ET 80 (4, '69) 125. BODE, E. L. The First Easter Morning (1970) 26-27. *SCROGGS, R., and GROFF, K. I., "Baptism in Mark: Dying and Rising With Christ" JBL 92 (1973) 531-48. MAHONEY, R., Two Disciples at the Tomb (Bern 1974) 147-49, 203, 219.

16:6-7   EGGER, W., Frohbotschaft und Lehre (Frankfurt 1976) 89.

16:6 LIGHTFOOT, R. H. Locality and Doctrine in the Gospels (1938) 57ff. HAHN, F. Christologische Hoheitstitel (1963) 200, 204. MOULE, C. F. D. The Significance of the Message of the Resurrection for Faith in Jesus Christ (1968) 25, 72, 87, 93. BODE, E. L. The First Easter Morning (1970) 27-31, 165-71. VAN IERSEL, B., "Besuch am Grabe" Schrift 7 (1970) 15-17. *LOCATELLI, A., " 'È risorto, non è qui' (Mc.16,6): La risurrezione di Cristo è anche motivo di credibilità" ScuC 101 (1973) 251-80. WANKE, J., Die Emmauserzählung (Leipzig 1973) 30. MAHONEY, R., Two Disciples at the Tomb (Bern 1974) 149-57. CROSSAN, J. D., "Empty Tomb and Absent Lord" in: W. H. Kelber (ed.) The Passion in Mark (Philadelphia 1976) 148f, 151.

16:7-8 RAWLINSON, A. E. J. St Mark (1925) 267-71. *CATCHPOLE, D., "The Fearful Silence of the Women at the Tomb: A Study in Markan Theology" Journal of Theology for Southern Africa 18 (1977) 3-10. RIST, J. M., On the Independence of Matthew and Mark (Cambridge 1978) 89-91.

16:7.11 SWIDLER, L., Biblical Affirmations of Woman (Philadelphia 1979) 222, 234.

16:7 LIGHTFOOT, R. H. Locality and Doctrine in the Gospels (1938) 36ff, 55ff, 59ff, 73ff. STONEHOUSE, N. B. The Witness of Matthew and Mark to Christ (1944) 27, 39, 47, 77, 81, 91, 113ff, 170f, 173ff. KUEMMEL, W. G. Verheissung und Erfüllung (1953) 70-72. STRECKER, G. Der Weg der Gerechtigkeit (1962) 48, 94, 97f. MEYE, R. P. Jesus and the Twelve (1968) 80-85. ODENKIRCHEN, P. C. "Praecedam vos in Galilaeam' (Mt 26, 32 cf. 28, 7.10; Mc 14, 28; 16, 7 cfr. Lc 24, 6)" VerbDom 46, 1968) 193-223. MOULE, C. F. D. (ed.) The Significance of the Message of the Resurrection for Faith in Jesus Christ (1968) 4, 5, 71, 73, 79, 84, 92. PESCH, R. Naherwartungen (1969) 30, 57, 62, 84, 85, 101. MARXSEN, W. Mark the Evangelist (1969) 75ff, 97f, 111ff, 186. KASTING, H. Die Anfänge der Urchristlichen Mission (1969) 38f, 82-84, 93f. GRASS, H. Ostergeschehen und Osterberichte (1970) 18n2, 19n1, 23n1, 23, 80, 81, 108, 119n2, 120n3, 301. BODE, E. L. The First Easter Morning (1970) 31-37, 43-44. WEEDEN, T. J. Mark - Traditions in Conflict (1971) 111-17. WILCOX, M., "The Denial-Sequence in Mark 14:26-31, 66-72" NTS 17 (1970-71) 428f. SCHENKE, L., Studien zur Passionsgeschichte des Markus (Würzburg 1971) 371ff, 433, 437-41, 454ff. BROWN, R. E. et al., Peter in the New Testament (Minneapolis 1973) 69-75. HOFFMANN, P., "Mk 8, 31. Zur Herkunft und markinischen Rezeption einer alten Überlieferung" in: P. Hoffmann (ed.) Orientierung an Jesus. Für J. Schmid

(Freiburg 1973) 201f. WANKE, J., Die Emmauserzählung (Leipzig 1973) 8, 52, A.389. BARTSCH, H. W., "Der ursprüngliche Schluss der Leidensgeschichte" in: M. Sabbe (ed.) L'Evangile selon Marc (Gembloux 1974) 421. DAVIES, W. D., The Gospel and the Land (London 1974) 230, 230n.26, 255, 264, 409-13 passim, 424-38 passim. PERRIN, N., The New Testament (New York 1974) 148-51. *STEIN, R. H., "A Short Note on Mark xiv.28 and xvi.7" NTS 20 (1974) 445-52. ALSUP, J. E., The Post-Resurrection Appearance Stories of the Gospel-Tradition (Stuttgart 1975) 90ff. POKORNY, P., " 'Anfang des Evangeliums'. Zum Problem des Anfangs und des Schlusses des Markusevangeliums" in: R. Schnackenburg (ed.) Die Kirche des Anfangs. Für H. Schürmann (Leipzig 1977) 117-20. FRIEDRICH, G., "Die Bedeutung der Auferweckung Jesu nach Aussagen des Neuen Testaments" in: Auf das Wort kommt es an (Göttingen 1978) 366. ERNST, J., "Die Petrustradition im Markusevangelium - ein altes Problem neu angegangen" in: J. Zmijewski/E. Nellessen (eds.) Begegnung mit dem Wort. Für H. Zimmermann (Bonn 1980) 58. MALBON, E. S., "Mythic Structure and Meaning in Mark" Semeia 16 (1980) 103-107. TANNEHILL, R. C., "The Gospel of Mark as Narrative Christology" Semeia 16 (1980) 83f.

16:8 LIGHTFOOT, R. H. Locality and Doctrine in the Gospels (1938) 2ff, 29f. STONEHOUSE, N. B. The Witness of Matthew and Mark to Christ (1944) 89, 92, 101, 107, 165. PARKER, P. The Gospel Before Mark (1953) 117ff. MOULE, C. F. D., "St. Mark 16:8 Once More" NTS 2 (1955-56) 58ff. ENSLIN, M. S., The Literature of the Christian Movement (New York 1956) 387f. BAUMBACH, G. Das Verständnis des Bösen in den synoptischen Evangelien (1963) 197ff, 201ff. PRYKE, E. J., "IΔE and IΔOY" NTS 14 (1967-68) 418f. ALAND, K., "Bemerkungen zum Schluss des Markusevangeliums" in: E. E. Ellis/M. Wilcox (eds.) Neotestamentica et Semitica. In Honour of M. Black (Edinburgh 1969) 157ff, 175-78. MOULE, C. F. D. (ed.) The Significance of the Message of the Resurrection for Faith in Jesus Christ (1968) 25, 71, 102. PESCH, R. Naherwartungen (1969) 54, 66, 67, 69, 70, 147, 150, 233. MARXSEN, W. Mark the Evangelist (1969) 76ff, 85, 88, 91, 208. *LUZARRAGA, J. "Retraduccion semitica de phobeomai en Mc 16, 8" Biblica 50 (4, '69) 497-510. MEYE, R., "The Ending of Mark's Gospel" BiRe 14 (1969) 33-43. GRASS, H. Ostergeschehen und Osterberichte (1970) 16, 17, 19, 21 n3, 23, 27n2, 182. BODE, E. L. The First Easter Morning (1970) 37-48. *ALAND, K. "Der wiedergefundene Markusschluss? Eine methodologische Bemerkung zur textkritischen Arbeit"

ZThK 67 (1, '70) 3-13. SCHENKE, L., Studien zur Passionsgeschichte des Markus (Würzburg 1971) 457ff. *VAN DER HORST, P. W. "Can a Book End with GAR? A Note on Mark xvi.8" JThS 23 (1, '72) 121-24. KÜMMEL, W. G., Einleitung in das Neue Testament (Heidelberg 1973 *(17)*) 71f. LANGE, J., Das Erscheinen des Auferstandenen im Evangelium nach Mattäus (Würzburg 1973) 203f, 374, 452, 455-60, 470, 483. WANKE, J., Die Emmauserzählung (Leipzig 1973) 71, 75. ALAND, K., "Der Schluss des Markusevangeliums" in: M. Sabbe (ed.) L'Evangile selon Marc (Gembloux 1974) 437-41. MAHONEY, R., Two Disciples at the Tomb (Bern 1974) 156-58. METZGER, B. M., The Early Versions of the New Testament (Oxford 1977) 315. POKORNY, P. " 'Anfang des Evangeliums'. Zum Problem des Anfangs und des Schlusses des Markusevangeliums" in: R. Schnackenburg (ed.) Die Kirche des Anfangs. Für H. Schürmann (Leipzig 1977) 115-17. SWIDLER, L., Biblical Affirmations of Woman (Philadelphia 1979) 201, 205.

16:9ff   LIGHTFOOT, R. H. "St. Mark's Gospel - Complete or Incomplete?" The Gospel Message of St Mark (1950) 80-97, 106-16. *DUNN, J. W. E. "The Text of Mark 16 in the English Bible" ET 83 (10, '72) 311-12.

16:9-20   LIGHTFOOT, R. H. Locality and Doctrine in the Gospels (1938) 1ff. STONEHOUSE, N. B. The Witness of Matthew and Mark to Christ (1944) 88ff. KLOSTERMANN, E. Das Markusevangelium (1950) 172-74. FEINE, P., und Behm, J., Einleitung in das Neue Testament (Heidelberg 1950) 62f. STREETER, B. H. The Four Gospels (1951) 70f, 335-60. CARRINGTON, P. The Primitive Christian Calendar (1952) 227-30. SCHMID, J. Das Evangelium nach Markus (1958) 313-16. TAYLOR, V., The Text of the New Testament (London 1961) 36f, 89f. METZGER, B. M., The Text of the New Testament (New York/London 1964) 226-29. QUESNELL, Q. This Good News (1964) 167f. *WAGENAARS, F. "Structura litteraria et momentum theologicum pericopae (Mc 16, 9-20)" VerbDom 45 (1, '67) 19-22. BEYSCHLAG, K., Clemens Romanus und der Frühkatholizismus (Tübingen 1966) 287f. BIEDER, W., Die Verheissung der Taufe im Neuen Testament (Zürich 1966) 207-12. STUHLMACHER, P. Das Paulinische Evangelium (1968) 254. MOULE, C. F. D. (ed.) The Significance of the Message of the Resurrection for Faith in Jesus Christ (1968) 4. KAMPHAUS, F. Von der Exegese zur Predigt (1968) 64-66. KASSING, A. Auferstanden für uns (1969) 94-98. ALAND, K. "Bemerkungen zum Schluss des Markusevangeliums"

Neotestamentica et Semitica, eds. E. E. Ellis and M. Wilcox (1969) 157-80. KASTING, H. Die Anfänge der urchristlichen Mission (1969) 38-40, 46, 82. WILCKENS, U. Auferstehung (1970) 85-87. ZIMMERMANN, W.-D. Markus über Jesus (1970) 179-81. GRASS, H. Ostergeschehen und Osterberichte (1970) 15f, 188, 255nl, 289n2. EVANS, C. F. Resurrection and the New Testament (1970) 67ff. LOHFINK, G. Die Himmelfahrt Jesu (1971) 119-20. *ELLIOTT, J. K. "The Text and Language of the Ending to Mark's Gospel" ThZ 27 (4, '71) 255-62. *TROMPF, G. W. "The First Resurrection Appearance and the Ending of Mark's Gospel" NTS 18 (3, '72) 308-30. HAY, D. M., Glory at the Right Hand (Nashville 1973) 83f. *TROMPF, G. W., "The Markusschluss in Recent Research" AusBR 21 (1973) 15-26. ALAND, K., "Der Schluss des Markusevangeliums" in: M. Sabbe (ed.) L'Evangile selon Marc (Gembloux 1974) 435-70; reprinted in: Aland, K., Neutestamentliche Entwürfe (München 1979) 246-83. BARTSCH, H. W., "Der ursprüngliche Schluss der Leidensgeschichte. Überlieferungsgeschichtliche Studien zum Markus-Schluss" in: M. Sabbe (ed.) L'Evangile selon Marc (Gembloux 1974) 411-33. FARMER, W. R., The Last Twelve Verses of Mark (New York 1974); *review*: BIRDSALL, J. N., JThS 26 (1975) 151-60. HUBBARD, B. J., The Matthean Redaction of a Primitive Apostolic Commission: An Exegesis of Matthew 28:16-20 (Missoula 1974) 137-49. ALSUP, J. E., The Post-Resurrection Appearance Stories of the Gospel-Tradition (Stuttgart 1975) 117ff. CONZELMANN, H., und LINDEMANN, A., Arbeitsbuch zum Neuen Testament (Tübingen 1975) 59. FULLER, D. O. (ed.) Counterfeit or Genuine? Mark 16? John 8? (Grand Rapids 1975). MARTIN, R. P., New Testament Foundations I (Grand Rapids 1975) 217-20.

16:9-20 MITTON, C. L., "Some Further Studies in St Mark's Gospel" ET 87 (1976) 297-301. LUBSCZYK, H., "Kyrios Jesus. Beobachtungen und Gedanken zum Schluss des Markusevangeliums" in: R. Schnackenburg (ed.) Die Kirche des Anfangs. Für H.Schürmann (Leipzig 1977) 133-74. METZGER, B. M., The Early Versions of the New Testament (Oxford 1977) 163, 234. PESCH, R., Das Markusevangelium II (Freiburg 1977) 556 (lit!). HENDRIKX, H., The Resurrection Narratives of the Synoptic Gospels (Manila 1978). HUG, J., La finale de l'évangile de Marc (Mc 16, 9-20) (Paris 1978). GNILKA, J., Das Evangelium nach Markus II (Einsiedeln/Neukirchen 1979) 352. (lit!). SCHMITHALS, W., Das Evangelium nach Markus (Gütersloh/Würzburg 1979)

718 (lit!). SWIDLER, L., Biblical Affirmations of Woman (Philadelphia 1979) 203, 205.

16:9-14   ALAND, K., "Der Schluss des Markusevangeliums" in: M. Sabbe (ed.) L'Evangile selon Marc (Gembloux 1974) 446-48.

16:9-11   SWIDLER, L., Biblical Affirmations of Woman (Philadelphia 1979) 203, 208, 279.

16:9   RUDOLPH, K., Die Mandäer I (Göttingen 1960) 97. HAHN, F. Christologische Hoheitstitel (1963) 205. METZGER, B. M., "St. Jerome's explicit references to variant readings in manuscripts of the New Testament" in: E. Best/R. McL. Wilson (eds.) Text and Interpretation. Studies in the New Testament presented to Matthew Black (Cambridge 1979) 182. SWIDLER, L., Biblical Affirmations of Woman (Philadelphia 1979) 223.

16:12   HAHN, F. Christologische Hoheitstitel (1963) 124. WANKE, J., Die Emmauserzählung (Leipzig 1973) 15.

16:14-20   WEBER, GPM 1949/50, 153ff. WENDLAND, GPM 9 (1954/55) 137ff. Herr, tue meine Lippen auf, ed. G. Eichholz (1957) 168-72. WENDLAND, H.-D. GPM 9/2, 137-42. HARDER, GPM 15 (1960/61) 157ff. SCHMIDT, L. "Erhöht und gegenwärtig zugleich" in: Kleine Predigt-Typologie III (1965) 343-46. WEBER, O. Predigtmeditationen (1967) 138-42. KAMPHAUS, F. Von der Exegese zur Predigt (1968) 103-112. DAHINTEN, G. GPM 27 (1973) 258-66.

16:14-19   MICHEL, H.-J., Die Abschiedsrede des Paulus an die Kirche Apg 20:17-38 (München 1973) 57, 59.

16:14-18   HENSS, W., Das Verhältnis zwischen Diatessaron, Christlicher Gnosis und "Western Text" (Berlin 1967) 13f.

16:14-15   HAACKER, K., "Bemerkungen zum Freer-Logion" ZNW 63 (1972) 125-29. SCHWARZ, G., "Zum Freer-Logion - ein Nachtrag" ZNW 70 (1979) 119.

16:14   HAHN, F. Christologische Hoheitstitel (1963) 204. MOULE, C. F. D. (ed.) The Significance of the Message of the Resurrection for Faith in Jesus Christ (1968) 87. HENSS, W., Das Verhältnis zwischen Diatessaron, Christlicher Gnosis und "Western Text" (Berlin 1967) 13f, 55. LUTHER, M. Predigten über die Christus-Botschaft (1966) 188-195. METZGER, B. M., "St. Jerome's explicit references to variant readings in manuscripts of the New Testament" in: E. Best/R. McL. Wilson (eds.) Text and Interpretation. Studies in the New Testament presented to Matthew Black (Cambridge 1979) 182f.

16:15-20   ALAND, K., "Der Schluss des Markusevangeliums" in: M. Sabbe (ed.) L'Evangile selon Marc (Gembloux 1974) 446-48. "Abendmahl" in: TRE 1 (1977) 216.

16:15-18   HAHN, F. Das Verständnis der Mission im Neuen Testament (1965) 50, 52, 53f, 60, 62.

16:15-16   EGGER, W., Frohbotschaft und Lehre (Frankfurt 1976) 49. TREVIJANO, ETCHEVERRÍA, R., "La misión dela Iglesia primitiva y los mandatos del Señor en los Evangelios" Salmanticensis 25 (1978) 5-36.

16:15   BEYSCHLAG, K., Clemens Romanus und der Frühkatholizismus (Tübingen 1966) 276f, 279. HAHN, F. Das Verständnis der Mission im Neuen Testament (1965) 10. KASTING, H. Die Anfänge der Urchristlichen Mission (1969) 38-40. KÜMMEL, W. G., Einleitung in das Neue Testament (Heidelberg 1973 *(17)*) 71f.

16:16-18   HENNECKE, E., und SCHNEEMELCHER, W., Neutestamentliche Apokryphen I (Tübingen 1964) 343.

16:16   KAESEMANN, E. Exegetische Versuche und Besinnungen (1964) II 97. New Testament Questions of Today (1969) 99. KASPER, W. (ed.) Christsein ohne Entscheidung oder soll die Kirche Kinder taufen? (1970) 65f. ALAND, K. Taufe und Kindertaufe (1971) 45-46.

16:17   HARRISVILLE, R. A., The Concept of Witness in the New Testament (Minneapolis 1960) 71ff. DUNN, J. D. G., Jesus and the Spirit (London 1975) 246.

16:19-20   GOLLWITZER, H., Veränderung im Diesseits (München 1973) 168.

16:19   HAHN, F. Christologische Hoheitstitel (1963) 124, 130. HAHN, F. Das Verständnis der Mission im Neuen Testament (1965) 54. JANSSEN, E., "Testament Abrahams" in: W. G. Kümmel (ed.) Jüdische Schriften aus hellenistisch-römischer Zeit III (Gütersloh 1975) 220. LOHFINK, G. Die Himmelfahrt Jesu (1971) 119-21. SCHMITHALS, W., "Zur Herkunft der gnostischen Elemente in der Sprache des Paulus" in: B.Aland et al. (eds.) Gnosis. Festschrift für Hans Jonas (Göttingen 1978) 403.

16:20   "Berufung" in: TRE 5 (1980) 697. HAHN, F. Das Verständnis der Mission im Neuen Testament (1965) 54.

 **AN EXEGETICAL BIBLIOGRAPHY OF THE NEW TESTAMENT—MATTHEW, MARK**

Composition by Omni Composition Services, Inc., Macon, Georgia
typeset in Times Roman by Janet Middlebrooks on an A/M Comp/Set
5404 phototypesetter and paginated on an A/M Comp/Set 4510

Binding and title pages designed by Haywood Ellis

Production specifications:
text paper—60# Warren's Olde Style
end papers—100# Warren's Old Style

Printing (offset lithography) by Omnipress of Macon, Inc., Macon, Georgia
Binding by John H. Dekker and Sons, Inc., Grand Rapids, Michigan